For Reference

Not to be taken from this room

The SCRIBNER ENCYCLOPEDIA *of*
AMERICAN LIVES

THE SCRIBNER ENCYCLOPEDIA OF AMERICAN LIVES

The *Scribner Encyclopedia of American Lives* presents original scholarly biographies of notable Americans.

The series consists of two branches. Chronologically organized, one branch includes volumes on figures who have died since 1981. Each concise summary of achievements ranges from 1,000 to 6,000 words and usually includes a photo of the individual. Also detailed, wherever possible, are family background; education; names of spouses with marriage and divorce dates; addresses of residences; and cause of death and place of burial. Volumes include:

The second branch is the *Scribner Encyclopedia of American Lives: Thematic Series*. These subject-oriented sets extend the coverage of the original series to high-interest fields of endeavor or periods in history. In order to appropriately document the selected subject, profiles cover both living and deceased individuals. Volumes include:

Sports Figures

The 1960s

A cumulative index for both branches appears in thematic volumes after Sports Figures and in chronological volumes after Volume 5.

The SCRIBNER ENCYCLOPEDIA *of*

AMERICAN LIVES

VOLUME EIGHT

2006–2008

ARNOLD MARKOE
EDITOR IN CHIEF

KAREN MARKOE
GENERAL EDITOR

KENNETH T. JACKSON
CONSULTING EDITOR

CHARLES SCRIBNER'S SONS
A part of Gale, Cengage Learning

GALE
CENGAGE Learning

Detroit • New York • San Francisco • New Haven, Conn • Waterville, Maine • London

**The Scribner Encyclopedia of American Lives,
Volume Eight**

Arnold Markoe, editor in chief

Project Editor: Neil Schlager

Rights Acquisition and Management: Jennifer
   Altschul, Kelly Quin

Composition: Evi Abou-El-Seoud

Manufacturing: Wendy Blurton

Imaging: Dean Dauphinais, John Watkins

Product Design: Pam Galbreath

For product information and technology assistance, contact us at
Gale Customer Support, 1-800-877-4253
For permission to use material from this text or product,
submit all requests online at **www.cengage.com/permissions**.
Further permissions questions can be emailed to
permissionrequest@cengage.com

While every effort has been made to ensure the reliability of the information
presented in this publication, Gale, a part of Cengage Learning, does not guarantee the
accuracy of the data contained herein. Gale accepts no payment for listing; and
inclusion in the publication of any organization, agency, institution, publication, service,
or individual does not imply endorsement of the editors or publisher. Errors brought to
the attention of the publisher and verified to the satisfaction of the publisher will be
corrected in future editions.

Library of Congress Cataloging-in-Publication Data

The Scribner encyclopedia of American Lives / Arnold Markoe, editor in chief; Karen
Markoe, general editor; Kenneth T. Jackson, consulting editor.
   p. cm. --
Includes bibliographical references and index.
ISBN 0-684-80492-1 (v. 1: alk. paper)
ISBN 978-0-6843-1575-1 (v. 8: alk. paper)
   1. Contents: v. 1 1981–1985 2. United States -- Biography -- Dictionaries. I. Markoe,
Arnold. II. Morkoe, Karen. III. Jackson, Kenneth T.

CT213.S37 1998
920.073--dc21   98-33793

Gale
27500 Drake Rd.
Farmington Hills, MI, 48331-3535

This title is also available as an e-book.
ISBN-13: 978-0-6843-1600-0 ISBN-10: 0-6843-1600-5
Contact your Gale, a part of Cengage Learning sales representative for ordering
information.

Printed in the United States of America
1 2 3 4 5 6 7 12 11 10 09

Editorial and Production Staff

PROJECT EDITOR

Neil Schlager

SCHLAGER GROUP INC. EDITORIAL STAFF

Kathryn Bianchi

COPY EDITORS, RESEARCHERS

*Rob Arlt, Jessica Hornik Evans,
Harrabeth Haidusek, Elizabeth Henry,
Carol Holmes, Georgia S. Maas,
Jason Miller*

PROOFREADERS

Dorothy Bauhoff, Amy Unterburger

COMPOSITOR

Integra Software Services

PROJECT MANAGER

Tracie Moy

PUBLISHER

Frank Menchaca

Contents

Preface

This is the eighth volume in the *Scribner Encyclopedia of American Lives* (SEAL) series. The first volume in the series, published in 1998, covered the years 1981 to 1985, taking up where Scribner's celebrated *Dictionary of American Biography* left off. In the present volume, comprising biographical essays on 310 notable Americans who died between 1 January 2006 and 31 December 2008, the sweep of American history is once again on display. There are now 2,917 entries in the series.

As in the preceding seven SEAL volumes, essays are intended for general readers as well as for students and scholars. The entries are arranged in alphabetical order, and each opens with a brief paragraph noting the subject's outstanding achievements. The length of articles depends primarily on the significance of their subjects. Where information is accessible, entries include dates of birth and death; names and occupations of parents; number of siblings; educational institutions attended and degrees granted; names of spouses and dates of marriages and divorces; number of children; cause of death and place of burial; and as a guide for further study, a selective annotated bibliography. A photograph of the subject accompanies many entries. The volume also includes a directory of contributors with their institutional affiliations as well as an occupations index and an alphabetical listing of SEAL entries; both indexes are cumulative.

Determining the subjects for inclusion was challenging given the limitations of space. Extensive lists of famous Americans who died in the years 2006, 2007, and 2008 were compiled from a variety of sources, including obituaries from nationally distributed periodicals. The final list of subjects was chosen with the understanding that other observers might have made different, equally valid selections. Among the list of particularly notable Americans, President Gerald R. Ford commanded the most extensive entry in this volume. Additional obvious choices were the soul singer James Brown and the operatic soprano Beverly Sills; the engaging television reporter and moderator of NBC's *Meet the Press* Tim Russert; U.S. Senators Jesse Helms, Howard Metzenbaum, and Lloyd Bentsen; the liberal economist John Kenneth Galbraith and the conservative economist Milton Friedman; the journalists Molly Ivins and David Halberstam; the actors Charlton Heston, Shelley Winters, and Paul Newman; the literary giants Norman Mailer and Kurt Vonnegut; the reformers Betty Friedan and Jane Jacobs; and in the memorable nickname category, First Lady Claudia "Ladybird" Johnson and the oral historian Louis "Studs" Terkel.

Other notables remembered on these pages are the Pulitzer Prize–winning historian Arthur Schlesinger, Jr., and the Nobel Prize–winning biologist Joshua Lederberg, both former consultants to SEAL; George Carlin, the comedian and wordsmith whose "seven dirty words" barred by the Federal Communications Commission formed the basis of a lawsuit that reached all the way to the U.S. Supreme Court; Michael DeBakey, the pioneering heart surgeon whose patients included presidents Johnson, Kennedy, and Nixon and the Shah of Iran; Mark Felt; Associate Director of the Federal Bureau of Investigation, who three decades after the Watergate break-in disclosed that he had been "Deep Throat"; William F. Buckley, Jr., a leading voice of the modern American conservative movement, television host of the long-running public affairs television program *Firing Line*, author or editor of fifty books, and intrepid sailor; and Robert Rauschenberg, painter, sculptor, printmaker, photographer, and performance artist, one of the world's foremost and most prolific postmodernists.

Most of the men and women represented in this volume were recognized during their lifetimes by their peers, but not always by the general public. Some came as immigrants, including Hungarian-born Tom Lantos, Holocaust survivor and U.S. congressman; and Romanian-born George Palade, the Nobel Prize–winning cell biologist. We recognize, however, that the women and minorities included in this volume do not statistically represent their numbers in the overall population. In the main, the productive lives of our subjects occurred in the last half of the twentieth century, a time when the discriminatory barriers of race and gender were first seriously confronted but not eradicated.

The contributors to this volume included journalists, freelance writers, and members of the academic community. All had in common a respect for language and an enthusiasm for research. In some cases we were able to enlist authors who had previously written full-length biographies to write SEAL entries for those same subjects. The book has gained from the experience and skill of its contributors, many of whom have been with us since publication of the first volume in this series. As editors, we have often worked together in the past and happily chose to do so again. We trust the result of our collaboration will provide a valuable resource and a spur to further study.

An undertaking of this scope requires a steady and skillful hand at the helm. We are especially indebted to project editor Neil Schlager, who deftly coordinated this work. We have benefited from his counsel and superb organizational skills. Our longtime colleague Richard H. Gentile provided expert guidance on a broad array of subjects. William Gargan generously shared with us his extensive knowledge of literary matters. Peter Brancazio had answers when we had questions about science. We also gratefully acknowledge the assistance of Matt Wasniewski of the U.S. House of Representatives Office of History and Preservation and Betty Koed of the U.S. Senate Historical Office. At Cengage Gale, we wish to thank in particular Tracie Moy, who provided help and support throughout the entire project.

Arnold Markoe, Editor in Chief
Karen E. Markoe, General Editor
Kenneth T. Jackson, Consulting Editor

A

ABERCROMBIE, Thomas James (*b.* 13 August 1930 in Stillwater, Minnesota; *d.* 3 April 2006 in Baltimore, Maryland), award-winning writer and photographer for *National Geographic*, considered the magazine's expert on the Middle East.

Abercrombie was the second child born to J. A. D. Abercrombie, a civil engineer, and Beth (McSevany) Abercrombie, a homemaker. Abercrombie was born in a small lumber town along the Saint Croix River, one of the earliest settled towns in Minnesota following treaties with local Native American tribes. In Stillwater High School, from which he graduated in 1948, he took to photography and found his path, professionally and personally, for it was there that he met his future wife, Marilyn "Lynn" Bruette whom he married on 7 June 1952. After a quick stint in the U.S. Army, where foot problems kept him from serving, Abercrombie entered Macalester College in Saint Paul, Minnesota, where he studied art and journalism. The desire to become a news photographer outweighed his academic dedication, however, and he took a job in 1952 as a photographer at the *Fargo Forum* in North Dakota before finishing school. He had no firm plans but hoped to get on at the *Saint Paul Tribune*.

A year later Abercrombie moved to Wisconsin to work for the *Milwaukee Journal*, which had a strong reputation in photojournalism circles. There he began earning his reputation for adventuresome risk taking to tell stories with his camera. For example, he wanted so badly to photograph a sunken freighter that he donned diving gear and tied a rope around his waist, attached the rope to his car bumper, and plunged into Lake Michigan—just to test the waterproof, acrylic housing he had built for his Leica camera. His wife was at the wheel with orders to pull him out of the drink if necessary.

In 1954 Abercrombie won the University of Missouri Newspaper Photographer of the Year Award. In 1958, at *National Geographic*, he won the Magazine Photographer of the Year Award, the first person to win both honors. For his writing, the Overseas Press Club awarded him its Best Magazine Reporting Award in 1974.

National Geographic hired Abercrombie in 1956. His first assignment was a story on Captain John Smith's travels around the Chesapeake Bay. Abercrombie called it a local story, which for the magazine was anything in the English-speaking world. His first foreign assignment, as well as his first venture out of the United States, was Lebanon. He was slated as the story's photographer but ended up writing the piece as well. The experience was also his first encounter with the Muslim world, which would dominate the body of his work, and philosophy, in the years to come. Abercrombie was swiftly promoted to the foreign editorial staff, made up of the magazine's best field men, equally adept with pen and camera.

In 1957 Abercrombie was the first journalist to journey to the South Pole, planting the *National Geographic* flag there after winning a lottery to make the trip. That honor was more than he bargained for, as his party was stranded for three weeks at the bottom of the world when the plane suffered engine trouble. The cold must not have bothered him much, for his next stories for the magazine included Alaska's statehood and ice fishing, for which he shot fish under the ice. Over the next few years Abercrombie traveled from Brazil to Cambodia, from Easter Island to Iraq, and to points in between.

1

It was in 1966 in Saudi Arabia that Abercrombie broke through the veil of Muslim life. He was the first Western photographer to produce pictures of the hajj in Mecca and was himself deeply touched by the event and converted to the Muslim faith. He took the Muslim name Omar and personally made the hajj four times.

In the Saudi desert Abercrombie also made other discoveries. He chased rumors into the desolate Empty Quarter to find the Wabar meteorite. Later he located one of the trains blown up by Lawrence of Arabia right where it had been lying in the sand for decades. Abercrombie's understanding of the Koran and his personal insight gave him a perspective of the region that would serve him for the rest of his career. He had a knack for listening, in addition to his keen eye. Coupled with a habit of "going native," he was able to unfold not only the scenes of life in the eighty countries he visited but also the psychology of the people he met.

Abercrombie became friends with the Saudi royal family, interviewed Yasser Arafat several times, and dived with Jacques Cousteau. Nevertheless, Abercrombie had a touch with common people, too. When he was on a visit with a sheikh in Arabia, with his wife at his side, their host offered thirty camels for Lynn Abercrombie, whom the host thought was the journalist's daughter. Abercrombie countered with fifty camels and kept his wife. She often accompanied Abercrombie on trips but spent most of the early years raising their two children, a son and a daughter. Another son died in childhood in 1958. An accomplished photographer in her own right, she would eventually shoot magazine assignments written by her husband.

Abercrombie nearly met his fate on several occasions. For instance, he nearly fell to his death from a cable car in Venezuela, only to be caught by the belt by his guide. His camera hit the bridge of his nose and left a scar that he would carry for the rest of his life. The dented camera was part of the vast collection kept in his Maryland home. He almost died when he fell off a yak in the Afghan mountains. An angry mob in a napalmed Cambodian village would have killed him had he not convinced them he was French. Caught in the middle of a civil war in Yemen, he had to purchase two Kalashnikov rifles, which he expensed as car insurance. In addition, he nearly succumbed to typhoid on a trip to Tibet.

A fully loaded Land Rover was Abercrombie's usual transport, though he also traveled by horse, camel, yak, and Cessna. He would spend weeks outfitting for his months-long excursions, sometimes packing gold bars for use in far-flung corners of the globe. His medical kit was a virtual hospital in a toolbox and came into use more than once; he tended to wounded victims of an earthquake in Iran and amputated frozen gangrenous toes of a pilgrim in Tibet.

Abercrombie's reputation was built through his knowledge of the people, places, and politics of the Middle East. He used anthropology, religion, and geography threaded in with familiar, first-person style to weave the fabric of the region.

First with his camera, then with his pen, he told of ancient Egypt and the cradle of civilization in the Tigris-Euphrates Valley and lifted the veil on the pilgrimage to Mecca and the oil-rich region's rush from feudalism to the twenty-first century.

Abercrombie thought that his best piece was "The Sword and the Sermon" (July 1972), an all-encompassing look at the history and culture of Islam. Many others point to his truly epic later work, "Ibn Battuta, Prince of Travelers" (December 1991), with the photographer Jim Stanfield, tracing the fourteenth-century journeys of the Muslim world's equivalent of Marco Polo. They spent eighteen months following the trails on which Battuta spent thirty years. They "journeyed the length and breadth of the area where Islam still thrives today, from south of the Sahara to Tashkent and Samarkand, Sri Lanka, Indonesia and China."

In 1994 Abercrombie retired from the magazine to his waterside home in Shady Side, Maryland. There he took to more tinkering, rebuilding a telescope to view the night sky and building a skipjack workboat, which he never finished. He also taught geography at George Washington University, an opportunity to continue weaving tales of the world as he had come to know it. He died on 3 April 2006 following heart valve surgery at Johns Hopkins University. His remains were cremated.

One of Abercrombie's friends, the former White House press secretary Marlin Fitzwater, painted this picture of Abercrombie for a reporter: "A rare combination of a physical man . . . who knows how to work with wood . . . all the physical things of life. And yet his writing was as gentle as a flower."

★

Researchers will find Abercrombie's forty-year body of work in *National Geographic* the best record of his life. Leah Bendavid-Val et al., eds., *Odysseys and Photographs: Four National Geographic Field Men* (2008) includes a detailed essay on Abercrombie by Gilbert M. Grosvenor, the magazine's former editor, and numerous photographs emblematic of Abercrombie's work. For a memorial story on Abercrombie, see Don Belt, "Thomas Abercrombie: A Geographic Life," *National Geographic* (Aug. 2006). Obituaries are in the *Washington Post* (6 Apr. 2006) and *New York Times* (16 Apr. 2006). Patricia A. Leone produced a documentary about Abercrombie, *White Tiger: The Adventures of Thomas J. Abercrombie* (2004).

E. B. Furgurson III

ADAMS, Edie (*b.* 16 April 1927 in Kingston, Pennsylvania; *d.* 15 October 2008 in Los Angeles, California), Tony Award–winning musical actress, television and film comedian, cigar promoter, and wife of the comedian Ernie Kovacs.

Edie Adams. **MICHAEL OCHS ARCHIVE/GETTY IMAGES**

Of Welsh descent, Adams was born Edith Elizabeth Enke, the only child of Sheldon Enke, a banker, and Ada (Adams) Enke, a music teacher. When Adams was two, her father lost his job during the 1929 Wall Street crash and moved the family from Kingston to Grove City, Pennsylvania, and then to Tenafly, New Jersey, where he became a salesman. While Adams was a child, her grandmother taught her sewing; her mother gave her singing and piano lessons. She later explained that according to Welsh tradition, young women were expected to sing.

While attending Tenafly High School, Adams joined the choir and the glee club and sang in the school's operettas. At age fifteen she won a baton-twirling contest. Because of her strict Presbyterian upbringing, she did not see her first movie until she was sixteen, when she watched a Jeanette MacDonald musical. Adams's ambition was to become an opera singer.

After graduating in 1945, Adams moved to New York City. She briefly attended the Traphagen School of Fashion Design and then the Juilliard School of Music. At Juilliard she was trained as a classical vocalist for four years, graduating with a BM, and she studied acting at the Columbia University School of Drama. Encouraged to enter the Miss U.S. Television pageant in 1950, she adopted her mother's maiden name and won the title. Despite her classical

background, she decided to make a career through popular songs, dropping her soprano voice two octaves, and by impersonations, being an excellent mimic (especially, later, of Marilyn Monroe).

Adams appeared in several television variety shows and nightclubs. In 1951 she auditioned for and became a part of *The Ernie Kovacs Show*, originally called *Ernie in Kovacs-land*. The program began in Philadelphia, running in the morning, and in 1952 moved to New York City, airing first in the morning and then at night. The show lasted two years and reappeared in 1955 and 1956. The program was groundbreaking. Written and produced by Kovacs, the comedy show was uninhibited and highly inventive. Critics called it "wacky and zany." With an innocent face, Adams was the perfect foil to Kovacs's mustached, cigar-smoking satirist. The show featured ingenious pranks and sound effects, pantomime sketches, and occasional custard pies. Kovacs appeared as Percy Dovetonsils, Uncle Gruesome, and the Kapusta Kid. Adams and Kovacs were part of the Nairobi Trio, costumed apes with derbies, playing xylophone, mallet, and finger bone. Often the show teased naturalistic assumptions about time and space, with such skits as Kovacs vacuuming the studio's ceiling. Adams and Kovacs were married on 12 September 1954 and had a daughter.

During the 1950s Adams appeared twice on Broadway. In 1953 she won the Best Newcomer Theatre World Award for *Wonderful Town* and introduced the songs "Ohio" and "A Little Bit of Love." In 1957 she won a Tony Award for Best Featured Actress in a Musical, playing the beguiling Daisy Mae in *Li'l Abner*, based on Al Capp's satirical comic strip.

To pursue their film careers, Adams and Kovacs moved in the late 1950s to Los Angeles, where Kovacs was killed in a car crash on 13 January 1962. While winning a custody battle over Kovacs's two daughters from his first marriage, Adams was confronted with a bill for $520,000 in back taxes owed by Kovacs's estate; she paid the bill in full by tirelessly working in films, on television, and in Muriel Cigar commercials. For the next nineteen years, Adams appeared as a sultry vamp, asking with a come-hither whisper and a wink, "Cigar? Cigarette? Tiparillo?" and "Why don't you pick one up and smoke it sometime?" "I was always the cartoon sex symbol," Adams told the *Chicago Tribune*. To her surprise, she found people took her seriously "although I was trying to be satirical and funny."

Serious film roles included a spurned secretary in *The Apartment* (1960) and a lonely wife in *The Best Man* (1964), and straight-faced comedy roles in *Lover Come Back* (1961), *It's a Mad, Mad, Mad, Mad World* (1963), and *Under the Yum Yum Tree* (1963). On television Adams hosted *The Edie Adams Show* (1963–1964), a musical variety show featuring the musical greats Count Basie, Duke Ellington, Sammy Davis, Jr., and Stan Getz; it was nominated for five Emmy Awards. On 16 August 1964 Adams married the photographer Martin Mills, and they had one son before they divorced in 1971.

Also during the 1960s Adams began her career as a businesswoman, lending her name to Edie Adams Cut and Curl Beauty Salons and a line of cosmetics. Her natural talent at sewing allowed her to design many of her costumes, and she rented them to revues, television shows, and movies. When she appeared on Jack Paar's talk show with her own fringed slacks, the style caused a sensation and was widely imitated. Later, in the 1980s and 1990s, she designed party gowns sold at Neiman Marcus stores under the Bonham label.

On 4 June 1972 Adams married the trumpeter Pete Candoli, and they toured as a nightclub act; the couple divorced in 1988. During the 1970s and 1980s, Adams appeared on many television shows, including *The Bob Hope Show*, *Fantasy Island*, *General Electric Theater*, *The Love Boat*, and *Murder, She Wrote*. In 1982 Adams bought a 160-acre almond grove in Bakersfield, California, and she toured in light operas and musicals, including *The Merry Widow* in 1986 and *Mame* in 1988. She also toured as a guest speaker, showing highlights of the Kovacs show; in 1984 she was a consultant for the television movie *Ernie Kovacs: Between the Laughter*.

From the 1990s Adams continued to tour in cabarets and musicals, including *Hello, Dolly* in 1991. She also appeared on television, with roles in the 1993 miniseries *Armistead Maupin's Tales of the City* and on the soap opera *As the World Turns*. She tirelessly promoted the memory of Kovacs in her 1990 memoir, personal appearances, and packaged videocassettes.

At the age of eighty-one, Adams died at her Los Angeles home of complications from pneumonia and cancer. She is buried in Forest Lawn Memorial Park in the Hollywood Hills section of Los Angeles. Through almost six decades, Adams's career as a singer, an actress, and a businesswoman may be best summed up by a remark by the comedian Groucho Marx, who said, "There are some things Edie won't do, but nothing she can't do."

★

Adams's memoir, written with Robert Windeler, is *Sing a Pretty Song: The "Offbeat" Life of Edie Adams, Including the Ernie Kovacs Years* (1990). See also Diana Rico, *Kovacsland: A Biography of Ernie Kovacs* (1990). An obituary is in the *New York Times* (16 Oct. 2008).

Patrick S. Smith

ADAMS, VICTORIA ALMETER JACKSON GRAY

SEE *Gray Adams, Victoria Almeter Jackson.*

AGEE, Philip Burnett Franklin (*b.* 19 July 1935 in Tacoma Park, Maryland; *d.* 7 January 2008 in Havana, Cuba), Central Intelligence Agency (CIA) agent who subsequently led a reviled and respected career as a writer and critic of America's intelligence apparatus.

Agee was the second of two children born to "Bill" Burnett Franklin, who ran a uniform and linen service for area businesses and military establishments, and Helen (O'Neill) Agee, who worked in the business with her husband and was also active in an associated statewide franchise association. He was raised in Tampa, Florida, member of a well-off Catholic family.

In 1952 Agee graduated from the all-male Jesuit High School of Tampa and matriculated to the University of Notre Dame. Initially a business major, in 1956 Agee graduated cum laude with a BA in philosophy. Resisting recruiting overtures from the CIA (a close family friend and CIA employee recommended him), he instead entered the University of Florida Law School. Following an unsuccessful semester and facing the draft, in 1957 Agee joined the CIA by enlisting in the U.S. Air Force as a radar mechanic. In 1959, after intensive military and CIA training, he was commissioned as an officer in an Air Intelligence Service Squadron. That same year he married Janet Wasserberger. The couple would go on to have two sons.

Agee's major assignments took him to Quito, Ecuador, in 1960; Montevideo, Uruguay, in 1964; and Mexico City in 1967; with interim assignments in Washington, D.C. In Latin America, he weathered the tedium of preparing watchlists of suspected subversives for the secret police. One day in a Montevideo police station, Agee heard the cries of a man undergoing torture and was told that he had been the source for the victim's arrest. From that point on, his moral opposition to CIA covert activities grew. In early 1969, after his assignment at the Mexico City Olympics, he resigned from the CIA.

His marriage to Wasserberger breaking up, Agee chose to remain in Mexico and study Latin American history at the National Autonomous University of Mexico. His romance there with "Muriel," an older American expatriate who loved Che Guevara and hated the CIA for murdering him, influenced his decision to write a tell-all book. For the next five years, he scoured major libraries and documentation centers in Cuba, France, and England for material for his book, even as his family and friends in the United States were under constant surveillance by the CIA. By his side during these years was Angela Camargo Seixas, lover, helpmate, and surrogate mother to his children in France and England, who as a young Brazilian university student had been brutally tortured by CIA-trained secret police and to whom Agee dedicated *Inside the Company: CIA Diary*.

When *Inside the Company* was published in 1975, it found a readership ready for such a public excoriation of

America's intelligence service. As such, the book was an immediate success, selling in the hundreds of thousands in its English-language version and—after being translated into more than twenty-seven languages—selling in the millions the world over. Agee's book differed from similar works in that he did not submit his manuscript to the CIA for review, thus avoiding the censorship imposed on those books by the agency. Indeed, Agee's *Inside the Company* was a distinctly risky work. In it, he revealed the names, profiles, and postings of active agents.

Later, with the journalist and peace activist Louis Wolf, Agee continued to expose agents in *Dirty Work: The CIA in Western Europe* (1978) and *Dirty Work 2: The CIA in Africa* (1979). In 1978 Agee and Wolf also began to expose agents through a publication called the *Covert Action Information Bulletin* until Congress in 1982 passed a law making it a crime to intentionally reveal the identity of covert agents.

Without the aid of his personal network, Agee would never have survived the machinations of the CIA. Immediately after the publication of *Inside the Company*, he was expelled or banned from one country after another. Finally, stripped of his American passport, he found that his ability to reside or travel outside of the United States was rapidly diminishing. In 1979, however, he married Giselle Roberge, a renowned American ballerina who had learned that German law allowed married foreigners to live in Germany with their families. Thereafter he divided his time between Hamburg and Havana, Cuba.

Agee was in great demand as a speaker, traveling widely when allowed. His stage manner was professorial, soft-spoken, and direct. His talks were erudite, analytical, and rich in anecdotal and historical materials, frequently supplemented with bibliographies.

Even given the severe restrictions placed upon him, Agee's ability to act swiftly and effectively against government propaganda was remarkable. For example, on 6 February 1981, the Ronald Reagan administration began a disinformation campaign regarding communist intrusions in El Salvador. Just two weeks later, on 20 February 1981, Agee held a long press conference in Amsterdam in which he provided fifty pages of material exposing the counterfeit nature of the CIA's claims. That very day the U.S. government published a white paper justifying its intervention in El Salvador. In June 1981 Agee, cooperating with the journalist Warner Poelchau, published *White Paper Whitewash*, a careful dissection of the fabricated nature of the report.

In 2000 Agee opened a successful travel business, cubalinda.com. He was also engaged in a Canadian petroleum start-up company in Latin America. He penned a series of essays on the origins of the first Gulf War, the George W. Bush administration's efforts to undermine Hugo Chavez's election victories in Venezuela, and the history of America's ill-conceived policies regarding Cuba. Any time the press reported on newly declassified information documenting CIA misdeeds, Agee's name usually came up. Perhaps most famously, the law created by Congress in 1982 largely in response to Agee's activities—the Intelligence Identities Protection Act—was frequently invoked during the investigation and prosecution of Vice President Dick Cheney's chief-of-staff, I. Lewis "Scooter" Libby, for his role in the politically motivated outing of a CIA agent named Valerie Plame.

Agee died from complications associated with surgery for ulcers. His cremated remains were shared by his wife, Giselle, and his two sons. Agee saw the actions he took against the CIA as the inevitable outcome of a profound moral struggle. He attributed his ethical impulse in no small measure to his Jesuit education. Until the declassification and release of his government documents and the opening of his personal files and manuscripts to scholarly inquiry, any final estimate of Agee's legacy will remain appropriately cloaked in the riddling variations of a modern enigma.

Though there is no biography of Agee and the disposition of his manuscripts is as yet unresolved, a detailed account of his life and work from 1969 to 1987 can be found in Agee, *On the Run* (1987). A treatment of his CIA training and service can be found in the aforementioned Agee, *Inside the Company: CIA Diary* (1975). Obituaries are in the *New York Times* and *Washington Post* (both 10 Jan. 2008).

Joseph G. Flynn

ALLYSON, June (*b.* 7 October 1917 in New York City; *d.* 8 July 2006 in Ojai, California), actress in Broadway musical theater and Hollywood films.

Allyson was born Eleanor ("Ella") Geisman. She was the daughter of Arthur Geisman and Clare (Provost) Geisman. Allyson's father left her and her mother when she was six months old, and her mother turned to engraving cards for a living. Nearly paralyzed in a bicycle accident at age eight, Ella wanted to dance like Fred Astaire and taught herself to do so after regaining her health. After three years at Theodore Roosevelt High School in the Bronx borough of New York City, she dropped out briefly to appear in the Broadway show *Sing Out the News* (1938). She returned to high school after the show was finished and graduated the next year with the highest scholastic grade in the school. Her unforgettable trademark was a husky voice that made her sound like she had a perpetual head cold. She adopted the name June Allyson (Allyson was the name of a relative) once she started acting in films.

Allyson rejected early movie offers to appear in several Broadway productions but finally began her film career with the 1943 release of *Best Foot Forward* starring Lucille

June Allyson, 1944. **FPG/HULTON ARCHIVE/GETTY IMAGES**

Ball. Allyson subsequently signed a contract with Metro-Goldwyn-Mayer (MGM), and on 1 October 1945 she made the front cover of *Life* magazine as the star of the movie *Her Highness and the Bellboy* (1945). *Life*, arguably the most popular American magazine at the time, described Allyson as a star but also noted that the movie's script was mediocre. Unfortunately, this notion would too often characterize Allyson's career. She acknowledged that she did not read scripts before accepting roles, and so she often appeared in forgettable movies. However, she gave convincing dramatic performances in *Music for Millions* (1944) and *The Sailor Takes a Wife* (1945). These performances were lauded by critics including the *New York Times* film critic Bosley Crowther. The *New York Post* described Allyson as 1944's "most promising" actress. She also sang several songs in *Till the Clouds Roll By* (1946), a sentimental film biography of the composer Jerome Kern.

For the next several years, Allyson remained an extremely popular actress, holding her own against the likes of Joan Crawford and Judy Garland and probably not being eclipsed until the rise of Marilyn Monroe in the early 1950s. In 1946 the Motion Picture Research Bureau named Allyson the "most typical American Girl," and in 1947 college newspaper editors voted her the most lovable female actress. She was in the top five in annual popularity polls for Rolfe Photoplays,

but her roles were not equal to her talent or accolades. She frequently played opposite Van Johnson—in *Till the Clouds Roll By, The Bride Goes Wild* (1948), and *Too Young to Kiss* (1951). In the latter movie she played a pianist pretending to be a thirteen-year-old girl in order to get a concert booking; *Time* magazine claimed that this role was her "perfect outlet."

In the early 1940s MGM tried to make it appear that Allyson was romantically involved with Johnson and with the actor Peter Lawford, but she was not. She dated the future president John F. Kennedy, but Dick Powell was her true romantic interest. Unfortunately, Powell was married to the actress Joan Blondell, and he was also considerably older than Allyson. Despite the opposition of studio executives, Allyson and Powell were married on 19 August 1945. Allyson even persuaded the MGM studio head Louis Mayer to give her away, and he did so, albeit reluctantly. Allyson became active in television after marrying Powell, who later installed her as host of the *June Allyson Show* (1959–1961). The program was a dramatic anthology, and Allyson always acted as the hostess and appeared in several televised plays.

Powell kept tight control of the couple's money and even vetoed Allyson's taste in furnishings for the new house he built in Bel Air, California. He had a son from a previous marriage, and he and Allyson adopted a daughter and had a son together.

In *The McConnell Story* (1955), a wartime love story, Allyson starred opposite Alan Ladd, who was also married to a controlling spouse. Around the same time, Powell started work as director of the *The Conqueror*, a spectacular of the life of Genghis Khan starring John Wayne; the film required tremendous preparation. Both Allyson and Ladd shared their professional quirks; in time dinners at the set turned into a deeper friendship. Eventually both actors' spouses and the press learned of the relationship, which Allyson in her autobiography, *June Allyson* (1982), claims did not get physical. Ladd left his wife, but Allyson stayed with Powell. However, marital discord continued as Powell became more involved in Four Star Productions, which he owned with the actor David Niven.

Eventually, the couple signed a divorce agreement, but while an interlocutory divorce was granted, the divorce was never finalized. (At the time, California had a two-stage divorce system designed to make quarreling couples think it over before officially terminating the marriage.) If the relationship with Ladd created tension, Powell himself joked that the actor Jimmy Stewart was "my wife's husband." Allyson appeared with the talented Stewart in perhaps her three best movies: *The Stratton Story* (1949), *The Glenn Miller Story* (1953), and *Strategic Air Command* (1955). Stewart brought out Allyson's most talented and dramatic side as she played the role of a wife waiting for her husband, most notably in *The Glenn Miller Story*. In 1954 she starred opposite William Holden in the well-received *Executive Suite*. She also appeared in *The Shrike* (1955), the only film in which she played a villain.

Soon after Powell completed *The Conqueror*, his health began to deteriorate. Although Powell was diagnosed with lung cancer, Allyson claimed that he did not know he was dying and indeed was making grandiose plans up until his death in 1963. Allyson was left a wealthy widow, and her desire to continue acting diminished. After Powell's death, she appeared in only a few movies, including *They Only Kill Their Masters* (1972) and *That's Entertainment III* (1994).

Allyson admittedly turned to alcohol after Powell's death. The Macy's department store chairman Jack Strauss and his wife, Peggy, were Allyson's best friends at that time. A brief marriage to Powell's barber, Alfred Maxwell, failed—some sources claim they married and divorced twice. Allyson later met the doctor and occasional actor David Ashrow at a party; they married on 30 October 1976.

Allyson appeared on Broadway in *Forty Carats* (1970) and a road version of *No, No, Nanette* (1971). In 1980 Allyson and Ashrow appeared in a production called *My Daughter, Your Son*. Soon after, Allyson published her autobiography, which describes her happiness with Ashrow. Allyson appeared in a few television movies and made one of her last acting appearances on *Murder, She Wrote* in 1984. She also appeared in commercials for Depend adult diapers in the mid-1990s. Allyson later remarked that Depend was a product that she felt needed awareness and was not embarrassed to be connected with. Allyson died of pulmonary respiratory failure and acute bronchitis at age eighty-eight in her home.

At the height of her career, Allyson claimed great popularity, but except for a Golden Globe Award for Best Motion Picture Actress in a Musical or Comedy (1952) for *Too Young to Kiss*, she never received an important industry award (although the MGM studio actresses were honored as a group in 1988 with a lifetime achievement award). None of her movies made the American Film Institute (AFI) list of the 100 most influential movies of all time. She would have achieved her dream of dancing with Astaire—in *Royal Wedding* (1951)—if she had not become pregnant. The famed director Alfred Hitchcock reportedly wanted Allyson to star in *Rear Window* with Jimmy Stewart, but MGM would not release her from her contract to work in a Paramount Pictures film. That movie made the classic AFI list. Allyson basically was happy to play the unassuming girl next door. She disliked what she believed were pretentious period costume dramas. Her supreme artistic moment may well have been at the end of the dramatic biographical film *The Glenn Miller Story*. As Helen Berger Miller, she waits on Christmas Day for word of her husband, the leader of the U.S. Army Air Force band, who has been lost in a fog for several days. Her husband's band plays live on the radio as the viewer watches a forlorn Allyson, waiting for the return of her husband. But it was, the audience knows, never to be.

★

Information about Allyson's life is available in her 1982 autobiography, *June Allyson*, written with Frances Spatz Leighton. It profiles many of the actors she met and includes personal recollections of her relationships, but it lacks much information on either her technique as an actress or technical cinematography issues. Obituaries are in the *New York Times* and *Los Angeles Times* (both 11 July 2006), and the London *Independent* and *Guardian* (both 12 July 2006).

John David Healy

ALPHER, Ralph Asher (*b.* 3 February 1921 in Washington, D.C.; *d.* 12 August 2007 in Austin, Texas), leading cosmologist at Johns Hopkins University who was generally overlooked for his significant contribution to the Nobel Prize–winning big bang theory of the universe and its origins.

Alpher was the youngest of four children born to Samuel Alpher, a Russian-Jewish immigrant and a home builder, and Rose (Maleson) Alpher. The young Alpher came of age during the Great Depression and started working at age twelve, earning fifty cents an hour as a stagehand to help support his family. He was a voracious reader who was known to challenge the rabbis at his Hebrew school. He was seen as a prodigy and graduated from Theodore Roosevelt High School at age sixteen. Alpher's mother died of stomach cancer a year later.

The Massachusetts Institute of Technology (MIT) offered Alpher a full scholarship but stipulated that he must not work. At the height of the Depression, his family was struggling; Alpher had to work to pay for his books and meals. His concerns were short-lived, however. MIT withdrew its scholarship offer without explanation after Alpher casually mentioned that he was Jewish. The aspiring teenager was devastated. "It was a searing experience," Alpher recalled, noting that "for Jews before World War II," life was "terrible." His dreams of MIT dashed, Alpher got a job and enrolled in night classes at George Washington University, first in chemistry; however, he changed his major to physics after hearing that there were no jobs for Jews in chemistry. He worked days at the Naval Ordnance Laboratory in Washington and later at the Johns Hopkins University physics laboratory on torpedo exploder devices and guided missiles. In 1943 Alpher graduated with a BS from George Washington University. Remaining at that institution, he received an MS in physics in 1945 and a PhD in physics in 1948. He married Louise Ellen Simons on 28 January 1942. They had two children.

While Alpher was trying to come up with a subject for his doctoral dissertation, his adviser, a Soviet defector named George Gamow, suggested that Alpher explore the big bang theory, which holds that the universe began billions of years ago in the explosion of a single, superdense point that contained all matter. The theory had been proposed twenty-five years earlier but was still controversial. The big bang theory is also referred to as big bang nucleosynthesis or primordial nucleosynthesis. Gamow believed that if a single atom had exploded and created the universe, then some physical evidence of it must remain. Alpher theorized that the expansion of the universe leaves behind radiation and that traces of the initial explosion could still be measured. His calculations marked the first major breakthrough in the big bang model in twenty years.

On 1 April 1948 Gamow and Alpher submitted their paper, titled "The Origin of Chemical Elements," for publication in the scientific journal *Physical Review*. Hoping to attract attention to their triumph, Gamow added to the paper the name of one of his friends, the famous physicist Hans Bethe, though Bethe had no hand in writing it. Gamow also wanted to play off the Greek letters alpha, beta, and gamma with their names, Alpher, Bethe, and Gamow. Alpher took issue with this ploy for publicity and felt that his name would be overshadowed by those of the two greater scientists, despite the fact that he had done most of the work on the paper.

The paper was a milestone in big bang theory. When news leaked that a twenty-seven-year-old novice had made a major breakthrough, word spread like wildfire throughout the scientific community. Alpher presented his case to a packed audience of 300 people. The reporters in the room seized on Alpher's assertion that the big bang had taken about 300 seconds. Alpher enjoyed national celebrity and academic interest for a few weeks, but as he suspected, he soon became overshadowed by his more illustrious "coauthors." The addition of Bethe's name to the paper virtually eliminated any chance that the unknown Alpher would receive recognition for his crucial role in the development of the big bang model.

As is common when new scientific theories are introduced, the paper raised questions in the academic community, and Alpher set about to answer them with Robert Herman of the Applied Physics Laboratory at Johns Hopkins University. The work that Alpher and Herman did in cosmic microwave background radiation, or CMB radiation, in the months after "The Origin of Chemical Elements" was published was arguably more important than the original work. Alpher and Herman published a paper predicting that the explosive moment of creation would have released an "echo" that should still be present in today's universe as radio waves. Unfortunately, they did not push radio astronomers to look for these sounds and were completely ignored. Faced with the overwhelming lack of interest that greeted his work, Alpher brought his research program to a halt in 1953. He left academia and took a job as a researcher with General Electric. Alpher worked at the General Electric Research and

Development Center in Schenectady, New York, starting in 1955. He became a professor of physics and astronomy at Union College in 1986 and retired in 2004.

Alpher did enjoy some kudos for his work, however belated. Steven Weinberg, a Nobel laureate physicist at the University of Texas, acknowledged Alpher in his authoritative book *The First Three Minutes* (1977). Weinberg described Alpher's research as "the first thoroughly modern analysis of the early history of the universe." When Arno A. Penzias and Robert W. Wilson won a Nobel Prize in 1978 for their work with CMB radiation and radio waves, they had never even heard of Alpher. When it was brought to their attention how much their work resembled Alpher's, they used their Nobel acceptance speech to set the record straight. Alpher suffered a heart attack one month later and was dogged by ill health for the rest of his life. Alpher later recalled the pain of being the forgotten man of big bang science. "Was I hurt?" he said. "Yes! How the hell did they think I'd feel?" Alpher died of respiratory failure at an acute care facility in Austin. His wife died in 2004.

In July 2007 Alpher was honored with the National Medal of Science at a White House ceremony in which he was cited for "his unprecedented work" and "for his prediction that universe expansion leaves behind background radiation and for providing the model for the Big Bang theory." It seemed like a belated effort from the science community to acknowledge the "forgotten father of the Big Bang." Alpher was too ill to accept the award in person. His other belated awards include a Magellanic Premium from the American Philosophical Society (1975), a John Price Wetherill Medal from the Franklin Institute (1980), and a National Academy of Sciences Henry Draper Medal (1993). Alpher was a fellow of the American Physical Society and the American Academy of Arts and Sciences.

★

Alpher is featured prominently in Steven Weinberg, *The First Three Minutes: A Modern View of the Origin of the Universe* (1977), and Simon Singh, *Big Bang: The Origin of the Universe* (2004). Alpher spoke with *Discover* (July 1999) for a lengthy feature article. Obituaries are in the *Washington Post* (14 Aug. 2007), *New York Times* (18 Aug. 2007), and *Daily Telegraph* (30 Aug. 2007).

Brenna Sanchez

ALTMAN, Robert Bernard (*b.* 20 February 1925 in Kansas City, Missouri; *d.* 20 November 2006 in Los Angeles, California), film director known for his innovative style and his renegade stance toward the American filmmaking establishment.

Robert Altman, 1983. AP IMAGES

Altman was the oldest of three children and the only son of Bernard Clement "B. C." Altman, an insurance salesman with a roving eye, a taste for whiskey, and wild ways, and Helen (Mathews) Altman, a level-headed woman from Nebraska whose ancestors came to America on the *Mayflower*. To keep peace in the family, Altman's mother converted to her husband's Catholic faith and became a devout follower. Altman attended Catholic schools in Kansas City. He was an indifferent student but expressed an early interest in sound recording and was the only avid filmgoer in the extended Altman family. A rebellious youngster, Altman was sent to Lexington, Missouri, to Wentworth Military Academy, which he attended through junior college. After graduating from Wentworth, he attended the University of Missouri for three years. He preferred partying to studying, eventually becoming a hard drinker like his father, but his conduct improved enough for him to enlist in the Army Air Forces in 1943. After his discharge in 1947, Altman moved to Hollywood, California, with his first wife, LaVonne Elmer (with whom he had one child). He got sporadic work as an actor, wrote a musical aimed for Broadway, and collaborated on several

scripts for the B thrillers, among them *Christmas Eve* (1947) and *Bodyguard* (1948).

In 1950, discouraged at being unable to secure a place for himself in the film industry, Altman returned to Kansas City. He divorced his wife that same year and began to work for a local production outfit, the Calvin Company, where for five years he scripted, edited, and shot over sixty industrial, educational, advertising, and employee training shorts. Altman claimed that his work at Calvin gave him a solid foundation in filmmaking. His goal was to break into features, and while at Calvin he wrote the screenplay for a locally produced film, *Corn's-A-Poppin'* (1951). At the end of 1955 Altman divorced his second wife, Lotus Corelli (with whom he had two children), and returned to Los Angeles to try his luck once again. This time he began to get steady work, in television, where over the next fifteen years he compiled a sizable portfolio directing and occasionally writing scripts for such series as *Alfred Hitchcock Presents*, *The Whirlybirds*, *The Gale Storm Show*, *The Millionaire*, *The Detectives*, *The Roaring Twenties*, *Bonanza*, and *Combat!*

Despite having to adhere to the formulaic patterns of series television, Altman was able to hone his maverick tendencies, bending the rules whenever he could. He had many run-ins with producers and coworkers, but he also had a gift for attracting loyal followers who shared with him a commitment to hard work and a taste for debauchery. When all was going well, Altman was a convivial taskmaster and group leader. He was quick to sense betrayal or disaffection, however, and over the years he compiled an extensive enemies' list. One by one members of his inner circle were either banished or chose to leave. In 1959, after five years of frustrating work in the television factories where he continued to feel like an undervalued outsider, Altman married his third wife, Kathryn Reed, with whom he had two children. Against the odds of his turbulent, mercurial personality, he remained married to Reed for the rest of his life.

At the same time as he was regularly employed in television, Altman managed to write, produce, and direct an obscure teen drama, *The Delinquents* (1957), and to cowrite, coproduce, and codirect a documentary, *The James Dean Story* (1957); in the documentary Altman made striking use of still photographs, disguising the fact that he was unable to interview most of the people who had been close to the actor. It was not until 1968, when he directed *Countdown*, a routine drama about astronauts starring James Caan and Robert Duvall, that Altman graduated at last to A-list features. The next year he directed *That Cold Day in the Park* (1969), a quirky, fatalistic story of sexual obsession.

In 1969, when Altman was forty-four and after more than a dozen prominent directors had rejected the script, he was given the chance to make a film that changed his life. *M*A*S*H* (1970), an episodic, antiwar dark comedy about a mobile army surgical hospital in the Korean War, set the stylistic and thematic models for the remaining thirty-six years of the filmmaker's career. All of the elements that were to define his directorial signature—a roving, obsessively zooming camera; freewheeling, seemingly improvisational performances; a narrative structure that is no more than a series of sketches; a blurred, multi-leveled soundtrack with overlapping dialogue; a cynical dismissal of figures of authority—are fully in place. The film offers ample evidence of misogyny, but it is critical of men as well. From the outset Altman was not a humanist, and his first hit is a curmudgeonly dark comedy bristling with resentment. (Altman and his cocreators disdained the cozy, sentimental television series that was "inspired" by their film.)

By design the film is not well made. Indeed, it is an assault on the balance, order, and good taste of the classical Hollywood style. The gross humor, the fraternity boy pranks, the bloody or dismembered bodies in the unit's makeshift operating room, along with the film's antiauthority sassiness and its view of war as a comedy of errors and mismanagement reflect the youth-oriented counterculture of the time. The film has not aged well—it has come to seem smug, mean-spirited, and juvenile—but in its day it was a cultural phenomenon that anointed Altman as the leading renegade filmmaker in America.

From 1970 to 1975 Altman worked nonstop, turning out a series of consistently idiosyncratic and flawed anti-Hollywood films. Frequently his intention was to overturn traditional genres. *McCabe and Mrs. Miller* (1971) is a moody, ribald, "new" Western about a gambler and a prostitute; the film undermines the myths of the old-fashioned pioneer sagas. The unheroic McCabe (played by Warren Beatty, who fought bitterly with the director) is a compulsive gambler-entrepreneur killed by rivals; Mrs. Miller (played by Julie Christie, who adored Altman) is a tough-talking, dope-taking Cockney madam. The blurred soundtrack and muted color give the film a fresh, art-house patina. As is often the case in Altman's work, storytelling is trumped by atmosphere, landscape, and weather. (The film ends in a snowstorm that covers the new, rough-and-ready frontier town with a blinding white blanket.)

Based on a Raymond Chandler novel featuring the fictional detective Philip Marlowe, *The Long Goodbye* (1973) is another Altman deconstruction. Mumbling to his cat and to himself, and without a trace of the gumshoe's patented hard-boiled style, Elliott Gould plays against the grain of such earlier Marlowes as Humphrey Bogart and Dick Powell. He seems to live in a world of his own, cut off from the bright contemporary Hollywood-Malibu world in which the film is set. Altman, more concerned with capturing reflections in windows and the quality of light on the ocean at sunset, treats the plot in a casual way, and the film ends on a brazen note that would have offended Chandler's gentlemanly code:

Altman's Marlowe, unlike Chandler's, kills a former friend who has set him up.

Nashville (1975) ended the first phase of Altman's career on a bravura note. Although it was hailed at the time as a major work about post-Watergate America, a searing referendum on the disillusioned state of the nation, the film endures as a stylistic rather than a thematic tour de force. All of the director's tricks—the sprawling, anecdotal narrative that weaves together the interlocking fates of many characters, the zooming camera, and the overlapping sounds—are on commanding display. The film's "higher meaning" remains elusive, however, even semicoherent. Although there is a political campaign in the background (an unseen presidential candidate is trying to garner support from country music stars) and the film ends in the assassination of a performer, no clear political statement is articulated. Altman is the master conductor of an intricately layered composition, encouraging his actors to fill out their characters, to write some of their dialogue, and (for those who could) to compose and perform their own songs. Pausing frequently for extended performances, *Nashville* is a musical (or at least an Altman antimusical) that achieves the contours if not the content of a national epic. It is the maverick director's greatest, most audacious sleight of hand, a mock profound work of sound and fury signifying if not exactly nothing, then at least nothing very much.

The acclaim for *Nashville* emboldened the director in an unfortunate direction, and from 1976 to 1980, operating on an anything-goes basis, he turned out ill-conceived follies for which he was able to engage many talented collaborators. *Buffalo Bill and the Indians; or, Sitting Bull's History Lesson* (1976), in which an invented hero performs in a Wild West touring show, is a heavy-handed lampoon about show business mythmaking. Altman's next project, *3 Women* (1977), is a pretentious allegory of psychological breakdown and transference conjured from the dream of a director whose treatment of women angered many feminists. Altman nonetheless sustains a bewitching atmosphere. The film is beautifully photographed, in the California desert, and Sissy Spacek and Shelley Duvall, the kind of unusual anti–movie stars Altman always favored, give riveting performances.

A Wedding (1978), a superficial ensemble comedy with even more characters than *Nashville*, reveals the director's pleasure in dismantling the rituals and etiquette of social convention. During a wedding in a well-to-do family, the matriarch expires, and after the ceremony the new bride and groom are mistakenly assumed to have been killed in a car accident. Altman reached his lowest point in *Quintet* (1979), another dream-derived parable, about a game of death set in an imaginary ice age.

Following a series of commercial and artistic disappointments, Altman was hired by Disney to make *Popeye* (1980), a musical film of the "Popeye" cartoons. As his employers should have known, Altman, with no gift for light fantasy, was the wrong man for the job. The script, by Jules Feiffer, has an inapt Freudian-based story line in which Popeye searches for his father. The sets radiate Germanic gloom. Altman treats the songs in a distracting, fragmented style. On the other hand, the scratchy, unmusical voices of Robin Williams (Popeye) and Shelley Duvall (Olive Oyl) are beguiling.

The failure of *Popeye* sent the director into a professional limbo that lasted a dozen years. He returned to television, made an inauspicious debut as a Broadway director, and directed a number of low-budget films based on plays. Unlike his episodic, multistranded mosaics of the 1970s, his work in the 1980s was notably claustrophobic. *Come Back to the Five and Dime, Jimmy Dean, Jimmy Dean* (1982), a film version of the play he had directed on Broadway earlier in 1982, is confined to a dime store in a small town in Texas. *Streamers* (1983) is set in army barracks. *Secret Honor* (1984) remains in the study of Richard M. Nixon as the former president implodes. Although Altman was hard on his screenwriters, often detonating their original structure and dialogue, in his play adaptations he was scrupulously faithful to the playwrights. The films have a tight, controlled, curiously detached quality, as if Altman is marking time, behaving himself until he can grab the chance to return to a larger canvas.

In 1992, with *The Player*, a sharp but good-natured parody of Hollywood insiders that begins with a virtuoso eight-minute tracking shot, the director made a triumphant comeback. Though filled with such distractions as dozens of famous players in cameo appearances, the film has a stronger narrative than any other Altman production. This deft, accessible, richly entertaining pop thriller in which a paranoid producer kills the wrong man—a screenwriter he thinks is sending him poison pen letters—put Altman back on top. For the last fourteen years of his career, Altman continued to work in his usual energetic, hit-or-miss fashion.

Short Cuts (1993), set in Los Angeles and considered by many to be Altman's masterpiece, is a long, expansive, complexly constructed chronicle of a large, nonethnic group of unhappy, mostly unfaithful married couples whose lives intersect. Though based on stories by Raymond Carver, the cynical, misanthropic, observant film, alternately brilliant and strained, is quintessential Altman. *Ready to Wear* (1994), a satire of behind-the-scenes warfare at a Parisian fashion show, received some harsh criticism for its purported misogyny; the film ends with an antifashion statement—models appear nude on the runway—that was hailed as both daring and contemptible. Nonetheless Altman directs with panache; the frequent fashion shows, like the extended musical sequences in *Nashville*, retard the plot but are wonderfully diverting. In *Kansas City* (1996) Altman often ignores a routine gangster-movie story set in

the 1930s to linger on first-rate jazz performances in smoky rooms. Critics decried *Dr. T and the Women* (2000) as further evidence of the director's misogyny, but in fact the film presents Altman in a more forgiving and sweet-natured mood than any of his earlier work.

In 2001, in another remarkable act of "recovery," Altman directed a British country-house murder mystery in an elegantly subdued manner. His trademark overlapping dialogue, densely composed group shots, and restless camera choreography do not detract from the engrossing plot of *Gosford Park* and its immaculate performances. Altman's final film, *A Prairie Home Companion* (2006), about the (fictional) last show of the beloved radio program, has the physical confinement of the director's work of the 1980s, the extended musical interpolations of *Nashville* and *Kansas City*, and Altman's usual large ensemble cast. On the other hand, it has none of the anger, self-importance, or grandstanding of the films that had made Altman Hollywood's leading contrarian. His final film is his most evenhanded and affectionate, a small-scale valentine to a group of idiosyncratic performers who do not want to stop making music. At the age of eighty-one, Altman died of complications related to cancer. His remains were cremated.

In 2006 Altman, the perennial outsider, received an honorary Academy Award for his body of work, a fitting tribute for a director whose substantial corpus is stronger than any individual film. During his career Altman was among the most problematic and controversial of major American film directors. Although he had a distinct personal style, he was at the same time a remarkably guarded, impersonal director whose work is free of autobiographical references—unless the irritating, garrulous characters who reappear in his ensembles and who seem trapped in their own obsessions can be said to be reflections of Altman. Nonetheless, Altman had a singular talent, and he made a handful of films that are likely to be treasured by historians and cinephiles for generations to come.

★

Patrick McGilligan, *Robert Altman: Jumping off the Cliff: A Biography of the Great American Director* (1989), is the standard biography. An obituary is in the *New York Times* (21 Nov. 2006).

Foster Hirsch

ANDERSON, Robert Orville (*b.* 13 April 1917 in Chicago, Illinois; *d.* 2 December 2007 in Roswell, New Mexico), oil industry executive credited with discovering Alaska's vast Prudhoe Bay oil field, civic leader, and philanthropist.

Robert O. Anderson. MICHAEL MAUNEY/TIME LIFE PICTURES/ GETTY IMAGES

Anderson was the son of Hugo A. Anderson and Hilda (Nelson) Anderson, both immigrants from Sweden. A prominent banker, his father helped finance ventures by friends who were entrepreneurs in the oil business. Anderson often said that his father was the first American banker "who loaned money on oil in the ground." Anderson attended the University of Chicago's Laboratory Schools, from elementary through high school, and then enrolled in a two-year college program in economics at the university. His original career goal was to become an architect. However, intrigued by his father's stories of wildcatters (those who drill wells in land not known to contain oil) who discovered oil fields in Texas and Oklahoma, he spent his summers in that region working as a roughneck (a worker on a drilling crew). By the time he graduated with a BA from the University of Chicago in 1939, Anderson had decided to make his career in the oil business. On 25 August 1939 he married his college sweetheart, Barbara Herrick Phelps; they would have seven children.

Anderson first went to work as an assistant to the president of American Mineral Spirits Company, a subsidiary of Pure Oil. With a $50,000 loan from a family friend, in October 1941 he and his brothers bought a run-down oil refinery in Artesia, New Mexico. He later discovered that the loan had been guaranteed by his father. In a classic case of being in the right place at the right time, Anderson's refinery rode a wave of war-generated demand for all sorts of petroleum products, most notably gasoline. When he heard that the Army Air Corps was looking for supplies of ninety-one-octane aviation fuel, Anderson convinced officials that his refinery could meet their needs even though it had never before produced this type of fuel. Given a thirty-one-day deadline to produce the specified grade of fuel or lose the contract, Anderson and his refinery employees managed to deliver on time.

During the early 1940s and into the mid-1950s, Anderson acquired and improved a number of older refineries throughout the Southwest. He also built a regional pipeline. Eager to find new sources of crude oil, he began wildcatting in the region and in 1957 hit pay dirt with his discovery of the vast Empire-Abo oil field in southeastern New Mexico. This find propelled Anderson into the top ranks of America's independent oil producers.

In 1963 Anderson merged his company into the Philadelphia-based Atlantic Refining Company and became a director on Atlantic's board. In 1966 he was asked to take over as chairman and chief executive officer. In those roles he negotiated two mergers that significantly bolstered the company's position in the American oil industry. First came a merger in 1966 with Richfield Oil, the end result of which was the creation of ARCO. Shortly thereafter he engineered the newly merged company's acquisition of Sinclair Oil, making ARCO America's seventh-largest oil company.

Under Anderson's leadership, ARCO in 1968 announced the discovery of the Prudhoe Bay oil field on Alaska's North Slope, the largest oil field in North America. When ARCO's geologists were ready to give up on their explorations in the area following a series of unsuccessful wells, Anderson insisted that one more exploratory well be drilled. It was this final well that led to the discovery. ARCO and a handful of other oil companies partnered on construction of the 800-mile Trans-Alaska Pipeline from Prudhoe Bay south to Valdez on Prince William Sound. In another significant first, he negotiated a contract in 1982 with the Chinese government that permitted ARCO to begin exploratory drilling for oil in the South China Sea.

In addition to his involvement in the oil industry, Anderson maintained extensive farm and ranch holdings in New Mexico, Texas, and Colorado. Those holdings covered roughly a million acres and were rivaled only by the famed King Ranch in Texas. When he retired from ARCO in 1986, he organized an independent exploration company called Hondo Oil & Gas Company, named for the Hondo River that flowed near his home in Roswell. Anderson served as Hondo's chairman and chief executive officer from September 1986 until February 1994. He retired from Hondo in 1996. Hondo, unlike the successful ARCO, struggled to survive. Anderson said the company was hurt by the purchase of a second California refinery in 1988, not long before gasoline demand took a serious hit during the economic recession of 1990–1991. To make matters worse, prices for natural gas declined sharply during this same period.

Throughout his life Anderson was deeply involved in civic and philanthropic endeavors, showing particular interest in environmental matters. He helped to establish Worldwatch Institute, an independent research organization based in Washington, D.C., that monitors and analyzes critical global issues affecting the environment. Anderson also was involved in the London-based International Institute for Environment and Development and the John Muir Institute of the Environment in Davis, California. He was also very closely identified with the Aspen Institute, serving as its president from 1957 to 1963 and as chairman from 1963 to 1987. Under Anderson's leadership the institute reached a number of important milestones: hosting a conference on climate change as early as 1962, developing artist and scholar residency programs, and opening a branch on Maryland's Eastern Shore.

During his tenure as CEO at ARCO, Anderson ensured that the company was a conscientious corporate citizen of Los Angeles, the city in which it was headquartered. In what was perhaps its most noteworthy contribution, ARCO donated $3 million toward the construction of a new building at the Los Angeles County Museum of Art. While at ARCO, Anderson also persuaded the company's board to help bail out two failing publications, the *Observer*, a London newspaper, and *Harper's*, a magazine based in New York City. The University of New Mexico's Anderson School of Management is named in his honor.

Anderson died peacefully at his home in Roswell of complications from a fall. He was ninety years old. One of America's most influential oil industry executives, Anderson will be remembered as the man behind ARCO's discovery of the vast Prudhoe Bay oil field on Alaska's North Slope. He is also noted for his contributions as a philanthropist, civic leader, and environmentalist.

★

Three biographies provide information about Anderson's life: Kenneth Harris, *The Wildcatter: A Portrait of Robert O. Anderson* (1987); Jack Raymond, *Robert O. Anderson: Oilman/ Environmentalist and His Leading Role in the International Environmentalist Movement: A Monograph* (1988); and Paul E. Patterson, *Hardhat and Stetson: Robert O. Anderson, Oilman and Cattleman* (1999). Obituaries are in the *Los Angeles Times* (5 Dec. 2007) and *New York Times* (6 Dec. 2007).

Don Amerman

APPLE, Raymond Walter ("Johnny"), Jr. (*b.* 20 November 1934 in Akron, Ohio; *d.* 3 October 2006 in Washington, D.C.), journalist, gourmand, and bon vivant whose high-profile tenure at the *New York Times* spanned forty-three years.

Apple was raised in a traditional and prosperous mid-American family with his sister. He was the son of Raymond Walter Apple, who managed grocery stores in northern Ohio that were founded by his wife's family (the Albrechts), and Julia (Albrecht) Apple. Apple's father assumed that he would enter the family business, yet Apple was a precocious child who frequented the Akron library and discovered that reporters were actually paid to travel and to write about and analyze a wider world. Apple attended Western Reserve Academy, a coeducational high school in Hudson, Ohio, where his peers inevitably nicknamed him "Seed." At Western Reserve Academy, Apple reported on sports and edited the school's yearbook. Following graduation, Apple attended Princeton University, where he became the classic underachiever; he spent long hours at the *Daily Princetonian* and was expelled in 1956

R. W. ("Johnny") Apple. THE NEW YORK TIMES/REDUX

for neglecting his academic responsibilities. To his father's dismay, Apple worked at the *Wall Street Journal* and was committed to journalism even before he served in the U.S. Army from 1957 to 1959. In the military he wrote speeches at Fort Monroe, Virginia, and moonlighted at the *Newport News Daily Press*. Afterward, he continued his education at Columbia University, graduating in 1961 magna cum laude with an AB in history.

In 1961 Apple rejoined the *Wall Street Journal*, where he covered business and the civil rights movement, but he quickly switched jobs to write for the nighttime newscast on the National Broadcasting Company. He then became an on-air correspondent for the *Huntley-Brinkley Report*, where he won an Emmy (1963) for his reporting on civil rights. Although Apple won accolades for his television reporting about the civil rights movement, which he believed to be the most important story of his career, print journalism beckoned. In 1963 he joined the *New York Times* metropolitan staff. Apple was a "hustler"; he worked longer and harder than anyone else and produced an amazing total of seventy-three front-page bylines within his first year at the newspaper. He was a "185 pound, water-cooled, self-propelled, semi-automatic machine," whose brash, almost arrogant behavior alienated many colleagues.

Apple's "incredible enthusiasm" for every story made him the protégé of Abe Rosenthal, the *New York Times* metropolitan editor. Rosenthal sent the young reporter to Albany, New York, as the bureau chief, perhaps to test his fiery spirit. In his new position, Apple covered Robert F. Kennedy's 1964 senatorial campaign and established a personal tie with the candidate. It became part of Apple's legend to claim that he was the one who informed Kennedy of the assassination of Martin Luther King, Jr., in 1968.

In 1965 the *New York Times* sent Apple to Vietnam. In 1966 he became Saigon bureau chief, leading coverage of the Vietnam War. Apple spearheaded the media assault on official reporting of the war and also claimed personal participation in combat against the Vietcong. On 7 August 1967 Apple became the first reporter to call the conflict a "stalemate"; he also claimed that South Vietnam lacked "the commitment . . . to work for its own survival." His reporting made him a Pulitzer Prize finalist for the first time; he later admitted that his failure to ever win this award was his greatest journalistic disappointment. Apple's Vietnam reportage did win the George Polk Memorial Award and the Overseas Press Club Award, both in 1967. Also, the redoubtable journalist James Reston, whom Apple idolized as a teenager, acknowledged that Apple taught a generation how to cover the Vietnam War.

After his work in Saigon, Apple globe-trotted and reported on political matters for four decades. Nicknamed "Johnny," Apple became famous for having a packed black bag always prepared, his personal pepper mill inside, as the reporter was ever searching for a perfect meal. He served as the *New York Times* bureau chief in Lagos, Nigeria; Nairobi, Kenya; Moscow, USSR; and Washington, D.C.; and seemingly met almost everyone of political or cultural importance. His reporting was memorable, his writing distinctive, and he spent off-hours visiting the museums, cathedrals, and restaurants of his beat. His outsized personality, termed both "insufferable and irresistible," dominated Timothy Crouse's *Boys on the Bus* (1973), a rollicking analysis of the 1972 presidential race, one of the ten campaigns Apple covered for the *New York Times*. As the newspaper's national political correspondent, his desire to pursue the Watergate story (a political scandal that plagued President Richard Nixon's second term) was denied by his bosses as a "fixation." Subsequently, *New York Times* Watergate coverage consistently trailed that of the *Washington Post*, but Apple memorably made the Nixon administration declare that all previous explanations of the scandal were "inoperative." Since Apple recognized the potential power of caucus voting during the 1972 presidential campaign, he was able to predict the unexpected rise of Jimmy Carter in 1976. His analysis of the Carter phenomenon led *More*, a journalism review, to call Apple the "most powerful political reporter in the United States." Apple enormously enjoyed such praise but modestly termed it "excessive."

Apple's tenure as *New York Times* bureau chief in London, England, from 1976 to 1989 served as "fertilizer" for his later career. He continued to secure scoops, including the first American interview with British prime minister Margaret Thatcher, but his focus gradually shifted toward cultural and social reportage. In England he mastered the rules of cricket, bought a home in the Cotswolds, and used his post to visit the great restaurants of Europe. After his first marriage to Edith Smith (they had married on 1 October 1966) ended in divorce, he married Betsey Pinckney Brown on 14 July 1982, and she became his devoted traveling companion. Together they collected Arts and Crafts vases and shared memorable feasts. Apple was a man whose personality and bulk filled any room, and it was as jovial "global-dining correspondent" rather than political sage that he endeared himself to a generation of *New York Times* readers. His expense account became the object of both humor and envy, and *Apple's Europe, an Uncommon Guide* (1986) was an indispensable travel guide for many Americans.

As chief correspondent and later bureau chief in Washington, D.C., Apple continued to write front-page articles of political analysis for the rest of his career. However, his "on the road" columns—examining architecture, English gardens, Scotch whisky, "Philadelphia Phoods," or the painted monasteries of Bukovina—became his favorite genre. He announced in 1994 that he would no longer cover the U.S. Congress, where partisanship had replaced compromise. He had no desire to become a *New York Times* editor—he was a writer not a manager—and when he passed retirement age, the newspaper named him associate editor so that he could keep his byline. His seventieth birthday party for fifty friends in a bistro in Paris, France, quickly became part of his expanding legend. Even before the long-anticipated *Apple's America: The Discriminating Traveler's Guide to 40 Great Cities in the United States and Canada* was published in 2005, his friend Joseph Lelyveld, a *New York Times* executive, asserted that Apple had actually become the "person he was pretending to be." Doubtless, the correspondent would have been delighted that he transparently appeared as the character Jimmy Pomegranate in *Black and White and Dead All Over*, a murder mystery written by his former *New York Times* colleague John Darnton in 2008. Apple died suddenly of complications from thoracic cancer at age seventy-one.

Apple's journalistic output appears in more than forty years of *New York Times* columns. Also, many of his articles appeared in other publications, including *Esquire, Saturday Review,* and *New Statesman.* He also wrote the introduction to *The Tower Commission Report* (1987) and contributed to several anthologies on the Watergate scandal.

★

Apple's travel books, *Apple's Europe, an Uncommon Guide* (1986) and *Apple's America* (2005), include significant information about his life. Insights into his personality can be gained from Timothy Crouse, *Boys on the Bus* (1973), and videos of Apple's twenty-four appearances on the *Charlie Rose Show.* An obituary is in the *New York Times* (5 Oct. 2006).

George J. Lankevich

ARIZIN, Paul Joseph (*b.* 9 April 1928 in Philadelphia, Pennsylvania; *d.* 12 December 2006 in Springfield, Pennsylvania), professional basketball player and member of the Naismith Memorial Basketball Hall of Fame.

Arizin was one of two children of Roger Arizin, who was French and who worked as a mechanic for the Pennsylvania Railroad, and Ann (Galen) Arizin, who was of Irish ancestry and who was a homemaker. A devout Roman Catholic, Arizin was a good student and attended La Salle High School—one of the oldest high schools in Philadelphia—which shared a campus with La Salle College until the 1960s. Arizin tried at least once to make the high school team, but he was cut. Nevertheless, he was determined to play the game he loved, and he played on intramural, church, and independent leagues in high school and continued doing so when he enrolled as a college freshman at Villanova University in the fall of 1946. Many years later Arizin recalled playing in six or seven leagues at once, often playing two games in a day. He did so, he said, "because he loved to play." During this time he developed a jump shot, more by accident than by intent. Many games were played on dance floors that were slippery, and Arizin found that if he jumped, he could get a better look

Paul Arizin, 1996. **ANDREW D. BERNSTEIN/NBAE/GETTY IMAGES**

at the basket and be better balanced. The shot he created had a very low trajectory because he played in venues with relatively low ceilings. This shot would be his trademark for the rest of his career and was nearly unstoppable because of his six-feet, four-inch frame. Another "trademark" was his grunting and wheezing due to a chronic sinus problem.

Many of the leagues in which Arizin played were filled with servicemen who had just returned from World War II, and the competition was fierce. The coach Al Severance of Villanova, who would become the winningest coach in school history, spotted Arizin when Arizin's independent league team lost to Severance's Villanova squad. Severance asked Arizin to join the Villanova varsity team. Arizin played sporadically in the beginning of his sophomore year (at this time freshmen were not eligible for varsity play) before becoming the starting center in midseason and leading the team in scoring with 267 points in twenty-four games, an average of 10.1 points per game.

The next season (1948–1949) Arizin averaged 22 points per game, including an 85-point game against an armed forces squad. He was playing forward and guard, more than center, a position more suitable for his height. Villanova had a 22–4 record, losing to the eventual champion Kentucky in the first round of the eight-team National Collegiate Athletic Association Tournament. The Wildcats of Villanova defeated Yale for third in the East. Arizin scored 30 points against Kentucky and 22 points against Yale.

In 1949–1950 Arizin led the nation in scoring, with 25.3 points per game and 735 points; he was named College Player of the Year by the *Sporting News*. In 1950 he graduated with honors from Villanova with a BS in accounting. He was then drafted, as a territorial pick, by the Philadelphia Warriors of the newly formed National Basketball Association (NBA). Arizin led a turnaround for the Warriors from a 26–42 record to a 40–26 record and first place in the Eastern Division of the NBA. Arizin scored 17.2 points per game, second on the team, and led with 9.8 rebounds per game. The Warriors lost to Syracuse in the first round of the playoffs.

The next year (1951–1952) Arizin led the NBA in eight categories, including minutes played, scoring average, and points. In one overtime game Arizin played sixty-three minutes, a record that stood for forty years. He also was the Most Valuable Player (MVP) of the All-Star game, but the Warriors finished with just a .500 record and lost in the first round of the playoffs. On 18 October 1952 Arizin married Maureen McAdams. They had five children, four sons and a daughter.

During these early years of the NBA, Arizin's jump shot became a model for players entering the league. Before the start of the NBA season in 1952–1953, Arizin enlisted in the U.S. Marines and fought in the Korean War, missing two seasons, but he did play service ball for the Quantico Marines, where he was voted Inter-Service MVP in 1954. He returned for the 1954–1955 season to average 21 points per game, second on his team and second in the league to Neil Johnston. Nevertheless, the Warriors again finished under .500 and failed to make the playoffs. In the 1955–1956 season Arizin averaged 24.2 points per game, second in the league; Johnston averaged 22.1; and the other three starters all averaged in double figures as the Warriors put together the best record in the NBA (45–27). They then beat Syracuse and Fort Wayne to win the NBA championship. Arizin averaged 28.9 points per game in the playoffs.

The next year Arizin led the league in scoring for the second time (25.6 points per game), but the Warriors finished third in the division and were eliminated in the first round of the playoffs. Arizin continued to average more than 20 points per game, but the Warriors remained a .500 club until 1959–1960, when Wilt Chamberlain joined the team.

For the next three years the Warriors were one of the top teams in the league, but they could never advance beyond the first round of the playoffs because of meeting and losing to the great Boston Celtics teams led by Bill Russell. Arizin became the fastest player (up to that time) to score 10,000 points and the third to score 15,000 career points. In 1962 Arizin retired (with a lifetime scoring average of 22.8 points per game) rather than move to the West Coast as the Warriors franchise relocated to San Francisco. Arizin became a full-time employee of IBM, where he worked for more than twenty-five years. For the first three of those years he also played and starred in the Eastern Professional Basketball Association for the Camden (New Jersey) Bullets, leading them to the 1964 league title.

Arizin was three times All-NBA first team, was a ten-time All-Star, and was selected to the NBA's Fiftieth Anniversary team of all-time greatest players in 1996. In 1978 he was inducted into the Naismith Memorial Basketball Hall of Fame. Arizin died in his sleep at his home in Springfield at the age of seventy-eight. He is buried in Saints Peter and Paul Cemetery in Springfield.

★

There are no biographies of Arizin. A lengthy and informative obituary is in the *Philadelphia Inquirer* (14 Dec. 2006).

Murry R. Nelson

ARNOLD, Richard Edward ("Eddy") (*b.* 15 May 1918 in Henderson, Tennessee; *d.* 8 May 2008 in Cool Springs, Tennessee), baritone singing star who sold over 85 million recordings during his seven-decade career.

Arnold was born to William Arnold, a dirt farmer, and Georgia (Wright) Arnold, a farm wife; Eddy Arnold was the last of four surviving children. Sometime after Arnold's father died on the boy's eleventh birthday, at the outset of the Great Depression, the family was forced to sell their farm at auction and to become tenant farmers on their own

Eddy Arnold. MICHAEL OCHS ARCHIVES/GETTY IMAGES

land. By the time sixteen-year-old Arnold dropped out of Pinson High School to work on the farm, he was performing at church and other community gatherings and had earned a local reputation as a fine singer. In 1937 Arnold struck out for Jackson, Tennessee, to pursue a career in music.

Almost immediately, Arnold landed a singing gig with a local country band with its own show on radio station WTJS. The pay was small but he took additional work at a funeral home to supplement his income. In 1938 the band moved to Memphis and radio station WMPS. Two years later, in January 1940, Arnold left Memphis for Nashville, Tennessee, the country music capital of the United States, to join the accordionist Pee Wee King and his famous Golden West Cowboys. It was the first big break of his young career.

Arnold played for three years with the King band, performing on radio station WMS on the *Grand Ole Opry* show, as well as performing with the nationally broadcast program's touring company. Calling himself the "Tennessee Plowboy," Arnold learned a great deal about the music business during these early years with Pee Wee King. On 28 November 1941 Arnold married Sally Gayhart. Two years later, he quit the Golden West Cowboys and assembled his own backup band. He remained with WSM and in 1944 was given his own segment on the *Opry*.

Exempt from military service in World War II because he was supporting both his wife and mother, Arnold saw his singing career blossom. He enjoyed more solo air time and in late 1943 negotiated a recording contract with RCA Victor. His first record, 1944's "Mommy, Please Stay Home with Me," sold 85,000 copies for the Bluebird label. Arnold's singing style was unusual for the country music of the day—a high baritone timbre instead of the more common nasal twang—and from the earliest days of his recording career he was popular among listeners of all ages. A string of hits followed: "That's How Much I Love You" (1946), "Bouquet of Roses" (1947), "Anytime" (1947), and "I'll Hold You in My Heart," this last remaining at number one on the *Billboard* charts for twenty-one weeks in 1947 and 1948. Under the shrewd management of "Colonel" Thomas A. Parker (with whom Arnold signed on in the fall of 1945 and who also oversaw the career of Elvis Presley), Arnold became RCA Victor's best-selling recording artist and a frequent guest on numerous radio programs. By the time he left the *Grand Ole Opry* in 1948, Arnold had become a household name.

His first television appearance was on *The Milton Berle Show* in 1949. Throughout the 1950s and 1960s Arnold guest starred on variety and talk shows such as *The Ed Sullivan Show*, *The Dean Martin Show*, and *Tonight Show*. From 1955 to 1957 he hosted *Eddy Arnold Time* on the Columbia Broadcasting System. In 1950 he even appeared as a "cowboy crooner" in two moderately successful films for Columbia Pictures, *Feudin' Rhythm* and *Hoedown*.

The mid-1950s, however, saw a shift in listening tastes away from country music and toward folk, rock and roll, and pop. In response, the canny Arnold abandoned the steel guitar and fiddle accompaniment that had been his staple and began recording with soft guitars, a string bass, and a harmonizing vocal group behind him. In public performance he left behind his string tie and Western wear for a business suit or tuxedo. His shift was successful. As one music critic wrote, "Arnold is bringing country music out of the hills and giving it a dressed-up universal appeal." Thus was born the more urbane "Nashville sound" that disappointed country music purists but that brought lushly orchestrated country ballads to a wider audience.

In the mid-1960s Arnold toured the United States with his seventeen-piece orchestra, traveling from the New York World's Fair (1964) to Carnegie Hall (1966) to the Coconut Grove in Los Angeles (1967). When his recording of "Make the World Go Away" topped the country charts and hit the Top Ten on the pop charts in 1965, he was firmly back on top. In 1966 Arnold was elected to the Country Music Hall of Fame, despite the protests of some critics who believed that he had moved too far from true country music to merit the honor. Arnold continued to tour and record, his last album, *After All These Years*, appearing in 2005. After a bad fall at his home, he died in a nursing facility two months after his wife. A public memorial for Arnold was held at the famous Ryman Auditorium in Nashville on 14 May 2008. He is buried in Woodlawn Memorial Park in Nashville.

As a pioneer of the crossover "countrypolitan" sound, Arnold was a relaxed, genial performer with a crooning, mellow style and a desire to reach the widest possible audience. During his decades-long career, he scored 148 charted country hits (thirty-seven of which also made it onto the pop charts) and reached the Top Ten in *Billboard* an amazing ninety-two times, hitting number one twenty-eight times.

★

Arnold's autobiography, *It's a Long Way from Chester County* (1969), is a pleasant read. For a complete treatment of Arnold's life and career, there is Michael Streissguth, *Eddy Arnold: Pioneer of the Nashville Sound* (1997), and Don Cusic, *Eddy Arnold: I'll Hold You in My Heart* (1997). For recording minutiae, Michael D. Freda, *Eddy Arnold: Discography, 1944–1996* (1997), is the authoritative source.

Michael Meckna

ARPINO, Gennaro Peter Arthur ("Gerald") (*b.* 14 January 1923 on Staten Island, New York; *d.* 29 October 2008 in Chicago, Illinois), dancer, cofounder, and chief choreographer for the Joffrey Ballet and a creative, exuberant popularizer of twentieth-century American ballet.

Gerald Arpino, 2006. AP IMAGES

Arpino was the youngest of nine children. His parents were Anna Santanastasio and Luigi Arpino. His father died when Arpino was seven, having lost most of his real estate and beauty salon holdings on Staten Island in the Depression. Arpino graduated from Port Richmond High School and entered Wagner College in 1940, though he quit two years later to join the U.S. Coast Guard.

In Seattle in 1945 he met Robert Joffrey, who was just then in the midst of a ballet class taught by Ivan Novikoff, an émigré from the Soviet Union. Arpino, instantly fascinated by both ballet and the young Joffrey, joined the class and later that year followed Joffrey when he went to study with the dance instructor Mary Ann Wells. Years after, Arpino said that it was from these two passions that the Joffrey Ballet company emerged. "Our company [was] born of our relationship. We became entwined in each other's desires to . . . see what American dance was about."

Wells instructed both young men in classical ballet and other forms of dance and encouraged them to experiment with choreography. Not long after, Wells urged them to study in New York, and in 1948—by which time Arpino had been discharged from the Coast Guard—he and Joffrey did just that, moving to New York for the summer session of George Balanchine's School of American Ballet and then to study with the dancers Gertrude Schurr and May O'Donnell. By 1951 Arpino was appearing as a soloist on and off

Broadway, and Joffrey had decided to form a ballet troupe with Arpino as a principal dancer. By 1953 they had founded the American Ballet Center as a feeder school, where Arpino also taught. In 1954 the Robert Joffrey Ballet debuted at New York's 92nd Street Young Men's–Young Women's Hebrew Association (Y).

In 1955 Columbia Artists Management approached Joffrey and suggested that his troupe tour under the auspices of Columbia's Community Concerts Series, and in 1956 the company—now the Robert Joffrey Theatre Dancers—set off on a five-week tour with Arpino as its lead dancer. Although at the time Arpino was not considered the troupe's cofounder, he made it patently clear that he did not agree. "Without one or the other of us, I don't think [the company] would have been manifested."

The company continued touring with Columbia for several years. By 1959 Arpino's dancing had become less showy and more mature. He also had begun "playing" with choreography, though it was only when his own early ballets, *Partita for 4* and *Ropes*, were performed at the 92nd Street Y in 1961 that critics began to take his choreography seriously. Following a serious accident in 1962, when he was dropped from a fair height, fell down steps, and broke and fractured parts of his lower spine, he seldom danced again, and soon became the company choreographer, creating such pieces as *Nightwings* (1966), *The Clowns* (1968), *Trinity* (1970), *Kettentanze* (1971), *Suite Saint-Saens* (1978), *Light Rain* (1981), *Round of Angels* (1983), and *Ruth: Ricordi Per Due* (2004). He also produced the successful rock ballet *Billboards* in 1993. Arpino was the first choreographer commissioned to create a ballet to honor the office of the president of the United States. He received a Dance Magazine Award in 1974 and honorary doctorates from Wagner College in 1992 and the College of Staten Island–City University of New York in 2001.

Robert Joffrey died in 1988, having named Arpino artistic director. By 1990 the company was undergoing one of its periodic bouts of financial distress and board conflict. Some of its board members wanted to remove Arpino from control. This led to a public controversy, with Arpino resigning and taking his and Joffrey's choreographies with him. His resignation was not accepted, however, and he retained directorship of the company. Continued financial concerns, though, prompted Arpino to permanently relocate the organization from New York to Chicago in 1995. In 2003 the director Robert Altman used Joffrey and Arpino as inspiration for his film *The Company*. In 2007 Arpino at last relinquished the title of director and became artistic director emeritus.

Arpino died, possibly of complications from prostate cancer. A memorial service was held for him at the Joffrey Tower in Chicago.

A handsome, dark-eyed, dark-haired man, Arpino was loved by most of those who worked with him. Many of his choreographies, like his personality and his dancing, were flamboyant and passionate. They were also very fast paced, his dancers styling themselves as the "Joffrey Jets." Other pieces, however, were brooding and mystical to suit the more solemn aspects of his personality, but all were composed with much help from the performers involved. As the dancer Pamela Johnson wrote when he died, "he made us reach far beyond ourselves to provide the animation and spirit to his mercurial, choreographic and creative genius." Several of his works, such as *The Clowns*, addressed modern social issues. At the time of his death, his nearly fifty choreographies represented more than one-third of the Joffrey canon.

Nevertheless, there was always some controversy among established critics about Arpino's work. Some were offended by what they regarded as its showmanship and trendiness, though the choreographer William Forsythe maintained that it was "extraordinarily well crafted and musical, way ahead of the garde who were principally choreographing ballet at the time." More important was that it accomplished one of the original criteria of the company vision. Christian Holder, a former Joffrey dancer, wrote that Arpino's dances "converted people who were not normally enamored of ballet into fans." Echoing this, the dance writer Anna Kisselgoff, writing in the *New York Times*, called Arpino "a very important choreographer" whose accessibility often "seduced" newcomers into loving ballet. William Como, in *Dance Magazine*, agreed: Joffrey and Arpino had "captured the imagination of a new, previously untapped audience, creating a love for ballet where none had existed. I cannot think of anything more important than that."

★

Some biographical information can be found in William Como, "Celebrating the Joffrey," *Dance Magazine* (Nov. 1981). The most complete biographical source to date is Sasha Anawalt, *The Joffrey Ballet: Robert Joffrey and the Making of an American Dance Company* (1996). The Kennedy Center's biography of Arpino, "About the Artist" (2004), is a reasonable fact sheet. A series of articles in the Arts section of the *New York Times* (May 1990) describes Arpino's argument with the Joffrey Board. Obituaries are in the Joffrey Ballet Chicago's official weblog, "J Pointe" (29 Oct. 2008), the *New York Times* (30 Oct. 2008), and the *Independent* (8 Nov. 2008).

Sandra Shaffer VanDoren

ASTOR, (Roberta) Brooke Russell (*b.* 30 March 1902 in Portsmouth, New Hampshire; *d.* 13 August 2007 in Briarcliff Manor, New York), thrice-married socialite, philanthropist, and writer; long-lived, witty, and energetic grande dame famed for her elegance, generosity, and joie de vivre.

Brooke Astor, 1997. © GREGORY PACE/CORBIS

Astor was the only child of John Henry Russell, Jr., a rear admiral's son and career naval officer who eventually became commandant of the Marine Corps, and Mabel (Howard) Russell, from a socially well-connected Washington, D.C., family. During her father's absence on sea duty, Astor spent her first three years in her grandmother's house. Much of her childhood was peripatetic, as her father's career took his family to Hawaii; Panama; Newport, Rhode Island; and from 1910 to 1913 to Beijing, China, where he commanded the American legation's guard. Astor's three years in China left her vivid memories of an exotic but turbulent country and of life in international diplomatic circles, where her witty, flirtatious, and attractive mother quickly became prominent. Astor adored her sometimes austere father, crediting him with teaching her discipline, endurance, and integrity, while Mabel Russell made her daughter a voracious reader, encouraging her to explore books that would challenge and stretch her mind and to keep a diary. After returning to Washington, D.C., in 1914, by way of Singapore, Hong Kong, Paris, and London, Astor attended the select Miss Madeira's School and then became a boarder at the Holton-Arms School, leaving in the summer of 1918.

A chance invitation to a Princeton senior prom introduced Astor, then sixteen, to graduating senior (John) Dryden Kuser, the well-read only son of a self-made millionaire and grandson of a U.S. senator. Kuser and his wealthy parents—who hoped the charming and well-mannered though inexperienced Astor would stabilize their erratic, hard-drinking son—paid court to Astor and her mother, who consented to the match while Astor's father was away in Latin America. The marriage, a major event on the Washington, D.C., social calendar, took place with great fanfare in April 1919 but almost immediately proved unhappy. After a disastrous honeymoon—"Dryden was oversexed and completely inexperienced, and I was hopelessly ignorant and unprepared," the bride recalled—Kuser soon took refuge in alcohol and infidelity, abusing his wife emotionally and physically and even breaking her jaw when she was six months pregnant in 1924 with their only child, Anthony. Naturally resilient and cocooned in what she later recalled as the greatest luxury she ever enjoyed, Astor chose to lead a largely separate life, frequenting literary and cultural circles, writing columns for *Vogue* and the *Pictorial Review*, and enjoying her own flirtations and affairs.

The death of his domineering father in 1929 emboldened Kuser to seek a divorce. His ex-wife settled in a stylish Gracie Square apartment in New York City, taking writing courses at Columbia University and enjoying an active social life in which theatrical and literary people featured prominently. In April 1932 she married Charles "Buddie" Marshall, a popular and respected stockbroker eleven years older than herself whom she had known well before her divorce, who finally decided to leave his wife and two children for her. Astor always claimed Marshall was the great love of her life. Anthony Kuser later took his stepfather's surname. Radiantly attractive rather than beautiful, Astor entertained extensively. Until 1939 the Marshalls rented an Italian summer house, the Castello, traveling widely in Europe while maintaining a New York apartment and, from 1935, a house at Tyringham, near Lenox, Massachusetts. During World War II Astor did volunteer work with paraplegic war veterans. In 1946 she became features editor at the Condé Nast magazine *House and Garden*. Astor's marriage to Marshall lasted until he died suddenly of a heart attack in November 1952.

Marshall's unexpected death left his devastated widow financially insecure. In October 1953 she became the third wife of Vincent Astor, heir to a New York real estate fortune, whose father died on the *Titanic*. His grandmother, Caroline Backhouse Astor, had dominated late nineteenth-century New York high society. Her difficult and reclusive grandson, already in poor health, proved a demanding, possessive husband who disliked large-scale entertaining, though he was devoted to his nieces and Brooke Astor's twin grandsons. The couple shuttled among luxurious homes in New York City; Rhinebeck on Hudson, New York; Arizona; and Maine, while Brooke Astor sat on several philanthropic

boards. She apparently made her curmudgeonly spouse's final years happy. The childless Vincent Astor died of heart failure in February 1959, leaving half his fortune, around $67 million, in trust to his widow, and the remainder to the Vincent Astor Foundation he had established in 1948 for "the alleviation of human misery."

The energetic, vital, Brooke Astor, who swam a daily thousand strokes whenever she visited her country homes and well into her nineties loved dancing, was soon a fixture in top New York social, political, and cultural circles, particularly close to the brothers Nelson, Laurance, and David Rockefeller; the banker Douglas Dillon; and the former secretary of state Henry Kissinger. She became identified with the Astor Foundation, of which she took control, eventually giving away almost $200 million in foundation funds and more from her own resources, directed mostly within New York City, to both its major cultural institutions, especially the New York Public Library, and facilities for the poor and disadvantaged. Always elegantly dressed and often accompanied by her adored dogs, she visited every grant recipient, sometimes repeatedly. Economically administered by minimal staff, the foundation was considered a model small philanthropic organization, whose relatively modest grants often paved the way for other, larger donations. Astor also published two not entirely reliable memoirs and two novels. As her energy gradually declined with age, in 1997 she decided to close the foundation, distributing its remaining assets to past grant recipients.

The 2002 celebrations of Astor's hundredth birthday were relatively restrained, since her health and memory were failing. In 2006 her grandson Philip Marshall took his father, Anthony—her legal guardian—to court, alleging that he kept his mother isolated in her New York apartment and deprived of basic comforts, accusations that David Rockefeller, Kissinger, and Astor's longtime close friend Annette de la Renta endorsed. De la Renta was appointed guardian, replacing Astor's son, who soon faced criminal charges of fraud and misappropriation of his mother's assets, still unresolved in late 2008. Astor, suffering from Alzheimer's, returned to her Hudson Valley estate, Holly Hill, in Briarcliff Manor, where she died of pneumonia. After a funeral service at Saint Thomas Church, New York City, she was buried beside her third husband at Sleepy Hollow Cemetery, New York. Her epitaph reads: "I had a wonderful life." Tributes after her death mourned the passing of a unique, legendary New York icon, a monument in her own lifetime who embodied a bygone era's style and discipline.

★

Many of Astor's own papers were apparently shredded by her son before her death. The New York Public Library, one of her major philanthropic beneficiaries, holds the Vincent Astor Foundation archive. She published two memoirs, *Patchwork*

Child: Early Memories (1962; rev. ed., 1993) and *Footprints* (1980). There are also elements of autobiography in her two novels, *The Bluebird Is at Home* (1965) and *The Last Blossom on the Plum Tree: A Period Piece* (1986). Full-length biographies include Frances Kiernan, *The Last Mrs. Astor: A New York Story* (2007; with new afterword, 2008); and Meryl Gordon, *Mrs. Astor Regrets: The Hidden Betrayals of a Family beyond Reproach* (2008). Notable profiles include Brendan Gill, "A Party for Brooke," the *New Yorker* (21 Apr. 1997); and John Richardson, "The Battle for Mrs. Astor," *Vanity Fair* (Oct. 2008). The activities of the Astor Foundation are covered in Waldemar A. Nielsen, *The Big Foundations* (1972); and *The Vincent Astor Foundation: 1948–1997* (1998). Obituaries are in the *New York Times* (13 Aug. 2007); *Washington Post* (14 Aug. 2007); the *Times* (London) and *Independent* (both 15 Aug. 2007); and the *Daily Telegraph* (18 Aug. 2007).

Priscilla Roberts

AUERBACH, Arnold Jacob ("Red") (*b.* 20 September 1917 in New York City; *d.* 28 October 2006 in Washington, D.C.), basketball coach, general manager, and president who led the Boston Celtics to a record nine National Basketball Association (NBA) titles and retired as the winningest coach in NBA history.

Auerbach was the second of four children born to Hyman Auerbach, a Russian immigrant and founder of a dry-cleaning business, and Marie (Thompson) Auerbach, a cashier. Auerbach captained the handball and basketball teams his senior year at Eastern District High School in Brooklyn in New York City, making the all-Brooklyn second basketball team. He served as senior class president before graduating in 1935.

Auerbach played basketball at Seth Low Junior College in Brooklyn before William Reinhardt, coach for George Washington University in Washington, D.C., persuaded Auerbach to play for his team. Auerbach played guard for three seasons at George Washington, directing its fast-break offense to a 38–19 composite win-loss mark. He led the Colonials in scoring his senior year and earned a BS in physical education in 1940.

In 1940–1941 Auerbach coached basketball at Saint Albans Preparatory School in Washington, D.C., and in 1941 he earned an MA in education from George Washington. He married Dorothy Lewis on 5 June 1941 and had two daughters. Auerbach spent the next year at Roosevelt High School in Washington, D.C., where he taught history and hygiene and coached basketball and baseball. He entered the U.S. Navy in May 1943 and was stationed at Norfolk Naval Air Station in Virginia before his discharge as an ensign in 1946.

Arnold ("Red") Auerbach, 1977. PICTORIAL PARADE/GETTY IMAGES

The Washington Capitols of the newly formed Basketball Association of America named Auerbach as head coach in 1946, signing him to a $5,000 one-year contract. Auerbach coached Washington for three seasons, guiding the team to an impressive 123–62 mark, including playoff games. He deliberately kept one of his top five players out of the starting lineup and inserted him when the opponents began tiring. In Auerbach's first season the Capitols won forty-nine of sixty games, including twenty-nine of thirty home games; they won the first fifteen contests in his final campaign. Auerbach resigned because the owner Mike Uline declined his request for a three-year contract.

After briefly serving as assistant basketball coach at Duke University, Auerbach became head coach of the Tri-Cities Blackhawks of the NBA in 1949. The Blackhawks finished only 29–35 in Auerbach's lone season there. Auerbach resigned when the owner Ben Kerner traded a player without consulting him.

In April 1950 the Boston Celtics of the NBA designated Auerbach as head coach. Auerbach built the Celtics into the most dominant franchise in NBA history. The Boston media wanted him to draft the popular Holy Cross all-American guard Bob Cousy in 1950, but Auerbach selected the center Charlie Share instead. When the Chicago Stags folded shortly thereafter, Cousy ended up with the Celtics in a dispersal draft. Cousy provided Boston with an excellent playmaker to initiate a running game. The Celtics became a high-powered offense with Cousy, Bill Sharman at guard, and Ed Macauley at center, but the team needed a strong defensive rebounder and shot blocker to start the fast break. Boston lacked the defensive skills to become an NBA champion.

Auerbach realized that the center Bill Russell, who led the University of San Francisco to two straight National College Athletic Association championships, was the type of player Boston needed to make his fast-break offense work. Russell, a stellar rebounder and shot blocker, could sweep the defensive boards and deliver quick outlet passes to a streaking Cousy. Auerbach traded the high-scoring veteran Macauley and Cliff Hagan to the St. Louis Hawks for draft rights to Russell. The acquisition of Russell converted the high-scoring Celtics into a strong defensive team. During the 1956 draft Auerbach also selected the future Hall of Famers Tom Heinsohn and K. C. Jones. Russell and Heinsohn combined with Cousy and Sharman to make the Celtics one of the most formidable units in NBA history. Heinsohn eventually gave way to Tom Sanders and John Havlicek, while K. C. Jones and Sam Jones replaced Cousy and Sharman.

Boston dominated the NBA, winning eleven NBA championships over the next thirteen seasons. In 1957 the Celtics took the first of nine NBA titles under Auerbach. Boston captured eight consecutive NBA crowns from 1959 through 1966. No professional coach won as many titles in such a short time. During the thirteen-year span, the Celtics averaged fifty-five victories per season, never lost more than seven home contests in any single season, and consistently maintained a winning percentage well above .600. Under Auerbach the Celtics capitalized on a high-scoring backcourt, a strong defense, and a tough rebounding front line. Seven members of the 1960–1961 aggregate, including all five starters, eventually made the Naismith Memorial Basketball Hall of Fame.

Auerbach firmly controlled the Celtics and did not employ assistant coaches. He stressed the team concept and balanced scoring as opposed to individual stardom, never boasting an NBA scoring leader. Auerbach instilled in his players an intense desire to win and implored them to communicate with teammates. He masterfully recruited veteran NBA players who blended well with his team concept. He considered the team-oriented Russell superior to the more individualistic, high-scoring Wilt Chamberlain.

Auerbach ranked among the least popular coaches with fans, the media, rival players, and fellow coaches because of his assertive on-court behavior. He frequently baited referees and sometimes had himself ejected to motivate his team.

When his teams had clinched wins, he often alienated opponents and their fans by lighting up his victory cigar.

Auerbach retired as coach in February 1966, having compiled 938 wins and 479 losses during twenty regular seasons and ninety-nine wins and seventy losses in the playoffs. He became the first NBA head coach to record 1,000 career victories, and he mentored eleven consecutive NBA East All-Star squads. Auerbach was named NBA Coach of the Year in 1965 and was elected to the Naismith Memorial Basketball Hall of Fame in 1968. In 1978 a blue-ribbon panel selected him the NBA Silver Anniversary Coach. Two years later the Professional Basketball Writers Association of America named Auerbach the greatest coach in the history of the NBA. In 1996 an elite group of basketball experts named him one of the ten greatest coaches in NBA history. Having assumed the front-office position of general manager of the Celtics in 1964, Auerbach continued in that capacity after retiring as head coach. He selected Russell to succeed him in that position. Russell led Boston to NBA titles in 1968 and 1969 before resigning. Auerbach rebuilt the Celtics in the 1970s, naming Heinsohn as head coach and drafting the center-forward Dave Cowens. Heinsohn directed Boston to NBA titles in 1974 and 1976.

Auerbach, named NBA Executive of the Year in 1980, erected another formidable team in the 1980s by acquiring perhaps the strongest forecourt in NBA history to that point. In 1978 he drafted Larry Bird, arguably the most popular and talented player in the Celtics' franchise history. The Indiana State University star was only a junior and could not join the Celtics until 1979. During the 1980 draft, Auerbach sent the veteran Bob McAdoo to the Detroit Pistons for a number-one draft pick and traded that selection to the Golden State Warriors for the veteran center Robert Parish and another draft choice. Auerbach picked the power forward Kevin McHale of the University of Minnesota. Auerbach possessed exceptional ability to acquire gifted players. Bird, Parish, and McHale embellished Auerbach's legacy, leading Boston to NBA championships in 1981, 1984, and 1986. Bird rivaled Earvin "Magic" Johnson of the Los Angeles Lakers as the premier NBA superstar for over a decade. Auerbach appeared to solidify the Celtics' dominance by drafting Len Bias of the University of Maryland as the second pick in 1986, but the All-American died two days later of a cocaine overdose.

Auerbach served as general manager of the Celtics from 1964 until 1984 and then was president of the club. The Celtics won an unprecedented sixteen NBA titles during his stints as coach and general manager but did not capture any championships after 1986. Auerbach recruited some of the sport's best team-oriented and championship-driven players, molding exceptional individual talent into his team concept. His acquisitions of Cousy, Heinsohn, Russell, Sam Jones, K. C. Jones, Cowens, Bird, and McHale staked his indelible claim to fame. Auerbach died of a heart attack at age eighty-nine. He is buried in King David Memorial Garden in Falls Church, Virginia.

Auerbach left many major legacies. He helped the NBA lower racial barriers, recruiting the highest percentage of black participants in professional sports. Chuck Cooper of Duquesne University joined the Celtics in 1950 as one of the first African-American NBA players and was followed by Russell, Sam Jones, K. C. Jones, Satch Sanders, and Willie Naulls in the 1950s and 1960s. In 1965 the Celtics featured the NBA's first all-black starting five. Several Celtics drew upon Auerbach's leadership skills to coach NBA teams. Russell, Heinsohn, Sanders, Cowens, K. C. Jones, and Don Cheney later coached the Celtics, while Cousy, Sharman, Don Nelson, and Bird coached other NBA clubs. Still others coached college teams. Auerbach also conducted numerous clinics abroad for the U.S. State Department, spreading the NBA internationally.

★

Auerbach's publications include *Winning the Hard Way* (1966), with Paul Sann; *Basketball for the Player, the Fan, and the Coach* (1975); *Red Auerbach: An Autobiography* (1977), with Joe Fitzgerald; and *On and Off the Court* (1985), also with Fitzgerald. The best biography of Auerbach is Dan Shaughnessy, *Seeing Red: The Red Auerbach Story* (1994). Informative articles include Frank Deford, "A Man for All Seasons," *Sports Illustrated* (15 Feb. 1982), and Irv Goodman, "The Winning Ways of Red Auerbach," *Sport* (Mar. 1965). Obituaries are in the *New York Times* and *Boston Globe* (both 29 Oct. 2006).

David L. Porter

AVIS, Warren Edward (*b.* 8 April 1915 in Bay City, Michigan; *d.* 24 April 2007 in Ann Arbor, Michigan), founder of Avis Rent-A-Car and head of other commercial enterprises.

Avis grew up in a town near the center of the American automobile industry. His father worked for a lumber company. As a young man Avis investigated car dealerships for fraudulent inventories and also worked on commission for a drug firm before becoming a bomber pilot during World War II. He carried a motorcycle in the bomb bay so he would have a way to get around at his destination. Having risen to the rank of major in the Army Air Force, after the war he became a partner in a Ford dealership in the Detroit area.

 As a frequent air traveler who was annoyed at having to wait for taxis at airports, he decided to address the problem of the lack of ground transportation for arriving airline passengers. Avis set out to create an airport car-rental service. Beginning in 1946 at Willow Run Airport in Ypsilanti,

Michigan (serving the Detroit area), and soon adding a facility at Miami Airport, he established Avis Airlines Rent-A-Car, the first car-rental operations to be located at airports. He obtained new cars from Ford and made agreements with the airlines to use their ticket counters so passengers could arrange the car rental upon arrival. The only other major car rental company at the time was Hertz, but that company scoffed at the idea of leaving cars at the airports rather than at downtown garages. (Hertz claims to have tried it briefly before World War II.) Avis also arranged to "piggyback" a credit card to rent Avis vehicles by asking airlines to drop an Avis card into the airlines' credit-card bills.

From an initial investment of $85,000 ($10,000 of his own, the rest borrowed), the business expanded to other major cities through a licensing system and within a decade was second only to Hertz. To further the business Avis even gave away licenses to prospective managers on the basis of a handshake deal. In 1948, when the business expanded outside airports to locations near major hotels, he dropped the word "Airlines" from the company name. Avis Rent-A-Car grew so rapidly that Avis felt he had to sell the business so that it could reach full potential. In 1954 the Boston financier Richard S. Robie purchased the company for $8 million. In 1963 the company launched an advertising campaign with the slogan "Avis is only number 2.... We try harder." Over the years the company went through many corporate management forms, including ownership by ITT Corporation and Beatrice (part of the Beatrice Foods company). In 2006 Avis Budget Group became the parent company of Avis Rent-A-Car System. The company slogan remains "We Try Harder."

After selling the company he founded, Avis turned his attention to writing books about business and personal fulfillment. "An identity crisis coupled with substantial means led me into pathways that finally emerged on the broad avenue of personal fulfillment," he later wrote. He set up what he termed "shared participation" groups. In week-long sessions at various hotels, Avis would gather a group of people who appeared to have little in common; he came up with what he saw as unlikely pairings for roommates. The groups normally began these sessions by subjecting each other to ridicule, but eventually, according to Avis, they would try to establish a community with shared goals. Avis argued that modern American capitalism was failing because of its individualism. Although he acknowledged that starting an enterprise from nothing required the personality of a "Western gunslinger," he contended that to get to the next level of operation required employees who could define and execute a common set of goals. Avis thought Japanese society was a better model for this type of business expansion. He believed it was time to change American culture from a conflict society to a problem-solving society.

In 1977 Avis started a new business, Avis Teleflorist, but he ran into legal difficulties. His former rental-car company unsuccessfully sued him under the Lanham Act, claiming that consumers would be confused by the Avis name as to which company was providing the floral services. He bought other businesses and sold them when they became too big for personal attention. He once bought a bank and then sold it because he found banking "boring." In his autobiography Avis wrote that for the businessperson starting out, "ignorance is bliss. If an entrepreneur knew all the pitfalls he might stumble upon, he would never get started."

Avis lived in high style throughout his life, shuttling between his horse farm in Ann Arbor, a villa in Mexico, and Europe. "If I want to do it, I do it," he told an interviewer. He spent time in New York, where he bought buildings for their landmark value first and their economic value second. He also invested in technology and sporting goods firms. Avis had three children by his first wife, Suzanne Packer, whom he divorced; on 3 January 1981 he married Yanna Elbim, a French actress and singer. Remaining active until his final years, he died at age ninety-two of natural causes. He is buried in Elm Lawn Cemetery in Bay City.

Based on a simple idea—that travelers ought to be able to find transportation easily at airports—Avis created a company that remains a world leader in the car-rental business. He amassed a personal fortune by selling the company and then moving on to other successful business ventures, becoming known as part of the jet set of celebrities from the entertainment and business worlds. His name remains synonymous with the car-rental business.

★

Avis was coauthor, with Robert R. Blake and Jane S. Mouton, of *Corporate Darwinism: An Evolutionary Perspective on Organizing Work in the Dynamic Corporation* (1966). He discusses the importance of cooperation in *Shared Participation: Finding Solutions to Personal, Business and Community Problems* (1976) and offers business advice, based on his own success, in *Take a Chance to Be First: The Secrets of Entrepreneurial Success* (1986). Obituaries are in the *New York Times* (25 Apr. 2007) and *Wall Street Journal* (28 Apr. 2007).

John David Healy

B

BAKKER, TAMMY FAYE

SEE *Messner, Tamara Faye LaValley ("Tammy Faye")*.

BARBERA, Joseph Roland (*b.* 24 March 1911 in New York City; *d.* 18 December 2006 in Los Angeles, California), animator who, with William Hanna, created such popular cartoons and characters as Tom and Jerry, Huckleberry Hound, the Flintstones, the Jetsons, and Scooby-Doo.

Barbera, the second of three sons, was the son of Vincent Barbera, a barber, and Francesca (Calvacca) Barbera, a homemaker. Soon after Barbera's birth, the family moved to the Flatbush section of Brooklyn. As a child Barbera contributed cartoons to school publications; an avid reader, he also considered a writing career, and he was an amateur boxer at Erasmus Hall High School. On graduation from Erasmus Hall in 1928, he worked at Manhattan's Irving Trust Bank while trying to find work as a cartoonist. He sold cartoons to *Collier's* magazine and decided to pursue animation after being inspired by the Walt Disney cartoon short *Skeleton Dance*, even trying unsuccessfully to set up a meeting with Disney.

Barbera worked briefly for Fleischer Studios while on vacation from Irving Trust; laid off from the bank during the Great Depression, he got a job at Van Beuren Studio in 1932 as an animator and scriptwriter. When the studio closed in 1936, he moved to Terrytoon Studios in New Rochelle, New York. That same year he married his first wife, Dorothy Earl; they had three children. In 1937 he was offered a position at Metro-Goldwyn-Mayer (MGM) Studios in Culver City, California, and he headed west.

It was at MGM that Barbera met Hanna, who was working there as a writer and director. The two collaborated on theatrical shorts called "The Captain and the Kids," based on *The Katzenjammer Kids* comic strips, then decided to create their own characters. The result was *Puss Gets the Boot*, a 1940 short about a cat frustrated in his attempts to catch a clever mouse. *Puss* proved to be a hit, the animals were rechristened "Tom" (the cat) and "Jerry" (the mouse), and Barbera and Hanna had their first big success. Over the next seventeen years, Tom and Jerry cartoons received fourteen Oscar nominations for Best Cartoon Short Subject, ultimately winning seven, more than any other animated series.

During World War II, Barbera worked on animated training films. In 1943 *Yankee Doodle Mouse* became the first Tom and Jerry cartoon to win an Oscar, though it was the short's producer, Fred Quimby, who accepted the award. The actor and dancer Gene Kelly asked to use Jerry in a dance sequence in the musical comedy *Anchors Aweigh* (1945); the mix of live action and animation dazzled audiences.

In 1956 Barbera and Hanna became the joint heads of MGM's animation division, but the division closed the following year. Undeterred, the two started Hanna-Barbera Productions (the name order decided by a coin toss) to create cartoons for the new medium of television. To make it cost effective, they used "limited" animation techniques, which used fewer drawings; instead of the 20,000 to 30,000 required for a Tom and Jerry short, they could create a cartoon of the same length with 3,000 drawings.

Joseph Barbera. © INTERFOTO PRESSEBILDAGENTUR/ALAMY

The Tom and Jerry cartoons had little dialogue, as they revolved around chase sequences, but Barbera and Hanna realized that for a cartoon to work on a smaller screen, they needed stronger story lines. Their first television series, *The Ruff and Reddy Show* (1957), followed the adventures of a dog and cat who were friends, not adversaries, with other cartoons filling out the half hour, a formula used in subsequent series. The next year saw the launch of *The Huckleberry Hound Show*, which featured a blue dog with a southern accent. The show quickly drew viewers beyond its presumed child audience, and in 1959 it became the first cartoon show to win an Emmy for Distinguished Children's Programming.

Building on their success, Hanna-Barbera created such shows as *The Quick Draw McGraw Show* (1959) and *The Yogi Bear Show* (1961), a *Huckleberry Hound* spin-off about a bear living in "Jellystone Park." The studio's next move was an ambitious one—creating a prime-time animated series that would appeal to children and adults. Drawing inspiration from *The Honeymooners*, a live-action comedy series about two families in New York City, the men hit upon the idea of having two families living in a "modern" Stone Age, surrounded by contemporary appliances given

a prehistoric touch, such as a vacuum cleaner that was actually a mastodon.

The show's original name, "The Flagstones," was too close to the surname of the leads in the newspaper comic *Hi and Lois* (Flagston), so the series was renamed *The Flintstones*. The show's protagonists were Fred Flintstone and his best friend, Barney Rubble, who work together at a local quarry. In typical sitcom fashion, plotlines revolved around domestic issues with the men's wives, Wilma Flintstone and Betty Rubble. Fred's exuberant catchphrase, "Yabba-dabba-do!," was coined by the actor who voiced the character, Alan Reed, who thought it sounded better than the "Yahoo!" called for by the script. Barney was voiced by the legendary vocal talent Mel Blanc. *The Flintstones* debuted 30 September 1960, and despite initial poor reviews (the *New York Times* called it an "inked disaster" and the male characters "unattractive, coarse and gruff"), it became a hit that ran for 166 episodes over six seasons.

The success of *The Flintstones* made Hanna-Barbera a household name, though the constant workload led to the end of Barbera's marriage. Barbera divorced in 1963; he then married Sheila Holden, a bookkeeper and cashier at the legendary Hollywood restaurant Musso and Frank's. Meanwhile, Hanna-Barbera was on a roll, producing such series as *Top Cat* (1961) and *The Magilla Gorilla Show* (1964). *The Jetsons* (1962) was initially a rare failure; the half-hour sitcom, set in a gadget-laden future, fared poorly in its 'original prime-time slot, but it found new life when rerun on Saturday mornings. The team also produced adventure-oriented series, including *The Adventures of Jonny Quest* (1964) and *Space Ghost* (1966). Two especially successful series were *Scooby-Doo, Where Are You?* (1969) and *Josie and the Pussycats* (1970), based on a comic book about an all-female rock band.

In the 1970s the studio began producing animated specials based on classic literature, such as *Oliver and the Artful Dodger* (1972). They also worked on live-action projects, including *The Banana Splits Adventure Hour* (1968), which mixed live-action sequences with cartoons and adventure serials. The studio also produced the feature film *Charlotte's Web* (1973), based on the classic children's book. The studio's biggest success in the 1980s was *The Smurfs* (1981), based on the little blue humanoid characters in a Belgian children's book series.

In 1991 Hanna-Barbera was acquired by Turner Broadcasting (and later acquired by Time Warner), with Barbera and Hanna continuing to serve as advisers and executive producers on many projects, chiefly new versions of previous hits like *The Flintstones* and *Scooby-Doo*, which also became live-action films. Barbera's last directorial credit was for *The Karateguard* (2005), the first theatrical Tom and Jerry short in more than forty-five years.

Barbera lost his longtime partner in 2001 when Hanna died at age ninety. Barbera's death came five years later, when he died at his home in Los Angeles of natural causes at age ninety-five. Barbera's work, especially during the Hanna-Barbera years, proved that animated cartoons, initially seen as entertainment filler, could be the basis of a multimillion-dollar empire. By dropping in contemporary and pop culture references, Barbera and his colleagues also showed how cartoons could appeal to both young and older audiences alike; *The Flintstones*, in particular, is considered a precursor of such shows as *The Simpsons*. The influence of Barbera's work and characters is seen both in the number of animators who continue to cite him as a key figure in the history of animation and the enjoyment his characters continue to bring to audiences today.

★

Barbera told his own story in *My Life in 'Toons: From Flatbush to Bedrock in under a Century* (1994). Michael Mallory, *Hanna-Barbera Cartoons* (1998), looks specifically at the work of Hanna-Barbera Productions. An obituary is in the *New York Times* (19 Dec. 2006).

Gillian G. Gaar

BARNES, Clive Alexander (*b.* 13 May 1927 in London, England; *d.* 19 November 2008 in New York City), prolific performing arts writer and critic who covered the theater and broadened appreciation of dance in both Europe and the United States.

Barnes was the only child of Arthur Lionel Barnes, an ambulance driver who abandoned the family when Barnes was seven, and Freda Marguerite (Garratt) Barnes, a theatrical press agent's secretary who encouraged her son's early interest in the theater by occasionally providing him with tickets. Educated at a boarding school, Barnes went on to the University of London, where he planned to prepare for a career in psychiatry. Instead he was called up to serve in the Royal Air Force from 1946 to 1948. He studied English at Saint Catherine's College, Oxford University, where he helped revive a ballet club and edited the school's quarterly journal. He graduated from Oxford with a BA in 1951.

Barnes began working as a planner for the London County Council, reportedly at the insistence of his first wife, Joyce Tolman, whom he had married in 1946. He was often quoted as saying that she had kept after him to find "an honest job." The marriage ended around the time that Barnes signed on as music and television critic for the *Daily Express*, a London tabloid.

On 26 July 1958 Barnes married his second wife, Patricia Winckley. They had a son and a daughter. After divorcing again, Barnes went on to marry the journalist

Amy Pagnozzi on 26 July 1985. On 24 July 2004 he married Valerie Taylor, a former soloist with Britain's Royal Ballet.

Having dreamed of being a dance critic since he was eighteen, Barnes eventually established himself in the profession by objecting to the fact that most London dance criticism was being written by music critics and by making dance his primary specialty. He began writing about dance for the *New Statesman*, and he published *Ballet in Britain Since the War*—the first of his many books—in 1953, when he was twenty-six. In 1956 Barnes began reviewing dance, theater, television, and film for the *Daily Express* and in 1959 started reporting for the *Spectator*. He became the *Times* of London's full-time dance critic in 1961. Barnes never tried to come across as either a highbrow or an arbiter of taste. Describing himself as "your typical working-class overachiever," he wrote that the function of a critic "is certainly not to lay down the law . . . [but] to stimulate thought and opinion."

While in London, Barnes began freelancing for the *New York Times*, moving to the United States in 1965, when he was hired as the publication's chief dance critic. Two years later he began doubling as its chief theater critic. He eventually became a U.S. citizen.

In 1977 editors for the *New York Times* decided that one person should no longer cover theater and dance; Barnes then moved to the *New York Post* and managed to continue writing about both disciplines for thirty years. Meanwhile he also wrote for *Dance Magazine* and contributed to major dance publications in Britain, France, and Italy.

Through the years Barnes reviewed and reported on a wide array of young theater and dance talent. Many dancers and choreographers have counted Barnes among their earliest supporters. He did the first television interview with the ballet great Rudolf Nureyev in 1962 and continued to cover him for many years. In *Nureyev* (1982), Barnes's biography of the dancer, Barnes attributes what he called "the dance explosion" partly to the emergence of "ballet superstars," including the Russian performing artist. "Few men have left an impression so deep and so indelible on dance," Barnes wrote. In 1967 Barnes was also among the first to herald the talents of Mikhail Baryshnikov and was still writing about the dancer's performances thirty years later, not to mention his contributions as the artistic director of American Ballet Theatre.

The journalist also lauded the plays of Harold Pinter, Tom Stoppard, and David Mamet, along with the choreography of Merce Cunningham, Jerome Robbins, George Balanchine, Elliot Feld, and Twyla Tharp. While Barnes could be enthusiastic about the work he admired, he was no less passionate about pieces of which he disapproved. He called Tharp's *Re-Moves* "bad in a rather interesting way" and wrote that Nureyev's late-life performances had become "an embarrassment."

Dance Magazine published Barnes's column, "Attitudes," from 1989 until his death. In that forum Barnes emerged as a sort of elder statesman of dance, often recalling influential or historic figures, such as Gene Kelly and Lincoln Kirstein, commenting on such trends as video's role in dance, and speculating about which choreographers would survive in the twenty-first century. (He seemed to think that Martha Graham's creations would last and that Anthony Tudor's "would not be easy to maintain.")

Even though Barnes suffered various health problems in later years, he continued to file reviews for the *New York Post*. His last review ran on 31 October 2008, less than three weeks before he died of complications from cancer at Mount Sinai Hospital. The following night Broadway theaters momentarily dimmed their lights in his memory.

In its February 2009 edition, *Dance Magazine* published several tributes to Barnes. The Dance Theatre of Harlem founder Arthur Mitchell wrote, "Gifted with a prodigious memory, Clive's love for the performing arts and dance in particular graced him with a sharp third eye. He could see the essence of an artist."

★

A profile of Barnes is in *Current Biography* (1972). Obituaries are in the *New York Times* and *New York Post* (both 19 Nov. 2008) and the *Guardian* (21 Nov. 2008).

Whitney Smith

BASS, Perry Richardson (*b*. 11 November 1914 in Wichita Falls, Texas; *d*. 1 June 2006 in Fort Worth, Texas), businessman and wildcatter whose oil exploration made him rich and initiated his philanthropic endeavors.

Bass was the only child born to E. Perry Bass, a physician and oilman, and Annie (Richardson) Bass, a homemaker. Bass previewed his future career at a young age, when his father gave up a successful medical practice to make his mark as a wildcatter (a person who drills for oil in territory not known to contain it), gaining and losing many fortunes. Likewise, Bass's uncle Sid Richardson was involved in the oil business. With a $40 loan from Bass's mother, Richardson earned millions of dollars from two successful wildcat strikes in West Texas. When Bass's father died in 1933, Richardson became a father figure to Bass.

Also in 1933 Bass graduated from the Hill School, a boarding and college preparatory school in Pottstown, Pennsylvania. Afterward, Bass attended Yale University, where he studied geology and nurtured his interest in shipbuilding and sailing. In 1935 he won the International Snipe Class Racing Championship, held at White Rock Lake in Dallas, in a boat he built himself. He graduated from Yale in 1937 with a BS in geology.

Shortly after graduating, Bass started working for Richardson to learn the oil business. His first job for Richardson, however, was to supervise the construction of a house on Saint Joseph Island (also called San Jose Island) off the coast of Rockport, Texas, in the Gulf of Mexico. Bass's work for Richardson was interrupted by World War II, during which he designed and built fireboats. He married Nancy Lee Muse on 28 June 1941; they had four sons: Sid, Edward, Robert, and Lee.

Bass resumed his partnership with Richardson after the war, and together they expanded their holdings beyond oil interests to include ranches and real estate. They maintained a successful business relationship in part because of their very different business styles. While Richardson focused on ideas, Bass excelled at tackling the details of the business and was a skilled problem solver. This collaboration brought both men immense wealth. In 1957 *Forbes* magazine listed Richardson as one of the wealthiest people in America.

When Richardson died in 1959, his estate and business were burdened with tax problems and poorly structured oil leases. These problems could have resulted in the loss of his entire fortune, but Bass was able to prevent this from happening. However, he almost did not have the opportunity to do so, as Richardson's original will left his holdings, except $200,000 intended for his sister, to charity. While Richardson was still alive, Bass asked John B. Connally, a political troubleshooter for Richardson and friend of the Bass family (as well as future Texas governor), to persuade Richardson to change his will. Richardson agreed to Connally's advice, leaving $2 million to each of Bass's four sons. In 1960 Bass formed Bass Brothers Enterprises to manage this money as well as the 25 percent stake in Sid Richardson Energy Services that Bass owned as a result of his partnership with Richardson. In 1961 Bass was named to the National Petroleum Council, and throughout the 1960s he remained active in the oil business.

In 1969 Bass semiretired and turned Bass Brothers Enterprises over to his oldest son, Sid. Bass continued as a director of the business, but Sid took over the day-to-day operations. Under his father's leadership, Sid diversified the company and grew the family fortune. With Sid in charge of Bass Brothers Enterprises, its business endeavors included buying large, struggling companies and making them successful. One of the company's most sensational buys was their purchase of 25 percent of Walt Disney Company stock in 1984, which they sold for $2 billion in 2001. Over the years the Bass Brothers Enterprises' diverse investments turned a multimillion-dollar oil fortune into a multibillion-dollar business concern.

During this period Bass spent much of his time sailing, for pleasure and competition, including serving as navigator on Ted Turner's *American Eagle* when it won the World's

Open Racing Championship in 1972. He was a member of the Fort Worth Boat Club, the New York Yacht Club, and the Royal Ocean Racing Club of London.

Bass was also a passionate conservationist and outdoorsman, and he spent much of his free time fishing at Saint Joseph Island, the entirety of which he inherited from Richardson. In 1977 Bass was appointed to the Texas Parks and Wildlife Commission (TPW), and later he served as chairman (1979–1983). During his time with TPW, Bass championed laws to protect coastal fishing. He also arranged for a ban on commercial fishing of redfish and speckled trout, resulting in a resurgence in both cases. After his term as chairman, he served as chairman emeritus and continued to attend nearly every TPW meeting. Through his efforts, TPW created the most successful state waterfowl stamp program in the country, constructed the first marine hatchery in Texas, and engineered the passage of the Wildlife Conservation Act, which established statewide game laws and limits.

Bass also spent much of his retirement giving away portions of his immense fortune. In addition to his work as director of the Sid Richardson Foundation (1959–2006), Bass donated $20 million to Yale University to build the Nancy Lee and Perry R. Bass Center for Molecular and Structural Biology in 1991. For their fiftieth wedding anniversary, Bass and his wife gave fifty individual gifts of $1 million to various organizations. Perhaps the most visible impact that Bass made with his philanthropy was the revitalization of Fort Worth. In the 1980s much of downtown Fort Worth was abandoned and desolate. The Bass family owned much of the downtown area property and invested millions of dollars for more than ten years to rejuvenate the city. Their efforts led to the development of Sundance Square, comprising fourteen city blocks, which reinvigorated downtown Fort Worth and became a national model for urban renewal. The culminating event in Fort Worth's resurgence (for the Basses) was the opening of the Nancy Lee and Perry R. Bass Performance Hall in 1998, which is home to the Van Cliburn International Piano Competition.

After a three-year illness, Bass died of natural causes in his home in Fort Worth and was buried in a private ceremony. At the time of his death the Bass family fortune was estimated at $9 billion.

Though Bass created his massive wealth in the West Texas oil fields, he did not fit the mold of the stereotypical Texas wildcatter. Bass was a very private man; he refused interviews regarding his business holdings and investments, a practice continued by his sons. Though he did not speak openly about his business ventures, his actions spoke volumes. Creating quite a stir on Wall Street, Bass Brothers Enterprises bought and sold companies. Its business dealings elicited fear and respect; for example, Texaco offered the company $400 million to terminate a takeover attempt. Bass was asked at his seventieth birthday celebration (one of the few times he was quoted) what he was most proud of—he replied that he was most proud of his sons. Together, Bass and his sons were able to amass one of the largest family fortunes in U.S. history.

As Bass did not conduct interviews, little printed matter about his life is available. The Fort Worth Public Library has a vertical file of material on the Bass family as well as a genealogy, *The Richardson-Bass Family and Their Roots*, by Justin Dinsdale (1998). In the memoir *In History's Shadow: An American Odyssey* (1993), John B. Connally offers some insight into the relationship between Richardson and Bass. Obituaries are in the *Fort Worth Star-Telegram*, *Dallas Morning News*, and *New York Times* (all 2 June 2006). The *Fort Worth Business Press* ran a series of articles and editorials about Bass in its 5 June 2006 issue.

Michael C. Miller

BAUGH, Samuel Adrian ("Sammy") (*b.* 17 March 1914 in Temple, Texas; *d.* 17 December 2008 in Rotan, Texas), record-setting pro football player and Hall of Famer generally credited with popularizing the forward pass in the National Football League (NFL) during his time with the Washington Redskins.

Baugh was born to James Valentine Baugh (better known as J. V.) and Catherine Lucinda (Ray) Baugh, who began their marriage as farmers. After the family relocated to Sweetwater, Texas, J. V. took up work as a "checker" on the Atchison, Topeka & Santa Fe railroad and fronted for a gambling house.

Baugh, a serious student, wanted nothing to do with his father's somewhat shady doings and led an exemplary life. He began to play organized football in the fourth grade. Because he was tall and lanky—he eventually grew to six feet, two inches and 180 pounds—Baugh was used as an end. Soon, however, his coaches noticed that when he tossed the ball back to the player who passed to him, Baugh did so better than the passer himself. They quickly moved him to the tailback position—one that involved passing, running, and kicking. Baugh could do all three, a true triple-threat.

Baugh proved a fine all-around high school athlete. At Sweetwater High School, he led his team to the Texas state quarterfinals his junior year and to the semifinals his senior year. Sought also as a pro baseball prospect, he signed a minor league contract with the St. Louis Cardinals after high school and played one season.

Baugh matriculated at the University of Texas at Austin but could not find a job to help pay his tuition. The Longhorns' baseball coach, the legendary "Uncle Billy" Disch, did

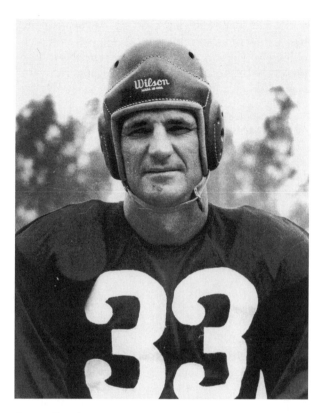

Sammy Baugh. PRO FOOTBALL HALL OF FAME/NFL/GETTY IMAGES

not think Baugh was sturdy enough to play Southwest Conference (SWC) football, but he lent Baugh enough money to enroll at Texas Christian University (TCU) in nearby Fort Worth.

Freshmen at the time were not eligible for varsity competition, so no one particularly noticed Baugh until his sophomore season (1934). As a part-time starter in coach Leo ("Dutch") Meyer's wide-open offense, Baugh passed for 883 yards and eleven touchdowns. This performance served to further enhance the SWC's long-standing reputation as an "aerial circus." In his junior year, Baugh put up even more impressive numbers—1,240 passing yards and eighteen touchdowns—and was named All-American. His senior year was similarly notable: 1,261 yards and ten touchdowns and another nod as All-American for the passer now known, thanks to the *Fort Worth Star-Telegram* sports editor Flem Hall, as Slingin' Sammy Baugh.

Many of Baugh's gridiron performances in the SWC would become the stuff of legend. During the 1936 Sugar Bowl against Louisiana State University (LSU), Baugh braved the wind and rain to punt a heavy, sodden ball fourteen times for a 44.6-yard average. He also intercepted two LSU passes as TCU scored a 3–2 victory. In the 1937 Cotton Bowl, Baugh's passing—including a fifty-yard scoring toss—led TCU to a 16–6 win over Marquette.

Baugh left TCU in the spring of 1937 with a BA and a slew of SWC offensive records to become the number-one draft choice of the NFL's Washington Redskins. The Washington franchise, which had recently moved from Boston, was owned by George Preston Marshall, a laundry tycoon, self-styled actor, and promoter extraordinaire. Marshall wanted to show the team's fans that he had chosen a real-life cowboy to lead his squad. He advised Baugh to arrive wearing a ten-gallon Stetson and fancy, high-heeled cowboy boots. That Baugh owned no such attire did not stop Marshall, who simply said, "Go out and buy some, I'll pay you when you get here." When Baugh stepped off the airplane at a D.C. airport, he was dressed as Marshall had directed. When asked about the boots, he replied, "The damn things pinch my toes."

Baugh's legendary skill as an accurate passer followed him to training camp. One day, coach Ray Flaherty, giving Baugh instructions on a particular pass pattern, said, "When [the receiver] makes his cut, I want you to hit him right in the eye." Baugh, according to NFL folklore, rejoined, "Which eye?"

As a rookie, Baugh took the Redskins to the NFL title game versus the Chicago Bears. On a blustery winter day in Chicago, he threw touchdowns of 35, 55, and 78 yards and passed for 354 yards total to defeat the Bears 28–21.

On 12 April 1938, Baugh married Edmonia Gary Smith. The couple had four sons and a daughter.

For the next eight years, Baugh directed Washington to winning records and more often than not a first- or second-place finish. In 1940 Baugh and the Redskins suffered the humiliation of a 73–0 championship loss to the Bears. Early in the game, when the score was still 0–0, the Redskins end Charley Malone dropped a sure touchdown pass. Afterward, Baugh was asked what he thought the score would have been if the usually reliable Malone had made the catch. He deadpanned, "Seventy-three to six."

Two years later, the Redskins got a measure of revenge, defeating the Bears 14–6 in the 1942 championship game. In 1945 the Washington squad went down to a title-match defeat, 15–14, against the Cleveland Rams when a Baugh pass out of his own end zone dinged off the goal post. The rules of the day called for a two-point safety, the margin of the Rams' victory.

Though he was known as a quarterback, Baugh also played eight years as a single-wing tailback and eight as a T-formation quarterback. His passing was equally skillful from both formations. He led the NFL in passing seven times, a record that stood for decades. His 1945 season completion percentage record (70.33) finally fell in 1982 to the Cincinnati Bengals' Ken Anderson by the slimmest of margins (70.55).

Not just a passer, Baugh held the career punting average (45.1 yards per kick) for decades. In 1943 he led the league in passing, punting, and interceptions made. He was also an outstanding quick-kicker.

In 1940 Baugh purchased a ranch near Rotan with money that he had earned by starring in the twelve-part Republic Pictures film serial *King of the Texas Rangers*. Baugh retired following the 1952 season, after which he tried his hand at a number of coaching jobs—with the New York Titans (later the New York Jets) and the Houston Oilers (later the Tennessee Titans) of the American Football League (AFL), and Hardin-Simmons and Tulsa on the collegiate level—but mostly he was happy to remain on his 20,000-acre ranch.

Dick McCann, the Redskins' general manager during Baugh's tenure, once wrote, "Sammy Baugh was the best, is the best, and will always be the best. There are throwers and passers, and then there's Sammy Baugh."

The last of the Pro Football Hall of Fame's 1963 charter class died at Fisher County Hospital in Rotan of complications of Alzheimer's, double pneumonia, kidney problems, and low blood pressure. His son David said, "It wasn't the same old Sam we all knew; he just finally wore out."

At the funeral service at First Baptist of Rotan, Baugh's coffin was draped with his saddle (he truly was a working cowboy) and chaps. He was taken to Belvieu Cemetery in Rotan by hearse but carried to his grave site in a horse-drawn wagon. One friend dressed as a football referee, another as a cowboy.

Baugh's impact on the passing game will be recalled every time an NFL quarterback cocks back his arm and throws downfield.

★

Baugh's life and career are discussed in Arthur Daley, *Pro Football Hall of Fame* (1963); Don Smith, *The Quarterbacks* (1963); George Sullivan, *Pro Football's All-Time Greats* (1968); and Myron Cope, *The Game That Was* (1970). Obituaries are in the *Washington Post*, the *New York Times*, and *USA Today* (all 18 Dec. 2008).

Jim Campbell

BAVARIA, Joan (*b*. 29 August 1943 in Shelburne Falls, Massachusetts; *d*. 18 November 2008 in Marblehead, Massachusetts), founder of Trillium Assets Management, one of the first investment firms to focus on socially responsible investments, and a founding member of Coalition for Environmentally Responsive Economies (CERES), a global partnership among leading companies, environmental groups, and institutional investors.

Bavaria was born Joan Crocker in the town of Shelburne Falls, in the Berkshire Mountains of Massachusetts, where

her family ran a bakery. Growing up in a religious family, Bavaria and her three sisters attended Sunday school, and she sang in the church choir. Her parents emphasized always doing what is right—a tenet Bavaria would follow all her life, saying that doing right was always its own justification. Like most of her family, she was interested in art. After high school graduation in 1961, Bavaria entered the Massachusetts College of Art but left to marry her high school sweetheart, Frederick Clark. Over the next three years, she had two sons, got divorced, and, needing to support herself and her sons, found a job.

In 1969 Bavaria started a job as an investment officer at the Bank of Boston, where she received solid on-the-job education in financial management. In those days, she said, women were being added to trust companies because women would manage money for less pay than men, and she was mainly assigned by her male superiors to wealthy women clients.

In working with her clients Bavaria learned that many investors wanted to integrate social and environmental concerns with their investment goals. Some of her clients were even more interested in the social and environmental values of the companies they wished to invest in than they were in the companies' financial returns. They asked questions about environmental practices, charitable giving, corporate ethics, and even how companies treated their employees. Because investment companies were ill equipped to deal with these questions, she began her own research into the social values of publicly traded companies.

In 1981 Bavaria cofounded and served as president of the Social Investment Forum, an organization of research, advisory, banking, and community loan fund organizations dedicated to the growth of socially and environmentally responsible investing. She would always stress collaboration between individuals and organizations—one of her goals was to bring about a more socially responsible financial industry. A year later, in 1982, Bavaria realized that there were enough people interested in socially responsible investing to start such an investment firm, and she cofounded Trillium Asset Management Corp. (formerly known as Franklin Research & Development, which she helped form as a spin-off from Franklin Management), an independent firm focusing on investing in socially responsible companies. She named the company "Trillium" to symbolize three aspects of sustainability: ecology, economy, and equity. She defined sustainability as a system that thinks about the environmental and social costs of economic activity and at the same time considers the viability of economic institutions.

Trillium Asset Management was the first U.S. firm focusing on socially responsible investments, and it built its reputation on that concept. Trillium worked with clients who shared Bavaria's belief that active investing could provide solid financial returns and at the same time promote social and economic justice. It managed the portfolios of individuals and institutions; many of these were nonprofit or religious organizations. Client portfolios contained stocks, money market funds, bonds, and community investments of various sorts—all depending on the client needs. The firm did most of its own research and published a newsletter each quarter on its website along with opinion pieces about socially responsible investing. Every year it donated 5 percent of its pretax profits to charitable causes.

Bavaria was one of the first investment professionals to foster shareholder advocacy as a means of change in capital markets on a whole range of issues, including the antiapartheid movement in the 1980s through to the issue of climate change in 2008. She was also one of the first investment managers who realized the role of microfinance in helping alleviate poverty in underserved communities. Early on, Trillium directed a portion of its clients' assets to microfinance and community development funds.

Nonetheless, the company remained focused on building the portfolios of its clients. "We have to be competent advisers," Bavaria said. "We would get fired if we didn't produce financial outcomes." By 2008 the company had just under $1 billion in assets under its management and offices in Boston; Durham, North Carolina; San Francisco; and Boise, Idaho. Founding and then leading Trillium would be a lasting legacy for anyone, but Bavaria was known to one and all for her energy, vision, and ability to bring people together.

In 1989, while heading Trillium, Bavaria launched CERES, another collaborative effort. CERES's mission was to move companies, financial markets, and policy makers to find solutions to sustainability issues like global climate change. Under her guidance, CERES launched three initiatives that had a worldwide impact: the CERES Principles, a corporate environmental code of conduct; the Global Reporting Initiative, which became the de facto international standard for corporate sustainability reporting, used by over 1,000 countries worldwide; and the Investor Network on Climate Risk, an alliance of investors dedicated to addressing climate change.

After divorcing Clark, Bavaria married Jesse Collins. Following a prolonged battle with cancer, Bavaria passed away at her home. To honor her, Trillium and CERES created the Joan Bavaria Awards for Building Sustainability in the Capital Markets, honoring those who help move capital markets from a focus on short-term profits toward one that balances financial prosperity with social and environmental health. Throughout Bavaria's career she was honored numerous times. In 1999 she was named one of the Heroes of the Planet by Time.com. She also received the City of Göteborg (Sweden) International Environmental Prize (2004), the Botwinick Prize in Ethics from the Columbia School of Business (2005), and the Charles R. Schwab IMPACT Award for vision and leadership (2008). She served on the advisory boards of the Union of Concerned Scientists and the Greening of Industry Network and many other financial and environmental organizations.

Tributes to Bavaria, her photo, biographical information, a YouTube video of her speech at the inaugural Joan Bavaria Awards ceremony in April 2008, and information about the Social Investment Forum, Trillium Assets, and CERES can be found on the CERES website (http://www.ceres.org/joan). An excerpt from Bavaria's acceptance speech of her Botwinick Prize in Business Ethics at Columbia's Social Enterprise Conference (7 Oct. 2005) gives insight into her management of Trillium, "of what I do, and why I do it" (http://www6.columbia.edu/cfmx/web/alumni/news/article.cfm?a=87). Bavaria was profiled in Sandra Waddock, *The Difference Makers* (2008). An interview by L. J. Rittenhouse, author of "Do Business with People You Can Tru$t" (which includes information about Bavaria), as part of the online 2004 Annual Report of Cinergy Corp., *Global Warming: Can We Find Common Ground*, gives Bavaria's investment philosophy and her management views. An obituary is in the *Marblehead Reporter* (26 Nov. 2008).

Julianne Cicarelli

BAVASI, Emil Joseph ("Buzzie") (*b.* 12 December 1914 in New York City; *d.* 1 May 2008 in San Diego, California), baseball executive under whose tenure as general manager the Brooklyn and Los Angeles Dodgers captured eight National League pennants and their first four World Series titles.

Bavasi was the son of Joseph Bavasi, a French immigrant and newspaper distributor, and Sue Bavasi. He grew up in Scarsdale, New York, and graduated from Bronxville High School in Bronxville, New York. His sister nicknamed him "Buzzie" because, as he put it, he was "always buzzing around." He graduated in 1938 with a bachelor's degree in political science from DePauw University in Greencastle, Indiana, where he was catcher for the baseball team and roomed with the son of the National League president Ford Frick.

Upon Frick's recommendation, in 1939 the Brooklyn Dodgers owner Larry MacPhail hired Bavasi as traveling secretary. In 1940 he was named business manager of the Dodgers' Americus, Georgia, farm team of the Class D Georgia-Florida League and then, from 1941 to 1942, of the Durham, North Carolina, team of the Class B Carolina League. In 1941 Bavasi married Evit E. Rice, with whom he had four sons; two of them became baseball executives like their father. During World War II, Bavasi served in the U.S. Army in North Africa and Italy, winning a bronze star as a machine-gunner. In 1946 the

Dodgers president Branch Rickey named him general manager of the Nashua, New Hampshire, team of the Class B New England League.

Bavasi expedited the integration of minor league baseball. The Dodgers, who had broken the color barrier by signing Jackie Robinson several months earlier, sent the former Negro League players Roy Campanella and Don Newcombe in 1946 to Nashua. When the manager of a competing team hurled racial epithets at the pair, Bavasi challenged him to a fight. Few other racially motivated incidents occurred. Bavasi smoothed the players' integration into the predominantly French-Canadian community of Nashua, boosted attendance through his imaginative promotional skills, and befriended the manager Walter Alston.

Bavasi served as general manager of the Montreal Royals of the Class AAA International League from 1948 to 1950, and in 1949 was named Minor League Executive of the Year. In November 1950 he was named general manager/executive vice president of the Brooklyn Dodgers, replacing Rickey after a boardroom battle won by Walter O'Malley.

During Bavasi's eighteen years with the team, the Dodgers won eight National League pennants and four World Series. Bavasi built a talented farm system and hired Alston as manager in 1953. Brooklyn fielded the superstars Robinson, Campanella, Newcombe, Pee Wee Reese, Duke Snider, and Gil Hodges. Their 1955 World Series win, over the New York Yankees, was the only title they won while in Brooklyn.

Following the 1957 season, O'Malley moved the Dodgers to Los Angeles. Bavasi remained with Los Angeles until 1968. The Dodgers, featuring the pitchers Sandy Koufax and Don Drysdale and the shortstop Maury Wills, won World Series titles in 1959 over the Chicago White Sox, in 1963 over the New York Yankees, and in 1965 over the Minnesota Twins. The *Sporting News* named Bavasi the 1959 Major League Executive of the Year.

Club owners guarded the reserve clause and they controlled contract negotiations. "We operated by the Golden Rule," Bavasi said. "He who has the gold, rules." Noted for his candor and flair, he dealt tenaciously with players in contract talks, tightly controlled the purse strings, and did not believe in incentives clauses. During spring training in 1966, Koufax and Drysdale tried to negotiate together with Bavasi for a three-year, $1 million package with the help of an agent, but Bavasi insisted on dealing with them directly and eventually gave them much smaller raises in separate one-year contracts totaling $225,000, $130,000 for Koufax and $105,000 for Drysdale. He refused to grant Wills, who stole 104 bases in 1962, an incentive clause in his contract. The advent of free agency and player agents soured Bavasi on the business aspect of baseball. He resigned in 1968 because O'Malley intended to pass control of the Dodgers over to his son Peter.

Bavasi led the campaign for San Diego to acquire a major league baseball team and convinced National League owners that its growing population could support a major league franchise. He owned one-third of the expansion San Diego Padres from their inception in 1969 through January 1974 and served as club president until September 1977. San Diego finished last its first six major league seasons and ranked last in National League attendance. Bavasi operated the Padres on a shoestring and often met payroll by selling players of any value. The club nearly moved to Washington, D.C., in 1973, but Ray Kroc of the McDonald's restaurant chain bought the Padres for $12 million in January 1974 and retained Bavasi as president. In 1977 Bavasi's son Peter became general manager of the Toronto Blue Jays, making the two men the first father and son to run different major league teams at the same time. Bavasi resigned from the Padres in September 1977 without attaining a winning season.

In 1978 the California Angels hired Bavasi as executive vice president and general manager. The owner Gene Autry wanted immediate results and to rely less on player development. Although Bavasi allowed Nolan Ryan to become a free agent, he traded top prospects for the stars Rod Carew in 1979, Fred Lynn in 1981, and Reggie Jackson in 1982. The Angels, led by Don Baylor, won their first West Division championships in 1979 and 1982. By the time Bavasi retired to his hilltop home in La Jolla, California, in August 1984, he had built the foundation for the 1986 club that nearly reached the World Series.

From 1978 to 1999 Bavasi served as a member of the Veterans Committee of the National Baseball Hall of Fame. He was inducted into the San Diego Padres Hall of Fame in 2001 and the San Diego Hall of Champions Breitbard Hall of Fame in 2007. He died in San Diego at the age of ninety-three.

Bavasi championed the acceptance of black players in organized baseball, guided all three major league teams in Southern California, assembled an expansion team in San Diego, and saw power shift from management to the players with the arrival of free agency. Drawing on his many years involved with the game, he was an often-quoted baseball storyteller.

★

Bavasi's candid autobiography, *Off the Record* (1987), coauthored with John Strege, is filled with whimsical first-person anecdotes. Steve Daly, *Dem Little Bums: The Nashua Dodgers* (2002), details Bavasi's Nashua years. Peter Golenbock, *Bums: An Oral History of the Brooklyn Dodgers* (1984), remains the most exhaustive, scholarly history of the Brooklyn years, while William F. McNeil, *The Dodgers Encyclopedia* (1997), is the definitive franchise history. David Porter and Joe Naiman, *The San Diego Padres Encyclopedia* (2002), describes Bavasi's tenure with San Diego, and Ross Newhan, *The California Angels*

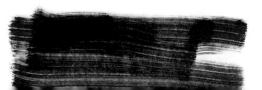

(1982), reviews the early years of that club. Obituaries are in the *New York Times* and *San Diego Union-Tribune* (both 2 May 2008).

David L. Porter

BEARD, Ralph Milton, Jr. (*b.* 2 December 1927 in Hardinsburg, Kentucky; *d.* 29 November 2007 in Louisville, Kentucky), college and professional basketball player whose playing career was overshadowed by his involvement in point shaving.

Beard was the older of two sons of Ralph Beard and Pauline (Sheeran) Beard. His father was a professional golfer and hardware-store owner. After Beard's parents divorced in 1937, his father moved to Dallas. His mother then supported the family by cleaning houses, and Ralph delivered newspapers to help make ends meet.

In 1941 Pauline Beard moved her family to Louisville, where she took a job at an aircraft factory so that Beard could attend Male High School. Beard became a star on the basketball, football, baseball, and track teams and captured the state championship in the half-mile race. He led his school to the 1945 state championship in

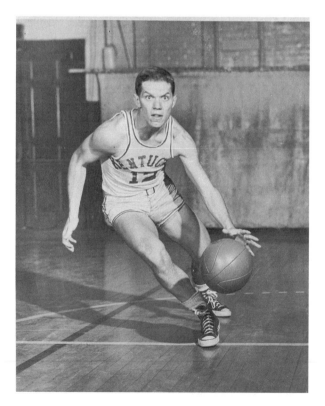

Ralph Beard, 1949. AP IMAGES

basketball. After graduating from high school, Beard went to the University of Kentucky to play basketball and football. After suffering a shoulder injury in his third game, he gave up football.

Beard started for the Kentucky Wildcats for four seasons. Russell Rice, a longtime observer of Kentucky basketball, noted that the five-feet, ten-inch, 175-pound Beard had "speed, aggressiveness, shooting ability, and desire." Beard's college teammate and future Kentucky coach Joe B. Hall called him "the most competitive person I ever knew." He could run opponents with less conditioning into the ground.

Beard averaged 9.3 points per game in 1946 and helped Kentucky to a 28–2 record and the National Invitation Tournament (NIT) title. His free throw provided the game-winning point in Kentucky's 46–45 win over Rhode Island in the NIT title game.

Beard teamed with six-feet, seven-inch Alex Groza to provide college basketball's most potent inside-outside tandem. Beard was a consensus All-American in 1947, when Kentucky went 34–2. However, the Wildcats were unable to defend their NIT title, falling to Utah 49–45 in the championship game. Beard had a miserable game, scoring only one point, ending his season averaging 10.6 points per game.

Beard had his best season in 1948, averaging 12.5 points for the team known as the Fabulous Five. Coached by Adolph Rupp, Kentucky easily handled all three of its tournament opponents to capture the school's first National Collegiate Athletic Association (NCAA) title. Beard scored 15 points against Columbia, 13 in a win over defending champion Holy Cross, and 12 in a 58–42 title win over Baylor. Kentucky finished the season 36–3, and Beard unanimously was voted first-team All-America.

In 1948 eight teams—some college, some Amateur Athletic Union (AAU)—were invited to the Olympic basketball trials. Kentucky won its first two games before losing to the AAU Bartlesville (Oklahoma) Oilers 53–49 in the title game. Beard scored 23 points against the Oilers, prompting their coach, Bud Browning, to proclaim him "absolutely the best basketball player I ever saw." The five Oilers and five Kentucky starters, along with four others, were selected for the Olympic team. After an early loss to Argentina, the United States cruised to a gold medal, defeating France 65–21 in the final.

Kentucky lost only once in the 1949 regular season, a 42–40 setback to St. Louis. So confident was Rupp that he accepted invitations to play in both the NIT and NCAA tournaments, which were held in consecutive weeks. Kentucky, however, was stunned in its NIT opener, a perplexing 67–56 loss to poorly regarded Loyola of Chicago. Beard scored 15 points.

The Wildcats regrouped and successfully defended their NCAA title. Groza dominated inside, scoring 82 points in wins over Villanova, Illinois, and Oklahoma A&M. Beard scored a modest 15 points in the three games, only 3 in the 46–36 championship win. He ended the season averaging 10.9 points per game and was consensus All-American. Beard concluded his Kentucky career with 1,514 points in 139 games, an average of 10.9 per game.

After graduating with a degree in education in 1949, Beard turned professional. He, Groza, and three other former Kentucky teammates played for and were part owners of the expansion Indianapolis Olympians in the National Basketball Association (NBA). Beard averaged 14.9 points per game in 1949, but the team's record was a dismal 18–62. The Olympians improved to 39–25 the following season and captured the Western Division regular-season title before losing to Anderson in the play-offs. Beard averaged 16.8 points per game and scored 6 points in the inaugural NBA All-Star game.

In October 1951 Beard, Groza, and a third Kentucky player, Dale Barnstable, were indicted for accepting money from gamblers to influence the outcome of games at Kentucky during the 1948–1949 season, including the NIT loss to Loyola. The three men cooperated with authorities, pleading guilty in April 1952. They were sentenced to probation.

Beard, along with Groza, was banned for life from the NBA and forced to sell his interests in the Olympians at a substantial loss. A talented baseball player, he was also banned from playing professionally in that sport. A short-lived attempt to play with Jersey City of the American Basketball League ended when that minor league, under pressure from the NBA, disbanded rather than allow players tainted by the scandal to suit up. The scandal contributed to the breakup of his marriage to Marilyn Beard, and his ex-wife won custody of their child, Ralph Beard III.

Beard was drafted into the U.S. Army and served two years (1955–1957), much of it in Japan. On 18 March 1955 Beard married Bettye Scott, with whom he had three children. After being honorably discharged from the military in 1957, Beard went into sales, ending up as general manager of Gould's Pharmaceuticals in Louisville. He also scouted for the American Basketball Association's Louisville Colonels and the NBA's Indiana Pacers in the 1970s. Beard was a member of the Beargrass Christian Church. He died of congestive heart failure, and his body was cremated.

Beard's legacy remains controversial. He was inducted into the University of Kentucky Athletic Hall of Fame, and his number 12 jersey was retired. However, he was denied induction into the Naismith Memorial Basketball Hall of Fame. Beard acknowledged taking money from gamblers but insisted that he had never shaved points. In 1995 he told the *New York Times*: "I was totally innocent of influencing games. I never had two dimes to rub together. . . . I took the money, and that was it. I always gave 101 percent on the court."

★

The best study of the point-shaving scandals is Charles Rosen, *Scandals of '51: How the Gamblers Almost Killed College Basketball* (1978). The Rupp years are examined in Tev Laudeman, *The Rupp Years: The University of Kentucky's Golden Era of Basketball* (1972); Russell Rice, *Adolph Rupp: Kentucky's Basketball Baron* (1994); and Tom Wallace, *Kentucky Basketball Encyclopedia* (2002). Obituaries are in the *New York Times* and *Louisville Courier-Journal* (both 30 Nov. 2007).

Jim Sumner

BENCHLEY, Peter Bradford (*b.* 8 May 1940 in New York City; *d.* 11 February 2006 in Princeton, New Jersey), novelist and nonfiction writer who gained fame and fortune for his novel *Jaws* and who subsequently became an advocate for sharks and other marine life.

Peter Benchley, 1976. **BERNARD GOTFRYD/HULTON ARCHIVE/ GETTY IMAGES**

Born on New York City's Upper East Side, Benchley was the grandson of Robert Benchley, a wit and one of the founders of the Algonquin Round Table, and the son of the novelist, playwright, and screenwriter Nathaniel Goddard Benchley and Marjorie (Bradford) Benchley. At home, he not only drew inspiration from his father's career but was also exposed to writers and artists, most of whom he recalled were "sensitive and feeling and concerned." As a result, Benchley observed, "I guess it was inevitable that I should end up as a writer."

He attended Phillips Exeter Academy, an exclusive and demanding preparatory school in Exeter, New Hampshire. In 1957 he entered Harvard University, where he graduated cum laude in 1961 with an English degree. After graduating, Benchley and a friend embarked on a trip around the world. Benchley's odyssey spawned his first book, the memoir *Time and a Ticket* (1964). The book, which drew mixed reviews, nevertheless sold well. One reviewer found *Time and a Ticket* unimpressive. But another writer for the *New Yorker* called Benchley a "fine reporter."

In 1963, prior to the publication of *Time and a Ticket*, Benchley worked for the *Washington Post* as a reporter and an obituary writer. He also wrote the children's book *Jonathan Visits the White House*. Published in 1964, the story concerns a young boy and his puppy and their visit to the Oval Office.

Benchley left the *Washington Post* and was hired by *Newsweek* magazine as an associate editor in New York City, where he was given a number of different assignments. In time he became the magazine's television critic, a post he did not savor. In February 1967 Benchley was engaged as a speechwriter for President Lyndon B. Johnson. He was a low-level aide but appreciated the opportunity to see the inside of the White House. After less than two years, Benchley was fired when Richard M. Nixon entered the White House in January 1969. He returned to Manhattan, and for a few years he attempted to support his family as a freelance writer. Matters improved for Benchley when he interested a senior editor at Doubleday in a novel about a great white shark that surfaces at a resort off the South Shore of Long Island and brings mayhem and death. After some discussion, the involved parties agreed on the title *Jaws*.

The novel's action takes place during the summer tourist season in the ocean surrounding the fictitious island Amity, located off the eastern end of Long Island. A swimmer is killed by a great white shark, and the sheriff, who wants to close the beach, is overruled by town authorities who fear the loss of tourist business. The shark attacks continue, the sheriff prevails, and the beaches are closed. Eventually the shark is killed by an experienced fisherman who loses his life in the struggle.

Published in 1974, *Jaws* was on the *New York Times* best-seller list for over forty weeks. Reviews, though, were a mixed bag. Most critics praised the menacing environment

Benchley had created and concluded that the great white shark was, in the words of one critic, rendered "with exhilarating and alarming skill, and every scene in which" the shark "appears is imagined with a special pitch of intensity."

On the other hand, some critics found Benchley's human characters uninteresting and shallow and noted weaknesses in the plot. Some reviewers believed that the end of *Jaws*—the fisherman's boat sinks, and the fisherman dies in his battle with the great white—was too reminiscent of the closing pages of Herman Melville's *Moby Dick*. Benchley, though, denied any such allusion. "It isn't that kind of book, really," he asserted, "It's a story, not an allegory."

Benchley drew for his novel on stories he had absorbed as a youngster on Nantucket Island, south of Cape Cod, Massachusetts. For years he had also reflected on an article he had kept from the *New York Daily News* about the capture of a 4,550-pound great white shark off Long Island. "I would brandish it at the first hint of disbelief that such an animal could exist," he wrote in *Shark Trouble: True Stories About Sharks and the Sea* (2002). Moreover, he read most of the available literature about sharks.

Benchley calculated that the aggregate income from book sales (the novel sold over twenty million copies), movie rights (Benchley cowrote the screenplay of the hugely popular movie *Jaws*), paperback rights, and book club syndications furnished him with a sufficient income to write freely for a decade. He was apprehensive, though, that *Jaws* might stimulate "would-be Hemingways" to kill sharks. His fears were not unfounded. And in fact, over the years following *Jaws*, Benchley became a staunch conservationist. His conservation ethic is a major factor in his 1991 novel *Beast*.

The beast in the title is a giant oceanic squid that lives in the waters surrounding Bermuda. The animal attacks and sinks boats, eating the human occupants, because its natural prey has been exhausted by overfishing. "What had killed Bermuda's fishing industry," Benchley wrote, was fishermen who "treated the ocean as if it were a deep pit to be strip-mined." The *New York Times* reviewer offered praise for the novel, declaring that *Beast* offered "diverting, suspenseful, informative entertainment."

Among Benchley's other books are *The Deep* (1976); *The Island* (1979); *The Girl of the Sea of Cortez* (1982); *Q Clearance* (1986); *Rummies* (1989); and *White Shark* (1994).

Benchley gave escapist pleasure to millions of readers. In addition, recognizing that the ocean was his milieu and sharks his major area of interest, he became a knowledgeable naturalist and steadfast conservationist. He said of himself, "What I have become, to the best of my ability is a shark protector, a shark advocate, a shark appreciator, and above all, a shark respecter."

Benchley was a member of the National Council of Environmental Defense and a spokesperson for its ocean program. He was also a member of the board of advisers of the Underwater Exploration Institute. Benchley journeyed around the globe crafting undersea documentaries where he swam with sharks and whales, including killer whales. He also lectured on marine conservation and hosted wildlife programs on television, including "The Making of Steven Spielberg's Jaws" (1995) and "The Shark Is Still Working" (2006).

He was a recipient of the Lowell Thomas Gold Award for adventure-travel writing by the Society of American Travel Writers (2003 and 2004) and the David B. Stone Award by the New England Aquarium (2005). Benchley married Wendy Wesson in September 1964. They had three children. Benchley died of pulmonary fibrosis at his home in Princeton.

★

For biographical information on Benchley, see David Doubilet, "Remembering Peter Benchley," *National Geographic* 210, no. 1 (July 2006). Obituaries are in the *Los Angeles Times, New York Times,* and *Washington Post* (all 13 Feb. 2006).

Richard P. Harmond

BENTSEN, Lloyd Millard, Jr. (*b.* 11 February 1921 in Mission, Texas; *d.* 23 May 2006 in Houston, Texas), secretary of the Treasury of the United States, U.S. senator and representative, businessman, Texas county judge, and decorated World War II veteran.

Bentsen was one of three boys and one girl born to Lloyd M. Bentsen, Sr., and Edna Ruth (Colbath) Bentsen in Mission, Texas. Growing up on a Rio Grande valley farm in the 1920s, Bentsen learned to speak both English and Spanish. During his youth the family's means were modest, but his father, Lloyd, Sr., and his uncle, Elmer, eventually developed vast ranching, farming, real estate, and banking enterprises in southern Texas.

Bentsen attended the University of Texas at Austin and earned his law degree in June 1942. At the age of twenty-two, he volunteered for the army and received officer and combat intelligence training. In 1943 he attended flight school and married Beryl Ann (nicknamed B. A.) Longino of Lufkin, Texas, on 27 November 1943. The couple would have three children. Bentsen commanded a B-24 bomber squadron and flew thirty-five missions over Germany and Italy. On one fateful mission, he safely returned his crippled plane and crew. He earned the Distinguished Flying Cross, the Air Medal with three oak clusters, and received the rank of major.

After the war Bentsen returned to the Rio Grande valley and opened a law practice in McAllen, Texas. Soon he entered elective politics, winning the 1946 race for

Lloyd Bentsen, 1993. TERRY ASHE/TIME LIFE PICTURES/GETTY IMAGES

county judge of Hidalgo County. Two years later he won a seat in the U.S. House of Representatives as a Democrat. At twenty-seven years old Bentsen was the youngest member of Congress in 1949. The speaker of the house, Democrat Sam Rayburn of Texas, recognized Bentsen's potential for leadership and brought the young congressman into his circle. In his first House term, Bentsen's vote against the poll tax—used to keep African Americans from voting—was unusual for a southern congressman. He also sided with Rayburn in supporting the 1952 Democratic presidential nominee, Adlai Stevenson, while many of his congressional colleagues supported the Republican nominee, Dwight D. Eisenhower.

After serving in the House for three terms, Bentsen decided not to run for reelection in 1954. Rayburn had hoped that Bentsen would follow in his path to become Speaker. However, Bentsen desired to leave Congress and enter business. With financial support from his father and uncle, Bentsen began the Consolidated American Life Insurance Company in Houston. Later, he bought out Lincoln

Liberty Life Insurance of Nebraska and developed Lincoln Consolidated, a financial services company. Bentsen continued as a significant adviser to and fund-raiser for moderate Texas Democrats during his years in business.

Bentsen played a role as a key member of the Texas governor John Connally's inner circle during the 1960s. Connally encouraged Bentsen to challenge the incumbent Democratic Texas senator Ralph Yarborough in the 1970 Democratic primary. Despite polls showing that very few Texas voters recognized his name, he challenged Senator Yarborough in the Democratic primary. Yarborough, anticipating an autumn race against the Houston Republican congressman George H. W. Bush, was unprepared for Bentsen's challenge.

Bentsen surprised Yarborough when he unleashed a series of television commercials linking the incumbent to urban riots and violence while targeting the senator's opposition to the Vietnam War. In the ads, Bentsen accused Yarborough and liberal Democrats of spawning crime, looting, and burning. Scenes of clashes between police and protesters from the Chicago Democratic convention in 1968 and of police spraying tear gas on demonstrators flashed across the screen. Bentsen also accused Yarborough of favoring forced busing to integrate schools while opposing voluntary prayer in public schools. In a surprising upset, Bentsen won the hard-fought primary against Senator Yarborough, united Texas Democrats behind his candidacy, and defeated Congressman Bush in November.

Bentsen, almost forty-nine years old, returned to Washington, D.C., with fifteen years of experience in business and finance. As a senator, he valued bipartisanship, compromise, and strategy. He maintained one of the best-run offices in the Senate. Known since his House days for his disciplined campaign organizations, Bentsen scrupulously separated his personal and election finances. Although he entered the Senate with a reputation as a fiscal conservative, his personal fairness and knowledge of finance and economic policy earned him the respect of both labor and management groups.

Bentsen's intellect and tactical brilliance also impressed Senate colleagues. As a freshman senator on the U.S. Senate Committee on Commerce, Science and Transportation, he successfully maneuvered the Employee Retirement Income Security Act, a long-stalled pension reform bill, to passage. He served on the U.S. Senate Committee on Armed Services early in his career; then, in 1973 he joined the U.S. Senate Committee on Finance. In 1975, before he had completed his first Senate term, he announced his candidacy for the presidency. Bentsen's campaign gained little momentum and Governor Jimmy Carter of Georgia won the Democratic nomination and the presidency. However, Bentsen easily won reelection to the Senate over the Republican nominee Alan Steelman.

Bentsen supported President Carter's arms control efforts. Bentsen often said his proudest accomplishment in the Senate was pension reform. As a member of the Committee on Finance and the Joint Economic Committee, he also believed in using the tax code to provide incentives for a variety of activities—to save, invest, produce oil, and make college loans. In 1978, despite opposition from his constituents, Bentsen supported Carter in pushing for passage of the controversial Panama Canal treaties, which handed control of the Panama Canal to Panama.

Bentsen's stature in the Democratic Party continued to grow during the presidency of Ronald Reagan (1981–1989). In 1982, when he ran for reelection against Representative James Collins, his organization assisted other Texas Democrats in a well-funded and coordinated statewide campaign. As a result, many new Democratic candidates won statewide offices, including Governor Mark White and Treasurer Ann Richards. Bentsen led the Democratic Senatorial Campaign Committee for the national party from 1983 to 1985, and was a prospective vice-presidential nominee in 1984. In 1987 he became chairman of the Committee on Finance. Continuing to advocate policies of fiscal responsibility, tax reform, and workers' rights, Bentsen became increasingly interested in trade policy and expanding the United States' foreign markets.

As senator, Bentsen became a powerful force on behalf of oil and gas industries, and his knowledge of tax law brought him influence and leverage among the financial titans of Wall Street. Although labeled by the media as the consummate Beltway insider, Bentsen avoided impropriety throughout his career, even during the savings and loan scandal of the late 1980s that tarnished several of his Democratic colleagues. Perhaps his biggest embarrassment took place in 1987, when he was to host a $10,000-a-plate breakfast for lobbyists. Following a media firestorm—the political satirist Mark Russell labeled the event "Eggs McBentsen"—Bentsen canceled the breakfast and refunded the money.

In 1988 Governor Michael S. Dukakis of Massachusetts, the Democratic nominee for the presidency, selected Bentsen to be his vice-presidential running mate. The two faced the Republican ticket of Vice President George H. W. Bush and Senator Dan Quayle. The only vice-presidential debate of the campaign produced an exchange that would become one of the most noteworthy in presidential campaign history. Seeking to allay concerns about his youth and inexperience, Quayle remarked, "I have as much experience in the Congress as Jack Kennedy did when he sought the presidency." Bentsen icily replied, "Senator, I served with Jack Kennedy. I knew Jack Kennedy. Jack Kennedy was a friend of mine. Senator, you're no Jack Kennedy." Despite Bentsen's memorable performance, the Bush-Quayle ticket won the election. However, Bentsen earned widespread admiration for his efforts and leadership and was easily reelected to the Senate by Texans. Bentsen was widely recognized as one of the most powerful and respected members of the Senate.

Following the 1992 presidential election, President-elect Bill Clinton, whom Bentsen knew from their work together on the centrist Democratic Leadership Council, invited the senator to serve as his secretary of the Treasury. Bentsen announced his resignation from the Senate and became treasury secretary in January 1993.

As treasury secretary, Bentsen accomplished many goals he had been working toward in the Senate. Initiatives included expanding American trade markets through the passage of the North American Free Trade Agreement and General Agreement on Tariffs and Trade measures. Bentsen pushed for legislation to reduce the federal deficit while increasing spending on education and training. Secretary Bentsen also served Clinton as an adviser and legislative strategist on nonfiscal issues.

During his tenure at the Treasury, Bentsen faced criticism over the role of the department's Bureau of Alcohol, Tobacco and Firearms in a seige and botched raid of the Branch Davidian complex outside Waco, Texas. Seventy-six people died during the raid, including more than twenty children. He also faced questions about the Treasury's supervisory role in handling a failed Arkansas savings and loan involved in the Whitewater investigation.

Bentsen served as treasury secretary until December 1994 and resigned to return to Houston. He continued his life outside the Senate as a partner in the Verner, Liipfert, Bernhard, McPherson, and Hand law firm; as an adviser to the Beacon Group, an investment bank; and as a member of several corporate boards. Bentsen kept up a full schedule until 1998 when he suffered a stroke.

In 1999 President Clinton awarded Bentsen the United States' highest civilian honor, the Presidential Medal of Freedom. "A man of courage, wisdom, and civility, Lloyd Bentsen has set the highest standard for public service," states the citation.

Bentsen passed away on 23 May 2006 at his home in Houston at the age of eighty-five following complications from his stroke in 1998.

★

Bentsen donated his public papers to the Center for American History at the University of Texas at Austin in 1996. The Bentsen Collection is especially valuable for its energy and trade issues, tax and banking policy, and the shaping of the federal budget. The Center for American History also has extensive clippings and stories on Bentsen. For information about Bentsen's life and career, see *Profiles in Power: Twentieth-Century Texans in Washington* (2004), edited by Kenneth E. Hendrickson, Jr., Michael L. Collins, and Patrick Cox. Obituaries are in the *New York Times* and *Washington Post* (both 24 May 2006).

Patrick Cox

BENZER, Seymour (*b.* 15 October 1921 in New York City; *d.* 30 November 2007 in Pasadena, California), geneticist, physicist, and molecular biologist whose pioneering research on the physical links among genes, the brain, and behavior launched the field of neurogenetics.

Benzer, one of four children and the only son of Mayer Benzer and Eva (Naidorf) Benzer, Jewish immigrants from Poland, grew up in the Bensonhurst section of Brooklyn, New York. As a young boy he believed, judging from the character of his own neighborhood, that the world was divided into two types of people, Jews and Italians. His father worked in the garment industry and briefly owned his own business; his mother, a skilled dressmaker, owned her own shop before she got married. During the Depression the family struggled economically, though Benzer recalled a stable, mostly carefree childhood. He attended public schools and spent his summers in the Catskill Mountains, where he enjoyed catching frogs and dissecting them. He turned the family basement into a rudimentary laboratory in which he conducted experiments. In 1934 he was given a microscope as a bar mitzvah present, "and that opened up the whole world," he said. In 1938 he graduated from New Utrecht High School and then entered Brooklyn College.

Benzer intended to study biology, but put off by the department's insistence that he take an introductory survey course before going into the more advanced classes, he ended up majoring in physics. On 10 January 1942 he married Dorothy ("Doty") Vlosky, a nurse, with whom he would have two daughters. Following graduation that year, Benzer enrolled as a graduate student in physics at

Seymour Benzer, 2006. AP IMAGES

Purdue University in Indiana, where he worked on a secret military project to develop robust crystal detectors to receive very-high-frequency microwaves. He earned an MS in 1943 and a PhD in 1947. Purdue immediately hired Benzer as an assistant professor of physics, but by then Benzer's interest in biology had been renewed by the physicist Erwin Schrödinger's 1944 book about viruses, *What Is Life?* In summer 1948 Benzer took a course on bacteriophage (the simplest kind of gene that reproduces itself) at Cold Spring Harbor Laboratory on Long Island, New York. "Three weeks of that, and I was converted," he later told an interviewer. That fall, Purdue granted him a yearlong leave to work at Oak Ridge National Laboratory in Tennessee on the phenomenon of photoreactivation in bacteriophage. Benzer extended his leave to spend the next two years, 1949 to 1951, as a research fellow in the lab of the biophysicist Max Delbrück at the California Institute of Technology (Caltech). In summer 1951, with the help of a Fulbright fellowship, he went to Paris for a year to work at the Institut Pasteur with the biologists André Lwoff and François Jacob and the biochemist Jacques Monod. During his stay there, Benzer conceived and developed an ingenious method for attacking a problem of bacterial physiology up to then considered almost impossible.

In 1953 Benzer returned to Purdue, and within months of James D. Watson and Francis Crick's discovery of the double-helix structure of deoxyribonucleic acid (DNA), he began a strictly genetic experiment to show the sequence of the genes on the chromosome, working with mutations of a bacteriophage that infected *Escherichia coli*. When two strains of the virus infected *E. coli*, their offspring contained new genes that combined elements of the same gene from both parents. He analyzed thousands of these recombination events and made the seminal discovery that a single gene could be cut and dissected into hundreds of parts, shattering the commonly held idea that the gene was indivisible. With each round of experiments, Benzer went deeper into the fine structure of the gene, with the intent of mapping it as far as it could be taken. More than any scientist, Benzer's mapping of the fine structure of the gene of a bacterial virus not only gave physical meaning to the nature of the gene but also bridged the gap between classical genetics and the new science of molecular biology.

Benzer spent a sabbatical year, 1957 to 1958, in Cambridge, England, working with Crick and the biologist Sydney Brenner to understand how DNA's one-dimensional structure of bases related to protein's one-dimensional sequence of amino acids. The experiments involved using protein bacteriophage mutations and doing fine-structure mapping, Benzer's specialty. Crick and Brenner later used Benzer's work to establish the triplet nature of the genetic code.

By the early 1960s Benzer had become interested in the roots of behavior, inspired partly by Dean Wooldridge's 1963 book, *The Machinery of the Brain*, and partly by observing the very different personalities of his two daughters as they grew up. While on sabbatical from 1965 to 1967 at Caltech, where he joined the lab of the psychobiologist Roger Sperry, Benzer worked with the fruit fly *Drosophila melanogaster* to answer the question, How do genes influence behavior? He never left Caltech; he never took another sabbatical; and he never touched a phage again.

Appointed James Griffin Boswell Professor of Neuroscience in 1967, Benzer developed a counter-current device that allowed him to sort flies according to behavior and isolate mutant strains. Using fruit flies as a model system to study the effect of mutations with specific behavioral abnormalities within large populations, Benzer first measured the flies' response to light; later, he and his students measured strains that slept and woke intermittently, mutants that died early, and homosexual flies. By systematically screening for these mutants, they identified the genes that affected the flies' circadian rhythms and other genes responsible for courtship, memory, learning, and longevity. As the story goes, when Benzer told Delbrück about the biological clock behavioral mutants, Delbrück replied that it was impossible. Benzer countered, "But, Max, we found the gene, we've already done it." Benzer's work with fruit flies, which he continued until his death, led directly to the modern field of *Drosophila* neurogenetics.

Among the many honors and awards Benzer received over the course of his career are the Lasker Award (1971), the National Medal of Science (1983), the Wolf Foundation Prize in Medicine (1991), the Bristol-Myers Squibb Award for Distinguished Achievement in Neuroscience Research (1992), the Crafoord Prize (1993), two Gairdner International Awards (1964 and 2004), and the $500,000 Albany Medical Center prize in medicine and biomedical research (2006). He was a member of the National Academy of Sciences, the American Academy of Arts and Sciences, the American Philosophical Society, and the Royal Society (London).

On 11 May 1980 Benzer, who had been widowed two years before, married Carol Miller, a neuropathologist, with whom he had a son; he also had two stepsons. He died at age eighty-six of a stroke at Huntington Hospital in Pasadena. He was cremated, according to his wishes.

Benzer made enormous and lasting contributions to physics, molecular biology, and neurobiology. His work on semiconductors at Purdue (1944 to 1953) contributed to the subsequent development of transistors. In his molecular biology period (1950 to 1966), Benzer elucidated the fine structure of the gene, and his research in this field helped lay the groundwork for an unprecedented era of genetic mapping and genetic engineering. In his neurobiology period (1967 to 2007), Benzer pioneered behavioral genetics from the organism down to the molecular level. Widely heralded as the father of neurogenetics, Benzer's fundamental work opened the field to exploration of models for Alzheimer's, Huntington's chorea, Parkinson's, and other neurodegenerative diseases of the human brain.

★

The Seymour Benzer Papers are at the Institute Archives, California Institute of Technology, Pasadena, California. The archives also contain an oral history interview with Benzer, conducted in eleven sessions from 1990 to 1991 by Heidi Aspaturian. Jonathan Weiner, *Time, Love, Memory: A Great Biologist and His Quest for the Origins of Behavior* (1999), focuses on Benzer's breakthrough work on genes and behavior. Frederic Lawrence Holmes, *Reconceiving the Gene: Seymour Benzer's Adventures in Phage Genetics* (2006), reconstructs Benzer's work in phage biology, drawing on the scientist's own records, and discusses the creativity of his research. Obituaries are in the *Boston Globe* (2 Dec. 2007) and *New York Times* (8 Dec. 2007).

Judith R. Goodstein

BERG, Patricia Jane ("Patty") (*b.* 13 February 1918 in Minneapolis, Minnesota; *d.* 10 September 2006 in Fort Myers, Florida), champion golfer and one of thirteen founders of the Ladies Professional Golf Association (LPGA) in 1950.

Berg was the daughter of Herman Berg, who owned a grain company in Minneapolis and who had been a semiprofessional baseball player. Her brother, Herman, Jr., was a fine golfer. In her youth she played golf at the Interlachen Country Club in suburban Edina, Minnesota. At age eight she was the quarterback on a Minneapolis neighborhood football team, the Fiftieth Street Tigers, whose coach and tackle, Charles "Bud" Wilkinson, would become a College Football Hall of Fame coach for the University of Oklahoma. Introducing Berg at a team practice years later, Wilkinson said, "This is the kind old lady who taught me how to play football." Torn clothing and various bruises prompted Berg's mother to persuade her to take up speed skating. In her early teens she turned to golf, which she found, she said later, to be a "great challenge for me. So much to do with tempo, rhythm, balance. I learned so much about patience. That's the key, patience. Then concentration and confidence." At sixteen she won the Minnesota City Championship, and at eighteen she was a member of the U.S. Curtis Cup team of amateur women golfers that retained the cup in a tie with the Great Britain and Ireland team at Gleneagles, Scotland.

Patty Berg, 1963. PA PHOTOS/LANDOV

Only five feet, two inches tall, Berg won ten of the thirteen tournaments in which she played in 1938, including the U.S. Women's Amateur, and again played for the Curtis Cup team that defeated Great Britain and Ireland at the Essex Country Club in Manchester, Massachusetts. Berg was named the 1938 Associated Press Female Athlete of the Year, an award she would also win in 1943 and 1955. In 1940, having attended the University of Minnesota since 1938, Berg turned pro, signing a contract with Wilson Sporting Goods to promote its golf equipment at clinics and exhibitions; out of loyalty to her sponsor, she declined to autograph a golf ball unless it was a Wilson ball. In 1941 she won the women's Western Open; her prize was a $100 war bond. As an officer in the U.S. Marine Corps Women's Reserve during World War II, she worked in recruitment and public relations and taught Marine Corps history at Camp Lejeune, North Carolina. In the first U.S. Women's Open Championship, in 1946, she defeated Betty Jameson (5–4) in the match-play final. One of thirteen founders of the LPGA in 1949, she was elected president of that organization. That year the first women's pro golf tour held fourteen events with $50,000 in total prize money; Berg was the leading money winner with $16,011.

Of her sixty career victories, Berg is credited by the LPGA as having won a record fifteen major titles, including eight that either were considered majors at the time or were later declared majors. Beginning in 1941 she won fifty-seven tournaments as a pro, including four Titleholders and three Western Opens. As an amateur, she had won three Titleholders championships, in 1937, 1938, and 1939. On the LPGA tour she was a three-time winner of the Glenna Collett Vare Trophy for lowest scoring average in 1953, 1955, and 1956; she was the leading money winner in 1954, 1955, and 1957. At the time of her death, her sixty victories put her at fourth on the career list, behind Kathy Whitworth, Mary "Mickey" Wright, and Annika Sorenstam. In her prime she often was overshadowed by Mildred "Babe" Didrikson Zaharias, who concentrated on golf after having earned two 1932 Olympic track-and-field gold medals. Zaharias won three U.S. Women's Opens. "Patty got kicked under the rug because of Babe," said Wright, whom many expert observers consider the best woman golfer ever and who rated Berg the best woman golfer she ever saw. "Number one, Patty had a good grip," Wright said. "She hit the ball solidly, she hit the ball high. She knew more golf shots than any other woman, before or after."

Berg, a member of the World Golf Hall of Fame, was one of the six inaugural inductees into the LPGA Hall of Fame. She was also a member of the LPGA Teaching and Club Professional Hall of Fame, the Women's Sports Hall of Fame, the Professional Golf Association of America Golf Hall of Fame, and the U.S. Marine Corps Sports Hall of Fame. Among her many honors, she received the Bob Jones Award for sportsmanship from the U.S. Golf Association. She continued to be a role model for younger pros and at clinics and exhibitions. Berg never married. She was a devout Catholic who rarely missed Sunday mass and was a member of an order of lay nuns. "My life," she often said, "has always been God, family, golf." When she spoke at golf gatherings, her advice to listeners was, "Keep your clothes ironed and your shoes clean. Be on time. Never criticize another person or a rival company. Know your lines." Many of her lines were supplied by the comedian Bob Hope, whose writers often sent her material. "She was quite hysterical, with a great sense of humor," Sorenstam said of Berg's patter at a clinic. "And she was a pioneer."

In her later years Berg lived in Fort Myers, where a plate near her front door proclaimed, "Golf is the worst damn game you'll ever love." In 1993 the Patty Berg Cancer Center was dedicated at the Southwest Florida Regional Medical Center as Berg continued to promote golf. "She never met a stranger," the golfer Nancy Lopez said. "She was the greatest ambassador the LPGA ever had." At age seventy-six, with the camera rolling during a 1994 video for the U.S. Golf Association centennial, she made a fourteen-foot, right-to-left putt, but the producer told her, "Sorry, Patty, we didn't get it that time." She made that same putt four times in a row until they got it. At age seventy-nine she said,

"I haven't retired. I'm still going to the golf course, still doing clinics and exhibitions. And I'm still taking lessons." In 2000 *Golf Digest* named her the forty-eighth-best golfer (men and women) of all time. She died of complications from Alzheimer's disease at the Hope Hospice in Fort Myers. She is buried at Fort Myers Memorial Gardens.

★

James Hahn and Lynn Hahn, *Patty! The Sports Career of Patty Berg* (1981), is a biography for young readers. For statistical information on Berg's career, the *LPGA Media Guide* (1998) is the definitive source. Obituaries are in the *New York Times*, *Minneapolis Star-Tribune*, and *Washington Post* (all 11 Sept. 2006).

Dave Anderson

BISHOP, Joey (*b*. 3 February 1918 in New York City; *d*. 17 October 2007 in Newport Beach, California), stand-up comedian and television and motion-picture actor who was part of the Rat Pack of the 1960s and whose late-night talk show for a time challenged *The Tonight Show* with Johnny Carson for ratings dominance.

Joey Bishop, 1964. CBS/LANDOV

Bishop was born Joseph Abraham Gottlieb. His father, Jacob Gottlieb, was a mechanic, and his mother, Anna (Siegel) Gottlieb, was a homemaker. Bishop was the youngest of five children. Soon after his birth, Bishop's family moved to Philadelphia, Pennsylvania, where he was raised. The family lived over a bicycle shop that his father ran, while he also worked as a machinist at Fidelity Machine Company. The Gottlieb children all worked to help their family. Bishop sold fruit, was a soda jerk, and made sandwiches at a delicatessen. He quit high school in order to pursue his dream of being in show business. As an adult he remembered being a happy child who did not mind having to work. When he became a star, he often used his influence and money to help childhood friends, as well as his siblings.

As a teenager Bishop and a few friends formed a comedy act, an unpolished mixture of fast talk and some songs. None of the members of the act considered his last name to be snazzy enough for show business, so they took the last name of a friend and dubbed themselves the Bishop Brothers. They found work in small nightclubs in Philadelphia, New York, and Chicago, but the group shrank to a threesome, then to a twosome, and eventually to just Joey Bishop. During this period he developed his trademark understated rejoinders; he said he wanted his audience to feel it was listening in on his remarks, rather than feeling he was demanding that it laugh. It was while performing at the Chez Paree in Chicago in the 1940s that someone called Bishop "The Frown Prince of Comedy" because of his sad visage while he delivered his jokes and impressions.

On 14 January 1941 he married Sylvia Ruzga of Oak Park, Illinois. In April 1942 Bishop was drafted into the army and stationed at Fort Sam Houston, Texas, for over three years, where he won a welterweight boxing title in the Eighth Service Command. On 4 August 1947 Bishop's only child, a son, Larry, was born.

Bishop and the singer and actor Frank Sinatra had crossed paths occasionally as each went from city to city to perform in clubs and theaters. Sinatra found Bishop's straightforward honesty appealing, and in 1952 he asked Bishop to be his opening act during his latest tour. This was a big boost for Bishop because it drew him the notice of America's top-performing venues. Even so, Bishop fretted that television would cost him his audiences because people could see televised comics for free, but people had to pay to see him.

In 1958 Bishop chose to forgo about $200,000 in income from clubs to perform for $850 per week on the game show *Keep Talking* on the Columbia Broadcasting System (CBS), where his quick wit and everyman persona were displayed to advantage. The gamble paid off in more than a decade of television work, including becoming a guest host on *The Jack Paar Show* (formerly *The Tonight Show*) in 1959. In 1958 he broke into motion-picture acting in a part in *The Naked and the Dead*. By then Bishop was a big draw in Las Vegas, Nevada, where in 1960 Sinatra chose to film

the motion-picture *Ocean's Eleven* with some of his buddies, including Bishop, Dean Martin, Sammy Davis, Jr., and Peter Lawford. They became known as the Rat Pack, and as a team they had an immensely popular Las Vegas showroom act, with the quiet and understated Bishop acting as the glue that held them together.

During the 1960s Bishop had a series of television shows, each titled *The Joey Bishop Show*. He and the actor Danny Thomas had been friends since the 1940s, and Thomas had become one of the television industry's most powerful people. Acting as producer, Thomas sold *The Joey Bishop Show* to the National Broadcasting Company (NBC); it premiered 20 September 1961, with Bishop portraying a publicity agent named Joey Barnes. The show did well in the ratings, but Bishop hated it, and throughout his life he refused to allow that season of his show to be rerun. The next season Bishop brought in new writers and turned Joey Barnes into a television talk-show host. In the spring of 1964, NBC canceled the show, which CBS then added to its Sunday night lineup. In spring 1965 CBS canceled the series. Bishop became the preferred substitute for Johnny Carson on *The Tonight Show* (so named again after Paar left it), and this inspired the American Broadcasting Company (ABC) to give Bishop his own weeknight talk show, again *The Joey Bishop Show*, beginning 17 April 1967. It became popular for its tackling social issues and competed well against *The Tonight Show*, but when *The Merv Griffin Show* also came on opposite Bishop, his show tanked in the ratings and Bishop himself ended it on 24 November 1969.

This marked the end of Bishop's remarkable climb to the top of show business, but he did not disappear from it. He had been wise with his earnings and could afford to do whatever he wanted, including becoming a skilled boater; he was credited at least twice with saving the lives of other boaters with his boat *Sonuvagun II*. He appeared on Broadway in *Sugar Babies* in 1981, and he remained a huge draw in Las Vegas. He made numerous appearances on television series and occasional appearances in movies, including *Mad Dog Time* (1996), which was directed by his son, Larry.

Bishop stood out from among many of his fellows in the 1950s and 1960s by usually keeping his acts family friendly and by avoiding racial jokes. He even asked Sinatra and Martin to stop calling each other "dago" during their Las Vegas act, which they agreed to do. His sad, world-weary onstage persona and humor made him a voice for many Americans who were just trying to get by day after day. Bishop's wife, Sylvia, died of lung cancer in September 1999. The last surviving member of the Rat Pack, Bishop died from multiple causes at his home at age eighty-nine. He was cremated and his ashes were scattered in the ocean.

★

Michael Seth Starr, *Mouse in the Rat Pack* (2002), focuses on Bishop's show business career. In the Home Box Office movie *The Rat Pack* (1998), Bishop was portrayed by Bobby Slayton. Obituaries are in the *Los Angeles Times* and *New York Times* (both 19 Oct. 2007).

Kirk H. Beetz

BOYD, Edward Francis (*b.* 27 June 1914 in Riverside, California; *d.* 30 April 2007 in Los Angeles, California), African-American sales manager for the Pepsi-Cola Company who, with his team of black salesmen, broke color barriers in the corporate world.

Boyd was one of four children born to Robert Boyd, a barber, and Emma (Barrett) Boyd, a realtor. As members of one of the few black middle-class families in the region, the Boyds taught their children never to underestimate what they could accomplish, even in the face of stereotypes and racism. Emma, especially, was a vocal opponent of racial stereotypes and was never afraid to stand her ground. As noted in Stephanie Capparell's *The Real Pepsi Challenge: The Inspirational Story of Breaking the Color Barrier in American Business* (2007), whenever Emma received a threatening phone call from a person who opposed her public stance on racial equality, she would reply, "I'm ready for you; come on over."

Emma's successful realty company, Boyd & Boyd Real Estate, was often under attack for its policy to sell land to any person regardless of race. Robert also ran his own business, a successful chain of barbershops. Boyd shared his parents' determination for success. He sang in the choir at his high school, from which he graduated in 1932. He also sang in the choir at Riverside Junior College and at Riverside's small opera company, and he worked as a singer at the Mission Inn, a stylish hotel in Riverside.

Boyd transferred from Riverside Junior College to the University of California, Los Angeles (UCLA), where he earned a bachelor's degree in international relations and public and personnel administration in 1938. In college Boyd's noted charisma and talent for singing and performing earned him a place in Hollywood. There he garnered small roles—some of which were cut from the final film version— and singing parts in films such as *Jezebel* and *Top of the Town*. However, performing in Hollywood films was not as fulfilling as Boyd might have thought. The only roles reserved for African Americans were those of subservient, stereotypical black characters. Eventually, after a makeup director commented that Boyd's skin did not seem dark enough to play an African American, Boyd could no longer stand the racist environment and stopped performing in films. Although he quit acting, Boyd joined the Screen Actors Guild (SAG), where he sat on the board of directors for two years. Upon graduating from UCLA,

Boyd took a paid position in the SAG personnel department. Later he accepted a personnel job with the National Youth Administration, a part of President Franklin D. Roosevelt's Works Progress Administration created to rebuild the U.S. economy during the Great Depression. While these positions helped pave Boyd's way into a professional life, it was his next job with California government war housing programs that thrust him into the center of U.S. racial tensions.

Upon entering World War II in 1941, the United States lost many male workers to the military. This shortage improved opportunities for African Americans to gain employment, and numerous blacks (many from the South) relocated to the West Coast for the war effort. Many white workers also relocated to the region. It was Boyd's job to place these new residents into war housing dormitories. Assigning black and white workers to the same buildings brought hostility from whites throughout the community, but Boyd nonetheless fought passionately for integration. It was while working in this position in 1944 that Boyd married Edith Jones, the daughter of an attorney who was one of the first African-American graduates of the Ohio State University Law School. The couple was married for sixty-three years and had three sons and one daughter.

Soon after they married, the couple moved to New York City, where Boyd worked as a housing specialist with the National Urban League and Edith became a librarian for *Time* magazine. In 1947 he took a position as assistant sales manager for the Pepsi-Cola Company. Pepsi was experiencing a dramatic drop in sales when Boyd was hired. Charged with attracting African-American customers, Boyd first endeavored to hire twelve black salespeople. It did not take long for Boyd and his sales team to succeed in their efforts; however, Boyd accomplished more than just increased sales for Pepsi. By targeting African-American customers on the business and marketing side, he initiated what is known as niche or target marketing.

By hiring articulate, highly educated salesmen, Boyd challenged racial discrimination in the corporate world and defeated the all too present stereotype of the unintelligent black man. In 1948 Boyd pioneered the "Leaders in Their Fields" series of advertisements for Pepsi that depicted African Americans in a positive light. The twenty African Americans profiled in the advertisements, including middle-class professionals and black university students, were intended to portray success and differed dramatically from the roles Boyd once played in movies.

During this period, with civil rights laws more than a decade away, Boyd and his sales team rode on segregated trains, struggled to find hotels that allowed blacks, were threatened by the Ku Klux Klan, and were insulted by some of their Pepsi colleagues. Although Boyd was successful in his sales campaign, he was dismissed by a new Pepsi president in 1951 because of fears that Pepsi was becoming known as a "black drink" that might be rejected by whites. After leaving Pepsi, Boyd headed food relief missions in Egypt and Gaza, worked with the Society of Ethical Culture in New York, and trained high school students in leadership. Upon retiring in 1981, he started a 120-acre alpaca farm in Sullivan County in New York. Boyd died at age ninety-two from complications of a stroke. When racial stereotyping and discrimination was the norm, Boyd and his family defied expectations. From his parents Boyd learned that black did not mean sub-servient, a message he passed along to countless others in his professional life, most publicly through his work with Pepsi.

★

Comprehensive biographical information on Boyd is available in Stephanie Capparell, *The Real Pepsi Challenge: The Inspirational Story of Breaking the Color Barrier in American Business* (2007). An interview with Boyd and Capparell aired on *Tavis Smiley* on the Public Broadcasting Service on 27 Feb. 2007; the transcript is available at http://www.pbs.org/kcet/tavissmiley/archive/200702/20070227_edwardboydstephan.html. Obituaries are in the *Los Angeles Times* (5 May 2007) and *New York Times* (6 May 2007).

Candice L. Mancini

Peter Boyle. CBS/MONTY BRINTON/LANDOV

BOYLE, Peter Lawrence (*b.* 18 October 1935 in Norristown, Pennsylvania; *d.* 12 December 2006 in New York City), versatile supporting actor best known for comic roles in Mel Brooks's *Young Frankenstein* and in the television sitcom *Everybody Loves Raymond*.

Boyle was one of four children born to Francis Xavier ("Pete") Boyle and Alice V. Boyle. He grew up in Phila-delphia, Pennsylvania, where his father became a local television celebrity hosting an afternoon program for chil-dren, *Uncle Pete Presents the Little Rascals*. Boyle attended Saint Francis De Sales School and then West Philadelphia Catholic High School for Boys. There, after dabbling in football, he turned to the stage and school musicals. At seventeen he entered the De La Salle Christian Brothers, a religious order dedicated to teaching, spending three years in religious training while earning his bachelor's degree in English from La Salle University, Philadelphia, in 1957. Recognizing his fading attraction to the brothers, Boyle left the order in 1958 and a year later graduated from the U.S. Navy Officer Candidate School. A nervous break-down ended his military career, and he started training as an actor in New York City with Uta Hagen as his coach. Like many aspiring actors, Boyle paid for acting lessons through jobs sorting mail, waiting tables, and performing in television commercials; in one airline ad

he appeared as the harried father racing with his family through an airport.

Prematurely bald, Boyle from the start played characters advanced beyond his real age. With an assist from Elaine May, he made his theatrical debut in 1967 as Murray the Cop in the road company production of Neil Simon's *The Odd Couple*. Leaving the show in Chicago, he joined the Second City improvisational team and appeared in Haskell Wexler's *Medium Cool* (1969). The realist film captured the anti–Vietnam War sentiment espoused by Boyle and other actors with whom he protested U.S. involvement. His break-through in film came with his appearance as the title char-acter in *Joe* (1970). A conniving, loudmouthed pipefitter, Joe convinces a corporate executive to go on a murderous ram-page against the hippies that ends in the death of his rebel-lious daughter. Provoked by the inflammatory and racist language and the graphic violence, audiences yelled to the character onscreen: "Go get them, Joe," and conversely, "We're going to get you, Joe." Alarmed by the impact, the performer for a time eschewed roles in violent movies, including the lead in the Oscar-winning *French Connection* (1971). Instead, opposite Robert Redford, he played a slick manager of a senator's campaign in *The Candidate* (1972) and then, with Robert Mitchum, appeared as a mobster in *The Friends of Eddie Coyle* (1973).

The following year brought career and life-altering events for Boyle. Looking for a brawny actor who could sing and dance, Mel Brooks cast him as the Monster in *Young Frankenstein* (1974), a spoof of the horror films of the 1930s. Boyle had none of the legendary lines of the movie, but in top hat and tails he starred in the memorable "Puttin' on the Ritz" dance scene, twirling a cane, tapping his feet, and grunting the lyrics. On the set and in his monster costume, Boyle met the *Rolling Stone* magazine reporter Loraine Alterman. Their relationship led to marriage in 1977, with the famed musician John Lennon serving as the couple's best man. The Boyles raised two children, Lucy and Amy.

A cameo as Wizard in Martin Scorsese's *Taxi Driver* (1976) preceded a long list of movie parts varying in style, size, and quality. Still, Boyle's biggest roles calibrate the range of his acting talents. He was one of the comically inept heist gang in *The Brink's Job* (1978), a lawyer for the gonzo journalist Hunter S. Thompson in the comedy *Where the Buffalo Roam* (1980), an arrogant, crooked boss of a space center in the sci-fi movie *Outland* (1981), a singing mental patient who thinks he is Jesus in the comedy *The Dream Team* (1989), and the malicious, redneck father in the drama *Monster's Ball* (2001). In lesser roles, he appeared in *Beyond the Poseidon Adventure* (1979), *Malcolm X* (1992), *While You Were Sleeping* (1995), and in *The Santa Clause* series of movies (1994, 2002, 2006).

On the small screen he earned an Emmy nomination for the 1977 film *Tail Gunner Joe*, playing the controversial senator Joseph McCarthy. In 1990 Boyle suffered a stroke that left him speechless for six months, after which he resumed his career. In 1996 he won his lone Emmy Award for Outstanding Guest Actor in a Drama Series for his role in an episode of *The X Files* series. Between film and television roles, Boyle also appeared onstage, notably opposite Tommy Lee Jones in Sam Shepard's off-Broadway drama *True West* (1980).

In 1996 the sixty-one-year-old actor found the role that extended his career for ten years and endeared him to television audiences worldwide. The comedian and producer Ray Romano was searching for a performer to play the grouchy father in his proposed sitcom series *Everybody Loves Raymond*. Arriving at the audition after several misadventures in Los Angeles traffic and with his teenage children critiquing his driving, the agitated Boyle quickly convinced Romano that he was right for the Frank Barone role, nagging father to Raymond and gruff husband to Marie (Doris Roberts). The cast and crew soon became family. Watching old movies together each Sunday night and going on monthly excursions cemented their relationships. Forced to commute each month from New York City to the Warner Bros. studio in Burbank, California, Boyle still counted himself lucky to be working with the ensemble cast. Thanks to their cohesive performances and incisive scripting by Philip Rosenthal, the Columbia

Broadcasting System program soared in the ratings and for almost a decade stayed near the top.

Frank Barone and his "holy crap" became part of the American cultural landscape. The actor sometimes relished the fact that *Everybody Loves Raymond* was also the most popular show in Pakistan, partly because the audience saw Frank Barone as "the typical Pakistani father." Despite the rave reviews, Boyle was the only member of the cast who never won an Emmy for the show. Coming full circle, his last professional appearance was in a commercial, this one for Alka-Seltzer with his television wife Marie Barone played by Roberts listening as he invoked the memorable tagline, "I can't believe I ate that whole thing." A consummate character actor, Boyle capped his career with a paradox: Frank Barone, the beloved curmudgeon.

In 1999 Boyle suffered a heart attack on the *Raymond* set, but he recovered rapidly. In 2001, however, he was diagnosed with multiple myeloma complicated by heart disease, and he gradually succumbed to the illnesses. Boyle died at age seventy-one at New York Presbyterian Hospital. Hundreds of colleagues and friends attended his memorial service, including the entire cast of *Everybody Loves Raymond*. His body was cremated.

★

New York Times critic J. Hoberman, "Off the Hippies: 'Joe' and the Chaotic Summer of '70" (30 July 2000), examines the significance of Boyle's first starring role in *Joe*. James Robert Parish in his biography of filmmaker Mel Brooks, *It's Good to Be the King* (2007), labels one chapter "A Monster Hit" and describes how the producer Gene Wilder connected Boyle to the Monster role in *Young Frankenstein*. Steve Lopez, "Sweet and Sourpuss," *Entertainment Weekly* (12 Jan. 2001), provides a short but comprehensive overview of Boyle's career. An obituary and an appended obituary are in the *New York Times* (14 Dec. 2006 and 23 Dec. 2006, respectively).

Gerard Molyneaux

BRADLEY, Edward Rudolph ("Ed"), Jr. (*b.* 22 June 1941 in Philadelphia, Pennsylvania; *d.* 9 November 2006 in New York City), television news reporter and anchor, White House correspondent, and documentary host for Columbia Broadcasting System (CBS).

Bradley was the only child of Edward Rudolph Bradley, Sr., and Gladys (Gaston) Bradley. His parents divorced when he was a small child, and his father moved to Detroit. As a youngster Bradley often spent his summer months in Detroit with his father, where the elder Bradley was in the vending machine business and also owned a restaurant. Bradley attended private Catholic grade schools and St. Thomas More Roman Catholic High School in Philadelphia. In 1964 he received a BS from Cheyney State College

Ed Bradley, 1983. CBS PHOTO ARCHIVE/GETTY IMAGES

(now Cheyney University of Pennsylvania). After a brief stint as an elementary school teacher, Bradley entered the broadcasting field, first as a radio disc jockey and then as a radio news reporter for WDAS-FM in Philadelphia. He joined WCBS Radio in New York City in 1967 and then became a stringer for CBS's Paris bureau in 1971.

The next year Bradley was transferred to the CBS Saigon bureau and was wounded while in Cambodia covering the military conflict there. He returned to the United States and was assigned as a White House correspondent in 1974. Returning to Southeast Asia, he reported on the fall of the Cambodian and Vietnamese capitals. He was one of the last American news reporters evacuated when Phnom Penh fell to the Communists in 1975.

Bradley returned to the United States and remained in Washington, D.C., from 1976 to 1978, when he began anchoring the *CBS Sunday Night News.* In 1981 he left to replace Dan Rather on American television's most celebrated weekly news and public affairs series, *60 Minutes.* Quickly becoming recognized as a master interviewer, Bradley could coax information out of a variety of sources, especially through the relationships he had developed and particularly with those in the entertainment field. He loved jazz and became closely involved in stories focusing on music and musicians. His friends in the music world included the jazz musician Wynton Marsalis, the soul and

jazz group the Neville Brothers, and the jazz promoter and producer George Wein.

Over the next several years, Bradley pursued a number of journalistic interests and activities. For example, he hosted *Jazz at Lincoln Center Radio,* a weekly show broadcast over 240 radio stations. He also conducted entertaining yet revealing interviews with the singers Bob Dylan, Jimmy Buffett, and Michael Jackson, who at the time was awaiting trial for child molestation. As an investigative reporter, Bradley explored charges of sexual abuse in the Catholic Church, prison labor in China, and the Columbine school shootings in Colorado, and also interviewed important news figures, such as the Oklahoma City bomber Timothy McVeigh and the convicted murderer Jack Henry Abbott. Bradley returned to Southeast Asia for a documentary titled "The Boat People." At one point he was caught on camera in a heroic effort to assist Vietnamese refugees off the coast of Malaysia in the South China Sea. That particular *CBS Reports* documentary, airing 19 January 1979, received the Overseas Press Club's Edward R. Murrow Award, the International Festival of the British Academy of Film and Television Arts Award, and the Alfred I. du Pont–Columbia University Award.

Bradley's best-remembered on-camera interactions came with the singer Lena Horne and the retired boxer Muhammad Ali. For the Horne feature, Bradley strolled hand in hand with Horne through Central Park in New York City and asked some rather personal questions. During an interview with Ali, who suffered from Parkinson's disease and had to be assisted by his wife, Ali pretended that he was asleep and even dreaming, feigning multiple boxing jabs before punching Bradley lightly with his eyes still closed. Ali then laughed out loud with his wife and the rest of his family at the interviewer's stunned response when Bradley realized that Ali was pretending.

Bradley befriended many of the subjects of his stories and was held in high esteem, even among interviewees who had been involved in some unsavory event or business. His interview with the ill-fated 1988 presidential candidate Gary Hart was one such prominent example. Hart had dropped out of the presidential race because of allegations of impropriety with a former model, Donna Rice.

Bradley's *CBS Reports* documentary program "Blacks in America: With All Deliberate Speed" (1979) examined progress by African Americans since 1954, when the U.S. Supreme Court ruled against segregation in schools. Bradley also won praise for revisiting the 1955 Mississippi murder case of fourteen-year-old Emmett Till; Bradley's efforts on the Till case helped to reopen some civil rights cases.

Over the course of his career, Bradley received nineteen Emmy Awards, including a Lifetime Achievement Award in 2003. One of his last reports for *60 Minutes* cast doubts on the prosecutor's case concerning allegations of rape against Duke University lacrosse players. The report concentrated on the evidence, with falsely accused athletes appearing with their families and describing the conduct of their trials and the effects on them. That program aired on 15 October 2006. Bradley's final report, presented on 29 October 2006, investigated an explosion at an oil refinery.

Bradley was married three times but had no children. He married Diane Jefferson right after college in 1964; the couple divorced in 1967. His second marriage, to the singer Priscilla Coolidge in 1981, ended in divorce in 1984. His final marriage was to the artist Patricia Blanchet in 2004. Bradley died at age sixty-five of complications from chronic lymphocytic leukemia at Mount Sinai Medical Center in New York City. He had previously undergone a quintuple bypass operation on his heart in 2003 and had been diagnosed with leukemia years earlier. An infection complicated his medical condition and contributed to his death. A memorial service filled with jazz music was held on 21 November 2006 at Riverside Church in New York City.

★

Excerpts from some of Bradley's key *60 Minutes* television interviews are in Frank Coffey, *60 Minutes: 25 Years of Television's Finest Hour* (1993). For a brief profile, see James Brady, "In Step with Ed Bradley," *Parade* (24 Mar. 1996). Reflections on Bradley's career and personal influence are in *NABJ Journal* (Winter 2006). An obituary is in the *New York Times* (10 Nov. 2006).

Michael D. Murray

BRECHT, George (*b.* 27 August 1926 in New York City; *d.* 5 December 2008 in Cologne, Germany), experimental visual and performing artist of the 1960s and founding member and primary innovator of a performance art collective known as Fluxus. His musical scores and art objects extended the nonauthorial voice in art begun by Marcel Duchamp and John Cage.

Brecht was born George Ellis MacDiarmid to a father also named George Ellis MacDiarmid, a professional flute player who performed in the Metropolitan Opera Orchestra. When the elder MacDiarmid succumbed in 1936 to alcoholism, George and his mother left New York City and moved to Atlantic City, New Jersey, where George attended Atlantic City High School. He enlisted in the U.S. Army in 1943 at the age of seventeen and was stationed in the Black Forest in southern Germany. In 1945 he changed his last name to Brecht, a clear reinvention of self and a considerable break with his past.

Brecht returned to the United States in 1946, studied briefly in Mexico, and then enrolled in the Philadelphia College of Pharmacy and Science, where he graduated with a BS in chemistry. For about twenty years after that, Brecht was employed as a research chemist and was granted five patents and two shared patents for health and hygiene inventions.

Brecht was influenced by the paintings of Jackson Pollock and Robert Rauschenberg, especially the latter's *Growing Painting* (1953), an assembly of dirt, seeds, and pigment in a six-foot wooden box. He began to paint with bed sheets, marbles, and pigments using a variety of chance operations. Brecht's pamphlet, "Chance Imagery," described chance operations and random number systems as they can be applied to the creation of art.

Brecht married his first wife, Marceline Allemand, around 1951. Three years later, his only son was born in New York City. Brecht had met the artists Robert Watts and Allan Kaprow at Rutgers University in New Brunswick, New Jersey. They convened weekly at a Howard Johnson's restaurant, at least once with John Cage.

Brecht enrolled in Cage's famous Experimental Music Composition class at the New School for Social Research in New York City. Cage's procedures for "found sound" and his Zen-based chance operations resonated strongly with Brecht. Brecht studied the relationships of Cage's art to Marcel Duchamp's earlier *Readymade* creations. During Cage's class, Brecht composed a piece that described a concerted action by individuals in an everyday context. The piece, titled *Timetable Music*, involved Cage's class traveling to Grand Central Station and using the local train schedules to time their auditory and visual perceptions.

Brecht remembers the inspiration for another piece during the spring of 1960: "waiting . . . behind my English Ford station wagon, the motor running and the left-turn signal blinking, it occurred to me that a truly 'event' piece could be drawn from the situation." This epiphany led to *Motor Vehicle Sundown (Event)*, which listed instructions for mundane actions to be performed by drivers of twenty-two automobiles gathered in a prearranged public space at sunset.

In 1959 Brecht's art was featured in a solo show, Toward Events: An Arrangement, at the Reuben Gallery in Greenwich Village. Here, Brecht continued his relationship with Kaprow, then a painting professor at Rutgers University and founder of the Happening and Un-Art movements. As an art form, assemblage continued the Cubist collage tradition, in some ways resembling the surrealistic boxes of Joseph Cornell, but Brecht's work invited the spectator to touch the sculpture, move its pieces, and interact with it in a playful, less egotistical manner. In 1961 *Repository*, his first "event/score," was displayed at the Museum of Modern Art's historic Art of Assemblage show, curated by the renowned art historian William Seitz. In his "Notes on Shipping and Exhibiting the Repository to Seitz," Brecht states he is less interested in the work itself than when someone becomes physically involved with it, when someone might freely open the cabinet, or when parts might be lost or destroyed: "When (if) parts disappear, replace these with parts that seem equivalent. If no equivalent parts are available, substitute something else, or nothing at all, if you'd rather. No catastrophes are possible."

Also in 1961 Brecht joined the Lithuanian artist George Maciunas and the Cage classmates Jackson Mac Low, Robert Watts, Alison Knowles, Yoko Ono, and La Monte Young in concerts of performance art, forming an artists' collective that would become known as Fluxus. Brecht's most productive years were 1960 to 1963. He wrote over 150 event/scores, titles in black type on small heavy-stock cards, with accompanying instructions and observations on them, mostly for Fluxus. Brecht never emphasized the newness or radical quality of his work. He believed his scores did not exist without a witness to observe them.

In 1963 Brecht launched the Yam Festival with Watts, a display of "art that could not be bought." It included mailings, Fluxboxes (assemblage), Fluxkits (do-it-yourself assemblage), and event/scores. In 1964 Brecht divorced his wife and began to prepare for a move to Europe. Cage inveighed upon his friend for nearly a year, trying to dissuade the move. But Brecht was resolute, and in 1965 he moved to Rome with his partner, Donna Jo Brewer.

Within a year, Brecht and Brewer moved to Villefranche-sur-mer in southern France. There Brecht opened a "workshop," La Cédille qui sourit ("The cedilla that smiles"), with the artist Robert Filliou. They also founded the Eternal Network: La Fête Permanente, a loosely defined art collective. Brecht and Filliou collaborated on puzzles, articles, and a few films, notably the *Hommage à Méliès*. This center for artistic and linguistic studies quickly closed, and during the next few years, Brecht moved to London and Düsseldorf before settling in Cologne in 1971. This marked the beginning of what he referred to as his period of "accelerated creative inactivity." Perhaps the greatest project during this time was the Landmass Translocation Project, sponsored by the Brecht and MacDiarmid Development Corporation, which proposed to relocate the Isle of Wight in the Azores.

Between 1971 and 2001 Brecht's creative output dwindled to several more sets of puzzles, some Fluxboxes and Fluxkits, and a few mechanical constructions. His early work enjoyed greater and greater acceptance. He exhibited in a 1972 London show called the Book of the Tumbler on Fire. In 1972 and 1977 his work was displayed in Kassel, Germany, as part of the Documenta exhibitions. In 1975 Brecht collaborated with the British artist Patrick Hughes to compile a list of aphorisms titled *Vicious Circles: A Panoply of Paradoxes*, released in boxes. In 2002 he married Hertha Klang in Cologne. In 2005 the Ludwig Museum in Cologne organized an exhibit of Brecht's collected works, titled George Brecht Events: A Heterospective. This exhibit traveled to the Museu d'Art Contemporani de Barcelona in 2006.

Brecht died in his sleep at age eighty-two in his apartment in Cologne during a period of failing health.

Brecht's art diminished the role of the artist and exalted that of the spectator by searching for beauty in the most normal and mundane parts of life. He wrote that his art ensures "that the details of everyday life, the random constellations of objects that surround us, stop going unnoticed."

★

Brecht, with Filliou, wrote *Games at the Cedilla, or the Cedilla Takes Off* (1967), with insight into Brecht's time in France. Brecht explained Fluxus in "Something About Fluxus," *Fluxus Newspaper* 4 (June 1964). H. Martin, *An Introduction to George Brecht's Book of the Tumbler on Fire* (1978), has interviews and an anthology of texts by Brecht. Anna Dezeuze, "Brecht for Beginners," *Papers of Surrealism* 4 (winter 2005), provides more insight into Brecht and his artwork. Obituaries are in the *New York Times* (15 Dec. 2008) and the *Guardian* (9 Jan. 2009).

James McElwaine

BRENNER, Charles (*b.* 18 November 1913 in Boston, Massachusetts; *d.* 19 May 2008 in New York City), internationally acclaimed psychoanalyst, author, and academician who was a significant leader in the evolution of Freudian concepts and who won renown for his "modern conflict theory."

Brenner was one of two sons born to Sam, a lawyer and an immigrant from the Ukraine, and Ann, a schoolteacher. He completed his studies at the Boston Latin School at the age of fourteen and attended Harvard University, graduating cum laude with a degree in chemistry in 1931. Brenner earned his MD in 1935 from the Harvard Medical School, and continued his studies with a residency and an internship in Boston. That same year, he wed Erma, to whom he would be married for sixty-six years until her death in 2001. The couple would have two daughters.

Brenner served as a neurologist at the College of Physicians and Surgeons at Columbia University in New York, where he published on drug treatments and surgical lobotomies. He continued his training at the Boston Psychoanalytic Society and Institute and decided to enter the field of psychiatry following his mother's treatment for hysteria. At the time, psychoanalysis was still in its formative period in the United States and was essentially led by those who were devoted to the Freudian approach. Brenner, too, decided to focus on Freudian theory.

From 1944 to 1950, Brenner held the position of associate attending psychiatrist at the Montefiore Medical Center in New York. In 1947 he became a member of the New York Psychoanalytic Society and Institute. His first book, *An Elementary Textbook of Psychoanalysis* (1955), exceeded the million mark in sales, becoming the best-selling text on psychoanalysis by someone other than Sigmund Freud and emerging as the standard reference for training programs in the United States and elsewhere.

Beginning in 1957 and for much of his career, Brenner worked at the New York Psychoanalytic Society and Institute both as an instructor and as a training and supervising analyst. He was president of the New York Psychoanalytic Society and Institute from 1961 to 1963, and with Dr. Jacob A. Arlow wrote a book titled *Psychoanalytic Concepts and the Structural Theory* (1964) in which they expound the Freudian concept that the purpose of psychoanalysis is to bring the unconscious to a conscious level. The book has been credited with facilitating the emergence of modern psychoanalysis.

Brenner was president of the American Psychoanalytic Association from 1967 to 1968, and maintained a long-standing relationship with the *Psychoanalytic Quarterly*, becoming a member of the journal's editorial board in 1972 and an associate editor and treasurer from 1981 until his death.

In his third book, *Psychoanalytic Technique and Psychic Conflict* (1976), Brenner discusses a number of ways in which familiar aspects of analytic technique can be applied to the various modes of expression and the resulting consequences of psychic conflict. In *The Mind in Conflict* (1982) Brenner put forward an assortment of inventive theoretical concepts, assimilating them in the context of conventional structural theory and established psychoanalytic technique. Although considered essential reading for the serious clinician, this book has also proven to be of interest to nonanalysts.

Brenner first presented his modern conflict theory in a paper titled "The Mind as Conflict and Compromise Formation" (1994) published in the *Journal of Clinical Psychoanalysis*. In it, he proposed a model of the mind in which psychological conflict is the result of the incompatibility of competing wishes. This conflict would in turn force the individual to make the best possible compromise in order to satisfy one's drives, while simultaneously taking into account one's emotions and defense mechanisms. Brenner's proposal did not sit well with many of his colleagues, who considered it contrary to Freud's model in which the id, ego, and superego are essentially at war.

In 1998 Brenner collaborated with a number of colleagues to launch a two-year telemedicine course in psychodynamic psychotherapy meant to determine its efficacy in teaching residents. Though Brenner formally retired in 2001, he continued teaching classes at the New York Psychoanalytic Society and Institute.

Brenner's last book, *Psychoanalysis or Mind and Meaning* (2006), is an account of his over sixty years of experience studying and practicing psychoanalytic theory and methodology. As part of his long and illustrious career, Brenner wrote numerous articles (the last one approximately a year before his death), became a distinguished lifetime member of the Association for Psychoanalytic Medicine, was a well-known participant in all New York psychoanalytic circle debates, and, with his wife, was a longtime supporter of the Pacella Parent Child Center of the New York Psychoanalytic Society and Institute.

Brenner died at age ninety-four at New York-Presbyterian/Weill Cornell Hospital following an emergency medical procedure to relieve internal bleeding. He will be remembered as a kind, generous, supportive professional; an opinionated, outspoken, and energetic proponent of all things Freudian; and an insightful scholar who served as an inspiration to all.

Biographical information is found in Sander M. Abend, "Charles Brenner: An Appreciation," *Psychoanalytic Quarterly* (1984). A tribute can be found in Henry F. Smith, "Charles Brenner (1913–2008)," *Psychoanalytic Quarterly* (2008). Obituaries are in the *New York Times* (22 May 2008), *Boston Globe* (23 May 2008), and *San Diego Union-Tribune* (27 May 2008).

Adriana C. Tomasino

BREWER, Teresa (*b.* 7 May 1931 in Toledo, Ohio; *d.* 17 October 2007 in New Rochelle, New York), one of America's most successful pop singers of the 1950s, who reemerged in the 1970s as a jazz singer.

Brewer, born Theresa Breuer, was the oldest of five children and the only girl. Her father was a glass inspector for a glassmaking company in Toledo, and her mother was a homemaker. As a toddler she showed both an interest in and a talent for music, an aptitude unique in her family. When Brewer was two years old her mother took her to audition for a local radio show, *Uncle August's Kiddie Show*, which invited her to perform. Her parents also invested in tap dance lessons.

By age five Brewer had graduated to the national stage, touring the United States with the road company of *Major Bowes Amateur Hour*, one of America's most popular radio programs of the period. Over the next seven years she both sang and danced as a member of the Bowes tour and on the regular weekly radio show. Accompanying her on out-of-town travels was her Aunt Mary, with whom the singer developed a close relationship. At age twelve she returned to Toledo to concentrate on her schooling while continuing to perform locally, including on her own radio show. Her musical success took her away from Toledo before she could finish high school.

Teresa Brewer, 1956. AP IMAGES

When she was sixteen Brewer was flown to New York City for an appearance on the popular radio talent show *Stairway to the Stars.* This appearance led to a weeklong engagement at New York's Latin Quarter nightclub, for which the club owners decided that "Teresa Brewer" looked more professional on a marquee than "Theresa Breuer." While in New York she worked in a number of clubs and appeared on several talent shows, making a name for herself in the New York market. In 1949 she married Bill Monahan, with whom she would have four daughters.

During an appearance at the Sawdust Trail, a small club near Times Square, the owners decided to place a loudspeaker near the club's entrance so that passersby could hear Brewer sing. Intrigued by the unique voice on the loudspeaker, Richie Lisella, a talent agent, decided to come inside. After hearing a full performance, Lisella offered to represent her, and she readily accepted. He soon negotiated a recording contract for her with London Records.

Brewer's first three singles on the London label did little to expand the singer's audience, but in late 1949 she recorded "Copenhagen" with the Dixieland All Stars. Selected for the flip—or B—side of the single was a tune called "Music! Music! Music!," which the record company considered a throwaway. To the surprise of almost everyone, it was that song that won the public's heart, selling well over a million records.

In 1950 and 1951 Brewer released a series of hits for London, including "Choo'n Gum," "Molasses, Molasses," and "Longing for You." In 1951 she left London to sign with Coral Records, a subsidiary of Decca Records. During her decade with Coral, she released a series of hit records, including "Gonna Get Along Without Ya Now" (1952), "Dancin' with Someone" (1953), "Baby, Baby, Baby" (1953), "Skinnie Minnie" (1954), "Let Me Go, Lover" (1954), "Tweedlee Dee" (1955), "Bo Weevil" (1956), "Teardrops in My Heart" (1957), and "You Send Me" (1957). Brewer's biggest hit, "Till I Waltz Again with You," released in 1952 and reaching number one in 1953, was produced by Bob Thiele, an up-and-coming record producer with Coral/Decca. The two enjoyed a successful professional relationship, a collaboration that produced such hits as "Ricochet" (1953) and "Jilted" (1954).

In 1953 Brewer appeared in the movie *Those Redheads from Seattle* but turned down Paramount Pictures' subsequent offer of a movie contract. In 1956 the demands of caring for three children under the age of six prompted the singer to cut back on personal appearances. Television, she discovered, offered a way for her to reach her fans without giving up valuable time with her family. During the latter half of the 1950s, Brewer made frequent appearances on popular variety shows, including those hosted by Perry Como, Arthur Godfrey, and Ed Sullivan. In 1958 she gave birth to her fourth daughter.

The changing musical trends of the 1960s brought Brewer's days on the top of the popular music charts to an end. However, she continued to make regular appearances on television variety shows and in 1962 signed a recording contract with Philips Records, ending her longtime run with Coral. Her four-year association with Philips produced four albums and roughly a dozen singles.

Brewer largely abandoned the music scene during the latter half of the 1960s, devoting her time and energy to her family. In the early 1970s she renewed her professional relationship with Thiele, signing with his label, Flying Dutchman Records. During this phase of her career, she worked in a wider range of musical genres, including jazz, rock, and country. Her newfound interest in jazz led to successful album collaborations with Count Basie, Earl "Fatha" Hines, Bobby Hackett, and Ruby Braff.

In 1972 Brewer divorced Monahan and not long thereafter married Thiele, under whose guidance she continued to experiment with a variety of musical styles. Her rock album, *Teresa Brewer in London* (1984), included a rock version of "Music! Music! Music!" Her 1983 single "No Way Conway" earned her a spot on the country charts. In support of her recording career, she continued to make live appearances throughout the 1970s and 1980s. *Memories of Louis* (1991), a tribute album to the jazz trumpeter Louis Armstrong, was released in 1991 and included backup performances by such jazz greats as Dizzy Gillespie, Wynton Marsalis, and Yank Lawson.

In the years following Thiele's death in 1996, Brewer showed little interest in recording or personal appearances, preferring instead to spend time with her four daughters and their families. Late in her life, she was diagnosed with a rare degenerative brain disorder, progressive supranuclear palsy. She died at her home of complications of the disorder.

The diminutive Brewer achieved popular success in the 1950s singing cheerful songs in her distinctly perky voice. She was able to reinvent herself in the 1970s as a jazz singer, collaborating with some of the greatest American jazz musicians. A favorite of adoring fans, she was also a devoted mother who kept her feet on the ground during the years of her greatest success. She had the rare ability to remain herself while adapting to different musical styles.

★

A fairly comprehensive biography of Brewer, as well as lists of her songs and albums, is available online from the Teresa Brewer Center, http://www.teresafans.org/. Obituaries are in the *New York Times*, *Washington Post*, and *Variety* (all 18 Oct. 2007).

Don Amerman

James Brown. DAVID CORIO/MICHAEL OCHS ARCHIVES/GETTY IMAGES

BROWN, James Joseph, Jr. (*b.* 3 May 1933 (?) in Barnwell, South Carolina; *d.* 25 December 2006 in Atlanta, Georgia), prolific singer-songwriter who, during a more than fifty-year career, changed the face of American entertainment by creating a style of music known as funk.

Brown was born in a one-room shack and was the only child of Joseph Gardner Brown, a filling station attendant, and Susie (Behlings) Brown. Brown's parents separated when Brown was four years old, and he was sent to live with his aunt, who operated a brothel in Augusta, Georgia. His clothes were so tattered that he was booted out of school in the seventh grade, and he earned pennies by shining shoes, picking cotton, washing dishes and cars, and dancing for the soldiers who passed through town during World War II. Meanwhile he taught himself to play the harmonica and learned to play the piano, the guitar, and the drums from others.

Brown seemed headed for a life of crime. In 1948 he was found guilty of petty theft after breaking into a car. He spent the next three years in a juvenile detention center in Toccoa, Georgia, where he sang in a gospel quartet and realized that he might have a future as an entertainer. After his release he became a member of a group led by Bobby Byrd, a gospel and rhythm-and-blues performer. Byrd's

troupe was known as the Gospel Starlighters when it performed before church congregations and as the Flames when it performed rhythm and blues. Initially Brown played the drums for Byrd and was one of the group's vocalists, but Brown's commanding voice, his hyperactive dancing, and his authoritative stage presence thrust him to the forefront. Soon he was the group's lead vocalist and star performer.

In 1953 Brown married Velma Warren, the first of his four wives. His initial success came a short time later when the Flames recorded "Please, Please, Please" (1956), a gospel-inspired rhythm-and-blues song, in the basement of a Macon, Georgia, radio station. The cut earned local airplay and, after hearing it, a talent agent signed Brown and the Flames to a contract with Federal Records, a subsidiary of King Records. "Please, Please, Please" was rerecorded the following year in a professional studio in Cincinnati. This version reached number five on the rhythm-and-blues charts.

Initially "Please, Please, Please" appeared to be a one-hit wonder for Brown and the Flames. They recorded nine follow-up singles, and each flopped miserably. "Try Me" (1958), however, a gospel-oriented ballad, became a number-one rhythm-and-blues hit. In the meantime Brown perfected his unique, electrifying stage presence. While onstage he endlessly spun and shuffled about, performing splits and dropping to his knees as if about to propose marriage. He also developed one of his classic stage routines. As he seemingly finished performing, he crumpled to the ground from exhaustion. The show's master of ceremonies tossed a cape over him and began to escort him offstage, but Brown flung it off and, with a burst of newfound energy, continued performing. This "act" was repeated over and over, much to the delight of the audience.

By this time the Flames had changed their billing to James Brown and the Famous Flames—and more hits followed. "Think" (1960), featuring a Latin beat, became a Top Ten rhythm-and-blues hit while landing on the Top Forty pop chart. (Brown would earn the distinction of being the performer with the most singles on the *Billboard* Hot 100 chart who never achieved number one.) He also began appearing at New York City's famed Apollo Theater. One such performance, on 24 October 1962, was recorded and released as an album. Simply titled *Live at the Apollo*, it became the number-two album on the pop charts. Meanwhile "Prisoner of Love" (1963), a ballad recorded with an orchestra, became Brown's initial Top Twenty pop hit.

Brown now was a national figure. He and the Famous Flames toured endlessly, playing to thousands of frenzied fans, and Brown and Byrd established Fair Deal, a production company that promoted Brown's music beyond the African-American market. Another single, "Out of Sight" (1964), made it to number twenty-four on the pop charts. In this song Brown first united rhythm and blues, soul music, and soul jazz, resulting in a new sound that was raw and cadenced—a sound that came to be known as funk. Brown also appeared in *The T.A.M.I. Show* (1964), a concert film featuring some of the era's leading American and British rock groups. In the film Brown memorably sashays across the stage on one foot, and Mick Jagger attempts to duplicate his moves.

"I Got You (I Feel Good)" (1965) and "Papa's Got a Brand New Bag" (1965) both became Top Twenty pop hits and number-one rhythm-and-blues hits. For the latter Brown earned his first Grammy Award, for Best Rhythm and Blues Recording. Yet another hit, "It's a Man's Man's Man's World" (1966), unites anguishing screams and throbbing blues. It was Brown's unique brand of funk, however, combined with his vocal styling, that quickly entered the mainstream of American music. It influenced other performers, including David Ruffin, Edwin Starr, the Isley Brothers, Sly and the Family Stone, George Clinton, Miles Davis, and a prepubescent Michael Jackson, and such African artists as King Sunny Adé, Fela Kuti, and Youssou N'Dour.

At this time the civil rights movement was gathering force in the United States, and Brown employed his celebrity to produce thoughtful, racially motivated recordings. "Don't Be a Dropout" (1966) stresses the importance of remaining in school. "Say It Loud—I'm Black and I'm Proud" (1968) became a rallying cry for African-American self-esteem. In April 1968 Brown was scheduled to perform in Boston when he learned of the assassination of Martin Luther King, Jr. Rather than cancel the show, he agreed to have it broadcast on television and implored viewers to exercise restraint in response to the murder. This action was credited with helping to spare Boston from the riots that gripped other American cities. At the urging of President Lyndon B. Johnson, Brown gave a benefit concert in Washington, D.C., during which he stressed that rioting was not a solution to the ills of African Americans. In 1969 *Look* magazine dubbed Brown "the most important black man in America."

That same year Brown divorced Warren, and in 1970 he wed his second wife, Deidre Jenkins. By this time he had created an entertainment industry empire. He owned a Learjet, a publishing house, and three radio stations. In his youth Brown shined shoes at one of them, Augusta's WRDW. This period saw additional groundbreaking recordings and hits, including "Cold Sweat" (1967), which some historians cite as the first true funk song; "Give It Up or Turnit a Loose" (1968); "Licking Stick-Licking Stick" (1968); "I Got the Feelin'" (1968); "Mother Popcorn" (1969); "Funky Drummer" (1969); "Get Up (I Feel Like Being a Sex Machine)" (1970), featuring the debut of Brown's new backup band, the J.B.'s; "Super Bad, Pts. 1 (1970); "Hot Pants" (1971); "Make It Funky" (1971); "Get on the Good Foot, Pt. 1" (1972); and "The Payback, Pt. 1" (1974). Brown recorded three Christmas albums, wrote music for two blaxploitation features, *Slaughter's Big Rip-off* (1973) and *Black Caesar* (1973), and performed at the 1974 Muhammad Ali–George Foreman "Rumble in the Jungle" fight in Zaire. Brown's personal life was unsettled, however. The Internal Revenue Service ordered him to pay $4.5 million in overdue taxes, and his private jet and radio stations had to be put up for sale.

Brown's popularity declined in the wake of the disco mania of the mid-1970s. Brown experimented with the music on several albums, including *The Original Disco Man* (1979). While he failed to become a disco superstar, he was still considered an iconic figure within the realm of popular music. With Cab Calloway, Aretha Franklin, and Ray Charles, Brown appeared onscreen in *The Blues Brothers* (1980)—a film that not only paid him homage but also resulted in a career rebirth. Meanwhile he divorced Jenkins in 1981 and three years later wed Adrienne Lois Rodriguez.

Brown then teamed with the rapper Afrika Bambaataa and produced "Unity" (1984), a single. A second Grammy, this one for Best Rhythm-and-Blues Vocal Performance, came for "Living in America" (1985), which he performed onscreen in *Rocky IV* (1985). In 1986 Brown became one of the initial inductees into the Rock and Roll Hall of Fame. His contributions were acknowledged by a new generation of music makers. The drum break from the version of "Give It Up or Turnit a Loose" that appeared on *In the Jungle Groove* (1986), a compilation album, was astoundingly popular during breakdances; the song was labeled "the national anthem of hip-hop" by Kurtis Blow, one of the first successful mainstream rap artists. Hip-hop performers from Public Enemy to L. L. Cool J also recognized Brown's influence.

Despite this acclaim and Brown's continuing to tour and cut records, his later years were mired by brushes with the law and headline-making scandals. Brown was arrested twice in 1986, for operating a car without proof of insurance and for speeding while trying to elude the police. The following year he was charged with beating his wife. In 1988, while reportedly under the influence of illicit drugs, he disrupted a seminar in an office next to his Augusta headquarters. He was pursued by the police in a high-speed car chase and subsequently received a jail sentence. A year after his 1991 release, however, he earned a Grammy Award for Lifetime Achievement. Then in 1993 he received the Rhythm & Blues Foundation's Lifetime Achievement Award. A bridge in Steamboat Springs, Colorado, was dubbed the James Brown Soul Center of the Universe Bridge, and a section of Ninth Street in Augusta was renamed James Brown Boulevard.

Brown's life remained an amalgamation of triumph and tragedy. His third wife died in 1996. Two years later Brown was placed in a ninety-day drug rehabilitation program after firing a rifle and leading police on another car chase. Then in 2000 he was charged with attacking an electric company repairman with a steak knife. In 2001 he wed Tomi Rae Hynie, with whom he had one son; their union was controversial, as Hynie was allegedly married to someone else at the time of the wedding. In 2003 Brown was a recipient of the Kennedy Center Honors and earned a BET Award for Lifetime Achievement. The following year *Rolling Stone* magazine ranked Brown seventh on a list of the 100 Greatest Artists of All Time and listed six of his singles on its registry of the 500 all-time greatest songs. Nevertheless, that year he was taken into custody and charged with domestic violence against Hynie.

In 2006 Brown performed across the globe in what was billed as his "Seven Decades of Funk World Tour." One appearance, at the Oxegen music festival at the Punchestown Racecourse in County Kildare, Ireland, attracted a record crowd of 80,000. That November, Brown was inducted into the U.K. Music Hall of Fame.

Upon returning to his home in Beech Island, South Carolina, Brown became ill. On 24 December he entered Atlanta's Emory Crawford Long Hospital. He was suffering from pneumonia and died there of congestive heart failure the following day. On 28 December his body, which had been transported to New York City and placed in a gold casket, was carried in a glass-walled, horse-drawn carriage to the Apollo Theater, where thousands of fans paid him

tribute. A private service was held on 29 December in North Augusta, South Carolina, and on 30 December a second public memorial took place at the James Brown Arena, Augusta's civic center (which recently had been renamed for the entertainer). Brown's remains initially were housed in a temperature-controlled room at his residence but were removed to an undisclosed location. On 10 March 2007 they were buried in a crypt located at the home of Deanna Brown Thomas, one of Brown's daughters. Most reports state that Brown had eight children, eight grandchildren, four great-grandchildren, and at least three illegitimate children.

In a career that spanned more than five decades, Brown recorded dozens of hit records and attracted countless fans on his tours. Even more significantly, he was a music industry innovator. He created a unique style of music that was most commonly known as funk and that influenced performers across the globe. It was appropriate that his many nicknames included "Soul Brother No. 1," "the Godfather of Soul," and "the Hardest-Working Man in Show Business."

Brown published two autobiographies, *James Brown: The Godfather of Soul* (1986), with Bruce Tucker, and *I Feel Good: A Memoir of a Life of Soul* (2005). Other books on Brown include Anne Danielsen, *Presence and Pleasure: The Funk Grooves of James Brown and Parliament* (2006); Don Rhodes, *Say It Loud!: My Memories of James Brown, Soul Brother No. 1* (2008); James Sullivan, *The Hardest Working Man: How James Brown Saved the Soul of America* (2008); and Nelson George and Alan Leeds, eds., *The James Brown Reader: 50 Years of Writing About the Godfather of Soul* (2009). Obituaries are in the *New York Times* (26 Dec. 2006) and *Rolling Stone* (10 Jan. 2007).

Rob Edelman

BROWNE, Roscoe Lee (*b.* 2 May 1925 in Woodbury, New Jersey; *d.* 11 April 2007 in Los Angeles, California), pioneering African-American actor, director, writer, and poet.

Browne was the second youngest of six children born to Sylvanus Browne, a Baptist minister, and Lovie Lee Browne. Browne grew up in Woodbury, where he attended high school. He expressed no recollection of racism, even though he stated there were a few students who displayed hostility toward him. He speculated that one reason may have been that he did better in French than they did, despite the fact that two of them had French nannies. Browne served in the army during World War II, and on completion of his service he attended Lincoln University in Pennsylvania, graduating in 1946 with a bachelor's degree.

Roscoe Lee Browne, 1985. RON GALELLA/WIREIMAGE/GETTY IMAGES

first role was as the Soothsayer in *Julius Caesar*. Browne performed with the company for seven years, playing roles in *Titus Andronicus*, *The Taming of the Shrew*, and *Romeo and Juliet*. His most noted role with the company was as the Fool in a production of *King Lear*.

Browne made his Broadway debut in 1960, performing in *A Cool World*, which closed after only one day. He acted in other Broadway shows during the 1960s, but most of them failed. An original off-Broadway production of *The Blacks* (1961) by the French writer Jean Genet featured Browne as the lead character. In 1965 he played a slave named Babu in the poet Robert Lowell's adaptation of *Benito Cereno*, a novella by Herman Melville. Browne made his stage directorial debut with *A Hand Is on the Gate: An Evening of Negro Poetry and Folk Music* (1966), which he also wrote. He starred in the production with Cicely Tyson and James Earl Jones. Browne also wrote *Behind the Broken Words*, a series of poetry readings that he regularly performed with the actor Anthony Zerbe over the course of three decades. Browne's stage work also included a role on Broadway in *My One and Only* (1983), written by the entertainer Tommy Tune. Additionally, Browne wrote poetry and short stories.

Browne made his film debut in *The Connection* (1962). He subsequently performed in numerous films, including *Terror in the City* (1964), *The Comedians* (1967), *Topaz* (1969), *The Liberation of L. B. Jones* (1970), *The Cowboys* (1972), and *Sweet Deadly Dreams* (2002). When Browne's character, Jedediah Nightlinger, in *The Cowboys* was criticized for speaking too well, Browne remarked to the *Washington Post* that if he had said, "'Yassuh, boss,'" to his costar John Wayne, "then the critic would have taken a shine to me."

Browne's mellifluous voice was much in demand; he narrated movies such as *Babe* (1995) and documentaries such as *One Shot: The Life and Work of Teenie Harris* (2001). Browne also gave voice to characters in cartoons such as *Spider-Man* (1995–1999), *Treasure Planet* (2002), and *Static Shock* (2003, 2004). Some sources describe Browne as a voice artist, and he recorded numerous taped readings and audiobooks, including *Norma Millay Reading from Collected Poems, Edna St. Vincent Millay in the Coolidge Auditorium* (1968), *Audio Bible* (1991), and *The Poetry of Robert Frost* (2001). His spoken word performances included roles in symphonic works with the Los Angeles Philharmonic and the Boston Pops.

He appeared as a series regular in television programs including *McCoy* (1975–1976), *Soap* (1980–1981), and *Falcon Crest* (1988). Browne also appeared as a guest star on *The Defenders* (1962), *The Invaders* (1968), *Good Times* (1974), *Father Dowling Mysteries* (1990), *Law & Order* (1992, 2003), and *Will & Grace* (2004), among others.

Browne received numerous honors for his performances, including an Obie Award for best actor in 1965 for *Benito Cereno*, a Los Angeles Drama Critics Award for best

An accomplished track star, Browne won the 1949 Amateur Athletic Union 1,000-yard title, and while running for the New York Pioneer Club, he won two American indoor championships. In 1951 he gained international fame when he won the 800-yard dash in Paris, France, winning the world championship. The next year, after winning the 880-yard run at the Millrose Games in New York City, he was felled by a career-ending injury. His fame enabled him to obtain a job as a wine sales representative for the Schenley Import Corporation; he worked for the company from 1946 to 1956.

In 1956, at a dinner with friends, Browne announced that he wanted to become an actor. His friends expressed skepticism, as it was very difficult for African Americans to become successful in acting at the time. The next day, Browne auditioned for the theatrical producer and director Joseph Papp, who had recently formed the New York Shakespeare Festival Company and wanted to include black actors in the company. Browne was hired, and his actor in 1970 for *The Dream on Monkey Mountain*, an Emmy Award for outstanding guest performer in a comedy series in 1986 for *The Cosby Show*, a Los Angeles Drama Critics Circle Award in 1989 for *Joe Turner's Come and Gone*, and an Antoinette Perry Award (Tony) nomination for best performance by a featured actor in a play for *Two Trains Running* (1992).

Browne was one of the black actors who broke barriers in the traditionally white theater world in the 1950s and 1960s. Not only did he act in the New York Shakespeare Company (known for Papp's practice of color-blind casting), but he also performed in the Broadway production of *The Ballad of the Sad Café* (1963), in which his understudy was a white actor, a practice unheard of at the time. Browne never married. He died of cancer at age eighty-one at Cedars-Sinai Medical Center in Los Angeles.

★

For further information about Browne's life and career, see Everett Evans, "A Growing Presence," *Houston Chronicle* (6 Jan. 1991); and "Long-Running Duet Is Poetry in Motion," *Chicago Tribune* (4 Feb. 1998). Obituaries are in the *New York Times* and *Los Angeles Times* (both 12 Apr. 2007).

Jennifer Thompson-Feuerherd

BRUCCOLI, Matthew Joseph (*b.* 21 August 1931 in New York City; *d.* 4 June 2008 in Columbia, South Carolina), prolific editor, writer, and publisher of literary scholarship and texts, known especially for restoring F. Scott Fitzgerald's fading reputation in the 1960s.

Bruccoli was the son of Joseph M. Bruccoli and Mary (Gervasi) Bruccoli, a homemaker. His father served in World War I and was severely wounded in France; Bruccoli founded the Joseph M. Bruccoli Great War Collection, held at the University of Virginia and the University of South Carolina, in his father's honor upon the older man's death in 1965. The elder Bruccoli, who ran a drugstore but may have been an undiagnosed dyslexic, did not enjoy books but encouraged his son's love for them.

Bruccoli's interest in the author F. Scott Fitzgerald began in 1947 when he heard a radio dramatization of Fitzgerald's story "The Diamond as Big as the Ritz." After finding a copy of Fitzgerald's *The Great Gatsby*—now taught in schools across the nation but hard to find at the time—Bruccoli was entranced by the writing. He graduated from the prestigious Bronx High School of Science in 1949 and majored in English at Yale University, receiving a BA in 1953. He briefly attended Cornell University, where his professors included the novelist Vladamir Nabokov, but transferred to the University of Virginia, where he earned his MA in 1956, with a

thesis on Fitzgerald's fiction, and a PhD in 1961. Bruccoli studied there under the textual scholar Fredson Bowers.

In 1957 Bruccoli married Arlyn S. Firkin, who received her bachelor's degree at Randolph-Macon Women's College that year. The Bruccolis had four children. He and his wife began collecting Fitzgerald books and memorabilia, even when the couple's finances were tight.

After teaching as a graduate student, Bruccoli went to Ohio State University, where he was assistant professor from 1961 to 1963, associate professor from 1963 to 1965, and full professor from 1965 to 1969. Bruccoli joined the faculty at the University of South Carolina in 1969; there he held the position of Emily Brown Jeffries Professor of English. Also in 1969, Bruccoli met and became friends with Fitzgerald's daughter, Scottie Fitzgerald Smith, with whom he later collaborated on various projects.

He began the *Fitzgerald Newsletter* in 1958, issued textual studies and bibliographies of Fitzgerald from the 1960s through the 1980s, and edited little-known works by Fitzgerald and his wife, Zelda, from the 1960s forward. His 1981 biography, *Some Sort of Epic Grandeur: The Life of F. Scott Fitzgerald*, became a milestone in the field. Bruccoli's writing has been criticized for offering too many facts and not enough interpretation, but his drive for impeccable accuracy made his works invaluable. With Scottie Fitzgerald Smith and Joan P. Kerr, Bruccoli compiled *The Romantic Egoists*, published in 1974, a collection of pictures and news clippings from the scrapbooks of F. Scott and Zelda Fitzgerald.

Though best known for his work on Fitzgerald, throughout his career Bruccoli focused on many authors. He also wrote about Ernest Hemingway, including two books for Random House on the friendship between Fitzgerald and Hemingway. In 1969 he began editing the *Fitzgerald/Hemingway Annual*, including bibliography, criticism, and biographical notes concerning the two authors. He also published books about Stephen Crane, Joseph Heller, and James Dickey.

Not all of Bruccoli's subjects have received the literary fame of Fitzgerald—he also worked extensively on the fiction of John O'Hara and James Gould Cozzens, whom he felt to be underrated. For various projects he worked with O'Hara's third wife and with Cozzens himself. He also wrote about Ring Lardner. A longtime reader of detective fiction, Bruccoli wrote about Ross Macdonald (pen name of the author Kenneth Millar) and Raymond Chandler; he also wrote about the espionage novelist John le Carré. He and Richard Layman edited two crime fiction periodicals, *The New Black Mask from 1985 to 1987* and *A Matter of Crime* from 1988 to 1989.

A tireless editor, Bruccoli produced *The Letters of Vladamir Nabokov* (1989) and, with his wife, Arlyn, *O Lost*, the version of Thomas Wolfe's *Look Homeward, Angel* without the massive editorial cuts by the editor Maxwell Perkins.

Bruccoli even made videotapes, on Fitzgerald and on the profession of authorship, for Manly/Omnigraphics, issued in 1988. In 1988 Bruccoli won the Lucy Hampton Bostick Award, given annually to a writer from South Carolina, and in 1997 he won the University of South Carolina Alumni Association Award.

One of Bruccoli's lasting contributions is the *Dictionary of Literary Biography*, a reference series published by Gale Research and conceived by Gale's founder and president, Frederick Ruffner. In 1976 Bruccoli began to head the series with Frazer Clark, his partner in Bruccoli Clark Books, later Bruccoli Clark Layman. The first volume was published in 1978, and approximately 400 volumes, edited by hundreds and contributed to by thousands of scholars, had been produced by 2009.

Bruccoli officially retired in 2005 but continued working at the university until diagnosed with a brainstem tumor in 2008. He left his books and memorabilia to the Thomas Cooper Library at the University of South Carolina; the Arlyn F. and Matthew J. Bruccoli Collection is valued at nearly $2 million, and donations to the collection were requested in lieu of flowers for his funeral. He is buried in Hawthorne, New York.

A dedicated and prolific writer, editor, and publisher, Bruccoli often said that the only important job in scholarship is to publish so that others can share the information and insights. He was admired for his determination and drive, although the writer Gore Vidal dismissed him as a "scholar-squirrel." Some fellow literary professionals felt that Bruccoli was too zealous, publishing and restoring materials that did not do the authors justice; however, others were grateful for the wealth of material that he made available. His impact on both literary and popular culture is undeniable.

★

The Professions of Authorship: Essays in Honor of Matthew J. Bruccoli (1996), edited by Bruccoli, Richard Layman, and Joel Myerson, includes both an introduction by Myerson about Bruccoli's personality and scholarly habits and one by Layman, describing Bruccoli's history as a publisher. Chris Horn presents a pleasant, short article about Bruccoli with revealing quotations and anecdotes in "Collecting Fitzgerald: A Passion as Big as the Ritz," available on the website http://www.sc.edu/fitzgerald/collection/horn.html. An obituary is in the *New York Times* (6 June 2008).

Bernadette Lynn Bosky

BUCHWALD, Arthur ("Art") (*b.* 20 October 1925 in Mount Vernon, New York; *d.* 17 January 2007 in Washington, D.C.), humor columnist best remembered for spoofing the politicians and bureaucrats of Washington, D.C.

Art Buchwald, 1984. CBS/LANDOV

Buchwald was the youngest of four children of Joseph Buchwald, a drape maker, and Helen (Klineberger) Buchwald, who had worked in a factory before her marriage; both of Buchwald's parents were immigrants from Austria-Hungary. Shortly after Buchwald's birth, his mother was committed to a sanatorium for severe chronic depression. She remained institutionalized for the rest of her life. Buchwald never saw his mother and often felt guilty as a result. He later wrote that he was not permitted to visit his mother when he was a child. "When I grew up, I didn't want to. I preferred the mother I had invented the one I would find in the hospital." The expense of the private sanatoriums in which Buchwald's mother was placed before being transferred to a public hospital impoverished Buchwald's father, and the onset of the Great Depression made it impossible for him to recover financially.

Buchwald spent his first year at the Heckscher Foundling Home, where he was treated for rickets. Then he and his sister, who had osteomyelitis, lived at a boarding school for sick children run by Seventh-day Adventists in Flushing, Queens, New York. When Buchwald was five, his father noticed that his Jewish children were being exposed to

Christian dogma, and he removed them. They were boarded briefly by relatives in the Bronx, New York; then all four Buchwald children entered the Hebrew Orphan Asylum, which placed them with a foster family in Hollis, Queens. From age five to age fifteen, Buchwald lived with three different foster families in Hollis. He was never treated cruelly, but nowhere did he feel as if he belonged. "Laughter was the weapon I used for survival," he later wrote. At age fifteen he finally got out of foster care. His father and his sisters, who by then were working, rented an apartment in Forest Hills, Queens, from which Buchwald attended Forest Hills High School and worked at various part-time jobs himself.

When the Japanese attacked Pearl Harbor on 7 December 1941, Buchwald later wrote, "It dawned on me that the Japanese attack could be my ticket out of high school." Buchwald, then sixteen, tried to enlist in the army, but his father refused to sign the permission form. The following fall Buchwald ran away from home and joined the Marine Corps. He was assigned to the ground crew of the Fourth Marine Aircraft Wing. The assignment kept him from seeing combat (to his disappointment at the time), but it also kept him out of danger. He served in the Pacific and was eventually promoted to sergeant.

In 1946 Buchwald enrolled in the University of Southern California (USC) on the GI Bill. A year later USC discovered that he had not graduated from high school but allowed him to continue as a nondegree student. He wrote a column for the *Daily Trojan* and was the managing editor of USC's humor magazine. In the spring of 1948, after learning that he could attend school in Paris on the GI Bill, Buchwald hitchhiked to New York and sailed to France.

In Paris, Buchwald briefly enrolled in a French-language school but soon landed a job. He worked as a legman for *Variety*'s Paris stringer and then talked his way into a job at the *International Herald Tribune*, covering nightlife and reviewing films. His duties at the *Herald Tribune* eventually expanded to include reviewing restaurants and writing an interview column that turned into a humor column.

In late 1949 Buchwald met Ann McGarry, who was working in Paris as a publicist for the fashion designer Pierre Balmain. After two years of serious involvement, they were married in London on 11 October 1952. While they were living in Paris, they adopted three children.

Buchwald began to attract readers in the United States through the syndication of his column and occasional magazine articles (such as a spoof of big-game hunting for *Collier's* called "Coward in the Congo"). When Prince Rainier of Monaco married Grace Kelly, Buchwald wrote that he did not expect a wedding invitation, since the Buchwalds and the Grimaldis had been feuding for 500 years. That column got him a coveted invitation. The column that really brought him attention, though, came in 1957, when President Dwight D. Eisenhower visited Paris and Buchwald

lampooned the inane questions the White House press corps asked Press Secretary James Hagerty and the press secretary's equally inane answers. Hagerty denounced the column as "unadulterated rot," and the flap became international news.

In 1962, feeling that he had exhausted the comic possibilities in Europe, Buchwald returned with his family to the United States. Shortly after his return, he experienced a severe clinical depression. He suffered a second one in 1987. In both depressions, he was suicidal, and in both he was hospitalized for weeks. The first was characterized with nonstop crying. In the second, he was manic. He later wrote: "No one recognized my manic phase because people thought I was being funny. Then came the crash. I plunged into a terrible black inky lake."

Professionally, though, Buchwald did beautifully. His humor played even better against the backdrop of Washington than it had in Paris. His column appeared in hundreds of papers across the country, and after the *New York Herald Tribune* folded in 1967, the *Washington Post* became his home paper. A complete Buchwald column was usually far more humorous than any of its individual parts, so it is difficult to convey an individual column's full effect. In one column Buchwald revealed how to get on television during a presidential news conference: sit behind a reporter who is sure to ask a long-winded question. In another, citizens protested "the way churches are trying to turn Christmas into a religious holiday." And in the early 1970s, Buchwald revealed how Richard Nixon's national security adviser managed to travel so often to so many cities: There were actually five Henry Kissingers.

Buchwald won a Pulitzer Prize for commentary in 1982. His columns were collected in more than two dozen books, including *I Chose Capitol Punishment* (1963), *Washington Is Leaking* (1976), and *Whose Rose Garden Is It Anyway?* (1989). He also appeared frequently on radio and television.

Buchwald's writing was not confined to his column. He also published four novels: *A Gift from the Boys* (1958), *The Bollo Caper* (1974), *Irving's Delight* (1975), and *Stella in Heaven* (2000). A play, *Sheep on the Runway*, ran for ninety-seven performances on Broadway in 1970. He also wrote two well-received memoirs: *Leaving Home* (1993), about his early years, and *I'll Always Have Paris* (1996), about his time in France. The outside project for which he may be best known, however, is a treatment for a movie about an African prince who temporarily winds up in the Washington ghetto. For several years Buchwald's partner in the project, the producer Alain Bernheim, worked on developing it for Paramount Pictures. Paramount dropped the project, but in 1988 the studio released the movie *Coming to America*, in which Eddie Murphy plays an African prince who temporarily winds up in Queens. Buchwald and Bernheim were convinced that the film *Coming to America* had developed out of their project, and they sued

Paramount. In early 1990 a judge ruled in their favor. The penalty phase, in which they successfully challenged Hollywood accounting practices, did not conclude until 1992.

Also in 1992, after forty years of marriage, Buchwald and his wife separated. Contributing to their problems, Buchwald felt, were his two depressions and his wife's heart attack and subsequent bypass surgery. The separation was bitter, and Ann Buchwald decided to get a divorce. Then she was diagnosed with terminal lung cancer. Before she died in 1994, a rapprochement developed, and Buchwald dedicated *I'll Always Have Paris* to her.

After Buchwald had a stroke in 2000, he lived with his son. In 2005 Buchwald's health took a dramatic turn for the worse. His kidneys began to fail. A few days after his eightieth birthday, blood clots in his foot blocked circulation. Then his kidneys failed entirely. He began dialysis, and his lower leg was amputated. After the amputation he briefly continued dialysis but decided to end the treatment. On 7 February 2006 he checked into a hospice. There he entertained friends who flocked to his bedside to say goodbye. He did a radio interview, and media coverage began to snowball. He was interviewed for numerous media outlets. Miraculously his kidneys began to function again. After five months in the hospice, he checked out and went to Martha's Vineyard, Massachusetts, where he had a summer home. There he completed his final book, *Too Soon to Say Goodbye* (2006), which is part memoir, part thoughts on death and dying. Buchwald died of kidney failure at his son's home ten months after he had initially expected to die. He is buried in West Chop Cemetery in Vineyard Haven, Massachusetts.

For more than forty years, Buchwald performed the most difficult task in journalism: he wrote a consistently funny newspaper column. He combined a keen eye for the absurd with a great ear for dialogue, a solid grasp of current events, and a clear, colloquial writing style. He also had a strong understanding of human nature. His columns, as topical as they seemed when they were written, have stood up surprisingly well over the years.

★

The best sources on Buchwald's life are his own memoirs, *Leaving Home* and *I'll Always Have Paris*. Also valuable are Ann Buchwald, *Seems Like Yesterday* (1980), written with Buchwald, and Pierce O'Donnell and Dennis McDougal, *Fatal Subtraction: The Inside Story of Buchwald v. Paramount* (1992). Valuable articles include Sharon Waxman, "Washington's Hottest Salon Is a Deathbed," *New York Times* (26 Mar. 2006), and Joyce Wadler, "At Home with Art Buchwald: A Defiant Jester, Laughing Best," *New York Times* (27 July 2006). Obituaries are in the *New York Times* and the *Washington Post* (both 19 Jan. 2007).

Lynn Hoogenboom

BUCKLEY, William F(rancis), Jr. (*b.* 24 November 1925 in New York City; *d.* 26 February 2008 in Stamford, Connecticut), editor and founder of *National Review*, syndicated columnist, novelist, television host, and the intellectual father and leading voice of modern American conservatism in the second half of the twentieth century.

Buckley was the second of four sons and the sixth of ten children born to Aloise Steiner Buckley, the daughter of a prominent New Orleans banker, and William Frank Buckley, a wealthy, Texas-born oilman who made his fortune in Mexico and Venezuela. Christened William Francis at the insistence of a priest who demanded a saint's name for the baptism, Buckley at age five won his parents' approval to take Frank as his middle name in honor of his father, becoming—as the world would know him—William F. Buckley, Jr.

By the time he was fourteen, Buckley had accepted his father's beliefs as his own and, like him, would be a lifelong political and religious conservative. He embraced Roman Catholic doctrine as revealed truth and in later years, when English became the liturgical language in American churches, often arranged for private services in the traditional Latin. Like his siblings, he grew up to be a fervent anticommunist, free-market capitalist, and an antigovernment libertarian.

William F. Buckley, Jr., 2004. AP IMAGES

Buckley was first educated by private tutors in Venezuela and Paris, at a Jesuit school in London when he was seven, and thereafter with tutors at Great Elm, the family's forty-three-acre estate in Sharon, Connecticut, and their winter home in Camden, South Carolina. Fluent in Spanish and French before he learned English, he was taught to ride, play the piano, ski, and sail, all to a high level of expertise. His father oversaw it all, pressing books and ideas on his son and urging him to lead a useful, principled life. When absent, he directed Buckley's moral development through an endless stream of letters and notes—a practice that continued until his death in 1958.

At thirteen, Buckley entered the Millbrook School in nearby Millbrook, New York. Because of his dogmatic defense of his beliefs, he made few friends—"I am not very popular with the boys," he wrote his father—and throughout his schooling found it difficult to accept contrary viewpoints. He graduated as valedictorian in 1943. Too young for the service, he studied Spanish at the University of Mexico until he was drafted into the U.S. Army in 1944. His stateside service, Buckley said, was "brief and bloodless." He mustered out in 1946 as a second lieutenant and headed for Yale, where he excelled both academically and socially: as a star debater, a member of Skull & Bones (the secret senior society), and chairman of the *Yale Daily News*, a coveted editorial platform from which he delivered biting criticisms of the college, its policies, and its faculty.

Buckley graduated on 12 June 1950, receiving a BA with honors in history, political science, and economics. On 6 July 1950, he married Patricia Aldyen Austin Taylor of Vancouver, British Columbia, his sister Priscilla's classmate at Vassar and the daughter of one of the richest men in Canada. The couple were together for fifty-seven years and had one son.

The Buckleys settled in Hamden, Connecticut, a suburb of New Haven, and he returned to Yale as a part-time instructor in Spanish. At a publisher's urging, he expanded his Alumni Day speech—canceled at the last minute by the university president who deemed it inappropriately hostile to the institution—into his first book, *God and Man at Yale: The Superstitions of Academic Freedom* (1951), in which he argued Yale had lost its way, abandoning its Christian heritage for secularism, atheism, and communism; its former commitment to free inquiry and fundamental truths had given way to indoctrination and false doctrines. He called for a return to the virtues of the past. It was a "coruscating attack," a Yale historian wrote, that was met on campus with "fear, revulsion and damage control" and elsewhere sparked a national debate on the nature and limits of academic freedom.

God and Man at Yale launched Buckley's career as an intellectual gadfly and foreshadowed the lines of argument he would follow to revive American conservatism, which, in the early 1950s, was a moribund and deeply divided minority wing of the Republican Party. Over the next half century Buckley would change those perceptions by connecting the fundamental principles he had defended in *God and Man at Yale* to conservatism itself, particularly the value of religion as a guide to personal and social morality and the dangers to personal freedom inherent in statism and communism.

After a nine-month sojourn in Mexico as a Central Intelligence Agency (CIA) agent in 1951, Buckley returned to New York and began his defense of conservatism in earnest. He joined his brother-in-law and Yale classmate, L. Brent Bozell, in writing *McCarthy and His Enemies* (1954), a spirited defense of Joseph McCarthy, the senator from Wisconsin, who had sparked an anticommunist crusade during the Korean War. They argued his sometimes flawed methods served the greater good in protecting the nation from communism and thus were justified—an ends-and-means argument that would appear often in Buckley's later political writing and speeches.

In 1955, with the financial backing of his siblings, Buckley founded the biweekly *National Review* and built it into a flourishing journal widely perceived as the intellectual voice of conservatism in America. Confrontational in style, brightly written, witty, and often irreverent, it featured the varied interests and opinions of its founder and editor, who deemed himself a revolutionary against the liberal order of the day. By the end of the century its circulation averaged 152,000 subscribers.

In its first years, the magazine sometimes reflected Buckley's casually expressed racism, which was based on his conviction that among the world's peoples, whites were naturally the most advanced. He opposed *Brown v. Board of Education*, the 1954 Supreme Court decision ordering the desegregation of the nation's schools, on the ground that educational policy should be left to the states. Using a similar cultural argument, he vigorously defended southern segregationists who defied federal efforts to grant blacks equal rights, and he mocked—often in veiled racist language—many of the egalitarian demands of activists in the civil rights movement. He repeatedly defended the fascist dictator General Francisco Franco, calling him a national hero because he kept Spain safe from communism. In later years Buckley backed away from expressing such views but never apologized for them. In the eyes of some critics, they darken his otherwise bright legacy.

In 1960 Buckley helped to found Young Americans for Freedom, an organization for college-age conservatives that was influential in securing the Republican presidential nomination for Barry Goldwater in 1964. In 1962 Buckley undertook a syndicated twice-weekly column, "On the Right," that ran until 2008 and at its peak appeared in 315 papers, making it the second-most-read opinion column in the nation (behind that of Jack Anderson, an investigative reporter). In addition, Buckley was a prolific contributor to a broad range of popular magazines, including the *Atlantic Monthly, Esquire, Harper's, Life,* the *New Republic,* the *New Yorker,* the *New York Times,* and *Playboy.* (This last caused him some discomfort, but he justified his several essays on the ground they challenged publisher Hugh Hefner's "playboy philosophy" in the magazine's own pages and gave him a platform, otherwise unavailable, to spread his conservative views.) Gifted and witty, Buckley was in high demand as a speaker on university campuses and to conservative audiences until the end of the century.

In 1965 Buckley ran as a Conservative for mayor of New York City, losing by a wide margin to the liberal Republican candidate John Lindsay, but gaining material for his book, *The Unmaking of a Mayor* (1966). In 1966 he conceived and served as host of *Firing Line,* a one-hour public affairs television program broadcast locally on WOR-TV in New York, that featured discussions between Buckley and prominent public figures drawn from government, academia, or publishing. In 1977 *Firing Line* moved to the Public Broadcasting System (PBS) and more than 100 stations across the country. *Firing Line* ended in 1999 after 1,504 programs. What set it apart during its thirty-three-year run—in its time the longest running public affairs program with the same host on television—was its tone of civility, which was rarely breached by either Buckley or his guests—except once when the writer Gore Vidal accused him of being a crypto-Nazi and Buckley replied with a vulgarism and threatened to punch him out. Buckley later apologized to his audience (but not to Vidal) for his loss of control. The two men subsequently engaged in a bitter exchange of insults in *Esquire* that led to a series of lawsuits for libel and an out-of-court settlement; the two never reconciled.

It was an uncharacteristic behavioral lapse for Buckley, who as an adult had shed his youthful arrogance and with it the cruel condescension he had once directed at his ideological opponents. He was by nature and training a gentleman: unfailingly gracious, charming and civil, with a self-deprecating wit. As the years passed, he was increasingly tolerant of contrary views—although almost never swayed in argument to accept them. He numbered among his friends many of the most notable liberals of his time: John Kenneth Galbraith, Murray Kempton, Norman Mailer, Michael Harrington, and scores of others. Like his father, he was a complicated man.

Buckley wrote or edited more than fifty books, nineteen of them novels, most of them written in a two-month period each year when the Buckleys took up residence in Switzerland to ski. Among his nonfiction books were compilations of previously published opinion pieces recycled under such titles as *Up from Liberalism* (1959), *Rumbles Left and Right* (1963), and *Inveighing We Will Go* (1972). Buckley combined personal narratives with his love of the sea and his skill as a yachtsman to describe transoceanic voyages in such books as *Airborne* (1976),

Atlantic High: A Celebration (1982), and *Racing Through Paradise: A Pacific Passage* (1987). As he turned fifty, Buckley tried his hand at espionage fiction, creating the CIA agent Blackford Oakes in *Saving the Queen* (1976) and carrying his hero through eleven books in all, ending with *Last Call for Blackford Oakes* (2005). In a change of genre, Buckley wrote several romans à clef including *Brothers No More* (1995), and *The Redhunter: A Novel Based on the Life of Senator Joe McCarthy* (1999).

Buckley retired as the ranking editor of *National Review* in October 1990 but continued to turn out books at the rate of nearly one a year. In 1997 and 1998 he taught a weekly two-hour seminar on composition for twelve select students at Yale, and in 2000 the university awarded an honorary degree to its once-errant son ("[T]he most dangerous undergraduate ever to attend Yale," an alumnus had written in 1951). Buckley received some thirty honorary degrees in all, as well as sixteen major journalism and literary awards, a television Emmy for *Firing Line,* and in 1991 the Presidential Medal of Freedom from President George H. W. Bush.

Buckley transferred his controlling shares of *National Review* to a handpicked board of trustees in 2004 but remained the magazine's editor-at-large, contributing occasional opinion pieces until his death. He maintained his always busy schedule of radio and television interviews in that presidential-election year, appearing on such outlets as the Fox television network, PBS, National Public Radio, and the Rush Limbaugh program. He granted interviews to the *New York Times,* the Associated Press, the *New York Post,* and *Time;* published his memoir, *Miles Gone By* (2004); and continued churning out his syndicated column, "On the Right," that ended in 2008 with his 5,600th article.

In 2007 Buckley brought out his amusing history, *Cancel Your Own Goddam Subscription: Notes and Asides from National Review,* and his final roman à clef, *The Rake,* a story of a young, liberal presidential candidate with a libidinous past. He did so as his health began to fail. He needed a walker or a wheelchair to get around and was tethered to an oxygen tank because of emphysema, for which he had been diagnosed at the Mayo Clinic a year earlier.

On 15 April 2007 Buckley suffered the greatest loss of his life when his beloved wife, Pat, died at age eighty from an infection following a hospital stay at the end of a long and wasting illness. Without her, Buckley seemed "rudderless," a friend said, and there was a marked and swift decline in his health. Nonetheless, he completed *Flying High: Remembering Barry Goldwater* (published posthumously in April 2008) and resumed working on a long-postponed memoir of Ronald Reagan, which he did not live to finish. Buckley was found dead early in the morning in his Stamford study. The cause of death was either emphysema or age-onset diabetes or both. Like his wife, he was cremated, his ashes placed in a brass canister and, in a private ceremony, encased with hers in a large bronze crucifix crafted by the Connecticut modernist sculptor Jimmy Knowles. The crucifix stands in the middle of the lawn at their Stamford home beside Long Island Sound.

Buckley's memorial Mass was held at Saint Patrick's Cathedral on 10 April 2008, a service attended by 2,200 friends and admirers. His son, Christopher, and Henry Kissinger were the principal speakers. The service concluded, as Buckley had requested, with the brisk, joyful sounds of the third movement of Bach's Brandenburg Concerto no. 2 in F Major celebrating his life.

For nearly sixty years Buckley was the face and voice of conservatism, his intellect and erudition giving new meaning and strength to what had played a minor role in mid-twentieth-century American political life. His public advocacy of the conservative agenda made possible the election of President Ronald Reagan in 1980 and the Reagan Revolution that followed. He did not live to see its repudiation twenty-eight years later in the electoral victory of Barack Obama in 2008.

★

The papers of Buckley are in the Manuscripts and Archives of the Sterling Memorial Library, Yale University, New Haven, Connecticut. The broadcast archive of *Firing Line*, containing all 1,504 programs, is in the Hoover Institution Archives, Stanford University, Stanford, California. Autobiographies are Buckley, *Nearer My God: An Autobiography of Faith* (1997) and *Miles Gone By: A Literary Autobiography* (2004). A well-researched, thoughtful biography is John B. Judis, *William F. Buckley, Jr., Patron Saint of the Conservatives* (2001). A sympathetic assessment can be found in Linda Bridges and John R. Coyne, Jr., *Strictly Right: William F. Buckley, Jr., and the American Conservative Movement* (2007). Obituaries are in the *New York Times* (27 Feb. 2008) and the *Washington Post* and *Guardian* (London) (both 28 Feb. 2008).

Allan L. Damon

BUSCH, Frederick (*b*. 1 August 1941 in New York City; *d*. 23 February 2006 in New York City), novelist and educator best known for his novels *Girls* and *The Night Inspector* and for his creation of the Living Writers program at Colgate University.

Busch was born and raised in the New York City borough of Brooklyn; he had one brother. His father, Benjamin Busch, was a lawyer who fought in Italy during World War II, and his mother, Phyllis (Schnell) Busch, was a teacher and herself an author. Unlike many of his contemporaries who attended college in New York City, he went off to

Muhlenberg College, a Christian-affiliated institution in rural Pennsylvania. Later in life he would always express his gratitude to the teaching he received there, both in and out of the classroom. When he graduated with a BA in 1962, he already knew everything he would need for his future: he had a vocation—literature—and a future wife—Judith Ann Burroughs, whom he would marry the next year and with whom he would have two sons.

Busch began studying metaphysical poetry at Columbia University but soon realized that he was not interested in scholarship; he withdrew, as he would do from a similar program at New York University. Instead, he married Burroughs and went to work as a professional writer, first for the North American Precis Syndicate and then for Management Magazines. By 1966, however, he had returned to the study of literature, obtaining an MA from Columbia and beginning a thirty-seven-year career at Colgate University, marked by his founding of the Living Writers program, which brings both established writers and those relatively new to their careers onto Colgate's rural campus and, through webcasting, to students of contemporary literature around the world; he would ultimately become the Edgar Fairchild Professor of Literature.

Busch published some twenty-seven volumes in thirty-five years: sixteen novels, seven collections of short stories, and four works of nonfiction. Yet despite this enviable record, he never achieved the level of public recognition that enables some writers to be automatic best sellers. Part of the reason was that Busch never succeeded in creating a significant relationship with a single publisher, hindering the creation of consistent publicity campaigns for his work. Furthermore, his insistence that he needed to write in both long and short forms also slowed his rise to the top of the best-seller lists. For example, Busch's first novel, *I Wanted a Year Without Fall*, was published with the assistance of his friend the British writer Robert Nye, who read the manuscript in 1970 and sent it on to his own publisher, Calder and Boyars. The London-based firm agreed to publish the novel in 1971, as well as the collection *Breathing Trouble and Other Stories* that came out in 1973. Neither of these titles, however, was published in the United States. Finally, in 1974, Busch was taken on by New Directions, which published both a novel, *Manual Labor*, and a collection of linked stories, *Domestic Particulars* (1976). But New Directions would publish only one more of his titles, *War Babies* (1989); instead, over the next three years after the publication of *Domestic Particulars*, Busch would publish three books, each with a different publisher.

Perhaps his greatest hindrance to best-seller status was his insistence, in stories and novels alike, that people can never escape unhappiness. Main characters in three of his novels lose their children; those in two others are physically scarred by their experiences. His incursions into what he once called "the terrible darkness of night-time in the forest" give much of his work a profound power over readers, but they do not offer much solace. His characters dwell lovingly on the rare moments of happiness that they have experienced—in their work or in their family life—but tragedy hovers continuously over each of them. Busch called this doubleness "getting close to the dark, scary stuff, which is what writing is about, and yet . . . trying to make it useful to other people."

Contributing further to the difficulty many readers experienced in coming to terms with Busch's novels and stories was his preference for setting his fictions in rural upstate New York, where Busch lived for more than three decades. The main character in *Girls* (1997), considered by some critics his finest single work, even works at a college that is an exact topographical match for Colgate University. As he said in an interview with Donald Greiner, "I used to . . . [get] characters out to the country and away from the more complex cityscape to achieve . . . my own fictive terrain."

Surmounting these obstacles to the wider acceptance of his work, Busch gradually won over critics and readers alike. In 1986 he published *Sometimes I Live in the Country*, which won the National Jewish Book Award for Fiction and the American Academy of Arts and Letters Fiction Award; in 1991 he won the PEN/Malamud Award "for distinguished achievement in the short story"; his collection *The Children in the Woods* was nominated for a PEN/Faulkner Award in 1995, as was his novel *The Night Inspector* in 2000; and in 2001 he received the Award of Merit from the American Academy of Arts and Sciences.

As Busch's reputation among colleagues and readers grew, he began writing nonfiction as well. He published the collection *When People Publish: Essays on Writers and Writing* in 1986, and a dozen years later he released another collection of scholarly essays on writers he admired, *A Dangerous Profession: A Book About the Writing Life* (1998). The last book broke new ground in that he included an account of the challenges he faced in his own writing—considered one of the most honest assessments of the writer's life in contemporary letters. And, building on this innovative work, the next year he published *Letters to a Fiction Writer*, an anthology containing a wide range of advice from established writers of the twentieth century to beginning authors. Busch died of a heart attack.

Perhaps the quality that will make Busch's novels and stories live on through the twenty-first century is his ability to make the reader see both individual characters—always ambivalent, filled with hopes and fears that will both see fruition—and the larger world in which those characters pursue their strivings—filled with demanding social and political challenges. As Busch put it in an interview just a year before his death, "I see my . . . characters as dealing simultaneously with their personal history and with the present in which they are trying to make their way. So that the books are simultaneously about public and interior events." To capture both these worlds, and to do it in a language that fills the mind with the pictorial imagination of the author, is a rare accomplishment indeed.

★

For a full-length study of Busch's work through the middle of his career, see Donald J. Greiner, *Domestic Particulars: The Novels of Frederick Busch* (1988). For an extended interview, see Bruce W. Jorgensen, "'A Grammar of Events': A Conversation with Frederick Busch," *Literature and Belief* 7 (1987): 26–40. Obituaries are in the *New York Times* (25 Feb. 2006) and *Washington Post* (26 Feb. 2006).

Hartley S. Spatt

BUTCHER, Susan Howlet (*b*. 26 December 1954 in Boston, Massachusetts; *d*. 5 August 2006 in Seattle, Washington), four-time winner of Alaska's grueling 1,157-mile Iditarod Trail Sled Dog Race and the only female musher to win multiple times.

Susan Butcher, 1990. WILLIAM R. SALLAZ/SPORTS ILLUSTRATED/GETTY IMAGES

Butcher was the younger of two daughters born to Charlie Butcher and Agnes (Young) Butcher. Her father ran a chemical-products company, and her mother worked as a psychiatric social worker. An older brother died of leukemia before Butcher was born. Butcher grew up in Cambridge, Massachusetts, and by all accounts spent her childhood dreaming of life in a more rural, rustic setting. In elementary school she wrote an essay titled "I Hate the City." Butcher looked forward to summers spent at the family home on Eggemoggin Reach in Brooklin, Maine, where she reveled in the freedom of open spaces.

Early on, Charlie Butcher noticed his daughter's strong-willed independence. He encouraged her sense of adventure and self-reliance by including her in pursuit of his hobbies, sailing and carpentry. The Butcher clan spent several years working to restore an old sailboat. By the time Butcher was a teenager she had her own set of carpentry tools. At sixteen she applied to a boat-building school but was not admitted; she assumed the rejection was because she was a girl.

With a mild case of dyslexia, Butcher struggled through her years at the Warehouse Cooperative School near Cambridge. She loved animals and considered becoming a veterinarian but was nervous about continuing her education past high school. At seventeen Butcher left home, setting her sights on Colorado and its wide open spaces. She settled in Boulder, where she found work as a veterinary technician and befriended a sled-dog racer and breeder.

In 1973, while looking through a magazine devoted to mushing (racing with teams of sled dogs), Butcher read about the Iditarod and knew she wanted to compete. Within about two years she relocated to Fairbanks, Alaska, to dedicate herself to the sport. Once there, Butcher acquired a few dogs, then moved to an isolated area in the Wrangell Mountains of southern Alaska. Holed up in a small cabin, Butcher spent two years in solitude training the dogs. To survive in the Alaskan bush, Butcher had to chop firewood, hunt for food, and tote water from a creek. During the summers she headed to Fairbanks to earn money working on a musk-ox farm. Later, she supplemented her income working at a salmon factory.

In 1977 Butcher moved to Unalakleet, Alaska, and met the famed musher and kennel owner Joe Redington, Sr. She wanted to compete in the Iditarod but needed two more dogs. Redington agreed to give her the dogs if she would work at his kennel in Knik. Butcher competed in her first Iditarod in 1978, finishing nineteenth. In 1979 Butcher and Redington packed up a team of dogs and spent forty days working their way up to the top of Mount McKinley, North America's highest peak. They became the first people to mush to the summit.

In 1980 Butcher decided to move to Eureka, Alaska, to concentrate on training and to open her own kennel. Around this time she met David Monson, a lawyer, dog

musher, and sea fisherman. He stopped by to sell her some seafood-blended dog food. Butcher bought 10,000 pounds and told Monson to bill her sponsor; when the sponsor went back on the deal, Butcher ended up owing Monson thousands of dollars, which she paid off over the next few years.

In 1985 Butcher and Monson became a team in more than one sense: They got married and they joined forces to run the kennel. Monson's job was to line up sponsors and take care of office work. Butcher preferred to stay outdoors, training and caring for the dogs. At times they had up to 150 dogs on their property and earned money selling premier Alaskan huskies to buyers in the United States, Canada, and northern Europe. All the while, Butcher trained her race dogs seven days a week, covering fifty to eighty miles of wilderness each day. The couple continued to live in Eureka, in a remote, one-room cabin that had once been a blacksmith shop. Butcher built the kennel's outbuildings herself.

In the 1985 Iditarod, Butcher got off to a great start, reaching the first three checkpoints in first place. After a deranged moose attacked her team, killing two dogs and injuring thirteen, she was forced to drop out of the race. Long-shot racer Libby Riddles went on to win the race, becoming the first female Iditarod champion.

Butcher won her first Iditarod in 1986 and won again in 1987 and 1988, making her the first person, male or female, to win the race in three consecutive years. Butcher was unbeatable in 1988, winning every race she entered, including the Portage 250 and the Kusho 300. That same year her husband won the Yukon Quest Sled Race.

Known as "The Last Great Race on Earth," the Iditarod runs more than 1,150 miles from Anchorage to Nome over a route charted during the Klondike gold rush, a period in the 1890s of frenzied prospecting for gold in Alaska. Mushers, armed with a team of up to sixteen dogs, cross mountain ranges and frozen tundra. Temperatures reach seventy degrees below zero, and blizzards cause whiteout conditions. When Butcher raced, she liked to run next to the sled in an effort to stay warm and ease the dogs' workload. At rest stops she prepared food for the dogs and melted snow with fire so they could drink. There was rarely time to sleep.

In 1989, her dogs sickened by an infection, Butcher nevertheless managed to finish second. She won the Iditarod again in 1990, setting a new record of eleven days, one hour. In all, Butcher raced in seventeen Iditarods, finishing in the top five a dozen times. The five-feet, six-inch, 140-pound Butcher was an unlikely hero in the world of dogsled racing, a sport previously dominated by men. Yet she became the face of the sport, winning devoted fans with her amazing displays of strength and endurance, her toothy smile, and her trademark, no-nonsense braided hair.

In 1995 Butcher retired from racing to start a family but continued to operate her kennel. Butcher and Monson had two daughters: Tekla, named after one of her lead dogs, and Chisana, named for a tributary in the Alaskan range. In December 2005 Butcher was diagnosed with leukemia. Even as she went through treatments, she ran the Mayor's Midnight Sun Marathon in Anchorage to raise money and awareness for bone-marrow donation programs. She died of the disease in 2006.

To honor Butcher, Monson transported her ashes by dogsled 700 miles to her favorite rest stop on the Iditarod trail, a place called Old Woman, between Kaltag and Unalakleet. There, he spread some of her ashes. Speaking to the *New York Times* shortly after her death, Monson summed up his wife's legacy by observing, "She lived more in 51 years than some people do in 100." Butcher had become an ambassador for her sport and an inspiring symbol of women's grit and fortitude.

For a biography of Butcher, see Ellen M. Dolan, *Susan Butcher and the Iditarod Trail* (1993). For a detailed profile of Butcher's life, see Sonja Steptoe, "The Dogged Pursuit of Excellence," *Sports Illustrated* (11 Feb. 1991). Articles that chronicle her career are "Susan Butcher, 9 Dogs Mush to 2nd Win in Alaskan Race," *Washington Post* (19 Mar. 1987); Dan McDonnell, "Toughest Woman in the World," *Advertiser* (6 Mar. 1990); and Dick Heller, "Tough Butcher Conquered Iditarod Four Times," *Washington Times* (19 Mar. 2007). Obituaries are in the *Boston Globe* (1 Sept. 2006) and *New York Times* (7 Aug. 2006).

Lisa Frick

BUTLER, Octavia Estelle (*b.* 22 June 1947 in Pasadena, California; *d.* 24 February 2006 in Lake Forest Park, Washington), acclaimed author who transformed the literary genre of science fiction by introducing complex leading characters who were often alien, African American, and female.

Butler was the only child of Laurice James Butler and Octavia Margaret (Guy) Butler. Her father was a shoeshine man who died when Butler was a small child. She was raised by her mother and grandmother in a deeply religious environment in a racially mixed area of Southern California and attended public schools with a diverse student body. She was shy but extremely bright and loved to escape the loneliness and boredom of being an only child through reading at the Pasadena Public Library. Her mother, who worked as a domestic, struggled to make ends meet and often brought home books for her precocious daughter from the wealthier households where she

Octavia E. Butler. BETH GWINN/WRITER PICTURES

worked. Butler said she was a hermit during her adolescence and often felt like an outsider. This would be a reoccurring theme in both her adult life and her writings.

Butler wrote her first short story at the age of ten, and she wrote her first science-fiction story at twelve after seeing a B movie called *Devil Girl from Mars*. She thought that the story line of the film was silly and decided that she could do a better job herself. From an early age, despite struggling with dyslexia, she knew that she wanted to be a writer and nothing else. She was also fascinated by science fiction and the space race between the United States and the Soviet Union. The idea of traveling to other worlds became her muse.

Butler earned an AA from Pasadena City College in 1968 and later studied writing at California State University, Los Angeles, and at the University of California, Los Angeles (UCLA). She never completed her course work at UCLA, but she later credited two writing workshops with having the greatest impact on her literary career. From 1969 to 1970 she attended the Open Door Program of the Screen Writers' Guild of America, West, which was created to mentor African-American and Latino writers in Hollywood. There she met the noted science-fiction writer Harlan Ellison, who in 1970 encouraged her to attend the Clarion Science Fiction Writers' Workshop, then held at Clarion State College in Clarion, Pennsylvania. At Clarion she was under the tutelage of instructors such as the noted feminist speculative fiction writer Joanna Russ. Butler credited Russ with giving her the confidence to write science-fiction using her real name. At that time most female science-fiction writers wrote under male pseudonyms because publishers were reluctant to accept science-fiction works written by women.

Butler's first published story, "Crossover," appeared in the Clarion science-fiction anthology in 1971. It took five long years before she would be published again. She lived in Los Angeles, where she wrote every morning, but she had to take odd jobs to earn a living.

Her first novel, *Patternmaster*, was published in 1976. It became the first in a series of five books known as the Patternist or Patternmaster series, published throughout the mid-1970s and early 1980s. The books span the time from ancient Egypt to the far distant future and explore the morality of power and the psychological dimensions of enslavement. Butler's most famous book is *Kindred* (1979). The heroine is an African-American woman living in Los Angeles in the 1970s. She is married to a white man but must travel back in time to the antebellum South to save a white slave owner who is her ancestor. *Kindred* was one of Butler's best-selling novels. More than half a million copies had been sold by the time of her death, and it became a standard on many high school and college reading lists. She once stated, "Every story that I read [as a child], practically had as its main character a white man." She loved being a writer because she could finally "write herself into the story."

Butler wrote more than fifteen novels. Her last book was *Fledgling* (2005). Throughout most of her career Butler struggled to earn a living as a writer. Many of her books, such as those in her Xenogenesis trilogy (also called the Lilith's Brood series), were critically acclaimed but were not best sellers. Many publishers could not decide how to market her science-fiction novels, which often featured sexually ambiguous female lead characters and focused on complex social issues such as religious zealotry, racial and sexual identity, and the frailties of human nature. Butler's works predated the 1990s-era publishing boom of best-selling African-American authors such as Terry McMillan and E. Lynn Harris, whose books were based on more marketable themes such as romance and relationships.

Butler never changed her writing style to gain commercial success. Later in her career, however, her works did find mass appeal owing to a strong and loyal fan base. Many fans and critics cite Butler's earlier works as "prophetic overtures" that discussed the effects of deadly viral diseases and global warming long before such topics became mainstream concerns.

Butler received numerous awards throughout her literary career, twice winning both the Hugo Award from the World Science Fiction Society and the Nebula Award from the Science Fiction and Fantasy Writers of America for best

novel and best short story. She was also awarded the Langston Hughes Medal as well as a PEN Lifetime Achievement award in 2000. Perhaps the most life-changing honor that she received was the John D. and Catherine T. MacArthur Foundation Fellowship in 1995. The $295,000 "genius" grant afforded Butler a much-needed financial windfall. She was the first science-fiction novelist ever to receive the MacArthur grant. The award brought her greater national recognition and also bestowed newfound respect on the literary genre of speculative fiction.

In 1999, after the death of her mother, Butler moved from Los Angeles to Lake Forest Park near Seattle and purchased her first home. She was an extremely private person, and almost all of her time was devoted to writing. She was, however, a popular attraction on numerous national book tours and at science-fiction symposia, and she taught five times at the Clarion West workshop. Her writings inspired a new generation of women of color to enter the field of science-fiction writing. Butler never married and had no children. Although many in the gay and lesbian community embraced her as a literary icon, her personal life remained an enigma—as did that of many of her asexual female characters. Butler suffered from hypertension and other health problems and succumbed to injuries from a fall in front of her home at the age of fifty-eight. She was laid to rest at the Mountain View Cemetery and Mausoleum in Altadena, California.

Butler was the first African-American woman to establish a successful career in speculative fiction. Her stories explored not only the outer realms of time and space but also the concepts of race, power, religion, morality, and human nature.

★

A biographical profile of Butler is included in Paula Geyh, Fred G. Leebron, and Andrew Levy, eds., *Postmodern American Fiction: A Norton Anthology* (1998). A critical analysis of Butler's writings is in Patricia Melzer, *Alien Constructions: Science Fiction and Feminist Thought* (2006). Obituaries are in the *Seattle Post-Intelligencer* (27 Feb. 2006) and *New York Times* (1 Mar. 2006). An appreciation is in the *Women's Review of Books* 23, no. 3 (May–June 2006): 19.

F. Romall Smalls

BUTTONS, Red (*b.* 15 February 1919 in New York City; *d.* 13 July 2006 in Los Angeles, California), versatile actor and comedian.

Born Aaron Chwatt to Jewish immigrant parents and raised on Manhattan's Lower East Side, Buttons was the son of Michael Chwatt, a hatmaker, and Sophie Chwatt, a homemaker. An

Red Buttons, 1975. **HULTON ARCHIVE/GETTY IMAGES**

indifferent student, Buttons saw his parents summoned to Public School 104 on East Fourth Street so often that he observed, "they should have graduated with me." The family, including brother Joe and sister Ida, moved to the Bronx. At age twelve Buttons won an amateur contest at the Fox Corona Theater when he sang a high-pitched rendition of "Sweet Jennie Lee" dressed in a sailor suit.

Four years later, when Buttons was sixteen and a student at Evander Childs High School, he worked as a singer-bellhop at Ryan's Tavern, where he wore a uniform bedecked with multiple buttons. Coupled with his mop of red hair, he earned the permanent moniker Red Buttons. After high school, encouraged by his father, Buttons secured a job in the Catskill Mountains as a singing bellhop at the Beerkill Lodge in Greenfield Park, New York, for which he was paid $1.50 per week plus room and board. Since his voice was changing, Buttons switched from music to comedy and baggage to dishes. As a busboy, he filled fountain pens with cream for beverages during meat meals in defiance of kosher laws, charging up to a quarter per squirt. In the Borscht Belt, Buttons also mastered the art of stand-up comedy. Short, impish, and blessed with an infectious grin, Buttons teamed up with the tall Gentile Robert Alda, who played his straight man.

Back in New York City he became a club comic, playing weddings, bar mitzvahs, conventions, and picnics. In 1939

Buttons began working for Minsky's Burlesque. He was later spotted by the actor José Ferrer, who hired him to perform in the Broadway play *The Admiral Takes a Wife*, a comedy about life at a naval base in Hawaii that was scheduled to open in December 1941 but was canceled when Pearl Harbor was bombed. The following year Buttons did get his Broadway debut in a second play with Ferrer and his then wife Uta Hagen in *Vickie*. That same year, 1942, Buttons appeared in Minsky's *Wine, Women and Song*, which was the final burlesque show in New York City following a ban on all burlesque that was enacted by the administration of Mayor Fiorello LaGuardia. In 1943 Buttons joined the Army Air Corps and the cast of *Winged Victory*—first a play, then a movie—featuring many stars promoting the war effort.

After the war Buttons resumed his career on and off Broadway. His performance in the musical *Hold It* in 1948 caught the attention of television moguls and led to appearances on the new medium as a guest of the National Broadcasting Company (NBC) megastar Milton Berle. In one sketch, preparing to examine Buttons, Berle inadvertently ripped off his clothes along with funny undergarments to the surprise and delight of the audience. In an effort to compete with Berle, Columbia Broadcasting System (CBS) offered Buttons his own show in 1952. *The Red Buttons Show* had a sensational first season in which Buttons impersonated several stock characters: Rocky, the punch-drunk fighter; Mugsy, the juvenile delinquent; the Kupke Kid, a dumb nebbish; and Keeglefarven, a Teutonic lout. Between acts he would cup his ears and sing: "Ho-ho, hee-hee, ha-ha, strange things are happening." Young audiences loved this comic everyman, and his nonsensical song became a catchphrase. Buttons was on the cover of *Time* magazine and was awarded the 1954 Comedian of the Year by the Academy of Radio and Television Arts and Sciences. After the initial popularity of his show in its first season, the ratings dropped considerably. Following a three-year run on two networks—CBS and later NBC—and a revolving door of writers that Buttons hired and fired in an effort to enliven the show, it was canceled in 1955.

Resilient, Buttons turned to drama. The director Joshua Logan chose Buttons to play Sergeant Joe Kelly in the 1957 film adaptation of James Michener's novel *Sayonara*, in which his character defies army regulations to marry a Japanese woman (played by Miyoshi Umeki) during the Korean War. Unable to sustain married life together, they commit suicide. Both Buttons and Umeki won Oscars for their supporting roles in this award-winning film starring Marlon Brando. Buttons's success in a dramatic role led to other parts in film, including such notable movies as *Hatari!* (1962), *The Longest Day* (1962), *They Shoot Horses, Don't They?* (1969), *The Poseidon Adventure* (1972), and *It Could Happen to You* (1994). Buttons capped his film career with two documentaries: *Goodnight, We Love You* (2004) and *Sid Bernstein Presents* (2005).

Buttons returned to television in the late 1970s, making several guest appearances on the series *Love Boat*. He continued to work in television throughout the 1980s and 1990s as a recurring character on the drama series *Knots Landing* as well as on the situation comedy *Roseanne*. In 2005 he was nominated for an Emmy for Outstanding Guest Actor in a Drama Series for his portrayal of the elderly widow Mr. Rubadoux on the medical drama *ER*.

Buttons gained lasting notoriety for his frequent performances on the *Dean Martin Celebrity Roast*, which ran on NBC beginning in the early 1970s. His most memorable appearances from these roasts stemmed from Buttons's "Never Got a Dinner" routine in which he noted the many famous people who never got a roast with such lines as "Abe Lincoln, who said 'A house divided is a condominium,' never got a dinner." Buttons finally did get his dinner when the Friars Club honored him with a lifetime achievement award coupled with a roast. A consummate live entertainer, Buttons performed in Atlantic City, New Jersey, and Las Vegas, Nevada. At age seventy-six in 1995, drawing upon his early roots from the Borscht Belt and burlesque, Buttons starred in the autobiographical one-man show *Buttons on Broadway* to favorable reviews.

Buttons married three times. His first marriage to the stripper Roxanne Arlen, whom he met during his burlesque years, was annulled; his second marriage to Helayne McNorton ended in divorce. He married Alicia Prats in 1964, and they had two children. The couple separated in 2000. Buttons died of vascular disease at his home; his body was cremated.

In a variety of roles, Buttons demonstrated immense talent, versatility, pathos, and impeccable timing. Whether a desperate marathon dancer who succumbs to a heart attack, a prissy bachelor who survives disaster at sea, or a World War II paratrooper trapped in his parachute on a church rooftop in France, Buttons created indelible characters.

Useful sources are Steve Allen, *The Funny Men* (1956); Joey Adams and Henry Tobias, *The Borscht Belt* (1966); Joe Franklin, *Joe Franklin's Encyclopedia of Comedians* (1979); and Lawrence J. Epstein, *The Haunted Smile: The Story of Jewish Comedians in America* (2001). Obituaries are in the *Los Angeles Times*, *New York Times*, and *Washington Post* (all 14 July 2006).

Joseph Dorinson

C

CALDWELL, Sarah (*b.* 6 March 1924 in Maryville, Missouri; *d.* 23 March 2006 in Portland, Maine), conductor, stage director, and opera impresario who founded the Opera Company of Boston and who is regarded as one of the most adventurous and innovative producers in the history of American opera.

Caldwell was the only child of Edwin F. Caldwell and Carrie Margaret (Baker) Caldwell, a pianist and music teacher. Caldwell's parents divorced when she was an infant; she was raised by relatives while her mother studied at Columbia University for a master's degree in music. As a child Caldwell was gifted in mathematics and music. She started taking violin lessons at the age of four and was able to give recitals at the age of ten. When Caldwell was twelve years old, her mother married Henry M. Alexander, a professor of political science at the University of Arkansas. Subsequently the family moved to Fayetteville, Arkansas, where Caldwell graduated from Fayetteville High School in 1939.

Following her stepfather's suggestion, Caldwell enrolled at the University of Arkansas as a psychology major. In 1940 she transferred to Hendrix College, where she studied violin with David Robertson. In 1942 Caldwell earned a scholarship to attend the New England Conservatory, where she studied violin with Richard Burgin, concertmaster of the Boston Symphony, and viola with Georges Fourel. She took courses in conducting, stage design, and opera production under the guidance of Boris Goldovsky, head of the department of opera. Caldwell completed her studies at the conservatory in 1946. Thereafter she declined offers to play violin with the Minneapolis Symphony Orchestra and Indianapolis Symphony Orchestra and decided to explore the opera world instead. "My passion in life is opera," she explained in a 14 February 1976 interview for *Opera News.* "I turned them down because all my life I've loved both the theater and music."

In the summer of 1946 Caldwell accepted a scholarship to play viola at the Berkshire Music Center at Tanglewood, the summer home of the Boston Symphony. In 1947 at the Tanglewood Music Festival, Caldwell successfully staged her first opera production, Ralph Vaughan Williams's *Riders to the Sea*, which impressed Serge Koussevitsky, founder and director of the Berkshire Music Center and conductor of the Boston Symphony. The following year Koussevitsky invited Caldwell to join the Berkshire Music Center faculty. Caldwell accepted the position and remained on the faculty from 1948 to 1952. During this period she also became Goldovsky's assistant for the New England Opera Theater in Boston. Her role involved all facets of opera production; she served as stage director, orchestra conductor, chorus director, and libretto translator. In 1952 Caldwell was appointed director of the opera workshop department at Boston University. She served as director for eight years, during which she helped establish the university's department of music theater.

Supported by a small group of colleagues and friends and with a budget of $5,000, Caldwell founded the Boston Opera Group in January 1957. It was renamed the Opera Company of Boston in 1965. The company presented its inaugural performance at the Back Bay Theater in June 1958 with Jacques Offenbach's *Le Voyage dans la lune.* The production was so well received that in 1960 it was performed on a national tour and was subsequently presented at the White House to President John F. Kennedy and his wife, Jacqueline; the aviation pioneer Charles Lindbergh;

Sarah Caldwell, 1981. **BACHRACH/GETTY IMAGES**

and several American astronauts. After the Back Bay Theater was torn down to make way for an apartment building, Caldwell faced a constant problem: the lack of a proper venue in which to perform. The company had to present productions in various facilities, such as the Kresge Auditorium at the Massachusetts Institute of Technology in Cambridge and the Schubert Theatre in Boston. Finally, in October 1978 Caldwell's company acquired the B. F. Keith Memorial Theatre, later named the Opera House, in Boston. Unfortunately, over the years the company managed real estate issues poorly until it was $5 million in debt. This ultimately led to the sale of the theater in 1990, at which point the company basically ceased production.

Limited by production space and funds, Caldwell presented four or five productions a season. She was both stage director and orchestra conductor for most of her productions and also served as administrator, researcher, talent scout, and fund-raiser. Caldwell was able to present an adventurous repertoire that included the world premiere of Gunther Schuller's *The Fisherman and His Wife* (1970) and the American premieres of Arnold Schoenberg's *Moses und Aron* (1966), Sergei Prokofiev's *War and Peace* (1974), and Hector Berlioz's *Benvenuto Cellini* (1975). Caldwell's devotion to opera and deep knowledge in both music and stage attracted world-class artists to perform in her operas. Among them were the sopranos Beverly Sills and Joan

Sutherland and the tenors Plácido Domingo and Jon Vickers.

Caldwell made her Carnegie Hall debut in December 1974, conducting the American Symphony Orchestra with her own concert version of Prokofiev's *War and Peace*. On 10 November 1975 Caldwell conducted a New York Philharmonic Pension Fund concert, *A Celebration of Women Composers*. In the same year Caldwell became the subject of *Time* magazine's 10 November 1975 cover story, "Music's Wonder Woman." In the article she was called "the first lady of American opera" and "one of the great impresarios in all the American performing arts."

On 13 January 1976 Caldwell became the first woman to conduct at the Metropolitan Opera in New York City. The historic performance, Giuseppe Verdi's *La Traviata*, featuring Sills, received favorable reviews. In the summer of 1978 Caldwell conducted her first recording, Gaetano Donizetti's *Don Pasquale*, for the EMI Angel music label.

Caldwell was also active on the international stage. In the summer of 1981 she conducted performances of *La Traviata* with the Central Opera Theater in Beijing, China. In 1982 she staged Wolfgang Amadeus Mozart's *The Magic Flute* in Manila, Philippines. In 1983 she was appointed artistic director of the New Opera Company of Israel. In 1988 in Boston and in 1991 in Moscow, Russia, Caldwell and the Soviet composer Rodion Shchedrin initiated and organized Making Music Together, a festival involving several hundred Soviet and American performing artists.

Caldwell joined the faculty at the University of Arkansas as a distinguished professor overseeing the opera program at the music department in fall 1999. She was also involved with the International Music Preservation Project of the Library of Congress, an effort to transcribe and publish seventy-two ancient Chinese and Japanese musical scrolls found in Japan in the 1970s. In 2003 she took a leave of absence from the university because of poor health and moved to Freeport, Maine. Caldwell formally retired in 2004. Also in 2004 she returned to Boston to accept an award from the New England Opera Club, and Boston mayor Thomas M. Menino proclaimed 31 October 2004 "Sarah Caldwell Day."

Caldwell received thirty-five honorary degrees from various institutions, including Harvard University, Georgetown University, and the New England Conservatory. She also was the first recipient of the Kennedy Center Award for Excellence (1978). In January 1997 she received the National Medal of the Arts from President Bill Clinton.

Weighing more than 200 pounds and at only five feet, three inches tall, Caldwell was sometimes described as "eccentric" and "absent-minded." Caldwell never married. She was very close to her mother, and they lived together until Margaret's death in 1983. At the age of eighty-two Caldwell died from heart failure at the Maine Medical Center in Portland.

In an interview for the 1981 book *Particular Passions: Talks with Women Who Have Shaped Our Times*, by Lynn Gilbert and Gaylen Moore, Caldwell explained that her concept of opera "is of a total musical and theatrical experience, in which the theatrical elements and the musical elements are very carefully combined so that they enhance one another." "Opera is everything rolled into one—music, theater, the dance, color and voices and theatrical illusions," she stated in an interview for *Life* magazine in 1965.

Some critics believed that Caldwell was more talented in directing than in conducting. Her most vulnerable technical point in conducting was the balance. In extreme cases she fell so deeply into the events onstage that she simply forgot to conduct at all. Nevertheless, being a sensitive musician, Caldwell possessed highly sophisticated musical tastes. She was always conscious of sound quality and was intent on beautiful tone.

★

Caldwell's autobiography is *Challenges: A Memoir of My Life in Opera* (2008). The only full length-biography is Daniel Kessler, *Sarah Caldwell: The First Woman of Opera* (2008). Lynn Gilbert and Gaylen Moore, *Particular Passions: Talks with Women Who Have Shaped Our Times* (1981), and Joan Kufrin, *Uncommon Women* (1981), provide firsthand information about Caldwell and are based on interviews with her. Jane Weiner LePage included information about Caldwell in *Women Composers, Conductors, and Musicians of the Twentieth Century: Selected Biographies*, volume 2 (1983). Among numerous articles on Caldwell, the following earn their prominence: Dora Jane Hamblin, "She Puts the Oomph in the Opera," *Life* (5 Mar. 1965); Winthrop Sargeant, "Infinite Pains," *New Yorker* (24 Dec. 1973); Andrew Porter, "Caldwell in Command," *New Yorker* (6 Jan. 1975); "Music's Wonder Woman," *Time* (10 Nov. 1975); and Richard Dyer, "The Divine Sarah: Richard Dyer Salutes the Genius of Sarah Caldwell, Whose Pioneering Productions of *Moses und Aron* and *Benvenuto Cellini* Helped Put Opera on the Map in Boston," *Opera News* 68, no. 6 (1 Dec. 2003): 42–44. Obituaries are in the *New York Times* and *Boston Globe* (both 25 Mar. 2006) and *Opera News* (June 2006).

Di Su

CAREY, Ronald Robert ("Ron") (*b.* 22 March 1936 in New York City; *d.* 11 December 2008 in New York City), union leader who served two terms as president of the International Brotherhood of Teamsters and Warehousemen, significantly democratizing Teamsters Union operations, only to be ousted because of a financial scandal.

Carey was the second of five sons of Joseph Carey, a driver for United Parcel Service (UPS), and Loretta Carey. With forty-six years of service with UPS, Carey's father taught him about workers' rights and the importance of a democratic union.

Raised in western Queens, New York City, Carey attended the now defunct Haaren High School (because it had a swim team) on the west side of Manhattan, New York City. Rather than attending Saint John's University in Queens on a swimming scholarship, Carey joined the Marine Corps, serving between 1953 and 1955. At age eighteen he married Barbara Murphy, an upstairs neighbor, with whom he had five children.

Following in his father's footsteps, Carey became a UPS driver in 1956 in Queens. In 1958 he was elected a shop steward for Teamsters Local 804, one of the union's largest locals; a typical job site had between twenty and thirty shop stewards. Teamsters Local 804 consisted mostly of 7,000 UPS delivery drivers and sorters throughout the New York metropolitan area. In 1963 and 1965 Carey ran for Local 804 business agent but lost those elections. He nevertheless continued to take a labor relations course at night. In 1967 he became local president.

Throughout his career Carey displayed an independent streak, unwilling to sacrifice Local 804 member rights and demands to those of the powerful national union. In 1968 he led Local 804 on a nine-week strike against UPS, seeking greater benefits than those offered in a national contract. In 1974 he called his men out on an eighty-seven-day strike to protest UPS replacement of full-time workers with part-timers.

Carey delivered for his members. Local 804 became one of the first locals in the nation to guarantee a pension to members with at least twenty-five years of experience, regardless of retirement age. Avoiding Mafia affiliation common to some top Teamster leaders, Carey also garnered a reputation for fairness and honesty. His local had no no-show jobs. Other locals allegedly assigned members to nonexistent jobs in firms they had contracts with.

While building his power base, Carey announced in 1989 that he would seek the union presidency in an election more than two years away. He ran a no-frills campaign across the nation, visiting as many of the Teamsters' 635 locals and 1.4 million members as possible. Frugality and personal safety, given death threats, were the order of the day.

The December 1991 election marked the first time that Teamsters would vote directly, in a secret ballot, for top union leadership. An agreement the union signed with federal officials to settle racketeering charges mandated such a change. Carey ran on a reform platform. He promised to curb outsized union leader salaries and to eliminate double-dipping, or drawing salaries from several positions. In addition he vowed to cut union spending for operating expenses and high-priced junkets. Finally he stressed pushing union organizers to seek aggressively to organize nonunion workers and avoid internal battles caused by poaching more easily recruited dues-paying members from competing locals. Such a platform was bold given that four of the previous seven Teamsters international presidents had been indicted, and three went to jail.

Carey was endorsed by the Teamsters for a Democratic Union, an influential group of union reformers. Federal officials disqualified the candidacy of James P. Hoffa, son of the former president James R. Hoffa and a longtime union attorney, asserting that he did not meet union eligibility rules.

With Carey and his slate winning almost half the vote in a three-man race, reform began in earnest. Shortly after assuming office in 1992, Carey ordered the union to sell its two airplanes, and he cut his salary from $225,000 to $175,000. He also cleaned out the Teamsters' headquarters staff.

Despite being dogged by persistent but minor corruption charges, Carey forged ahead. He would eventually put sixty-seven of the union's more than 600 local units under trusteeship, as recommended by an independent review board. He failed in his effort to win member backing to increase union dues 25 percent to fund a depleted strike benefit fund.

In December 1996 Carey won a second term, narrowly defeating Hoffa 52 percent to 48 percent. However, in March 1997 Hoffa accused Carey of illegal reelection practices, charges that ultimately led to Carey's resignation.

In August 1997 Carey led a successful fifteen-day nationwide strike against UPS, increasing pay for part-time workers for the first time since 1982, getting pay increases for full-time workers, and winning UPS's assurance that it would pay into the union's multiemployer pension plan. Essentially UPS management had underestimated the Teamsters' ability to generate public support by successfully using media, including the Internet.

The contract accord seemed to mark the high point of the Carey administration. In late August 1997 a federal official sought to overturn the election, claiming that Carey and his associates illegally donated union money to several liberal causes in exchange for contributions to the Carey reelection campaign. Using union money to support a union candidate is illegal under federal law.

Carey testified that he knew nothing about the kickbacks and continued to proclaim his innocence, while taking a leave of absence in November 1997. In 1998 a court-appointed review board expelled Carey from the union. The board concluded that while Carey did not take part in the illegal payment scheme, he failed to exercise proper oversight in not discovering and stopping the fraud. In the wake of the scandal, Hoffa was elected Teamsters

Union president on 5 December 1998. Carey, meanwhile, continued to protest the board's banning him from the union. He died of lung cancer at New York Queens Hospital ten years after his ouster.

Carey was a bright star in organized labor during the 1990s, albeit for an abbreviated period. Organized labor's share of the workforce then continued its slow and steady decline that had begun several decades earlier. Management still had the upper hand in many industries. Carey stood firm against persistent corruption in the Teamsters Union. His national prominence would extend only for about seven years, falling victim to a campaign finance scandal of which Carey claimed ignorance.

Steven Brill, *The Teamsters* (1978), includes a chapter on Carey. See also Ann Hagedorn, "A Teamster Sets Out on a Tough Campaign for Union Presidency," *Wall Street Journal* (12 Nov. 1990). An obituary is in the *New York Times* (13 Dec. 2008).

Ira Breskin

CARLIN, George Denis Patrick (*b*. 12 May 1937 in New York City; *d*. 22 June 2008 in Santa Monica, California), comedian who wrote and performed monologues for live audiences and for record albums and television programs, occasionally appearing in comic roles in feature films and on television series.

Carlin was the second of two sons of Patrick Carlin, a newspaper advertising salesman, and Mary (Beary) Carlin, an office worker. Carlin's parents separated during his infancy, and Carlin grew up living in his mother's apartment in Morningside Heights, a neighborhood in Upper Manhattan. As a student Carlin expressed strong antipathy toward authority and religion, leading to his expulsion from two Roman Catholic high schools before he completed tenth grade. He credited his mother and other family members for instilling an "Irish love of language" in him. In anticipation of receiving his draft notice, Carlin enlisted in the U.S. Air Force at age seventeen and qualified as a radar technician. While stationed at Barksdale Air Force Base in Louisiana, he earned a high school equivalency diploma and found his first work as an entertainer, moonlighting as a disc jockey at KJOE, a Shreveport, Louisiana, radio station.

Carlin's difficulties with institutional authority continued throughout his military service. The subject of three courts-martial, he was classified an "unproductive airman" and given early discharge in 1957. Deciding to pursue a radio career, he remained at KJOE for two years

George Carlin, 2001. **BILL GREENBLATT/UPI/LANDOV**

and then took a job in Boston at WEZE, where he met Jack Burns, an aspiring comedian who became a friend and collaborator. Carlin credited Burns for introducing him to ideas that affected his outlook, changing him from a nominal political conservative into a liberal thinker and an advocate of libertarian causes. Carlin was fired from WEZE for "borrowing" the station's only mobile broadcast vehicle just as a major prison riot was breaking out in the Boston area.

Burns followed Carlin to KXOL in Fort Worth, Texas, where the pair ad-libbed jokes over the air and began to make appearances in front of live audiences. Moving to Los Angeles, they cohosted a morning drive-time show as the "Wright Brothers" and played club dates at night as "Burns and Carlin." While performing at Cosmic Alley, a Hollywood, California, espresso bar, they attracted the attention of several cutting-edge comedians, including Lenny Bruce and Mort Sahl, who recommended them to agents and bookers. Appearances at the Chicago Playboy Club and the Hungry i nightclub in San Francisco led to a national television debut on *The Tonight Show* in 1962. At the

threshold of success, however, the partners amicably dissolved the act. Preferring improvisational sketch comedy, Burns joined the Second City troupe in Chicago, while Carlin, at age twenty-five, had found his calling as a monologuist.

Clean shaven, in suit and tie, Carlin rapidly climbed the ladder of big-time show business, relying on stories about his Irish-American upbringing, including some fairly standard jokes about nuns with rulers. He created a distinctive signature to his act with material drawn from his experiences as a radio disc jockey and as a heavy viewer of daytime television (which he described as "an occupational hazard for stand-up comedians"). The acute intelligence underlying an often goofy delivery gained Carlin a place on the circuit of upscale big-city night spots where toleration of blue material, drug references, and political irreverence defined the fringes of American commercial entertainment. While taking advantage of these freedoms in the clubs, he mastered the art of tailoring his work for the short, sanitized sets allowed on television.

Carlin became a sought-after guest on prime-time network variety programs, making ten appearances on the top-rated *Ed Sullivan Show* between 1967 and 1971. He was seen even more frequently on late-night programs, such as *The Tonight Show Starring Johnny Carson* and *The Merv Griffin Show*. Carlin's stock characters, such as Al Sleet, the Hippy-Dippy Weatherman ("Tonight's forecast? Continuing darkness") and Biff Burns ("bringing you *Biff Burns' Sportlight Spotlight*, spotlighting sports"), walked a thin line between stoner spoofing, acting as if he were high on marijuana, and traditional slapstick, attracting fans of both. Carlin made the rounds of a rising star, playing game shows as a celebrity contestant, appearing as a guest on sitcoms, and making his Hollywood debut in *With Six You Get Egg Roll*, a 1968 comedy starring Doris Day. Comedy albums were the medium of choice for reaching mass audiences with nightclub-style material, and in 1967 Carlin released the first of his twenty-two stand-up comedy albums, *Take-Offs and Put-Ons*. His next record, *FM and AM* (1971), won a Grammy Award for Best Comedy Album. Carlin received five Grammy Awards during his career.

While rising to the top of a profession in which failure is the norm, Carlin struggled with his innate rebelliousness. The contrast between the glitzy world of show business and his own social circle, which he described as "somewhere between beatnik and hippie," became a source of increasing anxiety. "It became more of a strain for me to work for straight audiences. I took acid and mescaline. My sense of being on the outside intensified. I changed." This inner conflict surfaced permanently in the wake of Carlin's 1972 arrest in Milwaukee, Wisconsin, for public profanity after a performance of "Seven Words You Can Never Use on Television." Embracing the opportunity to promote First Amendment rights, he refused to drop the material and was arrested in three more cities. A recording of the monologue broadcast by the New York radio station WBAI drew a listener complaint to the Federal Communications Commission (FCC), which then levied a fine against the station for "indecency." WBAI's owner, the Pacifica Foundation, a nonprofit organization dedicated to free-speech rights, fought the fine until the U.S. Supreme Court ruled in favor of the FCC, establishing a precedent that has been cited in twenty-first-century broadcast censorship cases.

Refusing to be censored by others, Carlin refused to censor himself. Growing a beard and long hair, wearing what he pleased onstage, he freely addressed drugs, sex, politics, and whatever else moved him. He accepted fewer casino and nightclub bookings, preferring concert-style performances at theaters and on university campuses. Chosen to host the first episode of the National Broadcasting Company's *Saturday Night Live* in 1975, Carlin cemented his status as an "edgy" comedian who could still pass muster for network television. Even so, the limitations on language in broadcast television were putting the medium at odds with the direction that Carlin's career was taking. Carlin might have gradually withdrawn from television if not for the new opportunities for innovative stand-up comedy offered by Home Box Office, the premium pay-cable television service established in 1972. Not subject to FCC rules, and with no commercial interruptions to limit the length of a joke or a routine, Home Box Office offered a nurturing home for stand-up comedy, allowing Carlin at last to reach a television audience on his own terms. His first hour-long special, *On Location: George Carlin at USC*, premiered in 1977; his fifteenth, *It's Bad for Ya*, aired in 2008.

Although Carlin was often associated with a willingness to use "dirty" words and explore taboo subjects, many of his funniest, most enduring routines contain little of either. In "Baseball and Football," he compared the two sports, creating a twin conceit to examine a cultural paradigm and a conflict in the American psyche. "Baseball begins in the spring, the season of new life; football begins in the fall, when everything is dying," he said, opening the set. Carlin then dazzled the audience with a profusion of oppositions: Baseball is a nineteenth-century pastoral game played on a field in a park; football is a twentieth-century technological struggle waged on the gridiron of a stadium. The object in football is to capture territory; in baseball the goal is to be safe at home. Seventh-inning stretch versus two-minute warning. Baseball cap versus football helmet. In a tied game it is sudden death versus extra innings. As Carlin engaged the audience with these contrasts, baseball's innocence illuminated the dark implications of an America that had clearly chosen football as its favorite pastime.

A master of timing, Carlin enjoyed riding the laughter from a purely clever joke to mask the power of one carrying more clout, as in this meditation on oxymorons: "There's jumbo shrimp . . . and, of course, military intelligence." Carlin never tired of going after his two biggest targets, consumerism ("greed so greedy it requires extra syllables") and religion ("God. You know, the invisible old guy in the sky who loves you and wants your money"). Sharing intimations of mortality, he opened *Life Is Worth Losing* (2005) by describing himself as a "high-tech low-life" who was both "new wave . . . and old school," concluding a series of like oppositions with an intimation of mortality: "My inner child is outward bound."

In addition to his stand-up work, Carlin appeared in minor comic roles in ten feature films, including *Car Wash* (1976), *Dogma* (1999) and *Jersey Girl* (2004), and he occasionally attempted noncomic roles, as in *The Prince of Tides* (1991) and *The Streets of Laredo* (1995), a television miniseries. *The George Carlin Show*, a short-lived sitcom, had him playing a New York cab driver. Carlin was more successful offscreen in his screen ventures, playing the unseen narrator in the U.S. version of *Thomas the Tank Engine and Friends* (1991–1994) and the voice of Fillmore, a hippie-era Volkswagen van, in *Cars* (2006), an animated feature. Carlin was the author of three books: *Brain Droppings* (1997), *Napalm and Silly Putty* (2001), and *When Will Jesus Bring the Pork Chops?* (2004). Each spent time on the best-seller list of the *New York Times*.

Carlin met Brenda Hosbrook in 1961 and the couple married on 3 July 1963. They had a daughter and lived in an oceanfront home in Pacific Palisades, California. Their thirty-four-year marriage ended with Hosbrook's death in 1997. A second marriage, to Sally Wade, took place in 1998. Carlin had a history of cardiovascular disease, dating to a heart attack in 1977. This long-term condition was complicated by a variety of dependencies, including alcohol and cocaine. Carlin died of congestive heart failure at a Santa Monica hospital. His remains were cremated.

Carlin and Richard Pryor, as well as several other comedians, can be credited with reinvigorating the exhausted old craft of toastmasters and joke tellers with the political and cultural tensions that gripped the country during a period bracketed by President John F. Kennedy's assassination and the end of the Vietnam War. Combining the energies of a schoolyard wise guy and an impassioned satirist with a poet's appreciation for the music of language and the absurdity of life, Carlin helped to elevate stand-up comedy into perhaps the most formidable of commercial performance arts. A pioneer in the development of stand-up comedy as a form of personal artistic expression, Carlin contested the boundaries of commercial popular culture with material considered too cerebral, bawdy, or otherwise controversial for mainstream American show business. Carlin was posthumously awarded the Mark Twain Prize for American Humor, the nation's highest honor reserved for humorists, in a 2008 ceremony at the Kennedy Center in Washington, D.C.

★

Richard Zoglin, *Comedy at the Edge: How 1970s Stand-up Comedy Changed America* (2008), provides an enriching context for understanding Carlin's life. Although he never wrote an autobiography, Carlin gave notable in-depth interviews to magazines, including the *Progressive* (July 2001) and *Playboy* (21 July 2006). "George Carlin's Finale," an interview conducted just nine days before Carlin's death, appeared in *Psychology Today* 41, no. 5 (Sept.–Oct. 2008): 90–91. For a portrait of Carlin in midcareer, see William Grimes, "George Carlin, Small but Amusing," *New York Times* (21 Jan. 1992). An obituary is in the *New York Times* (24 June 2008).

David Marc

CASSINI, Oleg Lolewski (*b.* 11 April 1913 in Paris, France; *d.* 17 March 2006 in Manhasset, New York), urbane fashion designer whose seven-decade career provided tasteful and influential couture for Hollywood actresses and First Lady Jacqueline Kennedy.

Cassini was the son of Alexander Lolewski, a diplomat of the court of Czar Nicholas II of Russia, and Marguerite (Cassini) Lolewski, an Italian countess. Cassini's parents were stationed in Copenhagen, Denmark, and were vacationing in Paris when Cassini was born. A younger brother, Igor, became a syndicated society columnist for the Hearst newspaper chain under the name Cholly Knickerbocker. When the czar was overthrown in 1917 and the Communist regime seized the family's ancestral estate, Cassini's now impoverished family fled to Florence, Italy, where Cassini attended the English Catholic School. He then studied drawing and painting under Giorgio de Chirico at the Academia Bella Arte, graduating in 1934. While in Italy, the family began using his mother's maiden name.

Cassini's mother designed hats for the fashion salon of Countess Fabricotti. She and Oleg traveled to Paris to sketch the latest couture to be copied back in Italy. In late 1932 Cassini worked briefly as a sketch artist for the Jean Patou fashion house in Paris. In 1935 he moved to Rome to open his own design studio. With his adept sketching skills, he won five first prizes in the 1934 International Fashion Competition in Turin, Italy. In 1936 Cassini and his brother moved to New York City, where Cassini, starting from scratch, became a designer for various clothing firms. Through his brother's Hollywood connections, Cassini became a staff designer in 1938 and then an assistant costume designer under Edith Head at Paramount Pictures. He

Oleg Cassini. HULTON ARCHIVE/GETTY IMAGES

also worked for Twentieth Century–Fox during the late 1940s and early 1950s.

A natural athlete, Cassini excelled in tennis, skiing, golf, car racing, and horse riding; his memoir details the many sports tournaments that he won. After becoming a naturalized U.S. citizen in 1942, he enlisted in the U.S. Coast Guard and later transferred to the U.S. Army Cavalry Corps, thinking that it was more glamorous, and became a second lieutenant.

Throughout his life Cassini was famous for his fastidious taste, old-world sophistication, and clever wit. The ever-dapper Cassini was a true lady's man who accompanied many Hollywood actresses. "There were always beautiful girls," he wrote in his memoir. On 2 September 1939 he became the fourth husband (of nine) of the cough syrup heiress Merry Fahrney; they had no children and divorced in 1940. In his memoir he describes himself as "just another scalp" for her.

Cassini married his second wife, the actress Gene Tierney, on 1 June 1941; they had two daughters. Tierney insisted that all of her costumes be designed by her husband; he designed the costumes for ten of her films. The couple appeared together in *Where the Sidewalk Ends* (1950). Tierney played a fashion model, and Cassini played a dress designer. In his memoir Cassini notes that in Hollywood he became known as Mr. Gene Tierney. Cassini and Tierney divorced in 1947.

Cassini moved back to New York City in 1950 and opened a salon at 16 East Fifty-fifth Street, an address convenient to café society debutants, their mothers, and Broadway actresses. Arguably the first "celebrity designer," Cassini fashioned ready-to-wear A-line wardrobes in shapely fine silk, sheer organdy, and taffeta. Unlike most American designers, who simply copied French designs, Cassini eliminated superfluous details and accessories so that a woman's clothing would not overwhelm her personality. His understated and elegant dresses were characterized by clean lines, solid colors, and ease of movement. Cassini called his work of luxurious simplicity the "Grace Kelly look." In fact, he was briefly engaged to the beautiful and patrician actress, who left him to marry Prince Rainier of Monaco.

In mid-December 1960 Cassini was appointed the official couturier of the incoming first lady, Jacqueline Kennedy. The Cassini brothers had known her for years. Igor dubbed her the debutante of the year in 1948, and Oleg had designed dresses for her and the Kennedy clan. It was also announced that all bills would be paid for by Joseph P. Kennedy, Jacqueline Kennedy's father-in-law and Cassini's friend. For the next three years, Cassini designed and coordinated some 300 photogenic outfits that became internationally known as the "Jackie look."

The minimally simple but utterly chic wardrobe continued Cassini's earlier work and echoed designs by the French couturier Hubert de Givenchy (Jacqueline Kennedy's favorite designer), such as the pillbox hat and A-line dress in beige wool crepe that Kennedy wore on Inauguration Day. Immediately after the event, pillbox hats and A-line dresses were in vogue internationally. In October 1961 the fashion columnist Eugene Sheppard wrote that "the best known name in American fashion is now Oleg Cassini." The Jackie look would be adapted by later designers, such as Halston, Donna Karan, and Calvin Klein.

When his White House connection was abruptly severed by the assassination of President John F. Kennedy in late 1963, Cassini opened the House of Cassini on East Nineteenth Street in New York City and capitalized on his reputation. He began a licensing empire—the first for an American dress designer—and by the end of the decade had over forty franchise agreements with manufacturers of his signature A-line dresses, accessories, sunglasses, linens, jewelry, girdles, and even baby dolls. Before Cassini's association with the White House, his company earned about $2 million per year; by the end of 1964 the company was earning $20 million per year. At the time of Cassini's death, the House of Cassini was earning $600 million per year. In 1971 Cassini married Marianne Nestor, a former fashion model, who continued to run his company after his death. They kept their thirty-seven-year marriage secret so as to keep Cassini's playboy image alive.

Cassini also invented "trunk shows" in which the designer and his models would travel to department stores with trunks of clothes for ready-to-wear shows and customers would place orders. He also designed men's clothing, including a vogue for the so-called Nehru jacket, colored shirts and underwear, and a line of suits named after the television host Johnny Carson. In the 1980s and 1990s Cassini added lines for sports and travel. With a partnership with David's Bridal in the 1990s, Cassini became the leading bridal designer, perhaps because of his name recognition among mothers of brides. In 2003 the Council of Fashion Designers of America recognized him with the Board of Directors Special Tribute Award for his contribution to fashion. Cassini died at North Shore Hospital in Manhasset from a ruptured blood vessel in his head. He was ninety-two. He is buried in the Cemetery of the Holy Rood in Westbury, New York.

Cassini's seven-decade career as a celebrity designer brought worldwide recognition to American fashion. He was a pioneer of franchised and licensed American couture.

Cassini's memoir is *In My Own Fashion: An Autobiography* (1987). His account of dressing Kennedy is *A Thousand Days of Magic* (1995). See also Hamish Bowles, *Jacqueline Kennedy: The White House Years* (2001). An obituary is in the *New York Times* (19 Mar. 2006).

Patrick S. Smith

CHANDLER, Alfred du Pont, Jr. (*b*. 15 September 1918 in Guyencourt, Delaware; *d*. 9 May 2007 in Cambridge, Massachusetts), eminent business historian and author of *The Visible Hand: The Managerial Revolution in American Business* (1977), a landmark study of managerial capitalism that provided an influential framework for understanding the rise and structural transformation of the modern business enterprise.

Chandler was born near Wilmington, Delaware, to Alfred du Pont Chandler, a businessman, and Carol (Ramsay) Chandler, the daughter of a chemical engineer for DuPont. Chandler's well-connected relatives had intimate ties to the family that founded the DuPont chemical company—his great-grandmother, orphaned by a yellow fever outbreak, was taken in by the du Ponts—but none was related by blood. Chandler spent his first five years in Buenos Aires, Argentina, where his father worked for Baldwin Locomotive Works. When Chandler was eleven, the family returned to the United States, first settling in Philadelphia, Pennsylvania, and then in the rural hinterland of Wilmington. He took an early interest in history—at age seven, his father gave him an American history primer that he read obsessively—and grew up within the social ambit of Delaware's business and cultural elite, including the du Ponts and the Wyeth family of artists.

Chandler was educated at Philips Exeter Academy and, following in the footsteps of several of his forebears, Harvard University, where he studied history and was a member of the school's sailing team with his classmate John F. Kennedy. Upon graduating in 1940 magna cum laude with a BA, Chandler joined the U.S. Naval Reserve, analyzing aerial photographs of American air strikes in Germany and Japan during World War II and rising to the rank of lieutenant commander. On 8 January 1944 he married Fay Martin, an artist with whom he had four children. Decommissioned from the navy in 1945, Chandler enrolled in graduate school at the University of North Carolina at Chapel Hill to pursue an interest in southern history. After a year, however, he returned to Harvard, where he earned an MA in 1947 and a PhD in 1952 with a dissertation on his great-grandfather, Henry Varnum Poor, a nineteenth-century business analyst and founder of the financial data company Standard & Poor's, whose papers Chandler fortuitously discovered in the storeroom of his great-aunt's home. At Harvard, Chandler was influenced by the sociologist Talcott Parsons, whose structural-functionalist theories and interest in the ideas of the German sociologist Max Weber shaped his own distinctive approach to the problem of business institutions.

Chandler began his academic career at the Massachusetts Institute of Technology in Cambridge, where he taught from 1950 to 1963 while editing volumes of Theodore Roosevelt's correspondence and publishing several books, including his biography of Poor, *Henry Varnum Poor, Business Editor, Analyst, and Reformer* (1956), and his first major work, *Strategy and Structure: Chapters in the History of the Industrial Enterprise* (1962). *Strategy and Structure* examined the development of decentralized, multidivisional firms in case studies of four leading American companies—DuPont; the General Motors Corporation; Standard Oil; and Sears, Roebuck and Company—and included comparative analysis of the nation's seventy largest industrial corporations. During this time Chandler also assisted the General Motors Corporation executive Alfred P. Sloan with the writing of his 1963 memoir. That same year, Chandler joined the faculty of Johns Hopkins University, where he chaired the history department, coedited a volume of *The Papers of Dwight David Eisenhower* (1970), and cowrote *Pierre S. Du Pont and the Making of the Modern Corporation* (1971). Seeking relief from administrative and teaching duties that inhibited his research, Chandler moved to the Harvard Graduate School of Business Administration in 1971 to become the Isidor Strauss Professor of Business History, an appointment he retained in emeritus until his death.

At Harvard, Chandler produced *The Visible Hand*, a magisterial work that won both the Pulitzer Prize in History and the Bancroft Prize in 1978. The book built upon his earlier analysis of administrative innovation in *Strategy and Structure*, in which he argued that decentralized corporate decision making was an executive reaction to changing market conditions and that new procedures and policies imposed by top leaders determined corporate structures, summarized in the dictum "structure follows strategy." *The Visible Hand* focused on the key role of the professional managerial class in the rise of big business. In this career-defining work, Chandler presented the nineteenth-century railroad as a model for modern business administration and emphasized the influence of new communication and manufacturing technologies in the evolution of large-scale integrated firms. The book's title alludes to Adam Smith's "invisible hand," a precept of free-market capitalism that assumes a natural concordance between the interests of society and that of self-interested, profit-maximizing individuals. In matters of coordination and resource allocation, however, Chandler asserted that the "visible hand" of the salaried manager had replaced the impersonal force of the market. Chandler's next major work, *Scale and Scope: The Dynamics of Industrial Capitalism* (1990), compared the ascendency of American industrial corporations with those in Great Britain and Germany between 1880 and 1940 and post–World War II Japan. In addition to publishing numerous edited volumes and articles, Chandler wrote companion histories of important twentieth-century industries: *Inventing the Electronic Century: The Epic Story of the Consumer Electronics and Computer Industries* (2001) and *Shaping the Industrial Century: The Remarkable Story of the Modern Chemical and Pharmaceutical Industries* (2005). Chandler continued to write and publish long after retiring in 1989. He died at age eighty-eight of cardiac arrest at Youville Hospital in Cambridge, while still working on a biography of his maternal grandfather, William G. Ramsay, founder of DuPont's engineering department during the early twentieth century.

In a distinguished career spanning half a century, Chandler exerted a far-reaching influence on the study of corporate capitalism and was instrumental in founding the subdiscipline of business history, a marginal specialization in the 1950s. Breaking from stagnant biographical approaches to the study of business that pitted immoral "robber barons" against heroic "industrial statesmen," Chandler offered productive conceptual and comparative lenses through which to view business institutions and economic development in the United States and globally. His seminal work gained an interdisciplinary following among economists, political scientists, scholars of administration and organizational theory, sociologists, and historians. Chandler's scholarship is greatly admired for its prodigious historical detail, synthetic vision, and empirical rigor; however, its technological and economic determinism have been contested. Chandler was revered by his peers for his generosity and self-effacing manner as much as for his erudition and intellectual openness. His influence among business historians was so great that some have referred to the period before his arrival as B.C.: Before Chandler.

★

Chandler discussed his personal and intellectual development in a presidential address to the Business History Conference, published in *Business and Economic History* (1978). There is no full-length biography of Chandler, but a valuable overview of his life and work is presented in Thomas K. McCraw's introduction to *The Essential Alfred Chandler* (1988). For analysis of *The Visible Hand* and Chandler's contributions to the field, see Richard R. John, "Elaborations, Revisions, Dissents: Alfred D. Chandler, Jr.'s, 'The Visible Hand' after Twenty Years," *Business History Review* 71 (Summer 1997): 151–200; and Steven W. Usselman, "Still Visible," *Technology and Culture* 47, no. 3 (July 2006): 584–596. Obituaries are in the *New York Times* (12 May 2007), *Boston Globe* (14 May 2007), and *Harvard Gazette* (17 May 2007).

Josh Lauer

CHANDLER, Otis (*b.* 23 November 1927 in Los Angeles, California; *d.* 27 February 2006 in Ojai, California), publisher of the *Los Angeles Times* who transformed it from a provincial, partisan newspaper into an influential and respected institution of American journalism.

Chandler was the son of Norman Chandler and Dorothy (Buffum) Chandler, members of a newspaper dynasty that had published the *Los Angeles Times* since 1882, when Chandler's great-grandfather, Harrison Gray Otis, took part ownership. Otis led the *Los Angeles Times* with an iron hand for thirty-five years, ensuring that it became a powerful voice for his family's interests as well as other Southern California business interests. Otis's son-in-law, Harry Chandler, took over in 1914. Harry Chandler's son Norman became president and general manager in 1941.

Chandler and his older sister grew up on a ten-acre citrus ranch in Sierra Madre, California. Norman Chandler had worked on the family's Tejon Ranch when he was growing up and wanted his son, born into wealth and privilege, to know the importance of physical labor. Chandler was an active child, bicycling several miles to and from Polytechnic School in Pasadena. When he was nine he was thrown to the ground during a horseback riding lesson. Pronounced dead at one hospital, he was rushed by his mother to another, where a doctor revived him with a

Otis Chandler, 1973. **AP IMAGES**

shot of adrenalin to the heart. Later he said the incident heightened his sense of competitiveness.

After graduating from Phillips Academy in Andover, Massachusetts, in 1946, Chandler attended Stanford University. He took up the shotput and went on to break records and win championships, becoming captain of the track team. Two years later he was considered a sure bet to make one of three slots on the U.S. Olympic shotput team going to the games in Helsinki, Finland, but a sprained wrist forced him to sit out the trials. Fifty years later he called the missed opportunity "the biggest disappointment of my life." After earning his BA in 1950, he served in the U.S. Air Force in the San Francisco Bay Area. On 18 June 1951 he married Marilyn Brant, with whom he had five children. Upon returning home in 1953, he entered his father's seven-year executive training program to learn the newspaper business from the bottom up. He served in the pressroom, the mailroom, and the mechanical department as well as in production, circulation, advertising, and the newsroom. For the most part, he found the experience "grinding" but was hooked by his time in the newsroom. "I loved being a reporter," he said.

His mother had other ideas. In the 1950s "Buff" Chandler, a force in her own right in Los Angeles cultural circles, led a campaign to save the troubled Hollywood Bowl from the wrecker's ball. (Later she raised $20 million to finance creation of the Los Angeles Music Center; one of its main theaters was named the Dorothy Chandler Pavilion in her honor.) She urged her husband to turn the newspaper over to their son, and on 11 April 1960, at a luncheon of 700 civic and political leaders at the Biltmore Bowl ballroom in downtown Los Angeles, Norman passed the baton, making Chandler the fourth—and ultimately the last—member of his family to run the *Los Angeles Times*. Chandler's first reaction was to stand up and say, "Wow!"

Chandler, seeking to improve the paper's journalistic reputation, introduced major changes. Spending money to attract talent, he lured reporters from the big East Coast publications and expanded the national and foreign staffs. He opened bureaus in Tokyo, Rio de Janeiro, Mexico City, Hong Kong, Rome, Bonn, London, and Vienna, and added heft to bureaus in San Francisco and Washington, D.C. He snagged Jim Murray, one of the stars of the recently launched *Sports Illustrated*, to be the paper's premier sports columnist; he stole the iconic editorial cartoonist Paul Conrad from the *Denver Post*; and he persuaded Robert J. Donovan, Washington bureau chief of the *New York Herald Tribune*, to fill that post at the *Times*, helping to put the paper on the map in the nation's capital.

Chandler was a unique character as compared to the more traditional scions of newspaper families. At six feet, one inch and a muscular 200 pounds, he was big, blond, and broad-shouldered. Even his business suits could not hide the athlete underneath. He liked to surf, hunt big game, race Ferraris, buy antique cars, and throw a shotput with champion precision, often risking injury to enjoy, as he put it, "living on the edge." In 1990 a musk ox trampled him in the Northwest Territories of Canada, yanking his right arm from its socket. Although doctors told him the arm would be useless for the rest of his life, through rigorous exercise he gradually regained almost full use of the arm. As the *Christian Science Monitor* had observed ten years before, "If Otis Chandler hadn't existed, Ernest Hemingway would have created him. When he strides out of a meeting to shake hands, it is like looking up at a California redwood."

Aside from bulking up the newspaper's staff, circulation, and international prestige, Chandler brought a new sense of professionalism to the paper's administration and balance to its editorial content. In his first year he replaced twenty-two of twenty-three department heads. He also approved a hard-hitting series on the John Birch Society, an ultra-right-wing organization of which some of his relatives were members. He followed the news stories with an editorial calling the Birch Society an extremist group. Some in the family protested, and 15,000 readers canceled their subscriptions. The watershed series signaled to the political world that the *Times* would no longer serve as a voice for right-wing causes. The new policy's first test came in the 1962 California gubernatorial campaign. The Republican candidate, former vice president Richard Nixon, disoriented by the newspaper's turnabout, blamed the press for his loss to Democrat Pat Brown.

Chandler served as publisher until 1980, stepping down to become editor in chief of the Times Mirror Co., the paper's parent corporation, and chairman of the board. In 1986 he gave up those titles, ending his direct involvement in the company; he remained chairman of the company's executive committee, a largely ceremonial post. During his long association with the paper, the *Los Angeles Times* won sixteen Pulitzer Prizes. It often printed more news—and more advertising—than any other newspaper in the United States. Under his leadership the *Los Angeles Times* topped one million in circulation. He also expanded the Times Mirror Co. by purchasing *Newsday*, the *Baltimore Sun*, and the *Hartford (Connecticut) Courant* as well as broadcast and cable television stations and the book-publishing houses New American Library and Harry N. Abrams. Chandler divorced his first wife in 1978. On 15 August 1981 he married Bettina Whitaker.

In 1999 Chandler, with no remaining official ties to the paper but distressed by changes he and others viewed as damaging to its reputation, issued a statement strongly critical of the *Times* and Times Mirror executives. In 2000 the 160 descendants of Harry Chandler voted to sell Times Mirror, including the *Los Angeles Times*, to the Tribune Co. of Chicago, which published the *Chicago Tribune* and owned WGN Broadcasting as well as the Chicago Cubs. Chandler said he did not hear about the proposed sale until rumors of the deal reached him two days before it was made. The merger of the two entities was strained and ended in 2007 when the *Tribune* was sold to Sam Zell, a Chicago real estate developer. Amid declining ad revenues and circulation, Zell slashed the *Los Angeles Times* staff and closed the Washington bureau as well as several international bureaus, which had been Chandler's legacy.

Chandler died at his home of Lewy body disease, a degenerative brain disorder, at the age of seventy-eight. He was cremated.

On its April 1979 cover, the *Atlantic Monthly* depicted Chandler in a bathing suit, riding a surfboard made of newspapers through a huge wave of dollar bills. The image was striking, but the man was more complex. Not merely an heir who ascended to fame and fortune through the family business, he was also a visionary who guided a major institution to embrace change, becoming, in his biographer's words, "the last great newspaperman of the 20th century." Journalists and politicians hailed his skill, even as his fellow adventurers and athletes praised his daring. "People want to stay on the same lane in the freeway, in the same safe cocoon," he explained in 1985. "I don't."

★

For a biography of Chandler that also covers the history of the *Los Angeles Times*, see Dennis McDougal, *Privileged Son: Otis Chandler and the Rise and Fall of the L.A. Times Dynasty* (2001). Alex Beam, "The Last Great Newspaperman," *Stanford*

Magazine, July/August 2000, is a profile of Chandler. Obituaries are in the *Los Angeles Times* (27 Feb. 2006) and *New York Times* (28 Feb. 2006); the *Los Angeles Times* obituary offers an extensive and detailed biographical account.

Johanna Neuman

CHARISSE, Cyd (*b.* 8 March 1922 [according to some sources, 1921] in Amarillo, Texas; *d.* 17 June 2008 in Los Angeles, California), classically trained dancer noted for her roles in film musicals during the 1940s and 1950s.

Charisse was born Tula Ellice Finklea to Ernest E. Finklea, a jeweler, and Lela (Norwood) Finklea, a homemaker. Her brother's attempts to say "sister" resulted in the nickname "Sid." Her father loved music and ballet, and she took piano lessons and was encouraged to dance. It was suspected that she had had a slight case of polio that left a weakness in her back, and when she was six a doctor suggested she do more dancing to improve her strength. Charisse's first ballet instructor was Constance Ferguson, who had trained with the Russian star Maurice Koslov and retired to Amarillo. When Charisse was twelve, the family

Cyd Charisse. © INTERFOTO PRESSEBILDAGENTUR/ALAMY

took a summer vacation trip to Santa Monica, California, and while there she took lessons at the Fanchon and Marco Dance Studio in Hollywood. One of the teachers was Nico Charisse.

By age fourteen dancing had become her life, and Charisse knew that to improve she needed better teachers. She moved to Hollywood, where she boarded with a family, and attended the Hollywood Professional School. Her ballet teacher was Adolph Bolm, once a partner of the famed Russian ballerina Anna Pavlova. When Colonel Vassili de Basil of the world-renowned Ballets Russes de Monte Carlo visited the studio, Charisse assumed he was there to see Bolm. In fact he was interested in Charisse and offered her a contract to dance with the company. Her parents agreed, and in 1934, as a young teenager, she joined the company, acquiring the first of her pseudonyms, Felia Siderova, to blend in with the names of the mostly Russian company. She toured the United States with the company as a member of the *Swan Lake* corps de ballet, improving by practicing and observing other dancers. She acquired a new name, Maria Istomina, and went to England for the company's six-week engagement at Covent Garden, where the choreographer Michel Fokine gave Charisse her first solo part in his ballet *Paganini*. However, the company was disbanded when World War II began in Europe. Charisse married her former teacher Nico Charisse in Paris on 12 August 1939, and they returned to Los Angeles, where she began teaching in his dance studio. Their son Nico, known as Nicky, was born in 1942.

Contacts Charisse made while with the Ballets Russes led to her first role in the movies, under the name Lily Norwood, in a dance number in *Something to Shout About* (1943). Other small roles followed. Arthur Freed of Metro-Goldwyn-Mayer (MGM) was looking for a partner for Fred Astaire in *Ziegfeld Follies* (1946), and after seeing her dance, Freed hired Charisse for the film and signed her to a seven-year contract. He changed her name again, this time to her married name, with a more exotic spelling of her nickname. Other roles followed, including her first speaking part in *The Harvey Girls* (1946). She divorced Nico Charisse in 1947 and married the singer and night-club entertainer Tony Martin on 9 May 1948.

Her big break was as the exotic femme fatale dancing the "Broadway Melody Ballet" in *Singin' in the Rain* (1952). Although she had no lines, her steamy dancing with Gene Kelly spoke volumes. The following year she starred with Fred Astaire in *The Band Wagon* (1953). Their dance to "Dancing in the Dark," a romantic but innocent duet set in New York's Central Park, with Charisse wearing a prim shirtwaist dress, is a film classic. So, too, is the movie's sexy number "The Girl Hunt Ballet," a spoof of a Mickey Spillane crime novel in which Charisse wears a skimpy, sparkling red dress.

Charisse was slated to star with Kelly in *An American in Paris* but had to withdraw because of her pregnancy.

Tony Martin, Jr., was born in 1950. She starred with Kelly in *Brigadoon* (1954) and *It's Always Fair Weather* (1955) and again with Astaire in *Silk Stockings* (1957). Charisse played dramatic screen roles, but none was as memorable as her ballets in the musicals. When the Hollywood musical died out, she and her husband put together a successful song and dance act. She first appeared at the Riviera in Las Vegas in 1965 and then traveled to other cities, including a 1977 appearance at the London Palladium.

In the 1970s and 1980s Charisse made frequent guest appearances on such television series as *Hawaii Five-O*, *The Love Boat*, and *Murder, She Wrote*. She also acted in the theater. In 1986 she performed in *Charlie's Girls* in London and in 1992 made her Broadway debut in *Grand Hotel*. Playing an aging Russian ballerina, Charisse, who over the years had continued ballet lessons in Los Angeles with Tatiana Riobouchinska, was perfect for the role. The sixty-nine-year-old Charisse again danced on *pointe* and attracted sell-out crowds. In 2006 she was presented with a National Medal of Arts for her lifetime achievement in dance by President George W. Bush. She died at Cedars-Sinai Medical Center of a heart attack and is buried at Hillside Memorial Park, in Culver City, California.

During the heyday of the movie musical, Charisse was unique among the many MGM dancers in having been classically trained in ballet. Her most effective dances show the grace and elegance of that training, as well as her glamorous sex appeal. Whereas other top dancers, such as Ginger Rogers and Ann Miller, smiled through every dance routine, Charisse's sensuous seriousness was distinctive. Her beauty was part of her attraction, as well her long legs, said to have been insured by MGM for $5 million. Although not known for her acting ability and unable to carry a tune, as a dancer Charisse is regarded as a movie superstar.

An autobiography by Charisse and Martin, written with the aid of Dick Kleiner, *The Two of Us* (1976), provides many details of her early life and includes a comparison of the dancing styles of Astaire and Kelly. Ted Sennett, *Hollywood Musicals*, focuses on her ballet sequences with Astaire and Kelly. Obituaries are in the *New York Times* (18 June 2008) and London *Daily Telegraph* (19 June 2008).

Marcia B. Dinneen

CLAIBORNE, Anne Elisabeth Jane ("Liz") (*b.* 31 March 1929 in Brussels, Belgium; *d.* 26 June 2007 in New York City), cofounder with her husband Arthur Ortenberg of a fashion empire specializing in stylish yet affordable women's career apparel of colorfully tailored separates that could be mixed or matched.

Liz Claiborne, 2000. EVAN AGOSTINI/IMAGEDIRECT/GETTY IMAGES

Claiborne was born in Brussels but she was descended from a prominent New Orleans family whose patriarch, William C. C. Claiborne, was the first governor of Louisiana. Her father, Omer Villere Claiborne, was a banker stationed in Brussels and instilled in her a strong aesthetic taste while the family toured European museums; her mother, Louise Carol (Fenner) Claiborne, was a stylish homemaker who taught Claiborne sewing and impeccable grooming at an early age. She had one brother. Her parents did not believe she needed a formal education, and her mother tutored her at home where she spoke French first. Her English always had a faint accent. When she was ten in 1939, the Nazis were advancing in Europe, and her family fled back to New Orleans.

She attended Saint Timothy's, a boarding school then in Catonsville, Maryland, and spent summers with family in Baltimore or New Orleans. Rather than finishing preparatory school, she studied painting in Brussels as well as in Paris and Nice, France. Her parents expected her to become an artist. "I'm glad I had that training," she later said, "because it taught me to see, it taught me color, proportion, and many other things that I don't think I would have learned in design school."

In 1948 the nineteen-year-old Claiborne won a sketching contest sponsored by *Harper's Bazaar* magazine. Two years later her family was touring Manhattan when she announced that she was staying there to pursue a career in fashion. Her father let her out of the car, gave her $50, and wished her luck. While living with a relative in Manhattan, Claiborne worked as a fit model and as a sketch artist for the sportswear designer Tina Lesser. In 1950 she married Ben Schultz, a book designer; they had one son.

Claiborne continued to develop her design talent while raising her son. For the next nine years she apprenticed with dress designers, including Ben Reig and Dan Keller. Ironically, she preferred to wear slacks to work. While working at the Rhea Manufacturing Company, she met Arthur Ortenberg, a design executive. Following divorces from both of their spouses, Claiborne and Ortenberg were married on 5 July 1957; she gained two stepchildren through the marriage. From 1960 to 1975 she was the principal designer for Youth Guild, the junior dress division of Jonathan Logan, a major women's apparel manufacturer. She spent years unsuccessfully trying to convince the company's executives that there was a real need for mix-and-match coordinated sportswear that would appeal to the growing number of women, like herself, who were raising families and working. Although she was eager to start her own business, she could not afford to take that risk until her son and two stepchildren finished college.

Liz Claiborne Inc. was formed on 18 January 1976 with savings and the backing of a handful of investors. Her husband became the company's secretary and treasurer. Her designs for what she called "the Liz Lady" were affordable businesslike clothes worn to compete with men in the workplace. In fact, she strove to limit the price of an item to what she herself would pay for it. With an acute and accurate business sense, Claiborne became a role model—and her label a lifestyle brand—to countless professional women who wanted to break through the glass ceiling and to wear feminine clothing signifying strength and intelligence. Her formula was an instant success, and her company's sales were $2.6 million in its first year. From the beginning the Claiborne brand emphasized fit, color, comfort, and good value.

As a designer, Claiborne was not interested in being a trendsetter but placed practical concerns over catwalk glamour. Polyester crepe de chine and velour peasant blouses felt richly textured and were easily washed. High-waisted slacks that flared at the bottom were durable and remained flat in a suitcase. Sweaters had loosely draped necklines. Color schemes included bright reds, yellows, and royal blues. Such mix-and-match and color-coordinated separates were well tailored and comfortable, offering a variety of interchangeable possibilities suitable for the office or a casual evening.

"As a working woman with a child," she later said, "I didn't want to spend hours shopping. Things should be easy." Claiborne revolutionized the way department stores stocked women's clothing. Instead of having slacks and blouses in different departments, as was the norm, her executives worked with store managers to consolidate entire outfits in the same place, the Liz Claiborne boutique within the store. Her business model of responsive marketing initiated in the fashion world a computer program that charted and systematically updated sales, and she employed traveling consultants who provided her company with constant feedback, making it possible to fill or reduce merchandise orders rapidly. Her firm produced six lines of fashion each year to expedite inventory turnover and to respond to changing preferences for color and style. Consequently, time-pressed professional woman could quickly and easily assemble for themselves Claiborne outfits without help from salespeople at a time when most stores were understaffed.

In 1981 Liz Claiborne Inc. went public, raising $6 million to add a dress division. A shoe division was added in 1983, and in 1985 the company bought the Kaiser-Roth Corporation, which produced accessories such as scarves, belts, and handbags. By 1986 her triangular logo included perfume and men's sportswear. That year her company's retail sales reached $1.2 billion, and it was the first company started by a woman to be featured in the Fortune 500 of America's largest corporations.

Claiborne retired in 1989. That same year the Liz Claiborne and Art Ortenberg Foundation was established to provide substantial support for environmental and humanitarian causes. Claiborne died at New York–Presbyterian Hospital from abdominal cancer. She was seventy-eight. She is buried near two trees at the Triple 8 Ranch near Helena, Montana, where she and her husband had spent their summers.

★

Claiborne is profiled in Caroline R. Milbank, *New York Fashion: The Evolution of American Style* (1989); Irene Daria, *The Fashion Cycle* (1990); and Gene N. Landrum, *Profiles of Female Genius* (1994). An obituary is in the *New York Times* (28 June 2007).

Patrick S. Smith

CLARK, James Gardner ("Jim"), Jr. (*b.* 17 September 1922 in Elba, Alabama; *d.* 4 June 2007 in Elba, Alabama), controversial sheriff of Dallas County, Alabama, whose 1965 confrontations with civil rights demonstrators in Selma helped dramatize the denial of African-American voting rights.

Clark was born in Elba, the county seat of Coffee County, in rural southeastern Alabama. His father, James Gardner Clark, was a farmer and his mother, Ettie Lee Clark, was a homemaker. He had two siblings, a brother and a sister. He graduated from Elba High School in 1940. During World War II he served as a gunner and engineer on B-25 bombers in the Army Air Forces while stationed in the Aleutian Islands. Following his discharge, he attended the University of Alabama and then moved to Brown's Station in Dallas County where he farmed and raised cattle. He married Laura Louise Pepper and they had five children; their marriage later ended in divorce. In 1955 Clark was appointed sheriff on the death of the incumbent by his friend, Governor James "Big Jim" Folsom. He subsequently won full terms in 1958 and 1962.

Standing six feet, two inches tall and weighing 220 pounds, Clark was a stereotypical southern lawman. He cultivated a combative image by wearing a campaign jacket and military-style hat. The pistol, nightstick, and cattle prod hanging from his belt reinforced his reputation as a man willing to use force while carrying out his duties. He wore a white pin on his uniform bearing the word "Never." The slogan was Clark's response to the question, when would integration occur in Dallas County.

Clark gained national notoriety when civil rights forces chose Selma, Dallas County's largest town, as the site for a voter registration campaign. With only 300 registered voters among its 15,000 African-American citizens, Selma was a promising target for the movement. Sheriff Clark's reputation as an outspoken opponent of African-American rights figured prominently in Selma's selection. Civil rights strategists believed their demonstrations might provoke the short-tempered Clark into a violent reaction. A similar response by Birmingham, Alabama's Eugene "Bull" Connor swung public sentiment in favor of the 1964 Civil Rights Act. Movement leaders hoped that Clark would do the same for the voting rights legislation they sought.

Selma's mayor and police chief, fearing bad publicity if the sheriff lost his temper, tried to limit Clark's exposure, but they could not challenge his control of the Dallas County courthouse. During January and February 1965 civil rights organizers staged almost daily processions of prospective voters to the courthouse. Clark allowed only a handful of applicants to enter the building at one time. Several angry confrontations ensued between the sheriff and African-American demonstrators that were recorded by newspaper reporters and television crews. The most dramatic incident occurred on 16 February when the Reverend C. T. Vivian of the Southern Christian Leadership Conference denounced Clark as a bigot and a brute. Despite efforts by deputies to restrain him, the irate Clark punched the preacher and sent him sprawling down the courthouse steps.

When a column of 600 civil rights protestors paraded over the Edmund Pettus Bridge on 7 March 1965 on the first leg of a proposed march to the state capital in Montgomery, they were blocked by fifty Alabama state troopers and several dozen members of Clark's posse, many on horseback. When ordered to disperse, the marchers paused. The troopers fired tear gas into the crowd and the posse attacked with billy clubs. More than sixty people were injured in the resulting melee, which came to be known as "Bloody Sunday." Scenes from this attack, aired that evening on network television, triggered national outrage. Eight days after Bloody Sunday, President Lyndon B. Johnson went before a joint session of Congress to urge enactment of voting rights legislation. Martin Luther King, Jr., then led a successful march from Selma to Montgomery to rally support for the measure. When Johnson signed the Voting Rights Act on 6 August 1965, observers credited Clark with unintentionally aiding the bill's passage.

Wilson Baker, Selma's moderate director of public safety, opposed Clark's reelection bid in 1966. Newly registered African-American voters rallied behind Baker who defeated Clark by 500 votes. Following the election, Clark wrote *The Jim Clark Story: I Saw Selma Raped* (1967) in defense of his administration. In it he claimed that "Martin Luther King ruined Selma's way of life. We had a way of life we liked." Clark held a variety of jobs including selling real estate and mobile homes. In 1978 he was convicted of conspiring to import marijuana and served nine months in prison. Late in life, his health failed and he was confined to a nursing home in Elba where he died of complications from a broken hip on 4 June 2007. He is buried in the Evergreen Cemetery in Elba.

Clark was an unrepentant segregationist. In a 2006 interview with the *Montgomery Advertiser* he said, "Basically, I'd do the same thing today if I had it to do over again. I did what I thought was right to uphold the law." As sheriff, he expected his commands to be obeyed; when civil rights demonstrators defied his authority, he responded with force. Clark failed to understand that his heavy-handed tactics, when captured by the national media, reinforced the image of southern intolerance and undermined the cause he tried to defend.

★

Taylor Branch examines Clark's role in the Selma voting rights campaign in two volumes of the history of the civil rights movement, *Pillar of Fire: America in the King Years, 1963–65* (1998) and *At Canaan's Edge: America in the King Years, 1965–68* (2006). David J. Garrow, *Protest at Selma: Martin Luther King, Jr., and the Voting Rights Act of 1965* (1978), places the events in Selma in a larger historical and political context. *Bridge to Freedom, 1965*, episode six of the Public Broadcasting Service documentary series, *Eyes on the Prize* (1986), covers the protests at Selma. Obituaries are in the *Washington Post* and *New York Times* (both 7 June 2007).

Paul T. Murray

COFFIN, William Sloane, Jr. (*b.* 1 June 1924 in New York City; *d.* 12 April 2006 in Strafford, Vermont), liberal Protestant clergyman, Yale University chaplain, and longtime activist in the civil rights and peace movements of the twentieth century.

Coffin was born into a wealthy, prominent New York City family. His father, William Sloane Coffin, Sr., was an executive in the family's successful furniture business and was president of the Metropolitan Museum of Art. His mother, Catherine (Butterfield) Coffin, was born in Kansas City, Missouri, and performed postwar relief aid in France, where she first met her husband. Coffin's parents were married in 1919. Coffin, his older brother, and his younger sister regularly attended the Madison Avenue Presbyterian Church, where their uncle Henry Sloane Coffin was pastor.

Coffin's father died in 1933, and the family moved to Carmel, California. In 1937 Coffin returned to the East Coast and enrolled at Deerfield Academy in Massachusetts.

William Sloan Coffin, 1970. LEE BALTERMAN/TIME LIFE PICTURES/GETTY IMAGES

He remained for only a year and then moved with his family to Paris. At age fifteen he began receiving piano instruction from the noted music teacher Nadia Boulanger. The family fled to Geneva, Switzerland, when the German army occupied France. In 1940 Coffin and his family returned to the United States. He enrolled in the well-known Phillips Academy in Andover, Massachusetts, graduating in 1942.

After graduation Coffin attended Yale University's School of Music with every intention of becoming a concert pianist. The prospect of defeating the forces of fascism and the lure of patriotic duty, however, proved too intoxicating for Coffin. "My heart was still set on the front," he wrote in his memoir. "I couldn't bear the idea of a soft job while others were fighting." From 1943 to 1947 he served in the army, rising to the rank of captain. He served as a liaison to the French and Russian armies as part of the U.S. military's intelligence unit. While serving in this capacity, he heard firsthand stories of life under the dictator Joseph Stalin's rule in the Soviet Union. These tales shaped his views regarding Communism and inspired his initial support for America's cold war policies.

Coffin returned to Yale after receiving his discharge from the army and received a BA in 1949. Despite his interest in music, Coffin enrolled at Union Theological Seminary, where his uncle Henry served as president. Union Theological was renowned for shaping the views of some of Protestantism's most liberal and progressive ministers. The faculty boasted the likes of such professors as Reinhold Niebuhr, John Bennett, George W. Webber, and James Muilenberg. Coffin's developing religious views combined early twentieth-century Social Gospel activism with a cosmopolitan attentiveness for common-sense explanations to modern-day problems. "We must look for fresh, first-hand, personal material if we are to present Christianity as the most exciting proposition that ever confronted man," Coffin wrote in his memoir. However, the outbreak of the Korean War and Coffin's desire to fight the evils of Communism cut short his theological studies. After one year of study, he joined the Central Intelligence Agency (CIA). As a case officer in the CIA, Coffin spent three years in West Germany assigned to recruiting pro-Western Russian refugees and then training them to infiltrate the Soviet regime and overthrow Stalin's dictatorship.

By 1953, however, Coffin had grown wary of CIA activities and resigned. Instead of returning to Union Theological, he enrolled at Yale Divinity School. In 1956 he received a BD and was later ordained a Presbyterian minister. He was imbued with a sense of social justice and liberal Protestant reform idealism, reminiscent of Progressive Era Social Gospel adherents. Focusing on society rather than self, he wrote that "Self glorification—pride—be it individual or collective, is ... the root of all human evil [and] a state of being in which we are alienated from God."

On 12 December 1956 Coffin married Eva Anna Rubinstein, a ballet dancer and the daughter of the renowned pianist Arthur Rubinstein. The Coffins' marriage was tumultuous, marked by Coffin's extramarital affairs. The couple divorced in 1968. The marriage produced three children. The death of Coffin's son Alexander from a car accident in 1983 deeply affected Coffin's sense of remorse for placing his own activist commitments and dalliances above the needs and interests of his children. For all of his notoriety as a compassionate crusader for peace and justice, Coffin often ignored his family's needs. He barely managed the household finances, if at all, and his children often felt abandoned. In 1969 Coffin married Harriet Harvey Gibney; their relationship also ended in a bitter divorce in 1983. He then married Virginia Randolph Wilson in 1984; they divorced in 2006. Neither of the last two marriages resulted in children.

When Coffin returned to Yale as its chaplain in 1958, he rode onto campus atop his motorcycle and quickly adopted the mantra of a "Christian revolutionary." Coffin immediately became involved in a number of social justice activities. In 1960 he participated in international relief work. He led a group of students to Guinea in the summer of 1960 as part of Operation Crossroads Africa. In 1961 Sargent Shriver, President John F. Kennedy's brother-in-law, enlisted Coffin to establish training programs for the Peace Corps. Coffin took a temporary leave from Yale and supervised the building of a training camp in Puerto Rico.

Coffin's involvement in the civil rights struggles of this period began to define his role as a Christian revolutionary. In May 1961 he was arrested in Montgomery, Alabama, along with six others who participated in the second Freedom Ride—the first was in 1947—while riding aboard interstate buses challenging the segregation laws in the South. In the early 1960s he organized busloads of Freedom Riders, particularly college students, to challenge segregationist policies in the South. His actions also led to his appointment as a member of the Connecticut Advisory Board of the U.S. Commission on Civil Rights.

Coffin's increasing political activism took center stage during the Vietnam War. In 1965 he joined with a group of religious leaders to form the National Emergency Committee of Clergy Concerned About Vietnam. He was named executive secretary of the organization; the group began enlisting laypeople and changed its name to Clergy and Laity Concerned About Vietnam. Negotiating an end to the war was Coffin's primary objective: "We plead ... with our fellow clergy to support our government's effort to negotiate an end to the war and to prevent further escalation." However, as the war expanded, Coffin and his antiwar organization mobilized antiwar supporters, defended the rights of conscientious objectors, and endorsed acts of civil disobedience. Coffin even went so far as to suggest that Battell Chapel at Yale become a sanctuary for draft resisters.

Throughout the war years Coffin was a frequent speaker at antiwar rallies. In October 1967, during a protest in Boston, over 1,000 draft resisters turned in their draft cards during a church service led by Coffin. This action was a response to an open letter that Coffin had signed along with several well-known intellectuals. The letter was titled "A Call to Resist Illegitimate Authority." The federal government then issued indictments against Dr. Benjamin Spock, Marcus Raskin, Mitchell Goodman, Michael Ferber, and Coffin on charges of conspiracy to aid draft resisters. They were convicted in 1968, but the convictions were overturned in 1970. The Boston Five, as they were called, were constantly sought after as speakers for antiwar rallies. Coffin reflected, "Thanks to the United States Government the five of us had become celebrities." In 1972 he traveled to North Vietnam to accompany three prisoners of war on their return home. After the war ended, Coffin remained an outspoken supporter of amnesty for draft resisters.

Coffin finally left Yale in December 1975. Although Yale's president, Kingman Brewster, stood behind Coffin's right to free speech, it was apparent that Coffin's search for personal recognition, acerbic tone, and criticisms of wealthy alumni ultimately led to a parting of the ways. His impatient temperament, fearlessness, and liberal religious activities rubbed many of Yale's most notable donors the wrong way. Taking some time off, he began writing his autobiography, *Once to Every Man: A Memoir* (1977).

In 1977 Coffin returned to the pulpit as the senior minister at Riverside Church, one of the most progressive and prominent congregations in New York City, with a ready-made media outlet to satisfy his need for personal publicity. He urged his parishioners to support gay rights, end discrimination, root out poverty and homelessness, develop programs to address world hunger, and create a workable disarmament plan that all nations could adopt. In 1979 he was back in the headlines when he traveled to Iran and conducted Christmas services for the hostages held in the captured American Embassy. Shortly after his visit to Iran, he went to Nicaragua to protest U.S. military intervention in the battle against the socialist-led government of Daniel Ortega and the Sandinistas. Just as he had done with the Yale chaplaincy, Coffin made Riverside one of the most visible pulpits in the nation: a religious instrument for social and political causes. Like Yale, moreover, there were those on Riverside's board who questioned Coffin's public defense of homosexuality and wondered why he appointed Cora Weiss, a Jew, to run the church's disarmament program. Coffin, in turn, relished such controversy and often could be downright demeaning. According to his biographer Warren Goldstein, "He was nasty at times; his masculinity sometimes shaded into swagger; and he held an Ivy League disdain for fundamentalists."

Coffin's last venture into peace and justice activism involved the disarmament crusade when President Ronald Reagan's military buildup sparked fears of a second cold war. In 1987 Coffin resigned from Riverside Church and became president of the National Committee for a Sane Nuclear Policy, or SANE. (The organization became SANE/Freeze in 1988 and was renamed Peace Action in 1993.) Coffin had joined SANE in 1962, and when he became its leader, it was the largest peace and justice organization in the country. As SANE/Freeze leader Coffin argued that arms reduction, a safer environment, and economic justice are inextricably linked and that only by addressing arms reduction can sufficient resources be secured to work on the other two issues. He retired as president emeritus in 1993.

Coffin devoted the remaining years of his life to lecturing and writing. Not long before his death, he founded a peace coalition, Faithful Security, devoted to the abolition of all nuclear weapons. He died of congestive heart failure at his home in Strafford. A memorial service was held at Riverside Church. His remains were cremated, and he was buried in Strafford Cemetery next to his son Alex.

Garry Trudeau, the creator of the *Doonesbury* comic strip, previously had immortalized Coffin when he blended his character with that of Trudeau's Yale roommate Scotty McLennan, dubbing the fictitious clergyman "the Reverend Scot Sloan," the bearded, hippieish "fighting young priest who can talk to the young." From the late 1950s to the 1990s Coffin was "the voice" of liberal Protestantism in the United States and a prominent leader in causes for peace and justice.

★

Manuscript sources related to the Coffin family include the papers of Henry Sloane Coffin housed in the Union Theological Seminary Archives in the Burke Library of Union Theological Seminary, New York City, and the William Sloane Coffin, Jr., Papers, Manuscripts and Archives Division of Sterling Memorial Library, Yale University. Coffin's autobiography, *Once to Every Man: A Memoir* (1977), is filled with Social Gospel convictions and deep commitment to social justice and change. *The Courage to Love* (1982) is a compilation of Coffin's most important sermons. The best biography of Coffin is Warren Goldstein, *William Sloane Coffin, Jr.: A Holy Impatience* (2004). Coffin's involvement in the civil rights and anti–Vietnam War movements is ably captured in Jessica Mitford, *The Trial of Dr. Spock, William Sloane Coffin, Michael Ferber, Mitchell Goodman, and Marcus Raskin* (1969); Mitchell K. Hall, *Because of Their Faith: CALCAV and Religious Opposition to the Vietnam War* (1990); and Raymond Arsenault, *Freedom Riders: 1961 and the Struggle for Racial Justice* (2006). Obituaries are in the *New York Times, Los Angeles Times,* and *Newsday* (all 13 Apr. 2006).

Charles F. Howlett

COHEN, Paul Joseph (*b.* 2 April 1934 in Long Branch, New Jersey; *d.* 23 March 2007 in Stanford, California), mathematician who shook the world of mathematics with his resolution of the famous continuum hypothesis and proof that the axiom of choice is independent of the axioms of set theory.

Cohen's parents, Abraham Cohen and Minnie (Kaplan) Cohen, were poor Jewish immigrants who arrived in the United States from western Russia (now a part of Poland) in 1914. His father held various odd jobs, and his mother was a seamstress. Cohen was the youngest of four children. The family moved from Long Branch to Brooklyn, New York, where Cohen grew up. His parents separated when he was nine; they would later divorce. At this time he started reading an older sister's algebra text and various other mathematical texts, including one on calculus that she got for him from the library.

He attended one of New York City's most prestigious high schools, Stuyvesant High School. There he was a member of the mathematics team and became one of the forty Westinghouse Science Talent Search winners. He skipped a few terms and graduated in 1950 at age sixteen. Knowing that his family was too poor for him to attend a private college, Cohen attended Brooklyn College. However, after just two years there and before attaining a degree, he was invited to start graduate work in the renowned mathematics department at the University of Chicago. He obtained an MS there in 1954, and while working on his PhD he was an instructor at the University of Rochester (1957–1958). He obtained his PhD from the University of Chicago in 1958 in the field of analysis, the branch of mathematics dealing with limits. During the academic year 1958–1959 he taught at the Massachusetts Institute of Technology, and from 1959 to 1961 he was a fellow at the Institute for Advanced Study at Princeton. In 1961 he started teaching at Stanford University as an assistant professor, then in 1962 as an associate professor, and in 1964 as a professor. In 1963 he married Christina Karls, whom he had met in Sweden. They had three sons. Even after his retirement from Stanford in 2004, he continued teaching until his death.

In 1960 Cohen published a paper in the field of analysis titled "On a Conjecture of Littlewood and Idempotent Measures" in *American Journal of Mathematics* for which, in 1964, he was awarded the Bôcher Memorial Prize of the American Mathematical Society. The mathematician Harold Davenport stated that Cohen had solved a problem that a generation of British analysts had unsuccessfully tackled.

Describing himself as restless, Cohen shifted his attention from analysis to set theory and the foundations of mathematics. His results on the continuum hypothesis and the axiom of choice earned him the 1966 Fields

Medal of the International Mathematical Union (considered equivalent to the Nobel Prize) and the 1967 National Medal of Science.

Set theory and orders of infinity were introduced in the 1870s by the German mathematician Georg Cantor. Two infinite sets have different orders of infinity (cardinalities) if the first set can be put in a one-to-one correspondence with part of the second but the second cannot be put in a one-to-one correspondence with the first. In this case the cardinality of the first is smaller than the cardinality of the second. Cantor proved that the cardinality of the integers is smaller than the cardinality of the real numbers (also called the continuum). Furthermore, Cantor proved that given any infinity set there is a set with a larger cardinality. He labored, unsuccessfully, to show that there is no cardinality between that of the integers and that of the real numbers; that is, any infinite subset of the real numbers has the cardinality of the integers or of the real numbers. This became known as the continuum hypothesis.

A second troublesome problem arose out of the axiomatic treatment of set theory: Is it allowable to select a single element out of each of an infinite collection of possibly infinite sets? This selection procedure, used often in mathematical proofs and especially in analysis, is known as the axiom of choice.

For a half century little progress was made on the resolution of these two questions until Kurt Gödel stunned the mathematical world with the publication in 1930 of his incompleteness theorem, which stated that there are meaningful statements in mathematics that cannot be shown to be true or false. In 1938 he proved that it was not possible to prove that the continuum hypothesis is a consequence of the standard axioms of set theory. Cohen completed the work of Gödel on the continuum hypothesis. To do this Cohen invented forcing, one of the fundamental processes of set theory. Forcing is a method of taking a model satisfying the axioms of set theory and extending it to a so-called strange set that satisfies the original axioms and, in addition, some others. In this manner he proved that it is not possible to prove that the continuum hypothesis is false using the standard axioms of set theory. Thus, the continuum hypothesis is improvable, and it or its negation could be added to the axioms without leading to a contradiction. Furthermore, Cohen proved that the axiom of choice is also not provable.

Cohen published his findings in "The Independence of the Continuum Hypothesis" in 1963 and "The Independence of the Continuum Hypothesis, II" in 1964, with both articles appearing in the *Proceedings of the National Academy of Sciences*. In 1966 he published *Set Theory and the Continuum Hypothesis*, which consists of edited lecture notes of a course he gave at Harvard University in the spring of 1965. It starts with basic set theory and builds up to Gödel's proof and his own proof using the method of forcing.

For the remainder of his life, restless as always, Cohen sought simple solutions for some very difficult problems, among them differential equations, unified field theories, and the Riemann conjecture. He was versed in five languages other than English. He played the violin and the piano, and he sang in a chorus. He traveled extensively and was a dynamic and enthusiastic teacher. The difficult problems he solved are central to the foundations of mathematics. He died of a rare lung disease at age seventy-two.

For biographical information about Cohen, see Ben H. Yandell, *The Honors Class: Hilbert's Problems and Their Solvers* (2002); *More Mathematical People* (1990), edited by Donald J. Albers, Gerald L. Alexanderson, and Constance Reid; and Peter Sarnak, "Remembering Paul Cohen," *MMA Focus* 27, no. 9 (Dec. 2007): 21–22. Obituaries are in the *Stanford Report* (28 Mar. 2007), the *San Francisco Chronicle* (30 Mar. 2007), and the *New York Times* (2 Apr. 2007).

Howard Allen

COLLINS, Dorothy Yvonne Wiltse ("Dottie")

(*b.* 23 September 1923 in Inglewood, California; *d.* 12 August 2008 in Fort Wayne, Indiana), key player in the All-American Girls Professional Baseball League, the only professional league for women in the history of the sport, and the moving force behind the recognition of the league by the Baseball Hall of Fame in the 1980s.

Collins, an only child, was born in 1923 in Inglewood, a suburb of Los Angeles, to Eleanor Camille (Runswick) Wiltse, a homemaker, and Daniel Emerson Wiltse. Her father, a lead burner for Standard Oil Co. in El Segundo, California, guarded second base in a semipro league, playing with athletes such as Lou Novikoff, who later played for the Chicago Cubs. Both men, but especially her father, molded Collins into the fast-pitch softball player she would become.

Collins began her baseball career as a batgirl for the Mark C. Bloome softball team. Having practiced both her pitching and throwing skills from the age of six, Collins was more than ready to take the mound for the Bloome team in the middle of a seemingly hopeless game during the 1936 Southern California Girls' Softball League championship series. Undaunted by the crowd of thousands, the twelve-year-old Collins not only retired the side, she thereafter yielded only three runs and two hits to the opposing Beverly Hills Amazons and led her team to victory.

Dottie Collins. NATIONAL BASEBALL HALL OF FAME LIBRARY, COOPERSTOWN, NY

Dubbed the Cinderella of softball by local sports writers, Collins continued to hone her pitching skills throughout the 1930s. Collins began the 1937 season with Young's Market in the newly erected Fiedler Fairfax Field, built to accommodate the ever-growing crowds that watched the girls perform. In early 1938 Collins pitched for Cantlay Tanzola and was chosen as one of the top four pitchers in the American League to even the sides for the National League in an exhibition game. Later that year she joined the Beverly Hills Amazons and catapulted another team to the Southern California Girls' Softball championship. Ending the decade of the 1930s, she posted a 20 and 9 season with 151 strikeouts in 1939 and led still another team to championship status.

The 1940s brought Collins to the corridors of Hollywood when Warner Bros. honored her as the Million Dollar Baby of Softball to promote the movie *Million Dollar Baby* in 1941. A receptionist by day and Rosie the Riveter by night, Collins continued honing her baseball skills in the early 1940s until finally, in 1944, she was called up to the All-American Girls Professional Baseball League. Joining the newly formed Minneapolis Millerettes, Collins performed admirably with a 20–16 record and a 1.88 earned run average (ERA). Unfortunately, the Millerettes failed to thrive in Minneapolis, but in 1945 they moved to Indiana and became the Fort Wayne Daisies.

In her first season in Fort Wayne, Collins set the league milestone with seventeen shutouts. She also pitched two no-hitters in seventeen days; pitched two doubleheaders in eight days, with two other games in between; and in those eight days she pitched six complete games with a 5 and 1 mark during fifty-two innings of play. By the end of 1945, Collins had pitched 345 innings with 293 strikeouts and 111 bases on balls, finishing the season with a .83 ERA and a .744 winning percentage. Among the thousands of spectators in the stands, a young U.S. Navy man home on leave showed more than a sporting interest in Collins's exhibitions. Following her first doubleheader win in August 1945, she married Harvey Collins on 10 March 1946 at the home of her parents in Inglewood, a union that would last for more than fifty years.

Collins continued to play for the Daisies during her first two years of marriage, striking out 244 batters in 44 games in 1946 and breaking a string of losses by pitching her third extra inning game in 1947. In 1948 Collins stepped off the mound after the first game of an August doubleheader, having pitched through her fifth month of pregnancy. Patricia Collins, the only daughter of Harvey and Dottie Collins, was born in December 1948. A son, Daniel, was born in 1954.

In 1950 Collins posted a 13 and 8 record, even after being away from the game for more than a year. By the end of that season, Collins retired from baseball to concentrate on raising her family. She left the league with 1,205 strikeouts, a 1.83 ERA, and over 1,600 innings of play. She threw curveballs, fastballs, and changeups. She pitched underhand, sidearm, and was one of the few players to adapt to the overhand throw after the league banned underhand pitching in 1948, one of several changes made that year to put the official baseball stamp on the game that in five years had made the league internationally famous.

However, once the league disbanded after the 1954 season, the players and their accomplishments sank into obscurity for more than thirty years. In the 1980s Collins played a major role in reviving interest in the league and in preserving its history. After the first reunion of the All-American Girls Professional Baseball League in 1982, Collins helped to form a Players' Association in 1986 that officially came into being in 1987. From there, she worked tirelessly so that the women of the league received the recognition they deserved. In 1988 the first exhibit on women in baseball opened in the Baseball Hall of Fame in Cooperstown, New York. Fittingly, Collins pulled the curtain to open the display. Ted Spencer, vice president of the Hall of Fame, put it aptly when he said that Collins was "the guiding light, the heart and soul of the whole operation to make the exhibit a reality."

That exhibit inspired the 1992 movie *A League of Their Own*, a film that immortalized the league and brought the women the fitting tributes denied them for so many years. Collins acted as a spokesperson for the league, appearing at schools and various sports venues until shortly before her death from a stroke in August 2008. Collins is buried in Fort Wayne, Indiana.

In a sport typically dominated by men, Collins stands as a towering example of the rewards that can be reaped when dedication, talent, and passion combine. Collins served not only as an example for women in general but also as a mentor for youth sports in the years following her baseball career. She particularly helped to open opportunities for women in the 1950s and 1960s, a time when women otherwise would have had no chance to excel at sports. Finally, the important part Collins played in ensuring the history of the league cannot be overlooked. While the legacy of the league belongs to all the women who played professional baseball, that the league has a legacy at all is due in large measure to the efforts of Collins.

★

Carolyn Trombe, *Dottie Wiltse Collins: Strikeout Queen of the All-American Girls Professional Baseball League* (2005), is the prime source of information about the life and career of Collins. Other sources are the *Encyclopedia of Women and Baseball* (2006), edited by Leslie A. Heaphy and Mel Anthony May; and Merrie Fidler, *The Origins and History of the All-American Girls Professional Baseball League, 1943–1954* (2006). An obituary is in the *New York Times* (17 Aug. 2008).

Carolyn M. Trombe

COMDEN, Betty (*b*. 3 May 1917 in New York City; *d*. 23 November 2006 in New York City), librettist, lyricist, and screenwriter whose sixty-year professional collaboration with Adolph Green produced numerous hits for stage and screen, most notably the musical *On the Town* (1944).

Comden was born Basya Cohen, the second child of Leo Cohen, a lawyer, and Rebecca (Sadvoransky) Cohen, a teacher before her marriage. As a child growing up in the borough of Brooklyn, she changed her first name to Betty after being teased because the nickname for Basya sounded like "Bossie," the nickname for a cow. She attended the Ethical Culture School, a small, progressive private school, until her last two years of high school, which she completed

Betty Comden. MICHAEL OCHS ARCHIVES/GETTY IMAGES

at Erasmus Hall, a large public school. As a child she loved movies and music and frequently attended performances at the Brooklyn Academy of Music, where an uncle knew the manager.

She entered New York University (NYU), where she majored in dramatic arts and English, graduating with a BS in 1938. Her father died when she was halfway through NYU, and she moved to Manhattan with her mother and brother. Not long after her father's death, the family changed its name from Cohen to Comden. Because Cohen was not their original name—it had been chosen by an Ellis Island clerk who found the family name too unwieldy—they had long planned the change. They arrived at Comden by combining letters from Cohen and her grandmother's maiden name, Endem.

Comden met Adolph Green, her future writing partner, while she was a student at NYU, but it was not until after she graduated and they were both looking for work in the theater that she got to know him well. In 1939 their careers became linked when Judy Holliday, a friend of Green's, was asked to put together a cabaret act by the owner of the Village Vanguard, a small club in Greenwich Village. Holliday contacted Green; he in turn contacted Comden and two other friends; and an act, the Revuers, was born. Since they could not afford to pay for material, they wrote their own. During this period Comden and Green began to write together.

The composer Leonard Bernstein, also a friend of Green's, came to the Vanguard to see the group perform. Bernstein sat down at the piano, "and we were up till dawn," Comden later recalled. "I ran home and woke my mother and said, 'Mom, I've met a genius!' She said, '"That's nice."'" Bernstein became a theater colleague and close friend.

On 4 January 1942 Comden married Steven Kyle, a designer and businessman, with whom she would have two children. Six months after their marriage, he was drafted into the army, and for the next four years they were separated for long periods. Meanwhile the Revuers' success led to a movie offer, and they went to Los Angeles to appear in *Greenwich Village* (1944). But Green was cut entirely from the movie, and the others appeared only briefly. Holliday was offered a contract at Twentieth Century–Fox; the others were offered nothing. Although Holliday did not want to break up their act, the others persuaded her to accept.

Comden and Green returned to New York City. Shortly after their return, Bernstein invited them to write the book and lyrics for a musical based on the ballet *Fancy Free*, a collaboration between Bernstein and the choreographer Jerome Robbins. The result was *On the Town*, a rollicking musical about three sailors on shore leave who are determined to see all of New York City in twenty-four hours. The show was a smash hit. Among its famous songs is the classic "New York, New York," with the memorable lyrics: "The Bronx is up and the Battery's down, / The people ride in a hole in the ground, / New York, New York, / It's a helluva town!" In addition to their work as writers, they appeared onstage, Comden as Claire de Loone, the anthropologist, and Green as Ozzie, one of the sailors.

Their follow-up musical, *Billion Dollar Baby* (1945), with music by Morton Gould, was not nearly as successful. They received an offer from Hollywood, where they wrote screenplays for *Good News* (1947), with June Allyson and Peter Lawford; *The Barkleys of Broadway* (1949), with Fred Astaire and Ginger Rogers; and *On the Town* (1949), adapted from their own Broadway hit but minus most of Bernstein's score.

Their Hollywood work included the screenplays for two of the best movie musicals ever: *Singin' in the Rain* (1952), with Gene Kelly, Debbie Reynolds, and Donald O'Connor, and *The Bandwagon* (1953), with Fred Astaire and Cyd Charisse. The husband-and-wife writing team played by Oscar Levant and Nanette Fabray in *The Bandwagon* was based on Comden and Green, though in real life Comden and Green were never a couple.

Another of the team's standout movie musicals was *It's Always Fair Weather* (1955), about the reunion of three soldiers who discover they have little in common. They also wrote the screenplays for two nonmusicals, *Auntie Mame* (1958) and *What a Way to Go!* (1964).

While they were working in Hollywood, Comden and Green continued to write for Broadway: the sketches and lyrics for *Two on the Aisle* (1951), a revue starring Bert Lahr, with a score by Jule Styne, who became a frequent collaborator; the lyrics for *Wonderful Town* (1953), with a score by Bernstein; the lyrics for some of the songs for *Peter Pan* (1954), starring Mary Martin; and the book and lyrics for *Bells Are Ringing* (1956), with a score by Styne. *Bells Are Ringing* was written for Judy Holliday and contained the classic songs "Just in Time" and "The Party's Over"; Comden and Green also wrote the screenplay for the 1960 movie adaptation of the show.

As performers, Comden and Green starred in *A Party with Betty Comden and Adolph Green* (1958), which included many of their early sketches. They did an updated version of the show in 1977 and continued to perform it at various venues in subsequent years.

Other Broadway musicals included *Do Re Mi* (1960), lyrics only, with music by Styne; *Subways Are for Sleeping* (1961), book and lyrics, with music by Styne; *Hallelujah, Baby* (1968), lyrics only, with music by Styne; *Applause* (1970), book only; *On the Twentieth Century* (1978), book and lyrics, with music by Cy Coleman; and *A Doll's Life* (1982), book and lyrics, with music by Larry Grossman. Their final hit was *The Will Rogers Follies* (1991), lyrics only, with music by Coleman.

Over the course of their career, the pair won seven Tony Awards, and in 1991 they were honored by the Kennedy Center for lifetime achievement in the arts. Their partnership, which lasted more than sixty years until Green's death in 2002, has been called the longest ever in show business.

Outside of her partnership with Green, Comden played the Jewish mother in Wendy Wasserstein's off-Broadway play *Isn't It Romantic* (1983), made an uncredited appearance as Greta Garbo in the film *Garbo Talks* (1984), and appeared in the film *Slaves of New York* (1989). Her 1995 memoir, *Off Stage*, is unusual in that it deals primarily with her life outside of show business, including the heartbreak of her husband's premature death in 1979 from complications of pancreatitis, and her son's drug addiction, which led to his death from AIDS. She died of heart failure.

Comden and Green had an unusual gift for comedy. Their scripts were frequently laugh-out-loud funny, but the reason that the pieces worked so well was that they were unusually well-crafted. Their witty lyrics seamlessly fit the characters they were written for and worked perfectly with the music. Their best work remains remarkably fresh.

★

Comden and Green's papers are at the Billy Rose Theatre Division of the New York Public Library for the Performing

Arts, where a clip file is also available. Betty Comden, *Off Stage* (1995), is an unusual memoir, since it barely touches on her professional triumphs, but it contains a good deal of valuable information. For information on works by Comden and Green, see Alice M. Robinson, *Betty Comden and Adolph Green: A Biobibliography* (1994). An interview with the writing team is William Baer, "'Singin' in the Rain': A Conversation with Betty Comden and Adolph Green," *Michigan Quarterly Review* 41, no. 1 (Winter 2002): 1–22. An obituary is in the *New York Times* (24 Nov. 2006).

Lynn Hoogenboom

CRICHTON, (John) Michael (*b*. 23 October 1942 in Chicago, Illinois; *d*. 4 November 2008 in Los Angeles, California), prolific science-fiction and techno-thriller author; producer, director, and screenwriter for film and television; and physician, best known for his novel *Jurassic Park* and the hit movie it inspired, and for creating the long-running television series *ER*.

Crichton was one of four children born to John Henderson Crichton, a journalist, and Zula (Miller) Crichton, a homemaker. Raised in the Long Island village of Roslyn, New York, Crichton attended Greenvale and East Hills elementary schools and Roslyn High School. He revealed an early interest in books and planned on a career as a writer when he entered Harvard University as an English major in 1960. A dispute with the English Department led him to change his major to anthropology, and he graduated both summa cum laude and Phi Beta Kappa in 1964 with a BA. That year he was appointed Henry Russell Shaw Traveling Fellow, and in 1965 he served as visiting lecturer in anthropology at the University of Cambridge in the United Kingdom. While in Europe, Crichton met and married the first of his five wives, Joan Radam. They divorced in 1970.

By the fall of 1970, Crichton returned to Harvard and entered the medical school, supporting his studies with his writing. His first book, a novel about a robbery at a Spanish hotel titled *Odds On* (1966), was released under the pseudonym John Lange, and before graduating in 1969, he would publish four more novels under this and another pseudonym, Jeffery Hudson. (Both of these pen names allude to Crichton's extraordinary height, as he stood six feet, nine inches tall. Lange is a variant of *lang*, the German word for "tall," and Jeffery Hudson was the name of a famous seventeenth-century British dwarf.) The most successful of these early novels was a medical thriller titled *A Case of Need* (1968), which earned him an Edgar Award from the Mystery Writers of America in 1969 and

Michael Crichton, 2004. AP IMAGES

was subsequently turned into a film titled *The Carey Treatment* (1972), directed by Blake Edwards.

Following graduation from medical school, Crichton did postdoctoral work at the Salk Institute for Biological Studies in La Jolla, California, and it was there that he published his first successful novel under a shortened version of his own name. *The Andromeda Strain* (1969), a medical thriller about a killer virus from outer space, became a best seller and inspired both a 1971 film and a 2008 television miniseries, which aired only a few months before Crichton's death. In 1970 he published a non-fiction book critical of the health-care system titled *Five Patients*, which won the Association of American Medical Writers Award.

Although he remained interested in medical research throughout his life, the success of his fiction changed the course of Crichton's career, and it was fairly clear by this point that his future lay in publishing and in the movies. In 1970 he coauthored *Dealing* with his younger brother, Douglas, under the shared pseudonym Michael Douglas; a film version appeared in 1972. Also in 1970 he released

Grave Descend as John Lange. Two years later he published two more novels: *The Terminal Man* (1972; film adaptation 1974) and *Binary*, the final book under the pseudonym John Lange and the basis for the 1972 television movie *Pursuit*, which Crichton himself wrote and directed. During this time he also wrote the screenplays for several theatrical films, including *Extreme Close-Up* (1973), *Westworld* (1973), and Robin Cook's novel *Coma* (1978). As a novelist, he branched out into historical fiction by mid-decade with *The Great Train Robbery* (1975), a best seller about an infamous 1855 British gold heist, and *Eaters of the Dead* (1976), a novel set in the tenth century and based in part on true events. Both books would eventually be turned into films in which Crichton took a direct part. In 1979 he wrote the screenplay and directed the successful film adaptation of *The Great Train Robbery* starring Sean Connery. The script won the Edgar Award for Best Motion Picture Screenplay that year. Twenty years later in 1999, *Eaters of the Dead* became the basis for the film *The 13th Warrior*, directed by John McTiernan. Dissatisfied with the results, Crichton directed reshoots of some scenes though he goes unnamed in the film's credits. During this time he also tried his hand at marriage again, wedding Kathy St. Johns in 1978. The couple divorced in 1980.

Throughout the 1980s Crichton continued to pursue his triple role as a filmmaker, writer, and scientist. He directed three forgettable films: *Looker* (1981), *Runaway* (1984), and *Physical Evidence* (1989). At the same time he published four very different books, two novels—*Congo* (1980), about the search for diamonds in Africa, and *Sphere* (1987), about an undersea alien craft—and two nonfiction books—*Electronic Life* (1983), a layman's guide to computers, and a memoir titled *Travels* (1988). In 1988, too, he took up a one-year residency as visiting writer at the Massachusetts Institute of Technology. On the personal front, he wed twice during the decade: to Suzanne Childs, an attorney, in 1981 (marriage ended) and to Anne-Marie Martin in 1987, the latter producing Crichton's only child, a daughter named Taylor Anne, born in 1989.

If, for all his activity, the 1980s produced only mixed results, it seemed that Crichton could do no wrong in the 1990s. The decade began with the publication of the celebrated *Jurassic Park* (1990), an inventive novel that combined fact-based science and entertaining speculation. Using dinosaur blood found in a bug trapped in amber, a genetic engineering firm clones a variety of dinosaurs and places them on an island amusement park. When things go horribly wrong at the preserve, a paleontologist and his team are brought in to discover the problem. Several filmmakers, including Steven Spielberg, had learned of the book even before it was published, and a bidding war ensued. Spielberg won out when he agreed to Crichton's terms, including his insistence that he himself adapt

his own novel for the screen. Directed by Spielberg and written by Crichton and David Koepp, the film was released in 1993 and became the highest-grossing film in history at that time. It would also inspire two film sequels, *The Lost World: Jurassic Park* (1997), based on Crichton's follow-up novel, *The Lost World* (1995), and also directed by Spielberg and scripted by Crichton and Koepp, and *Jurassic Park III* (2001), with characters created by Crichton. Indeed, the success of the two novels and the film series even transcended popular culture and entered the realm of science itself when, in 2002, a genus of dinosaurs was named *Crichtonsaurus* in his honor. Two species bear the name: *Crichtonsaurus bohlini* (2002) and *Crichtonsaurus benxiensis* (2007).

As if the runaway success of the book and film versions of *Jurassic Park* did not keep him busy enough, Crichton continued to turn out material in various genres at a blinding pace. He produced two novels that were immediately adapted as big-budget theatrical releases: a thriller titled *Rising Sun* (1992) and *Disclosure* (1994), a legal drama about sexual harassment in the workplace. (Two of his earlier books were also adapted for the screen—*Congo* in 1995 and *Sphere* in 1998.) In 1994 he created, developed, and produced the hit National Broadcasting Company (NBC) series *ER*, which won for him Emmy and Peabody awards and ran for fifteen seasons until 2009. In 1996 he cowrote (with Anne-Marie Martin, his wife at the time) the screenplay to the film *Twister*. Finally, he published three additional novels over the next few years—a story about the airline industry titled *Airframe* (1996), an adventure tale titled *Timeline* (1999), and a science-fiction thriller about nanotechnology titled *Prey* (2002). During this busy decade the private Crichton even made social headlines when *People* magazine named him one of the "Fifty Most Beautiful People" of 1992, an ironic honor for a man who was self-conscious about his height.

By contrast, the final years of his life brought some disappointments and controversy. *Timeline*, his 1999 novel about time travel, spawned both a film adaptation in 2003 and a computer game company, Timeline Computer Entertainment, neither of which was well received. The film earned weak reviews, and Crichton's game company issued only one personal computer game titled *Timeline*, and it, too, failed to excite critics and consumers. In 2001 Anne-Marie, his wife of fourteen years, filed for divorce, and the two-year battle between them would result in one of the largest divorce settlements in history. In September 2002 he made headlines when he and his daughter were tied up and robbed at gunpoint at his California home.

The well-publicized robbery and divorce were followed by more negative attention for the reclusive writer when, in 2003, he gave several speeches sharply criticizing what he called "consensus science." Likening environmentalism to a religious movement rather than a scientific endeavor, he was especially critical of the furor over global warming. Crichton published *State of Fear* (2004), a novel in which ecoterrorists plan a mass murder to promote their view on climate change, and he later testified before Congress in 2005 about the partisan political ends of some environmental scientists.

In May 2005 Crichton married the actress Sherri Alexander, and the following year, he published his final novel, *Next* (2006), a tale of corporate greed and genetic experimentation gone out of control. In the spring of 2008 he was diagnosed with cancer and quietly began chemotherapy treatment. He unexpectedly succumbed to the disease in Los Angeles at the age of sixty-six. At his request, the family did not release details about the illness, funeral arrangements, and burial.

Crichton was the target of a fair share of criticism from, among others, book reviewers for his stock characters and wooden dialogue and scientists for his controversial stance on politically charged issues like global warming. To millions of readers and moviegoers, however, he was and remains the innovating creator of timely and thought-provoking fictional portrayals of science, technology, and politics.

★

The only autobiographical statements that the fiercely private Crichton provided came in his nonfiction book *Travels* (1988). Elizabeth A. Trembley, *Michael Crichton: A Critical Companion* (1996) and Kevin R. Grazier, *The Science of Michael Crichton* (2008), provide scholarly assessments of his life and work. Charles McGrath appraises Crichton's work and legacy in "Builder of Windup Realms That Thrillingly Run Amok," *New York Times* (5 Nov. 2008). Obituaries are in the *New York Times* (5 Nov. 2008), *Los Angeles Times*, and *Guardian* (both 6 Nov. 2008).

Leonard Mustazza

CROSSFIELD, (Albert) Scott, Jr. (*b.* 2 October 1921 in Berkeley, California; *d.* 19 April 2006 near Ranger, Georgia), test pilot and aeronautical engineer who was the first pilot to break Mach 2, chief design consultant and test pilot for the X-15, and system director for the Apollo Command and Service Module.

Crossfield's father, Albert Scott Crossfield, Sr., a chemist and entrepreneur, passed more than his name to his son; he passed on "a refusal to display physical or emotional weakness," which made the son boast later in his autobiography, "I have never experienced real fear in the air." From his mother, Lucia (Dwyer) Crossfield, the son inherited a stubborn determination that helped make his dream of building and flying the X-15 a reality.

Crossfield, like many test pilots, developed his love for flying while quite young. At the age of six he was stricken with rheumatic fever and remained an invalid for the next four years; bedridden, he began to read about the great flyers of the 1920s and to build models of their airplanes. By the time he was thirteen he had recovered his strength (though he remained small of stature, something that enabled him to fit in the cramped cockpits of the rocket planes), and he began taking private flying lessons. He would not officially "solo," however, until the conclusion of his Civilian Pilot Training class in the summer of 1941. By that time he was studying engineering at the University of Washington, having graduated from Boistfort High School in 1939, and was working part time at Boeing Aircraft to cover his expenses.

After the Japanese attacked Pearl Harbor in December 1941, Crossfield joined the U.S. Navy as an aviator; he was an instructor for most of World War II, although his unit spent the last seven months of the war preparing to support the invasion of Japan. Subsequently, he remained in the naval reserves, organizing the first naval aerobatics team in the Northwest while resuming his interrupted studies. He obtained his BS in 1949 and his MS in 1950, both in aeronautical engineering.

Crossfield began his career as a test pilot in 1950, joining the High Speed Flight Research Station of the National Advisory Committee for Aeronautics (NACA), which after the launch of *Sputnik* by the Soviet Union in 1957 would be incorporated into the National Aeronautics and Space Administration (NASA). When the Korean War began and American jets with straight wings began facing nimbler MIG-15s with swept wings, the tests gained swiftly in importance. Over the next four years he flew nearly all of NACA's experimental aircraft: the X-1, first aircraft to exceed Mach 1; the X-4, which was built without a horizontal stabilizer; the X-5, the first jet fighter with variable-sweep wings; and the delta wing XF-92A, which Crossfield would sum up in his autobiography as "under-powered, under-geared, under-braked, and over-weight." Most importantly, he performed nearly fifty flights in the Douglas D-558-II Skyrocket, studying the instability that airplanes develop at high speeds and high altitudes. On 20 November 1953 Crossfield flew into the record books by taking that plane beyond Mach 2 (twice the speed of sound), the first pilot to reach that speed.

The life of a test pilot who lives into his eighties is filled with near misses. Crossfield survived engine fires; failure of his oxygen supply; icing of his windshield so severe he had to remove his shoe and rub away the ice with his sock; landings that blew tires, collapsed his front wheels, even broke one plane in half; and most dramatically, an explosion during a ground test of the X-15 that hurled the plane's cockpit, with Crossfield in it, some twenty feet across the concrete.

Throughout these early years Crossfield was arguing the need for a plane that could go far faster and far higher than these early rocket planes; and in October 1954 NACA agreed, recommending the design and construction of what would become the X-15. The contract was awarded to North American Aviation, builder of the F-86 Sabre jet that had eventually tamed the MIG over Korea and, through its Rocketdyne division, of the engine that powered the Atlas missile (the rocket that would one day hurl John Glenn and the other Mercury astronauts into space). Crossfield left NACA in 1955 and went to work as a consultant with North American, shepherding the new plane from paper sketches to a rough mock-up to the finished product that he would fly to the edge of space.

As an engineer, Crossfield focused primarily on the safety of the pilot. He helped design the pressure suit that would be used in the X-15, succeeding so well that the suit was also used by the first astronauts; he worked on the plane's ejection seat, ensuring that pilots could survive ejecting at speeds in excess of 2,000 miles per hour; and he personally tested the revolutionary sidearm control, which replaced the traditional "stick" control, in a centrifuge at forces up to ten times the force of gravity. On 17 September 1959, less than five years from the initial recommendation that the X-15 be constructed, Crossfield finally lit off its rocket engines, fulfilling his dream. Crossfield would make thirteen powered flights in the X-15 before turning it over to NASA. Over the next decade other pilots would take it to a speed of Mach 6.7 and an altitude of sixty-seven miles above Earth's surface, still records for winged aircraft.

Crossfield remained with North American until 1967, serving as system director and later technical director for testing and quality control on the Apollo Command and Service Module and the Saturn V rocket's second stage. After the completion of these projects he moved on to private industry, working for Eastern Airlines and for Hawker Siddeley Aviation until 1975. In 1977 Crossfield became a technical consultant to the House Committee on Science and Technology. Upon his retirement in 1993, Crossfield was awarded the NASA Distinguished Public Service Medal. It was a worthy addition to his other honors, which include the Clifford B. Harmon Trophy (1960), the Collier Trophy (1961), the National Air and Space Museum Trophy (2000), and induction into the National Aviation Hall of Fame (1983), the International Space Hall of Fame (1988), and the Aerospace Walk of Honor (1990). He also served as a technical adviser on the Countdown to Kitty Hawk project in 2003, teaching a group of volunteers how to fly a replica of the Wright brothers' Flyer.

Crossfield was proudest, however, of his involvement with aerospace education. He created two award programs, the Teacher of the Year Award for teachers of aerospace education and the Education Award for senior members of the Civil Air Patrol. He continued to fly throughout his seventies and eighties, logging more than 200 hours a year. On 19 April 2006, returning from a speech to junior U.S. Air Force officers at Maxwell Air Force Base in Alabama, he ran into severe weather and was killed when his plane disintegrated.

Crossfield married Alice Knoph in April 1943, and they had six children. At the time of his death he lived in Herndon, Virginia. He is buried in Arlington National Cemetery.

★

For an autobiographical account of Crossfield's years as a test pilot up until 1959, see A. Scott Crossfield with Clay Blair, Jr., *Always Another Dawn: The Story of a Rocket Test Pilot* (1960). For additional detail about all the flights made in the X-15, see Milton Thompson, *At the Edge of Space: The X-15 Flight Program* (1992). An obituary is in the *New York Times* (21 Apr. 2006).

Hartley S. Spatt

CROWE, William James, Jr. (*b.* 2 January 1925 in La Grange, Kentucky; *d.* 18 October 2007 in Bethesda, Maryland), U.S. Navy admiral and chairman of the Joint Chiefs of Staff near the end of the cold war who the *New York Times* called "the most powerful peacetime military officer in American history."

Born in Kentucky, Crowe, an only child, had deep roots in Oklahoma, where his family participated in the land run of 1889. His father, William James Crowe, Sr., and homemaker mother, Eula (Russell) Crowe, were both graduates of the University of Oklahoma. The senior Crowe, an attorney who enlisted in the navy in World War I, practiced law in La Grange after his discharge but returned to Oklahoma early in the Great Depression. The family lived with his paternal grandparents until Crowe's father reestablished his legal practice. As a boy he sold magazines after school, but he was unaware of his parents' economic difficulties. In school he became involved in interscholastic debate, which gave him experience that proved valuable throughout his life.

After completing Classen High School in Oklahoma City in 1942, Crowe spent a year at the University of Oklahoma before accepting an appointment to the U.S. Naval Academy. Not always successful in constraining his rebellious nature, he claimed that while there he developed a talent for avoiding detection, which proved useful during Pentagon assignments. At Annapolis, Crowe excelled in debate, defeating teams from Princeton University and West Point. Because of wartime acceleration, members of

William J. Crowe, Jr. DIRCK HALSTEAD/TIME LIFE PICTURES/
GETTY IMAGES

Promoted to commander in 1962, the burly six-feet, two-inch officer put his career in jeopardy by applying for a program that sent officers to universities for advanced degrees. Turning down an opportunity to join the prestigious nuclear submarine program, Crowe entered graduate school at Princeton in the fall. During his second semester there he was ordered to report to the office of Admiral Hyman Rickover, where he incurred the wrath of the father of the nuclear navy when he opted to remain at Princeton rather than join the nuclear submarine program before completing his doctorate. By 1965 Crowe had earned a second MA and a PhD in politics, but when he returned to naval duty after three years in the civilian academic world, his future seemed doubtful. After staff and command positions in the submarine service at San Diego, in 1967 Crowe returned to the Pentagon, where he headed the U.S. Navy's East Asian and Pacific desk and was promoted to captain. The next year he acted as the navy's liaison to the State Department in developing a repatriation plan for the captured crew of the USS *Pueblo*, a surveillance ship seized by the North Koreans.

After three years in Washington, D.C., Crowe needed to command a major ship to achieve flag rank, but his lack of surface sea experience blocked such an assignment. He volunteered for Vietnam, where he served a year as adviser to the South Vietnamese riverine force in the Mekong Delta. His next assignment as deputy to a State Department official negotiating an end to the United Nations' trusteeship of Micronesia recognized Crowe's diplomatic skill, but it delayed whatever hope he had for achieving command of a major ship. He might have ended his naval career as a captain had it not been for the influence of Chief of Naval Operations Admiral Elmo R. Zumwalt, Jr., himself a naval maverick who insisted that naval selection boards consider service beyond sea duty in recommending the promotion of captains to flag rank. In 1974 Crowe was appointed rear admiral and ordered to Washington, D.C., where he held key staff positions utilizing his analytical and diplomatic talents. In 1976 he was assigned to head the U.S. Middle East Force from Bahrain, where he commanded four ships, the smallest fleet in the navy. The position gave him the command experience essential for further promotion and allowed him to exercise his diplomatic expertise, which again served the nation when he persuaded the Bahraini government to allow the U.S. Navy to retain its base there.

Advanced to vice admiral in 1977, Crowe was posted to the Pentagon as deputy chief of Naval Operations for Plans, Policy, and Operations. Three years later naval officials attempted to send him to a dead-end assignment in London and then into retirement, but General Bernard Rogers, the supreme commander of the North Atlantic Treaty Organization (NATO), insisted that Crowe be named the NATO commander in chief for southern

Crowe's Class of 1947 were commissioned after three years in June 1946. The twenty-one-year-old ensign finished 81st in a class of 816, about 20 behind the Georgia midshipman and future president Jimmy Carter.

The young naval officer's career began conventionally with sea duty aboard a destroyer-minesweeper and appeared promising when he qualified for the submarine service. His assignments alternated between sea duty aboard diesel boats and staff positions ashore. On 14 February 1954 Crowe married Shirley Grennell, an American Airlines flight attendant from Okeene, Oklahoma, whom he had met while on leave. Before 1960 the couple had two sons and a daughter. A few months after his marriage he was posted to the White House as assistant to President Dwight D. Eisenhower's naval aide and took night classes at the George Washington University Law School. He earned an MA from Stanford University in 1956. Four years later Crowe, now a lieutenant commander, received his only sea command as captain of the newly commissioned diesel submarine USS *Trout*.

Europe, a four-star command in Naples. Despite opposition from within the navy, Crowe was promoted to admiral and given the command in 1980. In 1983 naval officials denied him command of the Atlantic fleet because of his lack of sea duty but acquiesced in his appointment as commander in chief of the Pacific fleet. Headquartered in Hawaii, Crowe briefed President Ronald Reagan and Defense Secretary Caspar Weinberger on the military and political situation in the Far East. Impressed by the admiral's analysis, when the position of chairman of the Joint Chiefs of Staff opened in 1985, Reagan insisted on Crowe's appointment, ignoring opposition from the navy's civilian and military hierarchy.

Crowe had reached the highest uniformed position in the American military by an unorthodox career path, and throughout his four years as chairman he demonstrated the same breadth of vision and flexibility that characterized his previous assignments. During his tenure in the final years of the cold war, he developed direct contact with his Soviet counterparts, which lessened the threat of accidental conflict and promoted an easing of tension between the superpowers. He was also confronted with an increasing threat of international terrorism that required a balance between restraint and measured response. A year after he became chairman, Congress enacted the Goldwater-Nichols Department of Defense Reorganization Act, which significantly increased his power. Crowe used his new authority to streamline the chain of command to make the military more responsive. Never afraid to tell his superiors views they did not want to hear, Crowe expressed his concern about Reagan's proposal to eliminate all intercontinental ballistic missiles within ten years. The president quietly dropped the idea. President George H. W. Bush asked Crowe to serve a third term, but after forty-three years of active service, the chairman opted to retire from the navy on 30 September 1989. The sixty-four-year-old retiree divided his time between teaching geopolitics at the University of Oklahoma, offering his expertise to the Center for Strategic and International Studies in Washington, D.C., serving on corporate boards, and coauthoring his autobiography and another work in 1993.

Shortly after retirement he urged Congress to allow more time for sanctions and diplomacy to resolve the crisis produced by Iraq's invasion of Kuwait. During the election of 1992, the retired admiral endorsed and advised Bill Clinton in his bid for the presidency. Two years later President Clinton appointed Crowe ambassador to the United Kingdom. After retiring from that post in 1997, he chaired boards investigating the bombing of U.S. embassies in Kenya and Tanzania. Before he left office, Clinton awarded Crowe the Presidential Medal of Freedom. In 2004 Crowe joined other prominent retired diplomats and military leaders in criticizing President George W. Bush's foreign policy. Active until near the end of his life, Crowe, who was teaching courses at the U.S. Naval Academy in 2007, died of cardiac arrest at the age of eighty-two at the National Naval Medical Center. He is buried at the U.S. Naval Academy Cemetery.

Recognizing that mastery of the military arts was no longer enough to equip high-ranking officers to confront the political and diplomatic complexities of the modern world, Crowe pioneered a career path that eventually led him to the apex of the American military. His career after retirement from the navy was equally distinguished, revealing that the unorthodox skills he had developed in the service were also valuable in civilian life.

★

Crowe with David Chanoff, *The Line of Fire: From Washington to the Gulf, the Politics and Battles of the New Military* (1993), surveys the author's formative years and military career and analyzes issues confronting him as a senior military commander. Crowe, McGeorge Bundy, and Sidney D. Drell, *Reducing Nuclear Danger: The Road away from the Brink* (1993), reflects Crowe's ideas for reducing arsenals of nuclear weapons and preventing further proliferation. James R. Locher, *Victory on the Potomac: The Goldwater-Nichols Act Unifies the Pentagon* (2002), details Crowe's role in the passage of legislation designed to reform the military bureaucracy and strengthen the powers of the chairman of the Joint Chiefs of Staff. Arthur T. Hadley wrote a perceptive profile of Crowe in the *New York Times* (7 Aug. 1988). Obituaries are in the *New York Times* and *Washington Post* (both 19 Oct 2007) and *Newsweek* (20 Oct. 2007).

Brad Agnew

D

DANIEL, MARGARET TRUMAN

SEE *Truman, (Mary) Margaret.*

DARMAN, Richard (*b.* 10 May 1943 in Charlotte, North Carolina; *d.* 25 January 2008 in Washington, D.C.), budgetary and economic adviser to Presidents Richard Nixon, Ronald Reagan, and George H. W. Bush.

Darman was the son of Morton H. Darman, a textile manufacturer, and Eleanor Darman. Born in Charlotte, he had a brother and sister and grew up in Woonsocket, Rhode Island, attending Rivers Country Day School in Weston, Massachusetts, after the family relocated to Wellesley Hills. In 1960 he entered Harvard University where he fell under the influence of the dean of faculty, McGeorge Bundy, soon to become President John F. Kennedy's national security adviser. Darman would ever after look to Kennedy as an iconic politician, even though he personally favored the Republican Party. He took a BA in 1964 and went on to pursue an MBA from Harvard Business School, from which he graduated in 1967. On 1 September 1967 he married Katherine Emmett. They would go on to have three sons.

In 1970 he became deputy assistant secretary of Health, Education, and Welfare under Elliot Richardson. A policy adviser, he followed Richardson to the Justice Department when Richardson replaced the disgraced (following his involvement in the Watergate scandal) Richard

Kleindienst. Darman reportedly was instrumental in persuading Vice President Spiro Agnew to resign following allegations of tax fraud, but he followed Richardson out of the Justice Department when Nixon summarily removed Richardson during the so-called Saturday Night Massacre.

In 1974 Darman joined the Woodrow Wilson International Center for Scholars, a foreign policy think tank headquartered in Washington, D.C. Two years later he returned to government service to take part in Law of the Sea negotiations, but when the Democrat Jimmy Carter defeated President Gerald Ford in the election of 1976, Darman returned to scholarly pursuits. Asked to coach Ronald Reagan in the presidential campaign of 1980, he was executive director of the presidential transition team. When Reagan named James Baker White House chief of staff, Baker enlisted Darman as deputy. Darman soon assumed the role of gatekeeper to the president, briefing Reagan on whatever issues of the day he thought worthy of the president's attention. He also took part in legislative strategy sessions.

Because the House of Representatives was in Democratic control, little domestic legislation could be passed without careful bipartisan conversation. Reagan had argued that "government was not a solution, but the problem," and many of his advisers urged a lowering of taxes—some on the premise, much cherished among conservatives, that lower taxes would result in economic growth and a net increase in government revenues. Darman's strategy was always to counter what he saw as excessive tax cutting and counted on what he termed the "sensible center" to prevent a drastic change in policy. Secondary to this was an argument over the future of the Social Security system. Darman urged, and Reagan appointed, a bipartisan committee to consider a number of changes that ultimately resulted in 1983 in a number of revisions to the government pension plan. Darman's actions helped to keep Social Security out of the hands of those in the Reagan camp who loathed the program as a socialist enterprise.

For the presidential debates of 1984, Darman was tasked with preparing Reagan for his appearance with the Democratic challenger, Walter Mondale. The initial debate, however, did not go well—Nancy Reagan later complained that the president had been "brutalized with facts"—and Darman began to fear that he would not be brought back for the second administration. Reagan soon recovered his poise, won the election, and asked Darman to serve as deputy secretary of the Treasury.

In that role, Darman turned his energy to tax policy. Many of Reagan's supporters were converted blue-collar Democrats who regarded the tax system as the embodiment of the kind of government interference that retarded economic advancement. Darman saw himself as the champion of this sector of the voting public and lashed out at the "corpocracy" of "bloated, risk-aversive, inefficient and unimaginative" business managers. He eventually quarterbacked a tax reform package that—through the elimination of deductions and the altering of the tax brackets—became what he termed the largest tax increase in American history. This he accomplished with significant assistance from both Senatorial Republicans and House Democrats.

In April 1987, after the Democrats took control of the Senate, Darman resigned to become managing director of Shearson Lehman Brothers, a Wall Street broker. From 1987 to 1988 he also served as a contributing editor for *U.S. News & World Report*. When Vice President George H. W. Bush asked Darman in 1988 to help him prepare for his presidential debates against the Democratic candidate, Michael Dukakis, Darman accepted, despite the fact that the two men had enjoyed a less than warm relationship during the Reagan administration. Bush won the presidency in part because he had made Dukakis look weak and equivocal during these debates and in part because Bush had pledged to a cheering throng at the Republican convention "Read my lips—no new taxes."

During this first Bush administration, Darman turned his attention to reducing the federal deficit, which had greatly expanded during the Reagan years. Darman consulted with congressional leaders from both parties to fashion a deficit reduction plan, one that included a tax increase. To the consternation of his own party—and despite his stark campaign pledge—Bush signed the measure, a decision that not a few political observers would later pinpoint as the beginning of the end of his second term hopes. After Bill Clinton defeated Bush in the 1992 election, Darman again left public life to join the Carlyle Group, an investment concern, and AES, a power company.

In 1996 Darman penned a memoir, *Who's in Control?: Polar Politics and the Sensible Center*, describing his squabbles with others in the Reagan and Bush administrations, mostly over fiscal matters. He died of acute myelogenous leukemia.

Darman was a voice for moderation in an increasingly polarized political environment. If his debate preparation helped Reagan to win the White House, the tax code changes of the 1990s may have cost George H. W. Bush his reelection.

★

Darman's memoir is *Who's in Control? Polar Politics and the Sensible Center* (1996). Marjorie Williams, "The Pragmatist," *The Woman at the Washington Zoo* (2006), is an extensive profile of Darman. Obituaries are in the *Washington Post* and *New York Times* (both 26 Jan. 2008).

John David Healy

DASSIN, Jules (*b.* 18 December 1911 in Middletown, Connecticut; *d.* 31 March 2008 in Athens, Greece), film director whose promising career in Hollywood was cut short when he was blacklisted by the House Un-American Activities Committee (HUAC).

Dassin was born one of eight children to Jewish Russian immigrants Samuel Dassin, a barber, and Berthe Vogel, a homemaker. The family moved to New York City soon after Dassin's birth and settled in Harlem. Dassin attended Morris High School in the Bronx, graduating in 1929.

Dassin studied acting in Europe before returning to New York to work in the Yiddish theater. In 1933 he married the violinist Beatrice Launer. The couple would go on to have three children, including Joseph Dassin, who later became a popular French pop singer. They would divorce in 1962. In 1934 Dassin took acting work with Artef, the Yiddish theater collective, before turning his hand to directing. In 1939 he helmed a play on Broadway, *Medicine Show*. It was during this time, too, that Dassin joined the Communist Party, a decision he later ascribed to the devastating poverty he saw all around him throughout the Depression. He left the party in 1939 in protest of the Soviet alliance with Adolf Hitler, but by then the course of much of his future life and work was already set.

Dassin relocated to Hollywood in 1940 to pursue a career in directing and almost immediately found work in the major film studios. He worked for RKO, Metro-Goldwyn-Mayer (MGM), Universal, and Twentieth Century–Fox, serving as assistant at various times to the directors Garson Kanin and Alfred Hitchcock. Training as a director, Dassin directed his first short feature film for MGM in 1941, *The Tell-Tale Heart*, based on the Edgar Allan Poe story.

Jules Dassin, 1945. **HULTON ARCHIVE/GETTY IMAGES**

A year later, 1942, saw Dassin direct three full-length feature films for MGM: *Nazi Agent*, starring Conrad Veidt; *The Affairs of Martha*; and *Reunion in France*, featuring Joan Crawford and John Wayne. The film *Two Smart People* (1946), starring Lucille Ball, was Dassin's first crime movie, and it set the stage for the film noir classics that followed.

With *Brute Force* (1947) Dassin created what the film noir expert Eddie Muller called "the most explosive of example of the 'prison movie' subgenre of noir." The film announced Dassin's arrival as a major film noir director. With this film and the four to follow, Dassin crafted a dark and powerful version of Hollywood's bleakest film style. The story of a violent prison break that goes terribly wrong, *Brute Force* starred Burt Lancaster as the prisoner who will do anything to bust out and Hume Cronyn as the crypto-fascist prison guard who stands in his way. The violent climax to this "blackest of film noirs" was epitomized in the words of the prison's doctor: "No one escapes. No one ever escapes."

Next came the classic New York noir *The Naked City* (1948). One of the first major films to be shot on location—the film's cinematographer, William Daniels, won an Oscar for his photography—*The Naked City* climaxes with a brilliant chase across the Williamsburg Bridge.

For *Thieves' Highway* (1949), Dassin took noir on the road with a story of truckers in California who confront a crooked produce dealer. Starring Richard Conte and Lee J. Cobb, the film's portrayal of a dark world of corruption constituted what the film critic J. Hoberman called a "proletarian saga." A gritty, tough film, *Thieves' Highway* proved to be the last film Dassin would make in Hollywood before political turmoil derailed his career.

In Washington, D.C., and throughout much of the country, another "red scare" was in full swing. The House of Representatives had launched HUAC during World War II to root out Nazi sympathizers, but now the committee turned its attention to perceived communists. Called to appear, Dassin refused and was instead sent to London by the producer Darryl F. Zanuck to shoot what some would call his greatest film, *Night and the City* (1950). The story of a down-and-out wrestling promoter (played by Richard Widmark), *Night and the City* is a nightmare noir marked by haunting location shooting in London and Widmark's intense, terrifying performance.

In 1951 Dassin could no longer avoid HUAC's reach. The directors Edward Dmytryk and Frank Tuttle named Dassin as a former member of the Communist Party. Dassin was again subpoenaed by the committee in 1952, but again he refused to appear. He immediately found himself on the infamous "blacklist" and could find no work in Hollywood. In 1953 he moved his family to Paris.

When he arrived in France, he spoke little French and had few film connections, but luck was on his side. In need of work, he agreed to direct a low-budget French film called *Du rififi chez les hommes*, or, as it was released in the United States, *Rififi* (1955). The story of a jewel heist, *Rififi* is American film noir transplanted to a dark Paris. Dassin himself stars as an Italian safecracker. A high point in the film is the heist itself, which takes thirty minutes and was filmed without any dialogue. As the film critic Kenneth Turan once put it, *Rififi* is the "benchmark all succeeding heist films have been measured against." Indeed, everything from Brian De Palma's *Mission: Impossible* (1996) to the *Ocean's Eleven* films (2001–2007) have been influenced by it.

For *Rififi* Dassin was awarded the best director award at Cannes. One of the high points of his career, the moment was nevertheless marked by his sense of being a reluctant exile; when his director's prize was announced, the French flag was raised above him. Dassin later noted that it was the wrong flag: "I'm an American. It should have been an American flag."

It was at Cannes, too, that Dassin met the Greek actress Melina Mercouri, who would go on to star in many of his films. The couple married in 1966. In 1958 Dassin made his first film in Greece, *He Who Must Die*, an adaptation of a Nikos Kazantzakis novel. He returned to France to shoot *La Legge* (1959) starring Gina Lollabrigida, Marcello Mastroianni, Yves Montand, and Mercouri. It was his next film, however, the comedy *Never on Sunday* (1960), shot in Greece, that brought Dassin international recognition and his only Oscar nomination for direction (he was also nominated for the film's screenplay). The story of an American tourist, played by Dassin himself, who tries to reform a good-hearted prostitute, played by Mercouri, *Never on Sunday* was the director's biggest international success. Mercouri was nominated for an Oscar for Best Actress, the film was credited with increasing tourism to Greece, and its theme song became a radio hit.

By the late 1960s the political situation in the United States had changed enough that Dassin was able to return. In 1967 he directed *Illya Darling*, a musical comedy based on *Never on Sunday*, on Broadway. Mercouri starred in it and received a Tony Award nomination for her performance. A year later, Dassin directed his first film in the United States in eighteen years, *Uptight!*, a modern revision of a John Ford movie.

Dassin's final film, *Circle of Two* (1980) starred Richard Burton and was a box-office disaster. He never made another. After Mercouri's death in 1994, Dassin devoted himself to the Melina Mercouri Foundation, dedicated to petitioning the British government to return the Elgin Marbles to the Parthenon. He died at the age of ninety-six in a hospital in Athens after a brief illness. He was buried in Athens's First Cemetery beside his wife, Mercouri.

In the words of the film critic Hoberman, Dassin was "an American director who thrived in exile but never lost his American identity." He directed several classics of American film noir and, in spite of Hollywood's blacklist, made several important films in Europe while maintaining his artistic integrity.

★

An obituary is in the *New York Times* (1 Apr. 2008).

John Rocco

DAVIS, Raymond, Jr. (*b.* 14 October 1914 in Washington, D.C.; *d.* 31 May 2006 in Blue Point, New York), physical chemist, awarded the 2002 Nobel Prize in Physics for pioneering research to detect solar neutrinos.

Davis was the son of Raymond D. Davis and Ida Rogers (Younger) Davis. His father was a photographer at the National Bureau of Standards and later chief of the Photographic Technology Section. Davis's father, who was well known for his ingenuity in making his own apparatus, greatly influenced Davis's career in experimenting and designing the equipment he needed. Davis's mother gave him an appreciation for music. Davis had one brother, Warren, who was fourteen months younger and a constant companion as they grew up.

Davis was educated in the public schools in Washington, D.C. Following high school graduation he commuted to the University of Maryland, where he majored in chemistry, graduating with a BS in 1937. His first job was with Dow Chemical Co. in Midland, Michigan, where he stayed for one year. Davis returned to the University of Maryland to receive his MS in 1939. Following his graduation he went to Yale University, earning a PhD in physical chemistry in 1942. When he graduated from Yale, Davis entered the U.S. Army. His time in the army was largely spent observing chemical weapons tests at Dugway Proving Ground in Utah.

After his discharge from the army in 1945, Davis worked for Monsanto Chemical Co.'s Mound Laboratory in Miamisburg, Ohio, until the spring of 1948, when he joined Brookhaven National Laboratory in Upton, New York, where he stayed until his retirement in 1984. When Davis started at Brookhaven, the chemistry department chairman, Richard Dodson, suggested he go to the library to find a project. He read an article in a 1948 *Reviews of Modern Physics* issue by H. R. Crane titled "The Energy and Momentum Relations in the Beta-Decay, and the Search for the Neutrino" and decided that he had the background to experiment in neutrino physics, a new research area. Davis said of his years at Brookhaven that he was paid to do whatever he wanted to do.

Neutrinos had been predicted to exist since 1930, when the Austrian physicist Wolfgang Pauli had suggested them as an explanation for a discrepancy that was being observed in certain measurements with radioactive beta decays. Neutrinos were also thought to be emitted by the Sun in great numbers produced by solar fusion, although no one had detected them. A theory existed that collision with a solar neutrino could convert a chlorine nucleus into a radioactive argon nucleus.

Davis built a neutrino detector that used a 100,000-gallon tank filled with 615 tons of a chlorine-based dry cleaning solvent, perchloroethylene, to detect solar neutrinos by the chlorine-argon reaction. He developed a method to extract and count the radioactive argon atoms when they were formed in the detector. Davis situated the detector some 4,800 feet deep in the Homestake Gold Mine in Lead, South Dakota, to shield the detector from interference from other subatomic particles. Davis described neutrinos as "so tiny and fast that they can pass straight through everything, even the earth itself, without even slowing down."

From 1967 to 1985 Davis detected 2,000 neutrinos from the Sun in his apparatus. Unfortunately, the number of hits he was getting was only one-third of the predicted number based on atomic physicists' calculations. For most of three decades physicists tried to resolve this "solar neutrino puzzle." By the 1990s Davis's findings were confirmed by other scientists and physicists who had found there are actually three types of neutrinos reaching Earth from the Sun but only one of the types could be recognized by the neutrino detector. When Davis retired from Brookhaven in 1984 he joined the University of Pennsylvania as a research professor and continued his experiments to detect solar neutrinos.

The physicist Kenneth Lande, who collaborated with Davis, described him as the most optimistic person one could ever encounter. He said that Davis saw the neutrino study as a challenge and that the greater the challenge was, the more he enjoyed attacking it.

Davis shared the Nobel Prize in Physics in 2002 with the Japanese scientist Masatoshi Koshiba "for pioneering contributions to astrophysics, in particular for the detection of cosmic neutrinos" and with the American scientist Riccardo Giacconi for work that led to the discovery of cosmic X-ray sources.

From 1971 to 1973 Davis was on the National Aeronautics and Space Administration (NASA) Lunar Sample Review Board, where he was involved in the analysis of lunar dust and rocks that were brought back to Earth by the *Apollo 11* NASA mission to the Moon. Davis was also a member of the National Academy of Sciences and the American Academy of Arts and Sciences. In addition to his Nobel Prize, Davis won many awards, including the Tom W. Bonner Prize (1988) and the W. K. H. Panofsky Prize (1992) from the American Physical Society. He also received the 1999 Bruno Pontecorvo Prize from the Joint Institute for Nuclear Physics in Dubna, Russia.

Davis met his wife, Anna Marsh Torrey, at Brookhaven when they both started working there. They were married on 4 December 1948. Davis and his wife had five children. Davis died at his home of complications from Alzheimer's disease at age ninety-one.

Davis's unique background led him to create the detector that found solar neutrinos against enormous odds. His experiment to detect solar neutrinos was the first to prove that the energy received from the Sun is produced by the fusion reaction that transforms hydrogen into helium.

★

Information on Davis's research can be found in his "Solar Neutrinos. II. Experimental," *Physical Review Letters* 12, no. 11 (16 Mar. 1964): 303–305; and in "Solar Neutrinos: A Scientific Puzzle," coauthored by John N. Bahcall and Raymond Davis, Jr., *Science* 191, no. 4224 (23 Jan. 1976): 264–267. Autobiographical information on Davis is included in Tore Frängsmyr, ed., *The Nobel Prizes 2002* (2003). For summaries of his work and life refer to news releases published by Brookhaven National Laboratory (2002, 2006) and obituaries in the *New York Times* and *Boston Globe* (both 2 June 2006).

M. C. Nagel

DEAVER, Michael Keith (*b.* 11 April 1938 in Bakersfield, California; *d.* 18 August 2007 in Bethesda, Maryland), entrepreneur, lobbyist, and senior adviser and White House deputy chief of staff (1981–1985) best known for shaping the public image of President Ronald Reagan.

Deaver was one of three children born to lower middle-class parents Paul Sperling Deaver, a Shell Oil distributor, and Marian (Mack) Deaver, a reporter for a local paper in Mojave, California. He was a sickly child suffering from nephritis and was diverted from any type of sports activities. He graduated from San Jose State University in 1960 with a degree in political science and public administration. After traveling for a brief period, Deaver was drawn toward public service in the defense of his country, viewing it as a foundation for future endeavors. He joined the U.S. Air Force Reserve and served from 1961 to 1966.

After completion of this military service, Deaver utilized his academic training in political science and public administration to gain a position as field representative for the California Republican Party in charge of three assembly campaigns in the central coastal region. From this experience he first met Reagan.

Michael K. Deaver, 1985. DIANA WALKER/TIME LIFE PICTURES/ GETTY IMAGES

In 1967 with the Republican Party experience behind him, he joined Reagan's gubernatorial staff as an assistant cabinet secretary and then as a deputy chief of staff. He was responsible for scheduling special projects and for working with Reagan's wife, Nancy. On 17 January 1968 he married Carolyn Judy, who also worked for the governor. They had two children, a daughter and a son.

As Reagan's governorship ended in 1975, Deaver began to investigate other options. With two other Reagan staff members, Mike and Peter Hannaford, he launched Deaver and Hannaford, a public relations firm with offices in Sacramento, California, and Los Angeles. The company was responsible for booking Reagan's public appearances, researching and selling his radio programs, and ghostwriting a syndicated column. Another component of its responsibilities was the development of a lucrative business with international clients such as Guatemala, Taiwan, and Argentina.

In both of Reagan's presidential campaigns (1976 and 1980), Deaver was a prominent asset as a senior adviser, confidant, and friend. Following Reagan's election as president in 1980, Deaver joined the White House staff in January 1981. Over the next four years Deaver oversaw the Office of Presidential Appointments and Scheduling and the Office of Private Sector Initiatives as deputy chief of staff to James Baker III. Deaver was as an expert on the media and a master of memorable visuals, and he sought to highlight the president's appearance through the use of ideal settings and favorable camera shots. Two outstanding examples that provided Deaver the distinction as the master of the "photo op" were at the Great Wall of China and the cliffs at Normandy, France, for the fortieth anniversary of the D-Day invasion. He experienced one failure that occurred in the scheduling of President Reagan's visit to Bitburg Cemetery in Germany to place a wreath, when it turned out to be the burial site of forty-nine of Adolf Hitler's SS soldiers. Deaver did not foresee the opposition to the visit expressed by Jewish leaders and veterans. But when President Reagan would not alter the schedule, Deaver scheduled an additional site to commemorate Jewish victims of the Holocaust

When Reagan won reelection in 1984, Deaver took on the responsibility of the chairman of the inaugural committee. During that time the stress and pressure of the work began to take a toll, and he began to drink heavily. In 1985 he committed himself to a twenty-eight-day rehabilitation program at Havre de Grace, Maryland.

Upon resigning from his White House staff position in May 1985, Deaver sought out the lucrative world of consulting and opened his own public relations firm, Michael K. Deaver & Associates, in Washington, D.C. Even while he was under investigation for perjury, for lying under oath about his lobbying activities with the Reagan administration, his organization thrived and was a success. Both national and international clients were part of the organization's portfolio, including the countries of Canada, South Korea, and Saudi Arabia.

After what was believed to be a weak defense strategy, Deaver was convicted of perjury in 1987. He was sentenced to three years of probation, 1,500 hours of community service, and a $100,000 fine. He was also forbidden from lobbying any presidential administration for three years. The fine was paid, and he continued to proclaim his innocence. The 1,500 hours of required community service ultimately turned into a fifteen-year relationship as board chair with the Washington, D.C.–based substance abuse treatment rehabilitation program Clean and Sober Streets.

Launching a third career in 1992, Deaver served as executive vice president for Edelman, where he oversaw the management of public affairs programs for corporations such as United Parcel Service, Bacardi, and Fujifilm. In 1995 he was promoted to director of corporate affairs for Edelman's Washington office, providing strategic counsel to Nike, CSX, Nissan, and Microsoft. Over the next decade Deaver worked to elevate the global standing of the corporation. By 1996 he was able to restore his image and was back in good standing with the Republican Party.

Deaver received an award from Harvard University as the Heffernan Visiting Fellow in the spring of 2005. This was followed in 2006 with his induction into the National Capital Public Relations Hall of Fame as an image maker.

Deaver died of pancreatic cancer at his home at age sixty-nine. Despite his perjury conviction and his alcohol addiction, he remained well known on the Washington social scene. Following a funeral service at Washington National Cathedral, Deaver was buried at Zoar Golden Acres Cemetery in Bishopville, Maryland.

★

For more information about Deaver, see his autobiography *Behind the Scenes* (1987), which was penned with Mickey Herskowitz, as well as *A Different Drummer: My Thirty Years with Ronald Reagan* (2001) and *Nancy: A Portrait of My Years with Nancy Reagan* (2004). Obituaries are in the *New York Times* and *Washington Post* (both 19 Aug. 2007).

Ann E. Pharr

DeBAKEY, Michael Ellis (*b.* 7 September 1908 in Lake Charles, Louisiana; *d.* 11 July 2008 in Houston, Texas), internationally recognized cardiovascular surgeon, educator, inventor, and medical statesman renowned for his many firsts, including breakthroughs and developments in the treatment of cardiovascular disease and for performing the first successful implantation of a partial artificial heart.

DeBakey was born Michel Dabaghi, the eldest of five children of Orthodox Lebanese immigrants Shaker Morris, a pharmacist and businessman, and Raheehja Zorba. Precocious, he

Michael E. DeBakey. REUTERS/LANDOV

return from Europe, he earned an MS at Tulane and a year later joined the surgical faculty, a position he held until 1948. In 1939, with his mentor, the surgeon and medical researcher Alton Ochsner, DeBakey hypothesized a link between smoking and lung cancer.

During World War II, DeBakey volunteered for military service, in 1942 becoming a member of the Surgical Consultants' Division in the Office of the Surgeon General of the Army. Three years later he was appointed director and received the U.S. Army Legion of Merit for helping to create the mobile army surgical hospital (MASH) units that would be utilized to save many lives during the Korean conflict and Vietnam War. DeBakey later helped institute the Veterans Affairs (VA) Medical Center Research System. He held the rank of colonel in the U.S. Army Reserves.

In 1946 DeBakey returned to Tulane as an associate professor of surgery, and there he remained until 1948, when he was hired as the first chairman of the Department of Surgery at the Baylor University College of Medicine (later the Baylor College of Medicine).

Within the next two decades, DeBakey would be at the center of many firsts. He campaigned to develop a partnership between a network of Texas Medical Center hospitals and Baylor so that graduates would be able to continue their training in the area instead of going elsewhere. In the early 1950s he became the first to classify arterial disease by location, characteristic, and pattern; invented the Dacron and Dacron-velour artificial arteries or grafts, which he initially created on his wife's sewing machine; performed the first successful removal and graft replacement of an arterial aneurysm; and carried out the first successful endarterectomy to remove plaque from an artery. In 1955 he executed the resection of an aneurysm, and three years later the first successful patch-graft angioplasty. Also in the 1950s he joined the medical task force of the Hoover Commission on the Organization of the Executive Branch of the Government, and helped to establish the U.S. National Library of Medicine, serving on its first board of regents and on numerous occasions acting as chair and consultant.

In 1960 DeBakey began development of an artificial heart. In 1962 and 1963 he was given a $2.5 million grant to create an implantable version with no external connections. He was the first to utilize interactive telemedicine; was honored with an Albert Lasker Clinical Research Award (1963); performed the first aortocoronary artery bypass, later simply known as "bypass surgery" (1964), the same year that President Lyndon Johnson appointed him chairman of the President's Commission on Heart Disease, Cancer, and Stroke; and became the first to successfully transplant a partial-artificial heart (1966).

It was also during the decade of the 1960s that DeBakey and his team became among the first to record surgeries on film. DeBakey also attempted both heart and multiple transplantations (1968), but organ rejection problems forced suspension of this practice until better

played numerous musical instruments, participated in sports, and maintained a garden with his brother. He also learned how to sew, a talent that, not coincidentally, would later help him to create one of his many inventions. From childhood, DeBakey was interested in becoming a doctor.

DeBakey graduated from Lake Charles High School as valedictorian before entering Tulane University in 1926. There he would earn both a BS and an MD in six years, rather than the usual eight. During his time at Tulane, he played saxophone in the school's band and orchestra and proved to be an accomplished billiards player. Almost immediately prior to his graduation from the Tulane University School of Medicine in 1932 at the age of twenty-three, DeBakey invented the "roller pump," a component for heart-lung machines.

DeBakey was elected to the Alpha Omega Alpha honorary medical society, and continued his medical training by both interning and completing his surgical residency training in surgery at Charity Hospital in New Orleans, Louisiana. He received surgical fellowships at the University of Strasbourg in France and the University of Heidelberg in Germany. In 1936 DeBakey married Diane Cooper, with whom he later had four sons. Upon his anti-rejection drugs were developed in the 1980s. In 1969 he received the Presidential Medal of Freedom with Distinction from President Johnson. That same year he was named president of Baylor, a position he held until 1979, when he became chancellor. In January 1996 he was named chancellor emeritus.

In the early 1970s DeBakey founded and directed the Cardiovascular Research and Training Center at the Texas Medical Center. Two years later he provided the impetus for instituting the High School for the Health Professions in the Houston Independent School District, which was later named in his honor, and he was one of the earliest proponents for the creation of a program at Baylor for premed students as well. That same year, DeBakey's wife died of a massive heart attack. He was by her side at the time, unable to save her.

In 1974 DeBakey was honored as the first American foreign member of the Academy of Medical Sciences of the Union of Soviet Socialist Republics. Also in 1974 he married Katrin Fehlhaber, with whom he had a daughter. In January 1975 DeBakey was awarded a grant to launch the first National Heart and Blood Vessel Research and Demonstration Center. One year later, students from around the world created the Michael E. DeBakey International Cardiovascular Surgical Society, later known as the Michael E. DeBakey International Surgical Society.

DeBakey received over fifty honorary degrees, and the awards, accolades, scholarships and fellowships either established by him, or in his honor, are too numerous to name. At Baylor alone, the following have been named in his honor: professorship in pharmacology (1977); lectureship (by the pharmacology department) (1982); DeBakey/Bard chair in surgery (1990); and chair in pharmacology (1994). On 27 January 1999 the school christened the Michael E. DeBakey Department of Surgery. In 1978 the Trustees at Baylor established the Michael E. DeBakey Center for Biomedical Education and Research, and in 1985 the DeBakey Heart Center for Research and Public Education. DeBakey was also named the Olga Keith Weiss and Distinguished Service Professor in the Michael E. DeBakey Department of Surgery at Baylor and director of the DeBakey Heart Center for Research and Public Education there and at Methodist Hospital. On 23 April 2008 he received the Congressional Gold Medal, the nation's highest civilian honor.

DeBakey served an unprecedented three terms as consultant on the National Heart, Lung and Blood Advisory Council of the National Institutes of Health, was an adviser to almost every president over the course of fifty years, and helped establish health-care systems in Europe and in the Middle and the Far East. In May 1978, the king and the princess of Belgium commissioned a 300-pound bronze bust of DeBakey. It now stands in the lobby of the Methodist Hospital in Houston. In 1992 he was inducted into the Academy of Athens, an honor reserved for Greeks with the exception of Winston Churchill, Albert Einstein, and DeBakey himself.

A prolific writer, DeBakey published more than 1,600 scholarly articles, chapters, and books, as well as numerous popular works with various coauthors, including *The Living Heart* (1983), *The Living Heart Diet* (1984), and *The New Living Heart* (1997). He served on the editorial boards of many prominent medical and surgical journals including the *Annals of Surgery, Circulation*, the *Journal of Cardiovascular Surgery*, and the *Journal of Vascular Surgery*. He served as editor of the *Yearbook of General Surgery* for fourteen years.

In his lifetime, DeBakey had many high-profile patients, including Presidents John F. Kennedy and Lyndon Johnson, Russian President Boris Yeltsin, Marlene Dietrich, and the shah of Iran. He trained nearly 1,000 surgeons and performed some 65,000 cardiovascular procedures. After his death at the age of ninety-nine at the Methodist Hospital in Houston, on 15 July he became the first person ever to lie in state at the Houston City Hall Rotunda. A memorial service was held at the Co-Cathedral of the Sacred Heart. He is buried at Arlington National Cemetery.

DeBakey will be remembered as the "Texas Tornado," a dedicated and lifelong scholar, a compassionate and caring individual, a perfectionist who would accept nothing less than the best, and a true humanitarian whose contributions to the world spanned the better part of seventy-five years. Boris Yeltsin said it best when he called DeBakey "a magician of the heart" and "a man with a gift for performing miracles." To this day, the "magician" and his "gift" continue to save lives.

Biographical information about DeBakey's life and work is in Lawrence K. Altman, "The Doctor's World; Dr. DeBakey at 90: Stringent Standards and a Steady Hand," *New York Times* (1 Sept. 1998). Details about DeBakey's return to performing heart transplant surgeries can be found in Wayne King, "DeBakey Resumes Heart Transplant Surgery," *New York Times* (22 Feb. 1984). For DeBakey as patient, see Lawrence K. Altman, "The Man on the Table Devised the Surgery," *New York Times* (25 Dec. 2006), and for details of DeBakey's momentous consultation with Yeltsin, see Lawrence K. Altman, "In Moscow in 1996, a Doctor's Visit Changed History," *New York Times* (1 May 2007). Obituaries are in the *Houston Chronicle* (12 July 2008) and *New York Times* (13 July 2008).

Adriana C. Tomasino

d'HARNONCOURT, Anne Julie (*b.* 7 September 1943 in Washington, D.C.; *d.* 1 June 2008 in Philadelphia, Pennsylvania), art historian and museum curator who served for twenty-six years as director of the Philadelphia Museum of Art; one of the first women to head a major art museum in the United States.

D'Harnoncourt was the only child of Rene d'Harnoncourt and Sara (Carr) d'Harnoncourt, and a cousin of the orchestra conductor Nikolaus Harnoncourt. Her father, born in Austria, was the director of the Museum of Modern Art in New York from 1949 to 1968. Her mother had been editor of *Fashions of the Hour*, a magazine published by the Marshall Fields department store in Chicago. D'Harnoncourt grew up in the art world of New York, where she attended the prestigious Brearley School from 1949 to 1961. She then entered Radcliffe College, majoring in European and English history and literature. Elected to Phi Beta Kappa, she received her AB magna cum laude in 1965 and won the Captain Jonathan Fay Prize, Radcliffe's highest undergraduate honor, awarded for outstanding scholarly promise.

In 1965 d'Harnoncourt went to London to do graduate work in European art of the nineteenth and twentieth centuries at the Courtauld Institute of Art, receiving her MA with distinction in 1967. Her graduate thesis dealt with mid-nineteenth-century British painting, especially that of the Pre-Raphaelites. In conjunction with her studies she worked at London's Tate Gallery preparing catalog entries for their holdings of Pre-Raphaelite art.

Returning home in 1967, d'Harnoncourt joined the staff of the Philadelphia Museum of Art. For the next two years she was a curatorial assistant in the Department of Painting and Sculpture, where her abiding interest in the avant-garde artist Marcel Duchamp took shape. His last work, the complex construction *Étant donnés* (*Given*), had just been acquired by the museum, and it was the young assistant's job to install it. Her article with Walter Hopps, "*Étant donnés*... Reflections on a New Work by Marcel Duchamp," published in 1969 in the Philadelphia Museum of Art *Bulletin*, was the first of her numerous articles on the artist.

In 1969 d'Harnoncourt was appointed assistant curator of twentieth-century art at the Chicago Art Institute. There she met Joseph J. Rishel, assistant curator of European painting. They were married on 19 June 1971, the same year she was promoted to be associate curator of twentieth-century art. The couple had no children. When the Philadelphia Museum of Art called her back, in 1972, as their curator of twentieth-century art, her husband accompanied her, becoming curator of the Department of European Painting Before 1900. Continuing her work as a specialist on Duchamp, d'Harnoncourt organized, with the Museum of Modern Art (MOMA) curator Kynaston McShine, a major Duchamp retrospective exhibition, which opened in Philadelphia in 1973 and then traveled to MOMA and the Chicago Art Institute. Her essay for the exhibition catalog has been called one of the best introductions to the work of this controversial artist. She wrote many other essays for the cataloges accompanying the noteworthy exhibitions of modern art held during her ten years as curator. These include *Futurism and the International Avant-Garde* (1980)

and the show devoted to the scores and prints of the composer John Cage (1982).

Succeeding Jean Sutherland Boggs, d'Harnoncourt was appointed the George D. Widener Director of the Philadelphia Museum of Art in 1982. (There are rumors, never confirmed, that she had declined other offers to head MOMA and the National Gallery of Art.) She presided over a period of enormous change and growth at the museum. Capital campaigns were successfully launched between 1986 and 2001, and in 1989 a court decision allowed the museum to integrate into its other holdings the previously separately housed John G. Johnson collection of European paintings. As a result, between 1992 and 1996, ninety galleries were renovated and rehung. In 2000 d'Harnoncourt oversaw another renovation: twenty galleries set aside for modern art, making room for a growing collection of major works by contemporary artists. A blockbuster show of works by Paul Cézanne in 1996 began a series of popular exhibitions, such as the one in 2001–2002 devoted to the Philadelphia native Thomas Eakins. One of her notable achievements was her success in 2006 in keeping Eakins's famous painting *The Gross Clinic* from being sold out of the city by Thomas Jefferson University. Working with the Pennsylvania Academy of the Fine Arts, she headed a campaign that raised enough money to purchase it jointly. "It's a painting that really belongs in Philadelphia—his presence still radiates here," d'Harnoncourt noted.

In 1997 d'Harnoncourt became, as well as director, chief executive officer of the museum, assuming additional management and fiscal responsibilities. These included planning for the museum's 125th anniversary in 2001 and negotiating another long-range plan, initiated in 2004, for the acquisition of a building to house the museum's library and archives and its collections of prints, drawings, photographs, costumes, and modern design. The Perelman Building, with its state-of-the-art facilities, opened in 2007. At the time of d'Harnoncourt's death the following year, she was overseeing plans for a new underground museum wing, to be designed by the architect Frank Gehry.

In addition to her positions at the Philadelphia Museum, d'Harnoncourt served at various times on panels of the National Endowment for the Arts and on the boards of, among others, the Pennsylvania Council on the Arts, the Japan Society, and the John Cage Trust. She was a member of the Association of Art Museum Directors and of the American Philosophical Society, and was a fellow of the American Association of Arts and Sciences. Among her many honors, she was named an Officier de l'Ordre des Arts et des Lettres in France in 2002 and received an honorary LLD from Princeton University in 2005.

D'Harnoncourt died at the age of sixty-four at her home on Fitler Square. She had been recuperating from minor surgery and suffered cardiac arrest.

D'Harnoncourt was known by her colleagues for her impeccable scholarship, gracious manner, and ability to work harmoniously with the distinguished curatorial staff she had built. Under her management the Philadelphia Museum of Art developed and prospered as a vibrant asset to the cultural life of its city and the nation. The museum established the Anne d'Harnoncourt Memorial for Art Acquisitions in her honor, and Rishel selected Ellsworth Kelly's painting *Seine* (1951) as the first work to be so acquired.

★

"Anne d'Harnoncourt: A Master of the Graceful Sidestep," an interview by Dinitia Smith in the *New York Times* (30 May 1996), offers a picture of her life and work. "Anne d'Harnoncourt: Discerning Enthusiasm for Art," an appraisal by the *New York Times* art critic Roberta Smith (4 June 2008), assesses her life and accomplishments. Obituaries are in the *New York Times* and *Philadelphia Inquirer* (both 3 June 2008).

Eleanor F. Wedge

DIDDLEY, Bo (*b.* 30 December 1929 in Magnolia, Mississippi; *d.* 2 June 2008 in Archer, Florida), guitarist, singer, and songwriter who became a founding father of rock and roll music, famous for his dynamic beat and bold lyrics.

Diddley was born Ellas Otha Bates in Magnolia. (Bo Diddley was a childhood nickname.) His father, Eugene Bates, soon left, and his teenage mother, Ethel Wilson, moved downstate to McComb, Mississippi. A cousin, Gussie McDaniel, adopted Diddley, changing his last name to McDaniel and raising him with her own three children. She took them all to Chicago in 1934.

The McDaniels attended the formal Ebenezer Baptist Church, and when the seven-year-old Diddley showed an interest in music, the congregation scraped together thirty dollars to buy him a violin. The music for which Diddley truly yearned, however, was more down-home. Diddley recalled, "I'd stand by the window at the sanctified church, peep at 'em shaking their tambourines, and I'd say, 'One day I'm gonna get me something that sounds like that.'"

He attended grammar school and Foster Vocational School. At thirteen Diddley got his first guitar, at fifteen he began playing on street corners, and at sixteen he had a band, the Langley Avenue Jive Cats—Roosevelt Jackson on washtub bass, Jerome Green on maracas, and Diddley on guitar—playing storefront bars under the elevated trains. Diddley admired the pop styles of Louis Jordan and Nat Cole, but he idolized Muddy Waters and his electric blues. Offstage Diddley worked as a laborer and a truck driver. He

Bo Diddley. FRANK DRIGGS COLLECTION/GETTY IMAGES

also boxed seriously as a teenager, training at Eddie Nicholson's gym, but he quit before turning professional. He loved boxing for teaching him self-reliance, but he was glad he quit before getting injured. Wherever he went he ran into racial prejudice. When he found out that people thought he was "bad business," he told them, "Hey, I'm a man. I don't give a damn what color I am, I didn't ask to come into this world no way."

In 1946 Diddley married Louise Woolingham. They divorced a year later. He married Ethel "Tootsie" Smith in 1949 and had a son and a daughter. Their union came apart in the late 1950s. In the early 1960s he married Kay Reynolds.

In early 1955 Diddley signed with Chess Records, and in May, Chess released "Bo Diddley" backed with "I'm a Man," two rough-hewn self-portraits. Diddley sings nonsense rhymes on "Bo Diddley," strumming his guitar to a hypnotic four-four time that soon became famous as the "Bo Diddley beat." "I'm a Man" sounds at first like an old blues song, but Diddley's bold statement, "I'm a man, I spell it M-A-N!" heralded a new frankness among African Americans in public speech.

Diddley's recording raced up the charts in good company. Rock and roll broke through in 1955, the year of Ray Charles's "I Got a Woman," Fats Domino's "Ain't That a Shame," Chuck Berry's "Maybellene," and Little Richard's

"Tutti Frutti." White kids loved the exciting music, without caring (or often knowing) that the singers were black, and bought their records by the million. Diddley joined his fellow rock and rollers on the *Ed Sullivan Show* and on endless one-nighter tours that seldom were as glamorous as they seemed. Diddley and Berry were Chess's gold-dust twins, but Diddley never became a star as big as his rival. Berry was a clever lyricist and had a flash and glamour that short, stocky Diddley with his thick, black-rimmed glasses could not match. Some people talked of a feud, but Diddley recalled, "I never envied Chuck. He's a strange dude, but I can get along with anybody."

From 1955 to 1962 Diddley recorded steadily, with Chess releasing such songs as "Say, Man" and "You Can't Judge a Book by Looking at the Cover" as singles and then collecting them in popular albums. These albums included *Bo Diddley* (1958), *Go Bo Diddley* (1959), *Have Guitar Will Travel* (1960), and *Bo Diddley Is a Gunslinger* (1961). In 1956 the guitar-vocal duo Mickey and Sylvia made Diddley's song "Love Is Strange" a long-lived chart topper. The Beatles and the British invasion took over rock and roll in 1964, and though John Lennon and Mick Jagger often named Diddley among their major inspirations, Diddley slipped from his peak as a contemporary hit maker. *Bo Diddley's 16 All-Time Greatest Hits* (1964), forty-five minutes of stunning rock and roll music, may be the best introduction to Diddley's classic era.

Diddley's records overflow with ribald good humor. He clearly loved making records, and his pleasure comes through the medium. On "Say, Man," Diddley delivers comic insults ("You're so ugly your mother had to put a sheet over your head so sleep could slip up on you"), and on "Roadrunner" he laughs at a rival, "Gonna put some dirt in your eye!" Diddley talks freely to the listener. In Willie Dixon's "You Can't Judge a Book by Looking at the Cover," he commands, "You got your radio turned down too low. Turn it up!" In "Hey, Bo Diddley," he is like Old McDonald with "women here, women there, women, women everywhere."

Though the songs vary widely in style, every track is inimitably Diddley's because he founded his artistic vision on a firm belief in his own uniqueness. Diddley said in a 1970 interview, "I have my own way of expressing my soulful feelings. I never wanted to be like anybody else, can't copy anybody else. I got my own bag of tricks."

In the 1960s Diddley moved his family from Chicago to a pleasantly sprawling house in the San Fernando Valley near Los Angeles. From there Diddley flew all over the world, to Europe and Japan, playing at concert halls, festivals, and rock and roll revival shows. In 1971 the family moved to a ranch near Los Lunas, New Mexico, and seven years later to a farm near Archer, a small town outside of Gainesville, Florida. The moves mattered little to

his musical career: Diddley felt at home playing music on the road.

Diddley continued performing and recording into the first decade of the 2000s. He drew a wide variety of sounds from his signature red rectangular electric guitar, playing on the neck and tapping the body. He could even make his guitar talk like Donald Duck, creating phrases with sentencelike inflections. A master showman, Diddley mesmerized crowds by strumming endless one-chord grooves to the Bo Diddley Beat while chanting such simple lyrics as "Let's get it funky in here." An unusual feature of his road band was a woman guitarist-singer. The women changed over the years—Peggy Jones (Lady Bo), Norma-Jean Wofford (the Duchess), Cornelia Redmond (Cookie), and Debby Hastings—but they always played the same role: a sexy female foil for Diddley's earthy masculinity. After playing on bills with all of the great stars of blues, rhythm and blues, and rock, Diddley declared, "Still the only person I ever feared on stage is Ray Charles."

Diddley recorded more albums after his peak than before, but most of these recapped older songs or attempted newer styles that did not suit his sound. *Black Gladiator* (1970) may be his finest postpeak album, a record exploding with the energy of an artist at the height of his powers. The opening cut is "Elephant Man"; two other songs are "Power House" and "You, Bo Diddley" (as in "Who's the greatest man in town? You, Bo Diddley"). *Black Gladiator* also introduces Diddley the opera singer, a side of himself he had long concealed. Diddley asserted, "I've always had that voice. In Sunday-school choir, when I got to singing, the teacher would stop everything and tell me to hush up."

Like many black recording stars, Diddley felt that white-owned record labels cheated their artists with low royalties paid informally as cash handouts or as down payments on expensive cars. "The minute I said I didn't want a new Cadillac, Chess started saying, ... 'This black boy is getting smart.' ... But you danced to the tune they was playing, or you didn't dance at all." Fortunately, deep religious faith balanced his bitterness.

Diddley received many late-life honors for his contributions to contemporary music. In 1987 he was inducted into the Rock and Roll Hall of Fame, and in 1999 the Grammy Hall of Fame declared "Bo Diddley" a recording of "lasting historical significance." In 2004 *Rolling Stone* magazine ranked Diddley at number twenty on their list of the 100 Greatest Artists of All Time.

In May 2007 Diddley, who had long had diabetes and hypertension, suffered a stroke after a concert at Council Bluffs, Iowa. A heart attack soon followed. He never regained full health, dying of heart failure at his home in Archer. His funeral was in Gainesville, near his last home.

Through decades of music making, Diddley expressed a clear and earthy vision of life, drawn from his own experience, sustained by his confident personality, and driven home with his irresistably danceable beat. A master guitarist and a singer of great gusto, Diddley inspired generations of young musicians. In an obituary tribute, the Voice of America declared that "his influence was so widespread that it's hard to imagine what rock and roll would have sounded like without him." Jagger called Diddley "a wonderful, original musician and an enormous force in popular music."

★

Arnold Shaw, *Honkers and Shouters: The Golden Years of Rhythm and Blues* (1978), covers the period. See also Michael Lydon, *Boogie Lightning: How Music Became Electric* (1980). George R. White, *Bo Diddley: Living Legend* (1995), is a biography of Diddley. An obituary is in the *New York Times* (3 June 2008).

Michael Lydon

DITH PRAN (*b.* 27 September 1942 in Siem Reap, Cambodia; *d.* 8 March 2008 in Edison, New Jersey), photojournalist and human rights activist who coined the phrase "killing fields" and whose life was depicted in the 1984 Academy Award–winning movie *The Killing Fields*.

Dith Pran ©BETTMANN/CORBIS

Dith was born into a middle-class Cambodian family, one of six children to Dith Proeung, a public works official, and Meak Ep. In high school, he learned French and taught himself English. Dith married Ser Meoun and they had one daughter and three sons. After graduating high school in 1960, he enlisted as a translator for the U.S. Military Assistance Group in Cambodia; however, when Cambodia severed diplomatic relations with the United States in 1965, Dith took work as an interpreter for a British film company. He also worked at a hotel in Angkor Wat, a tourist destination near Siem Reap. In 1970, after war had brought tourism in Cambodia to a halt, Dith moved to Phnom Penh, the capital, where he worked as a guide and interpreter for foreign journalists.

In 1972 Dith met the *New York Times* reporter Sydney Schanberg. A year later he was on a monthly retainer for the *Times* and, alongside Schanberg, Dith defied the American embassy by traveling to Neak Luong to report on an American bombing raid that had resulted in heavy civilian casualties. The two men worked together to publicize the impending refugee crisis in Cambodia. On 12 April 1975, the Khmer Rouge (the Cambodian Communist party) occupied Phnom Penh, forcing the United States to evacuate Cambodia. Dith was able to send his wife and children

to San Francisco, but he chose to stay and work with Schanberg. By 17 April, the Khmer Rouge was in control of all Cambodia, which it renamed Kampuchea. When Schanberg and two other journalists, Al Rockoff and Jon Swain, were seized by soldiers, Dith persuaded the soldiers to allow him into their armored vehicle. After several hours he was able to negotiate the journalists' release by persuading the captors that the men were French neutrals. Schanberg and the others took refuge in the French embassy, but Cambodians were not allowed sanctuary there. Dith walked away from the embassy, discarded the money that Schanberg had given him, and destroyed any clothing or identification that might link him to foreigners. The Khmer Rouge purged the cities and sent educated citizens to the countryside, its goal being to turn Cambodia back to an agrarian country. The party called 1975 "year zero." Affecting traditional Cambodian dress and the speech of a peasant, Dith found work as an oxcart driver. In 1976 Schanberg won a Pulitzer Prize for his reporting from Cambodia, an award he accepted on behalf of Dith.

During the famine that overtook the country during the late part of the 1970s, Dith struggled to survive, sometimes eating only a tablespoon of rice a day. For a time he was a prisoner in the forced labor camp in Dam Dek, about twenty miles from Siem Reap. He ate snakes, insects, and bark and was almost killed for stealing rice from a field. In January 1979 Vietnam invaded Phnom Penh, forcing the Khmer Rouge to flee. Dith returned to Siem Reap, where he was able to locate the few surviving members of his family: his sixty-three-year-old mother and some nieces and nephews. His father had starved to death in 1975; the Khmer Rouge had executed his three brothers, and one sister was murdered with her husband and two children. Dith was unable to bring his mother to the United States, and she later died of malnutrition.

Dith discovered the "killing fields," where thousands of victims had been killed and dumped outside of Siem Reap. For a time, he served as administrative chief of the Siem Reap area, until the Vietnamese discovered that he had worked for foreigners and forced him to resign. Finally, in 1979, Dith was able to get a message to Schanberg that he was alive, and, after a harrowing six-week walk, he crossed into a refugee camp in Thailand. Severely malnourished after years of famine and starvation, Dith was reunited with Schanberg in October 1979. With help from the *New York Times*, Schanberg was able to bring him to the United States.

In 1985 Dith was appointed Goodwill Ambassador by the United Nations High Commissioner for Refugees. He became an American citizen in 1986, and in 1998 he received an Ellis Island Medal of Honor.

Dith divorced Ser Meoun and married Kim De Paul, with whom he founded the Dith Pran Holocaust Awareness Project to educate the world about the Cambodian genocide. Dith returned to Cambodia in 1989 to interview child victims. He also established an Internet site that featured the pictures of survivors in order to help reunite Cambodian families. In 1997 he published *Children of Cambodia's Killing Fields: Memoirs by Survivors.* De Paul and Dith separated, and he then lived with his partner, Bette Parslow. On 15 April 2008 the U.S. Senate passed Senate Resolution 515 posthumously in honor of Dith's heroic life and work against future genocides.

Dith's mission was to tell the world about the Cambodian holocaust, what he considered a tragedy with "universal implications." He called the Jewish writer and Holocaust survivor Elie Wiesel one of his heroes for his work in telling the world about the horrors that had unfolded under the Nazi regime. Dith's success is measured by the widespread use of the phrase "killing fields," and international awareness of the killing of two million Cambodians.

Dith was diagnosed with pancreatic cancer in January 2008 and died at the Roosevelt Care Center in Edison, New Jersey. His first wife, Ser Meoun, and companion Parslow were at his side. Funeral services were held in New Jersey on 6 April at the South Plainfield Funeral Home. Schanberg delivered the eulogy. Dith's body was cremated on 7 April at a private ceremony and his ashes sent to a Buddhist temple in Philadelphia pending a location for a final resting place in Washington, D.C.

★

A biography of Dith can be found in Sydney Schanberg, *The Death and Life of Dith Pran* (1985), which focuses on their time together in Cambodia and Dith's escape. Obituaries are in the *Washington Post* (30 Mar. 2008) and *New York Times* (31 Mar. 2008).

Jane Brodsky Fitzpatrick

DIXON, Frank J(ames) (*b.* 9 March 1920 in Saint Paul, Minnesota; *d.* 8 February 2008 in La Jolla, California), pioneer in the use of radioactive isotopes as tracers, regarded as a highly important scientist in developing the field of immunology, and creator of the Scripps Research Institute.

Dixon was the only child of James Frank Washington Dixon (better known as Frank J. Dixon, Sr.) and Rosa Augusta (Kuhfeld) Dixon. The elder Dixon was a machinist, though when their son was growing up, the couple owned the Criterion Cafeteria in Saint Paul. In 1938 Dixon entered the University of Minnesota intending to major in mathematics. When his adviser convinced him that math did not offer a financially profitable career, he switched to biology. After two years of undergraduate study, he was admitted to the university's medical school. In 1943 he graduated, having earned a BS, an MS, and an MD. From 1943 until 1946 Dixon served as a lieutenant in the U.S. Naval Reserve; attached to the Marine Corps, he served in the Japan-Pacific theater. On 14 March 1946 he married Marion Janet Edwards; their sixty-two-year marriage ended only with his death.

Following his discharge from the navy, Dixon worked briefly as a research assistant in the Department of Pathology at Harvard Medical School under Shields Warren. Through Warren (later an important member of the Atomic Energy Commission), he was able to obtain radioactive iodine that he used as a tracer in studying proteins important to immune systems. Following a short stint at the medical school of Washington University in St. Louis, he became head of the Pathology Department of the University of Pittsburgh School of Medicine in 1950. He left Pittsburgh in 1961 (taking four young colleagues with him) for the more salubrious climate of La Jolla, California. At the little-known Scripps Medical Clinic (with its attached La Jolla Institute of Allergy and Immunology), Dixon's task was to establish the Department of Experimental Pathology; this later became the Scripps Research Institute. In time, this institute, which he founded and headed until 1987, became the largest medical research institute in the United States. By the mid-1980s the institute was the annual recipient of major grants from the National Institutes of Health as well as from such private donors as Johnson & Johnson and Pittsburgh Paint and Glass.

The main thrust of Dixon's early research was to demonstrate that antigen-antibody clusters were filtered out in the kidney by the glomerulus, a fine bed of capillaries. Unfortunately, these clusters can sometimes cause clogs that shut down the kidney. By attracting white blood cells, an inflammation similar to lupus is produced. Moreover, the transfer of these antibody clusters to monkeys can result in sickness there as well. It was this pioneer work in demonstrating the key role played by the kidney in the body's immune processes that led to his receiving the prestigious Lasker Award (often called the American Nobel Prize). Dixon's work led to a breakthrough in understanding systemic lupus erythematosus. Dixon and the virologist Michael Oldstone studied chronic viral infections that can lead to blood vessel and kidney diseases. Their work overturned the standard belief that maternal viruses would not cause damage to the fetus.

In addition to serving on the board of directors of the Scripps Institute (he was the chair of the board for fourteen years), Dixon's scientific contributions were numerous. Many bacterial diseases are treated by injecting the patient with serum from animals that have been exposed to the disease. Sometimes this leads to serum sickness with such side effects as fever, joint pain, rashes, and an enlarged spleen. As these symptoms are similar to those of rheumatoid arthritis, rheumatic fever, and lupus, this discovery was crucial to further research on those and other illnesses. Thus Dixon was able to demonstrate that exposure to natural proteins and viruses were often the cause of previously unexplained diseases.

Over the course of his professional career, Dixon earned many awards. In addition to the Lasker prize, he was made an honorary fellow of the Royal College of Pathologists. The International Society of Nephrology gave him the Jean Hamburger Award. From the New York Academy of Medicine came the Paul Klemperer Award. The Lupus Foundation of America added a Distinguished Service Award, and the American Society of Pathologists awarded him the Gold-Headed Cane. During his long career, Dixon also served as president of both the American Association of Immunologists and of the American Association of Pathologists.

Despite a hectic professional career of more than sixty years as a scientist and administrator, Dixon enjoyed pursuits beyond the laboratory and boardroom. An avid mountain climber, he successfully scaled such peaks as Mount Whitney and the Grand Teton. Well into his seventies, he was a familiar figure to residents of La Jolla

as he ran an average of six miles per day. Following his retirement from active leadership of the Scripps Research Institute, he raised bonsai trees.

On 8 February 2008 Dixon died at his home of complications arising from aortic stenosis. He was survived by his wife, three children, and four grandchildren. Following cremation, his ashes were scattered over sites that had been important to him during his lifetime.

Dixon will be remembered for a number of crucial contributions to the field of immunology. A doctor who devoted his life to research rather than treating patients, he was probably the first to demonstrate the use of atomic isotopes as tracers in understanding the role of proteins in disease. He was a pioneer in explaining the importance of the kidney in cleansing the body of antigens as well as the disastrous consequences that could result when it malfunctioned in this role. His work led to a clearer understanding of a number of diseases as well as promising ways to treat them. Finally, his work in the creation of the Scripps Research Institute resulted in a lasting institution for understanding and treating diseases, which may well be his most important legacy to future generations.

★

Dixon's professional papers are in the possession of the Scripps Research Institute. Obituaries are in the *Los Angeles Times* (10 Feb. 2008) and *New York Times* (13 Feb. 2008).

Art Barbeau

DOUGLAS, Mike (*b.* 11 August 1925 in Chicago, Illinois; *d.* 11 August 2006 in North Palm Beach, Florida), host of a popular and long-running talk-variety television program that changed the character of daytime television.

Born Michael Delaney Dowd, Jr., Douglas was one of three children of Michael Dowd, a railroad freight agent, and Gertrude (Smith) Dowd, a homemaker. Showing vocal talent at a young age, Douglas was encouraged by his mother to sing in the church choir and at family gatherings. At age eleven he successfully auditioned for *The Irish Hour*, a radio series that aired on Chicago station WLS, and was asked back several times. As a teenager he spent school vacations entertaining passengers on the summer cruise ships that plied the Great Lakes. Intending to study accounting as a backup career, he enrolled at Oklahoma City University and worked as a singer at WKY to help meet costs. In 1943, during his freshman year, he met Genevieve Purnell, also a first-year student, and the couple married within months. They would have three daughters. During World War II, Douglas left school to attend a U.S. Navy officer-training program in Wisconsin

Mike Douglas, 1976. **CBS/LANDOV**

and briefly served in the Pacific. Discharged at war's end, he chose to seek a show business career rather than return to college and thus moved to Los Angeles.

In 1946 Douglas was hired as a vocalist by the bandleader Kay Kyser, who advised him to change his name and made him the featured singer in Mike Douglas and the Campus Kids. Two songs recorded by the group, "Ole Buttermilk Sky" (1946) and "The Old Lamplighter" (1947), made *Billboard* magazine's Top 100. Douglas appeared regularly on *Kay Kyser's Kollege of Musical Knowledge*, a long-running radio series, and after 1949, on the television version. His first film role was as the singing voice of Prince Charming in Walt Disney's *Cinderella* (1950), an animated feature.

The young singer seemed on a fast track to success when Kyser, a show business power with interests in broadcasting, film, and recording, suddenly announced in 1950 that he was leaving the entertainment industry to lecture on behalf of Christian Science, a religion he had adopted several years earlier. The loss of his patron could not have come at a worse time for Douglas. The "big band sound," for decades the signature genre of American popular music, was facing challenges from rock and roll music, which would bring about a sea change in public taste. Established singing stars such as Frank Sinatra and Bing Crosby remained popular with their followings, but the big band scene lost its vitality and was no longer capable of nurturing young talent. Douglas's career stagnated during the 1950s

as he pursued gigs at a shrinking list of nightclubs and hotel piano bars. He returned to Chicago, where a thriving radio and television production industry increased his chances for work. With his career at a low ebb in 1961, Douglas received a modest offer of steady work that turned out to be the greatest break of his professional life.

The broadcasting division of the Westinghouse Corporation, known as Group W, was expanding program production at its five television stations. The division hoped to gain new revenue by selling broadcast rights to stations in other markets (a process known as syndication). Unable to compete with the "Big Three" coast-to-coast broadcasting networks (American Broadcasting Company, Columbia Broadcasting System, and National Broadcasting Company [NBC]) in production of costly prime-time dramatic series, Group W focused its efforts on inexpensive talk-variety formats designed for marginal viewing hours, on the model of NBC's *The Tonight Show*. The company hoped to try the format in the late afternoon and was seeking a personality who would appeal to the older female viewers who were the main segment of the time period's audience. The producer Woody Fraser, familiar with Douglas's friendly, mellow style, offered him $400 per week to serve as the host of a Monday-through-Friday afternoon series to be broadcast live from KYW-TV, Group W's Cleveland station. *The Mike Douglas Show* premiered on 1 December 1961. It consistently won its time period in the ratings and in 1963 was added to the daily schedules of Group W's four other stations, with similar results.

Two events in 1965 facilitated the show's national distribution. First, production was moved to Philadelphia following a legal action (unrelated to the Douglas show) that awarded Group W a station license in the city. Just ninety miles from New York City, the new location provided easy access to stars and celebrities who could appear as guests. Second, Group W switched the program from live broadcasts to videotaped production following an on-air incident in which the entertainer Zsa Zsa Gabor called the comedian Morey Amsterdam "a son of a bitch," violating Federal Communications Commission (FCC) profanity standards. Group W's ability to "bleep out" lapses in acceptable language allayed the fears of station owners in socially conservative markets who had been hesitant to carry the series.

By 1967 *The Mike Douglas Show* had emerged as the first syndicated daytime series in television history to approach national exposure, attracting a daily audience of about 6 million homes via 171 stations (a figure that would eventually peak at 221 stations in the United States and Canada). Douglas won the first Emmy Award for Achievement in Daytime Programming that year, and his annual salary rose to $500,000, a twenty-five-fold increase from just four years earlier. A fixture at the top of the daytime ratings for most of its run, *The Mike Douglas Show* proved that independently produced and distributed talk-entertainment shows could successfully compete with network soap operas and game shows in afternoon television. In all, Douglas recorded more than 6,000 episodes in Philadelphia and (after 1978) Los Angeles. In retrospect, they constitute a remarkably wide-ranging archive of American popular culture.

A typical ninety-minute episode featured any combination of well-known singers, comedians, authors, actors, film directors, sports figures, and freelance celebrities, all of whom gladly accepted union-scale minimum compensation in return for opportunities to publicize their media products, or simply themselves, to a national audience. Interviewing some 30,000 guests during the show's twenty-one years on the air, Douglas maintained a relaxed style as he chatted with an assortment of starlets, intellectuals, political activists, rock stars, and anyone else who might have caught or been captured by sufficient public attention to gain a booking. A small sampling of the Douglas guest list includes Muhammad Ali, Fred Astaire, Lucille Ball, Truman Capote, Jimmy Carter, Johnny Cash, Ray Charles, Alice Cooper, Joan Crawford, Angela Davis, Aretha Franklin, Robert Frost, Judy Garland, Barry Goldwater, Andy Kaufman, Liberace, Richard Nixon, Richard Pryor, Kenny Rogers, Linda Ronstadt, Frank Sinatra, Jimmy Stewart, the Three Stooges, Barbra Streisand, Mother Teresa, John Travolta, Malcolm X, and Frank Zappa.

The show's innocent spirit is revealed by a 1978 clip in which three-year-old Tiger Woods shows his golf swing to Bob Hope. "I don't know what kind of drugs they've got this kid on, but I want some," Hope says to Douglas, who dutifully laughs at the joke. In addition to the diverse array of guests, Douglas had an equally diverse series of weekly cohosts, including Louis Armstrong, Bette Davis, George Carlin, Ralph Nader, Vincent Price, and, in the most extensive commercial television exposure they ever received together, John Lennon and Yoko Ono. At Lennon's suggestion, Black Panther Party leader Bobby Seale did a cohost stint as well. Dozens of rock bands that made only rare television appearances performed on the show, including the Beach Boys, the Kinks, the Rolling Stones, Jefferson Airplane, KISS, Moby Grape, Sly and the Family Stone, and Vanilla Fudge. African-American recording artists were presented so regularly that Motown Records founder Berry Gordy credited Douglas with a role in integrating American popular music. By bringing millions of stay-at-home viewers into contact with personalities, performers, and ideas they might have otherwise missed, *The Mike Douglas Show* anticipated a role for syndicated daytime television talk shows that was later developed further by Phil Donahue, Sally Jesse Raphael, Oprah Winfrey, Rosie O'Donnell, and others.

Douglas opened most episodes by singing a ballad but made no attempt to revive his singing career on a grander scale. He recorded several albums of easy-listening "standards" and Christmas tunes, which were aimed at his television audience. The title cut of *The Men in My Little Girl's Life* (1966), a sentimental reflection on fatherhood, put Douglas on the *Billboard* charts for the first time since 1947 and led to a performance on *The Ed Sullivan Show*. He also appeared as an actor, taking small guest roles in episodes of popular television series, including *Knot's Landing* and *The Mary Tyler Moore Show*.

In 1980 Group W declined to renew Douglas's contract, replacing the aging star with a fresh face, John Davidson. Douglas promptly formed a production company and kept *Mike Douglas* on the air until early 1982, ensuring Davidson's failure. Douglas tried to repackage the show in a sixty-minute format several months later, and when that project failed, briefly hosted *People Now*, a daily entertainment segment on the Cable News Network, then in its second year of operation. Accepting that his fortunes had once again taken an abrupt turn, Douglas retired to a home in Palm Beach Gardens, Florida, in 1985, playing golf daily and only occasionally making public appearances. He died on his eighty-first birthday following a brief hospitalization for dehydration.

★

Douglas's autobiography is *Mike Douglas: My Story* (1978). Mike Douglas, *I'll Be Right Back: Memories of TV's Greatest Talk Show*, written with Tom Kelly and Michael Heaton (1999), offers autobiographical information and reminiscences of his talk-show years and comments on the genre; the later book is freer of self-promotion and more genuinely self-amused. More revealing than either is an interview (21 Oct. 1998) Douglas gave to Julius "Jack" Kuney, a former Group W executive, the transcript of which is held by Syracuse University Library's Special Collections Research Center. In some sense, Douglas's guest list was his most significant life's work; the website of *The Mike Douglas Show*, http://mikedouglasshow.com, offers a searchable list organized alphabetically and by occupation. Obituaries are in the *New York Times* and *Washington Post* (both 12 Aug. 2006).

David Marc

DRINAN, Robert Frederick (*b.* 15 November 1920 in Boston, Massachusetts; *d.* 28 January 2007 in Washington, D.C.), five-term U.S. representative, first Catholic priest to serve as a voting member of the U.S. Congress, legal scholar, activist, and author.

Drinan was the son of James John Drinan and Ann Mary (Flanagan) Drinan. Along with his brother and sister, Drinan grew up in Boston's Hyde Park neighborhood. During his youth he played the clarinet, eventually

Robert F. Drinan, 1971. ©BETTMANN/CORBIS

performing with the Boston Civic Symphony. After graduating from Hyde Park High School in 1938, Drinan enrolled at Boston College, where he was a member of the debate team. In 1942 he earned an AB and an MA from Boston College; during the same year he entered the Jesuit order. In 1950 Drinan received an LLB and an LLM from Georgetown University Law Center. In 1953 he became an ordained Jesuit priest. From 1956 until his election to the U.S. Congress in 1970, Drinan served as the dean of the Boston College Law School.

Throughout his career Drinan combined his interests and background in law, public policy, and religion. A prolific writer, he authored numerous books and articles on human rights, the separation of church and state, international law, and U.S. foreign policy. Before his service in Congress, Drinan became a leading advocate for civil rights, calling for the desegregation of Boston public schools and urging Boston-area college students to participate in the civil rights movement. From 1962 to 1971 he chaired the Massachusetts advisory committee to the U.S. Commission on Civil Rights.

Despite never having held political office, Drinan entered the 1970 Democratic primary race for the Third Congressional District of Massachusetts. "Why?" Drinan

queried when asked to explain his reasons for entering the political arena. "Why not? Jesuit priests always have been avant-garde. Right?" Drinan's foray into politics—one that he considered a natural extension of his work on behalf of human rights—stemmed from observations he made on a trip to Vietnam in 1969. Greatly disturbed by the large number of political prisoners held in South Vietnam (contrary to U.S. State Department reports on the subject), Drinan later implored the Catholic Church to declare the Vietnam War "morally objectionable." The incumbent, Philip J. Philbin, a former football player at Harvard University, proved a formidable opponent for Drinan. Philbin's strong record of steering federal funds into the district and his careful attention to constituent services (which included weekly trips to the district) contributed to his almost three-decade tenure in the House. Philbin also reaped the benefits of the seniority system. By 1970 he had risen to become the second-ranking Democratic member on the House Armed Services Committee. Philbin's expansive congressional district stretched from the Boston suburbs of Brookline and Newton westward to the affluent towns of Concord and Lexington and even farther west to the majority blue-collar central Massachusetts mill towns of Leominster, Fitchburg, and Gardner. The diverse constituency encompassed a considerable Catholic (70 percent) and a sizable Jewish population.

Drinan's entry into the race provoked strong criticism. Conservative Catholics in the district were faithful to Philbin, while other Catholics believed that Drinan's quest for political office violated the separation of church and state dogma. However, Drinan capitalized on the growing antiwar sentiment present in much of the district. He called for an immediate withdrawal from Southeast Asia and labeled his opponent as "an unthinking rubber stamp" for the prowar, hawkish L. Mendel Rivers, chairman of the Armed Services Committee. Drinan's well-organized grassroots campaign, consisting mainly of students and antiwar volunteers, provided an invaluable base of support that helped him overcome not only the incumbent but also the entry of a third candidate in the campaign—Massachusetts State Senator Charles Ohanian. On primary day, Drinan captured a 46 percent plurality, in what the *New York Times* termed "one of the most notable upsets of the year." Refusing to accept defeat, Philbin launched a write-in campaign as an Independent in the general election, in which Drinan also faced the Republican nominee John McGlendon. Drinan narrowly won the election, earning 38 percent to McGlendon's 36 percent and Philbin's 26 percent. "Our father, who art in Congress" became an unofficial slogan for Drinan, who made history with his successful House campaign.

With his election to the Ninety-second Congress (1971–1973), Drinan became the first Catholic priest to serve as a voting member in Congress. (Gabriel Richard, a nonvoting delegate who represented the Michigan Territory during the Eighteenth Congress [1823–1825], was the first Catholic cleric to serve in the House.) Drinan received national media attention during his five terms in the House. Historically, clergy had served in Congress, but the arrival of a Jesuit priest caused a stir because of its rarity and the mixed response by Catholics across the nation. Drinan's atypical persona further contributed to the media blitz; he lived in a simple dormitory room among the Jesuit community of Georgetown University during his tenure in Congress. Even Drinan's choice of wardrobe provoked interest. "It's the only clothes I have," he remarked when asked about his decision to wear his clerical collar and black suit on the House floor. In his four subsequent elections, for the most part, Drinan failed to secure large margins of victory—enduring controversy about a priest serving in Congress prevented him from the comfortable reelection bids typically enjoyed by incumbents. Unopposed in his next three Democratic primaries, Drinan made modest gains in the general elections, earning 49, 51, and 52 percent of the vote, respectively. However, in 1978 he captured 65 percent of the vote in the primary and ran unopposed in the general election.

Drinan's appointment to the House Committee on Internal Security—formerly the House Un-American Activities Committee—during his first term in Congress added to his media spotlight. As an outspoken critic of the Committee on Internal Security and a tireless advocate for civil liberties, Drinan sponsored unsuccessful legislation to abolish the group and transfer its functions to the House Committee on the Judiciary as one of his first actions in Congress. Drinan actively pursued a spot on the controversial Committee on Internal Security with the intention of working for its demise. "I am seeking to collapse it from within," he declared. After the House passed a resolution in 1975 to terminate the committee, Drinan was appointed to the Committee on Government Operations, where he served for his final three terms in Congress. In 1977 Drinan became one of the first members of Congress to access his Federal Bureau of Investigation file under the newly implemented Freedom of Information Act. "A lot of Congressmen are afraid to ask for their files," Drinan stated. "They're afraid they don't have one." His extensive file included a series of his sermons.

During his decade in Congress, Drinan also served on the Committee on the Judiciary. He gained national fame as a member of the panel during its investigation of President Richard Nixon in the aftermath of the Watergate scandal, a political scandal that plagued Nixon's second term. Before the public backlash against Nixon gained momentum, Drinan introduced the first formal resolution for impeachment on 31 July 1973. He based his decision on Nixon's bombing of Cambodia, which he argued violated the U.S. Constitution and exceeded the president's legal power. "Can we be silent about this flagrant violation of the Constitution?," Drinan queried. He also asked, "Can we impeach a president for concealing a burglary but not for concealing a massive bombing?" Although his resolution never reached the House floor for a vote, Drinan continued his vocal opposition to the Nixon administration. He declared that members of the U.S. House must "search diligently into our convictions and our conscience as to what is our duty under the Constitution as we behold the unprecedented revelations which every day become more incredible." Less than a year later, the Committee on the Judiciary, chaired by Peter Rodino of New Jersey, held impeachment hearings concerning Nixon's role in the Watergate scandal. On 24 July 1974 the committee approved three articles of impeachment. Nixon resigned on 9 August 1974 before the House could reach a vote on the articles of impeachment.

As a member of Congress, Drinan used his political position to continue his mission to fight for social justice and world peace. He relentlessly criticized the Vietnam War and the draft; he also spoke out against world hunger and the escalating arms race between the United States and USSR during the cold war. Drinan participated in human rights missions to Argentina, Central America, Vietnam, and the Soviet Union during his decade in the House. On the domestic front, he successfully led the charge for the abolition of mandatory retirement based on age as a member of the House Select Committee on Aging. An unabashed liberal, Drinan did not always take legislative stances that coincided with the doctrine of the Catholic Church. His political decisions, including backing federal funding of abortion and opposition to constitutional amendments banning abortion and permitting prayer in public schools, generated mounting tension among some Catholic leaders who already disagreed with priests holding political office. In 1980 Pope John Paul II issued a directive barring priests from holding public office. "With pain and regret," Drinan announced his decision to abide by the Vatican decree and not to seek election for a sixth term. "It is just unthinkable," he remarked when asked if he considered leaving the priesthood. Drinan stated that he was honored to be a Jesuit priest and added, "As a person of faith, I must believe that there is work for me to do which somehow will be more important than the work I am required to leave." Drinan described his role in Congress as a "moral architect" and expressed gratitude for having the opportunity to serve in the House. Barney Frank won the election to succeed Drinan in the Ninety-seventh Congress (1981–1983).

After leaving Congress, Drinan returned to academia as a law professor at Georgetown University Law Center. He continued writing, publishing several books, including *Can God & Caesar Coexist? Balancing Freedom and International Law* (2004). He also served as president of the Americans for Democratic Action, giving speeches on world hunger, civil liberties, and the arms race. In 1998 Drinan testified before the Committee on the Judiciary during the impeachment hearings of President Bill Clinton. He characterized Clinton's misdeeds (having an affair with an aide) as private, not an official crime worthy of removal from office. During his life, Drinan earned many honorary degrees and awards, including the American Bar Association Medal (2004) and the Congressional Distinguished Service Award (2006). Drinan died at age eighty-five of pneumonia and congestive heart failure. He is buried at the Campion Center in Weston, Massachusetts. "He was a profile in courage in every sense of the word," longtime Massachusetts senator Edward Kennedy eulogized.

Drinan's decision to run for political office had deep ramifications in Massachusetts and across the country. His direct challenge of the long-standing tradition of Catholic priests shunning the political arena led to a national debate concerning the proper role of clergy in American society. A trailblazer in Congress and throughout his life, Drinan demonstrated an ability to adeptly balance his dual role as priest and politician. Characterized as "the conscience of the House of Representatives" and as "a man of faith who never stopped searching for the truth," Drinan is remembered as a political pioneer who passionately fought for world peace and human rights.

★

Papers covering Drinan's career from 1949 to 1997 are housed in the John J. Burns Library Congressional Archives, Boston College, Chestnut Hill, Massachusetts. The papers include correspondence, photographs, publications, audiotapes, videocassettes, and artifacts. No major biographies have been written about Drinan, but several secondary sources provide valuable details on his career. Robert David Johnson, *Congress and the Cold War* (2006), includes background information on Drinan's first congressional campaign. Shay Studley, "Jesuit Who Gave Up U.S. House Seat, Not Issues, Notes 50 Years as Priest," *Boston Globe* (28 June 1992), provides extensive coverage of Drinan's tenure in the House and his career after Congress. Obituaries are in the *Boston Globe* and *Washington Post* (both 29 Jan. 2007).

Kathleen Johnson

DULLES, Avery Robert (*b.* 24 August 1918 in Auburn, New York; *d.* 12 December 2008 in New York City), theologian, educator, author and, after 2001, cardinal in the Roman Catholic Church. He is best known for his 62 years of penetrating theological writings, including 800 essays and 24 books written after he entered the Society of Jesus in 1946.

Dulles was the second son of John Foster Dulles (later U.S. secretary of state under President Dwight D. Eisenhower) and Janet (Pomeroy Avery) Dulles. By all measures, Dulles's extraordinary remarkable life began within an extraordinary family of leaders. His grandfather, Allen Macy Dulles, a Presbyterian minister, cofounded the American Theological Society. Besides Avery's father (for whom Dulles International Airport is named), two other U.S. secretaries of state were his great-grandfather John W. Foster (under President Benjamin Harrison), and great-uncle Robert Lansing (under President Woodrow Wilson), while his uncle Allen Welsh Dulles later founded the U.S. Central Intelligence Agency under President Harry S. Truman. Young Avery completed primary school in New York City and his secondary school in Switzerland as well as at Choate. For college, he set aside his family's Presbyterian roots at Princeton to instead attend Harvard.

In 1936 Dulles entered Harvard College a confessed atheist and esthete, one who preferred the bars in Cambridge, Massachusetts, over its classrooms. But some bad experiences that first year, and a serious prank with his friends, saw all but himself expelled from Harvard. This led Dulles into serious introspection and more intense study in his sophomore year, leading to a BA Phi Beta Kappa in history and literature in 1940. His senior thesis on the Renaissance was recognized as the Phi Beta Kappa Prize essay of 1940 and was published by Harvard University Press in 1941.

While at Harvard, the atheistic Dulles converted to Christianity. In riveting detail, Dulles recounts this two-step conversion to theism, then Catholicism, in his 1946 autobiography, *A Testimonial to Grace*. In it, one sees a brilliant undergraduate in search of meaning, sifting dozens of ancient, medieval, and modern "isms," and finding clear flaws within each—Marxism, fascism, democracy. For eight months Dulles was tutored by Professor Paul Rice Doolin, a convert to Roman Catholicism, who immersed Dulles in seventeenth- and eighteenth-century French thinkers, bringing him to the brink of his first of two religious conversions—to philosophical theism, the belief that the order within nature must be the product of an intelligent will. Dulles reported this moment of revelation during a walk one rainy day in 1939 when he saw a bud on a tree and suddenly concluded that such complex life could not possibly exist without a willful creator. "That night for the first time in years, I prayed," and he never again "doubted the existence of an all-good, and omnipotent God." Within two years of that day, while starting Harvard Law School, Dulles's further theistic study drew him into the authoritative structure of the Roman Catholic Church, and he embraced Catholicism.

After eighteen months of law school at Harvard (1940–1941), then four years as an intelligence officer (lieutenant) in the U.S. Navy Reserve (1942–1946), Dulles began his long priestly journey on 14 August 1946, when he entered the Novitiate of the Society of Jesus in Poughkeepsie, New York. He completed his PhL at Woodstock College in 1951 and was ordained to the priesthood in the Fordham University Church by Francis Cardinal Spellman on 16 June 1956. He pursued further Jesuit training in Münster, Germany (1957–1958) and completed his Doctorate in Sacred Theology in 1960 in Gregorian University in Rome. Dulles chose the Jesuits to match his own gifts and temperament—an order known for its scholarship, boldness, evangelism, and heart for service.

Dulles was a lifelong teacher—first of philosophy at Fordham University in the New York City borough of the Bronx (1951–1953), then, after earning his doctorate, of theology at Woodstock College in Woodstock, Maryland (1960–1974), and Catholic University of America in Washington, D.C. (1974–1988). Upon his "retirement" at age seventy in 1988, he intended to return to Fordham for one year as the Laurence J. McGinley Professor of Religion and Society, but he remained at Fordham until his death in 2008. During these fifty-eight years, the tireless Dulles also held visiting posts at a dozen universities in the United States, the United Kingdom, Italy, and Belgium.

During this time, Dulles was also a gifted writer of 800 essays and 24 volumes translated into a score of languages. *A Testimonial to Grace* was rereleased and expanded on its fiftieth anniversary in 1996. His most used textbook was *Models of the Church* (1974), which was revised and translated many times, along with *Models of Revelation* (1983).

In 1956 Dulles's ordination made front-page news in the *New York Times*, which noted his conversion from a prominent Presbyterian family. Dulles again made history on 21 February 2001 in Rome, when he was one of forty-four priests summoned by Pope John Paul II to be elevated to cardinal. Dulles's ascension to that rank was extraordinary in many ways. His adult conversion to Catholicism, his advanced age of eighty-two, his Jesuit affiliation, the fact that he had never been an archbishop or even bishop—all made it remarkable that he was "the first American theologian to be elevated to cardinal." With modesty, Dulles later recalled "I enjoyed it, but that's not what really counts.... I'm not particularly made for ceremonies." This also made Fordham the first American university ever to have a resident cardinal on its campus. Pope Benedict XVI made it a point to meet Dulles privately during his whirlwind visit to New York on 19 April 2008.

As a person, Dulles was lean and handsome, six feet, two inches tall, with a broad brow and ready smile. He was soft-spoken and gracious. In his eighties, a return of childhood polio caused him to rely on a cane.

In his theology, Dulles was widely regarded as "the Dean of American Catholic theology," across many diverse specialties—ecclesiology (the study of the church), revelation, faith, apologetics, and ecumenism. Dulles served as president of both the Catholic Theological Society of America (1975–1976) and the American Theological Society (1978–1979). After the reforms of the Second Vatican Council in the 1960s, Dulles's special expertise was to harmonize orthodox theology with the church's attempts at reform, as well as timely social issues. His thirty-nine semiannual McGinley Lectures at Fordham addressed such challenging questions as the death penalty, evolution, Hell, forgiveness, human rights, even "Should the church repent?" In 2002, when a contentious conference of U.S. Catholic bishops grappled with dreadful allegations of sexual abuses by clergy, all eyes repeatedly turned to Dulles for guidance. He also had great respect for non-theologian priests, noting that "Unlike the theologian who studies the Word, the priest bears the Word." At his eulogy, the rector of his Jesuit community observed, "As a Jesuit, he was called to live at the heart of the Church and at the same time at the frontier"—to embody the church's central principles while sharing these with others at the periphery.

Dulles died at age ninety in the Fordham University infirmary in the Bronx. The cause of death was complications of the polio that he had contracted as a young man. He is buried in the Jesuit cemetery at the Shrine of the North American Martyrs in Auriesville, New York.

Throughout his career, Dulles inspired an ever widening circle of students and colleagues, readers of his books, then Catholic laity and the public at large. Dulles visibly used his illness during his final years to serve as inspiration to others; a clear example is the McGinley Lecture on the night of 7 November 2007. With his polio, Dulles sat on stage as his prepared forty minute message was read aloud. With penetrating insight, Dulles carefully defined grace, clarified its importance, applied the church's teaching to this timely question, and concluded that even non-Christian souls could conceivably be "saved" by the grace of Jesus. After this lecture, Dulles granted a personal audience to a line of 300 admirers and became a living example of the biblical story in Luke 8:40–48, where Jesus was pressed by a crowd but still offered a "healing touch."

★

More insight into Dulles and his life are in *A Testimonial to Grace, and Reflections on a Theological Journey* (1996); this edition is an expanded reprint to mark fifty years of the 1946 autobiography. *Models of the Church* (1974) is a great textbook and has been revised and reprinted in many languages. *Models of Revelation* (1983) has been twice revised. *Church and Society: The Laurence J. McGinley Lectures, 1988–2007* (2008) is a compilation of all thirty-nine public lectures. An obituary is in the *New York Times* (14 Dec. 2008).

Harold Takooshian
John J. Cecero

DUNHAM, Katherine (*b.* 22 June 1909 in Chicago, Illinois; *d.* 21 May 2006 in New York City), dancer, choreographer, activist, and educator who was a pioneer of the modern dance aesthetic and African-American artistic expression.

Dunham was the second of two children born to Albert Millard Dunham, an African American who ran a dry-cleaning business, and Fanny June (Guillaume) Taylor Dunham, an assistant school principal of French-Canadian and Native American ancestry. The family, which included her mother's three children from a previous marriage and her grandchildren, lived in Glen Ellyn, a suburb of Chicago. After her mother's death when Dunham was four, her childhood was marked by upheaval and financial difficulties. She and her brother went to live with various family members until settling with their father, whose discipline over the years became increasingly harsh, and his new wife in Joliet, Illinois.

Dunham discovered music and dance while living with her aunt and other relatives on her father's side. There were several musical performers in her father's family, and it was with them that Dunham first experienced the pleasure of melody and dance. Encouraged by her aunt, she began to study dance at age nine. At age seventeen she entered Joliet Junior College and then went on to the University of

Katherine Dunham. **AMERICAN STOCK/GETTY IMAGES**

Chicago on scholarship to study anthropology. She continued to take dance lessons, and eventually formed Ballet Nègre, a black student dance company that developed into the Katherine Dunham Dance Company. The company gave recitals in a storefront and offered lessons to city children. Dunham married Jordis McCoo in 1931; they divorced in 1938. She danced professionally in 1934 with the Chicago Opera and at the Chicago World's Fair.

Dunham's keen interest in anthropology led her to study the survival of African culture and ritual in the former slave societies of the New World. She wanted to know "what we are really like as against what we have been made into by slavery and colonialism." The slave owners of the Caribbean had allowed African culture to flourish more freely than did their U.S. counterparts. For example, U.S. slaves by and large were not allowed to own drums or other musical instruments. This was not the case in the Caribbean. And thus Dunham was driven to explore African culture as it had evolved on the islands.

After receiving her BA in anthropology from the University of Chicago in 1936, she won a fellowship to do fieldwork in African culture, particularly dance, in the Caribbean. This turned out to be a crucial point in her development. She spent eighteen months during 1935 and 1936 in Haiti, Jamaica, Martinique, and Trinidad, most of the time in isolated communities where African traditions and practices had survived almost untouched. In the exciting African-based forms of movement she encountered, she saw the elements of a new modern dance vocabulary. She began to codify this vocabulary, developing the Dunham technique, which became a pillar of twentieth-century modern dance. The technique, which encompasses polyrhythms, isolated movement of the limbs, body flexibility, articulation of the pelvis, and improvisation, continues to be taught widely.

Returning to Chicago in 1937, Dunham began work on a master's degree in anthropology from Northwestern University. She then made a pivotal decision: she turned down a Rockefeller Foundation grant in anthropology to pursue a full-time career in dance. She launched it successfully in 1938 for the Chicago Federal Theater Project with *L'Ag'Ya*, a ballet based on a Martinique fighting dance. Showing her particular combination of acute organizational skills and multiple artistic talents, Dunham formed the first African-American modern dance company, choreographed and directed the work, danced a feature role, and created the costumes. On 10 July 1941 she married John Pratt, a white Canadian designer who had worked with her on *L'Ag'Ya*. Thereafter he would design all her sets and costumes. They adopted a four-year-old girl in 1951. Pratt died in 1986.

From 1939 through 1945 Dunham turned her attention to the stage and films, taking her company to New York and then to Hollywood. Dunham choreographed a number for the popular Broadway musical revue *Pins and Needles*, which went into the show in 1939; then she and her entire company appeared, with the star Ethel Waters, in the 1940 black musical *Cabin in the Sky*, with choreography by George Balanchine. Though not credited for it, Dunham collaborated on the dances with Balanchine. This was followed by Sol Hurok's *Tropical Revue*, which opened in New York in 1943 and toured nationally until 1945, and *Bal Nègre*, which toured for nine months in 1946 before opening in New York to critical acclaim. She danced in the film *Star Spangled Rhythm* (1942) and performed with her company in *Stormy Weather* (1943), a smash-hit all-black musical film starring Lena Horne and Bill "Bojangles" Robinson. In 1945 she opened the Dunham School of Dance and Theater in New York. Dunham financed the school, which survived for thirteen years, with revenues from performing. At its peak it served 400 students with a faculty of 30. Among the noted actors and dancers who studied at the school were Eartha Kitt (who later joined Dunham's company), Marlon Brando, James Dean, Peter Gennaro, Chita Rivera, and José Ferrer.

Dunham broke new ground between 1947 and 1949 when she took her full company on tours of Mexico and Europe. She became a postwar sensation, with both critics and audiences hailing the originality and verve of her art of the black diaspora. The London *Observer* in 1948 compared the impact of her visit there to that of the fabled arrival of Serge Diaghilev's Ballets Russes in Paris in 1909. True to her dual interests, while in London she delivered a lecture, "The State of Cults Among the Deprived," before the Royal Anthropological Society.

Strongly drawn to Haiti, in 1949 Dunham purchased a home there that became her primary residence. She was ordained a priestess in the local vodun religion and made sizable charitable and cultural contributions to the Haitian people.

During the 1950s Dunham developed a worldwide following. She created dozens of new productions as the company traveled almost nonstop, performing in the United States, Mexico, Australia, New Zealand, and more than fifty other countries in Europe, North Africa, South America, and the Far East. She won her success in the face of widespread racism, mounting antidiscrimination protests, suing a Brazilian hotel that would not allow her to share a hotel room with her own husband because of their racial difference, refusing to perform before segregated audiences, and turning down a lucrative Hollywood contract because she would not replace darker-skinned dancers in her troupe.

Plagued by arthritis, Dunham ended her performing career and disbanded the company during the early 1960s. She found a rewarding alternative in 1964 when she began an eighteen-year association as an artist-in-residence on the campuses of Southern Illinois University. In 1967 Dunham

was assigned to the Edwardsville campus, not far from East St. Louis, one of the poorest and most violent cities in the United States. Appalled by the deprivation she saw, she took up residence with her husband in the ghetto and spent most of each year there into the 1980s. Despite a constant battle for funds, Dunham established a Performing Arts Training Center and a museum. She used the arts to combat poverty and urban unrest and to show ghetto youth the richness of their cultural heritage.

The institutions she created continue to thrive as the Katherine Dunham Centers for Arts and Humanities in East St. Louis, under the aegis of Southern Illinois University. The centers provide a curriculum in Dunham technique, ballet, percussion, and jazz dance as well as summer camps and a children's workshop with both artistic and educational programs. The Dunham Museum houses African and Caribbean sculptures, ceremonial costumes, paintings, musical instruments, and tapestries from Dunham's collection.

Dunham's relationship with the university gave her considerable freedom to pursue other projects. She directed the French singer Charles Aznavour in a musical comedy in Paris (1965), provided choreography for John Huston's film *The Bible: In the Beginning . . .* (1966), helped train the national ballet of Senegal (1966–1967), directed the world premiere of Scott Joplin's opera *Treemonisha* (1972), taught for a semester at the University of California at Berkeley (1976), and taped a performance of her *Rites de Passage* for the Public Broadcasting Service program *Divine Drumbeats: Katherine Dunham and Her People* (1980).

In 1992, at the age of eighty-two, Dunham drew headlines when she went on a forty-seven-day hunger strike to protest the U.S. policy of forced repatriation of Haitian refugees. She ended her fast at the request of the exiled Haitian president Jean-Bertrand Aristide.

Dunham was one of the recipients of the 1983 Kennedy Center Honors and in 1989 was awarded the Presidential Medal of the Arts. Among her many other accolades were fifteen honorary degrees, membership in the French Legion of Honor, and the Samuel Scripps Dance Prize. In 1987 the Alvin Ailey American Dance Theater in New York, which teaches her technique, presented *The Magic of Katherine Dunham*, a three-act production that reconstructed several of Dunham's dances and showcased her dance styles. Dunham was too frail to travel to an Oprah Winfrey show in California in the spring of 2006 where Oprah celebrated Dunham and others whose careers had impelled her forward as a young black woman. Soon after, Oprah was able to invite Dunham to a New York party where a film of the California show would be shown. Dunham was in a wheelchair, and Oprah went to her knees so that they could speak face to face, and she told Dunham how profoundly Dunham had inspired her. A few weeks later, on 21 May 2006, Dunham died peacefully in her sleep. Her remains were cremated, and disposition was private.

Dunham played a major role in twentieth-century modern dance. A pioneer, she created a new and influential vocabulary of movement based on Afro-Caribbean sources. Called the Dunham technique, it is taught widely to this day. She found great success as a choreographer, dancer, and actress on Broadway and in Hollywood films and as the director of the Katherine Dunham Dance Company, which toured the world for more than two decades. She gave freely of herself as a philanthropist, teacher, and writer. Born black in a severely racist society, Dunham was a triumphant champion of African, Caribbean, and African-American culture and a militant fighter against racism and injustice.

Dunham's two memoirs are *A Touch of Innocence* (1959), a chronicle of her early life told in a third-person narrative, and *Island Possessed* (1969), which covers the two decades of her life as a resident of Haiti. Her two works of Caribbean cultural research are *Katherine Dunham's Journey to Accompong* (1946) and *Dances of Haiti*. She also wrote *Kasamance: A Fantasy* (1974). Works by and about Dunham are gathered in VèVè A. Clark and Sara E. Johnson, eds., *Kaiso! Writings By and About Katherine Dunham* (2005). An early biography is Ruth Biemiller, *Dance: The Story of Katherine Dunham* (1969), and a later one is Joyce Aschenbrenner, *Katherine Dunham: Dancing a Life* (2002). Dunham's influence is discussed in Richard A. Long, *The Black Tradition in American Dance* (1989). Obituaries are in the *Chicago Tribune* (22 May 2006) and the *New York Times* and *Guardian* (both 23 May 2006). A series of thirty-four instructional videos illustrating the Dunham technique are available online from the Library of Congress Performing Arts Encyclopedia at http://www.loc.gov.

Donald L. Maggin

E

EAGLETON, Thomas Francis (*b.* 4 September 1929 in St. Louis, Missouri; *d.* 4 March 2007 in Richmond Heights, Missouri), three-term U.S. senator who was briefly the Democratic vice presidential nominee in 1972.

Eagleton was the younger of two sons born to Mark David Eagleton and Zitta Louise (Swanson) Eagleton. Eagleton's Swedish mother instilled in Thomas and his brother the importance of education. After Zitta died in 1948, Eagleton's father remarried and had another son. Born to Irish immigrants, Mark rose from poverty to become a successful trial lawyer. He was also elected to the local school and police boards. With his father's keen political interests, young Thomas was reared to develop his own affinity for politics. He attended the exclusive St. Louis Country Day School and was tutored in public speaking and public affairs. In 1940 he accompanied his father to the Republican National Convention, where Mark backed the Republican presidential nominee Wendell Willkie. In 1946 Eagleton and his father traveled to Fulton, Missouri, to hear Winston Churchill's historic Iron Curtain speech describing the emergent sphere of Soviet influence in Europe. Eagleton later remarked about his early attraction to politics, "I became fascinated. The way other kids wanted to be farmers or firemen or cowboys, I wanted to be a politician."

During his undergraduate years at Amherst College in Amherst, Massachusetts, Eagleton honed his political skills by becoming active in student politics. He served in the U.S. Navy as an apprentice seaman from 1948 to 1949. After graduating with honors from Amherst College with a BA in 1950, he spent the summer in Oxford, England, before returning to Massachusetts to attend Harvard Law School. He earned his law degree from Harvard, graduating again

with honors, in 1953. Eagleton next returned to St. Louis, where he was admitted to the bar and joined his father's law firm. For a short time he was the assistant general counsel for Anheuser-Busch, but soon he turned his attention toward political pursuits. In 1956 Eagleton married Barbara Ann Smith, who would remain his wife for more than fifty years. Three weeks after their wedding, Eagleton announced his intention to run for St. Louis circuit attorney. He was elected in 1957, becoming the youngest person to serve in the St. Louis circuit attorney position. The election also marked the beginning of an electoral winning streak that spanned his entire political career. Eagleton and his wife settled into their new life, and Eagleton worked long hours to reduce a tremendous backlog of casework. The couple had a son in 1959 and a daughter in 1963.

In 1960 Eagleton ran for Missouri attorney general. An intense campaigner, he worked himself to the brink of exhaustion. Eagleton's youthfulness, enthusiasm, and passionate speaking style served him well on the campaign trail. His election made him the youngest person to serve in the attorney general office as well as the first Roman Catholic to win statewide office in Missouri. As attorney general Eagleton took an interest in consumer protection. In response to citizen complaints about deceptive business practices, Eagleton sent warning letters to the offending companies. These persuasive letters, though not enforceable, often influenced the companies to improve their practices. The ambitious young politician next became Missouri's youngest lieutenant governor, elected in 1964. Under Missouri Governor Warren E. Hearnes, Eagleton became one of the most active lieutenant governors in the state's history, taking the lead on issues ranging from education to crime and delinquency.

121

Thomas F. Eagleton, 1972. AP IMAGES

On 11 September 1967 Eagleton announced his Democratic candidacy for the U.S. Senate, challenging incumbent Democratic senator Edward V. Long. A third Democratic candidate, the wealthy businessman and diplomat True Davis, also entered the race. Vastly outspent by his opponents, Eagleton relied on grassroots organization and a relentless campaign schedule. His platform focused on his strong opposition to the Vietnam policies of the Lyndon B. Johnson administration as well as the critical state of American cities, two issues that Eagleton believed were "inextricably intertwined." "We cannot spend some [$]30 billion . . . a year in Vietnam, go around policing the world, and still hope to have safe streets at home," he argued. Nearing the end of the primary campaign, Eagleton received a major boost when he was endorsed by most of the state's major newspapers. On 6 August 1968 he emerged victorious with 36.7 percent of the vote in the Democratic primary. Eagleton faced another difficult race in the general election against the Republican candidate Thomas B. Curtis, a long-serving member of the U.S. House of Representatives. In the November 1968 election, Eagleton narrowly defeated Curtis with 51 percent of the vote.

Eagleton, dubbed Missouri's "boy wonder," arrived in Washington, D.C., in late 1968. He quickly established a reputation in the Senate as a hard-working, driven, and passionate lawmaker, introducing legislation to address financial crises in inner-city schools. He engaged in efforts to reduce the defense budget, stating that the federal government needed to modify its spending priorities and provide more federal assistance to address racial injustice and urban unrest. In 1970 Eagleton accepted the unpopular chairmanship of the Senate District of Columbia Committee and addressed the issue of home rule for the district. He also championed environmental legislation, serving as one of the principal sponsors of the Clean Air Act of 1970 and the Clean Water Act of 1972. In 1971 he delivered the Democratic Party response to President Richard Nixon's State of the Union address.

In June 1972 Eagleton was thrust into the national spotlight when the Democratic presidential nominee George McGovern asked him to be his running mate. McGovern had been turned down by as many as six other individuals, including Senators Edward M. Kennedy and Gaylord Nelson, before offering the vice presidential nomination to Eagleton only minutes before the convention deadline. Within days of the nomination, news reports began to surface about the state of Eagleton's mental health. The story quickly became a media maelstrom. On 25 July 1972 the two candidates held a press conference during which Eagleton revealed that he had previously been hospitalized for "nervous exhaustion and fatigue" on three occasions and had received psychiatric counseling and electroshock therapy for depression. He explained that he had overworked himself in the past, but he assured voters that he had learned to pace himself. McGovern expressed his confidence in Eagleton and memorably insisted, "I am one-thousand percent for Tom Eagleton and have no intention of dropping him from the ticket." False news reports that Eagleton had been arrested for drunk driving added more fuel to the media frenzy. By 31 July 1972, with the story still dominating the news, McGovern asked Eagleton to withdraw from the ticket. What came to be known as the Eagleton affair left the first-term senator a national celebrity and garnered him a great deal of public sympathy. Reflecting on the ordeal years later, McGovern stated, "If I had it to do over again, I'd have kept him. I didn't know anything about mental illness. Nobody did."

Eagleton returned to the Senate, becoming a leading voice against the Vietnam War and unchecked presidential war powers. He considered his greatest legislative accomplishment his 1973 appropriations amendment that halted the bombing of Cambodia, an instrumental step toward ending U.S. involvement in Vietnam. Eagleton was also a leading sponsor of the War Powers Act, believing that Congress needed to reassert its constitutional authority to wage war. Although he was the principal author of the original bill, he voted against the final version in 1973. He contended that the amended bill no longer achieved its purpose because it gave the president leeway to deploy troops without congressional approval. On the Senate floor he argued that the bill would "make permanent by statute the President's current misuse of power through a procedure which seeks only to limit that misuse rather that to prohibit it altogether." His concern for the issue led him to write *War and Presidential Power: A Chronicle of Congressional Surrender* (1974).

Reelected in 1974 and again in 1980, Eagleton worked in the Senate for eighteen years. He was instrumental in the creation of the National Institute on Aging and played a significant role in the creation of social legislation regarding education, children with disabilities, health care, and services for older Americans. He was also the leading Senate proponent of the Inspector General Act of 1978, which established inspectors in federal agencies to investigate waste, fraud, and mismanagement. In 1984 Eagleton announced that he would not seek reelection, stating, "public offices should not be held in perpetuity." He also acknowledged his disdain for rampant campaign spending and partisan rancor and explained his frustration with the inefficiency of the Senate and the filibuster.

After retiring from the Senate in 1987 at age fifty-seven, Eagleton returned to St. Louis, joined the legal firm of Thompson Coburn, LLP, taught courses in public affairs at Washington University, and wrote a newspaper column for the *St. Louis Post-Dispatch*. He also coauthored a book for children titled *Our Constitution and What It Means* (1987). Targeting an adult audience, Eagleton wrote *Issues in Business and Government* (1991). A lifelong sports fan, he led the effort to move the Rams football franchise from Los Angeles to St. Louis in 1995. Eagleton remained active in politics, reasserting his constant concern about presidential abuse of war powers during the Iraq War and also leading a successful effort to pass a Missouri stem cell initiative. He was preparing a memoir in his final days. Eagleton died of heart and lung failure at age seventy-seven. He willed his body to Washington University for medical research.

Eagleton was admired for his integrity throughout his career. He consistently displayed a willingness to take unpopular stands. His advocacy of gun control legislation and opposition to capital punishment were not always popular positions for a candidate in conservative-leaning Missouri. Likewise, he took positions that were unpopular among his fellow Democrats. For example, he strongly opposed abortion, was critical of busing to achieve school desegregation, and supported the military draft based on his belief that "an all-volunteer army will be a poor boys' army." While in the Senate, Eagleton developed an unlikely friendship with his fellow Missouri senator, the Republican John Danforth. The two men held joint constituent meetings and worked side by side in the Senate for a decade. Upon Eagleton's retirement from the Senate, Danforth remarked, "what has set Tom Eagleton apart from the rest of us is . . . his moral passion, his capacity for outrage, his insistence that justice be done, that wrongs be made right."

With his good humor Eagleton was well liked among his colleagues, but he was also known for his intensity and his often anxious disposition. Throughout his political career Eagleton maintained a friendly and informal demeanor, insisting that everyone call him "Tom." Six feet tall, handsome, and gregarious, he was an appealing politician. Eagleton was known for his irrepressible sense of humor and self-deprecating manner. "He saw the ridiculous in things," Danforth commented.

The Thomas F. Eagleton Papers are housed at the Western Historical Manuscript Collection in Columbia, Missouri. Biographical sources include James N. Giglio, "'Tom, You're Not Going to Get [It] on a Silver Platter': The Inaugural Senate Campaign of Thomas F. Eagleton," *Missouri Historical Review* 102, no. 3 (Apr. 2008), an analysis that makes extensive use of Eagleton's papers. For tributes to the senator, see the Senate publication *Tributes to the Honorable Thomas F. Eagleton in the United States Senate, upon the Occasion of His Retirement from the Senate* (1986), a volume that also includes a lengthy collection of Eagleton's speeches arranged by subject. An oral history interview with Eagleton (1998) is available at the Western Historical Manuscript Collection in Columbia. Will Sarvis, "'I Enjoyed My Work in the Senate': An Oral History Interview with Thomas F. Eagleton," *Missouri Historical Review* 102, no. 1 (Oct. 2007): 42–57, also provides information about Eagleton's life. Obituaries are in the *New York Times* and *Washington Post* (both 5 Mar. 2007).

Mary Baumann

ELDER, Will (*b.* 22 September 1921 in New York City; *d.* 15 May 2008 in Rockleigh, New Jersey), comic book artist and illustrator who helped launch *Mad* magazine and created the naughty satire "Little Annie Fanny" for *Playboy*.

Elder (sometimes known as "Bill" and later nicknamed "Chicken Fat") was born Wolf Eisenberg, one of four children of Polish parents who were of modest means. His father, Morris, worked in a clothing factory as a suit-presser. His mother was a homemaker. As a young man, Elder developed a love for comics and comedy. His father made sure he saw the Sunday funnies by placing them on his son's bed. Elder pranks were notorious in the neighborhood, and he was known as a class clown. His sense of humor was offbeat and more than a bit macabre: He once "hanged" himself in a school closet, his face chalked white, and waited to be discovered by his teacher. For another gag, he spread meat and old clothes on some train tracks then screamed for help—a friend had fallen on the rails.

Elder attended the High School of Music and Art in New York City, where he met Harvey Kurtzman. Both would grow up to be artists for E.C. Comics, which during the 1950s featured gory and controversial stories. He continued his studies at the Academy of Design and graduated in 1940. Two years later Elder was drafted into the Army Air Forces, serving was a map designer. He was present at the storming of the beaches at Normandy and fought in the Battle of the Bulge. In 1946 he returned to New York and received his first professional assignment, with *Toytown Comics*, drawing the comic strip "Rufus Debree" about a garbage man who time-trips to the days of King Arthur. Next, Elder had a stint in advertising for a publishing house before reconnecting with Kurtzman and Charlie Stern, another school chum, to form the Charles William Harvey Studio. In 1948 Elder and John Severin of the studio worked for *Prize Comics Western*, providing cover illustrations and creating the feature "American Eagle." Also in 1948 Elder married Jean Strashun. They had a son and a daughter.

At the end of 1950 Elder joined Kurtzman at E.C. Comics, where he and Stern illustrated *Two Fisted Tales*, *Frontline Combat*, *Weird Fantasy*, and several science-fiction stories, including an adaptation of Ray Bradbury's "King of the Grey Spaces." Such dramatic fare was not quite the thing, however, to suit Elder's outrageous sense of humor. It was Kurtzman who provided that outlet by founding, in 1952, *Mad* magazine, in many ways the perfect outlet for Elder's talents. Indeed, Kurtzman later credited Elder with shaping the irreverent humor magazine into the outrageous cultural phenomenon that it would become.

Elder's forte was creating parodies of comic book icons such as Mickey Mouse, Popeye, and Archie. His taste for outrageous antics carried over, too. He sometimes inserted controversial signs and messages in his work for *Mad* and for *Panic*, a sister magazine to which he contributed from 1954 to 1956. For example, he once penned a derisive take on Clement Clarke Moore's "A Visit from Saint Nicholas" ("'Twas the Night Before Christmas") that denigrated Santa Claus; the mockery was reported in many newspapers as a scandal, and the issue was banned in Boston.

Elder's *Mad* covers were richly laden with details within details: On one typically dense example, a private investigator (P.I.) is covered in blood-red kisses by a red-headed femme fatale who wears a skull-and-crossbones tattoo on her arm. The P.I. holds a whiskey bottle with two yellow daisies. A green-faced witch lights sticks under his fingernails. A victim lies on the floor with a cleaver splitting his head, a flaming arrow through his temple, four swords in his chest, and a yellow and red dart piercing his skin. A black-masked hood points a gun at the P.I. while an old, wrinkled nanny pushes a baby carriage from which a

monstrous hand emerges holding an intravenous bottle filled with purple liquid. Two shrunken heads hanging from a miniature swing set stare ahead.

Elder went on to draw for Hugh Hefner's *Trump* magazine, but soon reunited with Kurtzman as a staff artist for the magazines *Help!* and *Humbug*. His parodies included "Around the World in 80 Days" and "Tarzan." With Kurtzman, he created the popular "Goodman Beaver" feature for *Help!*

Elder contributed to the early issues of *Cracked*, a *Mad* magazine imitator in 1959. He returned to advertising for a television spot and rendered the film poster for *Mr. Hobbs Takes a Vacation* (1962). In 1962 Elder returned to working with Hefner, becoming the lead artist on *Playboy's* "Little Annie Fanny," a sexually explicit parody of the famed comic strip *Orphan Annie*, which shared several characteristics with the "Goodman Beaver" feature. Elder worked on the irreverent feature until September 1988.

In the late 1970s Elder and Kurtzman created print ads for the American Broadcasting Company television network. As an illustrator, he painted book covers and movie posters, for example, for example, *Bank Shot* starring George C. Scott in 1974. From 1976 to 1985 he drew advertisements for *TV Guide*. In that latter year, Kurtzman and Elder returned to *Mad* magazine to produce covers and articles. The collaboration ended with Kurtzman's retirement in 1988. Elder soon followed suit.

In 2003 Elder was inducted into the prestigious Will Eisner Hall of Fame. The team of Kurtzman and Elder influenced such diverse comics creators as Art Spiegelman, Robert Crumb, and Tim Sale. In his last years Elder resided at the Jewish Home in Rockleigh. He died from complications due to Parkinson's disease.

There are no full-length biographies of Elder but many books about him and featuring his work. Useful among them are Elder and Kurtzman, *Will Elder: The Mad Playboy of Art* (2004), and Grant Geissman, *Foul Play!: The Art and Artists of the Notorious 1950s, E.C. Comics!* (2005). Obituaries are in the *Los Angeles Times* (17 May 2008) and *New York Times* (18 May 2008).

Vincent LoBrutto

ELLIS, Albert (*b*. 27 September 1913 in Pittsburgh, Pennsylvania; *d*. 24 July 2007 in New York City), psychologist who created rational emotive behavior therapy, the first form of cognitive behavior therapy, and was known as an advocate of sexual liberation.

Albert Ellis, 1970. ©BETTMANN/CORBIS

Ellis was the oldest of three children born to Henry Ellis, an insurance broker, and Hettie (Hanigbaum) Ellis, a home-maker. He was a sickly child, suffering from kidney and other ailments. His father frequently traveled on business, and he found his mother emotionally distant. When he was eleven years old his parents moved from his native Pitts-burgh to the Bronx, New York, then separated.

He attended City College (now part of the City Uni-versity of New York) and graduated with a BBA in business administration in 1934, but his subsequent efforts to start a business career during the Depression were unsuccessful. He married Karyl Corper, an actress, but the marriage was annulled in 1938. Around this time he discovered that he liked to write (though not fiction) and was fascinated by human psychology and sexuality. Friends sought out his advice, relying on his knack for psychological under-standing. In 1942 he enrolled at Columbia University to study for a PhD in clinical psychology; in 1943, having completed his MA, he went into private practice in psy-chotherapy and marriage counseling. Already willing to challenge received wisdom in the field, in 1946 he wrote an article claiming that the Minnesota Multiphasic Person-ality Inventory was the only pencil-and-paper personality test that had been sufficiently validated.

In 1947 he received his PhD from Columbia and began his training therapy under Richard Hulbeck of the Karen Horney Institute. Ellis considered Horney, the German psychologist, an important influence, along with the psychologists Alfred Adler, Erich Fromm, and Harry Stack Sullivan as well as the theory of general semantics developed by the scientist and philosopher Alfred Kor-zybski. Ellis continued his private practice in New York while working full time as a psychologist for the state of New Jersey, becoming its chief psychologist in 1950. He also taught at Rutgers University and New York University in the late 1940s.

In 1951 he published the first of many books, *The Folklore of Sex*, which initiated what would become the most notorious aspect of his career—the questioning of standard beliefs about sex. At that time he also became the American editor of the *International Journal of Sexology*, and he wrote a sympathetic introduction to Donald Webster Cory's *The Homosexual in America*. Ellis maintained that sexual mor-ality is a subset of general morality, which in his view meant that the only sex acts that are wrong are those involving force, fraud, irresponsibility, and so on.

Ellis had been trained in psychoanalysis, founded and developed by the Austrian Sigmund Freud in the late nine-teenth and early twentieth centuries. However, he became increasingly doubtful of Freud's wisdom and by 1955 was ready to propose his own approach, which at first he called rational therapy and then rational emotive therapy. The central idea came from the works of two Stoic philosophers of the ancient world, the Roman Marcus Aurelius and the Greek Epictetus, who argued that what bothers us is not what has happened to us but what we tell ourselves about what has happened to us. In keeping with this view, the painstaking exploration of childhood trauma required by Freudian psychoanalysis is unnecessary and can be replaced by questioning and challenging a person's current beliefs. (He also maintained that the Freudian distinction between "mature" and "immature" female orgasms was physiolog-ically untenable, as later studies in sexuality demonstrated.)

Another factor in the development of Ellis's ideas was his own teenage shyness. When he got older, he decided to take a direct approach to the problem by forcing himself to attempt conversation with every woman he saw sitting alone on a park bench. After 130 attempts, as he later reported, he had gotten only a single date; but he had not gotten arrested, and his shyness was gone. He thus con-cluded that questioning one's premises should be accom-panied by actual behavioral change.

Ellis brought out two more popular works that were controversial: *The American Sexual Tragedy* (1954) and *Sex Without Guilt* (1958). In 1957 he turned his rational emo-tive approach into a book of advice, *How to Live with a Neurotic*. In 1959 he founded the Institute for Rational Living to promote his therapeutic approach, and by 1968 it was chartered by the New York State Board of Regents as a training institute and psychological clinic; its name was later changed to the Albert Ellis Institute. A second marriage, to Rhoda Winter, ended in amicable divorce in 1958. In 1960 he gave what became a famous interview to the *Realist* in which he discussed words then considered unprintable. He held that such words should be used with deliberate thought and that sexual terms in particular should be used positively (if one had positive feelings about sex).

The energetic Ellis typically worked sixteen-hour days that included therapy, writing, and organizational tasks. He was president of the American Psychological Association's division of consulting psychology in 1962. Three years later he began a series of public rational emotive therapy sessions, held on Friday nights, with volunteers drawn from audiences that often numbered in the hundreds. He held these weekly sessions for more than forty years. From 1961 to 1967 he was a consultant in clinical psychology to the Veterans Administration. In 1966 he began living with his colleague Janet L. Wolfe in an open relationship that lasted until 2002. *A Guide to Rational Living* (1961) and *Reason and Emotion in Psychotherapy* (1962) presented his psychological approach in clear, nontechnical terms. He continued producing popular sex guides, such as *Sex and the Single Man* and *The Intelligent Woman's Guide to Manhunting* (both 1963). In *Homosexuality: Its Causes and Cure* (1965) Ellis took the then-radical stance that homosexual behavior as such is not a sign of mental illness, but that the avoidance of heterosexual behavior, whether for homosexual behavior or celibacy, is something to be cured.

In the 1970s he won recognition from several groups: the American Humanist Association named him Humanist of the Year in 1971, and he won the Distinguished Sex Researcher award from the Society for the Scientific Study of Sex in 1972, the Distinguished Professional Psychologist award from the American Psychological Association's Division of Psychotherapy in 1974, and the Distinguished Sex Educator and Therapist award from the American Association of Sex Educators, Counselors, and Therapists in 1976. He published *How to Master Your Fear of Flying* and *The Civilized Couple's Guide to Extramarital Adventure* (both 1972). He wrote *A New Guide to Rational Living* (1975, with Robert A. Harper) and other books in E-Prime, a modification of the English language developed by a follower of general semantics that lacks all forms of the verb *to be*. Ellis insisted that any awkwardness in the prose was more than compensated for by the elimination of the hidden assumptions contained in that seemingly simple verb. His teaching positions in the 1970s included United States International University, San Diego, and Pittsburg State University, Kansas.

In 1982 a survey of clinical psychologists ranked Ellis as the second-most influential psychotherapist in history, behind only Carl Rogers and immediately ahead of Freud. Continuing to receive accolades from his colleagues in the field, Ellis maintained his intense schedule through his eighties. In 1996 he again renamed his theory, this time as rational emotive behavior therapy (REBT), to emphasize the importance of behavioral change. In his Friday night sessions he could frequently be heard urging his clients to "Do REBT!"

In 2003 Ellis suffered from an infection that required the removal of his large intestine, followed by pneumonia. He was nursed back to health by Debbie Joffe, an Australian psychologist who became his wife in 2004. Perhaps as a result of his health problems, he fell into disputes with the board of the institute that bore his name. He was removed from the board, and his Friday night sessions were canceled. In 2006 a New York State Supreme Court judge ruled that the board had wrongfully ousted him and ordered him reinstated.

Ellis died of kidney and heart failure. He is buried in Woodlawn Cemetery in the Bronx.

Ellis was a leading figure in changing the practice of psychotherapy, from the seemingly interminable Freudian talking cure to a proactive approach in which patients are encouraged to challenge their counterproductive beliefs and take actions to change their lives. He and Aaron T. Beck, working separately, laid the foundations of what is now known as cognitive therapy, which emphasizes the role of thinking in people's behavior and feelings. He replaced the clinical-sounding terminology of traditional therapy with more vivid phrasing, such as "sex without guilt." As a sexologist, Ellis was in the forefront of the movement to accept consensual sex, in all its varieties, as a positive part of human nature and to abandon the view of female sexuality Freud and other male psychologists had established.

★

For Ellis's summation of his own life and work, see *All Out!: An Autobiography* (2007). In Ellis, *Rational Emotive Behavior Therapy: It Works for Me—It Can Work for You* (2004), he presents his own life as an example of how REBT can be helpful. For an examination of Ellis's influence, see Emmett Velten, *Under the Influence: Reflections of Albert Ellis in the Work of Others* (2007), and for a full-scale biography, see Velten, *Albert Ellis: American Revolutionary* (2009). In "Ageless, Guiltless," *New Yorker* (13 Oct. 2003): 42–43, Adam Green talks to Ellis about his life and ideas on the occasion of his ninetieth birthday. An obituary is in the *New York Times* (25 July 2007).

Arthur D. Hlavaty

EPSTEIN, Barbara Zimmerman (*b*. 30 August 1928 in Boston, Massachusetts; *d*. 16 June 2006 in New York City), book and magazine editor, one of the founders and the longtime coeditor of the *New York Review of Books*, the widely respected journal of critical comment.

Epstein, the younger of two daughters of Harry W. Zimmerman, a textile merchant, and Helen (Diamond) Zimmerman, a homemaker, grew up in Brookline, a suburb of Boston. She attended the prestigious Girls' Latin School in Boston and at the age of sixteen went on to Radcliffe College, from which she graduated with an AB in 1949. Her friend and classmate, the scholar and writer Alison Lurie, recalled meeting Epstein for the first time: "Bubsey" (as she was then called) sat smoking in the college cafeteria surrounded by a stack of books, making "scarily brilliant" comments in her characteristically soft voice.

After college Epstein went to New York to enter the world of publishing, at that time a very difficult task for a young woman without connections. After a year of persistent efforts, she landed a job as a junior editor at Doubleday & Company, where she won recognition for her work on the first American edition of *Anne Frank: The Diary of a Young Girl* (1952). From Doubleday she went on to editorial positions at E. P. Dutton, McGraw-Hill, and, in 1963, the journal *Partisan Review*. In 1954 she married Jason Epstein, a fellow editor at Doubleday who later became the editorial director of Random House. The couple had two children, Jacob, a writer and film producer, and Helen, a scientist and writer on public health issues.

The Epsteins' duplex apartment on New York's Upper West Side, where Barbara Epstein lived the rest of her life, became a center for gatherings of luminaries of the literary and publishing worlds. When the New York newspapers were shut down for almost four months by a printers' strike beginning in the winter of 1962, the publishing industry found itself threatened by the loss of publicity in the form of both advertisements and reviews in the weekly *New York Times Book Review*. At a dinner party at the Epsteins' one evening early in 1963, they and their guests, the poet Robert Lowell and his wife, the writer and critic Elizabeth Hardwick, came up with the idea to put out their own more serious and responsible book review. The *New York Review of Books* (*NYRB*) was soon launched, with Barbara Epstein and Robert B. Silvers, previously the editor of *Harper's* magazine, as coeditors.

Epstein and Silvers remained—uniquely, in the organization of most magazines—the sole chief editors for the next forty-three years. They alone selected the books to be reviewed and the writers of the reviews. By an informal agreement, Epstein handled the arts and literature, Silvers the sciences, history, and politics. But Epstein read every piece published in every issue of "the paper" (as she always called it). "We were such close partners in the way of sharing every commission, every manuscript, every decision," Silvers recalled shortly after her death. The founder-shareholders, not the publisher, always had entire control of editorial policy—another rarity in magazine publishing.

The first issue of the *NYRB* came out on 1 February 1963. "To the Reader," the editors' note that introduced

it, announced that the new journal would spend "neither time nor space...on books which are trivial in their intention or venal in their effects." On very short notice, pieces had been quickly submitted for that first issue by, among others, Hardwick and Lowell, the essayist Susan Sontag, the poet W. H. Auden, and the novelists Norman Mailer and Gore Vidal. None of the contributors was paid, as the journal had not yet obtained funding. On 1 June 1963 a second issue appeared, though by then the newspaper strike had ended. With its fourth issue (17 October 1963), the *NYRB* began appearing twice a month. Two years later it was operating in the black, and it remained so from that point on. From the start it was published in large format on newsprint, its original "drab glory" (as one source described it) enlivened with David Levine's signature caricatures, an NYRB feature from its early years; eventually it included more photographs. In 1993 Silvers and Epstein, with Rea Hederman, the journal's longtime publisher, edited *The First Anthology: 30 Years of the New York Review of Books*, a collection of twenty-three landmark articles, including pieces by the Italian author and scientist Primo Levi on his time in the Auschwitz death camp, the political theorist Hannah Arendt on concepts of violence, and Sontag on photography.

Epstein and Silvers endeavored to make the *NYRB* a forum for in-depth discussions of politics, books, art, and culture by the best thinkers and writers they could find. Generally seen as a voice of liberal opinion, the journal was accused by some critics of a "radical chic" attitude and elitism. On the other hand, *New York* magazine once called it "the nation's preeminent journal of ideas." In 2000 the *Columbia Journalism Review* ranked Epstein and Silvers among the ten best editors of their time. In November 2006 Epstein received (posthumously), together with Silvers, the National Book Foundation's annual Literarian Award for outstanding lifetime service to the American literary community.

In 1980 Barbara and Jason Epstein were divorced. She then lived for many years with her companion, the newspaper columnist Murray Kempton, until his death in 1997. Diagnosed with lung cancer in 2005, Epstein continued working at her desk at the *NYRB* until two weeks before her death of the disease. To date her name remains on the masthead of "the paper."

For decades Epstein occupied a place in the highest echelons of the New York publishing world. Never conforming to the stereotype of the remote, powerful, aggressive editor, she dealt deftly with writers and their writings. She often demanded three or more revisions of a piece before it met with her approval, but she did so in a gentle manner. In the 26 August 2006 issue of the *NYRB*, Silvers published eleven brief memoirs by writers who had known and worked closely with Epstein over the years. They wrote of her wit and charm, her modest manner, and her nurturing but perfectionist concern for their craft. Silvers hailed her for her "superb intelligence, an exquisite sense of language, and a strong moral and political concern to expose and remedy injustice."

★

Epstein left no autobiography; although encouraged to write one, she always maintained, "Oh, I couldn't do that." Nor is there, to date, any formal biography. A useful profile is David Remnick, "Barbara Epstein," *New Yorker* (26 June 2006). James Atlas, "The Ma and Pa of the Intelligentsia,"*New York* (18 Sept. 2006), is a detailed look back at the history of the *New York Review of Books* and the achievements of Epstein and Silvers. An obituary is in the *New York Times* (17 June 2006).

Eleanor F. Wedge

ERTEGUN, Ahmet Munir (*b*. 31 July 1923 in Istanbul, Turkey; *d*. 14 December 2006 in New York City), music industry executive and cofounder of Atlantic Records.

Ahmet Ertegun. MICHAEL OCHS ARCHIVES/GETTY IMAGES

Ertegun was one of three children born to Mehmet Munir Ertegun, a distinguished Turkish civil servant, and Hayrunisa Rustem (Temel) Ertegun, the daughter of a Sufi sheik. Mehmet, a graduate of Istanbul University, served as a principal legal adviser to Mustafa Kemal Ataturk, the founder of modern Turkey. In 1925, when Ertegun was two years old, Mehmet was named ambassador to Switzerland and moved his family to Berne, Switzerland. Over the next several years Mehmet held a series of increasingly important diplomatic posts, including service as the representative to the League of Nations and minister to Switzerland (1925) and as the Turkish ambassador to Paris, France (1929); London, England (1931); and finally Washington, D.C. (1935). In 1936, in accordance with a Turkish decree that surnames be added to the names of all citizens, Ertegun's father chose the name *Ertegun*, which means "living in a hopeful future." Growing up in embassies in Europe and the United States, young Ahmet quickly became cultured and urbane, learning to speak French and English fluently at a very young age.

Ertegun's lifelong fascination with African-American music, particularly jazz, began when he was only nine years old. While his father served as ambassador to the British Court of Saint James's, Ertegun's older brother, Neshui, took him to the London Palladium in 1933 to see the Duke Ellington and Cab Calloway orchestras. Ertegun fell in love with the unique sounds of the elegant musicians, and just three years later, when his father was transferred to the United States, he and his brother happily began to explore their love of American musical forms more intensively. They frequented record stores in the Washington, D.C., area and amassed an enormous collection of jazz and blues recordings. When Ertegun's mother bought him a record cutting machine when he was fourteen years old, he amazed his friends and family by writing and recording lyrics to classic instrumental jazz music, thus creating new songs. Even at a young age, his interest in the art and science of creating and recording music was evident.

After graduating from the Landon School in Bethesda, Maryland, in 1940, Ertegun attended Saint John's College in Annapolis, Maryland, where he studied classical philosophy. However, Ertegun's first love remained music. That year Ertegun and his brother began to stage concerts at the Washington, D.C., Jewish Community Center, one of the few venues they could find that allowed both black and white individuals to attend performances together. The concerts featured such jazz greats as Lester Young. Ertegun and his brother also traveled to New Orleans and to Harlem in New York City to listen to new music. On Sunday afternoons they often held open houses for visiting jazz musicians at the Turkish embassy.

Ertegun graduated from Saint John's College in 1944 with a BA. During the same year life changed drastically for the entire Ertegun family. Ertegun's father died at the age of sixty-one, and the family was forced to leave the embassy. His mother and his sister, Selma, returned to Turkey, but Ertegun and his brother chose to remain in the United States, living in part on the income derived from selling their vast record collection. Neshui soon moved to Los Angeles. However, Ahmet, who had enrolled in the medieval philosophy doctoral program at Georgetown University before his father's death, decided to stay in Washington, D.C., to continue his studies. Even so, Ertegun spent most of his time at Max "Waxie Maxie" Silverman's Quality Music Shop, learning the retail aspects of the record business.

By 1947 Ertegun had abandoned his doctoral studies for the music industry. With a $10,000 loan from his family dentist, Ertegun began Atlantic Records with his partner, Herb Abramson, in ground-floor rooms at the run-down Jefferson Hotel in Manhattan in New York City. The independent label, principally intended as an outlet for blues and jazz, struggled to survive in the music industry but finally produced a hit record in 1949 with Stick McGhee's "Drinkin' Wine Spo-Dee-O-Dee." As a result, Atlantic began to attract a variety of recognized names in the rhythm and blues (R & B) and jazz music fields over the next several years, including Ruth Brown, the Clovers, the Drifters, the Coasters, and, most important of all, Ray Charles. The fledgling company expanded through the 1950s, and Ertegun took on two new partners, Jerry Wexler as well as his older brother, Neshui; the latter went on to sign such jazz greats as John Coltrane and Charles Mingus. Meanwhile, Ertegun and Wexler had success developing albums for artists such as Bobby Darin and Ray Charles, and Ertegun even dabbled in composition, writing several songs under the pseudonym Nugetre (his last name spelled backward), including Ray Charles's hit "Mess Around." By the end of the 1950s Atlantic had become the premier label for jazz, blues, and R & B. Atlantic was also among the first recording companies to record in stereo sound, thanks in large measure to its brilliant and innovative recording engineer Tom Dowd. Darin's hit song "Mack the Knife" was the first of many recordings by an Atlantic artist to win a Grammy Award.

During the 1960s Ertegun experienced a variety of personal and professional opportunities and challenges. On 6 April 1961 he married Ioana Maria Banu, a Romanian refugee commonly known as Mica, who went on to become a respected interior designer. (The marriage was the second for both of them; Ertegun's 1952 marriage to Jan Holm was dissolved in 1961.) Meanwhile, business at the label could not have been better, nor his selection of artists and genres better timed. As the John F. Kennedy administration held out new promise for true civil rights reform in America, African-American soul music became a major force in entertainment, and Atlantic, a longtime supporter of black musicians, was uniquely poised to prosper from this social change. Partnering with smaller labels in Memphis, Tennessee, and Muscle Shoals, Alabama, Atlantic began issuing the works of top-selling artists such as Otis Redding, Aretha Franklin, Sam and Dave, and Wilson Pickett. At the same time Ertegun was also pursuing white music groups for the label, and he signed such diverse talents as Sonny and Cher; the Rascals; the Righteous Brothers; Cream; Buffalo Springfield; Crosby, Stills, Nash, and Young; and Led Zeppelin. In a little over a decade the tiny upstart label found itself successfully competing with major companies like Columbia Records and Radio Corporation of America (RCA) Records.

At the height of its success in 1967, Atlantic was sold to Warner Bros. Seven Arts for $17 million in stock. Four years later Ertegun and his brother used a portion of their share of the sale to cofound the New York Cosmos of the North American Soccer League; they brought some of the sport's most illustrious players, including Pelé and Franz Beckenbauer, to the team. At the same time Ertegun retained creative control of and administrative responsibility for Atlantic as president through a variety of corporate takeovers. In this capacity he made major successful business deals for the company in the 1970s, when he signed lucrative recording and distribution contracts with the Rolling Stones, Bette Midler, and Genesis. By 1974 he had been promoted to chairman and chief executive officer of Atlantic.

In 1983 Ertegun established yet another music industry institution when, with *Rolling Stone* magazine founder and editor Jann Wenner, Wexler, and others, he established the Rock and Roll Hall of Fame. As a board member, he was instrumental in the selection of Cleveland as the institution's home and of the famed Chinese architect I. M. Pei to design the building. The first inductees were honored in 1986, and the museum opened nine years later on 2 September 1995. Ertegun himself was inducted into the Rock and Roll Hall of Fame in 1987, and the main exhibition hall was named for him in 1995.

Indeed, throughout the 1990s and early in the first decade of the 2000s, Ertegun was honored by a number of organizations. In 1991 he received an honorary doctorate in music from the Berklee College of Music. In 1993 he was awarded the Grammy Trustees Award. The Library of Congress named him a Living Legend in 2000, and he and his brother were inducted in 2003 into the National Soccer Hall of Fame. Also the National Academy of Recording Arts and Sciences presented Ertegun with its first President's Merit Award to Industry Icons in 2005.

On 29 October 2006 Ertegun sustained a head injury when he fell at the Beacon Theatre in New York City while backstage at a Rolling Stones concert commemorating President Bill Clinton's sixtieth birthday. After months spent in a coma, he died in a New York hospital on 14

December 2006 at the age of eighty-three, and his body was returned to his native Turkey. With many political and show business dignitaries in attendance, he was buried in the family grave on 18 December 2006 in the Garden of Sufi Tekke in Sultantepe beside his brother (who had died on 15 July 1989 from complications following cancer surgery), father, and great-grandfather. Since then, a variety of musical tributes in honor of Ertegun have been held both in the United States and in Great Britain, including a memorial concert in New York City in April 2007 featuring Eric Clapton and Phil Collins and a special performance in London in December 2007 by the reunited musical group Led Zeppelin.

Ertegun was among the most important figures in the history of modern music recordings. Not only did he establish one of America's most important and enduring record labels, but, more important, he was also a courageous advocate for African-American performers at a time when they were virtually excluded from mainstream recording and radio airplay. His love of African-American music and his support of its performers made him an influential pioneer in the music industry.

Ertegun wrote a combination autobiography and history of Atlantic titled *What'd I Say: The Atlantic Story, 50 Years of Music* (2001). For a comprehensive overview of his life and his importance to the music industry, see Robert Greenfield, "Ahmet Ertegun (1923–2006): The Greatest Record Man of All Time," *Rolling Stone* (25 Jan. 2007). Available on DVD is a May 2007 edition of the Public Broadcasting Service television series *American Masters*, titled *Atlantic Records: The House That Ahmet Built* (2007). An obituary is in the *New York Times* (15 Dec. 2006).

Leonard Mustazza

F

FALWELL, Jerry Lamon (*b*. 11 August 1933 in Lynchburg, Virginia; *d*. 15 May 2007 in Lynchburg, Virginia), fundamentalist televangelist who founded the Moral Majority and played a central role in the culture wars of the late twentieth century.

Falwell, one of five children born to Carey Hezekiah Falwell and Helen Virgie (Beasley) Falwell, grew up in relatively prosperous circumstances. His father owned a string of general stores and other businesses, including a popular dance hall, and also sponsored cockfights and dogfights and trafficked in illegal liquor. A heavy drinker with an explosive temper, Carey Falwell, who had killed a younger brother, declared himself an atheist but underwent a dramatic deathbed religious conversion when Falwell was fifteen years old. Falwell's mother remained a gentle, devout Baptist who encouraged her gregarious son to attend church and pray regularly. Although known for pulling pranks, Falwell excelled academically and graduated from Brookville High School in 1951 as valedictorian.

Falwell enrolled in Lynchburg College as a pre-mechanical engineering major. In January 1952, inspired by a radio broadcast of the Reverend Charles Fuller's *Old Fashioned Revival Hour*, Falwell visited a Baptist church in Lynchburg where he underwent what he called a "conversion experience." Shortly thereafter, he transferred to Baptist Bible College in Springfield, Missouri, a fundamentalist and unaccredited institution. He became an enthusiastic student of the Bible and served as a weekend pastor in Kansas City. Resolving to become a minister, Falwell explained his own unlikely career choice, and much of life itself, as the result of a tug-of-war between God and the Devil.

Upon graduation from Baptist Bible College in 1956, Falwell returned to Lynchburg. There, over the opposition of the local Baptist minister, Falwell established his own thirty-five-member congregation, the Thomas Road Baptist Church, in an abandoned building owned by a bottling company. While his initial followers cleaned the old brick walls, Falwell visited as many as 100 homes a day recruiting new members. Aggressively employing the grassroots organizing tactics he had learned at Baptist Bible College, Falwell could be both gracious and persistent. He kept careful files and organized follow-up visits. Within six months he launched both a daily radio broadcast and a weekly television program to promote his church. By 1957 over 800 worshippers attended services. On 12 April 1958 Falwell married Macel Pate, his longtime sweetheart and church pianist, who helped him in his recruitment efforts; they had three children. By the 1980s Thomas Road Baptist was a megachurch, with a membership close to 20,000, a facility for drug- and alcohol-dependent men, a home for unwed mothers, a Christian elementary school, and a highly successful nationwide television broadcast titled *The Old-Time Gospel Hour*, which Falwell claimed reached eighteen million viewers a week. He himself served as chancellor and president of Liberty University (which he first established in 1971 as Lynchburg Baptist College) on a sprawling nearby campus.

Beginning in the 1970s Falwell and other religious conservatives had become engulfed in a bitter battle with social liberals, often referred to as the culture wars. In the 1950s and 1960s he had been critical of ministerial involvement in the civil rights movement, in part because of his own segregationist sympathies and in part because of his fundamentalist belief that the primary role of the

Jerry Falwell, 1980. **MARK MEYER/TIME LIFE PICTURES/GETTY IMAGES**

church was personal salvation, not social reform. By the mid-1970s, however, the rise of feminism, the movement for gay rights, the growing availability of pornography, and the widespread use of illegal drugs frightened him, and he became convinced that modern secularism threatened the American family. He expressed special alarm at the Supreme Court decisions in *Engel v. Vitale* (1962), which struck down state-mandated school prayer, and *Roe v. Wade* (1973), overturning certain state restrictions on abortion. Along with other social conservatives, he opposed the Equal Rights Amendment (ERA)—a constitutional amendment proposed in 1972 to guarantee equal rights regardless of sex but never ratified—which he believed would undermine religiously based family values and traditional sex roles. In 1977 Falwell traveled to Miami to support the entertainer Anita Bryant's campaign to repeal a Dade County, Florida, ordinance banning discrimination against gays.

In June 1979, acting as a private citizen but with the encouragement of Republican political strategist Paul Weyrich, Falwell announced the formation of the Moral

Majority, an organization said to have two million members dedicated to mobilizing inactive Christians against the forces of immorality. The Moral Majority focused national attention on gay rights, pornography, the Supreme Court's ban on prayer in public schools, abortion, and the ERA. The organization endorsed a balanced national budget and higher defense spending. Partially based on elements of biblical prophecy, the Moral Majority also lobbied for uncompromising support for Israel. Attempting to reach beyond the fundamentalist Protestant core of the Moral Majority, Falwell tried, with modest success, to establish working relations with Mormons, conservative Roman Catholics, and Orthodox Jews. In the 1980 presidential election the Moral Majority supported Ronald Reagan, a Republican, over the incumbent president, Jimmy Carter, a Democrat and himself a "born-again" Christian. Falwell and his colleagues claimed to have helped register four million new voters and to have urged ten million others to go to the polls. Reagan's landslide victories in 1980 and 1984 seemed to vindicate Falwell's strategy and to foreshadow a period of unprecedented fundamentalist influence in American politics.

Such influence seems to have been exaggerated. Falwell enjoyed access to President Reagan, and came in second only to the president in a 1983 *Good Housekeeping* poll of "the most admired man in America." Reagan opposed the ERA and endorsed constitutional amendments restoring prayer in public schools and banning abortion. The president appeared sympathetic to Falwell's view that the AIDS pandemic represented a biblical curse on those engaged in homosexual practices. Reagan's priorities, however, involved libertarian economics and defense, not social issues.

Moreover, Falwell's frequently strident and pious comments made him an easy target for critics. In 1983 *Hustler* magazine, owned by the pornographer Larry Flynt, published a parody in which Falwell supposedly confessed that his first sexual encounter had occurred in an outhouse with his own mother. Falwell sued. Although the lower courts found Flynt guilty of the intentional infliction of emotional distress, the Supreme Court, in a landmark decision in 1988, reversed that decision, asserting that the First Amendment requires public figures such as Falwell to prove "actual malice" before claiming damages for emotional distress. The minister collected no damages.

Other developments also distracted Falwell from his efforts in the mid-1980s. While continuing his evangelizing and voter registration efforts, he found himself increasingly consumed by administrative and financial pressures connected with his television ministry and by Liberty University. When a series of sexual and financial scandals surfaced in the operations of certain other high-profile televangelists, this development cast a shadow on them all. In 1987 the disgraced Jim Bakker, the Pentecostal "president for life" of

PTL (Praise the Lord) ministries, handed over his administrative obligations to Falwell, who, after seven months of trying to save the operation, despaired and abandoned the effort. In 1988 the Reverend Marion "Pat" Robertson, televangelist and head of the Christian Broadcasting Network, sought the Republican nomination for president even after Falwell had pledged his support to Vice President George H. W. Bush, who ultimately won the election. The cohesion within the religious right continued to fragment. In 1989, shortly after Bush assumed the presidency, Falwell officially disbanded the Moral Majority.

Although he retained a significant following, and Republican presidential hopefuls generally sought his blessing, Falwell confronted increasing criticism in the last two decades of his life. His participation in the production of *The Clinton Chronicles* (1994), an eighty-minute video linking President Bill Clinton to illegal drug trafficking and murder, was widely condemned. Much of the press ridiculed his "discovery" in 1999 that one of the characters on *Teletubbies*, a television program for toddlers, represented a homosexual scheme to undermine traditional family life. His statement that he believed that the Antichrist was a living male Jew brought charges of anti-Semitism. Appearing on Robertson's popular television program *The 700 Club* shortly after the terrorist attacks on 11 September 2001, Falwell expressed the opinion that pagans, abortionists, feminists, gays, lesbians, and others who had tried to distance the nation from God had indirectly facilitated the terrorists—a notion promptly repudiated by President George W. Bush, whom Falwell had supported in 2000. Falwell later admitted that he had "misspoken." In 2002 his description of the prophet Muhammad as a "terrorist" provoked riots in India and prompted one ayatollah in Iran to issue a fatwa calling for Falwell's death. Wearied by such controversy and in declining health, Falwell retreated more and more into his duties at Thomas Road Baptist Church and Liberty University. He died of cardiac arrhythmia in his university office and is buried on the campus.

However offensive his statements were to many Americans in the late twentieth and early twenty-first centuries, Falwell expressed a worldview common to millions of biblical fundamentalists. Taking advantage of cable television and other new technologies, he articulated those views with considerable force, and through the Moral Majority, he helped mobilize the voting strength of cultural conservatives during the culture wars.

★

Falwell: An Autobiography (1997), an updated version of *Strength for the Journey: An Autobiography* (1987), is a full and surprisingly reflective volume, but it should be supplemented by Macel Falwell, with Melanie Hemry, *Jerry Falwell: His Life and Legacy* (2008). The best study of the *Hustler* case is Rodney A. Smolla, *Jerry Falwell v. Larry Flynt: The First Amendment on Trial* (1990). Mel White, *Religion Gone Bad: The Hidden Dangers of the Christian Right* (2006), is among the most useful critical accounts because White, who is gay, was once an aide to Falwell. Susan Friend Harding, *The Book of Jerry Falwell: Fundamentalist Language and Politics* (2000), is an excellent cultural study. David John Marley, "Ronald Reagan and the Splintering of the Christian Right," *Journal of Church and State* (Autumn 2006): 851–868, is a compelling examination of the relationship between the president and his religious supporters. Obituaries are in the *New York Times* (15 May 2007) and *Washington Post* (16 May 2007).

William Howard Moore

FEIGNER, Eddie (*b.* 25 or 26 March 1925 in Walla Walla, Washington; *d.* 9 February 2007 in Huntsville, Alabama), professional athlete, proclaimed by the *Washington Post* "beyond dispute the greatest softball pitcher who ever lived."

Born to Naomi R. Feigner, a single mother, Feigner was adopted at birth by a devout Adventist family and named Myrle Vernon King. He was raised by his adoptive mother, Mary King. There apparently was not an adoptive father.

Eddie Feigner. HY PESKIN/TIME LIFE PICTURES/GETTY IMAGES

Feigner reminisced in 1997 that he knew "the hurt and rejection" of not knowing who his birth parents were. "I spent a lot of time by myself. I threw a ball against a wall . . . and skipped thousands of stones. All that gave me a strong arm." Expelled from one high school for "troublemaking," he later attended Walla Walla College Academy. He served in the Marine Corps during World War II, though he was discharged after a nervous breakdown. Upon his return to Walla Walla, his permanent residence for most of his adult life, he changed his name, taking his birth mother's surname and the first name of a deceased friend.

In 1946 Feigner began to pitch in exhibition games against other local teams in the Pacific Northwest, albeit with a twist—his team fielded only four players (pitcher, catcher, first baseman, and shortstop) against the opposing nine. In 1950 he dubbed his four-man team "The King and His Court," and they soon became the softball equivalent of the Harlem Globetrotters, barnstorming the world in red, white, and blue uniforms. Over the next fifty-five years Feigner, sporting his trademark flattop haircut, and his revolving cast of supporting players appeared in over 10,000 games in all fifty states and ninety-eight countries before an estimated 200 million spectators, logging over four million miles and winning 95 percent of the time, once including 187 games in a row. The four-man team mostly played local amateur All-Star teams, and by his own account Feigner pitched 1,916 shutouts, 930 no-hitters, 238 perfect games, and struck out over 141,000 batters. As he told *Time* magazine in 1963, his muscular right arm "never ceases to amaze even me."

In his prime Feigner threw softballs underhand at a recorded speed of 104 miles per hour, faster than any major league baseball pitcher has ever been timed. At the height of their fame, the King and His Court played in such venues as Yankee Stadium in New York City and the Houston Astrodome, and Feigner earned $100,000 a month, though he usually shared box-office receipts with local charities. In 1967, in a two-inning exhibition at Dodger Stadium in Los Angeles, Feigner struck out six major league baseball players in succession—Willie Mays, Roberto Clemente, Brooks Robinson, Willie McCovey, Maury Wills, and Harmon Killebrew—five of whom were later elected to the National Baseball Hall of Fame. "It was a mismatch," Feigner said later. "A baseball batter has no concept how to hit a fastball that rises like mine, or sliders and curves that break 18 inches." In 1972 *Sports Illustrated* named him the most underrated athlete of his generation, and in 1981, during the Major League Baseball strike, the King and His Court defeated Magic Johnson's All-Stars, a nine-player team that included several major leaguers, before a crowd of over 16,000 at the Silverdome in Pontiac, Michigan.

A showman at his sport, Feigner pitched some innings of each game blindfolded, from his knees or from second base, sometimes even behind his back or between his legs.

With a so-called free-swinging ball socket in his shoulder that allowed him to move his arm in a complete circle, he developed nineteen different windmill windups, fourteen delivery motions, and a variety of pitch speeds and pickoff moves. A skilled batter, he once hit over eighty home runs during a 250-game exhibition season. He also became an occasional guest on such television programs as *You Asked for It*, *The Today Show*, *The Tonight Show with Johnny Carson*, *I've Got a Secret*, and *What's My Line?*

As late as 2000, at the age of seventy-five, Feigner still pitched an inning per game while on tour despite having suffered a series of strokes and heart attacks. A day after throwing out the ceremonial first pitch at the Olympic softball competition in Sydney, Australia, in 2000, Feigner suffered a stroke and never pitched again. That same year the King and His Court was ranked by *Sports Illustrated* the United States' eighth greatest team of the twentieth century in any sport. Married four times and the father of three daughters and a son who was a onetime member of Feigner's touring team, Feigner died of respiratory complications related to dementia in Huntsville, at the age of eighty-one.

In 2002 David Schoenfield of ESPN.com named Feigner one of the ten greatest pitchers of all time, a list that also included Sandy Koufax, Randy Johnson, Lefty Grove, Bob Feller, and Walter Johnson. Still, Feigner's fame waned when fast-pitch men's softball was superseded by women's softball and men's slow-pitch softball, which he regarded as "a sissy game." As his teammate Jack Knight reminisced after his death, on the field Feigner was "a master showman, brilliant pitcher, creator of the most popular softball attraction in history" and "off the field, one tough son of a gun."

★

The fullest account of Feigner's life is his privately printed autobiography, *From an Orphan to a King* (2004), though it is a mostly anecdotal memoir not entirely reliable in all details. The best articles about Feigner in newsmagazines are "Man with a Golden Arm," *Time* (23 Aug. 1963) and Curry Kirkpatrick, "A King Without a Crown," *Sports Illustrated* (21 Aug. 1972). Obituaries are in the *Washington Post* (11 Feb. 2007) and the *New York Times* (13 Feb. 2007).

Gary Scharnhorst

FELKER, Clay Schuette (*b.* 2 October 1925 in Webster Groves, Missouri; *d.* 1 July 2008 in New York City), visionary magazine editor and founder of *New York* magazine who invigorated and expanded city life reporting, and by extension magazine publishing.

Felker had strong journalistic roots. He was born in 1925 in an affluent St. Louis suburb to Carl Felker and Cora (Tyree) Felker, professional journalists. His father was managing editor of the *Sporting News* for three decades. Before having Felker and his sister, his mother worked at the *St. Louis Post-Dispatch* as the women's editor. Such a position during the industry's rough and tumble era was a coveted posting for hard-driving female journalists.

Felker attended Duke University, but he left in 1943 to join the U.S. Navy; he became a writer for *Blue Jacket*, the navy newspaper. He returned to Duke and graduated in 1951, having edited the *Chronicle*, the school's student newspaper. Duke briefly expelled him for spending a weekend off campus with Leslie Blatt (some sources list a surname of Aldrich or Aldridge), a fellow student whom he later married.

After graduation Felker worked for *Life* magazine as a sportswriter and subsequently a political reporter in Washington. He joined *Esquire* as a features editor in 1957 and began hiring top-notch literary figures such Gore Vidal and Norman Mailer, encouraging them to incorporate their discerning perspective and critical eye when writing about cutting-edge political and social issues. When Felker was passed over for the role of top editor at *Esquire*, he left the magazine and began consulting for the *New York Herald Tribune*, editing the Sunday magazine supplement *Today's Living*, which he renamed *New York* in 1968.

Felker purchased *New York* from a failing *Herald Tribune* for about $1 million with the help of financial backers. Developing a new formula, Felker broke journalistic ground, becoming an early driving force of New Journalism. The vehicle for Felker became *New York* magazine, a stand-alone he launched in 1969 as founding editor. Through the revamped *New York*, Felker engineered his assault on conventional reporting that leveraged literary devices. He encouraged well-known writers to incorporate novelistic techniques and use unconventional perspectives to vastly expand the boundaries and focus of conventional urban journalism.

In addition to innovations in writing, Felker's *New York* surrounded text with bold graphics, the glitzy package setting the standard and becoming the prototype for future generations of glossy, design-centric city lifestyle magazines. Milton Glaser, the highly respected graphic artist, joined Felker as *New York*'s cofounder. He provided direct, innovative, and simple graphics as well as headlines that emphasized the freshness and uniqueness of the new publication that celebrated a Manhattan-centered New York.

Felker challenged and changed the rules. At *New York* he hired some of the nation's edgiest, young Turk journalists—Jimmy Breslin, Pete Hamill, Gloria Steinem, Hunter S. Thompson, and Tom Wolfe—and encouraged them to ignore hidebound publishing industry rules. He urged them to take full advantage of literary techniques

and analysis when focusing on unconventional subjects, often the intriguing backstory or the story behind the story.

Detail, insight, nuance, personality, and vignette supported and enhanced critical facts, what is and was the journalists' stock and trade. Glamour, glitz, intrigue, personality, and psychology became the centerpiece of edgy, insightful journalism that offered a "hip" insider's view of New York and its social scene. In fact, *New York* magazine pages captured the essence and high energy of New York during the incendiary period of the late 1960s and the 1970s.

Felker also understood and addressed readers' needs. When introducing a "best of" column that catered to readers' insatiable lust for insider deals and bargains, he created the prototype for yet another publishing industry standard—reader-service journalism, or "News You Can Use." Prior to the appearance of Felker's *New York*, city magazines generally featured monotonous arts, culture, entertainment, and event listings set in waves of gray agate type. Accompanying feature stories followed established journalistic convention, essentially presenting only the facts. Moreover, comprehensive listings were unwelcoming, almost intimidating, to the occasional reader. The staid layout, reminiscent of a telephone directory or the daily racing forum, and predictable graphics and advertisements enticed only the most ardent "culture vultures."

Expanding his publishing reach, Felker also bought the *Village Voice* in 1974 and created *New West*, a West Coast version of *New York*, both of which the publishing titan Rupert Murdoch ultimately gobbled up. By 1977 Murdoch won a bitter takeover battle with Felker for control of *New York*; however, Felker did not give up, serving as editor of such publications as *Adweek* and *Esquire*. He developed *Manhattan, inc.*, a business lifestyle magazine that survived the stock market crash of 1987 but folded three years later.

In 1994 Felker decamped to the West Coast—he was fascinated with the goings on in Silicon Valley—and joined the nearby University of California, Berkeley, Graduate School of Journalism as a lecturer, where he taught the course "How to Make a Magazine." In 1995 he established and endowed the Felker Magazine Center and became its director.

Felker and the writer Gail Sheehy, his third wife whom he had married in 1984, moved to Berkeley in 1995, while maintaining a Manhattan residence. Felker continued to teach while fighting throat and mouth cancer. Following his death at his home in Manhattan, Felker was celebrated at memorial services in New York at the Society for Ethical Culture and on the Berkeley campus. He was survived by his wife, Sheehy; a daughter; and a stepdaughter.

Felker reinvigorated magazine journalism, serving as a mentor to the edgy writers whom he celebrated and supported. His success in providing a commercially viable and reader-friendly forum for these writers expanded the scope and reach of American magazine publishing.

★

Marc Weingarten, *The Gang That Wouldn't Write Straight* (2006), provides an overview of Felker's role in the New Journalism movement. Obituaries are in the *International Herald Tribune, Los Angeles Times, New York Times, Washington Post* (all 2 July 2008), and the *Guardian* (30 July 2008).

Ira Breskin

FELT, (William) Mark (*b.* 17 August 1913 in Twin Falls, Idaho; *d.* 18 December 2008 in Santa Rosa, California), intelligence officer who achieved a prominent career in the Federal Bureau of Investigation (FBI) and was, famously, "Deep Throat" in the Watergate scandal.

Felt was the son of Mark Earl Felt, a building contractor, and Rose R. (Dygert) Felt. He attended Twin Falls High

Mark Felt, 1976. ©BETTMANN/CORBIS

School, graduating in 1931. Four years later he earned a BA from the University of Idaho. He worked his way through college waiting tables and stoking furnaces. After college, he hoped to move to Washington, D.C., and obtain a government position that would give him time to go to law school. He approached Idaho senator James K. Pope, and to his "great good fortune" was awarded a post as a correspondence clerk. He worked every day until a quarter to five o'clock, and then went to George Washington Law School, where classes ran from five until seven o'clock. He thrived on the pressure. He married Audrey Robinson in 1938, and they had two children. He received his law degree in 1940.

After passing the Washington, D.C., bar exam in 1941, Felt applied for a legal position with the Federal Trade Commission. He found his assignments a disappointment, so, following the advice of two friends who worked for the FBI, he applied for a position as a special agent. After a rigorous physical examination and full vetting of his background, Felt was admitted as a probationary candidate.

The training began with three weeks of schooling at the new FBI academy in Quantico, Virginia. Then, Felt underwent another thirteen weeks of education in Washington, D.C. During the week classes were held from nine in the morning to nine at night and on Saturdays from nine o'clock to six o'clock. On Sundays he attended five hours of classroom work. At Quantico, the candidates were drilled (and tested) in the bureau's rules and regulations. The only hiatus in this routine—aside from an hour's break for lunch and supper—was a daily session in the gym doing calisthenics and learning judo and disarming tactics. A week was spent on the FBI's firearms range. Agents were taught to fire the .38 caliber police revolver, the twelve-gauge shotgun, and other weapons.

During his FBI training stint in Washington, D.C., Felt learned the routine of FBI work. Among other areas, students were taught how to develop evidence and write reports. They were also introduced to the bureau's highly advanced laboratory. Following his training, Felt was first appointed to Houston, where he prepared reports that were succinct and relevant—just like his boss, J. Edgar Hoover, liked them. Though Felt was next transferred to San Antonio, Texas—where the work was grueling and required long hours—he paid his dues and in 1942 was transferred to Washington, D.C.

Here Felt was named to the bureau's Espionage Section and was instructed in counterintelligence techniques. After Germany surrendered to the Allies in May 1945, closing the European theater of World War II, the Espionage Section was closed down. In 1947 Felt was promoted from special agent to supervisor. Gradually, he moved up the FBI hierarchy. In 1962 he was promoted to second-in-command of the agency's training division in

Washington, D.C. Two years later Felt was chosen chief inspector of the Inspection Division. And in 1971 he was appointed deputy associate director. Since the associate director, Clyde Tolson, was in poor health, Felt was, in effect, the FBI's second in command—poised to play a crucial role in the Watergate scandal.

In the early hours of 17 June 1972, five intruders were apprehended by Washington, D.C., police at the Democratic National Committee's headquarters in the Watergate complex. They had bugging equipment, burglary tools, and a considerable sum of money. With the bureau's acting director, L. Patrick Gray (a loyalist of President Richard Nixon), frequently out of town, Felt took charge of the Watergate investigation. At the same time, a *Washington Post* editor assigned Bob Woodward and Carl Bernstein to cover the Watergate burglary.

While Felt was managing the FBI's investigation, the *Post* reporters were conducting their own probe. Both FBI agents and the reporters, Woodward and Bernstein, discovered that the money carried by the burglars came from a bank in Mexico City. Then bureau agents uncovered copies of checks amounting to thousands of dollars, including a check for $25,000 deposited in the account of one of the burglars, Bernard Barker, which was directly linked to Nixon's campaign—the Committee to Reelect the President. Moreover, in the address books of two of the burglars was the name of E. Howard Hunt (who had once worked for the Central Intelligence Agency) and the notation "W.H"—that is, the White House.

By mid-August, Woodward and Bernstein "were running out of steam," and it is debatable whether they could have gone much further in their inquiry. So Woodward contacted Felt—the two men had met earlier in 1970 and had remained in contact—and the latter agreed to confirm the reporter's findings, or warn him when he had taken a wrong turn. Thereafter, Felt agreed to provide some information (with their rendezvous taking place in a Washington, D.C., garage). Thus, Felt informed Woodward that the attempted burglary was part of an organized attempt to spy on the Democrats, and that H. R. Haldeman, Nixon's chief of staff, had acquired funds to bankroll the break-in.

This well-informed reporting in the *Washington Post* made it obvious that Woodward and Bernstein were receiving inside information. Nixon and his confidants suspected Felt, but they were unable to prove his involvement. Felt adamantly denied that he was divulging White House business to the press.

The *Washington Post* expose did not derail Nixon's 1972 presidential campaign, as he steamrolled over the Democratic candidate, Senator George McGovern of South Dakota. But the scandal took on new life when the Watergate burglars Hunt and G. Gordon Liddy, the architect of the break-in, were convicted. In early April 1973 Felt informed Woodward that the conspiracy reached into the White House, involving Charles Colson, Nixon's special counsel, and John Mitchell, chairman of the president's campaign. On 30 April, Haldeman and the presidential assistant John Erlichman resigned over the scandal. In May the Senate began hearings into the Watergate operation, and in late July 1974 the House of Representatives passed three articles of impeachment. Thereafter, on 9 August 1974, the president resigned, brought down by Felt and the dedication of two aggressive journalists.

Felt had retired from the FBI in June 1973. Over the course of the Watergate probe, he had resisted White House interference into the FBI's investigation and had preserved the integrity of the bureau. This was the reason he had adopted the persona of Deep Throat (the term referred to a pornographic film that had entered American popular culture, as well as the journalistic label, "deep background," of a story provided by a source anonymously). It is also likely that Felt was dismayed that Nixon had not nominated him to replace Hoover, who had died in May 1972.

Felt lived quietly in retirement until, on 10 April 1978, he was indicted for having approved illegal break-ins of the homes and families of the radical Weather Underground. Felt defended himself, asserting that the searches were warranted and noting that under similar conditions he would act similarly. In April 1981 President Ronald Reagan pardoned him. Felt's role as Deep Throat was disclosed by Felt himself in the July 2005 issue of *Vanity Fair*.

Felt died at a hospice near his home in Santa Rosa. He had been suffering from congestive heart failure. His remains were cremated. As Deep Throat, Felt made an enduring contribution to investigative journalism as the whistleblower behind the Watergate story.

★

Felt and John O'Connor, *A G-Man's Life* (2006), includes details of the Deep Throat activities. Additional information is in Bob Woodward, *Shadow: Five Presidents and the Legacy of Watergate* (1999) and Woodward and Carl Bernstein, *The Secret Man: The Story of Watergate's Deep Throat* (2005). Obituaries are in the *Washington Post* (19 Dec. 2008) and *New York Times* (20 Dec. 2008).

Richard Harmond

FENDER, Freddy (*b.* 4 June 1937 in San Benito, Texas; *d.* 14 October 2006 in Corpus Christi, Texas), Grammy Award–winning Tex-Mex singer-songwriter known for such songs as "Before the Next Teardrop Falls" and "Wasted Days and Wasted Nights."

Freddy Fender. MICHAEL OCHS ARCHIVES/GETTY IMAGES

Fender was born Baldemar Garza Huerta in El Jardin, an economically depressed barrio in San Benito. His father was Serapio Huerta, an immigrant from Soto La Marina, Mexico, and his mother was Margarita (Garza) Huerta. The Huerta family was very poor, and all members (including children) toiled as migrant farm workers in order to support themselves. Fender had two brothers and one sister. Serapio died of tuberculosis in January 1945, when Freddy was only eight years old. Fender attributes his father's death to icing down vegetables (cooling them by inserting ice chips into the produce cartons) while working at night.

Known as "Balde" as a child, Fender had his first exposure to music via the Spanish-language conjunto-style rancheras (a genre of traditional Mexican music) and polkas that were customary in San Benito and the entire South Texas area. His affinity for and knowledge of the genre grew as Fender observed celebratory events at which conjunto music was played, such as weddings. Through his travels as a migrant worker, Fender discovered blues music, played by fellow black agricultural workers. It would be from these musical experiences that Fender would incorporate blues, the newly emerging phenomenon of rock and roll, and conjunto into his music.

In 1954, at the age of sixteen, Fender dropped out of San Benito High School and joined the U.S. Marine Corps. After completing a three-year tour in Korea and being discharged from the service, Fender began his musical career performing in small bars and dance halls in Texas. Fender began his recording career with Falcon Records. Known as "El Bebop King," Fender recorded "No Seas Cruel," a Spanish-language cover of Elvis Presley's "Don't Be Cruel" in 1957.

On 9 August 1957 Fender married sixteen-year-old Evangelina "Vangie" Muniz, who became not only his wife but also his manager. The couple divorced in 1963 but later remarried in 1965. They had four children.

In 1959 Fender was signed to a recording contract with Imperial Records. By signing with a national label, Fender intended to increase his fan base beyond his Spanish-language audience. He ultimately changed his stage name from Baldemar Huerta to the Anglo-sounding name "Freddy Fender": he borrowed the name Fender from the type of guitar he played and used Freddy because it sounded natural with Fender.

In 1960 Fender released the song "Wasted Days and Wasted Nights," which became a regional hit. However, that same year Fender and his bass player were arrested for possession of marijuana in Baton Rouge, Louisiana. As a result Fender served almost three years of a five-year sentence at Angola, the Louisiana State Penitentiary, and his career was halted. Upon his release from prison in 1963, Fender stayed in Louisiana and attempted to revive his music career. Unsuccessful in his endeavors, Fender returned in 1969 to Texas, where he worked as a mechanic. After earning his general equivalency diploma, Fender enrolled at nearby Del Mar Community College in Corpus Christi (where he would make his home) to study sociology while performing music on weekends.

Fender reinvented himself musically in 1974, moving from his early rock-and-roll roots to country-style ballads. Huey P. Meaux, the head of Crazy Cajun Records, persuaded Fender to record the bilingual country single "Before the Next Teardrop Falls." The song became Fender's most successful hit; it reached number one on the pop charts in April 1975. Also in 1975 Fender was named male vocalist of the year by *Billboard* magazine, and "Before the Next Teardrop Falls" was named single of the year by the Country Music Association. This success prompted Fender to resurrect "Wasted Days and Wasted Nights," propelling the song to number one on the *Billboard* country singles chart and number eight on the pop charts. Fender became a superstar; he released two more Top Forty tracks, guest starred on television programs such as *The Dukes of Hazzard*, and appeared in national television advertising campaigns. Fender also performed in the actor and director Robert Redford's 1988 film *The Milagro Beanfield War* as Mayor Sammy Cantu.

In 1989 Fender formed the Tex-Mex group Texas Tornados with fellow Texas musicians Augie Meyers,

Doug Sahm, and Flaco Jimenez. The group produced four albums that were an upbeat mix of Tejano, blues, early rock and roll, and country songs recorded in both English and Spanish. The group won a Grammy Award in 1990 for its version of the song "Soy de San Luis." In 1998 Fender became a member of another group, Los Super Seven, along with members of the musical group Los Lobos and the singers Ruben Ramos and Joe Ely.

Despite Fender's commercial success, his personal life was mired in alcohol and drug abuse. Over the years his relationship with Vangie would become turbulent; their arguments mostly centered on Fender's substance abuse, which stemmed from years of working in nightclubs. His substance abuse came to an end only after Vangie dropped him off at a substance abuse facility in August 1985; he remained sober for the remainder of his life.

Fender's extended bout with drug and alcohol abuse would eventually cause his health to deteriorate. Apart from his battle with diabetes, his heroin use and needle-sharing led to a diagnosis of hepatitis C in the early 1990s. On 24 January 2002 Fender received a kidney transplant from one of his daughters, Marla, and on 2 January 2004 he underwent a liver transplant. In January 2006 Fender was diagnosed with lung cancer, and despite chemotherapy his condition deteriorated. Fender passed away from lung cancer at his Corpus Christi home at the age of sixty-nine. His funeral was held in his hometown of San Benito on 18 October 2008. He is buried in the San Benito City Cemetery.

With his distinctive fuzzy hair, handlebar mustache, and nasal singing voice, Fender was known as a pioneer in the Tex-Mex music genre; he took the genre out of the confines of South Texas by becoming a nationally and internationally recognized entertainer. Fender's bouts with drugs and alcohol are often viewed as a by-product of the entertainment lifestyle. However, after his superstardom in the 1970s, he earned the moniker of the "Comeback Kid" by becoming sober and resurrecting a successful recording career. Always laidback and humbled by his adversities, Fender created the Freddy Fender Scholarship Fund for low-income students; his philanthropy efforts have made him an enduring icon in Tejano music.

★

While no full-length biographies or autobiographies of Fender exist, background information can be found in Bruce Cook with Peter S. Greenberg, "Tex-Mex Troubadour," *Newsweek* (24 Nov. 1975); James Pinkerton, "No More Wasted Days and Nights: Ex-Prisoner Freddy Fender Has Come Full Circle," *Houston Chronicle* (2 Oct. 1994); and John Morthland, "Wasted Days," *Texas Monthly* (Oct. 2005). Obituaries are in the *Dallas Morning News* and *New York Times* (both 15 Oct. 2006).

Steven Wise

FERGUSON, (Walter) Maynard (*b*. 4 May 1928 in Verdun, now part of Montreal, Quebec, Canada; *d*. 23 August 2006 in Ventura, California), trumpeter and bandleader famous for his command of his instrument's highest register.

Ferguson's stellar career had an auspicious beginning. His mother, Olive, a professional musician and music teacher, started him on the violin and piano at the age of four. However, at the age of nine he heard a cornet player perform in church and persuaded his father, Percival ("Percy"), a school principal, to get him a cornet. His father bought him a trumpet instead, and he saw to it that his son received formal training at the French Conservatory of Music in Montreal. He also let the boy experiment with school instruments stored in the family home basement. This led to Ferguson's facility on the saxophone, euphonium, French horn, trombone, and other instruments. The young man quickly began to play dance and club dates with his older brother and only sibling, Percival, a saxophonist. By the age of fifteen Ferguson had formed his own band, which opened for visiting artists such as

Maynard Ferguson, 2000. **ANDREW LEPLEY/REDFERNS/GETTY IMAGES**

Dizzy Gillespie, Duke Ellington, and Woody Herman. During this period he attended Montreal High School. When he began working seven days a week from nine in the evening to three in the morning, however, his parents allowed him to drop out of school.

In 1948 Ferguson left Canada to tour with the big bands of, successively, Boyd Raeburn, Jimmy Dorsey, Charlie Barnet, and Stan Kenton. He stayed with Kenton from 1950 to 1953, during which time he took first place for lead trumpet in the *Down Beat* readers' poll for three years in a row. He next spent three years as the first-call studio trumpeter for Paramount Pictures in Hollywood, California. An excellent example of his work can be heard on the soundtrack of *The Ten Commandments* (1956). Ferguson then formed his own group, Maynard Ferguson and the Dream Band of Birdland, later shortened to Maynard Ferguson's Dream Band. With various changes in personnel, the band stayed together until 1967. Illustrative of his versatility, Ferguson was also a guest soloist with the New York Philharmonic Orchestra in 1960.

Later in the 1960s Ferguson experimented with consciousness-altering drugs at the Timothy Leary community in Millbrook, New York. Founded in 1963 by the psychologist, writer, and psychedelic drug advocate Leary, Millbrook was a rambling mansion on an estate near Poughkeepsie, New York, where for nearly five years Leary and his friends gathered to, in Leary's words, "Turn on, tune in, drop out." These experiences, paired with his increasing discontent with the course of musical taste in the United States, led Ferguson into voluntary exile. He spent a year in India at the Krishnamurti-based Rhishi Valley School near Madras (now Chennai), and he subsequently made annual pilgrimages to study at the guru Sai Baba's temple in Bangalore. Musically and spiritually refreshed, in 1968 he formed a sixteen-piece band made up of English musicians and developed a big band sound for pop and rock music. In 1970 he had a hit single with "MacArthur Park" from the album *M.F. Horn*, and in 1973, after several more albums that covered pop material, he moved to Ojai, California (near Los Angeles), with his wife of twenty-one years, Floralou, and four daughters.

Now more or less stable, he gradually replaced his English musicians with young Americans and trimmed his group to thirteen. A highlight of his career came in 1976, when he performed "Vesti la giubba" from Ruggero Leoncavallo's *Pagliacci* for the widely televised closing ceremony of the Olympic Games in Montreal, his hometown. In 1977 his version of "Gonna Fly Now," the theme song from the film *Rocky*, was nominated for a Grammy. In the mid-1980s he formed the popular septet High Voltage, which played in an electronically enhanced fusion style, and in 1988 he returned to acoustics with his Big Bop Nouveau Band, which toured and recorded until 1996. In

2005 he received his country's highest civilian honor, the Order of Canada.

A distinctive feature of a Ferguson performance during these later years was his playing of a variety of different instruments—soprano sax, valve trombone, French horn, and others—competently and in quick succession. He also invented or developed several instruments. His combination valve and slide trumpet, the Firebird, was born in the early 1970s and adopted by the trumpeters Don Ellis and Al Hirt. Ferguson himself can be heard playing it on the 1982 album *Hollywood*. Another of his instruments was the Superbone, a combination valve and slide trombone in one unit. Finally, he developed several trumpets and mouthpieces for the instrument maker Holton Leblanc.

"He was a kind man," recalled the pianist Earl MacDonald, "always jovial and a delight to be around. He traveled in the bus with the guys and didn't set himself apart." Ferguson died of kidney and liver failure at Community Memorial Hospital in Ventura. His body was cremated.

"Maynard enjoys the distinction of standing alone as the pioneer first able to use the top end of the trumpet as a bona fide arena for genuine jazz improvisation," observed Chuck Berg of the University of Kansas. Indeed, Ferguson's name is indelibly associated with the trumpet's high tessitura, with which he thrilled audiences beginning in the 1940s in Kenton's band. Double high Cs were a common feature of his style, and he frequently extended to the E-flat above that. This skill, in addition to circular breathing and a dazzling technical proficiency, can be heard on such pieces as "MacArthur Park," "Frame for the Blues" (1962), "Olé" (1977), and "Maria" (1977). His style was more complex, however. He reveals a sensitive middle range on Billy Strayhorn's "Lush Life" (1985) and a haunting lyrical skill on Jimmy Van Heusen's lament "But Beautiful" (1990). While "A Night in Tunisia" (1988) by Gillespie might have tempted him up to the stratosphere, he contributed instead a middle-range, off-mike muted solo. On "Londonderry Aire (Danny Boy)" (1977) he runs the gamut, but the poignant low notes are the most memorable.

Before a performance, Ferguson would send everyone away for a few minutes so that he could meditate, but not on anything so specific as high notes or breath control. He meditated on the idea of enjoyment. "To bring joy to people, that's what you're really doing," he said.

★

Ferguson's authorized biography, *M F Horn: Maynard Ferguson's Life in Music* (1997), by William F. Lee, is generously informative if tending toward the hagiographic. An excellent interview by Chuck Berg is in *Jazz Educators Journal* 22, no. 4 (June 1990): 26–30. Michael Meckna, *Twentieth-Century Brass Soloists* (1994), analyzes Ferguson's style and compares it with other jazz trumpeters. Two comprehensive obituaries are John

McDonough, *Down Beat* 73, no. 11 (Nov. 2006): 46–49, and Tim Weiner, the *New York Times* (25 Aug. 2006).

Michael Meckna

FIELDS, Freddie (*b*. 12 July 1923 in Ferndale, New York; *d*. 11 December 2007 in Beverly Hills, California), talent agent, movie producer, and cofounder of one of America's preeminent talent agencies.

Born Fred Feldman, Fields was the son of Jack Feldman, owner of the Queen Mountain House, a popular resort hotel in New York's Catskill Mountains, and Jeanette (Sewal) Feldman. A pioneer in the Catskills resort trade, his father booked big-name talent, including the entertainers Eddie Cantor and Al Jolson, to attract business. His older brother Shep Fields became the leader of a Big Band–era orchestra called Shep Fields and His Rippling Rhythm.

Jack Feldman's death in 1929 left his widow and five sons in dire financial straits. Fields's mother moved the family from town to town in pursuit of work and often juggled multiple jobs to keep her sons fed, clothed, and housed. Fields himself took on odd jobs at an early age in an effort to help out at home. At seventeen he left home and moved to Miami, where he worked for a short time as a bellhop. He then joined the Coast Guard. After leaving the service he gravitated to a job in show business with the New York talent agent Abby Greshler, handling bookings for the promising young comedy team of Dean Martin and Jerry Lewis.

In 1946 Fields left Greshler's agency and went to work for Music Corporation of America (MCA), a music publisher and talent agency, and gradually made his way into the top ranks of MCA agents. Also in 1946 he married the actress Edith Fellows, with whom he had a child; they divorced in 1955. On 13 February 1957 he married the actress Polly Bergen, with whom he had two children; their marriage ended in 1975. By 1960 he made the difficult decision to leave MCA and strike out on his own, launching Freddie Fields Associates. Two months after setting up his own shop, Fields was joined by David Begelman, a close friend and fellow MCA agent. Fields and Begelman adopted the company name Creative Management Associates, or CMA—intentionally close to MCA's well-known acronym. Over the next decade and a half, Fields was considered one of the most powerful agents in Hollywood and CMA one of the top-ranked talent agencies. Fields's list of clients at CMA included the directors Steven Spielberg, Woody Allen, George Lucas, and Francis Ford Coppola, and the actors Judy Garland, Robert Redford, Paul Newman, Henry Fonda, Barbra Streisand, and Jack Nicholson.

In 1969 Fields partnered with some of the biggest names in Hollywood, including Newman, Streisand, Sidney Poitier, Steve McQueen, and Dustin Hoffman, to establish First Artists, an independent production company. Of this collaborative effort, which lasted only about five years, Streisand recalled, "we lived through a very exciting time together," praising Fields as a "creative thinker."

Fields was an early supporter of the so-called back-end deal—a contractual arrangement in which film stars forgo up-front paychecks in favor of a percentage of the motion picture's gross (the amount of money it makes on ticket sales). Following Fields's advice, Natalie Wood opted for such a deal for her role in *Bob & Carol & Ted & Alice* (1969) and, according to Fields, made more money on that film than on any other project in her career.

When Begelman quit CMA in 1973 to join Columbia Studios, Fields was left to operate the popular talent agency on his own. Over the years he had lost much of his enthusiasm for the job, and he soon began negotiations to merge CMA with Marvin Josephson's International Famous Agency. The merger, an agreement for which was announced in early November 1974, became official on 1 January 1975. The new company was named International Creative Management (ICM). Under the terms of the merger agreement, Fields became president of ICM, while Josephson assumed the company's chairmanship. However, Fields had negotiated an escape clause into the merger agreement that allowed him to leave the new company after only six months. He took advantage of that option and left ICM to participate in an independent film production deal at Paramount. Over the next few years Fields produced a number of films, including *Lipstick* (1976), *Handle with Care* (1976), *Looking for Mr. Goodbar* (1977), *American Gigolo* (1980), *Wholly Moses!* (1980), and *Victory* (1981).

After his time at Paramount, Fields worked in motion-picture studio operations. From 1980 to 1982 he served as chief operating officer at MGM Film Company, and from 1982 to 1984 as president of worldwide production at MGM/UA entertainment. After leaving MGM/UA, Fields said he would never take on a studio job again. In a 1986 interview he explained, "It's a thankless job, from almost every point of view. . . . We were not a hot studio, and it was hard to get good material." On 12 July 1981 he married Corinna Tsopei, a former Miss Greece and Miss Universe, with whom he remained until his death.

Fields returned to independent film production and in 1989 enjoyed perhaps his greatest motion-picture triumph with the release of *Glory*, the inspiring story of the Civil War's first all-black volunteer company, led by Colonel Robert Gould Shaw, a white officer in the Union army. The film won a number of awards, including three Oscars. In the late 1980s Fields served as executive producer of two television shows, the *Montel Williams Show* and *Naked Hollywood*.

Fields died at his home of lung cancer. He is buried in Westwood Memorial Park in Los Angeles.

Fields left an indelible imprint on the American entertainment industry. Although he found success in many segments of the business, his achievements as an agent became legendary. *Variety* called Fields and his partner Begelman "perhaps Hollywood's first superagents." As cofounder of Creative Management Associates, Fields reigned as one of America's most powerful talent agents for close to fifteen years, pioneering and aggressively negotiating lucrative back-end deals for many of his big-name clients.

For an interview with Fields, see Claudia Eller, "A Former Agent's Field(s) of Dreams," *Los Angeles Times* (16 June 1995). Charles Champlin, "Fields: From an Agent to Passionate Producer," *Los Angeles Times* (20 June 1985), discusses the two main aspects of his career. Obituaries are in *Variety* (12 Dec. 2007) and the *Los Angeles Times* and *New York Times* (both 13 Dec. 2007).

Don Amerman

FIROR, John William, Jr. (*b.* 18 October 1927 in Athens, Georgia; *d.* 5 November 2007 in Pullman, Washington), major scientist in atmospheric research, director of the National Center for Atmospheric Research, and pioneer in researching the effects of human activity on climate change.

Firor was born to John William Firor, a professor of economics, and Mary Valentine (Moss) Firor, a homemaker; Firor was their second son and third child. After starting his university studies at the Georgia Institute of Technology (Georgia Tech), he suspended them in 1945 to perform military service. As an enlisted man, he was assigned to guard duty at the Los Alamos National Laboratory while the Manhattan Project was still in operation. This experience may have altered his career. When he returned to the university in 1946, he switched his major from engineering to physics and earned a BS from Georgia Tech in 1949. Firor married Carolyn Merle Jenkins on 25 September 1950. In 1954 he was awarded a PhD in physics from the University of Chicago. For his dissertation he studied cosmic rays using a neutron monitor that he designed.

In 1953 Firor joined the Carnegie Institution in Washington, D.C., specializing in research on terrestrial magnetism. He moved his family (two sons and two daughters) to Boulder, Colorado, in 1961, when he accepted the position of associate director of the National Center for Atmospheric Research (NCAR) at the High Altitude Observatory. His major research contributions were in high-energy astrophysics and radio astronomy. The NCAR was a good fit for Firor, whose interests were wide-ranging, and he encouraged scholars from diverse backgrounds to connect with each other. An accomplished pilot—he was licensed to pilot single-engine and multiengine planes, sailplanes, and balloons—he once flew a sailplane into a developing thunderstorm to measure hail and the growth of such storms. He was also interested in seismology and the structure of continents.

In 1968 Firor advanced to the position of director of the NCAR. When that organization merged with the University Corporation for Atmospheric Research (UCAR), it became necessary to share managerial duties; Firor was designated the executive director of the combined operation in 1974 and held that position until his official retirement in 1980. In the summer of 1979, a year before his retirement, his wife of twenty-nine years died. On 15 October 1983 he married Judith Eva Jacobsen, a geographer who specialized in population and gender issues.

If Firor had accomplished nothing in his life except his personal research and his management of NCAR, he would still merit respect as a major scientist, though the general public might never have heard of him. He came to the wider world's attention in 1990 with the publication of a major book. In *The Changing Atmosphere: A Global Challenge*, he shows how such problems as acid rain, ozone depletion, and greenhouse gases are interrelated. He was one of the first to demonstrate how extensively manmade products in the atmosphere contribute to global warming. Malcolm Browne, science writer for the *New York Times*, said that the book was "about as agreeable as a dose of ipecac," but he praised it as necessary and felt that Firor's work focused on the evidence in an evenhanded manner when it could easily have been a polemic. The book was awarded the Louis J. Batten Author's Award by the American Meteorological Society.

A dozen years later Firor teamed up with Jacobsen to write another book; *The Crowded Greenhouse* (2002) expands on the work that Firor had started. The book was designed to reach a wider audience and to integrate the evidence that had accumulated since the publication of *The Changing Atmosphere*. The work also demonstrates how political and economic considerations stall implementation of an urgent need to change. A major focus is that Earth's increasing population is the factor that ties all of the problems together. Probably because of Jacobsen's special interests, the book argues that improving the status of and empowering women could increase the chances that needed steps would be taken. Committed to actions as well as words, Firor was a founding member of the World Resources Institute, an environmental think tank, when that organization was created in 1982 and served on its board until 1999 (a record for longevity that will never be surpassed because term limits were later implemented).

Following his official retirement, Firor stayed on with NCAR as a senior research associate at the Foothills Laboratory, supervising and advising younger scholars with their work. A lifelong teacher, at various times in his career, he held visiting professorships at such institutions as the California Institute of Technology, the University of Wyoming, and the University of Minnesota. He was Senior Wirth Fellow at the University of Colorado at Denver. Firor was a fellow of the American Meteorological Society and the American Association for the Advancement of Science. In addition, he served as a member of the National Academy of Sciences' Committee on Data Interchange and was on the Organizing Committee of the Solar Physics Division of the American Astronomical Society. He chaired the National Aeronautics and Space Administration Space Applications Advisory Committee. Community minded, he served on many local and regional committees and boards in the Boulder area. Over the course of his long career, he contributed a number of articles to scholarly journals. Preceded in death by his second wife (Jacobsen died in 2004), Firor died of complications from Alzheimer's disease. His remains were cremated and scattered.

As a scientist Firor was dedicated to the pursuit and promulgation of knowledge. Knowing well that his conclusions on global warming would elicit attacks from politicians and from an important part of the business community, he spoke out on public policy issues, even though the benefits of his proposals could be enjoyed only by generations that he would not live to see. He was ahead of his time in arguing that scientists of a wide variety of specialties must work together and that both science and the social sciences could benefit from cooperation.

It is expected that Firor's personal and professional papers will be housed at UCAR. An obituary is in the *New York Times* (12 Nov. 2007).

Art Barbeau

FISCHER, Robert James ("Bobby") (*b.* 9 March 1943 in Chicago, Illinois; *d.* 17 January 2008 in Reykjavík, Iceland), child chess prodigy, eight-time U.S. chess champion, and world chess champion from 1972 to 1975 whose controversial and dramatic victory over the world champion Boris Spassky during the summer of 1972 riveted world attention and heightened awareness and appreciation for championship chess.

Bobby Fischer, 1972. © **INTERFOTO PRESSEBILDAGENTUR/ ALAMY**

Fischer was the son of Paul Felix Nemenyi, a Hungarian-Jewish chemical engineer and college lecturer who would later do work on the first atomic bomb, and Regina (Wender) Fischer, a Polish Jew born in Switzerland whose family moved to the United States shortly after her birth. In 1932 she moved to Berlin, Germany, where she met Hans Gerhardt Fischer, a German physicist. They married and migrated to the Soviet Union in 1933 and had a daughter in 1937. Regina Fischer returned to the United States in 1939 while her husband remained in Europe; he eventually settled in Chile. They would lead separate lives before divorcing in 1945. Although Hans Fischer was initially thought to be Bobby Fischer's father, this parentage came under scrutiny with revelations from *Philadelphia Inquirer* reporters in 2002 that the Federal Bureau of Investigation had amassed a 900-page file on Regina Fischer between 1943 and 1973. This file documented that Regina Fischer and Nemenyi had met at the University of Denver in 1942 and had begun an affair that led to the birth of Fischer. Nemenyi would provide child support for Fischer until Nemenyi's death in 1952. Regina Fischer held many jobs and lived in many places as she and her children eked out an existence without a male breadwinner. In 1949 she relocated her family to the New York City borough of Brooklyn to pursue a nursing career.

While their mother was preoccupied with her studies, the Fischer children would attempt various board games and puzzles. In May 1949 she bought a chess set from the candy store over which the family lived in a small apartment. Bobby soon became infatuated with chess, and his mother sought to place a short advertisement in the *Brooklyn Daily Eagle* seeking young opponents for her son. The newspaper's chess editor responded with information about a forthcoming simultaneous chess exhibition, to be given by a chess master. On 17 January 1951 Fischer participated and was quickly defeated but was noticed by Carmine Nigro, president of the Brooklyn Chess Club, who enrolled Fischer as a member and provided chess lessons and guidance for the next four years.

Fischer began to play chess at the Brooklyn Chess Club and other chess haunts in New York City while his mother worried about his obsession. In 1955 his initial efforts in U.S. Chess Federation tournaments were not impressive, but in 1956 Fischer, as he would later say, "suddenly got good." At age thirteen he became the youngest U.S. Junior Champion. After a tie for fourth at the U.S. Open Championship, he was invited to the prestigious Lessing J. Rosenwald Trophy Tournament in New York City. There, he played a brilliant game, dubbed by critics as the "Game of the Century." His play began to attract attention in Soviet chess circles. Fischer learned sufficient Russian to keep abreast of theoretical discoveries in Soviet chess periodicals. Assisting Fischer's chess progress was his friendship with Jack Collins, a skilled chess master and teacher who would mentor Fischer starting in June 1956 and, together with Collins's sister Ethel, provide a surrogate set of parents and a nurturing home away from home for Fischer.

Fischer's successes would continue in 1957 with a second victory in the U.S. Junior Championship, a tie for first in the U.S. Open Championship, and a surprising first place finish in the 1957–1958 U.S. championship tournament, where at the age of fourteen, he became the youngest ever American chess champion. In the summer of 1958 he visited the Soviet Union, accompanied by his sister after his mother had contacted the Soviet Chess Federation seeking an official invitation for her son. In a Yugoslav tournament held to determine qualifiers for the 1959 Candidates event to select a challenger for the world title, Fischer finished tied for 5th–6th, which enabled him to advance to the next stage in the FIDE (Fédération Internationale des Échecs) three-year elimination system. In 1958 Fischer received the title of international grandmaster of chess; at age fifteen he was the youngest grandmaster in chess history.

Fischer attended Erasmus Hall High School in Brooklyn but was an indifferent student, antisocial, with a disparaging opinion of schools and teachers. Once he turned sixteen, he dropped out to devote all his time to chess. A headstrong, willful adolescent, he became alienated from his strong-willed mother, who had become involved in activist causes including civil rights and nuclear disarmament, all the while raising funds to support her son's career.

By the early 1960s Fischer's mother and sister had moved out of their Brooklyn apartment. In 1961 his mother participated in a 5,000-mile "peace walk" from San Francisco to Moscow, during which she met and later married Cyril Pustan, an English scientist and peace activist. An unflattering portrait of Fischer in the January 1962 issue of *Harper's* magazine revealed a self-absorbed, misogynistic young man of narrow interests save for his passion for chess. In early 1962 he won the Stockholm Interzonal tournament by a decisive 2½ point margin, but in the Curacao Challengers tournament that spring he finished a disappointing fourth behind three Soviet grandmasters. This led to his angry denunciation of the FIDE qualifying system in a 20 August 1962 article in *Sports Illustrated*, "The Russians Have Fixed World Chess," charging collusion among Soviet players to thwart his hopes for the title.

Fischer abstained from participation in the next three-year world championship elimination cycle. In the 1963–1964 U.S. Championship tournament he established a record by winning every game, resulting in a perfect 11–0 score. After an extended transcontinental exhibition tour in 1964, he returned to international competition in 1965, participating in the Capablanca Memorial tournament in Havana, Cuba, by telephone and teletype from the Marshall Chess Club in New York City after the U.S. State Department refused him a visa to travel to Cuba.

After an eighth and final triumph in the U.S. Championship tournament in 1966–1967, Fischer returned to FIDE competition. At the Interzonal tournament in 1967 Fischer was leading the event after ten games when a bitter dispute with tournament officials arose. There followed another enforced absence from the international chess arena until 1970. He described this period as a time to "plot my revenge." From 1970 to 1972 he dominated international chess with the most overwhelming display of chess mastery ever achieved. Beginning with his appearance in the "USSR versus the Rest of the World" match in March–April 1970 to his defeat of Spassky in 1972, Fischer recorded 74 wins, 37 draws, and 6 losses for a percentage of 79, a sustained performance unparalleled in grandmaster chess. Fischer defeated two leading grandmasters by perfect 6–0 scores in match play in 1971 and defeated former champion Tigran Petrosian by 6½–2½ to qualify for his match with Spassky. At one stage during this period, Fischer won twenty consecutive games until a loss to Petrosian. Fischer was awarded the "Chess Oscar" by a group of chess journalists and officials each year from 1970 to 1972.

Fischer's participation in the world championship match with Spassky in 1972 was uncertain until the English businessman Jim Slater provided an additional $125,000 to double the prize fund. After losing the first game with a risky maneuver, Fischer forfeited the second game in a dispute concerning the existence of television cameras in the playing hall filming the match. He returned to play the third game in a small room behind the stage, televised for spectators by closed circuit camera. It resulted in Fischer's first victory ever over Spassky, and the champion never recovered. On 1 September 1972 Spassky resigned the twenty-first game, giving Fischer a 12½–8½ victory in their match and the world championship. For two months the Fischer-Spassky match had become a sporting drama that dominated world headlines and thrilled beginners and experts alike.

Upon his return to the United States, Fischer was given the key to New York City by Mayor John Lindsay. For a time Fischer seemed to revel in his celebrity status, but despite promises to be an active champion, he avoided chess competitions, rejecting countless lavish offers to play chess publicly. Scheduled to defend his title in 1975 against the Soviet challenger Anatoly Karpov, Fischer submitted a list of match conditions that was not accepted by the FIDE and forfeited his title.

In 1962 Fischer had become an associate of a fundamentalist Christian religious sect, the Worldwide Church of God, to which he tithed a significant part of his chess income. In 1977 he broke with the church, claiming he had been duped and defrauded. For the next fifteen years Fischer led the life of a nomad, residing in cheap hotels and flophouses, mainly in and around Los Angeles and Pasadena, California, occasionally staying for a time with chess friends, his tirades against FIDE, the media, and authority generally intensifying. He considered but ultimately rejected all efforts to draw him back to the world of competitive chess. Attempts to locate and interview him by journalists were fruitless. Rumors of Fischer sightings tantalized the chess world for years. Anyone in his circle of friends and acquaintances who revealed any information about him to the media was cut off from further contact. His fascination with the World War II German dictator Adolf Hitler and his anti-Semitism, neither ever clearly explained, increased. On 26 May 1981 Fischer was stopped by Pasadena police, fitting the description of a bank robber. He failed to provide them with identifying information and, after a brief tussle, was jailed for two days on vagrancy charges. After being released, he produced a self-published account of his experience, "I Was Tortured in the Pasadena Jailhouse."

In September 1992 Fischer resurfaced in Yugoslavia to meet his old rival Spassky in match play, advertised at Fischer's insistence as being for the world's championship. Fischer was enticed by a $5 million prize fund, raised by the Serbian banker and alleged arms broker Jezdimir Vasiljevic, with two-thirds going to the victor. At a press conference prior to the start of the match on 1 September 1992, Fischer defied United Nations and U.S. State Department sanctions against conducting economic activity in war-torn Yugoslavia by spitting on a U.S. Treasury Department communiqué warning him against such activities. Displaying sporadic vestiges of his old form, Fischer defeated Spassky ten wins to five with fifteen draws, but clearly his best chess years were behind him.

Fischer spent the next twelve years without permanent residence, living mainly in Hungary, the Philippines, and Japan. He championed a variant of chess called Fischer Random or shuffle chess, characterized by a computer-generated alignment of forces on the initial ranks of the chessboard. In 1988 Fischer patented an innovative digital chess clock that added time increments for each move made at the board. In 2001 he fathered a daughter with a young Philippine woman, Justine Ong. Some sources contend that Fischer secretly married Myoko Watai, who was president of the Japanese Chess Federation and his constant companion in his final years.

Fischer's denunciations of the U.S. government and world Jewry intensified; between 1999 and 2006 he appeared on at least thirty-four radio broadcast interviews, mainly in the Philippines, lashing out at his enemies, real or imagined, vociferously denying the existence of the Holocaust. On 11 September 2001, calling from Japan to an interviewer on a Philippine radio station, Fischer praised the terrorist attacks against the United States and openly called for the death of President George W. Bush and for a military coup.

Fischer was detained by Japanese authorities on 13 July 2004 at Narita Airport in Tokyo while en route to the Philippines, charged with traveling on an expired American passport. He was incarcerated for nine months in a Japanese detention facility while extradition to the United States was being considered. During this time he renounced his American citizenship and sought political asylum from several nations, all unsuccessfully. He was finally granted asylum and citizenship by the Icelandic parliament in March 2005 for "humanitarian reasons." On 24 March 2005 Fischer arrived in Iceland, where he lived quietly for the rest of his life. He died of kidney failure at the Landspitali hospital in Reykjavík and was buried at the Laugardaelir Church cemetery outside the town of Selfoss.

Fischer was one of the greatest chess players of all time, but his legacy remains that of a troubled, elusive genius trapped by his inner demons. His chess style was classical, aggressive, and direct, in pursuit of clear strategic themes, accurate in calculation and technically precise. He disdained draws and exhausted all winning possibilities in even barren positions. He played the board, not the man, and his behavior at the chessboard was always scrupulously correct. His approach to chess and the presentation of it was principled, never seeking financial reward if chess itself would be demeaned or its significance diminished. No player ever gave himself so totally to chess; as he himself said, "All I ever want to do, ever, is play chess," and "Chess is life." Chess provided Fischer his métier, his raison d'être, and perhaps even his sanity. Away from the chessboard he was unable to protect himself from the darker aspects of his character.

★

There is a vast collection of print material devoted to Fischer's life and career. The most detailed Fischer biography is Frank Brady, *Profile of a Prodigy* (1965; rev. ed. 1973), which terminates with the 1972 world championship match. A controversial and often unsympathetic account of the world championship match and Fischer's often manic behavior before and during it is Brad Darrach, *Bobby Fischer vs. the Rest of the World* (1974). The best and most recent account of the background and politics of that match is David Edmonds and John Eidinow, *Bobby Fischer Goes to War* (2004). For one of the best of the many articles depicting Fischer's final years, see Rene Chun, "Bobby Fischer's Endgame," *Atlantic Monthly* (Dec. 2002). See also Dirk ten Geuzendam, "They'll Do It Every Time: In the Footsteps of Icelandic Citizen Bobby Fischer," *New in Chess* no. 2 (2008). An obituary is in the *New York Times* (19 Jan. 2008).

Edward J. Tassinari

FOLKMAN, (Moses) Judah (*b.* 24 February 1933 in Cleveland, Ohio; *d.* 14 January 2008 in Denver, Colorado), renowned cancer researcher, surgeon, educator, and discoverer of breakthrough cancer therapy.

Folkman was the oldest of three children born to Jerome Folkman, a rabbi, and Bessie Folkman, a homemaker. When he was seven years old, Folkman accompanied his father when he visited the patients in local hospitals and decided that he wanted to become a doctor. He was also influenced by his mother, who regaled a deeply moved Folkman with stories of great scientists and their breakthroughs. Before he was a teenager, Folkman was conducting experiments in a basement lab. For his bar mitzvah, he received a 1,000-power microscope. As a high school student in Bexley, Ohio, Folkman volunteered in a hospital laboratory at the Ohio State University (OSU) and also won a science prize for keeping a rat's heart beating outside of its body.

In 1953, just three years after graduating high school, Folkman took his BA as a premed student from OSU. With Dr. Robert Zollinger (then president of the American College of Surgeons) as a mentor, Folkman performed surgery on dogs, and coauthored academic papers on liver cancer. Folkman relocated to Harvard Medical School, where he distinguished himself by codeveloping the first implantable pacemaker. Folkman received his MD with honors from Harvard in 1957 and went on to establish a surgical residency at Massachusetts General Hospital. In 1960 Folkman married Paula Prial. The couple would go on to have two daughters and a son. That same year, his life and new practice were interrupted when he was drafted to serve a two-year term in the National Naval Medical Center in Bethesda, Maryland. There, he carried on research to find a blood substitute that could be safely stored on ships at sea.

It was while Folkman and a colleague were testing synthetic blood on a rabbit's thyroid gland that, simply out of curiosity, they added cancer cells from mice to the blood substitute. The cancer cells in the rabbit grew for a period then stopped, though they continued to grow in the mice. Folkman hypothesized that the cancer cells required a constant blood supply. This chance discovery led to a lifelong pursuit to find ways to block blood vessel growth as a way to arrest the growth of tumors. Folkman's research opened up a new field of biology, angiogenesis: the study of blood vessel growth.

In 1964 Folkman was named chief resident at Massachusetts General Hospital. Three years later he was recruited by Children's Hospital in Boston, where he was appointed chief surgeon. He remained in that position until 1981, at which time he resigned to devote his time to his angiogenesis research and to the development of angiogenesis inhibition therapies. He was director of the vascular biology program at Children's Hospital Boston at the time of his death. In 1968 Folkman was named Andrus Professor of Pediatric Surgery and received an appointment as professor of cell biology, both at Harvard Medical School.

In 1971, in a paper published in the *New England Journal of Medicine*, Folkman presented his hypothesis that tumors need a dedicated blood supply to grow, and that tumors produce a "tumor angiogenesis factor" that stimulates the growth of the blood supply. That his ideas were not accepted by the scientific community did nothing to dissuade him from continuing his research. By 1984 Folkman and his team had identified and published information about a specific angiogenic factor. That discovery further convinced Folkman of the correctness of his theories.

By the mid-1980s researchers in Folkman's lab had discovered two natural proteins that acted to block angiogenesis: angiostatin and endostatin. In 1997 the group published its results and attracted considerable attention to the potential of antiangiogentic therapies in treating cancerous tumors. Researchers in both academic and commercial laboratories began an intense search for therapies involving angiogenesis. In 2004 the U.S. Food and Drug Administration (FDA) approved a commercial drug for use in cancer treatment based on angiogenesis research.

Folkman was the author of 389 peer-reviewed papers and 106 book chapters and monographs. Although it took decades for his efforts to be recognized by the scientific community, Folkman's tenacity ultimately won him widespread recognition. In addition to honorary degrees from fifteen universities, he received both national and international awards. Among his many honors, Folkman was elected to the National Academy of Sciences and the Institute of Medicine of the National Academy of Sciences. He was appointed by President George W. Bush to the National Cancer Advisory Board of the National Institutes of Health.

Folkman was also recognized as an exceptional teacher and mentor, and he was much in demand as a lecturer. He was on his way to a speaking engagement in Vancouver, Canada, when he died of an apparent heart attack in the Denver International Airport.

Bruce Zetter, the chief scientific officer at Children's Hospital, opined that Folkman's contributions "profoundly influenced both science and medicine." As a result of Folkman's persistence and dedication, more than 1,000 laboratories went on to pursue angiogenesis research. At least fifty angiogenesis inhibitor–based drugs were put into clinical trials and ten others received FDA approval. This branching research led to the discovering of other treatments, not only for cancer but also for heart disease, diabetes, and the eye disease macular degeneration, among numerous others.

For a summary of Folkman's life see "Children's Mourns the Death of Dr. Judah Folkman," from the pressroom of Children's Hospital Boston (15 Jan. 2008). Also see Nikhil Swaminathan, "Father of Breakthrough Cancer Therapy Dies," in *Scientific American* (15 Jan. 2008). Obituaries are in the *Boston Globe*, *New York Times*, and *Washington Post* (all 16 Jan. 2008).

M. C. Nagel

FORD, Gerald Rudolph, Jr. (*b.* 14 July 1913 in Omaha, Nebraska; *d.* 26 December 2006 in Rancho Mirage, California), U.S. congressman from Michigan, House of Representatives minority leader, vice president of the United States, and thirty-eighth president of the United States.

Gerald R. Ford, 1973. ALFRED EISENSTAEDT/TIME LIFE PICTURES/GETTY IMAGES

Ford was born Leslie Lynch King, Jr., the son of Leslie King, a wool salesman, and Dorothy (Gardner) King, a homemaker. The senior King physically abused his wife, who divorced him and moved with her son to Grand Rapids, Michigan, to live with her parents. There she married Gerald Rudolph Ford, a paint salesman. The couple renamed the young boy Gerald Rudolph Ford, Jr.—nicknamed "Junie"—and had three more sons.

Sports provided a driving force during Ford's student years. At South High School in Grand Rapids, which he graduated from in June 1931, Ford played varsity football and basketball and ran track. He focused his athletic energy especially on the gridiron, becoming something of a star. As a senior he captained an undefeated team that won the state football championship. For the rest of his life Ford maintained an avid interest in athletics, and *Sports Illustrated* later called him "the nation's most athletic president." He peppered political talk with sports metaphors, referring to "team players" and exhorting colleagues to "huddle" on issues. Ford's football position later assumed a metaphorical importance in his politics: he gravitated toward the center of the political spectrum, urging Republican moderation and seeking compromise with colleagues.

In 1931 Ford entered the University of Michigan, where he continued to play football center, earning All-Big Ten honors his senior year. In 1935 he graduated with a BA, having majored in economics. With the Detroit Lions and the Green Bay Packers offering him contracts, Ford might have become a professional football player in another era. At the time, however, the National Football League was a fledgling enterprise, and college ball represented the acme of a player's career. More important, Ford aspired to attend law school.

Ford landed a job as a Yale University assistant football coach and took law school classes part time, performing well enough to be admitted full time. In 1941 he graduated from Yale Law School in the top third of his class, while still working full time as a coach.

Returning to Grand Rapids, Ford partnered in a law firm. During World War II he enlisted in the navy and served in the Pacific aboard the USS *Monterey*, a light-aircraft carrier. In 1946 Ford left the navy as a lieutenant commander and resumed legal work in Grand Rapids.

The war profoundly changed Ford's political views from isolationism to internationalism. The Michigan Fifth District congressman Bartel Jonkman's rigid isolationism troubled Ford enough that in 1948 Ford challenged Jonkman in the Republican primary. The novice upset the four-term incumbent, and Ford coasted to an easy general election victory.

On 15 October 1948, less than a month before his election, Ford married Elizabeth "Betty" Bloomer, a Grand Rapids department store fashion designer. The couple moved to the Washington, D.C., area and started a family that grew to four children, three sons and a daughter.

In 1950 Ford won a seat on the House Appropriations Committee and developed expertise on the federal budget. He saw elegance in its numbers and vigilantly watched over government expenditures. His alarm over federal deficits reflected his fiscal conservatism, emphasis on small government, and support for the private sector. During the 1950s Ford's views meshed with those of President Dwight D. Eisenhower, a deficit hawk whom Ford considered the twentieth century's best president.

Ford cut an impressive figure on Capitol Hill. Just over six feet tall, he retained a football player's build and enjoyed the House's camaraderie. Colleagues appreciated his geniality, work ethic, and ability to forge friendships that transcended political squabbling. Ford liked to say that he had "many adversaries, but not one enemy" in Congress. In 1963 he gained added visibility when he

began serving on the Warren Commission investigating President John F. Kennedy's assassination.

His attributes and experiences made Ford a prime candidate for promotion, and opportunity came amid political disaster. After Senator Barry Goldwater's drubbing in the 1964 presidential election, Republicans looked for new congressional leadership. In January 1965 Ford became the new House minority leader, using the position to oppose President Lyndon B. Johnson's Great Society and Vietnam War policies.

Opportunity notwithstanding, political life took a toll on Ford's family. The minority leader traveled as many as 200 days a year, and his absence from home made his wife almost a single parent. Ford began eyeing retirement, and after the 1972 election he decided to seek only one more term.

Scandal provided Ford's next political opportunity. In the fall of 1973, after Vice President Spiro T. Agnew resigned amid corruption charges, President Richard M. Nixon appointed Ford vice president. In December 1973, by wide margins, both the House and the Senate approved Ford as the new vice president. He requested that his swearing-in ceremony take place on Capitol Hill, which he considered his home, and his inaugural address reflected his self-effacing style. He said, "I am a Ford, not a Lincoln. My addresses will never be as eloquent as … Lincoln's. But I will do my very best to equal his brevity and plain speaking."

As Watergate sank the Nixon presidency, Ford substituted as Republican Party leader for the politically paralyzed president. During his eight months as vice president, Ford racked up 500 appearances, visiting forty states. The grueling travel schedule kept Ford away from the scandal-tainted administration and allowed him to develop close relationships with the reporters who covered him.

When Watergate finally toppled Nixon, who resigned on 9 August 1974, Ford became an unelected president—the first president who had never run on a national ticket for either the presidency or the vice presidency. His inaugural address, which he delivered in the White House East Room just after Nixon left the White House grounds, contained the most memorable line of his presidency. Ford reassured the nation, "My fellow Americans, our long national nightmare is over."

Ford's presidency brought an immediate style change to the White House. He and his wife insisted that White House staff interact freely with the Ford family, forbidden behavior under Nixon. The first lady was outspoken on such women's issues as the Equal Rights Amendment and about such personal experiences as her breast cancer. To signal more relaxed relations with the media, Ford approved a revised seating arrangement for East Room press conferences. To add gravitas to his administration, he appointed the veteran politician Nelson Rockefeller,

New York's four-term governor, as vice president. Favorable media stories appeared, describing Ford as an honest, down-to-earth president who prepared his own breakfast of English muffins, and he enjoyed an approval rating above 70 percent.

Then came the Nixon pardon. On 8 September 1974, after just one month in office, Ford granted the former president a pardon for any crimes he might have committed while in office. Nixon opponents were outraged that Nixon would never face trial or punishment. Ford's approval rating dropped from 66 percent to 49 percent. Ford explained the pardon by expressing frustration at devoting much presidential attention to Nixon's legal problems when he wished to concentrate on policy issues involving the economy, the energy crisis, and diplomacy. Despite this explanation, his action's suddenness shocked Americans and ended his initial honeymoon with the media. Wounded by Watergate and hurt anew by the pardon, Republicans suffered stunning losses in the 1974 midterm elections; the Democrats gained forty-three seats in the House and three seats in the Senate. Ford's frustrations with the resurgent new Democratic Congress became a theme of his presidency.

The greatest policy challenge confronting Ford was inflation, which ran at 11 percent in 1974. Knowing the damaging effects of rampant price increases, Ford established reducing inflation as the foremost goal of his presidency. Toward that end he supported a tight Federal Reserve monetary policy. While the president could not determine monetary policy, he influenced fiscal policy, and Ford fixated on limiting federal spending. This combination of tight monetary and fiscal policies, the orthodox conservative formula for fighting inflation, provided the mainstay of Ford's anti-inflation strategy. Ford opposed large-scale new federal programs because they would not only swell budget deficits but also stimulate inflation.

That philosophy brought Ford into conflict with Congress. Liberal Democrats supported programs in the New Deal and Great Society traditions. Facing a Congress that passed legislation he considered costly, Ford issued sixty-six vetoes during his presidency. Congress overrode his vetoes only twelve times. Ford touted his veto strategy as one of his greatest achievements as president, for it allowed him to restrain federal spending (he estimated that the vetoes saved $43 billion) and to wield authority over Congress.

By reducing spending, Ford hoped to decelerate inflation. To further his mission to contain inflation, Ford held two economic summit conferences at the White House in September 1974 to solicit strategies for fixing the economy from the nation's top experts. From these conclaves he developed his first major policy initiative, an anti-inflation program that he unveiled on 8 October 1974 to a joint session of Congress. The centerpiece was a 5 percent surcharge on incomes. To supplement the program, Ford announced a voluntary citizens campaign to combat inflation, "Whip Inflation Now," which was to involve consumers and businesses in a massive effort to encourage people to shop wisely, conserve energy, and hold down costs and prices.

Congress gave the tax surcharge a chilly reception and never voted on it. More important, the economy deteriorated. By November 1974 the economy had plunged into a steep recession and needed stimulus rather than a tax increase. By January 1975 Ford tacked a new course. Abandoning the surcharge proposal and the Whip Inflation Now program, he promulgated a new program in his State of the Union address, asking Congress for an emergency antirecession tax cut of $16 billion. In March, responding to Ford's prodding, Congress passed a $23 billion tax cut, which Ford signed. In May 1975 the recession bottomed out with 8.9 percent unemployment, after which the economy began a slow recovery.

Deregulation constituted another of Ford's major economic initiatives. Convinced that federal regulations hamstrung businesses and raised operating costs and prices, Ford directed administration economists to study deregulating various industries. While Ford's term in office proved too brief to implement large-scale deregulation, succeeding presidents carried out initiatives that Ford recommended, such as airline deregulation, which President Jimmy Carter effected in 1978.

The most urgent facet of deregulation involved energy. Since 1971 domestic oil prices had been under price controls, part of the Nixon administration's wage and price control program to contain inflation. Oil producers responded to the disincentive of controlled oil prices by producing less oil. The result was energy shortages, which the 1973 Arab oil embargo exacerbated.

In his 1975 State of the Union address, Ford unveiled an energy program that proposed decontrol of domestic oil, removing price controls within three months. His comprehensive plan also would encourage alternative energy sources, such as coal and nuclear power, and establish a strategic petroleum reserve to store millions of barrels' worth of oil that the president could release during an emergency.

Throughout 1975 congressional Democrats fought Ford on decontrol. They feared that lifting price controls would worsen inflation and enrich the oil companies. The impasse led Ford to compromise. In December 1975 he signed the Energy Policy and Conservation Act, which continued oil price controls but provided for their gradual phaseout over thirty-nine months. This comprehensive energy bill established the right-on-red traffic law, which allowed motorists to turn right on a red light to conserve the gasoline wasted while cars idled. The legislation also established a strategic petroleum reserve and included corporate average fuel economy standards, designed to induce automakers to produce more fuel-efficient fleets.

During 1975 Ford also clashed with legislators over diplomacy. Hoping to stave off South Vietnam's collapse before advancing Communist North Vietnamese forces, Ford proposed a $722 million military and economic aid package to South Vietnam in April 1975. Congress rejected it. Two weeks later the North Vietnamese army overran Saigon, South Vietnam's capital, and Ford ordered an evacuation of the American embassy. Thousands of South Vietnamese fled to the safety of American aircraft carriers stationed offshore. This episode marked the emphatic end of America's decades-long commitment to the country, and Ford recalled it as one of his presidency's saddest moments.

Amid South Vietnam's ruins, Ford tried to redeem America's standing. He welcomed thousands of South Vietnamese refugees to the United States, despite congressional resistance and nativist resentment. In May 1975 Ford acted vigorously when Cambodian pirates seized the American merchant ship the SS *Mayagüez*, taking its thirty-nine crew members hostage. Ford ordered military reprisals, and the Cambodians released the Americans unharmed. After the *Mayagüez* crisis, Ford's public approval ratings spiked eleven points, surpassing the 50 percent mark for one of the few times in his presidency.

Ford also traveled abroad extensively. In 1974 he went to the Soviet Union to negotiate a framework for a second Strategic Arms Limitation Treaty with the Soviet president Leonid Brezhnev. On the same trip Ford became the first president to visit Japan. In 1975 he followed up on Nixon's China initiative to make only the second presidential visit to that country. Also in 1975 he met with leaders of America's industrialized allies—the United Kingdom, France, Italy, Japan, and West Germany—in France, and in 1976 in Puerto Rico, he hosted the heads of those countries as well as the Canadian prime minister. These meetings to discuss economic and trade policies marked the beginning of the G7 ("Group of Seven") summit talks, which have continued annually at different host sites.

In July 1975 Ford participated in the Conference on Security and Cooperation in Europe, in Helsinki, Finland. There he signed the Helsinki Accords, which he regarded as his crowning diplomatic achievement. Thirty-four nations as well as the Vatican signed the accords, which provided for the greater movement of people, ideas, and technology across Eastern European boundaries. By making the Iron Curtain more porous, the Helsinki Accords encouraged agitation within the Soviet Union's satellite countries, hastening the breakdown of Communism there.

Even so, the Helsinki Accords angered conservatives, who protested that the policies ratified the Iron Curtain. This conflict reflected Ford's uncomfortable relationship with the Republican right. As a traditional conservative, Ford had impeccable career credentials, advocating smaller government and lower federal spending. His support of détente, however, irritated cold war hawks, and his moderate leanings on social issues earned suspicion from social conservatives and evangelicals, whom the Grand Old Party (GOP, the Republican Party) started increasingly to count as a core constituency during the 1970s. The Republican right rallied around Ronald W. Reagan, the former California governor, who challenged Ford in the 1976 GOP primaries. Although Ford eventually won the nomination, the Reagan ruckus cost him dearly by dividing the GOP and diverting his energy and resources.

Following the Democratic National Convention in July, Ford trailed the Democratic nominee, the former Georgia governor Carter, by thirty-three points in a Gallup poll. The president's campaign strategists devised a plan. For the first part of the fall campaign, Ford stayed at the White House to concentrate on executive duties and to enhance his "presidential" image. His running mate, Senator Bob Dole of Kansas, stumped for him, making speeches attacking Carter. Ford hit the campaign trail in October, aided by an advertising blitz in the campaign's last days. A central element to Ford's strategy was challenging Carter to debate on national television, leading to three face-offs between the two men. Ford thus revived a practice not seen since the 1960 election and became the first incumbent president to engage in campaign debates.

By election day Ford had pulled even with Carter in the polls, making one of the greatest comebacks in presidential history, but a sluggish economy, with unemployment hovering at nearly 8 percent, and voter disenchantment over Watergate combined to doom Ford. He lost the popular vote by two points, 50 percent to 48 percent, and by a close Electoral College margin, 297 to 240.

Ford retired to Rancho Mirage, where he and his wife moved into a new home on a golf course. The couple spent summers in Beaver Creek, Colorado. In 1979 his memoir, *A Time to Heal*, appeared, and in 1987 he published another book, *Humor and the Presidency*.

Ford declined to run for president in 1980, but at that year's Republican National Convention, the nominee, Reagan, asked Ford to be his running mate. After considering the offer, Ford turned it down. Although Reagan had done little campaigning for Ford four years earlier, Ford more generously stumped on Reagan's behalf in 1980, arguing that Reagan would make a better president than Carter.

The former president supervised the activities of the Gerald R. Ford Foundation, which oversaw his presidential museum in Grand Rapids and presidential library in Ann Arbor, Michigan. Ford directed that the museum and the library be located at separate sites, the former in his hometown, the latter on the campus of his alma mater to aid scholarly activity.

Ford kept his pulse on politics by making appearances for Republican presidential candidates and attending all GOP conventions up to 2000. When President Bill Clinton tried to secure approval of the North American Free Trade Agreement in 1993, Ford came to the president's aid with strong arguments for it. He also criticized Clinton publicly for his behavior during the Monica Lewinsky sex scandal.

Accolades came after Ford left office. In 1999 he received the Presidential Medal of Freedom, and in 2001 the John F. Kennedy Foundation awarded him its Profile in Courage Award for the Nixon pardon. To Ford, some of the most personally meaningful honors came from his alma mater. In 1994 the University of Michigan retired his football jersey, and in 2000 the university renamed its school of public policy for him.

Golfing and swimming remained Ford's favorite recreational pursuits during retirement. After suffering a ministroke in 2000, he curtailed activity and public appearances. He died of cardiovascular failure at his Rancho Mirage home. At age ninety-three years and five months, he had lived longer than any former president. He is buried at his Grand Rapids presidential museum.

After Watergate, Ford was proud that no scandal had marred his presidency. He reflected, "In the relatively short period of time that I served, the major problem was to restore integrity and confidence to the White House, which we did." His congenial personality also helped to rebuild tattered relations between the president and Congress, despite political disagreements, and with foreign leaders, with whom Ford enjoyed stable friendships. Ford also steadied the shaky economy. While unemployment remained high, he presided over a dramatic drop in inflation, which was just 5.7 percent during 1976. Ford liked to emphasize long-term policies, and several key ideas—his focus on inflation, tax cuts, lower deficits, deregulation, and allied economic summits—later became policies that presidents of both parties embraced.

★

The Gerald R. Ford Presidential Library in Ann Arbor houses Ford's papers and those of administration members. His Grand Rapids museum contains exhibits and memorabilia on his life. Personal memoirs are *A Time to Heal: The Autobiography of Gerald R. Ford* (1979) and Elizabeth Ford, *The Times of My Life* (1978). A comprehensive account of Ford's life up to his presidency is James Cannon, *Time and Chance: Gerald Ford's Appointment with History* (1994). Thomas DeFrank, *Write It When I'm Gone: Remarkable Off-the-Record Conversations with Gerald R. Ford* (2007), contains Ford's reflections during retirement. A brief biography is Douglas Brinkley, *Gerald R. Ford* (2007). Administration

members' accounts include Robert Hartmann, *Palace Politics: An Inside Account of the Ford Years* (1980), and Ron Nessen, *It Sure Looks Different from the Inside* (1978). Scholarly analyses of Ford's presidency are Bernard Firestone and Alexej Ugrinsky, eds., *Gerald Ford and the Politics of Post-Watergate America* (1993); John Greene, *The Presidency of Gerald R. Ford* (1995); Richard Norton Smith's essay accompanying David Kennerly's photographs in *Extraordinary Circumstances: The Presidency of Gerald R. Ford* (2008); and Yanek Mieczkowski, *Gerald Ford and the Challenges of the 1970s* (2005). A topical treatment of subjects and events during Ford's presidency as well as biographies of Ford, Betty Ford, and Rockefeller are in Mieczkowski, "Gerald Ford," in Nancy Beck Young, ed., *The Encyclopedia of the U.S. Presidency* (2008). An obituary is in the *New York Times* (27 Dec. 2006).

Yanek Mieczkowski

FORD, Gwyllyn Samuel Newton ("Glenn") (*b.* 1 May 1916 in Sainte-Christine, Quebec, Canada; *d.* 30 August 2006 in Beverly Hills, California), sturdy, dependable Hollywood leading man who won stardom during the 1940s and 1950s and built a career playing average yet heroic characters.

Ford was the only child of Newton Ford, a mill owner and a railway executive, and Hannah (Mitchell) Ford, a homemaker. Ford's father was the nephew of Sir John Macdonald, a Canadian prime minister, and a descendant of Martin Van Buren, a U.S. president. At age four Ford debuted onstage in a community theater production of *Tom Thumb's Wedding* (1920). In 1922 his family moved to the United States and settled in Santa Monica, California. Ford became enamored with acting while attending Santa Monica High School, whose drama club eventually presented an annual Glenn Ford Award to the best actor in a school play.

Following his graduation in 1934, Ford worked as an assistant stage manager and acted and toured with local theater groups; his first professional stage appearance came in a 1935 production of *The Children's Hour*. Ford debuted onscreen as an emcee in *Night in Manhattan* (1937), a one-reel Paramount Pictures musical short. He then made his lone Broadway appearance in *Soliloquy* (1938), a melodrama that ran for two performances. To support himself when not acting, he worked as a roofer, a window installer, and a barkeep.

In 1939 Ford became a naturalized U.S. citizen. That same year the boyishly good-looking actor was given a screen test at Twentieth Century–Fox, where he made his first feature, *Heaven with a Barbed Wire Fence* (1939). Then he signed a long-term contract with Columbia

Glenn Ford. SILVER SCREEN COLLECTION/HULTON ARCHIVE/ GETTY IMAGES

Pictures. Harry Cohn, the studio chief, wanted to rename him John Gower, but Ford refused, agreeing to change only his first name. His father's birthplace was Glenford, a Canadian town, so Ford rechristened himself "Glenn."

At Columbia, Ford appeared in such luridly titled potboilers as *My Son Is Guilty* (1939), *Convicted Woman* (1940), *Men Without Souls* (1940), and *Babies for Sale* (1940). His assignments improved with his next several films. He was cast in *So Ends Our Night* (1941), playing a German-Jewish refugee; *Texas* (1941), portraying a cowboy along with William Holden (who became his best friend); *The Adventures of Martin Eden* (1942), as a struggling writer; and *The Desperadoes* (1943), as an outlaw who reforms. All of these roles were age appropriate for Ford, but he did not establish an identifiable screen persona.

In 1942, after America's entry into World War II, Ford joined the U.S. Coast Guard Auxiliary. The following year he became a U.S. Marine. On 24 October 1943 he married the tap dancer Eleanor Powell, whom he met at a war bond rally. She became pregnant while Ford was on leave and gave birth to a son in 1945.

While he was in the military, Ford constructed safe houses in France as havens for those eluding the Nazis, and he trained resistance fighters. After Germany's surrender,

Ford learned that 15,000 malnourished inmates were housed at Fernwald, a concentration camp near Munich, Germany. Disobeying orders, he organized the delivery of food and medical supplies to the inmates; he was responsible for saving over 5,000 lives.

Upon leaving the Marine Corps in 1945, Ford returned to Columbia and was assigned the male lead in *Gilda* (1946), a film noir. His character in *Gilda*—Johnny Farrell, a money-hungry gambler-adventurer who has a complex relationship with the title character—was unlike those Ford would later regularly play. While Ford was well cast, the film is best recalled for the steamy presence of Rita Hayworth's Gilda and her sultry rendition of "Put the Blame on Mame."

Despite Hayworth's kudos, Ford emerged a bankable leading man, capable of acquitting himself in a range of genres, from Westerns and crime dramas to romantic and domestic comedies. Over the next fifteen years Ford accepted starring roles in plenty of forgettable films and a few Hollywood classics. Rarely was he cast as a character like Farrell. He primarily played likable heroes, steady and secure, quietly authoritative and resolute.

After *Gilda*, Ford costarred in *A Stolen Life* (1946), cast as the love object of a pair of twins, both played by Bette Davis. Throughout the rest of the decade and into the 1950s, Ford was a constant presence in movie houses, appearing in four features each in 1948 and 1949, five features each in 1953 and 1955, and four features in 1958. Most were eminently forgettable, from *Gallant Journey* (1946) and *The Mating of Millie* (1948) to *Torpedo Run* (1958) and *It Started with a Kiss* (1959). Unlike his pal Holden, Ford never became a superstar. He was never an Academy Award winner or even a nominee.

Most of Ford's best films were celebrated for reasons other than his presence. In *The Big Heat* (1953), one of the last pictures Ford made while under contract with Columbia, he was solidly cast as a scrupulous cop who battles a crime syndicate. However, the film is best remembered for the director Fritz Lang's take on the nature of evil and the then-shocking sequence in which a menacing Lee Marvin tosses scalding coffee in the face of Gloria Grahame. Ford was equally effective as a dedicated high school teacher in *Blackboard Jungle* (1955), but this film is recalled for the actors playing Ford's charges, including the young Sidney Poitier and Vic Morrow, and for the presence on the soundtrack of Bill Haley and the Comets' "Rock Around the Clock." It was the first time rock and roll was heard in a motion picture.

While acquitting himself nicely in a pair of military comedies, *The Teahouse of the August Moon* (1956) and *Don't Go near the Water* (1957), Ford did some of his best work in three adult Westerns, all directed by Delmar Daves: *Jubal* (1956), playing a drifter turned ranch hand; *3:10 to Yuma* (1957), cast against type as a deadly (albeit charming) outlaw; and *Cowboy* (1958), playing a tough veteran trail boss. Ford gave perhaps his finest performance in *3:10 to Yuma*, one that is as multileveled as his character. Everyone fears Ford's cold-blooded killer, who is ornery and subtly sarcastic but also capable of great tenderness. Adding to the irony of the characterization are Ford's pleasant face and humane countenance, which served him well in his more heroic characterizations.

In 1958 Ford was commissioned a lieutenant commander in the U.S. Naval Reserve. The following year he and Powell divorced. Around this time Ford was named the number-one box-office draw in the Quigley annual survey of motion-picture exhibitors. Ford was still considered a second-tier star, even though he rated the lead roles in three high-profile remakes of Hollywood classics—*Cimarron* (1960), *Pocketful of Miracles* (1961), and *The Four Horsemen of the Apocalypse* (1962)—and continued to display his versatility in films from *Experiment in Terror* (1962), playing a tough Federal Bureau of Investigation agent, to *The Courtship of Eddie's Father* (1963), cast as a widower with a sweetly meddlesome son.

For years Ford lived on a small cattle ranch. In the mid-1960s he erected a lavish Beverly Hills home whose centerpieces were a facsimile of an English pub and an atrium with a 900-pound artificial sun. He personally installed the home's electrical wiring and air-conditioning units and worked on its plumbing. During this period he married for a second time, to the actress Kathryn Hays. They wed on 27 March 1966 and divorced three years later. In 1967–1968, in his capacity as a U.S. Navy reservist, Ford served two tours of duty in Vietnam.

In the early 1970s Ford's career as a big-screen leading man was on the wane, and he moved over to television. He appeared in a dozen made-for-television features and several miniseries, and he starred in two short-lived series: *Cade's County* (1971–1972), cast as a sheriff, and *The Family Holvak* (1975), playing a minister. On 27 March 1977 Ford married the model Cynthia Hayward, but the couple divorced seven years later. By now Ford's feature-film appearances were infrequent, with his most memorable being a cameo as Clark Kent's adoptive father in *Superman* (1978). That same year the Western Heritage Museum inducted Ford into the National Cowboy Hall of Fame. For his heroism during World War II he was awarded the Simon Wiesenthal Center for Holocaust Studies' Liberator's Award in 1985 and the French Legion of Honor in 1992. He retired in 1991, after being afflicted with blood clots in his legs. On 5 March 1993 he wed one final time. This marriage, to Jeanne Baus, a nurse, lasted barely six months.

In May 2006, on his ninetieth birthday, Ford was feted at Hollywood's Egyptian Theater. Ill health prevented him from attending. Later that year he died at his son's Beverly Hills mansion. Complications from a series of strokes were the cause of death. He is buried in a mausoleum at Woodlawn Cemetery in Santa Monica.

For an actor who neither won top-flight superstardom nor earned a single Academy Award nomination, Ford was a durable leading man who starred in dozens of films across several decades and even in a few bona fide classics. He was an expert at underplaying and was adept at performing both light comedy and high drama. The critic Philip French noted that Ford "never turned in an inadequate, unconsidered performance."

Ford's autobiography is *Glenn Ford, RFD Beverly Hills* (1970), a slim, 185-page volume written with Margaret Redfield. Obituaries are in the *New York Times* (31 Aug. 2006) and London's *Guardian* and *Daily Telegraph* (both 1 Sept. 2006).

Rob Edelman

FOSSETT, James Stephen ("Steve") (*b.* 22 April 1944 in Jackson, Tennessee; *d.* c. 3 September 2007 in California), adventurer known for breaking records in hot-air ballooning, aviation, and sailing.

Fossett was born in Tennessee but grew up in Garden Grove, California. Despite having asthma, Fossett began pushing himself to great physical feats at an early age. As an adolescent he discovered a passion for hiking. He recalled, "When I was 12 years old I climbed my first mountain, and I just kept going, taking on more diverse and grander projects." In his youth Fossett participated in many outings as a Boy Scout and later as an Eagle Scout. Earning the rank of Eagle Scout, a difficult achievement even for those who did not suffer from asthma, demonstrated Fossett's level of discipline, tenacity, and physical capabilities, which he carried throughout his life.

After graduating from Garden Grove High School in 1962, Fossett attended Stanford University, earning a BA in economics in 1966. Before graduating, he served as a student body officer, was president of various clubs, and engaged in outdoor adventures. As a senior Fossett swam to Alcatraz—an island in the middle of San Francisco Bay and the site of an infamous prison—to hang a banner reading "Beat Cal" on the wall of the prison, which had been closed for two years. In the summer following graduation, Fossett traveled to Europe, where he swam the Dardanelles (the narrow strait between Europe and Turkey), climbed the Matterhorn in the Swiss Alps, and scaled the Eiger, where he slid hundreds of feet down a glacier and nearly died.

Steve Fossett, 2006. AP IMAGES

In 1968 Fossett married Peggy Viehland from Richmond Heights, Missouri; the couple had no children. In the same year he earned an MBA from the Olin School of Business at Washington University in St. Louis. After earning his graduate degree, Fossett worked in computer systems, first for International Business Machines and then for Marshall Field's. It was not long before Fossett discovered that a career in financial markets better suited him. In 1980 he formed Lakota Trading, a Chicago-based trading firm. For fifteen years he worked the floor of the exchanges, compiling a highly successful trading record. Fossett proclaimed that floor trading came naturally to him: "I'm a very competitive person, and I'm also very methodical. Those two aspects are key to being successful in financial trading."

These traits are also key to successful outdoor adventuring. In the early 1980s Fossett resumed mountain climbing, teaming up with Pat Morrow, who was trying to become the first person to climb each of the seven summits (the highest mountain on each continent). Fossett eventually climbed six of the seven summits—all but Everest. In addition to mountain climbing, Fossett ran marathons, completed cross-country ski races, raced cars, and swam long distances. In 1985 he swam the English

Channel, from France to England, even as he claimed he was not a very strong swimmer.

As his business experienced greater success, Fossett devoted more time to adventure sports. In 1990 he moved from Chicago to Beaver Creek, Colorado, where he began spending half his time on his business and the other half on adventure sports. By now he had become a multimillionaire. In 1992 he completed the Iditarod Trail Sled Dog Race in Alaska. In 1993 and 1996 he drove the twenty-four-hour Le Mans sports-car endurance race in France. In 1994 he competed in the Route de Rhum, a top-level sailing event, placing fifth. In 1996 he entered the Ironman Triathlon in Hawaii. In 2004 he set the world record for fastest circumnavigation of the world, sailing with a crew of twelve. In all Fossett set twenty-one sailing records.

Of all his adventures, it was Fossett's experiences in hot-air balloons that perhaps gained him the most attention. In 1995 Fossett became the first person to fly across the Pacific Ocean in a balloon. This achievement gave him the confidence he needed to work toward completing the first solo balloon flight around the word. For seven years he worked toward this goal, and by 2001 he had attempted the feat five separate times. In an attempt in 1998, Fossett ran into a serious thunderstorm that ruptured his balloon. After falling 29,000 feet into the Coral Sea, 500 miles east of Australia, he amazingly escaped unharmed. Before he crashed, Fossett had traveled 14,235.33 miles, breaking a world record in solo hot-air ballooning.

After this feat Fossett joined Richard Branson and Per Lindstrand to compete in the ICO Global Challenger Round-the-World event in 1998. They got halfway around the world. Shortly after, on 1 March 1999, a balloonist pair, Bertrand Piccard and Brian Jones, captured one of Fossett's goals: They became the first to fly a balloon nonstop around the world. Nevertheless, Fossett did not abandon his dream to become the first solo balloonist to travel around the globe. On 1 July 2002 Fossett fulfilled this dream, making the 20,626-mile flight in thirteen days, eight hours, and thirty-three minutes.

Following this milestone, Fossett dedicated a lot of time to chasing aviation records. In 2005, piloting the GlobalFlyer, a single-engine jet aircraft designed by Virgin Atlantic, he became the first person to achieve a solo, nonstop flight around the world. In 2006 he broke the airplane nonstop flight distance record of 24,986 miles. Soon after, however, Fossett's record-chasing days would come to a halt.

On 3 September 2007 Fossett borrowed a single-engine airplane from Barron Hilton at Hilton's Flying-M Ranch in Nevada, fueling up for four to five hours of flight. When he had not returned six hours later, a search began. The search involved the Civil Air Patrol, the National Guard, and around 50,000 volunteers, who scoured high-resolution satellite images for signs of Fossett's plane. The $1.6-million search for Fossett represented the largest search-and-rescue effort for a single person in the United States.

On 27 November 2007 Fossett's wife petitioned the Cook County Circuit Court in Chicago to declare her husband legally dead. On 15 February 2008, among unfounded rumors that Fossett might have faked his own death, Fossett was legally put to rest. A year after his disappearance, Fossett's remains were found in a remote section of the Sierra Nevada in California near the wreckage of his plane. Before his September 2007 disappearance, Fossett had compiled an impressive 115 world records and world firsts.

Fossett's autobiography, *Chasing the Wind: The Autobiography of Steve Fossett* (2006), provides detailed information about his adventures and some personal information. Between 2006 and 2008 *Airport Journals* published eight articles about Fossett. Obituaries are in the London *Times* (18 Feb. 2008) and the *Economist* (21 Feb. 2008).

Candice L. Mancini

Bill France, Jr., 1997. AP IMAGES

FRANCE, William Clifton ("Bill"), Jr. (*b.* 4 April 1933 in Washington, D.C.; *d.* 4 June 2007 in Daytona Beach, Florida), longtime president of the National Association for Stock Car Auto Racing (NASCAR).

France was one of two sons born to William Henry Getty France, the legendary founder of NASCAR, and Anne (Bledsoe) France. The economic and social hardships of the Great Depression forced the Frances to relocate, and in 1934 they established a new home in Daytona Beach. With the elder France's involvement in racing, it is hardly surprising that stock car racing became the younger France's vocation and passion. France immersed himself in the landscape of racetracks and was a cheerful presence at the Daytona Beach Road Course. His apprenticeship was far from grand. He learned the ropes by working concession stands, selling tickets, and parking cars.

France attended Seabreeze High School in Daytona Beach, where he was an able but not stellar basketball player. Upon graduation in 1951, he stayed near home, attending the University of Florida in Gainesville for two years. After two years of service in the U.S. Navy, he returned to Daytona Beach and devoted the rest of his life to sustaining and capitalizing on his father's legacy.

The Frances' dream was to carve and craft a racetrack—and a pioneering sports entertainment complex—from an ugly stretch of terrain that was mostly swampland. France recalled that they worked "seven days a week for 13 months to build the speedway. We went from 7 in the morning to 7 at night, and worked in the winter until it got dark."

Although France tried car racing as a young man, he never took part in NASCAR racing as a career. However, he was an avid motorcycle enthusiast and had a love of off-road racing. He participated in the Baja 1000 in the early 1970s, and his encouragement helped the eventual growth of motocross at Daytona, in turn helping to create the cultural phenomenon known as the Daytona Beach Bike Week.

On 10 January 1972 control of NASCAR passed from Bill France, Sr., to Bill France, Jr. It is important to note that this transfer of power took place just as NASCAR was moving out of the shadows to establish itself as a major sports player. The sport had sufficient sponsors and spectators to launch the Grand National Circuit and, in the swashbuckling figure of the driver Richard Petty, had a genuine American folk hero.

By the end of the decade (18 February 1979), France had negotiated a broadcasting coup whereby one of the country's top television networks (Columbia Broadcasting

System) broadcast the Daytona 500 in its entirety. NASCAR's survival was tied to the business model of wooing and securing robust financial support. In 1986 France happily found a new major sponsor for stock car racing, the tobacco company R. J. Reynolds. As a result, the Grand National Circuit was renamed the Winston Cup Series. In 2004 France supervised a shift from the R. J. Reynolds Winston brand to a decade-long deal with Nextel worth $700 million.

France's thirty-one-year reign as NASCAR chairman was highlighted by key positioning moves that consistently elevated the prestige of and popular support for the sport. In 1989 every Winston Cup race was televised, and on 16 May 1992, at what was then the Charlotte Motor Speedway, NASCAR showcased its inaugural race under lights. In 1994 France was roundly criticized for straying into foreign territory, with his project of taking NASCAR to the fabled home of auto racing, the Indianapolis Speedway. In fact this move was a stroke of genius. With the successes enjoyed by the young, charismatic driver Jeff Gordon, France steered stock car racing into its position as a significant national sport.

In 1997 and 1998, under France's leadership, NASCAR opened three new tracks—California Speedway, Texas Motor Speedway, and Las Vegas Motor Speedway. In 2000 France handed over the day-to-day running of NASCAR to Senior Vice President Mike Helton.

Though France was plagued by a series of illnesses in the last years of his life, his contribution to the consolidation and expansion of NASCAR was monumental. France oversaw the drawing up of multiyear contracts—a staggering $2.4 billion—announced on 11 November 1999. These contracts, giving NASCAR long-term deals with the Fox, National Broadcasting Company, and Turner networks, were a testament to an extraordinary individual who masterminded the transformation of a regional sport into a national headline sport, with a February to November race series.

France was diagnosed with cancer in 1999. He continued as NASCAR's chairman and chief executive officer until passing on those titular roles to his son, Brian, in 2003. Thanks to France's shrewd business acumen, NASCAR, as an institution, remained essentially a "France" operation. At the time of France's death, the family still owned the Daytona Speedway, and with a controlling interesting the International Speedway Corporation, they effectively owned thirteen racetracks.

France married Betty Jane Zachary on 20 September 1957. They had two children, Brian and Lesa France Kennedy. A preeminent focus of the France family was their desire and ability to be successful as a team organization. Jane Zachary France was chair of the NASCAR Foundation, and Lesa France Kennedy served as president of the International Speedway Corporation.

France died of cancer during the running of the Autism Speaks 400 Nextel Cup Race at the Dover International Speedway. He was inducted into the International Motorsports Hall of Fame and the Motorcycle Hall of Fame in 2004. In 2006 his name appeared in the Automotive Hall of Fame. France is buried at Daytona Memorial Park in Daytona Beach.

France's leadership style has been described as being that of a "benevolent dictator." His management focus was a "three point philosophy: safety, low cost and competitive racing." The driver Jeff Burton said in reference to France, "Part of leadership is having the guts to make a decision and then having the guts to stand by it. That's what he did on a lot of occasions."

Obituaries are in *USA Today* and the *New York Times* (both 4 June 2007).

Scott A. G. M. Crawford

FRANK, (Israel) Reuven (*b.* 7 December 1920 in Montreal, Quebec, Canada; *d.* 5 February 2006 in Englewood, New Jersey), pioneer in television journalism and twice president of NBC (National Broadcasting Company) News.

Frank was the son of Moses Zebi Frank, a journalist, and Anna (Rivenovich) Frank, a homemaker. Frank grew up in Toronto, Canada. He had at least one sibling, a sister. After graduating from Harbord Collegiate Institute, a high school in Toronto, in 1937, he studied at the University of Toronto for three years. In 1940 he immigrated to the United States, earned a BS from the City College of New York in 1942, and became a citizen in 1943. He served in the U.S. Army from 1943 until 1946. Following his discharge, he married Bernice Kaplow on 9 June 1946; they had two sons. In 1947 Frank earned an MS in journalism from Columbia University.

Frank worked for three years as a reporter and night city editor for the *Newark Evening News* and then joined NBC in August 1950 as a television news writer. When Frank started working at NBC, fewer than 10 percent of U.S. households had television, the network consisted of only sixty local stations, and practically all Americans relied on newspapers or radio as their primary source of news. In March 1951 Frank became a writer for the *Camel News Caravan*, the fifteen-minute NBC evening news broadcast. Frank quickly became a "partisan" of television news because, as he explained, "television enables the audience to see things happen, and that is what newspapers and magazines and radio cannot duplicate."

Reuven Frank. NBC TELEVISION/ARCHIVE PHOTOS/GETTY IMAGES

In 1954 Frank left *Camel News Caravan* to work on documentaries and news specials for NBC. In 1955 he was awarded a Sigma Delta Chi Award for television writing for *The Road to Spandau*, a program about Nazi war criminals in Spandau prison. He also worked as a writer and producer of weekly newsmagazines, including the short-lived *Background* and the more successful *Outlook*, which premiered in April 1956 with Chet Huntley as host. During that summer, as producer of NBC's coverage of the Democratic and Republican national conventions, Frank paired Huntley with David Brinkley, the Washington reporter for the *Camel News Caravan*, as coanchors of the network's convention broadcasts. Their collaboration was highly successful, with Brinkley's dry wit and skepticism complementing Huntley's stolid, authoritative manner. On 29 October 1956 the *Huntley-Brinkley Report*, with Huntley reporting from New York and Brinkley from Washington, D.C., replaced the *Camel News Caravan*. Frank was the producer of the new program, and he decided only minutes before the premiere how each evening's broadcast would end. "Goodnight, Chet; Goodnight, David" became a phrase familiar to millions of Americans, and it marked a new era in television news. The anchors' distinctive styles made them a popular team,

as did their ability to report the news in a concise, engaging fashion. The *Huntley-Brinkley Report* became the most influential as well as the top-rated network newscast, a position it held until the mid-1960s.

Frank produced NBC's convention and election night coverage in 1960 and then left the daily responsibilities of the *Huntley-Brinkley Report* in 1962 to concentrate on documentaries. His most celebrated work was *The Tunnel* (1962), a program that showed West Berliners digging an escape route beneath the Berlin Wall, allowing fifty-nine East Germans to flee Communist rule. *The Tunnel* won many awards, including an Emmy for program of the year.

Frank resumed his duties as producer of the *Huntley-Brinkley Report* in 1963 to supervise the expansion of that newscast from fifteen to thirty minutes. In preparation for the transition, Frank wrote a memorandum that summarized his most important ideas about television news. "The highest power of television journalism is not in the transmission of information but in the transmission of experience," Frank declared. Newspapers reported about food shortages, while "television can show hunger," he explained. "We have found a dimension of information which is not contained in words alone." NBC staffers called this memorandum "The Bible," and portions have been printed in journalism textbooks. The first thirty-minute broadcast aired on 9 September 1963, with Huntley and Brinkley interviewing President John F. Kennedy.

Frank left the *Huntley-Brinkley Report* a final time in 1965 but continued to hold major news-producing and executive responsibilities at NBC. He became, in succession, vice president (18 January 1966), executive vice president (13 March 1967), and president (13 June 1968) of NBC News. He produced the network's coverage of the national party conventions in 1964 and 1968. When Huntley retired in 1970, Frank created the *NBC Nightly News*, with Brinkley sharing anchor duties with Frank McGee and John Chancellor. Frank, however, quickly became persuaded that this troika system did not work well and assigned McGee to the *Today* show, Brinkley to commentary, and Chancellor to the position of sole anchor.

Frank resigned the presidency of NBC News in January 1973 to concentrate on documentaries and newsmagazines. He created *Weekend* (1974–1979), which at first shared a time slot with another new NBC production, *Saturday Night Live*, and *NBC News Overnight*, a latenight newsmagazine show that aired during 1982–1983. Frank returned to the presidency of NBC News in 1982. His most notable decision during his second stint as president was to make Tom Brokaw the sole anchor of the *NBC Nightly News*, a position Brokaw held from 1983 to 2004. In 1984 Frank resigned as news president once more to make documentaries and retired from NBC in

1988. He died of complications from pneumonia at the age of eighty-five.

Frank was the most important figure in the development of NBC as a major news organization. For nearly half a century, he chose the journalists who sat in the NBC anchor chairs. His innovations in convention coverage, including a central network anchor booth and a team of floor reporters, helped define how television networks covered political conventions. Frank understood the visual power of television news, yet he also emphasized the importance of a compelling narrative. He wrote, "Every news story should, without any sacrifice of probity or responsibility, display the attributes of fiction, of drama." At times Frank seemed almost "a Talmudic figure," Brokaw recollected, "a wise and reserved man" who thought deeply about his profession. His importance came from translating those ideas into actions and policies and, in so doing, helping to invent television news.

★

Frank wrote a memoir of his years at NBC, titled *Out of Thin Air: The Brief Wonderful Life of Network News* (1991). Discussions of his work at NBC during the 1950s and 1960s are in Erik Barnouw, *Tube of Plenty: The Evolution of American Television*, 2nd ed. (1990), and James L. Baughman, *Same Time, Same Station: Creating American Television, 1948–1961* (2007). An obituary is in the *New York Times* (7 Feb. 2006).

Chester Pach

FRASER, Douglas Andrew ("Doug") (*b.* 18 December 1919 in Glasgow, Scotland; *d.* 23 February 2008 in Southfield, Michigan), American labor leader who was president of the International Union, United Automobile, Aerospace and Agricultural Implement Workers of America (UAW) and a professor of labor studies at Wayne State University.

Fraser was the son of Samuel Douglas and Sarah (Andrew Casey) Douglas. His father was a college-educated electrician and a trade unionist in Scotland; his mother was a homemaker. The family followed Samuel to Detroit, leaving Scotland in 1922 and passing through Ellis Island in April 1923.

Growing up during the Great Depression left a lasting impression upon Fraser. His family often struggled when his father was unemployed. Fraser attended union meetings with his activist father and soon developed a devotion to the labor movement. In 1934 he left high school, never to finish, and found work at a Ford Motor Company machine shop. Fraser's career in the labor movement began with this first job; he was soon fired for union organizing. "The best way to describe it," Fraser said of his reasons for joining the labor movement at Ford, "there was no dignity [for workers]." He subsequently had the same experience at his next job with the Ever Hot Heaters Company.

Fraser then landed a job at Chrysler Corporation's Dodge Main Plant in 1936. He moved to the corporation's De Soto plant one year later, earning $1.15 an hour as a metal finisher. He joined UAW Local Union 22 and soon became a steward, then chief steward and recording secretary for the local union. In 1943 Fraser was elected to the first of three terms as president of Local 227, including a term during which he was drafted and served in the U.S. Army, from 1945 to 1946.

Fraser sharpened his skills as a trade unionist in the 1950s. He became a UAW international representative in 1947 and was assigned to the union's Chrysler Department. In 1950 Fraser's performance as a negotiator during the 104-day strike against Chrysler attracted the attention of UAW president Walter Reuther. One year later Reuther asked Fraser to become his administrative assistant, a position he held until 1959. Fraser became an important UAW leader during the 1960s and 1970s. Hoping to have a greater impact upon the union, he successfully ran for the position of Region 1A codirector in 1959. In 1964 Fraser was elected to the UAW Executive Board as a member at large, and in 1970 he was elected a UAW vice president.

While traveling to the UAW's Education Center at Black Lake in northern Michigan on 9 May 1970, Reuther died in a plane crash. Fraser and then UAW vice president Leonard Woodcock were both considered for the president's office. After a poll revealed that the International Executive Board favored Woodcock by thirteen to twelve, Fraser stepped aside and nominated Woodcock for UAW president, deciding that an internal political battle was not in the best interests of the union.

After Woodcock retired, Fraser was elected president of the UAW by acclamation in 1977. He was a hardworking, hands-on president, who was often inside an automobile factory, on the picket line, marching in support of the civil rights movement, or meeting with national political leaders. As president, Fraser was extremely popular with the UAW membership, and he was highly respected by automotive executives as well as civic leaders and international statesmen.

Fraser faced the greatest challenge of his career in 1979. The Chrysler Corporation was nearly bankrupt, and over 100,000 union jobs would be lost if the company failed. With the clout of the UAW behind him, he successfully lobbied Congress and President Jimmy Carter in support of $1.2 billion in federal loan guarantees for Chrysler. Fraser negotiated new contracts with the corporation; three times within fourteen months he persuaded UAW workers to give wage and benefit concessions to the company. As part of the negotiations, the union received a seat on the Chrysler Board of Directors, which Fraser held from 1980 to 1984. Chrysler CEO Lee Iacocca stated: "What Doug did was ground breaking. . . . Without him, we never would have survived."

Fraser loved being president of the UAW, but at the union's convention in 1983, following the unwritten rule that a member should not run for office after reaching the age of sixty-five, Fraser retired and passed the gavel to the incoming president, Owen Bieber. "He [Bieber] had a hell of a time getting it out of my hand," Fraser quipped.

Fraser retired from the UAW in 1983 and began a second career as an educator, becoming a professor of labor studies at Wayne State University in Detroit. During his years as an academic, he lectured at the University of Michigan; Harvard University; the University of California, Berkeley; the Massachusetts Institute of Technology; and other institutions of higher learning.

Fraser was also a family man. His first marriage was to Eva Falk in November 1938. They had two daughters and were divorced in May 1967. He married his second wife, Winifred Davis, on 28 July 1967 and helped raise his two stepdaughters. Fraser had several grandchildren.

Fraser retained a keen intellect throughout his life. He suffered from emphysema for many years but kept working until shortly before his death, spending time each week in his office at the Walter Reuther Library on the Wayne State University campus. He donated his body to the Wayne State University Medical School.

Fraser was arguably the most popular labor leader of his era. He was beloved by UAW members as well as highly respected by American corporate and elected leaders. As the later UAW president Ron Gettelfinger stated: "All anyone had to say was 'Doug,' and that was enough for everyone to know who you were talking about." Moreover, Fraser's legacy can be measured by his creative and pragmatic responses to the automobile industry's first major fiscal crisis and his unfailing determination and efforts to improve the lives of, and earn dignity for, all of America's workers and disadvantaged citizens.

★

The best sources for Fraser's career in the UAW are his UAW President, UAW Vice President, and WSU Professor Collections, along with oral interviews and various UAW publications and vertical file materials, held by the Archives of Labor and Urban Affairs, Walter P. Reuther Library, Wayne State University, Detroit. More information can be found in the article "Douglas A. Fraser," found in *Biographical Dictionary of American Labor*, 2nd ed. (1984). Gilbert J. Gall supplies more of Fraser's impact on the automotive industry in the article "Douglas Andrew Fraser" in *Encyclopedia of*

American Business History and Biography: The Automobile Industry, 1920–1980 (1989). An obituary is in the *Washington Post* (25 Feb. 2008).

Mike Smith

FREEDMAN, James Oliver (*b.* 21 September 1935 in Manchester, New Hampshire; *d.* 21 March 2006 in Cambridge, Massachusetts), lawyer, professor, and university president best known for his advocacy of liberal education and diversity during his tenure as president of Dartmouth College.

Freedman was the son of Louis Archer Freedman, a high school English teacher, and Sophie (Gottesman) Freedman, a bank bookkeeper. He and his sister grew up in a home of modest means that was filled with books and lively political discussions. He credited his father with inspiring his lifelong love of books and literature; he credited his mother with his ambition to succeed in a distinguished career, but he also believed her relentless focus on his success contributed to repeated bouts with depression during his youth and early adulthood. In high school he debated, edited the literary magazine, and served as president of the school's national honor society. After graduating third in his class in 1953, he went to Harvard College on full scholarship, earning an AB

James O. Freedman. DARTMOUTH COLLEGE LIBRARY

cum laude in English literature in 1957. He entered Harvard Law School but, depressed and unable to concentrate, quickly withdrew.

After a successful year working as a reporter for his hometown paper, the *Manchester Union Leader*, he entered Yale Law School, earning an LLB cum laude in 1962. Freedman then clerked for Judge Thurgood Marshall at the U.S. Court of Appeals for the Second Circuit in New York and practiced law for one year in New York. He married Bathsheba Ann Finkelstein in 1963; they would have a son and a daughter. In 1964 he joined the University of Pennsylvania faculty as assistant professor of law. As a young man, Freedman had dreamed of writing novels and essays or becoming a biographer or historian. He attributed his decision to teach to values of scholarship and learning he acquired as part of his Jewish identity and his experiences at Harvard. Known for his collegiality, Freedman built a solid reputation as a teacher and scholar in administrative law. Over the years he served as University of Pennsylvania ombudsman, associate provost, and associate dean before being named dean of the law school in 1979.

Freedman left Pennsylvania in 1982 to become president of the University of Iowa. During his five-year tenure there, he set out to improve standards at the medical and law schools and raise faculty salaries. He launched the university's largest fund-raising campaign and established a Center for Asian and Pacific Studies and the Iowa Center for the Book.

In 1987 Freedman was named president of Dartmouth College, making him the first Jewish president of the school and only the second Jewish president of any of the Ivy League colleges. Freedman arrived at Dartmouth during an era of increased national skepticism about undergraduate teaching and learning and fierce debates over diversity, particularly cultural pluralism in college curricula and "political correctness" in regulating student speech. Freedman believed fundamentally in the value of a comprehensive liberal education, not only as career preparation but also as preparation for citizenship and adult life. Freedman's vision for Dartmouth resulted in a new curriculum of greater breadth, helping the college to regain its ranking among the best American liberal arts colleges, particularly in teaching.

Freedman's tenure at Dartmouth was marked by controversies surrounding the *Dartmouth Review*, an off-campus, student-run newspaper whose editors voiced conservative political views. Contributors had been suspended for allegedly harassing a black music professor and were suspected of intentionally inserting an offensive quote from Adolf Hitler's *Mein Kampf* in the newspaper's masthead. The students maintained that this was an act of sabotage for which they were not responsible. The controversy, as well as the college's fraternity culture and its reputation

as a school inhospitable to women and minorities, had injured its prestige and alienated faculty. Freedman publicly denounced the *Dartmouth Review*, labeling it racist, sexist, and anti-Semitic. In response, the *Review* accused Freedman and the college administration of discrimination and of suppressing student speech. In November 1988 the college trustees circulated a letter to students and faculty deploring the *Review*'s depiction of Freedman with a Hitler mustache in a satirical cartoon.

In April 1994 Freedman was diagnosed with non-Hodgkin's lymphoma. He spoke at convocation that year about the challenge of dealing with cancer. By 1995, under his leadership, Dartmouth for the first time had enrolled more women than men and had conducted its most successful capital campaign to date, enabling major additions to academic and student facilities. In addition, Freedman had successfully overseen the most comprehensive restructuring of the undergraduate curriculum since the 1920s; the college installed the graduation requirements of the new curriculum in 1996.

Freedman stepped down from the presidency of Dartmouth in 1998, retiring to Cambridge, Massachusetts. He remained influential in higher education throughout his life as a writer and public speaker, and continued to be an avid book collector. In 2000 Freedman was elected president of the American Academy of Arts and Sciences; in 2003 the American Jewish Committee awarded him its National Distinguished Leadership Award. Freedman died of non-Hodgkin's lymphoma in his home and is buried in Lindwood Memorial Park in Randolph, Massachusetts.

As president of Dartmouth, Freedman was a controversial figure, earning praise from faculty and college trustees and criticism from many students and alumni. In his long and varied career, Freedman spoke and wrote persuasively about the values of the liberal arts and diversity. He defended affirmative action on college campuses in the midst of national efforts to curtail or end the policy. In his view, a critical part of education was to help college and university students distinguish between their constitutional rights to free expression and their moral responsibility to treat all members of the community with civility and tolerance.

★

Some of Freedman's papers are in the University Archives at the University of Iowa. The papers of George B. Monroe in the Dartmouth College Library contain correspondence between Monroe, who was chairman of the Dartmouth board of trustees, and alumni and others illustrating the controversies during the early Freedman administration (1988 to 1991). Freedman's memoir is *Finding the Words: The Education of James O. Freedman* (2007). He authored a legal work, *Crisis and Legitimacy: The Administrative Process and American Government* (1978), and two collections of essays and speeches,

Idealism and Liberal Education (1996) and *Liberal Education and the Public Interest* (2003), that lay out his views on liberal education, the university president's role, and issues of social justice. Obituaries are in the *New York Times* and *Boston Globe* (both 22 Mar. 2006).

Mildred Carstensen

FRIEDAN, Betty Naomi (*b.* 4 February 1921 in Peoria, Illinois; *d.* 4 February 2006 in Washington, D.C.), writer whose book *The Feminine Mystique* (1963) helped spark the women's liberation movement and whose activism helped found several important feminist organizations, including the National Organization for Women.

Born Bettye Naomi Goldstein, Friedan was raised in a middle-class Jewish family in a predominantly Protestant industrial city. Her father, Harry Goldstein, had immigrated from Russia around 1888 and worked his way up from peddling to owning a jewelry store in Peoria. Her

Betty Friedan. SUSAN WOOD/GETTY IMAGES

mother, Miriam (Horwitz) Goldstein, was a housewife from a prominent Peoria Jewish family; before her marriage to Harry, she had been the editor of the women's page of the Peoria newspaper. Friedan and her two younger siblings had a privileged childhood, although Friedan remembered her teenage years as lonely and isolating. A brainy girl with unconventional looks—dark hair, large eyes, and a prominent nose—Friedan did not fit traditional feminine roles and was not conventionally popular in school. Anti-Semitism, moreover, marred the family's life. The Goldsteins could not join the Peoria Country Club, and Friedan was rejected by the sororities that dominated social life at Peoria High School. The Depression further destabilized the Goldsteins' status: As the jewelry store's sales declined, the family fired its household help, and Miriam and Harry fought angrily over finances.

These tensions in the Goldstein household affected Friedan's later feminist politics. The experience of being a Jewish outsider gave her a political outlook that championed the weak and oppressed. And Miriam Goldstein's dissatisfaction with her husband's inability to provide for the household and with her own lack of paid employment led her daughter later to criticize gender roles that limited middle-class women to domestic work in their homes.

In the fall of 1938, Friedan entered Smith College. Because of her excellence in her coursework, her engagement in the campus literary scene, and her unconventional political positions, she became a prominent figure during her four years on campus. She founded a campus literary magazine, *Smith College Monthly*, and became editor in chief of the Smith student newspaper, *Smith College Associated News* (*SCAN*). As a psychology major, she worked with some of the leading figures in the field at the time, including Kurt Koffka and Kurt Lewin. Friedan also became radicalized during her years in college. At the suggestion of several professors, she spent the summer of 1941 at the Highlander Folk School in Monteagle, Tennessee, a school that had been established to teach protest strategies to working-class whites and African Americans. When she returned to campus, she used her position on SCAN to advocate leftist political positions, including opposition to U.S. intervention in World War II before December 1941.

Friedan entered graduate school in psychology at the University of California, Berkeley, in the fall of 1942. Although she studied with leading members of the discipline, including Erik Erikson, Friedan found her studies less engaging than those at Smith. She became involved in radical political circles at Berkeley, dating the physicist David Bohm, who worked on the Manhattan Project with J. Robert Oppenheimer and was a member of the Communist Party. Frustrated by the lack of intellectual stimulation at Berkeley, eager to engage more directly in radical politics, and afraid that her academic excellence would frighten potential spouses, Friedan left graduate school after one year.

She moved to New York City in 1943 and worked for three years at the Federated Press, a small leftist news agency that supplied articles to radical newspapers across the country. From 1946 through 1952 she was a reporter at the *UE News*, the official publication of the United Electrical, Radio, and Machine Workers of America, a radical union. While McCarthyism grew in the postwar era, Friedan continued to engage in radical politics, writing dozens of articles about workers' issues, including racial segregation and women's inequality.

While working as a labor reporter, she met Carl Friedan, a summer-stock theater producer who later became an advertising executive; the couple married in 1947. Betty Friedan used the name Goldstein professionally until 1952. The couple had three children and in 1950 moved from Manhattan to Parkway Village, an unusually integrated residential community in Queens. Friedan lost her job with the *UE News* in 1952, in part because she was pregnant with her second child, and entered a period of about two years when she did not work for pay outside her home. In 1956, the Friedans moved from Queens to suburban Rockland County, New York, first to a village called Sneden's Landing and then in 1957 to Grand View-on-Hudson.

Even as a housewife Friedan remained active in the public world. She was a community activist in Parkway Village and edited the community's newspaper from 1952 through 1954, years during which residents organized to fight rent increases in order to preserve the development's racial integration. In 1958, drawing upon the impressive numbers of intellectuals who lived in Grand View-on-Hudson, Friedan created an organization called the Intellectual Resources Pool to enrich the school curriculum. Perhaps most significant, from 1955 through the early 1960s, she worked as a freelance writer for magazines such as *McCall's* and *Ladies' Home Journal*.

It was Friedan's freelancing that gave her the immediate impetus to write *The Feminine Mystique*. After passing out a questionnaire at her fifteenth college reunion asking former classmates about their current lives, Friedan wrote an article for *McCall's* arguing that, contrary to contemporary popular belief, women were not wasting their time in college. Instead, women needed to embrace their education and find themselves as individuals rather than devoting themselves exclusively to housework. The popular women's magazines of the era rejected the article, leading Friedan to decide to make it into a book. She worked from 1957 until 1962 on what became *The Feminine Mystique*. Although the book drew on her experiences as a housewife, it also reflected Friedan's background in psychology as she urged women to reach their full potential as individuals, not just as housewives. *The Feminine Mystique* also reflected Friedan's experience as a

reporter for radical newspapers in its passionate descriptions of women's unhappiness and in its suggestion that women's colleges and magazines after World War II had conspired to create a "feminine mystique" that celebrated women's femininity and limited their lives to domestic concerns.

When it was published by W.W. Norton and Company in 1963, the book became a sensation. The initial print run of 3,000 quickly sold out, and Norton needed continually to order more copies. *The Feminine Mystique* was excerpted in major women's magazines and selected by the Book Find Club. Friedan went on a national press tour, unusual for authors at the time, and the publicity for the book made it a topic of controversy throughout the country. By 1964, *The Feminine Mystique* had sold 1.3 million copies and had become the number-one best-selling nonfiction book of the year. Friedan received hundreds of letters from women expressing gratitude to her and enthusiasm for the book's ideas.

In 1964, in the wake of *The Feminine Mystique*'s success, Friedan and her family moved back to New York City. While researching a new book on women and public policy, she became involved with a network of professional and union women and men, including the Women's Bureau official Catherine East and the activist and lawyer Pauli Murray, who were fighting sex discrimination at the Equal Employment Opportunity Commission (EEOC). In June 1966, Friedan, along with East and Murray, began recruiting women to establish a national advocacy organization to fight for women's equality; by October 1966, the National Organization for Women (NOW) was officially founded, and Friedan was elected its first president. In its first two years, the organization successfully pressured the EEOC to prohibit sex segregation in help-wanted ads and lobbied President Lyndon Johnson to extend affirmative action policies to include the hiring of women. With Friedan's flamboyant personality and celebrity status, the organization grew rapidly. Buoyed by its early success, Friedan pushed NOW in a more radical direction, shifting the focus from economic discrimination alone to that of women's status in society overall. In 1968 the organization adopted a Bill of Rights for Women written by Friedan that included support for abortion rights and for the Equal Rights Amendment, which had been defeated in Congress every year since its initial introduction in 1923.

At the same time that NOW was establishing itself as a successful lobbying force and moving to accomplish more radical goals, Friedan faced competition from young radical women. Disillusioned with their own treatment in the antiwar and student movements, young radical women began in the late 1960s to develop criticisms of the patriarchy that oppressed women. They attacked the ways that society exploited women's labor as domestic servants, caretakers, and sexual objects; radicals wanted to focus on concerns such as racism, rape, and lesbian rights. Friedan assailed radical women in interviews and speeches, arguing that they would alienate more conservative and traditional women from the Midwest and weaken the movement. Friedan particularly disapproved of radicals' championing of lesbian rights. She excluded lesbian rights from the NOW Bill of Rights for Women, and she fired NOW's national executive director for suggesting that the organization address lesbians' concerns. These actions alienated not only lesbians, many of whom left NOW altogether, but also many of their progressive sympathizers who remained in the organization. In 1970, NOW repudiated Friedan's actions. At the organization's 1970 National Convention, attendees voted to include lesbian rights as part of NOW Bill of Rights for Women. That same year, the executive board elected Aileen Clark Hernandez to serve as president.

Friedan's political defeats were matched by personal sorrow: After a tumultuous twenty-two-year marriage, she and Carl Friedan divorced in 1969. The following year, she began a long-term relationship with the writer and academic David Manning White, which lasted through the early 1980s.

Despite her defeat in NOW, Friedan was a powerful voice for women's causes throughout the 1970s. She organized the Women's Strike for Equality on August 26, 1970: Tens of thousands of women demonstrated throughout the country that day, including 50,000 women who marched down Fifth Avenue in New York City. She cofounded the National Association for the Repeal of Abortion Laws (NARAL) in 1969, and in the early 1970s she traveled throughout the country to speak on abortion rights. In 1971 she worked with other feminists, including Congresswomen Bella Abzug and Shirley Chisholm and the feminist leader Gloria Steinem to found the National Women's Political Caucus (NWPC), an organization designed to support female candidates for political office. In 1973 Friedan founded the First Women's Bank and Trust Company in New York City. The United Nations designated 1975 "International Woman's Year" and established an International Conference on Women's Rights in Mexico City as a result of Friedan's lobbying. She worked hard for the ratification of the Equal Rights Amendment, which passed Congress in 1972 but ultimately failed to receive ratification in 1982.

Even with Friedan's continued activism in the 1970s, her political positions and combative personality made her a controversial figure in the women's rights movement. The books on feminism that followed *The Feminine Mystique*—*It Changed My Life: Writings on the Women's Movement* (1976) and *The Second Stage* (1981)—inspired angry criticism from fellow feminists because they featured attacks on radical feminist activists. And although she

publicly renounced her position on lesbian rights at the National Women's Conference in Houston in 1977 and galvanized attendees, Friedan still remained outside the mainstream of organized feminism. Operating on her own in the 1980s and 1990s as feminism faced a more hostile conservative climate, she pursued the study of aging and of families. In 1993 she returned briefly to the best-seller list with *The Fountain of Age* and in 1997 published *Beyond Gender: The Real Politics of World and Family*. She died of congestive heart failure on her eighty-fifth birthday in Washington, D.C., and is buried in Sag Harbor Jewish Cemetery.

Friedan's writing and activism made her a central figure in American politics in the twentieth century. Millions of people read and responded to *The Feminine Mystique*; the book's insistence on women's right to individual growth provided an important spark for the Second Wave feminist movement. Friedan's activism, moreover, turned that movement into a meaningful political force. The organizations that she helped found and lead—NOW, NARAL, and NWPC—successfully promoted public policy that reshaped the workplace, the political landscape, and the social world of the late twentieth century.

★

Friedan's papers are available at the Schlesinger Library, Radcliffe Institute for Advanced Study, Harvard University. Among her most significant books are *The Feminine Mystique* (1963), *It Changed My Life: Writings on the Women's Movement* (1976), *The Second Stage* (1981), and *The Fountain of Age* (1993). Her autobiography is *Life So Far* (2000). Biographies include Daniel Horowitz, *Betty Friedan and the Making of the Feminine Mystique: The American Left, the Cold War, and Modern Feminism* (1998); Judith Hennessee, *Betty Friedan: Her Life* (1999); and Susan Oliver, *Betty Friedan: The Personal Is Political* (2008). See also Marcia Cohen, *The Sisterhood: The True Story of the Women Who Changed the World* (1988); Sylvie Murray, *The Progressive Housewife: Community Activism in Suburban Queens, 1945–1965* (2003); and Kirsten Fermaglich, *American Dreams and Nazi Nightmares: Early Holocaust Consciousness and Liberal America, 1957–1965* (2006). A collection of magazine interviews and profiles is *Interviews with Betty Friedan*, edited by Janann Sherman (2002). An obituary is in the *New York Times* (5 Feb. 2006). An oral history is in Jacqueline Van Voris, *The Smith Centennial Study* (1975).

Kirsten Fermaglich

FRIEDMAN, Milton (*b*. 31 July 1912 in New York City; *d*. 16 November 2006 in San Francisco, California), economist renowned for his advocacy of free-market theory and leadership of the Chicago School of monetary economics.

Milton Friedman, 1986. **GEORGE ROSE/GETTY IMAGES**

Friedman was the youngest of four children, and the only son, of two European Jewish immigrants, Jeno Saul Friedman and Sarah Ethel (Landau) Friedman. When Friedman was one year old the family moved to Rahway, New Jersey, where his father opened a trading business and his mother ran a dry-goods store below their home. During his childhood he went through a religious phase, but by the time of his bar mitzvah at age thirteen he was a self-proclaimed agnostic. Friedman excelled as a student and began high school early. In his senior year, his father died of a heart attack. Friedman's family encouraged him to continue his education despite this loss.

Friedman graduated from high school in June 1928 and was offered a scholarship to attend Rutgers University. He supported himself by waiting tables, clerking in a department store, and selling used textbooks and other supplies to Rutgers freshmen. He graduated from Rutgers with an AB in economics in June 1932 and received a scholarship to the University of Chicago master's degree program in economics. While at Chicago, Friedman met fellow student Rose Director, who had immigrated from

Charterisk, Russia, in the summer of 1914, just before the outbreak of World War I. After a somewhat awkward courtship, they married on 25 June 1938, and thus began a professional and personal partnership that would last until Friedman's death.

After receiving his AM in 1933, Friedman continued his graduate studies at Columbia University. He returned to Chicago in the fall of 1934, working as a research assistant and preparing for his doctoral examinations. Although academic jobs were scarce in 1935, the New Deal programs of the Franklin D. Roosevelt administration created a lucrative employment market for statisticians and economists in Washington, D.C. Friedman moved there to work for the National Resources Committee, a group commissioned to study consumer income and buying behavior.

In 1937 Friedman moved to New York to work for the National Bureau of Economic Research on a study of professional income, which eventually led to his doctoral work. Friedman and his colleague Simon Kuznets concluded that physicians exercised monopoly control over their services, thus inflating their incomes above those of other professionals—a claim that was highly controversial within the bureau and the medical community. Because of this controversy the study was not published until after World War II, which delayed the awarding of Friedman's doctoral degree.

In 1940 Friedman served as a visiting professor in economics at the University of Wisconsin at Madison. Internal disagreement within the university administration prevented Friedman from receiving a full-time position, so he and his wife moved back to Washington, where he worked as an aide to Secretary of the Treasury Henry Morgenthau. At the treasury Friedman developed a system for federal income tax withholding, creating the modern system of ongoing tax payments. Despite his successes he increasingly viewed his work at the treasury as mired in bureaucracy. In 1943 he took a position as an applied mathematician with the Statistical Research Group, a consulting group affiliated with Columbia University. The focus of his work was improving the effectiveness of military equipment during World War II. Rose Friedman at this time interrupted her career as an economist to care for the couple's daughter and son, born in 1943 and 1945, respectively.

Once the war ended in 1945, Friedman returned to teaching, accepting a one-year appointment at the University of Minnesota at Minneapolis. In 1946 he received his PhD in economics from Columbia University. That same year Friedman accepted a position teaching economic theory at the University of Chicago, beginning his long-term association with that institution. Friedman also taught courses in price theory and monetary theory as well as a workshop in money and banking. In addition to his academic work, in 1950 Friedman served as a consultant to one of the agencies responsible for implementing the Marshall Plan, the United States' program to rebuild Europe's economy after World War II.

During the 1950s and 1960s Friedman developed the theories behind what became known as the Chicago School of economics at the University of Chicago. He challenged the views of the English economist John Maynard Keynes (1883–1946), which were universally accepted at the time. Writing during the Great Depression (1929–1941), Keynes sought solutions to the problems of unemployment and a sluggish economy. In his 1936 book, *The General Theory of Employment, Interest, and Money*, he refuted laissez-faire capitalism (which calls for minimal interference by governments in economic affairs), the classic theory of the eighteenth-century Scottish economist Adam Smith. Keynes's book also questioned the necessity of balanced budgets and overall frugality in financial matters. Keynesian theory held that government intervention in markets was necessary to counteract the negative impacts that the cyclical nature of capitalism is bound to produce at certain times. For example, Keynesian economics argued that government spending would stimulate the economy in times of depression. Keynes also challenged what was then the traditional view of money supply, according to which an increase in the volume of money in circulation would increase prices or production. He theorized that increasing the amount of money in circulation would not result in a corresponding increase in spending; consumers would instead simply save the excess money and thus not fuel inflation.

Friedman challenged several aspects of Keynesian theory. In his essay "The Methodology of Positive Economics" (published in *Essays in Positive Economics*, 1953), he argued that economics must be based on facts, not suppositions, and must have predictive value. This argument opened the door for Friedman's subsequent questioning of many of Keynes's basic assumptions. In his book *A Theory of the Consumption Function* (1957), he challenged another of Keynes's main ideas. Evaluating the Great Depression, Keynes posited that a mature economy such as that of the United States developed a problem with excess savings, which meant that not enough money was circulating. According to Keynes, consumers alter their buying behavior based on short-term fluctuations in their earnings, thus creating the need for periodic injections of spending by the public sector. Friedman challenged Keynes's assumption by separating income into two types, "permanent" and "transitory." According to empirical evidence, he said, people make spending decisions based on "permanent" or long-range expectations of income rather than short-term ebbs and flows of money. Thus, whereas Keynes viewed demand as highly variable,

Friedman concluded, based on factual evidence, that it was quite stable.

Friedman also attacked Keynes's assessment of the role of money supply, and it is for this work that he and the Chicago School are best known. Friedman and coauthor Anna J. Schwartz conducted a historical analysis of the impact of money supply on the American economy from 1867 to 1960. Their 1963 work, *A Monetary History of the United States, 1867–1960*, completely refuted what was at the time the accepted explanation for the cause of the Great Depression: the excesses of capitalism, such as rampant speculation. Using historical data, Friedman and Schwartz demonstrated instead that the Depression was caused by poor monetary policy decisions resulting in a contraction of the money supply.

In great contrast to the U.S. economy of the 1930s, the post–World War II economy was booming and experiencing an associated rise in prices. Inflation, not unemployment, was the primary concern. During the Depression, Keynes postulated that increased government spending would increase overall demand, which would stimulate production and the need for more workers. At some point of full employment—but not before that point—increased spending would cause inflation. During the 1950s the economist A. W. Phillips developed the "Phillips curve," a graph that showed the corresponding tradeoff between inflation and unemployment, as a tool for public policy decisions. In his 1967 address to the American Economic Association titled "The Role of Monetary Policy," Friedman challenged the idea of full employment, advancing the concept of a "natural rate" of unemployment instead. In any economy, Friedman stated, there is at any given time a number of people who are looking for work; one cannot hope to eliminate this unemployed proportion entirely, and if the government attempts to do so, the result will be increasing inflation.

Friedman's academic reputation flourished during the 1960s and 1970s, particularly as the economy lapsed during the late 1970s into "stagflation," a situation in which high inflation was accompanied by unemployment and recession. This phenomenon supported Friedman's idea that there was not necessarily a tradeoff between inflation and unemployment. His public recognition increased as well, as he wrote extensively for general audiences and served as an adviser in matters of public policy. In 1962 Friedman published *Capitalism and Freedom*, which advocated a number of specific political actions, including elimination of the draft, school vouchers for public education, and floating exchange rates. Between 1966 and 1984 he wrote a regular column for *Newsweek* magazine, in which he stated his case for numerous political issues, such as the argument against increasing the minimum wage. Friedman was the chief economic adviser for Barry Goldwater's unsuccessful presidential campaign in 1964 and for Richard Nixon's successful 1968 bid.

Despite having open-heart surgery in 1972, Friedman pursued a vigorous schedule of academic and public involvement, including a March 1975 visit with the leader of Chile that received considerable criticism. The military commander Augusto Pinochet had taken over the Chilean government in a 1973 coup, and his ruling junta maintained control through brutal force. The Economics Department of the University of Chicago had a long-standing scholarship program for graduate students from Chile, and several of Friedman's former students attained positions in the Pinochet government. When another faculty member invited Friedman to travel to Chile as part of a weeklong seminar, which included a meeting with Pinochet, media reports that Friedman was personally advising the Pinochet regime led to public outcry and protests. Friedman received the Nobel Memorial Prize in Economic Science in 1976 and retired from the University of Chicago in 1977. The Friedmans moved to San Francisco, where Friedman served as a research fellow with the Hoover Institution at Stanford University until 2006. In January 1980 the Friedmans created a television series for the Public Broadcasting Service, *Free to Choose*, which was accompanied by a best-selling book, *Free to Choose: A Personal Statement*.

Friedman continued his political activity as well. He served as an adviser to Ronald Reagan during his 1980 presidential campaign and was a member of the president's Economic Policy Advisory Board during the Reagan administration. In 1988 Friedman received the Presidential Medal of Freedom as well as the National Medal of Science. He traveled extensively, including three trips to China to lecture and attend meetings on the country's economic development, as well as a tour of Eastern Europe in 1990, following the fall of the Berlin Wall and the breakup of the Soviet Union, to film an updated version of the documentary *Free to Choose*. In 1996 the Friedmans established the Milton and Rose D. Friedman Foundation, which is devoted to promoting parental choice in education. Together they published *Two Lucky People: Memoirs*, in 1998. Friedman died of heart failure.

Friedman, by refuting the reigning Keynesian ideology of his day, revolutionized economic thought and policy in the twentieth century. His message of free-market capitalism and individual economic freedom went against the political and academic mainstream during the 1950s and 1960s, an era of big government. Friedman's analytical work resulted in the framework for the monetary policy practiced by the Federal Reserve, in which the government intervenes in the market only to manage inflation, not to create jobs or raise wages. Perhaps most important, Friedman popularized economic principles and ideas, bringing complex academic concepts to the general public through his articles, books, and videos.

Many of Friedman's positions remain controversial. Conservative critics object to some of his more radical ideas, such as the legalization of drugs and prostitution. Critics on the left cite the negative effects of free-market capitalism's spread across the globe. Political debate continues on the merits of deregulation and privatization of government services, ideas that Friedman embraced. His absolute belief in private competition remains one of his most enduring legacies.

★

Friedman's papers are at the Hoover Institution at Stanford University. For information on his life and work, see Eamonn Butler, *Milton Friedman: A Guide to His Economic Thought* (1985), and Lanny Ebenstein, *Milton Friedman: A Biography* (2007). Milton and Rose D. Friedman, *Two Lucky People* (1998), is a book of memoirs. Career retrospectives include Lall Ramrattan and Michael Szenberg, "Memorializing Milton Friedman: A Review of His Major Works, 1912–2006," *American Economist* 52, no. 1 (Spring 2008): 23–39; and Anna J. Schwartz, "Milton Friedman and the Legacy of Milton Friedman," *Cato Journal* 28, no. 2 (Spring–Summer 2008): 263–274. Obituaries are in the *New York Times* and *Wall Street Journal* (both 17 Nov. 2006).

Karen E. Linkletter

G

GAJDUSEK, Daniel Carleton (*b.* 9 September 1923 in Yonkers, New York; *d.* 12 December 2008 in Tromsö, Norway), physician and researcher awarded the 1976 Nobel Prize in Physiology or Medicine with Baruch S. Blumberg for discoveries of new mechanisms for the origin and dissemination of infectious diseases.

Gajdusek was the older of two sons born to Karol and Ottilia (Dobroscky) Gajdusek. Gajdusek's father came to the United States from Slovakia as an adolescent youth. His mother's parents immigrated from Hungary. Gajdusek grew up in a polyglot neighborhood where his father had a butcher shop. The mixed immigrant culture in the Yonkers of his youth influenced Gajdusek's life and outlook.

Gajdusek's interest in science was inspired at a very early age by his mother's sister, Irene Dobroscky, who worked at the Boyce Thompson Institute for Plant Research in New York. She let young Gajdusek go with her when she explored the woods and fields looking for interesting specimens, and then took him to visit the laboratories and greenhouses where she worked. By the time he was ten years old Gajdusek wanted to be a scientist. Gajdusek received his early education in Yonkers. In later years he returned to visit the family home with his adopted children.

Gajdusek started studying at the University of Rochester in 1940, receiving a BS with honors in 1943. Following graduation from the University of Rochester, he went to Harvard Medical School, where he majored in pediatrics. Gajdusek was attracted to clinical pediatrics, living and working at Children's Hospital Boston much of his time at Harvard. Gajdusek graduated from Harvard Medical School in 1946. His postgraduate studies included work at Harvard, Columbia University, and the California Institute of Technology. He had a number of residencies, including one at Children's Hospital Boston. Gajdusek met many leading scientists during his academic career that inspired and influenced his life.

Drafted into the U.S. Army in 1951, Gajdusek was assigned to the Walter Reed Army Medical Service Graduate School as a research virologist. While still in the army, in 1952 and 1953, Gajdusek worked on epidemic diseases with Marcel Baltazard of the Institut Pasteur of Tehran, Iran, an experience that inspired him to look for infectious diseases in primitive, isolated populations to study. Gajdusek next went to Australia for postdoctoral work at the Walter and Eliza Hall Institute of Medical Research. These studies launched his work on child development and diseases within Australian aboriginal and New Guinean populations that ultimately led to his focusing on a unique disease of the brain called kuru that was discovered in the 1950s in an isolated Neolithic people living in the highlands of New Guinea.

Gajdusek identified kuru as a chronic degenerative disease and described his study of kuru in the *New England Journal of Medicine* in 1957. He determined kuru was unique to one New Guinea group and was spread through ritualistic cannibalism practiced when a member of the tribe died. Ending the cannibalism ultimately ended the disease. Gajdusek believed kuru was caused by a viral infection and took diseased brain samples to study in his lab at the National Institutes of Health in Bethesda, Maryland.

It took several years of injecting diseased brain tissue into animals before Gajdusek finally was able to reproduce the disease in a chimpanzee two years after injecting the animal and, therefore, proving it was an infectious disease. Gajdusek determined the incubation period is measured in years. He described the disease in 1966 in the journal *Nature* as a slow viral infection even though it had none of the inflammatory responses usually associated with viral infections. He identified similar agents as causing other diseases of the brain: Creutzfeldt-Jakob disease in humans and scrapie in sheep and goats. From 1970 until 1997 Gajdusek was head of brain studies at the National Institute of Neurological Disorders and Stroke at the National Institutes of Health.

In addition to the 1976 Nobel Prize that he shared with Blumberg, Gajdusek received many honors for his work, including a Gold Medal from the Slovak Academy of Sciences in 1996. He was a prolific writer. Gajdusek authored more than 1,000 papers published in journals of medicine, microbiology, immunology, pediatrics, and other sciences as well as papers on anthropology and linguistics.

Gajdusek has been described as energetic and intellectual, and also as eccentric. Gajdusek easily related to the Papua New Guinean tribes as he repeatedly visited among them. While he was on research trips, over a period of thirty years starting in 1963, Gajdusek brought back to the United States fifty-six young school-age Melanesian and Micronesian children. Although he claimed to have legally adopted all the children, there is documentation for only three children. Gajdusek had no interest in marrying, but he did like being a father to a family. His unique family style was based more on the kinship patterns and customs of the native culture where the children were born, than it was on American culture.

In 1996, while a college student, one of Gajdusek's boys confirmed allegations he had been sexually molested when he was a teenager in Gajdusek's family. Gajdusek did not deny the charges, defending his behaviors as normal in the cultures of the children's heritage. Following the advice of his lawyer, Gajdusek agreed to a plea bargain and subsequently served one year in prison from April 1997 to April 1998. He left the United States immediately on release to spend his last decade in Europe. Gajdusek spent time in Paris, Amsterdam, and Tromsö. He died of apparent congestive heart failure in his hotel room in Tromsö.

Gajdusek's discovery of a new mechanism for infection changed the scientific concept on how chronic brain diseases can develop. Although Gajdusek thought he had discovered a slow-acting virus, further studies led the neurologist Stanley Prusiner of the University of California, San Francisco, to identify the infectious agent as an unusual type of protein called a prion. The mechanism of infection of the misfolded protein is still not understood. What has been observed is that prions cause other proteins in the brain to change to similar proteins, disrupting the brain cells so they die. Since prions are proteins, the body does not recognize them as an infection and so there is no immune response as there would be for a virus infection. Prusiner was awarded the Nobel Prize for his work in 1997.

★

For information on Gajdusek's personal life, see Ceridwen Spark, "Family Man: The Papua New Guinean Children of D. Carleton Gajdusek," *Oceania* 77, no. 3 (1 Nov. 2007) and "Nobel Laureate Is Accused of Child Abuse," *New York Times* (6 Apr. 1996). Obituaries are in the *New York Times* (15 Dec. 2008) and *Los Angeles Times* (18 Dec. 2008).

M. C. Nagel

GALBRAITH, John Kenneth (*b.* 15 October 1908 in Iona Station, Ontario, Canada; *d.* 29 April 2006 in Cambridge, Massachusetts), prolific and influential liberal economist, economic historian, adviser and speechwriter to the Democratic presidents John F. Kennedy and Lyndon B. Johnson, and ambassador to India (1961–1963).

Galbraith was the third of five children (three daughters and two sons) born to William Archibald Galbraith, a

John Kenneth Galbraith, 1979. STEVE HANSEN/TIME LIFE PICTURES/GETTY IMAGES

farmer and a schoolteacher, and Sarah Catherine (Kendall) Galbraith, who worked in a dry-goods store until she married. Galbraith's parents were of Scottish descent and lived on a 150-acre farm in rural Ontario. His father was prominent and highly respected in community and Liberal Party affairs, serving as county auditor for decades and helping to found the local telephone and cooperative insurance companies. Galbraith's mother died when Galbraith was fifteen. During World War I his father abandoned the Liberals, rejecting their support for military conscription, and eventually helped form a Farmer-Labour alliance, which held power for four years before collapsing in 1923.

The youthful Galbraith put in long, hard hours on the family farm, later recalling, "A long day following a plodding, increasingly reluctant team behind a harrow endlessly back and forth over the uninspiring Ontario terrain persuaded one that all other work was easy." A voracious reader, Galbraith attended the one-room elementary Willey School, transferring at the age of twelve to Dutton High School, which he found uninspiring, particularly disliking the compulsory cadet corps. Gangling and awkward, at sixteen Galbraith was six feet, eight inches tall. After four years at Dutton, Galbraith spent a fifth year at the nearby Saint Thomas High School, graduating in June 1926. He then went on to Ontario Agricultural College at Guelph, majoring in animal husbandry and graduating with a BS in 1931. Motivated by demanding English teachers, Galbraith also began writing seriously, doing some freelance journalism and helping to found the college newspaper.

In 1931, as the Great Depression ravaged North American agriculture, Galbraith won a Giannini Foundation graduate research fellowship in agricultural economics to the University of California, Berkeley. He received his MS in 1933. Intellectually and socially, the institution transformed the unsophisticated farm boy. Taking numerous economics courses, often with famous and electrifying teachers, Galbraith soon became an outstanding student. He found the communist doctrines of Karl Marx less inspiring than those of the Norwegian immigrant and maverick sociologist Thorstein Veblen, whose *Theory of the Leisure Class* (1899) criticizes capitalism's frequent wastefulness and irrationality and conspicuous consumption by the wealthy. Throughout Galbraith's long career, his thinking owed much to Veblen.

Galbraith earned a PhD from Berkeley in 1934 and left in the fall to work in Harvard University's Economics Department as an instructor and a tutor. He worked closely with Professor John D. Black, coauthoring publications on manufacturing, productivity, consumer demand, and monopolistic competition, not just agricultural economics. Their writings discuss how economic systems work in practice, not just in theory, and how the real world often deviates from strict free-market models. Galbraith was initially influenced by Adolf A. Berle's book *The Modern Corporation and Private Property* (1932) and supported large-scale statist planning to combat the persistent depression. Unlike many Harvard economists, Galbraith already strongly supported the Democratic president Franklin D. Roosevelt's interventionist New Deal.

By 1936 Galbraith had also become enthralled with the British economist John Maynard Keynes, who advocated governmental countercyclical spending as the best means to achieve stable economic equilibrium and restore prosperity. Eager to study Keynes's theories more closely, Galbraith won a one-year Social Science Research Council fellowship to Europe in 1937 and studied at Cambridge University, where Keynes held a chair. On 17 September 1937 Galbraith married Catherine "Kitty" Merriam Atwater, the well-traveled daughter of a successful New York lawyer and a 1934 Smith College graduate who was working at Radcliffe on a PhD in comparative literature. The two eventually had four sons. Three days before his marriage, Galbraith became a U.S. citizen.

Cambridge made Galbraith a committed Keynesian. The young couple also traveled extensively in Europe. Supported by his socially adept wife, the once gauche Galbraith greatly enjoyed his new milieu, mingling comfortably with Britain's intellectual and political elites. Returning to Harvard, Galbraith taught for another year; denied tenure, in 1939 he switched to Princeton University for a year. A year later Galbraith moved to Chicago to work as an economist for the American Farm Bureau, but within a few weeks, in June 1940, he was summoned to Washington, D.C., to join the National Defense Advisory Commission, its mission to design potential domestic policies in case of war.

In April 1941 Galbraith moved as deputy administrator to the newly created Office of Price Administration, which became responsible for rationing and controlling prices after the attack on Pearl Harbor, when the United States entered World War II. Political pressure aroused by his strong defense of these policies finally forced Galbraith's resignation in June 1943. He briefly joined the Lend-Lease bureaucracy, but on the publisher Henry R. Luce's invitation, Galbraith soon moved to New York as an editorial writer for *Fortune* magazine. Almost two years later, in April 1945, Galbraith flew to Europe, temporarily commissioned as a colonel in the U.S. Army Air Forces, as a director of the U.S. Strategic Bombing Survey established to assess how effective the massive wartime aerial bombing raids had been in shortening the conflict and facilitating Allied victory. In fall 1945 he transferred to Japan. The survey's staff found that strategic bombing in Germany and firebombing and atomic attacks on Japanese cities had inflicted relatively little damage on war production capabilities in either country and had done little to accelerate the war's ending, conclusions that air force leaders resented, resisted, and refused to publicize.

Galbraith initially returned to the Luce publications, but in February 1946 became director of the State Department's new Office of Economic Security Policy, its mandate to design postwar reconstruction policies for Europe, Japan, and Korea. His major accomplishment was drafting a speech on German policy that Secretary of State James F. Byrnes delivered at Stuttgart, Germany, in September 1946, envisaging a united Germany reintegrated into Europe and the United Nations, with limits on industrial production and military forces, and acceptance of its post–World War II borders. This approach almost immediately fell victim to Washington policy makers' intensifying anti-Russian cold war mentality, and in early October, Galbraith, who had subsequently recommended improving German living standards and reducing occupation forces, resigned, to spend two more years in New York writing for *Fortune*.

In fall 1948 Galbraith returned to Harvard, gaining tenure in late 1949, after a battle during which several of the university's governing overseers questioned his New Deal record and Keynesian views. For his remaining career Galbraith was a Harvard professor of economics, enjoying uncustomary stability after numerous moves. Tragedy hit the family in May 1950, when Galbraith's second son died of leukemia at the age of seven. In January 1951 Galbraith purchased a three-story nineteenth-century family house on Francis Avenue, where he lived until his death. In 1947 he had bought a farm in Newfane, Vermont; later he also acquired an apartment in Gstaad, Switzerland.

Settled in Cambridge, Galbraith was an extremely popular teacher, his lectures marked by wry wit and self-assured showmanship. He also began writing prolifically, producing more than forty books—including three novels—and 1,000 articles over the next half century, in accessible, well-argued, and amusing though highly crafted prose that appealed to general readers, not just professional economists. Galbraith, a Keynesian New Deal liberal, eschewed mathematical economic models in favor of an approach melding sociological, historical, and political insights with economic thinking, an outlook clearly informed by his own varied government service. His sardonic satisfaction in publicly assailing the self-important and the wealthy soon won him both sometimes controversial media celebrity and a reputation for arrogance. His best-selling book *American Capitalism* (1952) was the first to win public acclaim; 400,000 copies were eventually printed. Galbraith argued trenchantly that the United States was no longer—if it ever had been—a free-market society, but was dominated by large organizations, including big business, labor unions, and government, whose operations massively distorted the supposedly automatic workings of classic laissez-faire principles.

The still more successful volume *The Affluent Society* (1958), in which Galbraith coined the phrase "conventional wisdom," sold over a million copies. His forceful and provocative contention that Americans enjoy "private affluence and public squalor" and his attacks on corporate encouragement of consumerism helped to frame contemporary political debate. Galbraith returned to these themes in *The New Industrial State* (1967) and *Economics and the Public Purpose* (1973), works that support government planning, including nationalizing defense and other industries and imposing wage and price controls, and that urge tax reform and income supports for the impoverished.

Energetic pursuit of extracurricular interests, especially politics and travel, supplemented Galbraith's heavy publishing schedule. A staunch Democrat, Galbraith advised the Democratic presidential candidate Adlai Stevenson in 1952 and 1956, and chaired the Democratic Advisory Council's economic panel from 1956 to 1960. He was an early supporter of the Massachusetts senator John F. Kennedy's 1960 presidential bid. After Kennedy's victory, Galbraith served on his foreign economic policy task force and assisted with speechwriting.

Kennedy rewarded Galbraith by appointing him ambassador to India, a country the Galbraiths had greatly enjoyed visiting in 1956. Galbraith served from March 1961 to June 1963, often bypassing the State Department and reporting directly to Kennedy. Despite his existing close friendship with the Indian prime minister Jawaharlal Nehru, U.S.-Indian relations were initially difficult because of American support for Pakistan and because of India's dissent from American actions in Laos and Berlin. Galbraith failed to prevent India's military takeover of Goa in 1961. He organized a widely publicized March 1962 state visit to India by First Lady Jacqueline Bouvier Kennedy, who charmed Nehru. Galbraith was instrumental in establishing an early computer science department at the Indian Institute of Technology in Kanpur, Uttar Pradesh. Relations improved during India's late 1962 border conflict with China, when Galbraith helped the ailing Nehru organize Indian defenses, facilitated American military aid, and supervised diplomatic moves aimed at preventing a Pakistani attack on India.

Galbraith also advised Kennedy on Vietnam. Galbraith was generally skeptical toward U.S. overseas bases and military commitments, an outlook he applied to Southeast Asia. In 1961 the Kennedy advisers General Maxwell D. Taylor and Walt W. Rostow visited South Vietnam, where antigovernment insurgency backed by North Vietnam was growing, and submitted a report recommending major American troop deployments. Late that year Kennedy, seeking a second opinion, dispatched Galbraith to Vietnam. Galbraith was highly critical of the existing South Vietnamese regime headed by President Ngo Dinh Diem and opposed sending American troops, advice Kennedy followed, authorizing only the use of helicopters and American advisers. Galbraith strongly advocated the opening of negotiations with North Vietnamese representatives and argued that if Vietnamese officials planned to overthrow Diem, the United States should not oppose this action.

Galbraith unsuccessfully opposed tax cuts that Kennedy contemplated, preferring to stimulate the economy through increased nonmilitary spending. Although shocked by Kennedy's November 1963 assassination, Galbraith, unlike many Kennedy New Frontiersmen, also genuinely respected and admired President Lyndon B. Johnson, Kennedy's successor; Galbraith endorsed Johnson's civil rights and anti-poverty programs, assisted with speeches (notably Johnson's speech on the Great Society), and proffered economic advice. In 1966, however, Galbraith broke with Johnson over Vietnam, testifying before Congress that the United States had no vital interests there. Elected president of Americans for Democratic Action in 1967, Galbraith publicly supported a bombing halt. The following year he supported the Minnesota senator Eugene McCarthy's antiwar campaign for the Democratic presidential nomination and in 1972 strongly endorsed the equally liberal Democratic candidate Senator George McGovern of South Dakota against the Republican president Richard Nixon.

By the early 1970s Galbraith had become a dedicated advocate of environmentalism and women's rights. In 1972, as president of the American Economic Association, he highlighted and sought to remedy discrimination against women in academe. Galbraith retired from Harvard in summer 1975, shortly afterward screening *The Age of Uncertainty*, a major television series on economics conceived and narrated by him. For three decades more he continued—albeit publishing fewer substantial full-length books except his memoirs—to write and speak profusely, finding prevailing late twentieth-century conservative, neoliberal, and free-market orthodoxies increasingly unattractive. Numerous honors, including a second Presidential Medal of Freedom in 2000—President Harry S. Truman had awarded his first in 1946—marked his later years. He was active almost until his death. In *The Culture of Contentment* (1992), *The Good Society: The Humane Agenda* (1996), and *The Economics of Innocent Fraud: Truth for Our Time* (2004), Galbraith sharply criticizes economic deregulation and the numerous financial scandals it facilitated, growing economic inequalities, global poverty, and the 2003 U.S. war with Iraq. After a two-week illness in 2006, he died of pneumonia at Mount Auburn Hospital in Cambridge.

Galbraith's public prominence and prestigious career failed to win him a Nobel Prize in economics. Many in his field, including such liberals as Paul Krugman, thought him a brilliant popularizer whose work was as much sociological as economic. With style, wit, and tenacity, throughout his long life Galbraith adhered faithfully to New Deal interventionist tenets and a liberal belief in state activism that often seemed old-fashioned in the late twentieth century. As the centenary of his birth approached and economic crisis engulfed the global financial system, it remained an open question whether Galbraith's outlook would gain renewed validity and acceptance.

★

Galbraith donated his personal papers to the John F. Kennedy Presidential Library in Boston. The U.S. National Archives II at College Park, Maryland, holds archival materials on Galbraith's service as U.S. ambassador to India. President Johnson's papers, at his presidential library in Austin, Texas, contain documents covering Galbraith's relationship with Johnson. Several of Galbraith's numerous books contain much autobiographical material, including *Ambassador's Journal: A Personal Account of the Kennedy Years* (1969), *A China Passage* (1973), *Annals of an Abiding Liberal* (1979), *A Life in Our Times: Memoirs* (1981), *Letters to Kennedy* (1998), and *Name-Dropping: From F.D.R. On* (1999). Over his long life Galbraith gave numerous interviews, the most significant of which are collected in James Ronald Stanfield and Jacqueline Bloom Stanfield, eds., *Interviews with John Kenneth Galbraith* (2004). The fullest biography is Richard Parker, *John Kenneth Galbraith: His Life, His Politics, His Economics* (2005), which should be supplemented by the less formal Peggy Lamson, *Speaking of Galbraith: A Personal Portrait* (1991). Studies of Galbraith as an economist include David A. Reisman, *Galbraith and Market Capitalism* (1980); Michael Keaney, ed., *Economist with a Public Purpose: Essays in Honour of John Kenneth Galbraith* (2001); and Conrad P. Waligorski, *John Kenneth Galbraith: The Economist as Political Theorist* (2006). Obituaries are in the *New York Times* and the *Washington Post* (both 1 May 2006). Galbraith recorded an extensive oral history for the John F. Kennedy Presidential Library and one on the World War II Office of Price Administration for the University of Arizona Library.

Priscilla Roberts

GALLO, Ernest (*b.* 18 March 1909 in Jackson, California; *d.* 6 March 2007 in Modesto, California), winemaker who, as cofounder and head of the E & J Gallo Winery, was a dominant force in establishing the modern American wine market.

Gallo was the eldest of three sons born to Italian immigrants. His father, Giuseppe ("Joseph") Gallo, met his mother, Assunta ("Susie") Bianco, while working as a wine merchant in California. Joseph purchased barrels of wine from small Central Valley producers such as the Bianco family and transported them via horse and cart to

Ernest Gallo. **STEVE KOSKO/MCT/LANDOV**

Modesto; by 1930 he had expanded the Modesto holdings to 230 acres.

When Ernest and Julio were not attending public school in Escalon and later Modesto, they worked in the fields beside their hard-driving father. Joseph, Sr., was a temperamental man who disliked dealing with buyers; in the summer before Ernest's senior year of high school, he persuaded his father to let him sell the family produce in Chicago. He proved himself a shrewd deal maker in a rough climate: "If you could get to the bank with the cash before [a buyer] could hold you up, you had a good day," Gallo recalled in a 1969 interview. Gallo graduated from Modesto High School in 1926 and spent two years at Modesto Junior College but did not receive a degree. His priority, as he stated in the same interview, was in taking classes that "would do me the greatest good" in terms of preparing for his livelihood: English, economics, and history.

He continued to travel to Chicago as a grape broker until 1932, and during this time he met Amelia Franzia, the daughter of a fellow broker. Gallo and Amelia married on 23 August 1931. The repeal of Prohibition made a significant impact on the Gallos' business. That year, 1933, with the country deep in the Depression, the price of grapes dropped significantly. Gallo would later say that he believed the repeal of Prohibition was an opportunity to enter the wine business, but the faltering economy took a toll on his father. On 21 June 1933, in what was ruled a murder-suicide, Joseph, Sr., shot and killed his wife and then himself.

Three months later, on 22 September 1933, Ernest and Julio founded the E & J Gallo Winery in a rented building and with equipment acquired on a trade acceptance basis. In their autobiography, *Ernest and Julio: Our Story*, the brothers remarked that they educated themselves in winemaking using pamphlets on fermentation and clarification that Ernest found in the basement of the Modesto Public Library. In its early years E & J Gallo Winery sold what Gallo described as "good sound common red wine" to bottlers across the country. In 1969 Gallo stated, "We adopted a policy of making the wine and selling it each year, turning it over. Each year we made a profit and increased the size of the plant." E & J Gallo Winery more than doubled its bulk wine output in its second year of operation.

In 1939 the E & J Gallo Winery started buying out its bottlers, eventually establishing its own glassworks in Modesto. The Gallo label first appeared in 1940 and the brand recognition that followed was largely a result of Ernest's tenacity in pursuing his stated aim of building E & J Gallo Winery into the Campbell Soup Company of the wine business—a difficult task at a time when Americans drank primarily beer and liquor. While Julio focused on viticulture, Ernest headed the company's financial and sales operations, combining his strengths as a deal maker with his

markets in San Francisco. After Joseph and Susie married in 1908, they ran a boardinghouse in Jackson, where Gallo was born. His younger brother Julio was born a year later, and young Ernest was sent to live with his maternal grandparents in Hanford, California, for five years. In 1917, when Ernest was eight years old, Joseph and Susie moved the family to Oakland, California, where they opened a boardinghouse and saloon. The following year, after passage of the Eighteenth Amendment signaled the start of Prohibition, criminalizing the manufacture, sale, and transportation of alcohol (Prohibition went into effect in 1920), Joseph sold the Oakland property and bought a ranch in Antioch, California. A third son, Joseph, Jr., was born in 1919.

In 1921 the Gallos moved to Escalon, California, where Joseph, Sr., bought a small vineyard. The grape business brought the Gallos modest prosperity during the Prohibition years. As the demand for wine grapes—and thus prices—increased across the United States, individuals, mostly European immigrants who could not buy wine, sought to make it legally themselves. (During Prohibition, home winemakers were allowed to make 200 gallons of wine per year.) In 1926 Joseph, Sr., sold the Escalon vineyard and bought forty acres of land in inherent abilities in marketing and distribution. He introduced a number of innovations, designing a distinctive bottle and creating racks that were backlit to showcase the color of the wine. He hired a sales staff to sell the Gallo brand exclusively, emphasizing product placement and distribution and generating sales data that enabled him to exploit untapped markets. He was the first winemaker to advertise wine in national markets.

In the 1950s Gallo's quest to create a mass market for wine led to the release of flavored "pop" wines including the fortified Thunderbird, which was criticized as being marketed to the lower-class consumer or "misery market," as well as popular sweet products such as Ripple and Boone's Farm. The release of the screw-top jug wines Hearty Burgundy and Chablis Blanc in the 1960s contributed to the perception of Gallo as a low-end producer, although these products were well received by consumers and critics alike as inexpensive but consistently drinkable table wines. Gallo reportedly kept a framed *New Yorker* cartoon in his office; it shows two couples drinking wine in a restaurant. The caption reads: "Surprisingly good, isn't it? It's Gallo. Mort and I simply got tired of being snobs." In 1966 E & J Gallo Winery was recognized as the nation's largest winery based on sales volume. The 27 November 1972 issue of *Time* magazine featured the brothers on the cover, with an accompanying article titled "American Wine Comes of Age."

Throughout the 1970s and 1980s E & J Gallo Winery continued its growth, acquiring smaller wineries, increasing capacity at the Modesto facility, and expanding its product base to include varietal wines, brandy, and nationally distributed brands such as Carlo Rossi and Bartles & Jaymes. It also released its first vintage and premium wines. In 1986 the Gallos brought a trademark-infringement lawsuit against their younger brother, Joseph, Jr., a dairy farmer and rancher who had begun marketing cheese under the Gallo name. Joseph, Jr., who was fourteen years old when Ernest was named his legal guardian after the deaths of their parents, brought a countersuit against his brothers claiming that they had conspired to cheat him out of one-third of the family business. The lawsuit made headlines and subjected the family and business operations to media scrutiny. Ernest and Julio prevailed in both suits and thereafter were estranged from Joseph, Jr. Julio died in an automobile accident in 1997; Ernest's wife died the same year.

The 1972 *Time* magazine article on the American wine industry referred to Gallo as "intense, crusty, and hard-driving"; associates described him as a gritty, reticent man, highly disciplined in both his personal and professional life, with an inquisitive mind and a dry wit. As head of E & J Gallo Winery, Gallo worked into his nineties, only relinquishing the post of chief executive officer to his son, Joseph E. Gallo, in 2001. (Gallo had another son who died in 1997.) In 2006 Gallo, whose estimated net worth was

$1.2 billion, was number 283 on *Forbes* magazine's list of the 400 richest Americans. He died at his home in Modesto at age ninety-seven, leaving behind the largest family-owned winery in the world. Gallo is buried at Saint Stanislaus Cemetery in Modesto.

At the time of Gallo's death, wine was a multibillion-dollar industry in the United States. Americans were drinking wine in record numbers, and E & J Gallo Winery was responsible for one in four bottles of wine sold in the country. Robert Mondavi, the Napa Valley winemaker and a friend of Gallo's since the 1930s, told the *San Francisco Chronicle* that Gallo was a "visionary" who transformed the United States into "a wine-drinking country."

★

In *Ernest and Julio: Our Story* (1994), written with Bruce B. Henderson, Ernest and Julio Gallo narrate, in alternating chapters, their classic American success story. A darker view of the business is given in Ellen Hawkes, *Blood and Wine: The Unauthorized Story of the Gallo Wine Empire* (1993). An interview by Ruth Teiser was recorded in 1969 for the California Wine Industry Oral History Series; the transcript is available at http://bancroft.berkeley.edu/ROHO/projects/food_wine/wine.html. Obituaries are in the *San Francisco Chronicle* (6 Mar. 2007) and *New York Times* (7 Mar. 2007).

Melissa A. Dobson

GEERTZ, Clifford James (*b.* 23 August 1926 in San Francisco, California; *d.* 30 October 2006 in Philadelphia, Pennsylvania), eminent cultural anthropologist best known for his influential social and cultural theory of interpretive (or symbolic) anthropology applied to Indonesian and Moroccan cultures.

Geertz was the son of Clifford James Geertz, a trader and civil engineer, and Lois (Brieger) Geertz, a former semi-professional tennis player. His parents divorced when he was three, and subsequently Geertz was raised by a distant relative in rural northern California. Having grown up in the Great Depression, Geertz learned early that his intelligence would be his only possible passport out of poverty. He was motivated during his early years at Santa Rosa High School; Geertz was the editor of his school newspaper and literary magazine and, with the encouragement of a high school English teacher, aspired to become a journalist and novelist.

He volunteered for the U.S. Navy from 1943 to 1945, serving in the Atlantic operations as an electronic technician. He sailed on the USS *St. Paul*. After World War II he returned to California, where he was uncertain about his next move. His former high school English teacher saw academia as the next logical step for Geertz; the great boom in American higher education was underway, and the GI Bill was helping to put thousands of veterans onto college campuses.

In 1946 Geertz was accepted to Antioch College in Yellow Springs, Ohio, where he majored in English and met Hildred Storey, a fellow English major whom he married in 1948. Geertz described the cold war culture at Antioch as "utopian, experimental, nonconformist, painfully earnest, desperately intense, and filled with political radicals and aesthetic free spirits." It was a time when "everything could disappear in a thermonuclear moment." In such an environment, Geertz found his English major too "constraining" and became discouraged with journalism after an internship with the *New York Post*. He switched his major to philosophy, influenced by his philosophy professor George Geiger.

After Geertz received a bachelor's degree in philosophy in 1950, Geiger encouraged his former student to consider anthropology. Geiger, at the time, was in contact with the Harvard University anthropology professor Clyde Kluckhohn, who was developing an experimental, interdisciplinary department called "social relations," in which cultural anthropology was connected not with archaeology and physical anthropology but with psychology and sociology.

Both Geertz and his wife applied to Harvard University, where they were accepted and studied anthropology, sociology, statistics, and social and clinical psychology. During this time he was also a research assistant at the Center for International Studies at the Massachusetts Institute of Technology (MIT) from 1952 to 1956, and he met Margaret Mead, whose work in Bali, Indonesia, greatly inspired Geertz.

Between 1952 and 1954 Geertz and his wife did their first fieldwork in Indonesia as two of five anthropologists, along with a team of two psychologists, a historian, and a sociologist, who were all assigned to go to the central Javanese village of Pare for a long-term intensive study. Geertz returned to Cambridge, Massachusetts, to write his thesis on Javanese religious life, and he earned a PhD from Harvard's Department of Social Relations in 1956.

In 1956 Geertz began his professional career as a research associate and instructor at Harvard. From 1957 to 1958 he was a research assistant at MIT and conducted fieldwork in Bali. On his return he moved to California, where he was a fellow at the Center for Advanced Study in the Behavioral Sciences in Stanford (1958–1959) and an assistant professor of anthropology at the University of California, Berkeley (1958–1960). In 1960 Geertz released his first major work, *The Religion of Java*, an ethnographic description of the variations, similarities, conflicts, and harmonies of Javanese religions.

From 1960 to 1970 Geertz taught at the University of Chicago, becoming a full professor in 1964. During this period he visited Morocco on four different occasions, studying the complexities of the Moroccan market—its genealogy, the religious and political structures that govern it, and its unwritten system of exchange, borrowing, security, and honor. He released five books that combine characteristics of more conventional ethnography with concerns about postcolonial economic and political development: *Agricultural Involution* (1963); *Peddlers and Princes* (1963); *The Social History of an Indonesian Town* (1965); *Person, Time and Conduct in Bali* (1966); and *Islam Observed: Religious Development in Morocco and Indonesia* (1968). In these works Geertz, unlike many of his contemporaries, chose not to concentrate on isolated, culturally primitive groups; rather, he focused on complex societies such as those in Indonesia and Morocco.

In 1970 he transferred to the Institute for Advanced Study as its first professor of the social sciences. He would remain there for the rest of his teaching career, along with appointments, among others, as the Eastman Professor at Oxford University (1978–1979) and visiting professor at Princeton University (1975–2000).

From 1970 to 1972 Geertz did extensive fieldwork in Java, Bali, Celebes, Sumatra, and Morocco. In 1973 he released his most influential book, *The Interpretation of Cultures*. It was lauded by the press and launched Geertz's innovative approach to anthropology as well as his status as one of the most important anthropologists for the next three and a half decades.

Geertz practiced anthropology at a time when it was being questioned about its colonial past and its ability to truly provide objective knowledge. Geertz wrote, "proposals for new directions in anthropological theory and method appeared almost by the month, one more clamorous than the next. I contributed to the merriment with *interpretive anthropology*." To arrive at this methodology, Geertz applied his education in English, philosophy, and the social sciences, emphasizing deep interdisciplinary readings to help break away from the anthropological emphasis on scientific inquiry and to introduce a more metaphorical and literary style. He had a semiotic concept of and interpretive approach to culture, seeing all human behavior as symbolic action. Geertz's most famous example of this methodology was his study of the Balinese cockfight. In his essay "Deep Play: Notes on the Balinese Cockfight," Geertz analyzes the kinship and social ties of the Balinese culture that are on display in the cockfight.

To Geertz the point of using a semiotic approach to culture was "to aid us in gaining access to the conceptual world in which our subjects live so that we can, in some extended sense of the term, converse with them." These meanings, he understood, were not indisputable. For Geertz the essential task of the interpretive anthropologist was "not to answer our deepest questions, but to make available to us answers that others . . . have given, and thus to include them in the consultable record of what man has said."

For the next thirty-five years Geertz practiced and honed his interpretive methodology, winning accolades beyond the confines of his discipline. He continued his fieldwork in Java and Morocco; authored and edited many prestigious books that have been translated into twenty-one languages; and wrote numerous articles, contributing frequently to the *New York Review of Books* and the *New Republic*. In 1988 he garnered the National Book Critics Circle Award in Criticism for *Works and Lives: The Anthropologist as Author*.

Toward the end of his career Geertz rallied against generalized theories in modern anthropology, arguing that circumstantial differences among ethnically diverse cultures—their unique time and space—prohibit any sweeping statements. At the same time, he was encouraged by the profession's continuing study of non-Western societies.

Geertz's marriage to Hildred Geertz, professor emeritus in the Department of Anthropology at Princeton University—with whom he coauthored two books and had two children—ended in divorce in 1981. He remarried in 1987 to the anthropologist Karen Blu. Geertz died after complications from heart surgery at the Hospital of the University of Pennsylvania in Philadelphia.

★

Geertz's memoir *After the Fact: Two Countries, Four Decades, One Anthropologist* (1995) is a strong source for information about his fieldwork and academic career. Other valuable works include Geertz's lecture for the American Council of Learned Societies, "A Life of Learning" (1999), and Fred Inglis's biography *Clifford Geertz: Culture, Custom, and Ethics*. (2000). Obituaries are in the *New York Times* (1 Nov. 2006) and *Washington Post* (2 Nov. 2006).

Joshua E. Polster

GIARDELLO, Joey (*b.* 16 July 1930 in New York City; *d.* 4 September 2008 in Cherry Hill, New Jersey), middleweight boxing champion from 1963 to 1965, member of International Boxing Hall of Fame.

Born Carmine Orlando Tilelli, Giardello was the third of six sons of Italian immigrants Joseph Tilelli, a New York City sanitation department foreman, and Anita Tilelli, a housewife. His father fought as a lightweight under the name Eddie Martin. Nicknamed "Chubby" as a boy by his family, Giardello, an indifferent student, developed his love for fighting in countless street fights, in altercations

with classmates, and while involved with youthful street gangs in his native Brooklyn. He attended P.S. 203 and the Brooklyn High School for Automotive Arts, then dropped out at age fifteen to enlist in the U.S. Army, joining the Eighty-second Airborne Division. Underage, he obtained a birth certificate from the cousin of a friend, acquiring the name Joseph Giardello.

Giardello boxed sporadically while stationed at Fort Bragg, North Carolina. In 1948 he went absent without leave (AWOL) and gravitated to Philadelphia where he worked for a time as a laborer digging sewer lines. Through a military acquaintance, he met the Philadelphia fight manager Jimmy Santore and the trainer Joe Polino who helped him get started as a professional boxer. On 2 October 1948 he scored a two-round knockout of Johnny Noel in Trenton, New Jersey, retaining as his ring name Giardello so as not to discredit his family name in case of defeat and also to confuse the military.

Giardello was undefeated in his first eighteen bouts before suffering his first loss on 16 January 1950. In July 1949 he returned to Fort Bragg to finish his tour of duty when it was learned that he had four more months to complete a two-year enlistment. On 29 October 1950 Giardello married Rosalie Monzo, a young woman he had met in Philadelphia the year before. They would have four sons.

On 30 April 1951 Giardello gained his first win over a rated middleweight with a ten-round decision over contender Ernie Durando. Standing five feet, ten inches tall and weighing between 155 and 160 pounds, Giardello was a largely self-taught fighter, a slick boxer-puncher with a rapid-fire left jab who combined clever feinting and movement to pile up points without a destructive knockout punch. However, his penchant for late night celebrating with friends, avoiding training, and a lack of focus in the ring would hamper his career. In 1952 he began the first of a three-bout series with the welterweight contender Billy Graham, winning two of three decisions. On 19 December 1952 Giardello was awarded a ten-round split decision victory over Graham, but the New York State Athletic Commission Chairman Robert Christenberry changed one judge's scorecard, giving the decision to Graham. Giardello's managers sued to have the decision reversed, and on 17 February 1953 New York State Supreme Court Justice Bernard Botein ruled that Christenberry had exceeded his authority in reversing the original decision, thus returning the victory to Giardello.

Giardello continued to move up in the ratings in 1953, and he won three straight bouts by technical knockouts in early 1954 but later that year injured his knee. After defeating Ralph "Tiger" Jones on 24 September 1954, Giardello had knee surgery to repair torn knee ligaments. Shortly thereafter it was announced that middleweight champion Carl "Bobo" Olson had agreed to fight Giardello for the title in San Francisco in December, but on 29 October 1954 Giardello and two friends were involved in a violent altercation with an African-American attendant at a South Philadelphia gas station. On 27 November 1954 Giardello was arrested and charged with hitting the attendant with a crutch. He was tried and convicted in March 1955 and served three and a half months of a six- to eighteen-month sentence.

For a time, Giardello struggled to regain his ring form after his release from prison and considered retirement. Between July 1956 and June 1958, however, he was undefeated in seventeen bouts. After further erratic ring performances in 1958 and 1959, he finally fought for the title against champion Gene Fullmer at Bozeman, Montana, on 20 April 1960. After fifteen foul-plagued rounds with both fighters guilty of countless violations, the decision was a draw. After another period of indifferent results, Giardello defeated the former champion Sugar Ray Robinson on 24 June 1963 to earn a title bout with the middleweight champion, Dick Tiger, at Atlantic City, New Jersey, on 7 December 1963. For once Giardello trained diligently for this fight and, although a decided underdog, boxed masterfully to win a fifteen-round decision. At age thirty-three Giardello gained the middleweight championship.

Giardello defended his title against Rubin "Hurricane" Carter on 14 December 1964, winning a unanimous but controversial fifteen-round decision. The film *The Hurricane* was released in 1999. Portraying the life of Carter, who spent nineteen years in prison for the conviction of and eventual exoneration for a triple murder committed in Paterson, New Jersey, in 1966, the movie depicts the bout as one in which Giardello received a thorough beating and won a racially influenced decision. Giardello sued Universal Pictures, Beacon Communications, and Aloof Films, contending that the film conveyed a false impression of the fight, defaming him, and robbing him of his rightful legacy as champion. The suit was settled out of court six months later for an unidentified amount.

On 21 October 1965 Giardello lost his title to Tiger in a unanimous fifteen-round decision. After four more bouts Giardello retired in 1967. His record was 100 victories, 25 defeats, and 7 draws, with 32 knockouts.

After leaving the ring Giardello worked as an insurance salesman, a salesman for a chemical supply company, and an inspector in the New Jersey State Department of Weights and Measures. Giardello became actively involved as a fund-raiser and advocate for the mentally and physically handicapped after his second son was diagnosed with Down syndrome. In 1967 he met with Sargent Shriver and Eunice Kennedy Shriver to discuss plans for what became in 1968 the Shriver-Kennedy Foundation for the Special Olympics.

In 1993 Giardello was elected to the International Boxing Hall of Fame. He also was chosen for the National Italian American Sports Hall of Fame and the New Jersey and Pennsylvania boxing halls of fame. In declining health in his final years, he died from congestive heart failure and diabetes on 4 September 2008 at the Cadbury Rehabilitation Center in Cherry Hill, New Jersey. He is buried at Calvary Cemetery in Cherry Hill.

Giardello was a boxer with great natural talent, a long-time contender who fought all the leading fighters in his division. For years he was his own worst enemy with erratic ring performances, slipshod training, and alleged links to organized crime through a relative of one of his managers. But his fistic resilience and dogged tenacity would enable him to finally gain the middleweight championship. At his best, his performances can be compared to the finest middleweights.

For biographical information and career records about Giardello, see James B. Roberts, and Alexander G. Skutt, *The Boxing Register: International Boxing Hall of Fame Official Record Book*, 4th ed. (2006). An account of Giardello's career can be found in Peter Heller, *"In This Corner...!": 42 World Champions Tell Their Stories* (1994). Articles about Giardello during his career include Murray Goodman, "The Riddle of Giardello," *Sport* (Oct. 1954); Barney Nagler, "Giardello Stands for Trouble," *Sport* (May 1957); Stan Hochman, "The Joey Giardello Comeback," *Sport* (Apr. 1964); John Underwood, "A Mighty Desirable Fellow," *Sports Illustrated* (18 May 1964); and Joey Giardello, "I'm Young Again," *King* (June 1964). An obituary is in the *New York Times* (8 Sept. 2008).

Edward J. Tassinari

GIROUX, Robert (*b.* 8 April 1914 in Jersey City, New Jersey; *d.* 5 September 2008 in Tinton Falls, New Jersey), editor, publisher, writer, and trusted friend of great twentieth-century writers.

Giroux was born in 1914 in Jersey City, a port of entry and an industrial city located on the west bank of the Hudson River across from lower Manhattan. He was the youngest of five children of Arthur J. Giroux, a cabinetmaker and weaver, and Katharine (Lyons) Giroux, a teacher. He attended Regis High School in Manhattan, but facing the economic pressures of the Great Depression, he left school to accept a job at the *Jersey Journal*. Lillian R. Hull was Giroux's editor, and with her advice and help, Giroux won a scholarship to Columbia University to study journalism.

After taking an honors seminar with Raymond Weaver, the author of the first biography of Herman Melville and the first reader of the manuscript of *Billy Budd*, and after studying with Mark Van Doren, the noteworthy literary scholar and writer, Giroux dedicated himself to literature and editing. As editor of the campus literary magazine, the *Columbia Review*, Giroux published writings by fellow students such as John Berryman and Thomas Merton, but he also successfully solicited contributions from John Dewey, R. P. Blackmur, and Kenneth Burke. Giroux completed his BA at Columbia in 1936 and worked in market research and promotion with the Columbia Broadcasting System.

In 1940 Giroux became an editor at Harcourt, Brace, and Co., where Frank Morley, a seasoned editor, helped Giroux make his start in the publishing business. In 1942 military service interrupted Giroux's career, and he served in the navy aboard the *Essex*, an aircraft carrier in the Pacific, and rose to the rank of lieutenant commander. When the war ended, Giroux returned to Harcourt. During his years at that publishing house, he met and worked with many exceptional authors, including Virginia Woolf, William Saroyan, Edmund Wilson, Carl Sandburg, T. S. Eliot, Katherine Anne Porter, and Jack Kerouac.

In 1955, at the invitation of Roger Straus, John Farrar, and Sheila Cudahy, Giroux left Harcourt to become editor in chief at Farrar and Straus; in 1964 Giroux became a partner, and the first book to bear the imprint of Farrar, Straus, and Giroux was Robert Lowell's *For the Union Dead*.

Giroux's illustrious career as editor and publisher lasted more than half a century, and seven of the writers he worked with won the Nobel Prize: Eliot, Isaac Bashevis Singer, Derek Walcott, Nadine Gordimer, Seamus Heaney, William Golding, and Alexander Solzhenitsyn. Giroux gained fame for his refined taste, and he published the first books by Jean Stafford, Lowell, Bernard Malamud, Flannery O'Connor, Randall Jarrell, William Gaddis, Kerouac, and Susan Sontag.

Giroux's success was a result of dedication and service to the authors he worked with. He insisted that an editor had to have faith and confidence in the authors with whom he or she worked, and the editor had to be determined to produce the finest final product. Insightful compassion and dutiful helpfulness were the hallmarks of Giroux's conduct with authors, and in return he won their loyalty and respect. When Giroux took his new position at Farrar and Straus, many writers chose to move with him to the new publisher; moreover, various writers referred their friends and associates to Giroux.

Despite the successes and good relationships that Giroux enjoyed, he did face some disappointments. J. D. Salinger and Giroux agreed to publish *The Catcher in the Rye*, but Giroux's superiors at Harcourt found that the novel was unsuitable, and the book slipped out of Giroux's control. When Giroux published Kerouac's first novel, *The Town and the City* (1950), Kerouac dedicated the novel to Giroux, but Giroux subsequently lost the chance to publish

On the Road (1957). According to Giroux, Kerouac arrived at Harcourt with a manuscript under his arm. The manuscript looked like a roll of paper towels, and Kerouac unfurled the scroll across Giroux's desk. Surprised, Giroux suggested to Kerouac that such a manuscript could not be edited, and Kerouac became irritated and said that he would not allow editorial changes. Years later, Giroux regretted that he had not simply congratulated Kerouac on the completion of the work and invited him to celebrate. Editors at Viking were eventually able to persuade Kerouac to submit a traditional manuscript and cooperate in the editing process.

Giroux himself was a writer, and his works include *The Book Known as Q: A Consideration of Shakespeare's Sonnets* (1982) and *A Deed of Death: The Story Behind the Unsolved Murder of Hollywood Director William Desmond Taylor* (1990). In addition, Giroux edited collections of writings for authors such as Malamud, Elizabeth Bishop, and Lowell, and the introductions he composed for these volumes reveal Giroux's close connections with the writers. For literary journals such as *Kenyon Review* and *Sewanee Review*, Giroux wrote memoirs in which he recounted his associations with Eliot, Lowell, Ezra Pound, and others.

Giroux received numerous awards, including an honorary doctorate from Seton Hall University. New York University gave Giroux the Elmer Holmes Bobst Award in Arts and Letters. The National Book Critics Circle, in appreciation of Giroux's literary accomplishments, gave Giroux the Ivan Sandrof Award. The Philolexian Society, an alumni organization at Columbia University, awarded Giroux the Alexander Hamilton Medal in 1987, and in 2006 Giroux received the Philolexian Award for Distinguished Literary Achievement.

In 1952 Giroux married Carmen de Arango, who served as an adviser to the Holy See Missions Delegation to the United Nations. The marriage ended in divorce in 1969, and the couple had no children. Giroux is survived by three nieces.

In December 2008 a memorial service for Giroux was held at Saint Paul's Chapel on the campus of Columbia University.

★

Giroux, *The Education of an Editor* (1982), is a concise and lively description of Giroux's life and career. Giroux analyzes the publishing industry and explains the factors involved in successful editing. Donald Hall, "Robert Giroux: Looking for Masterpieces," *New York Times Book Review* (6 Jan. 1980), reviews Giroux's accomplishments and recognizes the quality of his personality and character. George Plimpton, "Robert Giroux: The Art of Publishing No. 3," *Paris Review* no. 155 (Summer 2000), is an interview that reveals Giroux's flair for storytelling and literary anecdotes. Patricia Mulcahy, "The Apprentice: Starting Out with Mr. G.," *Publishers Weekly* (15

Dec. 2008), provides the perspective of a book editor indebted to Giroux. Obituaries are in the *New York Times* and *Washington Post* (both 5 Sept. 2008).

William T. Lawlor

GITTINGS, Barbara (*b.* 31 July 1932 in Vienna, Austria; *d.* 18 February 2007 in Kennett Square, Pennsylvania), gay rights activist, library worker, and editor who helped start the gay rights movement before the Stonewall Rebellion in 1969.

Gittings was one of two daughters born to John Sterett Gittings, a member of the U.S. Diplomatic Corps, and Elizabeth (Brooks) Gittings. When the family returned from Europe, they moved to Montreal, Canada, where they lived until 1941, when they moved to Wilmington, Delaware. During this period Gittings attended Catholic schools, where she first recognized her lesbian feelings. In 1949, following graduation from Wilmington High School, Gittings started attending Northwestern University in Evanston, Illinois. While there she decided to find everything she could about homosexuality in both the Chicago Public Library and the library at Northwestern in order to understand herself better. She later recalled about this period, "I had to find [material] under headings like 'sexual perversion' and 'sexual aberration' in books on abnormal psychology. I kept thinking, 'It's me they're writing about, but it doesn't feel like me.'" Gittings dropped out of Northwestern before the end of 1949.

Around this time Gittings located a copy of Radclyffe Hall's *The Well of Loneliness*, a 1928 novel about lesbianism. Her father found the book hidden in her room and ordered her to burn it. She did not. During this period she also discovered the earlier writers Colette, Rosamond Lehmann, and Compton Mackenzie. While these writers' novels did not describe who Gittings was, they reflected her feelings better than any of the scientific papers that she had also been reading. She used them to start compiling a list of gay and lesbian writings. This list that started with a single page included over 600 entries when Gittings discontinued it in the 1970s. In 1951 Gittings moved to Philadelphia and started working at clerical jobs, something she did for the rest of her life while she was an activist. Gittings also started visiting lesbian bars in New York City. Another book she discovered was Donald Webster Cory's *The Homosexual in America* (1951). After writing to the publisher, she was able to meet with Cory. Cory told her about the Mattachine Society, an early gay men's group, in Los Angeles.

In 1956 Gittings traveled to Los Angeles and met with the group. They told her about another organization, the Daughters of Bilitis (DOB), a women's group that had recently been founded in San Francisco. It defined itself as "A Woman's Organization...Promoting the Integration of the Homosexual into Society." These two early groups called themselves not gay groups but rather homophile groups. The DOB founders were so impressed by Gittings that in 1958 they asked her to establish a New York chapter of the DOB. She was president of this chapter from 1958 to 1961. In 1961, at a DOB picnic in Providence, Rhode Island, Gittings met the woman who would become her life partner, Kay Tobin Lahusen. From 1963 until 1966 Gittings was editor of the DOB newsletter, the *Ladder*. In 1963 she met Frank Kameny of the Washington, D.C., Mattachine Society. He radicalized her. She began to believe that the way homophile groups were trying to achieve equality in society at the time, by staying in the closet and blending in with society, was wrong. She felt that it was important to come out of the closet, so she started putting photographs of lesbians on the cover of the *Ladder*. This decision was very radical since at that time, homosexuals could be arrested merely for being open about their sexuality. She also added the phrase "A Lesbian Review" to the *Ladder*'s cover. When she tried removing the phrase "For Adults Only" from its cover, and because of problems she had meeting deadlines, she was removed as editor.

In 1965 Gittings joined the first gay rights demonstrations, at the White House, the Pentagon, and Independence Hall. From 1965 to 1969 she attended the demonstration that was held yearly at Independence Hall on July 4. Most of these demonstrations were photographed by Lahusen. After the Stonewall Rebellion, the 1969 event that sparked the gay rights movement, Gittings began to get involved on a larger stage. In 1970 she became the first out lesbian on a nationally syndicated television show when she appeared on *The Phil Donahue Show*. Gittings also joined the American Library Association (ALA), even though she was not a librarian, and helped start its Gay Task Force. From that time until 1986, she was the task force's second coordinator. At ALA's 1971 convention she organized a "Hug-A-Homosexual" booth. It was shocking at the time. Gittings's last act as head of the task force was the permanent establishment of the Stonewall Book Awards for gay writing. In 2003 Gittings was made an honorary lifetime member of the ALA.

In 1972 Gittings sat on a panel at the American Psychiatric Association, where she spoke out against the association's listing homosexuality as a mental disease. She was joined by a masked gay psychiatrist who was afraid of revealing his identity. As the 1970s ended, she remained involved in gay organizations, sitting on the board of directors of the Delaware Valley Legacy Fund, a group that gives grants to gay, lesbian, bisexual, transgender, and intersex projects. Eventually Gittings and Lahusen moved to an assisted-living facility in Kennett Square, where

Gittings died of breast cancer. Her remains were cremated and given to Lahusen. Gittings's last bit of activism was to come out in the facility's newsletter with her partner.

Because Gittings was courageous enough to be out of the closet when it was dangerous to be so, she helped energize several generations of gay and lesbian activists, thereby advancing gay rights in America. In 2001 the collection of lesbian and gay material at the Free Library of Philadelphia was named the Barbara Gittings Gay/ Lesbian Collection.

★

Gittings's papers were donated by Lahusen to the New York Public Library in 2007. An extensive interview with Gittings about her life and activism is in Jonathan Ned Katz, *Gay American History: Lesbians and Gay Men in the U.S.A.* (1992). Gittings is listed in Paul Russell, *The Gay 100: A Ranking of the Most Influential Gay Men and Lesbians, Past and Present* (1995). Lahusen's biography of Gittings is in Vern L. Bullough, ed., *Before Stonewall: Activists for Gay and Lesbian Rights in Historical Context* (2002). For more information about Gittings and the history of the Daughters of Bilitis, see Marcia M. Gallo, *Different Daughters: A History of the Daughters of Bilitis and the Rise of the Lesbian Rights Movement* (2006). Obituaries are in the *Philadelphia Inquirer* (20 Feb. 2007) and *New York Times* (15 Mar. 2007).

Scott Sheidlower

GLUECKSOHN-WAELSCH, Salome (*b.* 6 October 1907 in Danzig, Germany; *d.* 7 November 2007 in New York City), biologist who was one of the pioneers in the fields of developmental genetics and molecular genetics.

Gluecksohn-Waelsch was the daughter of Ilya and Nadia Gluecksohn; her family was Jewish. As a young woman she studied chemistry and zoology in Konigsberg and later in Berlin. In 1928 she applied to become a graduate student under the noted biologist Hans Spemann (who later was awarded the Nobel Prize in Physiology or Medicine). He took her on as an assistant at a time when there were few women scientists; however, Gluecksohn was assigned to relatively unimportant tasks that were not always within her field of interest, embryological development. Despite that, she received her PhD from the University of Freiburg in 1932.

After graduation she was named a research assistant at the University of Berlin. When Adolf Hitler came to power in Germany the following year, one of his first acts was to order the removal of Jewish scientists and teachers from their positions. Gluecksohn's dismissal may have been a blessing in disguise; she and her husband, the biologist and physiologist Rudolf Schoenheimer, left for the United States before the worst atrocities of Hitler's Nazi regime unfolded. Arriving in New York City in 1933 during the depths of the Great Depression, Gluecksohn was unable to find a job. Finally, in 1936 she secured a position as a research associate in the laboratory of Samuel Detwiler at Columbia University. She later moved to the Columbia University laboratory of Leslie C. Dunn, whose research was more in line with Gluecksohn's interests; for the first year with Dunn, she worked without pay. In 1938 she made a major breakthrough that permitted her to trace the effects of genes from the embryo to the mature mammal.

Gluecksohn was naturalized as an American citizen in 1938. Her first husband, Rudolf, died on 11 September 1941; she married Heinrich Waelsch (another refugee from Nazi Germany) on 8 January 1943. He was a neurochemist at Columbia University. Until her death she used the name Gluecksohn-Waelsch. The couple had two children, a daughter and a son. Waelsch died in 1966.

Under Dunn, Gluecksohn-Waelsch investigated mice whose embryos did not develop properly, resulting in spinal problems and stunted tails. Though her academic training was in experimental embryology, she soon became frustrated with the standard approach to such work. Spemann's studies in Germany had been designed to manipulate the embryo and then look at the effect on resulting phenotypes. Gluecksohn-Waelsch was convinced that more could be accomplished by borrowing some of the insights of the noted American geneticist Thomas Hunt Morgan and looking at phenotypes that were caused by mutant genes. Until 1949 she worked on mice. In the first scientific paper she produced, she presented the initial programmatic statement on how the methodology of developmental genetics differed from the techniques of the experimental embryologist. This marked the start of the new science of developmental genetics. For the next decade and a half, she published a number of articles on how mutant genes affected the spine and other parts of the lower skeleton.

Despite her growing reputation in the field, Gluecksohn-Waelsch remained a research associate at Columbia until 1955; for the last three years she was officially a research associate in obstetrics. When the Albert Einstein College of Medicine was created at Yeshiva University in New York City in 1955, Gluecksohn-Waelsch became a founding member of the faculty with the title of associate professor of anatomy; beginning in 1958 she was professor of genetics there. From 1963 until 1976 she was head of the department of genetics at the College of Medicine. It was not until the 1970s that because of major developments, gene activity could actively be studied at the molecular level. Though Gluecksohn-Waelsch officially retired in 1978, she continued her research for at least another two decades, working in her laboratory at Yeshiva.

For years her research was supported by a small grant from the American Cancer Society. Among her other most important works were studies of the inheritance of different kinds of hemoglobin and how a lethal chromosomal defect affected the function of the liver. Well into the 1990s she was in her laboratory every day. Based on her experiences under Spemann and her frustration that after nineteen years at Columbia she was still a research associate, she became an active champion of careers in science for women. Recognition came slowly. In 1979 she was elected to the National Academy of Sciences. In the 1980s she became a fellow of the American Academy of Arts and Sciences and of the American Association for the Advancement of Science. The University of Freiburg awarded Gluecksohn-Waelsch an honorary doctorate in 1982, the fiftieth anniversary of her graduation. She accepted the degree in absentia and with reservations, feeling that the horrors of the Holocaust were ignored in the citation that accompanied the award.

In 1993 Gluecksohn-Waelsch was awarded the National Medal of Science. Columbia University gave her an honorary degree in 1995 and cited her creativity in an era when the work of women in all sciences was continually undervalued. That same year she became a foreign fellow of the Royal Society of the United Kingdom. She received the Thomas Hunt Morgan Medal for Genetics in 1999. She died at her home in Manhattan, still carrying the title of professor emerita of molecular genetics at the Albert Einstein College of Medicine; her body was cremated.

A refugee from Nazi Germany, Gluecksohn-Waelsch fought all her life for proper recognition of the work of women in science. One of her earliest accomplishments was to demonstrate that classical Mendelian genes directed the development of the embryo. In the course of her long and active life, she was one of the creators of two new fields of science. She was the first to propose that developmental genetics was a separate discipline. Living long enough to see important further changes, she became a pioneer in molecular genetics.

★

A summary of some of Gluecksohn-Waelsch's work can be found in the remarks of Lee M. Silver when Gluecksohn-Waelsch was presented with the Thomas Hunt Morgan Medal for Genetics in 1999; see *Genetics* 154, no. 1 (Jan. 2000): 1–2. An obituary is in the *New York Times* (15 Nov. 2007).

Art Barbeau

GOHEEN, Robert Francis (*b.* 15 August 1919 in Vengurla, India; *d.* 31 March 2008 in Princeton, New Jersey), president of Princeton University (1956–1972), humanitarian, and U.S. ambassador to India (1977–1980).

Goheen was born to Robert H. H. Goheen, a doctor, and Anne (Ewing) Goheen, a teacher. Goheen's parents were Presbyterian missionaries. In 1934, when Goheen was fifteen, he moved from India to the United States to finish high school at the Lawrenceville School in Lawrenceville, New Jersey, graduating with honors after two years in 1936. At age seventeen he entered Princeton University, following the family tradition: His brother graduated from Princeton in 1936, and their grandfather, Joseph M. Goheen, also a Presbyterian missionary in India, was a member of the class of 1872.

At Princeton, Goheen played varsity soccer and was elected to Phi Beta Kappa. He was active in the political and debating club Whig-Clio, the Quadrangle Eating Club (of which he was president), and the Inter-Club Committee. He graduated in 1940 with an AB with highest honors in the Special Program in Humanities and Classics. The subject of his senior thesis was the nature and object of tragedy, an interest he would pursue in graduate school. Upon graduation he received an M. Taylor Pyne Honor Prize, the highest general distinction awarded to an undergraduate.

In October 1941, after completing a year of graduate study in Princeton's Department of Classics and just months after marrying Margaret M. Skelly, Goheen entered the army. World War II was ramping up, and he joined the infantry as a second lieutenant but served in the Military Intelligence Service of the War Department in Washington, D.C. In April 1943 he joined the First Cavalry Division and went overseas as a research analyst until July 1945, supervising the preparation of strategic intelligence reports on the Pacific Islands. Ultimately he earned the rank of lieutenant colonel and was awarded the Legion of Merit and the Bronze Star.

Goheen returned to Princeton in 1945. Now a father of two (he and his wife would eventually have six), he worked as a part-time instructor and a tutor while earning his MA in 1947 and his PhD in 1948, both in classics. His dissertation, *The Imagery of Sophocles' Antigone: A Study of Poetic Language and Structure*, which was published by the Princeton University Press in 1951, was well reviewed. After a year at the American Academy in Rome, Goheen became a full-time classics instructor at Princeton and was named an assistant professor of classics in 1950. He was one of the first four Woodrow Wilson Fellows and from 1953 to 1956 was the first national director of the Woodrow Wilson Fellowship Program, which encourages young intellectuals to pursue careers in academia.

In November 1956 Goheen was called to a meeting with Princeton trustees for what he believed would be a conversation about what younger faculty members wanted in a new president. He was taken aback when the trustees unanimously elected him to the job. On 1 July 1957, at age thirty-seven, Goheen became the youngest president in the history of the university since the Revolutionary War. In an interview with the *New York Herald Tribune* the day before he took office, Goheen established the outlook of his presidency when he said, "The thoughtful, creative minds which we require in numbers in all important aspects of our national life cannot be mass produced."

During Goheen's fifteen-year presidency, Princeton changed and grew. The campus itself grew by thirty-eight buildings, increasing the university's indoor space by 80 percent. Goheen quadrupled the budget, doubled alumni giving, increased the number of faculty members by 40 percent, and enlarged the student body from 3,000 to 4,000.

Many have suggested that Goheen was responsible for steering Princeton clear of the violence and civil unrest that rocked so many other U.S. campuses in the 1960s. In 1965 he opposed opening Princeton to women but changed his position when he bucked conservative critics and introduced coeducation to the campus in 1969. "I was just plain wrong in 1965," he said "It's no use pretending you're not wrong when you are." Goheen hired Princeton's first black administrator and full professor and actively recruited talented minority students. Though he agreed with the youth who opposed the Vietnam War, he saw little point in angry protest. After the American invasion of Cambodia, Goheen addressed students, faculty, and staff with humor, urging civilized debate.

After retiring from Princeton in 1972, Goheen focused his energies on charitable and philanthropic causes. He became president of the Council on Foundations, a consultant organization for private foundations, which he believed to be "critical elements in the diversity, openness and innovative character of the American society." In opinion pieces published in the *Los Angeles Times*, he occasionally lamented the shortage of funds available to charitable groups.

In January 1977 Goheen became president of the Edna McConnell Clark Foundation. Fewer than five months later, President Jimmy Carter appointed Goheen ambassador to India, where he served from May 1977 through December 1980. Having been born and spent most of his youth in India, Goheen described his appointment as an opportunity to return to his first home.

India had detonated its first nuclear device in 1974, eleven years after the United States had signed a thirty-year contract to deliver enriched uranium fuel to generate nuclear power. President Carter charged Goheen with the task of persuading India to cease nuclear testing and to start talks with the United States. On 3 January 1978, two months before Congress passed the Nuclear Non-Proliferation Act of 1978, Prime Minister Morarji Desai of India and President Carter signed a joint declaration aimed at reducing the threat of nuclear war.

Goheen left India in December 1980, returning to Princeton to teach in the Woodrow Wilson School. He also worked for the Woodrow Wilson National Fellowship Foundation, directing the Andrew W. Mellon Fellowship Program in the Humanities. He died of heart failure.

Goheen remained altruistic throughout his life, serving on the boards of numerous organizations, including the American University of Beirut, the National Humanities Center in Research Triangle Park, North Carolina, and the Village Charter School in Trenton, New Jersey. He was active in the American Philosophical Society and was a founder of Princeton Future, a community organization concerned with the development of downtown Princeton. In 1978 Goheen also cofounded the National Humanities Center in North Carolina and served as a trustee. Twenty years later he was recognized for his role at the center with the annual Robert and Margaret S. Goheen Fellowship. The Robert F. Goheen Professorship in the Humanities at Princeton and the annual Robert F. Goheen Prize in Classical Studies were both established in his honor. For most of his life, Goheen was affiliated with Princeton. "There was, and I believe there still is, a peculiar atmosphere about [Princeton] that grabs many of us and never lets go," he said.

★

Goheen's papers are in the Seeley G. Mudd Manuscript Library at Princeton University Library. His impassioned opinion pieces in the *Los Angeles Times* (7 June 1972, 24 July 1973, 26 Jan. 1975, and 12 Nov. 1976) offer insight into Goheen's commitment to humanitarian issues. Obituaries are in the *Times of Trenton* (31 Mar. 2008) and *New York Times* (1 Apr. 2008).

Brenna Sanchez

GOULET, Robert Gerard (*b.* 26 November 1933 in Lawrence, Massachusetts; *d.* 30 October 2007 in Los Angeles, California), singer, actor, and entertainer best known for originating the role of Lancelot in the Broadway musical *Camelot*.

Goulet was the second child born to Joseph Georges André Goulet and Jeanette (Gauthier) Goulet, who moved from their native Canada to Massachusetts to work in the textile-mill industry. Goulet, whose father was also an amateur singer and performer, first performed at family gatherings and later in a church choir. When he was thirteen his father died, and he moved with his mother and sister to Girouxville, Alberta, Canada. The family later moved to Edmonton, Alberta, where Goulet made his first professional appearance at age sixteen as a singer with the Edmonton Symphony Orchestra. Never finishing high school, he worked as an announcer for radio station CKUA for two years. In 1951,

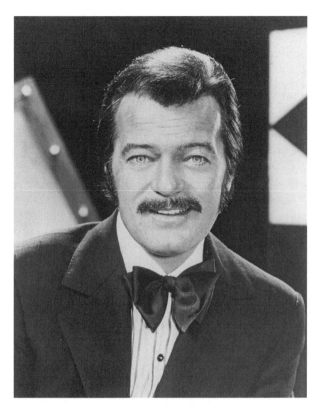

Robert Goulet. **MICHAEL OCHS ARCHIVES/GETTY IMAGES**

following an appearance in George Frideric Handel's *Messiah*, he won a scholarship to the Royal Conservatory of Music in Toronto, where he studied opera.

In 1952 Goulet appeared on *Pick the Stars*, a Canadian Broadcasting Company (CBC) program, and reached the semifinals. This success led to other TV appearances. Goulet eventually became the host of CBC's variety show *General Electric's Showtime*, continuing for three years while also working in theater and radio. A popular entertainer, he earned a reputation as "Canada's first matinee idol." In 1956 he married his first wife, Louise Longmore, with whom he had a daughter. The couple divorced in early 1963.

Goulet's big break came in 1959 when he met Alan Jay Lerner and Frederick Loewe, the lyricist-composer team best known for the 1956 musical *My Fair Lady*. The two were then working on *Camelot* (with Richard Burton as King Arthur and Julie Andrews as Queen Guenevere), and Goulet auditioned for the pivotal role of Sir Lancelot. His audition was so impressive that everyone listening burst into applause. After preview runs in Toronto and Boston, *Camelot* opened on Broadway on 3 December 1960. Reviews of the show were mixed, but critics praised Goulet's performance. The show proved to be a popular success, running for 873 performances and winning four Tony awards.

Camelot made Goulet an overnight star. Audiences loved his rendition of the emotional ballad "If Ever I Would Leave You," which was well suited to his rich baritone. The show's cast album topped the *Billboard* magazine charts for six weeks. Goulet received the Theatre World Award for his role, and in 1962 he signed a recording contract with Columbia Records. Although the *New York Daily News Magazine* hailed him as "just the man to help stamp out rock 'n' roll," his style of singing—that of a romantic crooner—was about to become distinctly unfashionable. He nonetheless enjoyed a measure of success in the 1960s, with eight albums landing in the Top Forty and the single "Forgive Me, My Love" reaching the Top Twenty. In 1963 he won the Grammy for Best New Artist. That year he married the musical theater performer Carol Lawrence, with whom he would have two sons. During the height of his popularity, he sang for Presidents Lyndon Johnson and Richard Nixon. He drew headlines for a rare gaffe on 25 May 1965, when he sang the wrong lyrics to the U.S. national anthem at the Muhammad Ali–Sonny Liston championship boxing match in Lewiston, Maine.

Goulet was not successful at translating his talents to the movies. His first "role" came in the 1962 animated feature *Gay Purr-ee*, as the voice of the male lead (a tomcat playing opposite Judy Garland's lead feline female). He then starred in the romantic comedies *Honeymoon Hotel* and *I'd Rather Be Rich* (both 1964) and the war drama *Underground* (1970). He was more successful on television, appearing on *The Ed Sullivan Show*, *The Patty Duke Show*, *Big Valley*, and others, as well as his own series, *Blue Light* (1966). He starred in musicals filmed for television, including *Brigadoon* (1966), *Carousel* (1967), and, opposite Lawrence, *Kiss Me Kate* (1968). He also continued working on the stage. He returned to Broadway in 1968 in *The Happy Time*, winning a Tony for his performance as the head of a family in Canada in the 1920s.

Goulet's record contract with Columbia ended in 1970. Although he recorded occasionally for other labels, he began to concentrate on live appearances, becoming a major concert attraction and a regular headliner in Las Vegas, where he would eventually live. In 1982 he was named Las Vegas Entertainer of the Year. He starred in a number of his own television specials and also appeared on such top-rated shows as *Mission: Impossible*, *The Love Boat*, and *Fantasy Island*.

He and Lawrence divorced in 1981, and her later memoir detailed an abusive marriage fueled by Goulet's alcoholism. Talking to the *New York Times*, Goulet admitted he had had a drinking problem but insisted it had not affected his work and defended himself against his ex-wife's charges. In 1982 he married Vera Chochorovska

Novak, a writer, artist, and photographer who later became his business manager.

The 1980s brought a resurgence in his professional popularity. While continuing to attract audiences to his concerts, he also began to gently mock his own smooth-singing, lounge persona, notably in the films *Atlantic City* (1980), in which he appeared as a singer, and *Toy Story 2* (1999), in which he was the voice of a lounge-singing penguin. He also played himself in the film *Scrooged* (1988) and episodes of the television shows *The Simpsons*, *Two Guys and a Girl*, and *King of Queens*, among others. He took on comedy roles in *Beetlejuice* (1988), *The Naked Gun 2: The Smell of Fear* (1991), and *Mr. Wrong* (1996). His light comedic touch worked well in commercials, as in a series of 1996 ESPN spots. He was even shown being stabbed in the eye and getting his hand chopped off in "Weird Al" Yankovic's 1992 video "You Don't Love Me Anymore." "If you can't laugh at yourself, you're a fool," Goulet told the *Orange County Register*.

Goulet continued his theatrical work in regional and touring productions and appeared on Broadway in *Moon over Buffalo* (1996) and revivals of *Camelot* (1993)—this time playing King Arthur—and *La Cage aux Folles* (2005). In 1993 the Royal Conservatory of Music in Toronto conferred on him an Honorary Fellowship, the school's highest honor. In 2005 he was given a star on the Hollywood Walk of Fame and the Shubert Walk of Fame in New Haven, Connecticut; in 2006 he was given a star on Canada's Walk of Fame, a rare honor for a person not born in Canada.

After surviving prostate cancer in 1993, he became a spokesman for early screening. He fell ill in September 2007 following a concert appearance and entered a hospital in Las Vegas, where he was diagnosed with idiopathic pulmonary fibrosis, a lung disease. In October he was transferred to Cedars-Sinai Medical Center in Los Angeles to receive a lung transplant, but he died before the procedure could take place. His cremated remains were given to his family. The night after his death, the lights were dimmed on Broadway theater marquees in his memory.

Although Goulet never became a major star—*Camelot* was the highlight of his career—his "old school" style survived changes in musical taste and eventually became popular again. He remained a household name for decades. Goulet was good-natured enough to poke fun at his own image and thus came to epitomize a very American type of entertainer—the genial, swingin' lounge singer, whose smooth style could always make the ladies swoon.

★

For anecdotes about Goulet and his work in *Camelot*, see Alan Jay Lerner, *The Street Where I Live* (1978), and Julie Andrews, *Home: A Memoir of My Early Years* (2008). A somewhat lurid account of the Goulet-Lawrence marriage is Carol Lawrence, *Carol Lawrence: The Backstage Story* (1990). Obituaries are in the *New York Times* (30 Oct. 2007) and *Los Angeles Times* (31 Oct. 2007).

Gillian G. Gaar

GOWDY, Curtis Edward ("Curt") (*b*. 31 July 1919 in Green River, Wyoming; *d*. 20 February 2006 in Palm Beach, Florida), sportscaster who was the first in his field to win a Peabody Award for Excellence.

Gowdy was the older of two children of Edward Gowdy, a dispatcher for the Union Pacific Railroad, and Ruth (Smith) Gowdy, a homemaker. The family moved to Cheyenne, Wyoming, when Gowdy was six. As a boy Gowdy followed the Chicago Cubs baseball team in the newspapers; he would make up games and practice broadcasting them in his room. His mother monitored his vocabulary growth and enrolled him in elocution classes, which he hated. He later acknowledged, however, that the classes gave him poise and confidence in his broadcasting career and made him learn typing (the only boy in his class). He began to play basketball in the third grade and became the top scorer in Wyoming in 1937, his senior year in high school. His mother persuaded the high school

Curt Gowdy, 1978. HEINZ KLUETMEIER/SPORTS ILLUSTRATED/ GETTY IMAGES

principal to bench Gowdy when his grades were failing. He graduated from Cheyenne High School in 1937 as a member of the National Honor Society.

Gowdy worked for a year as an electrician's apprentice for the Union Pacific Railroad before attending the University of Wyoming in Laramie. His first trip east of the Mississippi River, and to a big city, Chicago, came in the summer of 1938, with Thompson's Billiard Hall Class A softball team, which lost the national championship in the second round. At the university Gowdy started on the basketball team and played varsity tennis. He fished and hunted whenever possible, even when school was in session. He graduated with a BS in business in 1942.

Gowdy was in the Reserve Officers' Training Corps. After the Japanese attack on Pearl Harbor in 1941, he enlisted in the Army Air Forces to be a fighter pilot. He was called up in 1942 and sent to Camp Edwards in Massachusetts. With a ruptured disk in his back, he received a medical discharge in 1943, after some flight training in Alabama.

In 1943, recuperating from back surgery in Wyoming, Gowdy was asked to call a high school football game for a local radio station, KFBC. The team had only six players, with no roster, no numbered jerseys, and no markings on the field. The temperature was below zero. Gowdy stood on an orange crate to see and made up players' names. He began to read radio commercials, news, and local sporting events and wrote part time for the *Cheyenne Eagle*. He would re-create Major League Baseball games from telegraphs, memorizing ballpark dimensions to describe hits better and creating sound effects for crowd noise and hits.

In 1946 Gowdy was hired by KOMA, the Columbia Broadcasting System (CBS) affiliate in Oklahoma City, Oklahoma. His back problems continued, and he had spinal fusion surgery in 1946. He broadcast Oklahoma football games for KOMA from 1945 to 1949. Walter "Red" Barber, CBS's sports director, employed Gowdy intermittently for interviews and football and basketball games. In 1949 Gowdy was selected from 300 applicants to broadcast New York Yankees baseball games with Mel Allen. That winter Barber gave Gowdy his first regular radio show, *Football Scoreboard*. Gowdy also broadcast college basketball on television from Madison Square Garden in New York City. On 24 June 1949 Gowdy married Geraldine "Jerre" Dawkins; the couple had three children. In the spring of 1950 Gowdy announced the first nationally broadcast National Collegiate Athletic Association (NCAA) basketball games.

In 1951 Gowdy became the Boston Red Sox baseball franchise announcer on WHDH, signing a contract with the team, not the network. He never lost his Wyoming accent and stopped trying to lose it when he discovered that others had not been hired by the Red Sox because they had Boston accents. He spent the first winter memorizing the correct pronunciation of New England towns. Although the Red Sox never did well during Gowdy's years, he called his time in Boston the happiest fifteen years of his life. He was also the first radio announcer for the Boston Celtics basketball team (1951–1953). Gowdy broadcast college football in the fall and basketball in the winter for the National Broadcasting Company (NBC).

Gowdy missed the entire 1957 baseball season because of back pain so severe that he was immobilized in a plastic shell. He finally set up to broadcast both radio and television games from his home in Wellesley, a Boston suburb. In 1966 Gowdy left Boston for NBC's *Baseball Game of the Week* but maintained homes near Boston. In 1961 Gowdy partnered with Paul Christman to call television football games for the American Broadcasting Company (ABC). He bought WCCM, a radio station in Haverhill, Massachusetts, in 1963, when he thought his continuing back pain might end his broadcast career; he would eventually own six more stations, in New Hampshire, Florida, and Wyoming. In 1964 he hosted ABC's *Wide World of Sports*, which he helped develop with Roone Arledge.

In 1967 Gowdy called the first Super Bowl. In 1968 Gowdy was calling the New York Jets–Oakland Raiders football game when NBC infamously cut away to show *Heidi*, the classic children's story. No one heard Gowdy call the two touchdowns scored by Oakland in the final minute of the game. He recorded the game's end for broadcast the next day. He also called the historic Jets' upset victory in Super Bowl III in 1969, a game that put the American Football League on par with the National Football League.

In 1970 Gowdy became the first sportscaster to receive the George Foster Peabody Award for Excellence. He was inducted into the broadcasters' wing of the Baseball Hall of Fame in 1984 and the American Sportscasters Hall of Fame in 1985. In 1993 Gowdy wrote *Seasons to Remember: The Way It Was in American Sports, 1945–1960* with John Powers.

From 1964 to 1984 Gowdy hosted ABC's *American Sportsman*, for which he won six Emmys. His fishing guests included President Jimmy Carter, the baseball great Ted Williams and other sports figures, and the actors Bing Crosby and Peter O'Toole. Gowdy's love of the outdoors earned him the nickname "Cowboy," which he used as the title of his 1966 autobiography, *Cowboy at the Mike* (with Al Hirshberg). He hosted the Public Broadcasting Service's *The Way It Was* (1974–1978), reliving famous moments in sports history. A state park in Wyoming is named for Gowdy, for his love of the outdoors and his commitment to conservation as an advocate of "fish and release" to save the environment.

Gowdy died of leukemia at his home in Palm Beach. A funeral was held at Trinity Church in Boston on 25 February 2006. He is buried in Mount Auburn Cemetery in

Cambridge, Massachusetts. On 28 August 2006 he was honored with a pregame ceremony at Fenway Park.

Gowdy broadcast a total of sixteen World Series games, nine Super Bowls, eight Olympics, twelve Rose Bowls, and twenty-four NCAA Final Four championships in basketball. He won thirteen Emmys, including an award for lifetime achievement in 1992, and was inducted into twenty halls of fame. He called Williams's last at bat and Carl Yastrzemski's first. The ubiquitous announcer kept his unaffected voice throughout an international career spanning continents and decades.

★

Gowdy is included in Curt Smith, *The Storytellers: From Mel Allen to Bob Costas, Sixty Years of Baseball Tales from the Broadcast Booth* (1995). Gowdy's radio career is covered in Smith, *Of Mikes and Men: From Ray Scott to Curt Gowdy, Broadcast Tales from the Pro Football Booth* (1998), and Ted Patterson, *The Golden Voices of Baseball* (2002). Obituaries are in the *New York Times, Boston Globe,* and *Boston Herald* (all 21 Feb. 2006).

Jane Brodsky Fitzpatrick

GRAY ADAMS, Victoria Almeter Jackson (*b.* 5 November 1926 in Palmers Crossing, Mississippi; *d.* 12 August 2006 in Baltimore, Maryland), civil rights activist, cofounder of the Mississippi Freedom Democratic Party, and the first woman from Mississippi to run for the U.S. Senate.

Gray Adams was born in Palmers Crossing, an African-American village now part of Hattiesburg, Mississippi, to Mack and Annie Mae (Ott) Jackson; she had one younger brother. Gray Adams was three years old when her mother died, and she was raised on a farm by her paternal grandparents. At age seven, she moved for a while to Detroit with her father, who had remarried. She graduated from DePriest Consolidated School in Palmers Crossing and attended Wilberforce University in Ohio until she no longer had money for tuition. She later attended Tuskegee Institute in Alabama and Jackson State College in Mississippi, where she received her teaching certification. In the 1940s she taught school in rural Mississippi.

She married Tony West Gray, a military man, in Palmers Crossing. After living in Germany, they returned to segregated Fort Meade, Maryland, where she worked for the African-American-owned Beauty Queen Company. They had two sons (one died in 1997) and a daughter; they were divorced in 1964. Gray Adams returned to Mississippi to the house she inherited from her grandparents. She became the first franchise owner of Beauty Queen

in the South, eventually hiring twenty-five salespeople and leasing an office in the black section of Hattiesburg. Gray Adams married Reuben Ernest Adams, Jr., another military man, on 20 February 1966, and they had one son.

Gray Adams began her civil rights activism by teaching voter registration classes. When Student Nonviolent Coordinating Committee (SNCC) volunteers came to Hattiesburg in 1962, Gray Adams arranged for them to meet in her church, Saint John's United Methodist Church, which became a center for civil rights activity. In spring 1962 Gray Adams volunteered to take a voter registration test in Hattiesburg, which she failed. While African Americans were 30 percent of the Hattiesburg population, only fifty African Americans were registered voters, because of poll taxes, intimidation, impossible literacy tests (eventually made illegal by the Voting Rights Act of 1965), and economic reprisals for those who tried to register. By the end of 1962, Gray Adams gave up her business and became a salaried field secretary for SNCC, teaching basic literacy skills to draw people into the movement. In fall 1963 she was president of the Forrest County Voters League. She traveled to Dorchester, Georgia, for training, returning to Hattiesburg to establish the first literacy and citizenship education program that included black history. She wanted to teach people that voting could improve their lives.

The Mississippi Freedom Democratic Party (MFDP) was formed in April 1964 after 80,000 African Americans, excluded from voting, were registered for a mock election called the Freedom Vote. In July 1964 Gray Adams—barred from the official Democratic Party ballot—declared her candidacy as a member of the MFDP against the long-term incumbent, Senator John C. Stennis. Ignoring death threats and harassment, she knew she would not win but wanted to exercise her rights of citizenship by challenging segregationist politics, hoping to inspire other African Americans to get involved. She lost by a 30–1 margin, but in August, along with Fannie Lou Hamer, Gray Adams led a delegation to Atlantic City, New Jersey, to challenge the Democratic Party at their national convention. The MFDP claimed that the all-white contingent did not represent their state adequately. The all-white delegation, refusing to compromise, walked out of the convention. Gray Adams and twenty other MFDP delegates entered the convention center to take their place. Gray Adams was among the leaders who refused President Lyndon Johnson's request for a compromise that would seat two MFDP delegates but allow the all-white delegation to stay.

On 4 January 1965 hundreds of African Americans of all classes and ages stood silently in the tunnel leading to the House of Representatives as the congressmen walked into the session. Although the House voted not to seat the MFDP challengers, 149 representatives, over one-third of the total, voted for the MFDP. Gray Adams was one of the many civil rights activists invited to the inaugural celebrations for Johnson that January. The House scheduled hearings for fall 1965, and Gray Adams, Hamer, and Annie Devine became the first black women to be seated as guests on the floor of the House. The passage of the Voting Rights Act made the MFDP's challenge a moot point. By the 1968 convention, the Mississippi delegation was integrated.

In 1968 Gray Adams was involved in the Poor People's Campaign, run by the Southern Christian Leadership Conference (SCLC) using nonviolent demonstrations to end poverty in America. In the early 1970s, while living in Thailand with her husband, she founded the Afro American Women's Club (AAWC) in Bangkok, and she taught there as well. She was campus minister at the Interfaith Center at historically black Virginia State University in Petersburg for nearly thirty years beginning in 1969, and she taught and lectured at various colleges across the United States. She was national board member of the SCLC. In 2004 she helped found the Virginia Organizing Project, a grassroots political group dedicated to helping communities with issues such as racism, immigrant rights, child care, and education. From 2003 to 2006 she was chief adviser to Repaying Our Ancestors Respectfully, an organization dedicated to creating positive life choices for youth.

Among numerous awards, Gray Adams won the Martin Luther King, Jr. Community Service Award and the Fannie Lou Hamer Humanitarian Award. On 27 October 1989 Gray Adams received a distinguished service award from the Wilberforce University Alumni Association. On 4 November 1995 Gray Adams was honored with a resolution in the U.S. Congress for her lifelong humanitarian and civil rights work; on 19 August 2006 the Democratic National Committee passed a resolution honoring her life; and on 9 February 2007 she was honored by a resolution passed in the Virginia Senate.

Gray Adams died of lung cancer at her son Cecil's home in Baltimore. Services were held on 9 September 2006 at the Parkway Heights United Methodist Church in Hattiesburg. Her body was cremated. A national memorial was held on 23 September at the Northwood Appold United Methodist Church in Baltimore.

Gray Adams credited her Christianity and spirituality for inspiring and encouraging her lifelong involvement with civil and human rights. She was courageous in her civil rights activism, hoping to inspire people by demonstrating how education and civil involvement would improve their lives. She was a leader in changing politics in Mississippi and the United States at a time when it was a dangerous undertaking.

★

Gray Adams's papers are digitized in the Mississippi Digital Library at the University of Southern Mississippi, which includes photographs and her handwritten autobiography from

1945. Books with interviews and information on Gray Adams include Henry Hampton, Steve Fayer, and Sarah Flynn, *Voices of Freedom: An Oral History of the Civil Rights Movement from the 1950s Through the 1980s* (1990); Kay Mills, *This Little Light of Mine: The Life of Fannie Lou Hamer* (1993); John Dittmer, *Local People: The Struggle for Civil Rights in Mississippi* (1994); and Lynne Olson, *Freedom's Daughters: The Unsung Heroines of the Civil Rights Movement from 1830 to 1970* (2001). Gray Adams is featured in two films, *Freedom on My Mind* (1994), directed by Connie Field and Marilyn Mulford, and *Standing on My Sisters' Shoulders* (2002), directed by Laura J. Lipson, which documents the 1965 House of Representatives event. The 1995 resolution to Congress includes biographical information about Gray Adams's family. Jack Hitt, "Party Crasher," *New York Times* (31 Dec. 2006), describes Gray Adams's role at the Democratic Convention. Vicki Crawford, *Be Ye Doers of the Word, Not Just Hearers Only* (2007), documents Gray Adams's Christian faith and activism. Obituaries are in the *New York Times* (19 Aug. 2006) and *Washington Post* (9 Sept. 2006).

Jane Brodsky Fitzpatrick

GREENGLASS, Ruth Leah Printz (*b*. 30 April or 1 May 1924 in New York City; *d*. 7 April 2008 in New York City), provided testimony leading to the execution of her sister-in-law, Ethel Rosenberg, on espionage charges in 1953.

Greenglass, the oldest of four children born to Max Printz, a Hungarian immigrant, and Tillie (Leiter) Printz, an Austrian immigrant, in a Jewish section of Manhattan's Lower East Side, grew up in an impoverished household. Her father worked as a trimmer in a slaughterhouse. She frequented the Madison Settlement House, attended public schools, took college preparatory classes, and graduated from Seward Park High School at age sixteen. Encouraged by her mother to learn typing, she nonetheless briefly enrolled in 1942 in Brooklyn College. Withdrawing for financial reasons, she married her neighborhood sweetheart, David Greenglass, on 29 November 1942. They had two children.

During World War II the young couple, already sympathetic to communism, were much influenced by Greenglass's older sister, Ethel Rosenberg, and her husband, Julius. While Greenglass, an army machinist and vocal champion of left-wing causes, worked on the secret atomic bomb project at Los Alamos, New Mexico, his wife served as a stenographer for the United Electrical, Radio and Machine Workers of America. Encouraged by the Rosenbergs, she attended meetings of the Young Communist League (YCL), served briefly as president of the local Club Lincoln chapter of the YCL, and sold memberships in a communist book club.

Meanwhile, Julius Rosenberg had become involved in espionage. Apparently learning of the nature of his brother-in-law's work through Soviet contacts, Rosenberg asked Ruth Greenglass to approach her husband for information on the project. Uncertain, she flew to New Mexico in November 1944 to visit David Greenglass and to present Rosenberg's request. At first reluctant, Greenglass provided her with information for Rosenberg. In New York in January 1945, David Greenglass agreed to write up a report on the Manhattan Project, which he claimed Rosenberg indicated Ethel Rosenberg would type for Soviet agents. The two couples then planned for Ruth Greenglass to move to Albuquerque, New Mexico, where she worked as a clerk for the Office of Price Administration. Julius Rosenberg arranged for an espionage courier to pick up additional information from the Greenglasses there. The courier would present a portion of a torn Jell-O box matching one that Rosenberg had given the Greenglasses. In September 1945, when he and his wife were in New York, Greenglass provided Rosenberg still more information, which Rosenberg allegedly claimed Ethel Rosenberg would type. Julius Rosenberg or communist agents often provided the Greenglasses small sums of cash.

After the war the Greenglasses relocated to New York, and their relations with the Rosenbergs deteriorated. In the late 1940s Julius Rosenberg and David Greenglass launched a machine shop operation and several other unsuccessful small businesses. The two families quarreled over money. Both wives experienced emotional distress. Ruth Greenglass suffered a miscarriage and then gave birth to two children, the second after she was hospitalized from burns suffered in a household accident. With the onset of the cold war and the Soviet explosion of an atomic bomb in 1949, the British and American governments began a series of sensational investigations into espionage. The Federal Bureau of Investigation (FBI) discovered evidence against Julius Rosenberg, and Klaus Fuchs, a British physicist convicted of Soviet espionage, implicated Harry Gold, one of the couriers involved in the Greenglass-Rosenberg operation. Rosenberg explored the possibilities of fleeing the United States, and he provided funds for the Greenglasses to do likewise. They took the money, but did not leave the country. In 1950 both men were arrested. Rosenberg protested his innocence, but David Greenglass confessed and implicated others, including Julius Rosenberg. When questioned, Ruth Greenglass supported her husband's confessions, asserting that Julius Rosenberg had masterminded the espionage ring.

While the FBI knew that both the Rosenbergs and the Greenglasses had spied, they believed Julius Rosenberg had more extensive knowledge of Soviet espionage activities. They sought ways to exert pressure upon him to confess and implicate others. Knowing that the Rosenbergs were deeply attached to one another and had two young sons, prosecutors apparently reasoned that if they mounted charges against Ethel Rosenberg, her husband might cooperate. Already alienated from the Rosenbergs, the Greenglasses were receptive. Ruth Greenglass, almost certainly as deeply involved in espionage as Ethel Rosenberg, was never indicted. David Greenglass pleaded guilty and testified for the prosecution. Although she had not implicated her sister-in-law in the typing of her husband's notes during grand jury testimony, Ruth Greenglass told investigators a week prior to the opening of the trial that Ethel Rosenberg was the typist. Under intense cross-examination at the trial in New York in March 1951, Greenglass stood her ground. David Greenglass testified that his wife had an excellent memory and was almost certainly correct in her recollections. The Greenglasses' testimony constituted the strongest element in the case against Ethel Rosenberg who, along with her husband, was found guilty and sentenced to death. After highly publicized appeals, they were electrocuted in 1953.

After the trial the Greenglasses receded into virtual anonymity. Ruth Greenglass, a legal stenographer for the New York assemblyman Louis J. Lefkowitz, was fired. Her husband served ten years of a fifteen-year sentence prior to being reunited with his family and resuming work as a machinist. Federal officials gave the Greenglasses new identities, and they raised their children under assumed names in New York. Ruth Greenglass again became a legal secretary. The Rosenberg case became a cause célèbre for civil libertarians, who claimed that the Greenglasses had fabricated their testimony. In 1975 the Rosenberg sons insisted that their parents had been innocent but later conceded that their father had probably been guilty. In 1995 the National Security Agency released the Venona Cables, a set of decoded wartime Soviet intercepts that seemed to prove that the Rosenbergs had indeed been spies. David Greenglass in 1996 told a reporter that he had become uncertain of his testimony identifying his sister as the typist of the documents. Instead, he suggested that his wife had typed them. In June 2008, when the federal government released portions of the secret grand jury testimony, scholars discovered that Ruth Greenglass had died in April 2008.

★

The single best book on the case is Ronald Radosh and Joyce Milton, *The Rosenberg File: A Search for the Truth* (2nd ed., 1997). It should be supplemented by Sam Roberts, *The Brother: The Untold Story of the Rosenberg Case* (2003), which draws upon fifty hours of interviews with David Greenglass. Two books by John Earl Haynes and Harvey Klehr, *Venona: Decoding Soviet Espionage in America* (1999), and *Early Cold War Spies: The Espionage Trials That Shaped American Politics* (2006), are of considerable value. An obituary is in the *New York Times* (9 July 2008).

William Howard Moore

GRIFFIN, Mervyn Edward ("Merv"), Jr. (*b.* 6 July 1925 in San Mateo, California; *d.* 12 August 2007 in Los Angeles, California), singer, television personality, and entertainment industry mogul who earned his greatest popularity as host of *The Merv Griffin Show*, a long-running television talk show, and who created and produced *Jeopardy!* and *Wheel of Fortune*, two of the most successful game shows in television history.

Griffin was the only child of Mervyn Edward Griffin, Sr., a stockbroker, and Rita (Robinson) Griffin, a homemaker. When Griffin was four years old his aunt, Claudia Robinson, taught him how to play the piano, and on weekends he staged shows on the porch of his family's home. He began singing while in his teens. After graduating from San Mateo High School in 1942, Griffin attended San Mateo Junior College and the University of San Francisco. He dropped out of college in 1944 and, at his father's urging, took a job as a bank teller. On his first day at work, Griffin discovered that the teller toiling at his side had held that position for thirty years—and was still working for a meager salary. He promptly quit and was determined to break into the entertainment industry.

Merv Griffin, 1982. AP IMAGES

In 1945 Griffin was hired as a vocalist at KFRC, a San Francisco radio station. He was sold to the public as "America's new romantic singing star" and "the young romantic voice of radio," but his weight—he had ballooned to 240 pounds—worked against him when the RKO studio considered signing him to a movie contract. After being rejected for the movies, Griffin lost weight and would spend the rest of his life gaining and losing pounds.

In 1948 a slimmed-down Griffin was signed as a vocalist by the bandleader Freddy Martin. Griffin performed with Martin's orchestra at Los Angeles's Coconut Grove nightspot, earning $150 a week. He recorded "I've Got a Lovely Bunch of Coconuts," a novelty ditty that he sang with a faux English accent and that rose to number one on the Hit Parade. In addition, Griffin appeared on the *Freddy Martin Show* (1951), a musical television program. While performing in Las Vegas, Nevada, Griffin was spotted by the entertainer Doris Day, who recommended him to Warner Bros. He left Martin's band and made his screen debut in a supporting role in *Cattle Town* (1952), an undistinguished Western, and appeared unbilled as an announcer in *By the Light of the Silvery Moon* (1953), a Day musical comedy. Griffin was heard but not seen in *Trouble along the Way* (1953), a John Wayne vehicle, and *The Beast from 20,000 Fathoms* (1953), playing announcers. He had his one lead role opposite Kathryn Grayson in *So This Is Love* (1953), a biography of the opera singer Grace Moore. After supporting roles in *The Boy from Oklahoma* (1954) and *Phantom of the Rue Morgue* (1954), Warner Bros. released Griffin from his contract.

With his budding screen career over, Griffin turned to television and radio. He cohosted *Summer Holiday* (1954), a Columbia Broadcasting System (CBS) television summer replacement show, and briefly hosted *Look Up and Live* (1954–1979), a CBS Sunday morning religious show. Occasionally he appeared as a radio singer and host. On 18 May 1958 Griffin wed Julann Elizabeth Wright. The following year the pair had a son.

Griffin eventually became a familiar face on television game shows as a host of *Keep Talking* (1958–1960) and *Play Your Hunch* (1958–1963). Even more significant, he occasionally guest-hosted *The Jack Paar Tonight Show* (1957–1962). Upon Paar's retirement, Griffin lost out to Johnny Carson as the new *Tonight Show* host. As a consolation, the National Broadcasting Company (NBC) cast him in *The Merv Griffin Show* (1962–1963), a daytime gab fest modeled after *The Tonight Show*, but the program was canceled after six months. A couple of years later Griffin began his lengthy stint on a new *Merv Griffin Show* (1965–1986), which was syndicated for most of its run. His guests included not only movie stars but also classical musicians (Pablo Casals), civil rights leaders (Martin Luther King, Jr.), historians (Ted Sorensen, Will Durant, and Ariel Durant), politicians (Robert F. Kennedy and Richard

Nixon), writers and journalists (Truman Capote, Norman Mailer, Malcolm Muggeridge, and Adela Rogers St. John), antiwar activists (Abbie Hoffman), and unconventional entertainers (Richard Pryor, George Carlin, and Dick Gregory). On occasion the show attracted controversy. For example, it earned censure in some circles in 1965 when the philosopher Bertrand Russell delivered a scathing indictment of America's then-escalating involvement in the Vietnam War.

Meanwhile Griffin began conjuring up ideas for game shows. His first was *Word for Word* (1963–1964), a crossword puzzle–based program, which he also hosted and which lasted for one season. Then he achieved a phenomenal success with *Jeopardy!* (1964–1975, 1978–1979, 1984–), which over the years ran on the NBC and the American Broadcasting Company networks and in syndication. Griffin followed up with the equally popular and lucrative *Wheel of Fortune* (1975–). The shows were produced by his own company, Merv Griffin Enterprises, which he founded in 1964.

Griffin also began expanding his growing media empire by purchasing radio stations and media-related companies. One of them, Teleview Racing Patrol, evolved into the primary outlet for the closed-circuit broadcasting of horse races to offtrack betting sites. Meanwhile, in 1976 Griffin and Wright divorced. The reason cited was "irreconcilable differences."

Across the years Griffin produced other game shows, but none was as successful as *Jeopardy!* and *Wheel of Fortune*. In 1986 he sold his production company to Columbia Pictures Television for $250 million but shrewdly kept a portion of the *Jeopardy!* and *Wheel of Fortune* profits. At the time the transaction was the largest purchase of an entertainment enterprise owned by one individual. Griffin continued creating questions for *Jeopardy!* and puzzles for *Wheel of Fortune* and earning royalties on the *Jeopardy!* theme music he authored—most famously, the thirty-second melody heard during "Final Jeopardy." Griffin reported that he composed the melody in approximately thirty minutes and estimated that over the years it had earned him between $70 million and $80 million.

Even after divesting himself of his production company, Griffin was compelled to keep working. Most significantly, he purchased real estate. He acquired the Beverly Hilton Hotel for $100.2 million and refurbished it for an additional $25 million. At the Beverly Hilton he eventually opened the Coconut Club, a posh dance club modeled after the old Coconut Grove.

Griffin additionally purchased and sold over twenty hotels and resorts, from the Hilton Scottsdale Resort and Villas in Arizona to Ireland's Saint Clerans Manor, an eighteenth-century estate, which Griffin transformed into a boutique hotel. Griffin attempted to take control of Resorts International, which ran casinos and hotels in the United States and the Caribbean—an action that resulted in a dispute with the real estate mogul Donald Trump. In 1988 Griffin finally acquired Resorts for $240 million. His business dealings, combined with the astounding success of *Jeopardy!* and *Wheel of Fortune*, made Griffin one of America's richest citizens, with his worth estimated at well over $1 billion.

After his divorce Griffin never remarried but for many years was seen in public in the company of his close friend, the actress Eva Gabor. First Lady Nancy Reagan, with whom he shared a birthday, was another good friend. However, among the Hollywood crowd it commonly was assumed that Griffin was gay. In 1991 Griffin was sued for $200 million by Brent Plott, a former bodyguard, who claimed that he was Griffin's lover. Also in 1991 the dancer, choreographer, and television host Deney Terrio filed an $11.3 million sexual harassment suit against Griffin. Both cases were thrown out of court.

In 1994 Griffin entered the Broadcasting & Cable Hall of Fame. In 2005 he received a lifetime achievement award from the Academy of Television Arts and Sciences and a comparable honor from the Museum of Television and Radio. Later in life he also became a racehorse owner, raising Thoroughbreds at his La Quinta, California, ranch. In 2005 Stevie Wonderboy, a colt Griffin named for the singer Stevie Wonder, earned a first-place finish in the Breeders' Cup Junior.

In the mid-1990s Griffin was diagnosed with prostate cancer. He was treated for the disease, which went into remission. In July 2007, while Griffin was in production on *Merv Griffin's Crosswords* (2007–2008), a new syndicated game show, the cancer recurred. The eighty-two-year-old Griffin entered Cedars-Sinai Medical Center in Los Angeles, where he died. He is buried in Westwood Village Memorial Park in Los Angeles.

Most individuals are fortunate to flourish in one chosen field. Griffin, however, was a success in many fields. He was a big-band singer with a number-one hit record; a talk-show host who, for a time in the 1960s, was second only to Carson in popularity; a canny businessman whose holdings included hotels, resorts, and racehorses; and the creator of two astoundingly successful and lucrative television game shows.

★

Griffin published an account of his life, *Merv: An Autobiography* (1980), written with Peter Barsocchini. Also with Barsocchini, he wrote *From Where I Sit: Merv Griffin's Book of People* (1982). Two decades later he authored *Merv: Making the Good Life Last* (2003), written with David Bender. Obituaries are in *Variety* (12 Aug. 2007) and the *New York Times* (13 Aug. 2007).

Rob Edelman

H

HALBERSTAM, David (*b*. 10 April 1934 in New York City; *d*. 23 April 2007 in Menlo Park, California), Pulitzer Prize–winning reporter for the *New York Times* in South Vietnam and prolific author of best-selling books on history and sports.

Halberstam was the son of Charles Halberstam, a military surgeon, and Blanche (Levy) Halberstam, a schoolteacher. Halberstam and his older brother moved frequently during their childhood before their family settled in West-chester County, New York, after World War II. Charles Halberstam's assignments took the family to many loca-tions, including Austin, Texas; Rochester, Minnesota; and Winsted, Connecticut, before his death when Halberstam was sixteen. Halberstam's mother helped her sons appre-ciate the importance of education. After graduating from Roosevelt High School in Yonkers, New York, in 1951, Halberstam enrolled at Harvard University. He held the prestigious position of managing editor of the daily news-paper, the *Harvard Crimson*, and earned a BA in 1955.

Because of his experience at the *Crimson*, Halberstam could have found employment at one of the nation's most prominent newspapers. Instead he decided to accept a position as a reporter for the *West Point Daily Times Leader*, the daily newspaper with the smallest circulation in Mississippi. He wanted to cover racial issues at a time when the civil rights movement was emerging as a powerful force in the South. When an editor refused to publish his story about a white supremacist organization, Halber-stam resigned and joined the staff of the *Nashville Tennes-sean* in 1956. He also wrote occasional articles for the *Reporter*, a magazine with a national readership. His writ-ings impressed James Reston, the chief of the Washington

bureau of the *New York Times*, who offered Halberstam a job. Halberstam worked for only a few months in Wash-ington in 1961 before the *Times* sent him to the Congo, a nation where United Nations peacekeeping troops were trying to quell a civil war. For a year Halberstam covered what he described as a "bewildering war" that produced "real tragedy" for civilians as well as bizarre scenes, such as bursts of antiaircraft fire from a genteel restaurant where soldiers and civilians were eating lunch.

In September 1962 Halberstam became the *New York Times* correspondent in South Vietnam. He arrived at a time when the United States was increasing the number of its military advisers and expanding its arms assistance to the South Vietnamese government in its war against the National Liberation Front (NLF), a coalition of revolution-aries under Communist leadership. Officials in the John F. Kennedy administration tried to conceal information about the growing U.S. military involvement in South Vietnam for fear that public debate might complicate efforts to win an important victory in the cold war. In February 1962 the State and Defense departments had instructed U.S. officials in South Vietnam not to disclose the number of Americans involved in specific combat operations or to allow reporters into battle areas if they were likely to write critical stories. The South Vietnamese government imposed far more restrictive policies. Halberstam arrived in Saigon on the day of a farewell party for a *Newsweek* magazine reporter, who was being expelled for stories about the inadequacies of the government's war effort.

U.S. officials in Saigon at first praised Halberstam's reporting, but their attitude soon changed. Like other Amer-ican correspondents, Halberstam decided that he could not cover the war "from Saigon briefing rooms" and started

David Halberstam, 2005. © **PORTER GIFFORD/CORBIS**

traveling to battle areas. Instead of the optimism that pervaded the public statements of generals and diplomats, he found a sober and even pessimistic outlook among U.S. advisers in the field, who were familiar with the boldness and tenacity of NLF guerrillas and the lethargy and ineffectiveness of South Vietnamese troops. His stories revealed that Americans in South Vietnam were divided over how the war was going. His reporting about these differences rankled members of the Kennedy administration and the South Vietnamese government of President Ngo Dinh Diem, leading to new restrictions on news coverage of combat operations in late 1962. Halberstam was so furious that he wrote a letter of protest to Frederick E. Nolting, Jr., the U.S. ambassador in Saigon, declaring that he had become an "angry man."

The South Vietnamese defeat at the battle of Ap Bac in January 1963 heightened tensions between Halberstam and other U.S. journalists on one hand and high-ranking U.S. officials in Saigon on the other. In his article about the battle, Halberstam declared that government forces had suffered their worst defeat in a year—even though they possessed superior numbers and had attacked at a place of their choosing—because they "lost the initiative from the first moment and never showed much aggressive instinct." Halberstam reported only the judgments of American advisers who had been at Ap Bac; nevertheless, General Paul D. Harkins, the commander of U.S. military forces, believed that such assertions damaged South Vietnamese morale, and he chided reporters "for doing a disservice to the thousands of gallant and courageous men who are fighting in the defense of their country." Halberstam, however, did not question the desirability of halting Communist expansion in Southeast Asia. Instead he thought that the Diem government was not sufficiently popular, strong, or effective to win the war, and he worried that U.S. efforts to stifle or to discredit reporting about the government's failings would only make Diem less likely to implement necessary reforms. The dispute over policy became personal. Some U.S. officials reportedly hated Halberstam. In turn he made little effort to disguise his contempt for Harkins, whose hand he refused to shake at a social occasion.

During the Buddhist crisis of May–August 1963, Halberstam's reporting challenged South Vietnamese policy more forcefully than ever before. The crisis began when government troops shot demonstrators who opposed a ban on the display of religious flags. The unrest continued as Diem rejected U.S. counsel to lift the ban. On 11 June, after receiving a panicked telephone call, Halberstam rushed to a Saigon intersection and saw an elderly Buddhist monk burn himself to death in protest. "I was too shocked to cry, too confused to take notes or ask questions, too bewildered even to think," he later recollected. Few Americans had followed developments in South Vietnam closely, but this horrifying and sensational event attracted public attention.

As the crisis deepened, government officials tried to intimidate Halberstam and other Western reporters. During another Buddhist demonstration on 7 July, plainclothes South Vietnamese police assaulted Halberstam and eight other journalists. Government authorities also tapped Halberstam's telephone and intimated that he might be assassinated. The harassment failed to deter Halberstam. In mid-August the *Times* carried his front-page story about the substantial gains that NLF armed forces had made during the past year in the Mekong Delta. Harkins's staff tried to refute Halberstam's article but could find mistakes only in some details. Eight days later the *Times* carried another front-page article by Halberstam; the article alleged that the South Vietnamese secret police, disguised as regular army troops, were responsible for raids on Buddhist pagodas, despite Diem's assurances that he would take no new repressive actions. Fearing for his life, Halberstam took refuge in the residence of the chief U.S. information officer in Saigon.

The turmoil in South Vietnam persuaded some U.S. officials in Saigon and Washington that Diem should relinquish power. Kennedy was undecided about whether the United States should authorize a coup, but he thought that Halberstam's blunt reporting only complicated U.S. efforts. In October, Kennedy failed to persuade Arthur Ochs Sulzberger, the publisher of the *New York Times*, to recall his reporter. Halberstam remained in his assignment until the end of the year, covering the 1 November 1963 coup that deposed Diem and Diem's subsequent assassination. In 1964 Halberstam shared the Pulitzer Prize for international reporting with Malcolm Browne of the Associated Press. A year later he published *The Making of a Quagmire*, a history of U.S. involvement in Vietnam during the Kennedy presidency as well as a memoir of his reporting. The *Times* sent Halberstam to Warsaw in 1965, but the Polish government expelled him at the end of the year for publishing "slanderous articles." He then reported from Paris for several months in 1966. While in Poland, he married Elzbieta Czyzewska on 13 June 1965; the marriage ended in divorce in 1977. On 29 June 1979 he married Jean Sandness Butler; they had one daughter.

In 1967 Halberstam left the *Times* to work as a contributing editor for *Harper's* magazine. He also devoted much of his time to writing books, publishing *One Very Hot Day* (1968), a novel about Vietnam, as well as *The Unfinished Odyssey of Robert Kennedy* (1969) and *Ho* (1971), a portrait of the Vietnamese leader Ho Chi Minh. Halberstam left *Harper's* in 1971 and the next year published *The Best and the Brightest*, one of the most influential books ever written about the reasons for U.S. involvement in the Vietnam War. Halberstam offered memorable portraits of the architects of American intervention in the war to show that "for all their brilliance and hubris," these policy makers had "been unwilling to . . . learn from the past and . . . had been swept forward . . . by the sense of power and glory, omnipotence and omniscience of America in this century." The book was a best seller and a finalist for the National Book Award, and its title added an ironic phrase to contemporary English usage. In 1979 Halberstam published another major work, *The Powers That Be*, a rich, sprawling study of four media giants—Time Inc., Columbia Broadcasting System, the *Los Angeles Times*, and the *Washington Post*—and their effects on politics and contemporary American life. It was also a finalist for the National Book Award.

During the 1980s Halberstam began writing about sports and sports history. In *The Breaks of the Game* (1981), he chronicled a season of the Portland Trailblazers, a professional basketball team that granted him privileged access. He also wrote about four rowers who hoped to compete in the Olympics in *The Amateurs* (1985) and about the classic baseball rivalry between the New York Yankees and the Boston Red Sox in *Summer of '49* (1989). By the early 1990s his practice was to alternate a book on sports with one on politics, national security, or social issues.

In 1993 Halberstam published *The Fifties*, a book that called attention to the complexities of a decade that many people remember as a time of simplicity and serenity. His next book, *October 1964* (1994), an absorbing story of the 1964 World Series and the end of a great New York Yankees dynasty, was followed by *The Children* (1998), a study of the civil rights movement in Nashville, Tennessee.

Halberstam became even more prolific in his final decade, producing seven books between 1999 and 2007, including *Playing for Keeps: Michael Jordan and the World He Made* (1999); *War in a Time of Peace* (2001), a study of national security policy following the cold war; *Firehouse* (2002), a gripping portrait of firefighters involved in the 11 September 2001 rescue efforts in New York City; and *The Education of a Coach* (2005), a profile of Bill Belichick, the brilliant but aloof coach of the New England Patriots football franchise. Halberstam's final book, *The Coldest Winter: America and the Korean War* (2007), published posthumously, provides portraits of both political and military leaders as well as ordinary soldiers. The book was a finalist for the Pulitzer Prize in history.

In 2007, on his way to an interview with the former quarterback Y. A. Tittle, Halberstam was a passenger in a car that was involved in an accident. He suffered internal injuries and was pronounced dead at the scene. He had planned to interview Tittle as part of his research for a book on the famous football championship game in 1958 between the New York Giants and the Baltimore Colts.

Halberstam was a towering figure, both literally and figuratively, in American journalism for almost half a century. More than six feet tall and with a deep, resonant voice, he was an imposing presence. He had strong opinions, and he was unwilling to back down on issues he considered important. While at times his anger may have produced excesses—the journalist William Prochnau described him as "relentless, single-minded, obsessive; defensive, thin-skinned, quick to take offense"—his courage and persistence in Vietnam made both the public and government policy makers aware of the perils of the growing U.S. commitment. As a writer Halberstam had tremendous range. His subjects included President Lyndon B. Johnson and the basketball great Michael Jordan, civil rights and civil war. He was a master of individual portraiture. He wrote about uncommon leaders and common citizens, but almost always to probe connections between people and the institutions or culture that shaped their lives and that they in turn influenced. In his final public presentation, just two days before his death, he gave a speech titled "Turning Journalism into History." He turned journalism into history in his own career, making notable contributions to both fields.

★

Halberstam's papers are in the Howard Gotlieb Archival Research Center at Boston University. There is no biography, but a brief account of Halberstam's early life is in William Prochnau, *Once upon a Distant War* (1995). For information on Halberstam's reporting from Vietnam, see William M. Hammond, *Public Affairs: The Military and the Media, 1962–1968* (1988), and Clarence R. Wyatt, *Paper Soldiers: The American Press and the Vietnam War* (1993). An obituary is in the *New York Times* (24 Apr. 2007).

Chester Pach

HARDWICK, Elizabeth Bruce (*b.* 27 July 1916 in Lexington, Kentucky; *d.* 2 December 2007 in New York City), author, literary and social critic for the *Partisan Review*, cofounder of the *New York Review of Books*, and the first woman to receive the George Jean Nathan Award for dramatic criticism.

Hardwick was born to Eugene Allen Hardwick, who ran a plumbing and heating business, and Mary (Ramsey) Hardwick, a homemaker. Hardwick was the eighth of eleven children in the Presbyterian Scottish family. After attending Henry Clay High School, Hardwick enrolled in

Elizabeth Hardwick. AP IMAGES

the University of Kentucky, earning an AB in 1938 and an MA in 1939, both in English. Declining a fellowship to Louisiana State University, Hardwick instead accepted admission to Columbia University's PhD program in 1939 but dropped out in 1941, reasoning that a doctorate was not worth pursuing because women were rarely offered top teaching positions.

In 1945 Hardwick published her first novel, *The Ghostly Lover*. Philip Rahv, editor of the *Partisan Review*, invited Hardwick to join the left-leaning journal that became fiercely anti-Stalinist in 1937, when it began publishing again after a hiatus in 1936. Hardwick herself had engaged in communist activities in college, and her anti-Stalin stance was apparent in her reviews. In 1946 she began a regular column, "Fiction Chronicle," reviewing Richard Wright's *Black Boy*.

Also in 1945 Hardwick won the first of her three O. Henry Memorial Awards, the most prestigious award for short fiction, receiving third place for "The People on the Roller Coaster." She was included in the O. Henry Award collection again in 1946 and 1995. In 1947 she won a Guggenheim Fellowship for fiction. In summer 1948 Hardwick was selected for Yaddo, an artists' community, where she became further acquainted with the recently divorced poet Robert Lowell, whom she had first met at a party given by Rahv in Greenwich Village, New York City, in 1946. Shortly after their stay at Yaddo, Lowell was admitted to an asylum near Boston. Hardwick visited him there, and despite disapproval from Hardwick's parents, the couple married on 28 July 1949 at the home of Lowell's parents in Boston. Lowell spent the first year of the marriage in a psychiatric clinic in New York City. Lowell's mental illness produced a turbulent marriage.

Lowell taught for a term at the University of Iowa. Between 1950 and 1953 he and Hardwick traveled to and lived in various European cities, including Amsterdam, Netherlands; Florence, Italy; Vienna, Austria; and Salzburg, Austria. Lowell had an affair and another breakdown in Austria in 1953, and he and Hardwick returned to the United States. From 1954 to 1957 they sojourned in Ohio, Iowa, and Indiana, but were based in Boston starting in 1954, where their only daughter was born. In 1955 Hardwick published her second novel, *The Simple Truth*.

In 1960 Hardwick and Lowell moved to the Upper West Side of Manhattan in New York City, where Hardwick lived until her death. That year her story "The Purchase" appeared in *Best American Short Stories*, and in 1962 *A View of My Own: Essays in Literature and Society* was published. In 1963 a long printers' strike in New York City shut down the book reviews of the *New York Times* and the *Herald Tribune*. Hardwick cofounded the *New York Review of Books* (*NYRB*), which Lowell financed. *NYRB* became a standard of intellectual discourse and was still being published at the time of Hardwick's death. The first issue contained one of

Hardwick's most famous essays, "The Gang," a spoof of Mary McCarthy's *The Group* (1963); Hardwick published the essay under the pen name Xavier Prynne.

In 1969, while she was teaching at Barnard College, Hardwick became the first woman to receive the George Jean Nathan Award for excellence in drama criticism. She left Barnard in 1970 to join Lowell, who was teaching at Oxford University in England. A pattern had developed wherein Lowell would suffer a manic episode, publicly commit adultery, and then reconcile with Hardwick. In 1972 Hardwick finally filed for divorce when she discovered that Lowell had a son with Lady Caroline Blackwood. (Lowell documented the public breakup in his 1973 poem "The Dolphin").

In 1974 Hardwick published a collection of *NYRB* essays titled *Seduction and Betrayal: Women and Literature*, exploring and exposing her public betrayals by Lowell as well as unconventional views of literary heroines. By 1976 Hardwick and Lowell had reconciled and summered together in Maine. The next year they traveled together to Moscow and again spent the summer together. Lowell died in September 1977. In 1978 Hardwick returned to teaching at Barnard, and in 1982 she began teaching writing at Columbia.

In 1977 Hardwick was elected to the American Academy of Arts and Letters, an honor society of artists and writers. Her autobiographical third (and final) novel, *Sleepless Nights*, was published in 1979 to mostly positive reviews; it was nominated for a National Book Critics Circle Award. Hardwick's collection of essays *Bartleby in Manhattan and Other Essays* (1983) won universal acclaim for her as a major essayist. Another collection of essays, *Sight-Readings: American Fictions*, was published in 1998. In 2000 Hardwick wrote a biography of Herman Melville for the Penguin Lives series.

After retiring from both Barnard and *NYRB* in 1985, Hardwick was selected as editor of the first *Best American Essays* in 1986. Hardwick served on the board of the National Book Critics Circle, was on the advisory committee for the National Book Award, and was a judge for the PEN/Faulkner Award for Fiction. In 1993 Hardwick received a Gold Medal from the American Academy of Arts and Letters. The award is considered the highest recognition of artistic merit in the United States.

Hardwick died at Saint Luke's–Roosevelt Hospital after being hospitalized for an infection. A memorial service was held in New York City on 16 December 2007. She was cremated and her ashes are in possession of her family.

Hardwick was an integral member of the *Partisan Review* intellectuals, known for their leftist politics, hard drinking, cigarette smoking, and sexual exploits. Other members of the group included McCarthy, Hannah Arendt, and Diana Trilling. These prefeminist women were accepted in the group and worked and wrote alongside the men. Hardwick succeeded in her goal of becoming a "New York Jewish intellectual" and never identified herself as a southern writer. She earned acclaim for her essays and her hard-hitting literary and theater criticism rather than for her fiction.

★

Hardwick's papers are in the Washington University in St. Louis Libraries (1930–1981) and in the Harry Ransom Humanities Research Center at the University of Texas at Austin (1934–1991); the University of Texas collection includes manuscripts. A 1984 interview with Hardwick is in George Plimpton, ed., *Writers at Work: The Paris Review Interviews, Seventh Series* (1986). David Laskin, *Partisans: Marriage, Politics, and Betrayal Among the New York Intellectuals* (2000), chronicles the lives of Hardwick and others within the *Partisan Review* group. Obituaries are in the *New York Times* (4 Dec. 2007) and the *Los Angeles Times* (5 Dec. 2007).

Jane Brodsky Fitzpatrick

HART, Kitty Carlisle (*b.* 3 September 1910 in New Orleans, Louisiana; *d.* 17 April 2007 in New York City), singer, actress, television panelist, arts advocate and administrator, and New York society matron known for her sparkling personality.

Kitty Carlisle Hart, 1962. **CBS PHOTO ARCHIVE/GETTY IMAGES**

Hart was born Catherine Conn, the only child of Joseph Conn, a gynecologist, and Hortense (Holtzman) Conn. Hart's father died when Hart was ten, and she was raised by her mother, an ambitious woman who had grand designs for her daughter. Although the Conn family was well-to-do and prominent in New Orleans society, Hart's mother wanted a more cosmopolitan setting for her tall, slim, attractive daughter. In 1921, soon after the death of her husband, Hart's mother, an adventuress with an affected but ingratiating manner and a formidable ability to insinuate herself with the rich and famous, took Hart to Europe, where they hobnobbed with royalty. Living in the cheapest rooms in the best hotels in London and Paris, the two women led a strange, peripatetic life. They were like characters in a Henry James novel, eager to be Europeanized; Hart's mother was determined to remove from her pliant daughter any trace of her New Orleans origins or her Jewish heritage. Hart had an unaffectionate mother often given to volcanic rages, but her devotion to her daughter was absolute. She enrolled Hart in the finest private schools in Switzerland, London, Paris, and Rome, and honed her social skills in order to prepare her for a magnificent royal marriage.

When Hart failed to secure a wellborn husband, she decided to pursue a career in show business as a singer and an actress—at the time Broadway showgirls frequently married into money. She studied at London's Royal Academy of Dramatic Art and at the Théâtre de l'Atelier in Paris, but her practical mother insisted that she also take courses at the London School of Economics.

The lingering impact of the Wall Street crash eventually put an end to the Conns' European sojourn. In 1932 the women returned to America, hoping to launch Hart in a career on Broadway. They took up hotel living once again. Now the family breadwinner, expected to make good on her mother's investment in her, Hart changed her name to the euphonious Kitty Carlisle and began an arduous round of auditions. She got work quickly. After apprenticing at the Bucks County Playhouse in New Hope, Pennsylvania, she was cast in a leading role in a musical comedy, *Rio Rita*, presented between film screenings at large movie palaces. The grueling job was short on prestige and glamour, but performing far more than the standard eight-shows-a-week Broadway schedule, Hart exhibited a quality she had inherited from her mother that was to sustain her throughout her life: stamina.

Hart soon graduated to Broadway, where on 14 October 1933 she made her debut as Count Orlofsky in an adaptation of the Johann Strauss operetta *Die Fledermaus* called *Champagne, Sec*. Against her mother's wishes, the next year she accepted a contract at Paramount Pictures, where she was cast as the ingenue in *Murder at the Vanities* (1934) and in two lackluster Bing Crosby vehicles, *She Loves Me Not* (1934) and *Here Is My Heart* (1934). On-screen Hart was

curiously muted. She was stiff, and her eyes were inexpressive. In 1935 she was loaned out to Metro-Goldwyn-Mayer to costar in the only film that she would be remembered for, *A Night at the Opera*, a Marx Brothers vehicle. Lacking the kind of screen presence that would allow her to hold her own against the mayhem of the Marxes, Hart is no more than decorative in her role of a young opera performer. In the film she sings a charming duet with Allan Jones, "Alone," and operatic fragments from *Il Trovatore* and *I Pagliacci*.

In 1935, when her contract with Paramount was not renewed, Hart, downhearted, returned to New York City. She was soon back in action, however, winning the lead in *White Horse Inn* (1936), a spectacular operetta that played for six months at the mammoth Center Theatre in Rockefeller Center. The following season Hart played three roles in *Three Waltzes* (1937), another European-flavored operetta extravaganza. She also began to be heard regularly on radio and to make many personal appearances, but she was not a star. She auditioned for but was not cast in major roles in the important musicals of the era. As an avid New York partygoer, however, Hart got to know all the major Broadway composers. In 1940 she returned to Broadway as the star of *Walk with Music*, a short-lived musical composed by Hoagy Carmichael with lyrics by Johnny Mercer. Reuniting with Jones in 1943, Hart attempted a feeble comeback in movies in *Larceny with Music*.

In 1946, six months after meeting the Pulitzer Prize–winning playwright Moss Hart at a dinner party given by the playwright Lillian Hellman, Hart finally fulfilled her mother's wish: She married well—to Broadway if not European royalty. She dedicated herself to being a good wife to Moss Hart, seeing him through recurrent bouts of crippling depression, and a devoted mother to their two children. As the playwright's wife she was a gracious hostess in a resplendent apartment at 1185 Park Avenue in New York City and at a farm in Bucks County, and a much-sought-after guest at glittering parties and receptions. Though acting was no longer her primary focus, she also continued to perform. She appeared in stock, often in plays by her husband, such as *Lady in the Dark* and *The Man Who Came to Dinner*. In 1948, while pregnant, Hart appeared on Broadway in Benjamin Britten's opera *The Rape of Lucretia*. Directed by her husband, Hart made her sole Broadway appearance in 1954 in a nonsinging role, as the lead in a light comedy, *The Anniversary Waltz*.

Hart had her greatest show business success when she appeared on television as a panelist on *To Tell the Truth*. She made her debut in 1956 and was the only panelist to remain with the show through all its versions; her last appearance was at the end of the show's marathon run, in 2002. As a quick-witted panelist with a radiant smile and elegant taste in clothing, she paraded the sophistication in which she had been schooled by her mother. Her national fame led to a career on the lecture circuit in which she achieved particular success talking to women's clubs.

When her husband died prematurely of a heart attack in 1961, Hart was faced with the challenge that her mother had endured—shouldering the burdens of being a single parent. In 1962 she bought an imperial-sized apartment at Madison Avenue and East Sixty-fourth Street, where she lived for the rest of her life. At fifty-six she made her debut at the Metropolitan Opera in 1966 as Count Orlofsky in Garson Kanin's production of *Die Fledermaus*—an achievement she was certain her mother, who had died in 1957, would have been proud of.

Hart began to branch out into arts administration and public service. In 1966 her good friend Nelson Rockefeller appointed her to chair a conference on women. In the 1970s she began to serve on the boards of numerous New York cultural institutions, and in 1976 she became chair of the New York State Council on the Arts, a position she held for twenty years. "Governor, darling," was the way she addressed all the politicians to whom she reported. As chair she traveled the state, visiting and evaluating theater and opera companies, art galleries, museums, and symphony and chamber orchestras. She was a passionate and fair-minded arts advocate who sometimes funded avant-garde groups with which she was not personally sympathetic. In 1991, in recognition of her many years of tireless service, Hart was awarded the American National Medal of Arts by the National Endowment for the Arts in Washington, D.C.

Hart continued to make sporadic appearances in theater and films. On Broadway in 1983 she succeeded Dina Merrill in a hit revival of the Richard Rodgers and Lorenz Hart musical *On Your Toes*. She had a cameo as herself in Woody Allen's *Radio Days* (1987), and she was a New York society hostess in *Six Degrees of Separation* (1993). Her crowning success as a performer, however, did not come until she was in her eighties, when she began to appear in a one-woman show in which she reminisced about and sang songs by the famous composers she had known, including George Gershwin, Irving Berlin, Kurt Weill, and Cole Porter. Although she herself had had no significant part in the golden age of the Broadway musical, she was one of the last surviving links to its fabled history.

Until her last performance in December 2006, when she was ninety-five, she brought a remarkably well-preserved version of "Kitty Carlisle" onto the stage. With her upswept, raven hair immaculately in place and her legs, which she always proudly displayed, still in shape, she had grown into a stately beauty. In fact, in her ninth and tenth decades, Hart was more attractive and more talented than she had been as a starlet at Paramount or as a Broadway ingenue. In old age she had the carriage and the glamour of the kind of star she always conceded she had not been in her younger years. She sang better than she had ever sung. Her low tones, always her strongest register, were richer than ever before, and she handled lyrics in a way that revealed unexpected acting skill. Her meditative, wrenching version of Weill and Maxwell Anderson's "September Song" regularly received a standing ovation. Hart died of complications from pneumonia at her home in Manhattan, New York City. She is buried in Ferncliff Cemetery and Mausoleum in Hartsdale, New York.

Hart's trim figure, which she maintained through a strict regimen of daily exercise, her zest for performing, and her active social life became an inspiration for senior citizens throughout the country. "She had a long run, and a wonderful life," her son announced at the standing-room-only memorial in her honor at the Majestic Theater on Broadway on 12 June 2007. Hart was recognized as having had "one of the greatest third acts in the cultural history of Manhattan." In the end her greatest role was the one for which her mother had trained her well: playing herself, or at least the self she showed to the world—a charming, urbane, vivacious woman who acted as if her own life was the best party to which she had ever been invited.

★

Hart's memoir, *Kitty: An Autobiography* (1988), is an entertaining, reasonably candid self-portrait. An obituary is in the *New York Times* (18 Apr. 2007).

Foster Hirsch

HARTACK, William John ("Bill"), Jr. (*b.* 9 December 1932 in Colver, Pennsylvania; *d.* 26 November 2007 in Webb County, Texas), American Hall of Fame Thoroughbred jockey and record-tying five-time winner of the Kentucky Derby.

Hartack was born in mining shack 371, the son of William Hartack (originally Valentin Hartuk), a coal miner from Czechoslovakia, and Nancy (Rager) Hartack, a member of the Pennsylvania Dutch community. His mother died in a car accident in 1940, a wreck that also injured his father and infant sister. Hartack and his older sister were cared for by a couple and attended grade school while their father recuperated. About a year later the family's bungalow burned down, and they moved to a farm near Belsano, Pennsylvania. Hartack worked on the farm and attended Black Lick Township School. Considered too small for high school sports, Hartack acted as timer at basketball games. After his graduation, a jockey agent, Andy Bruno, encouraged the five-foot, four-inch, 114-pound Hartack to work at a horse racing track.

At Charles Town Race Course in West Virginia, Hartack was hired by the trainer Norman "Junie" Corbin and

Bill Hartack, 1964. AP IMAGES

choose mounts (Jimmy Jones of Calumet Farms had first call on Hartack's services) and soothe the feelings of ruffled clients. Lang described Hartack as "particularly rude if he hasn't won. He's the most competitive athlete I ever saw." Hartack himself said, "I want to win so badly that anything or anybody who takes my mind off winning bothers me. I tell them so. They dislike me for it."

In 1955 Hartack led the nation's jockeys with 417 victories, the second-highest total in Thoroughbred racing history. Placing second in the Kentucky Derby, Hartack won the Preakness on Fabius and led all jockeys in races won and purse earnings in 1956. In 1957 he won the Kentucky Derby on Iron Liege, 341 races to lead the nation for a third consecutive year, and a record 43 stakes races; he earned $3,060,051 in purses, becoming the first jockey to earn $3 million in a single year, a record that stood for the next decade. Hartack won the 1958 Florida Derby on Tim Tam but later broke his left leg, relinquishing his ride on this eventual Kentucky Derby winner to Ismael Valenzuela.

On 21 February 1959 Hartack was set to ride Greek Circle, owned by Fred W. Hooper, the president of the American Thoroughbred Owners Association, at the Hialeah track in Florida. Hartack pronounced the horse unfit just prior to the race and refused to ride, despite the track veterinarian's contrary opinion. Hialeah scratched Greek Circle from the race and refunded his bettors $136,089, negating a new track pari-mutuel betting record. (In this type of betting pool, those who bet on the top three finishers share the total amount bet minus a percentage for the track management.) When questioned by Hooper, Hartack simply said, "the horse is sore." Later that year he was inducted into the National Museum of Racing's Hall of Fame. At twenty-six he was the youngest jockey to be enshrined.

In 1960, with 307 wins, he led all jockeys in victories for the last time. That year he won the Kentucky Derby on Venetian Way and the Belmont on Celtic Ash. Hartack broke Kentucky Derby records in 1962, winning on Decidedly, and in 1964, winning on Northern Dancer. He repeated his Kentucky Derby and Preakness victories in 1964 on Northern Dancer and in 1969 on Majestic Prince. In 1963 the National Jockeys Hall of Fame at Pimlico enshrined Hartack. Just thirty-one at the time, he already ranked seventh in lifetime wins and fourth in earnings with $18 million.

In September 1964 Hartack resigned his membership and vice presidency of the Jockeys' Guild to protest that organization's decision not to support Valenzuela when trainer Les Lear, breaking an oral agreement, replaced Valenzuela with Willie Shoemaker for the Arlington Futurity at Arlington Park in Illinois. Controversy and his increasing weight resulted in fewer mounts for Hartack. Moving to Hong Kong in 1975, he rode at Happy Valley Race Course

quickly advanced to the position of exercise boy. In the winter of 1951–1952 an owner hired him to work her horses at Miami's Tropical Park race track. Hartack recalled that "almost all had some traits I had to cope with"; ever analytical, Hartack used this experience to quickly size up mounts and determine how to handle them in a race. Corbin encouraged Hartack to get his father's signature on a jockey's contract. Though reluctant, he went home to do so and while there read in a Pittsburgh newspaper that he was scheduled to ride the horse Hal's Play at West Virginia's Waterford Park the next day. After finishing last in that race on 9 October 1952, he rode Nickleby to victory five days later in his third race, launching his jockey career.

In 1953 Hartack won 350 races, second only to Willie Shoemaker's record 485 victories that year. He bought a 175-acre farm near Charles Town for his father to manage. Corbin, short on funds in 1954, sold Hartack's contract to Ada L. Rice for $15,000. Hartack boarded Corbin's horses for free at his farm and rode for Rice's trainer, the future Hall of Famer Tom Kelly, until the contract expired in the fall of 1955.

When Hartack decided to freelance, Corbin asked John Charles "Chick" Lang, Jr., to be Hartack's agent, a position he held until 1960. The diplomatic Lang contributed greatly to Hartack's success through his ability to until a protruding piece of metal on the racetrack rail cut a nerve in his foot. He retired from riding in 1981.

Hartack used race film and the *Daily Racing Form* to study his own riding, his opponents, and horses. During race warm-ups, he assessed his horse's tendencies and current condition. Because he whipped left-handed with a sideways motion, his use of the whip was sometimes hidden from spectators. The *Lexington Leader* observed that "Hartack's style of riding is a terrible thing to behold, but it certainly photographs well at the finish."

After his retirement Hartack worked at California tracks as a placing judge, paddock judge, and patrol judge, which involved film analysis. He commented on races for the American Broadcasting Company television network from 1983 to 1986, broadcasting Triple Crown races with the sports announcer Howard Cosell. In November 1985 Hartack passed the California exams to become a track steward, and Tampa Bay Downs offered him a position. His fellow steward John Hanley commented on Hartack's integrity and thorough preparation, noting that "when it comes to spotting nuances the camera has recorded, Bill Hartack's the best I've ever seen." Hartack worked as state steward at Chicago area tracks until 1993 and as steward at the Fair Grounds in New Orleans and various other tracks until his death. Hartack, who never married, maintained a permanent residence at Miami Springs, Florida. Nearby Hialeah High School honored him for his many contributions to area youth programs. In 2008, after his death, the Hawthorne Race Course inaugurated the Bill Hartack Memorial Handicap in his honor.

Hartack died of natural causes due to heart disease while on a hunting trip. He is buried in Iberia Cemetery in Iberia, Missouri, in a plot owned by his longtime friend Gary Condra.

Between 1952 and 1974 Hartack won 4,272 (then ranking second to Willie Shoemaker) of 21,535 races in the United States and total purses worth $26,466,758. He won five of his first nine Kentucky Derbys, tying Eddie Arcaro's record set in twenty-one attempts. Sports journalists and racing enthusiasts regard Hartack as one of the greatest jockeys of all time. Despite Hartack's famously difficult temperament, many admire him for his prowess and judgment in the sport of Thoroughbred racing as well as for his adherence to his principles.

★

Frank Eck, "New Golden Boy," *Saturday Evening Post* (3 May 1958), provides a wealth of information on Hartack's early life. "Bully and the Beasts," *Time* (10 Feb. 1958), features Hartack on its cover and describes his early life and career. A series of articles in *Sports Illustrated* cover his racing career: Joe Hirsch, "The Front Runner" (17 Sept. 1956); William Leggett, "Just Call Me Bill" (13 Apr. 1959); and Jack Olsen, "Whatever Happened to Bill Hartack?" (24 June 1963). Two examinations of Hartack's temperament and its effect on his racing career are Pat Rogerson, "Bill Hartack: Racing's Bad Boy or Rare Fighter for Principle?" *Morning Telegraph* (16 Jan. 1965), and Jennie Rees, "Combativeness Left Derby's Top Jockey 'Almost Forgotten,'" *Louisville Courier-Journal* (1 May 1994). For his career after retiring from riding, see Bill Mooney, "Call Me Steward," *Thoroughbred Times* (17 Apr. 1987). Obituaries are in the *Daily Racing Form* and *New York Times* (both 28 Nov. 2007).

Steven P. Savage

HARTFORD, (George) Huntington, II (*b.* 18 April 1911 in New York City; *d.* 19 May 2008 in Lyford Cay, Bahamas), heir to the A. & P. supermarket fortune and patron of the arts.

Hartford was the second of two children born to Edward Hartford and Henrietta (Guerard) Hartford. His older sister, Josephine, was born in 1904. His father was one of the three sons of George Huntington Hartford, who was one of the principal founders of the Great Atlantic & Pacific Tea Company (A. & P.) in 1859. Edward Hartford, unlike his two brothers, John A. Hartford and George L. Hartford, had little involvement in the supermarket company that had made his family one of the nation's richest. Instead he established a reputation as an inventor, winning a patent for an automobile shock absorber.

After the death of his father in 1922, Huntington Hartford, who never used "George," moved with his mother to Seaverge, an estate in Newport, Rhode Island. Shortly thereafter, his mother enrolled him in the prestigious St. Paul's School in New Hampshire, where he was ostracized by other students as a member of the nouveau riche. After high school he attended Harvard University, graduating in 1934 with an AB in English literature. During his college years he met Mary Lee Epling, whom he married on 18 April 1934; they divorced in 1939.

After college Hartford took a job clerking for the family company, which was headquartered in New York City. He had difficulty taking the job seriously and often took time off, which earned him a warning that his job was in jeopardy. When he defied his uncles and took off another day to attend the Harvard-Yale game in November 1934, his brief career with A. & P. came to an abrupt end. In 1940 he had a brief stint as a reporter for a New York City newspaper called *PM* but lost that job when he failed to meet his deadline for filing a story. During World War II Hartford served in the U.S. Coast Guard Reserve from 1942 to 1945, becoming a lieutenant. He briefly commanded a supply ship, an assignment that ended after he grounded the vessel twice over a short period.

Hartford, like his father, had little to do with the company that had brought his family such great wealth. In the late 1940s he opened a model agency, through which he met his second wife, Marjorie Steele, whom he married on 10 September 1949. That year he also established the Huntington Hartford Foundation, an artists' retreat near Los Angeles. He produced a handful of motion pictures, one of which, *Face to Face* (1953), was made to showcase the talents of his wife. In 1954 he converted an old movie theater into the Huntington Hartford Theater, the first legitimate stage theater in Los Angeles. In a departure from his other pursuits, from 1956 to 1962 he did graduate work in neurology at Columbia University.

Hartford became an eager—if not particularly discriminating—collector of art. He had little use for modern or abstract art and viewed the paintings of Pablo Picasso and Willem de Kooning as "vulgar" and "meaningless." Hartford was also outspoken in his condemnation of such popular twentieth-century American writers as William Faulkner and Tennessee Williams, whose work he considered immoral.

Hartford's second marriage ended in an expensive divorce in 1960. The final settlement called for Hartford to establish trust funds of $1 million each for his two children with Steele, Catherine and John. Catherine reportedly struggled with drug problems for years and was found dead on a beach in Hawaii in 1988.

To keep financing his lavish lifestyle, Hartford in 1959 sold off $40 million of his shares in A. & P. Among other projects funded by this new infusion of cash was an art museum he built in 1964 on Columbus Circle in New York City. The Gallery of Modern Art (also known as the Huntington Hartford Museum) was designed to showcase artworks of the nineteenth and twentieth centuries but only those of a more traditional, figurative nature and not avant-garde abstract art, which he criticized in a 1964 book, *Art or Anarchy?* A financial disaster, the museum closed after only five years. Beginning in the early 1960s he served on the advisory committee of the John F. Kennedy Center for the Performing Arts in Washington, D.C., and as an honorary chairman of New York's Lincoln Center for the Performing Arts, as well as on other arts-related advisory boards.

Another project that cut deeply into Hartford's wealth was his purchase of Hog Island, near Nassau in the Bahamas. He bought roughly 80 percent of the island's property and embarked on a project to turn it into a lavish resort with gambling. He renamed it Paradise Island, but it turned out to be an enormous waste of money when authorities turned down his request for a gambling license. Another costly project was his launch of a glossy arts-and-entertainment magazine called *Show*, which eventually shut down in 1973.

Hartford married Diane Brown, a model, on 6 October 1962, with whom he had a daughter, Cynara Juliet. The marriage ended in divorce in 1970. On 21 May 1974 Hartford married a hairdresser, Elaine Kay, who was forty years younger than he. Although the marriage officially ended in divorce seven years later, the couple continued to live together in a New York apartment for several years. According to some reports, Hartford may have become a heavy drug user during this period.

After being evicted from his longtime New York City apartment in the mid-1980s, Hartford moved to a townhouse in the city's Murray Hill neighborhood. He lost this property when he filed for bankruptcy in 1992. In 2004 Hartford's daughter, Juliet, took him to the Bahamas, where he spent the remainder of his life, dying at the age of ninety-seven in his Lyford Cay home. No cause of death was indicated.

Hartford's costly attempts to establish himself as an arbiter of contemporary culture, through a museum, theater, and magazine, ended in failure. This self-styled patron of the arts was not noted for his discerning taste, though he did travel in circles where wealth played a part in culture. The excesses of Hartford's personal life, most of which were covered widely by the press, left the public with an impression of a spendthrift playboy.

★

For a biography of Hartford, see Lisa R. Gubernick, *Squandered Fortune: The Life and Times of Huntington Hartford* (1991). Obituaries are in the *New York Times* and *Washington Post* (both 20 May 2008).

Don Amerman

HARTIGAN, Grace (*b*. 28 March 1922 in Newark, New Jersey; *d*. 15 November 2008 in Baltimore, Maryland), important female abstract expressionist painter and intimate of the artists Jackson Pollock, Willem de Kooning, and others of the New York School.

Hartigan was one of four children born to Mathew A. Hartigan, a banker, and Grace (Orvis) Hartigan, a conservative woman who refused even to allow her daughter to listen to opera on the radio. Her grandmother—along with a schoolteacher aunt, one of the two most significant influences of her early life—taught her folk stories and Irish songs. While confined to bed for more than a year because of pneumonia, the seven-year-old Hartigan taught herself how to read and draw. For a time Hartigan dreamed of becoming an actress, and she was entranced by the caravans of gypsies who would made camp in the countryside near Melbourne, New Jersey. In 1940 she graduated from Millburn High School in Millburn, New Jersey.

When she was eighteen she married Bob Jachens and relocated with him to Chicago, where she worked at mechanical drafting. They had one son and divorced in 1947. After the couple returned to New Jersey, Hartigan studied at the Newark College of Engineering before she and Jachens moved to New York's Lower East Side in 1945. There she met the painter Milton Avery and through him the abstract expressionists Mark Rothko and Adolph Gottlieb. Through a brief relationship with the painter Henry Jackson, she came to know Pollock and through him de Kooning. In 1948 she had her first show with some of the abstract expressionists at New York's KOOR Gallery. A year later she painted in the Mexican Art Colony at San Miguel Allende, where Mexican folk art and the surrealist work of Arshile Gorky and Joan Miró were among her inspirations. Back in New York, she showed in the "New Talent" Show curated by the influential art critic Clement Greenberg and the art historian Meyer Schapiro. From 1950 to 1960, the height of her prominence, her paintings sold so readily that, she said, she was not able to keep even one in her own possession.

In 1959 she married the gallery owner Robert Keene. They divorced in 1960, and later that year she married the epidemiologist Winston Price. In 1960 she invented the new medium of watercolor collage, which involved using washes to create a form and then tearing the form into pieces and reassembling them. In 1965 she served as the first director of the Maryland Institute College of Art.

In the 1950s Hartigan favored the vigorous swatches of paint used by the gestural painters de Kooning and Pollock. In her piece "Giftwares" (1955) she showed amid the brightly colored swatches of paint such offerings as lamps, saucers, glasses, and various knickknacks. In 1952 she focused on the works of the old masters, reinterpreting paintings and prints of Albrecht Dürer, Peter Paul Rubens, and Giovanni Battista Tiepolo, among others. That same year Alfred J. Barr, Jr., purchased for the Museum of Modern Art her *Persian Jacket*, in which she fused the traditional with the modern. In 1952 and 1953 she integrated text from the poems of Frank O'Hara, a close associate of several of the abstract expressionists, into her paintings.

After the heyday of abstract expressionism, Hartigan continued to evolve in unexpected ways. She felt no affinity with pop art, which she decried for its lack of "content and emotion." In the 1970s her art reflected her interest in the women's rights movement. Through her images, she explored Baltimore's urban communities, such as Fells Point with its ethnic neighborhoods. She also incorporated elements of the ancient and modern work that she encountered in museums, such as classical Greek pottery and Paleolithic cave paintings. In the 1980s she did a series of monumental "Paper Dolls," based on Tom Tierney's book *Glamorous Movie Stars of the Thirties* (1978), in which she partially submerged the figures by her powerful brushstrokes. In the late 1980s she did a series on "American Places," documenting the "glitter and trash" of West Coast Americana.

In 1982 Hartigan acknowledged her alcoholism, and a year later she stopped drinking. She died of liver failure at Loren Mays Chapel Nursing Home.

Hartigan never succumbed to the detached, hard-edge, cool approaches so favored by the pop artists, post-painterly abstractionists, and photo-realists in vogue in the 1960s, 1970s, and 1980s. Rather, whatever her subject matter, she kept to the fluid, painterly ways she had adopted when she had been part of the abstract expressionist circle. Hartigan's work is in many museums in the United States, including the Hirshhorn Museum and Sculpture Garden, the Museum of Fine Arts in Boston, the Brooklyn Museum of Art, the National Museum of Women in the Arts, and the Walker Art Center.

★

Documenting some of the fascinating aspects of Hartigan's early life is Julie Haifley, "Grace Hartigan Interview, 1979 10 May," conducted for Archives of American Art. Also useful in following the artist's stylistic progression is Robert Saltonstall Mattson, *Grace Hartigan: A Painter's World* (1990). An exhibition catalog is Sharon L. Hirsh, "Grace Hartigan, Painting Art History, Carlisle, PA" (2003). Obituaries are in the *Baltimore Sun* (16 Nov. 2008) and *New York Times* (18 Nov. 2008).

Abraham A. Davidson

HASKINS, Donald Lee ("Don") (*b.* 14 March 1930 in Enid, Oklahoma; *d.* 7 September 2008 in El Paso, Texas), coached Texas Western College to the 1966 National Collegiate Athletic Association (NCAA) basketball title and helped integrate college basketball by becoming the first coach to use an all-black starting lineup in an NCAA championship game.

Haskins was the son of Paul Haskins, a truck driver and semipro baseball player, and Opal (Richey) Haskins, a homemaker. He honed his basketball shooting skills by playing with Herman Carr, a black basketball player, in an Enid park. Haskins, who stood six feet, one inch tall, graduated in 1948 from Enid High School, where he gained All-State honors as a baseball pitcher and basketball guard his senior year.

Haskins entered Oklahoma A&M (now Oklahoma State) University in 1948 and played guard under the legendary basketball coach Hank Iba. He disliked Iba's demanding workouts, tight control, and defensive style, but eventually respected his toughness and insistence on team play. Oklahoma A&M won two Missouri Valley Conference (MVC) titles, finished second nationally in 1948–1949, and placed fourth in 1950–1951. Haskins made second team All-MVC as a senior for the 23–7 Aggies in 1952–1953.

Haskins married Mary Louise Gorman on 14 March 1951. They had four sons. Haskins left Oklahoma A&M in 1953 and played for the New Mexico team Artesia REA Travelers of the National Industrial Basketball League from 1953 to 1955. He completed his undergraduate degree at West Texas State College in 1958.

In the mid-1950s Haskins began coaching high school sports in Texas. He became basketball coach in 1955 at Benjamin High School, boasting a 21–10 win-loss record. Besides driving a school bus, he coached the six-man football and girls' basketball teams. Haskins compiled a 114–24 mark the next four years at Hedley High School, winning three district titles, a regional crown, and the school's first state tournament. In 1960–1961 his Dumas High School squad finished 25–7 and won the district and regional championships.

From 1961 to 1998 Haskins coached basketball at Texas Western College (renamed the University of Texas at El Paso in 1967). He posted winning records his first fifteen seasons. Texas Western finished 18–6, 19–7, and 25–3 his first three campaigns, setting school victory records each season. Haskins, nicknamed "The Bear" for his burly physique and gruff demeanor, exhibited Iba's discipline and intensity. The driven, highly competitive, demanding coach stressed hard work and defense, maximized his personnel, capitalized on his team's strengths, and taught masterfully. His tenacious, relentless teams consistently ranked among national leaders in fewest points allowed.

Haskins especially recruited black players from inner cities. Nolan Richardson already played for the Miners when Haskins arrived. Haskins added center Jim Barnes and guard Nate Archibald in the 1960s and guard Tim Hardaway and forward Antonio Davis in the 1980s.

Texas Western finished 23–1 in 1965–1966 and entered the NCAA tournament ranked third nationally. The Miners featured an all-black starting lineup—center David Lattin, forwards Nevil Shed and Harry Flournoy, and guards Bobby Joe Hill and Orsten Artis, with black players Willie Cager and Willie Worsley as key substitutes. Texas Western won its first three tournament games and defeated the University of Utah 85–78 in the semifinals. Adolph Rupp's top-ranked 27–1, all-white University of Kentucky squad, however, was favored in the title game. The Miners, led by Hill, won the NCAA championship, upsetting Kentucky 72–65, who shot under 40 percent for the first time all season.

The game marked the first national crown for any Miners aggregate. No team with an all-black starting lineup previously had taken the national basketball crown. Haskins remarked, "I played my five best players, who happened to be blacks." The victory made Haskins an instant hero in El Paso, but sparked racial bitterness. Haskins received several death threats and much hate mail. "That next year was about the saddest and toughest of my life," he recalled. *Sports Illustrated* and the author James Michener criticized Haskins and his program. That season was chronicled in Haskins's autobiography written with Daniel Wetzel *Glory Road* and in a 2006 film of the same title.

The 1966 national title game, however, triggered the desegregation of major southern college basketball teams and accelerated the integration in college basketball elsewhere. Haskins declined numerous job offers from more prestigious, visible, and well-endowed schools because he liked El Paso too much.

The University of Texas at El Paso (UTEP) joined the Western Athletic Conference (WAC) in 1970. Haskins served as assistant coach under Iba for the 1972 U.S. Olympic basketball team. UTEP dominated the WAC from 1983 to 1992, averaging twenty-four wins, capturing five consecutive WAC championships, and making eight NCAA tournament appearances, including seven straight in nine years. His 1988–1989 team, led by Hardaway and Davis, finished 26–7, while his 1992 aggregate upset top-seeded University of Kansas 66–60 in the Midwest regional semifinals of the NCAA tournament.

Haskins found recruiting more difficult after 1992 because the NCAA reduced the number of his UTEP basketball scholarships for several minor rules violations. He lost thirteen of his fifteen scholarship players within two years. Top-notch players considered Haskins too discipline-oriented and defense-minded and disliked UTEP's isolated location. Haskins went without a twenty-win season his last four seasons through 1999 and did not have an NCAA tournament appearance his final seven years. He suffered a heart attack in January 1996 and missed the remainder of that season. In September 1997 UTEP's facility was renamed Don Haskins Center. He died of congestive heart failure and is buried at Concordia Cemetery in El Paso, Texas.

During thirty-eight years at UTEP, Haskins recorded 719 wins, 353 losses, 7 WAC championships, 16 20-victory seasons, and just 5 losing campaigns. Only eighteen NCAA Division I coaches compiled more career victories. His teams fared 14–13 in fourteen NCAA tournaments and appeared in seven National Invitation Tournament tournaments. Haskins was inducted into the Texas Sports Hall of Fame in 1987 and the Naismith Memorial Basketball Hall of Fame in 1997. He mentored Richardson, Tim Floyd, and other coaches and ranked among the game's best defensive mentors. The 1966 championship game remained his biggest legacy, helping integrate college basketball.

★

His autobiography, *Haskins: The Bear Facts* (1987), as told to Ray Sanchez, relates his life story. Dan Wetzel, "Not Your

Ordinary Bear," *Basketball Times* (1 Apr. 1998), reviews his career. Ray Sanchez, *Basketball's Biggest Upset* (1991), and Frank Fitzpatrick, *And the Walls Came Tumbling Down* (1999), recount his 1966 NCAA championship season. See also *USA Today* (24 Mar. 1992; 28 Feb. 1995; 12 Jan. 2006). An obituary is in the *New York Times* (8 Sept. 2008).

David L. Porter

HAYDEN, Melissa ("Milly") (*b.* 25 April 1923 in Toronto, Ontario, Canada; *d.* 9 August 2006 in Winston-Salem, North Carolina), ballet dancer and teacher who enjoyed an unequaled twenty-two-year career with the New York City Ballet.

Hayden was born Mildred Herman to Jacob Herman, a businessman, and Kate Herman; Hayden's parents were Russian immigrants, and Hayden and her two sisters grew up in a middle-class home. Her interest in dance emerged at age twelve, when she started taking ballet classes with Boris Volkoff in Toronto. After graduation from high school, she went to New York City, where she studied with Anatole Vilzak and Ludmila Schollar and also with George Balanchine at the School of American Ballet. Hayden began a five-month stint in the corps de ballet

Melissa Hayden, 1961. AP IMAGES

at Radio City Music Hall in order to support herself and to pay for her classes.

In 1945 Hayden was accepted into the corps of Ballet Theatre (later the American Ballet Theatre), where Antony Tudor advised her to change her name to Melissa Hayden. She was quickly given solo roles and danced with the company for several seasons before finances caused the organization to suspend operations temporarily. Hayden was then invited to go on a tour of South America with a group formed by Alicia Alonso. While she was in South America, she received a telegram from Balanchine inviting her to join the New York City Ballet, and she became a charter member in 1949. She went back to Ballet Theatre from 1953 to 1955 but then returned to New York City Ballet, where she was made a principal dancer and where she remained until her retirement in 1973.

Hayden's first performing experience with Balanchine occurred when he set *Theme and Variations* for Ballet Theatre, but Hayden realized early in their relationship that she was not his favorite kind of dancer, possibly because Balanchine liked to mold a dancer and she was already trained. In Hayden's first years in the company, William Dollar, Frederick Ashton, Jerome Robbins, and John Cranko created ballets for her, but Balanchine did not. She inevitably danced roles that had belonged to someone else, often Maria Tallchief. It was for this reason that, frustrated, Hayden had left Balanchine to return to Ballet Theatre in 1953.

Hayden realized that she missed the excitement and the newness that Balanchine projected, so she returned to him in 1955, when he choreographed a role for her in *Pas de Trois*; in subsequent years he choreographed roles for Hayden in *Agon, Stars and Stripes, Liebeslieder Waltzer,* and *A Midsummer Night's Dream.* Always a dramatic, womanly figure in a company that emphasized youth, Hayden once said, "You make yourself a Balanchine dancer by dancing his ballets."

One of Hayden's signature roles was that of Clorinda, a Saracen girl who disguises herself as a warrior on horseback and is killed by her lover in Dollar's ballet *The Duel.* In Robbins's *The Cage* she was the demonic, stamping initiate who kills her man, but in his *Afternoon of a Faun* she was an almost poetic young dancer. She was sexy in Ashton's *Illuminations* and sassy in Balanchine's *Stars and Stripes.*

Hayden appeared as a guest artist with the National Ballet of Canada, the Royal Ballet of London, the Chicago Opera Ballet, the Boston Ballet, the Pennsylvania Ballet, and the San Francisco Ballet. Volkoff must have recognized the abilities of his student—her physical endurance, her "steely spine," and her innate dramatic sense—and he obviously trained her well. She was a dependable dancer, with an amazing sense of balance, and could accomplish anything any choreographer threw at her. Watching Hayden, an audience always felt a sense of security, sure that she knew what had to be done and that she would do it. With each passing year she was able to grow even more, developing the spontaneity that comes only with experience yet retaining her strength in every role until her last performance.

Hayden was in *Limelight* (1952), a Charlie Chaplin film, and was a major dancer on television with both André Eglevsky and Jacques d'Amboise as partners, thereby introducing ballet to a wide audience. She was also among the first to give lectures and demonstrations on ballet to schoolchildren.

For the 16 May 1973 gala in honor of Hayden's retirement, Balanchine choreographed *Cortège Hongrois*, in which Hayden's partner was d'Amboise. The two of them had danced together for over twenty years, during which d'Amboise's youthful buoyancy and Hayden's mixture of passion and glamour made them a beloved pair. On the same evening Hayden received New York City's Handel Medallion, the city's highest cultural award.

After her retirement Hayden took a position as artist in residence at Skidmore College in Saratoga Springs, New York, where she worked to build a strong dance division and to separate it from physical education. She also opened her own school. Unable to accomplish her goals, she left in 1976 to become artistic director of the Pacific Northwest Ballet Company in Seattle. The last twenty-three years of her life were spent teaching at the North Carolina School of the Arts in Winston-Salem. Hayden married Donald Hugh Coleman in 1954 and had two children, a son and a daughter. She died of pancreatic cancer at the age of eighty-three.

Hayden's attributes rendered her an American prima ballerina, even in a company that did not recognize such a title. Perhaps referring to what one critic labeled as her "glorious classical carriage and elegant extensions," her colleagues at Skidmore called Hayden "the world's own Sugar Plum Fairy."

★

The Jerome Robbins Dance Collection of the New York Public Library for the Performing Arts contains a great deal of material on Hayden, including clippings, programs, photographs, and interview transcripts. Hayden wrote three books: *Melissa Hayden: Off Stage and On* (1963), *Ballet Exercises for Figure, Grace, and Beauty* (1969), and *Dancer to Dancer: Advice for Today's Dancer* (1981). For additional information, see John Gruen, *The Private World of Ballet* (1975), and Robert Tracy, *Balanchine's Ballerinas: Conversations with the Muses* (1983). See also Robert Greskovic, "Some Artists of the New York City Ballet," *Ballet Review* 4, no. 4 (1973). For a tribute to Hayden, see Lincoln Kirstein, "Melissa Hayden: A Tribute," *Dance Magazine* (Aug. 1973). An obituary is in the *New York Times* (10 Aug. 2006).

Dawn Lille

HAYES, Isaac Lee, Jr. (*b.* 20 August 1942 in Covington, Tennessee; *d.* 10 August 2008 in Memphis, Tennessee), Academy Award–winning composer, singer, and actor who was an important creative force in the southern soul music of the mid-1960s and 1970s.

Hayes was born on a sharecropper's farm, the second child of Isaac Hayes, Sr., and Eula (Wade) Hayes. His mother died when he was eighteen months old, and his father left Hayes and his sister to be raised by their maternal grandparents. When Hayes was seven, the family moved north to Memphis in the hopes of finding greater opportunity, and his grandfather found work at a tomato-canning factory. Following a period of failing health, Hayes's grandfather died. Hayes was only eleven years old, but to help the family survive, he worked a number of jobs: picking cotton, pumping gas, running errands, and occasionally shining shoes on Beale Street.

As a student at Manassas High School, Hayes cultivated an interest in music that had begun when he was five. His grandparents had encouraged him to sing in church, and he later visited a juke joint operated by an aunt. Hayes taught himself rudimentary piano and learned

Isaac Hayes. MICHAEL OCHS ARCHIVES/GETTY IMAGES

to play saxophone in the school band. He secretly dropped out of high school in order to concentrate on earning money. A delegation of his teachers broke the news to his grandmother and encouraged Hayes not to give up on his education, even collecting some hand-me-down clothes to help him persevere in school. While he was still in his teens, however, he found himself married with a child, working as a meatpacker during the day, dropping in and out of classes, and playing as many music gigs as he could. Hayes earned his diploma with the class of 1962, and his dedication to literacy education later in life reflected his gratitude to his teachers at Manassas.

Although he had won several scholarships to study vocal music in college, Hayes continued to pursue his career in Memphis. Singing and playing both saxophone and piano, he worked with a variety of local musical groups. One job took him to the Plantation Inn across the river in west Arkansas, playing piano in a band led by Floyd Newman. As the staff baritone saxophonist at the Stax studio, Newman brought Hayes into what was already becoming known as the home of the Memphis soul sound. When the house band's keyboardist Booker T. Jones was scheduled to resume his music studies at Indiana University, Jim Stewart, co-owner of Stax, invited Hayes to become a session player. His first paid sessions were with Otis Redding in early 1964, and he began to spend most of his time at the studio. Meanwhile his first marriage ended, having given him two daughters.

At Stax, working with the lyricist David Porter, Hayes began a songwriting career that by 1966–1967 would provide the legendary label and its notable stars memorable hits, including "Hold On, I'm Coming" and "Soul Man" for Sam and Dave and "B-A-B-Y" and "Let Me Be Good to You" for Carla Thomas. In all, the Hayes-Porter team penned some 200 songs in addition to their work as arrangers and producers in the studio. Hayes's work as player and creative force put him at the epicenter of the southern soul sound during its most productive era. Following a raucous Stax party, Hayes, with the bassist Donald "Duck" Dunn and the drummer Al Jackson, remained in the studio through the rest of the night and recorded tracks for what would be his first album release, *Presenting Isaac Hayes* (1967). In 1966 Hayes married Emily Ruth Watson, and they would have three children before their divorce in 1971.

The year 1968 was fateful. Not only had Stax lost its most successful performer when Redding and most of his band died in a plane crash at the end of 1967, but the management of the label was in the throes of significant change pending a sale to Gulf and Western. The assassination of Martin Luther King, Jr., had a profound effect on local race relations and members of the Stax staff, including Hayes, who remembered, "It affected me for a whole year. I could not create properly. I was so bitter and so angry." Nevertheless, without a contract in hand, and with the

encouragement of a local disc jockey, Hayes set out to record some of the vocals he had been performing in local Memphis venues. He wanted to become successful and powerful enough that his voice would make a difference. The result was *Hot Buttered Soul* (1969), released on a newly created subsidiary label, Enterprise. The collection pointed toward a new direction in black music: silky, sensual vocals accompanied by lengthy "raps" and lush string arrangements. The album went triple platinum and remained on the pop charts for eighty-one weeks. For the next five years, Hayes continued to record for Enterprise, delivering seven number-one rhythm-and-blues (R & B) albums.

The film *Shaft*, for which Hayes had scored the soundtrack, premiered in 1971. The release of the theme song single and a double album soundtrack proved to be a defining moment in Hayes's career. If the period marked a new era of black power, Hayes was an icon with his shaved head and his muscular frame draped in gold chains (an antithesis of the symbols of slavery). The album hit number one on both the pop and R & B charts, making it the number three R & B album of the 1970s, remaining on the charts for sixteen months. Hayes's performance at the subsequent Academy Awards and the honor of becoming the first African-American composer to win the Oscar for best song from a motion picture marked the height of his career. The album won two Grammys and earned Hayes awards in the United States and abroad. His next effort, the Grammy-winning *Black Moses* (1971), featured creative packaging with bold photographics on a four-part foldout (a first for any album by a black artist), and launched an extended tour in the United States and Europe.

On 18 April 1973 Hayes married for the third time, to Mignon Harley; the couple had two children prior to their divorce in 1986. Hayes continued to record for Stax/Enterprise until the mid-1970s. In 1975 he launched his own record label, Hot Buttered Soul, and released several albums reflecting his contribution to the disco style of the era. However, several business setbacks caused him to file for bankruptcy, and he saw his personal possessions, including his gold records, sold at auction to satisfy Internal Revenue Service liens.

Determined to recover from bankruptcy, Hayes signed with Polydor Records and worked at Master Sound Studios while living in Atlanta for a time. He recorded four albums, including *For the Sake of Love* (1978) and *Don't Let Go* (1979), each of which saw some chart success and spawned hit singles. In spite of some album releases in the late 1980s for Columbia, Hayes's music career languished.

In late 1991 Hayes and Barry White traveled to Africa's Ivory Coast to shoot a video to accompany White's comeback album. The following year Dionne Warwick and Hayes were invited by Ghana's cultural minister to visit the Cape Coast and Elmina slave castles. Moved by the experience, Hayes began new philanthropic work in earnest, working and touring to raise African Americans' consciousness of their connections with Africa and to raise funds for schools and economic development. He created the Isaac Hayes Foundation, with the mission of promoting literacy, music and nutrition education, and self-esteem. He also became spokesperson for Applied Scholastics' World Literacy Crusade. In 1998 he officiated at the groundbreaking of the Neko Tech school in Ada, Ghana.

The mid-1990s signaled a return to form for Hayes. Two new albums for Virgin Records posted respectable sales and good reviews. In addition Hayes found unlikely stardom—and new generations of fans—as one of the founding actors in the animated series *South Park*. Providing the voice of "Chef" McElroy from 1997 to 2006, he added suggestive soul songs to the irreverent comedy of the series. His film career extended into the next decade, including a role in *Hustle and Flow* (2005).

In 1993 Hayes began to develop an interest in Scientology, joining in 2005. While his departure from *South Park* has been linked to an episode that made fun of his beliefs, he and his fellow Scientologist Lisa Marie Presley established a mission in Memphis that supports learning initiatives and promotes benefit concerts for the children of their hometown. Hayes was involved in Scientology-related events for the rest of his life.

Hayes was elected to the Rock and Roll Hall of Fame on the first ballot in 2002. In 2005 he married for the fourth time, and he and Adjowa had one son. The next year he suffered a stroke, but he soon seemed to have recovered fully. He continued to be involved in numerous creative and philanthropic activities, including a role in *Soul Men* (2008), a film with Samuel L. Jackson and Bernie Mac, and his first new studio album since 1995. Hayes was found unresponsive at his home on the floor next to his treadmill. Physicians declared him dead from a stroke. He is buried in Memorial Park Cemetery in Memphis.

The musical achievement of Hayes is considerable. Not only did he help establish the sound of southern soul music in the 1960s, but in the 1970s he redefined the possibilities of black music in the form of sweet soul, disco, and rap while becoming the first person of color to win an Academy Award in a nonacting category. His career extended to film and television, and he found success across the media during five decades. The father of twelve children, Hayes was a philanthropist dedicated to the welfare and education of children in the United States and in Africa. His emergence as a living icon embodying the essence of soul fueled African-American self-esteem in the late twentieth century.

★

For insightful commentary on Hayes's life and work, see Peter Guralnick, *Sweet Soul Music: Rhythm and Blues and the Southern Dream of Freedom* (1986). Gerri Hirshey, *Nowhere to Run: The Story of Soul Music* (1984), offers an introspective interview with Hayes after his bankruptcy. Rob Bowman, *Soulsville, U.S.A.: The Story of Stax Records* (1997), provides the most extensive coverage of Hayes's work at Stax. Obituaries are in the *Washington Post*, *Los Angeles Times*, and *New York Times* (all 11 Aug. 2008), as well as *Billboard* (23 Aug. 2008).

James F. Smith

HEINZ, W(ilfred) C(harles) (*b.* 11 January 1915 in Mount Vernon, New York; *d.* 27 February 2008 in Bennington, Vermont), sports reporter, author of books about sports, and novelist.

The only child of Frederick Louis Sylvester Heinz, a salesman, and Elizabeth (Thielke) Heinz, a homemaker, Heinz grew up in the New York City suburb of Mount Vernon. The genesis of his abiding love of athletics

W. C. Heinz, 2002. AP IMAGES

remains something of a mystery. Many years later, in an interview for *Sports Illustrated*, Heinz was unable to pinpoint its beginning, though he suggested that it might have originated with his father's vivid account of the boxer Jack Dempsey's legendary 1923 fight with Luis Firpo, his own love of baseball cards, and even a few impromptu experiences with fisticuffs in the schoolyard.

As passionate as Heinz was about sports, he was an equally eager reader. As a young man he concluded that he might combine these two enthusiasms by writing about athletics, a decision that may have been influenced by his own limited physical prowess.

After graduating from Mount Vernon High School, Heinz enrolled at Vermont's Middlebury College, where his extracurricular activities included a stint as sports editor for the school newspaper. During his freshman year, he met and fell in love with Elizabeth "Betty" Bailey. The couple married in January 1941.

Heinz graduated from Middlebury in 1937 with a BA in political science. It was the middle of the Great Depression, and there were few jobs to be had. With help from a family friend, Heinz finally landed a job as a messenger for the *New York Sun*.

Heinz practiced writing in his spare time, and his persistence was eventually rewarded when the *Sun*'s editor offered him a job as a cub reporter. During this early stage of his career, Heinz learned the essentials of reporting through assignments that ranged from covering local politics to reporting on the city's crime. It was as a war correspondent, however, that Heinz first distinguished himself. In 1943 he became the newspaper's junior war correspondent, and a year later was assigned to England to cover the Allies' preparations for their invasion of Nazi-occupied France.

Upon his return to New York in 1945, Heinz asked to be assigned to the *Sun*'s sports desk, an assignment the newspaper at first resisted but eventually granted. Drawing on the best of what other sportswriters had to offer, he gradually developed a writing style that was distinctly his own and is credited with pioneering what came to be known in the 1970s as "new journalism." This form of journalism, found mostly in magazine articles, blended the immediacy of conventional news reportage with literary techniques previously used almost exclusively in works of fiction.

In 1947 Heinz and Betty had their first child, Barbara. Shortly after her birth, the Heinzes left Manhattan and relocated to Old Greenwich, Connecticut. In 1951 Betty gave birth to their second daughter, Gayl.

In 1948 the *Sun* gave Heinz a sports column of his own, "The Sport Scene." He covered a wide variety of sports but concentrated on boxing and horse racing. In his spare time, Heinz wrote magazine articles and short stories on a freelance basis.

Now at the fore of mid-twentieth-century sportswriters, Heinz continued to write for the *Sun* until the newspaper went out of business in 1950. Turning down offers from a number of newspapers, he chose instead to freelance on a full-time basis, contributing articles about sports and other topics to a number of the era's most popular magazines, including *Life, Look, Collier's, Cosmopolitan*, the *Saturday Evening Post, Argosy, Esquire, True*, and *Ring*. In 1958 Heinz published his first novel, *The Professional*, an exploration of the relationship between a boxer and his trainer. The legendary writer Ernest Hemingway was so impressed with it that he sent a congratulatory telegram from Cuba.

Although he is best remembered for his sports writing, Heinz covered a wide array of other subjects, including the civil rights struggle in Selma, Alabama, and a profile of a surgeon for *Life*. His work on the latter piqued Heinz's interest in medicine, in turn leading him to write two novels with medical themes: *The Surgeon* (1963) and *Emergency* (1974). A collaboration with H. Richard Hornberger, a surgeon from Maine, produced what was undoubtedly Heinz's most famous novel, *MASH* (1968), a dark comedy about a group of frontline surgeons serving in the Korean War. This Heinz-Hornberger collaboration was published under the pseudonym Richard Hooker.

In addition to his four novels, Heinz wrote, edited, or otherwise contributed to a number of nonfiction books about sports. Among the most celebrated of these are *The Fireside Book of Boxing* (1961), an anthology of stories about prizefighting edited by Heinz; *Run to Daylight* (1963), written with the coach of professional football's Green Bay Packers, Vince Lombardi; and *What a Time It Was: The Best of W. C. Heinz on Sports* (2001).

In 1964 Barbara Heinz died of an infection at the age of sixteen. Two years later Heinz and his family moved to Dorset, Vermont, where they lived for the next several decades. In her later years, Heinz's wife suffered from Alzheimer's disease. She died in 2002. In his final years Heinz lived in an assisted-living facility in Bennington, Vermont, and it was there that he died at the age of ninety-three.

Hailed as the "heavyweight champion of the word" in a lengthy 2000 profile in *Sports Illustrated*, Heinz was the sort of writer who served as a model for others. Although his distinctive writing style has been widely imitated, it has never truly been duplicated and stands as an example of the best sports reportage and commentary ever committed to paper.

★

Some of Heinz's best writing can be found in *What a Time It Was: The Best of W. C. Heinz on Sports* (2001). Also valuable is Jeff MacGregor, "Heavyweight Champion of the Word," *Sports Illustrated* (25 Sept. 2000), which offers an excellent profile of Heinz's life and writing career. Obituaries are in the *International Herald Tribune Online* (27 Feb. 2008), *New York Times* (28 Feb. 2008), *Los Angeles Times* (1 Mar. 2008), and *Washington Post* (5 Mar. 2008).

Don Amerman

HELMS, Jesse Alexander, Jr. (*b.* 18 October 1921 in Monroe, North Carolina; *d.* 4 July 2008 in Raleigh, North Carolina), television broadcaster, conservative ideologue, U.S. senator (1973–2003), and chairman of the Foreign Relations Committee.

Helms was the son of Jesse Alexander Helms, Sr., a police officer and a firefighter, and Ethel Mae (Helms) Helms, a homemaker and a distant cousin of her husband's. Helms grew up with his older brother and younger sister in Monroe, a small town of about 4,000 inhabitants twenty-five miles east of Charlotte, North Carolina, in a devoutly Baptist family whose antecedents were eighteenth-century English and Scottisch-Irish immigrants to the Carolina backcountry. Like most southern towns of the 1920s and 1930s, Monroe was strictly segregated by race. At six feet, four inches tall, Helms's father was a dominating figure. He exercised an especially firm hand with Monroe's African-American population, and he maintained the racial hierarchy through intimidation and, if necessary, brute force.

Jesse Helms. MCT/LANDOV

Like his father, the young Helms was tall; as an adult he measured six feet, two inches. He was also extroverted and effusive, and he strongly respected order. In school he became a successful member of the Monroe High School band as a tuba player. Growing up in the Great Depression, Helms worked as a paperboy, a drugstore clerk, and a helper in the local newspaper, and he began writing sports stories while still in high school. After graduating from high school in 1938, Helms had little money for college, but he earned a small scholarship to the nearby Wingate Junior College. After one year there he earned another scholarship to the Baptist Wake Forest College.

Helms had less interest in his studies, however, than in a newspaper career. A need for money and his restless energy forced him to work at part-time jobs, including one at the *Raleigh News and Observer*. He also provided sports stories about Wake Forest for local newspapers, such as the evening *Raleigh Times* and the *Henderson Daily Dispatch*, as well as the *Charlotte News* and the *Charlotte Observer*. In the autumn of 1941, he dropped out of college and became a news reporter and an assistant city editor for the *Raleigh Times*, an evening newspaper. Helms reported enthusiastically, and vigorous, accessible prose became his trademark. The onset of World War II had turned Helms's life upside down. While working in Raleigh, Helms met and fell in love with Dorothy "Dot" Coble, a Raleigh native and a newspaper reporter. They married on 31 October 1942. They had two children and adopted a third. After the Japanese attack on Pearl Harbor on 7 December 1941, Helms was rejected for military service because of a hearing defect, so he joined the navy as a recruiter. He was stationed in North Carolina during the war and soon discovered radio journalism, a career that he would pursue after the war.

When the war ended in 1945, Helms went to work for the radio station WCBT in Roanoke Rapids, North Carolina, about fifty miles northeast of Raleigh, and three years later he joined WRAL radio in Raleigh. Helms pioneered radio news broadcasting in postwar North Carolina, and working under WRAL's owner, the conservative lawyer A. J. Fletcher, Helms became a conservative ideologue. Especially crucial was Helms's experience in the highly charged U.S. Senate campaign of 1950, which pitted the fabled southern liberal and former University of North Carolina president Frank Porter Graham against the conservative challenger in the Democratic primary, the Raleigh lawyer Willis Smith. Despite knowing and admiring Graham, Helms supported Smith's successful campaign, and he volunteered to conduct opposition research, do media work, and give political advice.

Helms became Smith's administrative assistant and right-hand man, and he served in that capacity until Smith's sudden death on 26 June 1953. Over the next twenty years, Helms continued a career as a conservative organizer who was especially adept at crafting an effective media message. From 1953 to 1960 he worked as executive director of the North Carolina Bankers Association, and he used that office as a platform for anticommunism, opposition to New Deal regulation and social programs, and, increasingly, hostility to federal intervention in civil rights. Helms also made his first foray into elective politics when he was elected to two terms on the Raleigh City Council (1957–1961). He also transformed the publication of the North Carolina Bankers Association, the *Tarheel Banker*, into a mouthpiece for his conservatism. After the *Brown v. Board of Education* decision of 1954, Helms took aim at what he believed was the increasingly "socialist" federal government. In December 1958 he wrote that he worried less about integration than about "the destruction of the fundamentals that made this government unique in all history." Federal intervention in the South, he wrote in the *Tarheel Banker*, was "exactly in tune" with Karl Marx's predictions: government-required integration amounted to socialism. "The cackles you hear," he said, have "a Russian accent."

Fletcher, who had obtained a license for a new television station in 1955, sought to make WRAL-TV a flagship for his brand of conservatism, with Helms as his main mouthpiece. Beginning in 1958, Helms hosted weekly television broadcasts on WRAL-TV that had a sharply conservative edge to them. In November 1960 he joined WRAL-TV as executive vice president. He also began broadcasting editorials, known as "Viewpoints," that were only several minutes long and that were aired twice a day, five days a week. Reaching WRAL's large viewing area, between November 1960 and February 1972, Helms would eventually broadcast 2,732 "Viewpoint" editorials. These fashioned a sharply framed conservative message of opposition to the main elements of the 1960s revolution in civil rights, the counterculture, the revolt on college and university campuses, and the secularization of life. On all of these issues, Helms pounded away, confounding liberals but energizing conservatives in the state.

Helms's television career provided a basis for a future political career. A lifelong Democrat, Helms switched to the Republican Party in 1970. He then ran for the Republican nomination for the U.S. Senate. The last Republican senator from North Carolina had been elected in 1898, yet Helms realized that the election of Richard Nixon to the presidency with considerable southern support marked a significant political realignment in North Carolina. Partly as a result of Nixon's 1972 landslide victory, in which he carried North Carolina by more than 70 percent over the Democrat George McGovern, Helms was swept into the U.S. Senate. Arriving in Washington, D.C., in January 1973, Helms soon established himself as a leading conservative in the Senate, where he took aggressive stands on such issues as busing for school desegregation, bans on school prayer, and legal abortion. During the 1980s and

1990s, Helms focused on the emerging issue of homosexuality. Along with the Religious Right, Helms strongly condemned homosexuality as sinful, and he was the Senate's leading opponent of gay rights. In the Senate, Helms rarely won the votes that he forced; instead, through skillful parliamentary maneuvering, he required his fellow senators to go on record on various issues. In the Senate, Helms quickly attracted the attention of "movement conservatives" around the country, and he enjoyed a large following from a gathering national conservative constituency.

Helms was especially effective at constructing this constituency through the use of political advertising and fundraising. In 1973 his political advisers organized the North Carolina Congressional Club to retire his campaign debt, and "the Club" became his main political organization during the next two decades. Congressional Club managers began employing direct-mail fund-raising—one of the first political organizations to make full use of this new technology, which identified and regularly communicated with supporters for funds. By the late 1970s the Club had succeeded in raising tens of millions of dollars that were used to support Helms and other conservative candidates around the country.

Helms eventually served five terms in the Senate, but his elections were always rancorous affairs, won only through the use of extravagant amounts of money fueling sharply focused and negative television advertising—tactics that eventually became standard in American politics. In 1984 Helms defeated a popular challenger, Governor James Hunt, by inundating the airwaves for months with attacks that sought to cast Hunt as a political opportunist and a "flip-flopper." Helms defeated Hunt through heavy advertising, while he also benefited from Ronald Reagan's landslide win in the presidential election of 1984. Similarly, in 1990 Helms defeated another potent challenger, the African-American Harvey Gantt, through a television campaign that portrayed Gantt as a liberal and, late in the campaign, raised ugly racial themes that appeared to sway the electorate in Helms's favor.

Foreign policy had long interested Helms. In the 1970s and the 1980s, he was a staunch opponent of the Soviet Union, and he favored support for authoritarian regimes in Latin America and Africa (which were also white minority regimes) in order to forestall the spread of Soviet influence. In the 1970s and the 1980s, Helms became the strongest supporter in the Senate of anticommunist dictatorships in Chile and Argentina. As the white minority regimes in Rhodesia and South Africa became increasingly besieged by black liberation movements and international disapproval, Helms remained a stolid supporter. In the 1970s he favored lifting economic sanctions imposed on the breakaway government of the white Rhodesian prime minister Ian Smith. Similarly, in the 1980s he opposed efforts, eventually successful, to impose strong sanctions on the white minority

South African government. In Central America, Helms also supported right-wing forces in El Salvador, despite their record of human rights abuses. With the breakup of the Soviet Union, Helms had positioned himself as ranking minority member of the Foreign Relations Committee, a post he assumed in 1987. When the Republicans were swept into control of Congress in 1994, Helms became chairman of this committee, arguably the most important committee in the U.S. Senate.

Helms's last decade in the Senate was concerned primarily with foreign policy. Although still a much-admired leader of the American Right, he no longer engaged in the kind of legislative tactics that characterized the first part of his political career. President Bill Clinton was in the White House during most of Helms's time as foreign relations chair, and Helms opposed most of Clinton's foreign policy efforts. A pronounced opponent of Fidel Castro's Cuban Communism, Helms sponsored passage of the Helms-Burton Act (1996), which imposed strong sanctions on the island republic. Helms remained a steadfast opponent of the United Nations (UN)—and of multilateralism generally—and he favored making the United States the only superpower in the world. He led efforts to limit American contributions to the UN, though he particpated in an agreement—embodied in the Helms-Biden Act of 1999—that resulted in reforms at the UN and restored American funding. A steadfast opponent of détente and negotiations with the Soviets, he continued to oppose arms control. Helms thus tried to block passage of the 1992 Chemical Weapons Convention (it was ratified nonetheless) and helped to defeat the Comprehensive Test Ban Treaty in 1999.

During his last years in the Senate, Helms particpated in a highly publicized alliance with the rock star Bono in support of debt relief and funding to fight AIDS in Africa. Although Helms had long opposed any efforts to support black Africa, Bono's appeal to help the children on a biblical basis reached Helms. Still Helms maintained a strongly antihomosexual view of AIDS in the United States, and he continued to reaffirm his belief that the spread of the epidemic was largely the responsibility of gays in America. Helms retired from the Senate after the conclusion of his fifth term in 2002. Helms is buried in Oakwood Cemetery in Raleigh.

In any assessment Helms must be regarded as a major figure in the rightward political turn of the United States occurring during the last third of the twentieth century. He helped to define and to communicate issues that brought together elements of a conservative coalition that included white southern opponents of the civil rights movement, libertarians, opponents of an expanded federal government, anticommunists, and the Religious Right. Helms contributed to building the basis for President Reagan's victory in the 1980 presidential election and to expanding the political power of conservatism during the next generation. He also helped to lead a conservative foreign policy that was rigidly anticommunist and favored the unbridled exercise of American power abroad.

A large collection of Helms's papers is housed at the Jesse Helms Center in Wingate, North Carolina. For biographies of Helms, see Ernest Furgurson, *Hard Right: The Rise of Jesse Helms* (1986), and William A. Link, *Righteous Warrior: Jesse Helms and the Rise of Modern Conservatism* (2008). See also Bryan Hardin Thrift, "Jesse Helms's Politics of Pious Incitement: Race, Conservatism, and Southern Realignment in the 1950s," *Journal of Southern History* (1 Nov. 2008). An obituary is in the *New York Times* (5 July 2008).

William A. Link

HELMSLEY, Leona (*b.* 4 February 1920 in Marbletown, Ulster County, New York; *d.* 20 August 2007 in Greenwich, Connecticut), real estate billionaire known as the "Queen of Mean" for her ill treatment of employees, ludicrous pettiness, mindless cruelty, and overarching greed, which ultimately led to her downfall and time in federal prison.

Helmsley was very evasive about her life. She changed her name several times and told varying facts about her age, birthplace, and career. Official records show that she was born Leona Mindy Rosenthal in a rural hamlet north of New York City. Her parents were Polish-Jewish immigrants. Her father, Morris Rosenthal, was a hatter, and her mother, Ida (Popkin) Rosenthal, was a homemaker whom Helmsley described as a tyrant. Helmsley had two older sisters and a younger brother. Except for Helmsley, the family was sickly: Her father died at age fifty-two of heart disease.

Helmsley attended elementary school and junior high school in Bensonhurst, New York. She attended Abraham Lincoln High School in New Jersey for a semester or so. Although Helmsley claimed that she attended Hunter College in Manhattan, New York City, for two years, there is no record of her being there. She took to calling herself Leona Mindy Roberts and later claimed to be a model.

In 1938 Helmsley married a lawyer, Leo Panzirer, ten years her senior. In 1940 their son was born. The couple divorced in 1952. In 1953 Helmsley married, later divorced, remarried, and in 1960 again divorced Joseph Lubin, a garment industry executive. It is not clear where her son was during these years. Helmsley later said that she and her son did not speak for several years. Helmsley worked for Lubin in his sewing factory.

Leona Helmsley, 1990. DMI/TIME LIFE PICTURES/GETTY IMAGES

In 1962 Helmsley joined Pease & Elliman, a prestigious real estate firm, where, she said, she took five years off her age and faked her typing test in order to land a secretarial job. In 1964 she was promoted to real estate broker. Helmsley excelled as a broker. Under the name Leona Roberts, she sold luxury cooperative apartments on the Upper East Side of Manhattan. Sometimes using pressure tactics, she had become a millionaire by 1969.

Helmsley then set her sights on Harry Helmsley. He was married and was ten years her senior, but he was also wealthy and was regarded as the real estate king of New York. In his heyday he would control and manage properties such as the Empire State Building, the Flatiron Building, and six Manhattan hotels, including the Helmsley Palace.

Leona would tell the *New York Times* that she met Harry Helmsley when he heard of her real estate acumen. Other times she would offer more romantic versions of their meeting. Harry Helmsley never said how he met his wife. He clearly respected her business ability; he hired her at an annual salary of $500,000.

It was clear to onlookers that the Helmsleys were madly and passionately in love. In 1972, after divorcing his wife of thirty-four years, Harry Helmsley married Leona Mindy Roberts. After she married, Helmsley started assuming power in the Helmsley organization. Soon the couple were part of the "beautiful people" known for dancing the night away and for extravagant, "I'm just wild about Harry" birthday parties that Leona threw every year for Harry.

Helmsley became the public face of the Helmsley Palace Hotel. For over ten years an advertising campaign pictured her in a diamond tiara and regal dress, proclaiming her the "queen" and her hotel "the only palace in the world where the Queen stands guard." Later the campaign featured other Helmsley hotels, and Helmsley became the empress.

Helmsley showed a much darker side to those who had to deal with her professionally. She earned a reputation for her hair-trigger temper, petty cruelty, and very foul mouth. She screamed at, demeaned, and fired people on the slightest whim. To avoid her, employees arranged a warning system when she left home to go to one of the hotels.

On 31 March 1982 Helmsley's son died of a heart attack. Helmsley promptly sued her son's estate for money and property, evicting her son's widow and the couple's four children. Helmsley's continued lawsuits eventually wiped out her daughter-in-law's finances.

In 1982 the Helmsleys' downfall began. Always reluctant to pay their bills, the Helmsleys delayed paying a group of contractors working on an $8 million remodel of the Helmsleys' personal mansion in Connecticut. Finally deciding that they had no other choice, the contractors started legal proceedings. Discovering that their work was being billed as business expenses, they bundled up their invoices and sent them to the *New York Post*. The *Post* story led to a federal criminal investigation, aided by numerous witnesses describing the Helmsleys' shady dealings. In 1988 the Helmsleys were indicted on extortion and several tax-related charges.

Over the years Harry Helmsley had begun to appear mentally enfeebled and suffered a stroke on top of a preexisting heart condition. He was ruled mentally and physically unfit to stand trial. Leona Helmsley, branded the "Queen of Mean" and a public symbol of arrogance and greed, faced the 1989 trial alone. On 30 August she was found guilty of conspiracy, tax evasion, and mail fraud, and was sentenced to eighteen months in federal prison.

Harry Helmsley, his memory virtually gone after a series of strokes, spent most of his final years in Arizona. He died in 1997, leaving his wife his entire fortune, estimated to be in excess of $5 billion. She spent her final years in virtual isolation with her Maltese dog, Trouble. At age eighty-seven, Helmsley died of congestive heart failure at her summer home in Greenwich. She is buried next to her husband at Sleepy Hollow Cemetery in Sleepy Hollow, Westchester County, New York.

Helmsley left most of her money to her charitable trust, $15 million to her brother, $12 million to her dog, Trouble, and $10 million each to two of her grandchildren; she disinherited the other two grandchildren. In 2008 a judge ruled that Helmsley was mentally unfit when she executed her will. Trouble's money was reduced to $2 million; $6 million went to the two disinherited grandchildren, and the rest went to Helmsley's charitable trust.

★

Biographies of Helmsley include Michael Moss, *Palace Coup* (1989), and Richard Hammer, *The Helmsleys: The Rise and Fall of Harry and Leona Helmsley* (1991). An interview with Helmsley in *The Playboy Interviews: Movers and Shakers* (2007), edited by Stephen Randall and the editors of *Playboy* magazine, provides insight into Helmsley's personality during her trial. An obituary is in the *New York Times* (21 Aug. 2007).

Julianne Cicarelli

HERBERT, Donald Jeffrey ("Don") (*b.* 10 July 1917 in Waconia, Minnesota; *d.* 12 June 2007 in Bell Canyon, California), best known as Mr. Wizard, the host of a pair of children's television broadcasts on which he taught science to members of the baby boom generation.

Don Herbert. AP IMAGES

Herbert developed an early interest in drama and garnered the lead in a theatrical production at Central High School in La Crosse, Wisconsin. Early on Herbert began to put together the pieces that would form his unique adult career. In athletics Herbert earned a letter on the school's football team. He graduated in 1935 and entered La Crosse State Teachers College (now the University of Wisconsin–La Crosse) as a general science and English double major. In 1938 he became director of the Pioneer Players. The next year he inaugurated the Lawson Summer Theater and married the art historian Maraleita Dutton. Herbert adopted three children during the course of this marriage. He earned a BA in science and a BA in English in 1940.

In the early 1940s Herbert continued his quest to become an actor and worked in stock companies and summer theater, where he once performed opposite the future First Lady Nancy (Davis) Reagan. An interest in magic and hosting events created another imprint of the Mr. Wizard persona. In 1942 Herbert worked as a guide for the famed Rockefeller Center in New York City. His acting career was curtailed when he joined the army during World War II. In 1944 Herbert learned to be a pilot during stays at bases all over the southern United States. During 1945 he piloted a B-24 four-engine bomber, and he and his crew flew more than fifty-six missions over Germany,

northern Italy, and Yugoslavia. Herbert received two major military medals for his courageous actions.

As a civilian following the war, Herbert relocated to Chicago and put his efforts into radio as a writer, actor, and teacher at the Chicago Radio Institute. He advanced to radio director at the Community Fund of Chicago and developed programming from interviews he conducted on a tape recorder. In 1949 he acted in children's radio programs, including *It's Your Life*. The experience significantly helped to birth his signature character, Mr. Wizard. He touted his concept to television: a show where he would perform science experiments. In 1950 Herbert developed a nascent version of a science display show, but no one in the medium was interested. Then WMAQ, the Chicago affiliate of the National Broadcasting Company (NBC), accepted the idea and premiered the weekly half-hour *Watch Mr. Wizard* series on 3 March 1951, sponsored by the Cereal Institute. Herbert, working with a young male assistant, performed impressive science experiments that could be duplicated by the home viewers. Before the year was over, a young female assistant was added to the cast.

By 1952 Herbert had become a national star, and feature stories appeared in such leading magazines as *TV Guide*, *Pageant*, and *Science Digest*, and in Herbert's own publication, *Mr. Wizard's Science Secrets*. Herbert was the "progress reporter" on *General Electric Theater*. Mr. Wizard Science Clubs were formed, and a *Billboard* magazine survey indicated that Mr. Wizard was a leader in children's programming. Major magazine coverage continued to grow as the science clubs hit the 5,000 mark.

In 1954 Herbert won the distinguished Peabody Award for excellence in children's programming. Mr. Wizard created and presented hundreds of science trials live during 547 episodes; the show ended with a cancellation in 1965.

Refusing to be thwarted, Herbert began producing science films geared to junior and senior high school students. He embraced his fourth medium by penning books about his field. In 1969 Herbert established a Mr. Wizard Science Center on the outskirts of Boston. He had become so famous that he was invited repeatedly to appear on day and evening network television programs, including the *Today Show*, the *Skitch Henderson Show*, the *Mike Douglas Show*, the *Merv Griffin Show*, and the *Tonight Show*. Revisits continued into the 1970s on the *Mike Douglas Show* and the *Merv Griffin Show*, and Herbert made new appearances on the *Virginia Graham Show*, the *Regis Philbin Show*, and the *Dinah Shore Show*.

In 1971 Herbert relocated to Camarillo, California. In 1972 he married a second time, to Norma Kasell. In the 1980s his fame brought him to the *Today Show* with Connie Chung and *Late Night with David Letterman*. He was also a celebrity on the game show *Hollywood Squares*.

Herbert so believed in science and the media of television and film that he continually reinvented Mr. Wizard. For the 1971–1972 season NBC aired *Watch Mr. Wizard*, albeit for a brief period because of changing demographics and the hard economic times of the early 1970s.

In 1983 Herbert tried the cable television stakes, entering with *Mr. Wizard's World*. Geared for a new generation raised on television and video games, the program found its home on Nickelodeon, where it aired three times a week. The show ran for seven years. From 1990 to the dawning of the new century, reruns were shown.

Always nurturing his brand and iconic status, Herbert in 1994 developed another series, this one in fifteen-minute spots, *Teacher to Teacher with Mr. Wizard*. The spots paid homage to science teachers by allowing them to present their projects to a still newer audience. Having come full circle starting with the boomers, Mr. Wizard was now delighting and educating their children.

For over fifty years Mr. Wizard Studios compiled and archived science and technology data to be made available for television shows, publishing enterprises, educational science reports, and magazine articles. Herbert was a kind and generous man who shared his vast knowledge with the media world. He died of multiple myeloma shortly before his ninetieth birthday.

Captain Kangaroo, Buffalo Bob Smith, and Mr. Rogers were stalwarts of children's programming, but only one character created interactivity with television and the secrets of the universe—Herbert's Mr. Wizard.

★

There is no autobiography or full biography of Herbert. Obituaries are in the *New York Times* and *Los Angeles Times* (both 13 June 2007).

Vincent LoBrutto

HESTON, Charlton (*b.* 4 October 1923 in No Man's Land, unincorporated territory near Evanston, Illinois; *d.* 5 April 2008 in Beverly Hills, California), actor, union leader, and political activist renowned for his larger-than-life screen portrayals.

Of Scottish descent, Heston was born John Charles Carter, the elder of two children of Russell Whitford

Charlton Heston. © **DOUGLAS KIRKLAND/CORBIS**

Carter, a mill operator and salesman, and Lilla (Charlton) Carter. Heston's contact with his father largely ended with his parents' divorce in 1933. Most of his boyhood—a happy period—was spent in the forest country of northern Michigan, but this idyll ended with the divorce and the family's return to the Chicago area. There Heston's mother settled in suburban Wilmette, Illinois, and married Chester Heston, from whom the actor took his official surname. A third child was born of that marriage.

Young Heston attended the nearby New Trier High School. There he enrolled in the drama program and also starred, at the age of seventeen, in a silent 16-millimeter film version of *Peer Gynt*, directed by a talented independent filmmaker, David Bradley. In 1941 a scholarship enabled Heston to enroll in Northwestern University's drama program, where he studied all aspects of theatrical craft and met Lydia Clarke, the love of his life. They were married on 17 March 1944 and remained together for sixty-four years.

Following Heston's U.S. Army Air Forces service in the Aleutians (1944–1946), the couple moved to New York City, residing in the Hell's Kitchen neighborhood and subsisting on modeling work while seeking theatrical roles. A surprise opportunity took them to North Carolina to manage the fledgling Asheville Community Theater, where their year of producing and directing amateur performances provided invaluable experience. Back in New York, Heston landed the small role of Proculeius in Katharine Cornell's Broadway production of *Antony and Cleopatra*. On the strength of its long run (including a midwestern tour), Heston got to play leading roles in a summer stock theater in Mount Gretna, Pennsylvania, where in 1948 he performed ten plays in eleven weeks. Again in New York, Heston found rapid success in the exciting new arena of live television drama, with parts in five Shakespearean plays in the Columbia Broadcasting System's *Studio One* productions, including the network's first coast-to-coast dramatic telecast. He also starred in a more sophisticated independent film for Bradley, *Julius Caesar* (1950). The production, already the young actor's second try at the role of Mark Antony, was inventively filmed amid Chicago's public spaces and attracted serious attention in Hollywood. Soon Heston, overcoming an instinctive disdain for the movies, signed a five-picture contract with the veteran Paramount producer Hal Wallis, who had also discovered Burt Lancaster and Kirk Douglas.

Heston's first Hollywood film role was as a gangster in the crime drama *Dark City* (1950) directed by William Dieterle. The director Cecil B. DeMille, noticing the actor's authoritative mien on the Paramount lot, cast him as the circus manager in *The Greatest Show on Earth* (1952), which became a major hit and won the Academy Award for Best Picture. Now an established star, with a lean, muscular physique and a hard (if not conventionally handsome) face, Heston played leading roles in a variety of films of the early 1950s: *Ruby Gentry* (1952), during which his costar Jennifer Jones broke her hand while slapping Heston's angular face; *The President's Lady* (1953), in which Heston played Andrew Jackson, a role he repeated in *The Buccaneer* (1958); *Secret of the Incas* (1954), whose fedora-wearing archaeologist helped to inspire the later Indiana Jones character; *The Naked Jungle* (1954), in which Heston battles an army of ants on his Amazon plantation; *The Private War of Major Benson* (1955); and *The Far Horizons* (1955), in which Heston played the explorer William Clark, of the famous Lewis and Clark expedition.

DeMille gave Heston his most famous role when he cast the actor as Moses in *The Ten Commandments* (1956), an enormous spectacle filmed partly in Egypt and Sinai. Although critics ridiculed aspects of DeMille's old-fashioned staging and his invented story of Moses' early life, the film achieved enormous rapport with audiences—a rapport that it has retained in regular Easter-Passover telecasts into the twenty-first century. Heston, who at thirty-one is curiously more convincing as the aged lawgiver than as the young prince of Egypt, largely escaped criticism (though *Time* said that he was "ridiculously miscast"). The image of the bearded patriarch extending his rod over the Red Sea and the sound of his formidable bass demanding of Pharaoh, "Let my people go!" gained Heston permanent iconic status in the American cultural pantheon. As the French critic Michel Mourlet later put it in *Cahiers du cinéma*, "Charlton Heston is an axiom. He constitutes a tragedy in himself, his presence in any film being enough to instill beauty.... His eagle's profile, the imperious arch of his eyebrows, the hard, bitter curve of his lips... the contempt of a god imprisoned, quivering with muted rage."

Heston gained the respect of the noted director William Wyler while working on a Western, *The Big Country* (1958), and was thus cast in the coveted lead role of *Ben-Hur* (1959), the story of a young Jew who overcomes enslavement and family tragedy to triumph through a famous chariot race and a transformative encounter with Christ. The challenging Roman production schedule had Heston shuttling between the film's three production units working on the main story, the naval battle, and the chariot race. This time nearly unanimous critical praise accompanied box-office success. The film won an unprecedented eleven Academy Awards, including Heston's Oscar as best actor. The performance also cemented Heston's image as an epic-scale figure, a tradition he maintained over a decade of stardom as a medieval warrior in *El Cid* (1961) and *The War Lord* (1965), as John the Baptist in *The Greatest Story Ever Told* (1965), as Michelangelo in *The Agony and the Ecstasy* (1965), as General Gordon in *Khartoum* (1966), and as Mark Antony in *Julius Caesar* (1970). Even in his supporting parts later in his career, Heston was routinely sought for such historical figures as

Cardinal Richelieu, Brigham Young, and Henry VIII. More stentorian than subtle, Heston's performances in these roles won him few additional acting honors.

Filmmakers of the Vietnam War era took advantage of Heston's hard-edged persona in such dystopian fictions as *The Omega Man* (1971), in which Heston fends off crazed nocturnal humanoids as the last survivor in a deserted Los Angeles; and *Soylent Green* (1973), in which he is a policeman in a future society in which human corpses are recycled as food; but above all *Planet of the Apes* (1968), in which Heston's cynical astronaut lands on a world where talking apes have supplanted a mute and servile human race. Hunted, stripped, and abused, Heston's first line, "Take your stinking paws off me, you damn dirty ape!" won applause from another large movie audience and pointed the way toward a harsher screen persona of later years. Seeking to avoid not so much typecasting as entrapment, Heston appeared in only the first of the five sequels to *Planet of the Apes*—and then only to destroy the world by detonating a doomsday device.

The year 1968, when Heston also gave a subtle portrayal of a broken-down cowboy in *Will Penny* (his favorite performance), marked the last of his great screen work. His stardom continued through several empty big-budget 1970s spectaculars, such as *Skyjacked* (1972), *Airport 1975* (1974), *Earthquake* (1974), and *Midway* (1976), after which most of his screen roles were character parts. His deeply felt but underbudgeted first directorial effort, *Antony and Cleopatra* (1973), failed for want of an adequate Cleopatra to play opposite his Antony.

Statesmanship beckoned when stardom faded. Heston had long displayed a strong sense of professional and public responsibility. His professionalism was legendary, and he reportedly never missed a day of shooting. He stood up for unappreciated directors, providing Orson Welles with his last Hollywood opportunity in *Touch of Evil* (1958), in which Heston played a Mexican detective, and rescuing the talented but self-destructive Sam Peckinpah on *Major Dundee* (1965) by placating a mistrustful studio. Heston picketed for civil rights even when the studios preferred to shun controversy, and he was one of the most prominent Hollywood figures to join the March on Washington, D.C., led by Martin Luther King, Jr., in 1963. As early as 1968 Heston commented in mock frustration, "I'm not an actor anymore.... I'm an activist." For such work Heston was honored with the academy's Jean Hersholt Humanitarian Award in 1977 and numerous other professional tributes. He was president of the Screen Actors Guild (SAG) for an unprecedented six terms (1965–1971) and an early chairman (1971–1982) and then president (1983–2002) of the American Film Institute, which he had helped to create through his previous work with the National Endowment for the Arts.

As with one of his SAG predecessors Ronald Reagan, Heston's political orientation shifted rightward in the 1970s. (Or, as Heston put it when finally registering as a Republican in 1987, "the Democratic Party moved, I didn't.") Lacking Reagan's genial personality, the plainspoken Heston sometimes found himself embroiled in bitter controversy, as when a 1982 union dispute with the liberal actor Ed Asner became an occasion for ugly public name-calling. Heston founded an opposition faction, Actors Working for an Actors Guild, dedicated to maintaining SAG's professional focus in a time of increasingly generalized political activism. Actors Working for an Actors Guild won major concessions from the union in 1984. Heston's support of right-to-work legislation actually drew a motion of censure from several thousand SAG members in 1986. In later years Heston's public persona was regularly associated with his political stands that now mixed inextricably with his heroic screen image. When the novelist Gore Vidal, who had contributed marginally to the script of *Ben-Hur*, gained a degree of notoriety with his oft-repeated claim to have injected a homoerotic subtext into the story behind Heston's back, the point had less to do with the movie than with an attempt to ridicule an actor widely perceived as straitlaced and behind the times.

The rightward trend culminated with Heston's role as president of the National Rifle Association (1998–2003), for which his outdoorsman's lifestyle and rugged individualism made him a natural spokesman. (Heston had actually supported gun-control legislation as late as 1968, around the time he considered running for office as a Democrat.) His oft-repeated taunt that he would give up his gun only when it was pried "from my cold, dead hands" became almost as famous as his screen roles. Controversy aside, he continued to receive public accolades, including the Kennedy Center Honors (1997) in the presence of President Bill Clinton, whom he had harshly criticized, and the Presidential Medal of Freedom from President George W. Bush (2003). Amid all his public engagements, Heston continued to act and occasionally to direct. *Mother Lode* (1982), a film about a crazed Klondike miner, gave him free rein to portray a Scotsman. He submitted to self-parody in *Wayne's World 2* (1993), appeared in *True Lies* (1994) because the director needed "the only person who could plausibly intimidate Arnold Schwarzenegger," and achieved his last significant success as the Player King in *Hamlet* (1996), an uncharacteristic comic role. Heston also made numerous audio recordings, including a set of Bible readings that enjoyed lasting popularity.

Heston's theatrical career has been insufficiently acknowledged. An icon of the screen, he retained the actor's passion for the stage and especially for the great Shakespearean roles. Macbeth was a particular favorite: He played the role four times including a notable Los Angeles production costarring Vanessa Redgrave. He returned to Broadway only once, immediately following *Ben-Hur*, to star in an ambitious but unsuccessful verse drama, *The Tumbler* (1960), directed by

Laurence Olivier. Most of Heston's stage work was saved for California as a means of keeping in touch with his family between films. He played Thomas More, the uncompromising hero of Robert Bolt's play *A Man for All Seasons*, no fewer than six times and always maintained (against the critical consensus) that his full-blooded approach to the role was preferable to that of Paul Scofield, who had triumphed in the original production. In connection with a London staging (which won the aged playwright's approval), Heston also created a telefilm version costarring Vanessa Redgrave and John Gielgud (1988). In 1988 Heston was invited to stage Herman Wouk's play *The Caine Mutiny Court-Martial* in China with a Chinese cast, an experience Heston describes in *Beijing Diary* (1990), illustrated with photographs by Lydia Heston, who had become an accomplished professional photographer and publicist.

Heston published two memoirs. *The Actor's Life* (1978) consists of extracts from his personal journals and is a valuable primary source on Hollywood moviemaking from 1956 to 1976. *In the Arena* (1995) is a more conventional autobiography. Family concerns strongly color both volumes. Despite stresses—both husband and wife were treated for substance addiction problems—the Hestons' marriage endured for sixty-four years. Their son, Fraser Clarke Heston, who appeared as the infant Moses in *The Ten Commandments*, became a screenwriter and a producer, collaborating with his father on several projects. The Hestons also adopted a daughter. Heston was diagnosed with Alzheimer's disease in 2002 and gradually withdrew from public life. He died at home of undisclosed causes, and his remains were cremated.

★

Aside from his two substantial memoirs, Heston's publications include a selection of family correspondence, *To Be a Man: Letters to My Grandson* (1997); a pictorial career survey, *Charlton Heston's Hollywood: 50 Years in American Film* (1998); and a collection of opinion pieces, *The Courage to Be Free* (2000). Emilie Raymond, *From My Cold, Dead Hands: Charlton Heston and American Politics* (2006), is a substantial and sympathetic appraisal of Heston's political influence. Movie-oriented books include Jeff Rovin, *The Films of Charlton Heston* (1977); Bruce Crowther, *Charlton Heston: The Epic Presence* (1986); and Michael Munn, *Charlton Heston* (1986). Academic film criticism includes Michel Mourlet, "In Defence of Violence," in Jim Hillier, ed., *Cahiers du cinéma: 1960–1968—New Wave, New Cinema, Reevaluating Hollywood* (1986); and Marc Jancovich, "'Charlton Heston Is an Axiom': Spectacle and Performance in the Development of the Blockbuster," in Andrew Willis, ed., *Film Stars: Hollywood and Beyond* (2004). See the notable appreciations by Richard Corliss in *Time* (6 Apr. 2008) and by Stanley Fish in the *New York Times* (13 Aug. 2008). Obituaries are in *Variety* (5 Apr. 2008) and the *New York Times* (6 Apr. 2008).

John Fitzpatrick

HIGHTOWER, Rosella (*b.* 30 January 1920 near Ardmore, Oklahoma; *d.* 3 or 4 November 2008 in Cannes, France), internationally acclaimed ballerina who established a prestigious dance school in Cannes.

Hightower was born on the family farm run by her father, Charles Edgar (C. E.) Hightower, of Choctaw ancestry, and her mother, Eula May (Fanning) Hightower. Because declining agricultural prices at that time made earning a living from the land difficult, when Rosella was five the family moved to Kansas City, where her father obtained work with the railroad. Her mother also found work, and her father's teenage sisters joined the family to care for Rosella, an only child. Her aunts took her to vaudeville shows, operas, and other entertainment. She began taking ballet classes at the age of eight. Years later she recalled attending a 1933 performance of the Ballets Russes, which prompted her to decide on a life in ballet.

Hightower pursued her goal with determination. Her dance instructor, Dorothy Perkins, recognized Hightower's innate ability and, confined to a wheelchair herself, used

Rosella Hightower, 1949. **LIPNITZKI/ROGER VIOLLET/GETTY IMAGES**

Hightower to demonstrate movements to the rest of the class. In 1934 Perkins recommended her fourteen-year-old protégée as an instructor for preschool dance students. That summer, at Perkins's insistence, Hightower persuaded her parents to allow her to travel to New York City in the summer to study with Michel Fokine, the renowned Russian choreographer and dancer. For the next four years she spent part of each summer there, striving to improve her technique. In 1937 Colonel W. de Basil's Ballets Russes performed in St. Louis. When Hightower learned that its director, the Russian choreographer and dancer Léonide Massine, intended to form his own company, she went to St. Louis and insisted that she be auditioned. Believing that Massine had invited her to Monte Carlo to join his new company, Hightower, after completing high school in Kansas City, sailed alone for Europe in 1938.

The aspiring dancer reached Monte Carlo and discovered that she had to compete against 200 others for one of sixty positions. Determined to earn a slot in the Ballet Russe de Monte Carlo, she arrived at rehearsals early, left late, and worked with an intensity that characterized her entire career. Her presence long after other dancers had left the studio attracted Massine's notice. He began using her to try new movements and demonstrate them. After the company's European tour began, Hightower was offered a position in the corps de ballet. Observing the principal dancers and choreographers and performing in a variety of ballets, Hightower grew professionally. Against the advice of family and friends, she married the Russian dancer Mischa Resnikov; they divorced less than a year later. After playing London, the company debuted at the Metropolitan Opera in New York City on 13 March 1939.

By the beginning of the company's second season, Hightower was a soloist on its European tour. Days before the London opening, World War II broke out. Hightower and other Americans returned to New York, where Massine reassembled the troupe. On the third day after the delayed opening, Hightower filled in for an injured dancer and received an encouraging review from the *New York Times* dance critic, John Martin, who proclaimed her "somebody to be watched." Joining Ballet Theater (as American Ballet Theater was then known) in late 1941, she advanced quickly, and in October 1943 Martin wrote that she had come "into her own as one of the finest of young ballerinas." After the war she joined the Original Ballet Russe (as the de Basil troupe was then calling itself) and toured the Western Hemisphere as a principal dancer. In March 1947 in New York, when the legendary ballerina Alicia Markova became ill, Hightower assumed the title role in *Giselle*, which she had never danced, after only five hours of rehearsal. The *New York Times* proclaimed Hightower a star, and for the next thirty years her skill and artistry justified the designation.

After the performance, the Marquis George de Cuevas, a wealthy Chilean-born patron of the arts, offered Hightower star billing in a company he was forming. Seizing the opportunity to work with the Russian choreographer Bronislava Nijinska, Hightower accepted de Cuevas's offer and began a professional association with him that continued, with a brief interruption, until his death in 1961. In France in 1948 as the leading ballerina of de Cuevas's Grand Ballet de Monte Carlo (at times known as the Grand Ballet de Marquis de Cuevas), Hightower electrified Paris with her style, musicality, and balance. On 6 May 1952 Hightower married Jean Robier, a company set designer. At the peak of her career, Hightower earned rave reviews for a wide range of roles performed throughout the world. She took time off for a brief return to Kansas City and the birth of her daughter, Dominique, on 18 February 1955, as well as a tour with American Ballet Theater. In November 1955 she resumed her role as leading ballerina of de Cuevas's company, now located in Cannes, which became Hightower's permanent home. During the company's last major production, *Swan Lake*, Hightower danced with the Kirov Ballet star Rudolf Nureyev, who had defected from the Soviet Union in 1961. By that time she had begun to attract notice as a choreographer.

In 1962, after de Cuevas's death, Hightower established the Centre de Danse Classique, a ballet school, in Cannes, which became known as École Superieure de Danse. Although she continued to dance occasionally until 1977, Hightower considered her tour of China with the Grand Ballet de Classique in 1965 the end of her performing career. Although her school occupied much of her time, she also directed the Marseille Ballet (1969–1972) and the Ballet de Nancy (1973–1974). The French government awarded Hightower its most prestigious honor, naming her a Chevalier of the Legion of Honor, in 1975. She was selected as the director of the famed Paris Opera Ballet, serving from 1980 to 1983 and successfully instituting needed reforms. In 1983 she turned her duties in Paris over to Nureyev and later agreed to direct La Scala Ballet in Milan (1985–1986).

Returning to Cannes in late 1986, she devoted her attention to her school. The school's prestige brought its founder designation as Commander of the Legion of Honor. Recognition also came from Oklahoma: The state government commissioned a painting of her and four other world-renowned Oklahoma ballerinas of Native American ancestry. In 1997 the governor proclaimed the five dancers "Oklahoma Treasures." In 2001, at the age of eighty-one, she turned her school over to a former student. Seven years later she suffered a series of strokes and was found dead in her home.

An artist who seemed to defy time and gravity, Hightower graced the dance world for more than a half century as a performer, choreographer, and administrator. Her influence will extend far into the future through the world-class school of dance that she founded.

★

Lili Cockerille Livingston, *American Indian Ballerinas* (1997), provides the most comprehensive account of Hightower's formative years and career. A chapter devoted to her in John Gruen, *The Private World of Ballet* (1975), is based on a personal interview. Another valuable interview, conducted while she was director of the Paris Opera Ballet, is Bruce Merrill, "Rosella Hightower," *Dance Magazine* (July 1981). Obituaries are in the *New York Times* (5 Nov. 2008) and *Washington Post* (8 Nov. 2008).

Brad Agnew

HILL, Oliver White, Sr. (*b.* 1 May 1907 in Richmond, Virginia; *d.* 5 August 2007 in Richmond, Virginia), pioneering civil rights attorney who filed a school desegregation suit in Prince Edward County, Virginia, that became part of the U.S. Supreme Court's 1954 *Brown v. Board of Education* decision.

Hill was born Oliver White. His father, William White, abandoned the family when Hill was an infant. His mother, Olivia Lewis, was a domestic worker and later a school employee. After living for a while with his grandmother, he joined his mother, who had remarried to Joseph Hill, and took his stepfather's last name. The family moved from

Oliver W. Hill. © BETTMANN/CORBIS

Roanoke, Virginia, to Washington, D.C., where Hill graduated from Dunbar High School and entered Howard University. His interest in law began during his sophomore year of college, when a relative gave him an annotated copy of the U.S. Constitution. When he read the document, he found no mention of segregation. In a 2004 interview, Hill recalled how this discovery shaped his subsequent career: "I decided the only thing for us to do was for somebody to carry a case back to the Supreme Court and convince them that they ought to reverse Jim Crow," referring to the system of southern segregation made possible by state and local laws.

After earning an AB from Howard University in 1931, Hill enrolled at Howard University's law school, where the dean, Charles Hamilton Houston, challenged his students to devise legal strategies to attack segregation. He graduated in 1933, ranking second in his class behind his good friend and future Supreme Court justice Thurgood Marshall. The two men had much in common. As Richard Kluger noted in *Simple Justice*, his history of the school desegregation cases, "each was large, outgoing, and fun-loving and had a highly pragmatic mind that leaped at Charles Houston's conception of the black lawyer as a social engineer."

In 1934 Hill married Beresenia Walker, with whom he had one son. He initially struggled to establish a legal practice and worked at a variety of jobs. In 1939 he returned to Richmond, the location of his professional activity over the next sixty years. His first major civil rights suit involved the equalization of teachers' salaries. Working with Marshall, at that time a National Association for the Advancement of Colored People (NAACP) Legal Defense Fund lawyer, and Marshall's colleague William H. Hastie, Hill sued on behalf of black teachers who were paid far less than their white counterparts. He prevailed in the case of *Alston v. the School Board of Norfolk*, which eventually led to improved salaries for all of Virginia's black teachers. This was the beginning of a decade-long campaign to force Virginia school districts to live up to the letter of the "separate but equal" doctrine, which the Supreme Court had instituted with its 1896 decision *Plessy v. Ferguson*. The *Alston* decision was followed by demands for bus transportation for black schoolchildren and improved facilities and equipment for jim crow schools. Hill and his partner, Spottswood W. Robinson III, filed dozens of suits against recalcitrant Virginia school districts.

In 1943 Hill was drafted into the U.S. Army, where he served in France with the Corps of Engineers. After his discharge, he resumed his civil rights work. His most famous case began in 1951, when black students at Robert R. Moton School in Farmville, Virginia, walked out of classes to protest the school's deplorable conditions. Barbara Johns, the fiery leader of the boycott, had written to Hill, asking him to represent her fellow striking students. Hill was impressed by their fighting spirit and agreed to sue the Prince Edward County school board.

The case of *Davis v. County School Board of Prince Edward County* came to trial in February 1952. Hill and his cocounsels, Robinson and Robert L. Carter, presented expert witnesses to document the appalling state of Prince Edward County's black schools and the harmful effects of segregation on African-American children. Lawyers for the school district claimed that progress was being made to improve the schooling of black youth and that any attempt to dismantle segregated education would have disastrous consequences. As expected, the judges unanimously ruled in favor of the defendants.

Hill and the NAACP appealed the *Davis* verdict to the U.S. Supreme Court. Their case was combined with similar cases from Kansas, South Carolina, Delaware, and the District of Columbia under the heading *Brown v. Board of Education*. On 17 May 1954, Chief Justice Earl Warren delivered the Court's historic ruling that "in the field of public education, the doctrine of 'separate but equal' has no place. Separate educational facilities are inherently unequal." Virginia authorities, however, refused to implement the Court's mandate and launched a campaign of "massive resistance." In 1959, rather than integrate, Prince Edward County officials closed all public schools. White parents sent their children to hastily organized private academies; black children were left without any education. Not until 1964 did public schools reopen on an integrated basis.

In addition to his legal work, Hill was active in Democratic Party politics. In 1948 he became the first African American elected to the Richmond City Council since Reconstruction (1865–1877). During the administration of President John F. Kennedy, he served briefly in Washington, D.C., as assistant commissioner in the Federal Housing Administration. Hill continued working at his law firm until his retirement in 1998. The following year, at the age of ninety-two, he received belated recognition for his contributions to the cause of racial justice when President Bill Clinton honored him with the Presidential Medal of Freedom, the nation's highest civilian award. He was also awarded the 2005 Spingarn Medal by the NAACP. Richmond's Oliver Hill Courts Building is named in his honor. Hill died in his home; he is buried in Richmond's Forest Lawn Cemetery.

Hill's lengthy career illustrates that under the right circumstances, the law can be a powerful instrument for social change. He was part of a remarkable generation of African-American lawyers, including Houston, Marshall, Hastie, Robinson, and Carter, that fundamentally reshaped the legal understanding of civil rights and laid the foundation for the modern civil rights movement.

★

Hill's autobiography, *The Big Bang: Brown vs. Board of Education and Beyond* (2000), is filled with personal anecdotes.

For a full account of Hill's role in the Prince Edward County case, see Richard Kluger, *Simple Justice* (2004). A brief review of the highlights of his career is found in Julian Bond, "Interview with Oliver W. Hill," *Virginia Quarterly Review* 80, no. 1 (Winter 2004): 9–15. Obituaries are in the *New York Times* (6 Aug. 2007) and *Washington Post* (7 Aug. 2007).

Paul T. Murray

HILL, Philip Toll ("Phil"), Jr. (*b.* 20 April 1927 in Miami, Florida; *d.* 28 August 2008 in Monterey, California), racecar driver who was the first American to win the Formula One World Championship.

Hill was born in Miami but grew up in Santa Monica, California, where his father had moved to become postmaster. Life for Hill and his two younger siblings was difficult emotionally because his parents did not have a successful marriage; the children were essentially raised by the wealthy older sister of Hill's mother. Recognizing Hill's love of cars—he had known how to drive since the age of nine—Hill's aunt bought him an old Model T Ford when he was twelve; in 1959 Hill inherited her house, and it would remain his residence for the rest of his life. He attended Hollywood Military Academy from 1935 to 1938 and then enrolled in Santa Monica High School, from which he graduated in 1944. Hill hung out with the wealthy set and would race cars with George Hearst on the publishing magnate's estate. Sinus trouble kept Hill from other athletic pursuits, so he spent much of his time poring over English car books and magazines, and turning old cars into "stop light drag racers."

Hill tried to fulfill his father's ambition for him, studying business administration at the University of Southern California from 1945 to 1947. When his old friend Hearst asked him to help prepare a midget car for racing, however, Hill dropped out of school and became first a mechanic and then a driver. He bought a racer of his own, an MG, in November 1947 and soon was competing in rallyes (as they were then styled). He spent 1949–1950 studying auto mechanics in England and attended his first Formula One race; looking back, he declared, "The limit of my ambition then was some day to become mechanic to a great racing driver." He returned home with a larger, faster car, a Jaguar XK120, and traded that in for an Alfa Romeo; in 1951, after his parents died, he added a Ferrari. That year he won his first major race, the Del Monte Trophy race at Pebble Beach, California; he would win it twice more in the next four years, establishing himself as a professional racecar driver.

In the early 1950s Hill also began a career as a restorer and would pursue that interest for three decades after his racing career ended. In 1955, with his restoration of his parents' 1931

Pierce-Arrow Cabriolet, he won Best in Show at the Pebble Beach Concours d'Elegance, a prize he won again in 1977 with a 1927 Packard 343 Murphy Convertible. In later years Hill and Vaughn, his company, would be known as the premier restorers of vintage Rolls-Royce motorcars.

In 1954 Hill raced in the Carrera Panamericana, finishing second. That effort brought him to the attention of Ferrari, for whom he would have his greatest successes. His first race as an official member of the Ferrari team was at Le Mans, France, in 1955, and his first win came in the Swedish Grand Prix for sports cars in 1956; he was becoming known as a driver who could go fast but who did not cause a mechanical failure in the process—a rare combination in those days of rear-wheel-drive vehicles driven "pedal to the metal." In November 1957 the Ferrari team, locked in a battle for the road-racing championship with Maserati, sent three cars to the season-ending race in Caracas, Venezuela; Hill and his codriver Peter Collins won the race, earning Hill a promotion to the Formula One team. Ironically Collins would crash and die in Hill's first Formula One event. In the intervening three years before he won a Grand Prix race, Hill continued his string of road-racing successes, winning twice at Sebring, Florida, and once at Le Mans. Finally, at the penultimate event of 1960, Hill won the Formula One race at Monza, Italy; he was the first American to win there in forty years.

The most significant year of Hill's racing career was 1961. Competing against other carmakers as well as his own teammates, Hill won at Sebring and at Le Mans; he won the pole position, given to the fastest driver, in five of his seven Formula One races. He broke the track record at Nürburgring, site of the German Grand Prix, and in six of the seven races he finished third or better, earning enough points to become world champion. No American had ever won that title, and no other American-born driver won it during Hill's lifetime. Unfortunately Hill's victory was marred by the death of Wolfgang von Trips, his closest rival for the title, at Monza in October.

Hill's amazing streak continued through the first half of 1962. He won at Le Mans and at Nürburgring, finished second at Sebring, and placed second or third in races in Monaco, Belgium, and Holland. However, a string of mechanical failures denied him a second straight world championship, and an ill-advised move to another factory team cost him any further victories on the Formula One circuit. He continued to race sports cars for several more years, with his last victory coming at Brands Hatch in England in 1967. In 1968 he allowed his international racing license to lapse, effectively retiring from competition.

In addition to his restoration business, Hill pursued a thirty-year career as a columnist for *Road & Track* magazine. He began acquiring antique clocks and player pianos, amassing a prize-winning collection. On 5 June 1971 he married Alma Varanowski, a teacher who had knocked on his door in Santa Monica one day asking for a donation to her school project; they had two children. Hill's son also became a racecar driver, winning the Barber Dodge Pro racing championship in 1997. Hill was inducted into the International Motorsports Hall of Fame in 1991. He battled Parkinson's disease for many years, finally succumbing to respiratory failure.

Hill forged a reputation as one of the world's premier long-distance road racers. In 1961 he set a mark for racing accomplishments in a single year that was not equaled during his lifetime.

Hill's authorized biography is William F. Nolan, *Phil Hill: Yankee Champion*, rev. ed. (1996). See also "Hamlet in a Helmet," *Automobile Quarterly* 1, no. 1 (1962). Obituaries are in the *Los Angeles Times* and *New York Times* (both 29 Aug. 2008) and the *Guardian* (30 Aug. 2008).

Hartley S. Spatt

HINCKLEY, Gordon Bitner (*b.* 23 June 1910 in Salt Lake City, Utah; *d.* 27 January 2008 in Salt Lake City, Utah), apostle and president of the Church of Jesus Christ of Latter-day Saints during its remarkable expansion at the dawn of the twenty-first century.

Hinckley, the oldest of five children born to Bryant Stringham Hinckley and Ada (Bitner) Hinckley, grew up in a prominent family in the Church of Jesus Christ of Latter-day Saints (LDS). His father was a highly respected Mormon educator and author, his mother a former English teacher who filled their home with books. Hinckley attended public schools and LDS High School. He went on to the University of Utah, earning a BA in 1932 with a major in English and a minor in ancient languages. In 1933 he began a two-year LDS mission in England. Although he preached in the streets of Preston, Lancashire, and at Speakers' Corner in Hyde Park, London, in letters to his father he expressed doubts about his success. Bryant Hinckley, who was subsidizing his son's mission, urged him to persist.

Hinckley's experiences in England sparked a life-long interest in public relations. In a report to LDS leadership in 1935, he urged the church to improve its printed and audiovisual materials. Shortly thereafter the LDS president appointed Hinckley executive secretary of a newly created Radio, Publicity, and Mission Literature Committee. Hinckley then began the preparation of a variety of widely used handouts and radio scripts on Mormon history and teachings. He organized the LDS exhibits at the San Francisco World's Fair in 1938–1939, directed translations of the Book of Mormon and the missionary's handbook into thirteen languages, and oversaw the activities of thousands of Mormon missionaries overseas. On 29 April 1937 Hinckley married Marjorie Pay, with whom he had five children. Most of Hinckley's LDS work was unpaid, and he supported his family through board service on a variety of publishing, broadcasting, insurance, utility, and banking enterprises in Salt Lake City.

Hinckley began to move into the upper echelons of the church hierarchy in the late 1950s. In 1958 he was appointed an assistant to the Quorum of the Twelve Apostles, the second level of administration within the church. President David O. McKay ordained him as a member of the Quorum in 1961. As one of the Twelve Apostles, Hinckley assumed much of the responsibility for the church's expansive work in Asia. In 1981, when all members of the three-man First Presidency, the church's highest authority, became seriously ill, President Spencer Kimball called on Hinckley for assistance as a counselor and the following year elevated Hinckley himself to the First Presidency. Careful not to overstep his authority, Hinckley adroitly handled much of the day-to-day business of the church for Kimball, as well as his two successors, Ezra Taft Benson and Howard Hunter. In 1995 Hinckley was ordained president of the church.

As an Apostle, member of the First Presidency, and LDS president, Hinckley proved an energetic moderate with a gift for public relations. He created considerable goodwill by encouraging non-Mormons to access the vast LDS genealogical archives in Utah that were opened for general use in the 1970s. Hinckley embraced the 1978 "revelation" of Kimball that reversed an earlier prohibition against persons of African ancestry holding the LDS priesthood. He worked to improve the racial image of the church internationally, especially in light of Mormon missionary efforts in Africa. He sought to blunt ridicule of the church by academics and social activists. In 1985 he admitted his role in purchasing and attempting to suppress documents forged by Mark Hofmann, who was seeking to disparage Joseph Smith, the nineteenth-century founder of the Mormon faith. In 1990 Hinckley attended a ceremony dedicating a monument in southern Utah marking an 1857 massacre of non-Mormons by LDS faithful. When DNA experts produced studies in the 1990s and early 2000s debunking claims by Smith that American Indians were descended from the ancient Hebrews, Hinckley dismissed the genetic evidence as inconclusive.

Hinckley sought to play down LDS theological differences with traditional Catholics and Protestants, his partners in the bitter culture wars of the late twentieth century. In the new LDS logo, he emphasized the words "Jesus Christ" rather than "Latter-day Saints." In conjunction with conservatives from other faiths, between 1974 and 1981 he helped block passage of the Equal Rights Amendment, a constitutional proposal introduced in 1972 to guarantee equal rights regardless of sex. He joined with Phyllis Schlafly, a Catholic, and with conservative Protestant groups in their concerns over such issues as illegal drug use, pornography, abortion, and same-sex civil unions and marriage. He affirmed the divinity of marriage, condemned premarital and extramarital sexual relations by heterosexuals, and forbade homosexual sex altogether. The soft-spoken, avuncular Hinckley appeared on several popular news programs, including *60 Minutes, Larry King Live,* and *The News-Hour with Jim Lehrer.* During the 2002 Winter Olympics in Salt Lake City, Hinckley's easy humor and courtesy helped soften the image of the Mormon faith. In 2004 President George W. Bush awarded Hinckley the Presidential Medal of Freedom.

Eighty-five years old when he became the leader of the Mormon church, Hinckley proved more energetic than any of his recent predecessors. His public relations skills and interest in missionary work coincided with a remarkable expansion in the church. As president he continued his world travels, Over his lifetime, he logged close to a million miles and visited dozens of countries. He created a Perpetual Education Fund to provide foreign-born LDS students with loans for postsecondary training. Because certain Mormon ceremonies could take place only in temples, as opposed to regular meetinghouses, Hinckley took considerable pleasure in performing 92 dedications for new or remodeled temples. Under his presidency the number of temples worldwide expanded from 47 to 124 (excluding the rededicated temples); LDS membership rose from nine million to twelve million, with over 50 percent of the faithful residing outside the United States. Stricken with cancer in 2007, Hinckley died at home and is buried in the Salt Lake City Cemetery.

Hinckley's energies, his soft-spoken style, and his public relations skills facilitated an extraordinary global expansion of the Mormon church. By establishing closer ties with conservatives from other faiths during the culture wars, he helped bring LDS into the mainstream of American life.

★

The fullest authorized Hinckley biography is Sheri L. Dew, *Go Forward with Faith: The Biography of Gordon B. Hinckley* (1996). Richard N. Ostling and Joan K. Ostling, *Mormon America: The Power and the Promise* (1999), and Harold Bloom, *The American Religion* (2006), are informative on the Mormon church and its role in American life. Obituaries are in the *Deseret News* (27 Jan. 2008) and *New York Times* (29 Jan. 2008). *An Ensign to the Nations* (1997) is a well-done LDS film focusing on the global expansion under Hinckley.

William Howard Moore

HO, Donald Tai Loy ("Don") (*b.* 13 August 1930 in Honolulu, Hawaii; *d.* 14 April 2007 in Honolulu, Hawaii), singer and entertainer who blended traditional Hawaiian and pop music.

Ho was the second of nine children born to James Ah You Hoy, of Chinese and Hawaiian descent, and Emily "Honey" (Lemaile Silva) Ho, of Hawaiian and Portuguese descent. In the early 1930s the family moved from the Kakaako district of Honolulu to the city's Kaneohe neighborhood and opened a restaurant called Honey's. After the Japanese attack on the U.S. naval base at Pearl Harbor in 1941, thousands of American servicemen arrived on the island. His parents obtained a liquor license and prospered from their many customers in the military.

Ho's parents held him back a year from entering school. Larger and more mature than his classmates, he excelled at basketball and football. As a teenager Ho attended Kamehameha Schools, a military school with a curriculum that emphasized Hawaiian culture. He believed that his experience playing quarterback on the school football team taught him leadership skills; he graduated as valedictorian in 1949. He then attended Springfield College in Springfield, Massachusetts, studying physical education for one year. One of three nonwhites on campus, Ho felt isolated. After encountering racism while on a car trip

Don Ho, 1977. AP IMAGES

through the South, Ho decided to transfer to the University of Hawaii. He earned a BS in sociology in 1954 and received a second lieutenant's commission as a member of the Army Reserve Officers' Training Corps. On 22 November 1951 he married his high school sweetheart, Melvamay Wong, with whom he had six children.

In 1954 Ho enlisted in the U.S. Air Force. He was sent to pilot training at Columbus Air Force Base in Columbus, Texas, where he learned to fly small planes. He then transferred to Bryan, Texas, to gain experience as a jet-fighter pilot. Because the close of the Korean War (1950–1953) had reduced the need for such skills, he became adept at piloting large military transport planes around the Pacific Ocean. Stationed in Travis, California, Ho became the commander of the first all-Hawaiian crew. Despite the steady pay, Ho resigned his commission in 1959, the year that Hawaii gained statehood, and went home to run the family business.

Ho was alert to the needs of his growing family, including paying the mortgage on their house. At his father's suggestion, he began to perform on an electric Hammond chord organ at Honey's as a way to boost business. He soon formed a band of skilled musicians to play an array of popular music styles, including Hawaiian, country, war songs, blues, and ballads. The band became known as Don Ho and the Aliis. Sonny Chillingworth, an experienced Hawaiian slack key guitarist, became one of the band's mentors. They developed a crowd-pleasing habit of calling visiting entertainers and beautiful young women up to the stage.

Ho's fame quickly spread. In 1960 he signed a performing contract with Duke Kahanamoku's famous supper club in Waikiki, then emerging as the center of Hawaiian tourism. Although he revered Kahanamoku, Ho insisted that his portion of the nightclub be called Honey's after his parents' lounge in Kaneohe. Audiences packed the club to hear him perform. The veteran music producer Sonny Burke recorded *The Don Ho Show—Live from Hawaii* for Reprise Records, which became Ho's first major hit. A second album, *Don Ho—Again* (Reprise) bolstered this growing fame. He mixed traditional Hawaiian tunes with such pop songs as "La Bamba," "Hang on Sloopy," and "Taste of Honey." To promote the album and expand his fame, Ho played in nightclubs in San Francisco, opening and closing his sets with the song "Night Life." He would sit casually at center stage behind his organ, lead the band, take requests, and call out "Suck 'em up" periodically to encourage patrons to drink, an exhortation that reflected drinking customs in Hawaii and China. His beach-boy party atmosphere resonated with young, affluent Americans attracted to surfing, beach volleyball, and tanning.

In 1965 Ho signed a ten-year contract with Duke Kahanamoku, which granted the Duke 15 percent of Ho's earnings. Ho became the headliner at the Waikiki nightclub. Celebrities such as Frank Sinatra, Desi Arnaz, Ava

Gardner, Jack Lemmon, Bill Cosby, Marlon Brando, and Gene Hackman came to hear his shows. Ho attained national fame with the release of the drinking song "Tiny Bubbles," which was also the name of another hit album. He was now a big draw at such famous nightclubs as the Coconut Grove in Los Angeles and the Royal Box at the Americana Hotel in New York City.

Sinatra became a major supporter, helping Ho to win coveted nightclub engagements at Las Vegas casinos. He became notorious for throwing beautiful women into swimming pools, including, on one occasion, Jacqueline Kennedy. His new mainland fame persuaded Ho to break up the Aliis so that he could use new songs and bigger bands and compete with Wayne Newton, Dean Martin, and Sinatra, some of the most popular singing stars of the day.

With fame came television contracts. Ho hosted the National Broadcasting Company television special *Hawaii-Ho*, which offered a tour through five segments of Hawaiian history. The Singer Company sponsored the show, promoting it through 2,500 stores selling Hawaiian clothing, souvenirs, and Ho's albums. Jetting around the country to perform for eager audiences, Ho became the emblem of Hawaiian style: a handsome crooner and a master storyteller. He turned up in television shows that took up Hawaiian themes, with cameo roles on *The Brady Bunch*, *Charlie's Angels*, *Batman*, and *I Dream of Jeannie*. From 1976 to 1977 he hosted his own American Broadcasting Company variety show, *The Don Ho Show*. He was also a frequent guest on television talk shows including *The Tonight Show Starring Johnny Carson* and shows hosted by Perry Como, Mike Douglas, and Merv Griffin.

Politicians also wanted a piece of Ho's fame. President Richard Nixon invited Ho to play at the celebratory party for the *Apollo 13* astronauts in Los Angeles after their voyage circling the Moon in 1970. In 1982 Ho's endorsement helped the Democratic candidate George Ariyoshi win the governor's race in Hawaii.

Ho continued recording albums in the 1970s and 1980s and played larger venues as Hawaiian tourism became industrialized. His gimmicks included kissing grandmas during his shows and introducing his children into his routines. He also opened his own restaurant, the Island Grill, in the Aloha Tower Center Marketplace in Honolulu.

Between 1982 and 1992 Ho had two children with Patti Swallie as well as two children with Liz Guevara. However, he remained married to Melvamay Ho, who died of lupus in 1999. Suffering from heart problems, Ho underwent experimental stem-cell surgery in Bangkok, Thailand, in 2005. He married his longtime executive producer, Haumea Hebenstreit, on 12 September 2006. After his death from heart failure the following year, his ashes were spread over the ocean in a traditional Hawaiian ceremony.

As an entertainer Ho popularized Hawaiian music and culture and brought a wider awareness of Hawaii to his mainland fans. In doing so he anticipated the modern multiculturalism of twenty-first-century America.

★

For an autobiographical account, see Ho and Jerry Hopkins, *Don Ho: My Music, My Life* (2007). Obituaries are in the *New York Times* and *Honolulu Star-Bulletin* (both 16 Apr. 2007).

Yunxiang Gao

HUFFINGTON, Roy Michael (*b.* 4 October 1917 in Tomball, Texas; *d.* 11 July 2008 in Venice, Italy), independent oilman, philanthropist, and ambassador to Austria.

Huffington was born Roy Michel Huffington, the son of Roy Mackey Huffington, an oilman, and Bertha (Michel) Huffington, who became an office clerk. He had a younger sister. Tombal was an agricultural community at the time but in 1933 earned the nickname "Oil Town USA" when the Humble Oil and Refining Company discovered oil there. The family moved to Dallas during the Depression, where at age fourteen Huffington delivered newspapers to support the family after his father died in an oil field accident while working in Venezuela. Tired of being called "Michelle" by his classmates, he changed his middle name from Michel to Michael. Huffington graduated from North Dallas High School and enrolled in Southern Methodist University (SMU), where he earned a BS in geology in 1938. He went on to graduate studies at Harvard, earning an MA (1941) and PhD (1942) in geology.

When the United States entered World War II, Huffington enlisted in the navy, serving from 1942 to 1945 on the USS *Hornet* aircraft carrier as an ensign to the lieutenant commander. He used his training in geology to interpret photographs for military intelligence. Huffington received the Bronze Star for heroism in combat; his unit received the Presidential Unit Citation for extraordinary heroism in action. He remained a member of the U.S. Naval Reserve until 1954.

After the war Huffington worked for Humble Oil, which later became known as ExxonMobil, as a senior geologist and exploration division geologist for ten years. On 26 October 1945 he married Phyllis Gough, a fellow SMU graduate; they had a son and daughter. The couple lived in New Mexico and Midland, Texas, while Huffington worked as a field geologist in Louisiana, Texas, and other oil-rich areas.

In 1956, not quite forty years old, Huffington decided to start his own independent company, Roy M. Huffington, Inc. (Huffco). He launched a career as a wildcatter, a speculator in drilling in unproven areas of suspected oil production. One of these areas was Indonesia, where Huffington began exploring for oil in 1968 through a joint production contract with the Indonesian government. Huffington made his fortune in 1972 when he discovered natural gas on the island of Borneo; this strike resulted in a twenty-five-year joint venture with Pertamina, the government-owned energy company. The Indonesian venture not only revealed Huffington's savvy as a wildcatter but also displayed his innovative approach to business negotiations. Traditionally, the major oil companies claimed ownership of the natural resources discovered and paid royalties and taxes to the home government. Huffington employed an unusual approach that involved the sharing of profits and technology with the nation in which the resource was found.

After his discovery in Indonesia, Huffington persuaded Japanese utilities to invest in liquid natural gas pipelines and plants and obtained subsidies from the U.S. government to build tanker ships to transport fuel. Huffco joined forces with Mobil Oil Indonesia to expand that country's natural gas production. Mobil agreed to relinquish its claims to Indonesian gas in exchange for a production-sharing agreement with Huffco. This agreement allowed for the extraction of natural gas from remote areas, which would then be converted to liquid natural gas by exposure to extremely low temperatures. Conversion to liquid form allowed the gas to be transported more easily, making Indonesia the world's largest liquid natural gas supplier. The agreement also involved infrastructure development and job training. Despite his remarkable success in Indonesia, Huffington also faced his share of setbacks; in 1968 the Federal Power Commission ruled that Huffco was charging too much for natural gas and required Huffington to refund overages to his customers.

Huffco profited tremendously from the boom in oil and gas prices that followed the Yom Kippur War between a coalition of Arab nations and Israel. In October 1973, on the Jewish holiday of Yom Kippur (the Day of Atonement), Syria and Egypt launched an attack against Israel. The following day, the Organization of Petroleum Exporting Countries announced that they would no longer ship oil to countries that supported Israel during the conflict. Energy prices rose sharply as a result, and producers such as Huffco scrambled to find new sources of now highly profitable oil and gas. But prices collapsed in the 1980s, and by 1986 oil prices were close to their 1973 levels (adjusted for inflation). Huffington's Indonesian agreement helped him to survive this change in market conditions;

the firm locked in a 20 percent stake in the Indonesian joint venture, which had protected profits. While other energy firms struggled, Huffco prospered. In 1990 Huffington sold Huffco to a Taiwanese consortium (Chinese Petroleum) for $600 million.

Huffington turned his attention to politics. Following his support of George H. W. Bush's 1988 presidential campaign, the new president named Huffington U.S. ambassador to Austria, a position he filled from 1990 to 1993. His primary interest was in developing business relationships with former Eastern bloc nations, which were eager to jump-start their economies following the collapse of the Soviet Union. He also financed the political campaigns of his son, Michael Huffington, who won a California seat in the House of Representatives in 1992 but lost in his bid for a Senate seat in 1994.

Noted for his philanthropic contributions, Huffington was an avid supporter of his alma mater, SMU, establishing endowments worth over $20 million; SMU renamed its Department of Earth Sciences after Huffington in his honor. He received an honorary doctorate from SMU in 1990 and distinguished alumni awards from SMU and Harvard Business School. The Austrian government awarded him the Grosse Goldene Ehrenzeichen (Grand Decoration of Honor in Gold) for his services as ambassador. Huffington was an honorary life trustee of the national board of the Asia Society and a trustee of the George H. W. Bush Presidential Library at College Station, Texas. He founded the Huffington Foundation, which contributed to local Houston charities, and with his wife established the Huffington Center on Aging at Baylor College of Medicine in Houston.

Huffington died of pulmonary embolus while on vacation in Italy. He is buried in Glenwood Cemetery in Houston.

Huffington established a new business model for the oil and gas industry in the late 1960s and early 1970s. American petrochemical companies had a history of protecting their own domestic interests and establishing "turf" when encountering new oil and gas reserves on foreign soil. Early on he understood the global nature of his business, and his more cooperative methods of resource development made him a standout in the industry. He epitomizes the early icons of entrepreneurial capitalism in America: the self-made man turned generous philanthropist.

★

Material on Huffington is hard to come by. Obituaries are in the *Houston Chronicle* (14 July 2008), *Washington Post* (15 July 2008), *New York Times* (17 July 2008), and *Los Angeles Times* (19 July 2008).

Karen Linkletter

HUMBARD, (Alpha) Rex Emmanuel (*b.* 13 August 1919 in Little Rock, Arkansas; *d.* 21 September 2007 in Atlantis, Florida), evangelical preacher and pioneer of televangelism whose Sunday morning services from the Cathedral of Tomorrow in Cuyahoga Falls, Ohio, were broadcast on more than 1,500 television and radio stations worldwide in ninety-one languages from 1952 to 1999.

Humbard was one of six children born to the Pentecostal preachers Alpha Edward Humbard and Martha Bell (Childers) Humbard. He grew up traveling across the country with his parents—primarily in the South and Midwest—playing the guitar as a part of his family's itinerant ministry. The Humbard family eventually settled in Dallas, and it was there that Rex met Maude Aimee Jones, whom he later married in 1942. The couple settled in Akron, Ohio, where they raised four children.

Young Rex began his career in the broadcast media in 1922, when at age thirteen he started singing gospel music for KTHS Radio in Berryville, Arkansas. These broadcasts

Rex Humbard, 1976. AP IMAGES

served primarily as advertisements for his father's weekly camp meetings. However, it was not until thirty years later, after he had started his own evangelical ministry, that Humbard conceived of using the broadcast media to spread the message of Jesus Christ. According to his autobiography *Put God on Main Street*, Humbard came up with the concept of television evangelism (later known as televangelism) in 1952, while watching a live broadcast of a Cleveland Indians–New York Yankees baseball game through a storefront window in downtown Akron. "At that moment," he wrote, "God placed upon my heart a burden to build a church known as the Cathedral of Tomorrow."

It would be a few years before the $4 million, 5,400-seat cathedral, which many religious scholars point to as America's first megachurch, was built. In the meantime Humbard broadcast his religious services from an old movie theater in Akron, a decision with which his father staunchly disagreed. While the two remained close, father and son parted ways professionally over Humbard's decision to embrace modernity and take the message of Christianity to the airwaves.

Finding a media partner in this endeavor proved difficult, and Humbard was turned down twelve times before he finally found a station that agreed to broadcast his services. The Federal Communications Commission (FCC) gave what it called "public service credit" to stations that provided religious organizations with free airtime, but many stations were hesitant to include evangelical groups for fear that the conservative tone of evangelical theology might alienate viewers or listeners. The Midwest, however, had experienced a recent influx of evangelical Christians from the South, many of whom had moved to northeastern Ohio during World War II to work in rubber factories. Humbard's sermons proved to be very popular with this local audience.

In 1960, two years after the Cathedral of Tomorrow opened, the FCC changed its policies so that stations could receive public interest credit for airtime that was sold to religious groups rather than given to them. Public interest credit was an essential part of the license renewal process, and the opportunity to turn a profit while earning this credit proved to be very attractive to station managers, even those concerned about the tone of evangelical broadcasts. Humbard began purchasing commercial airtime on stations across the United States and eventually around the world. By 1980 Humbard's simple, nondenominational message that "God loves you"—a harbinger of the "light" theology that would come to characterize the modern-day megachurch—could be heard on 226 television stations in the United States, 650 television stations in other countries, and more than 700 radio stations worldwide.

However, Rex Humbard Ministry, Inc., began to experience financial trouble in the 1970s. In 1973 the ministry was forced to sell a girdle factory in the Brooklyn borough of New York City that it had purchased in 1965. The initial purchase had generated unwanted publicity for the ministry, because some religious leaders believed it was inappropriate for a church to own a for-profit business that did not involve religion. At various times Rex Humbard Ministry, Inc., also owned a plastics company; advertising agency; skyscraper in downtown Akron; and Mackinac College, a liberal arts institution in Michigan that Humbard eventually turned into a vacation resort.

Also in 1973 Humbard was ordered by a court in Ohio to refund more than $12 million in unregistered securities that he had been collecting from investors since 1959. According to the *New York Times*, Humbard borrowed $500,000 from the Teamsters Pension Fund, which was managed by the International Brotherhood of Teamsters president Jimmy Hoffa, to help with this repayment. When the debt was finally repaid in December 1975, Humbard burned the last bill before an audience of congregants and viewers in a gesture that he said would "tell our critics that we didn't go under."

Nevertheless, financial mismanagement continued to plague the ministry, and by 1977, when Humbard spoke at the funeral of Elvis Presley, who professed to be a great admirer of Humbard's weekly broadcasts, the ministry was nearly $9 million in debt. In 1983 Humbard resigned as pastor of the Cathedral of Tomorrow and moved to Florida, where he continued to record broadcasts of his religious services until the mid-1990s. While in Florida, Humbard also served on the board of directors that reorganized Jim Bakker's "Praise the Lord" (PTL) ministry after Bakker resigned from the organization amid a sex scandal in 1987. The Cathedral of Tomorrow complex was eventually sold in 1994 to the ministry of Ernest Angley, an evangelical preacher whose claim that HIV and AIDS can be cured through prayer has generated controversy.

Humbard died at age eighty-eight of natural causes. He was a religious pioneer whose creative use of the television medium compelled thousands—perhaps even millions—of people around the globe to convert to evangelical Christianity. Although his work foreshadowed the ministries of evangelical leaders such as Jerry Falwell and Pat Robertson, Humbard did not link his work to that of the Religious Right, as Falwell and Roberson did. "For me to preach about the Vietnam War," Humbard told a reporter in the early 1970s, "would be like going to a blacksmith to get a tooth pulled." Years later, following the rise of the Moral Majority, a political action group founded by Falwell, Humbard reportedly remarked that "if Jesus were preaching today, he would never get into politics."

★

Comprehensive information about Humbard's life is available in his three autobiographies, *Put God on Main Street: An*

Autobiography (1970), written with Joyce Parks; *Miracles in My Life: Rex Humbard's Own Story* (1971); and *The Soul-Winning Century: The Humbard Family Legacy* (2006). Information on Humbard's career is available in Megan Rosenfeld, "Rex Humbard and His Mass Media Mission," *Washington Post* (23 Jan. 1980). Obituaries are in the *Washington Post* and *New York Times* (both 23 Sept. 2007).

Maura Jane Farrelly

HUNT, E(verette) Howard, Jr. (*b.* 9 October 1918 in Hamburg, New York; *d.* 23 January 2007 in Miami, Florida), prolific American novelist and U.S. Central Intelligence Agency (CIA) operative, best known for engineering break-ins at Democratic Party National Committee headquarters in the Watergate complex in Washington, D.C., during the 1970s, ultimately resulting in Richard Nixon's resignation as president of the United States.

As the only surviving child of Everette Howard Hunt, a lawyer and insurance industry lobbyist, and Ethel Jean

E. Howard Hunt, 1982. AP IMAGES

(Totterdale) Hunt, a church organist and conservatory-trained classical pianist, Hunt was raised mainly in Hamburg, a suburb of Buffalo, New York. Graduating from high school in 1936, he enrolled at Brown University. He graduated with a BA in English in 1940 and then finished his formal education in 1941 at the U.S. Naval Academy in a program leading to service as an ensign on a destroyer in the North Atlantic Ocean.

In 1942 an injury caused by a fall aboard the destroyer ended his navy career. After short stints of work with various branches of Time, Inc., he joined the Office of Strategic Services (the agency in charge of covert operations and intelligence gathering during World War II), serving in China until the end of the war in 1945. He had begun moonlighting as a novelist in the early 1940s, writing two books, one about convoy duty in the North Atlantic Ocean and the other about airmen on Guadalcanal in the Solomon Islands. These works were unlike the pulp spy fiction he later produced (more than seventy books written under his name and at least four pseudonyms). Although these early efforts were not commercially successful, they earned Hunt positive critical attention and a Guggenheim Fellowship in creative writing in 1946.

After failing as a screenwriter in Hollywood, California, he obtained a job in Paris, France, in 1947 with the Economic Cooperation Administration (ECA). With ECA, Hunt oversaw the Marshall Plan (the post–World War II effort by the United States to rebuild Europe), as an assistant to Averell Harriman, the plan's European administrator. According to the Hunt biographer Tad Szulc, although Hunt worked at ECA ostensibly as a state department officer, he "actually . . . belonged to the year old CIA station" in France. No matter Hunt's actual career status, in 1949 he moved from ECA in Paris to the U.S. Office of Policy Coordination, the covert operations branch of the CIA in Washington, D.C., where he helped establish its psychological warfare department. In 1950 he set up the CIA agency station in Mexico.

During the next several years Hunt was involved in the CIA's overthrow of a leftist government in Guatemala and was stationed in Japan and Uruguay (serving for three years as station chief in the latter country) before returning to Washington, D.C. There he became involved with the 1961 Bay of Pigs invasion (a failed attempt by the U.S. government to overthrow Fidel Castro's regime in Cuba), charged with organizing a shadow Cuban government with various Cuban exiles. In 1973 Hunt published *Give Us This Day: The Inside Story of the CIA and the Bay of Pigs—By One of the Key Organizers*. His career suffered, like that of so many others, because of the unsuccessful invasion; according to the journalist Tim Weiner, Hunt spent the rest of the 1960s "carrying out desultory propaganda tasks at the agency, among them running news

services and subsidizing books that fell stillborn from the press."

Disheartened with the CIA, Hunt resigned from his position on 1 May 1970 and worked for a year with an agency-related public relations firm. During this time, he came to know President Nixon's chief counsel, Charles Colson. (Both Hunt and Colson were involved in Brown University alumni activities.) Hunt worked as a $100-a-day consultant for the White House special investigation unit, later characterized as "a subterranean department of dirty tricks." The unit was assigned to stopping leaks of government secrets to the media. One such leak had occurred in 1971, when the national security analyst Daniel Ellsberg released the Pentagon Papers (a classified U.S. government report that detailed internal affairs concerning the Vietnam War) to the *New York Times*. After the unit's formal dissolution in fall 1971, Hunt continued to work for the Nixon administration.

As part of his secret operations, Hunt supervised the burglary of the office of Ellsberg's psychiatrist in Beverly Hills, California, in hopes of obtaining compromising information. He also traveled to New England to seek possibly scandalous information on Senator Edward M. Kennedy, a potential 1972 campaign opponent; offered "hush money" to a Colorado lobbyist whose memo about corporate dealings with the Nixon administration had been leaked to investigative journalists; and discussed with a colleague "ways of getting rid of the pesky" columnist Jack Anderson. He also organized the break-in and bugging of the Democratic National Committee offices at the Watergate complex, the deed for which he would become best known.

The first Watergate break-in effort, which took place the night of 28 May 1972, proved ineffective. During a second attempt on the night of 16 June 1972, the perpetrators were caught in the act. One of the apprehended conspirators had Hunt's White House telephone number in his address book, thus linking him to the crime. Nixon was overwhelmingly reelected in November 1972, but official investigators and journalists connected Hunt and the Watergate break-ins to Nixon and his reelection campaign. Attempted cover-ups were unsuccessful; shortly after the failed break-in, Nixon was recorded saying, "This fellow Hunt, he knows too damn much." Nixon ultimately resigned. Despite subsequent cooperation with various investigative bodies, Hunt was convicted of wiretapping, conspiracy, and burglary; he was sentenced to thirty-three months in prison.

After his parole Hunt continued to write spy novels. Conspiracy theorists focused on Hunt in 1978 when the Liberty Lobby (a right-wing group) printed an article in its newspaper *Spotlight* accusing him of being involved in President John F. Kennedy's assassination in 1963. Hunt sued the organization in 1981 and won substantial damages; however, the judgment was overturned on appeal in

1985 due to a jury instruction error. Until his death Hunt vigorously denied any involvement with the Kennedy assassination.

Hunt married Dorothy L. Wetzel, a divorcee and fellow ECA employee, on 7 September 1949. They had two daughters and two sons. In 1972 Dorothy died in an airplane crash in Chicago, carrying $10,000 in cash. According to Hunt, Dorothy was in possession of family money for an investment; others believe that the money was extorted by Hunt (with Dorothy's help) from the White House as part of a blackmail attempt to cover his legal bills. In 1978 he married the divorcee Laura E. Martin, a Spanish teacher, with whom he had two children. In his later years Hunt suffered from ill health; he required a leg amputation and was confined to a wheelchair. He died from pneumonia at age eighty-eight and is buried in Hamburg.

According to a *New York Times* obituary, Hunt had "a checkered career." A former U.S. ambassador who knew him said that Hunt "went from one disaster to another until he hit Watergate." In regard to his posthumously published memoir (written with Greg Aunapu), *American Spy: My Secret History in the CIA, Watergate, and Beyond* (2007), a favorable reviewer characterized Hunt as "the CIA's Forest Gump . . . a genial incompetent" whose "moral compass malfunctioned . . . with such dreadful consequences to him . . . and to the country he loved."

★

Hunt's two memoirs—*Undercover: Memoirs of an American Secret Agent* (1974) and *American Spy*—include significant information about his life yet are not always consistent in their accounts. Dated but useful in relating Hunt's life is Szulc, *Compulsive Spy: The Strange Career of E. Howard Hunt* (1974). Attorney Mark Lane, who represented Liberty Lobby in the second trial for Hunt's lawsuit (which overturned the original libel award), speculates about Hunt's involvement in the Kennedy assassination in *Plausible Denial: Was the CIA Involved in the Assassination of JFK?* (1991). There is an excellent lengthy obituary by the intelligence specialist Tim Weiner in the *New York Times* (24 Jan. 2007).

Daniel J. Leab

HUNT, Lamar (*b.* 2 August 1932 in El Dorado, Arkansas; *d.* 13 December 2006 in Dallas, Texas), founder of the American Football League, founder and owner of the Kansas City Chiefs, and sports promoter who was inducted into three professional sports halls of fame.

Hunt was the youngest of seven children of Haroldson Lafayette (H. L.) Hunt, Jr., an oilman, and Lyda (Bunker) Hunt, a schoolteacher. (They were known as the "First

Lamar Hunt, 2004. DAVE KAUP/REUTERS/LANDOV

Family," since H. L. also had eight children with two other women.) The elder Hunt had used his gambling winnings to purchase oil leases and was named the world's richest man by *Fortune* magazine in 1948. The family moved to Tyler, Texas, and then to Dallas, where the office of Hunt Oil Company was established.

As a child Hunt's nickname was "Games" due to his interest in inventing and playing new games. He attended high school at the Hill School in Pottstown, Pennsylvania, and was captain of the varsity football team during his senior year. After graduation in 1952, Hunt attended Southern Methodist University (SMU), from which he received a BS in geology in 1956. He was a third-string tight end on the SMU football team, played very sparingly, and was nicknamed "Poor Boy" by his teammates. Shortly after graduation Hunt married Rose Mary Whittle; they had two children and divorced in 1962. He married the schoolteacher Norma Lynn Knobel in 1964, and they also had two children.

Sharing his father's competitive nature, Hunt wanted to bring professional football back to Dallas, but he was rebuffed when he approached the National Football League (NFL) about acquiring an expansion franchise. He also attempted to purchase the Chicago Cardinals in 1959 and move them to Dallas but was again turned down. Realizing that several other people were also trying to purchase the Cardinals in order to bring professional football to their cities, Hunt approached those other businessmen to organize a new football league. The American Football League (AFL) was established in August 1959, and each owner paid $25,000 for his franchise, with Hunt forming the Dallas Texans. Hunt also served as the league's president for its ten-year existence. The original eight owners called themselves the "Foolish Club," knowing that they would likely lose money as well as face intense competition and pressure from the NFL. The NFL retaliated against the AFL by awarding an expansion franchise to Dallas (the Cowboys) to directly compete with the Texans for fans and revenue, and the NFL also awarded a team to Minnesota (the Vikings) to prevent them from joining the AFL. The NFL even offered Hunt a franchise as well as a share of the Cowboys, but he refused to abandon the other AFL owners.

As head coach Hunt hired Hank Stram, whom he knew from Stram's one year as offensive coach at SMU. Even though the Texans won the AFL championship after their third season, Dallas could not support two teams, so Hunt moved the franchise to Kansas City, Missouri, in 1963, where they became the Chiefs. The AFL secured a five-year $36 million national television contract with National Broadcasting Company (NBC) in 1965, which led teams to spend more freely on college talent and begin to sign top NFL players to future contracts. The television contract, the raid on players, and the AFL's increasing success in the important New York market (where the Jets had signed the quarterback Joe Namath from Alabama) led the NFL to realize that the AFL was not going to die, and they approached Hunt about a merger. Hunt met with NFL executives in April 1966 to negotiate the terms, and he succeeded in preserving all of the AFL franchises. The two leagues agreed to an interleague championship game, a common draft, and interleague preseason play beginning in 1967, with a full merger of all AFL teams into the NFL to take place in 1970.

After the Chiefs won the franchise's second AFL championship in 1966, they lost to the NFL's Green Bay Packers in the first NFL-AFL Championship Game (later referred to as Super Bowl I). Kansas City won a third AFL championship in 1969 and then defeated the heavily favored Minnesota Vikings in January 1970 in Super Bowl IV, the last game prior to the merger. Coupled with the Jets' victory in Super Bowl III a year earlier, the AFL was able to join the NFL as an equal partner, with each league having won two Super Bowls. Hunt was credited with coining the name "Super Bowl" for the championship game, inspired by the Super Ball that his children played with, and he also suggested using Roman numerals. Hunt was inducted into the Kansas City Chiefs Hall of Fame in 1970 and was the first AFL figure inducted into the Pro Football Hall of Fame (1972). He was president of the NFL's American Football Conference (AFC) from 1970 until his death, and in 1984 the NFL created the Lamar Hunt Trophy in his honor, presented annually to the AFC champion. Hunt's AFL forced the NFL to expand and brought professional football to areas of the country that had been ignored.

Although Hunt was primarily associated with football, he was also involved in the family oil business (including Placid Oil and Penrod Drilling), real estate ventures, and other professional sports. He built two Kansas City–based theme parks, Worlds of Fun (1973) and Oceans of Fun (1982), as well as SubTropolis, a 1,100-acre cave designed to be an underground business complex. In 1966 Hunt purchased a minority interest in the newly established Chicago Bulls basketball team, an investment that would pay off much later when Michael Jordan helped the team win six championships. In 1967 he founded the Dallas Tornado of the United Soccer Association (later renamed the North American Soccer League, or NASL), and the team won the NASL championship in 1971. Hunt promoted soccer tirelessly, and even though both the Tornado and the NASL folded in the early 1980s, he left a strong legacy of youth soccer in Texas. For his efforts, Hunt was inducted into the U.S. Soccer Federation Hall of Fame (1982), and the U.S. Open Cup was later renamed the Lamar Hunt U.S. Open Cup in his honor. Hunt also became owner of three franchises in Major League Soccer (MLS), and his Kansas City Wizards won the MLS championship in 2000. He received the Medal of Honor from the National Soccer Hall of Fame in 1999.

In 1967, at a time when there was a split in tennis between professional and amateur players, Hunt established the World Championship Tennis (WCT) tour, which consisted of a circuit of related events culminating in a final playoff. He obtained a television contract with NBC and reached an agreement with the rival International Lawn Tennis Federation, which led to the beginning of true open professional tennis. The WCT's final season was 1989, after which the Association of Tennis Players (the players' union) started its own tennis tour. Hunt was inducted into the International Tennis Hall of Fame in 1993.

Hunt and two of his brothers (William Herbert Hunt and Nelson Bunker Hunt) found themselves in the news during the 1970s and 1980s when they were accused of attempting to corner the world silver market. Lamar Hunt became involved in the purchasing of silver later than his brothers, but in 1988 a court ordered the Hunt brothers and other defendants to pay over $130 million in damages to Minpeco S.A., a commodities concern owned by the government of Peru that had lost money due to the Hunts' silver speculation. Although all three brothers' trusts declared bankruptcy, Lamar Hunt was the only one not to declare personal bankruptcy.

Hunt was diagnosed with prostate cancer in 1998, which was initially treated with chemotherapy. He underwent surgery to remove the prostate gland in 2003, but the cancer later spread, and he died in 2006 at age seventy-four. He is buried at Sparkman/Hillcrest Memorial Park in Dallas. Among his numerous awards were induction into the NFL Alumni Association's prestigious Order of the Leather Helmet (1981); the state sports halls of fame of both Texas (1984) and Missouri (1995); the business halls of fame of both Texas (1997) and Kansas City (2004); and the Lifetime Achievement Award from the U.S. Soccer Foundation (2005). In 2008 Hunt's bust was added to the "Hall of Famous Missourians" at the state capitol in Jefferson City.

A humble, soft-spoken man who mingled with fans, flew coach, and drove an old car, Hunt publicly listed his telephone number in the phone book until his death. He insisted on being cited in the team media guide as the *founder* of the Chiefs rather than the *owner*, and he left daily management of his sports teams to his professional employees. Hunt was involved with six different professional sports leagues and seven sports franchises, five of whom won thirteen championships, and he is the only person to have been inducted into three professional sports halls of fame. He anonymously lent and donated many pieces of art to the Dallas Museum of Art, generously donated to his alma mater, SMU, and also helped fund-raise for Saint Mark's School of Texas and for the Fellowship of Christian Athletes, both of whose boards he served on.

★

Information on Hunt, the AFL, and the Chiefs is in Joe McGuff, *Winning It All: The Chiefs of the AFL* (1970). His contributions to football, soccer, and tennis are detailed in Michael C. Miller, "Lamar Hunt: Dallas Sports Czar," *Legacies* 17 (Spring 2005): 56–65. The most thorough account of the Hunt family history is Harry Hurt III, *Texas Rich: The Hunt Dynasty from the Early Oil Days Through the Silver Crash* (1981). Obituaries are in the *Kansas City Star* (14 Dec. 2006) and the *New York Times* and *Washington Post* (both 15 Dec. 2006).

John A. Drobnicki

HUNTINGTON, Samuel Phillips (*b*. 18 April 1927 in New York City; *d*. 24 December 2008 on Martha's Vineyard, Massachusetts), eclectic Harvard University political scientist and public intellectual, best known for his controversial 1990s prediction of an impending global "clash of civilizations."

Huntington, the only child of Richard Thomas Huntington, who published hotel trade journals, and his wife Dorothy Sanborn (Phillips) Huntington, a short-story writer, grew up in New York City's Astoria, Queens, and the East Bronx. A precocious student, Huntington graduated from Stuyvesant High School in 1943, aged sixteen. He completed a BA "with exceptional distinction" from Yale University in two and a half years, majoring in international relations. He served briefly in the U.S. Army, and in 1948 earned an MA in American political history from the University of Chicago. He transferred to Harvard University in fall 1948, winning acclaim for writing his PhD dissertation on U.S. regulatory agencies in four months in 1950, during which time he also developed diabetes. In June 1950 he joined the teaching faculty in Harvard's Department of Government. Throughout his lengthy academic career, Huntington invariably made undergraduate teaching a high priority. Emulating his Harvard mentor Professor William Y. Elliott, an inveterate consultant to Washington officials, through his writings and personal advice, Huntington always sought to influence top policy makers and public opinion.

The bespectacled, balding Huntington's unassuming appearance and reticent manner belied his readiness to advance iconoclastic ideas that questioned accepted conventional wisdom and frequently provoked heated academic and popular debate. A prolific and original writer, over more than fifty years he produced or coauthored seventeen books and dozens of articles, spanning a wide range of topical and often controversial issues. All his major books attracted public attention and fierce criticism. Though diverse in subject, all addressed broad issues with important policy implications. Huntington's writings also defied easy classification as liberal or conservative, since he professed broad adherence to liberal principles, but combined these with a conservative emphasis, derived from the eighteenth-century British thinker Edmund Burke, on the importance of political institutions, stability, and order. Like many midcentury American liberals, Huntington staunchly supported his country's anticommunist cold war stance. The son of a Baptist father and atheist mother, by his own choice an Episcopalian, he was heavily influenced by the arguments of the Protestant theologian Reinhold Niebuhr that, in an imperfect world, well-meaning men might often be forced to employ flawed instruments and acquiesce in unattractive methods and seemingly immoral policies in pursuit of desirable objectives.

Huntington's first major book, *The Soldier and the State* (1957), argued that the loss of the free security the protection of the Atlantic and Pacific oceans had given the United States until the early twentieth century meant the country needed a professional military dedicated to protecting the national interest. Denied tenure at Harvard in 1958, largely because many colleagues found these views disturbing,

Huntington spent four years at Columbia University, as associate professor of government and deputy director of the Institute of War and Peace Studies. While there he published *The Common Defense* (1961), a book focusing upon policy making within the U.S. defense bureaucracy, and—with Zbigniew Brzezinski, a fellow colleague whom Harvard had also rejected—*Political Power: USA/USSR* (1964), a comparison of the two leading cold war antagonists. In 1963 Harvard invited Huntington back with tenure, where he remained, eventually becoming Albert J. Weatherhead III University Professor, until retiring in 2007. He was also a founder and from 1978 to 1989 a director of the Weatherhead Center for International Affairs. From 1989 to 1999 he served as director of Harvard's John M. Olin Institute for Strategic Studies. On 8 September 1957 Huntington married Nancy Alice Arkelyan, whom he met when both were working on the Democratic candidate Adlai Stevenson's 1956 presidential campaign. The couple had two sons, Timothy Mayo and Nicholas Phillips.

Huntington's next major book, *Political Order in Changing Societies* (1968), a monumental tome, queried the orthodoxy of then popular modernization theory, that economic growth would automatically generate democratization and liberalization in developing countries. He suggested that strong political institutions, whatever their nature, were more salient factors in ensuring steady progress and stability. *American Politics: The Promise of Disharmony* (1981) argued that the United States was almost unique in experiencing periodic outbursts of "creedal passion," rooted in its Puritan heritage: times such as the Great Awakening and the 1960s, when demands that the country live up to professed American ideals became overwhelming. These were normally followed by relapses into indifference and conservatism. Deprecating pleas by American leaders that other nations should emulate their own country's experience, Huntington warned that little in the U.S. pattern was likely to resonate with developing countries. In 1970 Huntington was a cofounder with Warren Demian Manshel of the influential journal *Foreign Policy*. In 1988 he was president of the American Political Science Association.

Huntington's political interests were not simply academic. Huntington was brought up and always remained a New Deal Democrat, supporting President Harry Truman's 1948 reelection campaign and civil rights position, and writing speeches for Democratic presidential candidates, Stevenson in 1956 and Hubert Humphrey in 1968. He was also much involved in Massachusetts Democratic politics, advising Senator Edward M. Kennedy, Boston's mayor Kevin White, and other prominent state figures. In the 1970s Huntington advised Brazil's government on how to implement gradual liberalization. Between 1966 and 1969 he chaired the Vietnam subcommittee of his own government's Southeast Asia Development Advisory Group. Initially, he strongly supported U.S. intervention in Vietnam; a

secret report he wrote in 1967, however, argued that military pacification would not succeed, and only a policy of decentralized accommodation involving all parties, including the Vietcong, would bring peace to Vietnam. During Jimmy Carter's presidency, as a consultant to the National Security Council in 1977 and 1978, Huntington successfully advocated a harder line against Soviet expansionism, including boosting defense spending and establishing a Persian Gulf rapid reaction force. On the Harvard campus, Huntington's Vietnam involvement and views on development made him the target of antiwar protestors. Rancor lingered into the 1980s, when political opponents twice blocked his election to the National Academy of Sciences.

Undeterred by such attacks, in his later years Huntington continued to generate controversy. A 1993 *Foreign Affairs* article, later expanded into the best-selling volume *The Clash of Civilizations and the Remaking of World Order* (1996), gainsaid optimistic liberal believers in globalization and universal democratization and predicted that the post–cold war world would be dominated by conflicts between different cultures, especially the West and Islam. Hostile critics bitterly assailed Huntington's analysis as a simplistic reworking of the earlier prophesies of Western decline popularized by Oswald Spengler and Arnold Toynbee, but many viewed the 11 September 2001 terrorist attacks by fundamentalist Muslims on New York and Washington as proof of its validity. Ironically, Huntington himself privately opposed the 2003 American-led war against Iraq. Huntington's last book, *Who Are We? The Challenges to America's National Identity* (2004), claimed that erosion of its once predominant Anglo-Protestant culture by unassimilated Hispanic immigration and elite support for multiculturalism threatened his own country's national coherence and sense of identity. In poor health for several years, Huntington died of congestive heart failure complicated by diabetes in 2008 in Oak Bluffs, Martha's Vineyard. He was buried in a family ceremony at West Tisbury cemetery on Martha's Vineyard on 30 December 2008. On 22 April 2009 a public memorial service was held at the Memorial Church of Harvard University. For over half a century he had been among the most provocative of American intellectuals, a formidably confident scholar defying categorization as he refused to respect the conventional pieties of either left or right.

★

Huntington donated his papers to the Harvard University Archives, Cambridge, Massachusetts. Significant profiles of Huntington include Robert D. Putnam, "Samuel P. Huntington: An Appreciation," *PS* 19, no. 4 (Autumn 1986): 837–845; and Robert D. Kaplan, "Looking the World in the Eye," *Atlantic Monthly* (Dec. 2001): 68–82. Insightful interviews with Huntington are in the *Guardian* (21 Oct. 2001); *Pew Forum* (18 Aug. 2006); *New Perspectives Quarterly* 24, no. 1 (Winter 2007);

and *Islamica Magazine* 17 (2008). Huntington's most controversial scholarly works are discussed at length in William B. Skelton, "Samuel P. Huntington and the Roots of the American Military Tradition," *Journal of Military History* 60, no. 2 (Apr. 1996): 325–338; Glenn E. Perry, "Huntington and His Critics: The West and Islam," *Arab Studies Quarterly* 24, no. 1 (Winter 2002): 31–48; and Ervand Abrahamian, "The US Media, Huntington and September 11," *Third World Quarterly* 24, no. 3 (2003): 529–544. Much of the criticism of Huntington's nomination to the National Academy of Sciences was published as "Academia, Journalism, and Politics: A Case Study: The Huntington Case," in Serge Lang, *Challenges* (1998). Obituaries are in the *New York Times*, *Daily Telegraph* (both 28 Dec. 2008); London *Times*, *Washington Post* (both 29 Dec. 2008); *Economist* (30 Dec. 2008); and *Guardian* (1 Jan. 2009).

Priscilla Roberts

HURWICZ, Leonid (*b*. 21 August 1917 in Moscow, Russia; *d*. 24 June 2008 in Minneapolis, Minnesota), economist whose pioneering work into mechanism design and incentive compatibility earned him a share of the 2007 Nobel Memorial Prize in Economic Science.

Leonid Hurwicz, 2007. **ERIC MILLER/REUTERS/LANDOV**

Hurwicz (pronounced HER-which) was the older of two sons born to Polish-Jewish parents who came from Congress Poland, a part of Poland then within the Russian Empire. Displaced after World War I, his parents left Poland and settled in Moscow; in 1919, fearing Bolshevik persecution, they moved back to what is now independent Poland to live in Warsaw. Originally intent on becoming a lawyer like his father, Hurwicz entered Warsaw University to study law, earning an LLM in 1938. During his second year of law school, Hurwicz took some obligatory economics classes and became interested in the subject. His father, sensing his son's shifting interests, suggested that Hurwicz pursue an advanced degree at the London School of Economics, which he entered in 1938.

After a year at the London School of Economics, where he studied under the noted Hungarian economist Nicholas Kaldor, Hurwicz was forced to leave England when his visa was not renewed. He moved to Geneva, Switzerland, where he enrolled as a part-time student at the Graduate Institute of International Studies, attending seminars taught by the famous economist Ludwig von Mises. Hurwicz arrived in Switzerland in August 1939, less than a week before Germany invaded Poland and World War II began. Hurwicz's family again fled from Warsaw to Russia, where his father was immediately arrested and interned in a labor camp while his mother and brother were sent to a different camp in Siberia. Alone and destitute, Hurwicz made arrangements to immigrate to the United States; he would live in Chicago with cousins who were funding his travel. After several false starts that put him in Spain and Portugal, the twenty-three-year-old Hurwicz arrived at his cousins' home in 1940, sleeping on their couch and auditing classes that von Mises was teaching at the University of Chicago. Later that year the rest of his family joined him.

Once Hurwicz was in the United States, he began to enjoy some success. In 1940 he landed a one-semester research assistantship with Paul Samuelson (winner of the 1970 Nobel Memorial Prize in Economic Science) at the Massachusetts Institute of Technology. After Hurwicz completed his assignment in Massachusetts, he returned to Chicago and in 1941 became a research assistant to the noted economist Oskar Lange at the University of Chicago. As his contribution to the war effort, Hurwicz taught electronics to the U.S. Army Signal Corps members at the Illinois Institute of Technology; from 1942 to 1944 he was a member of the faculty of the Institute of Meteorology at the University of Chicago and taught prospective army and navy inductees statistics, mathematics, and physics needed to analyze weather data. Hurwicz hired a teaching assistant, Evelyn Jensen, who was at the time an undergraduate in economics at the university. They were married in 1944 and went on to have four children. From January 1942 until June 1946 Hurwicz was also a research associate at the Cowles

Commission for Research in Economics, which was then at the University of Chicago but is now the Cowles Foundation at Yale University. His advisers at the commission were Tjalling Koopmans (who became a Nobel laureate in 1975) and Jacob Marschak, an expert in econometrics.

Hurwicz left the commission for short-term academic assignments at Iowa State College and the University of Illinois. He returned to the commission on a full-time basis in October 1950 while also becoming a visiting professor at the University of Chicago. A lifelong liberal who served as a Eugene McCarthy delegate to the 1968 Democratic Party Convention, Hurwicz did not get on with the libertarian Milton Friedman (who won the Nobel Memorial Prize in Economic Science in 1976), then the driving force at Cowles. Hurwicz left Chicago in 1951 to become a professor of economics and mathematics in the School of Business Administration at the University of Minnesota. He stayed at Minnesota for the remainder of his academic career except for several visiting appointments of varying duration at a number of institutions, including Tokyo University, Renmin University of China, University of Michigan, Harvard University, and Northwestern University.

Although he never earned a formal degree in economics, Hurwicz became well versed in the subject as well as skilled in mathematics by virtue of his academic experiences. Using his keen intellect and vivid imagination, he combined his knowledge of economics and mathematics with the emerging field of game theory in a series of pathbreaking articles and papers published from the mid-1950s through the early 1970s. In that body of work, he formulated the concepts of mechanism design and incentive compatibility as alternative means for solving vexing economic problems in ways that synchronized individual gains and societal benefits rather than trading off one against the other. In an interview with Professor George Feiwel, Hurwicz characterized his research as an interest "in studying how one can construct efficient mechanisms that have the decentralization features similar to a market economy but that do not necessarily resemble a market."

Broadly defined, a mechanism is a process, a procedure, or an institution designed to resolve a situation in a way that is mutually acceptable to all participants, while incentive compatibility is a mechanism characteristic that induces those affected to be truthful and forthcoming in their dealings with one another so that the outcome is perceived as just and impartial. Consider the parent who has to divide a single candy bar between two squabbling children. The wise parent will have the first child cut the candy bar and let the second child have first choice of the pieces. The first child is incentivized to cut the candy bar as equitably as possible since the second child chooses first and will almost certainly pick the larger piece. The outcome is mutually satisfactory to all—parent and children—inherently fair, fully participative, and readily acceptable. These are precisely the

characteristics that help the mechanism of a competitive market garner such affection among mainstream economists. To generate the desired outcome, however, the unfettered interactions of buyers and sellers must transpire in an economic environment that includes a large number of buyers and sellers, none of whom has the power to influence market price. In addition the actions of any particular market participant must be independent of what others do, and all market players must have similar information about market conditions. Of course, this environment is not always satisfied in real-world markets. When such a situation arises, there is a tendency to rely on government regulations to create a fair and socially desirable market. Regulations, however, only incentivize market participants to corrupt the regulators in hopes of creating a market outcome that promotes self-interest at the expense of societal well-being. With the use of extremely abstract mathematics, Hurwicz was able to fashion incredibly practical mechanisms to produce beneficial outcomes even when market conditions are less than ideal.

The process of salary arbitration in Major League Baseball owes its existence to Hurwicz's work. Not all major leaguers are eligible for arbitration, but those who are find a mechanism that incentivizes truthfulness and expedites settlements. Under existing rules, the team owner and the player must submit to arbitration regarding what each considers to be a fair salary, and the arbiter is required to select one of those claims to settle the dispute. This procedure forces each market participant to be honest in assessing the worth of the player. If the owner grossly underestimates the player's value or the player grossly overestimates his worth, the arbiter will most likely pick the salary figure of the other participant. The mechanism used in Major League Baseball encourages each participant to be honest and realistic, resulting in initial salary estimates that are close in value, in contrast to a traditional negotiation process in which the parties begin far apart and argue to a resolution that neither one finds just. Other mechanisms that reflect Hurwicz's insights include the open-auction approach the government uses in allocating cell phone bandwidth and the "cap-and-trade" system that uses financial incentives to assign costs to polluting as a way to control emissions.

Hurwicz continued researching and publishing well into his eighties, and though nominated for the Nobel Memorial Prize in Economic Science, he did not receive the award until the last year of his life. He was the oldest person ever to win a Nobel in any field at the time. Too frail to travel to Sweden to accept the prize in person, Hurwicz received his award from the Swedish ambassador to the United States on 10 December 2007 in a public ceremony held in Ted Mann Concert Hall on the campus of the University of Minnesota. Hurwicz died of renal failure the following June.

The academic world has long valued Hurwicz's contributions, but the potential of mechanism design and incentive compatibility for practical purposes has yet to be realized fully. Hurwicz received many awards prior to the Nobel Prize. In 1947 he was elected a fellow of the Econometric Society, becoming its president in 1969. He was inducted into the American Academy of Arts and Sciences in 1965 and into the National Academy of Sciences in 1974. In 1977 he became a distinguished fellow of the American Economic Association, and in 1990 President George H. W. Bush presented him with the National Medal of Science in Behavioral and Social Science. Hurwicz served on the United Nations Economic Commission in 1948, the U.S. National Research Council in 1954, and the National Science Foundation Commission on Weather Modification in 1964. He became a distinguished scholar of the California Institute of Technology in 1984.

An extensive interview in which Hurwicz discusses his contributions to modern economics (as well as those of Kenneth Arrow) is in George R. Feiwel, *Arrow and the Ascent of Modern Economics* (1987). For a nontechnical description of mechanism design, see the Introduction in Hurwicz and Stanley Reiter, *Designing Economic Mechanisms* (2006). A tribute by Eric S. Maskin, one of the Nobel cowinners with Hurwicz, is in the *Guardian* (21 July 2008). Obituaries are in the *New York Times* (26 June 2008), the *Telegraph* (27 June 2008), and the *Independent* (17 July 2008).

James Cicarelli

HUTTON, Betty (*b.* 26 February 1921 in Battle Creek, Michigan; *d.* 11 March 2007 in Palm Springs, California), actress who was the original "blonde bombshell" of Hollywood musicals of the 1940s and 1950s.

Born Elizabeth June Thornburg, Hutton was the second daughter of Percy Thornburg, a railroad brakeman, and Mabel (Lum) Thornburg, then a homemaker. When Hutton was two, her father abandoned the family for another woman; her mother suffered from acute alcoholism, a disease that later plagued Hutton. To earn money, her mother opened an illicit speakeasy in their basement, and Hutton began her career at age three, singing to customers on the lap of her mother, who played the piano. "We'd operate until the cops got wise," Hutton told *Time* magazine in 1950. "Then they'd move in and close us down, and we'd move somewhere else." In 1929 the family finally settled in Detroit, where Hutton's mother worked on an automobile assembly line. Hutton and her sister also danced and sang on street corners for coins after public school.

In 1936, at age fifteen, Hutton quit ninth grade and sang in a local nightclub, claiming that she was eighteen.

Betty Hutton. © JOHN SPRINGER COLLECTION/CORBIS

There she was discovered by the bandleader Vincent Lopez, who hired her as his lead singer and changed her last name to Hutton. One night in 1938 she thought she was about to be fired and got drunk; while performing, she turned somersaults, hopped on musicians' laps, tore up sheet music, mugged at the audience while singing, thereby creating her energetic and madcap persona.

In 1940 George "Buddy" De Sylva, a Broadway and Hollywood producer and songwriter, cast Hutton in his musical *Two for the Show*, to rave reviews. The next year Hutton was the second lead to the legendary Ethel Merman in *Panama Hattie*; on opening night Merman demanded and got Hutton's only song. (Hutton's revenge would come eight years later when she played Annie Oakley in the film version of the role that Merman originated onstage.) When De Sylva became an executive producer at Paramount Pictures, Hutton went with him to Hollywood, California.

From 1941 to 1952, when she left in a contract dispute, Hutton was Paramount's leading lady in musicals, comedies, and biopics. Like Paramount's star Bing Crosby, Hutton also had hit songs—mostly novelty tunes—on the pop charts, including one song in 1941 ("Not Mine"). A musicians' union strike in 1942 prevented recording for the next two years, but Hutton eventually had six top-ten songs during her tenure at Paramount. Also in 1942 Hutton was one of the first singers to sign with the newly formed Capitol Records; later, in a management dispute, she signed with Radio Corporation of America Victor. Most of her signature songs were composed by Frank Loesser.

For Hutton's first film, *The Fleet's In* (1941), her ballad "Not Mine," by Johnny Mercer and Victor Schertzinger, was a dreamy croon that was deliberately undercut by mopes. Loesser's novelty songs for Hutton often included tongue-twisting lyrics that she sang with alternating belts and whispers. Hutton's manically energetic and vividly humorous antics earned her the nickname the "blonde bombshell" during World War II, a term later applied to such actresses as Marilyn Monroe for their sex appeal. Other nicknames for Hutton included the "blonde blitz" and the "funny firecracker."

Hutton's fourth film was Preston Sturges's screwball comedy *The Miracle of Morgan's Creek* (1944). She played a woman who could not recall the father of her sextuplets; the film, which somehow passed the censors, was a satire on American motherhood and small-town values. One scene was particularly challenging, and it included five minutes of rapid-fire dialogue, which Hutton later said that she memorized "like a song, learning the lines rhythmically." The film was a great success, as was *The Incendiary Blonde* (1945), a biopic about the Prohibition-era nightclub queen Mary "Texas" Guinan. During filming Hutton cracked three ribs while being tossed by acrobats. Also in 1945 Hutton starred in *The Stork Club*, playing a hat-check girl who suddenly becomes wealthy when a patron leaves her money in his will. The rags-to-riches story, parallel to her own biography, memorably featured Hutton singing Hoaglund "Hoagy" Carmichael's "Doctor, Lawyer, Indian Chief."

In 1945 Hutton supplanted Dorothy Lamour as Paramount's number-one female box-office attraction. On 2 September 1945 she married the camera manufacturer Ted Briskin; they had two daughters. Briskin did not approve of Hutton's film career, and the rocky marriage ended in divorce in 1951.

De Sylva continued to cast Hutton in rags-to-riches films, including *Cross My Heart* (1946) and *The Perils of Pauline* (1947). The latter film is a biopic of Pearl White, who began as a garment sweatshop worker and became the queen of silent-film serials. *Red, Hot and Blue* (1949) featured Loesser's songs, including a manically comic four-minute number summarizing William Shakespeare's *Hamlet*.

Hutton's greatest success was *Annie Get Your Gun* (1950), which had begun as Irving Berlin's 1946 Broadway hit starring Merman. Paramount lent Hutton to Metro-Goldwyn-Mayer (MGM) after Judy Garland had a nervous breakdown during the filming of the Technicolor musical. The story line is a fictionalized embroidery of the romance between the Wild West sharpshooters Annie Oakley and

Frank Butler (played by Howard Keel). The musical allowed Hutton to be robustly earthy with the song "Doin' What Comes Naturally," breathlessly tender with "They Say It's Wonderful," laughably ornery with "Anything You Can Do, I Can Do Better" and "You Can't Get a Man with a Gun," and electrically heartfelt with "There's No Business Like Show Business." Hutton was nominated for a Golden Globe Award, and she won the Most Popular Female Star Award from *Photoplay* magazine.

As a part of Paramount's loan agreement with MGM, Hutton was paired with MGM's Fred Astaire in Paramount's *Let's Dance* (1950). Loesser's songs were tailored to Hutton's comic antics but not to Astaire's sophistication, resulting in clashing styles of the two leads. That year Hutton made $260,000. The studio had difficulty finding vehicles for her. Billy Wilder's *Sunset Boulevard* (1950) wickedly alluded to the studio's problem in a dialogue sequence in which a screenwriter pitches a baseball story to a Paramount producer who counters, saying, "Of course, we're always looking for a Betty Hutton. Do you see it as a Betty Hutton?"

In 1952 Hutton received top billing over Charlton Heston, Jimmy Stewart, and Lamour in Cecil B. DeMille's circus spectacular *The Greatest Show on Earth*, which won the Academy Award for Best Picture that year. Hutton played a lovelorn trapeze artist, fighting to star in the center ring by doing increasingly daring high-wire acts; Hutton performed most of her character's stunts. Also that year she starred in *Somebody Loves Me*, a biopic of the singer Blossom Seeley. Vocal surgery prevented Hutton from displaying her usual over-the-top style, and her singing was warm and mellow. Dance sequences were choreographed by Charles O'Curran, whom she married on 18 March 1952; they had no children.

Hutton insisted that her next film be directed by her husband, but Paramount refused. She then made a career-destroying decision by walking out on her contract, and no other Hollywood studio would hire her until 1957, when she appeared in the unsuccessful United Artists release *Spring Reunion*, her last film.

Hutton successfully appeared in one-woman concerts in Europe, New York City, and Las Vegas, Nevada. In 1954 she starred in the original and live television musical *Satins and Spurs*, about a rodeo performer. During rehearsals she fired her husband as choreographer, and they divorced in 1955. Soon after, on 8 March 1955, she married the recording company executive Alan Livingston, who had been her lover for over a year. They had no children and divorced in 1960. Two months later, on 24 December 1960, Hutton married the jazz trumpeter Pete Candoli; they had one daughter but divorced in 1967. "My husbands all fell in love with Betty Hutton," Hutton once said. "None of them fell in love with me."

For the 1959–1960 television season, Hutton starred in the comedy series *The Betty Hutton Show*, and she replaced Carol Burnett in 1965 in the Broadway musical *Fade Out, Fade In*. In 1980 Hutton appeared briefly on Broadway again in a revival of *Annie*. During the 1960s alcohol and pills took over her life. "Uppers, downers, inners, outers—I took everything I could get my hands on," she later remarked. A falling out with her children and a suicide attempt eventually resulted in a nervous breakdown. In 1967 she filed for bankruptcy and entered a rehab program run by the Reverend Peter Maguire, a Portsmouth, Rhode Island, priest who employed Hutton as a cook and a housekeeper in his parish's rectory and whom Hutton credited for saving her life.

Maguire helped Hutton enroll in Salve Regina University in Newport, Rhode Island, where she earned a BA in 1978 and an MFA in 1982. She then taught acting and singing, and she worked as a charity counselor and a casino hostess. When Maguire died in 1999, Hutton moved to Palm Springs, where she retired. She died of complications from colon cancer at the age of eighty-six. She is buried in Desert Memorial Park in Cathedral City, California.

Hutton brought a singular and vivacious vitality to Hollywood musicals and comedies during the 1940s and 1950s. She is best remembered as the blonde bombshell who starred in *Annie Get Your Gun*.

A biography of Hutton is Eldon Griffiths, *The Hutton Story* (1998). Tony Barbon directed the documentary film *Private Screenings: Betty Hutton* (2000). Also see *Time* magazine's cover story of 24 Apr. 1950. An obituary is in the *New York Times* (14 Mar. 2007).

Patrick S. Smith

HYDE, Henry John (*b.* 18 April 1924 in Chicago, Illinois; *d.* 29 November 2007 in Chicago, Illinois), sixteen-term U.S. representative; author of the Hyde Amendment banning federal funding for abortions; House Judiciary Committee chairman during the impeachment proceedings against President Bill Clinton; chairman of the House International Relations Committee.

Hyde grew up in Depression-era Chicago. His parents—Monica (Kelly) Hyde and Henry Clay Hyde, a coin collector for a local telephone company—lost their Evanston home during the economic upheaval, and the family resorted to living above a bar on Howard Street in Chicago. Hyde had one brother and one sister. He attended local parochial schools—Margaret Mary Catholic Elementary School in West Rogers Park and Saint George High

Henry J. Hyde. **AP IMAGES**

School in Evanston—performing janitorial work to pay the tuition that his family could not afford. Growing to a stout six feet, three inches, Hyde became an All-Chicago basketball center, earning a scholarship to attend Georgetown University in Washington, D.C., in 1942. Hyde left college in 1944 and was commissioned as an ensign in the U.S. Navy where he was assigned to the Seventh Fleet and saw combat during the invasion of the Philippine Islands. He was discharged as a lieutenant junior grade in 1946, though he remained in the naval reserve until he retired as a commander in 1968. Hyde returned to Georgetown, earning a BS in 1947. Two years later he graduated with a JD from the Loyola University School of Law in Chicago. Hyde was admitted to the Illinois State Bar in January 1950, and he subsequently entered private law practice as a trial lawyer. He married Jeanne Simpson on 8 November 1947, and they raised four children: Henry, Jr., Robert, Anthony, and Laura. Jeanne Simpson Hyde passed away in 1992.

Hyde was raised as a Democrat in an era when that party began to dominate Chicago politics. What he perceived as the excesses of the New Deal and Franklin Roosevelt's underestimation of the "communist threat" turned him toward the Republican Party. "I thought the party of the working man was being taken over by a well-off academic elite that thought 'left was beautiful,'" he once recalled. He explained, in part, that he "became concerned during [World War II] about the far Left and the inordinate influence it was having with the Roosevelt administration," particularly First Lady Eleanor Roosevelt, whose columns he edited as a part-time proofreader for the *Chicago Sun-Times*. He cast his ballot for Dwight D. Eisenhower in 1952 and, beginning in 1958, served as a delegate to Illinois state Republican conventions.

In 1962 local Republican leaders persuaded Hyde to make his first run for elective office against popular Democrat Roman Pucinski for a U.S. House seat representing the northwestern suburbs of Chicago. Far from being a sacrificial lamb, he went on the attack deriding Pucinski's campaign as a "street-corner medicine show." On election day Hyde garnered 47 percent of the vote and came within 10,000 votes of beating the two-term incumbent. In 1966 Hyde won election to the Illinois house of representatives, where he developed a reputation as a skilled debater, opposing the Equal Rights Amendment, supporting the death penalty, and proposing stricter penalties for drug use. In 1971 and 1972 he served as majority leader.

In 1974 Hyde set his sights on national office when Republican Representative Harold R. Collier, a nine-term U.S. House veteran from the western suburbs of Chicago, announced his retirement. The district encompassed portions of Cook and Du Page counties, O'Hare International Airport, and towns such as Berwyn, Cicero, Park Ridge, and Oak Park. He defeated his Democratic opponent Edward V. Hanrahan and in his subsequent fifteen reelection campaigns, large majorities (between 61 and 75 percent) returned Hyde to the House in a district that drew in middle-class whites and remained conservative as reapportionment pushed the bulk of the district westward and enveloped towns such as Wheaton.

Hyde was one of just a handful of Republican freshmen who took the oath of office for the Ninety-fourth Congress in early January 1975. He received assignments on the Judiciary Committee and the Banking, Currency, and Housing Committee. In the Ninety-seventh Congress (1981–1983), he left Banking for a seat on the Foreign Affairs Committee (later renamed International Relations Committee from 1995 to 2007). Hyde also served for six years on the House Permanent Select Committee on Intelligence, rising to the post of ranking minority member in the 100th and 101st Congresses. He played a prominent part in the televised Iran-Contra hearings in 1987, defending the Ronald Reagan administration and Oliver North from his seat on the House Select Committee to Investigate Covert Arms Transactions with Iran.

In 1976 Hyde became the congressional hero of the right-to-life movement when he attached a last-minute rider to the annual appropriations bill for the Department of Labor and the Department of Health, Education, and Welfare, prohibiting the expenditure of federal Medicaid funds for abortions. On 24 June 1976 Hyde offered a simple one-sentence amendment on the floor: "None of the funds appropriated under this Act shall be used to pay for abortions or to promote or encourage abortions." Coming just three years after the controversial *Roe v. Wade* 410 U.S. 113 (1973) Supreme Court decision legalizing abortion, Hyde saw his measure as a litmus test for congressional sentiment on abortion. Hyde emerged as his party's most articulate spokesman on the issue, declaring, "we who seek to protect that most defenseless and innocent of human lives—the unborn—seek to inhibit the use of Federal funds to pay for and thus encourage abortion as an answer to the human and compelling problem of an unwanted child."

The Hyde Amendment, as it subsequently became known, passed the House with the full appropriation measure. Though the Senate rejected the provision, a conference committee of House and Senate negotiators agreed to it—except in cases where women sought abortions because of rape, incest, or when the mother's life was endangered by carrying the fetus for the full term. Lower federal courts blocked implementation of the Hyde Amendment, but the Supreme Court in *Harris v. McRae* 448 U.S. 297 (1980) upheld its constitutionality by a 5–4 margin, arguing that the federal government was not constitutionally obligated to fund either elective or medically required abortions. Over the next several decades, pro-choice advocates assailed the amendment as denying equal protection under the law because it disproportionately affected poor and minority women who relied on Medicaid funds for medical procedures. In subsequent Congresses, Hyde sought to prohibit federal financing of abortions for armed service members, and he was a leading proponent of a bill that banned partial birth abortions in 2003.

Hyde was a stalwart conservative, whose voting record mirrored the politics of his constituency and received high ratings from conservative voting analysis organizations. Yet he demonstrated an intellectual flexibility that made him stand out. When presented with evidence that challenged his position, Hyde reconsidered—as he did in 1982 when Congress reauthorized the Voting Rights Act of 1965. Hyde objected strenuously to "preclearance" provisions that required some states to seek U.S. Department of Justice approval prior to enacting any changes in their electoral processes. Testimony by witnesses before his committee, detailing insidious tactics used to discourage black voters, persuaded him to support preclearance. "You're being dishonest if you don't change your mind after hearing the facts," Hyde noted.

In January 1995, when Republicans organized the House for the first time in forty years, Hyde became chairman of the influential, historically partisan, Judiciary Committee. The central battle on Judiciary during Hyde's tenure came with consideration of articles of impeachment against President Bill Clinton. When reports about the president's relationship with Monica Lewinsky, a young White House intern, became public in early 1998, Hyde initially remarked that Clinton would not be impeached for a "peccadillo." But over time, he became convinced that the president's actions necessitated an impeachment inquiry—believing that Clinton had perjured himself and obstructed justice in making evasive responses under oath in a private lawsuit against the president by Paula Jones and then in grand jury testimony that was part of Independent Counsel Kenneth Starr's investigation.

Hyde emerged as the public face of the impeachment process, as Republicans sought to minimize the polarizing role of Speaker Newt Gingrich of Georgia and other party leaders with acerbic styles. Operating with unusual latitude, Hyde invoked the bipartisan work of the 1974 Watergate proceedings. But his committee's actions failed to foster comity between Republicans and Democrats. On party line votes the panel released to the public the uncensored Starr Report, with its unseemly details about the president's affair, and blocked a proposal by a senior Democrat to limit the length of the inquiry. Late in the process, Hyde and Republicans on his committee voted down a Democratic motion to censure Clinton for "reprehensible behavior." Hyde warned Republican leaders against such a course because it "fails to meet constitutional muster."

Hyde's personal life was scrutinized amid the impeachment saga. On 16 September 1998 the online magazine *Salon* revealed that Hyde had a lengthy extramarital affair with a young married mother in the 1960s. He admitted the affair but dismissed it as a "youthful indiscretion.... Dredged up now . . . to intimidate me, and it won't work."

On 11–12 December 1998 Hyde's Judiciary Committee approved four articles of impeachment on a party line vote. On 18 December 1998 Hyde addressed the full House from the well: "Sexual misconduct and adultery are private acts. . . . The matter before the House is a question of lying under oath. This is a public act. . . . This is called perjury." The following day, largely along party line votes, the House passed two articles of impeachment: alleging that President Clinton had suborned perjury in his 17 August testimony before the Starr grand jury; and that he had obstructed justice. Two articles—alleging that the president had perjured himself in testimony related to the Jones lawsuit and that he had abused his power—failed to pass.

Public opinion remained decidedly in the president's favor even as the House moved toward impeachment. By the time Hyde, acting as the lead manager of a team of House trial prosecutors, began to lay out the monthlong case for impeachment before the U.S. Senate on 7 January 1999, acquittal had become a foregone conclusion. On 12 February the Senate acquitted Clinton on both articles—falling well short of the two-thirds vote required to impeach the president.

In 2001, bowing to Republican Conference rules limiting chairmen to three terms leading a panel, Hyde traded his Judiciary gavel for that of the International Relations Committee. It traditionally was a far less contentious panel—with moderates from both parties gravitating toward it. Hyde sought to rehabilitate his image as a bipartisan deal maker, which, even he acknowledged, was damaged by the impeachment episode. With the ranking Democrat on the panel, Tom Lantos of California, Hyde led the effort to expand international relief for the HIV/AIDS epidemic. He steered to passage the U.S. Leadership against HIV/AIDS, Tuberculosis, and Malaria Act of 2003, which provided $15 billion to fight the disease over five years.

In 2005 Hyde announced his retirement from the House at the conclusion of the 109th Congress in early 2007, due to his declining health. He remarried in November 2006 to his longtime chief of staff, Judy Wolverton. In November 2007 President George W. Bush awarded him the Presidential Medal of Freedom for his work championing a "culture of life." Hyde was so weakened by open-heart surgery earlier that year, his son accepted the award on his behalf. Weeks later, Hyde passed away from complications of his surgery. He is interred at Assumption Cemetery in Wheaton, Illinois.

Temperamentally, Hyde was never completely in sync with the cohort of Republican revolutionaries of the 1990s. A cigar-wielding raconteur, he was a throwback to an earlier time when behind-the-scenes dealing and networking advanced legislative goals. A generation older than Gingrich and his acolytes, he did not embrace the incendiary tactics they employed to recapture the majority. He refused a higher rung on the leadership ladder, describing it once as "onerous" and seeming to prefer independence to toeing the party line. Upon his death, colleagues recalled that Hyde's service, in the words of Lantos, "transcended partisan political considerations and was reminiscent of an era of congressional collegiality." Belying that reputation, however, Hyde's House career pivoted on his unbending positions on polarizing political issues. His inability to navigate the partisan shoals—particularly during the Clinton impeachment—revealed as much about fissures in the American electorate as they did the record of his leadership style.

★

Hyde's manuscript collection is in process at the Center for Public Service, Loyola University Chicago, http://www.luc.edu/ic/publicservice.shtml. The center was scheduled to open to the public in 2009. Hyde published several books of essays, including, *For Every Idle Silence* (1985), ruminations on the nexus of religion and politics. The Hyde Amendments—and how the debate over them played out in the federal courts—are treated in David J. Garrow, *Liberty and Sexuality: The Right to Privacy and the Making of Roe v.*

Wade (1994). Aspects of Hyde's role in the impeachment saga are covered in several books—the most thorough of which remain journalistic accounts. Peter Baker, *The Breach: Inside the Impeachment Trial of William Jefferson Clinton* (2000), is a standard account of the impeachment episode. Steve Gillon, *The Pact* (2008), portrays Hyde as a tenacious advocate for impeachment. Bob Woodward, *Shadow* (1999), depicts Hyde as a partisan who did not waver in his public stance on impeachment and its necessity, but who privately sought a way to defuse the process by instigating for a censure plan. Nicol Rae and Colton Campbell, *Impeaching Clinton: Partisan Strife on Capitol Hill* (2004), a political science analysis, addresses committee composition, partisanship, and Hyde's role in the impeachment process. Obituaries are in the *Chicago Tribune, New York Times,* and *Washington Post* (all 30 Nov. 2007).

Matthew A. Wasniewski

I

INGRAM, Vernon Martin (*b.* 19 May 1924 in Breslau, Germany (now Wrocław, Poland); *d.* 17 August 2006 in Boston, Massachusetts), scientist and professor who has been called the father of molecular medicine.

Growing up in Breslau, Ingram demonstrated an aptitude for the sciences and an inquisitive nature. For instance, when the Nazis outlawed radio receivers, the young Ingram built his own so that he could listen as world events unfolded. In 1938, when Ingram was fourteen, his family fled to England, leaving Breslau, which was quickly becoming a Nazi stronghold. Once in England, Ingram took a job at a chemical factory, where he helped to make drugs for the war effort. In 1941 Ingram enrolled in Birkbeck College at the University of London. Birkbeck College, which offered classes on weekends, was the only college that remained open in London during World War II; even after the library suffered a direct hit from German bombers, teaching continued. In 1945 Ingram received a BS, completing a program that focused on math, zoology, and chemistry. Following graduation, Ingram immediately entered Birkbeck's physical organic chemistry doctoral program, earning a PhD in 1949. In 1950 Ingram married Margaret Young; although the marriage would end in divorce, the couple had two children, a son and a daughter.

After completing his PhD, Ingram traveled to the United States, where he served two yearlong postdoctoral research appointments. The first was at the Rockefeller Institute in New York City, where he studied protein preparation and crystallization. His second appointment was at Yale University in New Haven, Connecticut, where Ingram focused on peptide chemistry. By 1952 Ingram was homesick for England and began applying for

positions there. After sending thirty-two letters of interest, Ingram finally landed a position as a protein biochemist at the Medical Research Council's Research Unit for the Study of the Molecular Structure of Biological Systems in Cambridge University's Cavendish Laboratory. By September 1952 Ingram was back in England.

During his six years working in the Cavendish Laboratory, 1952 to 1958, Ingram completed his best-known and most significant work. Colleagues introduced Ingram to Frederick Sanger's research on the complete amino acid sequence of insulin; the research proved that proteins have definite structures. Ingram was encouraged to apply Sanger's method to hemoglobin. Hemoglobin, however, is much larger than insulin, so to apply Sanger's method, Ingram first had to devise a way to get the hemoglobin into a manageable size. Ingram used trypsin, a substance found in the digestive system, to break down the hemoglobin proteins, developing the first two-dimensional protein analysis. Ingram then used both electrophoresis, a process that uses an electric field to move particles through a medium, and paper chromatography, a technique that separates mixtures, to produce a unique pattern, or "fingerprint," for hemoglobin. Using this method, Ingram was able to show that the hemoglobin from a healthy individual and the hemoglobin from someone with sickle-cell anemia differ in only one of the twenty-six peptides. The discovery that one single gene abnormality could cause such complex illnesses stunned the scientific and medical communities.

In 1958 Ingram moved his family from Cambridge, England, to Cambridge, Massachusetts, when he accepted a position in the Biochemistry Department of the Massachusetts Institute of Technology (MIT). The position was supposed to last only a year, but Ingram liked MIT so much that he decided to stay. Ingram continued his research on hemoglobin, collaborating with the Columbia University professor Paul Marks. While at MIT, Ingram discovered that he had a passion for teaching as well. In addition to teaching at MIT, he taught part time at Columbia, and from 1985 to 2001 he and his second wife, Elizabeth Hendee, whom he married in 1984, served as housemasters of Ashdown House, a graduate dorm at MIT.

During the 1980s Ingram's focus shifted to neuroscience research inspired by a conversation with Hendee, a physician's assistant, about Down syndrome and Alzheimer's disease. By the time people with Down syndrome reach forty, they have typically developed Alzheimer's disease. Ingram and his colleagues used this connection to examine the development of Alzheimer's and to create possible treatments. In Alzheimer's the peptide beta-amyloid is overproduced. When overproduced, the peptide folds over itself and collects, forming plaque. Ingram's experiments involved developing a peptide that attached to beta-amyloid to prevent it from folding and creating compounds that destroy the plaque.

In August 2006 Ingram fell in the hallway of his lab at MIT, severely breaking his arm. After surgery he suffered a pulmonary embolism and died a short time later at the age of eighty-two.

Ingram's impact is evident through his numerous awards, including his election to the National Academy of Sciences in 2002, and his numerous publications. His discoveries helped prove the direct relationship between the linear peptide chain and the linear DNA chain. Also Ingram's work with proteins would have implications for other diseases, such as prion disease, or transmissible spongiform encephalopathies, which affects the brain and nervous system, and Huntington's disease, a neurological disease characterized by dramatic body movements and the deterioration of mental abilities. Ingram also had a tremendous impact on his students. Throughout his career he continually gave credit to his colleagues and his students.

★

Brief biographies of Ingram are in *A Dictionary of Scientists* (1999) and the *Proceedings of the National Academy of Sciences* 101, no. 40 (5 Oct. 2004): 14323–14325. Obituaries are in the *Boston Globe* (10 Sept. 2006) and the *Lancet* (30 Sept. 2006).

Lisa A. Ennis

IVINS, Bruce Edwards (*b.* 22 April 1946 in Lebanon, Ohio; *d.* 29 July 2008 in Frederick, Maryland), a microbiologist with the U.S. Army Medical Research Institute of Infectious Diseases, Ivins aided federal investigation of the 2001 mail anthrax attacks; then, accused of having committed them, he killed himself.

Bruce E. Ivins, 2003. REUTERS/USAMRIID/LANDOV

Ivins was the youngest of three sons of Thomas Randall Ivins and Mary Johnson Knight Ivins. His father, a pharmacist who had attended Princeton University, owned a drug store; his mother stayed at home but did volunteer service. The family attended Lebanon Presbyterian Church.

In school in Lebanon, Ivins became interested in science, winning state science fair prizes and being inducted into the National Honor Society. He also joined the pep club and current events club, sang in the school choir, starred in the senior class play, and ran on the track and cross-country teams. Still, former high school classmates said he did not mesh socially and never dated. Even four decades later, a classmate said Ivins "was bitter about being excluded."

During the fall of 1964, Ivins started at the University of Cincinnati. There he received a BS with honors in 1968, an MS in microbiology in 1971, and a PhD in microbiology in 1976, after which he went to a postdoctoral fellowship at the University of North Carolina (UNC). Ivins began his professional research in Legionnaires' disease and cholera, but in 1979 began work with anthrax, a disease of animals and people caused by a spore-forming bacteria that can be used as a biological weapon.

Around 1975 Bruce and Diane Ivins married, staying together until his death; approximately ten years after their marriage, they adopted twins, a boy and a girl. Ivins worked as a civilian microbiologist at the U.S. Army Medical Research Institute of Infectious Diseases (USAMRIID) in Fort Detrick, Maryland, starting in 1987, finally serving as a senior defense researcher. There he worked over a decade to develop a vaccine against mixed strains of anthrax.

Reports of Ivins's personality are contradictory. One colleague said Ivins was "intense about his work, but a popular guy." When colleagues left USAMRIID, Ivins wrote and performed humorous songs about them. Others felt he was "odd" and "thin-skinned." Neighbors were more unanimously positive: Ivins volunteered at the American Red Cross of Frederick County; his whole family attended Saint John the Evangelist Roman Catholic Church, at which he played keyboard for an informal mass.

The bioterrorist act of delivering anthrax in letters through the postal system killed five people and infected seventeen more, including Senate Majority Leader Tom Daschle (Democrat, South Dakota), postal workers, and members of the print and television news media. The letters were mailed from 18 September to 9 October 2001, not long after the 11 September attacks on the World Trade Center and the Pentagon; the handwritten letters all read, "Death to America, Death to Israel, Allah is great." The Federal Bureau of Investigation (FBI) investigation, called Amerithrax, soon determined that a disgruntled American scientist, rather than al-Qaeda, sent the letters. Ivins participated in early investigations concerning the mailed anthrax.

At a ceremony at the Pentagon on 14 March 2003, Ivins received the Decoration for Exceptional Civilian Service, the highest honor for nonmilitary employees of the U.S. Department of Defense. The Amerithrax investigation was then focused on Steven Hatfill, another scientist at Fort Detrick. However, on 27 June 2008 Hatfill won a $5.8 million civil settlement against the U.S. Department of Justice for harassing him.

Nancy Haigwood, who met Ivins when they were both at UNC, felt stalked by him and sent his name to the FBI as a suspect in 2002, and the U.S. Army said that in 2001 Ivins had tested for anthrax outside his secure lab and not reported the spill. In 2006 when Edward Montooth took over the FBI investigation, attention focused primarily on Ivins; in May 2007 Ivins hired the lawyer Paul F. Kemp to represent him.

By November 2007 Ivins was the FBI's leading suspect in the anthrax attacks. Ivins spent the spring of 2008 in an inpatient clinic for alcoholism after what may have been a suicide attempt. Jean C. Duley, a social worker who counseled him there, said Ivins planned to kill his coworkers and acquired a restraining order against him in July 2008. On 10 July police searched his house and found guns and a bullet-proof vest. Ivins voluntarily entered the Sheppard Pratt psychiatric hospital in Baltimore that day; he was released on 24 July.

After an overdose of prescription Tylenol with codeine, Ivins was found unconscious in his home on 27 July 2008. He was taken to Frederick Memorial Hospital, where he died two days later. Using laboratory blood tests, the state medical examiner determined the cause of death without an autopsy. Ivins was cremated and his ashes scattered, per his request.

Evidence of Ivins's guilt is evocative but far from conclusive. Some suspected motives involve his work with anthrax: Perhaps he wanted the vaccine he developed to be widely used as a result of the attacks. A document from the Department of Justice states that at the time of the attacks, Ivins was "sole custodian" of a flask of the same strains of anthrax; however, his attorney, Kemp, stated that over 100 people had access to the flask. Also uncertain is whether Ivins had the ability to create the spores in the letters, which had been made into a dry powder to spread easily. One source stated that Ivins worked with liquid anthrax and could not have aerosolized his specimens. However, others stated that Ivins definitely could have produced the aerosolized spores by himself.

Doubtless, Ivins, who had a history of alcoholism and depression, exhibited odd behavior, including a strange obsession with Kappa Kappa Gamma sorority and deep mood changes. These could indicate a mind capable of sending the anthrax letters or simply one unable to endure the ordeal of investigation by the FBI.

Also beyond doubt is the protracted and clumsy nature of the Amerithrax investigation. The FBI and the Department of Justice did learn much that can help in any future incidents of bioterrorism but may have missed the window in which guilt for this one could be determined.

★

On Ivins's death, news stories rather than obituaries were published. Joby Warrick, Marilyn W. Thompson, and Nelson Hernandez, "A Scientist's Quiet Life Took a Darker Turn," *Washington Post* (2 Aug. 2008), draws together many facts concerning Ivins. Eric Lipton, "In Anthrax Scientist's E-Mail, Hints of Delusions," *New York Times* (6 Aug. 2008), focuses on Ivins's mental problems in mid- to late 2000. Scott Shane, "Portrait Emerges of Anthrax Suspect's Troubled Life," *New York Times* (3 Jan. 2009), gives many details about Ivins's life and the investigation. A short formal obituary (in addition to a news story) is in the *Frederick News-Post* (1 Aug. 2008).

Bernadette Lynn Bosky

IVINS, Molly Tyler (*b.* 30 August 1944 in Monterey, California; *d.* 31 January 2007 in Austin, Texas), newspaper columnist and best-selling political humorist who became one of the nation's best-known liberal commentators.

Molly Ivins, 1996. **CBS/LANDOV**

master's degree from the Columbia University Graduate School of Journalism in New York. The turning point of her political awareness was the civil rights movement of the 1960s. "I believe all Southern liberals come from the same starting point—race. Once you figure out they are lying to you about race, you start to question everything," Ivins said.

Her first newspaper job was at the *Houston Chronicle*, where her contemporaries remember her for persuading editors to write a long story on local poverty, then considered a daring topic. That was followed by a stint at the *Minneapolis Star-Tribune*, where she was that city's first female police reporter. She returned to her Texas home in 1970 to work at the liberal weekly *Texas Observer*. It was there she began covering the Texas Legislature, which she called "the finest free entertainment in Texas. Better than the zoo. Better than the circus." When the Citizen Conference on State Legislatures ranked the Texas body thirty-eighth out of the fifty states, Ivins's response was "My God! You mean there are twelve worse than this?" Her trademark humorous writing style and skewering wit proved to be a poor match with her next job at the *New York Times*, where she moved in 1976. During posts in New York City; Albany, New York; and Denver, she complained she found the *Times* "no fun," telling interviewers her editors changed such phrases as "squawked like a $2 fiddle" to "as an inexpensive instrument," and a man with "a beergut that belongs in the Smithsonian" to "a man with a protuberant abdomen." Finally, in 1980, when she described an annual New Mexico chicken slaughter as a "gang pluck," a phrase the paper did not print, the *Times* recalled her and assigned her to cover New York City Hall. She left the paper in 1982.

From there, Ivins moved to the *Dallas Times Herald*, where she developed a passionate following with a thrice-weekly column she wrote until the paper folded in 1991. She provoked controversy with an insult to a local politician, saying, "If his IQ slips any lower, we'll have to water him twice a day." The *Times Herald* erected billboards reading "Molly Ivins Can't Say That, Can She?" That became the title of her first book, a collection of her columns and essays published in 1991 by Random House, which remained on best-seller lists for a year. It also garnered critical praise, with Allen Lacy of the *New York Times Book Review* saying "she expresses her opinions firmly, with brio and a lot of irreverence." Ivins remained one of her newspaper's most popular columnists, with readers threatening to cancel subscriptions whenever she went on vacation, her former editor told *People* magazine. From there, her national profile grew with appearances on *60 Minutes* on CBS and *The MacNeil/Lehrer News-Hour* on PBS. Ivins went from Dallas to the *Fort Worth Star-Telegram*, where she worked until 2001. She became a nationally syndicated columnist with her column picked up by nearly 400 newspapers. During her career, she authored or coauthored ten books and was a three-time finalist

Ivins was born the middle of three children to James and Margot Milne Ivins. Jim Ivins was a naval officer who became a corporate attorney and executive and moved the family to an upper-middle-class suburban section of Houston. Margot was a "steel magnolia" type of southern woman, Ivins would later say. Her father was a staunch conservative, and family members told journalists they remembered frequent dinner-table debates between father and daughter. Her younger brother recalled that she earned the nickname "Mole" because she spent hours burrowing into books. Ivins enrolled at the Saint John's School in Houston, where she was the editor of the student newspaper. She was a six-footer who played basketball in defiance of Texas standards that revered cheerleading over athleticism. "I should confess that I've always been more of an observer than a participant in Texas Womanhood: the spirit was willing but I was . . . ineligible on grounds of size early," she wrote in the introduction to her first book. "You can't be six feet tall and cute, both." She graduated with an AB from Smith College in Massachusetts in 1966, following her mother and grandmother. From Smith she went to Paris, where she studied for a year at the Institute of Political Science, taking cooking lessons while not in class. She then obtained a for the Pulitzer Prize for commentary. She never married and had no children. Her final column, dated 11 January 2007, was devoted to criticism of President George W. Bush's plans to send more troops to Iraq. "Every single one of us needs to step outside and take some action to help stop this war. Raise hell," she wrote. Ivins died of breast cancer at her home in the Travis Heights neighborhood of South Austin and was cremated.

Though vilified by many conservatives and occasionally criticized for factual inaccuracies, Ivins gained respect from targets on both sides of the aisle. She frequently professed her love for politicians as a group and said none stayed angry at her for long. She sided with poor, middle-class, and marginalized people in her columns, jabbing at mostly Republican policies that tended to favor corporate interests and the wealthy. She saved some jabs for President Bill Clinton, too, calling his 1996 decisions to shrink federal welfare programs "welfare 'deform.'" While chronicling George W. Bush's rise through Texas politics in the 1990s, she coined the oft-repeated nickname "Shrub," referring to his status as offspring of his father, President George H. W. Bush. Of her own writing style, Ivins told *People* magazine: "Satire is traditionally the weapon of the powerless against the powerful. I only aim at the powerful." Though she often excoriated the second President Bush, he issued a fully sympathetic statement upon her death: "Molly Ivins was a Texas original.... I respected her convictions, her passionate belief in the power of words and her ability to turn a phrase." Among her legacies were support for the American Civil Liberties Union, to which she devoted her time and money, and support for the brand of independent journalism practiced by the *Texas Observer*, where she remained a board member and fund-raiser until her death.

Her final book, *Bill of Wrongs: The Executive Branch's Assault on America's Fundamental Rights*, coauthored with her frequent collaborator Lou Dubose and published posthumously in 2007 by Random House, was perhaps her most outraged. She set out to write the book as a "joyful tribute" to her heroes who fought for the Bill of Rights, she wrote in the book's introduction. But after the attacks of 11 September 2001, she wrote, she found more people were failing to stand up for American rights. Yet she maintained her sense of humor: "If there ever was a group that knew how to survive political reverses, your Texas liberals are the past masters. I do not discombobulate easily." It was a fitting cap to the career of a writer who came to be mentioned alongside Mark Twain, Ambrose Bierce, Will Rogers, and H. L. Mencken as masters of the art of satire.

Ivins's books include *Molly Ivins Can't Say That, Can She?* (1991); *Nothin' but Good Times Ahead* (1993); *You Got to Dance with Them What Brung You: Politics in the Clinton Years* (1998); and *Who Let the Dogs In? Incredible Political Animals I Have Known* (2004). Those she coauthored with Dubose include *Shrub: The Short but Happy Political Life of George W. Bush* (2000); *Bushwhacked: Life in George W. Bush's America* (2003); and *Bill of Wrongs: The Executive Branch's Assault on America's Fundamental Rights* (2007). For biographical information, see the Gale Group's *Newsmakers 1993*. For a comparison of Ivins to Mark Twain and other leading satirists, see David Rubien, "Molly Ivins," http://archive.salon.com/people/bc/2000/12/12/ivins/index.html (12 Dec. 2000). Obituaries are in the *Austin American-Statesman*, the *Fort Worth Star-Telegram*, and the *New York Times* (all 1 Feb. 2007).

Leigh Dyer

J

JACOBS, Jane (*b*. 4 May 1916 in Scranton, Pennsylvania; *d*. 25 April 2006 in Toronto, Ontario, Canada), community activist and independent thinker who, through her landmark 1961 book *The Death and Life of Great American Cities*, profoundly changed the way people think about cities and helped to redefine urban landscapes in North America, especially in New York City.

Jacobs was born Jane Isabel Butzner, the third of four children of John Decker Butzner, a physician, and Bess (Robison) Butzner, a schoolteacher and a nurse. Jacobs's progressive parents encouraged her to think independently. An avid reader, Jacobs started writing when she was young, publishing two poems in a local paper at age nine. School bored her, however, and she was known more for her pranks than for her academic achievements.

After graduating from Scranton Central High School in 1933, Jacobs decided not to go to college. Instead she took a stenography class, spent six months with an aunt in rural North Carolina, and then worked for a year at the *Scranton Tribune* as an unpaid assistant to the women's page editor. Scranton, suffering from the Great Depression and a declining coal industry, offered few job prospects. In 1935 Jacobs left her hometown for New York City, whose size and energy had impressed her during a childhood visit.

Jacobs joined her older sister, living in a sixth-floor walk-up apartment in Brooklyn Heights, near the Brooklyn Bridge. When not looking for employment, Jacobs explored the city's neighborhoods. Upon discovering Greenwich Village, which was not fashionable at the time, Jacobs was enraptured by its crooked streets and hodgepodge architecture of row houses, tenement buildings, shops, and warehouses.

The two sisters soon moved to Morton Street, in the southwestern area of the Village.

Over the next five years, Jacobs held various secretarial jobs and sold freelance articles to *Vogue* and other magazines. She wrote about the city's fur, flower, and diamond districts. From 1938 to 1940 she studied at the University Extension (now the School of General Studies) of Columbia University but was rejected by Barnard College because of her high school grades. Jacobs never completed her college degree. Regarding formal education with indifference if not disdain, she declined many honorary degrees later in her life.

In 1940 Jacobs began working at *Iron Age*, a trade publication for the metals industry, first as a secretary and then as an associate editor. In 1943 she obtained a job as a writer for the Office of War Information. From the end of World War II until 1952, Jacobs worked as a reporter and an editor for *Amerika*, a State Department propaganda publication distributed in the Soviet Union.

Jacobs met Robert Hyde Jacobs, Jr., an architect specializing in hospital design, in 1944. They were married two months later, on 27 May. Jacobs credited her husband as the strategist behind her community activism and as a source of encouragement for her writing.

In 1947 the couple bought a dilapidated three-story house at 555 Hudson Street, with a retail space on the ground level, and renovated the building. It was from this vantage point that Jacobs observed the "intricate sidewalk ballet"—the famous passage in *Death and Life* describing daily city life—raised the couple's two sons and one daughter, and wrote her groundbreaking book.

The 1950s were a challenging time for American cities. The middle class was fleeing cities for suburbs, leaving the poor and minorities in decaying urban enclaves. The typical

Jane Jacobs, 1962. AP IMAGES

conference at Harvard University in 1956. Her speech led to an article in a series about cities in the magazine *Fortune.* Published in 1958, "Downtown Is for People" criticizes, among other schemes, the plans to raze eighteen blocks in New York City on Manhattan's West Side in order to build Lincoln Center. This article in turn led to a grant from the Rockefeller Foundation. Jacobs took a leave of absence from *Architectural Forum* and wrote *The Death and Life of Great American Cities* (1961) over the next two years.

In *Death and Life,* Jacobs debunks the prevailing theories and practices in city planning at the time, declaring in the first sentence that "This book is an attack on current city planning and rebuilding." Her criticism spares no one, indicting in short order the English urban planner Ebenezer Howard's Garden City (where the city's poor are transplanted to self-supporting small towns, with industry nicely tucked away nearby) and the Swiss-born French architect Le Corbusier's Radiant City (in which residential towers are widely set apart in a parklike city crisscrossed by expressways). Jacobs charges that conventional city planners are not interested in how cities actually work. The first chapters of her book identify characteristics of a great city—sidewalks where activity continues throughout the day and where parents and merchants keep a watchful eye on each other and especially on children, parks and public buildings that are integrated into the neighborhood life, and a diversity of resources, structures, and functions. The book then describes the conditions that make these characteristics possible. Jacobs states that a city district must mix residential, leisure, and commercial uses so that its streets are constantly busy; it must have blocks short enough to encourage a varied flow of pedestrian traffic; it must have old buildings with rents low enough to foster new enterprises; and it must have high population densities.

Jacobs also describes the problems cities face, including "border vacuums"—deserted areas surrounding self-contained places, such as railroad tracks and civic centers—and a sudden influx of money that can lead to wholesale destructions of communities in the name of urban renewal. In this wide-ranging book, Jacobs also proposes a few solutions to urban problems: how slums can "unslum," or regenerate, themselves, how public housing can be replaced by subsidized private dwellings, and how community leaders can have an effective voice and fight city governments. A city, she concludes, presents complex and interconnected problems that must be examined and understood from the ground up.

The power of *Death and Life* comes from Jacob's astute observations, the conviction of her flowing prose, and her ability to persuade readers to see her point of view. Her ideas, which might seem commonsensical in retrospect, were controversial and radical in the early 1960s. Although others had objected to urban renewal policies, it was *Death and Life* that made people look closely at their

solution in dealing with these troubled areas was to bulldoze entire neighborhoods and rebuild, often with high-rise public housing projects. In 1952 Jacobs began working as an associate editor for *Architectural Forum,* an upscale trade magazine published by Time Inc. Two years later her editors sent her to report on a high-rise project in Philadelphia, Pennsylvania. Although her editors were in favor of this project, Jacobs noticed that the streets were empty and that the renewal plans actually made circumstances worse for the residents. Jacobs began talking to community leaders and visiting such places as East Harlem in New York City, where an influx of African Americans and Puerto Ricans was moving into deteriorating tenements. Robert Moses, a power broker who was responsible for massive public projects remaking New York City, wanted to demolish such neighborhoods. Jacobs became angry at what she observed.

In the Village, where a nine-block area southeast of Washington Square Park had been designated a slum and then torn down, Jacobs joined a hard-fought and ultimately successful grassroots effort to stop a roadway that Moses had wanted to build under the park. According to Jacobs, Moses screamed at a hearing, "There is nobody against this—nobody, nobody, nobody, but a bunch of, a bunch of mothers!"

Although she disliked public speaking, Jacobs agreed to her editors' request to speak at an urban design cities and that galvanized opposition to centralized city planning. In its transformative powers, *Death and Life* is often cited alongside two other books that successfully challenged the status quo of the era: Rachel Carson's *Silent Spring* (1962), about the environment, and Betty Friedan's *The Feminine Mystique* (1963), about women's role in society.

Jacobs's critics, on the other hand, called the book naive and simplistic, suggesting that her solutions, seen through the idealized prism of her favorite city neighborhoods, such as Greenwich Village and Boston's North End, were unworkable elsewhere. They also dismissed her as a "housewife" without academic credentials. Nevertheless, Jacobs's book helped set in motion a sea change in city planning. Within a few years New York City passed its landmarks preservation law (1965), and the U.S. Congress halted further construction of high-rise public housing (1968). In 1974 Congress discontinued urban renewal plans altogether.

After her book was published, Jacobs continued to fight city officials and developers on her home turf while giving her support and advice to those trying to save their neighborhoods elsewhere. In the early 1960s Jacobs led successful efforts to stop New York City from truncating the sidewalks on Hudson Street and from redeveloping the western side of the Village.

Jacobs's most difficult and longest battle, though, was against an old nemesis, Moses, who wanted to cut a wide swath through Manhattan to build a highway from the Holland Tunnel to the Williamsburg and Manhattan bridges. The Lower Manhattan Expressway would have displaced some 2,000 families and 800 small businesses and radically altered the neighborhoods of Hell's Hundred Acres (now SoHo), Little Italy, Chinatown, and the Lower East Side. From 1962 on, Jacobs and her supporters pressured politicians and staged demonstrations. Jacobs was arrested once, in 1968, for disrupting a hearing. She pleaded guilty to disorderly conduct and paid a fine, but in the end she won the battle. The expressway plan was finally abandoned in 1969.

Thanks to *Death and Life* and her activist work, Jacobs became a public figure, variously called "Queen Jane," "a prophet," and "a one-woman, runaway PTA meeting." Having left *Architectural Forum* in 1962, she started a second book, *The Economy of Cities* (1969), but needed six years to complete it. As the Vietnam War escalated in the 1960s, Jacobs also became active in the antiwar movement. The Jacobs family marched on the Pentagon in October 1967, when demonstrators clashed with soldiers. In 1968 the family immigrated from the United States to Canada, in part to shield their teenage sons from the military draft. The family settled in the Annex section of Toronto, near the University of Toronto, a neighborhood popular with American expatriates.

In many ways the Annex fit Jacobs's vision of an ideal urban neighborhood—mixed, multiethnic, and on a human scale—but she soon found that the problems that had beset New York City were now threatening Toronto. A highway approved in 1962, the Spadina Expressway, would cut through her new home. Her neighbors welcomed such a well-known figure in their fight against the expressway. The project was shelved in 1971.

Jacobs continued protesting against redevelopment plans in Toronto and continued to write. *Cities and the Wealth of Nations: Principles of Economic Life* (1984) argues that cities, not corporations or nations, are the fundamental drivers of economic growth. Using the same sweeping strokes with which she dismisses government-mandated city planning in her first book, Jacobs denounces tenets of modern economic thought, including the eighteenth-century philosopher Adam Smith's theories. Ever distrustful of big governments, Jacobs helped found Energy Probe in 1980 and advocated the privatization of public utilities.

Jacobs also wrote books on subjects other than cities and urban development. These include *The Question of Separatism: Quebec and the Struggle over Separation* (1980), which favors the French-speaking province's independence from Canada, and a children's book, *The Girl on the Hat* (1989). She edited a memoir by her grandaunt, *A School-teacher in Old Alaska: The Story of Hannah Breece* (1995). In *Systems of Survival: A Dialogue on the Moral Foundations of Commerce and Politics* (1992), which was a best seller in Canada, and *The Nature of Economies* (2000), fictional characters discuss the morals of work and the similarities between economies and ecosystems, respectively. (Jacobs told interviewers that since her childhood, she had discussed complex ideas in imaginary conversations with Thomas Jefferson, Benjamin Franklin, and the English historical novelist Alfred Duggan.) In her final book, *Dark Age Ahead* (2004), Jacobs sounds a pessimistic note about the future of North American civilization.

Jacobs died of a stroke at Toronto Western Hospital in 2006. The following year in the United States, the Rockefeller Foundation established the Jane Jacobs Medal, an annual prize to recognize work in improving the urban environment in New York City.

Jacobs, who became a Canadian citizen in 1974, was much admired in her adopted country. She was appointed an officer of the Order of Canada in 1996 (the year of Robert Jacobs's death). The following year a symposium called "Ideas That Matter" was held in Toronto to discuss her philosophies. That event grew to encompass a quarterly journal and an annual prize in Jacobs's name.

★

Jacobs's papers are collected at Boston College's John J. Burn Library. Alice Sparberg Alexiou, *Jane Jacobs: Urban Visionary* (2006), gives an overview of Jacobs's life and work. Timothy

Mennel, Jo Steffens, and Christopher Klemek, eds., *Block by Block: Jane Jacobs and the Future of New York* (2007), collects short essays about Jacobs by writers including Adam Gopnik and Tom Wolfe. Obituaries are in the *New York Times* (25 Apr. 2006) and the Toronto *Globe and Mail* (26 Apr. 2006).

Jeffrey H. Chen

JASTROW, Robert (*b.* 7 September 1925 in New York City; *d.* 8 February 2008 in Arlington, Virginia), physicist, astronomer, and author who served for twenty years as the head of the National Aeronautics and Space Administration's (NASA) Goddard Institute for Space Studies.

Jastrow was the son of Abraham Jastrow, a car salesman, and Marie (Grünfeld) Jastrow, who in her eighties published two memoirs of her experiences as a Jewish immigrant in New York in the early twentieth century. He had one sister. After graduating from Townsend Harris High School in Queens, New York, he earned his AB (1944), MA (1945), and PhD (1948) in theoretical physics from Columbia University. From 1948 to 1953 he held postdoctoral fellowships at the University of Leiden in the Netherlands; the Institute for Advanced Study in Princeton, New Jersey; and the Radiation Laboratory at the University of California, Berkeley. He then spent a year as an assistant professor of physics at Yale University. From 1954 to 1958 he was a consultant in nuclear physics at the Naval Research Laboratory in Washington, D.C. In 1958 he joined the recently formed NASA as the first head of its Theoretical Division, overseeing research in cosmology, astronomy, and planetary science.

At NASA Jastrow helped plan out the future of the space science program. In 1961 he founded and became head of the Goddard Institute for Space Studies, the primary research group of the Goddard Space Flight Center in Greenbelt, Maryland, and attracted top scientists to work at the institute in New York City. The Goddard Institute worked on projects such as the Pioneer, Voyager, and Galileo robotic probes that were launched into the solar system. Jastrow also oversaw other research in astrophysics and planetary science. Influenced by his NASA colleague Harold Urey, a Nobel laureate, Jastrow became a proponent of lunar exploration, arguing that understanding the moon was critical for identifying the origins of the earth and the other planets. Jastrow became the first chairman of NASA's Lunar Exploration Committee, a working group of academic and NASA scientists that exchanged ideas and evaluated and recommended experiments to be performed in space. In 1969 NASA asked Jastrow, working with five other scientists, to summarize the agency's massive studies of Moon rocks brought back by astronauts of the Apollo

mission. Early in his career Jastrow demonstrated a gift for explaining complex and sophisticated topics in science to the public, as for example in his 1967 book *Red Giants and White Dwarfs: The Evolution of Stars, Planets, and Life*. In 1967 he married and divorced Ruth Witenberg; he did not remarry.

During his two decades as the head of the Goddard Institute, Jastrow was an adjunct professor of astronomy at Columbia. From 1974 to 1992 he was an adjunct professor of earth sciences at Dartmouth College. In 1984 he became one of the founders of the George C. Marshall Institute, a group that takes stands on debated issues in science policy and examines how such policy affects the public. From 1992 to 2003 Jastrow was chairman of the Mount Wilson Institute, which runs the Mount Wilson Observatory in California. He was also a member of the board of governors of the National Space Society.

During the 1980s Jastrow was vocal in debates on ballistic missile defense. A supporter of President Ronald Reagan's Strategic Defense Initiative (also known as Star Wars), he explained his views in *How to Make Nuclear Weapons Obsolete* (1985). As an author and commentator on the space program, astronomy, earth science, and national security, Jastrow popularized science by hosting more than 100 television programs on Columbia Broadcasting System and also appeared on National Broadcasting Company programs such as the *Today* show. His articles appeared in many major newspapers and magazines as well as scholarly journals, including the *New York Times*, *Time*, *Reader's Digest*, *Foreign Affairs*, *Commentary*, the *Atlantic Monthly*, and *Scientific American*. He was noted for the clarity and immediacy of his writing, for example describing the fifty pounds of lunar rock and soil brought back by the *Apollo 11* astronauts as a "Rosetta Stone" to the history of the solar system.

Jastrow received many honors over the course of his career, including a Columbia University medal for excellence (1962), the Arthur S. Flemming Award for outstanding service to the U.S. government (1968), a NASA medal for exceptional scientific achievement (1968), and the Columbia University Graduate Faculties Alumni Award (1967).

Toward the end of his life Jastrow voiced skepticism about the human impacts on climate change. He argued that natural processes rather than human activity had led to global warming. Known for his embrace of hard work, Jastrow expected the same from the people who worked for him. He was considered a mentor by many former students, who kept in touch with him. He died at age eighty-two of complications of pneumonia.

Jastrow is remembered for his achievements in the fields of astronomy, physics, and cosmology, especially as a central figure in the U.S. lunar exploration program. A public intellectual, he was committed to bringing science to ordinary people. Through his best-selling books and television appearances, he connected with the public in ways that few scientists set out to master. He was also committed, especially in the later decades of his life, to protecting science from being politicized.

★

Among Jastrow's books are *Astronomy: Fundamentals and Frontiers* (1972), with Malcolm H. Thompson; *Until the Sun Dies* (1977); *God and the Astronomers* (1978); *The Enchanted Loom: Mind in the Universe* (1981); *Journey to the Stars: Space Exploration, Tomorrow and Beyond* (1989); and *Origins of Life in the Universe* (2008), with Michael Rampino. An undated interview with Jastrow appears at the website of the George C. Marshall Institute (http://www.marshall.org/). Obituaries are in the *New York Times* (12 Feb. 2008) and *Washington Post* (15 Feb. 2008).

Sheila Beck

JOHNSON, Claudia Alta Taylor ("Lady Bird")

(*b*. 22 December 1912 in Karnack, Texas; *d*. 11 July 2007 in Austin, Texas), first lady of the United States from 1963 to 1969, business entrepreneur, and environmentalist.

Johnson was the third child of Thomas Jefferson Taylor, a prosperous storekeeper, cotton grower, and landowner, and Minnie Lee (Pattillo) Johnson, the daughter of a wealthy Alabama family. The Taylors were the richest family in tiny Karnack (population 600), in East Texas near the Louisiana border, and lived in the town's largest structure, the two-story antebellum "Brick House." When Johnson was five her mother died of complications from a fall combined with a miscarriage. She and her brothers were cared for by her unmarried aunt, Effie Pattillo, who moved in with the Taylors. She had acquired the nickname "Lady Bird" when she was one year old after a family servant affectionately remarked that she was as "purty as a lady bird," the southwestern name for a ladybug. Over time her birth name, Claudia, all but disappeared as, despite her efforts to discourage its use, not only her family but all her friends and acquaintances called her Lady Bird. As an adult she was "Bird" to her husband and closest friends, "Mrs. Johnson" (the name she preferred) to her staff and business associates, and "Lady Bird" to the press and the nation at large.

Although well-cared for and enjoying the privileges of her family's wealth, Johnson was often left to herself and turned to her mother's books for companionship. Shy and wary of groups, she preferred long, solitary walks in the countryside, and when she was old enough she spent afternoons canoeing by herself or horseback riding on her father's lands, activities that led to her deep and lasting

Claudia ("Lady Bird") Johnson, 1962. HULTON ARCHIVE/ GETTY IMAGES

love of nature. She graduated third in her class from high school in Marshall, the county seat; her father felt she was too young for college and sent her instead to Saint Mary's Episcopal School for Girls, a junior college in Dallas. She then entered the University of Texas at Austin in 1930, earning a BA in history with honors in June 1933 and a second bachelor's, in journalism, also with honors, in 1934. Her postgraduate goal was to get far away from Karnack and find a new life.

That summer a mutual friend in Austin introduced her to Lyndon Baines Johnson (LBJ), then twenty-six. A former schoolteacher and now the executive secretary to the Texas congressman Richard Kleberg, Lyndon Johnson impressed her as "outspoken, straightforward, and determined." However, having just met him, she was wholly unprepared for his proposal of marriage the next afternoon, thinking at first he was joking. As she later said, "I knew I had met something remarkable, but I didn't quite know what." On 17 November 1934 they were married, and her husband took her from the backwater of Karnack to the nation's capital. The marriage produced two daughters and lasted until LBJ's death in 1973. In a partnership of opposites, Lady Bird remained somewhat timid but always gracious, whereas LBJ, as he came to be known by the public, was impulsive, demanding, and self-centered. Although he could be charming, he was also known for his sharp tongue and rough manner. Nonetheless, he was always the love of her life, and she of his. As one reporter wrote in a memoir: "In her realm, she had no peer; she knew it, he knew it, and so did everybody else."

LBJ's rise to power began in the spring of 1937, when Johnson used $10,000 of her inheritance to finance his successful run for Congress in a midterm election brought on by the death of the incumbent in Texas's Tenth District. He held the seat for ten years, then entered the Senate in 1949. During this time Johnson showed her business acumen, purchasing a nearly bankrupt Austin radio station, KTBC, in 1942. Using $21,000 of her inheritance and a $10,000 bank loan, Johnson, as a hands-on manager, turned a profit within six months and over the next two decades transformed her initial investment into the enormously profitable Texas Broadcasting Corporation, which controlled radio and television stations in eastern and central Texas.

As LBJ's political career developed, Johnson became increasingly self-confident in her role as a political wife. Overcoming her shyness, she spoke on his behalf in his campaigns for office and worked closely with him in organizing his congressional staffs. After LBJ volunteered for active naval duty in the Pacific following the Japanese attack on Pearl Harbor, Johnson was his surrogate, both in Washington and his home district, until President Franklin D. Roosevelt ordered all congressmen serving in the armed forces to return to the capital in July 1942. Following LBJ's heart attack in 1955, she assisted his Senate staff until he could return as majority leader.

In the 1950s the Johnsons branched out into real estate, purchasing grazing land and ranches in East Texas, and through an inheritance they acquired 3,600 acres of timberland in Alabama. Their showplace was the 438-acre Johnson Ranch on the banks of the Pedernales River near Stonewall, Texas, which they purchased from LBJ's aunt in 1951. Now a National Historic Park (a deeded gift from the Johnsons in 1972), the working ranch once served as the Texas White House.

When the Democratic presidential nominee John F. Kennedy selected LBJ as his running mate in 1960, Johnson campaigned energetically for her husband. He took office as vice president in 1961. Following Kennedy's assassination on 22 November 1963, LBJ became the thirty-sixth president. She campaigned for him again in his successful run for the presidency in 1964. Some of LBJ's biographers minimize Johnson's political role during his presidency by suggesting she was little more than the typical political wife, raising the children and serving as hostess for state dinners at the White House. However, in her time she was the most active first lady since Eleanor Roosevelt. As the president's partner and confidante, she worked quietly but forcefully on behalf of selected causes, setting an example for later first ladies.

In 1965 she traveled more than 1,600 miles through the South by train (the "Lady Bird Special") to gather support for the president's Great Society program after his signing of the Civil Rights Act of 1964 had angered many of the region's white voters. From 1963 to 1968 she served as honorary chairman of the Head Start Program, which was designed to prepare underprivileged children for school and which many people believe was the most successful of the Great Society programs. She took reporters on tours of poor neighborhoods and schools to publicize the administration's War on Poverty.

Her greatest influence, however, came in environmental legislation. Johnson created the First Lady's Committee for a More Beautiful Capital, which worked to clean up the city's slums and improve its parks, using both public and private funding. She urged Congress to spread this program across the nation. During the five years of LBJ's presidency, largely as a result of her lobbying behind the scenes, he signed more than 200 environmental laws, including the Wilderness Act of 1964 and the Wild and Scenic Rivers Program. Lady Bird also worked successfully to protect the California redwoods and to block dams in the Grand Canyon.

What she thought would be her greatest victory (what the Republicans initially dismissed as "Lady Bird's bill") was the Highway Beautification Act of 1965, designed to limit billboards along the nation's interstate highways. In the legislative battle that led to its passage, so many compromises were made on behalf of billboard companies that, even as he prepared to sign the measure, LBJ admitted to his wife that it was a failure and could be viewed only as a first step and not a solution. However, there were no second steps. At the time of Lady Bird's death there were more billboards—some 450,000 on major highways alone—than there were when the 1965 bill was signed into law.

When the Johnsons retired to their ranch and to a second home in Austin in 1969, the president having decided not to pursue another term, they were financially secure, in large part owing to Lady Bird's careful investing over the years. The foundation of their wealth was the Texas Broadcasting Corporation, which had developed from her 1942 radio station purchase. In 2003 she sold her 84 percent share in the corporation for $103 million.

In one of her first acts in retirement, Johnson established the Texas Highway Beautification Awards, and for the next two decades she presented personal checks to the winners. She took a leading role in beautifying a hiking and bike trail in Austin and in planning the Lyndon Baines Johnson Library and Museum in the same city. Following her husband's death from a heart attack on 22 January 1973, she continued to serve on a number of boards in Texas and Washington, including the University of Texas Board of Regents and the National Geographic Society. In

1982, on her seventieth birthday, she founded the National Wildflower Research Center (renamed the Lady Bird Johnson Wildflower Center in 1995) to encourage the propagation of native plants and wild flowers as an ecologically sound and low-cost way to beautify public and private spaces.

In 1970 Johnson published *A White House Diary*, a selection of entries from the diary she kept for five years. In 1988 she published *Wildflowers Across America*, written with with Carlton B. Lees. Among the many honors she received were the Medal of Freedom, presented by President Gerald Ford (1977), and the Congressional Gold Medal, presented by President Ronald Reagan (1988).

Johnson suffered strokes in 1993 and 2001, the second of which left her unable to speak, and she lost most of her eyesight to macular degeneration. She died of respiratory failure at her home in West Lake Hills, an Austin suburb. She is buried next to her husband in the small family cemetery beneath the live oak trees on the Johnson ranch in Stonewall.

At the time of her death, Johnson had become an American icon. She redefined the role of first lady and made her mark as one of the foremost environmentalists of the twentieth century. Her monuments are as varied as a grove named for her in the Redwoods National Forest, a park bearing her name on the banks of the Potomac River, and flower-bordered highways in Texas and a half-dozen other states. Her gift to the nation, the Lady Bird Johnson Wildflower Center in Austin, perpetuates her efforts to educate Americans about nature and to encourage the cultivation of native plants in their own backyards.

★

The Lady Bird Johnson Papers, including her correspondence and the unpublished pages of her diary, are in the Lyndon B. Johnson Library and Museum in Austin, Texas. Additional material concerning her years as first lady are in the "White House Social Files" in the Lyndon B. Johnson Papers and in the Library's Oral History Project. Legal papers and other documents related to the Taylor family and to Lady Bird Johnson's early life in East Texas and Alabama are in the Lewis L. Gould Papers at the LBJ Library. The only scholarly biographies are Lewis L. Gould, *Lady Bird Johnson and the Environment* (1988) and *Lady Bird Johnson: Our Environmental First Lady* (1999). See also Randall B. Woods, *LBJ: Architect of American Ambition* (2006) and *First Lady Lady Bird Johnson, 1912–2007: Memorial Tributes in the One Hundred Tenth Congress of the United States* (2008). Obituaries are in the *New York Times, Washington Post, Austin American-Statesman,* and *Dallas Morning News* (all 12 July 2007).

Allan L. Damon

JOHNSON, (Charles) Van Dell (*b.* 25 August 1916 in Providence, Rhode Island; *d.* 12 December 2008 in Nyack, New York), stage actor, movie star, and television performer, he became one of Hollywood's most important leading men of the 1940s, a romantic figure with a huge following of "bobby-soxers" but also a credible hero in several World War II pictures.

Johnson grew up in Providence, Rhode Island, under the strict care of his father, Charles Johnson, a plumber and later real estate salesman, who expected his son to pursue a conventional career. Home life was rather dreary for Johnson, whose mother, Loretta (Snyder) Johnson, an alcoholic, left the family when he was still a child. His reserved and rather dour Swedish father made it difficult for Johnson to share his feelings. The inhibited boy found an outlet in dramatic performances at Newport High School. Somewhat surprisingly his father tolerated his son's decision to move to New York City in pursuit of an acting career. Apparently, Charles believed that his son

Van Johnson, 1961. **DUFFY/GETTY IMAGES**

would eventually return home after realizing the futility of his ambition.

Johnson struggled to find his place in New York theater circles, but he did not choose the alternative—returning home in defeat. With some luck and a winning personality (he had a fresh, ingenuous look that led to his sobriquet, "the boy-next-door"), the hardworking and determined young man began to pick up jobs as a dancer-singer in acting troupes and Broadway revues such as *New Faces of 1936*.

By 1939 Johnson was in Hollywood taking a screen test for Warner Bros. But his sunny disposition seemed a mismatch with that studio's emphasis on tough-guy melodramas. When his contract was not renewed in the early 1940s, Johnson thought his Hollywood career was over. But then Lew Ayres, star of the popular Dr. Kildare film series, left for military service, and Johnson was picked as his replacement. Suddenly his strawberry blond hair and genial affect became an asset, and Metro-Goldwyn-Mayer (MGM) began a concerted effort to build him up as a major motion-picture star.

The early 1940s in Hollywood marked a great opportunity to create a new generation of stars, now in great demand because established stars such as Clark Gable and Jimmy Stewart were away at war. By 1943 Johnson was costarring with Irene Dunne and Spencer Tracy in *A Guy Named Joe*, playing a young pilot watched over by a guardian angel. This film introduced Johnson's signature style, his warm, open portrayal of all-American young men, sincere and reliable.

A devastating auto accident during the making of *A Guy Named Joe* nearly destroyed Johnson's career. He suffered significant head and facial injuries that left him badly scarred. Additionally, as a result of the accident, Johnson was disqualified from military service because he had to have a metal plate inserted in his head. Both of his costars refused to accept a replacement for Johnson, and the story of their loyalty to him as well as Johnson's gritty resolve to resume his career created such public sympathy and interest in him that he was propelled into several important films, especially *Thirty Seconds over Tokyo* (1944), the story of the Army Air Force's daring raid over Japan in April 1942 at a time when it was thought in both Japan and America that Japan was out of the reach of American bombs.

MGM alternated Johnson between serious roles in war pictures (*Battleground* in 1949 and *Men of the Fighting Lady* in 1954) with roles in lighthearted comedies in which he romanced the new leading ladies of the 1940s and 1950s, especially Esther Williams (*Easy to Wed* and *Easy to Love* in 1946 and 1953) and June Allyson (*Two Girls and a Sailor* and *Remains to Be Seen* in 1944 and 1953).

For Johnson, 1954 represented the end of his MGM period. Unlike many stars of his era, he never resented his studio's casting him in superficial and inferior roles. He remained grateful for the publicity department that had helped to engineer his achievement as one of the top box-office stars of the 1940s. But by the early 1950s, the Hollywood studio system was disintegrating as it confronted significant competition from television and a cadre of stars that had decided to become independent producers of their own work.

Johnson fit uneasily into this new terrain of freelance acting, regretting that as he aged he lost his appeal to young teenagers (the bobby-soxers of the 1940s). His audience had become somewhat disenchanted with Johnson when he married the actor Keenan Wynn's former wife, Eve. Johnson and the Wynns had been close friends, and the public presumed that Johnson had stolen Wynn's wife. In fact, the Wynns had been separated when Johnson proposed to Eve, and Keenan remained a lifelong friend of Johnson's. Eve Wynn had two sons from her marriage to Keenan Wynn; she and Johnson had a daughter in 1948.

Johnson's marriage, however, was not a happy one. While he initially welcomed his new wife's interest in managing his career, he ultimately chafed at her possessiveness, and she fretted over his reserved manner—perhaps a product of his troubled relationship with his father. Johnson gradually withdrew from his wife and stepchildren, having almost no contact with them after his divorce in 1968. At the same time, rumors of Johnson's homosexuality—never quite confirmed—added to the rather ambiguous nature of his private life.

Yet Johnson continued to perform well onstage and on-screen, achieving a comeback in 1985 in the Broadway hit *La Cage aux Folles* and in Woody Allen's acclaimed movie *The Purple Rose of Cairo*. Johnson had a lively and pleasant career appearing on the dinner theater circuit, where his fans of the 1940s came to see him and listen to his reminiscences about his heyday in Hollywood. He worked constantly in America and Europe when not living quietly by himself in Manhattan. He died, after having retired from screen work nearly fifteen years earlier, at Tappan Zee Manor, an assisted living residence in Nyack, New York, outside the city. He was cremated.

Besides his place in Hollywood history as one of the major stars of the 1940s, Johnson remains important for his creation of an American type: energetic, uncomplicated, and stalwart. He had an endearing quality that breaks through even in supporting roles—when he appears as the charming reporter in *Madame Curie* (1943) who is able to appeal to the austere scientist played by Greer Garson. Johnson is recognized for such unforgettable roles as the pilot Ted Lawson in *Thirty Seconds over Tokyo* and the mutineer Steve Maryk in *The Caine Mutiny* (1954), a complex role that Johnson believed had resurrected his career.

Ronald L. Davis, *Van Johnson: MGM's Golden Boy* (2001) is the only available full-length biography of Johnson. Scott Eyman, *Lion of Hollywood: The Life and Legend of Louis B. Mayer* (2005), places Johnson within an overview of Hollywood and its studios. Ned Wynn, *We Will Always Live in Beverly Hills: Growing Up Crazy in Hollywood* (1990), provides details of Johnson's personal life from the perspective of his stepson. Obituaries are in the *New York Times* (12 Dec. 2008) and *Los Angeles Times* (13 Dec. 2008).

Carl Rollyson

JONASSON, Olga (*b.* 12 August 1934 in Peoria, Illinois; *d.* 30 August 2006 in Chicago, Illinois), physician and educator who was a pioneer for women in surgery and who was the first female transplant surgeon.

Jonasson was the daughter of Olav Jonasson, a Lutheran minister, and Swea C. (Johnson) Jonasson, a nurse. When

Olga Jonasson. **ROBERTA DUPUIS-DEVLIN/UIC PHOTO SERVICES**

Jonasson was twelve, her family moved from Peoria to Chicago when her father accepted a position as pastor of Ebenezer Lutheran Church. Jonasson grew up watching her mother work in a local hospital and her father comfort the sick and the elderly. Deeply influenced by these experiences, Jonasson decided to pursue a medical career. At sixteen she graduated from North Park Academy. When her family moved to Connecticut, Jonasson stayed behind in Chicago and attended Northwestern University from 1951 to 1954. In 1954 she enrolled in the University of Illinois at Chicago and worked in a lab analyzing blood and urine samples. She finished her baccalaureate in 1956. After graduation she continued on to complete medical school, earning an MD at the University of Illinois College of Medicine in 1958. In medical school Jonasson became a member of Alpha Omega Alpha, the national medical honor society. She graduated with honors and began her internship at the University of Illinois.

During medical school and her internship, Jonasson decided that she wanted to be a surgeon. At the time, however, there were very few women surgeons, and to become a surgeon was very difficult, given the social views and mores of the late 1950s, when most people thought that women should remain at home while men worked. When Jonasson approached Dr. Warren Cole about entering a surgical residency, he thought the idea preposterous. Cole relented, however, and accepted Jonasson into the surgical residency program at the University of Illinois. Jonasson proved to be an exceptionally skilled and outspoken surgeon. By 1965 she was board certified. She was only the thirty-seventh woman to become a board certified surgeon among more than 14,000 male surgeons. After finishing her residency in 1964, Jonasson completed two fellowships. The first was studying immunohistochemistry at Walter Reed Hospital in Washington, D.C., and the second focused on transplantation immunobiology at Massachusetts General Hospital in Boston.

In 1966 Jonasson returned to Chicago, where she briefly served as a cardiovascular surgeon at Rush Presbyterian Hospital but resigned in 1967 to become a faculty member at the University of Illinois Hospital. It was during her tenure at the University of Illinois Hospital that Jonasson performed the first kidney transplant in Illinois and established the university's Division of Transplantation in 1968. Her reputation grew, and Jonasson became the first female member of the American College of Surgery Board of Regents in 1976; a year later she was named chief of surgery at Cook County Hospital, where she supervised 152 full-time and voluntary surgeons and 110 residents. In 1985 Jonasson chaired President Ronald W. Reagan's Task Force on Organ Transplantation, which stemmed from the National Organ Transplant Act (1984). The task force was charged with determining how to enact and enforce the act. The result was the nationwide Tissue Typing and

Histocompatibility Organization, which helps to match organ donors with possible recipients. Thus Jonasson was best known for her work with transplants, but her research interests also included the treatment of inguinal hernias in men and effectiveness of obesity surgery.

In 1987 Jonasson accepted the Robert M. Zollinger Chair of Surgery at Ohio State University. The position made her the first female to head a coeducational academic surgery department. Jonasson returned to Chicago in 1993 to take the position of director of education and surgical services for the American College of Surgeons. As an educator, Jonasson was known as a lively and rigorous instructor who often encouraged young doctors not to marry. As early as 1971 Jonasson was honored with the Outstanding Educator in America Award. She also began the annual Young Surgical Investigator Conference, a clinical trials methods course, a mentoring program for minority high school students, and a committee on women's issues. In recognition of her work with minorities, Jonasson was made an honorary member of the American College of Black Academic Surgeons. In 1988 Jonasson became an honorary member of the Royal College of Surgeons of England.

Jonasson was well known among her associates for her hospitality, her commitment to teaching, and her interest in community affairs. She often entertained large groups of friends, neighbors, and colleagues, at times hosting as many as sixty or seventy people for dinner. As a mentor to surgical students and residents, she held monthly meetings at her home for senior surgical residents. Dinner would be followed by a teaching and questioning session with an expert on a particular topic, to prepare residents for upcoming surgery exams. Jonasson regularly accompanied students and residents on teaching rounds at the University of Illinois Hospital and the West Side Veterans Administration Hospital. As an advocate for community causes, she helped to raise nearly $3 million to repair and restore the Church of the Epiphany in Chicago and volunteered hundreds of hours, working on interior projects at the church. Jonasson, who never married, died of T-cell lymphoma at Northwestern Memorial Hospital. She was seventy-two.

The impact of Jonasson's life is left not only in the lives of the patients she touched, her prolific volume of research, her students, her efforts to improve public health, and her role as a medical pioneer but also in the doors she opened for future women doctors, especially surgeons. As the first woman to be named to the American Surgical Association, the first woman to serve on the National Institutes of Health's Surgical Study Section, and a member of the American Board of Surgery, Jonasson achieved feats that are impressive for any person, male or female.

★

Jonasson's papers are housed at the University of Illinois at Chicago's University Library and include personal correspondence and photos. Tributes to Jonasson are in *Annals of Surgery* 244, no. 6 (Dec. 2006): 839–840 and the *American Journal of Transplantation* 7 (2007): 1882–1883. Obituaries are in the *Chicago Tribune* (12 Sept. 2006) and the *New York Times* (13 Sept. 2006).

Lisa A. Ennis

JORDAN, (William) Hamilton McWhorter (*b.* 21 September 1944 in Charlotte, North Carolina; *d.* 20 May 2008 in Atlanta, Georgia), political strategist and chief of staff to U.S. President Jimmy Carter.

The son of Adelaide (McWhorter) Jordan and Richard Lawton Jordan, he was born in Charlotte where his father was stationed during World War II. Jordan moved with his family to Albany, Georgia, his parents' hometown, not long after his birth. He was the middle child of three Jordan children, having an older brother, Lawton, and a younger sister, Helen.

According to his mother, a homemaker, Jordan got involved in school politics at a young age, either running for office himself or directing a campaign to get his cousin elected. His classmates at Albany High School voted Jordan as the graduating student "most likely to become governor."

Like most white Georgians of the mid-twentieth century, Jordan grew up in a segregated society and at least tacitly supported the status quo. His views on segregation changed dramatically after witnessing a December 1961 civil rights march in Albany that was led by the Reverend Martin Luther King, Jr. When city police surrounded the African-American demonstrators and herded them into a narrow alleyway, Jordan felt a deep sense of shame at seeing peaceful men, women, and children being treated like animals.

The summer after his graduation from high school, Jordan worked in the successful gubernatorial campaign of Carl E. Sanders. Considered a moderate on the issue of school integration, Sanders personally favored retention of the segregated school system in Georgia but felt that it was more important that Georgians avoid violence and obey the laws of the land.

Jordan enrolled at the University of Georgia in Athens and, true to form, was elected president of the freshman class. During the summer of 1966, he attended a luncheon at the Albany Elks Club and heard a speech by the gubernatorial hopeful Jimmy Carter, a fellow resident of southwest Georgia. Impressed by Carter's intelligence and moderate views on race, Jordan joined Carter's campaign staff and was disheartened when Carter came in third in the Democratic gubernatorial primary.

In 1967 Jordan graduated from the University of Georgia with a degree in political science. Although he had been rejected for military service because he had flat feet, he wanted to see firsthand what was going on in Vietnam, so he volunteered to work with a refugee resettlement organization in that Southeast Asian country. Ten months after his arrival in Vietnam, he was diagnosed with blackwater fever and had to return to the United States, but he left convinced that the war was a tragic mistake.

Back home in Georgia, Jordan struggled to recover from the debilitating illness. He was married to Nancy Konigsmark in 1970, but the marriage ended in divorce later that decade. When Carter decided to make another bid for the governor's seat in 1970, Jordan signed on as the candidate's campaign manager. This time Carter defeated Sanders in the Democratic primary and went on to top his Republican opponent in the general election. Jordan joined Carter's gubernatorial administration as executive secretary.

Jordan knew Carter could not be reelected as governor because of the state's one-term limit, so he began to secretly map out a plan that would culminate with Carter's election as president in 1976. In 1972 Jordan presented Carter with an eighty-page master plan that Jordan was convinced could put Carter in the White House if the strategy was followed to the letter. Against all odds, Jordan's plan propelled Carter into the national arena and won the South Georgia peanut farmer a 50 percent to 48 percent victory over the incumbent, Gerald Ford. Eugene McCarthy also ran that year as an independent candidate.

Carter put Jordan in charge of selecting and vetting candidates for the presidential staff. The end result was an administration top-heavy with Georgians, a situation that led to friction between Carter and many Democrats in Congress. Carter's "Georgia Mafia" rubbed the Washington establishment the wrong way, and Jordan found himself the target of criticism for his hard-partying ways. Jordan was a close adviser to Carter from the opening days of the administration, but it was not until the summer of 1979 that he was named White House chief of staff.

Carter's bid for reelection in 1980 failed, and Jordan returned to Georgia where he taught political science at Atlanta's Emory University during the 1981–1982 academic year and wrote *Crisis: The Last Year of the Carter Presidency*, a book chronicling the final year of Carter's term. In 1981 Jordan married the pediatric nurse Dorothy Henry, with whom he founded a summer camp for children with cancer in 1982. Years later the Jordans established Camp Kudzu—a summer camp for diabetic children—not long after discovering that their daughter, Kathleen, suffered from the disease.

Jordan was first diagnosed with cancer—non-Hodgkin's lymphoma—in 1985 and with the help of chemotherapy and radiation managed to survive multiple bouts with the disease—including melanoma and prostate cancer—over the next couple of decades. In 2000 he published *No Such Thing as a Bad Day*, a memoir in which he shared the story of his struggles with cancer. Six years later Jordan underwent surgery to drain a significant amount of fluid that had accumulated around his heart.

In 1986 Jordan made an unsuccessful bid to become Georgia's Democratic candidate for a U.S. Senate seat, losing to Wyche Fowler in the primary. From 1987 to 1990 Jordan served as chief executive of the Association of Tennis Players and campaigned tirelessly to give players a greater voice in the conduct of world competition. In 1992 he plunged back into the world of national politics when he signed on to help map campaign strategy for Ross Perot's third-party bid for the presidency.

Somewhat disillusioned by the partisan bickering that seemed to get in the way of any meaningful progress in Washington, Jordan joined with the former Carter aide Gerald Rafshoon and Doug Bailey, a former adviser to President Ford, to form Unity08, which hoped to put together a bipartisan team of presidential and vice presidential candidates to run in 2008.

On 20 May 2008 Jordan lost his battle with mesothelioma, a rare form of cancer. He died at his Atlanta home, surrounded by his family and friends. His body was cremated. He was survived by his wife, Dorothy; two sons, Hamilton, Jr., and Alexander; a daughter, Kathleen; a brother, R. Lawton Jordan, Jr.; and a sister, Helen Jordan Schroder.

Although Jordan's personal aspirations for higher office were frustrated, his management of Carter's 1976 presidential campaign was nothing short of brilliant. Jordan's road map to the presidency called upon Carter to write a book outlining his political philosophy, use his position as governor to cultivate ties with foreign leaders, and secure for himself a key role in the Democratic National Committee. Carter followed through on all of Jordan's suggestions and in November 1976 was elected president of the United States.

★

Hamilton Jordan, *Crisis: The Last Year of the Carter Presidency* (1982), offers behind-the-scenes insights into the Carter administration's efforts to free U.S. Embassy personnel held hostage in Tehran; Jordan, *No Such Thing as a Bad Day* (2000), chronicles Jordan's successful struggles against multiple bouts of cancer. Obituaries are in the *Atlanta Journal-Constitution* (20 May 2008) and the *New York Times* and *Washington Post* (both 21 May 2008).

Don Amerman

JORDAN, Winthrop Donaldson (*b.* 11 November 1931 in Worcester, Massachusetts; *d.* 23 February 2007 in Oxford, Mississippi), prize-winning American historian whose landmark work *White over Black* (1968) examines the origins of racial inequality and discrimination found in the attitudes of early European settlers in North America.

Jordan was the son of Henry Donaldson Jordan, a professor of history at Clark University, and Lucretia Mott (Churchill) Jordan, a descendant of the abolitionists James and Lucretia Mott. While he adhered to the family faith of Quakerism, Jordan was reluctant to follow in his father's career path as a historian. In 1953 Jordan graduated from Harvard University with an AB in social relations. Following graduation, Jordan considered a career in business, working as a management trainee for the Prudential Life Insurance Company.

Abandoning his interest in business, Jordan accepted a position teaching history in 1955 at Phillips Exeter Academy in Exeter, New Hampshire. Following a year at the school, Jordan entered graduate school to pursue his passion for colonial American history, earning an MA from Clark University in 1957 and a PhD from Brown University three years later.

In 1963 Jordan joined the history department at the University of California, Berkeley. In addition to his teaching duties, Jordan served as an associate dean for minority group affairs in the graduate school. In that capacity, Jordan was an advocate for student rights during the turbulent 1960s on the Berkeley campus. He was also a gifted, unassuming professor who listened to his students but demanded rigorous attention to primary sources.

His seminal work, *White over Black: American Attitudes toward the Negro, 1550–1812* (1968), received considerable critical acclaim and was selected for the National Book Award, Ralph Waldo Emerson Prize, Francis Parkman Prize, and Bancroft Prize. In this massive and eloquently written jargon-free study of some 650 pages, Jordan paid close attention to the role of sexuality in exposing the racist attitude of English settlers leading to the development of slavery in North America. In his review of the book for the *New York Times*, the historian C. Vann Woodward termed *White over Black* "a massive and learned work that stands as the most informed and impressive pronouncement on the subject yet made." Jordan was also one of the first professional historians to conclude that it was probable that Thomas Jefferson fathered children with his slave Sally Hemings, a claim now accepted by most scholars.

In 1982 Jordan left the Berkeley campus for the University of Mississippi. That same year he married native Mississippian Cora Miner Reilly. His earlier marriage to the poet Phyllis Henry, whom Jordan had wed during his undergraduate days at Harvard, produced three children but ended in divorce before Jordan's move to Mississippi. At the University of Mississippi, Jordan continued his fine teaching and scholarship. In addition to serving as F. A. P. Barnard Distinguished Professor and Professor of Afro American Studies, Jordan became in 1993 the first holder of the William F. Winter Professorship in History. In 1994 Jordan won a second Bancroft Prize for his book *Tumult and Silence at Second Creek: An Inquiry into a Civil War Slave Conspiracy* (1993).

In 2004 Jordan retired from the University of Mississippi, and two years later he was diagnosed with the neuromuscular disorder known as Lou Gehrig's disease, or ALS. He succumbed to the disease and a liver ailment at his home in Oxford. Two weeks before his death, Jordan was selected for the B. L. C. Wailes Award from the Mississippi Historical Society and was the first recipient of the award who was not a native of the state. In tribute to their mentor, Jordan's former graduate students produced a collection of essays titled *Affect and Power: Essays on Sex, Slavery, Race, and Religion in Appreciation of Winthrop D. Jordan* (2005).

Jordan's legacy as an American historian is evident in the distinguished scholars trained by the professor, while his *White over Black* remains essential reading for understanding the origins of racial discrimination against blacks in American history. *American Heritage* magazine rated *White over Black* as the second most important book on African-American history, second only to W. E. B. DuBois's *Souls of Black Folk* (1903).

For Jordan's scholarship and influence upon the historical profession, see *White over Black: American Attitudes toward the Negro, 1550–1812* (1968); *Tumult and Silence at Second Creek: An Inquiry into a Civil War Slave Conspiracy* (1993); David J. Libby, Paul Spickard, and Susan Ditto, eds., *Affect and Power: Essays on Sex, Slavery, Race, and Religion in Appreciation of Winthrop D. Jordan* (2005); and C. Vann Woodward, review of *White over Black*, the *New York Times* (31 Mar. 1968). Obituaries are in *American Historical Association Perspectives* (May 2007) and the *New York Times* (8 Mar. 2007).

Ron Briley

K

KANTROWITZ, Adrian (*b.* 4 October 1918 in New York City; *d.* 14 November 2008 in Ann Arbor, Michigan), preeminent cardiovascular surgeon noted for developing devices to prolong the lives of cardiac patients, including the implantable pacemaker, and for being the first to perform a human heart transplant in the United States.

Kantrowitz was the son of Bernard Kantrowitz, a general practitioner who ran a clinic in the Bronx, and Rose (Esserman) Kantrowitz, a costume designer for the Ziegfeld Follies. He had two brothers and a sister. At the age of three he expressed a desire to be a doctor, and he and his eldest brother, Arthur, who were both fascinated with the world of science, began their careers with experiments in their family kitchen. They once created an electrocardiograph from old radio parts, a prelude to their later groundbreaking collaboration.

Kantrowitz attended New York University, graduating with a degree in mathematics in 1940, and continued his studies at the Long Island College of Medicine, now part of the State University of New York (SUNY) Downstate Medical Center, receiving his MD in 1943 as part of an accelerated program in which doctors were trained to treat the troops during World War II. He developed an interest in neurosurgery while interning at the Brooklyn Jewish Hospital, publishing a 1944 paper in which he described having devised a new type of clamp to be used during brain surgery. He served for two years in the Army Medical Corps as a battalion surgeon and was discharged in 1946 with the rank of major. Upon his return, and as a result of a shortage of positions in neurosurgery, Kantrowitz decided to change his specialty to cardiovascular surgery. A year

later he became an assistant resident in surgery at Mount Sinai Hospital in Manhattan.

From 1948 to 1955 Kantrowitz held various surgical posts at Montefiore Hospital in the Bronx: assistant resident in surgery and pathology, cardiovascular research fellow (spending two years at the esteemed Case Western Reserve University Medical School in Cleveland, Ohio, where he studied cardiovascular physiology with Carl John Wiggers), and chief resident in surgery. On 25 November 1948 Kantrowitz married Jean Rosensaft, an administrator in the surgical research laboratories at Maimonides Medical Center in Brooklyn, New York. They had two daughters and a son, all of whom became doctors. On 16 October 1951, at the New York Academy of Medicine, Kantrowitz was credited with screening the world's first medical research film taken inside the living heart of a dog.

In 1952 Kantrowitz became an instructor of surgery at New York Medical College, remaining there until 1955, when he was hired as director of cardiovascular surgery at Maimonides Medical Center, where many of his breakthroughs would take place. With his colleagues at Maimonides, Kantrowitz developed the subspecialty of cardiothoracic surgery and became the director of that type of surgery as well. He was simultaneously employed as assistant professor and later associate professor of surgery at SUNY Downstate.

With Alan Lerrick, Kantrowitz coinvented a plastic heart valve in 1954 that would serve as an auxiliary pump, and in 1958 he developed an electronically controlled heart-lung machine. In 1959 he created a diaphragm booster heart that functioned as a second heart for a dog, relieving the natural heart of some of its work. In 1961–1962, in collaboration with General Electric,

Kantrowitz invented an implantable pacemaker, a device that has been used to prolong the lives of millions of people. In 1964, with Tetsuzo Akutsu, he devised a left ventricular assist device (LVAD), first used in humans in 1972 and often labeled his most significant invention. From 1964 to 1970 Kantrowitz held the position of professor of surgery at SUNY Downstate.

Kantrowitz and his brother Arthur, who had become a distinguished physicist, collaborated with their colleagues to devise a more advanced form of the artificial heart that existed at that time. On 4 February 1966 Kantrowitz carried out the world's second implantation of an auxiliary heart and performed another on 18 May 1966. Neither patient survived for very long, so he and his team decided to explore other avenues of research. On 29 June 1966 Kantrowitz had the opportunity to become the first surgeon to perform a human-to-human heart transplant in the world, but he was prevented from doing so by two elder doctors at Maimonides who noted that the donor child had not yet been declared brain-dead. Dr. Christiaan Barnard performed the landmark surgery on 3 December 1967 in South Africa. Only three days later, on 6 December 1967, Kantrowitz performed the second heart transplant in the world and the first in the United States, which was also the first pediatric heart transplant in the world. Although Barnard's patient died after two weeks and Kantrowitz's after six and a half hours, their groundbreaking surgeries paved the way for what would become routine transplants. Also in 1967 Kantrowitz invented the intra-aortic balloon pump, an instrument that reduced strain on the heart and functioned according to Kantrowitz's theory of "counterpulsation," deflating each time the heart pumped blood and inflating upon each relaxation of the heart.

In 1970 Kantrowitz left his post as director of surgical research and director of surgery and surgical services at Maimonides. He and his entire team relocated to Sinai Hospital (now known as Sinai-Grace Hospital) in Detroit, where he acted as both attending surgeon and chairman of the department of surgery. That same year he was appointed professor of surgery at Wayne State University School of Medicine, a position he held until 1993. From 1975 to 1983 he was chairman of the department of cardiovascular surgery, and from 1978 to 1993 he was director of surgical research.

In 1983 Kantrowitz and his wife founded LVAD Technology, Inc., a Detroit-based research and development company specializing in cardiovascular devices. Until Kantrowitz's death they remained active in the design of new instruments for use in cardiac patients. Among his other inventions were a mini-radio transmitter that would permit paralyzed patients to empty their bladders and other devices that would allow paralyzed patients to move their limbs through electronic triggering of muscles. In 2001 the American Society for Artificial Internal Organs presented Kantrowitz with its Lifetime Achievement Award.

Kantrowitz died of complications from congestive heart failure at the age of ninety at the University of Michigan Medical Center in Ann Arbor. He is buried in New Montefiore Cemetery in Farmingdale, New York.

Kantrowitz will be remembered as a driven and passionate professional, known to work six eighteen-hour days a week. When not working he enjoyed flying planes, sailing, and riding motorcycles. Described as an "engaging maverick," he was a brilliant, persistent, and inventive scholar, teacher, and surgeon. The more than twenty medical devices he developed have prolonged the lives of millions of patients, with his work having had a profound impact on cardiovascular and other areas of medicine.

★

Kantrowitz's papers are at the U.S. National Library of Medicine in Bethesda, Maryland. The competition to perform the first heart transplant is described in Donald R. McRae, *Every Second Counts: The Race to Transplant the First Human Heart* (2006). Obituaries are in the *New York Times* (19 Nov. 2008) and the *Washington Post* and *Los Angeles Times* (both 20 Nov. 2008).

Adriana C. Tomasino

KELLER, George Matthew (*b.* 3 December 1923 in Kansas City, Missouri; *d.* 17 October 2008 in Palo Alto, California), chairman of Standard Oil Company of California, architect of the merger that created Chevron, and noted San Francisco Bay Area philanthropist.

Keller was the son of George Matthew Keller and Edna Louise (Mathews) Keller. After his mother's death while he was in the first grade, he moved to Chicago to live with his aunt, who raised him and encouraged his fascination with science. Keller traced his interest in chemistry to the 1933 Chicago World's Fair, where he was entranced by the DuPont exhibit. After graduating first in his class from Fenwick High School in Oak Park, a suburb of Chicago, he enrolled at the Massachusetts Institute of Technology (MIT). In his sophomore year, following the nation's entry into World War II, he joined the U.S. Army, serving as an Army Air Forces meteorologist stationed in Labrador. He returned to MIT after the war to continue his studies. On 27 December 1946 he married Adelaide McCague; they had three sons. In 1948 he graduated with a BS in chemical engineering and then accepted a position with Standard Oil of California in San Francisco. The couple settled in San Mateo, California.

George M. Keller, 1984. ©ROGER RESSMEYER/CORBIS

Keller began his career designing refineries and moved up the corporate ladder quickly. In 1967 he was named assistant vice president of foreign operations, and the following year was tapped as assistant to the president of the company. Keller then moved into the executive suite, first as vice president in July 1969, then as director in August 1970, vice chairman in February 1974, and finally chairman of the board in 1981.

As chairman of Standard Oil, Keller distinguished himself through his willingness to take risks. In his first board meeting as chairman in 1982, he bid $600 million for offshore oil leases that led to the discovery of highly lucrative reserves off the coast of California. Concern for domestic oil production was especially high during the late 1970s and early 1980s, as war in the Middle East led the oil-producing Arab nations to punish pro-Israel countries by limiting their oil supplies. The United States experienced skyrocketing gas prices accompanied by rationing. There were calls for domestic production of oil to reduce dependency on foreign supplies; Keller's gamble on unproven offshore oil leases paid off in many ways. Standard Oil increased its reserves, and therefore its revenues, considerably, and the production in California meant reduced costs involved with transporting oil; offshore crude could be shipped to refineries by tanker rather than by multimillion-dollar pipelines.

However, the oil rush of the late 1970s and early 1980s resulted in a glut of oil reserves as Americans drove less and the price of oil declined. Oil companies scrambled to survive; many had invested in new exploration infrastructure during the boom years, only to find that they could no longer support these expenses. One of the companies in this situation was Gulf Oil. Founded in 1901, Gulf ran into trouble as gas prices plummeted in the 1980s. Eventually, T. Boone Pickens, the noted Texas oilman and corporate raider, targeted Gulf for takeover. Pickens and a group of investors purchased close to 9 percent of Gulf Oil, and then initiated a proxy battle, in which a minority group of owners in a corporation attempt to take control of the company. Gulf executives did not want to give in to Pickens, and contacted several other oil firms for possible offers to buy the company. Keller was one of the oil executives that Gulf chairman James E. Lee contacted.

Standard Oil analysts looked over Gulf's financial statements. Based on their assessment of the company's worth, Keller offered $80 a share for the firm, for a total purchase price of $13 billion, in what amounted to the largest takeover in corporate history at that time. On 5 March 1984 the Gulf board voted to sell the firm to Standard Oil. Chevron, the new name of the joined companies, engaged in oil and gas production, refining, and transportation as well as geothermal energy exploration and petrochemical manufacturing.

In the 1980s Keller's attitude regarding business relations with the Soviet-backed nation of Angola raised eyebrows. The Gulf–Standard Oil merger brought Gulf's existing activities in the sub-Saharan nation to Chevron's balance sheet. Tensions were high between the Soviet Union and the United States, and Angola was a Marxist state heavily dependent on Soviet military and financial support. Keller's decision to continue Chevron's activities in Angola provoked public protests, including the distribution of "Wanted" posters featuring Keller's picture.

Keller retired on 31 December 1988 and turned to philanthropic activity. As a practicing Catholic, Keller supported a number of causes that aligned with his beliefs. He was a trustee of the Notre Dame de Namur University in Belmont, an independent Catholic master's university in Northern California, and served as chairman of the board from 1982 to 1994. He served on the board of trustees for his alma mater, MIT, from 1981 to 1986, and was the chair emeritus of the Stanford Institute for Economic Policy Research from 1987 to 1988. He was on the board of directors for several corporations, including First Interstate Bancorp, Metropolitan Life Insurance Company, and the Boeing Company. In 1990 Keller and his wife established the George M. and Adelaide M. Keller Foundation, which focused on investing in a number of causes to prevent domestic abuse, including the Keller Center for

Family Violence Intervention at the San Mateo County Health Center.

Keller died at Stanford University Medical Center of complications from knee replacement surgery.

Keller's daring purchase of Gulf Oil launched a wave of megamergers in the petroleum industry that paved the way for the oil industry's control by a handful of highly profitable, powerful firms. In addition to his business savvy in engineering the merger that created Chevron, Keller was known for some rather controversial positions in the oil and gas industry. An advocate of government subsidies for the petrochemical industry during the 1980s, he argued that such subsidies would stimulate the development of domestic energy sources. He also recommended that the federal government set oil prices high enough to help energy companies climb out of a slump. In an industry that typically preferred little to no government regulation or intervention, Keller's positions were highly unusual.

★

Keller donated a small collection of papers to the University of Washington library. Obituaries are in the *Oakland Tribune* (17 Oct. 2008), *New York Times* (18 Oct. 2008), and *Washington Post* (19 Oct. 2008).

Karen Linkletter

KERR, Deborah Jane (*b.* 30 September 1921 in Helensburgh, Scotland; *d.* 16 October 2007 in Suffolk, England), stage, screen, and television actress who was best known for playing refined Englishwomen but on occasion broke out of this mold in spectacular fashion.

Kerr was the eldest of two children of Kathleen Rose (Smale) Kerr-Trimmer and Arthur Kerr-Trimmer, a World War I pilot turned naval architect and civil engineer who died when she was in her teens. As a youngster, Kerr relished performing plays and skits for her family. She studied at the Hicks-Smale Drama School operated by her aunt, Phyllis Smale, in Bristol, England, where her family had relocated, and won a scholarship to London's Sadler's Wells Ballet School.

At age seventeen, Kerr debuted professionally in the ballet *Prometheus*, but her five feet, seven inch height precluded a dancing career, so she decided to concentrate on acting. She began by reading children's stories on BBC radio programs and appearing in Shakespearean plays staged in Regent's Park in London. In 1940 the film director and producer Michael Powell hired her for a bit role as a hatcheck girl in *Contraband*, but the part ended up on the cutting room floor. Stardom came her way when the director and producer Gabriel Pascal signed her to a

Deborah Kerr. MICHAEL OCHS ARCHIVES/GETTY IMAGES

contract and cast her as Jenny Hill, a Salvation Army worker, in his screen version of George Bernard Shaw's *Major Barbara* (1941).

Kerr spent the years of World War II as a rising star of the British cinema. Easily her best wartime film was *The Life and Death of Colonel Blimp* (1943), in which she played three different characters, each representing the male ideal of a woman. She also made her West End debut as Ellie Dunn in a 1943 revival of Shaw's *Heartbreak House* and performed in France, Holland, and Belgium with the British army's entertainment service. In 1945, she married Anthony Bartley, a decorated Royal Air Force fighter pilot, and later became the mother of two daughters.

Meanwhile, Kerr's screen career progressed on an upward spiral when Pascal sold her contract to Metro-Goldwyn-Mayer (MGM). In *Perfect Strangers* (1945), released in the United States as *Vacation from Marriage*, her first MGM-British film, she played a married woman whose romantic spirit is rekindled by a wartime liaison. In *I See a Dark Stranger* (1946), released in the United States as *The Adventuress*, she was an Irish spy. In *Black Narcissus* (1947), her final film in England, she played a repressed nun. Then she relocated to Hollywood, and her first American film was a plum assignment: *The Hucksters* (1947), in which she was a dignified socialite war widow romanced by Clark Gable. She earned her first best actress Oscar nomination for *Edward, My Son* (1949), playing Spencer

Tracy's bitter alcoholic wife. This honor foreshadowed the five additional nominations she would receive during the next decade when she flourished as an A-list star and appeared in her best-remembered films.

Kerr began the 1950s inauspiciously, playing an Englishwoman wooed by various bachelors in *Please Believe Me* (1950), an undistinguished romantic comedy. Then she was window dressing in *King Solomon's Mines* (1950), *Quo Vadis* (1951), and *The Prisoner of Zenda* (1952), big-budget period epics that highlighted male derring-do. She was one of a host of American and British stars cast in *Julius Caesar* (1953), which served as a showcase for Marlon Brando's Mark Antony.

By this time, Kerr had earned a reputation for playing refined, always-chaste Englishwomen, the kind of woman for which a man would feel admiration and love rather than lust. Fearing that this typecasting would restrict her career, she hired a new agent, Bert Allenberg, who persuaded the powers at Columbia Pictures to cast her as the cynical, tough-minded adulteress in *From Here to Eternity* (1953). Her striking, change-of-pace performance was intensely believable and earned her a second Oscar nomination. Most memorably, her scorching lovemaking scene with Burt Lancaster, in which the two embraced on a beach with waves crashing around them, became one of the iconic images of world cinema.

Kerr debuted on Broadway in *Tea and Sympathy* (1953), playing yet another complex character defined by her sexuality: a boarding-school teacher's wife involved in an affair with an insecure student. Here, she uttered one of the era's more often-quoted lines. Just prior to the boy's sexual initiation, she declared, "Years from now, when you talk about this—and you will—be kind." Kerr eventually toured with the show and, in 1955, won the Sarah Siddons Award for her performance during its Chicago run.

She played another sexually motivated character in *The End of the Affair* (1955), in which she was cast as a repressed wife involved in an extramarital liaison in wartime London; she replayed her *Tea and Sympathy* character in the 1956 screen version. But Kerr continued accepting roles that were elegant, refined, and decidedly nonsexual. Even though she was no musical performer, her star status won her the coveted role of Anna Leonowens in *The King and I* (1956), the screen adaptation of the smash-hit Broadway musical. Her singing voice was ably dubbed by Marni Nixon, and her luminous performance won her a third Oscar nod. Nomination number four was for *Heaven Knows, Mr. Allison* (1957), a two-character story in which she played a nun stranded with a U.S. Marine on a Japanese-held island during World War II. While she was not nominated for her role in *An Affair to Remember* (1957), in which she and Cary Grant appeared as star-crossed lovers, the film became a favorite of romance movie aficionados. That year, *Photoplay* magazine dubbed her "the world's most famous actress."

Kerr earned her fifth and sixth Oscar nominations for *Separate Tables* (1958), in which she played an introverted spinster, and *The Sundownerss* (1960), in which she was cast as an Australian sheep farmer's unglamorous wife. She received three BAFTA (British Academy of Film and Television Arts) Award nominations, for *The End of the Affair*, *Tea and Sympathy*, and *The Sundowners*, and three Golden Globe nominations, for *Edward, My Son*; *Heaven Knows, Mr. Allison*; and *Separate Tables*. Her sole competitive win was the Golden Globe she earned for *The King and I*. Appropriately, she closed out the decade with the Golden Globe's Henrietta Award as 1959's "World Film Favorite—Female."

Kerr divorced Bartley in 1959 and, the following year, wed Peter Viertel, a novelist and screenwriter. During the 1960s she worked steadily, giving her best performance as a repressed Victorian-era governess in *The Innocents* (1961), an adaptation of Henry James's *The Turn of the Screw*. She earned a fourth BAFTA nomination for *The Chalk Garden* (1964), playing another governess, and had a tailor-made role in *The Night of the Iguana* (1964) as an impoverished sketch artist. Her other films—*Marriage on the Rocks* (1965), *Eye of the Devil* (1966), *Casino Royale* (1967), *Prudence and the Pill* (1968), *The Gypsy Moths* (1969)—were undistinguished. Realizing that Hollywood was not interested in developing multifaceted roles for middle-aged actresses, Kerr retired from full-time filmmaking after appearing as the wife of a troubled advertising executive in *The Arrangement* (1969), Elia Kazan's poorly received adaptation of his novel.

Kerr and Viertel settled into a comfortable life, residing in Marbella, Spain, and Klosters, Switzerland. She returned to acting on occasion, starring in a West End production of *The Day After the Fair*, an adaptation of a Thomas Hardy short story, in 1972 and the following year taking the play to the United States and Canada. On Broadway she played a middle-aged woman at a crossroads in her marriage in Edward Albee's *Seascape* (1975) and starred in revivals of *Candida* (1977) in London, *Long Day's Journey into Night* (1977) in Los Angeles, and *The Last of Mrs. Cheyney* (1978) on tour. She appeared in prestigious television projects, including *Witness for the Prosecution* (1982), in which she was cast as a nurse; *A Woman of Substance* (1984), for which she earned her lone Emmy Award nomination playing a department store tycoon; and *Reunion at Fairborough* (1985), in which she was cast as a woman who rekindles a romance with an old flame. She was a Welsh schoolteacher in a West End revival of *The Corn Is Green* (1985) and had one last screen role, playing a tea planter's repressed widow in *The Assam Garden* (1985).

In 1984 Kerr received a tribute at the Cannes Film Festival, and she was honored in 1991 with a special BAFTA Award. The Academy Award for Best Actress had eluded her throughout her career, but in 1994 she received an honorary Oscar for being "an artist of impeccable grace and beauty [and] a dedicated actress whose motion-picture career has always stood for perfection, discipline, and elegance." That same year, she was diagnosed with Parkinson's disease. Four years later, she was awarded a CBE (Commander of the Order of the British Empire).

When her health began to deteriorate, Kerr returned to England to be close to her children. She died in Suffolk, succumbing to Parkinson's disease, and was survived by her husband, her two daughters, one stepdaughter, and three grandchildren. Viertel outlived her by nineteen days, dying of cancer on 4 November. She is buried in a family plot in West Sussex.

Louis B. Mayer, the head of MGM, once declared that her surname rhymed with "star"—and Deborah Kerr was indeed a screen personality of the highest order. She exuded refinement in her early British films and in many of her best American films, and in *From Here to Eternity*, she displayed her versatility by playing against type. Overall, Kerr was one of a generation of actors who brought dignity and intelligence to some of the best-remembered post–World War II films.

Kerr is the subject of one substantive biography, *Deborah Kerr* (1977) by Eric Braun, and is cited in biographies of or memoirs by her various directors and costars, including Michael Powell, Stewart Granger, and Burt Lancaster. Obituaries are in *Variety* (18 Oct. 2007); the *New York Times*, *Washington Post*, *Los Angeles Times*, and *Independent* (all 19 Oct. 2007); and the *Daily Telegraph* (20 Oct. 2007).

Rob Edelman

KIDD, Michael ("Mike") (*b*. 12 August 1917 [?] in New York City; *d*. 23 December 2007 in Los Angeles, California), dancer, choreographer, actor, and director who left the world of classical ballet for Broadway and Hollywood.

Kidd was born Milton Greenwald to Abraham Greenwald, a barber, and Lillian Greenwald. His father was a Russian-Jewish immigrant. Kidd grew up in Brooklyn, New York City, where he graduated from New Utrecht High School and went on to major in chemical engineering at City College, supporting himself with a job as a copy boy at the *New York Daily Mirror*. His interest in dance began in high school, and he began to study with Blanche Evan. At the same time he became attracted to photography. He left college when he received a scholarship to the School of American Ballet, where one of his teachers was Muriel Stuart. He also studied with Anatole Vilzak and Ludmila

Michael Kidd. ©JOHN SPRINGER COLLECTION/CORBIS

Schollar. Kidd's older brother, Phil, was a talent booker for the Concord Hotel in the Catskills, and Kidd was known as Phil's "kid" brother—hence his stage name.

Kidd made his debut in 1937 in the chorus and as an understudy for Benjamin Zemach in *The Eternal Road*, a Max Reinhardt production. He then became a member of the American Ballet, under George Balanchine at the Metropolitan Opera House; he later joined Ballet Caravan. With Ballet Caravan, Kidd danced the title role in Eugene Loring's ballet *Billy the Kid*. He danced at the New York World's Fair in 1939 and at Radio City Music Hall in 1940, and he was a soloist for and an assistant director of Loring's Dance Players (1941–1942). At times Kidd also appeared as an actor and worked backstage. He joined Ballet Theatre (later American Ballet Theatre) in 1942.

A slight, compact, lithe dancer with a head of dark hair and deep-set, penetrating eyes, Kidd spent five years as a soloist with Ballet Theatre, where his muscular body and affinity for quick changes of direction, clarity of gestures, and bounciness endeared him to both critics and audiences. Among other works, he danced in Michel Fokine's *Petrouchka* (title role) and *Bluebeard*, in Antony Tudor's *Undertow* and *Pillar of Fire*, in Agnes de Mille's *Three Virgins and a Devil*, and as one of the sailors in Jerome Robbins's *Fancy Free*.

Kidd's first opportunity to choreograph and his only ballet was *On Stage!*, with music by Norman Dello Joio; Kidd created the production for Ballet Theatre on the recommendation of Antal Doráti, the musical director. What one critic described as "a poignant bit of whimsy," the ballet debuted at the Metropolitan Opera House on 4 October 1945. The story concerns a shy ballerina (danced by Nora Kaye) befriended by a stagehand (played by Kidd), who helps her overcome her fears. The work was really a lighthearted commentary on the dance world. Reviews of the production were mixed, with one critic viewing the ballet as a warm, engaging, human comedy and another suggesting that Kidd's gifts were "more suited to musical comedy than to ballet."

Kidd left Ballet Theatre in 1947 to choreograph the Broadway musical *Finian's Rainbow*, and he never looked back, declaring that he wanted a more rounded career than he could have had in ballet. He won a Tony Award for *Finian's Rainbow* and another for *Guys and Dolls* (1951), which cemented his fame as Broadway's leading choreographer. More Tony Awards followed, for *Can-Can* (1954), *Li'l Abner* (1957), and *Destry Rides Again* (1959), and Kidd was nominated six other times, including a nomination for his direction of Neil Simon's *The Goodbye Girl* (1993), one of several dramas he directed. *Li'l Abner*, which Kidd choreographed and in which he made his debut as director and producer, contained much stylized pantomime as well as what someone described as Evil Eye Fleagle's "slithering jitter step."

One writer, talking of Kidd's showstopping dances in *Can-Can*, noted his great theater craftsmanship, with staging that made use of dancers and movement to integrate scenic changes. Also acclaimed was Kidd's ability to re-create a given period via movement. His choreographic style featured energy, action, and fanciful groupings, and his ballet background served as a framework. All of his work included humor and earthiness, sometimes parody, because Kidd wanted his dances to be completely understandable and to elicit a response from the audience.

When Kidd went to Hollywood, California, many credited him with revitalizing the Hollywood musical. His first film, *Where's Charley?* (1952), was followed by *The Band Wagon* (1953), in which Fred Astaire and Cyd Charisse dance in Central Park to "Dancing in the Dark." Then came *Seven Brides for Seven Brothers* (1954), the dance scenes of which, particularly the barn raising, ensure Kidd a place in filmmaking history. Among other movies he created were *Guys and Dolls* (1955) and *Hello, Dolly!* (1969).

Kidd also acted and danced in several movies, most notably *It's Always Fair Weather* (1955), in which Gene Kelly issued an invitation to Kidd and Dan Dailey to join him in a number that the three performed with garbage can lids attached to their feet. Kidd was close to sixty when he appeared as a comic actor in three films. He was honored by the Film Society of Lincoln Center in 1994, received an honorary Academy Award in 1996, and was given a memorial tribute at the Academy Awards in 2008.

On television Kidd directed episodes of *Laverne and Shirley* and *All in the Family* and was nominated for an Emmy (with Peter Anastos) for *Baryshnikov in Hollywood* (1982). He spent many years commuting between the two American coasts, constantly mixing ballet, modern dance, jazz, and acrobatics, with forays into straight drama or comedy.

Kidd married Mary Heater, a dancer, in 1940; they had two daughters before their divorce. He married Shelagh Hackett, also a dancer, in 1970. They had a daughter and a son. Kidd died of cancer and is buried in Hollywood Forever Cemetery in Hollywood.

Kidd once said that he left engineering because it was devoid of any relationship to human emotions. The athletic energy behind his dancing and choreography went into creating unforgettable characters, with whom his audience could always identify and often laugh.

★

There is a great deal of material on Kidd in the Jerome Robbins Dance Collection of the New York Public Library for the Performing Arts. Noteworthy articles include John Martin, "Kidd from Brooklyn," *New York Times Magazine* (13 June 1954); John Newnham, "Kidd as an Actor," *Dancing Times* (Nov. 1955); and E. Coleman, "The Dance Man Leaps to the Top," *New York Times Magazine* (19 Apr. 1959). An obituary is in the *New York Times* (24 Dec. 2007).

Dawn Lille

KING, Coretta Scott (*b.* 27 April 1927 in Heiberger, Alabama; *d.* 30 January 2006 in Rosarito, Mexico), wife of Martin Luther King, Jr., and founder of the Martin Luther King, Jr., Center for Nonviolent Social Change after her husband's assassination in 1968, regarded by many as the matriarch of the civil rights movement.

King was the daughter of Obadiah Scott and Bernice (McMurry) Scott, landowning African-American farmers. King had an older sister and a younger brother as well as another sibling who died in childhood. As a child King performed farm chores at home and walked three miles to a one-room elementary school for black children. In 1945 she graduated as valedictorian from Lincoln High School in nearby Marion, Alabama, a rare and highly regarded public and missionary-supported institution with an integrated faculty. King leaped at the opportunity to escape the jim crow South and to enroll in the progressive Antioch College in Yellow Springs, Ohio, where her sister had preceded her.

Coretta Scott King. ARNOLD MICHAELIS/PIX INC./TIME LIFE PICTURES/GETTY IMAGES

King soon learned that the North was not free of racism. For example, the local public schools would not allow her to work with white students, so she had to practice teaching in the on-campus laboratory school. She joined the local chapter of the National Association for the Advancement of Colored People and served as a student delegate to the 1948 convention of the National Progressive Party.

After graduating from Antioch with an education degree in 1951, King earned a scholarship for further study at the prestigious New England Conservatory of Music in Boston. Meanwhile, Martin Luther King, Jr., was working on his doctorate at Boston University. In 1952 the two met though mutual acquaintances. On 18 June 1953 Martin Luther King, Sr., performed the couple's wedding ceremony at the Scott home. After completing their programs in Boston, the Kings moved to Montgomery, Alabama, where Martin became pastor of Dexter Avenue Baptist Church in September 1954. He soon stepped into leadership of the Montgomery bus boycott. Around this time King gave birth to her first child. About six weeks later the new mother was at home with the baby and a friend when a bomb exploded on the front porch, breaking out windows. Refusing to give in to violent intimidation, King remained in Montgomery with her husband,

even though her father offered her refuge. A son was born in 1957, just before his sister's second birthday.

After five years in Montgomery, the couple moved to Atlanta so that Martin could join his father as co-pastor of Ebenezer Baptist Church. Their third child, a son, was born in Atlanta in 1961, and a daughter came along just over two years later. Having given birth to four children in a span of just over seven years, King necessarily played a more supportive than active role in her husband's civil rights endeavors in this period.

In 1956 King sat by her husband as the U.S. Supreme Court struck down Montgomery's bus segregation. Many other courtrooms would follow. Although she had given up her dreams of a professional musical career, King often used her strong singing voice to support the movement at "freedom concerts" in New York and other cities.

King accompanied her husband to Ghana on the occasion of its independence from British rule in 1957, and two years later she traveled to India with him to learn firsthand about the nonviolent philosophy of the Indian resistance leader Mohandas Gandhi. On her own, King went to Switzerland in 1962 as a delegate to a women's conference on world peace.

Two episodes thrust King into the spotlight and cemented the emerging alliance of John and Robert Kennedy with the Kings and the civil rights movement. In 1960 Georgia officials imprisoned King's husband on trumped-up charges. The presidential candidate John F. Kennedy's supportive call to King received wide press coverage. Three years later President Kennedy and Attorney General Robert Kennedy called King to offer assistance while her husband was locked up in the facility where he would pen his famous "Letter from the Birmingham Jail." That same year the Kings stood together in front of massive crowds during the March on Washington, D.C.

King was with her husband in Oslo, Norway, when he received the 1964 Nobel Peace Prize, and she joined him at the controversial dinner in Atlanta celebrating his accomplishment. The next year she marched beside her husband and others in the Selma-to-Montgomery march. Several magazine articles by and about King appeared in the 1960s, often mentioning her religious faith as a source of strength for herself and her husband. Her marriage survived persistent rumors about her husband's womanizing during his travels.

With good cause, King had feared for the safety of her husband and her family ever since their home was bombed in Montgomery. On 4 April 1968 her fears were realized when her husband was assassinated in Memphis, Tennessee. Only two days later King held a press conference to appeal for nonviolence in the face of the civil disturbances that had arisen in several cities in response to the assassination. In those remarks she resolved to carry on her husband's work. True to her word, two days later she led a march in Memphis. On 9 April a huge, peaceful, three-part funeral in Atlanta brought dignitaries from around the nation and the world. King walked behind the mule-drawn wagon that carried her husband's casket. Atlanta mayor Ivan Allen, Jr., was supportive throughout the ordeal, and the former first lady Jacqueline Kennedy was among the many who called at the King home to offer personal condolences. Some financial support for King and the children came from an insurance policy that the singer and family friend Harry Belafonte had maintained on King's husband.

Barely two weeks after the funeral, King filled in for her late husband at an anti–Vietnam War rally in New York City. A few days later she was back in Memphis, helping to kick off the Poor People's March. In June she flew to California to be with the Kennedy family following Robert Kennedy's assassination.

King was only in her early forties and was just beginning her activism. For example, she helped lead a strike in South Carolina and spoke at Saint Paul's Cathedral in London in 1969. That same year she wrote her autobiography, which she revised in 1993. In the 1970s she endorsed George McGovern for president, served as a member of the U.S. delegation to the United Nations General Assembly, defended affirmative action, and helped lead the push for full employment legislation. In 1983 she spearheaded arrangements that brought a quarter of a million people or more to Washington, D.C., to commemorate the original March on Washington. She protested apartheid and was arrested at the South African embassy in Washington in 1985. The next year she traveled to South Africa to meet with Winnie Mandela, who at the time was married to the activist and later South African president Nelson Mandela. In the 1990s King attended Nelson Mandela's inauguration and continued her traditional civil rights work at home. She also spoke out endorsing homosexual rights and opposing both Iraq wars. These controversial positions, especially her gay rights stance, resulted in criticism from some black clergy, but King did not back down.

In 1968 and 1969 King was disappointed when the board of the Southern Christian Leadership Conference declined to endorse her ambitious proposal for a King Center. Undaunted, she pushed forward. Certainly, fundraising took longer than she expected, but in 1982 the $8 million Martin Luther King, Jr., Center for Nonviolent Social Change finally opened on Auburn Avenue in Atlanta, near Ebenezer Baptist Church. The center included an impressive tomb, exhibits, offices, a research center, and Martin's boyhood home. (The home was later transferred to the National Park Service.) In 1985 King established a joint venture among the center, the estate, and Stanford University to compile and publish her husband's papers. In addition to housing archives and historical displays, the

center also undertook a major role supporting and spawning workshops, institutes, conferences, and protests.

Soon after King's husband died, Congressman John Conyers (Democrat, Michigan) initiated the call to establish a holiday in honor of the slain leader. Informal commemorations of Martin's January birthday had begun as early as 1969, but the effort to establish a legal holiday consumed much of King's effort for the next fourteen years. Finally, in 1983 King joined President Ronald Reagan at the formal signing of the holiday act, even though she harbored resentment for his initial opposition to the legislation. Fittingly, King's final public appearance just about two weeks before her death was at a dinner in Atlanta on the occasion of the King holiday.

Although King was widely admired during her life and remained widely revered after her death, her career was not without controversy. To some critics she sometimes seemed too cool and calculating. What admirers regarded as her regal presence others called aloof. Much of the criticism focused on stewardship of the King Center in King's later years. Since her retirement in 1995 from active management, the center has been marred by squabbling among her four children. Dexter King led the center for about ten years, followed by a brief stint under his brother, Martin King III. The mother was unable to prevent the problems while she lived, and the rancor continued after her death. One historian noted that "the Center's earlier years under the leadership of Coretta Scott King had been its most effective."

In 1988 the King estate attempted to obtain control of papers that Martin had deposited with Boston University, but five years later the university prevailed in the controversial lawsuit and retained the papers. Disputes over media rights to the "I Have a Dream" speech and other utterances of Martin Luther King, Jr., also resulted in a lawsuit, which was settled. To some critics these and other episodes were evidence of an ongoing effort by King and her family to control and profit from her husband's reputation; to her defenders King was merely asserting her rightful responsibility to preserve her husband's legacy.

Also controversial was King's continued insistence that James Earl Ray had not acted alone in killing her husband. She testified to that effect in the conspiracy case against the restaurant owner Loyd Jowers. At one point King even called for Ray to be exonerated. In light of the Federal Bureau of Investigation surveillance of her husband and the continued delving into King's activities after 1968, it is not surprising that the King family would harbor doubts about the bureau's conclusions regarding the assassination.

By the 1990s King had become, in the eyes of many individuals, the principal living symbol of the generation that had led the fight against jim crow. A younger generation of African Americans, both prominent and obscure, credited her with inspiring them. Among those she influenced were President Barack Obama, who earlier in his career made the pilgrimage to her home in Atlanta to hear her stories about her husband and the movement; Secretary of State Condoleezza Rice, who met her at the White House; and Mayor Shirley Franklin of Atlanta. King became very close to the media mogul Oprah Winfrey and to the poet Maya Angelou, who called "Corrie" her "chosen sister."

In August 2005 King suffered a stroke, but her more serious health problem was ovarian cancer, which was not publicly announced. When traditional methods failed, she sought alternative treatments at a facility in Playas de Rosarito, Baja California, Mexico, where she died. Cause of death was cited as cardiorespiratory failure and cerebral vascular illness in conjunction with the cancer. King is buried next to her husband at the Martin Luther King, Jr., Center.

King was the first African American and the first woman to lie in state at the Georgia State Capitol Building. A limited service and another casket viewing followed at Ebenezer Baptist Church, but to accommodate the large crowd, her funeral was held at the New Birth Missionary Baptist Church in suburban Atlanta. The presence of George W. Bush and three former presidents (Jimmy Carter, George H. W. Bush, and Bill Clinton) attested to King's stature. A procession of civil rights movement veterans who had served alongside King's husband, including Andrew Young, John Lewis, Jesse Jackson, and Joseph Lowery, spoke at Ebenezer and New Birth. Senator Edward Kennedy's eulogy continued the King-Kennedy connection.

★

King's autobiography, *My Life with Martin Luther King, Jr.* (1969; rev. ed. 1993), is informative but limited because it is aimed at young readers. Octavia Vivian, *Coretta: The Story of Coretta Scott King* (2006), is a useful but uncritical and lightly documented biography. Many of the numerous works about Martin Luther King, Jr., contain valuable information about his wife. On the King Center controversy, see Joy T. Bennett, "Who Controls Dr. King's Dream?" *Ebony* (April 2008). An outpouring of obituaries and tributes followed in the year after King's death, among the most substantial and documented of which is Vicki Crawford, "Coretta Scott King and the Struggle for Civil and Human Rights: An Enduring Legacy," *Journal of African American History* 92 (Winter 2007): 106–117. An obituary is also in the *New York Times* (31 Jan. 2006).

Bradley R. Rice

KIRKPATRICK, Jeane Duane Jordan (*b.* 19 November 1926 in Duncan, Oklahoma; *d.* 7 December 2006 in Bethesda, Maryland), neoconservative academic-turned-diplomat and trailblazing feminist who served in President Ronald Reagan's cabinet and was the first woman to serve as U.S. ambassador to the United Nations.

Jeane J. Kirkpatrick, 1987. CYNTHIA JOHNSON/TIME LIFE PICTURES/GETTY IMAGES

Kirkpatrick was the elder of two children of Welcher F. Jordan, an oilman, and Leona (Kile) Jordan, a homemaker who kept books for her husband's business. Reared in Oklahoma during the infancy of its statehood, Kirkpatrick in her childhood was steeped in the pioneer culture that was characteristic of an earlier time in U.S. history. Precocious and politically minded by nature, she learned to read at age four and exhibited a unique thirst for learning by age ten.

At once the great-granddaughter of a Confederate soldier and the granddaughter of a Union officer, Kirkpatrick clung to her roots as a southern-born schoolgirl with youthful sympathies that leaned toward the Confederacy. She learned to appreciate the duplicity inherent in conflict, however, when in 1938 she was transplanted at age twelve to the town of Vandalia and later to Mount Vernon—both in Illinois, the home state of Abraham Lincoln.

As an adolescent in Illinois, Kirkpatrick studied piano. Entranced by the études of Johann Sebastian Bach, she elevated music to a niche on her short list of passions, alongside politics and academics. She graduated from

Mount Vernon High School in 1944 and spent the next two years at Stephens College in Columbia, Missouri, where she earned an AA in 1946. In September of that year, having gained admittance to both University of Chicago and Barnard College, she opted to continue at Barnard. At a time when women in academics were a rare breed and women in politics were practically nonexistent, Kirkpatrick was fortunate to study at Barnard under Dean Virginia Gildersleeve, who was the first American woman to sign a U.S. treaty.

After completing a BA in political science in 1948, Kirkpatrick enrolled at Columbia University, where she was awarded an MA in 1950 with a thesis on the rise of fascism. She spent 1952 and 1953 on a fellowship at the Institut des Sciences Politiques in Paris, developing a thesis on Communism and the French intellectual. She earned a PhD from Columbia in 1968 with her dissertation *Leader and Vanguard in Mass Society: A Study of Peronist Argentina*, which was published in book form in 1971.

As a research assistant at George Washington University in the early 1950s, Kirkpatrick established a friendship with the politico Evron M. "Kirk" Kirkpatrick, a prominent Democrat. The couple married on 20 February 1955. They had three sons. When the youngest entered preschool in 1962, Kirkpatrick resumed her career in academia, involving herself with writing and teaching as a member of the faculty of Washington's Trinity College for Women. In 1967 she joined the faculty at Georgetown University, where she achieved full professorship in 1973. She was only the second woman in the history of that school to earn tenure there and in 1967 was honored as the school's Thomas and Dorothy Leavey University Professor in recognition of her expertise in political theory, comparative government, and U.S. foreign policy. In 1978 she joined the American Enterprise Institute, where she was at the time of her death a senior fellow.

Although Kirkpatrick was catapulted into the echelons of Washington's Democratic Party elite by means of her husband's stature, her lifelong affiliation with that organization would fracture, if not crumble, by the late 1960s. Disillusioned and distraught at the violence she witnessed at the Democratic National Convention in Chicago in August 1968, Kirkpatrick embarked on sabbatical to southern France with her husband and sons in 1969. In 1972 her growing dissatisfaction with the party led her to shed ties with that group's failed antiwar presidential platform. She joined forces that year with her husband and other disaffected Democrats and founded the party spin-off Coalition for a Democratic Majority.

Further displeased with Jimmy Carter's Democratic presidential campaign in 1976, Kirkpatrick took the extreme measure of throwing her vote to the incumbent Republican, Gerald Ford, as a protest to Carter's foreign policy platform and despite Ford's link to the scandal-scorched Richard M. Nixon administration. Kirkpatrick later criticized the Carter administration for what she perceived as a weak foreign policy on multiple fronts, including the cold war, Iranian relations, Nicaraguan unrest, and her perception of the U.S. military as a stagnant force. At no time were her opinions more publicly pronounced than in November 1979, when *Commentary* published her controversial article "Dictatorships and Double Standards." In the treatise Kirkpatrick admonished relentlessly what she referred to as the Carter administration's "doublethink: It finds friendly powers to be guilty representatives of the status quo and view[s] the triumph of unfriendly groups as beneficial to America's true interest."

Labeled a neoconservative for her outspoken writings, Kirkpatrick remarked that any authoritarian right-wing government proffered the greater potential for democratic upheaval than any totalitarian government in a liberal state. This political posturing attracted the attention of the then California governor Ronald Reagan, a Republican, who solicited Kirkpatrick's active support for his 1980 presidential campaign. In accepting the offer, she officially severed ties with the Democratic Party and wielded her support as a member of the foreign policy advisory group for the Reagan campaign. In 1981 the newly elected president Reagan offered Kirkpatrick the U.S. ambassadorship to the United Nations (UN). It was a historic moment, as she was the first woman to be so honored. She was admitted simultaneously to the Reagan cabinet and was appointed to the National Security Council. During these years she was honored with the French Prix Politique (1984) and the U.S. Presidential Medal of Freedom (1985).

After Kirkpatrick relinquished the UN ambassadorship in 1985, her hands-on involvement in U.S. foreign policy endured for nearly a decade. Through 1987 she continued her service on both the Presidential Blue Ribbon Commission on Nuclear Products and Reagan's Presidential Commission on Space. She retained seats on the President's Foreign Intelligence Advisory Board (until 1990) and on the Defense Policy Review Board (until 1993). She served as chairperson of the Defense Department's Fail Safe and Risk Reduction Commission from 1991 to 1992.

Kirkpatrick's unyielding allegiance to the U.S. government bordered at times on the jingoistic. She viewed volatile protest against U.S. policy to be distasteful and inappropriate, and this theme underscored much of her writing. When nominated for an honorary degree by Brandeis University in the 1990s, she refused the honor, lambasting the school's administration for tolerating a protest by students who were antagonistic toward her politics. Decisive and caustic in her verbiage, she wrote a syndicated column for the *Los Angeles Times* between 1986 and 1997. Paradoxically outspoken in her beliefs, she never hesitated to voice her displeasure with any presidential administration or party platform, yet she decried what she dubbed the "blame America first" mentality. Following the death of her husband in 1995, Harvard University announced the endowment of a professorship by the grocery mogul Leo Kahn in October 1997. In establishing the Evron and Jeane Kirkpatrick Chair, Kahn cited Jeane Kirkpatrick's "rather . . . successful marrying of politics and academia."

As a septuagenarian and still politically influential, Kirkpatrick accepted an appointment from President George W. Bush in 2003 to head the U.S. delegation to the UN Human Rights Commission, and on 8 April 2004 she appeared before the Senate Armed Services Committee in opposition to the International Law of the Sea Treaty. In 2005 eight former UN ambassadors, including Kirkpatrick, joined forces in urging Congress to abandon its proposed scheme to withhold UN dues to force reform, citing the potential for building resentment and mistrust.

Kirkpatrick died in her sleep at her home in Bethesda of congestive heart failure. She was eighty. She is buried in Parklawn Memorial Park and Menorah Gardens in Rockville, Maryland.

An obituary in the *Wall Street Journal* praised Kirkpatrick for her ability to use "words as weapons." Critical to Kirkpatrick's legacy was her ability to pierce the gender barrier in the political arena of U.S. foreign policy. In *Political Woman* (1974), she bemoans the contemporary dearth of women in that arena; she followed with *The New Presidential Elite: Men and Women in National Politics* (1976). Kirkpatrick is credited with more than a score of published writings and books, including *The Presidential Nominating Process: Can It Be Improved?* (1980) and *The Withering Away of the Totalitarian State . . . and Other Surprises* (1990). Her final book, *Making War to Keep Peace*, was published posthumously in 2007. In it she defends the legality of the decision to invade Iraq in 2003 but elaborates on her disagreement with the action. Her honors include the 1988 Hubert H. Humphrey Award from the American Political Science Association, the Morgenthau Award from the American Council on Foreign Policy, the Gold Medal of the Veterans of Foreign Wars, and the Defender of Jerusalem Award.

★

Pat Harrison, *Jeane Kirkpatrick* (1991), offers a biographical snapshot of Kirkpatrick, embedded against the backdrop of world politics in her times. An obituary is in the *New York Times* (9 Dec. 2006).

Gloria V. Cooksey

KITT, Eartha (*b.* 17 January 1927 in North, South Carolina; *d.* 25 December 2008 in Weston, Connecticut), singer, songwriter, dancer, author, actor, and civil rights activist. Kitt was an exotic combination of cabaret and television talent, manifested in a multilingual, mixed-race sex symbol.

Eartha Kitt. ©JOHN SPRINGER COLLECTION/CORBIS

Kitt was born Eartha Mae Keith on a cotton farm outside a town called North in rural South Carolina. Her father, whom birth records identify as William Kitt, was a white sharecropper. Eartha's mother, Anna Mae Riley, had mixed black and Cherokee heritage. Kitt had two half sisters. When she was still a child, having been abandoned by her father and mother, Kitt was sent to New York City to live with Mamie Lue Riley, Anna Mae's sister.

Riley and Kitt did not get along well, but the former discerned Kitt's many talents, and she paid for piano lessons that ultimately helped Kitt attend Metropolitan High School, later known as the High School of the Performing Arts in New York. As life with her aunt deteriorated, Kitt found part-time jobs, dropped out of school, quit her jobs, and then reenrolled. When her aunt asked her to leave in 1943, Kitt found herself independent and jobless at sixteen.

In 1946 a chance encounter on a New York street with an entertainer inquiring for directions led to Kitt's audition for the prestigious Katherine Dunham Dance Company. "Kitty," as Dunham called her, won an immediate position with Dunham's "Sans Souci Singers," leaving on a nine-month tour of a new revue titled *Bal Negre*. In November 1946 the highly polished *Bal Negre* revue opened on Broadway and then launched into several extended European and South American tours in 1947.

In 1948 Kitt debuted as an uncredited dancer and actress in the Dunham Company in her first film, *Casbah*. During the second European tour of *Bal Negre* in

1948, Kitt appeared briefly at Carroll's, an alternative-culture nightclub in Paris. The next year she was offered a featured spot at Le Perroquet, a new cabaret in Paris, where she began to perfect her multilingual nightclub act. Here she cowrote a song called "C'est si bon" with the French composer Henri Betti. Kitt often improvised the "desir-ables" in this song, sometimes mangling together her own Franglais to the delight of her audiences.

In 1950 Orson Welles offered Kitt a role as Helen of Troy in his Parisian production of the Faust story *Time Runs*. Welles proclaimed Kitt to be "the most exciting woman in the world." Kitt wryly observed that was probably due to the fact that they never slept together.

In 1952 Kitt moved her cabaret to Istanbul, Turkey, appearing at Club Karavansari, where she added Turkish to her repertoire, thereby setting the stage for her first RCA recording, "Üska Dara (A Turkish Tale)," in 1954. Later in 1952 Kitt returned to the United States, opening at La Vie en Rose, a midtown Manhattan nightclub. That nightclub appearance was a failure, closing on the sixth day of a two-week run. Kitt rebounded from that into a show at the Blue Angel, a sister club to the Village Vanguard, singing there for a record twenty-five weeks. During that time, the producer Leonard Sillman saw her and cast her in his Broadway revue *New Faces of 1952*. After a successful 1954 movie remake of that review, Kitt was cast in Sillman's *Mrs. Patterson*. Her first major Broadway success earned her a Tony nomination.

More recordings in the 1950s followed, including among others "Monotonous," "I Want to Be Evil," and the enduring "Santa Baby." In between recordings, she acted in numerous movies—*Mark of the Hawk* (1957) with Sidney Poitier, *St. Louis Blues* (1958) with Nat King Cole, and *Anna Lucasta* (1959) with Sammy Davis, Jr. In the late 1950s Kitt insisted on guarantees in her contractual live performances that she would not play to segregated audiences, establishing a model for the next generation of entertainers.

In 1956 Kitt published her first autobiographical writing, *Thursday's Child*. She also starred in the 1957 Broadway production of *Shinbone Alley*, an important precursor to *Cats*. In 1960 she was honored with a star on the Hollywood Walk of Fame. She married John W. ("Bill") McDonald, a real estate financier and millionaire, on 6 June 1960. In 1962 they had a daughter. The McDonalds bought a mansion where Kitt kept chickens in her atrium, an eccentric tribute to her youthful servitude in South Carolina. They divorced in 1965.

Not only was Kitt fluent in ten languages, she was accomplished in multiple media, including her 1964 Emmy award nomination for *I Spy* and her 1967 "purr-fection" in the campy television series *Batman* as Catwoman, the caped crusader's growling and sexy arch-nemesis.

In 1968 Kitt accepted an invitation to a White House luncheon with Lady Bird Johnson. When the first lady asked Kitt about her feelings for the war in Vietnam, Kitt replied forthrightly: "You send the best of this country off to be shot and maimed. They rebel in the street. They don't want...to be shot in Vietnam."

Kitt's candor nearly derailed her career in the United States. A subsequent Central Intelligence Agency (CIA) memo called her "a sadistic nymphomaniac." Producers and entertainers shunned her outspokenness. Kitt returned to Europe undaunted and undiminished to continue working. Television, radio, and stage appearances throughout Europe, the Middle East, and Asia followed.

In 1974 Kitt toured South Africa, receiving preferential "white" treatment there on the basis of her mixed race. Her banishment by entertainers in the United States persisted, despite Kitt's protestations that her tour resulted in new African schools being built in Cape Town. Shortly after that tour, Kitt wrote her second autobiography, *Alone with Me* (1976).

In 1978 Kitt returned to the United States to star in *Timbuktu*, an African remake of *Kismet*, for which she received her second Tony nomination as well as an official "Welcome Home" from President Jimmy Carter. In 1988 she successfully upstaged Stephen Sondheim's *Follies* in London, bringing down the house with a spirited performance of "I'm Still Here," swathed in mink.

Kitt used that title as part of her third autobiography, *I'm Still Here: Confessions of a Sex Kitten* (1989). She remained active throughout the 1990s, costarring with Eddie Murphy in *Boomerang* (1992), recording the Grammy-nominated CD *Back to Business* (1994), appearing in the documentary *Unzipped* (1995), and initiating an annual appearance at the Café Carlyle in New York City that sold out for ten years in a row.

In 2000 Kitt provided the voice for Yzma, the monstrously eccentric diva, in Disney's *The Emperor's New Groove*. The next year she published her fourth book, coauthored with Tonya Bolden, *Rejuvenate! It's Never Too Late*. Two years later, at the age of seventy-six, she assumed Chita Rivera's role in a revival of the musical *Nine*. Despite being diagnosed with cancer in 2006, Kitt continued with performances at the Cheltenham (U.K.) Jazz Festival and with the Virginia Symphony Orchestra.

Kitt succumbed to colon cancer at her home in Weston. Her body was cremated. She created an enduring and versatile career that both challenged and caricatured many stereotypes. She was an atypical but highly effective feminist activist who furthered the art of entertainment and the cause of candor.

★

For information on Kitt's life and career, see her autobiographical works: Eartha Kitt, *Thursday's Child* (1956); *Alone with Me* (1976); and *I'm Still Here: Confessions of a Sex Kitten* (1989). Renee Montagne, "Eartha Kitt Still Sizzling," *Morning*

Edition, National Public Radio (31 Dec. 2007), features an interview with Kitt about her childhood and career. Obituaries are in the *New York Times* (25 Dec. 2008) and *Guardian* (London) (29 Dec. 2008).

James McElwaine

KNIEVEL, Robert Craig ("Evel"), Jr. (*b*. 17 October 1938 in Butte, Montana; *d*. 30 November 2007 in Clearwater, Florida), motorcycle daredevil who rose to fame through spectacular jumps, such as a failed attempt to cross the Snake River Canyon in Idaho in 1974.

Knievel was the son of Robert Knievel, a car dealer, and Ann Knievel. The couple divorced in 1940, partly because of the difficulties of surviving during the Great Depression. Knievel and his younger brother went to live with their paternal grandparents, Ognatius and Emma Knievel. They never again lived with their parents.

At age eight Knievel saw Joie Chitwood's Auto Daredevil Show when it came through Butte. The experience would set him on his career path. A legend to many rural

Evel Knievel, 1976. **TONY ESPARZA/CBS/LANDOV**

Americans, Chitwood used Ford flathead V-8–powered cars to jump from ramp to ramp, race through walls of fire, and accomplish other death-defying feats. After seeing the show, Knievel set up two doors on buckets, raced his bike up one ramp, flew through the air, and landed on the other door. Thirty years later boys inspired by Knievel would attempt similar jumps.

While Knievel soon graduated from bicycles to motorcycles, he did not think that he could make a living jumping motorcycles. A wild youth, he gained the nickname of "Evel" during one night that he spent in jail for leading police on a chase through Butte on his motorcycle. The motorcycle escapade was not Knievel's first but rather just one of the few times that the police were able catch the notorious rider. The jailer read through the list of prisoners and made a joke about Knievel being evil; the name stuck, though in a form that seemed less menacing.

Knievel made some money by participating in local professional rodeos and ski-jumping events. In 1956 he won a Montana ski-jumping title. Despite these successes, he could not earn a living. In Butte there simply were few jobs besides mining for a high school dropout, so Knievel turned to illegal ways of making money. In later years Knievel admitted to participating in a few robberies of businesses. He emphasized that he had never harmed anyone and that he did not target individuals. He eventually tried copper mining and served in the U.S. Army, but he continued to drift.

On 5 September 1959 Knievel married Linda Bork; they had four children. With a family soon on the way, Knievel took a more sober approach to life. After a brief stint as a player with the Eastern Professional Hockey League's Charlotte Clippers, Knievel returned to Butte to start the Bombers, a semiprofessional hockey team. Serving as owner, coach, general manager, promoter, and player, Knievel drew fans to the ice rink, but not enough to pay the bills. With the 1960 Winter Olympics scheduled to be held in Squaw Valley, California, Knievel managed to persuade the Czechoslovakian team to play an exhibition game against his Bombers in Butte. Knievel promised to pay room and board for the Czechs. When the gate receipts proved inadequate to cover the expenses of the Czechs, the U.S. Olympic Committee had to pay the bills to avoid an international incident.

Knievel next ran into trouble by opening the Sur-Kill Guide Service, promising to provide tourists with any animal they wanted to hunt. Knievel found these trophies by taking his hunters to hunt big game that happened to be protected within the confines of Yellowstone National Park. With game wardens closing in, Knievel shuttered the business. He then returned to crime in Butte, first by selling "protection" to businesses and then by cracking safes. By 1961 Knievel was providing well—albeit illegally—for his growing family. Resolving to change his ways and to make a contribution to society, he looked for a legal way of earning money.

Knievel turned to motocross. He found a sponsor and joined the circuit. While he made little money, his reputation grew with his victories. He appeared to be on the verge of stardom when he broke his collarbone and shoulder in a wreck. Informed by doctors that he could not race for months, Knievel had to find a new career. He became an insurance agent for Combined Insurance Company of America. A positive attitude, charm, and ferocious determination helped Knievel break every sales record in the company. When Combined refused to promote him, he left the business. Knievel's sales experience would later help him sell himself to the media as a stunt jumper. He moved to Moses Lake, Washington, to resume motocross racing and to take over a local Honda motorcycle dealership. In 1965 Knievel formed a traveling stunt show, Evel Knievel's Motorcycle Daredevils, and embarked on the career that would make him into a national hero.

To jump a motorcycle successfully, Knievel had to accelerate to a rate that was not too fast and not too slow. To do so he needed enough space to reach the proper speed. He had to hit the entering ramp at the right place, decrease his speed while flying through the air and keeping the machine from flipping, and then land on the correct spot. He then needed enough space to stop safely. If any step in the procedure went wrong, Knievel knew that he would wreck, but he hoped to control the crash enough to minimize the damage to his body. Occasionally Knievel would enter a site created for a jump, realize that the setup would result in a crash, but jump anyway to avoid disappointing the fans. With tickets sold and cameras filming, he could not walk away. Part of the allure in watching Knievel lay in anticipating that he would break something.

On 1 January 1968 Knievel put on his trademark white helmet and donned a white suit with red and blue highlights to jump his red, white, and blue motorcycle 140 feet over the fountains at Caesars Palace in Las Vegas, Nevada, while television cameras filmed the event. He immediately became a household name. Because he had crashed upon landing and had spent the next month in a coma with broken bones, including legs, an arm, pelvis, and a hip, he did not realize that he had become famous. Knievel's motorcycle had fishtailed and skidded upon landing, sending the stuntman slamming end over end on the asphalt like a rag doll. Assuming he survived, the fans eagerly awaited Knievel's next stunt. Five of the top twenty episodes of American Broadcasting Company's *Wide World of Sports* featured Knievel jumps.

Knievel's red, white, and blue wardrobe emphasized his genuine patriotism and added to his appeal. Knievel traveled the country in a flashy red tractor trailer. His image appeared on lunchboxes, toys, skateboards, radios,

toothbrushes, vitamins, knives, and many other products. The fame and the money put pressure on Knievel to devise ever more spectacular and dangerous stunts. In 1971 he jumped nineteen cars and 150 feet. On 8 September 1974 he captured the world's attention by attempting to jump the Snake River Canyon in Idaho in a custom, rocket-propelled motorcycle dubbed the Skycycle. Knievel did not expect to survive the jump. Much to his surprise, the rocket's parachute opened early, and he sailed to the bottom of the 400-foot basin, suffering only minor injuries.

Knievel continued to jump. In 1975 he crashed while trying to jump thirteen double-decker buses in London's Wembley Stadium. Five months later he successfully cleared fourteen buses at the King's Island amusement park near Cincinnati. In 1976 at the Chicago Amphitheater, Knievel cleared a tank containing thirteen sharks but broke both arms and his collarbone while striking a camera operator, who lost an eye. Since he had broken nearly forty bones by that point, Knievel decided that the time had come to quit. He remained a legend. Butte annually pays tribute to its favorite son with Evel Knievel Days that attract thousands to the city.

To the surprise of many fans, Knievel died not from injuries but of pulmonary fibrosis. The disease followed several strokes, diabetes, hepatitis C that resulted in a liver transplant, severe arthritis, and years of heavy drinking. His son Robbie Knievel also became a motorcycle daredevil and duplicated several of his father's feats, to the elder Knievel's pride and distress. Knievel is buried at Mountain View Cemetery in Buttte.

A larger-than-life character who wore a cape and walked with a diamond-studded cane, Knievel enjoyed all the perks of stardom. A notorious womanizer, Knievel claimed to have bedded more than 1,000 women. The behavior broke up his marriage to Bork in the 1990s; the two divorced in 1997. In 1999 he married Krystal Kennedy. The couple divorced several years later but were living together at the time of Knievel's death. Along the way Knievel had run through his entire fortune.

★

The best summary of Knievel's life is Ace Collins, *Evel Knievel: An American Hero* (1999), even though the book is filled with hero worship that prevents an objective portrayal of the stuntman. Several books that were published in Knievel's heyday contribute to the portrait of the motorcyclist. Marshall Spiegel, *The Cycle Jumpers* (1973), is a good biography. However, the book compares Knievel with the fifteen-year-old daredevil Gary Wells in an obvious attempt to attract the young readers who were the publisher's market. Joe Scalzo, *Evel Knievel and Other Daredevils* (1974), places Knievel in the context of some of the other jumpers of his era. *Absolute Evel: The Evel Knievel Story* (2005), a History Channel documentary, shows many of Knievel's jumps and is a good biography. An obituary is in the *New York Times* (1 Dec. 2007.)

Caryn E. Neumann

KNOTTS, Jesse Donald ("Don") (*b.* 21 July 1924 in Morgantown, West Virginia; *d.* 24 February 2006 in Los Angeles, California), wiry, bug-eyed, Emmy Award–winning comedian and actor who achieved iconic status as the bumbling but lovable Barney Fife on *The Andy Griffith Show*.

Knotts was the youngest of four sons of William Jesse Knotts, a farmer and miner, and Elsie L. (Moore) Knotts, who ran a boardinghouse in Morgantown. Shortly before Knotts's birth, his father, who was afflicted with schizophrenia, suffered a breakdown and remained bedridden until his death when Knotts was thirteen. Throughout his life Knotts suffered from hypochondria, shyness, and depression but remembered his family as being loving and having great humor. As a child Knotts learned magic and ventriloquism, later performing at parties and other functions. At Morgantown High School, Knotts blossomed—writing humorous columns for the student paper and

Don Knotts, 1965. CBS PHOTO ARCHIVE/GETTY IMAGES

sketches for school shows, performing in school programs and as a ventriloquist, and working at a local movie theater. These golden years were marred by the sudden death of one of his brothers from an asthma attack in 1942.

After graduation in 1942, Knotts went to New York City to try show business but returned to Morgantown to attend West Virginia University in the fall of 1942. Knotts joined the army on 21 July 1943 and entertained troops in the Pacific, in variety shows and a revue titled "Stars and Gripes." Knotts met the then prominent singer Lanny Ross, who encouraged Knotts to contact him after the war. Knotts left the service on 6 January 1946 with an honorable discharge. While finishing his degree at West Virginia University, Knotts performed at the university, in local venues, and later in the Pittsburgh area. He married Kathryn "Kay" Metz on 27 December 1947.

Knotts graduated with a BA in speech in 1948 and then borrowed $100 from his brother to move to New York City with his young wife. Knotts contacted Ross, who helped him get started. Knotts debuted on television on *Arthur Godfrey's Talent Scouts* (simulcast on radio and television), but his first regular job was as the folksy know-it-all Windy Wales on the radio program *Bobby Benson and the B-Bar-B Riders* (1949–1955). Between jobs Knotts performed comedy monologues at nightclubs, where he tested his new "nervous man" character. Knotts and his wife welcomed a daughter in 1954 and a son in 1957.

Knotts's early television career included *The Garry Moore Show* and *Search for Tomorrow* (1953–1955), which was Knotts's only noncomedic role. Knotts came to national prominence on the *Steve Allen Show* (1956–1960). Best remembered are his "Man on the Street" characters—always named Mr. Morrison with initials that matched their occupations. When Knotts played K. B. Morrison, who worked at a munitions factory, and was asked what his initials stood for, he said, "Kaboom!" Knotts debuted on Broadway in *No Time for Sergeants* (1955) and reprised his role in his film debut (1958). Andy Griffith and Don Knotts met during the play and formed the lasting friendship that would prove invaluable to both.

Knotts's most famous and favorite role was the bumbling deputy sheriff Barney Fife on *The Andy Griffith Show* (1960–1965, with later guest appearances and a 1986 made-for-television movie, *Return to Mayberry*). Knotts won five Emmys for outstanding supporting actor for his role as Barney Fife (1961, 1962, 1963, 1966, and 1967). Knotts explained his approach to playing Barney Fife: he thought of Barney as a kid, without the self-control of an adult.

Knotts guest-starred on television from the 1950s on but also made a comedy album, *Don Knotts: An Evening with Me* (1961), and did more films, such as *It's a Mad, Mad, Mad, Mad World* (1963) and *The Incredible Mr. Limpet*

(1964), in which he played his first starring role. After *The Andy Griffith Show*, Knotts starred in five movies for Universal, the most popular of which are *The Ghost and Mr. Chicken* (1966), *The Reluctant Astronaut* (1967), and *The Shakiest Gun in the West* (1968). During this period Knotts and his wife divorced.

The 1970s were busy for Knotts. He and Tim Conway teamed up for the first time in Disney's *The Apple Dumpling Gang* (1975), followed by five other Disney movies, most notably *No Deposit No Return* (1976), *Herbie Goes to Monte Carlo* (1977), and *The Apple Dumpling Gang Rides Again* (1979). Knotts and Conway reteamed in *The Prize Fighter* (1979) and *The Private Eyes* (1981). Knotts remarried on 12 October 1974, to Loralee Czuchna. Finally, Knotts returned as a regular on series television when he joined the cast of *Three's Company* (1979–1984) as the landlord Ralph Furley, a leisure-suited nerd who fancied himself a ladies' man.

Beginning in the 1980s, Knotts focused on regional theater but also performed live with Conway, attended events dedicated to *The Andy Griffith Show*, and authored *Barney Fife and Other Characters I Have Known* (1999). On television Knotts had a recurring role on *Matlock* as Matlock's (Griffith's) neighbor Les Calhoun (1988–1992). Knotts divorced a second time, in 1983. Around this time he met Francey Yarborough, who became his wife a couple of years before his death.

Knotts increasingly focused on voicing animation, most notably in *Chicken Little* (2005) and his last film, *Air Buddies* (2006). Macular degeneration eventually left him legally blind, so voice work enabled him to act to the end of his life. Knotts's final live-action appearance in a film was the pivotal role of the cantankerous television repairman in *Pleasantville* (1998). Knotts was recognized with a star on the Hollywood Walk of Fame in 2000. He died of aspiration pneumonia caused by lung cancer. He is buried at Westwood Village Memorial Park in Los Angeles.

Knotts was a master of broad physical comedy, but his best characters were more than funny—they were fully human. Because of Knotts's ability to combine farce and subtlety, Barney Fife is arguably the most perfectly drawn comic character in television history. Knotts's wife, Yarborough, said, "He saw poignancy in people's pride and pain and he turned it into something endearing and hilarious." Griffith summed up his friend's gift: "Don was a small man...but everything else about him was large: his mind, his expressions. Don was special. There's nobody like him."

★

Biographical information is in Knotts's autobiography, *Barney Fife and Other Characters I Have Known* (1999). Books on *The Andy Griffith Show* abound, but a good starting point is Richard Kelly, *The Andy Griffith Show* (1988). Steve Allen, *Hi-Ho, Steverino! My Adventures in the Wonderful Wacky World of TV* (1992), covers Knotts on *The Steve Allen Show*. Obituaries are in the *New York Times* and *Washington Post* (both 26 Feb. 2006).

Patricia L. Markley

KORMAN, Harvey Herschel (*b*. 27 February 1927 in Chicago, Illinois; *d*. 29 May 2008 in Los Angeles, California), comedian in television and movies, known for broad screwball characters and sketch comedy.

Korman was born to Cyril Raymond Korman, a salesman, and Ellen (Blecher) Korman, a homemaker. The family moved to Mississippi, where his only sibling, Faye, was born. In 1931 Ellen Korman took the children back to Chicago and the couple divorced; thereafter she worked in the garment district to help support the family. Korman later credited his inclination toward comedy to the pain and insecurity he felt growing up in a broken home but felt he benefited from the encouragement of his extended Russian-Jewish family.

Harvey Korman. CBS/LANDOV

Korman showed talent early, so his mother sent him to the Jack and Jill Players, a drama school for children. In 1939, at the age of twelve, he gave his first professional performance, in a radio commercial for toothpaste. A good student, Korman skipped a grade at Lowell Grammar School before attending Senn High School, where he studied drama. He entered Wright Junior College but left in 1945 to enlist in the U.S. Navy, serving until 1946. That year he enrolled at the Goodman Theatre School of Drama at the Art Institute of Chicago. After the regular three-year course and an extra year as an honor student, in 1950 Korman went to New York City to make it on the stage. By 1955 he was disheartened and gave up, moving to Los Angeles and becoming a salesman. He was soon drawn back to the theater and found critical success, though not regular employment. He returned to New York in 1956 and then to Chicago later that year, where, finally, positive notice for his role in the Samuel Beckett play *Waiting for Godot* led to regular work. Korman remained in Chicago, acting in and directing commercials as well as stock productions while caring for his dying mother. He married Donna Ehlert, a dancer and model, on 27 August 1960; they had a daughter and a son.

Seymour Berns of the television program *The Red Skelton Show* spotted Korman in the summer of 1960 and suggested he try Los Angeles again. Once there, Korman had some walk-on roles on television and in movies (including his 1961 film debut in *Living Venus*), but his big break occurred in 1963, when Berns recommended him for Danny Kaye's television variety show. Korman was a regular from 1964 until the show ended in 1967 and remained active on television and in films from then on. In the 1960s Korman played small parts in movies, most notably in *Lord Love a Duck* (1966), and guest-starred on television programs such as *Hazel* (1964), *The Lucy Show* (1964, 1965), and *The Munsters* (1964–1966). He started voicing animation, creating his first classic character, the Great Gazoo, for *The Flintstones*.

Admiring Korman on the Kaye show, the comedian Carol Burnett hired him for her new comedy-variety program in 1967. On *The Carol Burnett Show* she and Korman, with Vicki Lawrence, Lyle Waggoner, and Tim Conway, created a first-rate ensemble specializing in sketch comedy and spoofs of classic films, soap operas, and commercials. Backing Burnett, Korman raised the role of "second banana" to an art form.

Korman's most memorable feature films were directed by Mel Brooks: *High Anxiety* (1978), *History of the World: Part I* (1981), *Dracula: Dead and Loving It* (1995), and especially the Western comedy classic, *Blazing Saddles* (1974), in which he portrayed the hilariously diabolical Hedley ("no, not Hedy!") Lamarr. His other films include *The April Fools* (1969), *Huckleberry Finn* (1974), *Americathon* (1979), *Herbie Goes Bananas* (1980), three of the *Pink Panther* series (1981–1983), *Radioland Murders* (1994), and *Jingle All the Way* (1996). Korman's television movies include *Three's a Crowd* (1969), *The Love Boat* (1976), *Bud and Lou* (1978), *Alice in Wonderland* (1985), *Gideon* (1999), and *The Flintstones in Viva Rock Vegas* (2000). Critics often praised Korman's performances even though the movies themselves were mediocre.

Korman and his first wife divorced in 1977. On 8 September 1982 he married Deborah Fritz, with whom he had two daughters. In 1978, after ten seasons, Korman decided to leave *The Carol Burnett Show*. He starred in other series—*The Harvey Korman Show* (1978), *The Tim Conway Show* (1980–1981), *Eunice* (1982), *Mama's Family* (1983–1985; he also directed and coproduced several episodes), *Leo and Liz in Beverly Hills* (1986), and *The Nutt House* (1989)—but they lacked the appeal of the Burnett show.

Korman's television guest appearances included *The Wild Wild West* (1968), *The Hollywood Squares* (1969–1976, 1999–2003), *The Love Boat* (1982, 1983, 1985), *Diagnosis Murder* (1997), and *ER* (1998). In addition to *The Flintstones*, he voiced other animated programs, including *Garfield and Friends* (1994), *The Wild Thornberrys* (1999), *Hey Arnold!* (1997, 1999), *Buzz Lightyear of Star Command* (2000), and *The Ruby Princess Runs Away* (2001).

Korman formed a professional and personal bond with Conway that lasted until Korman's death. Audiences loved Korman's futile attempts to avoid laughing at Conway. From 1999 to 2007 the two comedians toured the country in *Together Again*, a sketch comedy revue reprising characters they had made famous that packed houses over 100 nights a year. In November 2001 the prime-time television special, *The Carol Burnett Show: Show Stoppers*, which reunited the original cast, was an enormous hit. Korman won four Emmys (1969, 1971, 1972, and 1974) out of seven nominations and one Golden Globe (1975) out of four nominations.

In January 2008 Korman underwent a successful operation on a benign brain tumor but suffered a ruptured abdominal aortic aneurysm after his release from the hospital. Readmitted to the University of California, Los Angeles, Medical Center, he remained hospitalized until his death from complications of the aneurysm on 29 May 2008. He is buried in Woodlawn Cemetery in Santa Monica, California.

Korman was tall (six feet, four inches), with wavy reddish hair, blue eyes, expressive features, a versatile voice, and a talent for accents. His characterizations were broad yet fundamentally truthful. His extensive training and approach to acting brought him limited critical success in serious roles but led to his enormous popularity as a comedian. As Burnett said of Korman, he "is not only the best there is in sketch comedy, he is also a brilliant actor." Brooks agreed: "Harvey was such a good solid actor that he could have done Shakespearean drama just as well and easily as he did comedy."

★

For information on Korman's life and career up through *The Carol Burnett Show*, see Mary Carpenter Good, *Harvey Korman: A Study of the Life and Career of a Television Comedy-Variety Performer* (1976), a master's thesis for California State University at Fullerton. Obituaries are in the *Los Angeles Times* and *New York Times* (both 30 May 2008).

Patricia L. Markley

KORNBERG, Arthur (*b*. 3 March 1918 in New York City; *d*. 26 October 2007 in Stanford, California), biochemist who won the 1959 Nobel Prize in Physiology or Medicine for his discovery of the key enzyme responsible for the synthesis of deoxyribonucleic acid (DNA) in the cell.

Kornberg was the youngest of three children of Joseph Kornberg and Lena (Katz) Kornberg, Jewish immigrants from Eastern Europe who owned a small hardware store. An excellent student, Kornberg graduated from public high school at age fifteen. He enrolled in the premed program at

Arthur Kornberg. AP IMAGES

City College of New York, commuting daily from Brooklyn to Manhattan on the subway. After obtaining his BS in 1937, he attended the University of Rochester School of Medicine on scholarship. Receiving his MD in 1941, he fulfilled his medical internship in Rochester, New York, and then served briefly as a medical officer in the U.S. Coast Guard before being commissioned as an officer in the Public Health Service. He was assigned to the National Institutes of Health (NIH) in Bethesda, Maryland, where he did research on vitamins in the nutrition section until the end of World War II. On 21 November 1943 Kornberg married Sylvy Ruth Levy, a biochemist who shared his research interests and who worked with him in the laboratory. They had three sons.

His research on vitamins led Kornberg to an interest in enzymes, large protein molecules that catalyze chemical reactions and that often require the assistance of certain vitamins called coenzymes. To gain more expertise on enzymes, in 1946 he trained with Severo Ochoa at New York University School of Medicine and in 1947 with Carl Cori and Gerty Cori at Washington University School of Medicine in St. Louis, Missouri. Kornberg then returned to NIH, where he served as chief of the enzymes and metabolism section from 1947 to 1952. During this time he became interested in the enzymes responsible for making nucleotides, the building blocks of DNA, which had recently been identified as the genetic material.

In 1953 he became the chairman of the microbiology department at the Washington University School of Medicine. There he made the momentous discovery of the enzyme called DNA polymerase, which is responsible for linking nucleotides together to form DNA. In 1959, just a year after his results were published, he was awarded the Nobel Prize in Physiology or Medicine, which he shared with Ochoa. Ochoa had discovered the enzyme that synthesizes ribonucleic acid, the molecule that works with DNA to produce proteins.

In 1959 Kornberg left St. Louis to establish the department of biochemistry at Stanford University in Stanford, California, which he headed until 1969. The department attracted a number of the leading names in the field. He continued to study the enzymes involved in DNA synthesis and in 1967 was able to copy the DNA of an entire virus. This important contribution to molecular biology, which received much publicity, was inaccurately presented in the press as creating life in a test tube. The true significance of Kornberg's enzyme research, and that of others at Stanford, was to give scientists the ability to recombine genes from different organisms, thus opening up the field of genetic engineering in the 1970s. In the 1980s Kornberg and his associates were able to duplicate the process by which DNA is actually copied in the cell, another important achievement.

Not only did Kornberg create a world-class research department, he was also an outstanding teacher. He mentored a number of researchers who would become noted biochemists; his 1980 textbook, *DNA Replication*, became a standard in the field. His later book *The Golden Helix: Inside Biotech Ventures* (1995) describes his experiences in the early 1990s as founder of the DNAX Research Institute of Molecular and Cellular Biology. Other significant works by Kornberg include *Enzymatic Synthesis of DNA* (1961), *DNA Synthesis* (1974), and *Genetic Chemistry and the Future of Medicine* (1988). In 1988 Kornberg retired from teaching but continued to be active in research at Stanford. He decided to change the focus of his work in 1990 to a study of the enzymes required for the metabolism of polyphosphates, which he discovered are important in bacterial growth and virulence. He continued this work until a week before his death, of respiratory failure, at the age of eighty-nine.

Kornberg dedicated his memoirs, *For the Love of Enzymes: The Odyssey of a Biochemist* (1989), to his wife Sylvy, who died in 1986, calling her "my great discovery." In 1988 he married Charlene Walsh Levering, a graphic artist; she died in 1995. Carolyn Frey Dixon became Kornberg's third wife in 1998.

Kornberg's three sons all chose science-related careers. Roger Kornberg won the 2006 Nobel Prize in Chemistry for his work on DNA replication in animal cells, and his father attended the awards ceremony. Thomas Kornberg discovered two other forms of DNA polymerase. Kenneth Kornberg, an architect, specialized in designing laboratories.

Arthur Kornberg made impressive contributions to the field of biochemistry in the second half of the twentieth century. He was involved in some of the key discoveries that led to genetic engineering, the human genome project, and gene therapy. His impact on the field was enhanced by his skills as an administrator, which allowed him to attract and retain an extremely gifted team of researchers, and his abilities as a writer, which ranged from the technical to the popular. *For the Love of Enzymes* is a classic in that few other scientists have been able to describe so well not only what they do but why they derive such pleasure from it. Kornberg's last book, *Germ Stories* (2007), a collection of poems about the microbial world for children, including his eight grandchildren, attests to his dedication to science and to his family.

★

The Stanford University Libraries Department of Special Collections and University Archives in Stanford, California, houses the Arthur Kornberg Papers. Kornberg's memoirs, *For the Love of Enzymes: The Odyssey of a Biochemist* (1989), contain useful biographical information. A biography, an extensive bibliography, and links to research articles, laboratory notes, and lectures are available online from the National Library of Medicine of the National Institutes of Health, *Profiles in Science*, "The Arthur Kornberg Papers," http://

profiles.nlm.nih.gov/WH. Obituaries are in the *New York Times* (28 Oct. 2007), *Nature* (6 Dec. 2007), and *Science* (7 Dec. 2007).

Maura C. Flannery

KRULAK, Victor Harold (*b.* 7 January 1913 in Denver, Colorado; *d.* 29 December 2008 in San Diego, California), decorated Marine Corps general and collaborator on development of the amphibious landing craft widely known as the "Higgins boat."

Krulak was the son of Morris Krulak, a businessman with interests in commercial jewelry and real estate, and Bess M. (Zall) Krulak, a homemaker. He grew up in Cheyenne, Wyoming, and attended Cheyenne High School through the tenth grade, when he transferred to Bobby Werntz Preparatory School in Annapolis, Maryland. After graduating from high school, he enrolled at the U.S. Naval Academy in Annapolis in the fall of 1930 at the age of seventeen. Diminutive in stature, standing roughly five feet, four inches tall and weighing only 120 pounds, Krulak was jokingly dubbed "Brute," a nickname that stuck with him for the rest of his life. As the years went by, the nickname, born in a moment of ironic jest, came to be a term of respect for Krulak's straightforward, no-nonsense style of leadership.

In 1932 Krulak met and started dating Amy Chandler, whose father, navy captain William D. Chandler, was temporarily based at the Naval Academy. The couple married in Washington, D.C., on 1 June 1936.

Upon graduation from the Naval Academy in 1934, Krulak was commissioned as a second lieutenant in the U.S. Marine Corps. After a series of brief stateside assignments with the U.S. Marines, he was posted to Shanghai in 1937 as an observer during the Second Sino-Japanese War. It was there that Krulak first saw and became intrigued with a landing craft used by the Japanese. Excited by the potential that such a craft could offer U.S. armed forces, he sent photographs and sketches of the boat back to Washington. Apparently no one in the nation's capital shared Krulak's enthusiasm, for he later discovered his communications about the landing craft were dismissed as rantings from "some nut out in China."

When he returned to the United States, Krulak built a balsa wood model of the craft, which featured a square-shaped bow that could be used as a retractable ramp to allow troops and equipment to exit the boat quickly. With model in hand, he visited the boatbuilder Andrew Higgins in New Orleans, and their discussions eventually led to construction of the Landing Craft, Vehicle, Personnel (LCVP), a modification of Higgins's Eureka boat design.

The LCVP, which was commonly referred to as the Higgins boat, was widely used in the Pacific theater during World War II and in the Allied invasion of Nazi-held France on D-Day.

At the outset of World War II, Krulak, now a captain, served briefly as an aide to General Holland M. Smith, commander of the Atlantic Fleet's amphibious corps. After completing parachute training, Krulak was ordered into the Pacific theater, where he first served as commander of the First Marine Amphibious Corps' Second Parachute Battalion. In the fall of 1943, Krulak, now a lieutenant colonel, led a raid on Choiseul Island, designed to divert Japanese attention from the U.S. invasion of Bougainville. At the end of the Choiseul operation, Krulak and some of his men were evacuated from the island in a PT boat commanded by John F. Kennedy. After the war ended, Krulak returned to the United States, where he first served as assistant director of the Marine Corps Senior School at Quantico, Virginia, and later as regimental commander of the Fifth Marines at Camp Pendleton in California.

Shortly after the start of the Korean War, Krulak served as chief of staff of the First Marine Division in Korea. The use of helicopters to carry troops and equipment to and from the battlefront, a concept he had first championed in the late 1940s, was successfully employed during the Korean War. In 1951 he returned to the United States, where he served until 1955 as secretary of the general staff at Marine Corps headquarters. Promoted to brigadier general in July 1956, Krulak became assistant commander of the Third Marine Division on Okinawa. Returning to the United States in 1957, he served as director of the Marine Corps Educational Center at Quantico until late 1959, when he was promoted to the rank of major general and took over command of the Marine Corps Recruit Depot in San Diego.

In 1962 President Kennedy appointed Krulak to serve as a counterinsurgency adviser to the Joint Chiefs of Staff. In early 1964 Krulak was promoted to the rank of lieutenant general and given command of all Marine Corps forces in the Pacific, a post he held until his retirement on 1 June 1968. During the Vietnam War, Krulak advocated greater efforts to win the hearts and minds of the South Vietnamese, a strategy that put him at odds with General William Westmoreland, the overall commander of U.S. forces in Vietnam. Krulak also called for intensive bombing of the North Vietnamese port of Haiphong to interrupt the flow of military supplies to the north. Krulak's suggestions were rejected.

During his lengthy military career, Krulak received a number of medals and decorations. His service in World War II earned him the Navy Cross, Purple Heart, Bronze Star, and Legion of Merit, and he received the Air Medal and a second Legion of Merit during the Korean War. His four years as commander of the Fleet Marine Force in the

Pacific earned Krulak a Distinguished Service Medal. In 2004 he received the Distinguished Graduate Award from the U.S. Naval Academy.

After his 1968 retirement from the Marine Corps, Krulak settled in the San Diego area and devoted much of his time to writing. For several years he wrote a syndicated column for Copley News Service, an organization he later served as president. Although he retired from Copley in 1977, he continued to make occasional contributions to the news service. Krulak also wrote a handful of books, the most notable of which is *First to Fight*, a history of the U.S. Marine Corps that was published in 1984.

Krulak, a resident of the Wesley Palms Retirement Community in San Diego, died in an area hospital of respiratory failure at the age of ninety-five. Predeceased by his wife, who died in 2004, Krulak was survived by three sons, Charles, Victor, Jr., and William, all of whom followed in their father's footsteps and graduated from the U.S. Naval Academy. All three also saw combat in Vietnam. Charles served as commandant of the Marine Corps from 1995 to 1999, while William and Victor both became clergymen. After funeral services at the Miramar Marine Corps Air Station chapel, Krulak's remains were interred at the nearby Fort Rosecrans National Cemetery.

Krulak will be remembered for his role in helping to develop the amphibious landing craft that played such a pivotal role in both the European and Pacific theaters of World War II and for his advocacy of using helicopters as attack platforms. Both of these strategies, which proved highly successful in battle, earned Krulak a reputation as a military innovator and visionary.

★

Victor H. Krulak, *First to Fight: An Inside View of the U.S. Marine Corps* (1984), chronicles the history and culture of this storied branch of the U.S. military. Obituaries are in the *Los Angeles Times* and *San Diego Union-Tribune* (both 31 Dec. 2008), the *Wall Street Journal* (3 Jan. 2009), and the *New York Times* (5 Jan. 2009).

Don Amerman

KRUSKAL, Martin David (*b.* 28 September 1925 in New York City; *d.* 26 December 2006 in Princeton, New Jersey), applied mathematician and mathematical physicist who made significant contributions to a number of fields, including plasma physics, astrophysics, nuclear fusion, and atmospheric and oceanic sciences.

Kruskal spent his childhood in New Rochelle, New York. He was one of five children born to Joseph Kruskal, a successful businessman and owner of a fur wholesale business, and Lillian (Vorhaus) Kruskal, a noted origami expert who established the Origami Center of America. He showed a keen interest in mathematics from an early age, taking pleasure in instructing his siblings and schoolmates in the subject. His two brothers, William Kruskal and Joseph Kruskal, Jr., also became noted mathematicians.

After graduating from Fieldston High School in Riverdale, New York, Kruskal entered the University of Chicago, where he earned a BS in 1945. Richard Courant, a New York University (NYU) professor and family neighbor, persuaded him to pursue graduate studies at NYU. He earned an MS in 1948 while working in Courant's Institute of Mathematical Sciences and a PhD, also from NYU, in 1952, with a doctoral thesis titled *The Bridge Theorem for Minimal Surfaces*. During his graduate studies he demonstrated an intense interest in a wide array of topics, a trait that, though perhaps slowing formal advancement, served him well throughout his career.

In 1950 Kruskal married Laura Lashinsky, with whom he remained until his death; they had three children. His wife, like his mother, became a widely recognized origami creator and teacher. Kruskal moved to Princeton, New Jersey, in 1951 to work on Project Matterhorn, the code name for an effort classified as secret by the U.S. government; upon declassification it became the Princeton Plasma Physics Laboratory. This laboratory was one of the first to pursue extensive research on the possibility of producing energy from controlled thermonuclear fusion for societal uses such as the generation of electricity.

For most of his career Kruskal remained at Princeton, where in 1959 he was appointed associate head of the Theoretical Division of Matterhorn and produced, with various colleagues, a number of important papers in plasma physics. He founded and served as the first chairman of the Program in Applied and Computational Mathematics at Princeton. A symbol of his breadth as a mathematical scientist came in 1959 with his appointment as lecturer in astronomy. A famous paper in 1960 laid the mathematical foundations for what became known as the "Kruskal coordinates," which paved the way theoretically to the study of black holes.

He was appointed professor of astronomy in 1961 and, after having served for twenty years as director of the Applied Mathematics Program, as professor of mathematics in 1979. His work moved more toward pure mathematics during the latter part of his career. The major discovery during this period began with a computer simulation with Norman Zabusky that led to the discovery of a type of nonlinear wave system called solitons. In 1974 Kruskal published a paper with Clifford Gardner and others that established the mathematical foundations for the study of solitons. The nonlinear nature of solitons required a new form of differential equations, and in subsequent years Kruskal worked out the mathematics to

describe the physical phenomenon. With his colleagues he developed the technique now termed the "inverse scattering transform," which turned out to be an important mathematical advance that could be applied to many systems in the natural world, such as the oceans and atmosphere.

The study of solitons also led to advances in plasma physics and some branches of optics. Kruskal and Gardner were honored in 2006 by the American Mathematical Society with its Steele Prize for a Seminal Contribution to Research. The society noted that "nonlinearity has undergone a revolution: from a nuisance to be eliminated, to a new tool to be exploited." In the latter part of his career he was widely recognized for his research and passion for "surreal numbers," numbers of either very large or very small dimension.

Although making significant advances in mathematics and physics, Kruskal was also known for his breadth of interests outside the sciences. He devised the "Kruskal count," a method for predicting the draw of cards from a deck. Although typically referred to as a card trick, the Kruskal count is based strictly on mathematical probability, a fact that baffled those who were known for ordinary card tricks. He also regularly wrote limericks to be read upon the introduction of guest speakers, and, taking up the interest of his mother and wife, he also created origami figures.

Among Kruskal's many awards and professional memberships were the American Mathematical Society Gibbs Lectureship (1979), National Academy of Sciences membership (1980), American Academy of Arts and Sciences membership (1983), Dannie Heineman Prize in Mathematical Physics (1983), National Academy of Sciences award in Applied Mathematics and Numerical Sciences (1989), and the President's Medal of Science, conferred in 1993 by President Bill Clinton at a ceremony in Washington, D.C. He also achieved international recognition, having been elected a fellow of the Royal Society of London, the Royal Society of Edinburgh, and the Russian Academy of Natural Sciences.

Upon retirement from Princeton in 1979, Kruskal assumed the David Hilbert Chair of Mathematics at Rutgers University. He remained at Rutgers for most of the remainder of his life and was active in research and publishing until just before his death, from a stroke.

Kruskal was known throughout his life for having diverse interests, a characteristic that early in his career some thought would hinder him from making major contributions in his field of specialization. Defying that notion, he became one of the most widely recognized and honored applied mathematicians and mathematical physicists of the last half of the twentieth century. He was a key member of the group that laid the theoretical foundations during the 1950s and 1960s for nuclear fusion and plasma physics. Credit for his work in this area was slow to come, however, because much of it was done on classified projects. Perhaps the greatest recognition came for his role in revealing solitons. While engaged in several of his major projects he also developed a type of mathematics called asymptotic analysis. In all his fields of interest, his intense focus on defining the dimensions of a problem and then persisting in working out the details, often going well beyond his theoretical specialized approach, was legendary.

★

For an account of his life, see the *Princeton Weekly Bulletin* (5 Feb. 2007) and Norman J. Zabusky and Robert M. Miura, "Martin David Kruskal," *Physics Today* 60, no. 5 (May 2007): 82–83. For a discussion of Kruskal's work on properties and representation of surreal numbers, see Robert Matthews, "The Man Who Played God with Infinity," *New Scientist* 147, no. 1993 (2 Sept. 1995): 36–41. Polly Shulman, "Infinity Plus One and Other Surreal Numbers," *Discover* 16, no. 12 (Dec. 1995): 96–106, also discusses surreal numbers, with comments by Kruskal made in conversation with the author. Obituaries are in the *New York Times* (13 Jan. 2007) and the *Society for Industrial and Applied Mathematics (SIAM) News* (11 Apr. 2007).

W. Hubert Keen

KUHN, Bowie Kent (*b.* 28 October 1926 in Takoma Park, Maryland; *d.* 15 March 2007 in Jacksonville, Florida), lawyer and Major League Baseball (MLB) commissioner whose dramatic fifteen-year tenure was marked by numerous advancements in the game as well as unprecedented labor problems.

Kuhn was the youngest of three children born to Louis Kuhn, an immigrant from Bavaria who worked as head office manager for Petroleum Heat and Power Company in Washington, D.C., and Alice Waring (Roberts) Kuhn. Kuhn's mother's family had strong ties to the Maryland area. Among her ancestors were five governors, two U.S. senators, and Jim Bowie, a hero of the Battle of the Alamo.

Kuhn attended Theodore Roosevelt High School in Washington, D.C., and grew up a Washington Senators fan. During school vacations he earned $1 per day tending the scoreboard at Griffith Stadium. The team owner's son, Calvin Griffith, Jr., was his supervisor. In his senior year Kuhn became class president, made honor society, and was voted most popular and most likely to succeed. At six feet, five inches tall, the teen played intramural sports but not interscholastic athletics. In his autobiography *Hardball: The Education of a Baseball Commissioner* (1987), Kuhn relates a story about Roosevelt High's coach, Arnold "Red" Auerbach, who later became a Naismith Memorial Basketball Hall of Fame coach and general manager of the Boston Celtics. Noting Kuhn's height, Auerbach asked Kuhn why he did not try out for the basketball team. Kuhn stated that he was a "lousy player," to which Auerbach replied, "You let

me be the judge of that." After a week of observing Kuhn, Auerbach agreed, telling Kuhn, "Son you were right and I was wrong."

After graduating from high school in 1944, Kuhn joined the navy's wartime V-12 program, which trained reserve officers. He was placed at Franklin and Marshall College in Pennsylvania. His commanding officer was Lloyd Jordan, who later became Harvard University's head football coach. Upon completion of his naval activities, Kuhn transferred to Princeton University in New Jersey and finished his coursework there. In 1947 Kuhn received a BA, graduating with honors in economics. He received a law degree in 1950 from the University of Virginia.

In September 1950 Kuhn began his legal career with Willkie, Owen, Farr, Gallagher & Walton. He was attracted to the firm because Wendell Willkie, President Franklin D. Roosevelt's 1940 opponent, was a political hero and because one of the firm's key clients was the National League of Professional Baseball Clubs. With a starting salary of $4,000, Kuhn took up residence in Manhattan, New York City.

In the summer of 1955 Kuhn met a young widow, Luisa Degener. They were married on 20 October 1956 at the farm of Degener's parents in Dutchess County, New York. The couple had two children together, in addition to Degener's two.

In 1965 the Milwaukee Braves received league approval to move to Atlanta, the team's third location in a thirteen-year span. Wisconsin and Milwaukee County sued to keep them. Kuhn represented the National League. In 1966 Kuhn argued before the Wisconsin Supreme Court, which decided in the league's favor.

On 4 February 1969 Kuhn was elected baseball commissioner and given a one-year, $100,000 interim contract. That year a dispute over pensions nearly stopped spring training. Kuhn averted a strike by reaching a settlement with the Players Association. Baseball's 100th anniversary season opened with expansion clubs in Montreal, Canada; San Diego; Seattle; and Kansas City, Kansas. The two leagues, each with twelve teams, were split into divisions.

In October 1969 the St. Louis Cardinals traded Curt Flood, Tim McCarver, Byron Browne, and Joe Hoerner to the Philadelphia Phillies for Dick Allen, Cookie Rojas, and Jerry Johnson. Flood refused to report based on the team's losing record, its poorly conditioned stadium, and the organization's dismal record on race relations. In December 1969 Flood wrote Kuhn a letter. He demanded that the trade be voided and that he be declared a free agent. Kuhn denied the request, noting that the reserve clause contained in all contracts prevented a player from playing on another team even after the contract had expired. On 16 January 1970 Flood filed suit against Kuhn and the league, contending that MLB's reserve clause violated federal antitrust laws. Kuhn testified against Flood, stating that MLB's actions were "for the good of the game" and that any alteration to the clause would lead to chaos. By a 5–3 decision, the U.S. Supreme Court ruled in the league's favor. In August 1970 owners elected Kuhn to a seven-year term with a contract valued at over a $1 million.

While Kuhn was in office, the league experienced growth as well as significant labor conflicts. On 13 October 1971, through Kuhn's work, the World Series held its first night game. The prime-time telecast increased television ratings and revenue for baseball. The first players' strike, a thirteen-day walkout, happened in 1972, in a dispute over pensions. Another labor dispute occurred when Kuhn ordered the Atlanta Braves to play Hank Aaron in their 1974 season-opening series in Cincinnati. Aaron was about to break Babe Ruth's career home-run record and the Braves wanted to bench Aaron until they got back to Atlanta so it would happen in front of the hometown fans. In the Kuhn-mandated Cincinnati contest Aaron tied Ruth's record; he broke it in Atlanta. In August 1975 Kuhn won a second seven-year term.

In June 1976, fearing free agency, the Oakland Athletics owner Charles Finley sold some of his best players. Citing the need for competitive balance among clubs, Kuhn voided the sales. It was the first time that a commissioner had nixed a cash transaction. Finley sued Kuhn and MLB in federal court and lost.

Kuhn barred Willie Mays from baseball in 1979 because the former ballplayer had worked with casinos. Kuhn did the same to Mickey Mantle in 1983. Both players were reinstated by a subsequent commissioner. In 1981 a fifty-day strike occurred as players opposed a plan to compensate teams losing free agents. After the strike ended, Kuhn declared a split-season format to determine post-season play.

Kuhn failed to receive a third term. When Peter Ueberroth took office in 1984, Kuhn returned to his former law firm, now called Willkie, Farr & Gallagher. In January 1988 he formed a law firm with Harvey Myerson. The firm did not succeed, and in December 1989 Myerson & Kuhn filed for bankruptcy. Kuhn, a resident of Ridgewood, New Jersey, moved to Ponte Vedra Beach, Florida.

Having been hospitalized with pneumonia, Kuhn died of respiratory failure at Saint Luke's Hospital in Jacksonville. He is buried in Quogue Cemetery in Quogue, New York. Nine months after his death, Kuhn was inducted into the Baseball Hall of Fame in Cooperstown, New York.

★

For additional information about Kuhn's life and career, see his memoir, *Hardball: The Education of a Baseball Commissioner* (1987). An obituary is in the *New York Times* (16 Mar. 2007).

John Vorperian

KUNITZ, Stanley Jasspon (*b.* 29 July 1905 in Worcester, Massachusetts; *d.* 14 May 2006 in New York City), poet, professor, and translator who was awarded many of the nation's highest literary honors.

Kunitz was the third child of Solomon Z. Kunitz and Yetta Helen (Jasspon) Kunitz. His father was a dress manufacturer who committed suicide just weeks before Kunitz was born; his mother was a Lithuanian immigrant who took over her husband's business after his death. When Kunitz was eight, his mother married Mark Dine. Dine died six years later, leaving Kunitz with a terrible longing for the "lost" father. After graduating as valedictorian from Worcester Classical High School, he went to Harvard College in 1922. He graduated summa cum laude in 1926, winning the university's Lloyd McKim Garrison Medal for Poetry, and went on to earn his AM in English from Harvard in 1927. He had hoped to teach at Harvard, but because of anti-Semitism he was not offered a position. Instead, he worked for a short while for a newspaper, the *Worcester Telegram*, before taking a position with the publishing house H. W. Wilson Company. Over a lifetime, he edited nine biographical dictionaries, including *Living Authors: A Book of Biographies* (1931), *Twentieth Century Authors* (1942), *European Authors* (1967), and *World*

Stanley Kunitz, 1986. ©CHRISTOPHER FELVER/CORBIS

Authors 1950–1970 (1975). He also served as an editor for the Yale Series of Younger Poets from 1966 to 1977.

While Kunitz was at Harvard, a visiting professor, Robert Gay, told Kunitz, "You are a poet—be one." This echoed advice from his high school mentor, Martin Post. The young poet approached his writing, as he noted later in his life, in a way that was more intellectual than emotional. Kunitz's earliest poems were published in some of the leading political and literary journals of the day, including *Poetry* and the *New Republic*. In 1930 he published his first collection, *Intellectual Things*. His title and his main theme were drawn from a line of the English Romantic poet William Blake (1757–1827): "The tear is an intellectual thing"; in this book he aimed to show that the "intellect and the passions were inseparable." His other influences at this point in his poetic career were the English Metaphysical poets John Donne (1572–1631) and George Herbert (1593–1633). The poems in this collection were complex, formal, and abstract, earning Kunitz a reputation as an intellectual poet.

One of the consistent subjects of Kunitz's work is the father he never knew. The poem "Three Floors" deals with his discovery of a photograph of his father; when he shows the picture to his mother, she rips it up and never allows the father's name to be mentioned again. In the poem "He," he writes: "She who has known him calls him stranger . . . / He steals within the heart, that humble manger / Where the white, astonished spirit kneels."

In 1930 Kunitz married Helen Pearce; they divorced in 1937. On 21 November 1939 he married Eleanor Evans, and they had one daughter, Gretchen. During World War II he served for two years in the U.S. Army, Air Transport, and earned the rank of staff sergeant. In 1944 Kunitz published his second volume, *Passport to the War*, a collection of interrelated poems. In 1945 Kunitz was awarded a Guggenheim Fellowship and went to live and write in Santa Fe, New Mexico. In 1946, with the encouragement of his friend, the American poet Theodore Roethke (1908–1963), he returned to the academic world to teach at Bennington College in Bennington, Vermont.

Over the next quarter-century he held teaching positions at the State University of New York at Potsdam; the New School for Social Research in New York City; the University of Washington, Seattle; Queens College in Queens, New York City; Vassar College in Poughkeepsie, New York; Brandeis University in Waltham, Massachusetts; Columbia University in New York City; Yale University in New Haven, Connecticut; and Rutgers University in New Brunswick, New Jersey. He refused offers of permanent positions at many of these institutions, explaining that for poets such a life can be "stultifying," dampening the creative impulse. As a teacher, he had a dramatic influence on many younger poets who would go

on to major careers of their own, including Tess Gallagher, Louise Glück, and Robert Hass.

Kunitz's *Selected Poems: 1928–1958* (1958) won the Pulitzer Prize in 1959. The poems in this collection, musing on love, life, and death, were technically accomplished, as Kunitz continued to write moving poems employing strict forms (in this book, quatrains, or four-line stanzas, with three metric beats per line). Following his divorce from his second wife, on 21 June 1958 he married the artist Elise Asher, with whom Kunitz spent the next forty-six years until her death in 2004.

In 1967 Kunitz traveled to the Soviet Union. He translated the works of the Russian poets Anna Akhmatova and Andrei Voznesensky, giving them a voice in the West. In 1971 Kunitz published his fourth volume, *The Testing-Tree*. This book, adopting a looser, less formal style written in the first person, marked a major change from his earlier work. In a 1974 interview Kunitz noted that, compared to the influential British poet T. S. Eliot (1888–1965), whose poetry he identified as impersonal, both he and Roethke took a more passionate approach to their art. Kunitz further explained that his goal was not to "spill everything out" in poems, but rather to enact through poetry "transformation, the ritual sense, the perception of a destiny." Acknowledging the English Romantic poet John Keats (1795–1821) as a major influence, Kunitz expressed his desire to move beyond this tradition to where the poet's "ego . . . [had] to be consumed in the fire of the poetic action." From 1974 to 1976 Kunitz was appointed the consultant in poetry to the Library of Congress, the precursor to the position of national poet laureate. His collected poems, *The Poems of Stanley Kunitz, 1928–1978* (1979), which brought together the poems in *The Testing-Tree*, *The Terrible Threshold: Selected Poems, 1940–1970* (1974), *The Coat Without a Seam: Sixty Poems, 1930–1972* (1974), and *The Lincoln Relics: A Poem* (1978), was honored with the prestigious Lenore Marshall Poetry Prize in 1980.

Kunitz, then in his seventies, had much more left to say. He published *Next-to-Last Things* (1985) and, in the following decade, *Passing Through: The Later Poems, New and Selected* (1995), which won the National Book Award. One of the recurring themes of Kunitz's work is rebirth, often achieved by means of a quest or night journey that takes the speaker of the poem on a descent into the underworld. The quest leads toward the understanding of simple truths about everyday life. In 1987 Kunitz was awarded the Bollingen Prize in Poetry from Yale University Library. That same year Governor Mario Cuomo appointed Kunitz to a two-year term as the official New York State Poet. In 1993 he was awarded the National Medal of Arts, the United States' highest government honor for artists and patrons of the arts.

Kunitz noted in a 1992 interview that he had spent much of his childhood alone in the woods near his home in

Worcester, communing with nature and sensing that it would be his destiny to become a poet. In keeping with that early love of nature, Kunitz divided his time between New York City and a house in Provincetown, Massachusetts, at the tip of Cape Cod. He created a celebrated garden there, and this, along with the ever-changing shore, inspired much of his work. In the poem "The Wellfleet Whale," first published in *The Wellfleet Whale and Companion Poems* (1983) and republished in *Passing Through*, he confronts a beached finback whale in its death throes: "[The whale] laboriously opened / a bloodshot, glistening eye / in which we swam with terror and recognition." This moment is like many others in Kunitz's work, vividly evoking the twin mysteries of life and death.

Kunitz noted that the act of creating a poem changes as one ages. In a 1995 interview with Mary B. W. Tabor in the *New York Times*, Kunitz noted, "In youth, poems come to you out of the blue. . . . But at this age . . . one has to dig." Kunitz felt that poems have to develop "organically," that the finest poems grow out of life itself; eventually the poet must give up his poem to the "printed page" for others to read and let the work take on a life of its own. His goal, as he explained in the interview, was to achieve "sparseness and rigor and a world of compassion" in his work. In 2000 Kunitz was appointed poet laureate of the United States, serving for one year. That same year *The Collected Poems* was published. In addition to his literary success, Kunitz was dedicated to promoting the work of other poets as well as bringing poetry to a wider public. Toward that end he was one of the founders of the Fine Arts Work Center, which offers residencies to writers and artists, in Provincetown and Poets House, a national poetry library and center for readings and other literary events, in New York City. Kunitz was also a member of the American Academy and Institute of Arts and Letters and the Academy of American Poets. In the year before his death he completed *The Wild Braid: A Poet Reflects on a Century in the Garden*, which he wrote with coauthor Genine Lentine. He died of pneumonia at his home in New York City. He is buried in Provincetown.

Kunitz's legacy is rich and varied. He is remembered for his dedication to the craft of poetry; his insistence on the importance of freedom of expression for writers; his generosity toward fellow writers and students through his work as editor, translator, teacher, and founder of organizations that support poets; for his artistry as a gardener; and not least for the poetry itself.

★

For a discussion of Kunitz's work, see Gregory Orr, *Stanley Kunitz: An Introduction to the Poetry* (1985). For a compilation of interviews with and essays about Kunitz, see Stanley Moss, ed., *Interviews and Encounters with Stanley Kunitz* (1993). Three interviews of particular interest are Cynthia Davis, "An Interview with Stanley Kunitz," *Contemporary Literature* 15, no. 1 (Winter 1974): 1–14; Peter Stitt, "An Interview with Stanley Kunitz," *Gettysburg Review* 5, no. 2 (Spring 1992): 193–209; and Mary B. W. Tabor, "A Poet Takes the Long View, 90 Years Old," *New York Times* (30 Nov. 1995). An obituary is in the *New York Times* (16 May 2006).

Jane Amler Lewis

L

LADER, Lawrence Powell (*b*. 6 August 1919 in New York City; *d*. 7 May 2006 in New York City), writer and activist who is considered the father of the abortion rights movement.

Lader was the son of Ludwig Lader and Myrtle (Powell) Lader. He attended Harvard University, where he studied journalism and was the editor of the *Crimson*, the daily student newspaper. Upon graduating from Harvard with a bachelor of arts degree in 1941, Lader enlisted in the U.S. Army, in which he became a lieutenant and served from 1942 to 1946. During World War II, he sent war reports to the *New Yorker*. He also contributed work to various magazines after the war, including *Look*, *Life*, and the *Saturday Evening Post*. In particular, he was a magazine foreign correspondent during the Arab-Israeli War in 1948 and a contributing editor for *Esquire*.

On 24 August 1942 Lader married Jean MacInnis, who kept her name and had a separate bank account, a radical step for a woman at the time. They divorced in January 1946. Lader later married Joan Summers on 27 September 1961, and they had one daughter. In addition to being a writer, Lader became involved in New York politics, working closely with the New York American Laborite representative Vito Marcantonio of East Harlem, New York City, one of the most leftist radical politicians of the time. In 1948 Lader ran unsuccessfully for New York State representative on the American Labor Party ticket.

Becoming interested in abortion rights, Lader published *The Margaret Sanger Story and the Fight for Birth Control* (1955), a biography of Margaret Sanger, one of the earliest birth control activists in the early twentieth century. "Working with her," he stated in a 1991 *New York Times* interview, "... convinced me that a woman's freedom ... could only be achieved when she gained control of her childbearing. I ... came to understand that birth control required abortion as a backup measure."

Recognizing the dearth of information on abortion, Lader published an article on abortion in the *New York Times* magazine in 1965. The article was followed by the book *Abortion* (1966). The book built upon the 1965 Supreme Court decision in *Griswold v. Connecticut*, which defined the right to privacy among adults engaging in consensual marital sexual relations, in particular in the use of contraceptives. Lader argued that the right to contraceptive privacy could be applied to abortion as well. Both *Griswold v. Connecticut* and Lader's *Abortion* were influential in the U.S. Supreme Court's decision in *Roe v. Wade* (1973), which overturned state and federal laws that outlawed or restricted abortion, thereby making it legal. Lader explains this political struggle in *Abortion II: Making of the Revolution* (1973).

In addition to his writings on abortion, Lader was also involved as an activist for abortion rights. After writing his *New York Times* article, he started receiving numerous letters from women seeking doctors who performed abortions, to which he responded. In 1969 he was one of the founders of the National Association for the Repeal of Abortion Laws, which became the National Abortion Rights Action League (NARAL), after abortion became legal in 1973. Later, the organization's name was changed to NARAL Pro-Choice America. The group's first battleground state in the fight to repeal abortion laws was New York, resulting in a victory in 1973.

However, believing that NARAL was not radical enough, Lader left the organization in 1976 to start a new group, the Abortion Rights Mobilization. Specifically, the group sued the Internal Revenue Service, trying unsuccessfully from 1980 to 1990 to remove the Catholic Church's tax-exemption status because of its participation in partisan politics against abortion laws. With the Abortion Rights Mobilization, Lader also worked to make the newly manufactured RU-486 pill (the so-called abortion pill) available in the United States. Indeed, the pill's manufacturer, Roussel Uclaf, did not want to sell RU-486 in the United States, and the U.S. government banned it. After illegally importing the drug into the United States in a strategy designed to get media attention, Lader set up a laboratory in Westchester, New York, to manufacture the drug and make it available to researchers. He wrote two books on the subject, *RU-486, the Pill that Could End the Abortion Wars and Why American Women Don't Have It* (1991) and *A Private Matter, RU-486 and the Abortion Crisis* (1995). In 2000 the U.S. Food and Drug Administration finally approved the drug. In recognition of his efforts to make the drug available, Lader was named the Feminist Majority's Feminist of the Year in 1992. Lader died at age eighty-six of colon cancer at his home in New York City.

In a turbulent era, when civil rights were being questioned and expanded to include new groups, Lader declared that women should have control of their bodies, including the right to have an abortion, at a time when even information on abortions was scarce. He fought tirelessly to make abortion rights possible, both through his writings and as an activist until his death, well earning the feminist and activist Betty Friedan's description of him as the father of the abortion rights movement.

Lader's papers can be found in the New York Public Library's archives. The collection includes material on the Abortion Rights Mobilization and NARAL and Lader's writings, correspondence, and reports. Insight into Lader's abortion rights activism is also available in Valerie Gladstone, "Long Island Q & A: Lawrence Lader, Writer Struggles Against Roadblocks to RU-486 Abortion Pill," *New York Times* (14 July 1991). Obituaries are in the *New York Times* (10 May 2006) and *Washington Post* (11 May 2006).

Michael Waldman

LAINE, Frankie (*b.* 30 March 1913 in Chicago, Illinois; *d.* 6 February 2007 in San Diego, California), chart-topping pop singer, entertainer, recording star, and songwriter whose career spanned seven decades.

Laine was born Francesco Paolo LoVecchio, the oldest of eight children of the Italian immigrants John LoVecchio, a barber, and Anna (Salerno) LoVecchio, who was a partner

Frankie Laine, 1952. **CBS PHOTO ARCHIVE/GETTY IMAGES**

in her father's grocery store in Chicago. Laine knew that he wanted a career in singing after joining a church choir in his youth. While still attending Lane Technical High School, he sang in local cabarets and nightclubs, with his first public appearance at the age of fifteen at the Merry Garden Ballroom on Chicago's North Side. When the Depression hit, Laine dropped out of high school to work full time to help support his large family.

In late 1930 Laine was laid off from his job and began traveling from town to town, auditioning at jazz clubs and supporting himself by working variously as a car salesman, a bouncer, and a marathon dancer. (He participated in fourteen dance marathons, and in 1932 in Atlantic City, New Jersey, he danced for 145 days straight, setting a world record.) After a brief stint in 1937 replacing the vocalist Perry Como in the band of Freddie Carlone in Cleveland, Laine headed to New York City. In 1938 he landed a singing job with radio station WINS, earning $5 per week. At this point he changed his name to Frankie Laine and also honed a new vocal style, eschewing the mellow crooning styles so popular at the time (for example, Bing Crosby, Russ Columbo, and Frank Sinatra). Laine began to "bend" notes (that is, singing around them instead of landing on them directly). He developed a quick vibrato and often sang against the tempo of a song. He explained himself by saying, "I just use my voice like a horn. I try to sing the way Louis Armstrong blows his trumpet."

Armstrong, Mildred Bailey, Billie Holiday, and other jazz greats influenced his style.

Back in Cleveland during World War II, Laine worked as a machinist making airplane parts. He sang over the roar of the factory and visited jazz clubs whenever he could. Requesting a transfer to the company's California plant to follow a girlfriend and also to pursue a singing career, Laine moved to Los Angeles in August 1943 and worked as a machinist until May 1945, when he was laid off at the end of the war.

Eking out a living doing radio and movie background vocals, Laine had his big break on 5 March 1946. He was singing for no pay at Billy Berg's Vine Street Club in Hollywood, California, when he was discovered by the composer Hoagy Carmichael, who was deeply moved by Laine's rendition of "Rockin' Chair." Carmichael persuaded Berg to hire Laine at $75 per week. A few nights later a Mercury Records executive caught Laine's act, and Laine's career was launched. "That's My Desire" was recorded on 15 September 1946 and quickly sold 1.3 million copies. Laine kept recording for Mercury until March 1951, following his first big hit with such gold recordings as "Shine" in 1948, "Lucky Old Sun" in 1949, "Mule Train" in 1949, and others.

Thus Laine suddenly became one of America's most popular entertainers and recording stars. He made feature appearances on such radio shows as *The Chesterfield Supper Club*, *The Big Show*, and *Philco Radio Time* (all in 1947). He played to full houses in large theaters all over the United States and unleashed an intense and personal style of delivery that included writhing, grimacing, and making other facial expressions while flailing his arms and stamping his feet. Compared more than once to a "windmill salesman" because of his gyrations, Laine persisted with this distinctive and highly emotive style.

In April 1951 Laine followed the record producer Mitch Miller to Columbia Records, where he continued until 1957, producing thirty-nine hit singles, among them "Jezebel" (1951), "I Believe" (1953), and his cover of the film title song "High Noon" (1955). He later recorded variously for Columbia, Mercury, Capitol, ABC Records, and other companies, selling over 100 million records (twenty-one of them gold) during his long career. His final album, *The Nashville Connection* (2004), took his career into the twenty-first century.

European tours in 1952 and 1954 (when he gave a command performance for Queen Elizabeth II of England) and in Australia and New Zealand in 1955 and 1956 increased Laine's popularity. In fact, over 300 Frankie Laine fan clubs sprang up, not only in the United States and England but also in such places as Cairo, Egypt; Malta; Iceland; Baghdad, Iraq; and Johannesburg, South Africa.

Riding his immense popularity, Laine appeared in seven movies from 1949 to 1956 (usually playing himself or a minor singing character) and performed the title songs of several other films, including *Gunfight at the O.K. Corral* and *3:10 to Yuma*, both in 1957. His robust, masculine voice lent itself naturally to the western idiom, and he sang the theme songs for the very popular western television series *Rawhide* (1959–1966) and Mel Brooks's Western movie spoof *Blazing Saddles* (1974).

Laine's movies naturally led to television appearances. From 1955 to 1956 on Columbia Broadcasting System, Laine hosted his own *Frankie Laine Show*, a variety hour, and he had guest spots on such popular late 1950s and early 1960s shows as *Perry Mason*, *Rawhide*, *Make Room for Daddy*, and *Bachelor Father*.

Laine was also a songwriter and lyricist, both solo and in collaboration. "We'll Be Together Again," composed in 1945 by Carl Fischer, features Laine's lyrics and went on to become a pop standard recorded by over 100 artists. Laine wrote "It Only Happens Once" in 1941, and he went on to work with such composers as Carmichael, Duke Ellington, and Mel Tormé. In 1996 he was presented with a Lifetime Achievement Award by the Songwriters Hall of Fame.

During this whirlwind career, on 15 June 1950 Laine married the actress Nan Grey, to whom he was devoted until her death in 1993. The two had no children of their own, but Laine helped to raise Grey's two young daughters from a previous marriage. On 5 July 1999 he married Marcia Ann Kline and was with her until his death of heart failure. His ashes were scattered with those of his first wife over the Pacific Ocean.

It is hard to overestimate Laine's popularity, which skyrocketed in the late 1940s and continued despite the advent of rock and roll in 1954 and the change in American musical tastes thereafter. His rich warm baritone voice and his abilities to express deep emotion unabashedly and sell a song completely made his name a household word in the United States and abroad for decades.

★

Laine's autobiography, *That Lucky Old Son* (1993), with Joseph F. Laredo, is an excellent source for anecdotes and details about Laine's colorful life in show business. For an in-depth, contemporaneous look at the Laine phenomenon in the 1950s, see Dean Jennings, "The Case of the Screaming Troubadour," *Saturday Evening Post* (11 Dec. 1954). Obituaries are in the *New York Times* and *Los Angeles Times* (both 7 Feb. 2007).

Michael Meckna

LAMB, Willis Eugene, Jr. (*b.* 12 July 1913 in Los Angeles, California; *d.* 15 May 2008 in Tucson, Arizona), physicist who was jointly awarded the 1955 Nobel Prize in Physics with Polykarp Kusch for independent research that led to discoveries of phenomena related to the interaction of electrons and electromagnetic radiation, profoundly advancing basic concepts in physics.

Lamb was the son of Willis Eugene Lamb, a telephone engineer, and Marie Helen (Metcalf) Lamb. He was educated in the Los Angeles public schools except for three years in the Oakland, California, public school system. In 1930 Lamb entered the University of California, Berkeley, graduating with a BS in chemistry in 1934. He continued at Berkeley as a graduate student but changed his major to theoretical physics. Lamb's graduate research focused on the electromagnetic properties of nuclear systems. His research was directed by J. Robert Oppenheimer, who was appointed in 1942 by President Franklin D. Roosevelt to head the Manhattan Project that developed the atomic bomb. Lamb received his PhD in 1938.

After receiving his PhD from Berkeley, Lamb joined the physics faculty at Columbia University as an instructor in 1938, rising through the ranks to full professor in 1948. Between 1943 and 1951 Lamb worked with the Columbia Radiation Laboratory, where his defense-related research focused on how to make shorter, higher-frequency microwave sources for radar. The research he did at Columbia led to his Nobel award in 1955.

While teaching a summer session course on spectroscopy at Columbia in 1945, Lamb read about German research in the 1930s which predicted that hydrogen atoms could be studied using three-centimeter-wavelength radiation. This was the same radiation with which he was working in the Radiation Laboratory. Lamb was also familiar with the theory proposed by the British physicist Paul Dirac in 1928, and for which Dirac received the Nobel Prize in Physics in 1933, relating to the fine structure exhibited in the spectral lines produced as hydrogen's one electron absorbs energy and achieves "excited" orbits when hydrogen atoms are exposed to radiation. Fine structure refers to the splitting of spectral lines. Dirac's theory was based on relativity and quantum theories.

Dirac's theory predicted that two of the excited states of the radiated hydrogen atoms would have exactly the same energy, but some physicists questioned that prediction. Numerous efforts had been made to use optical methods to test Dirac's theory of fine structures, but none provided conclusive results. In the summer of 1946, Lamb designed an apparatus with the Columbia graduate student R. C. Retherford to study the fine structure produced from optical radiation of hydrogen using very high-resolution radio frequency resonance methods adapted from his microwave research. In April 1947 Lamb succeeded in precisely identifying an extremely small but significant shift of energy in the hydrogen spectrum in different states, definitively answering the questions raised by physicists regarding Dirac's theory and fine structures. Lamb had discovered the quantum effect that would become known as the "Lamb shift."

Lamb reported his research in a series of papers published in the *Physical Review* from 1947 to 1953. These papers were widely acclaimed as classics by scientists working in atomic physics. From 1951 to 1956 Lamb continued his research as a member of the faculty at Stanford University. Between 1956 and 1962 he was a professor and fellow of New College at the University of Oxford in England. Following his tenure at Oxford, Lamb was Henry Ford II Professor of Physics and J. Willard Gibbs Professor of Physics at Yale University until 1974, when he became Regents' Professor of Physics and Optical Sciences at the University of Arizona, retiring from that position in 2002.

In addition to the Nobel Prize in Physics that Lamb won in 1955, he enjoyed numerous awards and accolades. In 1958 he was honored with a Guthrie Award from the Physical Society of London, and in 1992 he was awarded an Einstein Medal from the Society for Optical and Quantum Electronics. Lamb received a National Medal of Science, the nation's highest scientific honor, in 2000. In addition to his awards, Lamb was elected to the National Academy of Sciences, became a fellow of the American Physical Society, and was a foreign member of the Royal Society of Edinburgh. The Physics of Quantum Electronics organization presents an annual Willis E. Lamb Award for Laser Science and Quantum Optics for outstanding contributions in the field.

Lamb was described by William H. Wing, a physics professor at the University of Arizona and one of Lamb's postdoctoral students in 1968, as "a physicist's physicist." Wing added, "It was very important to him to get things right." Lamb died of complications from a gallstone disorder at the University Medical Center in Tucson. On 5 June 1939 Lamb married his first wife, Ursula Schaefer, a student from Germany. She died in 1996. On 29 November 1996 he married Bruria Kaufman; the marriage ended in divorce. In January 2008 Lamb married Elsie Wattson, whom he had met twenty-seven years earlier.

Lamb's discovery of the minute shift of energy in the fine structures of a hydrogen spectrum, the quantum effect called Lamb's shift, became a foundation for quantum electrodynamics, a key methodology for studies in modern particle physics. Lamb pioneered research that contributed to the discovery of the maser (microwave amplification by stimulated emission of radiation) and the optical version, laser (light amplification by stimulated emission of radiation). Lamb's Nobel Prize–winning experiment was actually the first demonstration of microwave-stimulated emission. Although the methodology behind the laser was invented in 1950 by the French physicist Alfred Kastler, who won the Nobel Prize for Physics in 1966, it was a former student of Lamb's, Theodore Maiman, who made the first working laser on 16 May 1960.

★

Obituaries are in the University of Arizona's *UA News* (16 May 2008), the *Washington Post* (19 May 2008), and the *New York Times* (20 May 2008).

M. C. Nagel

LANTOS, Thomas Peter ("Tom") (*b.* 1 February 1928 in Budapest, Hungary; *d.* 11 February 2008 in Bethesda, Maryland), Holocaust survivor and U.S. representative who chaired the House Committee on Foreign Affairs and crusaded for human rights.

Lantos was born to middle-class Jewish parents, Pal Lantos and Anna Lantos. The family was interred in concentration camps when the Nazis invaded Budapest in March 1944. The sixteen-year-old Lantos went to a forced-labor camp in nearby Szob, where he worked under brutal conditions repairing and maintaining a major railroad line. Lantos escaped twice. Following his initial capture, he was severely beaten. The second time he made it to Budapest, where he found shelter in a safe house operated by the Swedish diplomat Raoul Wallenberg. Lantos was blond and blue-eyed, and his "Aryan" looks served as a perfect disguise. Donning a military uniform, he ran errands for Wallenberg at great personal risk. "In retrospect, I was doing things I never should have done," Lantos once remarked, "because they took more courage than I'm sure I had."

At the end of World War II in 1945, Lantos discovered that most of his family had died in concentration camps. He did, however, manage to contact a childhood friend, Annette Tilleman, who had gone into hiding during the Nazi occupation. The two kept in touch when Lantos started school at the University of Budapest in 1946. A year later he was offered a Hillel Foundation scholarship to study at the University of Washington in Seattle. Lantos arrived in the United States penniless, yet he embraced his new life in the bucolic Seattle suburbs. "Getting beyond World War II, I felt like I was born again," he recalled in 1999. Lantos took on various odd jobs to pay for his studies, earning a BA in 1949 and an MA in economics from the same school in 1950.

On 13 July 1950 Lantos married Tilleman, who had immigrated to California. The couple eventually had two daughters. After receiving his PhD in economics from the University of California, Berkeley, in 1953, Lantos became an American citizen and taught for nearly three decades at San Francisco State University. He also worked as a television commentator as well as an economic consultant for several Democratic U.S. senators. In 1959 Lantos won his first elective office, to the Millbrae (California) School District Board of Trustees, serving until 1966.

In 1980 Lantos went unchallenged in the Democratic primary to face the freshman Republican U.S. representative William "Bill" Royer for a seat representing wealthy suburbs down peninsula from San Francisco, including the cities of San Mateo, Burlingame, and Hillsborough, California. Lantos proved an astute campaigner and an effective fund-raiser, tapping into a nationwide network of Jewish contributors. He barely prevailed, garnering 46 percent of the vote to unseat Royer, who received 43 percent. With Republican candidates riding on the coattails of the newly elected president, Ronald Reagan, Lantos was the only California Democrat to unseat a Republican incumbent. Royer tried to reclaim the seat in 1982; Lantos rebuffed the challenge and easily won reelection to the next twelve Congresses.

With his shock of white hair, piercing blue eyes, aquiline nose, and crisp Hungarian accent, Lantos brought a formal, courtly manner to the fast-paced atmosphere that often defines the House of Representatives. He replaced the desk in his office with settees and chairs, preferring low light and oriental rugs. Lantos's background, coupled with his notoriously sharp memory and professorial temperament, earned him the reputation as Congress's gentleman scholar. His committee assignments over the course of his career also reflected his legislative style and interests. Not one to seek passage of large amounts of legislation, he preferred more deliberative panels where he could bring issues important to him to the forefront; he was an active and career-long member of the Government Operations Committee and the Foreign Affairs Committee.

Lantos's investigation into allegations of government corruption initially thrust him into the national spotlight. From April to December 1989, as chairman of the Employment and Housing Subcommittee of the Government Operations Committee, Lantos conducted hearings investigating accusations of influence peddling and political favoritism by Housing and Urban Development officials during President Reagan's administration. Throughout the hearings Lantos earned praise from across the political spectrum for conducting a well-balanced and thorough investigation. The subcommittee's inquiry resulted in legislation aimed at curbing abuses in Housing and Urban Development and the appointment of a special prosecutor to look into criminal wrongdoing.

Lantos's contributions to U.S. foreign policy, however, became his lasting legacy during his nearly three-decade congressional career. The only Holocaust survivor to serve in Congress, he focused his efforts on shining a light on global human rights abuses. "My whole congressional career, if it has an overarching theme, it is an active involvement in human rights," he once reflected. Lantos credited Wallenberg as his inspiration. Lantos was gratified by his savior's heroism and haunted by Wallenberg's mysterious disappearance under the Soviet occupation of Budapest in 1945, and Lantos's first successful piece of legislation granted the Swedish diplomat honorary American citizenship. Wallenberg was only the second person (along with the former British prime minister Winston Churchill) to receive such an honor. In 1983 Lantos founded the Congressional Human Rights Caucus, with his wife serving as the caucus's volunteer director.

As he rose through the ranks on the Foreign Affairs Committee, Lantos was often the first member to address government oppression around the globe. He called for sanctions or military action against governments in the Soviet Union, China, Myanmar, Iran, Serbia, Rwanda, and Sudan for alleged abuses of their citizens. In April 2006 the seventy-eight-year-old Lantos was among five members of Congress who were arrested outside the Sudanese embassy in Washington, D.C., while protesting allegations of genocide in the country's embattled Darfur region. Lantos paid a fine for misdemeanor charges of disorderly conduct and unlawful assembly. "After the Holocaust that I have personally experienced ... we [must] put an end to this," he pleaded upon his release.

Lantos was particularly outspoken on the Middle East. A strong supporter of Israel, he often took a hawkish approach to Arab governments in the region. "We have been confronted by Ayatollahs from the Mideast and pretended they were accountants from the Midwest," he once admonished his colleagues. An early and outspoken critic of Saddam Hussein, Lantos likened the Iraqi dictator to Adolf Hitler and introduced a resolution to call him before an international war crimes tribunal. Lantos was among the eighty Democrats who voted to authorize President George H. W. Bush to use force against Iraq in January 1991 in retaliation for that country's invasion of its neighbor Kuwait. In 2002 Lantos was one of only a handful of Democrats to steer passage of a war resolution against Iraq. Lantos later retracted his support when he disagreed with how President George W. Bush's administration was conducting the war.

Lantos also proved that he was not beyond engaging Arab governments, believing that "dialogue is not appeasement." A leader in calling for sanctions against Libya in the early 1980s protesting that country's support of terrorist activities, Lantos later became one of the first lawmakers to advise lifting these restrictions. Believing that the longtime Libyan dictator Muammar Qaddafi was serious about dismantling his stockpiles of chemical, biological, and nuclear weapons, Lantos agreed to meet with him in 2004. The congressman won praise for his engagement with a former enemy. One San Francisco Jewish activist noted that "Tom could be very tough and direct. He made it a point to know most of these characters and talk to them."

In 2006, after Democrats won a majority in the House for the first time in more than a decade, Speaker Nancy Pelosi of California named Lantos chairman of the Committee on Foreign Affairs in the 110th Congress (2007–2009), a job that Lantos felt he had prepared his entire life to do. The new chairman vowed to bring his lifelong commitment to human rights to the forefront of American foreign policy. "Americans have demanded change in the way our country conducts itself in the world," Lantos announced. "Count on Congress to see [to] it."

Chairman Lantos had little time to legislate. In December 2007 he was diagnosed with a rare esophageal cancer. The grueling treatment schedule, set to begin the following January, convinced Lantos not seek reelection in 2008. "I will never be able to express fully my profoundly felt gratitude to this great country," he noted while announcing his impending retirement.

In early February 2008 Lantos checked into Bethesda Naval Hospital in Maryland after feeling poorly following a round of chemotherapy; he died there several days later. Congress memorialized him with a ceremony in Statuary Hall in the U.S. Capitol on 14 February 2008. Lantos is buried in the Congressional Cemetery in Washington, D.C. In June 2008 President George W. Bush posthumously awarded him the Presidential Medal of Freedom, the nation's highest civilian honor.

A self-proclaimed "American by choice," Lantos proved his great love for his adopted nation through nearly three decades of public service. Employing his scholarly and deliberative nature to awaken the conscience of an often pragmatic Congress, he profoundly affected the direction of U.S. human rights policy right up until the day he died. Once one of the oppressed, Lantos left a legacy of protecting those whose voices would be silenced.

★

Lantos's personal papers are housed at the University of California, Berkeley. An autobiographical account of Lantos's World War II experiences is in Steven Spielberg and Survivors of the Shoah Visual History Foundation, *The Last Days* (1999). See also Jon Marmor, "Against All Odds," *Columns* (Sept. 1999). Obituaries are in the *New York Times* and *Washington Post* (both 12 Feb. 2008).

Laura Turner O'Hara

LAUTERBUR, Paul Christian (*b.* 6 May 1929 in Sidney, Ohio; *d.* 27 March 2007 in Urbana, Illinois), chemist who shared a Nobel Prize for his pioneering work in the development of magnetic resonance imaging (MRI).

Paul C. Lauterbur, 2003. AP IMAGES

Lauterbur was the son of Edward Joseph Lauterbur, an engineer and part-owner of the Peerless Bread Machinery Company, and Gertrude Frieda (Wagner) Lauterbur, a homemaker. He had two brothers and a sister; his older brother died shortly after birth. Lauterbur attended parochial elementary school and the local public high school, but his later interests were influenced more by a favorite aunt, who was fascinated by natural history. In 1943 the Lauterbur family moved to a farm just outside of Sidney. There, Lauterbur nurtured his growing passion for all kinds of science by observing nature and experimenting in a self-created home chemistry laboratory.

In 1947 Lauterbur enrolled at the Case Institute of Technology (now part of Case Western Reserve University), an engineering school in Cleveland. His father recommended the school, noting that though he did not know what scientists did for a living, he did know that engineers could always get a job. Lauterbur chose to major in chemistry, however, and earned his BS in 1951. Upon graduation, he accepted a job with the Dow Corning Corporation in their laboratories at the Mellon Institute in Pittsburgh, where he pursued his interest in organosilicon chemistry. Despite his distaste for academics, he started taking graduate chemistry courses at the nearby University of Pittsburgh. He began to learn about nuclear

magnetic resonance (NMR), a new technology that used a magnetic field and radio waves to investigate the composition of chemical compounds.

In 1953 Lauterbur was drafted into the U.S. Army and assigned to the Scientific and Professional Personnel program at the Army Chemical Center in Edgewood, Maryland (now the Edgewood Chemical Biological Center). During his stint working in the center's Medical Laboratories, Lauterbur learned of a unit that had purchased an NMR machine and managed to obtain a transfer to that unit to help set it up. While still in the army he published four papers on his work with NMR, an unusual accomplishment for a soldier.

Lauterbur completed military service in 1955 and returned to the Mellon Institute, which bought an NMR spectrometer for his use. He experimented with different compounds, including carbon-13. In 1957 he published the first study of carbon-13 NMR in more than 100 compounds. This work gained Lauterbur respect in the NMR community and became the basis for his PhD dissertation. In 1962 Lauterbur received a PhD in chemistry from the University of Pittsburgh. Also that year he married Rose Mary Caputo, with whom he had two children. In 1963 he left the Mellon Institute to join the chemistry faculty at the State University of New York at Stony Brook. Lauterbur continued his NMR research, becoming increasingly interested in its possible biological applications.

In the summer of 1971 Lauterbur visited NMR Specialties, a small company in New Kensington, Pennsylvania, that manufactured NMR spectrometers. He observed experiments being conducted by Leon Saryan, a visiting researcher from Johns Hopkins University. Saryan was attempting to reproduce studies recently conducted by Raymond Damadian, a physician, at the Downstate Medical Center in New York City. Damadian reported observing unusually long NMR relaxation times in excised mouse tumors when compared to normal tissue. Lauterbur reasoned that the same must be true in the living animal and wondered if there was a way to use NMR to determine the location of tumors in a living body. It soon occurred to him that gradually altering the strength of the magnetic field of an NMR spectrometer might work. The nonuniform magnetic field that was created would cause different parts of the test object to emit radio waves of different frequencies, and the pitch of the signal would indicate its location. Lauterbur was certain this would allow for two- or even three-dimensional images of the object's internal structure. As he said in an interview decades later, he "made a leap of faith to the conclusion that the information could be recovered in the form of pictures."

Lauterbur conducted his own experiments at Stony Brook. In March 1973, in the journal *Nature*, he published the first nuclear magnetic resonance image: a cross-sectional view of two one-millimeter-diameter glass tubes of water in a bath of heavy water (D_2O). He named his technique *zeugmatography*. That same year, Lauterbur produced the first NMR image of a living creature, a clam. Meanwhile, the British physicist Peter Mansfield, also working with NMR, developed a mathematical method to rapidly extract images, a crucial step in making Lauterbur's technique practical and clinically useful. Mansfield was the first to use the technique on a human, producing an image of a student's finger in 1976.

By the early 1980s whole-body NMR imaging scanners began to appear in hospitals and research institutions. The technology gradually became known as magnetic resonance imaging (MRI), the word *nuclear* being dropped because of its negative connotation.

In 1984, following a divorce from his first wife, Lauterbur married Joan Dawson, a physiologist. They had one daughter. In 1985 both Lauterbur and his wife accepted positions at the University of Illinois at Urbana-Champaign. Lauterbur was appointed to three different professorships and became director of the Biomedical Magnetic Resonance Laboratory. He was affiliated with both the Beckman Institute and the Center for Advanced Study at the university.

In October 2003 Lauterbur and Mansfield shared the Nobel Prize in Physiology or Medicine for their discoveries concerning magnetic resonance imaging. The award was controversial, as Damadian declared he should have been included for his work with NMR. The medical community, however, agreed that Lauterbur's creation of an actual NMR image was the real scientific breakthrough.

Among Lauterbur's many honors and awards were the prestigious Albert Lasker Clinical Medical Research Award (1984), the National Medal of Science (1987), and the National Medal of Technology (1988). He was inducted into the National Inventors Hall of Fame for his work on MRI in 2007. Lauterbur's professional memberships included the National Academy of Sciences, the American Chemical Society, the American Physical Society, and the American Association for the Advancement of Science.

In his later years Lauterbur's research interest shifted to evolution and the origin of life. Although his health was failing, he continued working at the University of Illinois until his death. He died of kidney disease at his home. His body was cremated and interred at Graceland Cemetery in his hometown of Sidney.

Lauterbur has been described as a visionary and a scientific maverick. MRI has, arguably, become the most powerful and reliable tool in diagnostic medicine. It is highly effective in discriminating among different types of tissue and between healthy and diseased tissue, and can be used to examine almost all organs of the body. MRI is considered to be completely safe, being noninvasive and free of ionizing radiation. Upon Lauterbur's death,

Richard Herman, chancellor of the Urbana-Champaign campus, remarked that his "influence is felt around the world every day, every time an MRI saves [a] life."

★

Lauterbur contributed a short autobiography to Tore Frängsmyr, ed., *Les Prix Nobel: The Nobel Prizes 2003* (2004). A chapter is dedicated to him in James Mattson and Merrill Simon, *The Pioneers of NMR and Magnetic Resonance in Medicine: The Story of MRI* (1996). An article on Lauterbur and his Nobel Prize–winning research is in *Physics Today* 56, no. 12 (Dec. 2003): 24–27. Obituaries are in the *New York Times* and *Los Angeles Times* (both 28 Mar. 2007).

Victoria Tamborrino

LAWFORD, Patricia Kennedy (*b.* 6 May 1924 in Brookline, Massachusetts; *d.* 17 September 2006 in New York City), sister of President John F. Kennedy and wife of the actor Peter Lawford who established a relationship between the Kennedy administration and Hollywood.

Lawford, known as "Pat," was the sixth of nine children born to Joseph Patrick Kennedy, a businessman who was

Patricia Kennedy Lawford. JULIAN WASSER/TIME LIFE PICTURES/GETTY IMAGES

involved in politics as chairman of the U.S. Securities and Exchange Commission and the Maritime Commission and as a diplomat, and Rose Elizabeth (Fitzgerald) Kennedy, the daughter of John Francis ("Honey Fitz") Fitzgerald, U.S. congressman and mayor of Boston. The family moved to New York State in 1927. From 1937 to 1940 her father served as ambassador to Great Britain. Lawford attended a convent school outside London from 1938 to 1939. When she returned home to Bronxville, New York, she deliberately failed the entrance exam to Noroton, a rigid Catholic convent boarding school that her older sisters attended. Instead she went to Maplehurst, a nearby Sacred Heart school, to which she was chauffeured every day. In 1941 she entered Rosemont College in Philadelphia, a small Catholic women's school, where she became a tennis champion and directed and acted in college theater.

After graduating from college with a BA in 1945 she went to work for her brother Jack, as John F. Kennedy was called, on his 1946 campaign for the House of Representatives seat previously held by Honey Fitz Fitzgerald. In 1952 she worked on Jack's Senate campaign against Henry Cabot Lodge, Jr. Like her father, who amassed part of his great wealth through investing in and running Hollywood studios, she had both a skill for business and a fascination with Hollywood. She took a television job in New York City and in 1950 went to California to work as a production assistant on two radio programs.

She began dating the British actor Peter Lawford in November 1953, and after just two months she proposed marriage. Lawford hesitantly accepted. After her father obtained a Federal Bureau of Investigation report on his future son-in-law, the couple married on 24 April 1954. An estimated 3,000 spectators stood outside the church in Manhattan to get a glimpse of the couple. They would have four children. The Lawfords' beachfront Malibu mansion, once the home of the famed movie producer Louis B. Mayer, became a West Coast vacation spot for the Kennedy family, including the future president. Lawford served as the western head of the Joseph P. Kennedy, Jr. Foundation, dedicated to helping people with mental disabilities. It was named after her eldest brother, who was killed during World War II, and inspired by her eldest sister, Rosemary.

The Lawfords led a glamorous life with many acquaintances and friends in the entertainment industry, including Frank Sinatra. Both husband and wife developed heavy drinking habits and engaged in affairs. In 1958 the Lawfords paid $10,000 for the film rights to *Ocean's Eleven*, which were later bought by Sinatra. The 1960 movie starred Sinatra, Lawford, and others from the Hollywood "Rat Pack."

By the time of John F. Kennedy's 1960 presidential campaign, the Lawfords were the most celebrated couple in Hollywood. Peter Lawford became a U.S. citizen so he could vote for his brother-in-law. Together with Sinatra the couple held a fund-raising gala for Kennedy at the Washington Armory, with appearances by the conductor and composer Leonard Bernstein, the actors Laurence Olivier and Sidney Poitier, and the jazz vocalist Ella Fitzgerald. Lawford accompanied her brother at campaign events when his pregnant wife, Jacqueline Kennedy, was unable to attend.

In the summer of 1962 the Lawfords arranged a trip for President Kennedy to stay at Sinatra's Palm Springs home, where Sinatra had a helipad installed along with lodging for Secret Service agents. Pat's brother Robert F. ("Bobby") Kennedy, then attorney general, canceled the stay, infuriating Sinatra, who cut his ties with the Lawfords. Around this time Jimmy Hoffa, the president of the Teamsters union who harbored great bitterness toward Jack and Bobby Kennedy, hired a private investigator to bug the Lawford house for information on the Kennedys.

Lawford developed a close friendship with the actress Marilyn Monroe, whom she introduced to the president. Peter, whose affair with the actress Lee Remick had turned into a serious relationship, was then on a decline into alcoholism and drug abuse, though he remained the president's friend. The Lawfords agreed to stay married for Kennedy's sake until after his reelection in 1964; when the president was assassinated in November 1963, Pat moved with the couple's four children to New York City and became the first Kennedy to file for divorce. In New York she became a benefactor of arts organizations, befriending many artists and writers. She also continued to support her brothers' political activities, working on Bobby's 1964 New York Senate campaign and 1968 bid for the presidency and Edward ("Ted") Kennedy's Massachusetts Senate campaigns, appearing with Ted when his wife, Joan, could not. Though never comfortable on political platforms, she was always available for her brothers, whom she adored.

Lawford founded the National Committee for the Literary Arts, refurbished exhibits at the John F. Kennedy Library, and provided archival footage for the television special *The Kennedys*. After Bobby Kennedy's assassination in 1968, she put together a privately printed book of remembrances about him, *That Shining Hour* (1969). Pat saw Peter for the last time in September 1983, at their daughter Sydney's wedding; he died in December 1984 of kidney and liver failure. In 1986 she accompanied Senator Ted Kennedy on an official visit to Chile. In 1989 she was arrested for drunk driving after running into a telephone pole on Long Island; was inebriated at Rose Kennedy's 100th birthday celebration in July 1990. Her escort in her last years was Dotson Rader, who had been the companion of the playwright Tennessee Williams, one of her closest friends. She died of complications of pneumonia at her home in Manhattan. She is buried in Southampton Cemetery, Southampton, New York.

Emerging from a Catholic schoolgirl background, Lawford demonstrated her independent streak when she went against her father's wishes to marry a debonair Hollywood actor. Known for her beauty, sophistication, and skill—her father commented that she had "the best business head in the family"—she later struggled with a drinking problem. As the sister of a president and two prominent senators, she moved between the world of politics and Hollywood, bringing them together in ways that often piqued the interest of the press and public.

★

Biographical details can be found in Doris Kearns Goodwin, *The Fitzgeralds and the Kennedys* (1987); Rose Kennedy, *Times to Remember* (1974); Christopher Kennedy Lawford, *Symptoms of Withdrawal: A Memoir of Snapshots and Redemption* (2005); and Laurence Leamer, *The Kennedy Women: The Saga of an American Family* (1994). An obituary is in the *New York Times* (18 Sept. 2006).

Louise B. Ketz

LAY, Kenneth Lee ("Ken") (*b.* 15 April 1942 in Tyrone, Missouri; *d.* 5 July 2006 in Aspen, Colorado), businessman whose business practices harmed millions of consumers and resulted in one of the most costly bankruptcies in history, as well as in his indictment and conviction for crimes that he committed as the leader of Enron Corporation.

Lay was the son of Omer Lay, who was employed variously as a Baptist preacher, a feed store operator, and a tractor salesman, and Ruth E. (Reese) Lay, who worked in the feed store and was a homemaker. The family lived in poverty, and perhaps it was Lay's childhood of poverty that later compelled him in his relentless pursuit of wealth. Lay had an older sister and a younger sister. The feed store went out of business when Lay was still very young, and he and his parents moved in with relatives on a farm without indoor plumbing. Lay had to find work while he was still a child, and he learned to drive tractors to plow and harvest fields. His parents taught him the importance of hard work, and his father passed on an affection for intellectual pursuits.

Although Lay's schoolwork at David H. Hickman High School in Columbia, Missouri, from which he graduated in 1960, earned him a scholarship to the University of Missouri, it did not pay for all of his expenses, so Lay worked painting houses and took out loans. The professor and economist Pinkney Walker caught Lay's imagination

Kenneth L. Lay, 2001. **PAM FRANCIS/GETTY IMAGES**

with an introductory course, and Lay majored in economics. He graduated with a BA in 1964 and went on to earn an MA in 1965.

In 1965 Lay found a job with Humble Oil (later Exxon). In 1969 he taught night school at George Washington University while finishing work on his PhD in economics from the University of Houston, awarded in 1970. He had married Judith Diane Ayers in 1966, and they had two children. Meanwhile Walker was appointed to the Federal Power Commission, and in 1972 he made Lay his assistant. During his work for the government, Lay saw many business opportunities in energy markets, and in September 1973 he applied for a job with Florida Gas, where he began work as vice president of corporate planning in 1974. In 1976 he became the company's president.

In 1979 Lay moved on to a higher-paying position at the Continental Group. He had been having an affair with a legal secretary, Linda Ann (Phillips) Herrold, and in 1980 he asked his wife for a separation; this resulted in a bitter divorce that ended in 1982. Lay had a remarkably captivating personality; when all seemed hopeless, he would turn on his charm and win people over to his side. Thus in 1985 he, his new wife, his children, and their mother began mingling during holidays as if they were all friends.

Lay's winning personality may have brought him the greatest business success of his life. In 1984 he joined Houston Natural Gas (HNG) and helped his new employer buy Florida Gas. He became chief executive officer of HNG in 1985, and that year he made his coup. The pipeline company InterNorth was trying to prevent its takeover by the venture capitalist Irwin Jacobs, and in Lay its board of directors found a friendly, folksy, relaxed partner who helped them by merging HNG with Inter-North. They looted $230 million from the employees' pension fund to buy out Jacobs and then discovered that Lay had sneaked enough of his supporters onto the board of directors to make him chief executive officer of the merged companies; the former leaders of InterNorth were out of power.

The new company became Enron. With control of gas pipelines and supplies throughout the southeastern and western United States, Lay engineered one of the most complex cases of fraud in history; Enron created numerous dummy companies with which it traded energy supplies. These companies traded with one another, each time raising the cost of petroleum, natural gas, or electricity. When natural gas was deregulated in 1989, Lay turned the trading with dummy companies into a multibillion-dollar business, from which he and other members of management took hundreds of millions of dollars. Lay became internationally respected. In 1991, when President George H. W. Bush asked Lay to join the administration as secretary of commerce, Lay refused the job because it was beneath his dignity.

Lay's massive fraud required the cooperation of many employees. In 2000 Enron's energy traders defrauded millions of consumers in California and other western states, causing people to lose their homes, driving some to suicide, and destroying the life's savings of countless others because they could not pay their natural gas bills. Lay blamed those he had defrauded for their miseries.

By 2001 Enron's fake companies had accrued over $30 billion in debt. The corporation had been a gigantic Ponzi scheme, in which new shareholders in Enron paid for the excessive salaries and bonuses of those at the top of Enron's pyramid, with Lay himself at the apex. Enron could not pay its bills and went bankrupt. Lay and his wife claimed that they were broke, ruined by the collapse of Enron—even though they owned seven mansions and lived lives of enormous luxury and privilege.

On 7 July 2004 a grand jury indicted Lay for committing securities fraud, bank fraud, wire fraud, and criminal conspiracy and for lying to stockholders. Lay capitalized on his likableness, presenting himself to the public as a kind, regular guy who was as much a victim as the millions of people he had defrauded. Further, he insisted that Enron was a strong company ruined by government regulators. Lay's defense at his trial in 2006 was that there was nothing wrong with Enron—that only a few people had committed a few crimes that had nothing to do with him. The evidence against him, however, tied him personally to incidents of fraud, and during his testimony in his defense, he became imperious in his tone as each of his lies about his activities at Enron was exposed during cross-examination. Although the original indictment included eleven charges against Lay, only six remained by the end of his trial. On 25 May 2006 a jury found him guilty on all six counts. He faced $43.5 million in fines, as well as life in prison. Shortly after the trial and before he was sentenced, Lay died of heart disease. His remains were cremated.

Although Lay was one of the world's most celebrated businessmen, his legacy is unlikely to be favorable. He claimed that with Enron he was creating a new kind of business that would prosper for years to come, but it was just a fraud committed on a large scale.

★

For an explanation of Lay's business practices, see Bethany McLean and Peter Elkind, *The Smartest Guys in the Room: The Amazing Rise and Scandalous Fall of Enron* (2006). Brian Cruver, *Anatomy of Greed: The Unshredded Truth from an Enron Insider* (2002), presents informative details about Lay's behavior. For a well-researched analysis of Lay's character, see Evan Thomas and Andrew Murr, "The Gambler Who Blew It All: The Bland Smile Concealed an Epic Arrogance," *Newsweek* (4 Feb. 2002). Julian E. Barnes, "How a Titan Came Undone," *U.S. News & World Report* (10 Mar. 2002), provides an evenhanded account of the downfall of Lay and Enron. An obituary is in the *New York Times* (6 July 2006).

Kirk H. Beetz

LEAVITT, Harold Jack (*b*. 14 January 1922 in Lynn, Massachusetts; *d*. 8 December 2007 in Pasadena, California), prominent Stanford University management professor and author best known as a trailblazer in the academic field of organizational behavior.

Leavitt was born to Joseph Leavitt, a retail merchant, and May (Lopata) Leavitt, a homemaker. As the youngest of eleven children, Leavitt was keenly aware from an early age of the role that hierarchies played, an interest he would spend much of his life studying. In 1943 Leavitt earned a BS from Harvard University. He continued his studies and graduated with an MS from Brown University in 1944. While pursuing his doctoral degree, Leavitt served as an active duty personnel research officer in the U.S. Naval Reserve from 1944 to 1946. During the mid- to late 1940s, at a time when animals were studied to understand the role of human behavior and success was determined by ongoing statistical analysis, Leavitt's early research was breaking new barriers, especially since his work revolved around human subjects and their actions and reactions to scenarios that would lead to organizational success. Leavitt completed his PhD in industrial economics in 1949 at the Massachusetts Institute of Technology. It was around this time that Leavitt met and married his first wife, Gloria Rosenthal, a homemaker and liberal political activist. The couple had three children. Gloria Rosenthal Leavitt died in 1985.

Leavitt's findings would change the way organizational behavior is taught in business schools, both in the United States and internationally. His textbook, *Managerial Psychology*, first published in 1958 and still in use at the start of the twenty-first century in its fifth edition, has been translated into eighteen languages. In a 1986 interview for *Stanford Business* magazine, Leavitt jokingly remarked that despite its enduring success, *Managerial Psychology* was initially turned down for publication. Warren G. Bennis, professor of business administration at the University of Southern California, called Leavitt's research "beautifully inventive," and stated that his work illustrated that "a more democratic approach to communications was more likely to result in correct decisions, faster decision-making and better group morale."

Leavitt was a faculty member at the University of Chicago and at the Rensselaer Polytechnic Institute before being hired as a professor of industrial administration at the West Coast branch of Carnegie Mellon University. In 1966 Leavitt became professor of organizational behavior and psychology at the Stanford Graduate School of Business. During the 1970s Leavitt was influential in organizing the faculty in his department to develop a more creative curriculum for MBA students, so that the department and the school would attract the best and brightest in the field.

In 1986 Leavitt published *Corporate Pathfinders: Building Vision and Values into Organizations*. Throughout his career, Leavitt continued to examine and to observe how teaching in business schools ultimately affects students' lives and their future careers. He felt that many business schools did a magnificent job in teaching students about the different aspects of business, such as banking systems, financial markets, and the structures of an organization, but that these very same institutions failed to teach and acknowledge such necessary qualities as determination, leadership, imagination, and responsibility that must be present to be successful in business, or in any other field. During this time, Leavitt also noted that business schools had a tendency to hurt "well-proportioned young men and women, distorting them into critters with lopsided brains, icy hearts and shrunken souls."

Leavitt retired from Stanford in 1987 and moved to Pasadena, California. The following year *Managerial Psychology: Managing Behavior in Organizations* was published, and in 1989 the fourth edition of his *Readings in Managerial Psychology* was published. In these texts he offered suggestions as to how managers might best "negotiate their way through authoritarian mazes while maintaining personal integrity and... finding satisfaction in work." From 1987 until the time of his death, Leavitt was the Walter Kenneth Kilpatrick Professor of Organizational Behavior, Emeritus, at the Stanford Graduate School of Business. He also taught at the London Business School and at INSEAD, a graduate business school in Fontainebleau, France.

Jean Lipman-Blumen, an organizational sociologist/social psychologist and professor of organizational behavior at Claremont Graduate University in Claremont, California, became Leavitt's second wife, and, as a result, he became the father of three stepchildren.

Leavitt and Lipman-Blumen coauthored *Hot Groups: Seeding Them, Feeding Them, and Using Them to Ignite Your Organization* (1999), which has been translated into six languages and received the Association of American Publishers Professional/Scholarly Publishing Award for Excellence for "The Best Business Book of 1999." In it, the authors describe and examine "hot groups," which usually consist of small teams of intensely dedicated individuals who have a collective passion about a particular—and challenging—task. Although these groups generally are short-lived, the impact of the results produced is highly influential and extraordinarily beneficial to corporations and educational institutions. Leavitt and Lipman-Blumen emphasized that organizations, and the managers within them, should permit a wide-ranging view, so that these institutions are able "to recognize and harness" the energy and enthusiasm of hot groups before they dissipate.

As the link between the world of academia and the realm of business, Leavitt acted as a consultant to many corporations, including Bell Telephone Laboratories, the Ford Foundation, Kaiser Permanente, Varian Associates, and the Straits Times Press of Singapore. He also served on the advisory boards of the University of Southern California's Leadership Institute, Helsinki University of Technology's Euro-MBA Program, and the Institute for Advanced Studies in Leadership at Claremont Graduate University. In addition, Leavitt was the director of the Stanford Executive Program for several years, the first director of the Stanford–National University of Singapore Executive Program in Singapore, and the educational adviser to Thailand's Institute for Management Education.

Leavitt published papers in numerous scholarly journals, including the *Harvard Business Review*, the *Administrative Science Quarterly*, and *Management Science*.

In his last book, *Top Down: Why Hierarchies Are Here to Stay and How to Manage Them More Effectively* (2005),

Leavitt provides answers to those who predicted the end of hierarchies and the development of new ways of managing businesses. He studied the dynamics of group decision making and acknowledged the fact that hierarchies are an inevitable way of life in the business world. He concluded that often large groups of people work well when a chain of command is present. According to Leavitt, having a hierarchical arrangement was "the best method ever invented for solving large, complicated problems." He discusses the varied reasons human hierarchies exist and will continue to do so. "They thrive because they are efficient." However positive that argument may sound, Leavitt does not shy away from the troubling notion that hierarchies lead to the idea that "success deserves to be one's primary life-goal." As a matter of fact, notes Leavitt, "hierarchies satisfy our need for security, for a sense of identity...and for evaluation." He adds that organizational success is not achieved "battling against human hierarchies but rather in learning to modify them and tame them, and in helping people learn how to work effectively and meaningfully inside them."

Leavitt died of pulmonary fibrosis at Huntington Memorial Hospital at the age of eighty-five. A memorial service was held on 14 February 2008 at Stanford Memorial Church. He is buried at the Oak Tree Cemetery in Claremont, California.

Leavitt will be remembered as a brilliant professor, a prolific writer, and a warm, friendly, compassionate, and understanding human being. He captured the attention of his students, not only by his cheerful yet unassuming demeanor but also by the wealth of his experience from years of training and consulting. According to Robert Jaedicke (Stanford Graduate School of Business, dean emeritus), "Hal was the ultimate scholar, and he had the rare quality of being interested in your research and your problems—not just his."

Biographical information can be found at the Stanford Graduate School of Business website, "Stanford GSB News," http://www.gsb.stanford.edu/news/headlines/leavittobit.html (accessed 22 Jan. 2009). Obituaries are in the *Boston Globe* and *Los Angeles Times* (both 21 Dec. 2007).

Adriana C. Tomasino

LEDERBERG, Joshua (*b.* 23 May 1925 in Montclair, New Jersey; *d.* 2 February 2008 in New York City), molecular biologist who won a Nobel Prize in Physiology or Medicine (1958) for discovering mechanisms of genetic change in bacteria and who later served as president of Rockefeller University in New York City.

Joshua Lederberg, 1958. KEYSTONE/GETTY IMAGES

Lederberg was born, the oldest of three sons, to Zvi Hirsch Lederberg, a rabbi, and Esther Goldenbaum (Schulman) Lederberg, a homemaker, who were immigrants to the United States from what is now Israel. While Lederberg was still a baby, the family moved to New York City, where Lederberg attended public schools, graduating from Stuyvesant High School in 1940 at the age of fifteen. The following year he began studies in a premedical program in zoology at Columbia University. As an undergraduate he did research on the mold *Neurospora crassa* in Francis J. Ryan's laboratory. From 1943 to 1945 Lederberg also served in the U.S. Naval Reserve at Saint Albans Naval Hospital. After completing his BA in 1944, he enrolled in the College of Physicians and Surgeons, Columbia's Medical School. In 1946, however, he decided to take a leave of absence from these studies to do research at Yale University with Edward Tatum, Ryan's own mentor and another *N. crassa* investigator. This work went so well that Lederberg did not return to medical school but instead received a PhD from Yale in 1948.

During his time at Yale working with the bacterium *Escherichia coli*, Lederberg discovered that this organism has a sexual phase in which genetic information—that is, deoxyribonucleic acid (DNA)—can be transferred from one *E. coli* cell to another in a process called bacterial conjugation. This breakthrough was startling because, at the time, bacteria were seen as simple organisms that only reproduced by cell division. It was surprising then to discover that bacteria had sex, defined broadly as the movement of genetic material from one individual of a species to another. This finding brought bacteria closer to the center of investigations in molecular biology, where researchers were attempting to understand how molecules controlled cellular processes, including those underlying heredity. Bacteria subsequently became so pivotal to this research that it is difficult to appreciate how significant Lederberg's work was.

While at Yale, Lederberg met Esther Miriam Zimmer, another student in Tatum's lab. They married in 1946, and in 1947, when Lederberg was just twenty-two, he was hired as an assistant professor of genetics at the University of Wisconsin–Madison. There Zimmer completed her PhD in 1950, and she and Lederberg conducted research together. In 1952 Lederberg and his student Norton Zinder made another significant discovery about gene transfer in *E. coli* when they found that a virus called a bacteriophage could transmit DNA from one *E. coli* cell to another. In addition to conjugation, there was another means for genetic sharing in bacteria, and it was termed transduction.

This discovery opened up a new field in molecular biology because it meant that researchers could use viruses to change bacterial genes—that is, to transfer DNA from one bacterial cell to another. In the 1970s this development led to genetic engineering, in which specific genes were inserted into bacteria—for example, the gene for human insulin. From this practice came the production of the protein by bacteria and led to a whole new source of insulin for people with diabetes. In addition researchers found that viruses could also serve as vectors for the movement of new genes into animal and plant cells, thus broadening the biotechnology field considerably. This process is the means by which tomato genes, for example, can be routinely transferred into other plant species and sheep can be given genes so that they produce such proteins as human growth hormone.

Meanwhile Lederberg was becoming an administrator as well as a researcher. In 1957 he founded the Department of Medical Genetics at the University of Wisconsin. A year later he was lured to Stanford University's School of Medicine, where he became the first chair of its new Department of Genetics, thus fulfilling his dream of working in an environment where genetic and medical research could be closely tied together. In 1958 Lederberg received the Nobel Prize in Physiology or Medicine for his work on genetic recombination in bacteria. He shared the prize with Tatum and George Beadle, who were honored for research on the genetics of *N. crassa*.

While at Stanford, Lederberg continued studies on bacterial genetics, but he also began to broaden his investigations. He became director of Stanford's Joseph P. Kennedy, Jr., Laboratories for Molecular Medicine, where he initiated studies on the genetic and neurological bases of mental retardation. In 1961–1962 he served on President John F. Kennedy's Panel on Mental Retardation. Later Lederberg was chair of President Jimmy Carter's Cancer Panel. With the prestige that accompanied his Nobel Prize, Lederberg found that he had influence well outside genetics. In the late 1950s, when the U.S. space program got under way, he argued that biology should have a place in the field. Thinking like a bacteriologist, he warned that landing technology on the Moon or on Mars could cause contamination of these terrains with Earth organisms. As a member of the National Academy of Sciences' Space Science Board from 1958 to 1974, he also encouraged investigation of the possibility of extraterrestrial life. In preparation for the 1975 Viking mission, he helped in designing the instruments and procedures used to detect possible traces of life on Mars.

Lederberg's energy and inquiring mind also took him in other interesting directions. With Edward Feigenbaum, the chair of Stanford's Department of Computer Science, Lederberg helped develop DENDRAL, a computer program for exploring the composition of unknown chemical compounds from several types of laboratory data. DENDRAL was the first expert system specialized for scientific research, or a computer program that attempts to mimic the thought processes experts use in exploring a problem in their field. In the 1970s Lederberg helped to establish SUMEX-AIM, a national time-share computer network for biomedical research that was a forerunner of the massive computer interconnectivity used in the research community today.

Lederberg's last major geographic and professional move came in 1978, when he was appointed president of Rockefeller University, which specializes in graduate education and is one of the premier research institutions in the United States. With his immense energy and drive, Lederberg revitalized the university and stressed its commitment to his passion: the connection of basic research with medical studies. He encouraged research in such areas as heart disease, cancer, infectious diseases, and neurological problems. When he stepped down in 1990, the institution was at the pinnacle of its prestige. He stayed on at Rockefeller as university professor emeritus and Raymond and Beverly Sackler Foundation Scholar and continued to do research on DNA and on computer models into his eighties. In 1994 Lederberg headed the U.S. Defense Department Task Force on Persian Gulf War Health Effects, which investigated evidence for a syndrome or set of symptoms among veterans of this conflict. This appointment was the culmination of a long relationship with the Defense Department; Lederberg had been a member of the Defense Science Board since 1979.

In 1966 Lederberg and Zimmer divorced after twenty years of marriage and many years as research collaborators; they had no children. Two years later Lederberg married Marguerite Stein Kirsch, a psychiatrist. They had a daughter, and Lederberg was also stepfather to Kirsch's son from her first marriage. Lederberg died of pneumonia at New York–Presbyterian Hospital.

Lederberg is considered one of the leading scientists of the twentieth century because he helped to found the field of molecular biology through his work on bacterial genetics, which led ultimately to the development of biotechnology. In addition he was a significant voice in linking biomedical research to such fields as space science and computational analysis. He was always interested in making sure that the public understood the importance of scientific research, and with this aim in mind, he published a weekly column on science and society in the *Washington Post* from 1966 to 1971. During his long career, Lederberg wrote more than 300 articles that ranged from research studies to policy analyses. In addition he edited three volumes of papers dealing with microbial genetics (1951), emerging infections (1992), and biological weapons (1999). Just these three alone reflect the breadth of his interests and his commitment to giving science an important voice in society. Not surprisingly, Lederberg received a host of honors over the years. He was elected to the National Academy of Sciences in 1957 and to the Royal Society of London as a foreign member in 1979. President George H. W. Bush presented Lederberg with the U.S. National Medial of Science in 1989, and six years later Lederberg was given the Newell Award from the Association for Computing Machinery. In 2006 he received the Presidential Medal of Freedom from President George W. Bush.

The Rockefeller Archive Center houses many of Lederberg's papers, particularly relating to his tenure at Rockefeller University; there are also Lederberg papers at the Stanford University Archives and at the American Philosophical Society Library. See also István Hargittai, *Candid Science II: Conversations with Famous Biomedical Scientists* (2002). Obituaries are in the *New York Times* (5 Feb. 2008), *Science* (7 Mar. 2008), and *Nature* (27 Mar. 2008).

Maura C. Flannery

LEDGER, Heathcliff Andrew ("Heath") (*b*. 4 April 1979 in Perth, Australia; *d*. 22 January 2008 in New York City), actor best known for roles in films such as *Brokeback Mountain* and *The Dark Knight*.

Ledger was born to Kim Ledger, a mining engineer and auto racer, and Sally (Ramshaw) Ledger, a French teacher.

Heath Ledger, 2005. HUBERT BOESL/DPA/LANDOV

Known as Heath, he and his sister, Katherine, were named after the protagonists in Emily Brontë's classic novel *Wuthering Heights*. His parents divorced when he was a child; he had two half-sisters from his mother's second marriage, to Roger Bell. Ledger attended Guildford Grammar School in Perth and began performing in stage productions as a child. He also excelled at chess and sports, becoming Western Australia's junior division chess champion at age ten and participating in Australia's go-cart circuit and regional hockey competitions. His appearance at the age of ten in *Peter Pan* caught the attention of television producers, who cast him in a variety of children's shows in his native Australia in the early 1990s.

Ledger's first film role was an uncredited appearance in *Clowning Around* (1992), and he then appeared in the 1993 television series *Ship to Shore*. When he was sixteen he tried his hand in Australia's entertainment center of Sydney, landing a provocative role in the television series *Sweat* as a gay man involved in competitive cycling. He also appeared in several Australian films. In 1999 he made his debut in an American film in *10 Things I Hate About You*, a lighthearted teenage comedy. His next two films, *The Patriot* (2000) and *A Knight's Tale* (2001), put Ledger on the Hollywood map. Ledger once remarked that he believed Hollywood film studios were interested in him as the handsome, brooding male lead who could be taught to act with some time and effort. The media spotlight caused Ledger some discomfort, and this unease escalated with his rising popularity as he tried to avoid the prying eyes of the paparazzi.

A small yet powerful role as a prison guard in the 2001 film *Monster's Ball* changed Ledger's reputation from a performer who takes few risks to a serious dramatic actor willing to face challenges. Although he displayed his acting talents in several films over the next four years, including *The Four Feathers* (2002) and *Ned Kelly* (2003), none succeeded at the box office. The film that catapulted Ledger to worldwide acclaim was Ang Lee's 2005 *Brokeback Mountain*. That same year he appeared in *Lords of Dogtown*, *The Brothers Grimm*, and *Casanova*; but it was his performance as Ennis Del Mar, a cowboy torn between his secret love for another man and his public life as a husband and father, that established Ledger's talent and earned him an Academy Award nomination for Best Actor. Ledger's performance in *Brokeback Mountain* also earned him several awards for best actor, from the Australian Film Institute, Las Vegas Film Critics Society, New York Film Critics Circle, Phoenix Film Critics Society, and San Francisco Film Critics Circle (all 2005). It was on the set of *Brokeback Mountain* that Ledger met Michelle Williams, who played Del Mar's wife, Alma. Williams and Ledger were companions for several years and had a daughter.

Like many of his peers, Ledger often clashed with the paparazzi, finding them too intrusive into the private lives of celebrities. His romantic connections also seemed to fascinate the public. Defying the stereotype of the Hollywood heartthrob, Ledger gave a critically acclaimed performance in the 2007 film *I'm Not There*, in which he and several other actors portrayed imaginative manifestations of the singer-songwriter Bob Dylan. Ledger had also recently embarked on a new endeavor, directing music videos for the 2006 debut release of hip-hop musician N'Fa.

Ledger died in his New York City apartment at the age of twenty-eight. The cause of death was an accidental overdose of prescription drugs. At the time of his death he was completing the filming of *The Dark Knight* (2008), the sixth Batman film in a series that began in 1989. As the Joker, Ledger delivered a dark, searing performance that many critics and the public found as masterful as it was disturbing. In 2009 Ledger was awarded a number of posthumous best supporting actor honors for his performance, including the Academy Award, Golden Globe, Los Angeles Film Critics Association Award, British Academy Film Award, and Screen Actors' Guild Award, as well as the Australian Film Institute's International Award for Best Actor. Many of Ledger's friends, associates, and family members feared that his submersion in such a dark role played a part in his untimely death. Ledger himself

characterized the Joker as a "psychopathic, mass-murdering, schizophrenic clown with zero empathy." The depth to which Ledger internalized these qualities while preparing for the role led to bouts of insomnia that prompted Ledger to seek relief with prescription sleeping pills. At the time of his death, Ledger was working on another film, *The Imaginarium of Doctor Parnassus*, directed by Terry Gilliam and set for European release in late 2009.

While Ledger's career lasted a brief time, his impact on the international cinema community cannot be overestimated. Many film critics and historians posit that Ledger's role in *Brokeback Mountain* alone revolutionized filmmaking, due to its sympathetic and realistic portrayal of the love affair between two men. However, the breadth of Ledger's acting repertoire surpassed this one film role, and his legacy lies in the professionalism and commitment he dedicated to the craft of acting.

Ledger was cremated at Fremantle Cemetery in Perth and his ashes buried at Karrakatta Cemetery. A memorial service in his honor was held on 9 February 2008 at Pernhos College in Perth.

★

For a look at Ledger before *Brokeback Mountain*, see Kevin Sessums, "We're Havin' a Heath Wave," *Vanity Fair* (Aug. 2000). Two biographies of Ledger are John McShane, *Heath Ledger: His Beautiful Life and Mysterious Death* (2008), and Brian J. Robb, *Heath Ledger: Hollywood's Dark Star* (2008). Obituaries are in the *Los Angeles Times*, London *Times*, and *New York Times* (all 23 Jan. 2008).

Kimberly K. Little

L'ENGLE, Madeleine Camp (*b.* 29 November 1918 in New York City; *d.* 6 September 2007 in Litchfield, Connecticut), revered twentieth-century writer of young adult fiction.

L'Engle was the sole child of Charles Wadsworth Camp, a writer, and Madeleine Hall (Barnett) Camp, a pianist. She was named Madeleine L'Engle Camp for her great-grandmother and later took L'Engle as her professional name. L'Engle discovered her passion for writing at the age of five, and once she entered school, she often neglected assignments to pursue her creative writing. By the time L'Engle was twelve, her parents had temporarily relocated the family from New York to Switzerland, where L'Engle continued her education at an English boarding school before returning to the United States at fifteen to finish her secondary schooling at Ashley Hall in Charleston, South Carolina. In 1941 she graduated cum laude with an AB from Smith College.

Madeleine L'Engle. AP IMAGES

After graduation L'Engle moved back to New York City and began working in the New York theater world. She soon began publishing her written work. In 1944 L'Engle published a comedy, *18 Washington Square South, a Comedy in One Act*, followed by her first two novels, *A Small Rain* (1945) and *Ilsa* (1946). L'Engle married the actor Hugh Franklin on 26 January 1946.

Within a year of their marriage, L'Engle and Franklin purchased a farmhouse in Goshen, Connecticut; they made the move permanent in 1950. The couple had three children, and in 1960 the family returned to New York City, where L'Engle pursued writing and celebrated the publication of her first young adult novel, *Meet the Austins*, that same year.

L'Engle authored more than sixty books; perhaps her most popular work was *A Wrinkle in Time*, published in 1962 after a two-year struggle to find a publisher. The book won the American Library Association's Newbery Medal in 1963, but it was not without controversy. Many religious conservatives at the time (and in the years since) called for the book's banning, claiming that it celebrates a fantastic, mythical world where witches and other supernatural creatures exist and where God bears little resemblance to the deity of the Christian faith. L'Engle published *A Swiftly Tilting Planet*, a sequel to *A Wrinkle*

in Time, in 1978. Other notable works include *A Ring of Endless Light* (1980) and *The Other Dog* (2001).

Along with her prolific career of writing children's and young adult fiction, L'Engle also wrote several autobiographical treatments of her life, her Christian faith, and her philosophies on writing. She also enjoyed a successful public-speaking career, which began shortly after she met Canon Edward Nason West of the Cathedral Church of Saint John the Divine. L'Engle had begun delivering allegorical sermons at the behest of West in the mid-1960s, and she was so moved by her personal examinations of religion and creative expression that she took her show on the lecture circuit, delivering speeches to religious and lay audiences alike, while also publishing written work inspired by these religious sentiments.

The Genesis Trilogy adapts the biblical book of Genesis, rendering it accessible to readers more familiar and comfortable with a fictional style of narrative. *And It Was Good: Reflections on Beginnings* (1983), *A Stone for a Pillow: Journeys with Jacob* (1986), and *Sold into Egypt: Joseph's Journey into Human Being* (1989) form the trilogy, detailing the stories of such biblical figures as Jacob and Joseph, while also offering the reader an insight into L'Engle's own lifelong spiritual voyage, one she tried to reflect in some manner in all of her written works, whether children's books, poetry, or ruminations on her life and writing.

Keeping her creative writing at the forefront of her calendar and her life, L'Engle also devoted herself to public work until the final eight years of her life. Until the late 1990s L'Engle was the librarian and writer in residence of her church, Saint John the Divine in New York City. In her later years L'Engle also presided over the Authors Guild and carried a membership on the board of directors of the Authors League Foundation. She won the National Humanities Medal in 2004, but she was unable to accept the honor personally because of illness.

L'Engle died of natural causes at Rose Haven nursing home in Litchfield, where she had resided for three years preceding her death. A memorial service was held for her at the Church of Christ in Goshen on 15 September 2007. She is buried in Silver Lane Cemetery in East Hartford, Connecticut.

L'Engle devoted her life and work to the art of the written word, and she crafted much of her work in a manner that would be easily accessible to young readers. Hailed by critics and loved ones alike as blurring the lines between fiction and reality, L'Engle often frustrated family members who thought her candor about their lives eclipsed and censored her own foibles and personal problems. L'Engle rarely seemed ruffled by these criticisms, as she often said that she did not believe there was any difference between fiction and nonfiction. For L'Engle, those stories were fanciful, fantastic tales of science fiction, love, and the thrills and heartbreak of coming of age that continue to be beloved by millions of children and adults alike years after their initial publications.

★

The University of Southern Mississippi de Grummond Collection houses the Madeleine L'Engle Papers and is an excellent source for primary information. The collection includes correspondence between the author and the University of Southern Mississippi from 1973 to 1978. The University of Minnesota's Elmer L. Andersen Library also houses a collection of L'Engle's papers in its Children's Literature Research Collections, covering the years 1960 to 1990 and focusing on the actual writing process of ten of L'Engle's novels. L'Engle's quasi-autobiographical publications on her writing philosophies serve as the best resource for her life and career. *Madeleine L'Engle Herself: Reflections on a Writing Life* (2001), compiled by Carole Chase, includes transcripts from writing workshops L'Engle conducted, as well as her own recollections regarding her writing style and process and the creative life she chose for herself. *The Ordering of Love: The New and Collected Poems of Madeleine L'Engle* (2005) contains approximately 200 of L'Engle's original poems, crafted over the course her lifetime. Obituaries are in the *New York Times* and *Washington Post* (both 8 Sept. 2007).

Kimberly K. Little

LEONARD, John Dillon (*b*. 25 February 1939 in Washington, D.C.; *d*. 5 November 2008 in New York City), literary and cultural critic who was influential as the editor of the *New York Times Book Review* and as a reviewer and commentator in print and on television.

Leonard was born to Dan Leonard, a postal worker, and Ruth (Woods) Leonard. After his parents divorce, he was raised by his single mother, in Washington, D.C.; the Jackson Heights area of Queens, New York; and Lakewood, California. He had an inquisitive nature and, to fulfill his mother's promise to his father that she would raise him Catholic, at age fourteen he began to study the faith in depth. This religious self-education resulted in his becoming an atheist. After graduating from Woodrow Wilson High School in Long Beach, from 1956 to 1958 Leonard attended Harvard University. He dropped out to work for social causes, including as a community activist in Massachusetts, migrant worker organizer, and teacher.

During this time Leonard also wrote several magazine articles, one of which caught the attention of William F. Buckley, Jr., the publisher of the conservative magazine *National Review*. In 1959, fully aware of Leonard's left-wing politics, Buckley gave the young writer a summer internship as an editorial assistant, launching his career in journalism. That same year Leonard married Benigna Christiana Morison, daughter of the Pulitzer Prize–winning historian Samuel Eliot Morison; they had a son and a daughter. He then attended the University of California at Berkeley, earning a BA in English in 1962. While at Berkeley he served as the literary director for Pacifica Radio, the first listener-supported radio station in the nation, and became involved in the civil rights and anti–Vietnam War movements.

In September 1967 Leonard became an editor at the *New York Times Book Review*, a supplemental section of the paper's Sunday edition, and in 1969 became the *Times*'s daily book critic. In December 1970 the paper named him executive editor of the *Book Review*. Such a rapid rise to a position of authority was considered highly unusual in the newspaper business. Leonard clashed with *Times* management over politics but refused to modify the content of the *Book Review* to satisfy his superiors, who wanted to maintain a more centrist viewpoint. He made significant changes to the section, assigning reviewers to cover unknown women and minority authors in an era of budding feminism and civil rights awareness. The success of the novelists Toni Morrison, Gabriel García Márquez, Mary Gordon, and others rests in part on the attention Leonard gave them in the pages of the *Book Review*. Leonard also revamped the format, including photographs and visual images to make the section more appealing to a broader audience. At the same time, he often featured obscure books and authors on the cover, giving prominence to controversial material or what he considered hidden talent.

Because of continued friction with upper management of the *Times*, particularly the politically conservative editor A. M. Rosenthal, as well as his general unhappiness with being in any management position, in 1975 Leonard left his position as executive editor and resumed his role as a critic, this time writing daily columns not only on books but also on other aspects of American culture. After his divorce, Leonard married Sue Nessel on 6 November 1976. From 1977 to 1980 he had his own *Times* column, titled "Private Lives," in which he detailed his personal struggles with relationships and alcoholism.

Leonard left the *Times* in 1982 and became an active freelance writer and media personality. From 1984 until his death he was a television critic for *New York* magazine, and from 1995 to 1998 he and his wife served as co-literary editors at the *Nation*. For sixteen years his bearded, bespectacled face was a regular sight on the Columbia Broadcasting System television program *Sunday Morning*, where Leonard regularly reviewed television shows and movies for a popular audience. He also reviewed books for the National Public Radio program *Fresh Air* and wrote reviews and articles for *Harper's* magazine (where he was the regular book critic), *Salon*, the *Atlantic Monthly*, the *Village Voice*, the *New Republic*, the *Los Angeles Times Book Review*,

Newsweek, Vogue, Vanity Fair, and many other publications. He read voraciously—an average, he said, of five books a week. Leonard relished language and engaged in wordplay and complex syntax, becoming famous for his long sentences packed with allusions. His unique prose style often involved surprising combinations of literary and popular culture references. The novelist E. L. Doctorow said that Leonard used "club-sandwich sentences." For example, in a review of then-unknown author Fran Liebowitz, he wrote a mock recipe that called for adding "some Lenny Bruce and Oscar Wilde and Alexis de Tocqueville, a dash of cab driver, an assortment of puns, minced jargon, and top it off with smarty-pants. Serve without whine."

Leonard published ten full-length works of his own, including novels such as *The Naked Martini* (1964) and *Black Conceit* (1973), and literary criticism, notably *Smoke and Mirrors: Violence, Television, and Other American Cultures* (1997), an analysis of the ways in which television programs mirror larger concerns of American society. He received the National Book Critics Circle's Lifetime Achievement Award in 2006.

Leonard died at Mount Sinai Hospital in Manhattan of complications from lung cancer. He was cremated.

One of the hallmarks of Leonard's work is its blend of erudition and mainstream pop culture delivered with a wry sense of humor. Leonard's detractors complained that he tended to use a book review as a platform to air his own ideas rather than closely analyze the work under discussion. However, many authors who were the subjects of his reviews (including several who spoke at his memorial) noted that no one read their work more closely, or understood their intent more clearly, than Leonard. He delivered his opinions on film, television, and literature gracefully but forcefully, never shrinking from making bold statements, particularly when it came to his political views. He was that rare example of a critic who branched out from his early specialty to address the wide spectrum of American culture.

★

Meghan O'Rourke, "The Enthusiast," *Columbia Journalism Review* 45, no. 5 (Jan.–Feb. 2007), is a consideration of Leonard's career as a critic. Bill Kurtz, "Critics' Discomfort," *Quill* 86, no. 9 (Dec. 1998): 4, is based on an interview with Leonard and captures his philosophy of criticism. Obituaries are in the *New York Times* and *Washington Post* (both 7 Nov. 2008).

Karen Linkletter

LEOPOLD, Richard William (*b.* 6 January 1912 in New York City; *d.* 23 November 2006 in Evanston, Illinois), historian of American foreign policy.

Leopold was one of two sons born to Harry Leopold, Sr., a stockbroker, and Ethel A. (Kimmelstiel) Leopold. Growing up on Manhattan's Upper West Side, he attended the all-male Franklin School (successor to the Sachs School for Boys), then enrolled at Phillips Exeter Academy, from which he graduated cum laude in 1929. Entering Princeton University that year, Leopold received his BA in history in 1933. He was elected to Phi Beta Kappa and was awarded highest honors in history. He received an MA in 1934 from Harvard University and began teaching at Harvard in 1937; he earned his PhD in 1938.

The Social Science Research Council awarded Leopold a postdoctoral fellowship to support research for his dissertation, which was soon published as a volume of the Harvard Historical Studies under the title *Robert Dale Owen: A Biography* (1940; reprinted 1969). The book, centering on the life of the prominent nineteenth-century reformer, was awarded in 1940 the American Historical Association's John H. Dunning Prize, an honor given biennially to a budding historian for the best book on any subject pertaining to the history of the United States.

As a naval officer during World War II, Leopold was assigned to the Office of Naval Records and Library in Washington, D.C. There he helped organize official records concerning operations in the Pacific theater, a task that familiarized him with every military engagement there. In 1946 he returned to Harvard as assistant professor.

In 1948 Leopold joined the history department at Northwestern University as associate professor. He rose quickly, becoming full professor in 1953, acting department chairman in 1953 and 1954, and chairman from 1966 to 1969. In 1963 he was made William Smith Mason Professor of American History. He retired in 1980, becoming professor emeritus. Under his leadership at Northwestern the department became one of the nation's foremost, as he helped recruit such able scholars as Arthur S. Link and Clarence L. Ver Steeg. Moreover, he lectured to hundreds of students at a time and directed twenty doctoral theses.

In 1952, with his Northwestern colleague Link, Leopold edited *Problems in American History*, in which a series of leading scholars contributed sections combining narrative and primary sources. His next book, *Elihu Root and the Conservative Tradition* (1954), a volume in Oscar Handlin's Library of American Biography, presented a mixed portrayal of the American statesman, an individual who had served as secretary of both the War and State departments, senator from New York, and one of the creators of the World Court. On the one hand, wrote Leopold of Root, the cause of conservatism "can never do without his integrity and fair-mindedness, . . . his intuitive judgment and mastery of the facts, his respect for efficient administration and insistence upon balancing power with responsibility." On the other hand, Leopold maintained that the conservative cause "could benefit from a little more daring, imagination, and faith in the people than Root was able to contribute."

Leopold's magnum opus was *The Growth of American Foreign Policy: A History* (1962), a volume exceeding 850 pages and concentrating on the period from 1889, the year when Benjamin Harrison became president, to 1961. Leopold was careful to define "foreign policy" as "those objectives and aims set by the government for promoting the nation's interest and welfare in the world at large." He compared such a concept with "diplomacy," that is "the art or profession of transacting business among governments" and "foreign relations," which he saw as "the sum total of all connections—official, private, commercial, and cultural—among different countries and different peoples." He also contributed articles to such journals as the *Mississippi Valley Historical Review* (now the *Journal of American History*) and *World Politics*. Widely known for the rigor of his thinking, Leopold offered a review-essay on Alexander DeConde's *Encyclopedia of American Foreign Policy* (1978), titled "Historians and American Foreign Policy: An Encyclopedic Endeavor" and published in 1981 in the *Pacific Historical Review*, that remains a classic.

One of Leopold's major contributions centers on his government service. He spent countless hours on various advisory committees, among them those of the U.S. Army, Navy, and Marine Corps. In 1983 and 1984 the Department of the Navy awarded him citations of merit for his role in keeping the Naval Reserve Officer Training Corps on the Northwestern campus in 1968 during the height of student protests against the Vietnam War. He was also on advisory committees for the Atomic Energy Commission, the National Archives, the Central Intelligence Agency, and the papers of Woodrow Wilson. Leopold served as a member of the board of directors of the Harry S. Truman Library Institute. In 1969 he headed the American Historical Association–Organization of American Historians ad hoc committee appointed to investigate the accusation that the Franklin D. Roosevelt Presidential Library at Hyde Park, New York, was deliberately withholding materials from qualified scholars. A year later he wrote the committee's 448-page report exonerating the library of any misconduct.

Leopold received many honors. He held numerous offices in the Organization of American Historians (OAH), formerly the Mississippi Valley Historical Association, culminating in being elected president for the 1976–1977 term and receiving its Distinguished Service Award in 1992. In 1984 the OAH established the biennial Richard W. Leopold Prize for the best book written by an historian associated with government on some level and who covered foreign policy. In 1970 he was made president of the Society for Historians of American Foreign Relations (SHAFR), and in 1990 he received SHAFR's Norman and Laura Graebner Award for leadership in diplomatic history. Also in 1990

Northwestern University established the annual Richard W. Leopold lectureship, which brought prominent speakers to the campus. The Richard W. Leopold Professorship in American History was inaugurated at Northwestern in 1997.

Leopold ably represented a generation of scholars who saw themselves bearing high-level governmental and institutional responsibilities as well as professional ones. Few individuals so skillfully combined intellectual rigor in his field of study with such distinguished service to a broader community. He died at age ninety-four. His remains are interred at Chicago's Rosehill Cemetery and Mausoleum.

★

The Richard W. Leopold papers are located at Northwestern University. A good source of information about Leopold is Steven J. Harper, *Straddling Worlds: The Jewish-American Journey of Professor Richard W. Leopold* (2007). Obituaries are in the newsmagazine of the American Historical Association, *Perspectives* 45, no. 4 (Apr. 2007): 33–34; the Organization of American Historians *Newsletter* 35, no. 1 (Feb. 2007): 1, 12; and the Northwestern University *Observer* (11 Jan. 2007).

Justus Doenecke

LEVINE, Lawrence William (*b.* 27 February 1933 in New York City; *d.* 23 October 2006 in Berkeley, California), provocative American cultural historian and staunch defender of multiculturalism.

Born in the New York City borough of Manhattan in the midst of the Great Depression, Levine was the son of a Lithuanian Jewish father, Abraham Levine, who had immigrated to the United States in 1913, and a Russian Jewish mother, Ann (Schmookler) Levine, who was born in East Harlem, New York City, to immigrant parents. Together, Abraham and Ann operated a fruit and vegetable store in the Washington Heights section of northern Manhattan. Despite an imperfect grasp of English, Abraham nonetheless embraced many facets of American culture and society, expressing great admiration for President Franklin D. Roosevelt and the New York Yankees' first baseman Lou Gehrig. At the same time, he maintained numerous connections to his roots, including his lifelong membership in a fraternal organization composed of men from the small Lithuanian village of his birth. Levine explained that his parents did not raise him or his sister in an "either-or, cut-and-dried, black-or-white" way: "I could have both Moses *and* Lincoln as forefathers, both the Hebrew Torah *and* the United States Constitution for moral and legal touchstones."

Levine attended public schools, coming into contact with students from a great variety of ethnic backgrounds.

He later wrote, "the influences upon me...were not just East-European Jewish and Anglo American; they were also Greek American, Armenian American, German-Jewish American, African American, Irish American, Italian American, Chinese American." As a teenager in the late 1940s, Levine frequented Manhattan jazz clubs such as the Royal Roost and Birdland, where he heard legendary musicians such as Charlie Parker, Dizzy Gillespie, Thelonious Monk, Billie Holiday, and Lester Young perform. He and his friends were profoundly moved by these artists: "we not only found an art that touched us, we also saw a possibility of functioning in the outside society while retaining our individual and ethnic personas." Although he described himself as a less-than-serious high school student, Levine decided to enroll at the City College of New York (CCNY) in 1950, becoming a history major. He always felt indebted to CCNY for the opportunities it afforded him but also expressed a deep dissatisfaction with the history courses he took there. His professors required him to read thick textbooks that constructed what he believed were dry political narratives of "never-ending progress." In retrospect, Levine was confounded that he barely learned anything about "workers, slaves, immigrants, children, or women" or the peoples of Africa, Asia, or Latin America.

Despite his misgivings, Levine completed his bachelor's degree in history in 1955 and then enrolled at Columbia University to pursue graduate study. He obtained a master's degree in 1957 and then began work on a dissertation directed by Richard Hofstadter, one of the preeminent American historians of the post–World War II era. Levine took Hofstadter's suggestion to examine the last decade of the life of the great populist William Jennings Bryan. In such acclaimed works as *The American Political Tradition and The Men Who Made It* (1948) and *The Age of Reform: From Bryan to F.D.R.* (1955), Hofstadter had depicted Bryan as a buffoonish and intellectually limited evangelical. But Levine's dissertation, completed in 1962 and published in book form as *Defender of the Faith: William Jennings Bryan; The Last Decade, 1915–1925* (1965), challenged Hofstadter's assessment. Levine portrayed Bryan as a thoughtful, highly moral, and democratically minded reformer with a deep empathy for working people. This work signaled the direction of much of Levine's work to come, reflecting the openness and generosity of spirit with which he would approach the subjects of his writing. He sought not to pass judgment on Bryan but to understand the cultural context from which the politician emerged, leading Levine to become a top practitioner in the burgeoning field of cultural history.

Levine served as a lecturer at CCNY from 1959 to 1961 and an instructor at Princeton University in Princeton, New Jersey, from 1961 to 1962. After securing a position as an assistant professor at the University of California, Berkeley (UCB), in 1962, he married Cornelia Roettcher, a native of Berlin, Germany, on 29 May 1964. Cornelia had a son from a previous relationship, and the couple eventually had two more sons. Levine's political activism flourished in his early years at UCB. He participated in sit-in demonstrations orchestrated by the Congress of Racial Equality to influence stores to hire black employees. He defended students involved with the UCB free speech protests against the administration's attempt to ban on-campus political activities during the 1964–1965 academic year and joined civil rights protesters in the Selma to Montgomery marches in Alabama in March 1965. His activism inspired him to explore the African-American experience for his next major project, which culminated in the publication of the highly acclaimed *Black Culture and Black Consciousness: Afro-American Folk Thought from Slavery to Freedom* (1977). This landmark study was partly a response to social scientists such as Daniel Patrick Moynihan and Nathan Glazer who had disparaged African-American culture and values, and it offered a powerful analysis of black spirituals, folktales, proverbs, and jokes as evidence of a vibrant communal consciousness. Later commentators viewed the book as an important signpost in the emerging "cultural turn" in the humanities and social sciences, denoting an emphasis on culture and language over quantitative analysis. Its reception no doubt contributed to Levine being named a MacArthur Foundation "genius" fellow in 1983 and to his election to the American Academy of Arts and Sciences in 1985.

Levine's next book, *Highbrow/Lowbrow: The Emergence of Cultural Hierarchy in America* (1988), argued that the United States possessed a shared common public culture before the Civil War, but in the last three decades of the nineteenth century, elites divided culture into "high" and "low" categories, partly as a means of consolidating their identity apart from that of the "rabble." In Levine's estimation, the sacralized cultural forms—like Shakespearean drama and opera—became lifeless and routine as a result. Numerous literature, music, and history scholars have dissected and disputed Levine's argument, but *Highbrow/Lowbrow* remains a major touchstone for historical studies of American culture decades after its publication.

In the 1992–1993 academic year, Levine served as president of the Organization of American Historians and published *The Unpredictable Past: Explorations in American Cultural History* (1993), a collection of essays exploring facets of American cultural history. Taking early retirement from UCB in 1994, he decided to teach at George Mason University in Fairfax, Virginia, where he worked until close to the end of his life. During the 1990s Levine felt the need to respond directly to conservative critics of American higher education such as the philosopher Allan Bloom, who bemoaned the dilution of a "Western canon" by the inclusion of works outside the European tradition. The result was *The Opening of the American Mind: Canons, Culture, and History* (1996), in which Levine stated that Western civilization courses came from a relatively recent time period—dating from the World War I era—and that multiculturalism marked American culture's return to its more democratic and inclusive nineteenth-century roots. Levine's final book project, a collaboration with his wife titled *The People and the President: America's Conversations with FDR* (2002), compiled letters sent to Roosevelt in response to his radio fireside chats during the Great Depression. It fittingly continued Levine's lifelong ambition to restore the voices of those previously ignored in the historical record. Levine died of cancer at age seventy-three at his home in Berkeley.

Talkative and gifted with a sardonic wit, Levine was quick to wield humor to deflate pomposity. He was a memorable presence at academic conferences: his unruly gray mane, large circular wire-framed glasses, and wide-shouldered frame clad in black made him stand out in a crowd of his colleagues. Yet even the tweediest among them appreciated Levine's crucial role—along with other outstanding practitioners of his generation such as Eugene Genovese, Herbert Gutman, and Carroll Smith-Rosenberg—in forcing American historians to reconsider the way that they approached their craft. He employed highly imaginative methods and sources to restore the voices of common people previously thought unworthy of study by historians, reenvisioning American history as a far more inclusive and democratic practice than it had been previously.

A collection of transcripts of oral history interviews with Levine resides at the Regional Oral History Office at the Bancroft Library of the University of California, Berkeley. Autobiographical information is included in chapters 1 and 8 of *The Opening of the American Mind.* Obituaries are in the *New York Times* (28 Oct. 2006) and *Washington Post* (31 Oct. 2006).

Brendan P. O'Malley

LEVITT, Theodore (''Ted'') (*b*. 1 March 1925 in Vollmerz, Germany; *d*. 28 June 2006 in Belmont, Massachusetts), distinguished professor at Harvard Business School, former editor of the *Harvard Business Review*, and prolific author who profoundly influenced modern marketing thought and practice with such groundbreaking works as ''Marketing Myopia'' (1960), ''Globalization of Markets'' (1983), and *The Marketing Imagination* (1983).

Levitt was the son of Boris Levitt, a cobbler, and Rachel (Gruenebaum) Levitt. At age nine, shortly after Adolf Hitler's rise to power, Levitt fled Germany with his parents and three siblings. In 1935 the Levitt family immigrated to Dayton, Ohio, where some of their relatives lived.

Theodore (''Ted'') Levitt. **PHOTO BY RICHARD CHASE. COURTESY OF HBS ALUMNI BULLETIN.**

In Dayton, young Theodore quickly demonstrated his talent for writing. As a fifth grader at Emerson School, he cofounded a school newspaper, the *Emerson Owl*. In high school, Levitt worked as a reporter for the *Dayton Journal Herald*.

Levitt's high school education and budding reporting career were interrupted by World War II. Drafted into the U.S. Army, Levitt (who became a naturalized U.S. citizen in 1940) served in Europe. After the war, Levitt returned to Dayton and completed a correspondence course to obtain his high school degree. He then attended Antioch College and resumed his work at the *Dayton Journal Herald* as a sports writer. In 1948 Levitt married Joan Levy; the couple had five children. After graduating from Antioch College with a BA degree in 1949, Levitt began graduate studies at Ohio State University and obtained a doctorate in economics in 1951. That same year, Levitt began his first teaching position at the University of North Dakota. Five years later, he published his first article in the *Harvard Business Review*. It was titled ''The Changing Character of Capitalism.'' Levitt's article attracted the notice of Standard Oil Company executives and led to his working as an oil industry consultant in Chicago. Levitt would go on to write twenty-five more articles for the prestigious *Harvard Business Review*, earning him the distinction of tying with the management guru Peter Drucker as the most prolific contributor in the history of the *Harvard Business Review*.

In 1959 Levitt joined the faculty of Harvard Business School and quickly established himself as a rising star. In

1960 the *Harvard Business Review* published "Marketing Myopia," which would become Levitt's most famous article and one of the most widely reprinted articles in the magazine's history, selling more than 850,000 copies. In the landmark article, Levitt asked executives a potent question: "What business are you really in?" Levitt contended that companies (and indeed, entire industries) needed to define their businesses broadly if they hoped to achieve long-term success. For instance, railroads were not just in the railroad business; they were also in the transportation field. Likewise, Hollywood was not just about producing movies; it was about delivering entertainment. In Levitt's opinion, businesses often defined themselves too narrowly, because they were overly product-oriented, too focused on selling goods rather than on what consumers really wanted. Levitt dubbed this problem "marketing myopia," a short-sightedness that caused companies and industries to fall prematurely into a "shadow of decline." Levitt encouraged executives to avoid this malaise by becoming more customer oriented and putting marketing at the forefront of their thinking. By "marketing," Levitt made it clear that he did not mean "selling." As Levitt wrote, "Selling focuses on the needs of the seller, marketing on the needs of the buyer." Levitt was, in fact, arguing for an expanded idea of marketing.

Levitt won the *Harvard Business Review* McKinsey Award for "Marketing Myopia" in 1960. He would later win the McKinsey Award three more times in addition to garnering many other awards. In 1962 he won the Academy of Management Award for *Innovation in Marketing: New Perspectives for Profit and Growth* (1962), and in 1969 he was awarded the John Hancock Award for Excellence in Business Journalism. In 1970 Levitt was proclaimed "Marketing Man of the Year" with the receipt of the Charles Coolidge Parlin Award. He subsequently received the George Gallup Award for Marketing Excellence (1976), the Paul D. Converse Award of the American Marketing Association in recognition of his major contributions to the marketing field (1978), and the William M. McFeely Award of the International Management Council for outstanding contributions to management (1989).

While "Marketing Myopia" is Levitt's most famous article, "The Globalization of Markets" (1983), published in the *Harvard Business Review*, ranks as another of his most well-known works. In one indication of this article's extreme popularity, Levitt has often been credited with coining the term *globalization*, which appears in the article's title. Levitt and Harvard Business School representatives repeatedly emphasized that Levitt did not create the term and that it actually had been in use since the 1940s. Yet Levitt's article catapulted the term into widespread usage, in part because his predictions and comments in the text incited controversy. In the article, Levitt sweepingly announced that "the globalization of markets is at hand" and praised global corporations at the expense of multinational corporations. As Levitt contended, global corporations such as McDonald's or Coca-Cola were wise to operate with "resolute constancy . . . as if the entire world (or major regions of it) were a single entity." Achieving economies of scale, global corporations sold "the same things in the same way everywhere" and ignored regional differences. In contrast, Levitt stated that the multinational corporation foolishly went to the expense of adjusting its marketing practices in every country it served. Levitt argued that such customization was wasteful, unnecessary, and unimaginative. The spread of technology and explosion of mass media, Levitt contended, were among the factors making regions of the world more similar to each other, so corporations, in Levitt's eyes, now could offer the same product everywhere and still achieve great success. While Levitt sought to convey the benefits of a globalized, one-size-fits-all marketing strategy, critics contended that such an approach lacked cultural sensitivity, risked a loss of sales (due to displeased, unfulfilled customers), and accelerated a drift toward a worldwide homogenization of tastes and preferences that was not necessarily a positive development. This global standardization versus customization debate still continues, which explains the enduring appeal of Levitt's article.

In the same year that "The Globalization of Markets" appeared, Levitt published *The Marketing Imagination*, a collection of essays that he had written for *Harvard Business Review*. Among some of the included essays were "Marketing Intangible Products and Product Intangibles," "Differentiation—of Anything," "Relationship Management," and "The Marketing Imagination." The book became a best seller and ultimately was translated into eleven languages. Levitt became increasingly well known for his various contentions, such as his argument that "everything can be and is differentiable, even such 'commodities' as steel, cement, money, chemicals and grain." Just as "marketing myopia" became a buzzword, so too did "marketing imagination," which Levitt explained as "the starting point of success in marketing" as it facilitated "unique insights . . . to understanding customers, their problems, and the means to capture their attention."

Shortly after the resounding success of *The Marketing Imagination*, Levitt was asked by Harvard Business School dean John McArthur to serve as editor of the *Harvard Business Review*. Levitt accepted the offer despite the fact that he had once bluntly criticized the journal as "a magazine written by people who can't write for people who won't read." Determined to attract a broader readership to the *Harvard Business Review* and intent on making it easier to read, Levitt instituted several changes while serving as editor from 1985 through 1989. He especially focused on a shift toward shorter articles and the creation of executive summaries. His insistence on clear, crisp writing on the part of contributors became almost legendary. As staff members recalled, Levitt even posted notices in the bathrooms instructing contributors to "Write It Right and Write It Tight." Yet Levitt also was a strict editor of his own writings, admitting in 1983, "In the last twenty years, I've never published anything without at least five serious rewrites."

In 1990 Levitt officially retired, yet he maintained an active presence at Harvard Business School for years afterward, participating in such campus events as a colloquium on globalization in 2003. Levitt died at age eighty-one of prostate cancer at his home in Belmont. Commenting on Levitt's contributions to the Harvard Business School, Dean Jay Light praised Levitt for his "world-class leadership and research, his ability to generate ideas with impact," and his "remarkable talent for teaching them in an exciting way in the classroom." While Light extolled Levitt as a "giant in the history of Harvard Business School," John Quelch, associate dean of the school, hailed Levitt as "the most influential and imaginative professor in marketing history."

In his seminal article "Marketing Myopia," Levitt lamented that marketing in most organizations was still a "stepchild," ignored and not well understood. Over the course of his long, productive career, Levitt taught thousands of students, wrote influential articles for the *Harvard Business Review*, and authored eight books. Through his abundant scholarship and commitment to teaching, Levitt helped elevate marketing from stepchild status to a central role in business and society.

★

Information about Levitt's career as editor of the *Harvard Business Review* is available in Alison Leigh Cowan, "Harvard's Shrewd Blunder," *New York Times* (30 July 1989); and Stephen Brown, "Theodore Levitt: The Ultimate Writing Machine," *Marketing Theory* 4, no. 3 (2004): 209–238. Obituaries are in the *Harvard Business Review* and *BusinessWeek* (both 29 June 2006), *New York Times* and *Dayton Daily News* (both 6 July 2006), and *Advertising* Age (10 July 2006).

Janice M. Traflet

LEVY, Leonard Williams (*b.* 9 April 1923 in Toronto, Ontario, Canada; *d.* 24 August 2006 in Ashland, Oregon), historian who specialized in the formation of constitutional rights and who won a Pulitzer Prize in 1969 for his *Origins of the Fifth Amendment*.

Levy was the son of Albert Levy, a tailor, and Rae (Williams) Levy, a homemaker. He had one sibling, a sister. Levy attended Washington University in St. Louis in 1940 before switching to the University of Michigan. He attended classes at Ann Arbor until 1943, when he joined the U.S.

Army, in which he served as a sergeant until 1946. Under the GI Bill, Levy matriculated at Teachers College, Columbia University in New York City in 1946 and 1947, earning his bachelor's degree, and then the following year received a master's degree from Teachers College. Upon transferring to the graduate program in history at Columbia University, Levy needed only three years to complete his doctorate, working primarily with the historian Henry Steele Commager. A dissertation on the jurisprudence of Chief Justice Lemuel Shaw of the Supreme Judicial Court of Massachusetts became the subject of Levy's first book, *The Law of the Commonwealth and Chief Justice Shaw* (1957).

In 1951, the same year that he received his doctorate, Levy began teaching at Brandeis University, where he was to remain an ornament of its faculty and a key administrative figure until 1970. While holding the Earl Warren Chair in Constitutional History, Levy served as associate dean of the faculty and (from 1958 until 1963) as the first dean of the graduate school, and then (from 1963 until 1966) became dean of faculty. Reminiscences of his former students concur in describing a potent lecturer, a conscientious and demanding reader of written assignments and exam essays, and a challenging and inspiring mentor to graduate students. But the respiratory problems of Elyse Gitlow Levy, whom he married in 1944, required them to seek a much warmer climate. By the time he became the Andrew W. Mellon All-Claremont Professor of Humanities and History at the Claremont Graduate School in California, Levy had established a formidable body of scholarship that made him, according to Princeton's Stanley N. Katz, "one of the greatest constitutional historians of the twentieth century."

Perhaps Levy's most provocative and representative book is *Legacy of Suppression: Freedom of Speech and Press in Early American History* (1960), which torpedoed the effort of civil libertarians, seeking the authority of antiquity in the eighteenth century, to find historical warrant for their expansive views of the First Amendment. Instead the framers had a very restrictive sense of the scope of expression that the amendment protected, Levy argued. Though a champion of civil liberties, he was hardly pleased by the results of his inquiry; but he insisted on going where the evidence led him. Such an approach did not enchant Justice Hugo L. Black, who told a reviewer of *Legacy of Suppression* that "it is probably one of the most devastating blows that has been delivered against civil liberty in America in a long time." Three years later perhaps even greater controversy sprang from the publication of *Jefferson and Civil Liberties: The Darker Side* (1963). It served as a sort of prosecutor's brief by exposing the considerable gap between the third president's elegant claims for robust political dialogue and his sly and hypocritical repudiation of such democratic ideals in practice. Deliberately one-sided, the book consolidated Levy's reputation as an iconoclast within the liberal tradition.

By 1968 he was able to draw upon an enormously wide range of primary sources, stemming back to the Bible and fanning out to both sides of the Atlantic, to trace the evolution of the right against compulsory self-incrimination. With extraordinary skill and erudition, the author showed in *Origins of the Fifth Amendment: The Right Against Self-Incrimination* (1968) the significance of a very particular entitlement in the criminal courts—the right to avoid testifying against one's self, no matter how powerful the juridical force of the state. This time Levy's version of the past was reassuring for civil libertarians, though his masterly marshaling of evidence from a huge number of trial transcripts and political pamphlets is a more likely explanation for the award of a Pulitzer Prize in history for *Origins of the Fifth Amendment*. It remains the authoritative exploration of this particular feature of the Bill of Rights.

After moving to California in 1970, Levy returned to explorations of the First Amendment in particular. The growing influence of religion in the American polity may well have stimulated three books devoted to the legal dilemmas of faith. In *The Establishment Clause: Religion and the First Amendment* (1986), he argues that the framers intended to build what Jefferson had called "a wall of separation between Church and State." Their resistance to any sectarian or ecclesiastical support from the government therefore served as a historical reinforcement of the stance of modern liberalism. Starting with Moses and Jesus, Levy even produced huge histories of blasphemy, *Treason Against God* (1981) and *Blasphemy* (1993), that trace the melancholy fate of many of the victims of this accusation, down to the novelist Salman Rushdie. Though Levy was an insulated scholar in the final decades of his life, absenting himself from professional conferences, he was not indifferent to contemporary constitutional controversies. He took on the conservative reorientation of the Supreme Court in 1974 in *Against the Law: The Nixon Court and Criminal Justice* (1974), and he offered a vigorous riposte, extracted from eighteenth-century sources, to the emerging jurisprudence of Republican appointees to the bench in *Original Intent and the Framers' Constitution* (1988).

An insomniac who tended to read and write through the night, Levy calculated that if he could write at least one polished page per day, he could produce a book every year. Bequeathing a legacy of over three dozen works, he came remarkably close to that level of relentless intellectual activity, without compromising his own austere scholarly standards. Perhaps the best evidence of such rectitude occurred in 1985 when *Emergence of a Free Press* appeared. Its author admitted that *Legacy of Suppression* a quarter of a century earlier had suffered from a neglect of sources that testified to energetic and independent journalistic practice and not merely to the constraints of legal theory. "Seldom has a major constitutional scholar reversed his field under such brilliant light and with such a startling admission" was the reaction of the

television journalist Fred W. Friendly. The exactness and the scrupulousness of Levy's scholarship account for the dozens of times that it was cited in Supreme Court opinions.

Stocky, swarthy, and intense, Levy spoke crisply and wrote lucidly. He also enjoyed cultivating bonsai plants. After retiring from Claremont in 1990, he and his wife moved to Ashland, to be near their two daughters and their seven grandchildren. He died at age eighty-three after suffering a stroke. His body was cremated, and his ashes were buried in the garden near his home.

★

Levy revealed much about his scholarly career and his personality in "Anecdotage," which quotes Justice Black's low opinion of *Legacy of Suppression*, and in "Harvard University Press, et al., v. A Book." Both pieces are included in a collection of Levy's essays, *Ranters Run Amok* (2000). An important interview, "A Conversation with Leonard Levy," was published in *Journalism History* 7 (Autumn–Winter 1980): 96–103. A brief portrait of his Brandeis University years can be found in Abram L. Sachar, *A Host at Last* (1976). An obituary is in the *New York Times* (1 Sept. 2006).

Stephen J. Whitfield

LeWITT, Sol (*b.* 9 September 1928 in Hartford, Connecticut; *d.* 8 April 2007 in New York City), minimalist artist who placed great reliance on the concept underlying the execution of his open modular structures composed of identical cubes.

LeWitt's parents were Russian-Jewish immigrants. His father, a doctor, died when LeWitt was six. His mother, a nurse, took him to live with an aunt in New Britain, Connecticut. LeWitt graduated from New Britain High School. In 1949 he received a BFA from Syracuse University and then traveled to Europe, where he saw old master paintings. He served in the Korean War, stationed first in California, then in Japan and Korea. In 1953 LeWitt moved to New York City, where he enrolled in the School of Visual Arts and worked in the design department at *Seventeen* magazine doing pasteups and mechanicals. From 1955 to 1956 he worked for the architect I. M. Pei as a graphic designer. In 1960 LeWitt worked first at the book counter and then as a night receptionist at the Museum of Modern Art. During this time he met other young artists who favored minimalist and conceptual approaches, including Dan Flavin, Robert Mangold, and Robert Ryman.

LeWitt abandoned painting in 1962. That year he began making "relief constructions with nested enclosures projecting into space." His first solo exhibition was held in

1965 at the Daniels Gallery in New York City. In 1968 he made his first wall drawings. His work developed as "structures" (a term he preferred to "sculptures"), which took the form of towers and pyramids, some of which were monumental outdoor pieces, consisting of repetitive geometric forms based on the cube. These modular units, typically wooden and painted white, were open and closed in various places according to a mathematical formula worked out before the execution. LeWitt was usually not involved in the actual construction of the structure. He asserted that "art is information." He also produced numerous mural-size wall hangings showing geometric patterns. Some of these drawings were preparatory studies for the three-dimensional structures. The titles of the structures were prosaic notations of the numbers and arrangement of the cubes. LeWitt compared his method to that of an architect, who "doesn't go off with a shovel and dig his foundations and lay every brick."

LeWitt's repetitive forms conformed to the serial format of art found widely after the hegemony of abstract expressionism waned after about 1960. His repetition of cubes that are identical except for variations with solid and open faces recalls Andy Warhol's repetition of Campbell's soup cans and Marilyn Monroe heads and Ellsworth Kelly's row of colored squares of the same dimensions. Though the components of LeWitt's structures were chaste, unmodulated forms, the total effect could be engaging, even playful. LeWitt asserted that "conceptual artists are mystics rather than rationalists. They leap to conclusions that logic cannot reach." He also maintained that "irrational thoughts should be followed absolutely and logically."

LeWitt regarded himself as a conceptual artist and believed that an idea or a gesture was as significant as a sculpture or a painting. He valued ideas as opposed to the skills of the artist. Marcel Duchamp, the conceptual artist par excellence of the first half of the twentieth century, was a hero to LeWitt. In 1968 LeWitt buried a metal cube in the ground in the Netherlands and documented its disappearance from view. In 1980, in a work he titled *Autobiography*, he took more than 1,000 photographs of his Manhattan, New York City, loft (there was only one photograph of himself, which was out of focus), showing every detail, such as plumbing fixtures, wall sockets, and empty jars. He documented everything that happened to him while he took the pictures.

LeWitt married Carol Androccio; they had two daughters. In the 1980s, to get away from the hubbub of the New York art world, LeWitt and his family moved to Spoleto, Italy.

The artist knew renown during his lifetime. The Museum of Modern Art in New York City gave him his first retrospective in 1978–1979; it traveled to various American venues. A major exhibition, Sol LeWitt Drawings 1958–1992 (1992), originating in the Hague, traveled the next three years to museums in England, Germany,

Switzerland, Spain, France, and the United States. A retrospective in 2000 organized by the San Francisco Museum of Modern Art traveled to the Museum of Contemporary Art in Chicago and to the Whitney Museum of American Art in New York City. LeWitt's work is represented in many museums nationally and internationally, including the Museum of Modern Art in New York City, the National Gallery of Canada, the National Gallery in Washington, D.C., the Guggenheim Museums in New York City and in Bilbao, Spain, and the Fine Arts Museums of San Francisco. LeWitt died of cancer at age seventy-eight.

With his network of clusters of open and closed forms, LeWitt was among the minimalist sculptors who provided an interesting variation to the closed and few forms used by Donald Judd, Flavin, and Tony Smith.

The Museum of Modern Art, *Sol LeWitt* (1978), provides good coverage of LeWitt's drawings, 1962–1977, with the artist's commentaries. For further examples of LeWitt's work, see LeWitt, *Sol LeWitt: Twenty-Five Years of Wall Drawings, 1968–1993* (1993). San Francisco Museum of Modern Art, *Sol LeWitt* (2001), includes abundant illustrations, a full list of exhibitions, and writings by the artist. Nicholas Baume, ed., *Sol LeWitt: Incomplete Cubes* (2001), shows working drawings, models, and photographs of installations. Obituaries are in the *New York Times* (9 Apr. 2007) and the *Los Angeles Times* and *Washington Post* (both 10 Apr. 2007).

Abraham A. Davidson

LIBRESCU, Liviu (*b.* 18 August 1930 in Ploieşti, Romania; *d.* 16 April 2007 in Blacksburg, Virginia), acclaimed aeronautical engineer and professor who gave his life to save his students in one of the worst shooting massacres in U.S. history.

Librescu was born into a Jewish family, the only child of Isidore Librescu, a lawyer, and Mina Finkelstein Librescu, a homemaker. In 1940 Romania joined the Axis powers, and the Romanian government began implementing Nazi plans against the Jews. Librescu's father was sent to a labor camp, and Librescu and his mother went to the Jewish ghetto in Focşani, Romania. There the young man, already showing unusual aptitude in math and science, tutored students to support the family. Postwar commissions estimated that more than 350,000 Romanian Jews died during the Holocaust. Librescu's family, however, survived the Holocaust and was united after the war.

Librescu earned a BS in mechanics and aerospace engineering in 1952 from the Polytechnic University in Bucharest, Romania, and an MS from the university in

Liviu Librescu. LIBRESCU FAMILY/GETTY IMAGES

1953. He was then hired by the Bucharest Institute of Applied Mechanics, where he worked as a researcher until 1975. There he developed a particular expertise in the design of strong, light materials used in aircraft and ships.

Librescu delayed taking the exams for his doctorate until authorities relented on the requirement that students pass a test on Marxism, a theory with which he disagreed. Although he earned the degree in fluid mechanics from Romania's Academy of Sciences in 1969, he was forbidden to teach because he was Jewish and refused to join the Communist Party. In 1965 Librescu met his wife, Marilena Semian, a dentist, and they were married on 2 April 1966. They had two sons.

The family first sought to immigrate from Romania to Israel in 1975. Librescu was told that his application would not be considered unless he resigned from his job; he did so and then remained unemployed for three years. In 1976 he had his work smuggled to Norway, where his first book was published. The widely praised treatise on aerospace technology helped bring him to the attention of several Israeli groups, which lobbied for his right to emigrate. In 1978

Israeli Prime Minister Menachem Begin interceded with Romanian President Nicolae Ceauşescu on the family's behalf. Their immigration was also facilitated by Israel's monetary payments to the Romanian government.

The Librescus resettled in Israel in 1978 and eventually made their home in Ra'anana, a suburb north of Tel Aviv. In Israel, Librescu lived the academic life he had so long sought, teaching at the Haifa Technion and at Tel Aviv University, where he was professor of aeronautical and mechanical engineering from 1979 to 1986.

In 1985 Librescu accepted a one-year position in the Department of Engineering Science and Mechanics at Virginia Polytechnic Institute and State University in Blacksburg, Virginia (better known as Virginia Tech). Librescu and his family quickly grew comfortable in the university community and appreciated the natural beauty surrounding the school. Librescu's devotion to his teaching and research soon won him the respect of colleagues and students. At the end of the academic year, he was made a professor at the university, and the family decided to remain. He became an American citizen in 1995. Both of his sons graduated from Virginia Tech.

Librescu worked tirelessly as a teacher, a researcher, and a writer, and he won grants from the National Aeronautics and Space Administration and the Office of Naval Research. He wrote more than 100 chapters for books in his field, published nearly 250 articles in peer-reviewed journals, and served as a reviewer for more than thirty-five scientific journals. Librescu helped organize and spoke at scores of national and international conferences. He held visiting appointments at more than ten universities throughout the world, including the Università degli Studi di Roma and the Korea Advanced Institute of Science and Technology. Teaching and his students, however, always remained central to his work. It was his ultimate sacrifice for them that brought him to great renown outside the world of academic and professional engineering.

Librescu was teaching a solid mechanics class at Virginia Tech on the morning of 16 April 2007 when a mentally disturbed student, Seung-Hui Cho, began firing into classrooms at Norris Hall, home of the engineering science and mechanics program. Unknown to those in the building, two hours earlier Cho had killed two students in a dormitory. Carrying two semiautomatic weapons, Cho chained the main entrances of Norris Hall, leaving a note claiming that a bomb would explode should the doors be opened.

During a rampage that lasted fewer than fifteen minutes, Cho shot students and instructors in several classrooms. Surviving students testified that after hearing shots down the hall, Librescu blocked the door to his room with his body and yelled for his students to hurry to the windows and jump to safety. Of the sixteen students in his class that day, fifteen survived. Librescu braced himself against the door until Cho shot him five times through it, killing him. He was seventy-six years old. With the fatalities in the dormitory earlier that morning, Cho shot to death a total of twenty-seven students and five faculty members before committing suicide by shooting himself in the head.

Librescu was hailed as one of the heroes of the day, with his students attesting to his sacrifice on their behalf. One student wrote to Librescu's wife, "If your husband was not at the door, I don't know what would have happened to me or the other students." It was frequently noted that the professor, a survivor of the Holocaust, died on Holocaust Remembrance Day.

Librescu's body was flown back to Israel, where he was given a traditional Jewish burial in Na'arana, attended by his wife and his two sons. "The courses in aerodynamics have ended," Librescu's son said at the funeral. "On the 16th of the month, you started a new career, teaching a new subject—heroism—[which] millions of students are learning." Shortly after his death, the president of Romania awarded Librescu the Order of the Star of Romania, the nation's highest civil honor, for his life's work and his heroism at Virginia Tech.

★

Obituaries are in the *New York Times* and *Washington Post* (both 19 Apr. 2007).

Lauren Markoe

LIPSET, Seymour Martin (*b.* 18 March 1922 in New York City; *d.* 31 December 2006 in Arlington, Virginia), sociologist and political scientist whose academic work emphasized American exceptionalism and asserted that economic modernization was a prerequisite for democracy.

Lipset was born in Harlem to the Russian-Jewish immigrants Max Lipset and Lena (Lippman) Lipset. His mother came to America in 1907 and worked as a seamstress before she married and maintained a kosher household. Lipset's father was a printer and union member who was active in the revolutionary movement. He left czarist Russia in 1911 due to political oppression and pogroms directed against the Jewish population. Lipset asserts that the Judaism and Marxism of his parents were key factors in forming his worldview. Lipset graduated from Townsend Harris High School, which was the preparatory school for City College of New York (CCNY) in the late 1930s.

Although his family struggled economically and preferred that he study dentistry, Lipset's undergraduate studies were fueled by his passion for politics, and he focused on

history before settling upon sociology as a field of study due to the influence of his friend and the future president of the American Sociological Association Peter Rossi, who argued that social workers would be in demand as another depression would follow World War II. Lipset graduated from CCNY in 1943. During his college days Lipset was involved with a generation of New York City Jewish intellectuals who were anti-Stalin and championed the political ideas of Leon Trotsky. These college intellectuals, who were referred to as Alcove One because political groups at CCNY spent considerable time in partitioned areas off the large college cafeteria, included the literary critic Alfred Kazin and the political journalists Nathan Glazer and Irving Kristol, all of whom, including Lipset, moved to the political right in the 1960s.

According to Lipset, he and his socialist colleagues spent considerable time in their early college years investigating why the Bolshevik Revolution resulted in an oppressive society in the Soviet Union. They were also concerned with the failure of Social Democrats in Europe to pursue policies that furthered socialism by attacking capitalism and encouraging worker participation in political governance. The final political question that confronted young Lipset was how to explain why the United States failed to support a strong Socialist Party. These political dilemmas would provide the basis for much of Lipset's future academic scholarship.

Lipset credits *Political Parties* published by Robert Michels in 1911 with altering his political perspective. The book was introduced to the Alcove One group by Philip Selznick, whom Lipset would later follow into sociology graduate study. Michels proposed the "iron law of oligarchy," arguing that all political parties, including those on the political left, were primarily concerned with maintaining their power, status, and privileges rather than extending mass participation. Although while attending CCNY Lipset served as national chairman of the Young People's Socialist League, he describes the work of Michels as influencing him to abandon his faith in the ideas of Vladimir Lenin and Trotsky.

Following his graduation from CCNY during World War II, Lipset was deferred from military service due to his poor eyesight. He was offered a teaching position by the CCNY sociology department, but he would have to be enrolled in graduate school. At the urging of his friend Selznick, he approached the Columbia University sociologist Robert Merton to accept him as a student. Lipset began his graduate studies at Columbia in 1943 under Merton, whom he described as "the most important intellectual influence" upon his academic career. In 1945 Lipset married Elsie Braun, who shared his background and interest in Judaism and socialism.

In the late 1940s Lipset pursued a doctorate degree at Columbia University, while teaching at the University of Toronto. The result of his doctoral research was publication of *Agrarian Socialism* (1950) in which the sociologist studied the development of socialist democratic organizations among Canadian farmers in Saskatchewan in contrast with the North Dakota Nonpartisan League, which largely functioned within the Republican Party. Lipset concluded that the parliamentary system of Canada was more favorable to the growth of third political parties than the American presidential election on a national level. For his second book, which Lipset sometimes referred to as his second dissertation, the sociologist studied the International Typographical Union (ITU), with whom his father was associated. In *Union Democracy* (1956), Lipset argued that the ITU was able to avoid oligarchy by fostering a democratic system in which the rank and file of the union was able to select between competing elites.

Following the granting of his PhD in sociology from Columbia in 1949, Lipset began a distinguished academic career at some of the nation's leading institutions of higher learning. From 1950 to 1956 Lipset taught at Columbia before moving to the University of California, Berkeley, in 1956. While happy at Columbia, Lipset reported that he was somewhat intimidated as a colleague with such influential mentors as Merton. Nevertheless, Lipset asserted that he entered Columbia as a political activist but left as a scholar. During his decade of tenure at Berkeley, Lipset also served as director of the university's Institute of International Studies. Citing that he was becoming too involved with campus politics in his Berkeley position, Lipset accepted a position as George D. Markham Professor of Government and Sociology at Harvard University from 1974 to 1975, and from 1975 to 1990 the sociologist was the Caroline S. G. Munro Professor of Political Science and Sociology at Stanford University. Following his retirement from Stanford, Lipset served as Hazel Professor of Public Policy at George Mason University and was a senior fellow at the Hoover Institution.

Lipset was active in many scholarly, political, and Jewish organizations. He was the only person to have served as president of both the American Political Science Association (1979–1980) and American Sociological Association (1992–1993). A staunch supporter of Israel who worked to find a peaceful resolution to the Israeli-Palestinian conflict, Lipset was president of the American Professors for Peace in the Middle East, chair of the B'nai B'rith Hillel Commission and the Faculty Advisory Cabinet of the United Jewish Appeal, and cochair of the Executive Committee of the International Center for Peace in the Middle East. In addition, Lipset served as

director of the U.S. Institute of Peace; cochair of the Committee for an Effective United Nations Educational, Scientific and Cultural Organization; and consultant to the National Endowment for Democracy and the American Jewish Committee.

Best known for his scholarship, Lipset was the author or coauthor of twenty-five books, editor of another twenty-seven volumes, and produced more than 350 scholarly articles. Among his most influential books was *Political Man: The Social Basis of Politics* (1960). In this landmark study, which sold over 400,000 copies and was translated into over twenty languages, Lipset argued that the rise of a middle class, the growth of educational opportunities, and the viability of voluntary associations reduced class conflict and provided the foundation for a stable democracy. In *The First New Nation: The United States in Historical and Comparative Perspective* (1963), a finalist for the National Book Award, Lipset noted the similarities between the challenges facing the new American nation following independence and newly emerging nations nearly two hundred years later. In this book Lipset was concerned with Alexis de Tocqueville's question of why the United States was the first institutionalized mass democracy, and the sociologist credited George Washington with using his status to legitimize the new system of democratic politics. Lipset also emphasized the role of religion, describing the United States as the most religious and moralistic of developed nations.

In 1970 Lipset received the Gunnar Myrdal Prize for *The Politics of Unreason*, in which he denounced right-wing extremism and called for the end of ideological politics in the United States. Responding to growing campus unrest during the 1960s and 1970s, Lipset published *The Divided Academy: Professors and Politics* (1975), observing that professors were predominantly on the political left as creativity encouraged refuting the status quo, while those critical of business were inclined to pursue more intellectual endeavors. With *American Exceptionalism: A Double-Edged Sword* (1996) and *It Didn't Happen Here: Why Socialism Failed in the United States* (2000), Lipset emphasized the unique qualities of American democracy, asserting that waves of immigration, religious faith, and individualistic values weakened class solidarity and limited the role of state intervention in the economy. *The Democratic Century*, his final book, was published in 2004.

Lipset left the Socialist Party in 1960, moving into the more conservative wing of the Democratic Party and became one of the first intellectuals described as a neoconservative. Lipset's first wife, Braun, with whom he fathered three children, died in 1987 after numerous cancer surgeries, and he married Sydnee Guyer in 1990. Lipset suffered a stroke in 2001 while having heart valve surgery, resulting in immobility and reduced speech. Five years later, the renowned sociologist died from a second stroke at age eighty-four.

★

An autobiographical account of Lipset's life is available in "Steady Work: An Academic Memoir," *Annual Review of Sociology* 22 (1996): 1–27. For Lipset's key writings, see *Political Man: The Social Basis of Politics* (1959); *The First New Nation* (1963); *The Politics of Unreason: Right-Wing Extremism in America, 1790–1970* (1970); *American Exceptionalism: A Double-Edged Sword* (1996); and *It Didn't Happen Here: Why Socialism Failed in the United States* (2000). An obituary is in the *New York Times* (4 Jan. 2007).

Ron Briley

M

MAC, Bernie (*b*. 5 October 1957 in Chicago, Illinois; *d*. 9 August 2008 in Chicago), popular stand-up comedian who enjoyed success on television, in films, and as one of the Original Kings of Comedy.

Mac was born Bernard Jeffrey McCullough, the son of Mary McCullough, who was a single parent. Mac came of age among the masses of urban poor on Chicago's South Side and spent his earliest years in a rat-infested house in the Woodlawn community. Eventually the McCullough family, including Mac's mother, his aunt, his older brother, and his grandparents, moved to an apartment in the Englewood neighborhood located above the Baptist church where his grandfather was a deacon. At the age of five, Mac was inspired to pursue a show business career while watching Bill Cosby tell a funny story on *The Ed Sullivan Show* and seeing how Cosby's humor transformed his mother's tears to laughter.

When Mac was sixteen, his mother died of cancer. She was a major influence in his life, and her death had a great impact on him. While attending Chicago Vocational High School, from which he graduated in 1975, Mac met his future wife, Rhonda Gore. They were married on 17 September 1977 and eventually had one daughter. In the meantime Mac toiled as a street performer, spouting comic riffs in parks and on Chicago Transit Authority trains. Just before his twentieth birthday, he made his professional debut at the Cotton Club in Chicago. For the next few years, he passed his evenings performing stand-up at clubs and honing his comic delivery. At this point his material was raw, edgy—and decidedly not mainstream. During the day Mac supported his family by working at odd jobs, including delivery truck and school bus driver, furniture mover, and janitor.

Mac's breakthrough came in 1989, when Redd Foxx and Slappy White invited Mac to perform in Las Vegas, Nevada. The following year he won the top prize at the Miller Lite Comedy Search. A 1992 appearance on Home Box Office's *Def Comedy Jam* earned him further acclaim. His film debut came in a small role as a club doorman in *Mo' Money* (1992), and he followed up with parts in such black niche films as *Who's the Man?* (1993); *House Party 3* (1994); *Above the Rim* (1994); *The Walking Dead* (1995); *Friday* (1995), earning notice for his performance as a lascivious pastor; *Don't Be a Menace to South Central While Drinking Your Juice in the Hood* (1996); *Get on the Bus* (1996); *B*A*P*S* (1997); *How to Be a Player* (1997); *Booty Call* (1997); *The Players Club* (1998); and *Life* (1999). He briefly hosted *Midnight Mac* (1995), a late-night Home Box Office comedy and variety program, and from 1996 to 2000 he played Uncle Bernie on eleven episodes of the television sitcom *Moesha*.

With Steve Harvey, Cedric the Entertainer, and D. L. Hughley, Mac appeared in the country's top comedy clubs, with the quartet billed as the Original Kings of Comedy. They toplined a documentary, *The Original Kings of Comedy* (2000), which brought their brand of humor to a wider audience. Mac was one of an ensemble of stars cast in *Ocean's Eleven* (2001), a caper film, thus transcending the African-American humor niche and segueing into mainstream fare.

The same might be said for *The Bernie Mac Show* (2001–2006), Mac's greatest success. The series was a semi-autobiographical television sitcom that Mac developed and in which he starred, playing Bernie "Mac" McCullough, a

Bernie Mac, 2007. **SCOTT GRIES/GETTY IMAGES**

starring screen role, in which he played a former baseball star making a comeback. Mac also won the lead in *Guess Who* (2005), a remake of *Guess Who's Coming to Dinner* (1967), perfectly cast as a father who comically tussles with his daughter's Caucasian boyfriend.

In 2005 Mac revealed that he previously had been diagnosed with sarcoidosis, a rare autoimmune disease, and that the condition was in remission. Two years later, while a guest on the *Late Show with David Letterman*, he announced that he was forsaking the stand-up comedy grind to spend more time with his family and to focus on his screen career. Other movie roles came in the third entry in the "Ocean's" franchise, *Ocean's Thirteen* (2007), as well as *Pride* (2007) and *Transformers* (2007).

On 24 July 2008 Mac was admitted to Northwestern Memorial Hospital in Chicago, suffering from pneumonia. His condition quickly deteriorated, and he died of complications from pneumonia. More than 7,000 mourners attended his funeral on 16 August 2008 at Chicago's House of Hope church. He is buried at Washington Memory Gardens Cemetery in Homewood, Illinois. His final films were released posthumously: *Soul Men* (2008), in which he played a former Motown backup singer; the animated *Madagascar: Escape 2 Africa* (2008), in which he provided the voice of Zuba, a lion; and *Old Dogs* (2009), released more than a year after his death.

Mac was a product of mid-twentieth-century urban America. His poverty-stricken childhood and streetwise personality combined with his belief in the importance of self-reliance and strong parental role models to form the basis of his humor. He earned acclaim first by tickling the funny bones of African Americans who understood his worldview and eventually by appealing to mainstream audiences.

★

Mac authored two books. In *I Ain't Scared of You: Bernie Mac on How Life Is* (2001), cowritten with Darrell Dawsey, Mac offers his views on subjects ranging from sex and religion to marriage and child rearing. *Maybe You Never Cry Again* (2003), cowritten with Pablo F. Fenjves, is a memoir. Henry Louis Gates, *America Behind the Color Line: Dialogues with African Americans* (2004), includes an extensive profile of Mac. Obituaries are in the *Chicago Tribune* (9 Aug. 2008), *New York Times* (10 Aug. 2008), and *Chicago Defender* (13 Aug. 2008).

Rob Edelman

stand-up comedian who dispenses tough love to his sister's three children when he becomes their custodian. In this show Mac played a fully developed character rather than a comic foil who existed merely for laughs. In 2002 *The Bernie Mac Show* earned an Emmy Award for Outstanding Writing, a Peabody Award for excellence in broadcasting, and a Humanitas Prize for television writing that upholds human dignity. During the show's run, Mac earned two Emmy nominations as outstanding lead actor in a comedy series, two Golden Globe nominations as outstanding actor in a comedy/musical series, and four National Association for the Advancement of Colored People Image Awards and two nominations as outstanding actor in a comedy series.

Meanwhile Mac continued appearing in supporting screen roles, but now in a wider range of films: *What's the Worst That Could Happen?* (2001); *Bad Santa* (2003), earning praise as a comically villainous store detective; *Charlie's Angels: Full Throttle* (2003); *Head of State* (2003); and *Ocean's Twelve* (2004). The persona Mac honed on television, that of an ornery but endearing everyman who humorously deals with life's curveballs, was effectively employed in *Mr 3000* (2004), his first

MacDIARMID, Alan Graham (*b.* 14 April 1927 in Masterton, New Zealand; *d.* 7 February 2007 in Philadelphia, Pennsylvania), organic chemist who was awarded the Nobel Prize in Chemistry in 2000 for his pioneering work on plastics that conduct electricity.

MacDiarmid was the youngest of five children born to Archibald MacDiarmid, a marine engineer, and Ruby (Graham) MacDiarmid, the daughter of a surveyor. During the Depression, MacDiarmid's father was unemployed for four years, and the family was very poor. MacDiarmid went to the local school barefoot. Before going to primary school, he delivered milk by bicycle each day. During high school he delivered newspapers after school. Years later he attributed his intense work ethic to these difficult times and to his close family ties.

When MacDiarmid was about ten years old, he found one of his father's chemistry textbooks from the 1880s. He was so curious about chemistry that he borrowed *The Boy Chemist* from the library. MacDiarmid had to leave Hutt Valley High School at age sixteen, and by age seventeen he was supporting himself with a job as a lab boy in the chemistry department of Victoria University College. One work assignment had a lasting effect. A lecturer asked him to prepare beautiful orange crystals of sulfur combined with nitrogen. MacDiarmid later said that he was inspired to follow chemistry research because he liked ''pretty things.''

MacDiarmid studied part time at the university, where he supported himself as a live-in janitor, completing a BS in 1948. He then was appointed demonstrator in the undergraduate laboratories, earning an MS in 1950 with first-class honors in chemistry. MacDiarmid received a Fulbright Fellowship to the University of Wisconsin, where he received a PhD in inorganic chemistry in 1953.

Following graduation from the University of Wisconsin, MacDiarmid received a New Zealand Shell graduate scholarship to study at Cambridge University in England. He very briefly was a lecturer at Queens College of the University of Saint Andrews in Scotland, after which he accepted the position of instructor in the chemistry department at the University of Pennsylvania. He became a full professor in 1964. It was at the University of Pennsylvania that MacDiarmid grew to love teaching as well as sharing research with his students.

Serendipity played a large role in MacDiarmid's career. At the University of Pennsylvania he met the physics professor Alan J. Heeger, who asked MacDiarmid to make some $(SN)x$, a polymer, after reading about its conducting properties. Polymers, commonly called plastics, are molecules made of many repeating parts. MacDiarmid was interested because he had worked on a colorful, simple sulfur-nitrogen compound years earlier. Heeger and MacDiarmid finally succeeded in making the golden crystals and copublished articles about their work.

In 1975, while MacDiarmid was lecturing in Japan, he chanced to describe the colorful sulfur-nitrogen compound to the Tokyo Institute of Technology professor Hideki Shirakawa as the two enjoyed some green tea. Shirakawa showed MacDiarmid a sample of an unusual silvery film

that was polyacetylene, $(CH)x$, prepared by one of his foreign students who did not understand Japanese and who had prepared the polymer using 1,000 times more catalyst than the instructions called for. MacDiarmid invited Shirakawa to come to the University of Pennsylvania for a year to study the interesting result because the silvery color suggested that the polymer might conduct electricity. Shirakawa accepted the invitation.

Working together, MacDiarmid, Heeger, and Shirakawa found that the mystery polymer was not a good conductor and that making it more pure made it worse. Then they tried adding iodine as an impurity and found that this increased their polymer's conductivity 10 million times at room temperature. The impurity acted like a dopant in the polymer, making it possible for the carbon-based crystal structure to conduct electricity just as certain impurities make silicon-based crystals become semiconductors.

The three scientists published their results in October 1977. Because plastics were considered excellent electrical insulators, the idea that there could also be conducting plastics was at first received with skepticism by the scientific community. Within a few years not only was the discovery widely accepted but applications were developed for conducting polymers, changing the electronics industry forever. Applications include plastic-based batteries that make laptop computers possible and organic light-emitting diode displays used in flat-panel televisions and cellular phones.

In 2002 Heeger, MacDiarmid, and Shirakawa shared the Nobel Prize in Chemistry ''for the discovery and development of conductive polymers.'' MacDiarmid, an American citizen since the mid-1960s, was always in close contact with his New Zealand family. MacDiarmid paid for twenty-two members of his New Zealand family to travel to Stockholm, Sweden, for the Nobel award ceremony.

MacDiarmid received many honors. In 2000 the Royal Society of New Zealand awarded MacDiarmid the Rutherford Medal. In 2001 New Zealand's Victoria University created the Alan MacDiarmid Chair in Physical Chemistry, and in 2002 MacDiarmid became a member of the Order of New Zealand, an honor that is limited to twenty living people. He held leadership positions at the NanoTech Institute of the University of Texas at Dallas and the Jilin MacDiarmid Institute at Jilin University in Changchun, China. MacDiarmid was teaching himself Chinese when he died. MacDiarmid authored or coauthored over 600 papers and held twenty-seven U.S. patents.

MacDiarmid married Marian Mathieu in 1954. They had four children. She died in 1990. He married Gayl Gentile in 2005. MacDiarmid died after a fall in his home in Drexel Hill, a suburb of Philadelphia. He was dying of myelodysplastic syndrome, a leukemia-like disease, and was rushing to go to New Zealand to bid farewell to his family. MacDiarmid is buried in Arlington Cemetery in Drexel Hill.

David E. Daniel, president of the University of Texas at Dallas, described MacDiarmid as an intellectually adventurous person. MacDiarmid saw the future of science in the next generation and was as committed to teaching as he was to interdisciplinary research. In his lectures MacDiarmid enjoyed using quotations. One quotation that well describes his success comes from Louis Pasteur's 1854 address in Lille, France: "Chance favors only the prepared mind."

★

For a summary of MacDiarmid's life, see the *New Zealand Herald* (9 Feb. 2007). Obituaries are in the *New York Times* (8 Feb. 2007) and *Los Angeles Times* (9 Feb. 2007).

M. C. Nagel

McFALL, John Joseph (*b.* 20 February 1918 in Buffalo, New York; *d.* 7 March 2006 in Alexandria, Virginia), California Democrat who served eleven terms as member of the House of Representatives, from 1973 to 1977 as majority whip.

McFall was the son of Hope McFall and Norma (Dempsey) McFall. He grew up on his grandparents' farm in Manteca, California, after his father died in combat during World War I. After attending the public schools of Manteca, McFall enrolled in Modesto (California) Junior College, from which he graduated in 1936. Two years later he earned a BA in political science from the University of California, Berkeley. McFall went on to study law at the university's Boalt Hall School of Law, earning an LLB in 1941. He worked as an attorney in Oakland before serving in World War II as an army staff sergeant in the Security Intelligence Corps. After the war McFall resumed his law career and opened a practice in Manteca. He married Evelyn Anklam, a union that lasted fifty-one years until her death, and the couple had four children.

McFall's lengthy political career began in 1948 when he served as a councilman and mayor of Manteca. He used his local political experience as a springboard to state government, where he served three terms in the California assembly (1951–1956). Setting his sights on Congress, in 1956 McFall won the Democratic primary for California's Eleventh Congressional District, a predominantly agricultural area in north-central California, encompassing the Central Valley and Joaquin County. In the general election he squared off against the seven-term Republican incumbent Justin Leroy Johnson. McFall won the contest with 53 percent of the vote. In his subsequent reelection bids in the district, he typically won by sizable margins.

Initially assigned to the Public Works Committee during the Eighty-fifth Congress (1957–1959), and later to the Committee on House Administration for the Eighty-

seventh Congress (1961–1963), McFall relinquished these panels for a spot on the influential Appropriations Committee (the House committee responsible for federal funding) in 1963. In 1971 McFall earned a coveted spot as an Appropriations subcommittee chair, or "cardinal"—a title, borrowed from the College of Cardinals who elect and advise the pope, that suggested the power of the person holding the post to shape federal spending. From his position as chairman of the House Appropriations Subcommittee on Transportation, the California congressman steered millions of dollars in federal funding into his district for several major infrastructure projects. During his eleven terms in Congress, many of his legislative initiatives focused on preventing floods and achieving better irrigation for his agricultural district. "I've put a dam or project on every stream in [my] congressional district," McFall once boasted. Primarily concerned with bolstering the local economy and meeting the needs of his constituents, McFall earned the reputation as a moderate who rarely made waves in Congress. A consistent supporter of labor interests, McFall also demonstrated unwavering support for defense spending and the Vietnam War during the administrations of Lyndon B. Johnson (1963–1969) and Richard M. Nixon (1969–1974), even as the Democratic Party increasingly voiced its criticism of American foreign policy.

The mild-mannered McFall quietly rose through the political ranks during his twenty-two years in Congress. Once described as a member of "an older breed of Democrat, a man who surely feels more comfortable in a group of cigar smoking regulars or at a union meeting than before a college audience," McFall's membership on the Appropriations Committee increased his visibility and helped him build important coalitions in the House. When Representative Thomas "Tip" O'Neill of Massachusetts became majority leader, McFall emerged as a leading contender to replace O'Neill as the Democratic whip. The reform-minded Democratic Study Group unsuccessfully lobbied for a caucus vote for the powerful whip post, which traditionally is a position selected by the Speaker of the House and majority leader. Appointed House whip in 1973, McFall became the third-ranking Democrat in the House. "The job of the whip is to be loyal to the elected Speaker and to the elected majority leader," McFall noted, not to determine policy. "He is a bridge between the members and the leadership."

Despite his ascension to whip—historically a key stepping-stone to the speakership—McFall's political leadership was short-lived. The election of seventy-five freshman Democrats in the fall of 1974 (termed the Watergate babies in the wake of the scandal that led to President Nixon's resignation on 9 August 1974)—signaled a period of institutional reform for the House. Linked to the old guard and the traditional power base rooted in the seniority system, McFall faced a competitive race for the majority leader

318

position left vacant in 1976 when O'Neill replaced the retiring Carl Albert of Oklahoma as Speaker of the House. The four-way contest included two leading reformers in the House, Phil Burton of California and Richard Bolling of Missouri, as well as centrist Jim Wright of Texas. "They say I'm too nice a guy to get anything done," McFall remarked before the vote. "But have you ever known a Speaker or majority leader who wasn't a nice guy?" He managed only thirty-one votes on the first ballot; eliminated from the race as the last-place finisher, he subsequently backed the eventual victor (and future Speaker), Jim Wright, who won the majority leadership post by a single vote on the third ballot.

During the contest, McFall's candidacy was undermined by his connection with a growing scandal (dubbed Koreagate) involving a South Korean businessman and lobbyist, Tongsun Park. In December 1976, O'Neill announced that the new whip for the Ninety-fifth Congress would be John Brademas of Indiana. Beginning in February 1977 the House Committee on Standards of Official Conduct (also known as the Ethics Committee) led an eighteen-month investigation of allegations that Park—in collusion with high-ranking South Korean officials—orchestrated a scheme to use funds collected from inflated commissions of American rice sales to South Korea to bribe U.S. officials to support foreign policy initiatives favorable to South Korea. McFall's representation of an agricultural district with significant rice production and his spot on the prominent Appropriations Committee made him a prime target for the influence peddling plot. McFall proclaimed his innocence, insisting that Park was "nothing but a South Korean businessman who was interested in selling rice." On 4 October 1978 the Ethics Committee found McFall guilty on the least serious of three charges of breaking House rules—failing to report a $3,000 campaign contribution from Park—and recommended a reprimand by the House. On 13 October 1978 the House concurred, voting to reprimand McFall and two other California representatives, Edward Roybal and Charles Wilson, embroiled in the Koreagate scandal.

McFall, stressing his reputation for integrity and honesty, was relieved at the sanction, one of the mildest possible punishments imposed by the House. Asserting that he had been vindicated, he went on to characterize the reprimand as a "technical matter" and predicted that his constituents would back him at the polls. But McFall was unable to overcome the effects of the scandal. In the 1978 election, with only 44 percent of the vote, he lost to Republican Norman Shumway.

After leaving Congress, McFall worked as a lobbyist for the U.S. Railway Association until his retirement in 1987. He died of complications from a broken hip and Parkinson's disease.

McFall's involvement in scandal, though harmful, was not the only reason that he failed to ascend to majority leader, the second-most powerful position in the House. The large group of young Democrats that swept into Congress in the wake of the Watergate scandal challenged many of the long-standing institutional traditions, including the seniority system. With a rapidly changing environment in the House, McFall's ties to the old guard hindered his ability to lead his party and placed him in the unfamiliar position of having to win the approval of the majority of his Democratic colleagues rather than the support of the Speaker. McFall's career, therefore, suffered from a missed opportunity and reveals the changing leadership criteria of the House that emerged during the 1970s.

★

Papers covering McFall's congressional career (1957–1978), including correspondence, reports, case files, clippings, legislation, speeches, and photographs, are located in the Holt-Atherton Department of Special Collections, University of the Pacific, Stockton, California. Robert Boettcher, *Gifts of Deceit: Sun Myung Moon, Tongsun Park, and the Korean Scandal* (1980), offers important background information on the scandal that contributed to McFall's political downfall. Two contemporary newspaper accounts of the scandal are "4 Seeking House Leadership Post Press Claims in the Election Today," *New York Times* (6 Dec. 1976), and "McFall Admits He Got Cash from Park," *Washington Post* (5 Nov. 1976). Obituaries are in the *Los Angeles Times* (16 Mar. 2006) and *Washington Post* (15 Mar. 2006).

Kathleen Johnson

McKAY, James McManus ("Jim") (*b*. 24 September 1921 in Philadelphia, Pennsylvania; *d*. 7 June 2008 in Monkton, Maryland), television sportscaster who hosted *ABC's Wide World of Sports*, a popular weekly anthology of sporting events, and covered major sporting activities throughout the world.

McKay was born James Kenneth McManus (his legal name throughout his life), the younger of two children of Joseph F. McManus, a real estate appraiser and later a mortgage banker, and Florence (Gallagher) McManus. In 1935 the family moved to Baltimore, where McKay continued his Roman Catholic schooling, graduating from Loyola High School (now Loyola Blakefield) in 1939. At Loyola College he won induction into Alpha Sigma Nu, the national Jesuit honor fraternity. Earning a BA in social science in 1943, he was commissioned as a naval officer and served on a minesweeper, escorting convoys in the South Atlantic. Discharged at the rank of lieutenant in 1946, McKay returned to Baltimore and worked as a city reporter for the *Baltimore Evening Sun*. He married Margaret Dempsey, a colleague at the *Sun*, on 2 October 1948. Margaret

Dempsey-McManus became a well-known political columnist and authored several children's books. Sean McManus, one of the couple's two children, became head of Columbia Broadcasting System (CBS) Sports in 1996 and president of CBS News and Sports in 2005.

The *Sun* established Baltimore's first television station, WMAR-TV, in 1948, and McKay was transferred to the television operation to host *The Sports Parade*, a three-hour program presented live on weekday afternoons. Responsible for fifteen hours of programming each week, McKay and his crew combed the region in a remote truck, presenting sports events ranging from horse races to prep school lacrosse matches.

In 1950 McKay accepted an offer from CBS to host a local afternoon variety program in New York City. The show's producer thought *The Real McKay* a winning title for the series and imposed the name on McManus as a "casting decision." Although *The Real McKay* was short-lived, "Jim McKay" remained McManus's professional name for the balance of his career. Like many New York "announcers" in the early television era, McKay was on call for local and network assignments of every type, including stints as a game-show host (*Make the Connection*, 1955) and a dramatic actor (*The Verdict Is Yours*, 1957). McKay aspired to establish himself as a broadcast journalist, but CBS News was top-heavy with star reporters and commentators. Eventually he carved out a niche in the network's sports operations, gaining assignments that included national telecasts of such high-profile events as the Masters Golf Tournament, the Kentucky Derby, and CBS coverage of the 1960 Rome Summer Olympic Games.

In 1961 Roone Arledge, newly appointed as head of American Broadcasting Company (ABC) Sports, persuaded McKay to jump to the rival network, offering him a chance to become the primary on-camera personality in a new type of weekly sports series. "Jim's not just somebody yelling at you," Arledge said, explaining his choice of McKay. "He has a sense of . . . the drama of the moment [that] has more to do with intellect than voice." The program, *ABC's Wide World of Sports*, premiered for a four-episode test run in spring 1961 and was placed in a regular Saturday afternoon spot that fall. It remained on the network schedule for thirty-seven years, with McKay as host and principal commentator for a quarter of a century. Covering one or several events each episode, the show introduced American audiences to sports rarely presented on national television during the black-and-white broadcast era, including track and field, soccer, weightlifting, amateur wrestling, auto racing, and skiing. Virtuoso Olympic sports, such as gymnastics, figure skating, and competitive diving, gained their first U.S. mass followings from the exposure afforded them by the show, leading ABC to outbid competitors in an attempt to put its brand on the Olympic Games.

Arledge's success with ABC Sports was based in part on creating recognizable sportscaster "personalities," such as the highly opinionated Howard Cosell and the folksy Don Meredith. McKay emerged as the network's steadiest voice, always at the ready with background information and well-reasoned commentary. Although McKay had a prominent role in ABC Olympics coverage, Arledge passed over him for the anchor position in 1968 and again in 1972. When the Munich games were disrupted by terrorist violence, however, Arledge did not hesitate to make McKay the face and the voice of the network's coverage of the incident, even though experienced ABC international correspondents were available at the site. With the confidence of a veteran television newsman, McKay guided viewers through unfolding events, keeping a matter-of-fact tone and personalizing comment in measured doses. At the closing ceremonies, as others stumbled to find appropriate words, McKay touched the hearts of many viewers when he recited "To an Athlete Dying Young," a poem by A. E. Housman that he first encountered in high school. McKay received a telegram in Munich from Walter Cronkite of CBS News, the most widely respected figure in American broadcast journalism, congratulating him for "honoring yourself, your network, and your industry."

McKay's spontaneous performance under pressure at Munich brought him two Emmy awards that year (one for news and one for sports), as well as a George Polk Memorial Award for Journalism and an Officer's Cross of the Legion of Merit from the German Federal Republic. Thirty years later ABC granted McKay a waiver on his lifetime contract so that he could appear as a commentator for the National Broadcasting Company at the 2002 Salt Lake City Winter Games, allowing him the distinction of becoming the first (and only) sportscaster to participate in Olympic coverage for all three of the original broadcast networks.

Other honors afforded McKay include a Peabody Award (1989) and membership in the Olympic Order (1998), the highest honor given by the International Olympic Committee. In 1987 he was elected to the Jockey Club, the governing body of American horse racing, and he has twice received an Engelhard Award from the Thoroughbred Breeders of Kentucky for his broadcast work in horse racing. The recipient of twelve Emmys during his career, McKay was inducted into the Television Academy Hall of Fame in 1995.

After leaving the anchor spot at *Wide World of Sports* in 1986, McKay reduced his responsibilities, continuing to participate in ABC television coverage of his favorite sports events, including the British Open Golf Championship and Triple Crown horse racing. In 1993 he purchased a minority share of the Baltimore Orioles baseball team. McKay and his wife lived in a nineteenth-century country house in Monkton, a horse-breeding district north of

Baltimore, spending winters at a vacation home in Key Largo, Florida. McKay died at the age of eighty-six. No cause of death was announced. A funeral ceremony held at the Cathedral of Mary Our Queen in Baltimore was attended by leading figures in broadcasting, sports, and journalism. McKay is buried on the McKay family farm in Monkton.

Part of a team of sportscasters providing ABC's television coverage of the 1972 Summer Olympic Games in Munich, McKay was thrust into the position of a news anchor when eleven members of the Israeli Olympic team were taken hostage and killed by Palestinian gunmen. With little training and no experience in covering breaking international news stories, McKay earned the respect of colleagues and viewers for his professional poise and personal sensitivity during the two-day ordeal. A pioneer television sportscaster, McKay won the admiration of viewers and colleagues alike.

★

McKay wrote two memoirs, *My Wide World* (1973) and *The Real McKay: My Wide World of Sports* (1998). William Taaffe, "You Can't Keep Him Down on the Farm: ABC's Jim McKay," *Sports Illustrated* (18 July 1984), offers a picture of McKay at the peak of his career. *One Day in September* (1999), an Academy Award–winning documentary film, includes footage of McKay anchoring coverage of the Munich Olympics hostage crisis and a candid interview. Obituaries are in the *New York Times* (8 June 2008) and the *Guardian* (9 June 2008).

David Marc

McKUSICK, Victor Almon (*b*. 21 October 1921 in Parkman, Maine; *d*. 22 July 2008 in Baltimore, Maryland), considered the father of medical genetics for his pioneering work in analyzing inheritance patterns of human abnormalities and establishing information databases on inherited diseases.

McKusick was the son of Carroll L. McKusick and Ethel M. (Buzzell) McKusick, both schoolteachers who had become dairy farmers. McKusick and his identical twin brother, Vincent, who became chief justice of the Maine Supreme Court, were the youngest of five children. He attended a one-room elementary school, having the same teacher for seven of his eight years there, and graduated from a small local high school that provided almost no instruction in science. Several generations of his family had lived in the vicinity of his birth. His parents were educated and religious, and they created an intellectual home environment.

During his teen years, McKusick contracted a bacterial infection that led to ten weeks in hospitals in Maine and Massachusetts. He was successfully treated with sulfanilamide, which had only recently become available for treatment of bacterial infections. This experience with medicine as a patient led him to change his plans from pursuing a life in the ministry to pursuing a career in medicine. In 1940 he entered Tufts University, where he spent three years. When the Johns Hopkins University Medical School, having insufficient candidates to fill its classes during World War II, decided to admit students without the baccalaureate degree, McKusick seized the opportunity to enroll there, earning an MD in cardiology in 1946.

Awarded a prestigious internship in the Osler Medical Service at Johns Hopkins University, McKusick first served for two years as chief of cardiology at the U.S. Marine Hospital in Baltimore to fulfill his military obligation. In 1947 his first observation of an inherited intestinal condition in a patient led to his first publication in medical genetics, in collaboration with a Boston physician. On 11 June 1949 he married Anne Bishop, a physician completing her training in rheumatology at Johns Hopkins; the couple had two sons and a daughter. In 1950 he returned to the Osler Medical Service, and in 1954 McKusick accepted a faculty appointment at Johns Hopkins. He and his wife remained at Johns Hopkins as professors of medicine for their entire careers.

McKusick's abiding interest in collecting data, both from his own research and that of other scientists, on various inherited diseases, led to the publication in 1956 of his first book, *Heritable Disorders of Connective Tissue*. At that time, medical genetics had not emerged as a specialty, yet he observed the incidence of the same diseases in families and collaborated with other researchers to combine their data on inherited conditions. He was also highly productive in his early career in the field of cardiology. He adapted new technology, just developed by the Bell Telephone Laboratory for studying speech sounds, to the study of heart sounds. The technology enabled physicians to visualize on paper or on a screen the sounds they were hearing through the stethoscope. He published an extensive volume on heart sounds, *Cardiovascular Sound in Health and Disease*, in 1958. His work as a cardiologist also gave him ample opportunity to observe congenital heart conditions and other ailments associated with them.

The rich intellectual and research environment at Johns Hopkins enabled him to work with major medical and scientific researchers and world-renowned practitioners. One such collaborator and mentor was the biologist Bentley Glass, who helped McKusick gain insights into the genetic basis of the inherited diseases that he came to study as the central focus of his research. When he was charged to head a major unit at the medical school, he negotiated to add a Division of Medical Genetics, which became an internationally known center for the study of inherited diseases and hosted many specialists from various fields of medicine. He headed the division from 1957 to 1973 and again from 1985 to 1989. The range of McKusick's work on human inheritance, including research on the Amish populations of Pennsylvania, Ohio, and Indiana and of skeletal abnormalities, led to the publication in 1966 of *Mendelian Inheritance in Man*, later posted on the Internet as *Online Mendelian Inheritance in Man*. This resource continues to serve as a reference in medical research.

McKusick served as physician in chief of Johns Hopkins Hospital from 1973 to 1985. During the late 1980s, as information continued to accumulate on molecular genetics, he played a key role in formulating the conceptual framework for the Human Genome Project, the goal of which was to map and sequence the entire complement of human genes. During the 1990s, at a time when the use of deoxyribonucleic acid (DNA) analysis in law enforcement and the judicial system was just becoming established and needed a methodological framework, he chaired a National Research Council committee that formulated guidelines for the field.

McKusick received many honors during his career, including the Johns Phillips Award from the American College of Physicians (1972) for contributions to internal medicine, election to the National Academy of Sciences (1973), the William A. Allan Award from the American Society of Human Genetics (1977), the Lasker Award for Special Achievement in Medical Science (1977), and the National Medal of Science (2002). He was the author of more than 500 articles and seven books, and he received more than twenty honorary doctorates.

McKusick died of cancer at his home. He is buried in Pingree Cemetery in Parkman.

Deeply respected by his students and colleagues alike, McKusick was the widely recognized leader in establishing the field of medical genetics. He was a major contributor to advancing the practice of medicine based on the most recent scientific discoveries, especially in the field of genetics. His discoveries in human inheritance made major contributions to Mendelian genetics in the field of biology generally. He helped pave the way for the Human Genome Project for the mapping and sequencing of the entire human genome and led efforts to establish frameworks for the use of DNA in law enforcement and the legal system.

★

For articles on McKusick's contributions to medical genetics, see "The Gene Doctor Is In: The Physician Who Has Written the Book Linking Genes to Disease Explains How the Next Wave of Genetic Research Will Affect Our Lives," *Technology Review* (July 1997): 46–52, and J. Wheelwright, "Reading the Language of Our Ancestors: Getting Up to Speed on Medical Genetics through the Vision of Victor McKusick," *Discover* (Feb. 2002): 70–77. McKusick discusses his work toward the development of medical genetics in his article "Medical

Genetics: A 40-Year Perspective on the Evolution of a Medical Specialty from a Basic Science," *JAMA: The Journal of the American Medical Association* 270, no. 19 (1993): 2351–2356. Obituaries are in the *New York Times* and *Washington Post* (both 24 July 2008).

W. Hubert Keen

MAILER, Norman Kingsley (*b.* 31 January 1923 in Long Branch, New Jersey; *d.* 10 November 2007 in New York City), novelist, journalist, playwright, screenwriter, and poet who was one of the major writers of post–World War II America.

Mailer grew up in Brooklyn, New York City, doted on by his father, Isaac Barnett ("Barney") Mailer, an accountant, and his mother, Fanny (Schneider) Mailer, who ran a small business. He had one sibling, a sister. Mailer's mother and her sisters made the young Mailer feel special, and by his own account he grew up a "nice Jewish boy." Although

Norman Mailer. STR/AFP/GETTY IMAGES

Mailer's mother encouraged her nine-year-old son, a rambunctious boy, to fill up notebooks with his writing, he showed an aptitude early on for engineering. Mailer attended Boys' High School in Brooklyn, graduating in 1939. He enjoyed building model airplanes and in 1943 earned an SB in aeronautical engineering from Harvard University. Nevertheless, as an undergraduate he had already been drawn to writing courses and to a career as an author, winning a prize from *Story* magazine for his short story "The Greatest Thing in the World" as well as working on Harvard's literary magazine, the *Advocate*.

Drafted into the army in 1944, Mailer experienced a brief period of combat in the Pacific theater—enough to provide the basic material for his best-selling and critically acclaimed novel *The Naked and the Dead* (1948). This panoramic novel, written, as Mailer admitted, in imitation of his literary heroes John Dos Passos and James T. Farrell, follows in precise detail and riveting narrative pace the adventures of a platoon of U.S. soldiers, part of a reconnaissance team preparing for the invasion of a Japanese island. Mailer's ability to provide authentic portraits of Americans from all regions of the country was an impressive achievement for a young author not yet thirty. Quite suddenly the press and public treated him as an authority on American culture and history.

Although Mailer had written two unpublished novels, he was not prepared for his overnight success, noting in *Advertisements for Myself* (1959) that he had exhausted his store of experience in his first novel. He did not want to write about his childhood, family, or community. His idea of a writer was modeled on André Malraux, whose books about heroes and world-changing conflicts influenced Mailer's idea of what a great writer ought to accomplish.

Mailer's second novel, *Barbary Shore* (1951), set in a Brooklyn rooming house, was an attempt to deal with the postwar and cold war years, during which fears of Communist subversion wracked American politics. Mailer's hero found himself caught in the murky world of espionage. Unsure of how to develop a main character who was not himself, Mailer failed (in the estimation of most critics) sufficiently to develop the dilemma of a young man caught between warring ideologies, even though Mailer himself had become active in criticizing both the United States and the Soviet Union for engaging in a mutually destructive arms race.

Mailer's third novel, *The Deer Park* (1955), an ambitious dissection of Hollywood, was written in the romantic tradition of F. Scott Fitzgerald, yet once again Mailer seemed to have difficulty fashioning an entirely credible protagonist and narrator. Extensively revised before publication, the novel nevertheless received mixed reviews.

During this stressful period (1948–1964), when the novelist could not seem to find his own voice, Mailer led a troublesome and controversial life. He married Beatrice

Silverman in January 1944. In 1952 they divorced, ending an eight-year marriage that produced one child. On 19 April 1954 Mailer married Adele Morales, a painter, with whom he had two daughters. The stormy marriage fell apart in 1960 after Mailer stabbed his wife, on the eve of his announcement that he would run for mayor of New York City. Briefly detained in Bellevue Hospital in New York City for psychiatric evaluation, Mailer was released, and his wife decided not to press charges. The couple divorced in 1962. That same year a tempestuous marriage to the journalist Jeanne Campbell produced another daughter. Campbell and Mailer divorced in 1963, and in December of that year he married for a fourth time, to the actress Beverly Bentley. Although the marriage to Bentley began well and resulted in the birth of four children, it ended in an acrimonious divorce in 1980.

Beginning with *Advertisements with Myself*, a collection of Mailer's fiction and nonfiction, Mailer began to find his own voice by incorporating into his writings a commentary on his ups and downs as writer. This supple autobiographical voice began to make its way into both his reportage and his fiction—most notably in his landmark essay "Superman Comes to the Supermarket," an account of John F. Kennedy at the 1960 Democratic Convention, and *An American Dream* (1965), a first-person novel that draws on Mailer's war experience, his stabbing of his wife Adele, and his quest to remake himself into a redoubtable writer on the model of Ernest Hemingway. The culmination of this fruitful phase was the frenetic and inventive novel *Why Are We in Vietnam?* (1967) and what many consider Mailer's masterpiece, *The Armies of the Night* (1968). In *Armies of the Night*, Mailer appears as a comic yet profound character, "Mailer," providing his firsthand account of the March on the Pentagon to protest the Vietnam War as well as a sober and subtle analysis of how the media covered this event. This highly praised book won both the National Book Award and the Pulitzer Prize.

Mailer's energy in the 1960s seemed boundless. Not only did he resurrect his campaign for mayor of New York City, promoting the idea that New York City should become the fifty-first state and finishing fourth in the election of 1969, he also wrote, directed, and starred in three films: *Wild 90* (1968), *Beyond the Law* (1968), and *Maidstone* (1970). Although critics slighted these achievements, the films represented a raw spontaneity that Mailer found lacking in conventional, mainstream cinema. Mailer's movies express his fascination with gangsters, violence, filmmaking, and politics. *Maidstone* is of special value because of its autobiographical nature: Mailer plays the main character, a director running for president and the target of an assassination attempt, made all too real by the actor Rip Torn when he attacks Mailer with a hammer, drawing blood and curses in a much-discussed cinema verité scene.

In the 1970s Mailer and his work came under increasing attack from feminists. Spearheaded by Kate Millet's landmark book *Sexual Politics* (1970), critics condemned the male chauvinism of such novels as *An American Dream*, in which the narrator gets away with murdering his wife and also sodomizes her maid. Mailer's defense of himself and other male authors (notably D. H. Lawrence and Henry Miller) in *The Prisoner of Sex* (1971) displayed his prowess as a literary critic but did little to dispel his growing reputation as a sexist. His biography of Marilyn Monroe, *Marilyn* (1973), a fresh and daring reconsideration of a screen icon, was similarly dismissed as merely male exploitation of a popular subject.

Although Mailer continued to write superb journalism, including *The Fight* (1977), his shrewdly observed account of the George Foreman–Muhammad Ali heavyweight title match, his best work of the decade was *The Executioner's Song* (1979), written in a new, understated style. The book won for Mailer superb reviews and a Pulitzer Prize. His account of the murderer Gary Gilmore's life and the social and psychological dynamic of the Utah environment in which the executed man lived and died had a panoramic, epic quality not seen in Mailer's work since *The Naked and the Dead*. It is arguable that his work never again quite reached this peak achievement.

Reports of Mailer's private and public life, so often melded together in his published work and the subject of gossip columns and sensational stories in tabloids and in noisy public debates with feminists and his fellow authors, reached a kind of crescendo in 1980. In that year he divorced Bentley in September, married and divorced the singer Carol Stevens a month later, and then married Norris Church, a model and an artist, in November. Mailer had had a relationship with Stevens since 1969 and wanted publicly to acknowledge his affection for her and their daughter, even though he had fallen in love with and would remain married to his sixth wife to the end of his life. While this final marriage would prove long lasting and produce a son, Mailer continued to have affairs with other women.

In 1983 Mailer published his novel about Egypt, *Ancient Evenings*, over which he had labored for a decade, hoping to create a masterpiece. A few critics treated the work as such, but most viewed the novelist's foray into historical fiction as dull and self-indulgent. Nevertheless, the novel is a kind of key to Mailer's view of human psychology, also reflecting his concern with karma and a view of the human condition that provides a perspective on what he regards as the limitations of modern thought and feeling. This novel may yet occupy a higher place in Mailer's body of work than contemporary critics were willing to accord it. A short novel, *Tough Guys Don't Dance* (1985), an effort at a hard-boiled detective story, seemed a forced effort redeemed mainly by Mailer's

beautiful evocation of Provincetown, Massachusetts, which he had made his second home—a stark contrast to his brownstone Brooklyn Heights life.

Mailer published another ambitious novel, *Harlot's Ghost*, in 1991. It is a fascinating, if turgid, history of the Central Intelligence Agency. The novel is full of Mailer's pet theories about espionage and post–World War II American history, but it lacks a compelling shape. Indeed, the novel ends with the words "to be continued."

More satisfying is *Oswald's Ghost* (1995), which in some respects reprises the methods of *The Executioner's Song*. Mailer had access to important tape-recorded interviews with the major figures in the life of the Kennedy assassin Lee Harvey Oswald as well as material in the Soviet KGB archives. The result is a meticulous and dramatic portrayal of an assassin, an account that makes the scores of books arguing that Oswald did not shoot Kennedy seem farfetched. As with *Marilyn*, *The Executioner's Song* displays Mailer's ability to empathize with his main subject and show how an individual personality interacts with his era.

In the next decade Mailer published a short book attacking the Second Gulf War, *Why Are We At War?* (2003); *The Spooky Art: Thoughts on Writing* (2004); a collection of interviews, *The Big Empty* (2006); and work on screenplays. None of these efforts added much to his stature as a major American writer, although the ideas on which he elaborates, especially in *On God* (2007), made their way into his last major novel, *The Castle in the Forest* (2007), an in-depth exploration of the childhood of the World War II German dictator Adolf Hitler. The bibliography Mailer appended to his book shows his diligent research habits culminating in a powerful re-creation of the pre-twentieth-century world that shaped Hitler's consciousness. The figure of Hitler's father, Alois, dominates the narrative. Lusty and shrewd, he is fit for a Mailer hero. Less satisfying is Mailer's choice of a narrator, literally a devil assigned by Lucifer to intervene in human history and make sure that Hitler is aided in achieving his evil designs. While critics expressed some reservations about yet another foray into historical fiction, by and large they deemed *The Castle in the Forest* one of Mailer's best books in over a decade.

Mailer's last years were troubled with ailments, including gout and hearing loss. He had to walk with two canes and wear hearing aids. His final year was plagued with respiratory problems. Hospitalized in the fall of 2007, he succumbed to a kidney ailment and other physical problems. He is buried in Provincetown Cemetery in Provincetown.

While Mailer's published work is uneven and there is no critical consensus on his merit as a novelist, his contributions to American culture and to writing are indisputable. He reenergized American journalism with his deeply probing and imaginative explorations of American politics, and he maintained the novelist's right to explore the largest subjects. Indeed, he promoted the primacy of the novel in a time when films and other media were capturing public attention. Certain of his books—*The Naked and the Dead*, *The Armies of the Night*, and *The Executioner's Song*—are likely to remain in the canon. No account of the post–World War II cultural climate would be complete without acknowledging Mailer's central role in American literary history.

★

Mailer's papers, including manuscripts, letters, and other materials, are held by the Harry Ransom Center, University of Texas at Austin. Several of his books—notably *Advertisements for Myself*, *The Armies of the Night*, and *The Fight*—include significant autobiographical material. Noteworthy biographies include Hilary Mills, *Mailer: A Biography* (1982); Peter Manso, *Mailer: His Life and Times* (1985); and Mary Dearborn, *Mailer: A Biography* (1999). Carl Rollyson, *Norman Mailer: The Last Romantic* (2008), a revision of *The Lives of Norman Mailer: A Biography* (1991), covers Mailer's life and career up to and including *The Castle in the Forest*. Worthwhile collections of literary criticism include Leo Braudy, ed., *Norman Mailer: A Collection of Critical Essays* (1972), and Harold Bloom, ed., *Norman Mailer* (2003). Obituaries are in the *New York Times* and *Washington Post* (both 11 Nov. 2007).

Carl Rollyson

Delbert Mann. THE KOBAL COLLECTION/THE PICTURE DESK, INC.

MANN, Delbert Martin ("Del"), Jr. (*b.* 30 January 1920 in Lawrence, Kansas; *d.* 11 November 2007 in Los Angeles, California), Academy Award–winning motion-picture director and president of the Directors Guild of America (1967–1971).

Mann was the first of three children born to Delbert Martin Mann, a sociology professor, and Ora (Patton) Mann, a teacher and a social worker. Mann grew up in Nashville, Tennessee, after his father assumed a professorship at Scarritt College. While attending Hume-Fogg High School in Nashville, Mann developed an interest in theater and worked extensively with the dramatic club. During this time Mann met Fred Coe, a director at the Nashville Community Playhouse. The two became friends, and Mann acted in playhouse productions throughout college and began assisting Coe, earning the title of assistant director on some of the group's productions. After graduating from high school in 1938, Mann entered Vanderbilt University, where he majored in political science and minored in sociology and economics, graduating in 1941 with a BA. Mann's numerous campus activities included a stint as student body president. He also participated in extracurricular activities related to his love of theater.

On his first day at Vanderbilt, Mann met Ann Caroline Gillespie; the two served on many boards and committees together and were coeditors of the student newspaper. They eventually began dating and married on 13 January 1942.

During World War II, Mann served in the Army Air Forces and was assigned to the Eighth Air Force in England as the pilot of a B-24 bomber. While in England, Mann used many of his off-base passes to attend London theater, and his interest in the stage intensified. At breakfast one morning in 1944, Mann was seated next to a bombardier from another plane. As they talked about what they might like to do after the war, the crew member told Mann that he would like to be a poet; Mann replied that he would like to work in the theater. That day only one plane was lost in the bombing raids, and it was the one on which the bombardier served. That loss, and its representation of the fragility of life, motivated Mann to pursue his dream.

After completing his military service, Mann entered the Yale School of Drama, where he earned an MFA in directing in 1948. While he was at Yale, he narrowed his career focus to directing and took his first directing job in 1947 at the Town Theatre in Columbia, South Carolina.

There Mann succeeded Coe, who had left for New York City, where he would eventually join the National Broadcasting Company (NBC) television network.

In 1949, with Coe's recommendation, Mann joined NBC as a stage manager. Later that year Coe hired Mann as one of two alternating directors on a new dramatic anthology series called the *Philco Television Playhouse*. Later, when Goodyear became a sponsor, the program became the *Philco-Goodyear Television Playhouse*. For this series alone, Mann directed 108 live television dramas between 1949 and 1955. During its first two years, the program featured television adaptations of plays and novels; in its third season the repertoire expanded to include original scripts. Mann typically received his script on a Monday with thirteen days to rehearse and prepare for the live telecast.

Paddy Chayefsky was one of the writers for the *Playhouse*, and Mann directed seven of his scripts. Their third collaboration was *Marty*, which aired on 24 May 1953. The story of a lonely Bronx butcher and a plain, unmarried schoolteacher struck a chord with audiences and critics alike. The *New Yorker* called it "the most touching play we have watched . . . in five years of televiewing." The show went on to win the Sylvania Award and the Donaldson Award for Best TV Drama of 1953. When the production aired, Harold Hecht, the actor Burt Lancaster's film-producing partner, was among the viewers. Their company purchased the motion-picture rights to the story, hiring Chayefsky to write the script and Mann to direct. The 1955 film was recognized as the first major project to be adapted from television to film and won four Academy Awards, including Best Picture and Best Director for Mann, marking the first time that a director had won the award for his debut film. *Marty* also became the first American film to win the Palme d'Or (Golden Palm) at the Cannes Film Festival in France.

Throughout the 1950s Mann divided his work between television and film. For television he directed for such programs as *Omnibus*, *Producers Showcase*, *Playhouse 90*, and *Wide, Wide World*. Mann's productions include a musical version of *Our Town* (1955), which introduced the song "Love and Marriage"; *The Red Mill* (1958), which was the first Columbia Broadcasting System program to be filmed on videotape and which was completed despite a strike by technical employees; *The Plot to Kill Stalin* (1958), which generated a protest from the Russian government; a two-part color production of *What Makes Sammy Run?* (1959); and *The Tunnel* (1959), a Civil War story utilizing extensive special effects, described by Mann in his memoirs as "the most physically demanding episode we ever tried in a television studio."

For film Mann followed *Marty* with a series of dramatic adaptations from television and stage, including *The Bachelor Party* (1956) and *Middle of the Night* (1959), both of which were written by Chayefsky and originally directed for television by Mann. Mann directed the film versions of *Desire Under the Elms* (1958), Sophia Loren's first film made in Hollywood; *Separate Tables* (1958), which Mann took over after Laurence Olivier departed as director; and *The Dark at the Top of the Stairs* (1960). Among Mann's other film credits are the immensely popular Doris Day comedies *Lover Come Back* (1961) and *That Touch of Mink* (1962), along with such dramatic fare as *The Outsider* (1961), the story of Ira Hayes, the Native American who helped raise the flag at Iwo Jima, Japan, and *A Gathering of Eagles* (1963). With the producer Doug Laurence and the writer Dale Wasserman, Mann formed an independent production company in 1964 to produce films for Metro-Goldwyn-Mayer (MGM). For MGM, Mann directed the drama *Mister Buddwing* (1965), among other films. Mann's last feature film was *Night Crossing* (1981).

In 1959 Mann was elected to the board of directors of the Screen Directors Guild, renamed the Directors Guild of America in 1960. In 1967 he was elected the ninth president of the Directors Guild and served two terms in that office. Mann continued to work on behalf of the guild for the rest of his life and was a member of the guild's Health and Welfare Plan Board, Pension Plan Board, and Educational and Benevolent Foundation. The guild recognized Mann's service by presenting him with a Robert B. Aldrich Award (1997) and an Honorary Life Member Award (2002). Additionally, Mann served on boards at the Academy of Television Arts and Sciences and the Academy of Motion Picture Arts and Sciences. He was a trustee of Vanderbilt University, where he established and raised money for the Fred Coe Artist-in-Residence program. He also supported the Motion Picture and Television Country House and Hospital.

In 1967 Mann returned to television, directing forty television productions through 1994. His production of *Heidi* (1968) sparked a national furor when NBC started the film instead of showing the dramatic closing sixty-five seconds of a football game between the New York Jets and the Oakland Raiders. Mann directed a number of literary adaptations for television, including *David Copperfield* (1969) and *Jane Eyre* (1970). His production of *All Quiet on the Western Front* (1979) won a Golden Globe Award for Best Television Movie.

Despite beginning his career working on the stage, Mann did not work in that medium extensively after his success in film and television. Among his stage productions were a tour of *A Quiet Place* (1955) with Tyrone Power. *Speaking of Murder* (1956) and *Zelda* (1969) both had short Broadway runs. Mann withdrew as director of *Tovarich* (1962) prior to its Broadway opening. For the New York City Center Opera, Mann staged a production of *Wuthering Heights* (1959).

Mann and Gillespie remained married until Gillespie's death in 2001. They had one daughter and three sons.

Mann was tall and thin with a friendly disposition and what one of his sons described as "warm Southern-bred manners." Following Mann's death of pneumonia at the age of eighty-seven, a memorial service was held at his longtime church, the Beverly Hills Presbyterian Church, and his remains were cremated.

Mann began directing for television at the dawn of that medium's rise to mass prominence, and he demonstrated an ability to innovate with location photography, special effects, and other techniques not normally attempted during live broadcasts—techniques that would later become standard. During his film career, Mann exhibited a diverse range that encompassed drama and comedy alike. With a fine sense of detail, he was a director who used a nurturing approach to elicit sensitive and effective portrayals from his actors. In addition to his creative accomplishments, Mann's legacy includes a strong commitment to industry service. His decades-long leadership contributions to the Directors Guild and other organizations serve as a model for other industry professionals.

★

Mann's personal papers were donated to the Jean and Alexander Heard Library at Vanderbilt University and provide invaluable information about his life and career. Sara Harwell, ed., *The Papers of Delbert Mann: A Manuscripts Catalog* (1993), is a guide to the collection and includes essays from Mann, his wife, and several of his colleagues. Mann's autobiography, *Looking Back at Live Television and Other Matters* (1998), provides the director's personal account of his life and career. Obituaries are in the *New York Times* and *Los Angeles Times* (both 13 Nov. 2007). An oral history was recorded by the Academy of Television Arts and Sciences (1997).

Robert E. Davis

MATHIAS, Robert Bruce ("Bob") (*b.* 17 November 1930 in Tulare, California; *d.* 2 September 2006 in Fresno, California), track-and-field athlete who became the first winner of two Olympic gold medals in the decathlon, and a four-term member of the U.S. House of Representatives.

Mathias was the second child of four born to Charlie Milfred Mathias, a physician, and Lillian Harris Mathias, a homemaker. He was born a few months after the family moved to California from Oklahoma. Mathias was sickly as a child and suffered from anemia. His father, a former tackle on the University of Oklahoma football team, gave him iron pills and created a backyard track-and-field venue to help his son build up his strength. The regimen worked.

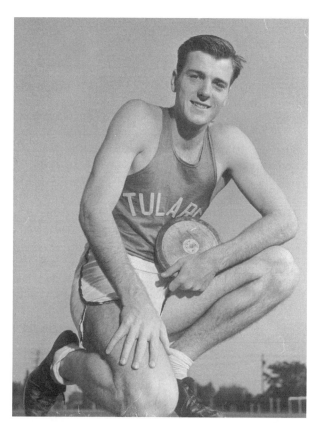

Bob Mathias, 1949. MICHAEL ROUGIER/TIME LIFE PICTURES/ GETTY IMAGES

By the time Mathias was twelve, he cleared the high jump at five feet, six inches.

Modest, clean-cut, and confident, Mathias was a basketball star at Tulare Union High School, where he averaged eighteen points per game in his senior year. He also played football as a running back and competed as a hurdler, sprinter, and thrower on the track-and-field team. When Mathias was seventeen, his track coach, Virgil Johnson, suggested that Mathias add the javelin and pole vault; in 1948, after Mathias's senior track season, Johnson told Mathias that if he worked hard he could probably make the 1952 Olympic team for the decathlon. At the time, neither of them was familiar with all ten events in the two-day competition. The first day of the decathlon includes a 100-meter sprint, long jump, shot put, high jump, and 400-meter relay. On the second day, an athlete must compete in the 110-meter hurdles, discus, pole vault, javelin, and 1,500-meter race. The winner of the Olympic decathlon is widely regarded as the world's greatest and most versatile athlete.

In June 1948 Mathias won the Southern Pacific Amateur Athletic Union (AAU) decathlon, which qualified him for the Olympic trials in Bloomfield, New Jersey. Having won at the trials, at the age of seventeen he went to the

1948 Olympics in London, England, four years before his coach originally thought he would be ready. In cold, rainy weather, Mathias earned 7,139 points in the event, winning the gold medal and becoming the youngest man ever to win an Olympic gold medal in track and field. Also that year he received the 1948 Sullivan Award, given to the top American amateur athlete. When a reporter asked what he would do next after such a stunning debut, the six-feet, two-inch, 190-pound athlete joked, "Start shaving, I guess." When he returned to his hometown, his plane had to circle the runway twice while officials cleared the crowd that had gathered to welcome him home.

In the fall of 1948 Mathias entered the Kiski School, a prep school in Saltsburg, Pennsylvania. The following year he entered Stanford University in California, where he starred on both the football and track-and-field teams. In track and field he won the 1949 and 1950 national AAU titles; in 1950 he had a world-record score of 8,042 points in the decathlon. On the football field, he had a ninety-six-yard kickoff return for a touchdown, which gave Stanford the win over the University of Southern California, and took his team to the 1952 Rose Bowl. In 1952, competing in front of a home crowd in Tulare, he won the combined AAU national and Olympic trials, setting a new world record for decathlon points and setting new personal bests in eight of the ten events.

Less than a month later, at the Helsinki Olympics in Finland, Mathias won his second gold medal in the decathlon, despite suffering from a pulled muscle in his thigh. He had grown since his previous gold medal; he was now six feet, three inches, weighing 205 pounds. He scored 7,887 points on a new International Association of Athletics Federations (IAAF) scoring system, setting a new world record for the event. The win made him the first athlete to play in the Rose Bowl and win an Olympic gold medal in the same year.

After his second Olympic win, having never been defeated, he retired from the decathlon. At the age of twenty-one he was a four-time national champion, three-time world record setter, and two-time Olympic gold medalist. Mathias later said of his two Olympic appearances: "There was no pressure the first time because I didn't know any better. Nobody thought I would even finish. The second time . . . everybody put pressure on me"— not least himself.

In June 1953 Mathias graduated from Stanford with a BA in education. That same month he married Melba Wiser, with whom he had four children. He then enlisted in the U.S. Marine Corps, serving for two and a half years as a goodwill ambassador to less-developed nations. On one visit to Formosa (also known as Taiwan), Mathias presented a javelin to a local teenager, C. K. Yang, who later broke the decathlon world record in 1963. In 1956, after three seasons without competing or training, Mathias won

the interservice decathlon (a competition among members of the armed services), scoring 7,193 points even though he did not run the 1,500 meters. The win showed that he could have been a contender in the 1956 Olympics.

Mathias was not allowed to compete in those Olympics because at the time Olympic competition was restricted to amateur athletes who had not made any money from their sport. In 1954 Allied Artists Pictures began production of a biographical film about Mathias. Unable to find an actor with his combination of good looks and athletic ability, they finally asked Mathias to portray himself in the film. The payment he received for working on the movie cost him his amateur status as an athlete.

Mathias continued to make film and television appearances and also established the Bob Mathias Sierra Boys Camp. From 1967 to 1975 he served four terms in the U.S. House of Representatives as a Republican for California's Eighteenth Congressional District. Gerald Ford, the future president who at that time was a Michigan congressman serving as Republican minority leader of the House, later said of Mathias, "You were initially attracted by his name, his presence, and appearance, but once you got to know him, it was his sound judgment that was very impressive."

As a legislator, Mathias worked to allay a dispute between the AAU and the National Collegiate Athletic Association. His work led to the Amateur Sports Act of 1978, which was passed after he left office. Mathias lost his seat when the Democrats swept the House in the wake of the Watergate scandal, which led to the resignation of President Richard M. Nixon in 1974. After leaving the House, Mathias served as the director of the U.S. Olympic Training Center in Colorado Springs, Colorado, from 1977 to 1983, and then was executive director of the National Fitness Foundation. Mathias and Wiser divorced in 1977. On 31 December 1977 he married Gwen Haven Alexander, who had a daughter from a previous marriage.

In 1996 a cancerous tumor was discovered in Mathias's throat. He died of cancer ten years later and was buried in Tulare.

If Mathias had won only one Olympic title, he would still be remembered as one of the greatest athletes of all time because he won so decisively and at such a young age. As Paul Helms of the Helms Athletic Foundation said, "We sent a boy over to do a man's job, and he did it far better than any man ever could." Mathias's second Olympic gold medal, and his world records, confirmed his place as the world's greatest all-around athlete. He was named to many athletic halls of fame, including the U.S. Olympic Hall of Fame and the U.S. National Track and Field Hall of Fame.

★

Mathias's autobiography is *A Twentieth-Century Odyssey: The Bob Mathias Story* (2000), written with Bob Mendes. For a discussion of the decathlon and Mathias's role in its history, see Frank Zarnowski, *The Decathlon: A Colorful History of Track and Field's Most Challenging Event* (1989) and *American Decathletes: A 20th Century Who's Who* (2001). Chris Terrence, *Bob Mathias: Across the Fields of Gold* (2000), includes many family photos and reminiscences by Mathias's friends. Obituaries are in the *New York Times* and *Los Angeles Times* (both 3 Sept. 2006). The Allied Artists film *The Bob Mathias Story* (1954), starring Mathias and his first wife as themselves, covers his life and Olympic career up to his enlistment in the Marines.

Kelly Winters

MENOTTI, Gian Carlo (*b.* 7 July 1911 in Cadegliano, Italy; *d.* 1 February 2007 in Monaco), Italian-born American composer best known for his operas of the 1940s and 1950s, and founder of the Festival of Two Worlds, based in Spoleto, Italy, and its American counterpart in Charleston, South Carolina.

Menotti was the sixth of eight children born to Alfonso Menotti, a coffee merchant, and Ines (Pellini) Menotti, who took part in the family business. From a very young age he was encouraged, particularly by his mother, to

Gian Carlo Menotti, 1991. AP IMAGES

cultivate his interest in music and composition. He and his siblings attended the theater, took music lessons, and staged their own puppet shows for which they would also write the music. By the age of eleven he had composed the music and libretto for a complete opera, *The Death of Pierrot*. After the family moved to Milan from their home in the Lake Lugano region, he went regularly to see operas at the city's famed La Scala. He enrolled at the Giuseppe Verdi Conservatory in 1924.

After the death of Menotti's father, his mother remarried. Menotti traveled with his mother to South America to try to rescue the family coffee business and then directly to Philadelphia, where in 1928 he enrolled at the Curtis Institute of Music. Ines Menotti had approached the famed conductor Arturo Toscanini, who recommended that her son hone his skills at Curtis. There Menotti studied composition with Rosario Scalero, and during these classes he met his fellow student Samuel Barber, who would become one of the most celebrated American composers. The two soon developed a romantic and professional relationship that would last for more than thirty years. Menotti spent most of his professional life in the United States and his libretti were mainly written in English, but he never relinquished his Italian citizenship.

Although it could have been a major barrier to their careers, Menotti and Barber never concealed their same-sex relationship. They shared a house in Mount Kisco, New York, which they called Capricorn, bought thanks to the patronage of Mary Curtis Bok, founder of the Curtis Institute. The press treated their relationship as an "open secret," entailing thinly coded references to homosexuality. For example, *Newsweek* once referred to Barber and Menotti as "the closest of friends for 30 years." Although Menotti and Barber collaborated on various projects, their careers sometimes put a strain on their relationship, as Barber was jealous of Menotti's commercial success.

In 1933 Menotti graduated from Curtis and moved to Vienna with Barber. The scenes of Austrian life that Menotti observed served as the basis for his first opera, *Amelia al Ballo*, a one-act work that opened in Philadelphia in April 1937. Dedicated to Bok, the opera enjoyed a successful run as *Amelia Goes to the Ball* at the Metropolitan Opera in New York on a double bill with Richard Strauss's *Elektra*; this success launched Menotti's career. *Amelia* was also scheduled to have an Italian premiere, but because of Menotti's refusal to join the ruling Fascist Party of Benito Mussolini, the Italian debut was canceled; the composer was largely neglected in his homeland until the end of World War II. Influenced by Scalero's opinion that opera was not a serious genre, Menotti at first considered himself primarily a composer of symphonies and concertos. He conceived *Amelia* as an entertainment, an opera buffa (comic opera), but the work's success changed his attitude toward the genre. He started working on a second opera commissioned by National Broadcasting Company (NBC) Radio, *The Old Maid and the Thief* (1939). As Menotti's audience continued to grow, the Metropolitan Opera commissioned a full-length opera, *The Island God* (1942), which, in contrast to *Amelia*, was a serious work. The public did not appreciate the change of genre, and the work was a failure. Embittered by this commercial disappointment, Menotti turned to the composition of the ballet *Sebastian* (1943) and the Piano Concerto in F (1945).

With a commission from the Alice M. Ditson Fund of Columbia University, Menotti composed *The Medium* (1946), a melodrama about a psychic medium who becomes the victim of her own frauds. This two-act "chamber opera" required fewer singers and a smaller orchestra than did Menotti's previous works. The influential *New York Herald Tribune* music critic, and a composer in his own right, Virgil Thomson, gave the opera a positive review. Yet commercial success did not come until a year later, when *The Medium* was shown on a double bill with Menotti's comic curtain raiser *The Telephone* (1947) at the Ethel Barrymore Theater on Broadway. Menotti invited Toscanini to the theater, and the conductor loved the production so much that he publicly endorsed it. Ticket sales soon skyrocketed, and the show was sold out for its entire eight-month run. Menotti directed the movie version of *The Medium* (1951), which won the Best Lyrical Film award at the 1952 Cannes Film Festival.

In 1950, as cold war tensions escalated, Menotti premiered his opera *The Consul* (1950), about a group of powerless citizens trying to get out of a totalitarian state. The opera earned the composer his first Pulitzer Prize and the Drama Critics Circle Award, shared with T. S. Eliot's *The Cocktail Party*. Menotti reached a wider audience with *Amahl and the Night Visitors* (1951), a Christmas story commissioned by NBC that became the first television opera. *Amahl* has been a Christmas-season favorite ever since. Menotti won another Pulitzer Prize in 1955 for *The Saint of Bleecker Street* (1954), which centers on the inner conflicts generated by the composer's religious upbringing and his subsequent loss of faith. The show enjoyed a Broadway run, though more limited than that of *The Medium*.

Menotti contributed the libretto to Barber's opera *Vanessa* (1958), which was performed at the Metropolitan under the direction of Menotti himself, with lavish sets by the noted photographer and stage designer Cecil Beaton. Menotti also wrote the libretto for Barber's *A Hand of Bridge* (1959), but the Met refused him as librettist for Barber's *Antony and Cleopatra*, based on William Shakespeare's play, preferring Franco Zeffirelli. Debuting in 1966, the work was a failure with critics and audiences. A revised version of the opera, with a reworked libretto by Menotti, premiered under Menotti's direction at the Juilliard School in 1975. As Menotti admitted, his rejection by the Met caused a crisis in his relationship with Barber.

In 1958 Menotti founded the Festival of Two Worlds, which represents one of the composer's most enduring legacies. His goal for the festival, based in Spoleto, was to foster artistic collaboration between Europe and the United States. The Spoleto festival soon attained an international reputation, and in 1977 Menotti created an American counterpart, Spoleto Festival USA, in Charleston, as well as an Australian branch in Melbourne in 1986. Although Menotti withdrew from Spoleto USA in 1993 because of administrative disputes, it continues to attract leading artists in the fields of music, theater, and dance.

Menotti's own reputation as a lyric composer started to decline in the 1960s, and later works such as *Maria Golovin* (1958); *The Last Savage* (1963); *La Loca* (1979); *Goya* (1986), written for Placido Domingo; and *The Singing Child* (1993) did not replicate the success of his earlier operas. Starting with *Martin's Lie* (1964), Menotti also composed a series of children's operas. In 1967 the Russian composer Igor Stravinsky personally asked Menotti to direct his own opera, *The Rake's Progress*, at the Hamburg Opera House in Germany.

In 1973 the relationship between Barber and Menotti ended, and they sold their Mount Kisco house. Menotti then decided to leave the United States for Europe, and in 1974 he bought Yester House in Scotland, the ancestral home of the Marquess of Tweeddale. That year he also adopted Francis "Chip" Phelan, a young American actor and figure skater. In 1984 Menotti was awarded the Kennedy Center Honor for lifetime achievement in the arts. In 1993 he became director of the Rome Opera, a post he left after two seasons over disagreements on financial management. He died at the age of ninety-five in Monaco, where he had a home.

Menotti is remembered as one of the leading composers of the twentieth century, and his operas successfully reached large audiences. He resisted the avant-garde musical currents of his time, preferring traditional harmony but emphasizing particularly dramatic moments with dissonance and polytonality. For Menotti, the connection with the audience was a paramount concern, and he embraced traditional theater as an integral part of his operas. The reason for his popularity resides in his effective blend of traditional opera form with twentieth-century dramatic situations.

★

John Gruen, *Menotti: A Biography* (1978) is the first biography devoted to Menotti; it reconstructs the composer's professional career and, albeit with some coyness, his private life. John Ardoin, *The Stages of Menotti* (1985) is a tribute to the composer that includes biographical information, interviews, plot summaries of his operas, and performance history. Michael S. Sherry, *Gay Artists in Modern American Culture: An Imagined Conspiracy*

(2007) contextualizes Menotti's contribution to American culture within the historical context of the cold war and its equation of communism and homosexuality fostered by anti-Communist paranoia. Obituaries are in the *New York Times* and *Washington Post* (both 2 Feb. 2007).

Luca Prono

MERRIFIELD, (Robert) Bruce (*b.* 15 July 1921 in Fort Worth, Texas; *d.* 14 May 2006 in Cresskill, New Jersey), chemist who received the 1984 Nobel Prize in Chemistry for his invention of an efficient method to synthesize proteins.

Merrifield's parents, George E. Merrifield and Lorene (Lucas) Merrifield, were native Texans who married in 1920. Their only son was born the next year, and in 1923 they moved to Southern California. They relocated frequently, particularly after the onset of the Great Depression. Merrifield attended nine different grade schools and two high schools before graduating from Montebello High School in 1939. He attended Pasadena Junior College for two years and then transferred to the University of California, Los Angeles (UCLA), where he received a bachelor's degree in chemistry in 1943.

Upon graduation from UCLA, Merrifield began working as a chemist at the Philip R. Park Research Foundation. After working there for a year on the synthesis of amino acids, the building blocks of proteins, Merrifield returned to UCLA for graduate work with the biochemist Max S. Dunn on pyrimidines, the chemical building blocks of nucleic acids—deoxyribonucleic acid (DNA) and ribonucleic acid (RNA). He had a position as a chemistry instructor at UCLA from 1944 to 1947 while doing graduate work. He worked with Dunn from 1948 to 1949. It was at UCLA that Merrifield met a fellow biochemistry student, Elizabeth ("Libby") Furlong, whom he married on 20 July 1949, the day after he received his PhD. The couple had five daughters and one son. Immediately after their wedding, Bruce and Libby set out for the Rockefeller Institute for Medical Research (later changed to Rockefeller University) in New York City, where Bruce was to spend his entire career. He had been offered a job as an assistant to D. W. Woolley, who had studied vitamins and was investigating a bacterial growth factor he had discovered earlier. This bacterial growth factor was believed to be a peptide, a string of different amino acids bonded together in a specific way and in a particular order, the sequence being crucial to the peptide's properties: changing the sequence altered the peptide's characteristics completely.

As an assistant to Woolley, Merrifield synthesized a number of these peptides but found the process extremely time-consuming and the yields extremely low. In one case, only 7 percent of the synthesis product was the peptide of interest. The problem was that it was difficult to get the amino acids to bind to each other in the right order and with the correct type of bonds. Out of his frustration with these methods, Merrifield decided to bind the initial amino acid to a solid plastic bead, wash off the chemicals involved in the resulting reaction, add the next amino acid and other needed reactants, bind the two amino acids, and repeat the process until he produced a peptide of the desired length and sequence. Merrifield suggested this approach to Woolley, who approved it the next day.

While Merrifield's method may seem rather simple and straightforward, it took almost four years of painstaking trial and error to find the best chemical makeup for the bead that served as the solid-state foundation for the reaction and also the most successful process to ensure that the amino acids bound to each other correctly. Finally, in 1963 Merrifield reported the synthesis of the 10-amino acid bradykinin, a hormone that influences blood pressure. Merrifield's experiment was a major accomplishment, although some chemists were unconvinced of his technique's merits, since it was impossible to test the product at each stage of the synthesis, as was done in traditional methods. However, the synthesized bradykinin was shown to have the same chemical makeup and activity as the natural hormone, so eventually Merrifield's work was hailed as a breakthrough. It led to a great deal of other solid-state chemical syntheses not only of peptides but also of other large molecules with building blocks that had to be bonded to each other in a particular chemical orientation and sequence. The technique eventually became important in producing sequences of nucleotides in DNA and RNA as well as complex sugar polymers.

Merrifield made two more especially significant contributions to the chemistry field in the 1960s. By 1965 it was possible to synthesize peptides in the 35–40 amino acid range. This achievement made it more feasible to synthesize entire proteins, although most are over 100 amino acids long. In 1966 Merrifield and his team managed to create the first synthetic protein, ribonuclease, which is 114 amino acids long. Like the natural product, ribonuclease was able to break down RNA. At the same time, Merrifield and John Stewart, his Rockefeller colleague, were attempting to automate the synthesis process. They built the first rather simple machine in 1965 and by 1969 had constructed a more sophisticated model that made synthesis much faster and produced higher yields.

In 1966 Merrifield was promoted to full professor at Rockefeller University, and he assumed management of Woolley's laboratory after Woolley's death later that year. Merrifield trained many strong researchers who went on to excel in various areas of biochemistry. One of these scientists, Stephen Kent of the University of Chicago, described Merrifield's lab as a "hotbed" of peptide science in the

1960s and 1970s. At Rockefeller, Merrifield became a John D. Rockefeller, Jr., Professor, the institute's highest academic rank. Although he officially retired in 1992, Merrifield continued to do laboratory work at Rockefeller until a few years before his death. After a long illness, Merrifield died at age eighty-four at his home in Cresskill.

Merrifield was described as a quiet and unassuming man. For more than half his life he suffered stoically with a disfiguring form of skin cancer attributed to radiation treatments he received for acne during adolescence. While Merrifield and his wife lived in New York City in the early years of their marriage, they moved to suburban New Jersey after the birth of their first two children. For thirty-seven years, Merrifield commuted with his fellow Rockefeller researcher Vincent Allfrey, with Merrifield driving and Allfrey reading books aloud.

Merrifield's development of the solid-state synthesis technique revolutionized many areas of chemistry, and variations of this process are now used on an industrial scale to produce pharmaceuticals, nutritional supplements, and other crucial chemicals. For his revolutionary work, Merrifield received the Lasker Award for Basic Research in 1969 and the American Chemical Society's Award for Creative Research in 1972. Finally, he was awarded the Nobel Prize in Chemistry in 1984. While the Nobel Prize is often shared by several recipients, Merrifield received a solo award, another indication of the significance of his contribution to the field.

★

Merrifield published a memoir, *Life During a Golden Age of Peptide Chemistry* (1992). Biographical information on him, along with the text of his Nobel Lecture (8 Dec. 1984), is available on the official website of the Nobel Foundation at http://nobelprize.org/nobel_prizes/chemistry/laureates/1984. Papers relating to Merrifield's research are in the Rockefeller University Archives in the Rockefeller Archive Center. Obituaries are in the *New York Times* (20 May 2006), *Nature* (15 June 2006), and *Science* (7 July 2006).

Maura C. Flannery

MESSNER, Tamara Faye LaValley ("Tammy Faye") (*b.* 7 March 1942 in International Falls, Minnesota; *d.* 20 July 2007 in Kansas City, Missouri), flamboyant, outspoken televangelist, singer, and motivational speaker, notorious for her role as the wife of the televangelist Jim Bakker, who retired in disgrace following financial and personal scandal in the late 1980s.

Messner was born to Carl LaValley, a truck driver and a Pentecostal minister, and Rachel (Fairchild) LaValley, a

Tammy Faye Messner, 1987. AP IMAGES

homemaker. After her parents' divorce when Messner was three years old, her mother married Fred Grover, a mill worker, expanding the family to a total of eight children, of which Messner was the eldest. A music lover from an early age, Messner started singing for church audiences at the age of three. Messner's religious convictions, instilled in her from an early age by her mother and her aunt, continued to intensify throughout her teenage years. She attended Falls High School in International Falls, Minnesota, and after graduating in 1960 began attending North Central Bible College in Minneapolis, where she met Jim Bakker; the couple married on 1 April 1961 and would have two children, a son and a daughter.

Soon after their marriage and Bakker's ordination as an Assemblies of God minister, the couple embarked upon a traveling ministry throughout the southern United States, focusing much of their work on children. These attempts to reach children soon caught the eye of Marion "Pat" Robertson, head of the Christian Broadcasting Network, who was interested in starting a children's show. The children's show morphed into an adult format, and the Bakkers appeared on the air on 28 November 1966 in the first episode of *The 700 Club*. They hosted the show until 1973.

In 1974 the couple launched the Praise the Lord (PTL) Network, one of the first and most financially successful television ministries. Messner was quite active in the television network; she cohosted the *Jim and Tammy TV Ministry Hour* and starred in her own show, *Tammy's House Party*.

Perhaps the best-known event in Messner's life followed the downfall of Bakker and his Christian television ministry, PTL. Bakker stepped down from the helm of PTL on 19 March 1987, as news of his extramarital affair with the church secretary Jessica Hahn became public. An indictment followed in December 1988, and in 1989 Bakker was found guilty of defrauding PTL members of over $150 million. A portion of this sum (estimated at $265,000) consisted of a bribe to silence Hahn. Bakker faced a forty-five-year prison sentence, but his parole came early, in 1994. Messner was frank and open about the role that Bakker's fall from grace played in her tranquilizer addiction during this time—she entered the Betty Ford Center in 1987 for this problem—although she maintained her own innocence in the debacle and never faced any formal criminal charges.

Messner and Bakker divorced in 1992. In 1993 Messner married Roe Messner, whom she and Bakker had known for years while Roe Messner assisted in the construction of Heritage USA, Bakker's dream of a Christian theme park, worship center, and living complex in Fort Mill, South Carolina. In 1996 Roe Messner was found guilty of bankruptcy fraud, a conviction that carried a twenty-seven-month prison sentence.

After her second wedding, Tammy Faye Messner reinvented herself as a television celebrity. She made cameo appearances on *Roseanne* and *The Drew Carey Show* during the 1990s. She also cohosted a talk show with Jim J. Bullock on the Fox network (*The Jim J. and Tammy Faye Show*) in 1996 and appeared on the VH1 reality show *The Surreal Life* in 2004. This appearance—and the documentary film *The Eyes of Tammy Faye*—introduced an entire new audience to another side of Messner, who wept openly on camera for those less fortunate than she, but outside of the context of a religious service.

Messner was a strong ally of America's gay and lesbian community, and her popularity escalated after the 2000 autobiographical documentary about her, *The Eyes of Tammy Faye*. The film's title plays on one of Messner's signature characteristics: Messner was often moved to tears in religious services or musical performances, and her mascara would stream down her face, drawing attention to her heavy eye makeup that was the hallmark of her personal style. The documentary represents another stage in Messner's life, contributing to her enormous popularity within the gay community. Messner believed that the appeal of the film stemmed from the message inherent within it and within her larger life: Once a person falls down, if that person trusts in a higher power, all things are possible. Messner attended numerous gay pride celebrations,

offering unconditional love and support to a community often demonized and ostracized by her fellow evangelicals. She felt a commonality between her treatment by the religious right and its treatment of the gay and lesbian community.

Messner continued to spread her Christian beliefs through public appearances and musical performances, even garnering an Angel Award from the Religion in Media group in 1985 for Best Female Vocalist for the religious album *In the Upper Room*. She recorded a total of twenty-five albums over the course of her singing career.

In 1996 Messner disclosed that she had been diagnosed with colon cancer, even enduring surgery in order to stop the disease. In 2004 she revealed the disease had moved into her lungs. By May 2007 Messner and her doctors had made the decision to end her cancer treatments, and Messner died of the disease at her home in Kansas City at the age of sixty-five. Her deep-seated religious beliefs sustained her to the end of her life, allowing her to face death unafraid. Her remains were cremated, and her ashes were buried in Kansas, along the Oklahoma-Kansas state line.

★

Messner wrote several autobiographical treatments on her life, including *I Gotta Be Me* (1978), *Tammy: Telling It My Way* (1996) and *I Will Survive—And You Will Too* (2004). Insight into her religious and philosophical beliefs, so central to an understanding of Messner as an individual, can be gleaned from one of her other books, *Run to the Roar: The Way to Overcome Fear* (1980). Numerous works exist on the rise and fall of Bakker and PTL, including Joe E. Barnhart and Stephen Winzenburg, *Jim and Tammy: Charismatic Intrigue Inside PTL* (1988); Larry Martz and Ginny Carroll, *Ministry of Greed: The Inside Story of the Televangelists and Their Holy Wars* (1988); Charles E. Shepard, *Forgiven: The Rise and Fall of Jim Bakker and the PTL Ministry* (1989); and Hunter James, *Smile Pretty and Say Jesus: The Last Great Days of PTL* (1993). Obituaries are in the *Los Angeles Times*, *Seattle Times*, and *New York Times* (all 22 July 2007).

Kimberly K. Little

METZENBAUM, Howard Morton (*b.* 4 June 1917 in Cleveland, Ohio; *d.* 12 March 2008 in Aventura, Florida), Democratic legislator from Ohio known for his liberalism and combative style during his nineteen years in the U.S. Senate.

Metzenbaum was the second son of Charles Metzenbaum, a wholesale jobber, and Anna Klafter, a store clerk. Both parents were the Ohio-born children of Eastern European

Howard Metzenbaum. **TERRY ASHE/TIME LIFE PICTURES/ GETTY IMAGES**

Jewish immigrants. As his parents struggled to eke out a living in a lower-middle-class household in the Glenville section of Cleveland, Metzenbaum sold magazines and delivered groceries. Too young to drive, he nevertheless acquired a car and used it to ferry patrons to a nearby racetrack. This illicit enterprise was shuttered abruptly when his father sold the car to pay the mortgage. Metzenbaum's childhood left him with a strong sense of class consciousness as well as a burning desire to get ahead. For him, there was no contradiction between an ambition for material success and a conviction that the government should be used to benefit the less fortunate.

At Ohio State University, Metzenbaum made ends meet by selling chrysanthemums outside the stadium on football Saturdays, running a bicycle rental business, and playing trombone in a youth band. After graduating with a BA in 1939, he continued on in the university's law school, from which he earned his JD in 1941. Metzenbaum returned to Cleveland to enter politics and to take up a practice as a labor attorney. Poor eyesight prevented him from enlisting to fight in World War II.

Metzenbaum soon discovered that Cleveland's major law firms refused to hire Jewish attorneys, one of many religious slights that he would endure in his lifetime. He worked at small law firms in exchange for a desk and telephone. At a time before tax preparation businesses were commonplace, Metzenbaum and a partner spotted a need. They opened twenty-three offices around Cleveland to prepare taxes for low-income customers. Soon, Metzenbaum had enough capital to open his own firm, Metzenbaum and Gaines, with his friend Sam Gaines.

Metzenbaum had political ambitions, too. In 1942 he won election to the Ohio House, a seat he held until 1947. He then moved to the Ohio Senate, where he remained until 1951. He joined the leftist National Lawyer's Guild and, in 1944, cofounded the Ohio School of Social Sciences to foster dialogue between organized labor and business. Despite later rumors, there is no evidence that Metzenbaum ever belonged to a communist organization. On 8 August 1946 he married Shirley Turoff. The couple went on to have four daughters.

With the end of World War II, Metzenbaum guessed that an unprecedented travel boom would begin. Additionally, the price controls that had been instituted during the war were now inoperative, and the demand for new cars soon exceeded the supply. To capitalize, Metzenbaum joined with Sidney Moss to create a rental company called Drive-a-Car, which, when sold, would become Avis. He continued to work as an attorney, typically representing injured union members in worker's compensation cases, but this work brought in comparatively little money. In 1947 Metzenbaum and Ted Bonda spotted an opportunity to develop parking lots at airports. Within twelve years, Airport Parking Company of America (APCOA) had grown into the largest parking lot business in the United States. When the company was sold years later to International Telephone & Telegraph (ITT), Metzenbaum received $6 million and joined the board of ITT. Despite publicly supporting unions, Metzenbaum built his empire without union labor, thereby fueling charges of hypocrisy.

In a state known for being relatively conservative, Metzenbaum spent much of his life going against the grain. He devoted countless hours of his law practice to fighting the restrictions instituted by country clubs and the like against African Americans and Jews. Shocked by the violence visited on civil rights activists in the 1964 Selma-to-Montgomery march, Metzenbaum joined the second Alabama march in 1965. Upon returning home safely, he donated $10,000 to the Lawyers Constitutional Defense Committee, which recruited attorneys to handle voting rights cases pro bono. He soon became the group's chairman. That same year, President Lyndon B. Johnson appointed Metzenbaum to a commission overseeing enforcement of the 1964 civil rights legislation.

On 17 September 1968 Metzenbaum announced that he was retiring from business to focus on the challenges facing the nation and world. Resigning as chairman of the board of ITT, he continued as senior partner at his law firm. In 1969, Metzenbaum's company ComCorp had purchased the six-newspaper *Sun* chain. Metzenbaum served as publisher for a few years before selling the chain to Booth Newspapers. In 1970 he declared his candidacy for the U.S. Senate. He ran against the military hero and astronaut John Glenn in the Democratic primary, a contest few observers expected Metzenbaum to win. The state of Ohio had never elected a Jew as senator or governor. During the campaign, newspapers in the state commonly referred to Metzenbaum as a "millionaire Jewish businessman." However, the election was held just days after Ohio National Guardsmen killed four students during a Vietnam War protest at Kent State University. The antiwar Metzenbaum won an upset victory over the military hero in the only election that Glenn would ever lose in his home state. Metzenbaum then went down to defeat against Robert Taft, Jr., the scion of a distinguished Ohio political family, in the general election.

In 1973, when President Richard M. Nixon named Senator William B. Saxbe as his new attorney general, Ohio's Democratic governor John J. Gilligan chose Metzenbaum to fill Saxbe's remaining term in the U.S. Senate. Gilligan would later lament the appointment as one of his worst acts as governor after Metzenbaum blundered badly in the 1974 election for the seat. Again running against Glenn in the Democratic primary, Metzenbaum charged that the astronaut had never held a job. He had intended to refer to Glenn's lack of *business* experience, but few observers understood that distinction. Glenn responded with an emotional speech about the costs born by those in the military and promptly won the election. The two men, quite unalike, would have a distinctly frosty relationship for the rest of their political careers.

Metzenbaum returned to the U.S. Senate by defeating Taft in 1976, a bad year for Republicans who could not escape the shadow of Watergate. "Headline Howard," as he was nicknamed for his love of publicity, proved to be consistently liberal. He fought the deregulation of gas and oil prices, called for tighter oversight of the insurance industry, and promoted national health insurance. He championed the feminist movement and promoted workplace equality. In 1982, during his successful reelection bid, Metzenbaum's voting record received a 100 percent score from the liberal Americans for Democratic Action but a grade of only 7 percent from the pro-business U.S. Chamber of Commerce. Despite ample evidence, however, many Ohio voters simply did not see Metzenbaum as a liberal, instead viewing him as someone willing to fight for the interests of ordinary Americans. "Metz" won his last election in 1988 when he scored a wider margin of victory in traditionally Republican Ohio than that enjoyed by the Republican presidential nominee, George H. W. Bush.

Toward the end of his life, Metzenbaum argued that he had disproved the adage that one had to go along to get along, and his unwillingness to accept the unwritten quid pro quo traditions among senators often put him at odds with his colleagues. Senator Ted Stevens of Alaska condemned Metzenbaum for violating the basic rule of the Senate by not being a gentleman. Lacking much of an ego and impervious to criticism, Metzenbaum attributed his success in the chamber to a willingness to make people angry. His skill, guile, and endurance enabled him to work effectively in a deliberative body that, throughout most of his career, was run by Republicans. He employed sneak attacks, unlimited amendments, and filibusters to block bills. He also posted a staffer in the Senate in the early morning hours so that no other senator would be able to sneak through a bill. During his time in the Senate, Metzenbaum sponsored or cosponsored thirty-seven bills that were eventually signed into law. His most significant achievements include requiring companies to give employees sixty days' notice of an impending plant shutdown, protecting workers' health and life insurance benefits at companies that enter into bankruptcy, and mandating nutrition labels on foods.

On 29 June 1993 Metzenbaum announced his retirement upon the end of his term. He died at an assisted living facility in Aventura, a suburb of Miami, Florida, following years of poor health and is buried in Cleveland Heights.

★

The only biography of Metzenbaum can be found in Tom Diemer, *Fighting the Unbeatable Foe: Howard Metzenbaum of Ohio, the Washington Years* (2008). Despite the title, the book covers Metzenbaum's entire life. An obituary is in the *New York Times* (14 Mar. 2008).

Caryn E. Neumann

MEYER, Raymond Joseph ("Ray") (*b.* 18 December 1913 in Chicago, Illinois; *d.* 17 March 2006 in Wheeling, Illinois), legendary college basketball coach who won a total of 724 games at DePaul University and was inducted in the Naismith Memorial Basketball Hall of Fame in 1979.

Meyer was the youngest of ten children of Joseph Meyer, a candy wholesaler, and Barbara (Hummel) Meyer, a homemaker. He attended Quigley Preparatory Seminary High on Chicago's North Side. During that time he also became involved with coaching the girls' team in the parish. From that experience he changed his mind about becoming a priest and decided to pursue a career in basketball. He also ended up dating and marrying a member of the girls' team, Margaret Mary ("Marge") Delaney, though the wedding was not until 27 May 1939. Meyer transferred to Saint Patrick's High School, where his squad won the Catholic high school national title. Meyer then went on to Northwestern University in the fall of 1934. His time at Northwestern lasted less than a week, as he dropped out to help his widowed mother during the worst period of the Great Depression.

In the fall of 1935 Meyer enrolled at the University of Notre Dame on a full scholarship, except for books (which he borrowed). He was elected captain of the Notre Dame basketball team both his junior and senior years, an honor not repeated until the 1970–1971 season, when Austin Carr was elected captain for the second year in a row. Meyer had a number of injuries, most notably a dislocated elbow, which prevented him from playing regularly, but he graduated cum laude with a BA in 1938 and became a social worker in Chicago. After a year he was offered and took various positions in basketball, most notably as an assistant coach for his alma mater, Notre Dame. It was while in this position that he was offered and took the job as head coach of DePaul University in Chicago, beginning in the spring of 1942.

Meyer was fortunate to have a young, awkward player on the DePaul squad named George Mikan. He had been a student at Quigley, as Meyer had, and had also decided against the priesthood and sought a basketball scholarship to Notre Dame. The coach there, George Keogan, Meyer's mentor, had thought Mikan too undeveloped to play major college basketball, and Mikan had enrolled at DePaul. Mikan and Meyer learned and worked together, shaping Mikan's skills to perfection and the DePaul team's success. In their four years together, DePaul won eighty-one games, lost only seventeen, and won the National Invitational Tournament (NIT) in 1945. Mikan went on to greatness as a professional player, while Meyer remained at DePaul for thirty-eight more seasons. For a couple seasons (1945–1947) Meyer was an adviser and unofficial coach of the Chicago American Gears of the National Basketball League (NBL), a team that featured Mikan and Dick Triptow, both former DePaul captains, and the Gears won the 1946–1947 NBL title before the team was disbanded the next season.

Over the next thirty years, until the 1974–1975 season, DePaul was a respectable program, usually winning more than they lost, but only winning twenty games twice in any season during that span. Following the college basketball season, Meyer also coached the College All-Stars, who played the Harlem Globetrotters on a national tour. As part of this job Meyer got to coach top graduating seniors, but the National Collegiate Athletic Association (NCAA) disbanded the tour in 1961, ruling that the seniors would lose scholarships for the remainder of their college time if they played. Meyer was still recruiting almost exclusively from the Chicago area, since DePaul had no dormitories and little to offer students in scholarships. That began to change in the late 1970s, when Meyer recruited some top Chicago talent and was able to provide full scholarships and new dormitory space.

Meyer's 1975–1976 team was a breakthrough squad, winning twenty games and losing nine, including an upset victory over Virginia in the first round of the NCAA tournament. The rest of the 1970s through the mid-1980s saw DePaul and Coach Meyer consistently at the top of the college basketball world. In the 1977–1978 season the Blue Demons of DePaul won twenty-seven games and lost just three. In the NCAA tournament, they defeated Creighton and Louisville before losing to Notre Dame, whom they had beaten earlier in the season, in the NCAA Midwest Regional Final.

Over the next four years DePaul lost a total of twelve games while winning 105 times. Meyer had recruited his first superstar since Mikan in Mark Aguirre. Aguirre was an All-American, and his presence was an impetus for other top players to come to DePaul. Terry Cummings followed, as did Dave Corzine, Clyde Bradshaw, Curtis Watkins, Skip Dillard, and Tyrone Corbin. During these years DePaul was ranked first in the country a number of times but was unable to make a long run in the NCAA tournament. In 1978–1979 they were 22–5 entering the tournament and defeated the University of Southern California, Marquette University, and the University of California, Los Angeles, before losing in the NCAA semifinal game to Indiana State, led by Larry Bird, 76–74. DePaul did defeat the University of Pennsylvania, 96–93, to finish third in the country, but this would be as close as Meyer would ever get to an NCAA title.

In each of the next three seasons, DePaul entered the NCAA tournament with only one loss, but the team was eliminated in the first round of the tournament. The following year (1982–1983) the Blue Demons went only 17–11 in the regular season and were relegated to the NIT tournament, which was now a second-class event. Nevertheless, they pulled together to finish second in the tournament, losing 69–60 to Fresno State in the finals.

In Meyer's last year (1983–1984), his team went 26–2, and they were a top seed in the NCAA tournament once again. After defeating Illinois State, they lost in overtime to Wake Forest, and Meyer's distinguished coaching career ended when he was at the age of seventy. He became a special assistant to the DePaul president on athletics and later became a regular broadcaster of DePaul games, as his son, Joey, succeeded him as DePaul's coach. Meyer's wife died a year after he retired. He became estranged from DePaul after his son was fired as the coach in 1997. Eventually, DePaul and Meyer reconciled, and he was honored in 2003 by having the basketball court at DePaul named in his and his wife's honor, as well as a new university fitness center named after him. In 1979 he entered the Naismith Memorial Basketball Hall of Fame. Meyer's overall coaching record (all at DePaul) was 724 wins and 354 losses. He and his wife had six children. Meyer died at age ninety-two of congestive heart failure and was buried at All Saints Cemetery in Des Plaines, Illinois.

★

For details about Meyer's life and career, see his autobiography, *Coach* (1987), written with Ray Sons. An obituary is in the *New York Times* (18 Mar. 2006).

Murry R. Nelson

MEYERSON, Martin (*b.* 14 November 1922 in New York City; *d.* 2 June 2007 in Philadelphia, Pennsylvania), city planner, educator, intellectual, public servant, internationalist, and president of three universities.

The only child of Samuel Meyerson, an engineer, and Etta (Berger) Meyerson, a teacher, Meyerson met his wife of almost sixty-two years, the former Margy Ellin Lazarus, while working in Chicago where she was a graduate student in sociology. Married on 31 December 1945, they had three children.

After earning a BA in classics at Columbia University in 1942, Meyerson started graduate work in city planning at Harvard University. In 1944 he worked for the Philadelphia City Planning Commission and in 1945–1946 was a Wheelwright Fellow in the School of Design at Harvard University. In the fall of 1947 he assumed his first academic position, becoming an assistant professor of social sciences at the University of Chicago. During his stay in Chicago he also worked for the planning board of the Michael Reese Hospital. In 1949 he received a master's degree from Harvard. He returned to Philadelphia in 1952 as associate professor of city and regional planning in the Graduate School of Fine Arts of the University of Pennsylvania (Penn), later renamed the Penn School of Design.

Meyerson found Penn's third campus, selected in 1878 for its then bucolic location across the Schuylkill River from downtown Philadelphia, "choked with traffic and crowded with noisily distracting commercial uses." This was a time of university expansion; Penn's building program to the north and west was pushing out working-class and poor black residents in adjacent neighborhoods. As head of planning and development for the Chicago Housing Authority and adviser to the South Side Planning Board, Meyerson had been involved in efforts to stabilize and upgrade the University of Chicago's Hyde Park and Kenwood neighborhoods. At Penn, where activist students joined with the community to oppose the university's expansionist aims, Meyerson drafted pointers in 1956 for avoiding what he described as inevitable islands of development in a "sea of residential slums" and recommended

establishment of a "West Philadelphia planning and development corporation led by" the university. The proposal was adopted by President Gaylord Harnwell in 1959 to engage area educational and medical institutions with the community under the aegis of the West Philadelphia Corporation.

Meyerson had meanwhile returned to Harvard in 1957 as a tenured professor of city planning and urban research—a field that was only beginning to be recognized at universities and had yet to award a PhD. Two years later he became the first director of the Massachusetts Institute of Technology and Harvard Joint Center for Urban Studies, which was created to bring together faculty from several fields to investigate theoretical and applied problems at home and abroad. After serving as acting dean of Harvard's Graduate School of Design, he moved to the University of California at Berkeley as professor and dean of the first College of Environmental Design in the country (1963–1966). Universities across the nation were in an uproar, especially after changes to draft exemptions, and Meyerson was soon at the heart of the fray. He found himself catapulted into the position of acting chancellor, vacated by then chancellor Edward Strong in 1965 at the height of the Free Speech movement, and received the credit for restoring calm on campus.

When Meyerson returned as president-elect to give the commencement address at Penn in the summer of 1970, he was greeted by students wearing black armbands to protest the Vietnam War. Similar unrest had occurred during his tenure in Buffalo, New York (1966–1970). He became president shortly after that private university merged with the State University of New York, a change he consolidated while overseeing construction of a new second campus. His skills in negotiating student unrest remained a major reason for his selection as Penn's fifth president and served him well during the tumultuous days of expansion and revolt of the 1970s. Penn was one of the few campuses to avoid major violence, despite protests and sit-ins culminating in a student takeover of the main administration building in 1978. Returning late at night to campus from abroad, Meyerson dealt directly with the students' demands concerning tuition fee increases, reductions of academic and recreational offerings, and those of a vocal cohort of black students. Concessions made by the administration led to the resignation of the provost, the university's chief academic officer, when the faculty in turn revolted against lack of consultation and a perceived usurpation of their role.

On arrival at Penn, Meyerson set up a far-reaching educational development commission whose final report, "Pennsylvania: One University" (1973), drew on existing strengths and set the directions for future initiatives that continued to be implemented in the new millennium. His proposals for coherence and integration resulted in a major undertaking, the replacement of separate undergraduate colleges for men and women into the Faculty of Arts and Sciences (later renamed the School of Arts and Sciences) in 1974. Also subsumed were the social sciences, including economics, the former Graduate School of Arts and Sciences, and the College of General Studies. Funds were reallocated and undergraduate education received new emphasis, as did intrauniversity cooperation and the establishment of endowed professorships. The Landscape Development Master Plan sought to integrate Penn's twelve schools, all uniquely located on its single urban campus. Initiatives to cut expenditures by outsourcing some non-academic costs were two decades ahead of their time, but Meyerson's proposals for "selective excellence," "responsibility center budgeting," and a highly successful capital campaign, "The Program for the Eighties," improved Penn's finances and provided the basis for progress in less tumultuous years that followed.

In implementing his programs, Meyerson sought out and supported people of extraordinary talent. He nurtured some dozen university presidents, including several who had worked with him as staff, and influenced planners and scholars in his field. He was principal author, with Edward C. Banfield, of *Politics, Planning, and the Public Interest: The Case of Public Housing in Chicago* (1955)—a seminal work that emphasizes the place of a design as it relates theory to practice in urban management and politics—and *Boston: The Job Ahead* (1966). He was principal author, with Barbara Terrett and William L. C. Wheaton, of *Housing, People, and Cities* (1962). His portrait at Penn depicts him at the heart of the green, redesigned campus, holding *Gladly Learn and Gladly Teach: Franklin and His Heirs at the University of Pennsylvania* (1976), itself a historical account by portrait, coauthored with Dilys Pegler Winegrad, of the evolution of his beloved Penn.

Throughout his career Meyerson worked on urban, regional, national, and cultural development for governments and organizations abroad. He was tapped by the United Nations Mission on Urbanization and Industrialization in Japan, was a United Nations adviser in Yugoslavia after the Skopje earthquake (both 1963), and in Indonesia and West Africa. As emeritus president (1981–2007), Meyerson continued to chair or advise an astounding number and variety of educational and scientific institutes, universities, and foundations. In Philadelphia he was a member of the executive committee of the American Philosophical Society and headed the selection committee for the Philadelphia Liberty Medal. The Penn Trustees named the Meyerson Building in the Penn School of Design (1983) and established the Martin and Margy Meyerson Professorship in Urbanism (1988) in recognition of his past and continuing service. He was honored for his longstanding national and international contributions in the award of twenty-three honorary doctorates and the medals of the cities of Parma, Italy, and Skopje. He was

decorated a Knight-Commander of the Republic of Italy in 1988 and received the Order of the Rising Sun from the emperor of Japan in 1989. The Philippine Women's University cited the achievements of "that remarkable couple" in establishing the Martin and Margy Meyerson Chair for International Relations (1993). Myerson died of prostate cancer near his home in Philadelphia at age eighty-four.

★

The Meyerson Papers are at the University Archives and Records Center, University of Pennsylvania, UPT50 613M. Obituaries are in the *New York Times* and *Los Angeles Times* (both 7 June 2007).

Dilys Pegler Winegrad

MICHAELS, James Walker (*b.* 17 June 1921 in Buffalo, New York; *d.* 2 October 2007 in New York City), journalist and magazine editor whose editorial leadership of *Forbes* magazine between 1961 and 1999 transformed business journalism.

Michaels, one of three children of Dewey Michaels and Phyllis (Boasberg) Michaels, spent his childhood in upstate New York and then attended the Culver Academy, a military school in Indiana. He went on to Harvard University, graduating with a BS in economics in 1943. Because of his poor eyesight, Michaels was not allowed to serve in the U.S. Army during World War II. Instead, he signed up to drive an ambulance for the British army in its Burma campaign. As a result of that experience, Michaels developed an interest in international affairs. After the war he landed a $35-a-week job with a major news wire, United Press, which sent him to Calcutta and Delhi, India, to cover the movement toward Indian independence from Britain and the fighting between religious factions in Kashmir that followed. Michaels was the first journalist to report on the 1948 assassination of the Indian independence activist Mohandas K. Gandhi.

Upon his return to the United States, Michaels worked briefly for the *Buffalo News* before taking a position in 1954 at what was then a little-known investment magazine called *Forbes*. The magazine had been around since 1917, but it had few readers beyond the Wall Street financial community.

Michaels's first task at the magazine was to write about mutual funds. He quickly moved up the ranks, becoming editor in 1961. At the time business journalism tended to be dry, and business reporters rarely questioned the pronouncements of the companies they were covering. Under Michaels's leadership, *Forbes* reporters became much more probing and their writing livelier. The magazine's chief competitors, *Fortune* and *Business Week*, were both forced to follow suit to meet the expectations of a growing community of consumers of business news. As readership grew, Michaels cultivated and reacted to the magazine's audience by developing sections on law, taxes, science, medicine, and leisure. He insisted on tweaking nearly every piece published in *Forbes* throughout his tenure as editor. Under his guidance stories became shorter and blunter, more interpretive and even opinionated, provided the reporter was able to back up his or her judgment with facts. When Michaels arrived at *Forbes*, its circulation was 130,000. By the time he retired in 1999, it had grown to 785,000.

Business leaders, many of whom had grown accustomed to being lionized on the pages of America's business magazines, often found their decisions questioned and lampooned by the journalists at *Forbes*. The magazine remained staunchly and unabashedly pro-business and—more controversially—pro-wealth, which put it at odds with much of mainstream journalism in the 1960s and 1970s. In 1982 *Forbes* began publishing an annual list of the 400 richest Americans, according to net worth. Nevertheless, Michaels believed the primary obligation of business reporters was to serve as watchdogs for investors, and for that reason he was determined to curtail some of the boosterism that had previously characterized business journalism. According to Arthur Jones, the author of a 1977 biography of *Forbes*'s publisher, Malcolm Forbes, "No other magazine or newspaper in the country so boldly holds the corporations accountable to the investors."

According to those who worked for Michaels, his editorial standards could be as blunt and uncompromising as the articles found within the pages of his magazine. Michaels himself was known to take pleasure in a rumor circulating in the journalism industry in the 1970s that he had fired a reporter on Christmas Day, and that the reporter's wife had been pregnant at the time. "It might have been Christmas Day," he told the *New York Times*. "But it wasn't, actually. I think it was some time during the holiday season."

At the same time, Michaels mentored many young reporters who went on to leave their mark on the field of business journalism. Among them were Norman Pearlstine, who became managing editor of the *Wall Street Journal*, editor in chief of Time Inc., and eventually content officer at Bloomberg LP, and Allan Sloan, an editor and columnist at *Newsweek* and *Fortune*. Sloan said that Michaels, always focusing on the interests of small investors, believed in "throwing rocks and being irreverent." He also insisted on originality and beating other publications to the punch. In 1969 *Forbes* was one of the first publications to report on the investment strategies of Warren E. Buffett, a Nebraska money man who by 2007 had become, according to the magazine, the richest person in the world. Michaels rarely socialized with the wealthy people he reported on, believing such activity would compromise his editorial integrity.

In 1983 *Adweek* named him Editor of the Year, and in 1994 he was given the Loeb Lifetime Achievement Award. Michaels had three children with his first wife. On 29 June 1985 he married his second wife, Jean Briggs, a senior editor at *Forbes*. After his retirement in 1999 and until his death, he oversaw efforts to bring *Forbes* content to television and the Internet. He admitted this was an odd pursuit for someone who never watched television and paid little attention to popular culture. Michaels died of pneumonia.

★

For a tribute to Michaels, see Steve Forbes, "James W. Michaels," *Forbes* (29 Oct. 2007). Michaels's role at *Forbes* is discussed in Arthur Jones, *Malcolm Forbes: Peripatetic Millionaire* (1977). Obituaries are in the *New York Times* (4 Oct. 2007), *Washington Post* (7 Oct. 2007), and *Times* of London (10 Oct. 2007).

Maura Jane Farrelly

MIDDLEBROOK, (Helen) Diane Wood (*b.* 16 April 1939 in Pocatello, Idaho; *d.* 15 December 2007 in San Francisco, California), biographer, professor, and feminist who authored books on the poets Anne Sexton, Ted Hughes, and Sylvia Plath and the jazz musician Billy Tipton.

Middlebrook was the eldest of three daughters born to Thomas Wood, a pharmacist, and Helen Downey Wood, a homemaker who later became a licensed practical nurse. The family moved from Pocatello to Spokane, Washington, when Middlebrook was five. Because of her mother's ill health, Middlebrook played the role of surrogate mother and developed a strong sense of authority at an early age. She was determined to be a poet and a writer, despite the opposition of her father, who demanded that she pay her own way through college.

Middlebrook attended North Central High School in Spokane, graduating in 1957. She began attending Whitman College in Walla Walla, Washington, and then transferred to the University of Washington in Seattle, receiving a BA in English in 1961. In 1966 she joined the faculty at Stanford University as an assistant professor and one of the first women in the English department. Two years later she received a PhD from Yale University, having written her doctoral dissertation on the poets Wallace Stevens and Walt Whitman under the direction of the formidable scholar and literary critic Harold Bloom.

Middlebrook married three times, first to Michael D. Shough, in June 1960. After their marriage was dissolved in 1963, she wed her second husband, Jonathan Middlebrook, whose name she assumed for her own professional life. They married on 15 June 1963, when they were both graduate students at Yale, and divorced in 1972. They had one daughter, Leah, who became a professor of literature.

For over three decades Middlebrook was a highly popular teacher at Stanford, respected by her colleagues and adored by her students. She was especially admired by those who shared her passion for poetry, which she taught in various courses and wrote about in *Worlds into Words: Understanding Modern Poems* (1978). She also wrote poetry, a practice that gave her a "hands-on" understanding of the genre.

In the late 1970s Middlebrook was enlisted to help develop Stanford's fledgling Center for Research on Women—now the Michelle R. Clayman Institute for Gender Research—founded in 1974 under the direction of Myra Strober. As the center's director from 1977 to 1979, Middlebrook became a feminist scholar and a leading force in establishing feminist studies at Stanford. In 1985 she and Marilyn Yalom, the center's deputy director, coedited *Coming to Light: American Women Poets in the Twentieth Century*, based on a notable 1982 Stanford conference of women poets and critics.

From 1977 Middlebrook was intimately connected with Carl Djerassi, a Stanford professor of chemistry credited with the invention of the contraceptive pill for women. Married on 21 June 1985, Middlebrook and Djerassi established in San Francisco and London residences that became international meeting places for their many friends, and especially for writers. Middlebrook also played a major role in the Djerassi Resident Artists' Program, founded in 1979 after the suicide of Djerassi's daughter, who had been a painter.

Middlebrook is best known for her work as a biographer. In 1980 she was tapped by the Anne Sexton estate to write a biography of the poet. Although Middlebrook was not initially a great Sexton fan, she spent a decade immersing herself in the life of a writer whom she came to consider as not only gifted but also important. Sexton's transition from "Housewife into Poet" (a chapter heading), her history of mental breakdown, and her eventual suicide in 1974 were all relevant to the problems American women were facing in the second half of the twentieth century. Middlebrook cultivated many of her ideas in the context of the Biographers' Seminar, which she ran at Stanford throughout the 1980s with the law professor Barbara Babcock.

A controversial aspect of *Anne Sexton: A Biography* (1991) was Middlebrook's use of Sexton's tape-recorded conversations with her psychiatrist, Dr. Martin Orne. After the book was published, other psychiatrists questioned the ethics of allowing posthumous access to private records when the patient had not explicitly given consent. The public discourse pitting Orne, Linda Sexton (the poet's daughter), and Middlebrook against their critics helped to make the biography a *New York Times* best seller. *Anne Sexton* received a Commonwealth Club of California Gold Medal in nonfiction and was a finalist for both a National Book Award and a National Book Critics Circle Award.

Following *Anne Sexton*, Middlebrook wrote another biography, *Suits Me: The Double Life of Billy Tipton* (1998). The book explores the curious trajectory of a cross-dressing female jazz musician who convinces the world—including five wives—that she is a man.

Middlebrook then returned to literature, examining the marriage of the poets Sylvia Plath and Ted Hughes in the dual biography *Her Husband: Hughes and Plath—A Marriage* (2003). The book maintains that marriage was central to the two poets' adult sense of self: For Hughes, the psychic connection to Plath endured until his death in 1998, long after the breakdown of their marriage and her 1963 suicide. Moreover, Middlebrook argues that their convulsive marriage had beneficial effects on their poetry. *Her Husband* was a *Los Angeles Times* best seller, a finalist for a Bay Area Book Reviewers Award in nonfiction, and a recipient of France's Prix du Meilleur livre étranger (Prize for Best Foreign Book).

Middlebrook took early retirement from Stanford to devote herself more fully to biography and to the sophisticated life she and Djerassi enjoyed in San Francisco and London. In London, Middlebrook established a salon for women writers in 2003, cohosted with the poet Sarah Greenberg, and then another in 2004 in San Francisco, cohosted with Yalom. The authors Kamy Wicoff, one of Middlebrook's former Stanford students who had helped found the London salon, and Nancy Miller, a professor at the City University of New York Graduate Center, started a third "Diane Middlebrook salon" in New York City.

Soon after retirement Middlebrook discovered that she had cancer; subsequently she underwent numerous medical interventions in San Francisco, New York, London, and Germany. Middlebrook died of cancer at the age of sixty-eight. Her ashes were scattered on the property of the Djerassi Resident Artists Program.

Middlebrook's openness in discussing her condition and her hunger to stay alive were inspirational to many who heard her speak publicly about her disease. During the last years of her life, Middlebrook worked on a biography of the Roman poet Ovid; she said that writing about Ovid, whom she passionately admired, sustained her in her fight against death and oblivion. Titled "Young Ovid" at Djerassi's suggestion because Ovid's youth is the portion of the biography that Middlebrook was able to complete, the work was scheduled for publication in 2009.

★

Obituaries are in the *Stanford Report* (15 Dec. 2007), *San Francisco Chronicle* (16 Dec. 2007), *New York Times* (17 Dec. 2007), *Guardian* (18 Dec. 2007), and *Independent* (19 Dec. 2007).

Marilyn Yalom

MILLER, Stanley Lloyd (*b.* 7 March 1930 in Oakland, California; *d.* 20 May 2007 in National City, California), chemist who pioneered studies of the origin of life on Earth when he synthesized simple organic compounds under conditions that simulated Earth's primitive atmosphere.

Miller was the younger of two sons born to Nathan Harry Miller, an attorney and deputy district attorney, and Edith Levy Miller, a homemaker. Miller's father died when he was fifteen years old. Miller attended the University of California, Berkeley, receiving a BS in 1951. That same year he started graduate school at the University of Chicago, where he attended a lecture by the Nobel laureate Harold C. Urey on the possible emergence of life on Earth in a particular primitive atmosphere.

Miller contemplated Urey's lecture, and a year and a half later he asked Urey's permission to write a doctoral thesis based on it. Miller proposed using a simulation of the Earth's primitive atmosphere as Urey had described and experimenting to see if he could create organic compounds such as those that could have led to the emergence of life on Earth. At first Urey was not interested, but then he eventually agreed.

In 1953 Urey and Miller designed an instrument intended to simulate the ocean-atmosphere system that Urey envisioned had existed on primitive Earth. The apparatus was built to simulate the evaporation of water from oceans into a primitive Earth atmosphere of methane, ammonia, and hydrogen. No oxygen was added to the vessel. An electric spark simulated lightning. The amount of time allotted, pressure within the vessel, and electric discharge were varied over three trials. The results were evaluated using paper chromatography, the best analysis method available in 1953. Miller detected glycine, the simplest amino acid (and one that is found in proteins), and twelve other amino acids. Urey was so impressed with the results of Miller's experiments that he suggested Miller publish them. Miller included Urey as a coauthor on his article, but Urey removed his name from the manuscript, stating that he already had a Nobel Prize. Miller sent the article, titled "A Production of Amino Acids Under Possible Primitive Earth Conditions," to *Science* magazine in February 1953.

At first the magazine editors disregarded the article. Urey was furious and urged Miller to withdraw his writing and resubmit it to the *Journal of the American Chemical Society*. On this news, *Science* editors quickly decided to publish the article. The result was a great deal of excitement not only in the scientific community but also in the general media. The possibility that an electric spark could form what was called a "prebiotic soup" became the subject of comic strips, cartoons, movies, and novels.

Continuing his education, Miller received his PhD from the University of Chicago in 1954. Following his

graduation Miller held a fellowship at the California Institute of Technology for one year. From 1955 to 1960 he served as an instructor and then an assistant professor in the department of biochemistry at the College of Physicians and Surgeons at Columbia University in New York City. In 1960 he joined the faculty of the newly formed chemistry department at the University of California, San Diego. He became a full professor of chemistry and biochemistry in 1968.

Other scientists repeated Miller's origin of life experiment with the same success, but none was able to take the next step to show how the amino acids created in Miller's experiment might have combined into living cells. However, Miller collected evidence to support his earlier work when he analyzed material collected from a meteorite that crashed in Australia in September 1969. He found the same amino acids on the meteorite as were created in his experiment, suggesting that these chemicals were formed in the solar system about 4.5 billion years ago.

Miller continued research into the chemical origins of life for four decades at the University of California, San Diego. He remained active in academia even after his first stroke in November 1999, not officially retiring until 2007. Following his retirement Miller suffered a series of additional strokes and was moved to a nursing home in National City. He died of heart failure at Paradise Hospital in National City at the age of seventy-seven. His remains were cremated.

Miller's most important contribution to science is his origin of life experiment. His work not only popularized the idea that life began in a primitive Earth's atmosphere but also gave respectability to the scientific study of the origin of life. Called the father of origin of life chemistry, Miller is also credited with promoting interdisciplinary research at the University of California, San Diego.

Although Miller's colleagues at the University of California, San Diego, believed his work was a significant contribution to science, he never received the Nobel Prize. Miller did earn recognition as a member of the National Academy of Sciences, and he received the Oparin Medal from the International Society for the Study of the Origin of Life (ISSOL) in 1983. He was ISSOL president from 1986 to 1989. Miller was also made an Honorary Counselor of the Higher Council for Scientific Research of Spain in 1973.

Biographical information is available in Kim McDonald, "Father of 'Origin of Life' Chemistry at UC San Diego Dies," University of California, San Diego *News Center* (21 May 2007). Information on Miller's research is available in his "Production of Amino Acids Under Possible Primitive Earth Conditions," *Science* 117 (Feb. 1953): 528–529; and Jeffrey L. Bada and Antonio Lazcano, "Prebiotic Soup—Revisiting the

Miller Experiment," *Science* 300 (2 May 2003): 745–746. Obituaries are in the *San Diego Union-Tribune* and *Los Angeles Times* (both 24 May 2007).

M. C. Nagel

MOFFO, Anna (*b*. 27 June 1932 in Wayne, Pennsylvania; *d*. 9 March 2006 in New York City), opera singer whose soprano voice and physical beauty enchanted audiences at New York's Metropolitan Opera as well as international opera houses.

Moffo was the daughter of Nicolas Moffo, an Italian-American shoemaker, and Regina (Cinti) Moffo, a homemaker. Music was part of the Moffo household, and she began singing during her childhood. At age seven she sang "Mighty Lak' a Rose" for a school assembly. She also performed at weddings and funerals, and although she took piano lessons, she did not study voice. Graduating from Radnor High School as valedictorian in 1951, Moffo was offered an opportunity to take a screen test. At that time her career choice leaned toward becoming a nun, a

Anna Moffo, 1972. AP IMAGES

leaning her parents supported. However, with an operatic repertoire of just one aria, "Un bel di" from Giacomo Puccini's *Madama Butterfly*, she auditioned for the Curtis Institute of Music in Philadelphia, where all students admitted attend on full scholarship, and was accepted. She majored in voice, studying with Eufemia Giannini-Gregory, and continued her study of piano. She graduated with high honors and won a Fulbright grant for advanced vocal study in Italy.

Moffo enrolled at the Accademia di Santa Cecilia in Rome, where she studied with Luigi Ricci and Mercedes Llopart. In 1955 she made her debut in the role of Norina in Gaetano Donizetti's *Don Pasquale* in Spoleto, Italy. In 1956 Moffo took a chance and auditioned for the role of Cio-Cio-San for a television production of *Madama Butterfly*, singing her "lucky" aria "Un bel di." She was initially turned down because of her height—at five feet, seven inches she was considered too tall for the role—but finally, impressed by her lyric soprano voice, the director-producer Mario Lanfranchi hired her. The production made her a star in Italy and led to a number of engagements in European opera houses.

Lanfranchi, who became her mentor and business manager, encouraged Moffo to extend her range to include the higher coloratura roles. She eventually learned eighty operatic roles. In 1957 she appeared as Nannetta in Giuseppe Verdi's *Falstaff* at Milan's La Scala. On 14 November 1957 Moffo made her American debut singing Mimi in Puccini's *La Bohème* with the Chicago Lyric Opera. On 8 December 1957 she married Lanfranchi. The following year she debuted at the Vienna State Opera and in the summer of 1959 at the Salzburg Festival. She debuted at New York's Metropolitan Opera on 14 November 1959, singing Violetta in Verdi's *La Traviata*, which became her signature role. Although critical reaction was mixed, audiences loved her, and everyone appreciated her beauty. That spring she joined the Metropolitan's American tour, again singing Violetta as well as Marguerite in Charles Gounod's *Faust*. On 1 October 1960 Moffo sang with the San Francisco Opera as Amina in Vincenzo Bellini's *La Sonnambula*. With the Metropolitan for the 1960–1961 season, she sang three new roles: Gilda in Verdi's *Rigoletto*, Adina in Donizetti's *L'Elisir d'Amore*, and Liu in Puccini's *Turandot*.

In addition to starring in operatic productions, Moffo became involved in television and film. Produced by Lanfranchi and aired in Italy, *The Anna Moffo Show*, a weekly program devoted to opera, ran from 1960 to 1973. Moffo appeared in more than twenty films: some were operas, such as the critically acclaimed *La Traviata* (1967), and others demonstrated her acting ability in straight dramatic roles. In America she appeared frequently on television shows, such as Ed Sullivan's *Toast of the Town, The Bell*

Telephone Hour, and *The Dean Martin Show*. Moffo traveled worldwide giving recitals and sang on a number of critically acclaimed recordings, two of which were nominated for Grammy awards. In fifteen years she sang more than 200 times at the Met.

Her extensive singing engagements and traveling began to have an effect on her voice and health. Many have argued that Lanfranchi's efforts to promote Moffo and push her into coloratura roles ruined her voice. Others have noted that she operated on instinct, not technique, which made her best performances spontaneous and compelling, yet dangerous to the voice. Moffo herself said the failure of her voice was a case of too much too soon. She divorced her husband in 1972. In 1974 her heavily promoted recording of Jules Massenet's *Thaïs* was a disaster, as it demonstrated her vocal breakdown. Most critics thought her career was over.

Moffo withdrew from performing and recording and started voice lessons, in an attempt to rebuild her voice. At age forty-one she was too young to be a "has been." Her teacher, Beverley Johnson, worked with Moffo to build physiological technique, focusing on breath support; meanwhile her health improved. On 14 November 1974 Moffo married Robert W. Sarnoff, the chairman of RCA Victor, and in 1976 she resumed her career, both in the opera house and recitals. Her final appearance at the Metropolitan Opera was on 15 March 1976, singing Violetta, and was not well received. However, Moffo continued to sing in other opera houses. In 1978 she sang Verdi's *Stiffelio* with the Opera Company of Boston, but her career as a singer was essentially over. For the rest of her life, Moffo continued to be active in promoting opera. She died of a stroke and is buried at Kensico Cemetery in Valhalla, New York.

For her time Moffo, as an American-born soprano, was a rarity in the world of opera. At the height of her career her voice was characterized as warm and rich. Moffo learned and sang an astounding number of roles, but she became most famous for Violetta in *La Traviata*, which she sang eighty times at the Metropolitan Opera alone. Some of her recordings have become classics. Also famed for her beauty, Moffo was named one of the ten most beautiful women in Italy. The combination of physical and vocal beauty made Moffo a star for twenty years in the world of opera.

★

The only biography of Moffo is Mario G. Genesi, *Anna Moffo: Una Carriera Italo-Americana* (2002), in Italian. Jerome Hines, *Great Singers on Great Singing* (1982), contains a chapter on Moffo, as does Clyde T. McCants, *American Opera Singers and Their Recordings: Critical Commentaries and Discographies* (2004), which also includes a comprehensive Moffo discography. A detailed discussion of her vocal problems is in Stephen E.

Rubin, "A Troubled Prima Donna Tries for a Comeback," *New York Times* (15 May 1977). Obituaries are in the *New York Times* (11 Mar. 2006) and *Boston Globe* (17 Mar. 2006).

Marcia B. Dinneen

MONDAVI, Robert Gerald (*b*. 18 June 1913 in Hibbing, Minnesota; *d*. 16 May 2008 in Yountville, California), vintner, entrepreneur, and patriarch of the Robert Mondavi wine empire.

Mondavi was one of four children, two daughters and two sons, of Cesare Mondavi and Rosa (Grasso) Mondavi, penniless Italian immigrants from Sassoferrato, in the Marches region of Italy. His father was an iron miner before opening a grocery store and saloon in Virginia, Minnesota; his mother ran a boardinghouse for Italian laborers. When Prohibition threatened Cesare Mondavi's saloon business, he noted a loophole in the law that allowed

Robert Mondavi. LEE LOCKWOOD/TIME LIFE PICTURES/
GETTY IMAGES

individuals to produce up to 200 gallons of wine for personal consumption and became a wholesale grape buyer, shuttling to California to buy grapes for Minnesota winemakers.

In 1923 the Mondavi family moved to Lodi, California, then the leading wine-grape region in the United States. Mondavi, who liked to be called "Bob," and his younger brother, Peter, helped in the family business. He attended Lodi Union High School, where he was a football star and went on to play rugby at Stanford University, intending to study business or law. But after his father suggested there was going to be a future in wine, Mondavi took chemistry classes and also a few winemaking courses at the University of California at Berkeley. After graduating from Stanford in 1936 with a BA in economics, he took a job at Sunnyhill, a small winery in California's Napa Valley. On 27 January 1940 Mondavi married his high school sweetheart, Marjorie Declusin, and settled in the Napa Valley town of Saint Helena; the couple had two sons and a daughter.

The condition of California winemaking was dismal at the time. Prohibition had devastated the industry, and domestic wines were "the stuff of skid-row jokes," according to one critic. By 1940 Mondavi was the manager at Sunnyhill, and in 1943 he persuaded his family to buy the Charles Krug Winery, then the oldest operating winery in Napa Valley. The Mondavi sons ran Krug for twenty-three years, with Robert traveling and handling sales, and Peter in Napa running the winery. But the brothers had opposing temperaments: Robert was dogged and unpredictable, Peter was reserved and systematic. The two even used different pronunciations of the family name—Robert said Mon-DAH-vi, Peter used Mon-DAY-vi. Their feuding became explosive after their father, who had always kept the peace, died in 1959. In 1965 an argument between the brothers about money ended in a fistfight. The family rallied behind Peter and, at age fifty-two, Robert was discharged from the family business. Lawsuits and court battles raged on for thirteen years, with Robert finally receiving $5 million for his shares in the Krug winery.

Jobless and broke, Mondavi quickly found investors and within a year had bought his own vineyard and grown, harvested, and fermented his first Robert Mondavi vintage. By 1967 he had built an expansive, mission-style winery on the land. But while his wines were well received and praised by critics, Mondavi's business was dying on the vine. His investor-partners sold their controlling shares to the Rainier Brewing Company of Seattle, which was itself bought and sold to even bigger conglomerates, and drained the winery of cash. By 1977 Mondavi was able to buy back the Rainier stake.

Now in control of his own business, Mondavi went in two equally successful directions. In a partnership with Baron Philippe de Rothschild's Château Mouton-Rothschild, he developed his high-end wines under the stamp Opus One, selling them for as much as $350 per bottle. At the same time he released a line of low-priced wines under the name Woodbridge. Both were well received. Mondavi purchased other wineries and introduced new lines of coastal wines and Italian varietals. In a 1981 interview Mondavi said, "Fifteen years ago, California didn't belong [with] the fine wines of the world. Now, we...produce outstanding wines, [giving] better value than the Europeans, who are limited by classification[s] and government restrictions."

In 1979, after more than thirty-five years, Mondavi's marriage ended in divorce, and in 1980 he married Margrit Biever, a Swiss-born woman who had worked at the winery. Mondavi's three children worked for the family business; his sons became cochairmen of the company. Mondavi began criticizing his sons for focusing on low-end wines and forsaking the signature brand. History began to repeat itself when a rift developed in the family. "With success," he wrote in his autobiography *Harvests of Joy*, "there always comes a day of reckoning."

During the 1990s Mondavi retreated from the business, spending most of his time, and money, on philanthropy. He got behind a controversial plan to build a $50 million cultural complex in Napa. In 2001 he and his wife donated $25 million to the University of California at Davis to establish the Robert Mondavi Institute for Wine and Food Science, but they could scarcely afford to make good on the gift. Other family members were also spending away the family fortune. Meanwhile, cheaper brands and tough competition drove company shares way down.

After a second split in the family, the winery's board forced the Mondavis to cede control of the firm. The company, then the sixth-largest U.S. winery, was sold in 2004 for $1 billion. Forty years after their bitter split, Mondavi went back to winemaking, briefly, with his brother, Peter. Using equal amounts of grapes from the Robert Mondavi and Peter Mondavi family vineyards, the brothers produced one small barrel of wine. It fetched more than $400,000 for charity at the 2005 Napa Valley Auction.

Into his nineties Mondavi traveled the world as an ambassador for wine. He died peacefully at home at the age of ninety-four. He was buried at Saint Helena, California.

For all of his family and professional troubles, Mondavi's contribution to American culture was significant. Once considered undrinkable, California wines are now among the world's premier labels, and Mondavi is largely credited for the shift. By bringing European winemaking traditions to California, making quality wines for a reasonable price, and marketing them brilliantly, he turned the world's attention to Napa Valley as America's "wine country."

★

Mondavi's autobiography, written with Paul Chutkow, is *Harvests of Joy: My Passion for Excellence* (1998). For a biography of Mondavi and a view of his empire written before his death, see Julia Flynn Siler, *The House of Mondavi: The Rise and Fall of an American Wine Dynasty* (2007). Obituaries are in the *Washington Post* and *Los Angeles Times* (both 17 May 2008) and the *New York Times* (21 May 2008).

Brenna Sanchez

MONTGOMERY, Gillespie V. ("Sonny") (*b.* 5 August 1920 in Meridian, Mississippi; *d.* 12 May 2006 in Meridian, Mississippi), fifteen-term U.S. representative from Mississippi, chairman of the House Committee on Veterans' Affairs, and author of the Montgomery GI Bill of Rights.

Montgomery was the only child born to Gillespie Montgomery, a gasoline and oil wholesale businessman, and Emily (Jones) Montgomery. Montgomery's father suffered from tuberculosis, and the family relocated to Phoenix, hoping that the illness would abate in a dry climate. After his father's health improved, the Montgomerys moved to Memphis, Tennessee, but when the tuberculosis recurred, they returned to Meridian. Montgomery's father died when his son was just ten years old. Emily Montgomery remarried, and during the Great Depression the family struggled

G. V. ("Sonny") Montgomery, 2001. AP IMAGES

to make ends meet. Montgomery attended several public schools as the family relocated to Hattiesburg, Mississippi, before his wealthy aunt offered to send the young teenager to the McCallie School—a military boarding academy in Chattanooga, Tennessee—from which he graduated in 1939.

McCallie's regimen profoundly influenced Montgomery, accentuating his boyhood desire to serve in the military. In the fall of 1939, when he enrolled at Mississippi State College in Starkville, he began two years of compulsory service in the Army Reserve Officers' Training Corps. In college Montgomery majored in business, played varsity basketball, participated in track and field, and was elected president of the student body in his senior year. With U.S. intervention in World War II in late 1941, Montgomery remained in the Reserve Officers' Training Corps, attending officer candidate school and graduating from college with a bachelor's degree in business in May 1943 with a commission as a second lieutenant in the army.

During World War II, Montgomery served in the Twelfth Armored Division in Europe. As a general's aide, he delivered messages and monitored troop and tank movements in the field. Montgomery won several commendations, including the Bronze Star for subduing a German machine-gun nest as Allied forces approached the Rhine River. Later, as a member of the Mississippi National Guard, he was activated during the Korean War as an officer in the Thirty-first Infantry Division. After leaving active duty, Montgomery remained in the guard, retiring at the rank of major general in 1980.

After being honorably discharged in 1946, Montgomery sold sporting goods and worked as a car salesman before launching a successful business specializing in credit life insurance, first in Meridian and then statewide. Beginning in the early 1950s, Montgomery became interested in politics. His insurance connections gradually formed the building blocks of his future political network. In 1955, by fewer than 100 votes, Montgomery won election to the Mississippi State Senate, representing Lauderdale County.

In 1966, when the freshman Republican representative Prentiss Walker left the House to run for the U.S. Senate, Montgomery vied for the open seat. He narrowly captured the Democratic nomination and prevailed in the general election with a 58 percent majority. Montgomery won his subsequent fourteen reelection campaigns handily—usually with 80 percent of the vote or more. In the post–civil rights era, however, the solidly Democratic South trended Republican. In his last election, Montgomery won with 68 percent of the vote.

When Montgomery entered the House in 1967, he was assigned to the Agriculture Committee—a panel long dominated by southerners with farm-based constituencies. In 1969 he secured a post on the Veterans' Affairs Committee. Two years later he left the Agriculture Committee after earning a spot on the Armed Services Committee. He remained on both panels until his retirement, eventually chairing Veterans' Affairs and rising to the third-ranking position on Armed Services.

Montgomery staked out as position as a hawk on most military matters, strongly supporting U.S. Vietnam War policies. Montgomery chaired the Select Committee on Military Involvement in Southeast Asia (1969–1971) and the Select Committee on Missing in Action in Southeast Asia (1975–1977). In 1990 he led a congressional delegation to North Korea when the Communist government in Pyongyang turned over the remains of U.S. service members killed in the Korean War. Working closely with the Republican representative Gerald Solomon of New York, Montgomery authored a 1988 law conferring presidential cabinet status on the Veterans Administration.

In 1981 Montgomery ascended to the chairmanship of the House Veterans' Affairs Committee. He led the panel for fourteen years, longer than any chairman since the committee was reorganized in 1947. His crowning achievement came in 1984 with the enactment of an updated GI Bill of Rights. A veterans' benefits bill had existed since the Servicemen's Readjustment Act of 1944 (known popularly as the GI Bill of Rights). It was revised during the Korean and Vietnam wars. After a drop in recruiting enrollments during the late 1970s, Montgomery argued that a "new GI Bill is absolutely essential if we are to maintain quality in our armed services in the quantity needed for a strong and sound national defense." Montgomery worked diligently for several years to overcome the skepticism of House leaders and appropriators. Known as the Montgomery GI Bill, the Educational Assistance Act of 1984 increased the educational incentives for new recruits, assuring individuals who contributed $100 per month from their own pay a matching $300 per month in federal educational benefits. Within three years, more than half a million service members availed themselves of its benefits. It was later regarded as a key tool to recruit and retain the all-volunteer military that defined the U.S. defense apparatus in the late twentieth century.

Montgomery was a prototypical conservative Democrat, strong on defense and to the right on many social issues. He personified a group whose numbers had declined in the South since the 1960s, and he was more ideologically attuned to Republicans than to his own party. In the early 1980s he facilitated meetings of a group of southern conservatives—dubbed the Boll Weevils, after the tiny beetle that infests cotton plants—who sided with the Republican president Ronald W. Reagan's economic initiatives and massive military buildup. Montgomery developed an abiding friendship with President George H. W. Bush (a fellow freshman House member in 1967). A lifelong bachelor who had no children of his own, Montgomery often joined the Bush family for holidays.

In 1997 Montgomery retired from the House and operated a lobbying firm for seven years before retiring to Meridian in 2004. On 9 November 2005 President George W. Bush awarded Montgomery the Presidential Medal of Freedom, noting his work as a "tireless advocate" for servicemen and servicewomen. His death from natural causes came six months later, following a long recuperation from surgery for a bowel obstruction. He is buried at Magnolia Cemetery in Meridian.

Montgomery's military service, an experience shared by many of his generation, had a formative influence on his future legislative agenda. His genial approach toward colleagues and low-key legislative style allowed Montgomery to work effectively across the aisle. Though he remained cordial with Democratic leaders, his brand of southern conservative politics often aligned him with Republicans who shared his approach to defense issues broadly and his emphasis on veterans' issues particularly.

★

Montgomery's papers are housed at the Mississippi State University Libraries, Congressional and Political Research Center Collections. Montgomery also coauthored a memoir, *Sonny Montgomery: The Veteran's Champion* (2003), with Michael B. Ballard and Craig S. Piper. Obituaries are in the *Washington Post* and *New York Times* (both 13 May 2006).

Matthew A. Wasniewski

MORRIS, Henry M(adison) (*b*. 6 October 1918 in Dallas, Texas; *d*. 25 February 2006 in Santee, California), hydraulic engineer, eminent scholar, and religious leader who is considered the father of modern creation science.

Morris was the eldest of three sons born to Henry Morris, Sr., a businessman active in real estate, and Emily Ida (Hunter) Morris, a professional pianist. In late 1927 the family moved to Houston, where Morris attended Johnson Junior High School before finishing his secondary schooling at San Jacinto High School, from which he graduated in 1935. That fall Morris enrolled at Rice University, where he graduated with honors in 1939 with a BS in civil engineering. Morris married Mary Louise Beach on 24 January 1940 in Houston; the couple had six children. Following graduation, he was at first employed by the Texas Highway Department and later worked as assistant hydraulic engineer in various positions from 1939 until 1942. Morris began his teaching career in 1942 when he returned to Rice University as an instructor in civil engineering, a position he held until 1946.

Also in 1946 Morris moved to Minneapolis, where he was instructor and later assistant professor of civil engineering at the University of Minnesota, a position he held until 1951. Continuing his scientific studies at the University of Minnesota, he earned his MS (1948) and a PhD (1950) in hydraulics engineering with minors in geology and mathematics.

In 1951 he relocated to the University of Southwestern Louisiana, Lafayette, where he served as professor and head of the department of civil engineering, as well as acting dean of engineering, until 1956. Morris became professor of applied science at Southern Illinois University from 1956 to 1957. In 1957 he accepted a position as professor of hydraulic engineering and chairman of the department of civil engineering at Virginia Polytechnic Institute and State University (Virginia Tech) in Blacksburg, where he remained until 1970.

During his academic life Morris authored a college-level textbook, *Applied Hydraulics in Engineering* (1963), which became a popular and widely used text in many universities around the world. In his years at Virginia Tech, the civil engineering program became one of the most outstanding and largest of its kind in the nation.

As a child Morris was not interested in religion, but in the late 1930s, while a student at Rice University, he began studying the Bible, which transformed his life as he acknowledged its teachings as the infallible and literal word of God. His comprehensive approach to research and his strong commitment to biblical truths and creationism are best seen in his prolific writings. Morris's combination of hydraulic engineering with his belief in studying the Bible in its literal, historical, and theological dimensions led him to explore the relationship between science and religion and how the Genesis flood might be explained in scientific terms. At the same time, his background provided intellectual underpinnings for attacks from evolutionists as he examined the origins of life from both the scientific and religious viewpoints.

Working as a young engineer in the early 1940s, Morris became interested in biblical apologetics as it relates to the literal interpretation of the Bible by science. His first apologetic work, *That You Might Believe*, was written in 1946 to explain his faith in opposition to the theory of evolution. Following this work are his two most popular apologetic works, *The Bible and Modern Science* (1951) and *The Genesis Flood: The Biblical Record and Its Scientific Implications* (1961). *The Genesis Flood*, coauthored with the theologian John C. Whitcomb, Jr., has been acclaimed as the most influential contribution to strict creationism since the 1920s. Because of this popular and groundbreaking work, both creationists and opponents of creationism regard Morris as the father of the modern creationist movement. In 1963 Morris and a group of like-minded scientists founded the Creation Research Society (CRS), whose mission was to institute scientific

support for the Genesis creation story; a quarterly journal was published by the society. Morris served as president of CRS from 1967 to 1973, providing leadership and research for *creation science*, a term he coined.

In 1970 Morris retired from his high-profile and distinguished position at Virginia Tech to devote himself even more fully to biblical research and writing and to pursue his activities in creationism full time. He moved to San Diego, where he cofounded with Tim LaHaye the Christian Heritage College (now San Diego Christian College), a four-year, private liberal arts college emphasizing religious education. In that same year Morris founded the Institute for Creation Research (ICR), which is a graduate school and research organization where creation scientists engage in study and research. It was established as part of the Christian Heritage College after breaking away, following an organizational split, from the CRS. The ICR became the world's leading center for strict creationism. In 1981 ICR was reorganized as an independent entity. Morris served as president of ICR from 1970 to 1995, when his son, John D. Morris, succeeded him as president. In 2006 the board of directors for ICR approved its relocation to the newly established Henry M. Morris Center for Christian Leadership in Dallas. In January 2007 Henry M. Morris III, the eldest son, took over as chief executive officer, while John D. Morris continued as president. The creation museum, which is a part of ICR, remained in San Diego.

Morris's creationist views were politically and culturally influential, especially among religious fundamentalists in the United States, despite overwhelming rejection by the world's scientific community. Morris dismissed Judeo-Christian allegorical or symbolic interpretations of the Bible and centuries of textual and historical biblical criticism. To defend the biblical prescription that Earth was created 6,000 years ago in six days, Morris ignored widespread acceptance of radiometric dating and the physical evidence for a 4.5-billion-year-old planet. Challenging the validity of evolution, he claimed that all humans descended directly from Adam and Eve. Contrary to a large body of geological scholarship, Morris defended the account in Genesis of a flood that covered the entire Earth and furthermore that 600-year-old Noah, his family, and a few animals were the flood's only survivors. In sum, the great majority of scientists asserted that Morris misrepresented, omitted, or denied all evidence that did not conform to his literal reading of the Bible.

Despite the hostile environment of public debates in the field of the creation-evolution controversy, Morris was a soft-spoken man known for his personal gentleness and his ability to work with others, which moved most people to admiration even among his fiercest critics and opponents. Among the relatively few scientists and scholars who accepted Morris's views of biblical creationism and science was John Sanford, a Cornell University professor. Sanford mentioned in the *Los Angeles Times* (3 Mar. 2006) that although he himself believed in the theory of evolution, Morris had influenced his thinking in a major way, noting that Morris would be remembered "as one of the high-impact individuals of his generation."

Morris earned numerous prizes and honors. He was a fellow of both the American Association for the Advancement of Science and the American Society of Civil Engineers; in 1983 he was elected fellow of the CRS. He held membership in a number of institutions, including the Geological Society of America, the American Society for Engineering Education, and the Engineers Council for Professional Development. He held honorary doctorates from Bob Jones University (1966) and Liberty University (1989). He was the first president of the Transnational Association of Christian Colleges and Schools, an accrediting agency.

After he retired as president of ICR, Morris continued to write and to serve as president emeritus until his death. Morris died at the age of eighty-seven after a series of strokes and is buried in Greenwood Cemetery, San Diego. Morris wrote more than sixty books during his lifetime, interweaving science and theology to address various topics of creation, evolution, and the Christian faith. Morris's legacy as a biblical scholar, along with his many significant accomplishments, will continue to have a profound impact around the world.

★

Remarks on parts of his life are included in some of Morris's writings, including *The Bible and Modern Science* (1951) and *A History of Modern Creationism* (1984). Many personal insights are also provided in Ronald L. Numbers, *The Creationists* (1993), J. Gordon Melton, *Religious Leaders of America: A Biographical Guide to Founders and Leaders of Religious Bodies, Churches, and Spiritual Groups in North America* (1999), and Gerald Bergman, "A Short History of the Modern Creation Movement and the Continuing Modern Cultural Wars," *Journal of American Culture* 26, no. 2 (June 2003): 243–262. Obituaries are in the *San Diego Union Tribune* and *Washington Post* (both 1 Mar. 2006), the *Los Angeles Times* (3 Mar. 2006), the *New York Times* (4 Mar. 2006), and the London *Times* (27 Mar. 2006).

Hope E. Young

MOTT, Stewart Rawlings (*b.* 4 December 1937 in Flint, Michigan; *d.* 12 June 2008 in Mount Kisco, New York), politically progressive, offbeat philanthropist who financially supported a wide variety of progressive causes and candidates.

Mott was born one of three children to Charles Stewart Mott, a wealthy automobile executive and for a time General Motors' largest stockholder, and Ruth Rawlings. "Young Stewart," as he was known around the Detroit area, went to various local schools before entering Deerfield Academy in Massachusetts at the age of thirteen. He later attended the Massachusetts Institute of Technology for three years, after which he spent a year hitchhiking around the world. Upon returning to the United States, he enrolled at Columbia University's School of General Studies, earning two BA degrees, one in business administration and one in comparative literature. At Columbia he also began work on an MA in comparative literature.

From an early age Mott had displayed an interest in his father's business and various philanthropic ventures. After a stint (1963–1964) teaching English at Eastern Michigan University, Mott began his own career in philanthropy by founding a branch of Planned Parenthood in Flint, Michigan. His work for that organization as well as arguments over the direction of the family foundation led to a serious breach between father and son. The two did not speak for over a year. Mott moved to New York City and used his trust funds to become an activist in a number of causes.

During the 1970s his advocacy group People Politics supported organizations for women, African Americans, young people, and groups investigating political and business scandals. In 1968 he took out ads in the local papers to pledge $50,000 for a then nonexistent Nelson Rockefeller presidential candidacy on the Republican ticket provided others would contribute double that amount. Mott then bankrolled Democratic Senator Eugene McCarthy's challenge to President Lyndon Johnson. Four years later Mott was the largest contributor to Democratic Senator George McGovern's losing race for the presidency, support that earned him a place on Richard Nixon's famed "enemies list." When Congress in 1974 passed legislation to curb large political gifts to candidates, Mott joined with conservatives to challenge the restrictions, most of which the U.S. Supreme Court ruled constitutional. Mott was limited in how much he could contribute to Representative John Anderson's independent run for the presidency in 1980, a limitation that, it has been said, hampered Anderson. In 1979 Mott married Kappy Wells, a sculptor. The couple would go on to have a son. They divorced in 1999.

Politics was not the only reason for Mott's widespread media coverage. In Washington, D.C., he threw a party at which guests rode an elephant on the sidewalk while wearing gold sashes that read in French "shame on those who think badly of this." His passion for urban gardening drew attention when he was thrown out of his Park Avenue apartment for installing a rooftop "farm" that included large plots to raise food, compost piles, and a chicken coop. Moving to a midtown high-rise he announced with great fanfare the cultivation of more than 8,000 square feet of penthouse terraces with over 400 plant species including seventeen types of radishes; by 1975 the plan had failed. He was somewhat notorious, too, for speaking all too candidly about his sex partners and his parents (describing his father as "a zoo keeper" and his mother as "a nice lady who did nothing with her life").

After this series of events and failures Mott lowered his profile, toning down his public comments. He continued to support left-leaning causes, but with "seed grants" rather than large cash outlays. For the last thirty years of his life, he worked through the Stewart R. Mott Charitable Trust and vehicles such as the Fund for Constitutional Government to concentrate, as the trust's website put it, on small, "strategic investments" designed "to build capacity and create fund-raising leverage" in such areas as arms control, family planning, reproductive rights, government reform, public policy, and civil rights. In 1974 Mott bought a historic house in Washington, D.C., which became known as Mott House and that served as his home as well as the trust's offices.

From the time he was young, Mott spent part of each year at the impressive family home in Bermuda, where as an adult he arranged for grants for local social activists and became an honorary member of the island's Progressive Labor Party. Among his numerous residences was one in the posh community of North Salem, New York, and it was not far from there that he died in the emergency room of the Northern Westchester Hospital in Mount Kisco, following a yearlong battle with cancer.

The high points in Mott's political career came early on, when his contributions made a difference despite the fact that he routinely backed losing candidates. The activities of his later life, less well known, helped a variety of small groups, many of them on the political fringe, to survive. Mott was viewed all too often as an eccentric, but he was far from a dilettante. Still, given Mott's exceptional wealth, it seems not unfair to say that his career should have had more of an effect on the U.S. political scene. He remains an attractive and interesting, if unusual, footnote.

★

A fascinating insight into Mott's career until 1971 and his relationship with his father can be found in E. J. Kahn, Jr., "Profiles: Blue Chip off the Old Block," *New Yorker* (27 Nov. 1971). Obituaries are in the *Washington Post* (13 June 2008), the *New York Times* and *Los Angeles Times* (both 14 June 2008), and the Bermuda *Royal Gazette* (8 Aug. 2008).

Daniel J. Leab

MULLIGAN, Robert Patrick (*b.* 23 August 1925 in New York City; *d.* 20 December 2008 in Lyme, Connecticut), director of television dramas and feature films, best known for *To Kill a Mockingbird* (1962), a movie that won four Academy Awards.

Robert Mulligan. LEE CELANO/WIREIMAGE/GETTY IMAGES

Born in the Bronx borough of New York City, Mulligan was the oldest of three boys, including Richard and James, raised by Robert Edward, a policeman, and Elizabeth (Gingell) Mulligan. At the age of fourteen he entered Saint Ann's Academy for seminary training. During World War II, however, he enlisted in the navy and served as a radio operator before returning to the States to work as a copy clerk for the *New York Times*. In 1948 Mulligan graduated from Fordham University with a BA. Four years later, in 1952, he married the actress Jane Lee Sutherland. The couple would go on to have two sons and a daughter. They divorced in 1968.

Mulligan got his start in television as a messenger with the Columbia Broadcasting System (CBS). He was later noticed by the director Robert Stevens and went on to serve first as a production assistant then as a director of live dramas produced for *Studio One*, *Playhouse 90*, and the *Philco Television Playhouse*. Between 1954 and 1959, Mulligan distinguished himself as a versatile and prolific director who in one two-year span directed or worked on one hundred television dramas, including *Billy Budd*; *Ah, Wilderness!*; *The Human*

Comedy; *What Every Woman Knows*; *A Catered Affair*; and *Tales of Two Cities*. His direction of David Susskind's acclaimed production of *Member of the Wedding* (1958) preceded his helming of *The Moon and Sixpence* (1959), for which he won his only Emmy. Based on the short novel by Somerset Maugham, the drama starred the British actor Laurence Olivier in his first television appearance.

Even as he was delivering live television dramas every two weeks, Mulligan was establishing his reputation as an actor's director, helping stars such as Paul Newman, Rosemary Harris, Sidney Poitier, Steve McQueen, Karl Malden, Jessica Tandy, Hume Cronyn, and Judith Anderson to successfully make their move to the new medium. In his lone Broadway production, Mulligan directed George C. Scott and Uta Hagen during the short run of the drama *Comes a Day* (1958).

Mulligan had worked with the producer Alan Pakula at CBS, and when Pakula made his move to Hollywood, Mulligan followed suit. In 1957 Mulligan and Pakula teamed up for Mulligan's first feature film, *Fear Strikes Out* (1957), based on the life of the Boston Red Sox outfielder Jimmy Piersall.

In 1960 Mulligan directed Tony Curtis, first with Debbie Reynolds in the comedy *The Rat Race* (1960) as young performers struggling to make it in New York, and then as the title character in *The Great Imposter*, both mildly successful both critically and at the box office. Two movies for Universal starring Rock Hudson, *Come September* (1961) and *The Spiral Road* (1962), were less noteworthy but were preamble to Mulligan's best work.

Determined to resist studio control of his scripts and casting, Mulligan formed an independent film company with Pakula as producer. They turned to Harper Lee's best-selling novel *To Kill a Mockingbird*, Mulligan telling Pakula that he was ready to "pawn his belongings to get the film rights." During the negotiations, Mulligan persuaded Lee by promising that Gregory Peck would play Atticus Finch, the Alabama lawyer who defends a black man falsely accused of raping a white woman. Under Mulligan's sensitive directing, the film's young actors blossomed as performers, their development an initial display of Mulligan's talent for cultivating the performances of children and young adults in a number of films to follow, notably *Up the Down Staircase* (1967), *Summer of '42* (1971), *The Other* (1972), and *The Man in the Moon* (1991), this last with a fourteen-year-old Reese Witherspoon in her first film. For his part in *To Kill a Mockingbird*, Peck won his only Oscar. Nominated in eight categories, including Best Director, the film won awards for Best Adapted Screenplay, Best Art Direction, and Best Set Decoration.

The remainder of Mulligan's movies were met largely with critical indifference, a tepid response spawned in part by Mulligan's eclectic choice of films and by his resistance to imposing his stamp upon them. For his part, Mulligan

believed that the impact of a director on his or her work was "way overrated" by film critics, seeing himself instead as a collaborator with his writers, actors, and crew. The critic John Belton spoke for those critics among whom Mulligan's understated style did find favor when he celebrated "films as astonishing for their stylistic subtly as for their emotional power."

Indeed, for such critics and some audiences, "underrated" was the operative description for films such as *Love with the Proper Stranger* (1963), with Steve McQueen and Natalie Wood coping with an unwanted pregnancy, and *Inside Daisy Clover*, the 1966 exposé of Hollywood, again with Wood, and *Up the Down Staircase* (1967), with Sandy Dennis as a high school teacher pitting her idealism against her students' world of drugs and violence. While directing these urban-based films, Mulligan also completed *Baby the Rain Must Fall* (1965) with McQueen as an ex-con, seemingly doomed by parental abuse and stuck in small town Texas. In their last collaboration, Pakula and Mulligan presented Peck in a Western-horror vehicle, *The Stalking Moon* (1969) in which he saves a child from a savage murderer. Critically disparaged at the time, later reviews would hail the movie as "Mulligan's unsung masterpiece."

On 21 December 1971 Mulligan married Dennis. Professionally, the early 1970s brought no change in Mulligan's eclecticism as director nor to the divided reviews received by his films. To some, *Summer of '42* (1971) was too pastoral and sentimental; for others it examined the angst of a lonely adolescent falling into love for the first time. In a rare departure from his customary behind-the-scenes role, Mulligan provided the opening voice-over that captured the teenager's confusion. A year later, Mulligan took a darker look at youth in the gothic horror movie *The Other* (1972), about twin boys living on a New England farm who discover their potential for murder. To cast the film, Mulligan interviewed 200 sets of twins to discover the right boys then taught them how not to "act" for the camera. He also employed his stylistic hallmark, the subjective camera, as he said, "to put the audience into the body, the soul, the mind and the imagination of a ten-year-old boy—visually." With a reversal worthy of Alfred Hitchcock, he then shifted the perspective and shattered his viewers' assumptions.

Bloodbrothers (1979) revisited the father-son clash on display in *Fear Strikes Out* and featured Richard Gere as an adolescent trying to escape the teeming streets of New York. Mulligan's last film, *The Man in the Moon* again reveals his compassion for children as well as his admiration for their resilience in the face of pain. Mulligan died at his home in Lyme, the cause apparently heart failure. Despite his many achievements, Mulligan remains a director in need of rescue. With the choice of Mulligan's films to inaugurate "American Auteurs," a yearlong celebration of great film artists, the Film Society of Lincoln Center seems to have launched that reevaluation of the director and his work.

★

An assessment of Mulligan's work can be found in John Belton, *Cinema Stylist* (1983). A review of his career as well as an outline of the controversy among critics regarding Mulligan's standing among directors is in John Wakeman, *World Film Directors, Vol. II* (1988). A further summary of Mulligan's career can be found in Charles Denny, *International Dictionary of Films and Filmmakers,* 4th ed. (2000). An obituary is in the *New York Times* (23 Dec. 2008).

Gerard Molyneaux

MURRAY, Elizabeth (*b.* 6 September 1940 in Chicago, Illinois; *d.* 12 August 2007 in Granville, New York), acclaimed abstract artist and painter renowned for her use of bold and vivid colors and emotionally charged, complex works of art whose subjects include relationships, everyday life, and the nature of art itself.

Murray was one of three children born into a working-class family that had faced homelessness for brief periods due to the ill health of her father. As a result, the family found it necessary to move to Bloomington, Illinois, to live with Murray's grandmother. Her passion for art was evident from the start, and Murray's interest in it was encouraged by her parents, Lester and Dorothy Murray, as well. She loved to draw constantly and was inspired by comic books and newspaper comic strips from an early age. She attributed her enduring sense of the physicality of color to an experience of having watched a nursery school teacher use a thick red crayon to cover a blank sheet of paper. By the time Murray was in the fifth grade, she was selling her drawings to classmates for a quarter each, and she even wrote to Walt Disney asking for a job. At that time her dream was to become a commercial artist.

With the help of an anonymous gift from a high school teacher, Murray began her studies at the Art Institute of Chicago in 1958. It was here that she was initially exposed to various works of artistic splendor, especially a Paul Cézanne still life that would ultimately change her own life. She would later say that that particular painting was "the first in which I lost myself looking," and "I just realized I could be a painter if I wanted to try." Willem de Kooning, Max Beckmann, and the surrealists were also particularly significant for Murray during those years. She earned her BFA from the Art Institute in 1962. It was her continued fascination with Beckmann, however, that helped her make the decision to attend Mills College in

Oakland, California, for her graduate studies, especially since he had taught at that Bay Area school for a semester. At that time Murray met Jennifer Bartlett, an undergraduate student whom she was to mentor, and who would eventually become Murray's lifelong best friend.

During these years all of the elements for which Murray's art ultimately became known were at their developing stages, such as her use of unconventional shapes, vivid color, unusual, extravagant paint surfaces, and emotionally complex narratives that were implicitly autobiographical in nature. She then became interested in the work of Jasper Johns and Robert Rauschenberg. After marrying Don Sunseri, a sculptor and former classmate from the Art Institute of Chicago, and graduating from Mills College with her MFA in 1964, Murray and her husband decided to move to Buffalo, New York, the next year. Murray taught at a small Catholic college in the area before the couple relocated to New York City in the fall of 1967. There Murray was exposed to the work of Brice Marden, Richard Serra, and Ellen Phelan, as well as to such artists as Robert Moskowitz, Susan Rothenberg, and Joel Shapiro, who had combined abstraction and imagery much like her friend Bartlett.

Murray's first child, a boy, Dakota, was born in 1969, and in 1972 Murray made her debut with *Dakota Red* in the Contemporary American Painting exhibit at the Whitney Museum of American Art. Murray and her husband divorced in 1973, just prior to her work being exhibited at the Paula Cooper Gallery in SoHo. Her first solo show at that gallery was in 1976.

In the early 1980s Murray met and married Robert ("Bob") Holman, a poet and performer, who would found and become the proprietor of the Bowery Poetry Club, a performance arts venue in New York City. They had two daughters, Sophie and Daisy. Murray's first solo museum show in New York City, Elizabeth Murray: Paintings and Drawings, covered a little over a decade of her work and took place at the Whitney Museum of American Art from 21 April to 26 June 1988.

In the 1980s and 1990s Murray designed two large murals for the New York subway system—one at the 59th Street and Lexington Avenue station in Manhattan and the other at the 23rd Street and Ely Avenue station in Queens. In 1995 Murray curated the exhibition Artist's Choice—Elizabeth Murray: Modern Woman for the Museum of Modern Art (MoMA) in New York, and since that year, Murray had been represented by the Pace-Wildenstein Gallery.

Murray received many awards, including the Skowhegan Medal in Painting (1986), the Larry Aldrich Prize in Contemporary Art (1993), the John D. and Catherine T. MacArthur Foundation Fellowship, or "genius grant" (1999), which incidentally helped to establish the Bowery

Poetry Club. Murray's *The Lowdown* was chosen as the 2002 Spoleto Festival USA official poster art, as well.

Over the years Murray taught at a number of schools, including the University of Buffalo, Bard College, Yale University, and the California Institute of the Arts in Valencia. In addition, Murray was appointed distinguished lecturer in painting at Brooklyn College in Brooklyn, New York.

In 2006 there was a major retrospective showing of Murray's paintings from 1963 to 2005 at MoMA in New York City. As of 2008 Murray remained only one of four women to be so honored. She also was asked to select an artist for the 2006 AXA Artist Award, and she served on the boards of both the Andy Warhol Foundation and the Foundation for Contemporary Arts. Murray's work is featured in numerous collections, including her alma mater, the Art Institute of Chicago, the Museum of Contemporary Art in Los Angeles, and MoMA.

Murray died at the age of sixty-six of complications from lung cancer at her home in Granville. A "Praise Day" was held in her honor at the Bowery Poetry Club on 30 August 2007, and later that fall, a private memorial was held at MoMA.

Murray will be remembered as one of only a handful of contemporary women artists who blazed the trail for other young women artists, an amazingly complex painter who permitted herself to become vulnerable in her work, the unofficial art teacher at the Downtown Community School, and for her exuberant energy, magnanimous spirit, unpretentious character, bold blue eyes, and prematurely white hair, and, most of all, for her witty sense of humor, once even calling herself the "James Joyce of painting."

★

For biographical material about Murray's life and work, see Robert Storr, *Elizabeth Murray* (2005); Robert Hughes, "Abstraction and Popeye's Biceps," *Time* (13 July 1987); Michael Brenson, "Review/Art: A Look at a Decade of Elizabeth Murray's Works," *New York Times* (22 Apr. 1988); and Carol Kino, "A Visit with the Modern's First Grandmother," *New York Times* (2 Oct. 2005). For information about Murray's 2005 exhibit, see Hilton Kramer, "Caution to Viewers: Murray's Paintings May Induce Vertigo," *New York Observer* (30 Oct. 2005). A tribute is given by Verlyn Klinkenborg in "Appreciations: Elizabeth Murray," *New York Times* (13 and 14 Aug. 2007). Obituaries are in the *New York Times* (13 Aug. 2007); *Chicago Tribune* and *Los Angeles Times* (both 16 Aug. 2007); *Villager* 77, no. 12 (22–28 Aug. 2007); and *Downtown Express* 20, no. 16 (31 Aug.–6 Sept. 2007).

Adriana C. Tomasino

N

NELSON, (John) Byron, Jr. (*b*. 4 February 1912 in Waxahachie, Texas; *d*. 26 September 2006 in Roanoke, Texas), record-setting professional golfer who is counted among the best golfers of the twentieth century.

Nelson was the son of John Byron Nelson, Sr., a cotton farmer, and Madge (Allen) Nelson, a schoolteacher and later a homemaker. Nelson had two siblings. When he was eleven, his family moved to Fort Worth, Texas. He barely survived typhoid fever, and he lost nearly half his body weight to the disease, which left him unable to have children. At age twelve he started caddying at Glen Garden Country Club, as did the famed golfer Ben Hogan, whom Nelson beat by a stroke in the 1928 Glen Garden Caddie Tournament. Nelson did not like school, and that same year he dropped out, halfway through tenth grade.

Throughout Nelson's youth and his first years on tour, money was in short supply, and Nelson held several jobs. He was a file clerk for the Fort Worth–Denver City Railroad from the fall of 1928 throughout most of 1930, when he was let go. He next worked for *Southwest Builders* magazine, until it went defunct in 1930. With work hard to find during the Depression, Nelson turned pro on 22 November 1932, with $500 in support from backers in Fort Worth. At a Sunday Bible study in 1933, Nelson met Louise Shofner. They were married on 24 June 1934.

Nelson next worked in the pro shop at Texarkana Country Club in Texarkana, Texas, in 1933 and then as an assistant pro at Ridgewood Country Club in Ridgewood, New Jersey, for two years. Following his stint at Ridgewood, Nelson took the head professional job at the Reading Country Club in Reading, Pennsylvania, until 1940, when he accepted an offer to be head professional

at Inverness Golf Club in Toledo, Ohio. He stayed at Inverness until 1944, when after some member dissatisfaction over the money he was making on tour, in addition to what the club members were paying him, he had a perfect excuse to resign. He tendered his resignation, realizing that he did not want to be a club professional all his life.

In a short professional career, Nelson won fifty-two tour tournaments and twelve additional tournaments, and in 1945 he had one of the greatest years of all time, winning a record eighteen tournaments, eleven of them in a row. During that year he also registered a record stroke average of 68.33; the record stood for fifty-five years. His prodigious achievements earned him the nickname "Lord Byron."

Often overlooked because of his impressive streaks of 1945, Nelson's accomplishments in 1944 and 1946, the year of his retirement, were also impressive. His streaks during the war years have at times not been fully appreciated because many professional golfers were in the service, but it should be noted that many tour players, including Sam Snead and Hogan, had rejoined the tour in 1944.

Many tour tournaments were canceled in 1942 and 1943. Nelson tried twice to enlist in the armed forces but was rejected for a condition that kept his blood from coagulating properly. During the two-year tour hiatus, Nelson, mostly with his good friend Harold McSpadden, crossed the country, giving exhibitions for the Red Cross, for the United Service Organizations, and at rehabilitation centers.

When the tour reopened in 1944, Nelson entered twenty-one of the twenty-three scheduled tournaments, winning eight. In 1946 he won six times. Early in 1946 Nelson began thinking of retirement. He had long felt that his main interest in being a professional golfer was as a means to fulfill a lifelong aspiration of owning a ranch.

Byron Nelson, 1937. ©BETTMANN/CORBIS

Soon after his retirement, Nelson and his wife bought a 630-acre ranch in Roanoke.

The succeeding years of ranching, exhibitions, and television work were wonderful for the couple until 1985, when after a succession of strokes, Nelson's wife died on 4 October, ending a marriage that had spanned over fifty years. Devastated by his wife's death and suffering drastic weight loss, Nelson finally turned his situation around and began to play again. When he was invited to play in a 1986 tournament in Dayton, Ohio, he contacted a young advertising writer named Peggy Simmons, whom he had met at the same tournament in 1981. She came to see him play, they remained in contact, and six months later she moved to Texas, where they married on 15 November 1986.

Nelson's long, fluid swing is considered the model of the modern way to strike a golf ball. Nelson learned that using the big muscles in the hips and legs could be a more reliable, powerful, and effective way to hit a golf ball than the more wristy method that had been employed in the era of hickory shafts. Nelson was particularly noteworthy for the way his swing was more upright and along the target line. His swing served as the model for the mechanical testing robot that came to be known as "Iron Byron."

In 1968 Nelson became the first player to have a Professional Golfers' Association (PGA) event named after him, the Byron Nelson Classic. Following his playing career, Nelson played a significant role in the development of Tom Watson and Ken Venturi as world-class players, and starting in 1957, he was for several years a successful television golf commentator, often teamed with Chris Schenkel.

Nelson's fifty-two tour championships ranked him sixth all time at the time of his death. Of these victories five were in majors: the Masters in 1937 and 1942, the U.S. Open in 1939, and the PGA Championship in 1940 and 1945. Nelson played on Ryder Cup teams in 1937 and 1947 and was nonplaying captain in 1965. He won the Vardon Trophy in 1939 and 1945, and he was PGA Tour Money Winner in 1944 and 1945. Nelson died at his home in Roanoke. He is buried in Roselawn Memorial Park in Denton, Texas.

Nelson's many distinctions and honors include the Bob Jones Award and induction into the World Golf Hall of Fame (both 1974). In 1994 Nelson won the Old Tom Morris Award, and in 1997 his career accomplishments, both on and off the course, were recognized with the PGA Tour Lifetime Achievement Award. In 2000 *Golf Digest* ranked Nelson as the fifth-greatest golfer of all time, behind Jack Nicklaus, Hogan, Snead, and Bobby Jones. In 2006 Nelson was posthumously awarded the Congressional Gold Medal, the highest award bestowed by the legislative branch of the U.S. government.

★

Nelson's 1993 book *How I Played the Game* is a humble, plain-spoken autobiography emphasizing the Christian beliefs and virtues that guided Nelson throughout his life. Nelson also penned *Winning Golf* (1946). For additional biographical information, see Ralph Hickok, *New Encyclopedia of Sports* (1977), and David L. Porter, ed., *Biographical Dictionary of American Sports: Outdoor Sports* (1988). Obituaries are in the *Christian Chronicle* (26 Sept. 2006), *Dallas Morning News* (27 Sept. 2006), and *Guardian* (28 Sept. 2006).

Jim Castañeda

NEWELL, Peter Francis ("Pete"), Jr. (*b.* 31 August 1915 in Vancouver, British Columbia, Canada; *d.* 17 November 2008 in Rancho Santa Fe, California), college basketball coach who was the first to win the sport's "triple crown" with victories in the National Invitational Tournament (NIT), the National Collegiate Athletic Association (NCAA) tournament, and the Olympics.

Newell was the fifth of eight children born to Peter Francis Newell, who worked for the Knights of Columbus, and

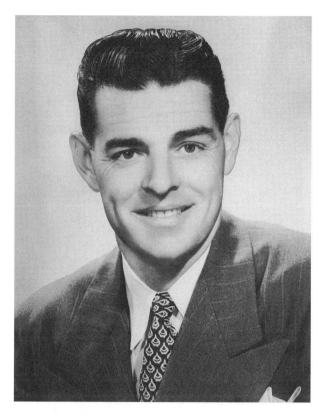

Pete Newell, 1950. AP IMAGES

In February 1942 Newell enlisted in the U.S. Navy and was assigned to the Great Lakes Naval Air Station, just north of Chicago. On 4 August 1942 in Chicago, he married Florence O'Connor, whom he had met when he was in high school. She attended the nearby Catholic Girls High School. The Newells had four sons during their forty-two-year marriage, which ended with Florence Newell's death in 1984.

During World War II, Pete Newell served in the Pacific with an amphibious unit. In 1946 he was discharged as a lieutenant, junior grade, and returned to California. With the recommendation of Needles, his former coach at Loyola, Newell was offered the position of head basketball and baseball coach at the University of San Francisco (USF) for the 1946–1947 season. He also coached golf and tennis, and the tennis team won the NCAA championship in 1949.

Newell's first teams at USF went 13–14 and 13–11 before a breakthrough season (1948–1949), in which they went 25–5 and capped the season by winning the NIT in Madison Square Garden in New York City. At the time, the NIT was recognized as the top tournament in college basketball. The next year the USF Dons went 19–6 before losing to City College of New York, the eventual champion, in the 1950 NIT.

At the end of the season, Newell accepted the position of head basketball coach at Michigan State University (MSU), which was entering the Big Ten that year. Newell left USF with a record of 70–37. At Michigan State he emphasized the defensive play that had brought success at USF but that was not practiced as much in the Midwest at that time. In four years at MSU, Newell had a record of only 45–42 but laid a solid foundation for his successor, Forrest "Fordy" Anderson.

Newell expected to remain at MSU for many years, but he accepted the head coaching job (and the position of assistant baseball coach) at the University of California, Berkeley (Cal), so that he and his wife could return to their home state to raise their family. Cal had been a West Coast power but had fallen on hard times, and Newell's 1954–1955 team won only one conference game before Newell turned the team around. Over the next five years, his teams went 17–8, 21–5, 19–9, 25–4, and 28–2. In 1959 Cal won the NCAA championship. The team finished second in 1960, losing to the great Ohio State team of Jerry Lucas and John Havlicek, though Newell was named the NCAA Coach of the Year. The last four years his teams won the Pacific Coast Conference, and Newell's Cal squads won their last eight games against John Wooden's University of California, Los Angeles, squads. At age forty-six Newell quit at the top of his coaching career because his doctor warned him that his coffee drinking, heavy smoking, and poor eating and sleeping habits during the season were severely impairing his health. Newell would

Alice (Heffron) Newell, a homemaker. Newell's father was transferred to Los Angeles when Newell was just a year old, and his mother took him to auditions for film roles. He appeared in small film roles (mostly in *Our Gang* comedies) from the age of three until the age of seven or eight. Newell attended Saint Agnes High School, where he played football, basketball, and baseball, graduating in 1934.

After high school Newell worked as a janitor before getting a job as a deck cadet for the Dollar Steamship Line, sailing across the Pacific. After two years, in the fall of 1936, he enrolled at Loyola University of Los Angeles (now Loyola Marymount), where he played basketball under Coach Jimmy Needles, who was the first American Olympic basketball coach when basketball became a medal sport for the 1936 Berlin Olympics. A teammate was Phil Woolpert, who would later be Newell's assistant coach at the University of San Francisco and succeed him as head coach in 1951. In 1939 Newell graduated with a BA in political science and then took a coaching position at Saint John's Military Academy in Los Angeles, a position he kept for two years. Newell coached football, basketball, baseball, and track, and his teams were undefeated in all four sports for those two years. During the summer of 1940, Newell played minor league baseball at Pine Bluff (in Arkansas), hitting .217 as an outfielder.

step down as coach and become Cal's athletic director. Newell's coaching record at Cal was 119–44.

Though he had retired, Newell reluctantly agreed to coach the 1960 U.S. Olympic basketball team; at the time, professionals were not allowed to play on such teams. Newell led the team—later referred to by some as the Original Dream Team because of its great players—to a gold medal in Rome, with the closest game a twenty-four-point victory over the Soviet Union. The top three scorers on the team were Oscar Robertson, Jerry Lucas, and Jerry West.

Newell served as athletic director at Cal until 1968, and during that time he also served on the NCAA Basketball Tournament Committee and the U.S. Olympic Committee, chairing the Olympic Basketball Coach Committee in 1964 and 1968. Newell resigned from Cal in 1968 and accepted the position of general manager of the San Diego Rockets of the National Basketball Association (NBA) in June of that year. He remained in the position for three years but stepped down rather than move to Houston with the franchise in 1971.

From 1972 to 1976 Newell was the general manager of the Los Angeles Lakers, acquiring Kareem Abdul-Jabbar in 1975. Abdul-Jabbar would lead the Lakers to five NBA championships in the 1980s, after Newell had retired. In late 1977 Newell agreed to serve as consultant and scout for the Golden State Warriors and kept the position until 1985, when the club was sold. During that time Newell also established what came to be known as his "Big Man's Camp," which he ran at no charge for various NBA big men. He established it informally in 1976 and maintained contact with the summer program until his death. From 1991 to 2000 Newell worked as a West Coast scout for the Cleveland Cavaliers. He died at age ninety-three of heart failure and was buried in Holy Cross Cemetery in Los Angeles.

In 1978 Newell was elected to the Naismith Memorial Basketball Hall of Fame. His coaching record was 234–123. In 1987 the court at Cal's Harmon Gym was renamed Pete Newell Court.

★

Newell coauthored a number of basketball coaching books. Bruce Jenkins, *A Good Man: The Pete Newell Story* (1999), is a biography of Newell. Obituaries are in the *New York Times*, *Los Angeles Times*, and *San Francisco Chronicle* (all 18 Nov. 2008).

Murry Nelson

NEWMAN, Arnold Abner (*b.* 3 March 1918 in New York City; *d.* 6 June 2006 in New York City), photographer credited with introducing the "environmental portrait."

Arnold Newman, 2002. AP IMAGES

Newman was the second of three sons of Isidore (also rendered as Isidor) Newman and Freda (Perell) Newman. In 1920 the family moved to Atlantic City, New Jersey, where his father, previously a clothing manufacturer, opened a dry-goods store. Not long after the stock market collapse of 1929, the store failed, and his father turned to leasing small hotels. In 1934 the family moved to Miami Beach, where his father could operate hotels year-round. After graduating from Miami Beach High School in 1936, Newman accepted a working scholarship to study art at the University of Miami in nearby Coral Gables. He attended classes during the day and worked in the evening. When his father fell ill after Newman's sophomore year at Miami, he dropped out of school to help support the family.

Newman, who had been interested in painting and photography since his boyhood, took a job with a Philadelphia-based chain of portrait studios. There he shared an apartment with his boyhood friend, Ben Rose. Newman befriended a number of photography students at the Philadelphia Museum School of Industrial Arts (later renamed the Philadelphia College of Art). These friends exposed Newman to an experimental approach to photography that was then being taught at the school by Alexey Brodovitch. Captivated by these new ideas, he spent much of his spare time experimenting with his camera. In December 1939 Newman accepted a job as manager of a portrait studio in West Palm Beach, Florida.

During a June 1941 visit to New York City, Newman was introduced to the photographers Beaumont Newhall and Alfred Stieglitz, who were impressed by Newman's work and encouraged him to continue with his experimental approach to photography. Robert Leslie, owner of the A.D. Gallery, offered to exhibit photographs by Newman and Rose. Newman moved to New York, and not long after the September 1941 gallery exhibit, the city's Museum of Modern Art began purchasing some of Newman's prints.

While still in New York in early 1942, Newman began laying the groundwork for what came to known as environmental portraiture, a movement in photography that he pioneered. Newman's portraits sought to capture the essence of his subjects and their work by careful selection of the background and objects against which each subject was posed. His early portraits in this style focused on fellow artists, including Marcel Duchamp, Piet Mondrian, and Marc Chagall. Many of Newman's portraits show artists standing before notable examples of their work; one of his most famous portraits shows the composer Igor Stravinsky sitting at rest before his grand piano. An important aspect of the environmental approach was to photograph subjects in their own homes or workspaces rather than his studio.

In the fall of 1942 Newman returned to Miami Beach and opened up his own business, Newman Portrait Studio, which he operated for the next four years. He made frequent visits to New York City and continued to take photographic portraits of influential figures in the art world. The Philadelphia Museum of Art in 1945 held an exhibition, Artists Look Like This, of Newman's portraits.

In 1946 Newman moved his business to New York City, opening a portrait studio that he shared with Rose. Brodovitch, who was now art director of *Harper's Bazaar*, was impressed by Newman's work and commissioned him to shoot portraits for the magazine. Soon other magazines, including *Fortune*, *Holiday*, *Life*, and *Look*, were clamoring for his work. His first assignment for *Life* was a portrait of the playwright Eugene O'Neill. *Life* ran four covers by Newman in 1947 alone. In 1948 he relocated his New York City studios to West 67th Street, which would remain his professional headquarters throughout his career. That year he began accepting advertising assignments. Although a number of magazines and advertising agencies sought to sign Newman to an exclusive contract, he chose to remain a freelancer. On 6 March 1949 Newman married Augusta Rubenstein, whom he met in New York City, where she was working for the Haganah, the underground organization that helped to establish the State of Israel. The couple had two sons.

In 1952 Newman won the plum assignment of shooting cover photographs of the presidential candidates Dwight Eisenhower and Adlai Stevenson for *Life*. Over the years he traveled on assignment to shoot portraits of such diverse figures as the artists Pablo Picasso and Albert Giacometti; the Israeli prime minister Yitzhak Rabin; the PLO leader Yasser Arafat; the German industrialist Alfried Krupp; the French president Charles de Gaulle; the Russian composer Igor Stravinsky; and the Spanish dictator Generalissimo Francisco Franco (Newman was the first to photograph Franco out of uniform). Of the portrait of Krupp, the *New York Times* observed that he "is made to look like Mephistopheles incarnate: smirking, his fingers clasped as he confronts the viewer against the background of an assembly line in the Ruhr."

Newman shared his insights into photographic portraiture with colleagues and students. In 1965 he was named an adviser to the photography department of the Israel Museum in Jerusalem. In 1968 he began teaching a master class in photography at Cooper Union in New York City. In the 1970s he was invited to lecture in Venice, and he lectured and exhibited in 1980 at the Rencontres Internationales de la Photographie in Arles, France, with which he was involved for the next several years. In 1986 the San Diego Museum of Photographic Arts organized a retrospective exhibit of his work titled Arnold Newman, Five Decades. Over the next six years the exhibit traveled to major cities in the Americas and around the world.

Newman was the recipient of numerous international awards, including the 1996 Honor Award from the American Society of Media Photographers, which in 2007 established the Arnold Newman Award, given annually to "a contemporary environmental portrait photographer whose imagery is grounded in the traditions and values that Newman pioneered." In 2002 he received the Lifetime Achievement Award from the Professional Photographers of America. He was honored in 2004 by the Royal English Photographic Society, which awarded him its Centenary Gold Medal, as well as an honorary membership. Not long before his death, Newman received the National Arts Club's Gold Medal for Portraiture. His photographs are part of the permanent collections of many of the world's major museums.

Newman died at the age of eighty-eight at Mount Sinai Medical Center in New York City while recovering from a stroke.

Newman was known for his artistic integrity and craftsmanship. With his carefully composed portraits—his best-known photographs were in black and white, though he also took notable color portraits—Newman managed to capture the very essence of his subjects, who include some of the most influential figures of the twentieth century. He pioneered a style and techniques that shaped the character of modern portrait photography.

★

Arnold Newman, *One Mind's Eye: The Portraits and Other Photographs of Arnold Newman* (1974), is a collection of some of his most noted works. Robert A. Sobieszek, *Arnold Newman* (1982), from a series called The Great Photographers, offers a biography, examples of his photographs, and a chronology of his work. Philip Brookman, *Arnold Newman: The Early Works*, (2007) is a collection of photographs taken before Newman achieved recognition for his portraiture. Many of Newman's photographs can be viewed at http://www.arnoldnewmanarchive .com. Obituaries are in the *New York Times* (7 June 2006) and *Guardian* (12 June 2006).

Don Amerman

NEWMAN, Paul Leonard (*b.* 26 January 1925 in Shaker Heights, Ohio; *d.* 26 September 2008 in Westport, Connecticut), iconic motion-picture luminary as well known for his philanthropic activities as for his steely blue eyes and magnetic on-screen presence.

Newman grew up in Shaker Heights, an affluent Cleveland suburb. He was the younger of two sons born to Arthur Newman, the owner of one of the country's largest sporting

Paul Newman. ©JOHN SPRINGER COLLECTION/CORBIS

goods stores, and Theresa (Fetzer) Newman, a housewife who also worked with her husband. His mother, a theater aficionado, encouraged him to pursue acting. While attending Shaker Heights High School, from which he graduated in 1943, he appeared in school theatrical productions and played football, baseball, and basketball.

Having briefly attended Ohio University at Athens, Newman entered the Navy Air Corps with the intention of becoming a pilot. However, after a test revealed that he was colorblind, he became an aircraft radio operator and saw action in the Pacific theater. At war's end, he enrolled in Kenyon College in Gambier, Ohio. He was more interested in drinking and brawling than studying, however, and his barroom fisticuffs got him booted off the Kenyon football team. But he acted in school plays—it was here that he became enamored of the theater—and graduated in 1949.

Newman appeared in summer stock in Williams Bay, Wisconsin, and in repertory in Woodstock, Illinois. On 6 December 1949 he married Jacqueline Witte, an actress; they had three children, two girls and a boy. He abandoned the theater in May 1950, upon the death of his father, and returned to Cleveland to manage the family business. A year-and-a-half later, he asked his brother to replace him and enrolled in the Yale University drama school. He remained in New Haven, Connecticut, through the summer of 1952 and then set out for New York.

Newman's breakthrough came almost immediately. He was cast in a supporting role as a well-heeled Midwesterner in the Broadway production of William Inge's *Picnic* (1953). During the show's fourteen-month run, he understudied the show's lead, Ralph Meeker, and even took over for Meeker for a two-week stint. While appearing in *Picnic*, he took up a study of Method acting with the directors and acting teachers Elia Kazan and Lee Strasberg at their legendary Actors Studio.

By this time, Newman was attracting interest from Hollywood. He initially declined all film offers, preferring to concentrate on a stage career. However, he was not hostile to acting on screen and decided to head to California upon realizing that Hollywood's open door soon might slam shut permanently. He made his screen debut as a toga-clad Greek in *The Silver Chalice* (1954), but the film might easily have sabotaged his career. *The Silver Chalice* earned disastrous reviews, and his wooden performance was equally panned. Years later, when it was set for broadcast on Los Angeles television, Newman purchased a newspaper ad in which he apologized for the film.

Newman soon returned to New York where he won raves on Broadway playing a thug who holds a family hostage in *The Desperate Hours* (1955). Other noteworthy roles came on television: a broken-down prizefighter in the *Playwrights '56* production of Ernest Hemingway's "The Battler" (1955); the title character in Gore Vidal's "The Death of Billy the Kid" (1955), which aired on *Philco*

Television Playhouse; his lone singing role in a musical adaptation of Thornton Wilder's *Our Town* (1955), presented on *Producers' Showcase*; a star pitcher tending to a terminally ill teammate in the *United States Steel Hour* production of Mark Harris's *Bang the Drum Slowly* (1956); and a faded football hero in "The 80-Yard Run" (1958), broadcast on *Playhouse 90*.

But Newman was not done with movies. He redeemed himself with two follow-up features: *Somebody Up There Likes Me* (1956), offering a vibrant performance as the boxer Rocky Graziano; and *The Rack* (1956), playing a GI accused of collaborating with the enemy. Even at this early stage of his career, he refused to exploit his looks to win roles as stock heroes, choosing instead to tackle parts that were more layered.

In 1957 Newman (along with John Kerr and Anthony Perkins) won the Golden Globe Award as the screen's "Most Promising Newcomer—Male." Meanwhile, he divorced Witte and, on 29 January 1958, wed the actress Joanne Woodward, whom he had met while she was an understudy in *Picnic*. Their marriage produced three daughters.

Newman continued to add credits to his filmography, appearing in *The Left Handed Gun* (1958), a screen adaptation of "The Death of Billy the Kid"; William Faulkner's *The Long Hot Summer* (1958)—the first of ten films in which he costarred with Woodward—playing a predatory Southerner; and Tennessee Williams's *Cat on a Hot Tin Roof* (1958), cast as the sexually repressed Brick Pollitt. He then returned to Broadway, playing the drifter-gigolo Chance Wayne in Williams's *Sweet Bird of Youth* (1959).

A series of memorable movie roles came in the 1960s, the decade that fully established Newman as a celluloid superstar. Among the first was one of his all-time best: Fast Eddie Felson, a cocky, self-destructive pool shark, in *The Hustler* (1961). He followed with *Sweet Bird of Youth* (1962), reprising his role as Chance Wayne; *Hemingway's Adventures of a Young Man* (1962), appearing as his character from "The Battler"; *Hud* (1963), portraying an amoral Texan; *Harper* (1966), playing a sardonic private investigator; *Cool Hand Luke* (1967), playing a rebellious convict; and *Butch Cassidy and the Sundance Kid* (1969), famously pairing with Robert Redford as affable turn-of-the-twentieth-century outlaws.

Newman was now at his zenith as a screen idol. In 1963 he placed ninth on Quigley Publications' annual list of Top Ten Money Making Stars. In 1964 and 1966 he earned the Golden Globe's Henrietta Award as "World Film Favorite—Male." He placed third on the Quigley list in 1967, second in 1968, and first in 1969 and 1970. Ever-committed to expanding his talent, he directed his first feature, *Rachel, Rachel* (1968), a low-budget drama starring Woodward as a repressed schoolteacher. A political liberal and fervent anti-Vietnam War activist, he vocally supported Minnesota Senator Eugene McCarthy's unsuccessful bid for the 1968 Democratic Party presidential nomination. He expressed his pride at being included on President Richard Nixon's "enemy's list," and was chosen by President Jimmy Carter as a delegate to a United Nations General Assembly conference on disarmament.

In the late 1960s Newman and his agent, John Foreman, formed the Newman-Foreman Company, a production company. Playing a race-car driver in *Winning* (1969), Newman-Foreman's first project, Newman became enamored of auto racing. He began his racing career in 1972, won a national amateur title four years later, and in 1979 placed second in the Le Mans twenty-four-hour race. He also was co-owner of the Newman/Haas Indy racing team. In the meantime, he directed and starred in *Sometimes a Great Notion* (1971), based on a Ken Kesey novel, and directed *The Effect of Gamma Rays on Man-in-the-Moon Marigolds* (1972), an adaptation of Paul Zindel's play. Although he kept acting, the quality of his screen roles diminished somewhat. Easily his greatest success during the 1970s was the Oscar-winning *The Sting* (1973), in which he played a con artist and was reteamed with Redford. He was an architect in *The Towering Inferno* (1974), an all-star-cast disaster film, and he re-created his *Harper* character in *The Drowning Pool* (1975). That year, he was feted by the Film Society of Lincoln Center.

As he entered his fifties, Newman began reshaping his screen image by playing character parts. Two typical roles of this period were a comical William F. Cody in *Buffalo Bill and the Indians, or Sitting Bull's History Lesson* (1976) and an ill-mannered hockey player-coach in *Slap Shot* (1977). On 28 November 1978 Newman's eldest child and only son, Scott, died of an overdose of Valium and alcohol at the age of twenty-eight. Newman would go on to establish the Scott Newman Center, to publicize the perils of drinking and drugs.

Newman began the 1980s by directing *The Shadow Box* (1980), a made-for-television adaptation of Michael Cristofer's play about hospice patients. He won kudos playing an innocent man maligned by the media in *Absence of Malice* (1981) and a hard-luck, ambulance-chasing lawyer in *The Verdict* (1982). Also in 1982 Newman and his friend, the writer A. E. Hotchner, started Newman's Own, a company that manufactured a line of foods, including cookies, lemonade, wine, spaghetti sauce, organic figs (called Fig Newmans), and, most notably, salad dressing. Profits from the enterprise—which, in his lifetime, reportedly amounted to over $250 million—went directly into his charitable ventures, including the Hole in the Wall Gang Camps, which he and Hotchner founded to provide a free camping respite for seriously ill children and support for their families and health-care providers.

In 1984 Newman was the recipient of the Golden Globe's Cecil B. DeMille Award. Two years later, he earned a Screen Actors Guild Life Achievement Award and an honorary Academy Award "in recognition of his many and memorable and compelling screen performances and for his personal integrity and dedication to his craft." Such an honor usually is afforded to screen legends who have failed to win an in-competition Oscar; he previously had earned six nominations, for *Cat on a Hot Tin Roof*; *The Hustler*; *Hud*; *Cool Hand Luke*; *Absence of Malice*; and *The Verdict*. Nevertheless, a year later, he took home the best actor statuette for *The Color of Money* (1986), in which he reprised the role of Fast Eddie Felson. By that time, he had earned three BAFTA (British Academy of Film and Television Arts) Award nominations and one win (for *The Hustler*) and seven Golden Globe nominations along with one win (for directing *Rachel, Rachel*).

Newman returned to directing with a screen version of Williams's *The Glass Menagerie* (1987). He began the 1990s in fine style, playing a stuffy Midwesterner in *Mr. & Mrs. Bridge* (1990) and a comically corrupt business mogul in *The Hudsucker Proxy* (1994). Without question, his finest late-career role was in *Nobody's Fool* (1994), in which he was cast as a hard-luck denizen of a dreary small town and for which he earned his final best actor Oscar and Golden Globe nominations. That same year, he was the Jean Hersholt Humanitarian Award-winner for his philanthropic endeavors. And in 1995, on his seventieth birthday, he raced at the Daytona speedway in Daytona, Florida.

Newman remained a beloved and respected actor as he entered old age. In 2002 he returned to Broadway one final time, earning his lone Tony Award nomination as the stage manager in a revival of *Our Town*.

One last noteworthy film role came in *Road to Perdition* (2002), in which he played a crusty crime boss and which brought him best supporting actor Oscar, BAFTA, and Golden Globe nominations. He was Emmy-nominated for acting in the television version of *Our Town* (2003)— he previously was nominated for directing *The Shadow Box*—and won an Emmy and Golden Globe for his supporting performance as an aged rapscallion in *Empire Falls* (2005), a television miniseries. At the time, he still was entering races. In 2004 he competed in the Baja 1000. The following year, he raced in the 24 Hours of Daytona. Appropriately, he provided the voice of a 1951 Hudson Hornet in *Cars* (2006), an animated feature. His final screen credit came as the narrator of *The Price of Sugar* (2008), a documentary about the exploitation of Haitian sugarcane workers.

In May 2007 Newman announced his retirement from acting, declaring that he had lost confidence in his capacity to effectively create a characterization. The following June, it was reported that Newman—a former chain smoker—had contracted lung cancer, and had known about the disease for a year and a half. Three months later, he died at his Westport farmhouse. After a private funeral service in Westport, his remains were cremated.

With James Dean, Montgomery Clift, and Marlon Brando, Newman was thrust into the public consciousness during the 1950s, when handsome rebel hero actors were all the rage in American popular culture. The following decade, he ably filled a void created by the death of Dean and the decline of Brando and Clift. He remained a respected film star for decades not only because of his smoldering good looks and legendary blue eyes but also for his nuanced but powerful flair for playing a range of emotionally complex characters. No mere screen icon content to wallow in vanity, he was just as famed for his philanthropic activities as for the scope of his screen career.

★

Newman has been the subject of numerous books. They include Michael Kerbel, *Paul Newman* (1974); Charles Hamblett, *Paul Newman* (1975); Lionel Godfrey, *Paul Newman, Superstar: A Critical Biography* (1979); J. C. Landry, *Paul Newman* (1983); Joe Morella and Edward Z. Epstein, *Paul and Joanne: A Biography of Paul Newman and Joanne Woodward* (1988); Elena Oumano, *Paul Newman* (1989); Stewart Stern, *No Tricks in My Pocket: Paul Newman Directs* (1989); Eric Lax, *Paul Newman: A Biography* (1996); Lawrence J. Quirk, *Paul Newman* (1996); and Daniel O'Brien, *Paul Newman* (2005). With A. E. Hotchner, he authored *Newman's Own Cookbook* and *The Hole in the Wall Gang Cookbook* (both 1998) and *Shameless Exploitation in Pursuit of the Common Good* (2003). Obituaries are in the *New York Times*, *Washington Post*, and *Chicago Tribune* (all 27 Sept. 2008), and the *Los Angeles Times* (28 Sept. 2008).

Rob Edelman

NICHOLAS, Fayard Antonio (*b.* 28 October 1914 in Mobile, Alabama; *d.* 24 January 2006 in Los Angeles, California), the elder of the two tap-dancing Nicholas Brothers.

Born to the musicians Ulysses Nicholas and Viola (Harden) Nicholas, Nicholas was the oldest of three children. His father, a drummer, led a pit band called the Nicholas Collegians. The band performed at the Standard Theatre, the premiere black vaudeville house in Philadelphia, Pennsylvania. As a child Nicholas would sit by his father's drums and watch soft-shoe and tap dancers perform, learning their moves and imitating them later at home. He would teach the routines to his younger brother, Harold, and together they first appeared on stage at the Standard in early 1929. "We looked like kids," Nicholas recalled, "but we danced like men." The brothers proved to be tremendously popular, combining their talents with youthful charm, and their

Fayard Nicholas, 1994. ©ANNIE GRIFFITHS BELT/CORBIS

balletic movement of the "class act" and the athleticism and fast-paced rhythm of the "flash act." Their signature move, the flying split, exemplified this combination, as the brothers would drop down (or leap from an elevated platform) into a full split and then, seemingly without effort, rise up again, using only the strength of their legs. Nicholas, the taller of the two, used his longer limbs to great effect, employing elegant arm and hand gestures and keeping his wrists fluid and his long fingers splayed and reaching, creating what one dance critic called "peculiar poetry."

The brothers made several short films in the early 1930s, beginning with *Pie, Pie Blackbird*, and traveled to Hollywood, California, to make their first feature film together, *Kid Millions*, in 1934. Twentieth Century–Fox signed them to a five-year contract, and Nicholas would thereafter consider Los Angeles his home, although the brothers divided their time between stage and film work. The Nicholas Brothers' film appearances included *Down Argentine Way* (1940). (They were so popular that some newspapers would list the showtimes of their films followed by the time that the Nicholas Brothers' routine started so that moviegoers could arrive just to watch their dance numbers.) They also appeared in *Orchestra Wives* (1942) and *Stormy Weather* (1943), which provided their most famous routine. In the routine, set to Calloway's "Jumpin' Jive," the brothers begin by singing with Calloway before tapping, jumping through the orchestra, and building to a series of flying splits, each brother leapfrogging the other repeatedly down an oversized staircase. The famed dancer Fred Astaire called this sequence "the finest piece of tap dancing ever filmed."

While on tour in Chicago, Nicholas met the DePaul University student Geraldine "Geri" Pate. They married in 1942 and had two sons but would divorce amicably in 1955. At the onset of World War II, Nicholas served as a member of a black auxiliary of the Hollywood Victory Committee before being inducted into the army in July 1943. After completing boot camp in Mississippi, Nicholas was transferred to a United Service Organizations unit in Fort Huachuca, Arizona, and after his service the brothers continued with their film work and their touring schedule. In 1948 they danced with Gene Kelly in *The Pirate* and gave a Royal Command Performance with Ellington's orchestra for England's King George VI; the performance spearheaded a three-year tour of Europe. Upon returning to the United States, the brothers discovered that popular styles were changing. Music was moving from swing to rock, and dance was moving from tap to modern. Because they were less in demand in America, the brothers returned to Europe. In 1958 a homesick Nicholas separated from his brother and returned to California, where he taught at the Los Angeles Inner City Cultural Center and, although age and arthritis made dancing increasingly difficult, performed occasionally as a solo act. In 1967 Nicholas converted to the Baha'i faith. On 17 September 1967 he

act was in great demand. By December 1931 Nicholas's parents had abandoned their own careers to dedicate themselves to managing the careers of their sons, relocating to New York City, in the Sugar Hill section of Harlem. The brothers made a few appearances on the Broadway stage, but the bulk of their work was in Harlem's most popular nightclub, the Cotton Club. Dancing to the music of Duke Ellington or Cab Calloway, the crowd-pleasing Nicholas Brothers frequently closed the shows, a situation that created late nights for the two youngsters. Often they would not get to bed until five or six a.m. and then would sleep until three p.m., when they would study with private tutors. They would return to the club at midnight.

As the brothers matured, their dancing became based less on their precocious talents and more on their superb combination of athleticism and artistry. Nicholas described the Nicholas Brothers' dance style as "classical tap," and their work combined elements of several styles of African-American tap dance. They did excellent close floor work, or pure tap dancing, and brought in the humor of black comedy dance. They had the formal attire and graceful, married the singer Barbara January, with whom he had one child; they had a happy marriage until her death in 1998. Nicholas married a third time, to Katherine Hopkins, in June 2000.

Through the 1960s and 1970s the brothers reunited occasionally to appear on television variety shows, such as *Hollywood Palace* and *The Jacksons*, but Nicholas mostly taught and choreographed while his younger brother pursued a solo career. With a resurgence of interest in tap in the 1980s, Nicholas's services became more in demand. He shared a Tony Award for choreography for *Black and Blue* (1989), one of many awards he earned either alone or with his brother, including an Ebony Lifetime Achievement Award (1989), the Kennedy Center Honors (1991), and a star on the Hollywood Walk of Fame (1994). At the age of ninety-one, Nicholas died at his home of pneumonia and complications from a stroke. He is buried at Pierce Brothers Valhalla Memorial Park in North Hollywood.

One of the greatest tap dancers who ever lived, Nicholas left a legacy not just as a performer but also as an ambassador of his art. Always accessible to interviewers and historians (even giving one interview from his hospital room while recovering from a 1998 stroke), Nicholas appeared in over twenty documentaries, either alone or with his brother, and he frequently spoke at schools and dance festivals, providing inspiration for performers and valuable first-person accounts of life in African-American dance.

★

The definitive biography of the Nicholas Brothers and analysis of their work is Constance Valis Hill, *Brotherhood in Rhythm* (2000). Their role in black Hollywood society is explored in Donald Bogle, *Bright Boulevards, Bold Dreams: The Story of Black Hollywood* (2005). Nicholas also contributed to Rusty E. Frank, *Tap! The Greatest Tap Dance Stars and Their Stories: 1900–1955* (1994), a collection of dancers' oral histories. An obituary is in the *New York Times* (26 Jan. 2006).

Malcolm Womack

O

O

O'BRIEN, (William) Parry, Jr. (*b.* 28 January 1932 in Santa Monica, California; *d.* 21 April 2007 in Santa Clarita, California), world record-setting shot-putter and Olympic champion who revolutionized the sport.

O'Brien was the only child of William Parry O'Brien, a movie studio electrician and former minor league baseball player, and Hazel Agnes (Tobin) O'Brien, a homemaker. O'Brien developed an interest in the shot put at the age of fourteen during a Canadian vacation, where he passed the time tossing large riverbed stones for distance.

O'Brien attended Santa Monica High School, where he excelled in football, as an end on a team that won the state championship. He also participated in track and field as a shot-putter, a discus thrower, and a sprinter. Following graduation, O'Brien attended the University of Southern California (USC) on a football scholarship but lost interest in football after suffering a serious injury. Wilbur Thompson, the 1948 Olympic gold medalist in the shot put, observed O'Brien working out with the USC track team and persuaded him to devote his full attention to shot-putting, a sport for which the self-described "soloist" was well suited.

At six feet, three inches tall and 220 pounds, O'Brien possessed the physique of a "whale," the name given to the weight men of track and field, combined with determination and a willingness to embrace the unorthodox. As a nineteen-year-old sophomore at USC in 1951, O'Brien came in second at a meet in Fresno, California, tossing the shot well below his previous distances. At three o'clock the next morning, his father discovered him putting the shot in a vacant lot behind the house. O'Brien's strong work ethic pushed him to toss the sixteen-pound shot 150 times per day—a feat that left his hands bleeding.

Competing at the National Collegiate Athletic Association meet in Seattle later in 1951, O'Brien fell one inch short of first place and soon after lost at another meet. His put of 55 feet, 9.25 inches earned a victory at his first national Amateur Athletic Union meet in 1951 and ended Jim Fuchs's streak of eighty-eight consecutive victories.

Determined to increase the distance of his throws, O'Brien began to alter the accepted style, which had the putter stand at the rear of the ring, rock back on his right leg, swing his left leg in front for balance, hop across the seven-foot circle, and heave the shot. Instead he turned his right foot and torso toward the back of the circle so that his back faced the direction of the throw. Crouched low over his right leg, he kicked his left leg, starting a 180-degree spin that built up momentum prior to the put. Despite criticism from the track-and-field community, he continued to perfect his new style with a goal of breaking the sixty-foot mark. O'Brien's Phi Kappa Psi fraternity brothers recalled that he chalked a shot put circle in an alley next to the fraternity and practiced into the night. Adjacent to the USC campus sat the Los Angeles Coliseum, site of the 1932 Summer Olympics. Occasionally O'Brien sneaked into the Coliseum after dark to toss his shot and to gather inspiration from the light of the Olympic flame tower.

The mental approach taken by O'Brien also followed the unorthodox. He took a class in Hindu religion and studied yoga, believing that it enhanced his power to concentrate and visualize his throw. Prior to meets he sought energy and motivation by listening to African chants, Afro-Cuban drums, Tibetan bells, and recordings of his own voice. At meets he enjoyed "psyching out" his opponents by walking around with a snarl, slipping into a competitive trance, and sipping on a mysterious liquid. When asked by competitors what was in the drink, he responded, "It's an energy-giving substance." Though the beverage was actually a mixture of honey and water, the other shot-putters wondered what edge O'Brien may have achieved during an era when commercially available energy drinks did not exist.

At the 1952 Summer Olympics in Helsinki, Finland, O'Brien set an Olympic record with a put of 57 feet, 1.5 inches. In 1953 he set a world record with a throw of 59 feet, 0.75 inches. A toss of 60 feet was considered highly unlikely, but O'Brien broke this barrier on 8 May 1954 with a throw of 60 feet, 5.25 inches. This spectacular sports achievement received less acclaim than would have been expected because the Oxford student Roger Bannister had broken the four-minute mile two days earlier. O'Brien dominated shot-putting from July 1952 to June 1956, winning 116 consecutive meets and improving the world record sixteen times. O'Brien won another gold medal at the 1956 Olympics, earned a silver medal in 1960, and finished fourth in 1964 in Tokyo, Japan, where he served as the American flag bearer. As a discus thrower, O'Brien won two collegiate titles.

Over a long track-and-field career, O'Brien won seventeen national Amateur Athletic Union titles in the shot and one in the discus, including nine straight indoor shot titles and five straight outdoor titles. While in Mexico City to participate in the 1955 Pan-American Games, which he won in the shot, O'Brien married Sandra Cordrey, whom he had met at USC. He also won the 1959 Pan-American championship. In 1960 he married Arden, with whom he had two daughters.

O'Brien's image was twice on the cover of *Sports Illustrated* (21 March 1955 and 31 August 1959) and once on the cover of *Time* (3 December 1956). O'Brien won the Sullivan Award as the nation's best amateur athlete in 1959. In 1974 the National Track and Field Association inducted him into its Hall of Fame. He was inducted into the U.S. Olympic Hall of Fame in 1984. In the 1990s O'Brien took up competitive swimming and in 2007 died of a heart attack while swimming at a meet in Santa Clarita.

After retiring from track-and-field competition in 1966, O'Brien worked in civil engineering, banking, and real estate in Southern California. In the world of shot-putting, O'Brien stands out for longevity, determination, and the application of intelligence to physical ability, resulting in the revolutionary throwing technique known as the "O'Brien glide" or the "O'Brien technique."

★

O'Brien tells his own story in Lewis H. Carlson and John J. Fogarty, eds., *Tales of Gold* (1987). Cordner Nelson, *Track and Field: The Great Ones* (1970), Jack Drees and James C. Mullen, *Where Is He Now? Sports Heroes of Yesterday—Revisited* (1975), and *Lincoln Library of Sports Champions*, 8th ed. (2007) include chapters on O'Brien. Obituaries are in the *Los Angeles Times* and *New York Times* (both 23 Apr. 2007).

Paul A. Frisch

O'DAY, Anita (*b.* 18 October 1919 in Chicago, Illinois; *d.* 23 November 2006 in Los Angeles, California), a true giant of jazz who belongs on the upper echelon of jazz singers alongside such iconic figures as Ella Fitzgerald, Sarah Vaughan, and Billie Holiday.

O'Day was born Anita Belle Colton. Her father was a printer, and her mother worked at a meatpacking plant. She was on her own from the age of twelve and worked her entire professional life under the name "O'Day" from the pig Latin for "dough"—meaning money—in hopes of getting some. In addition to working dance marathons during the Great Depression, she supported herself by dancing in nightclubs (in "a scanty costume," she reported many years later in her memoir, *High Times, Hard Times*, 1981). Early on she came into contact with such other showbiz hopefuls as the pop singer Frankie Laine and the

Anita O'Day. **MICHAEL OCHS ARCHIVES/GETTY IMAGES**

comic mastermind Lord Buckley. In her late teens she began absorbing the influences of her key inspirations, Ella Fitzgerald, Billie Holiday, Louis Armstrong, and, most of all, Martha Raye. Although known primarily as a Hollywood comedienne rather than a singer, Raye possessed a hip, scat-inflected, highly musical vocal style that led O'Day to say to herself, as she recalled in 1996, "Now there's *my* singer! I saw her in a movie and she was my favorite. I liked her rhythm, freedom and sound."

O'Day was married and divorced quickly as a young woman to a percussionist named Don Carter. There was another brief marriage later to the golfer Carl Hoff. However, it was the Chicago drummer Gene Krupa who gave O'Day her first important professional break when he signed her as a vocalist with his nationally known big band in 1941. He teamed her with Roy Eldridge in a "daring interracial voice-and-trumpet duet" on one of the best-known songs of the entire swing era, "Let Me Off Uptown." O'Day stayed together with Krupa until he was temporarily put out of a commission on a narcotics possession charge and forced to disband; she rejoined him after he recovered in 1945. In the interim, she sang with the younger, pianist-bandleader Stan Kenton, and she helped give the father of "progressive jazz" (as he was known) one of his most important chart hits, "And Her Tears Flowed Like Wine."

O'Day was somewhat less visible in the postwar, post–big band era, recording a set of sessions for Bob Thiele's Signature label that were better known on LP reissues than they were at the time, as well as a largely forgettable series of pop singles for London Records. She began to reemerge as a major jazz singer in the 1950s after starting to work with the pioneering producer Norman Granz, who was responsible for a series of classic recordings, first singles and 10-inch LPs released on the Mercury and Clef labels and eventually 12-inch LPs on Verve Records.

Between 1952 and 1962 O'Day recorded sixteen masterpiece albums (eventually collected into a boxed set by Mosaic Records), using every conceivable context, from the Oscar Peterson Quartet to Billy May's string orchestra, and repertoire ranging from Broadway's mainstream (albums of classic songs by Cole Porter and Richard Rodgers and Lorenz Hart) to jazz's avant-garde periphery (wordless "instrumental" compositions by Jimmy Giuffre and Johnny Mandel, among others). The Verve albums constitute the sweet spot of her career, upon which the larger part of her overall reputation rests. She also enticed several generations of fans at the Newport Jazz Festival in 1958 with her remarkable reconstruction of the 1920s chestnut "Tea for Two," as documented in the concert film *Jazz on a Summer's Day* (1960).

She was largely absent from the scene in the mid- to late 1960s with the encroaching dominance of rock and roll; she was also preoccupied with ridding herself of a

decade-long heroin habit, although she would continue to drink heavily. O'Day gradually established herself as an elder stateswoman of jazz in the 1970s, 1980s, and 1990s; her pitch was erratic and her enthusiasm declined with her health, but her high rhythmic style never failed her.

In the late 1990s O'Day (who had lived for most of the decade in a trailer park) was nearly derailed for good when a routine hospitalization went wrong and almost put her entirely out of commission. The one good thing to happen from the traumatic experience was that, somehow, she was cured of her dependence on alcohol. There was a major appearance at the JVC Jazz Festival and a new manager, Robbie Cavolina, who began filming concert appearances and interviews with her. Her performances were strong at the start of the millennium, but she quickly declined once again. She was still touring as late as 2004, and she recorded one final album (*Indestructible!*, 2006) under Cavolina's supervision, but by now she could no longer remember lyrics and seemed to be in a permanent daze. By November 2006, when she died of pneumonia in a Los Angeles hospital at age eighty-seven, Cavolina was well on his way to finishing his documentary, *Anita O'Day: The Life of a Jazz Singer* (2007). O'Day is buried in Hollywood Forever Cemetery in Hollywood, California.

O'Day was so intrinsically cool that she did not even have to play it cool. Taking more risks than any high-wire walker, she played fast and loose with the harmonies and rhythms of her source material, deconstructing and reimagining her songs from their foundation elements outward. Her modus operandi was predicated on pure unrepressed spontaneity; everything seemed to happen ad lib, with as little preparation as possible; even her classic arrangements ("Honeysuckle Rose" and "Sweet Georgia Brown") that she kept doing for a half century, seemed completely fresh with spur-of-the-moment invention. Her vocal style stressed rhythm above everything. The tone of her voice was sweet enough, but she would happily sacrifice whatever beauty there might be in an extended legato note for the more strongly swinging momentum of a series of jazzy staccato bursts. Between her dedication to the twin gods of improvisation and swing, O'Day may have been the most firmly committed of all vocalists to the ideals of jazz.

O'Day enjoyed what was easily the longest career of the great jazz singers. In her early days, at the nadir of the Great Depression, she sustained herself through dance marathons; ten years later, at the height of the swing era, she was singing in the same ballrooms with the big bands of Krupa and Kenton; sixty years after that, when the main venue of pop music was no longer ballrooms at all but YouTube and Facebook, O'Day was still going strong.

During most of her career, the music press was quick to point out that O'Day was the foremother of a school of jazz singing that extended principally to her two successors in the Stan Kenton Orchestra, June Christy and Chris

Connor. Yet it became gradually clear that O'Day was much more than that—she was a true giant of jazz who belonged with such iconic figures as Fitzgerald, Vaughan, and Holiday.

If she was too often excluded from the pantheon, it is not only partly because she was the only Caucasian to even be considered for inclusion but also because she was perhaps too idiosyncratic and eccentric to be fully appreciated even by the cast-off characters who populated the jazz world. O'Day was somehow both subtle and over the top, blessed with amazing musical taste, but as her manager Joe Glaser once famously put it, "a million bucks worth of talent, but no class." As appealing as her voice was, her primary strengths were not in the timbre of her voice—she never had a pure, perfect sound like Fitzgerald or Vaughan—but in her amazing timing and rhythmic exhibitionism. As her somewhat younger colleague Ernestine Anderson once observed, "I listen to Anita for speed. She can sing faster than any jazz singer I know and will still make sense."

★

O'Day's memoirs are in *High Times, Hard Times* (1981), written with George Eells. The life and music of O'Day is chronicled in "Anita O'Day: High Times and Hard Times," National Public Radio *Jazz Profiles*, http://www.npr.org/programs/jazzprofiles/archive/o'day_a.html (accessed 18 Dec. 2008) and the documentary film *Anita O'Day: The Life of a Jazz Singer* (2007), directed by Robbie Cavolina and Ian McCrudden. Obituaries are in the *Washington Post* and the *New York Times* (both 24 Nov. 2006) and the *Guardian* (27 Nov. 2006).

Will Friedwald

ODETTA (*b.* 31 December 1930 in Birmingham, Alabama; *d.* 2 December 2008 in New York City), folk singer, known for her powerful renditions of African-American work songs, spirituals, and blues, who supported the civil rights movement and sang at the 1963 March on Washington.

Odetta was born Odetta Holmes, the daughter of Reuben Holmes, a steel mill worker, and Flora (Sanders) Holmes, a housekeeper. Reuben Holmes died when Odetta was a toddler, and her mother then married Zadock Felious; after the marriage Odetta took his last name. In 1937 the family, including Odetta's younger sister, moved to California, where her mother found work as a maid. Traveling by train from Alabama, the Felious family and other African-American passengers were ordered to move into a segregated car; Odetta later described this incident as her

Odetta. ©CHRISTOPHER FELVER/CORBIS

"first wound." The family settled in a multiracial Los Angeles neighborhood. Following the attack on Pearl Harbor, Odetta saw Japanese-American neighbors sent to internment camps—a "second wound."

The Felious home was filled with all kinds of music, from big bands to the Metropolitan Opera to the Grand Ole Opry. The young Odetta banged on the piano, pretending to play, and tried to compose without knowing musical notation. A teacher heard Odetta sing and urged her mother to give her daughter voice lessons. At the age of thirteen, she began studying classical music. She also developed acting skills during four years with the Turnabout Puppet Theatre in Hollywood, California. At first Odetta aspired to be "another Marian Anderson," but she eventually realized that her color made an operatic career unlikely. Soon the young singer discovered her own distinctive voice. In an interview with the *New York Times*, Odetta recalled, "I adored Marian Anderson...but I didn't want to be anybody else." Classical music was "a nice exercise, but it had nothing to do with my life."

After graduating from Belmont High School in 1947, Odetta continued studying music at Los Angeles City College. In 1949 she joined the chorus of the West Coast company of *Finian's Rainbow*. This tour brought her to San

Francisco, where she discovered folk music in the city's bohemian coffeehouses. She described those days to a *New York Times* interviewer: "We would finish our play, we'd go to the joint, and people would sit around playing guitars and singing songs and it felt like home." On her return to Los Angeles, a friend gave her a guitar, which she named "Baby," and taught her three basic chords. Soon Odetta was appearing at political meetings and benefits. Her first professional performances took place in San Francisco nightclubs, including appearances at the hungry i and a long engagement at the Tin Angel. A club manager suggested that she use only her first name; for the rest of her life she was known simply as "Odetta."

Although she sang songs from many musical sources, Odetta's repertoire drew heavily on the African-American tradition. Prison work songs, such as "Water Boy" and "Take This Hammer," became her trademark. In an interview with the Visionary Leadership Project, she said that performing these songs allowed her to express "my concerns, my fury, my hate, my resentment" at the treatment of her people. "I could sing those songs and no one would know where I began and the prisoner left off." In their lyrics she found an affirmation of the daily struggle of African Americans to be free of racial oppression.

With her powerfully expressive voice, her classic African features, and her close-cropped "natural" hair, Odetta created a distinctive stage presence. In 1953 she left the West Coast for an engagement at Chicago's Gate of Horn. She then moved on to New York City for a booking at Manhattan's Blue Angel. Her career blossomed with an assist from Harry Belafonte. An appearance in 1959 on Belafonte's Emmy Award–winning television show *Tonight with Belafonte* gave her national exposure. She sang at the Newport Folk Festival and in concert at Carnegie Hall. In 1960 Odetta was described in *Time* magazine as "the most exciting female folk singer in the U.S."

Odetta's concert tours and many recordings made her a prominent figure in the folk music revival of the late 1950s and early 1960s. Her first solo album, *Odetta Sings Ballads and Blues*, was released in 1956. It featured such signature songs as "Another Man Done Gone," "Jack O' Diamonds," and "Easy Rider." When a young Bob Dylan heard this album in a Minnesota record store, he decided to take up folk music. In a 1978 *Playboy* interview, Dylan remembered, "The first thing that turned me on to folk singing was Odetta." After listening to her songs, "I went out and traded my electric guitar and amplifier for an acoustical guitar, a flattop Gibson." Odetta returned the favor by recording an album of Dylan compositions in 1965. Janis Joplin was another popular singer influenced by Odetta. Joplin "spent much of her adolescence listening to Odetta. . . . Legend has it that Janis discovered she could sing when she mastered an Odetta song."

Odetta's career took off at a time when the civil rights movement was gaining national prominence. Her first solo album included the "Freedom Trilogy," a medley of three freedom songs rooted in the African-American experience: "Oh Freedom," "Come and Go with Me," and "I'm on My Way." During the 1960s Odetta frequently appeared at rallies and benefit concerts for the movement. Martin Luther King, Jr., dubbed her "the queen of American folk music." She performed her trilogy at the 1963 March on Washington and during the 1965 Selma-to-Montgomery March. When asked by an interviewer to describe the role of song in the civil rights struggle, she affirmed, "It was central. It was music from those who went before. The music gave them strength and it gave us strength to carry it on." Singing protest songs may not bring change by itself, she observed, but "it can bring people together." When the historian Douglas Brinkley asked Rosa Parks which songs of the civil rights movement mattered most to her, she replied, "Essentially, all of the songs Odetta sings."

In 1959 Odetta signed with Vanguard Records and over the next decade recorded seventeen albums for Vanguard and other labels. With folk music's waning popularity in the 1970s, Odetta's recording output declined. Although she continued to tour and perform widely, she released only two albums between 1969 and 1986. Odetta enjoyed a revival of her career in last decades of her life. Her 1999 album *Blues Everywhere I Go* was nominated for both a Grammy and a W. C. Handy Award. In 2001 her recording *Looking for a Home*, a collection of fifteen songs popularized by Leadbelly, received another Handy Award nomination. *Gonna Let It Shine*, a live album of holiday songs, garnered another Grammy nomination as the best traditional folk recording of 2007. Despite health problems, Odetta continued performing until a few months before her death.

Odetta also acted in stage productions of *The Crucible* and *The Effect of Gamma Rays on Man-in-the-Moon Marigolds*. She appeared in films as well, including the 1961 movie *Sanctuary*, and the 1974 television feature *The Autobiography of Miss Jane Pittman*.

In 1994 Odetta was named an "elder" at the International Women's Conference in Beijing. President Bill Clinton honored her with the National Medal of the Arts and Humanities in 1999. On meeting Odetta for the first time, Clinton remarked, "I've loved your music since I was a southern boy in Arkansas. . . . You were a major inspiration to me." Odetta received a Lifetime Achievement Award from the International Folk Music Alliance and in 2003 was named a Living Legend by the Library of Congress.

Odetta married and divorced Don Gordon. She had a relationship with Gary Shead. The blues musician Iverson "Louisiana Red" Minter was also a former companion. Odetta adopted two children. She died of heart disease complicated by kidney failure. Her remains were cremated, and her ashes were scattered in New York's Central Park, not far from her Manhattan apartment. A memorial concert drew a capacity crowd of 2,500 to New York's Riverside Church on 24 February 2009. Pete Seeger, Harry Belafonte, and Maya Angelou were among those paying tribute. At the conclusion of the four-hour celebration, the audience rose to its feet in a spirited rendition of Odetta's signature song, "This Little Light of Mine."

In a musical career spanning nearly six decades, Odetta was a powerful voice interpreting the African-American experience in song. She expressed her people's sorrows and aspirations and used her music as a force for social change. Odetta helped to popularize many of the folks songs now considered standards and was a role model for a generation of young folk musicians.

An early profile is in *Time* (5 Dec. 1960). The memorial concert is covered in the *New York Times* (26 Feb. 2009). Obituaries are in the *New York Times* and *Time* (both 3 Dec. 2008).

Paul T. Murray

OERTER, Alfred Adolph ("Al"), Jr. (*b.* 19 August 1936 in Astoria, New York; *d.* 1 October 2007 in Fort Myers, Florida), discus thrower and four-time Olympic gold medalist.

Oerter was born to parents of German and Czech descent, Alfred and Mary (Strup) Oerter. He was raised on Long Island at West Islip. At Sewanhaka High School this physically dominating athlete first used his power as a sprinter and then discovered that his commanding stride made him a better miler. However, at the age of fifteen he threw a discus for the first time and found that his large hands, long arms, and athletic torso made him a natural in this event. Oerter recalled this pivotal moment: "One day . . . an errant discus came skipping in front of me. . . . I threw the discus back. . . . [My] coach came running over and said, . . . 'You're now my discus thrower.'"

Standing six feet, four inches tall and eventually weighing 280 pounds, Oerter had the ability to apply force over a long range of movement and was ideally suited for the discus. In 1954 he set a national high school record of 184 feet, 2 inches. He accepted a scholarship to the University of Kansas, where he came under the tutelage of the master coach Millard "Bill" Easton. Oerter was a successful student-athlete at Kansas, perhaps in part because his scholarship was academic, not athletic, thus allowing him to concentrate on his studies and on discus throwing rather than being pressured to try out for the

Al Oerter, 1960. AP IMAGES

football team. His size, build, and athleticism would have made him an enticing prospect for any college football coach.

In his freshman year at Kansas, Oerter threw 171 feet, 6 inches; a year later he was a Big Seven champion. His early 1956 form was competitive but inconsistent. While he eventually made the U.S. Olympic team for the 1956 Melbourne Olympics, he was not favored to do well. In many respects he was a raw sophomore student, with no international experience, and in his U.S. teammate Fortune Gordien he was up against the world record holder. However, Oerter's first toss was monumental, measuring 184 feet, 10.5 inches. It was a career best for him and won him the gold medal by a margin of five feet.

On his return to University of Kansas, Oerter won outdoor discus Big Seven titles in 1957 and 1958. In 1959, following his college graduation with a business degree, he took a position with the Grumman Aircraft Company. Oerter's athletic success following the Melbourne Olympics is all the more surprising because in 1957 he was in a near-fatal automobile crash.

At the 1960 Rome Olympics, Oerter again demonstrated his tenacity and a singular ability to rise to the occasion. With one throw to go, Oerter's fellow American

Richard "Rink" Babka was leading by fifteen inches. Babka had beaten Oerter at the U.S. trials earlier in 1960. Nevertheless, Oerter did not succumb to the pressure and unleashed yet another personal best of 194 feet, 2 inches to secure his second gold medal.

It was only following his victory at Rome in 1960 that Oerter finally and firmly established himself as a world record holder, with his premier performance being a throw of 206 feet, 4 inches in 1964. In many respects Oerter's display at the 1964 Tokyo Games was as notable for its theater and drama as it was for its athleticism. With less than a week to competition day, Oerter ripped cartilage in his lower ribcage. Oerter "showed up for the Games covered with ice packs and bandages and full of pain killers." Nevertheless, yet again Oerter showed that in the face of both adversity and superior athletic performances by other athletes, he could produce a fantastic result. His fifth throw of 200 feet, 1.5 inches was sufficient to earn him a third Olympic gold.

In 1968 Oerter's third-place finish at the U.S. Olympic Trials won him a ticket to his fourth consecutive Olympics. However, at thirty-two years of age and with a number of health issues—most seriously, chronic back problems—Oerter was not considered a favorite in the event. However, Oerter's mind-set, his ability to focus, and his memories of past Olympic successes all helped him to deliver a series of Olympic record throws, resulting in a heave of 212 feet, 6 inches and his fourth Olympic gold medal.

It is hardly surprising that after four Olympic gold medals, Oerter continued to focus on the challenges of elite competition. In 1980 he threw a personal best of 227 feet, 11 inches and was a reserve for the 1980 team that boycotted the Moscow Olympics. One can only speculate as to how Oerter would have fared in Moscow. The winner of the 1980 Moscow Olympics was Viktor Rashchupkin of the Soviet Union, with a distance of 218 feet, 7 inches.

At age forty-seven Oerter would have participated in the 1984 Olympics but for a leg injury. He gave up track-and-field competition for good in 1987 after "the drug culture had taken over." One of the high points of his life occurred when he completed his last throw at the Eugene trials for the ill-fated 1980 Olympics team. There would be no final gold medal for him, as he finished fourth. However, the crowd gave him a five-minute standing ovation. Oerter noted, "That had never happened to me before."

Oerter married Corinne Benedetto in 1958. They had two daughters before divorcing in 1975. In 1983 Oerter married Cathy Jo Campbell.

Oerter worked for Grumman as a computer specialist for more than twenty-five years. In his later years he was a motivational speaker with sponsorship from Reebok. He was inducted as a founding member into the National Track and Field Hall of Fame in 1974 and was elected to the U.S. Olympic Hall of Fame in 1983. Oerter died of heart failure.

Although Oerter is revered as an iconic athlete—at the time of his death only Carl Lewis had equaled his four consecutive Olympic gold medals—his enduring legacy may be more about defying the societal constraints regarding age and vocation. He competed well into middle age, and then, when athletics lost its allure, he immersed himself in a program called Art of the Olympians, a unique vehicle to give fellow Olympians an outlet for their artistic visions. He was a significant fund-raiser and public relations spokesperson for this organization. Oerter developed an end-of-life passion for abstract art, and his canvases are all about light, bright colors, space, and surreal shapes. Sport, sinew, and gold medals are nowhere to be seen.

★

Bud Greenspan, *100 Greatest Moments in Olympic History* (1995), offers information on Oerter's athletic achievements. Obituaries are in the *New York Times* (2 Oct. 2007) and the *Independent* (4 Oct. 2007).

Scott A. G. M. Crawford

OLDS, Robin (*b*. 14 July 1922 in Honolulu, Hawaii; *d*. 14 June 2007 in Steamboat Springs, Colorado), U.S. Air Force (USAF) general officer and fighter pilot who was the only fighter ace to shoot down aircraft in both World War II and the Vietnam War.

Olds was the son of Robert Olds, a career army pilot who attained the rank of major general, and Eloise Olds, a homemaker; Olds's mother died when Olds was four. He had a brother who died in childhood and two half brothers. His love of flight began early, when his father, a World War I veteran, took him up in an open cockpit biplane. Graduating from Hampton High School in Hampton, Virginia, in 1939, Olds attended Millard Preparatory School in Washington, D.C., and then entered the U.S. Military Academy at West Point in 1940. While he was there, his warrior spirit, confidence, and leadership ability became evident, particularly on the football field. Playing both offensive and defensive tackle, Olds earned All-America status in 1942; he was inducted into the College Football Hall of Fame in 1985. With war raging, Olds graduated from West Point in June 1943, a year early, earning his pilot's wings at the same time. Olds completed fighter training in Glendale, California, and was assigned to the 434th Fighter Squadron in Lomita, California. His father, who died prematurely in late 1943, was an aide to and a disciple of the former Air Service chief Billy Mitchell. As such he instilled in the younger Olds the importance of constant innovation for the effective use of airpower.

Olds and his unit arrived in mid-May 1944 at Royal Air Force (RAF) Wattisham, an RAF station in Suffolk, England. In a P-38, the first of many aircraft that Olds nicknamed "Scat," Olds flew over beachheads, escorted bombers, and conducted fighter sweeps in advance of D-Day and the invasion of Normandy. His prowess for aerial combat became evident when he shot down five German fighters in August 1944. Olds later shot down seven more fighters while flying the P-51. He also supported the invasion of Holland and participated in the Battle of the Bulge, tallying 107 total combat missions by the war's end. In March 1945, at the age of twenty-two, the talented Olds was given command of the 434th. Olds was rebuffed, however, when he insisted that a small number of P-51s could do more damage to a target requiring precision attack than could a 1,000-ship multiengine bomber armada; heavy bombers were considered the raison d'être for an independent postwar air force, and Olds's idea was considered "heresy." Such doctrine, especially the USAF strategic nuclear role, remained supreme throughout the cold war.

Willingness to go against established protocols led to conflict with superiors and increasing frustration and flamboyance for Olds. Nevertheless, Olds continued to receive prestigious assignments. In early 1946 he joined the USAF's first jet squadron, flying P-80s at March Field, California; he then helped form the first jet aerobatics team, the precursor to the renowned Thunderbirds. Olds took second place in the 1946 Thompson Trophy jet aircraft contest at the National Air Races in Cleveland. Superior jet piloting skills led to selection as an exchange officer with RAF No. 1 Squadron in 1948. Flying the Gloster Meteor, Olds became the first non-Commonwealth pilot honored with command of an RAF squadron. Olds married the actress Ella Raines early in February 1947; they had two daughters before divorcing in 1976. In 1978 Olds married Morgan Barnett, but they divorced after fifteen years.

Olds took command of the Seventy-first Fighter Squadron, an air defense unit at Pittsburgh, but was repeatedly refused the opportunity to fly and fight in Korea. Promoted to colonel in 1953, Olds served staff assignments before returning to flying status in Germany in 1955. The following year he took command of the Eighty-sixth Fighter-Interceptor Group and then served at the Pentagon from 1958 to 1962. Olds graduated from the National War College in 1963 and took command of the Eighty-first Tactical Fighter Wing (TFW) at RAF Bentwaters but was removed because he formed an unauthorized F-101 aerial demonstration team. Olds was transferred to South Carolina and then trained to fly the F-4 Phantom. In September 1966 he took command of the lethargic Eighth TFW at Ubon Air Base, Thailand, as the war in Southeast Asia escalated.

At the Eighth TFW, Olds reunited with his friend Daniel "Chappie" James, Jr., who would become the first African-American four-star USAF general. Because of their work hard–play hard ethos and aggressive "take it to the bad guys" approach to aerial warfare, the two became known as "Blackman and Robin," a play on the short-lived but popular contemporary television show *Batman and Robin*. Olds also grew a large, nonregulation mustache as an act of defiance that won the adoration of subordinates and the ire of superiors.

Ever the tactician, Olds devised Operation Bolo, an effort to ambush North Vietnamese MiG fighters, who had increased attacks against the less agile F-105 fighter-bombers. In early January 1967, using F-105 call signs, code words, and flight profiles, Olds led his F-4 air superiority fighters over North Vietnam. The unsuspecting MiGs fell for the trap, with Olds, flying *Scat XXVII*, destroying one of the seven jets his unit shot down that day; it was the most successful American air battle of the war. In May 1967 Olds downed three more enemy fighters. Near the end of his Southeast Asia tour, Olds received the Air Force Cross, a valor award second only to the Medal of Honor, for his leadership in a mission against Hanoi. Having flown 152 combat missions, Olds returned to the United States to serve as USAF Academy commandant of cadets. He was promoted to brigadier general, but his maverick attitude prevented further advancement. Serving in aerospace safety roles near the end of the Vietnam War, Olds was sent to Southeast Asia to discover why USAF fighter losses had mounted. His report was blunt, and when his offer to fix the problem by returning to operational flying at a reduced rank was rebuffed, Olds retired on 1 June 1973. Until his death he campaigned for the advancement of tactical airpower. In 2001 Olds was inducted into the National Aviation Hall of Fame. Olds suffered from advanced prostate cancer and died of congestive heart failure. He is buried at the USAF Academy.

Olds believed that effective tactical airpower was an important instrument of national policy. Frustrated by the USAF's cold war focus on nuclear warfare, Olds sacrificed career advancement by remaining an outspoken advocate for enhanced fighter capabilities and better pilot training. In the end his vision was vindicated by the stunning success of the 1991 Desert Storm air campaign over Iraq.

★

The Air Force Historical Research Center, Maxwell Air Force Base, Alabama, has official interviews and records. For additional information, see John Darrell Sherwood, *Fast Movers: Jet Pilots and the Vietnam Experience* (2000), and Walter Boyne,

"The Robin Olds Factor," *Air Force Magazine* 91, no. 6 (June 2008): 44–48. Obituaries are in *Steamboat Pilot and Today* (16 June 2007) and the *New York Times* (20 June 2007).

William E. Fischer, Jr.

OLITSKI, Jules (*b.* 27 March 1922 in Snovsk, Russia; *d.* 4 February 2007 in New York City), painter who rose to prominence in the 1960s with his abstract color-field paintings.

Olitski was born Jevel Demikovsky in Ukraine, then part of the Soviet Union, at a time of great turmoil in the aftermath of the Russian revolution. He never knew his father, a government official who was executed by the Communists a few months before his birth. His mother, Anna (Zarnitsky) Demikovsky, and grandmother immigrated with him to the United States in August 1923, settling in Brooklyn, New York. In 1926 his mother married Hyman Olitsky, a widower with two sons. Olitski graduated from Samuel J. Tilden High School in 1940. Although his family did not encourage his interest in art, Olitski won a scholarship to study drawing at the Pratt Institute in 1939 and an art prize at graduation.

From 1939 to 1942 Olitski studied drawing and painting at the National Academy of Design; from 1940 to 1942 he studied sculpture at the Beaux-Arts Institute of Design. In 1942, shortly after he gained U.S. citizenship (taking his stepfather's surname), he was drafted into the U.S. Army. He studied at Purdue University from 1942 to 1945; sometime before his discharge in 1945, he married Gladys Katz, with whom he had a daughter. The couple divorced in 1951.

Olitski traveled to Paris in 1949 to study at art schools on the GI Bill. For the next two years he began the process of defining himself as a modernist through formal and informal study. He admired the paintings of Jean Dubuffet and was fascinated by the ideas of the noted American critic Clement Greenberg, who later became a champion of Olitski's work. He also met other young artists and participated in his first group exhibition, Americans in Paris, held in December 1950 at the Hacker Gallery, New York, with paintings that a critic described as having "a savage vigor." He followed with his first solo show of semiabstract paintings at Galerie Huit in Paris in 1951.

He returned to New York in 1951, earning a BA (1952) and an MA (1955) in art education from New York University. He taught at the State University College at New Paltz from 1954 to 1955 and the following year joined the faculty at C. W. Post College of Long Island University, in Greenvale, New York, where he eventually became the chairman of the Fine Arts Division. In 1956

Olitski married his second wife, Andrea Hill Pierce, with whom he had a second daughter; the couple divorced in 1973. In 1963 he joined the faculty at Bennington College, in Bennington, Vermont, remaining there until 1967.

Olitski met Greenberg for the first time in 1958, when the critic saw his solo show at the Iolas Gallery in New York. (In the exhibition catalog, his name was misspelled with an "i" at the end, and from then on Olitski used that spelling.) The critic admired the thickly painted, textured canvases, and with Greenberg's influence Olitski gained representation by the gallery French & Co. His paintings were presented there that December in a group show that included works by David Smith, Morris Louis, and Kenneth Noland, artists who became important colleagues.

In contrast to his earlier style of applying paint to create thick surface textures, in 1960 Olitski adopted the technique of staining favored by Noland and Louis, among others. In these paintings large areas of bare canvas are surrounded by thin applications of color pushed to the edges of the canvas. He began to pour the paint directly onto the canvas rather than apply it with a brush. He showed seventeen of these stain paintings at French & Co. in spring 1961 and more such paintings that October at Poindexter Gallery. From 1961 to 1964 Olitski experimented widely with this technique, from using water-based acrylics to thinned Magna acrylic applied with household items. His compositions at this time featured a central core with bands of concentric color moving outward toward the boundaries of the image.

In spring 1964, during a conversation with the sculptor Anthony Caro and Noland, Olitski spoke of his desire to spray paint into the air and somehow have it remain as such on the canvas surface. He sprayed his first painting with a spray gun he had rented from a hardware store. By the spring of 1965 he was using an industrial spray gun powered by an electric air compressor to spray directly onto a canvas spread out on the floor. He began to use guns that had a number of different nozzles for greater control and switched to water-based Aqua-tec acrylics. These spray paintings have delicate surfaces of airy color, with only a few brushstrokes at the edges or corners of the canvas.

The stark simplicity and immediacy of color in these works, as well as the unusual method of paint application, catapulted Olitski to fame. His work was included in Greenberg's 1964 influential traveling exhibition, Post-Painterly Abstraction, and then in the art critic Michael Fried's seminal 1965 exhibition Three American Painters: Noland, Olitski, and Stella. In 1966 Olitski, along with Helen Frankenthaler, Roy Lichtenstein, and Ellsworth Kelly, represented the United States in the XXIII International Biennale Exhibition of Art in Venice. In 1967 he received his first solo museum exhibition at the Corcoran Gallery of Art in Washington, D.C., winning the Corcoran Gold Medal and the William A. C. Clark Prize. "I think of painting as possessed by a structure," stated Olitski in his Biennial statement, "but in a structure born of the flow of color feeling."

In 1966 Olitski moved to New York City, finally able to support himself through his art. In 1969 he became the third living artist to have a one-man exhibition at the Metropolitan Museum of Art; the show, which included his experiments with metal sculptures, was not well received critically. In 1973 he had his first retrospective at the Museum of Fine Arts in Boston, which included sculptures as well as paintings. The critics panned the show, finding his work too pretty and lightweight.

In 1973 Olitski purchased a home on an island on Lake Winnipesaukee in New Hampshire, where he continued to live until the end of his life. He painted in his island studio from late spring through late fall and spent winters in his second home in the Florida Keys. On 29 February 1980 Olitski married Joan Fourgis Gorby, known as Kristina.

Although he never regained much critical attention from the New York art world, Olitski maintained his representation by major New York galleries, and collectors continued to buy his work. An artist with a strong work ethic, he continued to create art in a variety of media throughout his life. He died at eighty-four of complications from prostate cancer at the Memorial Sloan-Kettering Cancer Center in New York City. He is buried in the Jewish Community/Congregation Shir Heharim Cemetery in Brattleboro, Vermont.

Kenworth Moffett, *Jules Olitski*, is the exhibition catalog for the retrospective at the Museum of Fine Arts, Boston (1973). Moffett, *Jules Olitski* (1981), is a monograph. Michael Fried, "Three American Painters: Stella, Noland, Olitski," an influential essay written for the 1965 exhibition organized for the Fogg Art Museum at Harvard University, is reprinted in Fried, *Art and Objecthood: Essays and Reviews* (1998). *With Love and Disregard: New Paintings by Jules Olitski—An Eightieth Birthday Celebration* (2002) and *Jules Olitski: The Late Paintings—A Celebration* (2008) feature the artist's later works. Obituaries are in the *New York Times* (5 Feb. 2007) and *Washington Post* (7 Feb. 2007).

Leigh Bullard Weisblat

OLSEN, Tillie Lerner (*b.* 14 January 1912 or 1913 in Omaha, Nebraska; *d.* 1 January 2007 in Oakland, California), socialist activist and proletarian writer who, despite a meager literary output, exerted an important influence on the development of feminine consciousness and as a chronicler of the working class.

Tillie Olsen. ©CHRISTOPHER FELVER/CORBIS

Olsen was born in either 1912 or 1913; no birth certificate exists. She was the second of six children born to the Russian-Jewish immigrants Samuel Lerner and Ida (Beber) Lerner, who settled in Nebraska after fleeing to the United States following the unsuccessful 1905 Russian rebellion against the czar. Samuel Lerner took jobs ranging from packinghouse worker to candy maker. His socialist activities, which caused him to be blacklisted in the early 1920s, left a deep impression on his young daughter. As a youngster, Olsen, afflicted often with childhood illnesses and very shy because of a stutter, attended Lake School through the eighth grade and took care of her brothers and sisters at home.

In 1925 Olsen entered Omaha Central High School and was dismayed by the social distinctions she found there. During her high school years she read voraciously and spent her small amounts of free time at the Omaha Carnegie Library. When she was fifteen Olsen bought some ten cent books containing a serialized story, *Life in the Iron Mills* by Rebecca Harding Davis. Inspired by this work, Olsen took to heart its twin messages: "Literature can be made out of the lives of despised people" and "You, too, must write."

Because of Depression-era difficulties, Olsen was forced to leave high school after the eleventh grade in 1929 to help support her family. During a series of low-skilled, low-paying jobs, such as pork trimmer in a meatpacking plant, she formed friendships with some Communist female co-workers. She joined the Young Communist League in 1931 and was sent to the Communist Party School in Kansas City, Kansas. She found employment in a tie factory, where she contracted pleurisy. Olsen's involvement in a strike in Kansas City landed her in jail, but by the age of eighteen she had found her literary themes, the horror and reality of poverty-stricken, working-class life and the hidden potential inside each human being.

In jail Olsen became ill with incipient tuberculosis, and in 1932 the Communist Party sent her back to Omaha and then to Faribault, Minnesota, to recuperate. During her recovery, Olsen began her only novel, *Yonnondio: From the Thirties*, which she abandoned in 1937 and did not publish until 1974. At the end of 1932 in Minneapolis, she gave birth out of wedlock to a daughter. In the spring of the following year she left Minnesota for California, committed to being a political activist, a writer, and a mother.

In late 1933 Olsen and her daughter settled in San Francisco, where Olsen gained employment with the *Waterfront Worker*, a union publication. The same year, she met Jack Olsen, a fellow Communist activist, with whom she was arrested on a vagrancy charge on 5 July 1934, following a violent clash during the San Francisco Maritime Strike. During this period of ardent activism appeared her first published works, two poems ("I Want You Women Up North to Know" and "There Is a Lesson"), a short story ("The Iron Throat"), and two essays. "The Iron Throat," which later was incorporated into *Yonnondio*, gained a great deal of attention among literary critics. Editors and literary agents took up Olsen's cause, and she was eventually released from jail. In 1935 she was even invited to speak at the American Writers Congress in New York City, where she joined more famous celebrities of the left, including the writers Richard Wright and Theodore Dreiser.

In 1936 Olsen began living with Jack Olsen, and by 1937 she was pregnant with her second child, born in 1938. In 1943, after the birth of her third child, she married Jack Olsen in San Francisco before he was drafted. While he was away, Olsen raised three daughters and still found time to support activist causes. While her children were in school, Olsen was president of the Parent Teacher Association and brought to court the case that established teachers' tenure in California. She also helped to form a separate women's division of the International Longshoremen's and Warehousemen's Union. In the next few years Olsen continued to organize unions. Another child was born in 1948.

In 1953 Jack Olsen was subpoenaed to appear before the House Un-American Activities Committee and was subsequently blacklisted as a member of the Communist Party, thereby losing his union job. He eventually found employment as a printer's apprentice while his wife was fired from every job she undertook because of her "subversive" activities.

In 1954 Olsen began to write in earnest. She took an evening creative writing class at San Francisco State College, where she received encouragement. She never completed the course but was so confident in her ability that she applied for the prestigious Wallace Stegner Creative Writing Fellowship at Stanford University. She won the fellowship and attended Stanford in 1955–1956, sharing the writing workshop table with such notables as James Baldwin, Bernard Malamud, Flannery O'Connor, and Katherine Ann Porter. Prompted by a Ford Foundation grant in literature in 1959, Olsen gained more time for writing, completing the short story "Tell Me a Riddle," which won the O. Henry Award in 1961 for the best American short story. It became one of four stories that comprised *Tell Me a Riddle* (1961), the collection upon which much of Olsen's reputation rests, and was made into a well-regarded motion picture in 1980.

In addition to writing, Olsen served as a teacher in many places: visiting professor and writer in residence at Amherst College in Massachusetts (1969), visiting professor at Stanford (1972), writer in residence at the Massachusetts Institute of Technology (1973), and distinguished visiting professor at the University of Massachusetts, Boston (1973–1974). She also received many awards, including the American Academy and National Institute of Arts and Letters Award for distinguished contribution to American letters (1975), followed by a Guggenheim Fellowship (1975). In 1977 she became a Copeland Fellow at Amherst. In 1980 she traveled as an international visiting scholar to Norway and was named Radcliffe's centennial lecturer. Olsen was named Bunting Fellow at Radcliffe College in 1985. She served as Hill Visiting Professor at the University of Minnesota in 1986 and as Gund Professor at Kenyon College, Ohio, in 1987.

When Jack Olsen died on 26 February 1989, Olsen was being feted with still more honors. In 1989 she was honored at a special session of the Modern Language Association. She also received the Mari Sandoz Award from the Nebraska Library Association in 1991 and the Rea Award for the Short Story in 1994.

In 1998 Olsen moved from San Francisco to Berkeley, California. Olsen died at age ninety-four at Kaiser Oakland Medical Center, following a long bout with Alzheimer's disease. Her body was cremated and her ashes interred in Fernwood Cemetery, Mill Valley, California.

Olsen published only a small volume of material: a collection of short stories (*Tell Me a Riddle*), a book of essays and speeches given between 1962 and 1972 (*Silences*; 1978), and one unfinished novel (*Yonnondio*). Olsen wrote about working-class families, their struggles, and their hopes for fulfillment. She focused especially on the relationship between mothers and their children. In all of her works Olsen tries to show how, through individual and community strength, human dignity gives rise to hope. The writer Alice Walker described Olsen as "a writer of such generosity and honesty she literally saves our lives."

★

Olsen's papers are archived at Stanford University in its Special Collections at the Green Library and in the Berg Collection in the New York Public Library. The foremost source for information about Olsen's life and career is Constance Coiner, *Better Red: The Writing and Resistance of Tillie Olsen and Meridel Le Sueur* (1995). Much autobiographical material may be found in an extensive interview with Anne-Marie Cusac in *Progressive* (Nov. 1999). Obituaries are in the *New York Times* (3 Jan. 2007) and *Washington Post* (4 Jan. 2007).

John J. Byrne

O'NEIL, John Jordan ("Buck"), Jr. (*b.* 13 November 1911 in Carrabelle, Florida; *d.* 6 October 2006 in Kansas City, Missouri), baseball player, manager, coach, and scout who was a star in the Negro American League during the 1940s and who was the first African-American coach in Major League Baseball after the elimination of racial segregation in the sport.

O'Neil, a grandson of slaves, was the second of three children born to John Jordan O'Neil, Sr., a sawmill machine operator, and Louella O'Neil, a cook and homemaker. In 1923 the family, which included his older sister and younger brother, moved to Sarasota, Florida, where his father was a foreman in the celery fields and his mother secured employment as a cook for the Ringling family of the Ringling Brothers Circus. Eventually his parents opened their own restaurant, aptly named O'Neil's.

O'Neil attended Sarasota's segregated African-American grade school, where he learned the value of education from Principal Emma Booker. Young John, who developed an early love of baseball from his father, worked in the celery fields until he voiced a desire to play professional baseball. At twelve years old O'Neil played semiprofessional baseball with the Sarasota Tigers, traveling around Florida. In 1924, with his father's approval, he enrolled in secondary school at Edward G. Waters College in Jacksonville, Florida, where he earned a baseball and football scholarship and played baseball under coach Ox Clemons.

After receiving his high school diploma and completing two years of college at Edward G. Waters College (the institution had curriculums for both high school and college), O'Neil left school in 1930 and continued to pursue his baseball career, playing with semiprofessional

Buck O'Neil, 1942. **NATIONAL BASEBALL HALL OF FAME LIBRARY/MLB PHOTOS/GETTY IMAGES**

teams until he joined a professional baseball team, the Miami Giants, in 1934. The same year he gained his lifetime nickname "Buck" from a co-owner of the team, Buck O'Neal. For the next two years (1935–1936) he played with the New York Tigers and the Shreveport Acme Giants before signing with the Memphis Red Sox of the Negro American League (NAL) in 1937. Later that season he moved to the Zulu Cannibal Giants, a traveling team that offered more money than traditional professional teams.

In 1938 O'Neil joined the Kansas City Monarchs, the premier team of the NAL. He remained with the franchise through 1955, with time out (1943–1945) for service in a U.S. Navy construction battalion during World War II. Before O'Neil entered the military, the Monarchs won four consecutive NAL pennants (1939–1942), with O'Neil anchoring first base. In 1942 he made his first of three appearances on the West team (1942, 1943, 1949) in the East-West All-Star Classic, and he culminated the season with a batting average of .353. Also in 1942 he led the Monarchs to a four-game sweep of the vaunted Negro National League champion Homestead Grays (which featured the power tandem of Josh Gibson and Buck Leonard) in the first Negro World Series played between the two leagues.

O'Neil returned home after World War II, and on 17 January 1946 he married Ora Lee Owen in Memphis, Tennessee. In the spring he resumed his place in the Monarchs lineup and won the 1946 NAL batting title. O'Neil also helped the Monarchs win another pennant before the team lost a hard-fought seven-game Negro World Series to the Newark Eagles. Following the series, O'Neil joined the American baseball player Satchel Paige's All-Stars and barnstormed coast-to-coast against the American baseball player Bob Feller's All-Stars in a fall exhibition tour. After the exhibition tour, O'Neil made his first excursion to Latin America, where he played with Almendares in the 1946–1947 Cuban winter baseball league. He later played with Obregón in the 1951 Mexican winter baseball league.

In 1948 O'Neil became a player-manager for the Monarchs and remained in that capacity until leaving the franchise. In his first season as manager, the Monarchs won the split season's second-half title before dropping a seven-game play-off to the Birmingham Black Barons for the NAL pennant. Subsequently, he guided the Monarchs to three additional NAL titles, including his final season with the Monarchs (1955), and managed the West squad in four straight East-West All-Star games (1951–1954). During his tenure as manager of the Monarchs, O'Neil was a father figure to the young players under his charge.

After the color line in baseball was eliminated with Jackie Robinson's entrance into Major League Baseball in 1947, the quality of the NAL declined with the exodus of many young African-American players to the major leagues. O'Neil was not offered an opportunity to make the transition due to his older age, but he did pioneer the entrance of African Americans into the major leagues as scouts and coaches. In 1956 he joined the Chicago Cubs as a scout, and in 1962 with the Cubs he became the major leagues' first African-American coach.

In his latter years, as a leading advocate for preserving the history of the Negro Leagues, O'Neil was a visible personage of racial dignity in this role. He was appointed to the National Baseball Hall of Fame's Veterans Committee in 1981 and served until 2000. In 1988 O'Neil became a special scout for the Kansas City Royals in his adopted hometown, where he and his wife of fifty years lived until her death in 1996. O'Neil and his wife had no children. His charismatic appearance in the director Ken Burns's 1994 award-winning television series *Baseball* for the Public Broadcasting Service thrust him to national prominence, and his presence at a plethora of venues fostered pride in African Americans and enhanced white Americans' awareness of this part of baseball history. O'Neil was a founding father of the Negro Leagues Baseball Museum in Kansas City and served as chairman of the board from its inception in 1990 until his death from heart failure at the age of ninety-four. He is interred in Forest Hills Cemetery in Kansas City, Missouri.

The eloquent and esteemed baseball ambassador was honored by the National Baseball Hall of Fame at Cooperstown, New York, in 2008, when he posthumously became the first recipient of the Buck O'Neil Lifetime Achievement Award. Also, a life-size bronze statue of O'Neil was unveiled during the same induction ceremony. At the ceremony, baseball commissioner Bud Selig stated, "He's in Cooperstown where he belongs."

O'Neil's autobiography *I Was Right on Time: My Journey from the Negro Leagues to the Majors* (1996), written with Steve Wulf and David Conrads, is an excellent source of information. Another valuable work is Joe Posnanski, *The Soul of Baseball: A Road Trip Through Buck O'Neil's America* (2007), written about the last year of O'Neil's life, which provides insight into his values and character. Several books include profiles of O'Neil, including James A. Riley, *The Biographical Encyclopedia of the Negro Baseball Leagues* (1994), and Brent Kelley, *The Negro Leagues Revisited: Conversations with 66 More Baseball Heroes* (2000). Obituaries are in the *New York Times* (7 Oct. 2006), *Newsweek* (16 Oct. 2006), and *Jet* (23 Oct. 2006).

James A. Riley

OWENS, Alvis Edgar ("Buck"), Jr. (*b.* 12 August 1929 in Sherman, Texas; *d.* 25 March 2006 in Bakersfield, California), country singer and songwriter and cohost of the television variety show *Hee Haw.*

Owens was the second of four children born to struggling sharecroppers Alvis Edgar Owens, Sr., and Maicie (Azel) Owens. Early on, he adopted his nickname, "Buck," from the family mule. During the 1930s dust storms brought on by severe drought and poor land management rendered farming nearly impossible in the northern Texas region where the Owens family lived. In 1937 ten members of the Owens clan piled into the family's 1933 Ford sedan and headed west in search of a better life. The trailer hitch broke in Arizona, so the family settled near Mesa and went back to farming, laboring on various fruit and dairy farms in Arizona, and also traveling to California's San Joaquin Valley to pick crops. Music provided an escape from the reality of the family's difficult existence. Owens's father played the harmonica, his mother played the piano in church, and two uncles were handy with the guitar.

Owens first played the mandolin and took up guitar as a teen. His mother showed him a couple of chords and he learned the rest on his own. He spent his summer vacations toiling in the hot, dusty fields and became determined to

Buck Owens, 1970. CBS/LANDOV

find another path through life. By the time he was a teenager, Owens knew he would rather pick guitar indoors than pick crops outdoors. As he later put it in an interview: "I hated being poor. . . . I remember as a little kid saying, 'Boy, when I get big I ain't never gonna be poor again.'"

As a teen, Owens teamed with the guitarist Theryl Ray Britten and began performing at local honky-tonks and roadhouses, much to his parents' dismay. They did not like their young son hanging out where people were drinking. In 1945 the duo snagged a spot on a local radio station with a fifteen-minute show called *Buck and Britt*. In ninth grade Owens dropped out of school to work and play music full time. To make a living he delivered messages for Western Union, washed cars, and loaded and unloaded fruit. In time, Owens joined a local band called Mac's Skillet Lickers. On 13 January 1948 he married Bonnie Campbell, the group's singer. They had two sons before divorcing in 1953. To support his family, Owens hauled produce by day and played music at night. Married and divorced a total of four times, Owens had a third son with his second wife, Phyllis, whom he divorced in 1972. He had a marriage of a few days to Janna Jae Greif in 1977. He married Jennifer Smith on 21 June 1979.

In 1951 Owens relocated to Bakersfield—home of an emerging honky-tonk scene—to see if he could make his mark on the music world. In Bakersfield Owens made a

name for himself as a guitarist with the bandleader Bill Woods and his Orange Blossom Playboys. Under Woods's direction, Owens took on vocals. Eventually, Owens gained a local following and formed his own group, Buck Owens and the Schoolhouse Playboys.

In the mid-1950s Owens began commuting to Los Angeles to work as a studio musician for Capitol Records. During this time he contributed to songs recorded by Gene Vincent, Stan Freberg, Del Reeves, and Wanda Jackson. In 1957 Capitol Records finally offered Owens a solo deal. Two years later he made his first waves with a song called "Second Fiddle," which peaked at number twenty-four on the *Billboard* country chart. In 1959 he followed with "Under Your Spell Again," which hit number four.

Around 1962 Owens formed another band, the Buckaroos, which included a little-known bass player named Merle Haggard, who went on to become a country music legend in his own right. Fronting the Buckaroos, Owens became one of the most famous country music acts of all time and is credited—along with Haggard and Tommy Collins—for developing the "Bakersfield Sound," a flinty, hard-nosed style of country that included a gritty, steel pedal guitar, driving drum beats, and tight vocal harmonies. This style of country music was in direct contrast to the smooth and highly polished, string-laden tracks most Nashville artists were producing at the time.

Between 1959 and 1974 Owens released forty-five songs that made the country Top Ten; twenty of them hit number one. He wrote most of his own songs and during the 1960s sold more than one million records a year. His long streak of number-one hits included "Act Naturally" (1963), later recorded by the Beatles; "Love's Gonna Live Here" (1963); "I've Got a Tiger by the Tail" (1964), later recorded by Ray Charles; "Buckaroo" (1965); and "Waitin' in Your Welfare Line" (1966).

During the mid-1960s Owens spent most of his time on the road. He performed at Carnegie Hall in New York City, the Fillmore Auditorium in San Francisco, and the London Palladium. In 1968 he played a concert at the White House for President Lyndon Johnson. As his fame grew, Owens moved from radio to television and appeared on many popular variety shows. From 1966 to 1972 he hosted *Buck Owens' Ranch Show*, which was taped in Oklahoma City and reached 100 markets. In 1969 he joined the singer-songwriter Roy Clark as cohost of the Columbia Broadcasting System television show *Hee Haw*, which featured country music and comedy. Filled with corny one-liners, the show delivered laughs by playing up the rural stereotype of the overall-wearing, straw-chewing hillbilly. Owens soon became better known for his aw-shucks television personality than for his hard-core country roots, and his record sales declined.

By the late 1970s Owens had pulled away from the recording industry and spent his time on other entrepreneurial ventures, including real estate, printing presses, and television and radio stations. The death of Don Rich—his confidant and guitar player—in 1974 was a contributing factor to his withdrawal. In 1987, however, the country musician and Owens devotee Dwight Yoakam lured Owens back into music by suggesting he play a duet with him at county fair in California. The following year they recorded a duet of Owens's 1972 song "Streets of Bakersfield," which became a number-one hit.

In 1996 Owens opened Buck Owens' Crystal Palace, a restaurant, club, and museum, in Bakersfield and spent the next decade playing weekend shows there. That same year he was inducted into the Country Music Hall of Fame and the Nashville Songwriters Hall of Fame. He died in his sleep hours after finishing a show at his concert hall. He is buried at Greenlawn Southwest Mortuary and Cemetery in Bakersfield.

Owens is remembered as the man who put the hard-driving twang back into country music. His gritty, California brand of country was a departure from the mainstream Nashville sound of the day. He is also remembered as the host of *Hee Haw*, which ran for two decades in syndication. His songs have been recorded by country and rock musicians who value the hard-driving, honky-tonk style that was Owens's signature.

★

David Toop, "Myths of the Honky-Tonker: Buck Owens," *Times* (London) (25 Mar. 1989) is a nice sketch of Owens's life. Gerald W. Haslam, *Workin' Man Blues: Country Music in California* (1999), contains a chapter on Owens. A rich and detailed profile, including photos, can be found at Owens's Crystal Palace website, http://www.buckowens.com. Obituaries are in the *New York Times* (26 Mar. 2006) and *Washington Post* (26 Mar. 2006 and 27 Mar. 2006).

Lisa Frick

P

PAGE, Bettie Mae (*b*. 22 April 1923 in Nashville, Tennessee; *d*. 11 December 2008 in Los Angeles, California), a top pinup model of the 1950s who is credited as a pioneer of the sexual revolution and who became a pop culture icon decades after she stepped away from the spotlight.

Even from the time of her childhood, Page's life was itinerant and tumultuous. The second of six children, she moved frequently in Texas, Oklahoma, and Tennessee with her father, Walter Roy Page, an often unemployed auto mechanic, and mother, Edna Mae Pirtle, a homemaker and beautician. After Page's parents separated, her impoverished mother sent her and her younger sisters to live in a Nashville church orphanage for two years. When her father moved back to the house, he sexually abused Page, as she recounted in interviews decades later.

Despite these difficulties, Page excelled at school. She was active in drama and newspaper groups at Hume-Fogg, a Nashville high school for the academically gifted. In 1940 she graduated second in her class, winning a scholarship to George Peabody College for Teachers (now part of Vanderbilt University), also in Nashville. She graduated in 1944 with a BA in education.

In February 1943 Page married Billy Neal, a navy draftee. Their relationship proved to be stormy. In 1945 the couple moved to San Francisco, where Neal was stationed prior to shipping out for the Pacific in 1945. Working as a secretary, Page explored her childhood dream of Hollywood stardom. Following an unsuccessful screen test in Los Angeles, she took modeling classes because, as a model, nobody would hear her southern accent. In March 1946 Page and her younger sister

Goldie stood trial for assaulting their landlord and received thirty-day suspended sentences, the first of several brushes with the law.

Shortly after Neal was discharged in 1946, the couple separated. The next year Page moved to Miami, where a job with a furniture importer led to a four-month stint in Haiti. By fall 1947 Page was in Manhattan, but she was sexually assaulted and moved back to Nashville. In a matter of weeks she returned to New York City.

Page left New York in 1950 for Florida and then Atlanta, where she had a brief reunion with Neal but after which the two finally divorced. By summer she was back in New York State, where she joined the Greenbush Summer Theater in Rockland County. She moved back to New York City in the fall.

In October 1950, while at Coney Island, Page met Jerry Tibbs, a New York police officer and amateur photographer. He introduced her to private camera clubs, where photographers took pictures of models, sometimes nude, in rented studios or discreet outdoor locations. Tibbs also suggested to Page that she wear her black bangs straight down, across her forehead. This became Page's signature look, even after her modeling career ended seven years later.

Page's work with the camera clubs led to appearances in cheesecake magazines. She also posed for Irving Klaw, whose store and mail-order business, Movie Star News, sold movie stills and racy photos of women in bondage. After Page appeared in Jerald Intrator's *Striporama* in 1953, Klaw filmed Page in two feature films of burlesque acts, *Varietease* in 1954 and *Teaserama* in 1955. Page continued to model in New York and Miami. The Miami-based photographer Bunny Yeager took some of Page's best-known photos, including the January 1955 *Playboy* centerfold.

Bettie Page. MICHAEL OCHS ARCHIVES/GETTY IMAGES

In the meantime Page still dreamed of mainstream success. She took lessons with the renowned acting teacher Herbert Berghof and appeared in television commercials and shows, off-Broadway plays, and summer stock.

In her photos Page projects an image of complete comfort with her sexuality—alternately naughty and playful but never debauched, even in her more risqué poses. These photos were taken and distributed at a time when overt displays of sexuality were taboo in polite society. Senator Carey Estes Kefauver of Tennessee, who in the early 1950s had investigated organized crime, comic books, and juvenile delinquency in well-publicized hearings, turned his attention to Klaw's bondage photos in 1955. He subpoenaed both Page and Klaw. Klaw pleaded the Fifth Amendment; Page was never called to testify.

In December 1957 Page left New York and her modeling career. Later in her life she explained that she needed a change. She started a new chapter in her life devoted to religion, but she remained rootless.

Over the next few years, Page's religious quest took her cross-country, starting in Key West, Florida, where she taught fifth grade for three months and was married, briefly, to Armond Carlyle Walterson in 1958 and 1959. She then attended Bible schools and camps in Los Angeles, Chicago, Indiana, and Portland, Oregon. She had hoped to become a missionary, but her application was rejected.

In 1963 Page moved back to Nashville to take care of her dying father. She remarried Neal but they separated one month later. She returned to George Peabody College for Teachers for a master's degree but gave up after a year and a half. Page moved back to Miami, where in February 1967 she married Harry Lear, a telephone line electrician. As she attempted to impose religious discipline on Lear and his two children from his first marriage, Page's behavior became more erratic. After Lear divorced her in 1972, Page brandished a gun at a religious compound. Three months later she held the Lears at knifepoint. She was committed to Jackson Memorial Hospital, the first of her several stays in mental institutions.

In 1978 Page moved to California. The following year she stabbed her landlords, an elderly couple, in Lawndale. Found "not guilty by reason of insanity," she spent two years in Patton State Hospital in Highland, California. In 1982 Page committed an even more violent knife attack on her housemate in Santa Monica. She was tried for attempted murder and was again found insane and sent to Patton State, where she was diagnosed as a paranoid schizophrenic. She was released in 1992. Until her death from a heart attack, Page lived in almost complete seclusion in Los Angeles, granting few interviews and then only on the condition that her face not be shown. Page is buried in Westwood Village Memorial Park Cemetery in Los Angeles.

During her years of religious fervor and mental illness, Page's place in American culture continued to evolve. Collectors of her cheesecake and bondage pictures kept her work in demand. In the 1970s erotic artists such as Olivia De Berardinis and Robert Blue started reinterpreting Page's images.

In his 1980 best seller, *Thy Neighbor's Wife,* Gay Talese pays tribute to Page as a harbinger of the sexual revolution. In the 1980s the cartoonist Dave Stevens introduced Page to a new generation of fans in his Rocketeer comic books. Her images were repackaged on all manner of merchandising. Page, who made her own costumes, continued to exert her influence on fashion and popular culture, as reflected in films such as Quentin Tarantino's *Pulp Fiction* (1994).

★

An authorized biography of Page is in Karen Essex and James L. Swanson, *Bettie Page: The Life of a Pin-Up Legend* (1995). Well-documented accounts of Page's mental illness and criminal history are in Richard Foster, *The Real Bettie Page: The Truth about the Queen of Pinups* (1997). A feature-length film about Page's life and work is Mary Harron, *The Notorious Bettie Page* (2005). Obituaries are in the *New York Times* and *Los Angeles Times* (both 12 Dec. 2008).

Jeffrey H. Chen

PAIK, Nam June (*b*. 20 June 1932 in Seoul, Korea; *d*. 29 January 2006 in Miami, Florida), artist and composer who blended music, visual media, and technology to become the first video artist.

Paik was the fifth son born to a Korean textile manufacturer. As a child he studied piano and composition. The approaching Korean War (1950–1953) forced his family to flee in 1949 to Hong Kong and then to Japan. He attended the University of Tokyo, where he studied music history and art history, earning a degree in aesthetics in 1956 with a thesis on the Austrian-born American composer Arnold Schoenberg (1874–1951). He then moved to West Germany to continue his studies in music history at the University of Munich and in composition at the Freiburg Conservatory.

While in Germany, Paik began to use tape recorders as instruments in his compositions. During summer music studies in Darmstadt, he met the American composer John Cage (1912–1992), who would become an enormous influence on his work. Cage brought "found sounds" (prerecorded

Nam June Paik, 1984. © **CHRISTOPHER FELVER/CORBIS**

sounds discovered and then used in new works) and extended silence into musical compositions. Paik built on Cage's ideas by creating musical sculptures, adding random objects such as a telephone, brassiere, lightbulbs, radios, and barbed wires to pianos. From 1958 to 1963 he presented his "Action Music" performances—sound forms such as the destruction of a violin or the overturning of a piano—and musical sculptures at the Studio for Electronic Music, founded at the offices of West German Radio in Cologne.

In the 1960s Paik became closely associated with the Fluxus movement organized by the Lithuanian-born artist George Maciunas in 1961. Fluxus challenged the conventions of high art, rejecting the view of artists as elite creators standing apart from the common folk. Instead, Fluxus called for simplicity, spontaneity, and ingenuity in works combining many artistic media. Paik began to participate in Fluxus events throughout Europe. Reflecting Fluxus thought, Paik experimented with collages and found objects—ordinary, everyday objects that could be incorporated in a work of art. In 1962 Maciunas performed Paik's *One for Violin Solo* by destroying a violin.

In 1963, with his first one-man exhibition, Exposition of Music—Electronic Television, at the Galerie Parnass in Wuppertal, Germany, Paik became the first artist to display abstract forms on a television set as part of a work of art. The video sculpture installation included pianos, noise machines, and, scattered around the gallery space, thirteen "prepared" televisions—functioning and semidefective sets transformed by altered electronics to receive new signals. Paik had spent months deciphering Japanese and German electronics handbooks to adapt the televisions for this purpose. Joseph Beuys, a German sculptor friend of Paik's who briefly joined the Fluxus movement, "played" one of the pianos with an ax.

Paik subsequently traveled to Japan to collaborate with electronics engineer Shuya Abe in the construction of *Robot K-456*, a remote-controlled robot made of found parts that walked, talked, and defecated beans. In 1969 Abe and Paik would develop one of the first video synthesizers, producing an array of electronic forms and colors, at the Experimental Workshop at the WGBH television station in Boston.

Paik and his robot moved to New York City in 1964 to work with Maciunas and other Fluxus artists. During this time he met and married a fellow Fluxus member, Shigeko Kubota, a Japanese-born visual and performance artist. Paik constantly varied his pieces and adapted them to given circumstances. He also collaborated with Charlotte Moorman, a cellist and proponent of new music, in a famous performance of Cage's *26'1.1499 for a String Player*. In the piece, performed at the Cafe au Go-Go in New York City in 1965, Moorman played a cello that was in fact a half-dressed Paik, who questioned why serious music always had to be played by serious-looking people dressed in black. In 1967 the two spent a night in jail for a performance in the nude of Paik's *Opera Sextronique*. Paik's collaborations with Moorman continued for years. In 1969 he created *TV Bra for Living Sculpture*, a blending of sound and video technology, live performance, and sexuality. Moorman performed unclothed except for her cello and two miniature televisions covering her breasts. The cello sounds were processed into video images that played on the television screens.

Increasingly focused on television, Paik wanted to exploit the medium as though it were a musical instrument through retuning, altering circuits, and distorting images, as he did using magnets in his 1965 *Magnet TV*. Paik, credited with coining the term *information highway*, wanted to overturn the passive, one-way flow of information typical of the electronic media. He described his work as "time art" (rather than a genre such as sculpture) and his goal as changing the attitude of the viewer within time. Instead of using modern technology, he often laboriously transformed old objects by hand.

In 1965 Paik obtained one of Sony's first portable video cameras and reportedly produced his first work in the medium on the same day. In such works as *Video Fish* (1975) and *TV Garden* (1982), he created the template for the video artists who followed him by abandoning both narrative structure (the components of storytelling) and editing. With *Time Is Triangular* (1993), he created a blizzard of pulsating, morphing images shown on an array of monitors.

Paik's reputation became established with the 1982 retrospective of his work at the Whitney Museum of American Art in New York City. During the Whitney show, Paik staged a collision between *Robot K-456* and a car, calling this event *The First 21st Century Disaster*. New York's Guggenheim Museum presented the last major retrospective of Paik's work, The Worlds of Nam June Paik, in 2000. His works are part of the permanent collections of many major museums in the United States and around the world.

Paik was partially paralyzed by a stroke in 1996 and died of related causes ten years later. Some of his ashes were placed at the Bongeun Temple in Seoul, with the remainder divided between Germany and the United States. A Buddhist memorial service was held on the forty-ninth day after his death to wish him a good afterlife.

Never bound by any convention, Paik used his work to reflect his humanity rather than his national roots. In his optimistic vision, the human spirit triumphs over the machine. Technology, for Paik, was a benign power that could enhance understanding and communication among cultures. The originator of video art, he celebrated new opportunities for creative play and artistic adventure, redefining the genres in which he worked.

★

The best summary of Paik's life is John G. Hanhardt, *The Worlds of Nam June Paik* (2003), an exhibition catalog that accompanied the Paik retrospective at the Guggenheim Museum. Useful personal information is in *Shigeko Kubota: My Life with Nam June Paik* (2007), a memoir by Paik's wife. Edith Decker-Phillips, *Paik Video* (1998), is an excellent and heavily illustrated biography up to 1984. Toni Stooss and Thomas Kellein, eds., *Nam June Paik: Video Time, Video Space* (1993), contains essays on Paik's work as well as several interviews with the artist. *Nam June Paik: Video Works, 1963–88* (1988) focuses on Paik's video sculptures and installations and includes biographical essays. Obituaries are in the *Boston Globe* and the *Times* of London (both 31 Jan. 2006).

Caryn E. Neumann

PALADE, George Emil (*b*. 19 November 1912 in Iaşi, Romania; *d*. 7 October 2008 in Del Mar, California), cell biologist who won the 1974 Nobel Prize in Physiology or Medicine for his contributions to imaging cellular structures and discovering their functions.

Palade was the only son of Emil Palade, a professor of philosophy at the University of Iaşi in Romania, and Constanta (Cantemir) Palade, a former schoolteacher; he had two sisters. Palade attended the Liceul Al Hasdeu, from which he graduated in 1930 with the equivalent of a high school and early college education. He went on to the University of Bucharest, where he completed the

George E. Palade, 1966. **AP IMAGES**

undergraduate premedical course and enrolled in the medical school at the university. While pursuing his medical degree, he did research part time in the anatomy department and wrote a dissertation, required for the MD, on the structure and function of porpoise kidney tubules. Laboratory work so interested him that by the time he became a doctor in 1940 he had decided to pursue a career in research rather than practice medicine.

Soon after graduating, Palade entered the Romanian army medical corps where he served until 1945. However, all through this period he continued to work part time at the University of Bucharest Medical School, as instructor (1941) and then as assistant professor (1941–1945). Following his discharge from military service, he was made an associate professor. On 12 June 1941 he married Irina Malaxa. The couple would go on to have two children. In 1946 Palade and his family left Romania so that he could take up a two-year fellowship in New York. By the time his fellowship expired, a Communist regime had come to power in Romania and, just as significantly, Palade had become deeply involved in research. For these reasons he decided to remain in the United States; he became a naturalized citizen in 1952.

When he first arrived in the United States, Palade worked for a few months in Robert Chambers's laboratory at New York University. There he heard Albert Claude lecture on electron microscopy and was so excited by the possibilities of this instrument that a subsequent conversation with Claude led to an invitation for Palade to join Claude at Rockefeller Institute for Medical Research in New York (later Rockefeller University). It was there that Palade's cellular research, for which he became so well-known, began in earnest. He focused on the cytoplasm, the part of the cell outside the nucleus where the genetic material, the DNA, resides. He was interested not in genetics, but in how the cell uses genetic instructions to carry out its business.

Palade first worked on developing cell fractionation methods. The object of his research, the animal cell, is too small to see with the naked eye, yet has an extraordinarily complex internal structure, which at the time was just being more fully revealed by electron microscopy (EM). However, EM images give little hint at what functions are performed by these structures called organelles, the cell's little organs. Breaking cells down and subsequent fractionation—that is, separating out the different organelles—would allow researchers to study each type of organelle on its own and discover their specific functions. This was the great cell biology project of the 1950s, and Palade was a leader in the field.

Fractionation was difficult to achieve because, if the techniques for breaking up the cells were too vigorous, the organelles themselves were destroyed. Therefore a great deal of painstaking trial-and-error research was necessary to

come up with a consistently successful approach to disrupting the cells. Next came the problem of separating the organelles from each other, an even more difficult task inasmuch as they were all made of similar membranous material. Fortunately, Rockefeller had the equipment and the researchers to successfully tackle the problem, and Palade, working with George Hogeboom and Walter Schneider, came up with the sucrose method for fractionating liver cells. The cells were suspended in a sugar solution so concentrated as to cause them to burst. Next the mixture was put into a centrifuge and spun until the organelles, which had slightly different densities, settled into separate layers in the sticky sugar mixture. After centrifugation, the layers could then be drained off one by one and studied individually.

By the late 1940s, however, Schneider and Hogeboom had moved on to other institutions, and Claude returned to his native Belgium in 1949. Of the original cell biology group at Rockefeller, only Palade and the electron microscopist Keith Porter remained. When the head of the Pathology Department where they worked retired, Herbert Gasser, the institute's director, became their mentor; neither Palade nor Porter was senior enough to head a laboratory. For his part, Gasser supported their research with sufficient resources for them to make significant progress.

Porter and Palade worked together on identifying cellular structures with EM; they painstakingly developed techniques that allowed for good imaging without destroying cell structures in the process. This was no mean feat because, in order to be visible with EM, cells had to be sliced thinly and then subjected to a series of chemical procedures. Added to this is that, if the cell structures are to be seen clearly, the slice has to be made at just the right angle, meaning that many slices had to be examined in order to find those that showed structures most clearly. Again, patient trial and error won out, and the Palade-Porter team produced an amazing series of cell images. In concert with this line of research, Palade also continued working out the function of these structures after separating them from other cell contents.

It was this combination of microscopy and biochemistry that made Palade's research so noteworthy and so productive. In 1949 he reported on the Golgi apparatus, a cluster of membranes involved in secretion of materials from the cell. He also worked on the mitochondrion, discovering its role in providing energy for the cell. He described small particles found throughout the cytoplasm, and these later became know as ribosomes when they were found to be made of RNA and protein. In addition, Palade and Porter studied the endoplasmic reticulum, a series of folded membranes in which synthesis reactions take place in the cell. It was not always easy to relate the structures seen with EM to the structures found in disrupted cells, so the accuracy of Palade's work indicates the care he took with it.

The success of his research led to Palade's promotion at Rockefeller, from assistant to associate member, and finally to professor in 1958. Palade described these years as those during which cell biology became a recognized discipline. He and Porter contributed to this development by helping to found the *Journal of Cell Biology*, of which Palade was editor, and the American Society of Cell Biology. Porter remained at Rockefeller until 1961, at which time he moved to Harvard University. By this time, Palade had been joined by Philip Siekevitz, who collaborated on the ribosome and endoplasmic reticulum work.

In 1969, Irina Palade died. A year later, Palade married Marilyn Farquhar, also a cell biologist, whom he had met when she was a postdoctoral researcher in his laboratory. She brought two children into the marriage. In 1973 Palade left Rockefeller for the Yale University Medical School. A year later, he was awarded the Nobel Prize in Physiology or Medicine along with Claude and Christian de Duve. At Yale, Palade continued his research on cellular structure and function by discovering the ways in which the structures he had worked on earlier, such as the Golgi apparatus and the endoplasmic reticulum, related to each other functionally. In 1990 Palade left Yale to become the first dean for Scientific Affairs at the School of Medicine at the University of California, San Diego. He was seventy-seven at the time and served in this capacity until 2001. In 2004 this institution named a building for him, and two years later further honored him by creating an endowed professorship in his name. Other accolades for Palade included the Albert Lasker Basic Medical Research Award and the National Medal of Science presented by President Ronald Reagan in 1986. In addition he was a member of the National Academy of Sciences.

Palade died at his home in Del Mar from the complications of Parkinson's disease.

Palade's contributions to cell biology helped to change every biologist's perceptions of the cell from a mere blob with a somewhat shadowy nucleus to an intricately built vessel of life. His scientific interests were matched by a love of learning in all fields. He was passionate about the arts, literature, and history. He was an impressive lecturer whose enthusiasm for the life of the mind was evident and well communicated. In all, Palade was a model of an engaged scientist who remained enthusiastic about the life of the mind throughout his long life.

★

An essay about Palade as well as his Nobel lecture can be found on the Nobel Prize website, http://nobelprize.org/nobel_prizes/medicine/laureates/1974/palade-autobio.html. An overview of Palade and his work can be found in Alan Tartakoff, "George Emil Palade: Charismatic Virtuoso of Cell Biology,"

Nature Reviews: Molecular Cell Biology (Nov. 2002). The Rockefeller Archive Center houses Palade's papers, particularly those relating to his tenure at Rockefeller University. Obituaries are in the *New York Times* (10 Oct. 2008), *Science* (31 Oct. 2008), and *Nature* (6 Nov. 2008).

Maura C. Flannery

PALANCE, Jack (*b.* 18 February 1918 or 1920 in Lattimer Mines, Pennsylvania; *d.* 10 November 2006 in Montecito, California), Academy Award–winning actor best known for his portrayal of villains in Westerns and film noirs.

Palance was born Vladimir Ivanovich Palahniuk to Ukrainian immigrant parents, Vladimir Palahniuk, a coal miner, and Anna Palahniuk. Raised in a coal-mining town with two siblings, Palance described his childhood as rough. He worked in the mines before winning a football scholarship to the University of North Carolina. A natural athlete, Palance was six feet, four inches tall. He soon left college to pursue another sport, boxing, in 1938. At the age of twenty Palance became a professional heavyweight boxer and fought under the name Jack Brazzo. He won his first fifteen fights

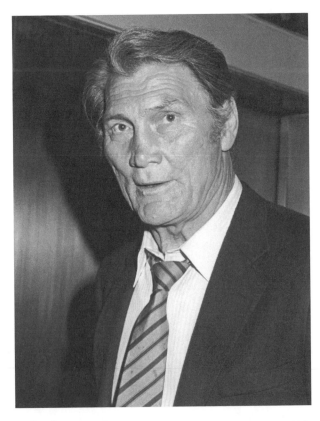

Jack Palance, 1983. RON GALELLA/WIREIMAGE/GETTY IMAGES

before facing Joe Baksi, a future heavyweight contender, in 1940. Palance lost the fight and left boxing because he came to believe that "you must be nuts to get your head beat in for $200." In 1942, after the United States' entry into World War II, he joined the U.S. Army Air Forces. A year later a B-42 bomber he was piloting crashed during a flight in California. Palance suffered severe burns to his face that required plastic surgery, a procedure that contributed to his gaunt, sharp looks and rugged profile.

After his plane crash, Palance left military service and attended Stanford University on the GI Bill. By this time he had changed his name to Walter Jack Palance. He first studied journalism at Stanford before being drawn to acting. He graduated from Stanford in 1947 with a BA in drama and that same year made his Broadway debut in a play called *The Big Two*. In 1948 he had roles in *Temporary Island* and *The Vigil*, but his first great acting break came as the understudy to Anthony Quinn in the touring company of the Tennessee Williams classic *A Streetcar Named Desire*. This led to his becoming the understudy for Marlon Brando during the play's Broadway run. As theater legend tells it, Palance got to play the famous role of Stanley Kowalski after a boxing match in which he punched Brando so hard in the face that the star had to go to the hospital. In 1949 Palance married Virginia Baker, an actress. The couple would have three children. They divorced in 1966. A second marriage in 1987 to Elaine Rogers also ended in divorce.

In 1950 Palance, under the name Walter Palance, made his first movie appearance in Elia Kazan's film noir *Panic in the Streets*. He played a gangster on the run infected with the bubonic plague. This first "heavy" role, combined with Palance's rich voice and striking, angular features, led to a quick succession of roles as villains or tough guys. As the film critic David Thomson describes it, Palance had a "flamboyant menace" that seemed to define his roles. Palance appeared in the war film *Halls of Montezuma* (1950) and was nominated for his first Oscar for his performance as a murderous husband opposite Joan Crawford in the classic noir *Sudden Fear* (1952). But it was his fourth film that seemed to cement Palance's place in Hollywood. Although he had only sixteen lines in the classic Western *Shane* (1953), Palance's role as the gunslinger Jack Wilson was a masterpiece of threatening villainy and almost overshadowed the film's star, Alan Ladd. For this memorable role, Palance received his second Oscar nomination and forever became an icon of the Western "bad guy."

After *Shane* and his two Oscar nominations, Palance found steady film and television work in a long string of villainous and dramatic roles. However, he always maintained that he thought he was better suited for comedy. In 1953 Palance starred in four other movies besides *Shane*: the crime drama *Second Chance*, opposite Robert Mitchum; the Western *Arrowhead*; *Flight to Tangier*; and *Man in the*

Attic. Throughout the 1950s he appeared in idiosyncratic roles, such as Attila the Hun in *Sign of the Pagan* (1954). In 1955 he broke out of his villain stereotype to play a tortured film star in Robert Aldrich's *The Big Knife*. That same year he also starred in *I Died a Thousand Times*, a remake of the Humphrey Bogart gangster classic *High Sierra*. Many war and crime films followed, including *Attack* (1956), *House of Numbers* (1957), and *Ten Seconds to Hell* (1959). He also appeared in many television roles, including *Requiem for a Heavyweight* in 1956, a role that won him an Emmy Award.

In the late 1950s Palance moved to Europe. He starred in many foreign films, specializing in war movies and spaghetti Westerns, as Westerns filmed in Italy were called, including Sergio Corbucci's leftist cult-classic *Vamos a matar, compañeros!* (1970; also known as *Compañeros!*). He also appeared in *Le Mépris* (*Contempt*, 1963), directed by the French New Wave director Jean-Luc Godard, and big-budget American Westerns such as *The Professionals* (1966), costarring Lee Marvin and Burt Lancaster.

Palance never stopped acting, even though he called much of his work "garbage." He became well known in the 1980s for hosting the television show *Ripley's Believe It or Not!* (1982–1986). In the late 1980s and the early 1990s Palance made a comeback in big Hollywood films with roles in *Young Guns* (1988) and Tim Burton's *Batman* (1989). But it was his portrayal of an old cowhand in the comedy *City Slickers* (1991) for which he finally won an Oscar, for best supporting actor. This role seemed to validate Palance's longtime feeling that he should have appeared in more comedies. During his famous Academy Award acceptance speech, he shocked and delighted the audience by doing one-handed push-ups. It proved to be one of the most memorable appearances in Oscar history.

In his last years he tended a cattle ranch in California and a farm near his birthplace in Pennsylvania. In contrast to his rugged and often villainous roles in films, Palance was a lifelong lover of nature, a painter, and a writer of poetry. In 1996 he published *The Forest of Love: A Love Story in Blank Verse*, and in 2003 he rereleased *Palance*, a country music album originally made in 1969. He died of natural causes at the age of eighty-seven and was cremated.

Palance's long career in movie and television is a testament to his strong acting talent and dynamic personality. He was an important actor who had an impact on American popular culture, particularly in his roles as villains. A complicated person, he sought to show other aspects of his talent and seized the chance late in his career. Palance was a dedicated and passionate actor who brought a rough vitality to several classic American films.

★

Palance's appearance on *Charlie Rose* (17 Feb. 1997), in which he discusses his Hollywood career and his book of poetry, is available from http://charlierose.com.view/interview/5701. An obituary is in the *New York Times* (11 Nov. 2006).

John Rocco

PALEY, Grace Goodside (*b*. 11 December 1922 in New York City; *d*. 22 August 2007 in Thetford Hill, Vermont), writer best known for her short stories and political activism.

Paley was the youngest of three children of Isaac Goodside (originally Gutseit), a physician, and Manya (Ridnyik) Goodside, a homemaker, both Jewish immigrants from Ukraine. During her childhood she heard many heated political arguments about Zionism, communism, and socialism among her relatives. After graduating from Evander Childs High School in New York, she attended Hunter College from 1938 to 1939, and later New York University, but did not complete a degree. She married Jess Paley, a movie cameraman, on 20 June 1942; they would have two children.

In 1939 Paley took a course with the British-born poet W. H. Auden, who was then teaching at the New School for Social Research in New York City, and began to write

Grace Paley, 2000. © CHRISTOPHER FELVER/CORBIS

poetry. During the 1950s Paley became politically involved and began as a writer to concentrate on the voices of her childhood. By exploring the world of Yiddishkeit—the sense of Jewishness among Yiddish-speaking Jews from Eastern Europe—she found her own voice. She turned to writing short stories and vignettes that portrayed families in all their messy glory, particularly the inner yearnings of young mothers. Her stories, filled with quiet fury, irony, warmth, and humor, resonated with the voices of her own parents, extended family, and children. No matter how angry her characters are with each other, there is always an underlying sense of caring for one's fellow human beings that permeates her work.

In 1959 Paley published her first collection of stories, *The Little Disturbances of Man*. The novelist Philip Roth noted that the stories offer "an understanding of loneliness, lust, selfishness ... that is splendidly comic and unladylike." The stories pose questions about what men and women expect from each other and from intimacy and marriage—not necessarily the same thing. In this collection the first of Paley's many independent women question the 1950s version of the American dream, in which women are dependent, their identities restricted to wife and mother.

During the 1960s Paley taught writing courses at Columbia University and Syracuse University and conducted summer writing workshops in Vermont, North Dakota, and California. In 1966 she joined the faculty of Sarah Lawrence College in Bronxville, New York, where she played a central role in developing the writing program; she retired in 1989. In 1961 she helped form the Greenwich Village Peace Center. After trying to block an Armed Forces Day parade in New York City in 1966, she was arrested and spent time in the Women's House of Detention; she later spoke out against conditions women inmates faced there. Her protests against the Vietnam War in 1969 took her to Hanoi, where she was part of a committee that freed three American prisoners. In 1973 she attended a World Peace Conference in Moscow to support human rights. She described herself as a "somewhat combative pacifist and cooperative anarchist." In 1972 Paley divorced her first husband and married the landscape architect and writer Robert Nichols.

Paley's second collection of short stories, *Enormous Changes at the Last Minute* (1974), reflects a darker assessment of the world. Critics noted that Faith Darwin, a recurring character in the stories, represents Paley in many ways. In Faith the reader finds a strong female character whose concerns move from family life to the implications of nuclear disaster for the whole world. The theme of injustice, with a particular concern for anti-Semitism, also runs through the book. A movie based on the book appeared in 1983. That year she began teaching at City College in New York City.

In Paley's third collection, *Later the Same Day* (1985), characters from a variety of ethnic backgrounds learn to listen to one another. Their seemingly simplistic conversations have deep undercurrents of political ideas. The proper role of the political in the personal, and vice versa, becomes a pressing issue. In the final story of the collection, "Listening," Faith Darwin realizes that she has paid such close attention to world causes that she has not listened to the voices of her friends in need.

Also in 1985 Paley published a collection of poems, *Leaning Forward*, and in 1991 a collection of poems and short stories, *Long Walks and Intimate Talks*. Her *Begin Again: New and Collected Poems* appeared in 1992, and *Collected Stories* in 1994. She published *Just As I Thought*, a book of essays, speeches, reviews, and poems written over three decades, in 1998. During these years Paley divided her time between New York's Greenwich Village and a house in Thetford Hill. She continued her political activism with opposition to the 2003 American invasion of Iraq.

Paley was a member of the National Institute of Arts and Letters and the American Academy and Institute of Arts and Letters. Widely recognized for her contributions to literature, she was awarded a Guggenheim Fellowship (1961), the Edith Wharton Award (1986), the Rea Award for the Short Story (1993), and the Lannan Foundation Literary Award for fiction (1997). She was named the first official New York State Writer (1986–1988) and also poet laureate of Vermont.

Paley died at the age of eighty-four of breast cancer. *Fidelity*, a book of poems she completed just before her death, was published posthumously in 2008.

Paley's fiction aimed to be, as she put it, "a history of everyday life." Written in a style of clarity and simplicity, her stories reveal a loving familiarity with women's inner struggles and family dynamics. She was particularly admired by critics and readers for her dialogue, which though concise and spare was evocative of deep and complicated feelings. As one critic observed, no author "captures the itch of the city, or the complexities of love between parents and children, or the cutting edge of sexual combat as well as Grace Paley does." For a small but rich body of work, Paley earned the respect of the literary community and the devotion of her readers.

★

Judith Arcana, *Grace Paley's Life Stories: A Literary Biography*, (1993), examines the life and work. For interviews with Paley, see Gerhard Bach and Blaine H. Hall, eds., *Conversations with Grace Paley* (1997), containing interviews with the author from 1978 to 1995; see especially interviews conducted by Frieda Gardiner and Maya Friedman. Obituaries are in the *New York Times* (23 Aug. 2007) and *Washington Post* (24 Aug. 2007).

Jane Amler Lewis

PARKS, Gordon Roger Alexander Buchanan

(*b*. 30 November 1912 in Fort Scott, Kansas; *d*. 7 March 2006 in New York City), acclaimed photographer, writer, composer, and filmmaker whose work captured twentieth-century African-American life as well as his own personal story.

Parks was the youngest of fifteen offspring of Andrew Jackson Parks, a tenant farmer, and Sarah (Ross) Parks. His mother instilled in him a sense of self-worth and a strong work ethic. From early on Parks, an African American, faced the seemingly insurmountable obstacles of poverty, segregation, and racism. The death of his mother while he was in his teens robbed him of any sense of security. His father sent him to Saint Paul, Minnesota, to live with a married sister, but after arguing with his brother-in-law Parks took to living in the streets. Although he never took lessons, he learned to play the piano and found work playing the instrument in a brothel. He attended Central High School in Saint Paul, but did not graduate.

In 1933 Parks married Sally Alvis. The union produced two sons and a daughter; his firstborn son, Gordon Parks, Jr., became a film director and died in a plane crash while filming in 1979. Leaving his family in Minnesota,

Gordon Parks, 1974. ALFRED EISENSTAEDT/TIME LIFE PICTURES/GETTY IMAGES

Parks took to the road to find work. He joined the Civilian Conservation Corps, played semiprofessional basketball, and worked as a waiter and busboy. In 1938, while working as a waiter and porter on the North Coast Limited, a train operating between Chicago and Seattle, he noticed a magazine that included photographs taken by members of the photography program of the Farm Security Administration (FSA), whose mission was to record images of rural poverty in America. He decided to become a photographer and purchased his first camera in a Seattle pawn shop.

Parks quickly mastered the fundamentals of photography. After he returned to the Midwest, the Eastman Kodak store in Minneapolis gave him his first exhibition, and an upscale Saint Paul women's clothing store hired him to shoot fashion stills. He soon relocated to Chicago, where he produced high-fashion photographs as well as images chronicling the city's South Side slum. In 1942 he was awarded a Julius Rosenwald Fellowship, which allowed him to move to Washington, D.C., to apprentice with the FSA's photography program. That year Parks took one of his best-known photographs, showing Ella Watson, an African-American cleaning woman, posing with broom and mop in hand in front of an American flag. He called it *American Gothic.*

The following year Parks became a correspondent with the Office of War Information (OWI) and photographed the training of the 332nd Fighter Group, an all-African-American troop. He then moved to Harlem in New York City. In 1944 he began photographing women's fashions for *Vogue,* which employed him for the rest of the decade, and shooting images of rural and industrial America for the Standard Oil company's Photography Project. He also published two photography instruction books, *Flash Photography* (1947) and *Camera Portraits: Techniques and Principles of Documentary Portraiture* (1948).

In 1948 Parks became the first African American to be hired as a staff photojournalist for *Life,* a national high-circulation magazine. His first assignments revealed the range of his talent: he photographed the latest Paris fashions and chronicled the Midtowners, a Harlem street gang. Between 1949 and 1951 he worked out of *Life's* Paris bureau. It was during this time that he composed his first piano concerto, Concerto for Piano and Orchestra (1953).

For the next decade and well into the 1960s, Parks photographed a range of celebrated individuals—Gloria Vanderbilt (with whom he enjoyed a decades-long friendship), Barbra Streisand, Aaron Copland, Muhammad Ali, Malcolm X—as well as ghetto dwellers far outside the American mainstream. His most famous photo essay for *Life,* published in 1961, spotlighted Flavio da Silva, a poor, ailing Brazilian boy in a Rio de Janeiro slum. By this time Parks was rated one of the leading photojournalists of the post–World War II era. Outside his work for publication, he took pictures of female nudes and idyllic nature scenes.

In 1961 he divorced his wife of nearly three decades and the following year married Elizabeth Campbell, with whom he would have a daughter.

At this point in his career Parks decided to conquer new artistic media. He directed a short documentary, *Flavio* (1961); wrote *The Learning Tree* (1963), an autobiographical novel about a young black boy in 1920s Kansas; published *A Choice of Weapons* (1966), the first of four memoirs; composed *Tree Symphony* (1967); published *A Poet and His Camera* (1968), a book of his poems and photographs; and directed two more documentaries, *Diary of a Harlem Family* (1968), a short, and the hour-long *The World of Piri Thomas* (1968), about the Hispanic writer-poet.

Parks became the first African American to direct a Hollywood-made feature when he helmed the screen version of *The Learning Tree* (1969). He also produced the film, wrote the screenplay, composed the score, and was its cinematographer. In 1970 he became one of the founders of *Essence,* a magazine with an African-American orientation, and was named its editorial director. He also published *Born Black* (1971), a compilation of essays and photographs.

Parks followed up *The Learning Tree* with an entirely different film, *Shaft* (1971), a landmark detective drama notable for its presentation of a new kind of African-American screen personality. The title character, a private eye, is no polite black man attempting to fit into a white world. Instead, he is a sexual, independent-minded, self-possessed man who exudes self-confidence and thrives in both the black and white communities. *Shaft* was a smash hit and helped launch the "blaxploitation" film genre, a union of the words *black* and *exploitation,* which primarily featured glorified portraits of drug dealers, pimps, and other wrongdoers. It was a designation that Parks disdained.

Parks followed *Shaft* with a sequel, *Shaft's Big Score!* (1972), which he wrote and directed and for which he composed the score. In 1972 he broke his ties with *Life* when it ceased publication as a weekly. He remained with *Essence* through 1973. That year he divorced his second wife and on 26 August married Genevieve Young. He then directed two films, *The Super Cops* (1974), a cop movie, and *Leadbelly* (1976), a biography of the folksinger Huddie Ledbetter. In 1979 he divorced his third wife.

Parks published a second memoir, *To Smile in Autumn* (1979), and a second novel, *Shannon* (1981), about Irish-American immigrants at the turn of the twentieth century. He directed one final film (this time for television), *Solomon Northrup's Odyssey* (1984), a fact-based account of a nineteenth-century African American who was born free but kidnapped and sold into slavery.

In 1987 the New York Public Library and Wichita State University's Ulrich Museum of Art coordinated the first of numerous retrospectives of Parks's photographs. The following year he was awarded the National Medal of Arts, presented to him by President Ronald Reagan. He eventually was granted several dozen honorary degrees from universities throughout the United States and England. In 1989 *The Learning Tree* was selected as one of the first twenty-five films to be preserved in the Library of Congress's National Film Registry.

But Parks's creative career was far from over. He composed the music and libretto for *Martin* (1989), a ballet that paid homage to Martin Luther King, Jr. Next came a third memoir, *Voices in the Mirror: An Autobiography* (1990). A book of photographs, *Half Past Autumn* (1997), was published in conjunction with a touring exhibition of his photographs organized by the Corcoran Gallery of Art in Washington, D.C. At age eighty-eight he made a cameo appearance in John Singleton's remake of *Shaft* (2000). He published one final memoir, *A Hungry Heart* (2005), and one last book of poetry and photos, *Eyes with Winged Thoughts* (2005).

Parks died at ninety-three of cancer at his Manhattan residence. He is buried beside his parents in Evergreen Cemetery in Fort Scott.

Parks came of age in an era when opportunities for African Americans were severely limited. Yet he refused to be stifled by these constraints. Despite his lack of training, he achieved success in several artistic disciplines, employing images and words to break open stereotypes to reveal truths. In all his work he celebrated freedom. His groundbreaking career inspired many African-American artists who came after him.

Parks's life and works are the subject of several books, including Midge Turk, *Gordon Parks* (1971); Terry Harnan, *Gordon Parks: Black Photographer and Film Maker* (1972); Martin H. Bush, *Photographs of Gordon Parks* (1983); Darlene Donloe, *Gordon Parks* (1993); Ann Parr, *Gordon Parks: No Excuses* (2006); and *Bare Witness: Photographs by Gordon Parks* (2007), an exhibition catalog with an introductory essay by Maren Stange surveying and analyzing Parks's work. Obituaries are in the *New York Times* and *Washington Post* (both 8 Mar. 2006).

Rob Edelman

PATTERSON, Floyd (*b.* 4 January 1935 in Waco, North Carolina; *d.* 11 May 2006 in New Paltz, New York), the first boxer in history to hold the heavyweight title twice; he later served as athletic commissioner for the state of New York.

Floyd Patterson, 1962. AP IMAGES

Patterson was the third of eleven children born to Thomas Patterson, a laborer, and Annabelle Johnson. The family moved from North Carolina to Brooklyn, New York, in 1936 to allow Patterson's father to find work (which he did, in construction, as a longshoreman, in sanitation, and in a fish market). Patterson became involved in gangs, and after a series of arrests for petty thievery was sent at age ten to the Wiltwyck School for Boys in Esopus, New York, a school for emotionally disturbed youths, where he learned to read and box. After Wiltwyck, he attended Public School 614, a vocational elementary school. Here he got the idea that he could use boxing to earn money for his family.

In 1949 he began working at Gramercy Gym with trainer Cus D'Amato (later Mike Tyson's trainer and manager), who gave him boxing equipment and taught him the fundamentals of the sport. In January 1950 Patterson entered and won his first Amateur Athletic Union (AAU) tournament in the 147-pound weight class. In the next year he won his weight class as a 160-pound fighter and went to Chicago to box in the national AAU Championships. In 1951 he won the Golden Gloves middleweight championship. Patterson, now sixteen, wanted to turn professional that year, but D'Amato would not let him, perhaps with the idea of saving him for the 1952 Olympics. The next year Patterson won the New York Golden Gloves light heavyweight title. On 2 August 1952, fighting as a middleweight, Patterson knocked out Vasial Tita one minute into the first round to win an Olympic gold medal in Helsinki, Finland. Patterson fought forty-four bouts as an amateur, winning forty, thirty-seven by knockout.

Patterson made his professional debut on 12 September 1952 as a light heavyweight, defeating Eddie Godbold by knockout in the fourth round. Over the next two years, he bested twelve more opponents, knocking out nine. On 7 June 1954 he lost a contested decision to former champion Joey Maxim, but went on to win sixteen consecutive bouts over the next twenty-four months.

In 1956 Rocky Marciano retired from the ring, leaving his title vacant. To win the championship, Patterson first defeated Tommy "Hurricane" Jackson by decision in twelve rounds. On 30 November 1956 he knocked out Archie Moore in five rounds, becoming, at twenty-one years, five months old, the youngest man ever to win the heavyweight title. That same year Patterson married Sandra Hicks on 11 February in a civil ceremony. After Patterson converted to Catholicism later that year, the two were married again in a religious ceremony on 13 July. The couple later had four children. They moved into an expensive home in Scarsdale, New York, until a racial incident forced them to relocate to Great Neck, Long Island.

Patterson became prominent during the heyday of New York boxing and was immensely popular with the crowd at Madison Square Garden. His troubled youth left him sensitive, introspective, and shy; his nickname was "Freudian Floyd." Admirers regarded Patterson as a perfect gentleman and noted that he had once stooped to pick up an opponent's mouthpiece in the middle of a round. Before bouts, Patterson prayed not for victory, but to avoid serious injury to his opponents or himself. His boxing method was unique. He held his gloves high in front of his face, then stunned opponents with lashing, unexpected hooks. At five feet, eleven inches tall, and usually weighing around 195 pounds, Patterson used speed, timing, and finesse to overcome his opponents. D'Amato carefully guided him through his career, but because of D'Amato's disputes with the boxing powers-that-be, top contenders such as Nino Valdes and Ezzard Charles would not fight Patterson.

Patterson successfully defended his championship four times in the two and a half years he held the title (November 1956–June 1959), starting with Jackson on 29 July 1957. He then beat two journeymen boxers and the English champion Brian London. In a stunning upset, however, Ingemar Johannson, the Swedish challenger and number-one contender for the title, knocked out Patterson in the third round on 28 June 1959. Deeply ashamed, Patterson wore disguises to avoid public criticism, a habit that by 1966 cost him $3,000 annually. Patterson made boxing history when he became the first to regain the heavyweight championship by knocking out Johannson in the fifth round of their rematch a year later on 20 June 1960. A second rematch followed on 13 March 1961, but Johannson survived only one round longer, losing by knockout in the sixth round.

In the next two years Patterson defended his title only once, stopping the lightly regarded Tom McNeeley in the fourth round on 4 December 1961. He could not avoid a more serious challenger, however, and on 22 September 1962 Patterson lost his crown when the glowering Sonny Liston knocked him out in the first round and then repeated this humiliation in their rematch nine months later.

No longer champion, Patterson stayed in the ring. He beat five opponents, the best known of whom was George Chuvalo. When Cassius Clay (later Muhammad Ali) upset Liston for the championship and then proclaimed his victory was due to Allah, Patterson took offense. A devout Roman Catholic and staunch integrationist, Patterson vowed to take the crown away from Ali (who had proclaimed himself to be a Muslim, not an American), and give it back to America. He insisted on referring to his opponent as Clay, which Ali called his "slave name." Such prefight posturing became politicized in the ring. Ali taunted Patterson throughout the bout, yelling, "Come on White America," at the defenseless contender. Black Muslim spectators at ringside shouted, "Play with that Uncle Tom!" Although Ali said later that Patterson had taken his best punches and proclaimed him a good man, many observers, including Joe Louis, felt that Ali deliberately refrained from knocking Patterson out until the twelfth round.

Patterson's advisers encouraged him to retire, and his wife, Sandra, divorced him in August 1966 after he insisted on staying in boxing. Still a contender, Patterson won his next three bouts, then fought to a draw with Jerry Quarry, only to lose in the rematch. After Ali was stripped of his title for draft evasion in 1968, Patterson lost a unification bout for the championship to Jimmy Ellis on 14 September 1968.

Patterson announced his retirement after the match with Ellis. Then, after a two-year layover, he resumed his career in September 1970. He won seven fights against little-known boxers before winning an unimpressive decision against the rugged Oscar Bonavena on 11 February 1972. Patterson's father had died two days before, and he acknowledged later that he had not been at this best during the bout. After a six-round win over Pedro Agosto on 14 July 1972, Patterson lost his last title match to Ali on 20 September 1972. He retired permanently after this defeat, with a professional record of fifty-five wins (forty by knockout), eight losses, and a draw.

Patterson, his second wife Janet, and their three children retired to their home in New Paltz, New York. In

1973 Patterson opened the Huguenot Boxing Club, a youth center intended to give youngsters an alternative to drugs; by 1988 the center had helped over 1,200 teenagers. Patterson was a member of the New York State Boxing Commission from 1977 to 1985, and used the position to push successfully for the adoption of a thumbless boxing glove for amateurs. In 1985 he was appointed head of the Off-Track Betting Commission in New York, and was named boxing commissioner for New York State ten years later. Patterson served until 1998 when he resigned after disclosing that he suffered from severe memory loss, probably caused by years of boxing. He was elected to the Boxing Hall of Fame in 1977 and to the Olympic Hall of Fame in 1987. He died of dementia pugilistica and prostate cancer at his home. He is buried in New Paltz Rural Cemetery.

★

Patterson's autobiography, coauthored with Milton Gross, is *Victory over Myself* (1961). Another biography is Jack Newcombe, *Floyd Patterson: Heavyweight King* (1961). Magazine articles include Gay Talese, "Portrait of the Ascetic Champ," *New York Times Magazine* (5 Mar. 1961), and Pete Hamill, "Floyd's Fight to Save His Pride," *Saturday Evening Post* (27 June 1964). See also "Floyd Patterson: Still Making a Mark in the Ring," *Ebony* (Mar. 1987), and "Boxing's Last Gentleman," *New Yorker* (31 July 1995). An obituary is in the *New York Times* (11 May 2006).

Graham Russell Gao Hodges

PELIKAN, Jaroslav Jan, Jr. (*b.* 17 December 1923 in Akron, Ohio; *d.* 13 May 2006 in Hamden, Connecticut), theologian and professor of history at Yale University whose analyses of the development of Christian doctrine over the centuries earned him the 2004 Library of Congress John W. Kluge Prize (shared with the philosopher Paul Ricoeur) for lifetime achievement in the human sciences.

Pelikan was the son of Jaroslav Jan Pelikan, Sr., a Lutheran pastor who served congregations in the Midwest, and the Serbian-born Anna (Buzek) Pelikan, a teacher. Pelikan's paternal grandfather, an immigrant from what is now Slovakia, was a Lutheran bishop. The oldest of three surviving children, Pelikan began to read at the age of two. Growing up in a polyglot household, he eventually mastered some dozen languages. In 1936, when his family moved to Chicago, he enrolled in Concordia Junior College in Fort Wayne, Indiana, a rigorously academic Lutheran institution that combined high school and the first two years of college. After graduating in 1942, Pelikan entered Concordia Theological Seminary in St. Louis. A talented musician who had been contemplating a concert career, he now devoted himself to theology. However, his lifelong love of music was reflected in several of his later writings, such as *Bach Among the Theologians* (1986).

While finishing undergraduate studies, Pelikan began work on his doctorate at the University of Chicago. In 1946 he received a BD from Concordia and was ordained a Lutheran pastor, but he served in the ministry only occasionally throughout his life. Also in 1946 he received a PhD from Chicago, with a dissertation on the relationship between the Lutheran and the Hussite reformations. On 9 June 1946 he married Sylvia Burica, a teacher of Latin, with whom he would have three children. That same year he began his academic career teaching church history at Valparaiso University in Indiana. From 1949 to 1953 he was back teaching at Concordia Seminary and in 1950 published his first book, *From Luther to Kierkegaard: A Study in the History of Theology*. In 1953 Pelikan became a professor of historical theology at the University of Chicago; two years later he commenced work as general editor of the first thirty volumes of an English translation of the complete writings of Martin Luther. In 1959, turning to the problem of ecumenism, which engaged him throughout his life, Pelikan published *The Riddle of Roman Catholicism*, urging dialogue between Catholics and Protestants. Published at the time of controversy over John F. Kennedy's presidential candidacy and at the beginning of Vatican II deliberations, the book became a best seller, popular despite some hostile responses.

Called to Yale Divinity School in 1962 as Titus Street Professor of Ecclesiastical History, Pelikan later joined the university's faculty of arts and sciences; in 1972 he was appointed Sterling Professor of History and Religious Studies. A fluent, forceful lecturer (who never lost his midwestern accent), he taught both graduate seminars and such undergraduate courses as a survey of Western civilization, popularly dubbed "Plato to NATO." Despite his academic prestige—he would eventually hold forty-two honorary degrees—Pelikan was an outgoing, informal, tweedy campus figure. Known to his colleagues familiarly as "Jary," he referred to himself with characteristic self-deprecating wit as someone who "was carrying on [his] private education in public"—and was known to take much pleasure in collecting figures of his namesake bird, the pelican.

While still in graduate school, influenced by the late-nineteenth-century work of Adolf von Harnack, one of the first theologians to apply modern research methods to the study of church history, Pelikan had begun to plan what would become his magnum opus. It was eventually published in five volumes, between 1971 and 1989, as *The Christian Tradition: A History of the Development of Doctrine*. Considered a magisterial work of scholarship, an astonishing feat for one person to have accomplished, it was also recognized as the first history of Christianity to treat the Eastern Orthodox contribution adequately. A prolific and efficient worker, Pelikan went on to write a total of some forty books, in addition to a formidable body of articles, translations, and editions—bringing to bear on the subject of church history his keen interest in literature, the arts, and natural science and distinguished by a clear, straightforward style, occasionally leavened with humor. He also wrote theological works addressed to more general audiences, among them *Jesus Through the Centuries: His Place in the History of Culture* (1985), which was translated into several languages and was later reissued in an illustrated edition, and *Whose Bible Is It? A History of the Scriptures Through the Ages* (2005).

Pelikan served Yale in several administrative posts: chair of the graduate program in medieval studies, director of the division of the humanities, and dean of the Graduate School of Arts and Sciences from 1973 to 1978. From 1980 on he was a member of the board of governors of Yale University Press. Besides these university affiliations, he was, variously, chair of the Fourth International Congress for Luther Research (1971), associated with the National Conference of Christians and Jews, and the first chair of the Council of Scholars of the Library of Congress (1980–1983). From 1994 to 1997 he was president of the American Academy of Arts and Sciences. Over the years Pelikan also lectured widely. In 1983, for example, he was invited by the National Endowment for the Humanities to deliver its twelfth annual Jefferson Lecture, subsequently published as *The Vindication of Tradition* (1984). In 1992–1993 he gave the prestigious Gifford Lectures at the University of Aberdeen, as had such theologians and philosophers as Paul Tillich, Reinhold Niebuhr, and John Dewey before him.

Pelikan's lectures were published in 1993 as *Christianity and Classical Culture*. Two years after his retirement from Yale in 1996 as professor emeritus, Pelikan joined the Orthodox Church of America and was chrismated at Saint Vladimir's Orthodox Theological Seminary in Crestwood, New York. He described the event as a homecoming, not just a conversion—rather like a pilot who has been circling an airport looking for a way to land. Pelikan's last book, *Acts* (2005), a commentary on the New Testament book, was dedicated to "my liturgical family at Saint Vladimir's." To the seminary he also donated his share of the Library of Congress Kluge Prize monetary award. At the age of eighty-two, Pelikan died of lung cancer at his home in Hamden, a suburb of New Haven, Connecticut. He is buried near his home.

"The Will to Believe and the Need for Creed" was the title of a lecture Pelikan gave at Yale in 2003, on the occasion of the publication of *Creeds & Confessions of Faith in the Christian Tradition*, a four-volume compendium of which he was coeditor (with Valerie Hotchkiss). Though an upholder of religious tradition, Pelikan took as his guiding principle a passage from Johann Wolfgang von Goethe's *Faust*, that what you inherit from your forebears you must repossess to make your own. He saw the creative use of tradition, a process of continuity and change, as central to the development of Christianity. Explaining his nonparticipation in twentieth-century religious debates because "there ought to be somebody who speaks to the other 19 centuries," Pelikan concluded that he was "filing a minority report on behalf of the past." For that "report," filed with immense labor and erudition, he was regarded by his peers as perhaps the greatest church historian of his time.

No complete biography of Pelikan exists, but "a kind of autobiography in small bites" (as his editor called it) appeared as *The Melody of Theology: A Philosophical Dictionary* (1988). "A Personal Memoir: Fragments of a Scholar's Autobiography" is included in *Orthodoxy and Western Culture* (2005), compiled by Saint Vladimir's Seminary to honor Pelikan's eightieth birthday. This volume also contains a biographical sketch and a forty-four-page bibliography of Pelikan's published work from 1946 to 2006. An earlier Festschrift, *The Unbounded Community* (1996), also has some biographical information and a bibliography of Pelikan's writings up to 1995, as well as the text of the citation he received with the award of the Kluge Prize. Interviews with Pelikan that record his views of his work and his principles of scholarly responsibility are in Patrick Granfield, *Theologians at Work* (1967), and "Talk of the Town," *New Yorker* (2 Feb. 1981). An obituary is in the *New York Times* (16 May 2006).

Eleanor F. Wedge

PEP, Willie (*b.* 19 September 1922 in Middletown, Connecticut; *d.* 23 November 2006 in Rocky Hill, Connecticut), featherweight boxing champion from 1942 to 1948 and 1949 to 1950, member of International Boxing Hall of Fame.

Born Guglielmo (William) Papaleo, Pep was one of three children of Sicilian immigrants Salvatore Papaleo, a construction worker, and Mary (Marchese) Papaleo, a homemaker. When Pep was a young boy his family moved to Hartford, Connecticut, where they lived in an unheated, cold-water tenement. To help his family, Pep earned money as a shoeshine boy in Hartford's north side. He learned to box in local gyms to protect himself and his turf after beatings from bigger boys. Pep began his amateur boxing career at age fifteen and dropped out of Hartford High School the following year. Pep won sixty-two of sixty-five amateur bouts and held the Connecticut amateur flyweight title in 1938 and amateur bantamweight title in 1939. One of his amateur losses was to a taller, heavier New York fighter boxing under the name of Ray Roberts, who

Willie Pep. **KEYSTONE/GETTY IMAGES**

later would be better known as Sugar Ray Robinson, the welterweight and middleweight champion of the world.

Pep turned professional in July 1940. Managed by Lou Viscusi and trained by Bill Gore, Pep was a lightning-quick boxing stylist, darting in and out of danger, peppering his befuddled opponents with rapid-fire left jabs and combinations while rarely being hit solidly. At five feet, five and one-half inches tall and weighing between 118 and 126 pounds, Pep won sixty-two consecutive bouts from the start of his career, defeating Albert "Chalky" Wright on 20 November 1942 for the New York State Athletic Commission version of the featherweight title. At the age of twenty, Pep was the youngest champion to win a boxing title in forty years. Pep suffered his first loss to the former lightweight champion Sammy Angott on 19 March 1943. He then went undefeated in his next seventy-three bouts, becoming undisputed featherweight champion with a twelve-round knockout of Sal Bartolo on 7 June 1946.

During World War II, Pep served in the U.S. Navy from June 1943 to February 1944 and in the U.S. Army

from March to October 1945, being discharged for a punctured eardrum in each instance. In January 1947 Pep was flying from Miami to Hartford on a National Air Transport Service chartered DC-3 when the plane crashed during a snowstorm in a wooded area near Bridgeton, New Jersey. Pep suffered a broken leg, cracked vertebrae, and a chest injury; he was hospitalized and placed in two body casts. He was told by doctors he would never fight again but returned to the ring less than six months later and successfully defended his title in August 1947.

Pep had a record of 134 wins, 1 loss, and 1 draw when he defended his title against Sandy Saddler on 29 October 1948. A tall, strong, hard-punching brawler, Saddler was badly underestimated by Pep and knocked him out in the fourth round to gain the title. Pep would regain the title from Saddler on 11 February 1949, winning a fifteen-round decision in a brilliant display of boxing skill despite suffering serious facial cuts. But in two subsequent title bouts against Saddler in 1950 and 1951, Pep would lose twice, unable to answer the bell in the eighth and tenth rounds, respectively, after suffering shoulder and eye injuries. Each succeeding bout with Saddler became more foul plagued with both fighters guilty of heeling, gouging, holding, tripping, butting, wrestling, and other illegal tactics. After their final bout, both fighters would be suspended by the New York State Athletic Commission. On 26 February 1954 Pep lost in a second-round technical knockout to a former sparring partner, Lulu Perez, amid rumors of a fixed result.

In the final years of his boxing career, Pep became a boxing nomad, fighting generally lesser opposition for meager purses in minor venues. His final chance against a topflight opponent ended in defeat against the featherweight champion Hogan "Kid" Bassey in a nontitle fight on 20 September 1958. After retiring in 1959, Pep made a comeback in 1965 at the age of forty-two, winning nine bouts before retiring for good in 1966 after a defeat. His record of 230 victories, 11 losses, and 1 draw rates among the finest in boxing history.

A fun-loving free spender and an inveterate gambler who enjoyed the nightlife, Pep would claim to have gone through over $1 million during his boxing career, much of which was squandered on slow horses, bad business decisions, and divorce settlements. Pep was married six times and was divorced five times. He had four children, two boys and two girls. After his boxing career ended he held many jobs, working as a nightclub manager, restaurant greeter, brewery customer relations representative, automobile salesman, courtroom deputy, tax marshal, inspector for the Connecticut state boxing and wrestling commission, as well as boxing referee, trainer, and manager. For a time he hosted a Hartford television show, *Pep Talks.* In 1973 Pep coauthored with Robert Sacchi *Willie Pep Remembers . . . Friday's Heroes,* a mixture of personal reminiscences of his own ring career and glimpses of the great and near-great fighters of the 1940s and 1950s when he was at his best. In July 1980 *Inside Sports* magazine published "The Fix," ostensibly a piece of fiction that contended a fighter, described only as "The Champ" but strikingly similar to Pep, deliberately threw a fight and bet against himself. Pep's lawsuit against Newsweek, Inc., publisher of *Inside Sports*, was unsuccessful.

Pep was elected to the Ring Boxing Hall of Fame in 1963, the National Italian American Sports Hall of Fame in 1977, and the International Boxing Hall of Fame in 1990. In 1987 he married for the final time, a marriage that lasted for the remainder of his life. In 2000 Pep was diagnosed with dementia pugilistica and spent the final years of his life in an Alzheimer's disease unit of the Haven Health Center in Rocky Hill. He died from Alzheimer's and is buried in Rose Hill Memorial Park in Rocky Hill.

Pep's unparalleled boxing skills would be recognized by boxing experts and opponents, yet his tendency to outbox and outthink opponents while avoiding crowd-pleasing slugfests did not endear his quicksilver style to many fans during his career. Nagging questions linked to his losses to Saddler and mediocre performances in defeats to lesser opponents dogged him throughout his boxing career. But in the final analysis, his sheer ring brilliance would be transcendent. His onetime amateur foe Robinson would call Pep the best boxer he ever saw and the noted sportswriter W. C. Heinz said Pep was the greatest creative artist he had ever seen in the ring. Based on many such opinions, his reputation remains secure.

★

For information about Pep's life, see Brian Hughes, *Willie Pep: The Will o' the Wisp* (1997). For basic biographical information and career records about Pep, see James B. Roberts and Alexander G. Skutt, *The Boxing Register* (2002). Pep provides a sometimes hazy look back at his career in *Willie Pep Remembers... Friday's Heroes* with Robert Sacchi (1973). A fond appreciation of Pep's talent can be found in W. C. Heinz, *Once They Heard the Cheers* (1979). An informative article about Pep at the height of his career is in Barney Nagler, "The Return of Willie Pep," *Sport* (May 1949), while a perceptive portrait of Pep in the final stages of his boxing career is in Steve Gelman, "Willie Pep's Art of Self-Defense," *Esquire* (Dec. 1965). Obituaries are in the *New York Times* (24 Nov. 2006), *Boston Globe* (25 Nov. 2006), and *The Ring 2007 Boxing Almanac and Book of Facts*.

Edward J. Tassinari

PICKETT, Wilson, Jr. (*b.* 18 March 1941 in Prattville, Alabama; *d.* 19 January 2006 in Reston, Virginia), singer who was one of the founders of the southern soul sound, blending gospel fervor with rhythm and blues and rock and roll, in American popular music during the 1960s.

Wilson Pickett. MICHAEL OCHS ARCHIVES/GETTY IMAGES

Pickett was one of eleven children born to Wilson Pickett, Sr., and Lena Pickett, who were sharecroppers in rural Alabama. When Pickett was young his grandfather, a Baptist preacher, encouraged him to sing in church but beat him for singing secular music. His mother was a strict disciplinarian whose beatings occasionally drove the boy to run and hide in the woods. Chafing under the yoke of white domination, Pickett came up with ways to ease his work in the cotton fields, for instance by having bags of picked cotton counted twice. On one occasion he questioned a white man for intruding on his family home without knocking. In 1955, at the age of fourteen, he was sent to Detroit to live with his father, who had left the family some years earlier.

In Detroit, Pickett did not attend school but instead joined the Violinaires, a gospel singing group. He began to develop a passionate style of delivery, patterned after the singing style of Archie Brownlee, of the Five Blind Boys of Mississippi, and Julius Cheeks, of the Sensational Nightingales. The Violinaires moved from performing at local churches to touring with more famous gospel groups such as the Swan Silvertones and the Soul Stirrers, which featured Sam Cooke on vocals. Inspired by Cooke, who had made a successful transition from gospel to secular music, Pickett joined a Detroit rhythm-and-blues group, the Falcons, when Joe Stubbs, their lead singer, left the group. The Falcons had already scored a hit record with "She's So Fine" in 1959. Pickett had the chance to work with

Eddie Floyd and Sir Mack Rice during his tenure with the group; he wrote and sang lead on the Falcons' 1962 single "I Found a Love," which enjoyed success on both the rhythm-and-blues and pop charts.

The Falcons' producer introduced Pickett to Lloyd Price, a successful performer who was establishing his own Double-L record label. Meanwhile in 1963 Pickett and his manager approached Jerry Wexler at Atlantic Records to negotiate a solo contract and gave him a demo recording of Pickett's song "If You Need Me." But instead of giving Pickett a contract, the record company gave him a cash fee, and the song was recorded by the Atlantic artist Solomon Burke. Although his own version of the song was released on Double-L, it was overshadowed by Burke's hit. Later that year he released "It's Too Late," and the song's success prompted Wexler to buy his contract from Price in 1964.

In spite of Wexler's efforts to put Pickett on the charts by teaming him with the producer Bert Berns and the songwriters Barry Mann and Cynthia Weil, his early recordings for Atlantic were unsuccessful. The defining moment in Pickett's career came the following year when Wexler was inspired by the music then being recorded at Jim Stewart's Stax studio in Memphis, Tennessee. Believing that the soulful "black" sound of Stax was a match for Pickett's vocal style, Wexler and Pickett traveled to Memphis for a recording session in May 1965. This session ensured the singer's place in the history of southern soul music. Collaborating with the Stax guitarist Steve Cropper and under the direction of Wexler, Pickett wrote and recorded "In the Midnight Hour," which became his first major chart success for Atlantic and his signature song. Pickett had two additional recording sessions at Stax prior to Stewart's falling out with Wexler and Atlantic in December 1965. Working with the Memphis Horns, a soul horn section that became famous for its work on Stax recordings, and the studio's house band, Booker T and the MG's, Pickett added to the canon of soul music with hits such as "634-5789 (Soulsville, USA)," "Ninety-nine and a Half (Won't Do)," and "Don't Fight It." In all, he compiled enough songs for his second Atlantic album, *The Exciting Wilson Pickett* (1966), the most popular release of his career.

Wexler arranged for Pickett's next recording sessions at Rick Hall's Fame Studios in Muscle Shoals, Alabama. Pickett had some initial misgivings about working at a recording studio next to a Deep South cotton field. But Hall put him at ease, and Pickett added to his reputation with hits such as "Land of 1,000 Dances," which reached number six on the pop charts—his career high—and "Mustang Sally," a cover of a song by former colleague Rice, both in 1966, and "Funky Broadway" (1967). Returning to Memphis in late 1967, Pickett recorded at American Studios with the famed Atlantic producer Tom Dowd. These sessions yielded successful collaborations with the songwriter Bobby Womack, including "I'm in

Love" (1967) and "I'm a Midnight Mover" (1968). Pickett returned to Fame Studios for sessions that produced a successful cover of the Beatles' "Hey Jude" (1968).

By the end of the 1960s black music was expanding in several directions. Pickett's recording sessions for Atlantic moved to Miami and ultimately to Philadelphia, where he worked with the legendary producers Kenny Gamble and Leon Huff on *Wilson Pickett in Philadelphia* (1970), which included two hit singles. A final session at Fame Studios produced his last Top Twenty pop hit, "Don't Knock My Love, Part 1" (1971), but by this time his tenure with Atlantic records was nearing its end. As the popularity of the "Philadelphia sound," funk, and ultimately disco began to overshadow that of southern soul, Pickett's recording career declined. He tried without success to modify his screaming and shouting style to keep pace with changing times; a recording contract with RCA lasted only from 1972 to 1975, yielding five albums that were commercial failures. An album released on his own Wicked label in 1978, *A Funky Situation*, was recorded back in Muscle Shoals in his old style but found only limited success.

Pickett rerecorded "In the Midnight Hour" at the Motown studios in 1987, but his recording career did not recover. However, in 1991 two encouraging events were the release of Alan Parker's film *The Commitments* (1991), which depicted a band of Irish musicians whose inspiration is Pickett's music and which brought his music to younger audiences, and his induction into the Rock and Roll Hall of Fame. In 1992 *A Man and a Half*, a compilation of his hits, was released. In 1993 he was featured in a documentary on soul music, *Only the Strong Survive*, directed by D. A. Pennebaker, and he received a Pioneer Award from the Rhythm and Blues Foundation. His last studio album, *It's Harder Now*, appeared in 1999 and earned Pickett his first Grammy nomination and three W. C. Handy Awards from the Blues Foundation. Also in 1999 Pickett was inducted into the Alabama Music Hall of Fame, receiving a Life Work Award for Performing Achievement.

Pickett was regarded as a volatile personality by friends and associates, earning the nickname "Wicked Pickett," or just "the Wicked." He had at least one marriage and four children. Although many details of his personal life remain unknown, frequent brushes with the law made other aspects public. His use of alcohol and drugs was complicated by his fondness for guns and his violent temper. As his recording career foundered, he was arrested several times between 1975 and 1996; in 1994 he served time in a New Jersey prison, followed by several years' probation, on a drunk driving conviction. He entered drug rehabilitation when cocaine possession violated the terms of his probation. Nevertheless, he remained a popular performer on the club and concert circuit throughout his career, and the income supported a comfortable lifestyle. By 1999 he had settled into a more tranquil life in Ashburn, Virginia, maintaining an active tour schedule until his health began to fail. Pickett was planning to reunite with old friends Burke and Don Covay in the Soul Clan and considering recording a gospel album, but he died of heart failure. He is buried in Louisville, Kentucky, next to his mother.

Pickett earned his place in American popular music history in the mid-1960s, when the black sound of southern soul was introduced to mass audiences. His raw gospel passion, infused with screams, was representative of this style of music, which coincided with the rise of African-American pride. Several of the songs he wrote and performed have become soul standards.

★

Gerri Hirshey, *Nowhere to Run: The Story of Soul Music* (1984), offers Pickett's own observations on his background and career. In *Sweet Soul Music: Rhythm and Blues and the Southern Dream of Freedom* (1986), Peter Guralnick provides a detailed discussion of the social and cultural context of the rise of southern soul. Rob Bowman, *Soulsville, U.S.A: The Story of Stax Records* (1997), documents Pickett's experience in the Memphis studio that would define his career. Hirshey, "Wilson Pickett, 1941–2006," *Rolling Stone* (9 Feb. 2006), updates her earlier discussion of Pickett's place in the history of soul. Obituaries are in the *New York Times* (20 Jan. 2006) and *Washington Post* (21 Jan. 2006).

James F. Smith

PITNEY, Gene Francis Allan (*b.* 17 February 1941 in Hartford, Connecticut; *d.* 5 April 2006 in Cardiff, Wales), noted singer-songwriter whose full-voiced, dramatic ballads and finely crafted melodies helped define mid-twentieth-century popular music in film, radio, and television.

Pitney was one of four children born to Harold F. Pitney, a lathe operator at a mill, and Anna Agnes Orlowski Pitney, a homemaker. Growing up in Rockville, Connecticut, Pitney was introduced to music in a way that was similar to many young popular artists. Gene learned to sing in school and church choirs and displayed an early affinity for piano, guitar, and drums. Pitney acquired recording technology; studied the music of the dominant rhythm-and-blues artists of the 1950s; formed his own high school rock band called Gene & the Genials; and wrote several songs for the Embers, a Hartford doo-wop group. After graduating from Rockville High School in 1958, Pitney enrolled in the Ward School of Electronics, now part of the University of Hartford. He also teamed up with a writing partner, Ginny Arnell. Together, they recorded several songs pseudonymously as Jamie and Jane for Decca Records. In 1959 Pitney released his first solo recording, "Cradle of My

Gene Pitney. CHARLIE GILLETT COLLECTION/REDFERNS/ GETTY IMAGES

Arms," for the tiny label Festival Records, under another pseudonym, Billy Bryan. Neither project yielded significant notoriety, but Pitney was on the brink of a decade-long rise to stardom.

Early in 1959 Pitney met Aaron Schroeder, a songwriter for Elvis Presley. With Schroeder, Pitney wrote a bubblegum single, "Rubber Ball," for the singer Bobby Vee and Liberty Records. Pitney was listed pseudonymously yet again, as Anne Orlowski. At the height of the success of "Rubber Ball," the singer Roy Orbison chose Pitney's song "Today's Teardrops" as the B side for his record "Blue Angel" (1960). Orbison's record became a Top Ten single, as did Pitney's "Hello Mary Lou," written for the singer Ricky Nelson's record "Travelin' Man" (1961). By late 1960 Pitney's songs had appeared on three Top Ten records in a two-year span. In 1961 Schroeder, who at the time was president of Musicor Records, asked Pitney to record "I Wanna Love My Life Away" under his own name. Pitney not only sang it but also performed all instruments except the electric bass, using the music layering process of overdubbing, available with the revolutionary technology of multitrack tape recording. The entire recording cost a total of $30, including the tape and the bass player's session fee. Musicor was able to release the demonstration recording itself—usually considered too utilitarian and straightforward—because of its careful production. The record sold modestly, but its production aesthetic of layered tracks, rather than a recorded ensemble performance, helped change pop music paradigms. Pitney's combination of writing, performing, and recording his own records recalled earlier experiments by seminal artists such as the guitarist Les Paul and the blues artist Chester Burnett ("Howlin' Wolf"). Pitney's work also prepared for future experiments by the musicians Brian Wilson, Jimi Hendrix, and Stevie Wonder.

In September 1961 Pitney recorded "Every Breath I Take," written by Carole King and Gerry Goffin. The record featured the music producer and songwriter Phil Spector's highly reverberant and intricately overdubbed "wall of sound" production style. Despite sluggish sales, the record achieved more professional acclaim and visibility for Pitney. Later in 1961 Pitney recorded "Town Without Pity," written for the movie of the same name by the film scoring team of Dmitri Tiomkin and Ned Washington. The movie was an adaptation of Manfred Gregor's controversial 1960 novel, *Das Urteil*. The film's brooding plot of post–World War II occupation, sexual provocation and abuse, outraged citizenry, and predatory courtroom action was melodramatically counterpointed by Pitney's tightly strung performance of the disaffected title song. Spector demanded multiple takes by Pitney at the vocal session, finally accepting the thirtieth attempt. This last take revealed a very strained and edgy timbre, instead of Pitney's usually pure voice, but one that complemented the film's jagged polarizations.

Pitney's collaboration with Spector continued with "He's a Rebel." Spector selected this song for his successful singing group the Crystals, despite the song's earlier acceptance as a featured debut for the singer Vicki Carr on a competing record label. Spector rushed his recording of "He's a Rebel" into production by actually recording the session vocalist Darlene Love and the singing group the Blossoms, not the Crystals (who were touring on the East Coast at the time). Released in August 1962 and attributed to the Crystals, the song rose to number one in the United States by November 1962. Simultaneously, Pitney recorded another of his signature songs, "Only Love Can Break a Heart," written by Burt Bacharach and Hal David. The song peaked at number two during the same period that "He's a Rebel" reached number one. During late 1962 Pitney sang another movie theme song, "The Man Who Shot Liberty Valance." Bacharach and David wrote the song for a film of the same name that was in production and directed by John Ford, but the song was not included in the film score due to a publishing disagreement. Nevertheless, the song achieved substantial success on the radio, and Pitney was at the top of U.S. popularity charts once again in 1963. For the next twelve months Pitney wrote or sang seven consecutive Top Ten hits. He recorded songs by some of America's best new popular songwriters, including Ellie Greenwich, Al Kooper, and Randy Newman. Pitney continued recording his own songs—"Mecca," "It Hurts to Be in Love," "True Love Never Runs Smooth," and

"I'm Gonna Be Strong"—and Bacharach and David's "24 Hours from Tulsa," a song that achieved considerable success in the United Kingdom, guaranteeing Pitney's European touring opportunities for the next three decades.

In early 1964 Spector introduced Pitney to a new, unknown team of English songwriters, Mick Jagger and Keith Richards of the Rolling Stones. When Pitney listened to their music, he heard the future of rock in it. He even performed the Rolling Stones's first recording in the United States, "That Girl Belongs to Yesterday." The same year that Pitney introduced the Rolling Stones to the United States, he was voted best popular singer (in Italian) in an Italian listeners' poll. Pitney's extraordinary musical diversity led the pop musicologist Mitchell Cohen to observe in the disc jacket information of the album *Gene Pitney: Anthology (1961–1968),* produced by Rhino Records (1986), "[Pitney is] an artist always willing to turn a new corner, always looking for where the next hit [is] coming from, and, more often than not, looking in the right places."

In 1966 Pitney married Lynne Gayton, his high school sweetheart. The couple had three sons. Soon after their marriage, Pitney and his wife moved to nearby Somers, Connecticut. There, Pitney focused on building his family and managing his promotional tours, located mostly in Europe, the United Kingdom, and Australia. Pitney's next career phase would entail touring six to ten months a year for the next twenty years and playing at sold-out international concert venues.

In 1989 Pitney collaborated with the U.K. pop singer Marc Almond (from Soft Cell, an early electronica band) on a remake of "Something's Gotten Hold of My Heart," originally recorded by Pitney in 1967. The remake paired Almond's 1980s black-leather style with Pitney's 1960s white-tuxedo style, resulting in an "odd couple" recording that reached number one on the U.K. music charts. The success reinvigorated Pitney's U.S. touring. Throughout the 1990s Pitney performed around the world. In 1995 the Public Broadcasting Service filmed a television special called *Gene Pitney on Stage.* In 2002 Pitney was inducted into the Rock and Roll Hall of Fame, with the "He's a Rebel" vocalist Love presenting. In 2006, while on tour in the United Kingdom, Pitney was discovered dead in his hotel suite in Cardiff, Wales, the day after performing to another full house. The cause of death was noted as arteriosclerosis. Pitney is buried in Somers Centre Cemetery in Somers. His career as a singer-songwriter spanned almost fifty years, including thirty-seven albums, fifty-three singles, sixteen Top Forty hits, four Top Ten hits, and nearly forty world tours. His music established dramatic teen balladry as an enduring component of twentieth-century popular culture.

Information about Pitney's life is available in Ed Ward, Geoffrey Stokes, and Ken Tucker, *Rock of Ages: The Rolling Stone History of Rock & Roll* (1986); Mark Ribowsky, *He's a Rebel: The Truth About Phil Spector—Rock and Roll's Legendary Madman* (1989); Dafydd Ress and Luke Crampton, *Rock's Movers and Shakers: An A to Z of the People Who Made Rock Happen* (1991); Jay Warner, *Billboard's American Rock 'n' Roll in Review* (1997); Brock Helander, *The Rockin' 60s: The People Who Made the Music* (1999); and Joseph A. Angiolillo, Jr., *Gene Pitney, His Climb to International Success* (2005). Obituaries are in the *New York Times* (6 Apr. 2006) and London *Daily Telegraph* (7 Apr. 2006).

James McElwaine

PLESHETTE, Suzanne (*b.* 31 January 1937 in New York City; *d.* 19 January 2008 in Los Angeles, California), actor of screen, stage, and television.

Pleshette was born to Geraldine (Kaplan) Pleshette, a former dancer who used the stage name of Geraldine Rivers throughout her career, and Eugene Pleshette, once manager of the New York and Brooklyn Paramount

Suzanne Pleshette. © **PHOTOS 12/ALAMY**

theaters during the 1930s. Pleshette believed that her attendance at the New York High School of the Performing Arts awakened her desire for a career in the performing arts. Even as she took the conventional route of college after graduation in 1955 (Pleshette attended Syracuse University and Finch College for one semester each), she soon found her way to New York's Neighborhood Playhouse School of the Theater, where she studied with the renowned acting teacher Sanford Meisner.

Pleshette took her first acting roles in 1957. In that year, she appeared in a television series, *Harbourmaster,* and also performed in the Broadway production of *Compulsion.* In February 1961 Pleshette replaced Anne Bancroft—in the role Bancroft originated on Broadway and for which she had won the 1960 Tony Award for Best Actress—as Annie Sullivan. Pleshette played opposite Patty Duke's Helen Keller in *The Miracle Worker.* In 1964 Pleshette married the actor Troy Donahue, but the marriage ended after only four months.

As for her career in motion pictures, Pleshette collaborated with a number of talented and prestigious filmmakers, including Alfred Hitchcock in 1963's *The Birds.* Her debut on the silver screen occurred in 1958, when she appeared in *The Geisha Boy,* one of Jerry Lewis's star vehicles. Other notable roles included *Youngblood Hawke* (1964), *A Rage to Live* (1965), *Nevada Smith* (1966), *Blackbeard's Ghost* (1968), *If It's Tuesday, This Must Be Belgium* (1969), *Support Your Local Gunfighter!* (1970), and *The Shaggy D.A.* (1976).

Acting took a back seat to domestic life in 1968, when Pleshette married for the second time, this time to Tom Gallagher, a businessman. Her retirement was short-lived, however. Within several months of her wedding, Pleshette was seeking out guest appearances on the talk-show circuit in an attempt to remain in show business, yet with a slower-paced workload. Johnny Carson obliged, inviting Pleshette to be his guest more than twenty times over a four-year span. Her appearances proved successful; as one such turn, with Bob Newhart, caught the eye of *The Bob Newhart Show*'s creators, the writers David Davis and Lorenzo Music. Pleshette's acerbic wit, quirky personality, and honesty about her marital life appealed to Davis and Music, who envisioned a fictional wife who did not fall into the stereotypical homemaker ideals so popular on the sitcoms of the 1950s and 1960s.

It was this role—that of Emily Hartley, wife of television's Newhart, in the situation comedy, *The Bob Newhart Show,* which ran from 1972 until 1978—that would become perhaps Pleshette's best known and most beloved. *The Bob Newhart Show* proved to be a watershed in Pleshette's career. Her performance as Emily led to two Emmy Award nominations in 1977 and 1978. (Her first Emmy Award nomination came from her guest-starring appearance in a 1962 episode of *Dr. Kildare.*) She soon landed roles in sitcoms in which she would play the starring role, including 1984's *Suzanne Pleshette Is Maggie Briggs* and 1994–1995's comedic *The Boys Are Back*. The 1980s also witnessed Pleshette's turn at television drama. She starred in 1986's *Bridges to Cross* and 1989's *Nightingales*. Among the other television programs on which Pleshette appeared were *Have Gun, Will Travel* (1959), *Naked City* (1959), and *Playhouse 90* (1959). She also portrayed the controversial New York hotel mogul, Leona Helmsley in 1991's *Leona Helmsley: The Queen of Mean*, a role that garnered Pleshette her fourth Emmy Award nomination the following year.

It is the role of Emily Hartley that remains Pleshette's legacy. For Bob Newhart's second series, *Newhart*, Pleshette made a surprise appearance as Emily Hartley in the closing moments of the series finale. Newhart's character of Dick Loudon, upon awakening from a blow to the head with an errant golf ball, discovers himself in the bedroom of Robert Hartley (Newhart's character in *The Bob Newhart* show), with Emily by his side. Critics and studio audience members alike were thrilled and shocked by the surprise ending that had been guarded by show producers and network executives in the days leading up to the finale. An emblematic role that shaped and defined her career, Emily Hartley remained the character with which Pleshette was most closely associated.

Following Gallagher's death in 2000, Pleshette married Tom Poston, one of her costars on Broadway in the 1959 production of *Golden Fleecing*. The couple remained married until Poston's death from respiratory failure on 30 April 2007.

Pleshette continued working throughout the early years of the twenty-first century, performing in a series of cameo appearances on the sitcom *Will and Grace* in 2002 and 2004. She also had a starring role in the 2002–2003 sitcom *Good Morning, Miami*. The official cause of her death at age seventy was respiratory failure, although Pleshette had battled health problems for several years preceding her death. She had spent the bulk of her sixties struggling with lung cancer, including enduring a grueling round of chemotherapy in 2006. A bittersweet footnote to her brilliant career as a comedian with impeccable timing lies in the fact that Pleshette was to be honored with a star on Hollywood's Walk of Fame on 31 January 2008, the date of her seventy-first birthday. Pleshette was buried at the Hillside Memorial Park Cemetery in Culver City, California, on 23 January 2008 following a memorial service in her honor.

★

Obituaries for Pleshette are in the *Los Angeles Times* (20 Jan. 2008) and the *Seattle Times, Washington Post,* and *New York Times* (all 21 Jan. 2008).

Kimberly K. Little

POLLACK, Sydney Irwin (*b.* 1 July 1934 in Lafayette, Indiana; *d.* 26 May 2008 in Pacific Palisades, California), producer, director, and actor for the large and small screens, and Academy Award winner.

Pollack was born the oldest of three children to first-generation Jewish Russian-Americans Rebecca Miller and David Pollack, a semiprofessional boxer and pharmacist. His brother, Bernie, designed film costumes and his sister, Sharon, taught dancing. Upon moving to South Bend, Indiana, the young Pollack saw his mother's emotional problems lead to alcoholism and to her death when he was sixteen. Against the wishes of his father, who wanted him to be a dentist, upon graduating from South Bend Central High School in 1952, Pollack fled Indiana for New York City and the chance to act. Having accepted a fellowship at the Neighborhood Playhouse, he came under the tutelage of the revered mentor Sanford Meisner.

Meisner's coaching would not only prepare Pollack for his performances but would also provide him a method for film directing. Barely nineteen years old, he assisted Meisner as tutor and by the age of twenty had made his Broadway debut in *The Dark Is Light Enough*. In 1958, in the midst of an army hitch, Pollack married Claire Griswold, another student of Meisner's; the couple would go on to have three children.

Sydney Pollack, 2006. MARIO ANZUONI/REUTERS/LANDOV

Back from the service, Pollack lowered his ambitions from star to character actor, realizing that he was "a character-looking kind of guy." He found roles on *Playhouse 90* and in series such as *The Twilight Zone* and *Have Gun, Will Travel*. During the 1959 production of the *Playhouse 90* version of *For Whom the Bell Tolls*, the director John Frankenheimer offered Pollack dialogue coaching jobs, first with two children for the televised *Turn of the Screw* (1959) and then for the movie *The Young Savages* (1961). That film's star, Burt Lancaster, connected Pollack to Lew Wasserman at Universal Studios and thereby launched a brief but prolific career in television directing. Pollack started inauspiciously, with the last episode of a canceled Western series. By the mid-1960s, however, he was helming episodes for *Ben Casey*, *The Alfred Hitchcock Hour*, and *Kraft Suspense Theater*. Thrice nominated for Emmys, he won in 1965 for "The Game" episode on *Bob Hope Presents the Chrysler Theatre*.

Pollack transitioned into feature films with his performance as Sergeant Owen Van Horn in *War Hunt* (1962), a film that also marked the debut of Robert Redford, who formed a long professional and personal bond with Pollack. Pollack's first film as director, *The Slender Thread*, featured Sidney Poitier as a crisis-phone operator trying to keep an overdosed Anne Bancroft alive until help arrives. Neither that film nor Pollack's next three—*This Property Is Condemned* (1966) with Redford and Natalie Wood, *The Scalphunters* (1968), and *Castle Keep* (1969) both with Burt Lancaster—proved box-office hits. However, the director had proven his versatility by wrangling stars; handling the drama, Western, comedy, and war genres; and establishing his antiracism, antiwar, and liberal credentials.

With *They Shoot Horses, Don't They?* (1969), Pollack vaulted to the next level as a Hollywood insider who combined commercial and art house sensibilities. The film garnered Oscar nominations, with Gig Young winning one for best supporting actor. Also in 1969 Pollack and Mark Rydell formed Sanford Pictures and cosigned a six-picture deal with the Mirisch Company. Of these, Pollack directed only one, *Jeremiah Johnson* (1972), a Western starring Redford as a murderous mountain man who finally comes to terms with the Crow tribe. Shot in Utah, the low-budget production drew favorable reviews for capturing the rugged lifestyle and was another box-office hit.

For *The Way We Were* (1973), Pollack teamed Redford and Barbra Streisand as a couple torn apart by the Hollywood Ten hearings. Despite some scathing reviews, the movie scored with fans and its title song won an Oscar. With a script by Robert Towne and Paul Schrader, Pollack went on location to Japan to film a gangster story, *The Yakuza* (1974), with Robert Mitchum. Post-Watergate America provided the setting for *Three Days of the Condor* (1975), a critically admired suspense thriller with Redford as a self-doubting Central Intelligence Agency operative sheltered from his pursuers by Faye Dunaway. With *The*

Electric Horseman (1979) with its theme of commercial exploitation, Pollack continued his collaborations with Redford as star and consultant. The film won good reviews and box office. In response to the glorification of journalism on display in Alan Pakula's *All the President's Men* (1976), *Absence of Malice* (1981) depicted the exploitation of a liquor warehouse owner (played by Paul Newman) by media minions bent on delivering a story.

Pollack's forays into producing and executive producing account for the gaps between his directing projects, but *Tootsie* (1982) and *Out of Africa* (1985) stand as two of his best and most popular directing and producing achievements. For *Tootsie* (1982), Pollack also brilliantly played the star Dustin Hoffman's agent in the feminist comedy about a struggling actor who cross-dresses his way to fame, falls in love with his costar, Jessica Lange, and taps into his sensitive side. The film earned over $180 million domestically, received ten Oscar nominations, and won the best supporting actress award for Lange. With big budget and stars, *Out of Africa* (1985) set Redford and Meryl Streep in Kenya as doomed lovers trying to overcome their differences. The star power, lush settings, and stirring music led to Oscars for best film, director, screenplay, cinematography, and score and to breathtaking box-office receipts. Pollack had reached his pinnacle.

Subsequently, only the adaptation of John Grisham's *The Firm* (1993), a corporate corruption thriller starring Tom Cruise, Gene Hackman, and Holly Hunter, met the Pollack standards. Forming the Mirage Production Company with the British producer-director Anthony Minghella and collaborating with George Clooney, Pollack continued to deliver highly regarded films, this time as producer: *Cold Mountain* (2003), *Michael Clayton* (2007), and *The Reader* (2008). As executive producer, he also underwrote dozens of movies for the big screen and television and served as a resource for needy independent filmmakers. His performances in Woody Allen's *Husbands and Wives* (1992), Stanley Kubrick's *Eyes Wide Shut* (1999), and *Michael Clayton* won critical applause and brought full circle the career of a mainstream Hollywood producer and director who began as an actor. Pollack died of cancer at his home in Pacific Palisades. Services were private.

In retrospect, Pollack gave audiences some of the biggest and most influential films of the 1970s, 1980s, and 1990s, gained the respect of critics, and became a champion of artists' rights. One of Hollywood's most financially successful moviemakers, Pollack agreed, "I've made personal films all along. I just made them in another form."

★

An overview and analyses of Pollack's directing methods can be found in Janet Maslin, "The Pollack Touch," *New York Times Magazine* (15 Dec. 1985). A critical commentary on a number of Pollack films appears in John Wakeman, ed.,

World Film Directors, Vol. 2, 1945–1985 (1987). A further retrospective and examination of his films can be found in Janet Meyer, *Sydney Pollack: A Critical Filmography* (1998). An obituary is in the *New York Times* (27 May 2008).

Gerard Molyneaux

POLSBY, Nelson Woolf (*b.* 25 October 1934 in Norwich, Connecticut; *d.* 6 February 2007 in Berkeley, California), political scientist, educator, and author of influential studies of political parties, Congress, the media, and the presidency.

Polsby was one of three sons of Daniel Polsby, a businessman and member of a Connecticut farming family, and Edythe (Woolf) Polsby (later Salzberger), an artist and art therapist. His father, who died when Polsby was twelve, nurtured his young son's interest in politics. Polsby graduated from Pomfret School, a private boarding school in Connecticut. When his family moved to the Washington, D.C., area, he enjoyed attending sessions of Congress during his visits on school breaks. Turning down offers from Yale and Harvard universities, he attended Johns Hopkins University in Baltimore because it was closer to Washington, where he could continue to observe the Senate at work. He earned an AB in political science in 1956 and an MA in sociology from Brown University in 1957. He then went on to Yale University, earning a second MA (in political science) in 1958 and a PhD, with a thesis on political power relationships, in 1961. On 3 August 1958 he married Linda Offenbach, with whom he would have two daughters and a son.

Polsby began his teaching career at the University of Wisconsin at Madison and Wesleyan University in Connecticut, where in 1967, after six years on the faculty, he attained full professorship. That year he joined the faculty of the University of California at Berkeley, where he remained for the rest of his career. As Heller Professor of Political Science and director of the Institute of Governmental Studies (1988–1999), he taught courses in American politics, Congress, and presidential elections and advised many graduate students who went on to become prominent scholars. He was known for holding three o'clock teas for graduate students and visiting professors, at which lively discussions contributed to the campus intellectual community. People wanted to know what Professor Polsby thought, and he was equally eager to promote the study and understanding of American politics among his students and colleagues.

Polsby's first influential works were *Politics and Social Life: An Introduction to Political Behavior* (1963), edited with Robert Dentler and Paul Smith, and an essay, "Institutionalization of the U.S. House of Representatives" (1968), published in the *American Political Science Review*, the journal of which he was managing editor from 1971 to 1977. Among his many other books are *Presidential Elections: Strategies and Structures of American Politics* (1964) and *American Governmental Institutions: A Reader in the Political Process* (1969), both written or edited with Aaron Wildavsky, and *What If? Explorations in Social-Science Fiction* (1966). *Presidential Elections* has been updated twelve times and remains the standard text used in the study of the topic. Over the course of his career he wrote many articles and opinion pieces for the *New York Times* and other major newspapers on such topics as the presidential nominating process and the news media. He maintained a lifelong interest in Congress, often writing about its inner workings.

Bipartisan in his irritation with politicians, Polsby was described by a colleague as someone who "could rip the bark off Bill Clinton just as easily as he could George Bush." Suspicious of the objectivity of reporters, he instead viewed the news media as just another interest group "attempting to make their product interesting" or, during presidential election years, in "the manufacture of a horse race." He was often sought out during campaigns for what he called "'the prof quote,' which is a ten-second answer to the question, 'Has anybody in history ever done this before?'" In a typically acerbic and evenhanded comment on the vice-presidential candidates in the 2000 race between George W. Bush and Al Gore, he noted that "[Richard] Cheney was picked to indemnify Bush against the charge that he was ignorant" and "[Joseph] Lieberman was picked to indemnify Gore against the charge that he was sleazy."

Polsby's last book was *How Congress Evolves: Social Bases of Institutional Change* (2004). In his last major article, "The Importance of Constituents," also published in 2004, he attributed the shift of power in the House of Representatives in the 1950s and 1960s to demographic changes; Republicans, drawn to the South in part, as he wryly noted, by residential air-conditioning, displaced traditional Democrats in conservative leadership. In 2008 the Institute for Governmental Studies began awarding the Nelson W. Polsby Grant for Public Affairs Research. His family also established the Nelson W. Polsby Memorial Graduate Student Fund to support University of California at Berkeley graduate students interested in the study of Congress. Over the years Polsby held visiting professorships at several universities, including Harvard, Stanford, and the Hebrew University of Jerusalem. He was a member of the Council on Foreign Relations, the American Academy of Arts and Sciences, and the American Association for the Advancement of Science. He was twice awarded a Guggenheim Fellowship (1977–1978, 1985–1986) and in 1985 was awarded Yale University's Wilbur Cross Medal.

Polsby died at his home of complications due to congestive heart failure on 6 February 2007. His remains were cremated.

Noted for his wit and vitality as well as his brilliance, Polsby was hailed for his clear-sighted approach to American politics. For him the workings of Washington and the role of the electorate were a vastly interesting and entertaining subject. He once commented that he had trouble believing "people paid you American money to study this stuff." A revered scholar, he influenced the way many people—readers, students, and colleagues—think about the American political system.

★

Polsby's papers are at the Bancroft Library, University of California at Berkeley. "Institutional Change in the U.S. Congress," an interview with Harry Kreisler in the *Conversations with History* series of the Institute of International Studies (Berkeley), provides biographical information and a personal account of his political science methods and political thinking. Obituaries are in the *Times* (London) and *Washington Post* (both 8 Feb. 2007) and the *New York Times* (9 Feb. 2007).

Louise B. Ketz

PRAN, DITH

SEE *Dith Pran.*

Kirby Puckett. MLB PHOTOS/GETTY IMAGES

PUCKETT, Kirby (*b.* 14 March 1960 in Chicago, Illinois; *d.* 6 March 2006 in Phoenix, Arizona), center fielder for the Minnesota Twins who helped lead the team to two World Series titles but whose career was cut short by glaucoma.

Puckett was the youngest of nine children of William Puckett, a postal worker, and Catherine Puckett. The family lived in a three-room apartment in the Robert Taylor Homes on Chicago's South Side. It was a rough neighborhood, but he stayed away from gangs, violence, and drugs by playing baseball. As he once told an interviewer, "If you ever wanted to find [me], you knew where to go—around the corner, where I'd be with my ball and bat and hitting and throwing against a wall." He graduated from Calumet High School in 1979, but having received no offers from teams, he went to work at a local Ford automotive plant. After working for a year, he attended a free-agent tryout for the Kansas City Royals. Instead of a professional contract, he was offered a baseball scholarship to Bradley University in Peoria, Illinois. There he played center field and worked on his offense. After a

year at Bradley, his father died, and he returned to Chicago. He enrolled at Triton Community College, where, though at five feet, eight inches he was small by baseball standards, he caught the eye of a Twins scout. He became a first-round draft pick for the Minnesota Twins organization and was sent to the minor leagues in 1982.

After two successful seasons in the minors and being chosen best major-league prospect, in 1984 he was called up to the majors. In his first game for the Twins on 8 May 1984 in Anaheim, California, he had four hits in his first five at bats, launching his career. His short stature and good-natured personality earned him the fan nickname "Puck," and his heavy build—during his playing career he weighed over 200 pounds—made him an unusual sight on the field. For his success as a hitter and a fielder, he was chosen to play on the American League All-Star Team in 1986 and for the next ten consecutive years. On 1 November 1986 Puckett married Tonya Hudson, with whom he had a daughter and a son.

The two high points of his twelve-season career with the Twins were leading the team to World Series championships in 1987 and 1991. In game six of the 1991 series against the Atlanta Braves, with the Braves leading three games to two, Puckett leaped above the center-field fence to make a catch, preventing a home run and saving the game for the Twins. Later, in the eleventh inning, Charlie Leibrandt was sent in to pitch for the Braves. Leibrandt was a seasoned and successful pitcher, but for Puckett it was an opportunity. He yelled to coach Rick Stelmaszek, "It's over, it's over." Taking his classic stance—bat cocked behind his head, front leg lifted high—he hit the ball into the left field stands to win the game. It is said that, as he rounded the bases, those sitting close to the field could hear him yell, "I said it was over," above the thunderous noise of 60,000 fans screaming "Kirby! Kirby!" Named Most Valuable Player, Puckett showed his ability to carry a team for a game, a season, or a series.

On 15 September 1995 Puckett was hit in the face by a fastball that shattered his jaw. The injury ended his season, but he recovered. During spring training in 1996, he was performing with his usual élan, hitting well, fielding perfectly, his energy and enthusiasm empowering the team. But when he woke up on 26 March, he was suddenly unable to see out of his right eye. He was diagnosed with glaucoma; despite several operations, he never regained the vision in that eye. Puckett's career ended at a point where he was hitting .326 for the spring and had just hit .314 for the season. Such an abrupt ending was psychologically stressful.

Although Puckett took a job with the Twins and proved to be a capable executive, his life took a dark turn. His marital problems became public when his wife accused him of a history of domestic violence and infidelity. The couple divorced in 2002. Later that year he was charged with sexually assaulting a woman in a Twin Cities restaurant; he was acquitted at trial in April 2003. His association with the Twins ended at that time.

In 2000 Puckett was inducted into the Baseball Hall of Fame. Standing before thousands of fans chanting his name, he thanked them, saying, "It may be cloudy in my right eye, but the sun is shining very brightly in my left eye." He enjoyed the life of a Hall of Famer, spending time with his fellow former players at baseball events and sponsoring charitable events. He served as a spokesman for the Glaucoma Foundation and was awarded the Roberto Clemente and Branch Rickey awards for community service. At age forty-five he suffered a stroke at his home in Arizona and died a day later. After his funeral in Wayzata, Minnesota, a huge crowd gathered at the Metrodome for a celebration of his career. Puckett was cremated.

Puckett retired from twelve seasons playing for the Twins with a .318 career batting average, 207 home runs, 1,085 runs batted in, and 134 stolen bases. His baseball career, tragically shortened by glaucoma, took him to two winning World Series tournaments and earned him a lasting place in Minnesota Twins history.

★

Puckett's autobiography is *I Love This Game!: My Life and Baseball* (1993). For details of Puckett's personal struggles, see Frank Deford, "The Rise and Fall of Kirby Puckett," *Sports Illustrated* (17 Mar. 2003). Obituaries are in the *New York Times* (7 Mar. 2006), *Chicago Tribune* (13 Mar. 2006), and *Sports Illustrated* (20 Mar. 2006).

Clark C. Griffith

R

———■———

RAUSCHENBERG, Robert (*b*. 22 October 1925 in Port Arthur, Texas; *d*. 12 May 2008 on Captiva Island, Florida), painter, sculptor, printmaker, photographer, and performance artist, regarded internationally as one of the foremost and most prolific postmodernist artists.

———

Born Milton Ernest Rauschenberg, the artist would change his first name to Robert in his early twenties. He and his sister grew up in a family of somewhat limited means. His father, Ernest Rauschenberg, of German and Cherokee descent, worked for a utilities company; his mother, Dora (Matson) Rauschenberg, was a homemaker. Both were strict fundamentalists, opposed to dissipations such as drinking and dancing. (In later life, their son indulged freely in both.) Rauschenberg began to draw at the age of ten and, although dyslexic, graduated from high school in 1943. He then entered the University of Texas at Austin to study pharmacology but was suspended within a year, allegedly for refusing to dissect a frog. In 1944 he was drafted into the U.S. Navy, where he spent his free time doing sketches of his fellow servicemen. His first sight of portrait masterpieces, on a visit to the Huntington Library in California, decided him to become a painter.

After completing his term of service, he enrolled at the Kansas City Art Institute in 1947. Aided by the GI Bill and work as a window dresser, by 1948 he was able to study in Paris at the Académie Julian. Within a year he left to join a fellow American student, Susan Weil, at Black Mountain College in North Carolina. From 1948 to 1949 he studied there with the Bauhaus master Josef Albers, whom Rauschenberg later acknowledged as his most important teacher; and he formed friendships that profoundly influenced his life and his art, notably with the painter Cy Twombly, the

musician John Cage, and the dancer Merce Cunningham. In 1949 Rauschenberg departed for New York, studying at the Art Students League until 1952.

In 1950 Rauschenberg and Weil were married; their son, Christopher (later a photographer), was born in 1951. The couple divorced in 1952. Between 1949 and 1951 they had experimented making images of themselves and of objects on light-sensitive blueprint paper. These were used as department store window decorations and were reproduced in a 1951 issue of *Life* magazine. That same year, the influential Betty Parsons Gallery gave Rauschenberg his first solo exhibition. In 1952 he began a series of all-white paintings, the surfaces enlivened only by shadowy reflections of passing viewers. All-black paintings, pasted over with crumpled pieces of newsprint, followed, and then a series of all-red paintings.

Rauschenberg and Twombly began a brief relationship in 1952, traveling together in Italy and North Africa. During this time, Rauschenberg made a number of constructions (subsequently destroyed) using odd bits of wood and stone, which are considered to have been precursors of his famous *Combines*. Returning to New York in 1953, the artist established himself in a downtown loft and started to develop a style very different from that of his contemporaries, the first-generation abstract expressionists. His *Erased de Kooning* (1953) expressed both the divide and the connection: a drawing given him by Willem de Kooning that Rauschenberg deliberately defaced in a gesture of negative tribute. Between 1954 and 1964 he worked on the *Combines*: part-sculpture, part-painting assemblages of found objects scavenged from city streets, much in the manner of Marcel Duchamp's "readymades." *Bed* (1955), one of his best-known pieces, was composed of an old quilt spread on a

Robert Rauschenberg. © **CHRISTOPHER FELVER/CORBIS**

frame, with a pillow, dribbled over with red paint. To some observers it suggested murder or rape, and it was a succès de scandale at his 1958 solo exhibition at the Leo Castelli Gallery, the artist's first and longtime dealer. Many years later, in 2005, a retrospective exhibition of the *Combines* opened to great acclaim at the Metropolitan Museum of Art.

As early as 1954 Rauschenberg's long and significant involvement with performance art had begun. From then until 1994 he worked frequently with the dance companies of Paul Taylor, Cunningham, and Trisha Brown, not only designing their sets and costumes but also devising choreography and occasionally dancing himself—as he did in *Pelican* (1963), in which he appeared on roller skates in a costume of his own making.

From 1955 to 1962 Rauschenberg and the painter Jasper Johns lived and worked together in a succession of New York studios, supporting themselves by doing window displays for Bonwit Teller and Tiffany & Co., while developing their quite different art styles. From 1958 to 1970 Rauschenberg did transfer drawings, made by rubbing or silkscreening images onto paper and then scribbling over them with pencil marks or paint. Among such works were his thirty-four drawings (1958–1960) that illustrate each of the cantos of Dante's *Inferno* and can be read as a scathing commentary on modern social ills. The series was exhibited first at the Castelli Gallery in 1961, and then throughout Europe and the United States. In 1964 Rauschenberg won the International Grand Prize for painting at the Venice

Biennale, the first American artist to do so. Since then his work has been exhibited regularly in galleries and acquired by museums worldwide.

From about 1959 much of Rauschenberg's visual art incorporated technological elements. One of the first such pieces was the sound-producing *Oracle* (1962–1965), made of found metal parts and five radios: the visual combined with the aural. In 1966 he and Billy Klüver founded Experiments in Art and Technology (E.A.T.), a nonprofit organization to bring artists and scientists together in an effort to "humanize" American technology. A later and important phase of his collaborative art making was his work with ROCI (the Rauschenberg Overseas Cultural Interchange), a privately funded venture to encourage world peace and understanding. Between 1984 and 1991 his travels with the ROCI participants took him all over the world, working with local artists and craftspeople. Another manifestation of his social concern was his founding, in 1970, of Change, Inc., an organization to help needy artists.

By 1970 Rauschenberg was dividing his time between the five-story Greenwich Village house he now owned—a center of lively art-world gatherings— and his property on Captiva Island, off Florida's Gulf Coast. There, over the years, he developed a thirty-five acre compound of residential buildings, a two-story studio, and his own graphics workshop. Printmaking had occupied a central place in Rauschenberg's oeuvre since 1962, when he began using the facilities of Tatyana Grosman's Universal Limited Art Editions. His thousands of prints have been arranged in series differing widely in method of reproduction and in theme. *Stoned Moon* (1969–1970), for example, is a series of lithographs commissioned by the National Aeronautics and Space Administration and celebrating the *Apollo 11* Moon landing. In contrast, *Hoarfrosts* (1974–1976) consists of images taken from mass media sources, transferred onto fabric, and veiled over with gauze. By the late 1970s, however, and for the rest of his life, the artist concentrated on exploring ways of combining printmaking techniques with his own photography, a medium he had been interested in since his Black Mountain days.

In 1976 the first of two mammoth retrospectives of his oeuvre in all media opened at the National Collection of Fine Arts in Washington, D.C. Twenty years later, in 1997, the Guggenheim Museum in New York mounted a showing of 400 of the artist's works—the largest solo exhibition it had ever held. Both retrospectives traveled throughout the country and in Europe. Among Rauschenberg's many awards and prizes were honorary doctorates in the fine arts from the University of South Florida (1976) and from New York University (1984). Elected to the American Academy and Institute of Arts and Letters in 1976, he was also a foreign member of the Swedish Royal Academy of Fine Arts (1980) and a commander of the Ordre des Arts et des Lettres, France (1992). In 1993 he was presented with the National Medal of Arts of the National Endowment for the Arts.

Some critics contend that there were no further radical experiments in his later work. Nevertheless, Rauschenberg's search for meaningful images and ways to combine them continued. From 1975 on, aided by a troop of studio assistants, he worked on projects of ever-larger scale. After a stroke in 2002 left his right side paralyzed he learned to work with his left hand instead. Since 1981 he had been adding to what became his *1/4 Mile or 2 Furlong Piece*, a conglomerate of hundreds of panels in various combinations of media. It was first shown at the Metropolitan Museum of Art in 1987 and was exhibited later in other museums at different stages in its growth. The kaleidoscopic assemblage has been described as a diary of Rauschenberg's commentaries on contemporary life. As he once declared, "[T]he artist's job is to be a witness to his time in history." At the opposite end of the scale was his 2007 series called *Runts* at a mere five by six feet the smallest works he had done for some time. By combining his own photographs with other images, and transferring them to polylaminate panels, he produced a somewhat nostalgic evocation of lost or threatened landscapes. At the New York opening of the exhibition of *Runts* at Pace-Wildenstein Galleries in January 2008 both Rauschenberg and his old friend Cunningham were present, sitting together in their wheelchairs, greeting friends and admirers.

Four months later, Rauschenberg died of heart failure at his Captiva Island home, leaving a multimillion dollar estate, much of it bequeathed to charitable organizations. His ashes were scattered throughout his beloved sanctuary. His survivors were his partner of twenty-five years, the artist Darryl Pottorf; his former wife and his son; and his sister. In October 2008 a memorial exhibition of his work was held at the Bob Rauschenberg Gallery in Fort Myers, Florida, and A Photo Tribute to the Life of Robert Rauschenberg opened at the Guggenheim Museum in New York.

Rauschenberg is considered to have produced the most innovative, groundbreaking art of the late twentieth century. He is recognized as a seminal figure whose enormous output was a precursor of the various movements that followed abstract expressionism: from pop art to the return of figurative, representational art. It has been said that he produced a body of work that altered our understanding of what art is. And though it is possible to describe the artist's almost sixty-year-long career as a series of discrete periods, in actuality all phases of his art connect and fuse into an organic whole. An artist in constant motion, his driving force was a desire to embrace all of life. "I'm for 'yes,'" he once said. "'No' excludes. I'm for inclusion." That generosity of spirit informed not only his art but also his lifelong concern for social justice and world peace.

★

Rauschenberg left no formal written autobiography, but there is a short autobiographical account in Andrew Forge, *Rauschenberg*

(1972). The standard, and exceptionally readable, introduction to his early life and career remains Calvin Tomkins, *Off the Wall: Robert Rauschenberg and the Art World of Our Time* (1980). An indispensable biographical source is Rauschenberg, Walter Hopps, Susan Davidson, and Trisha Brown, *Robert Rauschenberg, a Retrospective* (1997), the catalog from the Guggenheim retrospective exhibit. An important profile is John Richardson, "Rauschenberg's Epic Vision," *Vanity Fair* (Sept. 1997). An obituary is in the *New York Times* (14 May 2008).

Eleanor F. Wedge

RAWLS, Louis Allen ("Lou") (*b.* 1 December 1933 in Chicago, Illinois; *d.* 6 January 2006 in Los Angeles, California), singer who emerged from gospel music to become a successful performer blending rhythm and blues, soul, jazz, and pop; leading spokesperson and fund-raiser for the United Negro College Fund.

Rawls was born to Virgil Rawls, a Baptist minister, and Evelyn Rawls, a homemaker. When his father left the household, his mother went to the West Coast to find

Lou Rawls. AP IMAGES

work, and he was raised on Chicago's South Side by his grandmother, Eliza Rawls. By the time he was seven, Rawls was singing in the choir of Eliza's Greater Mount Olive Baptist Church, and as a teenager he performed with the church's West Singers as well as with pickup groups on his own. At the Young Men's Christian Club, Rawls mingled with other young gospel performers, including Sam Cooke, who would become a friend as well as a role model.

Following his graduation from Dunbar Vocational Career Academy, Rawls performed with various gospel groups, including the Pilgrim Travelers, through the mid-1950s. In 1956 he enlisted in the army, serving as a paratrooper with the Eighty-second Airborne Division. Following his discharge in 1958, he again joined the Pilgrim Travelers, who by this time were touring with Cooke during the early days of his pop-music career. In November, en route from St. Louis to a booking in Mississippi, Rawls, Cooke, and two others were in a car crash that killed the driver, left Cooke and his guitarist injured, and Rawls in a coma for nearly a week. After he regained consciousness, he experienced memory loss for three months and needed nearly a year to recover completely. During that time he made the decision to leave gospel music for a career in secular music where he "really wanted to do something good, to make a mark."

Since he had been based in Los Angeles during his last year with the Travelers, he began to perform there wherever he could get work and managed to appear in a small role on *77 Sunset Strip*, a popular television series. Rawls married his first wife, Lana Jean, in 1961; they would divorce in 1973. In 1962, during an engagement at Pandora's Box, a coffeehouse near the headquarters of Capitol Records, he was discovered by Nick Venet, who signed him to the label. His recorded his first Capitol album, *Stormy Monday* (1962), with the Les McCann Trio. That same year he sang on two popular singles by Cooke, "Having a Party" and "Bring It on Home to Me." On his second Capitol album, *Tobacco Road* (1963), Rawls was backed up by a big band led by Onzy Matthews. His *Live!* album (1966), his first gold record, captured Rawls's engaging stage presence, featuring extended monologues or "raps" used to focus club audiences on his musical repertoire of jazz and blues. Later that year Rawls released *Soulin'*, which included "Love Is a Hurtin' Thing," his first single to reach number one on the rhythm-and-blues (R & B) chart. In 1967 he earned his first Grammy (Best R & B Vocal Performance) for the single "Dead End Street." In all, he would record twenty-eight albums for Capitol before leaving the label in 1971 for MGM Records.

Rawls recorded *A Natural Man* (1971) for his new label, and the title song was a hit on both the R & B and pop charts. The album earned Rawls his second Grammy in 1972. However, he disagreed with MGM executives on the material he was offered, and after recording one more album he left the company. Following a brief association

with Bell Records, Rawls signed with Philadelphia International. Working with the legendary producers Kenny Gamble and Leon Huff, Rawls recast himself in the "Philadelphia sound" of soul. His first album for the label, *All Things in Time* (1976), was the most successful of his career, and the single "You'll Never Find Another Love Like Mine" topped the R & B chart and went to number two on the pop chart. He won his third Grammy for the album *Unmistakably Lou* (1977), and he continued to have commercial success with the other recordings he made during the late 1970s. He became a commercial spokesman for the Anheuser-Busch brewing company in 1979, and in turn the company helped Rawls by sponsoring a television show that would become his most significant legacy outside of music.

As a well-established and respected performer, Rawls used his fame to support his philanthropic work as a spokesperson for the United Negro College Fund (UNCF). Beginning in 1980 he hosted the Parade of Stars telethon, and over the next quarter-century the annual event, as overseen by Rawls, raised more than $200 million for the charity. Rawls, who did not have a college degree, thus enabled thousands of young African Americans to earn theirs. Although he continued to record, including albums on the Epic and the Blue Note labels, he did not seem concerned with the chart potential of those albums. Instead, he became an entertainment institution, concentrating on his work for the UNCF while touring and appearing in television shows and movies, including the Oscar-nominated *Leaving Las Vegas* (1995). He appeared in *Smokey Joe's Café* on Broadway in 1999, and he produced and appeared in another Broadway show, *Me and Mrs. Jones* (2001), filled with the Philadelphia sound of Gamble and Huff music. He also performed in numerous tours of American military bases over two decades.

Rawls married his second wife, Cici, in 1989; they were divorced in 2003. In 1989 Chicago's South Wentworth Avenue was renamed Lou Rawls Drive in his honor, and in 1993 Rawls attended the groundbreaking ceremonies for the Lou Rawls Theater and Cultural Center, built on the site of the Regal Theater on Chicago's South Side, where as a young man he had seen gospel and blues performers. In 2003 his album *Rawls Sings Sinatra*, with arrangements by the jazz saxophonist Benny Golson, paid tribute to Frank Sinatra, the popular and influential singer who had praised Rawls throughout his career.

In 2004 Rawls married his third wife, Nina Malek Inman, and in 2005 they had a son. Rawls also had three children from his earlier marriages. Wilberforce University awarded Rawls an honorary doctorate in 2004 for his "lifelong service to the education of historically disadvantaged populations." Late in the year he was diagnosed with lung cancer, which spread to his brain. In September 2005 he taped his final appearance for the 2005–2006 UNCF television special, and although he was gravely ill, he performed a stirring rendition of Sinatra's "It Was a Very Good Year." He died at Cedars-Sinai Medical Center. He is buried in Forest Lawn Memorial Park in Los Angeles.

Rawls sustained a successful performing and recording career for more than forty years. In more than forty albums, his style mirrors the diversity of African-American music, from blues, gospel, and soul to commercial pop and jazz. Yet Rawls was always true to his own style. His smooth, deep baritone was unmistakable, whether part of a commercial jingle or the national anthem. His lasting legacy is his work as honorary chairman of the UNCF and producer of the Parade of Stars telethons. The Lou Rawls Scholarship Foundation was established in 2007 to provide financial support for needy minority students seeking a college education.

Material on Rawls is scant. There are references to his work with the UNCF in an interview he gave to the *Arizona Republic* (25 Apr. 1997). Annette John-Hall, "Lou Rawls Puts Phila. Sound on Stage," *Philadelphia Inquirer* (28 Oct. 2001), discusses his production of *Me and Mrs. Jones*. Peter Guralnick, *Dream Boogie: The Triumph of Sam Cooke* (2005), discusses the friendship between Rawls and Cooke and Cooke's influence on Rawls. Obituaries are in the *Philadelphia Inquirer*, *New York Times*, and *Washington Post* (all 7 Jan. 2006).

James F. Smith

RICHARDS, (Dorothy) Ann Willis (*b*. 1 September 1933 in Lakeview, Texas; *d*. 13 September 2006 in Austin, Texas), political activist, politician, and the second woman to be elected governor of Texas.

Richards was the only child of Robert Cecil Willis, a truck driver and salesman, and Mildred Iona (Warren) Willis, a homemaker. She was raised in the small town of Lakeview, near Waco, Texas. When she was a teenager, the family moved to Waco. Richards graduated from Waco High School in 1950, attended Baylor University in Waco on a debate scholarship, graduating in 1954, and completed teaching certification requirements at the University of Texas the following year. She married her high school classmate David Richards in May 1953 and taught social studies and history at Fulmore Junior High School in Austin from 1955 to 1956 while her husband attended the University of Texas Law School.

As a young wife and mother of four children, Richards worked as a volunteer over the next several years on the campaigns of such progressive and populist Texas Democrats as U.S. Senator Ralph Yarborough, Congressman Henry B. Gonzalez, and Sarah Weddington, a member of

Ann Richards, 1992. AP IMAGES

the Texas House of Representatives who had successfully argued the *Roe v. Wade* decision before the U.S. Supreme Court in 1973. Richards later described Weddington as the first "out-and-out feminist activist" she had ever met. In 1974 she became Weddington's administrative assistant. In 1976 she was elected and in 1980 reelected to the Travis County Commissioners Court; and in 1982 she was elected Texas state treasurer, the first woman to be elected to statewide office there in over half a century, with the most votes of any statewide candidate. Her friend and the columnist Molly Ivins credited Richards's victory to her "hard hair," the distinctive white halo or bouffant "Dairy Queen hairdo" she wore for the rest of her life. "I take a lot of cracks about my hair," she once joked. "Mostly from men who don't have any."

As state treasurer Richards modernized the office and by her own estimate saved taxpayers $2 billion by maximizing state investments over the next eight years. However, the demands of her political career took a toll; she was treated for alcohol addiction in 1980. "I had seen the very bottom of life," she later reminisced. "I was…afraid I wouldn't be funny anymore….That I would lose my zaniness and my sense of humor. But I didn't. Recovery turned out to be a wonderful thing." Though she became a forceful proponent of Alcoholics Anonymous, allegations of illegal drug use dogged her for the rest of her life. Her political career also took its toll on her marriage, which ended amicably in February 1984.

In July 1984 Richards delivered one of the nominating speeches for Walter Mondale at the Democratic National Convention in San Francisco; and in 1986 she was reelected Texas state treasurer without opposition. In July 1988 she delivered the keynote address at the Democratic National Convention in Atlanta. She joked in her peroration, repeating a line from the cartoonist Bob Thaves, that "if you give [women] a chance, we can perform. After all, Ginger Rogers did everything Fred Astaire did. She just did it backwards and in high heels." Most famously, she ridiculed the Republican presidential nominee, her fellow Texan and Vice President George H. W. Bush, for his privileged upbringing. As she declared in her distinctive drawl to riotous laughter, "Poor George. He can't help it. He was born with a silver foot in his mouth." The address established Richards as a national political figure, and in 1989 she published an autobiography, *Straight from the Heart: My Life in Politics and Other Places.*

After the incumbent Republican governor of Texas declined to stand for reelection in 1990, Richards won the Democratic nomination for the office in a so-called mudslide against the sitting state attorney general and a former governor by eliciting the support of traditional Democrats, crossover Republicans, and young and minority voters. She was narrowly elected the forty-fifth governor of Texas the following December after a brawling campaign against the Republican nominee, the millionaire west Texas rancher and gaffe-prone political novice Clayton Williams, Jr.

As governor of the "New Texas," Richards reformed state regulatory agencies, invested in infrastructure, created a state ethics commission, and introduced a substance abuse program for prison inmates. She signed into law a state lottery, reformed school finance, and proposed the decentralization of educational policy making by delegating authority to individual school districts. She saved taxpayers by her own estimate some $6 billion through audits of every state agency, and she appointed more women and minorities to state office than any of her predecessors, including the first African-American member of the University of Texas Board of Regents, as well as the first disabled person to serve on the human services board, and the first teacher to lead the State Board of Education. Richards also transferred the Texas Music Office and the Texas Film Commission from the state Department of Commerce to the Office of the Governor, raising their profile and increasing the importance of the entertainment industry in the long-term economic planning of the state. As she explained in February 2005, "I've been a friend to Texas film since the number of people who cared about Texas film could have fit in a phone booth." She was active in such musical events as the Austin City Limits Music Festival and the South by Southwest Festival, and she was instrumental in the founding of the Texas Film Hall of Fame.

In the final months of her gubernatorial term, Richards vetoed a bill, passed by the Texas state legislature and endorsed by the National Rifle Association, that would have permitted Texas citizens to carry concealed weapons in public establishments. The advocates of the bill argued that the women of Texas deserved to carry guns in their purses to protect themselves. Richards replied that, while she was not a sexist, "there is not a woman in this state who could *find* a gun in her handbag." Her opposition to the legislation was critical in her unexpected defeat for reelection in 1994 by George W. Bush, managing general partner of the Texas Rangers baseball team and son of the vice president (subsequently elected president) she had ridiculed in her 1988 keynote address.

Richards taught political science as a visiting professor at Brandeis University in Waltham, Massachusetts, from 1997 to 1998 and served as a member of the university trustees from 1998 until her death. She spent the last years of her life working as a corporate adviser and political consultant. She served on the boards of J.C. Penney and the Aspen Institute, worked as a commentator on Cable News Network, endorsed Howard Dean's candidacy for president in 2004, and campaigned for John Kerry the same year against the incumbent President George W. Bush. After she was diagnosed with osteoporosis, she coauthored the book *I'm Not Slowing Down* (2004) to advise women at risk for the disease. In fall 2005 she also taught a class at the University of Texas at Austin on women and leadership.

In March 2006 Richards announced that she had been diagnosed with esophageal cancer. She died of the disease at her home in Austin six months later and is buried in the Texas State Cemetery in Austin. One of her daughters, Cecile Richards, who became president of Planned Parenthood in February 2006, said after addressing the Democratic National Convention in Denver in August 2008 that her mother "got us all into this, but she left a hell of a lot still for us to do."

Over the course of her career, Richards was honored with the Texas National Association for the Advancement of Colored People Presidential Award for Outstanding Contributions to Civil Rights, the National Wildlife Federation Conservation Achievement Award, the Orden del Aguila Azteca from the government of Mexico, and the Maurice N. Eisendrath Bearer of Light Award from the Union of American Hebrew Congregations. When Richards was asked after her retirement from politics to assess her career, she avowed that "the greatest part . . . was the opportunity to be in public service. . . . To try to make things better, whether they turned out in the fashion I expected them to or not." In all, as Sue Tolleson-Rinehart and Jeanie R. Stanley have remarked, "Her passage through the Texas political crucible is a case study not just for

Texans, but for all students of women's progress through electoral arenas."

★

Richards's memoirs, coauthored with Peter Knobler, are contained in *Straight from the Heart: My Life in Politics and Other Places* (1989). Mike Shropshire and Frank Schaefer, *The Thorny Rose of Texas: An Intimate Portrait of Governor Ann Richards* (1994), offers a sympathetic biography largely based on Richards's autobiography. Sue Tolleson-Rinehart and Jeanie R. Stanley, *Claytie and the Lady: Ann Richards, Gender, and Politics in Texas* (1994), present a scholarly account of the 1990 Texas gubernatorial election. Obituaries are in the *New York Times* and *Washington Post* (both 14 Sept. 2006).

Gary Scharnhorst

RINGO, James Stephen ("Jim") (*b*. 21 November 1921 in Orange, New Jersey; *d*. 19 November 2007 in Chesapeake, Virginia), college and professional football player, professional football coach, and an inductee in the Pro Football Hall of Fame whose play as an undersized lineman made him a leader on Vince Lombardi's Green Bay Packers teams.

Ringo was one of three children of James S. Ringo, an explosives professional, and Vera (Young) Ringo, a homemaker. When Ringo was a child, his family moved from Orange to Phillipsburg, New Jersey, where his father worked in a quarry. Ringo started his athletic career at Phillipsburg High School, playing varsity football, basketball, and track. Football was the most important. Ringo remembered that as far as notoriety went, "the other sports hardly existed." Phillipsburg's annual Thanksgiving Day game with Easton Pennsylvania's high school was a major community event.

Originally a fullback, Ringo switched to center at the suggestion of his high school line coach, Willard ("Wiz") Rinehart. He won All-State recognition as a senior in 1948. Ringo's play brought him to the attention of Floyd ("Ben") Schwartzwalder, the coach at nearby Muhlenberg College. When Schwartzwalder became the head coach at Syracuse University in 1949, he offered Ringo and several other local players scholarships. Ringo accepted and graduated from Syracuse in 1953 with a degree in sociology. As a student he met Elizabeth Martin. They were married in 1951 and had four children.

When Ringo arrived at Syracuse, the university's team was considered to be a minor eastern football power. Under Schwartzwalder the program grew. In Ringo's senior year Syracuse won the Lambert Trophy, symbolic of the best team in the East, and was invited to the Orange Bowl, where they lost to Alabama 61–6. Ringo enjoyed a solid college career at center. Roy Simmons, Sr., who played at Syracuse from 1922 to 1925 and was an assistant coach there from 1925 to 1970, described Ringo as the best center to ever play at the school. A knee injury during Ringo's senior year limited his mobility, though, and while he still won All-East honors, he was not selected as an All-American.

After the Orange Bowl, Ringo was chosen in the seventh round of the National Football League (NFL) draft by the Green Bay Packers. When he reported to camp for preseason practice, he was six feet, one inch tall, and he weighed 211 pounds. Because of his small size, Ringo became discouraged and went home. Neither his father nor his wife sympathized. They could not understand how anyone could turn down $5,250 for four months' work. Ringo returned to the Packers and made the team.

During Ringo's rookie season he suffered torn cartilage in his knee, a broken hand, and a broken cheekbone. He missed seven games with injuries, the only seven he would miss during his entire career. During the off-season Ringo lifted weights to build up to 235 pounds. He also received advice from teammate David ("Hawg") Hanner, a 260-pound defensive tackle, on how to handle larger players. Changes within the game also helped Ringo. During his rookie season many teams played a 5–2 defense, where a middle guard, often one of the largest players, would play directly opposite the center. As the 1950s progressed, teams switched to a 4–3, where the center was left uncovered. Not facing an immediate collision, Ringo could use his speed and technique to outmaneuver opponents.

While the Packers were not enjoying much success as a team, Ringo was soon recognized as one of their best players. He was named team captain in 1956, a position he held through 1963, and, beginning in 1957, became a regular participant in the postseason Pro Bowl game. In 1959, after a 1–10–1 season, the team named Vince Lombardi as its head coach. The Packers immediately improved. They had a 7–5 record in 1959, then played in the next three league championship games, losing to the Philadelphia Eagles 17–13 in 1960 and beating the New York Giants in 1961 and 1962. Ringo's quickness was ideal for Lombardi's offense, particularly the famous Packer sweep. With both guards pulling to lead the running back, Ringo had to use his speed to cut off the opposing defensive tackle.

Prior to the 1964 season Ringo wanted either a substantial raise or to be traded to another team. His wife had never liked the small-town atmosphere in Green Bay, Wisconsin, and Ringo felt being in a larger city would help him make future business contacts or pick up product endorsement work. According to Packer legend, Ringo showed up at Lombardi's office with an agent to help him negotiate. Lombardi left the room and immediately traded Ringo to the Philadelphia Eagles. Lombardi often repeated the story, no doubt to discourage other players from seeking higher pay, but Ringo denied most of the particulars and remained on good terms with his former coach. Ringo received a substantial raise when he joined the Eagles and saved money by commuting to games and practices from his Phillipsburg home.

Ringo played for the Eagles from 1964 through 1967 and remained a Pro Bowl performer. His final game was the 1968 Pro Bowl. He retired having played a then-NFL record 182 consecutive games, often overcoming injuries and infections to take the field. In 1981 Ringo was inducted into the Pro Football Hall of Fame. Rinehart, his high school coach who suggested he move to center, was his presenter. Ringo was subsequently chosen as the NFL's best center of the 1960s by the Pro Football Hall of Fame Selection Committee.

After leaving the Eagles, Ringo worked in construction one year with team owner Jerry Wolman, then entered the coaching profession as an assistant with the Chicago Bears. After three years in Chicago, Ringo joined the Buffalo Bills, where he helped guide the offensive line that let O. J. Simpson set a series of rushing records, and where he endured a 3–20 record as head coach in 1976 and 1977. Ringo later coached for the New England Patriots, Los Angeles Rams, and New York Jets, before finally returning to the Bills. In 1988, after being injured in a sideline collision, Ringo retired.

In 1987 Ringo's wife died of cancer. The following year he married Judith Lischer. They moved to Chesapeake, Virginia. Ringo was diagnosed with Alzheimer's disease in 1996. He died of pneumonia and was buried at Fairmount Cemetery in Phillipsburg, where the high school field house is named in his honor.

Ringo's football career was marked by durability and quiet leadership. Lombardi said, "A bigger man might not be able to make the cutoff blocks on our sweeps the way Jim does. The reason Ringo is the best in the league is because he's quick and he's smart." He is considered one of the best linemen to play the game.

Ringo's years at Syracuse University are covered in Ken Rappoport, *The Syracuse Football Story* (1975). Stuart Leuthner, *Iron Men: Bucko, Crazylegs, and the Boys Recall the Golden Days of Professional Football* (1988), contains an extensive interview with Ringo. Ed Gruver, "The Lombardi Sweep," *Coffin Corner* 19, no. 5 (1997), gives a detailed description of Ringo's assignments in the Packer offensive scheme. An obituary is in the *New York Times* (21 Nov. 2007).

Harold W. Aurand, Jr.

RIZZUTO, Philip Francis ("Phil") (*b.* 25 September 1917 in New York City; *d.* 13 August 2007 in West Orange, New Jersey), National Baseball Hall of Fame shortstop and broadcaster for the New York Yankees.

Phil Rizzuto. **PHOTOFILE/MLB PHOTOS/GETTY IMAGES**

Rizzuto, born in the Ridgewood section of Brooklyn in New York City, was one of five children of Fiore Francesco Rizzuto and Rose Angotti Rizzuto. Fiore, a construction worker and trolley car conductor for the Brooklyn Rapid Transit Company, moved the family to the New York City borough of Queens in 1929, just prior to the stock market crash that year. Rizzuto attended Richmond Hill High School in Queens, playing both baseball and football despite being considered undersized for the two sports at five feet, six inches and 150 pounds. It was at Richmond Hill that Rizzuto began to develop the skills that would characterize his career with the New York Yankees. His high school baseball coach, Al Kunitz, instilled in him a focus on "small ball," which included bunting, stealing bases, and hustling at all times.

In 1936 Rizzuto dropped out of high school to pursue a career in professional baseball. He failed in tryouts with the Brooklyn Dodgers and New York Giants, supposedly not getting much of an opportunity to demonstrate his skills because of his small size. This was one of many times in his life that he would rise to the challenge and overcome low expectations. In 1937 the New York Yankees scout Paul Krichell, whose previous discoveries included the baseball legends Lou Gehrig and Tony Lazzeri, signed Rizzuto as an amateur free agent. Rizzuto was assigned to the Yankees' Class D minor league team in Bassett, Virginia.

After moving steadily up the organizational chain, he was promoted to the Kansas City Blues of the American Association in 1939. It was while playing for the Blues that Rizzuto earned the nickname "Scooter." His Blues teammate Billy Hitchcock, watching Rizzuto run and noticing his short legs and choppy strides, reportedly proclaimed, "Man, you're not running, you're scootin'."

After two successful seasons with the Kansas City Blues, Rizzuto made his major league debut with the Yankees in the season opener against the Washington Senators on 14 April 1941. According to the *New York Times*, Rizzuto and his fellow rookie Gerald Priddy received a "huge floral horseshoe" prior to the game from residents of Norfolk, Virginia, where the two men had played for the local minor league franchise in 1938. Rizzuto went hitless in his first game, but he managed to turn two double plays as the starting shortstop. The game inaugurated a fifty-five-year relationship with the Yankees.

Rizzuto married Cora Esselborn on 23 June 1943. The couple had three daughters and one son. Like many men of his generation, Rizzuto enlisted in the military during World War II, serving in the U.S. Navy from 1943 to 1945 and missing three full baseball seasons in the prime of his career. He returned to the Yankees in 1946 and became an integral part of the team in the 1940s and 1950s. Throughout his career he was known as an outstanding defensive shortstop, superb bunter, and excellent base runner. Over the span of thirteen seasons (1941–1956), he was a five-time All-Star, with a lifetime batting average of .273. He played in nine World Series, winning seven, including five consecutive wins (1949–1953). Among his illustrious teammates were the Hall of Famers Bill Dickey, Joe DiMaggio, Yogi Berra, Whitey Ford, and Mickey Mantle. In 1950 Rizzuto won the Most Valuable Player Award with a .324 batting average, 200 base hits, 125 runs, and a .439 slugging percentage. Despite these honors Rizzuto was unceremoniously released from the Yankees during the 1956 season in order to make room on the roster for the veteran outfielder Enos Slaughter. Rizzuto played his last game with the Yankees on 16 August 1956.

As was indicative of the resiliency evident throughout his life, Rizzuto recovered from his release from the Yankees and began a career in sports broadcasting. He signed on as a radio and television broadcaster for the Yankees on 18 December 1956, teaming up with the legendary announcers Mel Allen and Red Barber. Reportedly, Rizzuto was warned by the sports journalist Howard Cosell, "You'll never last. You look like George Burns and you sound like Groucho Marx." Ignoring the critique, Rizzuto remained and flourished as a Yankee broadcaster for the next forty years.

In the broadcasting booth Rizzuto developed a unique style of storytelling rather than straight analysis, and he entertained audience members with anecdotes of his fear of lightning, love of cannolis, and family life. He livened

broadcasts with cries of "Holy cow!" and "What a huckleberry!," which became his signature phrases. Never one to hide his favoritism for the home team, he included on-air greetings to friends and fans. Rizzuto was famous for leaving Yankee games early to avoid traffic. Therefore, his various broadcasting partners, including Bill White, Jerry Coleman, Bobby Murcer, Tom Seaver, and Rick Cerone, were required to finish broadcasts on their own as Rizzuto traveled across the George Washington Bridge, which spans the Hudson River, to his home in Hillside, New Jersey.

It was during his time as a broadcaster that Rizzuto was elected to the Baseball Hall of Fame by the Veterans Committee on 25 February 1994. He had waited more than three decades for the honor and reveled in every aspect of the celebration. At the induction ceremony in Cooperstown, New York, Rizzuto delivered a humorous, rambling, anecdote-driven speech that is known as one of the longest as well as one of the most memorable in the long annals of the Hall of Fame. On 15 August 1995 Rizzuto briefly retired after the television network WPIX-TV would not allow him to miss a broadcast to attend Mantle's funeral in Dallas. Rizzuto eventually returned to the position and concluded his broadcast career after the 1996 season.

Rizzuto's entire life was a testament to the fact that diminutive size need not be a deterrent to greatness. On 4 August 1985 the Yankees held Phil Rizzuto Day to celebrate his career and officially retire his number ten jersey. During the ceremony he was presented with a plaque honoring his achievements that read, "A man's size is measured by his heart." Even beyond the baseball diamond and broadcast booth, he forged a presence in popular culture. He served as a mystery guest on the first episode of the television game show *What's My Line?* on 2 February 1950, provided play-by-play commentary for the singer Meat Loaf's 1977 song "Paradise by the Dashboard Light," and appeared in numerous advertisements for the Money Store.

Rizzuto died in his sleep at age eighty-nine from pneumonia. After Rizzuto's death, the Yankees owner George M. Steinbrenner issued a statement that read in part, "I guess heaven must have needed a shortstop.... [Rizzuto] was one of the greatest Yankees of all time and a dear, close friend of mine."

★

Information about Rizzuto's life is available in Dan Hirshberg, *Phil Rizzuto: A Yankee Tradition* (1993), a biography that chronicles Rizzuto's early life as well as his careers as a baseball player and radio broadcaster. Rizzuto's player file in the archives of the National Baseball Hall of Fame in Cooperstown, New York, contains newspaper and magazine clippings from publications such as the *New York Times*, *New York Daily News*, *New York Post*, *Sporting News*, *Baseball*

Digest, and *Saturday Evening Post.* Obituaries are in the *New York Times* and *USA Today* (both 14 Aug. 2007) and the *Boston Globe* and *Newsday* (both 15 Aug. 2007).

Jon S. Arakaki

ROACH, Maxwell Lemuel ("Max") (*b.* 10 January 1924 in Newland, North Carolina; *d.* 16 August 2007 in New York City), one of the greatest jazz percussionists, a founder of modern jazz, and a polymath whose reach extended well beyond jazz.

Roach was born to Alphonse Roach, whose last job was that of newsstand manager, and Cressie Roach. He had a brother who died in childhood. The family moved to Brooklyn, New York, when he was four. His mother was a gospel singer and his aunt a church pianist who taught him how to play, but at age twelve Roach turned from the piano to the drums. A prodigy who practiced incessantly,

Max Roach. RUBY WASHINGTON/NEW YORK TIMES CO./GETTY IMAGES

as a teenager he took any gig he could find and went to clubs to hear the latest jazz. At sixteen he substituted successfully for Duke Ellington's drummer. After graduating with honors from Boys High School in 1942, he performed with various groups, establishing himself as one of the up-and-coming young drummers of the day.

Roach's sixty-three-year career began during the era of bebop music. Bebop, the most important aesthetic upheaval in jazz history, originated in the dissatisfaction of a small group of musicians during the late 1930s with the prevailing swing aesthetic. The first bebop pioneers, including the trumpeter Dizzy Gillespie, the saxophonist Charlie Parker, and the drummer Kenny Clarke, found that they could not adequately express themselves with the rhythmic and harmonic materials at hand. They set out to transform these materials and encouraged previously unheard-of rhythmic freedom, radically changing the drummer's role from a timekeeper to an improvising voice. By mid-1943 Roach was recognized as the most gifted and original of the bebop drummers. He had moved quickly to its forefront with his muscular authority, the melodic intelligence of his phrasing, and his immense technical facility.

Between 1943 and 1949 he was in the bebop vanguard, participating in many historic engagements in clubs on New York's 52nd Street, the center of jazz, and playing on groundbreaking recordings. Roach participated in the first bebop record date with the saxophonist Coleman Hawkins's group in 1944 and took part in the 1945 session that produced one of the greatest of all jazz recordings, Parker's "Koko." He performed with the Gillespie-Parker quintet during their historic 1945 engagement at the Three Deuces Club, which, in Gillespie's estimation, was "the height of perfection of our music." From April 1947 to November 1949, Roach was a mainstay of Parker's classic quintets. During this period they recorded several Parker masterworks, such as "Parker's Mood" and "Embraceable You." While working in Parker's groups, Roach also recorded with the seminal Miles Davis nonet on *Birth of the Cool.* During the 1940s Roach was married to Mildred Roach, with whom he had a son and a daughter (Maxine became a successful viola player); the couple divorced in the late 1950s.

In 1950 Roach enrolled at the Manhattan School of Music. His percussion professor sharply criticized his mechanics, telling him that his posture was wrong and that he was holding the sticks incorrectly. As a result, Roach changed his major to composition, a decision that paid big dividends in later years. He studied there until 1952 but left without earning a degree. He received an honorary doctorate from the school in 1990.

Roach faced a weakened economy for jazz during the early 1950s. The rise of television, migration to the suburbs, and other sociological factors led to the end of all but a handful of the big bands. Hundreds of musicians found themselves out of work. Roach freelanced on both coasts and received a big boost when he signed with the music impresario Norman Granz, who recorded him frequently and hired him for lucrative concert tours. Roach founded the Debut label with Charles Mingus, the noted bassist, composer, and bandleader. They participated in what has been called "the greatest jazz concert ever" with Gillespie, Parker, and the pianist Bud Powell at Toronto's Massey Hall in May 1953, which resulted in the Grammy-winning recording *Jazz at Massey Hall*.

As jazz began to gather steam again, in 1953 Roach organized the first of his great small groups centered on Hank Mobley, an inventive saxophonist. He then found his greatest collaborator, the gifted young trumpeter Clifford Brown. Brown's playing exuded warmth and joy, and he exhibited a tremendous capacity for melodic invention, a rich, buttery tone, and fluency at any tempo. A recording, *Clifford Brown & Max Roach* (sometimes known as *Clifford Brown/Max Roach*), was released in 1955 and won a Grammy in 1999 when it was inducted into the Grammy Hall of Fame. Brown and Roach formed a quintet with Richie Powell (the younger brother of Bud) on piano, George Morrow on bass, and Harold Land on sax. Sadly, the Brown-Roach collaboration was cut short after little more than two years when Brown was killed in a car crash, along with Richie Powell and his wife, in June 1956. Brown and Roach left a brilliant recorded legacy, including such masterful tracks as "Dahoud" and "I'll Remember April." A critical consensus places the Brown-Roach quintet with the Davis–John Coltrane quintet and Ornette Coleman's quartet at the summit of jazz achievement for the 1950s.

Though devastated by the loss of his friend and collaborator and struggling during this period with a drinking problem, Roach carried on to the end of the decade with a stunning array of young talent. One of his collaborators was the vocalist Abbey Lincoln, whom he married in 1962; they divorced in 1970. In 1971 Roach married the writer Janus Adams; they had twin daughters and were divorced in 1984. Roach had also fathered a son with singer Barbara Jai (Johnson) in 1957.

Roach entered the struggles of the civil rights movement by composing and performing the searing multimedia piece "We Insist! Freedom Now Suite," with lyrics by Oscar Brown, Jr. Recorded in the summer of 1960, it was performed for the first time in January 1961 with narration by the actress Ruby Dee, Michael Olantunji's quartet of African drummers, and Roach's eight-piece band, featuring Lincoln and three dancers. The author Maya Angelou danced as a member of the troupe later in 1961. The suite, which dealt with racial injustice in both the United States and South Africa, had a major political and artistic impact. It and two other remarkable Roach political recordings, "Percussion Bittersweet" and "It's Time," were performed numerous times during the 1960s and beyond and became sources of inspiration for those engaged in the civil rights movement.

The success of "We Insist!" emboldened Roach to widen his horizons as he entered the final phase of his career and moved strongly beyond jazz percussion into the worlds of dance, education, gospel, drama, the jazz avant-garde, classical music, video art, and the spoken word. Between 1961 and 2003, he collaborated with the choreographers Alvin Ailey, Donald Byrd, and Bill T. Jones; built a degree program in Jazz and American Music at the University of Massachusetts at Amherst, where he was a full professor for six years during the 1970s; and composed music for productions of plays by Sam Shepard (for which Roach won an Obie Award in 1984), Eugene O'Neill, Amiri Baraka, and William Shakespeare.

Roach was showered with honors during his last decades. He was awarded eight honorary degrees; was named a MacArthur Fellow (known as the "genius" award), an honor that came with a cash prize of $372,000; and became an Officer of the French Ordre des Arts et des Lettres. He was given a posthumous lifetime-achievement Grammy Award in 2008. Roach remained physically fit until his late seventies and performed until 2003, when he was seventy-nine. He died from an Alzheimer's-related illness on 16 August 2007 at age eighty-three. Roach is buried in Woodlawn Cemetery in the Bronx, New York.

Max Roach's melodic imagination, immense technical facility, and passionate musical intelligence place him firmly in the pantheon of jazz percussion. Unique among outstanding jazz musicians, his artistic reach as composer and performer extended well beyond jazz to dance, the theater, musical education, spoken word performance, video art, gospel, and classical music. He began in the 1940s with Parker, Gillespie, and Davis as a bebop revolutionary, reached a summit of jazz accomplishment with the Brown-Roach quintet in the 1950s, and created his extraordinary achievements in a broad spectrum of the arts from 1960 to the end of his career in 2003.

★

For information about Roach's contributions to jazz, see Leonard Feather, *The Jazz Years: Earwitness to an Era* (1987); and Ira Gitler, *The Masters of Bebop: A Listener's Guide* (2001). Further analysis of jazz as well as biographical information is available in Bert Korall, *Drummin' Men: The Heartbeat of Jazz: The Bebop Years* (2002), and Brian Priestly, *Chasin' the Bird: The Life and Legacy of Charlie Parker* (2006). Alyn Shipton, *A New History of Jazz* (2001), and Geoffrey C. Ward and Ken Burns, *Jazz: A History of America's Music* (2000), which provide overviews of jazz and jazz musicians, contain significant references to Roach. Obituaries are in the *New York Times* (16 Aug. 2007), *Washington Post* (17 Aug. 2007), and *Guardian* (London) (18 Aug. 2007).

Donald L. Maggin

ROBINSON, Edward Gay ("Eddie") (*b.* 13 February 1919 in Jackson, Louisiana; *d.* 3 April 2007 in Ruston, Louisiana), football legend who was head coach of the Grambling State University Tigers from 1941 to 1997.

The son of Frank Robinson, a sharecropper, and Lydia (Stewart) Robinson, a domestic worker, Robinson graduated from McKinley High School in Jackson in 1937. Upon graduation he attended Leland College in Baker, Louisiana, graduating with a BA degree in physical education in 1941. Robinson subsequently attended the University of Iowa, receiving an MA in physical education in 1954. After graduating from Leland College, Robinson married Doris Mott on 24 June 1941 and worked at a feed mill in Baton Rouge, Louisiana, for twenty-five cents an hour.

A star football quarterback at Leland College, Robinson was hired by the Louisiana Negro Normal and Industrial Institute (officially renamed Grambling State University in 1946) in Grambling, Louisiana, as the head football coach in 1941. Once on the job, Robinson became a one-man "crew." He did not have a paid assistant coaching staff or groundskeepers. Before home games at a stadium that seated only 13,000 people, Robinson lined the field himself. When traveling to away games, he traveled on the team bus and always packed sandwiches for his players, because most white restaurants in the South refused to serve blacks.

From the beginning Robinson proved to be an excellent coach, but in his first year, the Tigers finished 3–5–1. In his second year, however, the team played nine games and won all of them. Throughout his career as the Tigers' head coach, Robinson had forty-five winning seasons and only eight losing seasons, three of which came at the end of his career. During his tenure Grambling won nine games in a season nine different times, ten games nine different times, and eleven games once. All together the Tigers won 408 games, losing only 165 (with 15 ties) under Robinson. Omitting ties, his winning percentage was .712. Upon his retirement following the 1997 season, he led the nation in the number of college football wins. His record was surpassed only by John Gagliardi, football coach at Saint John's University in Collegeville, Minnesota, with 453 wins in 2003. Robinson's Tigers won nine black college championships and seventeen titles in the Southwestern Athletic Conference. Over the years Robinson, nicknamed "Coach Rob," sent about 200 players into the National Football League (NFL). Notably, he trained the star running back Paul "Tank" Younger. In 1949 the NFL's Los Angeles Rams drafted Younger, who became the first player from a predominantly black college to enter the league. In 1963 Grambling's Junius "Buck" Buchanan was chosen first in the NFL draft, also a first for a player from a

historically black university. Another of Robinson's players, Doug Williams, became the first black quarterback to lead a team to the NFL Super Bowl and win.

While he excelled as a coach, Robinson emphasized that football players are more than just athletes, more than merely assets to be used and then discarded. He was especially proud that 80 percent of his more than 4,000 players graduated from Grambling. After playing college football, these graduates were educationally prepared to build good lives for themselves and their families. Robinson also believed that the daily practices and weekly games during the football season helped young men make a successful transition from adolescence to adulthood. He taught his players discipline, patience, and perseverance; as a surrogate father, he looked after their welfare off-season as well as during the season.

Robinson and his team factored into the civil rights movement, including its origins. Segregated and facing overt discrimination based on race, Robinson and his players persevered for many years. The national African-American community's spirit was buoyed by Grambling's success. Further, the players who went on to NFL careers helped break down the "whites only" nature of professional sports.

During the late 1990s Robinson began experiencing problems on and off the field. In 1995 he had a losing season; the Tigers were 5–6. Worse, in 1996 they went 3–8 as Robinson dealt with an investigation by the National Collegiate Athletic Association regarding recruiting violations. Also in 1996 four Tigers team members were arrested for rape. Soon after, alumni and other fans called for the legendary coach to resign from his position. The issue was addressed by the Louisiana governor Murphy J. Foster, who lobbied for Robinson's retention as coach. Foster's appeal was successful, and Robinson returned to coach the Tigers for another year. Unfortunately, Robinson's team went 3–8 again, and he was forced to retire. There is evidence that physical problems contributed to Robinson's departure from Grambling. Shortly after retiring in 1997 he was diagnosed by medical authorities with Alzheimer's disease. In his last years Robinson spent much of his time in hospitals and nursing homes. He died at age eighty-eight from a fatal heart attack classified as a complication of Alzheimer's disease. He is buried in the Memorial Gardens Cemetery at Grambling.

The unfortunately negative end of Robinson's career cannot obscure his status as one of the greatest coaches in college football history. In his fifty-six years at Grambling, he received more honors than any other coach. Robinson was awarded five honorary degrees, including one from Yale University. In 1966 the voting members of the Football Writers Association of America (FWAA) named him the coach who made the biggest impact on college football during the last quarter century. Also, FWAA created the

Eddie Robinson Coach of the Year Award in honor of his accomplishments. Robinson served as president of the National Association of Intercollegiate Athletics from 1966 to 1977. In 1979 he was inducted into both the Pop Warner Hall of Fame and the Sugar Bowl Hall of Fame. He won the Boy Scouts of America Silver Buffalo Award in 1985. Three years later he won the B'nai B'rith International Molder of Champions Award. In 1992 he was named to the Southwestern Athletic Conference Hall of Fame, and in 1997 he was inducted into the College Football Hall of Fame.

★

Robinson's autobiography, *Never Before, Never Again: The Stirring Autobiography of Eddie Robinson, the Winningest Coach in the History of College Football* (1999), written with Richard Lapchick, provides detailed information about Robinson's life. Information about Robinson is also available in O. K. Davis, *Grambling's Gridiron Glory: Eddie Robinson and the Tigers' Success Story* (1985), and Aaron S. Lee, *Quotable Eddie Robinson: 408 Memorable Quotes About Football, Life, and Success* (2003). The Eddie G. Robinson Museum at Grambling contains a wealth of material about Robinson's life and career, including documentation of his term as the Tigers' head coach. Obituaries are in *USA Today* (4 Apr. 2007) and the *Los Angeles Times* (5 Apr. 2007).

James M. Smallwood

RORTY, Richard McKay (*b.* 4 October 1931 in New York City; *d.* 8 June 2007 in Palo Alto, California), pragmatist philosopher, leftist social critic, and secularist reformer.

Rorty was the only child born into the intellectual, book-loving home of James Rorty, a journalist and poet, and Winifred (Rauschenbusch) Rorty, a journalist and sociologist, in Flatbrookville, New Jersey. His maternal grandfather was Walter Rauschenbusch, a Baptist minister and key proponent of the Social Gospel movement of Christianity that called for economic and social justice for the poor. Both his parents were socialist activists but strongly critical of the Soviet leader Joseph Stalin. Rorty's parents pushed him toward reasoned dissent and academic rigor. Like many bookish boys, he was the frequent target of schoolyard bullies. At fifteen he left high school early to enroll in Hutchins College at the University of Chicago, where he earned his bachelor's degree in just three years, graduating in 1949.

Remaining at Chicago to study philosophy, Rorty completed his MA in 1952. He wrote his thesis on the mathematician and philosopher Alfred North Whitehead under the direction of Whitehead's student and disciple Charles Hartshorne. Moving on to Yale University, he earned his PhD in 1956, with a dissertation on metaphysics titled "The Concept of Potentiality" supervised by Paul Weiss. On 15 June 1954 Rorty married Amélie Oksenberg, a Chicago alumna and Yale graduate student, who would become a prominent philosopher in her own right. They had one son.

After two years in the army, Rorty was assistant professor of philosophy at Wellesley College from 1958 until 1961, when he joined the philosophy department at Princeton University, serving as assistant professor until 1965, associate professor until 1970, and full professor until 1982. After his divorce in 1972 from his first wife, on 4 November of that year he married the bioethicist Mary Varney, with whom he had a son and daughter. While at Princeton he became internationally famous, primarily because of his magnum opus, *Philosophy and the Mirror of Nature* (1979). Increasingly disillusioned by what he saw as the insularity, arrogance, and irrelevance of philosophy departments, in 1982 he accepted an offer from the University of Virginia to become the William R. Kenan, Jr., Professor of Humanities and University Professor, which in effect made him his own one-person department. In 1998 he relocated to Stanford University as professor of comparative literature. He retired in 2005.

Despite having been taught by Hartshorne and Weiss, both distinguished nonanalytic philosophers, throughout the 1960s Rorty was considered an analytic philosopher, mainly because of his edited volume, *The Linguistic Turn* (1967). In subsequent books, articles, and speeches, he rejected the Anglo-American analytic philosophical tradition that dominated American philosophy departments from the 1940s to the 1990s. He saw this tradition as absolutist and dogmatic where it should have been relativist and flexible, or as too prone to try to define, clarify, and solve problems where it should have recognized them as indefinable, unclear, and insoluble. For Rorty, the value of a proposition was not to be determined by its truth or falsity, which are unknowable, but by its relative usefulness or uselessness, which are learned only in the practical arena of everyday life.

Among Rorty's major influences were Georg Wilhelm Friedrich Hegel; Charles Darwin; Walt Whitman; Friedrich Nietzsche; Marcel Proust; Martin Heidegger; Ludwig Wittgenstein; the American analytic philosophers Wilfrid Sellars, Donald Davidson, and Willard Van Orman Quine; the German hermeneutic philosopher Hans Georg Gadamer; Michel Foucault; Jacques Derrida; and the American liberal theorist John Rawls. As a result of these influences, he revived and redefined pragmatism, which was the classic American philosophy of Charles Sanders Peirce and John Dewey. Rorty held that the genuine mission of philosophy was practical and political, to promote socioeconomic progress away from the rule of the few toward the rule of the many. His book

Achieving Our Country (1998) calls for classlessness, fair distribution of wealth, and ever purer American democracy.

Rorty was a remarkably prolific writer. Among his major works are *Consequences of Pragmatism: Essays, 1972–1980* (1982); *Contingency, Irony, and Solidarity* (1989); and *Philosophy and Social Hope* (1999). His works are collected in four volumes of philosophical papers: *Objectivity, Relativism, and Truth* (1991); *Essays on Heidegger and Others* (1991); *Truth and Progress* (1998); and *Philosophy as Cultural Politics* (2007).

In his philosophy and his politics, Rorty aimed at fostering evolutionary democracy. He envisioned a world in which free individuals, united only by their common and mutually respecting humanity, would each create and continually re-create themselves. Some of Rorty's critics, proponents of a more scientific pragmatism, accused him of inconsistency, relativism, and subjectivism. But for him, philosophy was not a means to truth, either scientific or otherwise. He did not see philosophy as a mirror of nature but rather as a metaphor of the human condition, which would always evolve and could never be pinned down or exhaustively understood. Thus in his view any scientific attempt to solve nonscientific—that is, human—problems was wrongheaded. Even as he abandoned analytic philosophy, he retained one of its core beliefs—that universals do not exist.

Rorty's nonchalance, often mistaken for a cynical attitude, was legendary. He was modest, approachable, and generous. He was never afraid of controversy and often stirred it up deliberately. His brand of leftism angered many leftists, who considered him too patriotic or too elitist. He held a fluid view of what philosophy ought to be, and though he was sharply opposed to certain ways of thinking was very fond of entertaining his critics. He was suspicious of anyone who took philosophy too seriously and always tried to find the underlying humor in it.

Rorty was an admirer of nature, a hiker, an orchid fancier, and an avid birder. He died at home after a long struggle with pancreatic cancer.

★

Rorty's autobiography is the essay "Trotsky and the Wild Orchids" (1992), collected in his *Philosophy and Social Hope* (1999); autobiographical information is also found in Rorty, *Achieving Our Country* (1998). Major books about Rorty include Robert Hollinger, ed., *Hermeneutics and Praxis* (1985); Alan R. Malachowski and Jo Burrows, eds., *Reading Rorty: Critical Responses to Philosophy and the Mirror of Nature (and Beyond)* (1990); David L. Hall, *Richard Rorty: Prophet and Poet of the New Pragmatism* (1994); Robert Brandom, ed., *Rorty and His Critics* (2000); John Pettegrew, ed., *A Pragmatist's Progress* (2000); Alan R. Malachowski, ed., *Richard Rorty* (2002); Robert B. Westbrook, *Democratic Hope: Pragmatism and the Politics of Truth* (2005); and Neil Gross, *Richard Rorty: The Making of an American*

Philosopher (2008). The University of Virginia Archives has texts and recordings of some of Rorty's speeches. Obituaries are in the *New York Times* and *Washington Post* (both 11 June 2007), the *Guardian* (12 June 2007), and the *Los Angeles Times* (13 June 2007).

Eric v. d. Luft

ROSENTHAL, A(braham) M(ichael) (''Abe'')

(*b.* 2 May 1922 in Sault Sainte Marie, Ontario, Canada; *d.* 10 May 2006 in New York City), journalist who became the executive editor of the *New York Times*, widening its coverage and restoring its profitability.

Rosenthal was the youngest of the six children of Harry Rosenthal (who changed his name from Shipiatsky) and Sarah (Dickstein) Rosenthal, immigrants from Byelorussia to Canada. When Rosenthal was four years old the family moved to New York City and resided in the Amalgamated Houses, a fabled leftist community in the Bronx. His father, who had worked as a farmer and fur trapper in

A. M. Rosenthal. **THE NEW YORK TIMES/REDUX**

Canada, became a house painter. During the 1930s his father died in an accident; four sisters also died, and he himself was nearly crippled by osteomyelitis, a disease of the bone marrow. A series of operations at the Mayo Clinic in Minnesota, where he was a charity patient, enabled him to walk, but Rosenthal experienced lifelong pain in his legs. He was graded 4-F in the wartime draft, making him ineligible for service because of his medical condition.

After graduating from DeWitt Clinton High School, Rosenthal attended the City College of New York (CCNY). In 1944, only a few credits short of graduation, he joined the staff of the *New York Times* as a stringer (or correspondent) earning twelve dollars a week—the beginning of a fifty-five-year relationship with the paper. After covering everything from church services to crime scenes, Rosenthal was given the opportunity in 1946 to report on the United Nations (UN), which convened only one subway stop away from where he lived with his mother. He would remain on the UN beat until 1954. There were rumors that *Times* owner Arthur "Punch" Sulzberger vetoed more rapid advancement to foreign correspondent because of Rosenthal's troublesome temperament. In 1948 CCNY awarded him a BS, substituting his UN reporting for the normal graduation requirements. On 12 March 1949 he married Ann Burke, with whom he had three sons. Two years later he became an American citizen.

In 1954 the *Times* sent Rosenthal to India, where he began nine years of brilliant foreign reportage from four countries. He was enamored of India, writing about Jawaharlal Nehru, the charismatic founder of Indian democracy, that he "was mean...but he was beautiful." His next posting, in Poland, was cut short by an expulsion order from the communist regime that set a new standard for bluntness: Rosenthal had to leave because he was "exposing too deeply" the realities of Polish life and the "government cannot tolerate such probing reporting." His Warsaw dispatches, combined with a moving personal report from Auschwitz, the site of an infamous Nazi concentration camp during World War II, won him a Pulitzer Prize for international reporting in 1960. From subsequent postings in Switzerland and Japan, he continued to file fact-filled news reports and contribute scores of articles to the *Times* Sunday magazine and other national publications.

In 1963 Turner Catledge, then the paper's editor, brought Rosenthal back to Manhattan to become the metropolitan editor. Rosenthal adjusted quickly to editorial discipline and demonstrated what has been called his "obsessive" love for the paper, which would dominate his professional life. His first decision, to increase the stipend for the CCNY stringer, was a symbolic one, but his broader policy goal was to recruit better writers, give them freer rein, and improve the paper's readability; toward that end, he called the hiring of the reporter R. W. Apple the best

decision of his career. Teaming with his deputy, Arthur Gelb, the "Abe and Artie Show" brought "show biz snap and tension" to the paper's city desk and revived local news after years of decline. His abrasiveness—he characterized his editorial style as being a "Red Hot Mama"—often alienated both younger and older reporters as he molded coverage to his specifications, and by 1965 he had shattered the once sacrosanct seniority system. In April 1968, when he ventured out as a reporter covering the Columbia University student uprising, this unhappy experience confirmed a conservative bent in his politics.

Having risen to assistant and then associate managing editor, in July 1969 Rosenthal became the managing editor after Clifton Daniels's retirement. The paper's circulation and advertising lines had been declining for several years, and its financial situation was precarious as he assumed command. Rosenthal planned and implemented improvements designed to offer a "total range" of special services for *Times* readers. The "sectional revolution" he carried out during his first decade as editor included creation of an Op-Ed page (a page of columns appearing opposite the editorial page) and separate daily sections under the banners Sports, Science, Living, Home, and Weekend. Suburban and national editions of the *Times* were inaugurated as the paper expanded its audience. By 1986, as a result of his innovations, the *Times* had grown from 89 million advertising lines to 118 million, its revenues had soared from $238 million to $1.6 billion, and its circulation had passed 1 million daily and 1.6 million on Sunday. The redesigned six-column front-page format enhanced readability and saved money. Rosenthal was variously described as the "iron fist in the iron glove" and the paper's "radioactive core—dangerous and leaking energy"; yet by the end of Rosenthal's long tenure as managing editor, then executive editor, *Business Week* reported that the *Times* that he ruled was "flush with record profits."

Rosenthal was notoriously a hands-on editor. He personally approved all hires, promotions, raises, and assignments, and his many critics said that he played newsroom favorites. His authoritarian temperament drove dozens of independent reporters to leave the *Times*—a partial list includes such notable names as David Broder, Clyde Haberman, Seymour Hersh, Sidney Schanberg, Eileen Shanahan, Neil Sheehan, and Gay Talese—and in 1974 provoked a lawsuit over women's rights. His critics charged that he made the *Times* "an equal opportunity oppressor" and accused him of homophobia, sexism, and vendettas. Yet Rosenthal never lost his newsman's principles or his nose for hard news. As metropolitan editor he approved the first public analysis of Manhattan's gay community and as new managing editor he led the staff through the trauma of publishing the Pentagon Papers, a secret government history of the Vietnam War. Although the *Times* appeared to focus late on the Watergate scandal, it led subsequent investigations of the Central Intelligence Agency (CIA) and scooped the nation in reporting a CIA project using a ship, the *Glomar Explorer*, to recover a sunken Soviet submarine. During Rosenthal's long regime the *Times* won an unprecedented twenty-four Pulitzers, even though his newsroom was often an unhappy place.

In 1977, at Sulzberger's invitation, Rosenthal became executive editor of the *Times*. The position, which had been vacant since 1970, fulfilled his highest ambition. He quickly brought both the Sunday paper and the previously independent Washington bureau under his control. His policy remained constant: the *Times* must pilot "as close to the center as possible" and simultaneously offer a "total range" of coverage. Critics continued to accuse him of bias, especially in using the paper to enhance the careers of his favorites in the arts (such as the opera singer Beverly Sills) or defending the reputation of a friend (notably the novelist Jerzy Kosinski). Imperious, he acted on his own impulses, as in 1977, when he hired a new liberal commentator, the columnist Anna Quindlen, and in 1982, when he dismissed the investigative reporter Raymond Bonner for dispatches from Central America that undermined the policy of the administration of President Ronald Reagan. He never lost his eye for the main story. In 1986, when the space shuttle *Challenger* exploded shortly after liftoff, he immediately cleared his front pages to report the disaster and later sent a team of reporters to Florida to uncover what had caused it.

As he neared retirement age in 1986, Rosenthal hoped his achievements would exempt him from the *Times*' mandatory retirement age policy. He was chagrined when the publisher replaced him with Max Frankel. Part of Frankel's mandate was to make the newsroom a happier place; when Frankel later referred to his intention simply "to be not-Abe," Rosenthal wrote an angry riposte in the pages of *Vanity Fair*. Removed from the editor's desk, he began a new career as a *Times* columnist. His "On My Mind" column appeared on the Op-Ed page from 6 January 1987 to 5 November 1999. The headlines on both his first and last columns urged people to "Please Read This Column," and his opinionated, argumentative style was intended to "make other columnists kick themselves when they see what I am writing." Invariably he followed the friendly advice of his fellow columnist William Safire, "don't be objective." Although critics mocked his twice weekly offerings as "Out of My Mind," the column's emphasis on U.S.–Israel relations, human rights, Indian democracy, and religious freedom won him many loyal readers. It was notable that Rosenthal, though accused of homophobia during his editorial years, backed President Bill Clinton's policy on gays in the military and declared that AIDS was the primary story of the 1990s. In another striking move, Rosenthal, who had never considered himself Jewish and accepted the designation only because others so labeled him, embraced his heritage by becoming a bar mitzvah. He was divorced from his first wife in 1986 and married Shirley Lord on 10 June 1987.

In 1999 Sulzberger, even as he ended Rosenthal's column, continued to laud him as a "titan of American journalism." A disconsolate Rosenthal began to write a column for the *Daily News*, where he continued to offer neoconservative political views until 2004. After suffering a stroke in April 2006, he died in Mount Sinai Hospital. He is buried in Westchester County, New York. Rosenthal's tombstone affirms, "He kept the paper straight," reflecting his pride in the paper's record of delivering unbiased news.

★

As early as 1988 Rosenthal deposited his working papers and personal files in the archives of the *New York Times*, where they may be reviewed without restrictions. For information about Rosenthal's career, see Joseph C. Goulden, *Fit to Print: A. M. Rosenthal and His Times* (1988), which portrays him as a villain, and three histories of the *Times* in which he is a primary figure: Harrison E. Salisbury, *Without Fear or Favor: The* New York Times *and Its Times* (1980); Edwin Diamond, *Behind the Times: Inside the New* New York Times (1994); and Gay Talese, *The Kingdom and the Power: Behind the Scenes at the New York Times—The Institution that Influences the World* (2007). Obituaries are in the *New York Times* and *Boston Globe* (both 11 May 2006).

George J. Lankevich

ROSTROPOVICH, Mstislav Leopoldovich (*b.* 27 March 1927 in Baku, Azerbaijan; *d.* 27 April 2007 in Moscow, Russia), one of the twentieth century's most gifted cellists, prominent conductor, and dissident who defended artistic freedom in the Soviet Union toward the end of the cold war.

Rostropovich was born into a family of musicians. His father, Leopold Rostropovich, was a cellist who had studied with Pablo Casals, and his mother, Sofia Fedotova-Rostropovich, was a pianist. Rostropovich's sister, who was two years older, played the violin. The family lived in Azerbaijan at the time Rostropovich was born because his father was teaching at a conservatory there. However, his parents decided to move to Moscow in 1931, without jobs, for the sake of their children's education.

Rostropovich demonstrated musical talent early. He began to play the piano at age four and commenced formal cello studies with his father at age eight. Five years later he made his professional debut as a cellist in Slavyansk, Ukraine.

Mstislav Rostropovich, 1961. ERICH AUERBACH/GETTY IMAGES

In May 1943 Rostropovich entered the Moscow Conservatory. He studied the cello with Semyon Kozolupov and orchestration with the renowned composer Dmitri Shostakovich, with whom he became close friends. After graduating from the conservatory in 1946, Rostropovich began postgraduate studies there and eventually became a professor and head of the cello and string bass faculty. Meanwhile, Rostropovich's international concert career began to blossom. During the late 1940s and early 1950s he made trips to Finland, Norway, and Italy. He embarked on coast-to-coast tours of the United States in 1956 and 1959.

Rostropovich cultivated a lifelong passion for contemporary music, initially as a cellist and later as a conductor. By encouraging the development of new cello music, as Casals had, Rostropovich helped to pave the way for an increasing number of concert cellists.

In late 1947 a slim, twenty-year-old Rostropovich gave a performance that helped revive interest in Sergei Prokofiev's neglected Cello Concerto no. 1. The composer attended that concert, congratulated Rostropovich backstage, and promised to revise the piece for him. Rostropovich premiered the revised version, called Sinfonia Concertante for Cello and Orchestra, in 1952.

After meeting the British composer Benjamin Britten, the extroverted young Rostropovich asked Britten to write some new music for cello. Britten obliged by composing several pieces during the 1960s, including the Sonata in C, the Cello Symphony op. 68, and two suites. Britten and his partner, the tenor Peter Pears, became close friends of Rostropovich and performed with him at music festivals.

Rostropovich nurtured an even longer, deeper relationship with Shostakovich. In 1954 he played Shostakovich's Cello Sonata with the composer at the piano. Four years later Shostakovich gave him the manuscript to his Cello Concerto no. 1, and Rostropovich reportedly memorized it in four days. Through the years Rostropovich built a home near Shostakovich's residence, championed his works in the West, and recorded his symphonies and the opera *Lady Macbeth of the Mtsensk District.*

In May 1955 Rostropovich took four Moscow Conservatory cello students to Prague for a competition, and while there he met and fell in love with the well-known soprano Galina Vishnevskaya. It was a classic whirlwind romance. When they returned to Moscow, Vishnevskaya moved into the Rostropovich family apartment, and the couple quietly registered their marriage. They had two daughters.

By the late 1950s Rostropovich had become one of the most widely respected performing artists in the Soviet Union. In fact, he won a Stalin Prize complete with 50,000 rubles for his accomplishments as a concert artist. However, his relationship with Soviet authorities would not remain cordial over the long run.

In 1967 the dissident writer Aleksandr Solzhenitsyn heard Rostropovich play in the town of Ryazan. Rostropovich visited Solzhenitsyn and began a friendship that had tremendous impact on both artists. In 1969, when Rostropovich learned that Solzhenitsyn was ill, Rostropovich invited the writer to live with his family. Unfortunately, that gesture of hospitality coincided with the Soviet government's punitive measures against Solzhenitsyn, partly because of his novel *Cancer Ward* (1968). The Soviets had banned the book and were not pleased that a British firm had published it. Soviet officials demanded that Rostropovich and Vishnevskaya turn out Solzhenitsyn; they refused.

As a result, Rostropovich began to experience retaliation, especially after dispatching a letter in Solzhenitsyn's defense to various newspapers. In 1971 the Soviets kept Rostropovich from touring abroad for six months. On 26 May 1974 he left the Soviet Union and began a new life in the West. His exile would last for sixteen years.

Rostropovich and his wife settled in Paris but also spent a great deal of time in the United States. He eventually became a U.S. citizen. In 1977 Rostropovich accepted a position as chief conductor of the National Symphony Orchestra in Washington, D.C., and remained for seventeen seasons. It was with the National Symphony that he returned to Russia in 1990, to perform music by Shostakovich. That same year, the Soviet government, having stripped Rostropovich of his citizenship in 1978, reinstated it.

During the last two decades of his life, Rostropovich devoted an increasing amount of his time to philanthropy. In 1992 he founded the Vishnevskaya-Rostropovich Foundation, which helps to alleviate public health crises in Russia. In November 2006 he opened the Shostakovich Museum in the Saint Petersburg apartment where his beloved composer friend had once lived.

Rostropovich died in a Moscow hospital of intestinal cancer a month after his eightieth birthday. He is buried in Novodevichy Cemetery, where Prokofiev and Shostakovich are also buried.

Rostropovich's passion and virtuosity as a cellist survive him, thanks to his prolific series of recordings. Less obvious is the legacy he left by inspiring the creation of new music from some of the most important composers of the twentieth century.

★

Elizabeth Wilson, one of Shostakovich's students at the Moscow Conservatory, captures Rostropovich's passion for teaching and humanitarian issues in the *Rostropovich: The Musical Life of the Great Cellist, Teacher, and Legend* (2008). An obituary is in the *New York Times* (28 Apr. 2007).

Whitney Smith

Louis Rukeyser. AP IMAGES

RUKEYSER, Louis Richard (*b.* 30 January 1933 in New York City; *d.* 2 May 2006 in Greenwich, Connecticut), economic commentator, best-selling author, columnist, and lecturer who hosted the popular television financial program *Wall Street Week*.

Rukeyser was the second of four sons of Merryle S. Rukeyser, a financial columnist, and Berenice (Simon) Rukeyser. He graduated from New Rochelle High School in 1950 and then attended the Woodrow Wilson School of Public and International Affairs at Princeton University, where he studied public aspects of business. After earning an AB in 1954, he served in the U.S. Army for two years, principally in Darmstadt, Germany. He began his journalism career as an editor at the U.S. military publication *Stars and Stripes*. In 1956 Rukeyser joined the *Baltimore Sun* as a political and foreign correspondent. He was given assignments in Europe and Asia, including covering the Vietnam War. He won two Overseas Press Club awards for his news interpretation during these years. On 3 March 1962 he married Alexandra Gill, with whom he had three daughters.

In 1965 Rukeyser joined American Broadcasting Company (ABC) News as Paris correspondent and was soon named chief of its London bureau. In 1968 ABC

brought him to New York, where he became television's first commentator on national economic issues. He also hosted a regular series of radio and television commentaries on international and national affairs. His radio program, *Rukeyser's World*, won the George Washington Honor Medal from the Freedoms Foundation. In November 1970, while still working at ABC, Rukeyser began hosting *Wall Street Week*, created by the producer Anne Truax Darlington at Maryland Public Television and broadcast nationally on public television. On the show Rukeyser offered his thoughts on the week's economic events, investment advice, and the opinions and analysis of guests from the financial world. As Rukeyser's popularity grew, the show's regular guests also attained a certain amount of celebrity.

With a weak American economy, it hardly seemed an auspicious time for such a program. The Dow Jones had failed to achieve significant growth since 1968 (a trend that continued through 1983), mutual funds numbered a mere 323, and household ownership of equities was collapsing, decreasing from nearly 35 percent in 1968 to less than 15 percent by 1974. Nevertheless, Rukeyser captured viewers' attention with his witty, accessible commentary making Wall Street and personal investment understandable. By 1973 the show was so successful that he resigned from

ABC. The program enjoyed perhaps the largest audience ever in financial broadcast journalism; at its peak in the mid-1980s, it was carried by more than 300 stations and claimed total viewership of more than four million households—larger than the circulation of the *Wall Street Journal* at that time. Rukeyser's timing proved impeccable: from 1983 to 2000, the Dow surged from 1,000 to 10,000 and household ownership of equities climbed to more than 50 percent.

Rukeyser hosted the program for thirty-two years, until June 2002. *TV Guide* ranked it as one of the best programs of any kind, praising Rukeyser's opening remarks on the week's business events as "gems of wry commentary" and admiring "his airy and adroit handling" of his big-shot guests. Blending style with substance, in 1991 he was declared the "best dressed man in finance" by the Fashion Foundation of America. He loved to fly first-class and—perhaps surprisingly for someone who advised people on wise investing strategies—was an inveterate gambler. Notorious for his love of puns, he once famously commented on investing in a producer of hairpieces: "If . . . your money seems to be hair today and gone tomorrow, we'll try to make it grow by bringing you the bald facts on how to get your investments toupee."

In 2002 Maryland Public Television, facing increasing competition from a variety of business-oriented programs, especially those on cable channels, decided to bring in younger hosts for the show. The station decided to reduce Rukeyser's role to a five-minute commentary. In his last regular program, broadcast live, Rukeyser told his listeners he had been "ambushed." He was fired immediately. Within two months he re-created the program as *Louis Rukeyser's Wall Street* on the cable channel CNBC. The following year ill health forced him from the host's chair, with 31 October 2003 marking his last appearance. The show continued with guest hosts until 31 December 2004, when CNBC canceled it at Rukeyser's request. Maryland Public Television tried to continue his original program as *Wall Street Week* in collaboration with *Fortune* magazine, but it never drew more than a fraction of Rukeyser's audience and was dropped in June 2005.

In addition to his print, radio, and television journalism, Rukeyser published two best sellers, *How to Make Money in Wall Street* (1974) and *What's Ahead for the Economy: The Challenge and the Chance* (1983). From 1976 to 1993 he wrote a widely read and respected economic commentary for the Tribune Media Services, published three times a week, and from 1988 to 1991 he published several editions of *Louis Rukeyser's Business Almanac* (coauthored with John Cooney and George Winslow). He produced two newsletters, *Louis Rukeyser's Wall Street* and *Rukeyser's Mutual Funds*, both of which continue to be published. Rukeyser appeared as himself in two films, *Gordy* (1995) and *Big Business* (1988), and made guest appearances on Public Broadcasting Service's

Mister Rogers' Neighborhood and the Columbia Broadcasting System drama *Northern Exposure*. From these various pursuits, together with frequent lectures, Rukeyser reportedly earned well over $1 million annually by the 1990s.

Rukeyser was awarded nine honorary doctorates, the Gerald Loeb Lifetime Achievement Award for Distinguished Business and Financial Journalism, and the first Lifetime Achievement Emmy for Business and Financial Reporting. He died at home of multiple myeloma (bone cancer). He was cremated.

Rukeyser carved out new territory on television, laying the ground for the many financial programs that followed. An unlikely celebrity, he embraced his role as investment adviser both to Wall Street insiders and millions of ordinary viewers, whom he helped to understand the workings of the stock market (if not necessarily to get rich by playing it). For many people over the three-decade run of *Wall Street Week*, it became a ritual to tune in to Louis Rukeyser on Friday nights at 8:30.

John Brooks, "Onward and Upward with Wall Street: Gory Theatre, Soap-Opera Anguish," *New Yorker* 59 (14 Nov. 1983), details the origins of *Wall Street Week* and Rukeyser's skill as host. Obituaries are in the *Washington Post* and *New York Times* (both 3 May 2006).

Fred Carstensen

RUSSERT, Timothy John ("Tim"), Jr. (*b.* 7 May 1950 in Buffalo, New York; *d.* 13 June 2008 in Washington, D.C.), television news broadcaster and executive, National Broadcasting Company (NBC) News Washington bureau chief, and moderator of *Meet the Press*, the longest running television program in public affairs reporting.

Russert was born into a working-class, Irish-American home to Timothy John Russert, Sr., a sanitation worker who moonlighted as a delivery truck driver, and Elizabeth "Betty" Russert, a homemaker. He was educated by the Sisters of Mercy at Saint Bonaventure School and Canisius High School, where he edited the school newspaper and from which he graduated in 1968. The first person in his family to attend college, Russert pursued a degree in political science at John Carroll University, a Jesuit institution. He graduated with a BA in 1972 and went on to attend Cleveland-Marshall College of Law, completing a law degree in 1976. He was admitted to the bar in both Washington, D.C., and New York State and, beginning in 1983, served as an adviser to New York Governor Mario Cuomo, then as chief of staff for U.S. Senator Daniel Patrick Moynihan, also from New York.

Tim Russert, 2000. **ALEX WONG/NEWSMAKERS/GETTY IMAGES**

from key political players, Russert was thorough and meticulous, an enthusiastic but balanced interrogator. His strategy was to visually highlight and recite press accounts of a given guest's public pronouncements, usually as a prelude to tough follow-up questions or suggestions of politically motivated vacillating. As moderator, Russert played host to the most powerful and influential politicians of the day, including Vice President Dick Cheney, Arizona Senator John McCain, Massachusetts Senator John Kerry, Illinois Senator (and later U.S. President) Barack Obama, and former First Lady (and later U.S. Secretary of State) Hillary Rodham Clinton.

Perhaps Russert's most famous on-air moment came during the hotly contested and deeply controversial 2000 presidential cycle, during the coverage of which Russert abjured the more familiar high-tech news graphics and scrawled "Florida, Florida, Florida" on an unassuming white dry-erase board, a symbolic prelude to what would be that election's outcome. The dry-erase board was later acquired by the Smithsonian. In 2005 Russert received an Emmy Award. A year later he was inducted into the Broadcasting & Cable Hall of Fame. He was the author of two books, *Big Russ and Me* (2004) and *Wisdom of Our Fathers: Lesson and Letters from Daughters and Sons* (2005), both emphasizing themes of family and Russert's upbringing.

Professionally, Russert was not without his critics. During the 2003 lead-up to the Iraq War, a George W. Bush administration official suggested that the *Meet the Press* program was one of the White House's preferred outlets for information, leading some observers to suggest that Russert went easy on powerful Washington figures, especially Republicans. His "gotcha" interview style, too, came under frequent criticism as showy and television-friendly but without real substance or depth. He took criticism, as well, for his handling of his moderator duties, along with the NBC anchorman Brian Williams, during a Democratic presidential debate in October 2007. When then-candidate Clinton faltered in answering a question about driver's licenses for illegal aliens, it was said in some quarters that the moderators had gone too easy on Clinton opponents.

Also in 2007 Russert became the object of news himself, placed in an uncomfortable position when he was called to testify in a perjury trial involving a former aide to Vice President Cheney. Lewis "Scooter" Libby was accused of lying under oath to those investigating the leak of the name of an active Central Intelligence Agency agent, apparently an act of politically motivated revenge against her husband, a former U.S. ambassador and outspoken critic of Bush administration foreign policy regarding Iraq. Libby maintained that he had first learned the agent's name from Russert, a claim Russert denied.

In 1983 Russert married the journalist Maureen Orth, whom he had met years earlier at the Democratic National Convention. The couple would go on to have a son. The Russerts lived in Washington, D.C., and had a vacation home on Nantucket Island. But Russert retained family connections in and a close sense of identity with the city of Buffalo. He enthusiastically supported his hometown teams, perhaps especially the Buffalo Bills football franchise.

In 1984 Russert made the jump from Cuomo's office to NBC's news division. Among his early victories was engineering an interview with Pope John Paul II for the morning *Today* program. He rose quickly through the ranks of the network and by 1989 had been named Washington bureau chief.

Russert first appeared as a panelist on the long-running and popular Sunday-morning program *Meet the Press* in 1990. When he became moderator a year later, he took steps to shake up the traditionally staid program, adding a sense of immediacy, earnestness, and lightheartedness, without diminishing the broadcast's political importance. As a means of getting firsthand information

Russert served as member of the board of directors of the Baseball Hall of Fame and as national trustee for the Newseum in Washington, D.C. He was also on the steering committee for the Reporters Committee for Freedom of the Press and the Greater Washington Board for the Boys and Girls Clubs of America. He was a regular speaker on behalf of Boys and Girls Clubs and the importance of athletics in America. At the time of his death, he had received over forty honorary degrees and forged a pioneering path as a television newsman. As an index of popularity, he had been parodied on the comedy program *Saturday Night Live.*

Russert had become such a recognizable figure, in fact, that when he died suddenly of a heart attack at the offices of WRC-TV during a recording session for *Meet the Press,* there were expressions of incredulity both inside and out of journalism. A hard blow to broadcasting, his untimely death had unexpected effects throughout the news business. In an unusual move, some of the nation's obituary writers commented on the awkwardness of writing his death notice. The cause of Russert's death initiated a public discussion about the risks of heart disease.

Russert was buried at Rock Creek Cemetery in Washington, D.C. A public viewing of the body was held at Saint Alban's School. At the time of Russert's death, the presidential candidates Senators McCain and Obama commented on his leadership role in news, politics, and family life. Obama suggested that there was not a better interviewer and that Russert's importance was that he cared about American issues—and American families.

★

More about Russert can be found in Howard Kurtz, "In the Hot Seat: Tim Russert on His Ego, His Bias, His Father Worship and What He Really Thinks About Tax Cuts," *Washington Post* (May 2004). Obituaries are in the *Washington Post* and *New York Times* (both 14 June 2008).

Michael D. Murray

S

SCHEIDER, Roy Richard (*b.* 10 November 1932 in Orange, New Jersey; *d.* 10 February 2008 in Little Rock, Arkansas), actor best known for his roles in *Jaws*, *The French Connection*, and *All That Jazz*.

Scheider was one of two sons of Roy Bernhard Scheider, an auto mechanic and gas station owner, and Anna (Crosson) Scheider, who worked for the phone company. Scheider developed rheumatic fever at age six. Unable to partake in sports or other physical activities, he turned to literature and film as an escape. Once he was given a clean bill of health at seventeen, he exercised to lose weight and was briefly a welterweight boxer. He broke his nose during a bout, which left him with a distinctive look. Scheider began acting at Columbia High School in Maplewood, New Jersey, from which he graduated in 1950. After first attending Rutgers University, Scheider transferred to Franklin and Marshall College in Lancaster, Pennsylvania. He joined drama clubs at both colleges, twice winning the Theresa Helburn–John Baker Opdycke Acting Award at Franklin and Marshall. He also joined the U.S. Air Force Reserve Officers' Training Corps. He graduated in 1955 with a BA in history.

After college Scheider appeared on television in New York City and in summer stock theater at the Pocono Playhouse before entering the U.S. Air Force. He served for three years, rising to the rank of first lieutenant, and continued acting in training films. After his discharge, Scheider returned to New Jersey. In 1960 a role in a student production at Franklin and Marshall led to his professional debut in a 1961 New York Shakespeare Festival production of *Romeo and Juliet*, as Mercutio. Scheider then worked in various repertory companies along the East Coast. While appearing with the American Shakespeare Festival in Stratford, Connecticut, Scheider met Cynthia Eddenfield Bebout, an actress. The two married on 8 November 1962 and had a daughter in 1964. (In 1959 Scheider had been briefly married to a nurse whom he met while in the air force.)

During the 1960s Scheider had recurring roles in television soap operas, including *Love of Life*, *Search for Tomorrow*, and *Where the Heart Is*. In 1968 he won an Obie for Distinguished Performance in an off-Broadway production, *Stephen D.* He made his film debut in the 1964 low-budget feature *The Curse of the Living Corpse*, then moved on to higher-profile films, including *Stiletto* (1969), *Puzzle of a Downfall Child* (1970), and the critically acclaimed drama *Klute* (1971), which gave him his first major role, as a menacing pimp to a prostitute played by Jane Fonda.

His film breakthrough came in William Friedkin's *The French Connection* (1971), a gritty thriller in which he and Gene Hackman played New York City detectives uncovering a drug smuggling operation. Scheider received an Oscar nomination for best supporting actor. He then appeared in the thrillers *Un Homme est mort* (1972) and *The Seven-Ups* (1972) and the romantic comedy *Sheila Levine Is Dead and Living in New York* (1975). He then appeared in one of the most successful movies of all time, *Jaws* (1975), directed by then-emerging director Steven Spielberg, playing the police chief in a resort town terrorized by a great white shark. His character's remark on first seeing the shark, "You're gonna need a bigger boat," now regarded as a classic line, was an ad lib by Scheider. The film was a runaway success, becoming the first film to make $100 million at the box office and the first summer blockbuster.

Scheider continued working in thrillers, including *Marathon Man* (1976) and Friedkin's *Sorcerer* (1977), as well as

Jaws 2 (1978). He then tackled a musical, *All That Jazz* (1979), a surreal, semiautobiographical film by the director/choreographer Bob Fosse. He won the role of Joe Gideon, Fosse's alter ego, when Richard Dreyfuss left the film. Although he had no prior musical experience, Scheider's physical resemblance to Fosse and his lean physique made him credible in the role, which Scheider cited as his favorite. He received best actor nominations from the Academy Awards, BAFTA Awards, and Golden Globes.

In 1980 Scheider returned to the stage in the Broadway production of Harold Pinter's *Betrayal*, for which he won the Drama League of New York award for distinguished performance. During the 1980s he appeared in such films as *Blue Thunder* (1983) and *2010* (1984), a sequel to the sci-fi classic *2001: A Space Odyssey*. In 1986 he won the ShoWest Career Achievement Award. Scheider and his wife separated in 1984 and divorced in January 1989; he married the actress Brenda Siemer on 14 February 1989. The couple had a son and a daughter.

In 1993 Scheider took a leading role in the television series *SeaQuest DSV*, though his public disparagement of the show led to his being reduced to a "guest star" by the third season. Scheider's career never regained the heights he had enjoyed in the 1970s, as he moved from leading man to character parts. But he continued working until the year before his death, appearing on television (*Third Watch*, *Law & Order: Criminal Intent*), and in such films as *Naked Lunch* (1991), based on the William S. Burroughs book, *Romeo Is Bleeding* (1993), and *The Rainmaker* (1997). His last film, *Iron Cross*, in which he played a retired detective, was set for release in 2009; as he had not completed filming, the filmmakers created a prosthetic latex mask of Scheider's face and used computer-generated special effects imagery to "re-create" his character.

Scheider's oldest child, Maximillia, died in 2006. Scheider was diagnosed with multiple myeloma, a type of blood cancer, in 2004. He was seeking treatment for the disease at the University of Arkansas for Medical Sciences, where he died of complications from a staph infection.

★

A comprehensive examination of Scheider's career is Diane C. Kachmar, *Roy Scheider: A Film Biography* (2002). Obituaries are in the *New York Times* and *Los Angeles Times* (both 11 Feb. 2008).

Gillian G. Gaar

SCHEMBECHLER, Glenn Edward ("Bo"), Jr. (*b*. 1 April 1929 in Barberton, Ohio; *d*. 17 November 2006 in Southfield, Michigan), college football coach known for leading the University of Michigan Wolverines to national prominence.

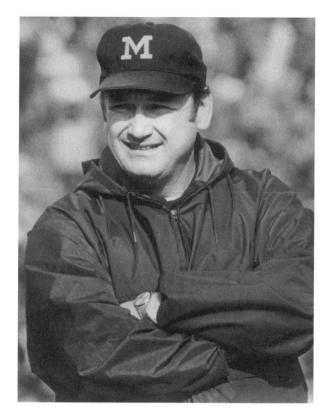

Bo Schembechler. PHOTO BY BOB KALMBACH, BL006733. COURTESY OF BENTLEY HISTORICAL LIBRARY, UNIVERSITY OF MICHIGAN.

Schembechler was one of three children of Glenn E. Schembechler, a fireman, and Elizabeth (Bing) Schembechler, a homemaker. While at Barberton High School he excelled at football, earning All-Ohio honors as a senior, and was also a left-handed pitcher on the baseball team. At five feet, eleven inches and 195 pounds, Schembechler was small for a lineman and so attracted little attention from the Midwest's traditional football powers. Instead, after graduating in 1947, he accepted a football scholarship to play for Sid Gilman at Miami University of Ohio.

After Schembechler's freshman year, Gilman accepted a job at the University of Cincinnati and was replaced by Woody Hayes. Hayes disdained trickery and the forward pass, instead favoring toughness, repetition of a few basic plays, and overpowering opponents through skillful execution. Although Hayes was noted for his temper tantrums, he bonded with Schembechler and became his mentor. As a senior in 1950, Schembechler started for the Miami of Ohio team that won the Mid-American Conference Championship, beating Gilman's Cincinnati team 28–0, and Arizona State 34–21 in the Salad Bowl.

Schembechler graduated in 1951 with a BS in education. He followed Hayes, who had been named the head coach at Ohio State University, serving as a graduate assistant coach. Schembechler earned an MS in physical education at Ohio State. He then entered the military, serving as a player-coach for the regimental football team at Camp Rucker, Alabama.

After being discharged in the summer of 1954, Schembechler began working as a full-time assistant coach. He was on the staff at Presbyterian College in South Carolina in 1954, Bowling Green University under Doyt Perry in 1955, Northwestern under Ara Parseghian in 1956 and 1957, and then returned to Ohio State to coach under Hayes from 1958 through 1962.

In 1963 Schembechler accepted the head coaching job at his alma mater, Miami of Ohio. He joined a large number of fellow alumni who had gone on to coaching success, including Carm Cozza, John Pont, Parseghian, Paul Dietzel, and Red Blaik. In six years at Miami of Ohio, he built a 40–17–3 record, including wins over the Big Ten Conference teams Indiana and Northwestern, and two Mid-American Conference Championships.

Schembechler's success attracted the attention of the University of Michigan. The Wolverines, one of college football's dominant teams, by 1968 were in something of a slump. Although they still regularly won most of their games, they had been to only one Rose Bowl as Big Ten champions since 1950. During the final game of 1968 they had suffered a humiliating 50–14 loss to Ohio State. In 1969 Schembechler was hired to turn the team around. He soon became convinced that the team had enough talent but lacked the discipline and toughness necessary to win championships. Schembechler put the players through grueling off-season workouts. Some left, unwilling to do the work. The Wolverine team shrank from 125 to 85 players. Schembechler's motto was, "Those who remain will be champions."

On 3 August 1968 Schembechler married Mildred ("Millie") Cunningham, a young widow with three sons. He adopted her sons, and they also had a son together.

Schembechler's Wolverines entered the last game of the 1969 season with a 7–2 record. Their opponent was Hayes's Ohio State Buckeyes. Hayes had won the national championship in 1968, was ranked number one in 1969, and had won twenty-two games in a row. Michigan upset the Buckeyes 24–12. The victory put Michigan into the 1970 Rose Bowl and began a ten-year period during which Hayes and Schembechler would struggle for Big Ten supremacy. Other than the Wolverines and Buckeyes, no Big Ten team would win a championship for a decade, and only once would the loser fail to finish in second place. The "Ten Year War" became one of the fiercest coaching rivalries in college football history, with Schembechler finishing with a 5–4–1 advantage.

Schembechler suffered a heart attack the day before the Rose Bowl. Michigan went on to lose to the University of Southern California. This began two trends for Schembechler:

one was recurrent heart problems, and the other was the Wolverines' difficulty in winning bowl games. Michigan represented the Big Ten in the Rose Bowl ten times and won only twice. Schembechler's overall bowl-game record was only 5–12. Some believed his desire to beat Hayes caused the team to peak too soon. Schembechler once said, "Me on one sideline, the 'Old Man' on the other. Those were the greatest ten years of my life." Others suggested that Schembechler's emphasis on defense and the running game, while an excellent strategy for beating weaker teams, was less successful against stronger opponents.

During his twenty-one years at Michigan, from 1969 through the 1990 Rose Bowl, Schembechler never had a losing season, finished in the nation's top ten sixteen times, and coached thirty-seven All-Americans. He was the Big Ten coach of the year seven times, and won national honors in 1969 and 1985. Schembechler also was a force for reform in the football community: He spearheaded efforts to make Big Ten teams eligible for more bowl games than just the Rose Bowl and to combat the use of steroids in college sports. In 1983 he was president of the American Football Coaches Association. His overall record was 194–48–5, or 234–65–8 including his years at Miami of Ohio. He was 142–24–3 in Big Ten play. Schembechler had a second heart attack in 1987, twice underwent quadruple bypass surgery, and because of these health concerns retired from Michigan in 1990 at the relatively young age of sixty.

In addition to coaching football, Schembechler was Michigan's athletic director from 1988 to 1990. A defining moment in that role came in 1999, when, just prior to the National Collegiate Athletic Association basketball tournament, the Michigan basketball coach Bill Frieder announced that he had accepted the head coaching position at Arizona State University for the following year. Schembechler fired him immediately, declaring that "a Michigan man is going to coach Michigan." The assistant coach Steve Fisher led Michigan to the national championship.

From 1990 to 1992 Schembechler served as president and chief executive officer of the Detroit Tigers baseball team. After a year as a football analyst with American Broadcasting Company (ABC) Sports, he then served as cohost of *Big Ten Ticket*, a pregame show on ABC's Detroit affiliate, until his death. Following the death of his wife in 1992, Schembechler married Cathy Aiken in 1993.

In retirement Schembechler was elected to the National Football Foundation College Football Hall of Fame and awarded an honorary doctor of laws degree by the University of Michigan. He received the Lifetime Achievement Award from the Walter Camp Foundation and saw Michigan's football building named Schembechler Hall.

Schembechler died after collapsing on the set of *Big Ten Ticket*. The cause of death was listed as congestive heart failure. He is buried in Forest Hill Cemetery in Ann Arbor, Michigan.

Schembechler's career as a football coach epitomized integrity, loyalty, and hard work. As he put it, "football is the American game that typifies the old American spirit. It's physical. It's hard work. It's aggressive. It's kind of a swashbuckling American sport." With his trademark blue baseball cap and tinted glasses, his gruff and straightforward personality, he was an important figure in sports for two decades.

★

Schembechler is the subject of several biographies and ghostwritten autobiographies. Joe Falls, *Man in Motion* (1973), and Schembechler and Mitch Albom, *Bo* (1989), are among the best. Schembechler with Dan Ewald, *Michigan Memories: Inside Bo Schembechler's Football Scrapbook* (1998), puts his career within the context of the overall history of University of Michigan football. Sally Pont, *Fields of Honor: The Golden Age of College Football and the Men Who Created It* (2001), discusses him within the circle of coaches who came through Miami of Ohio. Schembechler and John U. Bacon, *Bo's Lasting Lessons: The Legendary Coach Teaches the Timeless Fundamentals of Leadership* (2007), examines Schembechler's philosophy of coaching and leadership. Obituaries are in the *Washington Post* (17 Nov. 2006) and *New York Times* (18 Nov. 2006).

Harold Aurand, Jr.

Walter M. Schirra, Jr., 1962. REUTERS/NASA/LANDOV

SCHIRRA, Walter Marty ("Wally"), Jr. (*b.* 12 March 1923 in Hackensack, New Jersey; *d.* 3 May 2007 in La Jolla, California), one of the original Mercury Seven astronauts and the only astronaut to fly in all three of America's earliest manned space programs—Mercury, Gemini, and Apollo.

Schirra grew up in Oradell, New Jersey, where his parents, Walter Marty Schirra, Sr., and Florence Shillito (Leach) Schirra, settled a few years after World War I. His father, a civil engineer, was a pilot in the U.S. Army Signal Corps during the war and flew in numerous combat missions overseas. Before Schirra and his sister were born, his parents barnstormed around New Jersey performing flying stunts in a Curtiss Jenny biplane. With his father at the controls, his mother would wing-walk as part of the show.

As a boy Schirra enjoyed sports and studied the trumpet but was most interested in aviation. By age fifteen he could fly his father's plane. In 1940 Schirra graduated from Dwight W. Morrow High School in Englewood, New Jersey, and began studying aeronautical engineering at the Newark College of Engineering. In 1942 he was accepted into an accelerated program at the U.S. Naval Academy at Annapolis, Maryland, from which he received a BS in 1945. Upon graduation he was commissioned in the U.S. Navy and assigned to an armored cruiser, *Alaska*, but World War II ended shortly after he reached the ship.

On 23 February 1946, after a whirlwind courtship, Schirra married Josephine Cook Fraser. They had two children. That same year Schirra served briefly on the staff of the Seventh Fleet in the Pacific and was then sent to the Naval Test Station in Pensacola, Florida, for flight training. He became a navy pilot in 1948 and spent the next three years with carrier-based Fighter Squadron 71. In 1951 he was assigned as an exchange pilot to the U.S. Air Force 154th Fighter Bomber Squadron, where he flew ninety bombing and close-ground support missions over North Korea. Among the honors Schirra received for his military service were three Distinguished Flying Crosses and two Air Medals.

From 1952 to 1954 Schirra was a test pilot at the Naval Ordnance Training Station at China Lake, California, where he participated in the development of the Sidewinder missile. From 1954 to 1956 he was a project pilot for the F7U-3 Cutlass jet fighter and an instructor pilot. Schirra was operations officer for the 124th Fighter Squadron on the carrier *Lexington* in 1956 and 1957. In 1957 he attended Naval Air Safety Officer School at the University of Southern California, and the following year he completed test pilot training at the Naval Air Test Center at Patuxent River, Maryland, after which he was assigned there as a full-fledged test pilot.

In February 1959 Schirra learned he was being considered as a candidate for a program of the National Aeronautics and Space Administration (NASA) to send a man into space. At first Schirra was reluctant to leave the navy, but he eventually applied for the program. On 9 April 1959 seven men, including Schirra, were chosen to train as astronauts for Project Mercury, the first phase of the U.S. space program.

At NASA, Schirra specialized in developing environmental controls and life support systems for spacecraft and in testing and improving spacesuits. On 27 June 1962 he was chosen for Mercury 8, America's fifth manned space mission. On 3 October 1962 the *Sigma 7* spacecraft was launched at Cape Canaveral, Florida. During the six-orbit flight, Schirra turned off all control systems and allowed the capsule to drift for three hours, twenty-six minutes. He demonstrated that he could maneuver the craft without the help of ground control and could conserve a large portion of his fuel, two important steps that would help NASA plan longer, more complex flights. Schirra completed the mission with an almost flawless splashdown. For his work with Project Mercury, he received NASA's Distinguished Service Award.

In 1965 Schirra was assigned to his second space mission. *Gemini 6* was to be the first attempt to rendezvous in space with another orbiting vehicle, a crucial prerequisite for missions to the moon. Schirra was named pilot, and his copilot was the astronaut Thomas P. Stafford.

On 25 October 1965 *Gemini 6* was ready to launch when its unmanned rendezvous target exploded before reaching orbit, forcing the mission to be canceled. Less than six weeks later, NASA went ahead with *Gemini 7*, a planned fourteen-day endurance flight with the astronauts Frank Borman and James A. Lovell, Jr. *Gemini 6* was renamed *Gemini 6-A*, and the decision was made that it would rendezvous with *Gemini 7*. On 15 December 1965, eleven days after *Gemini 7* began its mission and three days after another postponed launch attempt, Schirra and Stafford finally lifted off. During a sixteen-orbit flight, Schirra brought *Gemini 6-A* alongside *Gemini 7*, close enough for the astronauts in the two spacecraft to see each other. The two ships then flew in close formation for several hours, perfecting the techniques that would enable later space vehicles to dock with one another during flights to the moon.

Schirra's third and final mission began on 11 October 1968, as he commanded *Apollo 7*, the first manned Apollo mission. The Apollo program had begun in tragedy when, on 27 January 1967, the three astronauts on the crew of *Apollo 1* were killed in a fire while testing the spacecraft on the launch pad. During the *Apollo 7* flight, Schirra and the pilots Donn Eisele and Walter Cunningham tested the spacecraft's systems, particularly those that had been redesigned after the *Apollo 1* fire. In their eleven days in space, they practiced several rendezvous and docking maneuvers

that would be used during a lunar landing, already scheduled for the following July. *Apollo 7* also provided the first live network television pictures from space, for which the crew received a special Emmy Award.

In 1969 Schirra retired from the navy and left NASA to begin an extensive business career. He moved from Houston to Colorado to become president of Regency Investors, Inc., a Denver-based leasing and finance company. In 1970 he formed ECCO Corp., an environmental control company in Englewood, Colorado. He was an executive or board member of numerous other companies until he retired in the late 1970s. Beginning in 1984, Schirra and his family lived in Rancho Santa Fe, California, a suburb of San Diego. In 1986 he was inducted into the National Aviation Hall of Fame.

Schirra was well known for his sense of humor and for his practical jokes, which he called "gotchas." Yet he was also described as tough, cool, decisive under pressure, and a perfectionist. Schirra died of a heart attack at Scripps Green Hospital in La Jolla. He was cremated and his ashes were committed to the sea from the USS *Ronald Reagan* on 11 February 2008.

Upon Schirra's death, one NASA official described him as a "pioneer of human spaceflight." He was unique in being the only astronaut to fly in each of NASA's early space programs. Each of his three successful space missions moved the United States closer to its goal of landing a man on the Moon.

★

Schirra tells his own story, with Richard N. Billings, in *Schirra's Space* (1988). Along with the six other original astronauts, Schirra provides personal narrative in M. Scott Carpenter, et al., *We Seven, by the Astronauts Themselves* (1962). He is profiled in H. V. Pat Reilly, *From the Balloon to the Moon: A Chronology of New Jersey's Amazing Aviation History* (1992), and Douglas B. Hawthorne, *Men and Women of Space* (1992). Obituaries are in the *New York Times*, *Washington Post*, *Los Angeles Times*, and *Houston Chronicle* (all 4 May 2007).

Victoria Tamborrino

SCHLESINGER, Arthur Meier, Jr. (*b.* 15 October 1917 in Columbus, Ohio; *d.* 28 February 2007 in New York City), leading public intellectual, historian, author, educator, and spokesperson for the Democratic Party tradition in the United States.

Schlesinger was the second of three children born to Arthur M. Schlesinger, Sr., a distinguished professor of history, and Elizabeth Harriet (Bancroft) Schlesinger, a teacher who became a civic advocate for education as well as a women's

Arthur M. Schlesinger, Jr., 1991. **FRANK CAPRI/SAGA/ARCHIVE PHOTOS/GETTY IMAGES**

historian. The couple's first child died in infancy; their second son was born in 1922. In 1924 his father, recognized as a pioneer of the "new social history," became a professor at Harvard University in Cambridge, Massachusetts. Schlesinger, a precocious student and voracious reader who received great intellectual stimulation from many of his father's Harvard colleagues, attended Peabody School, a Cambridge public elementary school, skipping two grades and moving on in 1929 to the Cambridge High and Latin School. In 1931 his parents transferred him to the elite New Hampshire boarding school Phillips Exeter Academy, from which he graduated with numerous prizes in 1933 at age fifteen. In tribute to his father, in his early teens Schlesinger changed his middle name from Bancroft to Meier, and thereafter never dropped the suffix "Jr."

In 1934 Schlesinger went with his family on a yearlong world tour. He then attended Harvard, graduating summa cum laude with a BA in history and literature in June 1938. His revised senior thesis, a biography of the nineteenth-century intellectual Orestes A. Brownson, was published the following year. By the time he reached twenty Schlesinger had decided to emulate his father and become a historian. As

World War II drew ever closer in Europe, Schlesinger was awarded a Henry Fellowship to Britain, to spend a year at Peterhouse College of Cambridge University. This experience afforded him a ringside view of the September 1938 Munich crisis, the Fascist victory in Spain, the German invasion of Czechoslovakia, and the outbreak of war. Schlesinger, who had already begun sporting what would become his trademark bow tie, moved in sophisticated circles in Cambridge, Oxford, and London, beginning numerous lifelong friendships with British students who soon became prominent in politics and academia. Talkative and opinionated, he was passionate about movies and the theater.

In September 1939 Schlesinger accepted a three-year appointment as a junior fellow of Harvard's Society of Fellows. Having predicted the summer 1939 Nazi-Soviet Non-Aggression Pact almost a year earlier, he returned from Europe convinced that fascism and communism had much in common, and that the United States should support neither. He was disillusioned by Britain's policies of appeasement toward Nazi Germany. The German blitzkrieg across Western Europe in spring 1940 made him an interventionist; nonetheless, he believed the United States should hold itself apart from the European conflict. He joined the American Defense, Harvard Group, speaking and writing forcefully in favor of U.S. aid to Britain, rearmament, conscription, and the need to prevent German domination of Europe, and making morale-boosting radio broadcasts to the United Kingdom in 1941. On 10 August 1940 he married Marian Cannon; they would have four children.

From 1942 to 1943 he served in the Washington-based Office of War Information, and then transferred to the Office of Strategic Services (OSS, the forerunner of the Central Intelligence Agency) as an analyst, spending the last two years of the war in Britain and France. In March 1945 he joined the armed forces as a private, continuing his OSS work and leaving as a corporal nine months later. His prewar and wartime experiences left Schlesinger deeply suspicious of communism and communists, in his own country and abroad.

Schlesinger's first major historical work, *The Age of Jackson*, appeared in September 1945. A best seller, it won him instant celebrity and a Pulitzer Prize. A prolific writer of highly readable history, he combined thorough research with narrative sweep and readability. He advanced the theory, first expounded by his father, that the underlying pattern of U.S. history is a cycle of periods of conservatism, in which the power of business becomes dangerously strong, followed at approximately thirty-year intervals by bursts of reform designed to remedy the previous abuses. Schlesinger, like his father a committed Democrat, gained recognition as the most distinguished American chronicler of what he saw as his party's laudable record of centrist liberalism.

As in his three-volume *The Age of Roosevelt* (1957, 1959, 1960), about Franklin Delano Roosevelt, he structured his historical narratives around the careers of strong, heroic leaders, statesmen who, in his view, inspired their followers and the American people to rise to new challenges and overcome them. His books stressed continuities in the American reform tradition, identifying connections among farmers, urban workers, and liberal intellectuals. In contrast to the prevailing historical theorists of his day, known as the consensus school, he adapted the progressive historians' view, highlighting the role of conflict in the development of American political institutions. Some critics noted that in practice Schlesinger's interpretation focused on conflict only within a broader consensus as to the acceptable range of alternatives open to the United States. In the periods he studied and wrote about, successful reformers accepted the capitalist economic system and the Constitution as givens, seeking merely to adapt them to changing circumstances.

After spending fifteen months in Washington, D.C., as a writer for *Fortune* magazine, Schlesinger joined Harvard's history department in September 1947. He remained active in the Democratic Party and wrote extensively over the years on political subjects for the *New York Times Magazine*, the *Saturday Evening Post*, *Harper's*, and the *Atlantic Monthly*. A centrist, Schlesinger rejected the extremes of conservatism and radical socialism or communism in favor of pragmatic liberalism, essentially policies of New Deal reform at home and cold war anticommunism abroad. Heavily influenced by the popular theologian Reinhold Niebuhr (1892–1971), he argued that practical politicians must be prepared to compromise and on occasion to use less than attractive means to attain at least part of their aims. He deemed it necessary for the United States to combat the evil of totalitarianism around the world, even at the risk of war. In 1947 he helped found Americans for Democratic Action, an organization of the anticommunist left.

During the 1950s Schlesinger, seeking another heroic Democratic leader, attached himself first to Adlai Stevenson, serving as a speechwriter for his 1952 and 1956 presidential campaigns against Dwight D. Eisenhower, and then to Senator John F. Kennedy. When Kennedy won the 1960 election, he appointed Schlesinger to the position of special assistant to the president. Schlesinger remained in that post until two months after Kennedy's assassination in November 1963, functioning as the president's contact to intellectuals and his liaison with Stevenson, who became ambassador to the United Nations. Schlesinger also advised Kennedy on Latin America, a long-standing interest of his own, and wrote some of his speeches. In 1961 he was among the few administration officials to oppose the disastrous Bay of Pigs invasion attempt in Cuba, aimed at overthrowing the government of Fidel Castro, even though afterward he publicly defended it. In 1962 Schlesinger resigned from his Harvard position. With Kennedy's encouragement, he gathered

material for a memoir of the Kennedy presidency, *A Thousand Days: John F. Kennedy in the White House* (1965), which received a Pulitzer Prize and National Book Award.

From then on Schlesinger, who in 1967 moved to New York City and accepted the Albert Schweitzer Chair in the Humanities at the City University of New York Graduate School, was closely identified with the Kennedy family. He supported Kennedy's younger brother Robert in his 1968 presidential bid, and remained close to Edward, the youngest Kennedy brother and long-term senator for Massachusetts. Ten years after Robert's 1968 assassination, Schlesinger published the massive *Robert Kennedy and His Times* (1978), which won the National Book Award. It has often been suggested that Schlesinger's political activities and his close association with the Kennedy family were detrimental to his later historical writing, and that he became effectively a "court historian." Schlesinger himself strongly denied this.

In 1970 Schlesinger was divorced from his first wife. On 9 July 1971 he married Alexandra Emmet Allan, who had a son from a previous marriage; the couple had another son in 1977. He continued writing short pieces on history and politics, many of which were later published in book form. Even so, despite his frequent promises to return to it, his history of the Roosevelt administration was never completed, the third volume ending in 1936. Critics also claimed his staunchly Democratic political views informed his interpretation of U.S. history; many assessed him as a partisan chronicler celebrating his own party's political tradition and achievements while reserving criticism for the Republicans.

An outstanding example of a public intellectual, over the years Schlesinger published several collections of essays on topical themes. Among them are *The Vital Center* (1949); *The Politics of Hope* (1963); *The Bitter Heritage* (1967), on Vietnam; and *The Crisis of Confidence* (1969). His early optimistic outlook on U.S. domestic and international policies gradually gave way to a qualified pessimism. Initially a supporter of the Vietnam intervention, he then turned against it. He watched apprehensively the growing strength of American conservatism. Schlesinger's study *The Imperial Presidency* (1973) warned of the dangerous increase in the powers of the presidency. In 1986 he published his collected historical essays, *The Cycles of American History* (1986). His controversial book *The Disuniting of America* (1991) challenged those who misrepresent the past in the interests of political correctness and the enhanced self-esteem of particular minority groups.

Schlesinger welcomed the election of President Bill Clinton in 1992, which he believed vindicated his cyclical interpretation of American history. When Clinton faced impeachment during his second term, Schlesinger publicly defended the president. In his later years he highlighted race as the major problem facing the United States, still described himself as a "New Dealer," and proclaimed the need for "affirmative government." In his final book, *War* and the American Presidency (2004), and assorted articles, Schlesinger condemned President George W. Bush for going to war in Iraq and for what he viewed as the administration's infractions on civil liberties within and beyond the United States.

Despite suffering from Parkinson's disease, until the end of his life Schlesinger remained politically engaged and maintained a glamorous social life. The first volume of his own memoirs, *A Life in the Twentieth Century: Innocent Beginnings, 1917–1950* (2000), covered his career to 1950. At the time of his death, of a heart attack, he was working on a second volume of memoirs and a compilation of selections from his diaries.

In his last two decades Schlesinger remained a mid-twentieth-century liberal centrist. One of America's foremost historians, he combined academic eminence with passionate political engagement. By the time of his death, Schlesinger had become an institution, an integral part of the liberal tradition he celebrated. He had not merely chronicled his country's history but become a colorful and engaging character in it, contributing to the historical narrative of the twentieth-century United States.

★

Schlesinger's personal papers are divided between the John F. Kennedy Presidential Library at Columbia Point, Boston, Massachusetts, and the New York Public Library. Selections from his diaries were published posthumously as *Journals 1952–2000*, edited by Andrew Schlesinger and Stephen Schlesinger (2007). Further biographical information on Schlesinger may be found in memoirs by his father, Arthur M. Schlesinger, Sr., *In Retrospect: The History of a Historian* (1963), and his first wife, Marian Cannon Schlesinger, *Snatched from Oblivion: A Cambridge Memoir* (1979). Schlesinger's ideological outlook and historical attainments are discussed in Stephen P. Depoe, *Arthur M. Schlesinger, Jr., and the Ideological History of American Liberalism* (1994); John Patrick Diggins, ed., *The Liberal Persuasion: Arthur Schlesinger, Jr., and the Challenge of the American Past* (1997); Marcus Cunliffe, "Arthur M. Schlesinger, Jr.," in *Pastmasters: Some Essays on American Historians*, edited by Marcus Cunliffe and Robin W. Winks (1969); Carroll Engelhardt, "Man in the Middle: Arthur M. Schlesinger, Jr., and Postwar American Liberalism," *South Atlantic Quarterly* 80, no. 2 (Spring 1981): 119–142; Daniel Feller, "Arthur M. Schlesinger, Jr.," in *Clio's Favorites: Leading Historians of the United States, 1945–2000*, edited by Robert Allen Rutland (2000); and James A. Nuechterlein, "Arthur M. Schlesinger, Jr., and the Discontents of Postwar American Liberalism," *Review of Politics* 39, no. 1 (Jan. 1977). Important interviews with Schlesinger are in Henry Brandon, *Conversations with Henry Brandon* (1966); John A. Garraty, *Interpreting American History: Conversations with Historians*, vol. 2 (1970); and Alejandro Benes, "The Guardian of Liberalism," *Cigar Aficionado* (1995). A notable piece in memory of Schlesinger is Ted Widmer, "Arthur of Camelot: Remembering Arthur Schlesinger, a Knight-Errant with Typewriter," *American Scholar* 76, no. 3 (Summer 2007): 115–118. Obituaries are in the *New York Times*, *Guardian*, and *Washington Post* (all 1 Mar. 2007). The Kennedy Presidential Library holds an oral history recorded by Schlesinger.

Priscilla Roberts

SCHOENFELD, Gerald (*b*. 22 September 1924 in New York City; *d*. 25 November 2008 in New York City), head of the Shubert Organization who played a major role in deciding what plays appeared on Broadway and who is credited with reviving commercial theater in New York City.

Schoenfeld was born the youngest son of a garment district entrepreneur who manufactured long-haired fur coats. He attended local schools, including Public School 87 on the Upper West Side of Manhattan. Schoenfeld earned a BS from the University of Illinois. After serving in the army during World War II, he decided to pursue a legal degree and graduated from New York University School of Law in 1949 under the GI Bill.

Schoenfeld did not come from a theatergoing family. Indeed, when he accepted a position as an attorney in June

Gerald Schoenfeld, 1977. AP IMAGES

1949 with the New York law firm of Klein & Weir, he had never even set foot in a theater. However, J. J. Shubert, one of three brothers who had built a theatrical empire, employed Klein & Weir for his legal needs. Over the next few years, the firm's attorneys either died or left to pursue other interests. By 1957 Schoenfeld was the only one left. When Shubert decided to hire a young lawyer with progressive views to serve as in-house legal aid, Schoenfeld proved the logical choice.

From Shubert, Schoenfeld learned the ropes of the theater business. Schoenfeld and his new partner, Bernard B. Jacobs, would sit alongside the theater legend all day long, seven days a week. They saw everything that landed on his desk. Schoenfeld described it as a total immersion in the theater business. It did not, however, prove to be an easy apprenticeship. Shubert, a man who cared not a whit for the opinions of others, proved a difficult employer. Schoenfeld tolerated the poor treatment because of his respect for Shubert's efforts to save commercial theater from the threats posed by the advent of motion pictures, the Depression, and, later, the coming of television.

When Shubert died in 1963, the company passed into the hands of his great-nephew, Lawrence Shubert Lawrence, Jr. He proved to be a poor manager. In 1972 Lawrence was ousted by the board of the Shubert Foundation, upon which Schoenfeld sat. Jacobs and Schoenfeld assumed leadership of the company. In 1973 a reorganization of the various Shubert subsidiaries resulted in the creation of the Shubert Organization. Jacobs took over the role of president, and Schoenfeld became chairman. Over the next twenty-four years, the two friends worked together so closely that they were generally known as "the Shuberts."

The two men took the Shubert Organization from near-bankruptcy to prosperity. So successful was the enterprise, in fact, that much of what is present-day Broadway is largely the creation of Schoenfeld and, to a lesser extent, Jacobs. At the time Schoenfeld and Jacobs took control of the Shubert theater group, audiences for commercial theater had dwindled to the extent that some observers doubted its continued survival. In 1972 the Shubert Organization was $2 million in debt, and half of its theaters stood empty. It took the Schoenfeld and Jacobs only two years to restore the company to financial stability by investing in plays and acting as producers.

More gregarious than his partner, Schoenfeld became the public face of the theater organization. He could often be found on opening nights in the center aisle, between rows five and eight. Schoenfeld would patrol the room, shaking hands, and making conversation. He picked the shows that would play in Shubert theaters, deciding when they would open and when they would close. He helped choose casts, occasionally luring Hollywood stars to play on Broadway. Meanwhile, Jacobs booked the theaters, helped develop new plays, and marketed the current ones. When

Jacobs died in 1996, Schoenfeld assumed some of his duties. By the time of Schoenfeld's death, Shubert operated sixteen theaters fully, and shared operation of another, making his organization by far the largest owner of legitimate theaters in New York City, or ones that relied upon actors using spoken words and natural movements instead of song and dance.

The Shubert Organization introduced new ways of attracting audiences into its theaters by promoting shows on television and by making it easier and more convenient for theatergoers to purchase tickets. Of course, much of Schoenfeld's success rested on his knack for backing hit plays, among them *Ain't Misbehavin'* (1978), *A Chorus Line* (1975), *Dreamgirls* (1981), *Glengarry Glen Ross* (1984), *Little Shop of Horrors* (1982), and *Sunday in the Park with George* (1984). Schoenfeld's Shubert Organization also produced *Cats*, which on 19 June 1997 became the longest-running Broadway musical to that date with performance number 6,138. Along the way, there were failures, too, notably *Chess* (1988), *Devour the Snow* (1979), and *Zoot Suit* (1979).

The bald, congenial Schoenfeld could be, at turns, affable and exasperating and often displayed a steely resolve. A skilled storyteller, he could dominate a room but could also be pompous. As a leader in the Broadway League (formerly the League of Broadway Theaters and Producers), Schoenfeld frequently clashed with union leaders during contract negotiations. Producers criticized him for bleeding individual shows with theater-operating costs. Always focused on profit, Schoenfeld often complained that his commercial theaters had to compete with nonprofit ones that enjoyed tax exemptions. Oddly enough, many of these same nonprofit theaters could attribute their existence to the nonprofit Shubert Foundation headed by Schoenfeld. As its leader, he gave away millions to support theater and, to a lesser extent, dance.

Schoenfeld's desire to make money has been cited by critics as his motivation for focusing on flashy British musical blockbusters instead of helping to develop American theater. In the early 1980s the playwright David Mamet confronted Schoenfeld and accused the producer of working to destroy the theater rather than creating anything. Despite this legendary clash, Schoenfeld went on to book eight of Mamet's productions.

At the time of his argument with Mamet, Schoenfeld had publicly backed the decision to demolish two theaters in Times Square to make way for a hotel as part of a revitalization project. Times Square and Broadway had garnered such a notorious reputation for drug use, prostitution, and crime that many would-be theatergoers were unwilling to brave the area. Schoenfeld had argued for a revitalization of the area since 1970. Viewing Broadway as an economic engine for New York City, he lobbied government to take action to clean it up. Seven years later, in 1977, he gathered the casts of twenty-five Broadway shows, members of trade unions, neighborhood residents, and members of the clergy to stage a three-day rally in Times Square against smut. Schoenfeld is widely credited with helping to reshape the Broadway district into a family destination.

In 2004 the Shubert Organization named its theater, formerly the Plymouth, on 45th Street between Broadway and Eighth Avenue for Schoenfeld. When Schoenfeld died of a heart attack at his Manhattan home at the age of eighty-four, the mayor of New York City, Michael Bloomberg, paid tribute to him. A memorial service at the Majestic Theater attracted everyone from actors to ushers to box-office staff.

★

There is no biography of Schoenfeld. He did contribute an introduction that is largely autobiographical to Maryann Chach, Reagan Fletcher, Mark Evan Swartz, and Sylvia Want, *The Shuberts Present: 100 Years of American Theater* (2001). A Schoenfeld-authored essay in Robert Viagas, *The Alchemy of Theatre: The Divine Science* (2006), discusses the importance of producers and the challenges of running theaters. The online Shubert Archive, http://www.shubertarchive.org/noflash.htm, contains the business and artistic records of the Shubert Organization. Obituaries are in the *New York Times* and *Newsday* (both 26 Nov. 2008).

Caryn E. Neumann

Viktor Schreckengost, 2006. AP IMAGES

SCHRECKENGOST, Viktor Sebring (*b*. 26 June 1906 in Sebring, Ohio; *d*. 26 January 2008 in Tallahassee, Florida), innovative industrial designer, artist, and teacher who became emeritus professor of industrial design at the Cleveland Institute of Art, serving on the faculty for seventy-eight years.

Schreckengost was one of six children, three boys and three girls, of Warren Schreckengost, a potter, and Ada Schreckengost [*sic*], a caterer for the Sebrings, who owned china factories in the Ohio town. The name *Schreckengost* is derived from German for "frightening guest," a reference to Viking raiders. Schreckengost learned to sculpt clay from his father. Two uncles and two younger brothers were also ceramists.

As a child Schreckengost began working at local potteries, where he learned the properties of materials. After graduating from high school in Sebring in 1924, Schreckengost studied at the Cleveland School of Art (later the Cleveland Institute of Art), with Frank Wilcox and Paul Travis. In 1929 Schreckengost visited a local exhibition of Viennese ceramics, where he became fascinated by the work of Michael Powolny, who taught in Vienna, Austria. Schreckengost won a scholarship and borrowed $1,500 from two owners of Gem Clay, an industrial ceramics manufacturer in

Sebring, enabling him to attend the Kunstgewerbeschule (Industrial Arts School) for a year to study with Powolny. While Schreckengost was at the school in Vienna, classmates spelled his first name with a *k*, a practice he adopted. At the school he received instruction from the Viennese architect and furniture designer Josef Hoffmann.

In 1930 Schreckengost started teaching industrial design at the Cleveland School of Art, where he founded the first program of industrial design in the United States three years later. He generally taught two or three days a week, devoting the rest of his time to design projects or to art. He viewed designing as a process of asking questions, and his classes were always casual. After almost eight decades, Schreckengost had trained more than a thousand students. He doubted he ever developed a teaching style, but considered his instruction effective.

Industrial designers have ranked Schreckengost among the most democratic industrial designers. He adapted items found in homes, yards, and garages. From 1938 to 1972 he designed forty-two different Murray bicycles for Sears, Roebuck and Co., including the Spaceliner, which was manufactured from the mid-1960s.

Schreckengost also excelled in dinnerware. His "Econo-Rim" china reduced the width of rims on plates and cups, easing storage and increasing their capacity. He changed the emphasis of American Limoges in Sebring from Victorian nostalgia to a contemporary look that was pleasing to middle-class customers. "Americana" and "Diana" became best-selling lines, and the "Floral Pattern" saved the company during the Depression, although critics felt that Schreckengost often sacrificed original shapes to decoration. During the 1930s he created Jiffy Ware ceramic food containers.

Schreckengost believed that form follows function. "The last thing I look at is aesthetics," he once told an interviewer. "The first thing I have to solve is the basic function of things." He would always ask himself, "How could I take it and make it simpler and take labor out of it, so it's cheaper?" His philosophy was that good design should not be available only to the wealthy. In 1930 Schreckengost and the engineer Ray Spiller designed the first cab-over-engine truck for White Motors. It added five feet to the hauling area. Historians of industrial design have called it "the greatest development in truck transportation." From the late 1930s, working for the Murray Ohio Company, Schreckengost created children's pedal cars shaped like racers, jet planes, and missiles.

The future first lady Eleanor Roosevelt commissioned Schreckengost's most famous ceramic piece, the art deco *Jazz* (1930–1931), a blue-and-black sgraffito glazed bowl depicting a night on the town. Working for Cowan Pottery, Schreckengost had drawn the project assignment from an office hopper. Other punch bowls followed. In 2004 Sotheby's auctioned one of the bowls, originally priced at $50, for $254,400. In 2008 a *Danse Moderne* plate, created as a companion piece for the *Night Club Jazz Bowl*, sold at auction for $55,000. Schreckengost's sister had introduced him to jazz recordings in the late 1920s, and he had made regular trips to New York City to visit the Cotton Club.

Many of Schreckengost's sculptures resemble caricatures. In *The Rape of Europa* (c. 1940), for example, the artist modeled Europa after the actress Josephine Baker. *Apocalypse '42* (1942) depicts a German soldier as Death and Adolf Hitler, Hirohito, and Benito Mussolini as the Four Horseman, all riding one terrified animal. In 1954 Schreckengost created the world's largest freestanding ceramic sculpture (34 feet x 17.5 feet), *Early Settler*, which is on permanent display at Lakewood High School in Lakewood, Ohio.

Schreckengost's "Beverly Hills" lawn chair, made in 1941, consisted of two pieces of colored, stamped steel on a tubular base. To mold the seat, Schreckengost cut a barrel to a suitable height, placed soft clay on top, and covered the clay with plastic. The playful designer promised a drink to every person who sat on the clay. He was satisfied after 428 impressions for his mold.

In 1943, at age thirty-seven, Schreckengost enlisted in the U.S. Navy. He helped perfect radar and design three-dimensional terrain models of Honshu and the Remagen Bridge. He left the military in 1946.

Schreckengost's students included Giuseppe Delena, a principal designer for Ford; Larry Nagode, chief designer at Fisher-Price; Joe Oros, designer of the 1965 Ford Mustang; Sid Ramnarace, also a designer of the Mustang series; and Jerry Hirschberg, creator of the 1971 Buick Riviera.

Because Schreckengost chose to live and work quietly in Cleveland Heights, Ohio, fame came late to the ceramist. In 2000 the Cleveland Museum of Art curated his first retrospective. Schreckengost made several personal appearances at the exhibit and in April 1991, at age ninety-three, traveled to Norfolk, Virginia, to address a chapter of the American Institute of Architects. The Viktor Schreckengost Foundation arranged more than 100 exhibits of his work, with at least one in each state, to celebrate his centenary in 2006. That year Schreckengost received the National Medal of Arts, the nation's highest cultural honor. *Crain's Cleveland Business* reported in 2005 that his designs had contributed more than $200 billion to the U.S. economy.

Schreckengost died at the age of 101 while wintering in Tallahassee. His first wife, Nadine Averill, an art student whom he married on 6 September 1935, died in 1975. In April 1991 Schreckengost married Virgene "Gene" Nowacek, a pediatrician. He had no children. Schreckengost is buried at Cleveland's Lake View Cemetery beneath a headstone of his own design.

Schreckengost revitalized American appliance and toy design, creating such diverse items as furniture, fans, lawn chairs, prosthetic devices, safer and cleaner printing presses, golf carts, baby strollers, and riding lawn mowers.

★

The Cleveland Institute of Art's Gund Library owns more than 450 slides depicting Schreckengost's work. Henry Adams, *Viktor Schreckengost and 20th-Century Design* (2000), provides biography and discusses the designer's works. Adams, *Viktor Schreckengost: American Da Vinci* (2006), edited by Sunny McClellan Morton, contains numerous illustrations and lists the institutions participating in the 100th anniversary exhibitions. For additional information, see Steven Litt, "Viktor Schreckengost Has Had a Huge Impact on American Culture," *Cleveland Plain Dealer* (23 July 2000). An obituary is in the *New York Times* (2 Feb. 2008).

John L. Scherer

SCHWARTZ, Anthony (*b.* 19 August 1923 in New York City; *d.* 15 June 2008 in New York City), sound archivist, electronic media specialist, and advertising consultant noted for the "Daisy" television commercial used in Lyndon B. Johnson's 1964 presidential campaign.

Schwartz, known as "Tony," was one of two sons of Samuel Schwartz, a civil engineer, and Esther (Levy) Schwartz, a writer. The family moved from Manhattan to Crompond, New York, shortly after he was born. By the time he was thirteen he had developed agoraphobia; he became keenly interested in the sensory realms of sound and image and enjoyed operating ham radios. A six-month period of blindness when he was sixteen deepened his connection to the auditory world. He graduated from Peekskill High School in 1941 and earned a BFA in graphic design from Pratt Institute in 1944. He went to work as a graphic designer for the U.S. Navy during World War II.

As early as the 1940s Schwartz started recording all kinds of sounds—events, people, music. As audiotape technology developed, so did his desire to experiment with sound and the audio world. Because of his agoraphobia, Schwartz confined his fieldwork to his neighborhood on Manhattan's West Side. An early result was the recording "New York 19," which documented the "music" he encountered on the streets, from street performers to the speech of immigrants to the sound of a pneumatic drill. Schwartz's early recordings of ambient sound and folk music led to the release of many albums under the Folkways Records and Columbia Records labels. One of these albums, *New York Taxi Driver*, was among the first 100 recordings inducted into the National Recording Registry. From 1945 to 1976 he also produced and hosted *Around New York*, a program on the public radio station WNYC.

In 1958 the Johnson & Johnson company approached Schwartz about creating ads using children as narrators. The resulting radio commercials are thought to be the first to use real children's voices. Schwartz soon broadened into general advertising, creating or consulting for radio and television ads for such clients as Coca-Cola, American Airlines, Chrysler, the American Cancer Society, and Kodak. In one notable use of sound, he created an ad for Coca-Cola in which the only thing one hears is the enticing sound of liquid being poured. He worked as an art director at ad agencies and then started his own agency, the Wexton Company, which later became Solow/Wexton. He also was the sound director for several Broadway plays. Schwartz married Reenah Lurie, who often worked with him on scriptwriting, on 27 September 1959; the couple had a daughter and a son.

While continuing to create product ads, from the 1960s to the 1980s Schwartz helped develop advertising campaigns for more than 200 political candidates, including Johnson, Edward Kennedy, Hubert Humphrey, Jimmy Carter, and Bill Clinton. Most candidates came to Schwartz's home to be filmed. The most famous and controversial advertisement on which he worked is known as the "Daisy ad," created for the 1964 Johnson campaign. It shows a little girl in a field picking petals off a daisy, counting out loud. An adult voice-over then begins a military-sounding countdown as the screen shows an atomic blast. President Johnson is then heard intoning the words, "These are the stakes—to make a world in which all of God's children can live, or to go into the dark. We must either love each other, or we must die." Although it never referred to Johnson's opponent by name, the ad suggested that the Republican candidate, Senator Barry M. Goldwater, would be a dangerous leader in a nuclear age. The "Daisy ad," which had a powerful impact, was aired only once as a paid advertisement. It has often been cited as the beginning of negative commercials. To the end of his career, Schwartz defended it, arguing that "there was nothing negative about it. Frankly, I think it was the most positive commercial ever made." In his book *The Responsive Chord* (1973), he wrote: "The best political commercials . . . do not tell the viewer anything. They surface his feelings and provide a context for him to express these feelings."

Early in his career Schwartz had created the first antismoking commercials, and in the 1980s he resumed his work in public interest advertising. He created many more influential antismoking commercials as well as ads for such causes as fire prevention, AIDS awareness, educational funding, and nuclear disarmament.

Schwartz taught media studies remotely, by means of a variety of technologies, at Fordham University, where he shared the Schweitzer Chair with Marshall McLuhan, Columbia University, New York University, Emerson College, and Harvard University. He was known to say that he had delivered lectures on every continent but Antarctica, all without leaving the house.

Schwartz received many awards for his work in commercials and sound recordings, including the Prix Italia for Best Documentary (1955); First Place for Commercials at the Cannes Film Festival (1963, 1967, and two later years) and the Venice Film Festival (1973); and Academy Awards in 1960 and 1973 for soundtracks for short films. For more than ten years he represented the United States and North America at the World Radio Festival in the Best Documentary category. The World Health Organization awarded him its first World No Smoking Day Medal (1988); he was also honored with the Distinguished Service Citation of the American Foundation for AIDS Research (1988) and with the 1990 International Radio Festival Award for Best Public Service Radio Ad. He was given honorary degrees by John Jay College (1977), Emerson College (1983), and Stonehill College (1986).

Schwartz died at his home of aortic valve stenosis.

Schwartz, known as "the wizard of sound," once said, "the best thing about radio is that people were born without earlids. You can't close your ears to it." The photographer Edward Steichen called Schwartz the man "who moved sound recording into the realm of the arts." He is considered a master of electronic media who left his mark on radio, film, television, and advertising.

★

The Schwartz Collection, a vast collection of audio and audiovisual materials assembled by Schwartz over his fifty-five-year career, as well as his commercials, is housed at the Library of Congress. Schwartz's book *Media: The Second God* (1981) was widely used in university media classes. Robert Shelton, "New York on Tape: A Young New Yorker with a Recorder Limns the City in Its Variety of Sound," *New York Times* (12 Apr. 1959), is an early assessment of Schwartz's work. Obituaries are in the *New York Times* and *Washington Post* (both 17 June 2008).

Joan Goodbody

SCHWARTZ, Melvin (*b.* 2 November 1932 in New York City; *d.* 28 August 2006 in Twin Falls, Idaho), physicist who was awarded the 1988 Nobel Prize in Physics for his part in generating a neutrino beam and the discovery of muon neutrinos.

Schwartz grew up in the Bronx, a borough of New York City, during the Great Depression. His parents, Harry Schwartz and Hannah (Shulman) Schwartz, struggled to make ends meet. In spite of the difficult economic times, Schwartz's parents instilled in him a strong sense of optimism and the importance of developing one's mind. At

Melvin Schwartz. © UPI PHOTO/CORBIS

the age of twelve Schwartz entered the Bronx High School of Science, where he became interested in physics.

After graduating in 1949, Schwartz entered Columbia University, which was renowned for its physics department. He earned an AB in physics and mathematics in 1953 and stayed on for graduate work, receiving his PhD in 1958. He became an assistant professor in the Columbia physics department in 1958, an associate professor in 1960, and a full professor in 1963. Schwartz married Marilyn Fenster on 25 November 1953. They had a son and two daughters.

In the late 1950s Schwartz took part in the daily coffee breaks at Columbia's Pupin Laboratory, where scientists gathered to discuss the problems of particle physics, a branch of physics that deals with subatomic matter and the energy associated with it. At the time physicists were frustrated by the limited means of studying the weak force, one of four basic forces in nature, along with gravitation, electromagnetism, and the strong force, and the most difficult to observe. The physicists at the lab were searching for a way to gain further empirical evidence on the weak force but were not optimistic about finding one.

Then Schwartz suggested that the solution to the problem was neutrinos, tiny, uncharged particles emitted by the sun in vast numbers. Neutrinos can pass through almost all matter and are detected only when the very rare event of a collision with an atomic nucleus occurs. His Columbia colleagues Leon Lederman and Jack Steinberger joined Schwartz in the pursuit of a neutrino beam. The interactions produced when a neutrino beam passes through matter involve only the weak force. Their breakthrough came after two years of work using the alternating gradient synchrotron located at the Brookhaven National Laboratory on Long Island, New York.

In their experiments, the team directed an energetic beam of protons at metallic beryllium. When the beam and the beryllium collided, subatomic particles, including neutrinos, were produced. To separate the neutrinos from other particles, the team created a 44-foot-thick, 5,000-ton steel wall made from old battleship plates that only the neutrinos could pass through. To detect the neutrinos after they passed through the steel, the team designed a neon-filled spark chamber in which they placed ninety aluminum plates. When the neutrinos interacted with the aluminum, charged particles were produced. These charged particles ionized the neon to form a spark—thus making the neutrinos detectable.

Until this time scientists knew of only one kind of neutrino, the electron neutrino; but a theoretical physicist, Gerald Feinberg, had hypothesized that a second neutrino, the muon neutrino, might also exist. If the neutrinos formed in Schwartz's team's experiment were like the neutrinos already known, a fast electron should also have been formed. The fact that no fast electron was found proved the existence of this second neutrino. Thus in June 1962 the team was able to declare success in devising a new way to study the weak force using a neutrino beam as well as in the discovery of the muon neutrino. (Researchers have since found a third type of neutrino.)

In 1966 Schwartz became a professor at physics at Stanford University in California. He was attracted to the position because a new particle accelerator had just been built at Stanford. In 1970 he founded a private company, Digital Pathways, Inc., to provide security in the management of computer data. Increasingly, he found the field of particle physics, with dozens of researchers working together at one time, too crowded to suit his style. Thus in 1983 Schwartz left Stanford to devote himself to his company. In 1988, twenty-six years after the success of their work on the weak force and discovery of the muon, Schwartz, Lederman, and Steinberger were awarded the Nobel Prize in Physics. The Nobel Committee noted that the team had presented "entirely new opportunities for research into the innermost structure and dynamics of matter."

In 1991 an old classmate persuaded Schwartz to return to physics as associate director of High Energy and Nuclear Physics at the Brookhaven lab and to Columbia as professor of physics. Ironically, at Brookhaven he was responsible for managing 300 to 400 scientists, successfully overseeing the building of a new atomic physics collider. William A. Zajc, one of the scientists who worked under him, described Schwartz as an "iconoclast" who trusted his own judgment.

Schwartz was a member of the National Academy of Sciences and a fellow of the American Physical Society. For his outstanding contributions to science, he was awarded Columbia's highest honor, the Alexander Hamilton Medal, in 1995. In 1997 he retired and moved to Ketchum, Idaho. He died at a nursing home in Twin Falls of complications of Parkinson's disease and hepatitis C.

Passionate about his field, Schwartz was an original thinker whose ideas and methods contributed to great strides in understanding the physical world. Many subsequent experiments in physics became possible because of his work. Schwartz earned the respect and admiration of his colleagues for his intellect, creativity, and enthusiasm for discovery.

★

For information on the work that led to the Nobel, see Bertram Schwarzschild, "Physics Nobel Prize to Lederman, Schwartz, and Steinberger," *Physics Today* 42 (Jan. 1989): 17–20. Obituaries are in the *San Francisco Chronicle* (29 Aug. 2006) and *New York Times* (30 Aug. 2006).

M. C. Nagel

SEAMAN, Barbara (*b.* 11 September 1935 in New York City; *d.* 27 February 2008 in New York City), author and pioneering advocate for women's health and reproductive rights.

Seaman was born into a leftist Jewish community (her parents had met at a Young People's Socialist League picnic and honeymooned in the Soviet Union), the oldest of three daughters of Henry Jerome Rosner, an assistant commissioner for New York's Department of Social Services, and Sophie Blanche (Kimels) Rosner, a high school English teacher.

Seaman left New York to attend Oberlin College in Ohio, where she was a Ford Foundation Scholar. In 1954 Seaman married Peter Marks, but the marriage was annulled after six months. In 1956 she graduated with a BA in history. A year later, on 15 January, she married Gideon Seaman, a psychiatrist. The couple would go on to have a son and two daughters. In 1957 Seaman expressed a desire to breast-feed her newborn son but was discouraged from doing so by her doctor. The baby nearly died from a laxative Seaman was prescribed without her knowledge. When two years later her aunt died from uterine cancer, she discovered that the high levels of estrogen in the commercial hormone replacement drug Premarin were a contributing factor.

From 1965 to 1969 Seaman wrote for the *Ladies' Home Journal* and *Bride's Magazine*, but she felt women's magazines were a ghetto. In 1967 she won a Sloan-Rockefeller Science Writing Fellowship at the Columbia University School of Journalism, where a year later she earned a certificate in science writing. A prolific freelance writer, Seaman became a member of the Society of Magazine Writers, through which she met the feminist activists Betty Friedan and Gloria Steinem. In 1966 she covered the founding of National Organization for Women (NOW) and in 1969 the National Association for the Repeal of Abortion Laws (NARAL). She became a contributing editor to *Ms. Magazine* and a writer for the *New York Times*, *Village Voice*, and *Washington Post*.

In 1969 Seaman's first book, *The Doctors' Case Against the Pill*, appeared, despite the attempt by a number of drug companies to block its publication. The book received somewhat mixed notices: *Science* gave it a positive review, whereas the *Journal of the American Medical Association* did not.

In 1970 Seaman penned a letter to Senator Gaylord Nelson of Wisconsin, declaring that she had been "horrified" to learn that doctors had not warned her aunt of the danger to her health posed by Premarin. Nelson was in the process of presenting his "environmental agenda," which included enhancing quality of life by encouraging family planning. The hearings that Nelson subsequently held were so raucous—interrupted by women, including Seamen, who were outraged at not being allowed to testify—that they soon became known as the "Boston Tea Party" of the women's health movement. Seaman was the first to publicize the dangers of the high estrogen level in birth control pills, including heart disease, stroke, and depression. As a result of the hearings, the U.S. Food and Drug Administration issued a warning concerning the possible health risks associated with birth control pills, a first for a prescription drug.

In 1971 Seaman became vice president of the New York City Women's Medical Center. A year later her second book, *Free and Female: The Sex Life of Contemporary Women*, made its appearance. From 1970 to 1971 she penned a syndicated column, "Your Mind, Your Heart," and between 1970 and 1973 she was child care and education editor for *Family Circle*. In 1973 she was honored by the Library of Congress for her work in raising awareness of the problem of sexism in the delivery of health care around the world.

That same year Seaman became a founding member of the New York Women's Forum and a member of the advisory board of the New York chapter of the NOW. A year later she cofounded the National Women's Health Network (NWHN), an advocacy group for women's health issues. She wrote two books with her husband, *How to Get off the Pill and Hormones and Be Better Than Ever* (1976) and *Women and the Crisis in Sex Hormones* (1977), about the side effects and use of contraceptives and hormones. The book prompted the Department of Health, Education and Welfare (HEW) to convene a task force, on which Seaman served, to study DES (diethylstilbestrol), a synthetic steroid that had been shown to cause cancer in the daughters of the women who had taken it to prevent miscarriages. In May 1978 Seaman was awarded an honorary doctor of humane letters from Oberlin College. She divorced her husband and, on 9 April 1982, married Milton Forman, a business executive. They were also divorced.

Virtually blacklisted by many magazines, including *Ladies' Home Journal*, *Family Circle*, and *Omni*, for her attacks on the pharmaceutical and medical industries, Seaman switched to biography for her next book, *Lovely Me: The Life of Jacqueline Susann*, in 1987. It received poor reviews but was made into a television movie, *Scandalous Me*, in 1998.

In 2000 Seaman was named by the U.S. Postal Service as an honoree of the 1970s women's rights movement stamp. In 2001 she compiled classic readings in women's health in *For Women Only!: Your Guide to Health Empowerment*. In 2003 *The Greatest Experiment Ever Performed on Women: Exploding the Estrogen Myth* was published. Seaman likened corporations' and the medical profession's treatment of women—in which women were given drugs without their knowledge or consent—to the kinds of experiments conducted by the Nazis. Though the dangers posed by estrogen treatments had been understood since 1940, she wrote, doctors had continued to prescribe

contraceptives containing high amounts of estrogen to treat hot flashes and to lessen the risk of pregnancy or miscarriage. In 2005 Seaman's research was vindicated when the large Women's Health Initiative Study was canceled because the risks of hormone therapy were discovered to outweigh its advantages.

In 2008 two more books on which she collaborated with Laura Eldridge were published posthumously: *The No-Nonsense Guide to Menopause* and *Body Politic: Dispatches from the Women's Health Revolution*.

Diagnosed in 2007 with lung cancer, Seaman refused treatment and died at home in Manhattan. A memorial service attended by over 300 people was held on 6 March 2008 at the Riverside Memorial Chapel. She was buried after a private funeral in the Trinity Church Cemetery on Manhattan's Upper West Side.

Seaman helped to change the focus of health reporting, thereby enabling both women and men to be well-informed by their physicians and to participate in decisions about their own medical care. She was often called the "Ralph Nader of the birth-control pill," after the well-known consumer advocate. When *The Doctors' Case Against the Pill* was reissued on its twenty-fifth anniversary in 1995, the magazine *Science* credited Seaman with successfully challenging the overwhelmingly male medical profession and helping to found the women's self-help health movement. Her work resulted in lower estrogen levels in birth control pills in the United States and the inclusion of patient information in drug prescriptions.

★

No biographies have been written about Seaman. Her papers (through 1983) are at the Schlesinger Library, Radcliffe Institute, Cambridge, Massachusetts. Obituaries are in the *Washington Post* (29 Feb. 2008), *New York Times* (1 Mar. 2008), and *CMAJ: Canadian Medical Association Journal* (8 Apr. 2008).

Jane Brodsky Fitzpatrick

SHELDON, Sidney (*b.* 11 February 1917 in Chicago, Illinois; *d.* 30 January 2007 in Rancho Mirage, California), novelist, film and television screenwriter, and Broadway playwright.

Born Sidney Schechtel, Sheldon was the son of Ascher "Otto" Schechtel and Natalia (Marcus) Schechtel, both of whom were of Russian Jewish ancestry. Sheldon's father managed a jewelry store in Chicago, and his mother was a homemaker. Although neither of his parents had been educated beyond the third grade, Sheldon was a voracious reader as a child and soon found himself drawn to writing. He attained professional status at the tender age

Sidney Sheldon. **JEFF KATZ/LIAISON AGENCY/GETTY IMAGES**

of ten when he sold one of his poems for the princely sum of $10.

Subject to extreme mood swings even as a teenager, Sheldon struggled with bipolar disorder for much of his life, although in later years the condition was successfully managed with medication. In Sheldon's 2005 memoir, *The Other Side of Me*, he revealed that he had considered suicide in his late teens while working as a delivery boy for a Chicago drugstore.

With a scholarship and supplementary earnings from odd jobs, Sheldon enrolled at Northwestern University in nearby Evanston in 1935 but was forced to drop out as the economic situation deteriorated during the Great Depression. Shortly thereafter he set off for New York City, hoping to establish himself as a songwriter. When that venture failed, he headed to Los Angeles to try his hand at screenwriting. Sheldon was hired as a script reader by Universal Studios and by 1941 had found modest success as a screenwriter. His budding career was soon interrupted by World War II. He served briefly in the Army Air Forces but was discharged for medical reasons and traveled again to New York City, hoping this time to find success in writing for the Broadway stage.

Sheldon's second attempt to make a name for himself in New York proved moderately successful. At various times during 1944, three musical hits—*Dream with Music, Jackpot,* and a revised staging of *The Merry Widow*—for which he received writing credits appeared on Broadway; however, only the revival of *The Merry Widow* ran for more than two months. The following year Sheldon shared writing credits with Mary Helen Fay and Ladislaus Bush-Fekete on *Alice in Arms,* which served as the vehicle for Kirk Douglas's Broadway debut but closed after only five performances.

Hoping he might have better luck writing once again for films, Sheldon in 1946 returned to the West Coast and was soon busy writing screenplays for a number of motion-picture productions, including *Easter Parade, Annie Get Your Gun,* and *The Bachelor and the Bobby-Soxer,* the screenplay for which won Sheldon an Academy Award in 1948. Between 1947 and 1962 he earned writing credits on an additional fifteen films produced or distributed by Metro-Goldwyn-Mayer (MGM) and Paramount. In the late 1950s Sheldon made a brief and successful return to Broadway. He collaborated with Dorothy Fields, Herbert Fields, and David Shaw to write the book for the musical *Redhead,* which starred Gwen Verdon. The writing team was rewarded for its efforts with a Tony Award in 1959.

Attracted by the growing popularity of television, Sheldon got involved in television production in a big way in the early 1960s. With William Asher he cocreated *The Patty Duke Show* and received writing credits for eighty-eight episodes of the show, which ran from 1963 through 1966. In 1965 Sheldon created *I Dream of Jeannie,* for many episodes of which he provided the scripts and also served as executive producer. Sheldon's other television credits include teleplays for several episodes of *Hart to Hart,* which ran from 1979 to 1981, and his novels, several of which were made into television miniseries and movies.

For a writer who is best known for his novels of mystery and romance, Sheldon got a relatively late start in those genres. He was in his early fifties when his first novel, *The Naked Face,* a mystery, was published in 1970. Although it was well received critically, being dubbed "the best mystery novel of the year" by the *New York Times* and earning its author an Edgar Allan Poe Award, it was not a commercial success when first released. His second novel, *The Other Side of Midnight* (1974), rocketed to the top of the best-seller list and firmly established Sheldon as a successful author.

Although they received little in the way of praise from book reviewers, most of Sheldon's subsequent novels managed to achieve best-seller status. Not surprisingly, these books, most of which featured strong women characters who managed to achieve success in a male-dominated world, were particularly popular with female readers. Among his many best-selling novels were *A Stranger in the Mirror* (1976), *Bloodline* (1977), *Rage of Angels* (1980),

Master of the Game (1982), *If Tomorrow Comes* (1985), *Windmills of the Gods* (1987), *The Sands of Time* (1988), *Memories of Midnight* (1990), *The Doomsday Conspiracy* (1991), *The Stars Shine Down* (1992), *Nothing Lasts Forever* (1994), *Morning, Noon, and Night* (1995), *The Best Laid Plans* (1997), *Tell Me Your Dreams* (1998), *The Sky Is Falling* (2001), and *Are You Afraid of the Dark?* (2004). Sheldon's autobiography, *The Other Side of Me*, was published in 2005.

In 1945 Sheldon married Jane Harding Kaufman, a New Yorker; the couple divorced two years later. In 1950 he met the actress Jorja Curtwright in the MGM commissary; the two dated for several months and in late March 1951 were married in Las Vegas. Shortly thereafter Sheldon and his second wife embarked on a three-month honeymoon tour of European capitals. Their marriage produced two daughters, one of whom suffered from spina bifida and died in infancy. On 11 May 1985, Jorja Sheldon suffered a massive heart attack and died. Sheldon married his third wife, the Bulgarian-born actress Alexandra Joyce Kostoff, on 14 October 1989.

In addition to being a strong advocate for freedom of the press, Sheldon was an active participant in a handful of charitable organizations that provide assistance for the homeless or promote literacy. He served as a national spokesman for the Freedom to Read Foundation, Libraries for the Future, and the National Coalition for Literacy.

Sheldon died in Rancho Mirage, with his wife, Alexandra, at his side. The cause of death was complications from pneumonia. He is buried in Westwood Memorial Park in Los Angeles.

Sheldon was an influential force in shaping America's popular culture during the latter half of the twentieth century. Although he will probably be best remembered for his novels, Sheldon's writing for motion pictures and television helped to shape both media and influenced the direction that both would take for subsequent decades.

★

An excellent source of additional information about Sidney Sheldon is his autobiography, *The Other Side of Me* (2005). Obituaries are in the *Los Angeles Times* and *USA Today* (both 31 Jan. 2007) and the *New York Times* (1 Feb. 2007).

Don Amerman

SHOULDERS, James Arthur ("Jim") (*b.* 13 May 1928 in Tulsa, Oklahoma; *d.* 20 June 2007 in Henryetta, Oklahoma), champion rodeo cowboy from the late 1940s through the 1960s who became the first nationally known rodeo star.

Shoulders was the son of Joe Louis Shoulders, an automobile repair mechanic, and Ellen (Draper) Shoulders, a homemaker. He was raised in town but spent time on his grandfather's farm. An athletic, wiry boy, he followed his older brother Marvin into rodeo and won his first bull-riding event at age fourteen at the Oilton Rodeo near Tulsa. By 1945, at age sixteen, he was considered a professional, so he joined the Cowboy Turtle Association in the same year that the group changed its name to the Rodeo Cowboy Association (later adding the word "Professional" to become known as the PRCA). Soon after he graduated from Tulsa's East Central High School in 1946, Shoulders hit the rodeo circuit full time and won $7,000 in his first full season.

Shoulders's career breakout came at the Madison Square Garden Rodeo in 1947, the same year he married his high school sweetheart, Sharon Heindselman. He won $5,000 and the bull-riding, bareback, and all-around titles while on his honeymoon, beginning not only his sixty-year marriage but also a six-decade endorsement relationship with Wrangler jeans. He claimed in an interview shortly before his death that it was "the longest running sports endorsement ever."

In 1949 Shoulders purchased a 5,000-acre cattle ranch near Henryetta, about fifty miles south of Tulsa. He and his wife raised four children, one of whom continued to run the ranch after Shoulders's death.

From 1949 to the late 1950s, during a period that some rodeo historians call the golden age of rodeo, Shoulders dominated the sport and became its public face. He won championships at all the marquee rodeos, including the Calgary Stampede in Canada and Cheyenne Frontier Days in Wyoming, and the big rodeos at Houston and Fort Worth, Texas, and Oklahoma City, Oklahoma. His won his first all-around PRCA world championship in 1949; at twenty-one he was the youngest man ever to win the title, a record that stood for forty years. He placed second in the all-around championship in 1950 and 1951 and won the title in four consecutive years from 1956 to 1959. He won the world championship of bull riding in 1951 and each year from 1954 to 1959; he won bareback bronco riding in 1950 and each year from 1956 to 1958. This total of sixteen PRCA world championships had not been matched as of 2009. In addition to his world titles, Shoulders finished second a combined ten times in bull and bareback riding. His last world championship came in 1959, but he continued to ride competitively as late as 1970.

Shoulders's greatest years were from 1956 to 1959, when he won the "triple crown" of bull-riding, bareback-riding, and all-around world championships three straight times followed by two of the three (all-around and bull) in 1959. His 1956 season earnings of $43,381 set a record that stood for eleven years. In Oklahoma his fame rivaled that of his fellow Okie Mickey Mantle, who won baseball's batting triple crown in 1956. In fact, Shoulders's 1956 earnings were comparable to those of Mantle. A 1957 *Time* magazine profile of Shoulders declared that "the scrawny cowpoke...had the casual swagger of a champ." He was also the subject of profiles in *Life* and *Sports Illustrated*.

Like all serious rough-stock riders, Shoulders suffered numerous injuries. At times, especially in 1952 and 1953, ailments slowed him down, but he had a reputation for tolerating pain and riding hurt. Already by 1957 he had suffered two breaks each of his collarbone, arms, legs, and ankles. A bull's horns fractured his face at Houston in 1960; he put off surgery until after the rodeo, telling the doctor, "I don't ride with my nose." One bull-riding champion told the *Tulsa World* that Shoulders "was probably the toughest guy I ever saw."

As a board member, Shoulders played a key role in the PRCA's effort to establish the official National Finals Rodeo (NFR) as the world series of rodeo. He presented President Dwight D. Eisenhower with the ceremonial first ticket to the new event. At the inaugural NFR in Dallas, Shoulders won the most money and his seventh, and last, bull-riding world title. The NFR became highly successful, running for many years in Oklahoma City and then moving to Las Vegas, Nevada, in the 1980s.

In the early 1960s Shoulders started a rodeo school, the first one for rough-stock riders. His school developed the mechanical bull that became a fad in western bars in the1980s. Shoulders also operated a successful rodeo stock contracting business. His bull Toronado became almost as famous as its owner, throwing off 220 attempts before Freckles Brown finally qualified on him in the first round of the 1967 NFR. With his fellow star Neal Gay, Shoulders owned the popular Mesquite Championship Rodeo near Dallas, which, unlike most rodeos, played weekly at the same location from spring through early fall.

Although endorsement deals for rodeo stars never reached the huge amounts offered in baseball, football, basketball, and golf, Shoulders profited nicely from his. He was most identified with Wrangler's cowboy-cut jeans, but he also had several other contracts, including Justin Boots. In the mid-1970s he joined other legendary retired athletes such as the baseball player and New York Yankees manager Billy Martin in a series of television commercials for Miller Lite beer. When Shoulders died, Wrangler issued a special line of cowboy shirts with a commemorative tag.

In recognition of his accomplishments, Shoulders was an inaugural member of the Pro Rodeo Hall of Fame in Colorado Springs, Colorado, and is honored in the Cowboy Hall of Fame at the National Cowboy and Western Heritage Museum in Oklahoma City. He is also a member of the Oklahoma Hall of Fame. Shoulders is the only cowboy in the Madison Square Garden Walk of Fame. Late in his life he continued to make appearances at rodeos, including the annual Navajo Nation Rodeo in 2005 and a special three-day festival in his honor in Tulsa in 2006.

Shoulders died at age seventy-nine from congestive heart failure. His funeral was held at the Henryetta rodeo arena named for him. Over a thousand people attended, including numerous world champion cowboys. He was buried wearing Justin boots, a bright red cowboy shirt, a world championship buckle, and, of course, Wrangler jeans, in Sonora Cemetery in Henryetta. A ceremony on the closing night of the NFR in December 2007, with Sharon Shoulders in attendance, honored the memory of the sixteen-time world champion.

Sometimes called the Babe Ruth of rodeo, Shoulders dominated the sport in the 1950s and remained a major competitor until 1970. He operated an influential rodeo school and was a major rough-stock contractor. As a member of the PRCA board, Shoulders was influential in establishing the National Finals Rodeo in 1958. Many modern PRCA and Professional Bull Riders (PBR) stars recognize that the sport's contemporary media success would not have been possible without the pioneering accomplishments of Shoulders and the other cowboys of rodeo's golden era. Shoulders won more Professional Rodeo Cowboy AssociationWorld Championship titles than any other competitor.

Gavin Ehringer, *Rodeo Legends: 20 Extraordinary Athletes of America's Sport* (2001) includes a chapter on Shoulders. His career is central to Gail Hughbanks Woerner, *Cowboy Up! The History of Bull Riding* (2001). Wayne S. Wooden and Ehringer, *Rodeo in America: Wranglers, Roughstock & Paydirt* (1996), provides a good historic overview of the sport. The National Cowboy and Western Heritage Museum in Oklahoma City and the Pro Rodeo Hall of Fame in Colorado Springs maintain biographical information on Shoulders. The Territorial Museum in Henryetta displays Shoulders memorabilia. *American Cowboy Magazine* (Sept./Oct. 2007) featured several articles in tribute to Shoulders following his death. Obituaries are in the *Daily Oklahoman* (21 June 2007) and *New York Times* (22 June 2007).

Bradley R. Rice

SHULMAN, Marshall Darrow (*b.* 8 April 1916 in Jersey City, New Jersey; *d.* 21 June 2007 in Sherman, Connecticut), scholar of the Soviet Union and foreign affairs, director of Columbia University's Russian Institute, ambassador, and a main adviser to Secretary of State Cyrus R. Vance in the Carter administration.

Shulman was one of two sons of Harry Shulman, an engineer, and Bessie (Waldman) Shulman, a homemaker and a volunteer for numerous charitable organizations. After graduating from Central High School in Detroit, Shulman attended the University of Michigan, where he was an editor of the student newspaper *Michigan Daily*, covering the stormy relations between Detroit's giant automakers and the United Automobile Workers of America. In 1937 he earned a BA and soon after worked for two years as a reporter for the *Detroit News*. During those years he also took courses in economics and government at the University of Chicago and in 1940 studied English literature at Harvard University.

During World War II, Shulman entered the U.S. Army Air Forces at age twenty-five and served for nearly five years, initially training as a glider pilot but later transferring to a psychological warfare program in Burma run by the Office of War Information. He was eventually awarded the Bronze Star. Toward the end of the war, while recovering from pneumonia, Shulman came to believe that the postwar years would be dominated by relations with the Soviet Union. "I didn't know anything about it," he told the *New York Times* in 1986. "I didn't even know the [Russian] language." Back home he enrolled in Columbia University's newly established Russian Institute, where he received an MA in 1948. Based on his journalistic experience, he was hired by the U.S. State Department in 1949 as an information officer for the U.S. Permanent Mission to the United Nations. From 1950 to 1953, during the Truman administration, he became Secretary of State Dean Acheson's special assistant and speechwriter and was part of a small White House team that drafted President Harry S. Truman's foreign policy speeches.

In 1948 Shulman married Elizabeth Van Anda Thomson, who died in 1956 and with whom he had two children. He married Colette Schwarzenbach in 1960.

When Dwight D. Eisenhower was elected president in 1953, Shulman moved to Paris, France, to conduct research for his doctoral dissertation on the French Communist Party and its relationship to the Soviet Union. In 1959 he earned his PhD from Columbia University, but not before he was hired by Harvard University as associate director of its Russian Research Center, where he served from 1954 to 1962. He also taught at the Fletcher School of Law and Diplomacy at Tufts University from 1961 to 1967. Shulman was then named director of the Russian Institute of Columbia University and Adlai E. Stevenson Professor of International Relations in 1967.

During this time of cold war passions between the United States and the Soviet Union, Shulman wrote *Stalin's Foreign Policy Reappraised* (1963), arguing for a less emotional response to the rivalry between the two superpowers. Later he and others developed the concept of what has been

termed "second track" diplomacy, a way of encouraging unofficial channels of communication between American and Russian intellectuals, politicians, scientists, and the like where they could discuss, away from the glare of headlines and denunciations, possible common denominators and seek mutual agreements on the most perilous situations, such as the threat of nuclear warfare. The Soviet-American Disarmament Study Group, a joint project with the American Academy of Arts and Sciences and the Soviet Academy of Sciences, was but one such example. "In all this no one on either side could transcend differences and bring the participants into a dialogue better than Marshall," said Robert Legvold, who succeeded Shulman as director of the Russian (renamed the Harriman) Institute at Columbia University.

When Jimmy Carter was elected president, Vance, his newly named secretary of state, asked Shulman to join him as an adviser with ambassadorial rank. There Shulman continued to express his views against nuclear war, in favor of arms limitations and the Strategic Arms Limitation Treaty II. However, when the Soviet Union invaded Afghanistan in 1979, President Carter, beset by hawkish pressure at home, turned toward a more confrontational stance, and Vance resigned in protest. Shulman remained at his post for a few more months to serve the new secretary of state, Edmund Muskie, but eventually Shulman left as well.

In his writings Shulman looked ahead, asking, "Is the Soviet system capable of change?" In a wide-ranging and thoughtful essay before the collapse of Communism and the Soviet state, Shulman perceptively noted that change could come about with "the emergence of new generations" and where "a vast generational shift is already in progress . . . free of the formative influences of the Revolution and the Stalinist terror." Until then "the best that can be hoped for in our relations with the Soviet Union . . . is a Cold Truce," much more preferable than "misperception and miscalculation in response to local crises." In a later essay he perceptively noted that because of new developments inside the Soviet Union and essentially economic considerations within the United States, "the prospect exists for a management of the competitive relationship that is less irrational, dangerous and costly than it has been for the past four decades."

Upon Shulman's death, Georgi Arbatov, the leading student of American studies in the Soviet Union, praised Shulman for having had the courage to speak against jingoists in both countries, saying that maybe "they" are not as "evil" as we think. Shulman, scholar and educator, reflected American opinion, in and out of government, which sought a less hostile, more moderate attitude in dealing with the Soviet Union, a stance that ultimately helped prevent war between the two nuclear-armed powers and allowed reformist tendencies within the Soviet Union to thrive.

Shulman died at his home of acute aortic stenosis leading to heart failure; his remains were cremated. His ashes are buried in Mount Auburn Cemetery in Cambridge, Massachusetts.

★

Shulman's papers are housed in Columbia University's Bakhmeteff Archive of Russian and East European Culture. In addition to *Stalin's Foreign Policy Reappraised*, Shulman wrote *Beyond the Cold War* (1966). Obituaries are in the *Los Angeles Times* (22 June 2007) and *New York Times* (23 June 2007).

Murray Polner

SHUMWAY, Norman Edward, Jr. (*b.* 9 February 1923 in Kalamazoo, Michigan; *d.* 10 February 2006 in Palo Alto, California), pioneering heart surgeon who developed and improved the procedures for heart transplantation and who carried out the first heart-lung transplant. He also developed processes for improving heart surgery and correcting various heart defects.

Norman E. Shumway. REUTERS/LANDOV

Shumway was born to Norman Edward Shumway, Sr., and Laura Irene (VanderVliet) Shumway. His parents operated a creamery in Jackson, Michigan, where Shumway was raised. In 1941 Shumway enrolled at the University of Michigan, intending to study law. His academic career was interrupted when he was drafted into the U.S. Army in 1943. Upon entering the army, he was given a career aptitude test. One part of the test asked him to designate a career choice of medicine or dentistry should he receive a passing score. Shumway chose medicine and passed the test. He was sent by the army to Baylor University in Texas for a nine-month-long premedical course; upon completion in 1945 he attended Vanderbilt University, earning his MD in 1949.

Shumway started his residency in surgery at the University of Minnesota, where he worked under F. John Lewis and C. Walton Lillehei, pioneers of open-heart surgery. Shumway was fascinated by their experiments and the results they achieved. He decided to give up his plans for neurosurgery and concentrate on the heart. His special interest was hypothermia—cooling the patient so that circulation could be stopped and the heart repaired.

Shumway married Mary Lou Stuurmans in 1951. The couple subsequently had four children. Also in 1951 he was drafted into the U.S. Air Force. He served as a flight surgeon for two years during the Korean War before returning to Minnesota to continue his doctoral studies. In 1956 Shumway earned his PhD in surgery from the University of Minnesota. He completed his surgical residency in 1957 and moved his young family to Santa Barbara, California. After leaving an unsuccessful partnership at a private surgical practice in Santa Barbara, Shumway interviewed for a position in the department of surgery at the University of California, San Francisco. During the interview he excitedly recounted his work with hypothermia in heart surgery only to realize his interviewer had fallen asleep. Shumway did not take the position.

In 1958 Shumway interviewed with Stanford University and accepted a position that entailed running the dialysis machine at night. He moonlighted as a freelance surgeon, and during the day he conducted hypothermia research on dogs' hearts. He was joined in the laboratory by a young surgical resident named Richard Lower. In 1959 Shumway and Lower began measuring how long a hypothermic heart could remain still (no circulation or beat) before it could be warmed back up and possibly restarted. They were able to stop dogs' hearts for more than sixty minutes and restart them without any negative side effects. These experiments opened up a world of possibility in surgical repairs of complicated heart defects.

Shumway and Lower speculated about other possible heart procedures that could be done during a one-hour-long surgery. It was Lower who suggested heart transplantation, though the idea was not new. Shumway and

Lower discovered that the transplant surgery itself was not technically difficult, but possible transplant rejection was the real challenge. They went on to perfect their surgical technique on dog test subjects and made important advances in overcoming transplant rejection. The dogs' survival rates slowly improved, and Shumway and Lower continued their research even after Lower completed his residency and moved to the Medical College of Virginia (MCV).

In 1965 Shumway was named head of cardiothoracic surgery at the Stanford University School of Medicine. At a press conference on 20 November 1967, he declared that he was ready to perform a human heart transplant. With over 70 percent of his dog test subjects surviving for more than a year after transplant, all Shumway needed was a human recipient and donor. The former proved easier to find than the latter, since the concept of brain death was not recognized in the United States at the time as a legal definition of death. In the United States a surgeon who stopped a beating heart to remove it from a brain-dead patient risked being charged with murder.

However, there were no such legal restrictions in South Africa. In 1966 the surgeon Christiaan Barnard spent several months at MCV observing Lower perform heart transplants in dogs. Barnard was determined to perform the surgery on humans. With far less experience with the procedure or its aftermath than Shumway or Lower and with mostly dismal results in his own laboratory experiments, Barnard nevertheless performed the first human-to-human heart transplant on 3 December 1967. His patient died from double pneumonia eighteen days after the surgery, and worldwide frenzy about the heart transplant ensued.

Shumway was in equal measures stung and relieved by word of Barnard's surgery; he detested publicity as much as Barnard craved it. He hoped Barnard's surgery would allow him to perform transplants quietly before publishing an academic paper about his experience. On 6 January 1968 he performed the first adult human-to-human heart transplant in the United States. To Shumway's chagrin, journalists were actually scaling the hospital's walls to get a glimpse of his patient, Mike Kasperak, who lived for fourteen days after the transplant. Kasperak died from various health complications mostly unrelated to the transplant.

Upon news of Shumway's successful surgery, medical centers around the world hastily performed heart transplant procedures—with dismal results. By the early 1970s, with 146 of 170 transplant patients dead, there was a strong call for a moratorium on heart transplants. Shumway and his team at Stanford refused to stop their work. He pioneered the use of cyclosporin, an antirejection drug that changed the face of organ transplants forever. He also perfected a simple way to sample tissues from a transplanted heart to detect rejection early before heart damage occurred. On 9 March 1981 Shumway and Bruce Reitz, a renowned

cardiac surgeon, carried out the world's first heart-lung transplant. The patient lived for five years and died of causes unrelated to the transplant. Shumway retired from his position at Stanford in 1993. He died of lung cancer at age eighty-three.

In addition to his pioneering efforts in heart transplants, Shumway worked on correcting many congenital heart defects as well as treating heart valve diseases in children and adults. His work saved and improved the lives of numerous people. Throughout his career, he remained a good-humored, down-to-earth, caring physician who was admired by colleagues and patients alike. He also oversaw the education of many heart surgeons in his long and distinguished career. A humble man, he delighted in merely being an assistant on the surgeries his residents performed. Contributing to Shumway's legacy, many of his trainees have become leading surgeons in their respective fields. Sara Shumway, one of Shumway's children, also followed his lead, becoming the vice chief of the division of cardiothoracic surgery and a professor of surgery at the University of Minnesota.

★

For a detailed account of Shumway's revolutionary surgical research and work beginning with his early career in Minnesota, see Donald McRae, *Every Second Counts: The Race to Transplant the First Human Heart* (2006). The Stanford School of Medicine has created a website dedicated to Shumway that includes a career time line and coverage of his 6 Jan. 1968 human heart transplant surgery; the site is at http://med.stanford.edu/special_ topics/ 2006/shumway/. Other biographical sources include Sara Shumway's tribute to her father in *Heart Failure Clinics* (2007) and obituaries in *Stanford Magazine* (May/June 2006) and the London *Guardian* (16 Feb. 2006).

Adi R. Ferrara

SILLS, Beverly (*b*. 25 May 1929 in New York City; *d*. 2 July 2007 in New York City), internationally known opera singer who reinvented herself as an arts administrator, first leading the New York City Opera and then Lincoln Center.

Born Belle Miriam Silverman in the Crown Heights section of Brooklyn, Sills was the daughter of Morris Silverman, an insurance broker whose family immigrated from Romania, and Shirley (Bahn) Silverman, who was born Sonia Markovna in Odessa, and developed a great love for music. Belle had two older brothers. As a young child, she took lessons in singing, tap dancing, and the piano. From early in her childhood, relatives called her "Bubbles" because she was born with a bubble in her mouth. When she was seven she

Beverly Sills, 1969. **AP IMAGES**

began calling herself Beverly Sills, at the suggestion of a family friend who thought it would look better than her given name on a theater marquee.

Sills studied voice with Estelle Liebling from 1936 until the teacher's death more than thirty years later. The young soprano became a regular on radio programs, including *Major Bowes' Capitol Family Hour*. She attended public schools and Erasmus Hall High School in Brooklyn, as well as the Professional Children's School in Manhattan.

By the time Sills was in her teens, she was already dreaming of being an opera star. She toured with the J. J. Schubert organization, performing in several Gilbert and Sullivan operettas in 1945, and in Franz Lehar's *The Merry Widow* the following year. Sills made her operatic debut singing the role of Frasquita the gypsy in a Philadelphia production of *Carmen*. During her early years as a professional opera singer, she became close friends with the tenor John Alexander, who taught her to study literature pertaining to an opera before playing a role in the piece. Early in her career she also began singing roles, such as Aida, that were not necessarily best for her voice over the long run. "I was still saying yes to everything," she wrote in her autobiography *Bubbles: A Self-Portrait*, "because I needed to earn a living and because I felt that the more people who heard me sing, the better."

It was in 1951 that Sills felt her operatic career truly began, with a tour organized by the impresario Charles Wagner. On that tour she sang the leading role of Violetta in many performances of *La Traviata*. She signed on again with the Wagner company to tour as Micaela in *Carmen*. In 1953 she made her San Francisco Opera debut as Helen of Troy in *Mefistofele*.

Sills's long, productive association with the New York City Opera (City Opera) began in 1955 when she debuted as Rosalinde in *Die Fledermaus*. When the conductor Joseph Rosenstock hired her, he said she had "a phenomenal voice, but no personality." Sills performed in City Opera's fall season and toured the following spring. During a stop in Cleveland, the company threw a party for the local press, and Sills met Peter Greenough, an associate editor of the *Cleveland Plain Dealer*, which was then owned by his family.

Sills and Greenough married on 17 November 1956 in a civil ceremony at Liebling's studio. Following their marriage she became stepmother to Greenough's three daughters. Sills has written that she spent much of the first year of their marriage on tour. During the late 1950s the couple moved from Cleveland to Boston, where Greenough began writing a financial column for a local newspaper. They had two children, Meredith "Muffy" Greenough, and Peter Greenough, Jr., known as "Bucky." Both faced major challenges from early childhood: Muffy had hearing impairments, and Bucky was mentally retarded. "The discovery of our children's problems seriously altered our lives," Sills wrote in *Bubbles: A Self-Portrait*. As a result, she began to regard her opera career "as a kind of refuge from personal problems."

Except for a two-year leave during the early 1960s, Sills performed steadily with New York City Opera, essentially becoming its unofficial leading lady for more than two decades. She sang the title role in *The Merry Widow*, Donna Anna in Wolfgang Amadeus Mozart's *Don Giovanni*, Marguerite in *Faust*, Cleopatra in *Julius Caesar*, the heroines in *The Tales of Hoffmann*, the title role in *Lucia di Lammermoor*, and Gaetano Donizetti's Tudor queens: Elizabeth I, Mary Stuart, and Anne Boleyn. In 1958 City Opera staged a season of American works. That April the company presented Douglas Moore's *The Ballad of Baby Doe* inspired by the life of the Colorado silver tycoon Horace Tabor, with Sills in the title role.

In 1964 Sills sang her first Queen of the Night in Mozart's *The Magic Flute*, a coloratura role noted for its high Fs. With characteristic candor, Sills has made no secret of the fact that she considered the role a bore. That year she made her New Orleans Opera debut, singing all the female leads in *The Tales of Hoffmann*. After she sang the role of Constanza in Mozart's *The Abduction from the Seraglio*, Winthrop Sargeant, music critic for the *New Yorker*, called her the prima donna of New York City Opera. Sills considered her portrayal of Cleopatra in a 1966 City Opera performance of *Julius Caesar* the "turning point" of her career.

Sills did not sing outside the United States until she was thirty-six years old, but at that point she gave a series of international engagements. She sang in Vienna, at La Scala opera house in Milan, and at Covent Garden in London. In 1970 she made her Israeli debut with the Israel Philharmonic in a concert version of *The Abduction from the Seraglio*. At her mother's insistence, Sills performed the engagement free of charge.

President Richard Nixon appointed Sills to the Council on the National Endowment for the Arts. In February 1971 the Nixons invited her to sing at the White House. Later she wrote that a zipper on her gown broke during the performance and that a cape First Lady Pat Nixon had suggested she wear because of the temperature in the room saved the day. In 1975 President Gerald Ford invited Sills back to the White House to sing during a state dinner honoring the prime minister of Great Britain.

Even though Sills was a quintessentially American opera singer, both because of her early performance history and because of her interest in American works, she did not debut at the Metropolitan Opera (the Met), one of the nation's leading opera houses, until she was forty-five. With typical bluntness, she said that Sir Rudolf Bing, the Met's longtime general manager, was instrumental in blocking her debut there. She said Bing objected to booking American singers at the Met, particularly if they had not studied abroad. However, after several attempts at making schedules coincide (and after Bing's departure in 1972), Sills finally made her Met debut on 8 April 1975, as Pamira in Gioacchino Antonio Rossini's *The Siege of Corinth*. Her later roles there included Violetta in *La Traviata*, the title roles in *Lucia di Lammermoor* and *Thais*, and Norina in *Don Pasquale*.

Through the years Sills developed a reputation as one of the best coloratura sopranos in the United States. She said she built a repertoire of about a hundred roles and performed fifty or sixty of them, either in opera or concert form. She wrote that during the late 1970s, she was among the world's three highest-paid opera singers. She developed a reputation for having solid technique, dramatic interpretations, and comic timing—a rare and distinctive combination. She also was respected for her interpretations of roles in the repertoire known as "bel canto," from the Italian for beautiful singing.

Nonetheless, by 1970 Sills had begun getting mixed reviews. She gave her last known operatic performance at New York City Opera in 1979 in Gian Carlo Menotti's *La Loca* and formally retired the following year. It was not long before it became clear that she had no regrets about retiring from her singing career. Sills said in a 1987 interview when she was fifty-seven. "I quit singing at fifty-one.... I sang 'Happy Birthday' for Isaac Stern and 'Jingle

Bells' for Ronald Reagan.... Other than that, I don't sing anymore—not even in the tub."

Meanwhile, Sills launched a second career as an arts administrator. In 1979 she began her ten-year tenure as the general manager of New York City Opera. At that company in the late 1980s, she oversaw an annual budget in excess of $20 million and took a hands-on approach to fund-raising, especially with major individual and corporate donors. "My pitch is that this is a unique company," she said in an interview with the *Memphis (Tennessee) Commercial Appeal*. "We help young American singers." Sills was certainly in a position to know, having been one of the singers whose careers were established with help from City Opera. In 1994 she became chairwoman of Lincoln Center, then served in the same capacity with the Metropolitan Opera from 2002 to 2005.

Sills was seventy-eight years old when she died at her home in Manhattan. Her manager, Edgar Vincent, said the cause of her death was inoperable lung cancer. She is buried at Kensico Cemetery in Valhalla, New York.

★

Sills's autobiographies include *Bubbles: A Self-Portrait* (1976); *Beverly: An Autobiography* (1987), coauthored with Lawrence Linderman; and *Bubbles: An Encore* (1981). She discusses her arts administration career in an interview with the *Memphis (TN) Commercial Appeal* (12 Feb. 1987). Obituaries are in the *New York Times* (3 and 4 July 2007).

Whitney Smith

SKIPPER, Howard Earle (*b.* 21 November 1915 in Avon Park, Florida; *d.* 2 January 2006 in Birmingham, Alabama), biochemist and cancer researcher who laid the foundation for chemotherapy.

Skipper was the son of Chesley Allen Skipper and Estelle (Wiggins) Skipper, both schoolteachers. His father was also involved in banking, real estate, and cattle ranching. As a high school student during the Great Depression, Skipper earned extra money by helping out on his father's cattle ranch and performing in diving exhibitions. After graduating, Skipper enrolled in the University of Florida in Gainesville on a football scholarship and also became captain of the swim team. Initially intending to become a lawyer, he soon discovered that his true fascination was with his chemistry and biology classes. He received a BS in 1938 and enrolled in a master's program at the university to study chemistry, biochemistry, nutrition, and biology. He earned an MS the following year and went on to earn his PhD in biochemistry and nutrition in 1941. He married Margaret Edwards, a law student at the university, on 24 August 1940; they would have a son and a daughter.

In June 1941, just two weeks after Skipper had completed his doctorate, he received a letter from President Franklin D. Roosevelt asking him to serve as second lieutenant in the Medical Research Division of the U.S. Army's Chemical Warfare Service (later the Chemical Corps). For the next two years Skipper was chief of the Toxicology Section at Edgewood Arsenal in Maryland. In 1943 Skipper was sent to serve as chief biochemist at the Australian Chemical Warfare Field Experimental Station in Queensland, Australia, and in 1944 he was named technical director of the Eastern Technical Unit of the Chemical Warfare Service in New Guinea and the Philippines, where he worked with a group of British and Australian scientists to research chemical warfare. He received an Army Commendation Medal for this research. Immediately following World War II, he went to Japan as part of a scientific research team assessing the status of Japanese research and development. He retired from the army with the rank of lieutenant colonel.

In 1946 Skipper established a cancer drug research group at the Southern Research Institute in Birmingham. He and his team began collaborating with the Sloan-Kettering Institute as well as the Division of Cancer Treatment of the National Cancer Institute to develop new drugs for the treatment of cancers. The team also worked to determine why certain existing drugs succeeded or failed at curing various cancers. In 1949 Skipper was named director and head of the Organic and Biochemical Divisions. While at the Southern Research Institute, he worked closely with his colleague Frank Schabel, a virologist. Together the two introduced the concept that a single cancer cell could multiply and ultimately lead to death from that cancer.

In 1955 the Southern Research Institute began a contract with the recently founded Cancer Chemotherapy National Service Center (CCNSC) to screen for new anticancer drugs by studying leukemias and solid tumors found in mice. Skipper's research on the metabolic activity of anticancer drugs in mice with tumors led to the development of chemotherapy for use in humans. He was the first to establish the idea that all cancer cells must be destroyed in order to ensure patient survival. Previously, scientists believed that removing or destroying most cancer cells would suffice because the immune system would kill off the rest, as in the case of bacterial infection. He was also the first to assert that administering certain combinations of anticancer drugs in the proper doses on a prescribed schedule ultimately improved chemotherapy's effectiveness and could eradicate certain cancers. Skipper's research demonstrated that drug resistance was lessened when several drugs were used at once.

In 1974 Skipper was appointed president of the Southern Research Institute in addition to his role, since 1964, as director of the Kettering-Meyer Laboratory at the institute. He was a gifted leader, assembling a superb team of scientists and guiding their research toward specific goals. He retired as president in 1980 but carried on with his research until 1989. In 1981 the institute named its new chemotherapy research building the Howard E. Skipper Chemotherapy Laboratory. In addition to his work at the Southern Research Institute, Skipper was a professor of experimental pathology and investigative medicine at the University of Alabama School of Medicine.

Over the course of his career, Skipper held a number of national offices. He served on the President's National Advisory Cancer Council from 1958 to 1960 and 1964 to 1968. He was chairman of the Cancer Chemotherapy Review Board of the National Institutes of Health from 1958 to 1960. Skipper received a number of awards and honors, including the Lasker Foundation's Albert Lasker Award for Basic Medical Research in 1974, and the Ernst W. Bertner Memorial Award from the University of Texas M. D. Anderson Cancer Center in 1975. In 1980 he was honored with the third Bristol-Myers Award for Distinguished Achievement in Cancer Research.

Skipper was admired by his colleagues not only for his brilliance but also for his modesty and humor. He died at age ninety.

With the Southern Research Institute for more than forty years, Skipper was one of the country's leading researchers in cancer chemotherapy research. His work furthered scientists' understanding of the relationships among cancer cells, normal cells, and anticancer drugs. His research led to the use of chemotherapy as a method for curing some cancers in humans. Because of his pioneering work, the prompt eradication of cancer cells has become the standard in the treatment of many cancers.

★

An autobiographical sketch by Skipper is in *Cancer* 54, no. S1 (1984): 1142–1143. Information about Skipper and his work is included in Gillian Goodrich, *Southern Research Institute: An Oral History* (1991), and John Temple Graves, *History of Southern Research Institute* (1955). Skipper's 1991 speech "A Few Recollections on the Cancer Research Program" offers insight into his work. Linda Simpson-Herren and Glynn P. Wheeler, "Howard Earle Skipper: In Memoriam," *Cancer Research* 66 (Dec. 2006): 12035–12036, provides biographical information. Obituaries are in the *Birmingham News* (4 Jan. 2006) and *Independent* (London; 12 Jan. 2006).

Nicole Mitchell

SMATHERS, George Armistead (*b.* 14 November 1913 in Atlantic City, New Jersey; *d.* 20 January 2007 in Indian Creek Village, Florida), lawyer and prominent U.S. congressman (1947–1951) and senator (1951–1969) who figured significantly in cold war developments, particularly relating to Latin America.

Smathers was one of four children born to Frank Smathers, a prominent judge, and Lura (Jones) Smathers, a homemaker. Because his father was advised to relocate to warmer climate to alleviate his arthritis, Smathers grew up in Florida, specifically in the "Miracle City" of 1920s Miami. There Smathers became a star athlete and a solid student at Miami High, from which he graduated in 1931. Smathers was directed toward the University of Florida by his father, who had already perceived a political future for his six-feet-tall, handsome son. Smathers's charisma and ability earned him a wide circle of friends who voted him student body president. These friends, who became leaders in state politics, business, and social circles, formed Smathers's political base in future years.

Having earned a sterling record at the University of Florida and aided by connections through his friends and family, Smathers was made an assistant district attorney after graduating from the University of Florida School of Law in 1938. On 9 March 1939 he married Rosemary

George A. Smathers. AP IMAGES

Townley; the couple would have two children. Serving the vast southern district of Florida, Smathers made himself a public figure by successfully prosecuting several noteworthy cases in the years leading up to 1941. At twenty-seven years old, with a young wife and son, he was not supposed to be put in harm's way immediately after Japan's attack on Pearl Harbor. However, at his urging, the U.S. Marine Corps inducted him as an officer in 1942. Service in the South Pacific took Smathers into a world he never forgot. Seeing firsthand the brutal consequence of a failed isolationist policy, the young Miamian became a devoted internationalist and consistently advocated a strong American presence abroad throughout his political career.

Returning home by 1946, Smathers immediately engaged in a political contest to win a seat in the U.S. House of Representatives. Facing Pat Cannon, a multiterm incumbent congressman, Smathers quickly took and maintained the offensive in the campaign. Railing against Cannon's outdated isolationist views and skewering his opponent's poor attendance record in the House, Smathers worked tirelessly to meet and sway voters. His good-looking image eventually grated on Cannon so that the incumbent groused of being pitted against "Gorgeous George" and his "Goon Squad" of old Miami school friends. Smathers's arguments, dash, and style easily won the election for him. He would never know political defeat.

As part of the vital "Class of 1946," Smathers joined a cadre of young politicians—the "GI Generation" that had experienced the Great Depression and won World War II. Next door to him in his new congressional offices was a rail-thin, sickly young Massachusetts lawmaker named John F. Kennedy. Kennedy and Smathers became, and remained, strong friends; Smathers soon introduced Kennedy to another friend he had made, Richard M. Nixon of California. What the GI Generation understood was that appeasement was a discredited policy and that isolationism had failed America. In the spring of 1947, with Britain bankrupt and Greece and Turkey facing dire circumstances, Smathers joined with his fellows in supporting the Truman Doctrine and eventually the Marshall Plan. Dovetailing with these legislative efforts was the publication of the famed "Mr. X" article—George F. Kennan's landmark "Sources of Soviet Conduct" (1947)—and the delivery of the Iron Curtain speech by Winston Churchill in 1946. What coalesced into the containment policy appealed to Smathers's thinking. Soviet Communism, aiming to strip individual liberty from societies in an ill-fated effort to undo capitalist excesses, was anathema to Smathers and many others. A steadfast refusal to appease Communist expansion and a desire to build a permanent internationalist feature into American foreign policy became hallmarks of Smathers and his generation—and broadly defined the cold war era.

Cold war politics drove American domestic and foreign affairs for over forty years, and they drove Smathers's most important and controversial campaign: the 1950 senatorial primary against Claude D. Pepper. Pepper, after his later 1962 election to the U.S. House of Representatives, was celebrated as a liberal icon most noted for his rock-solid defense of Social Security. In 1950 the then-senator Pepper was not as endearing a figure. Elected to the U.S. Senate in 1936 to fill an unexpired term, then elected twice more in 1938 and 1944, Pepper was a New Deal stalwart with a reputation of being something of a liberal maverick. Having alienated the Florida business community, having advocated an American welfare state, and continuing to harbor a nearly inexplicable belief in the potential friendliness of Soviet Russia, Pepper had placed himself in a precarious position in Florida politics.

With the blessing of President Harry S. Truman, whom Pepper had attempted to destroy politically in both 1944 and 1948, and with a solid record in the House, Smathers took the same offensive tactics into the 1950 campaign that he had used in 1946. His opponent had severe weaknesses; Smathers exploited them. While Pepper urged a deepening and broadening of the New Deal, Smathers correctly saw that the vast majority of the Florida electorate did not share this passion for unending reform. When Smathers began to announce a "Communist front a day" that Pepper had spoken for or supported, the senator had no defense—and while Smathers never labeled Pepper a "Communist," the clear perception left was of Pepper as at least an unwitting dupe.

Though Pepper swung back at Smathers, criticizing both his New Jersey birthplace and his wealthy upbringing, Pepper simply found himself out of step with Florida's voters. Still, the ferocity of the campaign—both Pepper and Smathers were master orators, and each possessed a unique presence and bearing—made the contest a national event. The tone of the campaign added attention to the miles-long caravans attending each candidate and the mass rallies held for them over the weeks, leading to the most infamous words Smathers never said. In what was termed the "thespian" speech, Smathers allegedly lambasted his opponent as someone who "habitually practiced celibacy before marriage" and whose sister was a "thespian in wicked New York City." Meant as a ruse among reporters following the campaign to illustrate the dramatic flair of the candidates, Smathers's supposed speech was said to be an attempt to sway unlettered rural Floridians. The joke eventually took on a life of its own and was accepted as fact for decades after the campaign, though all evidence indicates that Smathers never delivered the speech.

After his legendary victory over Pepper in 1950, Smathers often became the whipping boy for liberal writers who saw Pepper as their champion. However, in the U.S. Senate his ability and personality led him quickly up the Democratic ranks. Well within his first term, Smathers was recognized as being in the "Inner Circle" of leading senators, who were directed by the particular genius of Lyndon B. Johnson. Serving as one of Johnson's top lieutenants, Smathers typically was figured as the third-most powerful Democratic senator through most of his career, after Mike Mansfield. Following up on interests he had in the House, Smathers consistently called for increased American attention and aid to Latin America. Terming the region America's "best customers" and the hemisphere's "guards and tackles" in the cold war, Smathers had a passion that was driven by his Miami roots and lifelong friends as well as by practical foreign policy. Warning that military aid alone was wholly insufficient, he advocated American help with Latin American infrastructure, economic and educational development, and democratic reform. Short of strong U.S. commitment, Smathers worried that a Communist insurgency would attend discontent with dictators and lack of economic opportunities. His arguments were so powerful and consistent that Smathers became known as the "senator from Latin America." His fears were borne out in the Cuban Revolution.

While others hoped for the best from the Cuban revolutionary leader Fidel Castro in 1959, Smathers anticipated trouble. When Castro attached Cuba to the Soviet sphere in 1960, Smathers was not surprised. In the presidential contest that year, Smathers was close friends with Kennedy, Johnson, and Senator Stuart Symington of Missouri. Though he had served as an usher at Kennedy's wedding and remained a Kennedy intimate, Smathers hoped for a Johnson nomination. However, when Kennedy secured the nomination in Los Angeles, Smathers quickly volunteered to coordinate the campaign in the South. With Kennedy's defeat of Nixon, Smathers had uncommon access to the Oval Office.

Smathers urged Kennedy to take an active approach to Latin America and Cuba in particular. While Kennedy's administration instituted an economic embargo against Cuba, Smathers was unable to persuade the president to support the ill-fated Bay of Pigs invasion with air strikes. When the nation was alerted to the existence of missiles in Cuba in October 1962, Smathers reviewed Kennedy's speech with him and was the only nonpress individual in the Oval Office. Moreover, with the Alliance for Progress, Smathers hoped that long-term American aid for development of Latin America would take place. His hopes, like many, were dashed by the assassination of Kennedy and by the American war in Vietnam.

Like so many of his generation, Smathers vigorously supported the Vietnam War, believing that fight to be one opposing the extension of Soviet power. While the war in Southeast Asia escalated in the mid-1960s, Smathers—like all Americans—was faced with the struggle for racial equality. Though he played a key role in helping then-Senate majority leader Johnson pass the 1957 Civil Rights Act, Smathers did not support subsequent measures in 1960 and 1964. Consistently calling for the securing of voting rights for African Americans, he ironically did not support the final passage of the monumental 1965 Voting Rights Act, believing it to be too strong a federal measure.

When Smathers retired from the Senate in 1968, his legacy was that of a quintessential cold warrior and a symbol of the changing South. He lived out his private life, from 1969 to 2007, as a lobbyist and a lawyer, dividing his time between Washington, D.C., and Miami. He died at age ninety-three of complications following a stroke. He is buried at Arlington National Cemetery in Arlington, Virginia.

Smathers's political career was unique. Playing a vital role in shaping the post–World War II world in terms of cold war foreign policy and presidential politics, Smathers wielded tremendous influence and played a key role in national affairs.

Smathers's papers are in the Special Collections of the Smathers Libraries, University of Florida. The standard scholarly work on Smathers is Brian Lewis Crispell, *Testing the Limits: George Armistead Smathers and Cold War America* (1999). An oral history was compiled by Donald Ritchie of the Senate Historical Office and includes the 1989 interview with Smathers and the 1992 interview with Scott I. Peek, Smathers's administrative assistant. Smathers also contributed an oral history to the Lyndon Baines Johnson Presidential Library in Austin, Texas, and his close working relationship with Johnson is illustrated in additional recorded telephone conversations with the president, including those that occurred shortly after the assassination of President John F. Kennedy. Obituaries are in the *New York Times* and *Washington Post* (both 21 Jan. 2007).

Brian Lewis Crispell

SMITH, Anna Nicole (*b.* 28 November 1967 in Houston, Texas; *d.* 8 February 2007 in Hollywood, Florida), model, television personality, and celebrity widow of the Texas billionaire J. Howard Marshall II.

Smith was born Vickie Lynn Hogan, the only daughter of Donald Eugene Hogan, an itinerant laborer, and Virgie Mae (Tabers) Hogan, who later became a deputy sheriff. She had several half sisters and half brothers. Smith later described her childhood and adolescence as a "tough time." Her mother, who was sixteen years old when Smith was born, divorced her father two years afterward. Smith attended elementary school in Houston and was later

Anna Nicole Smith, 2005. **KEVIN WINTER/GETTY IMAGES**

sent to live with her aunt in Mexia, Texas, a former oil boomtown. Classmates at Mexia High School knew her as Nikki Hart, a name she adopted after her mother married Donald R. Hart and the first in a series of name changes. A yearbook picture portrayed her as an unsmiling but slim, attractive teenager with long dark-brown hair, giving little hint of her future blond, buxom, and glamorous appearance achieved with several breast-enhancement surgeries. She struggled with classes and dropped out of high school during her sophomore year. Smith began working as a waitress and breakfast cook at Jim's Krispy Fried Chicken in Mexia, where she met Billy Wayne Smith, a cook whom she married on 4 April 1985; she was seventeen and he was sixteen. The following year they had a son, Daniel Wayne Smith, but their marriage disintegrated. After separating from Billy Wayne in 1987 (divorce would come in 1993), she moved to Houston with her one-year-old son; there, she worked at Red Lobster and Wal-Mart before becoming a topless dancer. She later called exotic dancing a "really horrible" way of life but said she needed the money to support herself and her son.

While performing at Rick's Cabaret in 1991, she met the Texas oil billionaire J. Howard Marshall II, who was immediately attracted to Smith and wooed her. She quit topless dancing and began a two-and-a-half-year relationship with Marshall, her senior by sixty-three years. They were married on 27 June 1994; he was eighty-nine and she was twenty-six. In a 2002 interview on the Cable News Network (CNN) program *Larry King Live*, Smith said she was not physically attracted to Marshall but described their relationship as one of love and mutual respect, stating that Marshall devotedly took care of her and Daniel. According to court briefs, Marshall gave her $6 million in cash and gifts.

Aspiring to become a latter-day Marilyn Monroe, Smith embarked on a professional ascent that started when she responded to a newspaper advertisement seeking playmates (female models) for *Playboy* magazine. She became the cover girl for the March 1992 issue of the magazine, and in 1993 she was chosen as Playmate of the Year, which served as a springboard for her modeling career. While working as a model for Guess Jeans, she and Paul Marciano (one of the three brothers who created the clothing line) discussed possible stage names, ultimately choosing "Anna Nicole."

After Marshall died from pneumonia on 4 August 1995, Smith sought her husband's $1.6 billion estate in a legal battle that involved five courts and extended for more than thirteen years. The case generated national media attention and pitted her against her husband's son, E. Pierce Marshall, who depicted his young stepmother as an insensitive gold digger who was not legally entitled to his father's estate. A Texas probate court in Houston ruled in Marshall's favor, but a federal bankruptcy court ruled in Smith's favor, awarding her $449 million. However, in 2002 a California district court reduced the award to $88.5 million. On 30 December 2004 the U.S. Court of Appeals for the Ninth Circuit, based in San Francisco, reduced the award to zero dollars and ruled that federal courts lack jurisdiction in probate matters.

Marshall v. Marshall (Smith filed her briefs as Vickie Lynn Marshall) reached the U.S. Supreme Court in 2006. Sedately clad in a dark business dress with a scoop neckline, the blond widow brushed past a phalanx of reporters and photographers to take her place in the rear of the courtroom, with her son at her side. On 1 May 2006 the Supreme Court justices ruled in her favor; they sent the case back to the appeals court, deciding that Smith was entitled to continue pursuing the estate through federal courts. E. Pierce Marshall died a month after the ruling, and his widow took over the estate; the suit was still pending in the Ninth Circuit more than a year after Smith's death.

Smith pursued an entertainment career, appearing in films, including *The Hudsucker Proxy* (1994), *Naked Gun 33 1/3: The Final Insult* (1994), and *Skyscraper* (1996), which she also produced. She starred in a reality television series, *The Anna Nicole Show*, for the E! Entertainment Television cable network. Her performances were disparaged by critics, but her television series initially enjoyed high ratings and persisted for two years (2002–2004).

Smith endured an emotional toll from the drawn-out legal battle and mocking news coverage that frequently made her a tabloid punch line. She gained a significant amount of weight and became addicted to prescription pain medication and alcohol, prompting her to admit herself to the Betty Ford Center, an addiction treatment facility in Rancho Mirage, California. Smith's life was on an upswing when she gave birth to a daughter, Dannielynn Hope, on 7 September 2006, but tragedy struck three days later when her twenty-year-old son, Daniel, died while visiting his mother and newborn sister in the hospital. A seven-member jury concluded that Daniel died of an accidental drug overdose.

Smith, who was virtually inseparable from her son, was devastated by his death. "You were my rock...I wish he would have taken me instead," she wrote in Daniel's funeral program. Until her death five months later, Smith was haunted by nightmares that Daniel was lost and needed her help.

Smith was involved in a long-term relationship with her attorney, Howard K. Stern; they exchanged vows in a commitment ceremony on 28 September 2006. However, Smith's former boyfriend, the photojournalist Larry Birkhead, ultimately won custody of Dannielynn following Smith's death, after DNA paternity tests confirmed that he was Dannielynn's father. Stern did not contest the findings.

On 8 February 2007 Smith was found unconscious at the Seminole Hard Rock Hotel and Casino in Hollywood, Florida. Attempts to save her through cardiopulmonary resuscitation were unsuccessful, and she was pronounced dead at a hospital. Smith's death at age thirty-nine ignited international news coverage that continued for weeks, involving the investigation into her death, legal disputes regarding her estate, and the paternity battle over Dannielynn, her sole heir. Investigators stated that the death was an accident caused by a combination of toxic levels of the sedative chloral hydrate and various other prescription drugs. She was buried next to her son at Lakeview Memorial Gardens and Mausoleum in Nassau, Bahamas. Her coffin was draped in a pink blanket and contained the ashes of her late husband, Marshall. In a eulogy, Stern said Smith faced "more adversity in her life than most people would face in a hundred lifetimes....And Anna overcame everything. She was the toughest person you're ever going to meet."

★

Extensive details of Smith's well-publicized life are available on the Internet. Smith offers introspective glimpses of herself in a 29 May 2002 appearance on *Larry King Live*. Information about her life is also evident in episodes of *The Anna Nicole Show*. Briefs from her Supreme Court case—*Marshall v. Marshall*—provide biographical information as well as legal arguments. Obituaries and news coverage are in the *New York Times*, *Miami Herald*, and *Washington Post* (all 9 Feb. 2007).

Dave Montgomery

SMITH, Roger Bonham (*b.* 12 July 1925 in Columbus, Ohio; *d.* 29 November 2007 in Detroit, Michigan), executive who presided over General Motors during the 1980s and became associated with its decline despite efforts to improve the company's products and increase profits.

Smith was the third of four children of Emmet Quimby Smith, a banker who as a result of the Depression took a job with an auto-parts supplier in Detroit, and Bess Belle (Obetz) Smith, an Ohio school administrator until her marriage. Smith graduated in 1942 from Detroit University High School and then attended the University of

Roger B. Smith. **SHEPARD SHERBELL/CORBIS SABA**

Michigan, studying business administration. He served in the U.S. Navy from 1944 to 1946 and then returned to the university to earn his BBA in 1947 and MBA in 1949. He began his career at General Motors (GM), the only company for which he ever worked, in 1949 as an accounting clerk in the Detroit central office. Smith married Barbara Ann Rasch, a GM secretary, on 7 June 1954. They had four children.

Smith rose steadily up GM's "bean counter" ladder. In 1958 he became the head of his section and two years later took a financial job in GM's central New York office. He returned to Detroit in 1968 as general assistant comptroller and then rose to assistant general treasurer, treasurer, and vice president of financial staff, advancing in 1972 to vice president of the nonautomotive and defense group. There, faced with problems in two no longer profitable units (Frigidaire, an appliance division, and Terex, an earthmoving equipment maker), he sold them off, explaining "it's the GM spirit of things to say we can always fix something.... But what the fix should have been was to get rid of it."

By the end of 1974 he had become an executive vice president and a member of GM's board of directors. He was a prime mover behind the corporation's adoption of a policy of strategic planning and an overseer of GM's financial and insurance subsidiaries. In 1981 he became the tenth chairman of GM and its chief executive officer. At the time the corporation faced serious problems: In 1980 GM had lost over $700 million—its first such loss in six decades.

Smith understood that change was imperative. GM needed to meet the challenge of the Japanese imports and to overhaul its risk-averse bureaucracy. In addition, its half-century-old divisional autonomy needed to be reworked. However, despite nearly all his attempts to reorganize and reenergize the corporation, production methods remained the same, the quality of GM's products did not improve, and the automaker failed to maintain its share of the market. Rather than enhance the corporation's tarnished reputation, Smith's efforts had the opposite effect. As the Wall Street analyst Maryann Keller put it, "good ideas, poor execution."

The GM10 project, unveiled in 1984 and designed to reorganize the various GM divisions into two efficient, cost-effective groups—one building smaller cars, the other large cars—led to quality problems, design flaws, and a loss of brand identity as various models began to look alike. Because GM10 altered traditional relations at the corporation, it created more layers of bureaucracy; the new divisions duplicated some staff members while others were laid off as a cost-saving measure, souring labor relations.

By 1989 the corporation was losing an estimated $2,000 on each vehicle produced. That year it was estimated that GM10 had cost the corporation over $7 trillion. In

1992 *Fortune* magazine called GM10 "the biggest catastrophe in American industrial history." Smith said of his attempts to implement GM10, "I should have had the sense to see that this thing was not going well and to figure out why."

Smith hoped to modernize car production and save costs by using advanced technology to compete with Japanese cars built in automated plants. Working with the Japanese firm Fujitsu Fanuc, GM made substantial technology investments, with GMF Robotics becoming the world's largest robotics manufacturer. The corporation also acquired Electronic Data Systems (EDS) and Hughes Aircraft, but benefits from these acquisitions proved limited. Given the different corporate cultures of GM and EDS, the latter proved ineffective in standardizing the corporation's computer systems. Hughes's electronic wizardry did not transfer well to assembly lines: Workers reported that robots painted each other and welded car doors shut. GM soon removed some robotic systems from the plants.

With the acquisition of EDS in 1984, its founder, H. Ross Perot, became GM's largest stockholder, with a seat on the GM board. Representing a different mode of doing business, Perot became a vocal critic of Smith's management. Their irreconcilable differences resulted in vitriolic public and private exchanges. Perot was bought out in 1986 at a substantial premium over EDS's market share price. He denounced Smith for such an extravagant expenditure at a time when GM was closing plants and laying off workers. Perot's statements hurt GM's and Smith's image.

One of Smith's successes came in 1984 with the opening of the New United Motor Manufacturing, Inc., a joint venture with Toyota in Fremont, California. The small-vehicle plant has had high rates of productivity since it began. By the end of the decade, however, Smith's reputation suffered further damage with the release of Michael Moore's satiric documentary *Roger & Me* (1989), which highlighted GM layoffs in Flint, Michigan, once a center of GM car production, and the economic devastation resulting from GM's plant closures. Although some critics argued that the film took creative liberties with the truth and thus was not in the strictest sense a documentary, Smith could not escape the negative publicity the film focused on him. As an article in *Automotive News* put it, he became a "pop-culture punching bag."

In 1990 Smith pioneered the Saturn Corporation, whose well-received small cars demonstrated that GM could compete with Japanese imports. That year he retired on company schedule at age sixty-five. In subsequent years, the acquisition of EDS and Hughes proved to have been a positive move. GM's involvement with those entities led to the corporation's successful OnStar roadside assistance program; moreover, the sale of EDS in 1996 and of Hughes in 2003 produced massive profits. But during Smith's tenure GM's share of the market declined from 46 percent to 35 percent, and continued to go down after his retirement. Smith died at age eighty-two after a short illness.

Smith took the helm of GM at a time when U.S. automakers faced enormous challenges, and though he tried to modernize the company, overall it continued to falter. As a former GM officer put it, Smith "never could crack his own culture." Viewed by many as a sharp-tongued, often autocratic, imperious boss, Smith was also described as brilliant and dedicated. Many blame him for the decline of GM. He was a controversial figure in Detroit and nationally.

★

Doron P. Levin, *Irreconcilable Differences: Ross Perot Versus General Motors* (1989), deals with the feud between GM and Perot. For insight into GM and the U.S. auto industry during Smith's tenure as chairman, see Paul Ingrassia and Joseph B. White, *Comeback: The Fall and Rise of the American Automobile Industry* (1994); Alex Taylor III, "GM Gets Its Act Together, Finally," *Fortune* (5 Apr. 2004); and Paul A. Witteman et al., "Roger's Painful Legacy," *Time* (9 Nov. 1992). Jim Henry, "Smith's Diversification Strategy Created Saturn—and Lots of Problems," *Automotive News* (15 Sept. 2008), sums up the successes and failures of Smith's career. Obituaries are in the *New York Times* and *Detroit News* (both 1 Dec. 2007), and the *Times* of London (4 Dec. 2007).

Daniel J. Leab

SNYDER, Thomas James ("Tom") (*b*. 12 May 1936 in Milwaukee, Wisconsin; *d*. 29 July 2007 in San Francisco, California), news broadcaster who became a pioneer of late-night television talk shows.

Snyder was raised in a strongly Roman Catholic household. His father, Frank Snyder, was a peddler, his mother, Marie (Buettner) Snyder, a nurse. He graduated from the Jesuit-run Marquette University High School and then went on to Marquette University as a premed student but dropped out to take up a career in broadcasting.

In 1955 he got a job as a news correspondent at a Milwaukee radio station; he also worked as a radio disc jockey in Kalamazoo, Michigan. He then branched out into television reporting, working in several cities around the country until landing a job with KYW-TV in Philadelphia in 1965 as coanchor on the nation's first noon newscast. He was also a talk-show host for the station on its morning program, *Contact*. In April 1958 Snyder married Mary Ann Bendel, with whom he had a daughter; they divorced in 1975.

In 1970 Snyder was brought to Los Angeles by KNBC as a news anchor and host of an interview show, *Sunday.*

Tom Snyder, 1995. CBS/LANDOV

His next job, as host of National Broadcasting Company's (NBC) *The Tomorrow Show*, was the one through which he would achieve his fame. The program followed *The Tonight Show with Johnny Carson*, going on the air at one o'clock in the morning, a time slot in which other stations, if they were still on the air at all, showed old movies. But *Tomorrow*, which debuted on 15 October 1973, revealed that there was indeed an audience for television at that hour.

Tomorrow was unusual in that it had no live audience, studio band, or cohost. Snyder faced his guests one-on-one, gesturing with an ever-present cigarette in hand (guests occasionally requested cigarettes from Snyder) and often asking probing questions in an aggressive manner. The setting created an intimacy that made the show more akin to a televised conversation than a formal interview. As Snyder himself once noted, "a great interview is a conversation in which you keep your mouth shut and the subject tells the story." The show's informality was further enhanced by Snyder's frequent jokes to the off-camera crew. Because Snyder allowed his guests to talk at length, instead of pushing them to make clever quips, people who generally shunned the talk-show circuit jumped at the chance to appear on *Tomorrow*. But his interviewing style was a performance in its own right,

and he often went off on his own tangents, talking directly to the viewer. Some critics considered his interviewing style harsh and egotistical.

Snyder's spontaneous guffaws, and the contrast of his stark black eyebrows and graying hair, made him a prime target for parody. The best-known impersonation was by the comedian Dan Aykroyd on the sketch-comedy program *Saturday Night Live*. Snyder took no offense, telling the *New York Times*, "I was flattered. It wasn't a spiteful parody at all. And it was hilarious." It also enhanced his own popularity.

The show went back and forth between the coasts during its nine-year run. In 1974 it moved to New York City, where Snyder also coanchored WNBC's *NewsCenter 4*, NBC's *Sunday Night News*, and *NBC News Update*; that year *Tomorrow* won an Emmy for outstanding program and individual achievement. In 1977 the show returned to Los Angeles, then in 1979 went back to New York (where Snyder also hosted *Prime Time Sunday*). Guests from many fields came on the show, including the former Beatle John Lennon, the writer and philosopher Ayn Rand, and, in a prison interview, the convicted criminal Charles Manson. The comedian "Weird Al" Yankovic and the rock group U2 made their first U.S. television appearances on the show. Of the many musical acts that appeared on *Tomorrow*, the most notorious was the punk rock band the Plasmatics. During their March 1981 appearance, the lead singer Wendy O. Williams smashed a television set with a sledgehammer; two months later the band was back on the show blowing up a car.

In the early 1980s, in an attempt to stop a slide in ratings, NBC reworked the program as a more conventional talk show, renamed *Tomorrow Coast to Coast*. The gossip columnist Rona Barrett was added as a cohost, and the show was filmed before a live audience. The changes did not help, and the show's last broadcast was 28 January 1982. The network replaced it with a new, more traditionally formatted talk show, *Late Night with David Letterman*.

Snyder then worked as an anchor for WABC-TV's *Eyewitness News* in New York. In 1985 he returned to Los Angeles as a news anchor for KABC-TV and then in 1986 began hosting *Tom Snyder*, an afternoon talk show. There were plans to syndicate the show nationally, but he was beaten to the punch when Oprah Winfrey's afternoon talk show was picked up first. In 1987 he appeared as a guest host on Larry King's radio talk show, then hosted his own program, *The Tom Snyder Show*, for American Broadcasting Company Radio, which ran until 1992. In 1993 and 1994 he hosted a late-night program, *Tom Snyder*, for the cable channel CNBC.

In August 1994 CBS announced that Snyder would be returning to the network on *The Late Late Show with Tom Snyder*, which would follow Letterman's program. *The Late Late Show*, based in Los Angeles, debuted 9 January 1995.

Like *Tomorrow*, the *Late Late Show* had an intimate setting with no live audience, though it was simulcast over select radio stations, allowing viewers to call in. Snyder's opening comments were not the jokes favored by other talk-show hosts but instead a simple recounting of the events of his day, however ordinary. Before going into the show's first commercial break, he always told his viewers to "fire up a Colortini, sit back, relax, and watch the pictures now, as they fly through the air"—with "Colortini" a blending of *Colorcast*, a word from the early days of color broadcasting, and *martini*.

Snyder remained with the show through 26 March 1999, after which he retired. He then moved online, launching a website, www.colortini.com, where he regularly posted messages recounting his activities. But he abruptly pulled the plug on the site in 2005, announcing on 28 July that "the novelty of communicating this way has worn off." The following year, Snyder moved up the coast from Los Angeles to Belvedere, just north of San Francisco.

Over the years Snyder made several guest appearances as himself on television comedies and dramas as well as hosting specials. In his final decade he suffered from heart ailments and in 2005 was diagnosed with chronic lymphocytic leukemia, for which he underwent a variety of treatments. He died of complications associated with the disease at age seventy-one.

Although Snyder often said his role as a talk-show host was to keep the focus on his guests and not himself, he nonetheless became a personality in his own right. His work set a standard for thoughtful, in-depth interviewing—sometimes driven by his own distinct point of view—that influenced many in the profession, as can be seen in programs such as *Charlie Rose*. He also opened the way to talk shows in the "late-late" time slot.

★

For profiles of Snyder, see Mary Murphy, "Tom Snyder: TV's Child Faces the Future," *Esquire* (28 Mar. 1978), and James Wolcott, "Son of Kong," *New York* (11 Oct. 1982). Snyder's work is available on DVD in three collections: *The Tomorrow Show with Tom Snyder: Punk & New Wave* (2006) features interviews with and performances by Patti Smith, John Lydon, Joan Jett, and the Plasmatics; *The Tomorrow Show: Tom Snyder's Electric Kool-Aid Talk Show* (2006) features interviews with and performances by Tom Wolfe, Ken Kesey, Timothy Leary, and the Grateful Dead; and *The Tomorrow Show with Tom Snyder: John, Paul, Tom & Ringo* (2008) features interviews with John Lennon, Paul McCartney, and Ringo Starr. Obituaries are in the *New York Times* (30 July 2007) and the *Los Angeles Times* and *Washington Post* (both 31 July 2007).

Gillian G. Gaar

SONNENBLICK, Edmund Hiram (*b.* 7 December 1932 in New Haven, Connecticut; *d.* 22 September 2007 in Darien, Connecticut), internationally renowned cardiologist and professor, best known as a pioneer in the pathophysiology and treatment of congestive heart failure.

Sonnenblick was the son of Ira J. Sonnenblick and Rosalind (Helfand) Sonnenblick. He earned his BA summa cum laude from Wesleyan University in 1954, around the time that he met and married Linda Bland. They later had three daughters. After graduating cum laude with an MD from the Harvard Medical School in 1958, Sonnenblick commenced his medical and scientific career with his training in internal medicine at the Presbyterian Hospital in Manhattan. In 1960 he became an attending physician at the National Heart, Lung, and Blood Institute in Bethesda, Maryland. In addition, he conducted research there and simultaneously served as an associate professorial lecturer of physiology at the George Washington University School of Medicine. Sonnenblick occupied a number of roles after moving to Boston: assistant professor of medicine at the Harvard Medical School; codirector of the cardiovascular unit, senior associate in medicine, and physician at Peter Bent Brigham Hospital; and director of cardiovascular research in Brigham's Department of Medicine. From 1960 to 1962 he served as a senior assistant surgeon in the Commissioned Corps of the U.S. Public Health Service.

What was unique about Sonnenblick's research was that he applied the principles learned by other scientists from skeletal muscle to the heart. He and his colleagues then "demonstrated that the amount of blood pumped by the heart is dependent on muscle mechanisms." With Eugene Braunwald and John H. Ross, Sonnenblick provided many of the fundamental concepts in clinical use by cardiologists with regard to the measurement of cardiac function, and Sonnenblick is credited with first coining terms, such as *preload*, *afterload*, *contractility*, and *ejection fraction*.

In 1963 at Columbia University Sonnenblick was recognized as the first researcher to use an electron microscope to take images of the heart muscle under controlled conditions. He presented his groundbreaking work at what was then the most highly regarded meeting for scientists involved in biomedical research—the plenary session of the American Society for Clinical Investigation in Atlantic City, New Jersey. According to Braunwald, "a hush fell over the audience" as Sonnenblick revealed the results of his work. His findings about the structure and function of cardiac myocytes and the way in which the heart muscle contracts and relaxes would later help other scientists to develop a class of drugs known as angiotensin converting enzyme (ACE) inhibitors.

In 1975 Sonnenblick became distinguished university professor of medicine (cardiology) and chief of the Division of Cardiology at the Albert Einstein College of Medicine of Yeshiva University in the Bronx, New York—a position he held until 1996. In 1984 Sonnenblick became the director of the medical school's Cardiovascular Center, the same year he was appointed Olson Professor of Cardiology, an honor he held until 1995. In 1985 Sonnenblick was awarded the Distinguished Scientist Award by the American College of Cardiology.

Sonnenblick was also named the Edmond J. Safra Republic National Bank of New York Professor of Cardiovascular Medicine, the Charles and Tamara Krasne Faculty Scholar in Cardiovascular Research, and, later, chief emeritus of the Division of Cardiology at Albert Einstein. With William Frishman at Albert Einstein, Sonnenblick became an early advocate for the use of beta-blockers to treat heart failure. Until then, beta-blockers were considered too risky for the treatment of heart failure and had been prescribed only to lower high blood pressure.

In the late 1990s Sonnenblick was involved with the introduction of Bristol-Myers Squibb's Theragran Heart Right multivitamin. He noted, "a growing body of research shows us the link between vitamins, overall nutrition and heart health," adding that "clearly micronutrient supplementation can never replace a healthy diet or lifestyle, but, given the importance of cardiovascular nutrition, it only makes sense to take a supplement." Sonnenblick coauthored the book *Cardiovascular Pharmacotherapeutics* (2003) with his colleagues Frishman and Domenic A. Sica. The use of nutrients as adjunctive therapies for cardiovascular conditions is covered in this text, as are general pharmacotherapeutic topics.

The American Heart Association posthumously bestowed its Research Achievement Award, one of its highest honors, upon Sonnenblick "with distinct gratitude" at its 2007 Scientific Sessions at the Orange County Convention Center in Orlando, Florida. Richard N. Kitsis, a colleague at Albert Einstein, accepted the award for him, which recognized Sonnenblick's lifetime contributions to cardiovascular science and medicine. At the ceremony, Daniel Jones, the American Heart Association president, described Sonnenblick's "classic experiments" as having "helped [to] define the human heart as a self-renewing organ and not merely a pump." He continued by describing Sonnenblick as "one of the world's foremost cardiologists and investigators, rightfully regarded as an icon in the history of cardiovascular medicine."

During his illustrious career, which spanned almost half a century, Sonnenblick trained more than 300 researchers and cardiologists, authored nearly 700 papers in his field-related research, and served on the editorial boards of numerous journals within the cardiology field, such as *Cardiovascular Drugs and Therapy Journal*.

Sonnenblick and his wife were patrons of the arts, contributing generously to the Mark Twain House and Museum and the Wadsworth Atheneum Museum of Art, both in Hartford, Connecticut. One of their most notable donations was for partial funding of the choreographer George Balanchine's centennial celebration exhibition *Ballets Russes to Balanchine: Dance at the Wadsworth Atheneum*, which was held from 25 September 2004 to 2 January 2005.

Sonnenblick died of esophageal cancer at his home in Darien at the age of seventy-four. He will be remembered as a kind gentleman who genuinely cared for the welfare of others; a dedicated and inspiring teacher and mentor; a distinguished and an esteemed colleague, a warm and wonderful friend and family member; and one who will occupy, in Braunwald's words, "an honored place in the pantheon of the greatest heart and blood vessel physiologists of the 20th century."

★

For biographical information, see Albert Einstein College of Medicine of Yeshiva University, "Einstein's Dr. Edmund Sonnenblick to Receive High Scientific Honor from American Heart Association" (7 Aug. 2007); Karen Astle, "The Late Edmund H. Sonnenblick, New York Cardiologist, Receives Posthumous National Research Achievement Award," *Medical News Today* (5 Nov. 2007); and William H. Frishman, "A Tribute to Edmund H. Sonnenblick, MD: 1932–2007," *Cardiology in Review* 16, no. 1 (Jan./Feb. 2008): 1–3. An obituary is in the *New York Times* (27 Sept. 2007).

Adriana C. Tomasino

SPELLING, Aaron (*b*. 22 April 1923 in Dallas, Texas; *d*. 23 June 2006 in Los Angeles, California), television producer who created dozens of popular and trend-setting prime-time network series, including *The Mod Squad, The Love Boat, Dynasty*, and *Melrose Place*.

Spelling was the youngest of five children of David Spelling, a tailor born in Poland, and Pearl (Wald) Spelling, born in Russia. Growing up in a Yiddish-speaking, Orthodox Jewish family in the Oak Cliff section of Dallas, Spelling was teased and bullied at school because of his religion, slight build, and sensitive temperament, all factors contributing to what he called his sense of "foreignness" in the working-class neighborhood. At age eight he became traumatized by these experiences and was medically excused from school for an extended period. During his time at home Spelling became an avid reader, developing a taste for the short fiction of O. Henry, a popular turn-of-the-twentieth-century writer known for surprise endings. "I found that stories came

Aaron Spelling, 1996. **AP IMAGES**

naturally to me, and when I went back to school I used them as a means of defense," he told an interviewer.

Graduating from Forest Avenue High School in 1942, Spelling joined the U.S. Army Air Forces. He saw combat in Europe and received a Bronze Star, but details of his service record vary and some accounts are at odds with others. Spelling returned to Dallas in 1945 and enrolled at Southern Methodist University on the GI Bill (an education assistance program for World War II veterans). Majoring in journalism to reassure his doubting parents, he spent his college years preparing for a show business career by participating in drama productions, performing as half of a comedy team at campus parties, and joining the cheerleading squad. Although Spelling claimed repeatedly to have won the "Eugene O'Neill Award" in a national student playwright's competition in 1947, the existence of such a competition in the United States cannot be confirmed. He graduated with a BA in 1949.

Following an unsuccessful attempt to find a stage career in New York City, Spelling returned to Dallas and married Janice Carruth late in 1949. The couple moved to Los Angeles and divorced a few months later, but Spelling put down roots in Southern California. On 10 April 1953 he married Carolyn Jones, a Texas-born actress; they divorced in 1964.

Spelling's rise from obscurity to Hollywood power begins in the historic moment dividing the film and television eras. While working as an airline reservations agent, he was hired by a customer as a roadie for Ada Leonard's All-Girl Orchestra. When hauling the band instruments proved too arduous for Spelling, Leonard kept him on the payroll to scout prospective contestants for her "all-girl" talent contests, which aired on a Los Angeles television station. With a foot in the door of the show business world, Spelling made personal connections with established members of the film community who were accommodating themselves to the breakup of the studio system. The film director Preston Sturges hired Spelling to direct stage productions at his Hollywood dinner theater. A friendship with the actor Alan Ladd brought Spelling writing credits in two feature Westerns.

Jack Webb, a minor screen actor who had broken out in television as the star and producer of *Dragnet*, a prime-time cop show, cast Spelling in a small part that recurred over six episodes (1953–1955). This role led to dozens of appearances on series such as *I Love Lucy* and *Gunsmoke*. Seeing little possibility for moving beyond bit roles, however, Spelling attempted a career as a scriptwriter. Dick Powell, a studio-era star who became Spelling's patron and mentor, hired him to write for his Western anthology series, *Zane Grey Theater* (1956–1961), and also made him a staff writer at Four Star Productions, the company he had formed in partnership with the actors David Niven, Ida Lupino, and Charles Boyer. Four Star supplied thirty prime-time drama series to the networks, and Spelling wrote for many of them, including *The Dick Powell Theatre* and *Wagon Train*, graduating to line producer and executive producer under Powell's guidance. Beyond the skills that would bring him wealth and power, Spelling gained a sense of personal style from Powell and the other "old-Hollywood royalty" at Four Star.

Because the television Western, his early specialty, was in decline during the 1960s, Spelling redirected his efforts as a producer toward the urban crime story, a dominant genre in popular American literature and film that had yet to achieve its potential in television. In *Burke's Law* (American Broadcasting Company [ABC], 1963–1965), Spelling cast Gene Barry as a millionaire playboy chief of detectives who pursues criminals in a Rolls-Royce. *Honey West* (ABC, 1965–1966) starred Anne Francis in the title role as television's first female action hero. Although less than successful, these series were the origins of Spelling trademarks: over-the-top opulence; voyeuristic fantasies involving strong, capable women; and breaking the conventions of action-hero roles usually given to white, middle-aged men.

On 23 November 1968 Spelling married Carole Gene "Candy" Marer, with whom he remained for the rest of his life; they had a daughter and a son. That year also marked the debut of Spelling's series *The Mod Squad*

(ABC, 1968–1973), which marked a bold leap in American popular culture. Under the watchful eye of their old-school police captain, an unusual trio of detectives—a black man, an unmarried career woman, and an angry young white man—contribute their talents to fighting crime. When first proposed in 1958 by a former narcotics cop, the series concept was rejected as a violation of all the genre's proven rules. But in the midst of a period of cultural turmoil, Spelling resurrected it, seeing in *The Mod Squad* the very elements that were holding back the television cop show from becoming an effective marketing vehicle: youth, sex, and social relevance. The ABC president Leonard Goldenson, impressed by the show's ability to attract younger audiences, asked for more of the same, opening the network schedule to Spelling.

Now heading his own production partnership, Spelling delivered to ABC a succession of crime series built on *The Mod Squad* model, including *The Rookies* (1972–1975), *S.W.A.T.* (1975–1976), and *Starsky and Hutch* (1975–1979). *Charlie's Angels* (1976–1981) tripled the attraction of *Honey West* with three knockout female private eyes, inspiring imitators and the term *jiggle TV*. *Hart to Hart* (1979–1983) presented a contemporary partnership of married equals. Spelling added two more hits to ABC's prime-time schedule, the hour-long comedies *The Love Boat* (1977–1987), which presented stories of romance on a cruise ship, and *Fantasy Island* (1978–1984), about an enchanted resort where visitors' dreams could come true. With the 1978 premiere of *Vega$*, a private-eye series that made early use of the city as a glamorous setting for crime stories, Spelling was supplying approximately one-third of ABC's prime-time programming and helped lift the network to the top of the prime-time ratings for the first time in television history. Industry insiders referred to the network as the Aaron Broadcasting Company.

Spelling continued to produce crime shows such as *T.J. Hooker* (1982–1986) and *Matt Houston* (1982–1985), but by the late 1970s he had shifted his focus toward family sagas. *Family* (1976–1980), about middle-class suburbanites in Pasadena, California, was the first successful series in a new genre, the weekly nighttime soap opera. In 1978 the producer Lee Rich had a smash-hit with *Dallas* (CBS, 1978–1991), which defined the new genre's principal concern as exploring the decay of middle-class values in the face of conspicuous consumption. Spelling responded to the Ewing family of *Dallas* with the Carringtons of *Dynasty* (1981–1989), switching the locale to Denver and adding a special element of female ruthlessness as a signature feature. Other Spelling prime-time soaps (*The Colbys, Hotel*) were less successful, and some were major failures. But with a weekly audience of 40 million, *Dynasty* was an enormous franchise, commanding $235,000 for a thirty-second commercial spot

and establishing itself as a symbol of the glorification of shameless materialism.

By the end of the 1980s, Spelling's long relationship with ABC had run its course, and a string of failed projects led to a *Variety* headline proclaiming "Spelling Dynasty Dead." The master producer promptly bounced back with a pair of major hits for the new Fox network. Just as *The Mod Squad* and *Charlie's Angels* had revived the television crime show and led ABC to the top of the ratings, Spelling's comeback hits, *Beverly Hills, 90210* (1990–2000), a show about teenagers in which Spelling's daughter Tori Spelling starred in a major role, and *Melrose Place* (1992–1999), which focused on young adults, infused the prime-time soap opera with new energy and helped bring Fox to ratings parity with its established competitors.

Other notable Spelling productions were *7th Heaven* (1996–2006), a socially aware soap concerning the family of a Protestant minister (and winner of two Emmy Awards); *And the Band Played On* (1993), a Home Box Office film dramatizing the effects of the AIDS epidemic; and the television movie *The Best Little Girl in the World* (1981), about a teenage girl suffering from anorexia. He also produced the well-received feature-film comedies *Soap Dish* (1991) and *Mr. Mom* (1983). His final television series, *Charmed* (WB, 1998–2006), concerned three young witches who operate a detective agency. Spelling died of complications related to a stroke. He is buried in Hillside Memorial Park in Culver City, California.

Amassing a personal fortune in excess of $100 million and living in a 123-room house, believed to be the largest private residence in California, Spelling achieved enormous success as a producer. However, he was never a favorite of the critics. Tom Shales of the *Washington Post* spoke for many of his colleagues when he said that although some Spelling programs were better than others, "there is never great Spelling, only degrees of terribleness." Spelling himself characterized his work as "mind candy." However, the National Association for the Advancement of Colored People acknowledged Spelling's role in racially integrating television drama, giving him its Image Award a record six times. Over the course of a career that began with bit parts as an actor, Spelling was responsible for the production of thousands of hours of original television programming, as well as a dozen theatrically released feature films. He was a dominant influence on network television drama, shaping and reshaping trends and entire genres to the satisfaction of audiences numbering in the tens of millions. He was a major Hollywood player.

★

Aaron Spelling: A Prime-Time Life (1996), an autobiography written with Jefferson Graham, offers an account that is enjoyable for television fans but cannot be considered authoritative; it alters known dates (including the year of Spelling's birth) and ignores such issues as Spelling's unfounded claim that he spent a year studying at the Sorbonne. For a critical appraisal of Spelling's career, see David Marc and Robert J. Thompson, *Prime Time, Prime Movers: From* I Love Lucy *to* L.A. Law—*America's Greatest TV Shows and the People Who Created Them* (1995). Obituaries are in the *Dallas Morning News* (24 June 2006), *New York Times* (25 June 2006), and London *Daily Telegraph* (26 June 2006).

David Marc

SPILLANE, Mickey (*b*. 9 March 1918 in New York City; *d*. 17 July 2006 in Murrells Inlet, South Carolina), writer of crime fiction who became one of the best-selling authors of the twentieth century despite critical disapproval.

Spillane was born Frank Morrison Spillane, the only child of John Joseph Spillane, a bartender, and Catherine Anne (Morrison) Spillane. His father gave him the name "Mickey" after his baptismal name, Michael. Spillane graduated from Erasmus Hall High School in Brooklyn and in 1939 briefly attended what is now Fort Hays State University in Kansas. In 1940 he met Joe Gill, a writer of

Mickey Spillane. © **BETTMANN/CORBIS**

comic books and one of the more important contributors during the so-called Golden Age of comics. Through Gill, Spillane began to write comic books for Funnies, Inc., many of them unsigned. Turning out this work at a rapid clip proved useful when he turned to writing the kind of fast-paced, sensationalist fiction he would become famous for. The comic book character he created, Mike Danger, was an early version of the much more violent Mike Hammer, the hard-boiled detective at the center of much of his work.

Spillane joined the U.S. Air Force as a pilot one day after the attack on Pearl Harbor on 7 December 1941. He was disappointed not to see combat, instead being stationed in the United States to instruct other pilots. He left the air force with the rank of captain and in 1945 married Mary Ann Pearce, with whom he had four children.

Spillane once famously said that he was not an "author" but a "writer." He called himself a "money writer" because he wrote for money, not for critical acclaim. In 1947 Spillane needed $1,000 for a down payment on some land in New Jersey. To raise the cash he wrote his first novel, *I, the Jury*, which introduced Mike Hammer, in three weeks. It turned out to be a publishing phenomenon. The story of a detective out to avenge the murder of a friend, *I, the Jury* introduced a new level of sex and violence into popular fiction. In the words of the critic Geoffrey O'Brien, Spillane "opened the floodgates of sadism" into the genre. The *New York Times* called it a "spectacularly bad book." It went on to sell more than eight million copies, making Spillane both rich and famous. He once commented on his rejection by critics and the embrace of millions of readers by saying, "I have no fans. You know what I got? Customers. And customers are your friends."

Mike Hammer had his origins in the pulps, cheap magazines (such as the legendary *Black Mask*) published from the 1920s to the 1950s that featured crime, science fiction, and other kinds of stories. Hammer's other predecessors were Sam Spade, the creation of the novelist Dashiell Hammett, and Philip Marlowe, the recurring detective character in Raymond Chandler's novels. But where Spade was clever and Marlowe romantic, Hammer was brutal. In the thirteen Mike Hammer novels, delivered in intense first-person narration, Hammer is always out for some kind of violent revenge. As he says in *I, the Jury*: "I don't want to arrest anybody. I just want to shoot somebody." It was an attitude that seemed to connect with millions of readers. In *One Lonely Night*, Hammer says: "I lived to kill so others could live. . . . I was the evil that opposed other evil, leaving the good and the meek in the middle to inherit the earth!"

Spillane brought out a quick succession of Mike Hammer novels, all packed with his characteristic brand of shocking sex and outrageous violence: *My Gun Is Quick* (1950), *Vengeance Is Mine!* (1950), *The Big Kill* (1951),

One Lonely Night (1951), and *Kiss Me, Deadly* (1952). These books and another crime novel without Hammer, *The Long Wait* (1951), were each a stunning success in terms of paperback sales, making Spillane a celebrity. With popular fame came critical contempt. The critic Malcolm Cowley called Mike Hammer "a homicidal paranoiac." But there was no denying that the books had hit a cultural nerve.

At the height of his sales and early fame, Spillane stepped away from the spotlight and Mike Hammer. In 1952 he became a Jehovah's Witness and committed himself to his new religion, going door to door to talk to people about the Bible. He did not publish another Hammer novel for nine years but kept writing short fiction for magazines. From 1953 to 1954 he returned to his origins by writing for the Mike Hammer comic strip that ran in newspapers throughout the country. In 1953 Spillane sold the movie rights to his Hammer novels to the British producer Victor Saville, who quickly made a succession of unremarkable films based on the books. The major exception was the film noir masterpiece *Kiss Me, Deadly* (1955), directed by Robert Aldrich and starring Ralph Meeker as Hammer. Spillane's detective also appeared in a television series, *Mickey Spillane's Mike Hammer* (1956–1959), played by Darren McGavin. Stacy Keach played Hammer in a second television series by that title (1984–1987) and again in *Mike Hammer, Private Eye* (1997–1998).

Spillane returned to novel writing in 1961 with the non-Hammer murder mystery *The Deep*, and a year later he brought back his tough detective in *The Girl Hunters*. Critics seemed to soften their harsh tone, and Spillane slowly began to gain recognition as a storyteller. He no longer sold books in the numbers he reached in the 1950s, but he kept publishing. In 1963, declaring himself his favorite actor for the role of Hammer, he played the detective in the film version of *The Girl Hunters*. As he put it: "I am Mike Hammer!"

During the 1960s and early 1970s Spillane published fifteen crime books, including four Mike Hammer novels: *The Snake* (1964), *The Twisted Thing* (1966), *The Body Lovers* (1967), and *Survival . . . Zero!* (1970). By the mid-1960s Ian Fleming's James Bond novels were outselling Spillane's books. He was so impressed that he created a spy character named Tiger Mann in the novels *Day of the Guns* (1964), *Bloody Sunrise* (1965), *The Death Dealers* (1965), and *The By-Pass Control* (1966). Although Tiger Mann never achieved the fame of Bond, it was fitting that Spillane should challenge the British spy given that Mike Hammer's brand of violent justice was an important influence on Fleming's creation. The first Bond novel, *Casino Royale*, had appeared in 1953, six years after Spillane had unleashed Hammer on the polite world of cops and robbers.

After his 1962 divorce from his first wife, Spillane in 1965 married Sherri Malinou, a model and actress who

posed for the paperback covers of *The By-Pass Control* and *The Erection Set* (1972). Throughout the 1980s Spillane continued to write, enhancing his popularity by appearing in over 100 television commercials for Miller Lite beer, always spoofing himself and his famous character. On a bet from his publisher, Spillane wrote a children's book, *The Day the Sea Rolled Back* (1979), which won the Junior Literary Guild Award. He followed this up with another children's book, *The Ship That Never Was* (1982). Following a divorce from his second wife in 1982, in 1983 he married Jane Rodgers Johnson, who had two daughters from a previous marriage.

The second-to-last Hammer novel, *The Killing Man*, came out in 1989. Hammer made his last appearance in 1996 in *Black Alley*. The character had become an American archetype, a model that many subsequent characters in books, films, and television were based on. Critics no longer attacked Spillane. In 1995 he was awarded the Grand Master Award by the Mystery Writers of America. He died quietly at his home in South Carolina at the age of eighty-eight.

Mickey Spillane was an American cultural phenomenon. He once claimed that he was the most widely read writer in human experience, and sales numbers for his books suggest he was not exaggerating. He took the pulp world of detective fiction to new levels of violence and sex that shocked and delighted readers but initially repulsed critics. Spillane always believed that the early bad reviews he got actually helped sell his books. He called his fiction "the chewing gum of American literature," but it became a symbol of 1950s America and influenced figures from James Bond to Clint Eastwood's Dirty Harry and the comic book antihero the Punisher. Spillane's early Hammer novels rank with the top-twenty best sellers of all time, making him an important, if controversial, American writer.

★

For a discussion of the Mike Hammer character, see Max Allan Collins and James L. Traylor, *One Lonely Knight: Mickey Spillane's Mike Hammer* (1984). J. Kenneth Van Dover, *Murder in the Millions: Erle Stanley Gardner, Mickey Spillane, and Ian Fleming* (1984), compares three authors of popular detective and spy fiction. For an interview with Spillane, see Art Harris, "Mickey Spillane, Still Hammering," *Washington Post* (24 Oct. 1984). An obituary is in the *New York Times* (18 July 2006).

John Rocco

STAFFORD, Jo (*b.* Coalinga, California, 12 November 1917; *d.* 16 July 2008 in Los Angeles, California), versatile vocalist and prolific recording artist whose career spanned the big-band era into the 1970s.

Jo Stafford, 1951. © BETTMANN/CORBIS

Stafford's parents, Grover Cleveland Stafford and Anna York Stafford, moved from Tennessee to California in the early 1900s, attracted by the prospect of oil wealth. The wealth never materialized, but several talented daughters did. Stafford, the third of four girls, hoped for a career in opera, but the Depression made the investment in such a future impractical. She joined her older sisters, Pauline and Christine, in a vocal trio. The Three Stafford Sisters had their own radio program on KHJ in Los Angeles. They made their first commercial recording in May 1936 with the trumpeter Louis Prima for Brunswick, "Let's Get Together and Swing." The Three Stafford Sisters found additional work in the film studios, recording voice tracks. They sang a chorus of "Nice Work if You Can Get It" for the madrigal trio appearing on screen in *A Damsel in Distress* (1937).

After her sister Pauline married, Jo became the sole female voice in the Pied Pipers, an octet formed from a merger of two male ensembles, the Four Esquires and the Three Rhythm Kings. The Pipers devised arrangements using different combinations of voices to evoke the brass and reed sections of a big band. Axel Stordahl and Paul Wetstein (later Weston), staff arrangers for the bandleader Tommy Dorsey, heard the group and were impressed. Hired initially for a single appearance on Dorsey's Raleigh-Kool radio program, the Pipers were subsequently signed for a ten-week stint. However, the program sponsor took exception to their performance of the nonsensical song "Hold Tight (I Want Some Seafood, Mama)" and had them fired after just two weeks. The quartet remained in New York for several months, scuffling for work, and recorded four selections for Victor Records in June 1939 before returning to California. Four members of the octet left to find more secure livelihoods. Before their departure, the Pied Pipers recorded two selections for the Ammor label in Los Angeles. These titles also appeared on Varsity, a label based in the East and controlled by the U.S. Record Corporation in Scranton, Pennsylvania.

Only months later, Dorsey phoned Stafford from Chicago about hiring the quartet that remained—Stafford, John Huddleston, Billy Wilson, and Chuck Lowry. The Pied Pipers joined the band in Chicago in December 1939, making memorable recordings of "Once in a While" and "The Night We Called It a Day." They accompanied Frank Sinatra on selections such as "I'll Never Smile Again" and "There Are Such Things." Stafford discovered a song, "Little Man with a Candy Cigar," and asked Dorsey whether she could record it as a solo, a request Dorsey was happy to grant; Stafford's first recordings as a vocal soloist with Dorsey were that title and "For You," recorded in February 1941. That same year, Stafford and Huddleston were married.

Stafford remained with Dorsey until November 1942, when his well-known temper flashed over a trivial incident on the railroad platform in Portland, Oregon, and he fired Lowry. Finding Dorsey's decision capricious and unwarranted, the Pied Pipers quit as a unit, never even boarding the train.

In the spring of 1942 the songwriter Johnny Mercer was a partner in the establishment of Capitol Records, and was enthralled by Stafford. Once aware that Stafford was at liberty, he quickly signed the quartet. Stafford continued to record solo as well as with the Pipers, delivering the first of many high-charting recordings with "Old Acquaintance" and "How Sweet You Are," released back-to-back on a single 78 RPM record. Soon, Stafford went out as a single and June Hutton assumed her place in the Pipers. Stafford was also now single in another sense. Her marriage to Huddleston was dissolved in 1943. That same year, he left the quartet to join the war effort; the couple had no children.

More than three dozen of Stafford's Capitol recordings during the 1940s would chart in the Top Twenty. She was a presence on radio—not only as a guest on many different programs but also as one of the hosts in rotation of *The Chesterfield Supper Club*. She recorded for V-Disc, a record label produced by the government to provide recordings to service camps and troops overseas. Stafford became exceptionally popular among servicemen, many of whom no doubt associated her pitch-perfect and sweet, smooth voice with the home front. Stafford's appearance, too, reinforced this impression. Her good looks were not that of Hollywood Boulevard but rather were of the sort that evoked Main Street and resonated deeply with members of the armed forces, who christened her "G.I. Jo."

Paul Weston, who had left Dorsey only days after the Pied Pipers' arrival, was Capitol's director of Artists and Repertoire, and the in-house arranger. He and Stafford were married in 1952, and would have a son and a daughter. Weston was Stafford's musical director on the great majority of her sessions. While at Capitol, Weston and Stafford delved into neglected repertoire, including the collection *Jo Stafford Sings American Folk Songs*, in 1948. In 1949, with Gordon MacRae, Stafford recorded "Whispering Hope," a devotional song written in 1868 by Septimus Winner.

For all her popularity, Stafford appeared unidentified on some of her best-selling records. In March 1947 Jo made a satiric—and unplanned—record of "Temptation" with Red Ingle, a former Spike Jones musician known for leaving the dignity of many popular songs in shreds. Stafford assumed a hillbilly alter ego so convincing that Capitol released the record under the title of "Tim-Tay-Shun" and hid her identity behind the name of Cinderella G. Stump. The public was none the wiser at first; when word leaked that Stump was Stafford, sales of the record only increased.

Even better remembered are recordings that Stafford and Weston made for Columbia beginning in 1957 under the pseudonym of Jonathan and Darlene Edwards. Inspired by mediocre lounge performers, Weston and Stafford depicted a florid pianist with neither restraint nor taste, and a singer for whom correct pitch is more elusive than a winning lottery ticket. Anyone can sing badly, but Jo Stafford was one of the few whose musicianship was so consummate that she could sing badly *well*. Indeed, Stafford's only Grammy Award was for "Jonathan and Darlene Edwards in Paris" (1960).

Stafford and Weston had moved to Columbia Records in 1950, where she made a number of hits charting number one in *Billboard*, including "You Belong to Me" and "Make Love to Me." Other brisk sellers were "Shrimp Boats" and "Jambalaya." In 1955, Columbia awarded Stafford a platinum disc for sales of 25 million records in the previous five years. Highly regarded long-play albums in the 1950s and 1960s for Columbia, Capitol and other labels included *Swinging down Broadway* (1958), *Ballad of the Blues* (1959), and *Jo + Jazz* (1960).

In 1961 Stafford and Weston were in London filming a well-budgeted thirteen-week television series that featured top American and British performers. She gradually withdrew from music beginning in the 1960s to raise the couple's children. Approached with invitations to return to the recording studios, Stafford demurred. Asked why,

she quipped, "For the same reason that Lana Turner is not posing in a bathing suit anymore."

Weston died in 1996 and Stafford continued to live the quiet life, enjoying her family during the years that remained to her. She died of congestive heart failure at her home in Century City, in West Los Angeles. Services were private. She is buried in Holy Cross Cemetery in Culver City, California.

The writer and music historian Will Friedwald has described Stafford as the "Mona Lisa of pop music," her appeal as inscrutable and challenging to divine as the expression on the face of Leonardo da Vinci's subject, Lisa Gherardini. Stafford's unerring sense of pitch and the absence of affectation or idiosyncrasy in her singing was, for some, at the heart of her appeal. It also provided grist for her critics, who heard Stafford as emotionally detached from the lyrics; cold rather than cool. What she really did was to pare a song back to its very essence, making both singer and song timeless.

★

A good survey of Stafford's career with an emphasis on the 1950s and 1960s can be found in *Jo Stafford: The Portrait Edition* (Sony A3K 57836, three CDs). Her Capitol years are well represented on *Spotlight on Jo Stafford* (Capitol CDP 7243 8 29391), with liner notes by Tom Colburn, and *Jo Stafford: Capitol Collectors Series* (CDP 7 791638), annotated by Joseph F. Laredo. An affectionate portrait of Stafford (and Weston) is included in Gene Lees, *Singers & the Song* (1987). Obituaries are in the *New York Times* and *Guardian* (London) (both 19 July 2008).

Rob Bamberger

STAFFORD, Robert Theodore (*b.* 8 August 1913 in Rutland, Vermont; *d.* 23 December 2006 in Rutland), Vermont Republican who served as governor, U.S. representative, and U.S. senator, known for his advocacy of education and the environment.

Stafford, the son of Burt Linus Stafford, a prominent lawyer, and Mabel Rose (Stratton) Stafford, a homemaker, wanted to attend the U.S. Naval Academy, but his father proposed Middlebury College in Vermont for at least a year. He stayed and graduated in 1935; a star football player at the college, he was selected by *Sports Illustrated* for its Silver Anniversary Team. He attended the University of Michigan Law School but transferred to Boston University Law School to be closer to home as his father's health declined. He received an LLB in 1938 and on 15 October of that year he married Helen Kelley, with whom he would have four daughters. He joined his father's law firm and served as Rutland city prosecutor from 1938

Robert T. Stafford, 1987. AP IMAGES

to 1942. After the Japanese attack on Pearl Harbor in December 1941, he volunteered for the U.S. Navy, attaining the rank of lieutenant commander. After World War II he was asked to establish a navy reserve unit in Burlington, Vermont.

Stafford, taking advantage of political opportunities, climbed the political ladder. In 1946 he was elected state's attorney of Rutland County (1947–1951). Recalled to active duty during the Korean War, he served two years and retired as captain in 1953. Returning to Rutland, he accepted an offer to become deputy attorney general of Vermont. He was elected attorney general in 1954, lieutenant governor in 1956, and, in the closest race ever run for that office, governor in 1958. As governor he reduced the state debt with an austerity budget, began implementing the Little Hoover Commission's proposals for greater government efficiency, opposed Republican colleagues who wanted right-to-work laws, and promoted state parks and tourism.

In 1960 Stafford ran for Congress as a fiscal conservative and anticommunist, defeating the incumbent William H. Meyer who in 1958 had become the state's first Democratic congressman since the Civil War. Stafford served on the Armed Forces Committee and supported the country's foreign policies during the 1960s. His unassuming personal qualities—integrity, patience, and an ability to listen and work with colleagues—led to his election as vice chairman of the House Republican Conference Committee. He won that post despite having distanced himself in 1964 from the Republican Barry Goldwater's presidential campaign and despite his decreasing support for the Vietnam War. In 1967 he coauthored *How to End the Draft*; he recalled seeing "streams of dead and wounded" on his visits to Vietnam in 1966 and 1968 and having to face soldiers "who came back permanently crippled." He felt pressure from the public's reaction against the war as well as from his own daughters to end his support for the war, and in 1969 he voiced his opposition.

When the Vermont senator Winston Prouty died in September 1971, Stafford expected Governor Deane C. Davis, a Republican, to appoint him until a special election could be held to finish the term; but Davis hesitated for nearly a week, probably because of their differences on Vietnam. Stafford's support in the House for an all-voluntary army, however, led President Richard Nixon, in spite of Stafford's criticism of the Cambodian invasion in 1970, to request the appointment, as the Senate was about to vote on a draft bill. The president had the new senator flown to Washington, D.C., for the vote; the bill passed, paving the way for an all-volunteer army. Stafford thus had the rare opportunity to vote on the same bill as both a senator and a representative. Later in 1971 Stafford won the special election to serve the five years remaining in Prouty's term. The following year he cosponsored a draft-dodgers' amnesty bill. In 1976 President Gerald Ford, who had worked with Stafford in the House during the 1960s, seriously considered the Vermonter for the vice presidential nomination.

Throughout the 1970s Stafford served in relative obscurity in the Senate, overshadowed by his influential colleague George Aiken. During the 1980s, however, he was outspoken in his opposition to certain policies of the Republican Party and the Reagan administration. Ronald Reagan's landslide election in 1980 saw a Republican sweep of House and Senate. Stafford, the ranking Republican on the Environment and Public Works Committee, realized "a sense of urgency" for proposed legislation on environmental cleanup, known as Superfund, on which he had worked with the former committee chair Edmund Muskie, a Democrat from Maine. "Unless the Senate acts now," Stafford noted, "the legislation stands little chance when the new Republican-controlled Senate convenes in January." As the Congress approached the end of the session, the Senate had acted, but Stafford needed House support. Stafford, as a former member of the House, took advantage of a rarely used House privilege to speak on the floor, winning support for the original Superfund legislation, which, as Stafford had hoped, passed in 1980. He personally spent many hours with the environment committee's staff to broker the differences between industry and environmentalists and to obtain bipartisan support. Critics argued that he had compromised too much, and though he agreed, he knew that legislation is "the art of the possible." The committee's chief counsel emphasized: "I think it is safe to say that because of Bob Stafford there is a Superfund law today." Five years later Stafford played a central role in the renewal of the legislation with a larger appropriation than the administration had wanted, and Congress also enacted the Stafford Disaster and Emergency Assistance Act.

In 1981 Stafford became the chairman of the Committee on the Environment and Public Works and of the Subcommittee on Education in the new Congress, thus acquiring two crucial roles in areas in which the administration zealously sought change. He supported many of Reagan's domestic and foreign policies, especially in Central America, but he pushed for renewal of Superfund and blocked Reagan's proposals to weaken the Clean Air Act; earlier he had called the 1977 Clean Air Act his "proudest legislative achievement." He succeeded in gaining committee support for an acid-rain bill, but he could not get congressional approval. In 1988 he cosponsored a strengthened Clean Water Act and organized an overwhelming override of Reagan's veto of the legislation.

Stafford also thwarted other administration plans. He blocked efforts to cut federally funded education programs and led the way for legislation creating opportunities for the disabled and poor. Colleagues praised his role in what would be called the Robert T. Stafford Elementary and Secondary Act of 1987. Senator Claiborne Pell, Democrat from Rhode Island and chairman of the Education Committee, declared that "many of the programs in this bill would have been lost entirely if it had not been for his vigorous leadership." In 1988 the Senate renamed the Federal Guaranteed Student Loan program the Robert T. Stafford Student Loan program. At the time of Stafford's death, the program offered 14 million post-secondary students low-interest loans. In 1987 Stafford opposed the nomination of Judge Robert H. Bork to the Supreme Court, again disappointing the White House and Republican leaders in Vermont.

Once a conservative governor and congressman, especially on fiscal and military issues, Stafford became an influential leader of the liberal-moderate wing of the Republican Party during the Reagan years. A Vermont newspaper asserted: "He took Vermont and its priorities to Washington and quietly influenced the nation from a Vermont perspective." During his political career Vermont underwent enormous changes, as had he. Yet he and his staff may have lost touch with Vermonters when he sought reelection in 1982, winning only narrowly. His opponent represented the new liberal wave in the state, and Stafford was not liberal enough for the left at a time when many Vermont Republicans, following Reagan, were moving to the right. He retired from the Senate in 1989 and returned to Vermont. Still, as he noted before leaving Washington, "I think Vermonters appreciated that I could change with them."

In 2000 Vermont passed civil-union legislation affording same-sex couples the benefits and responsibilities of marriage, provoking bitter controversy in the state. The law's opponents especially targeted Republicans who had voted in favor of it. Stafford held a press conference with the Vermont congressional delegation and called for civil discourse on the issue in the state's heated gubernatorial campaign. "It occurs to me that even if a same-sex couple unites in love," he said, "what harm does that do any body or any society?" Stafford's statesmanship was a turning point in the reelection of the Democratic governor who had supported the legislation and an important moment in the national debate over civil unions.

Stafford's accomplishments came, a Vermont reporter observed, "without fanfare, without getting on the networks, without becoming a household name." The *New York Times* suggested that Stafford might give "the worst interview of any public official in the capital." Because he was "not an ink hound," his record was not well known to the American public or even his fellow Vermonters. Stafford died at a nursing home after a long illness. He is buried at Evergreen Cemetery in Rutland.

To date Stafford is the only Vermonter to have held every major statewide office. Throughout his career Stafford earned the respect and admiration of his colleagues. The political columnist David Broder, commenting on Stafford's pending retirement, wrote that "the Senate will be a louder and a lesser place for his departure." Stafford's fellow Vermonter, the Democratic senator Patrick Leahy, declared that Stafford was "the only person I've met in 14 years that every senator of either party has said, publicly and privately, that they are sorry to see him go." A distinguished Vermont statesman, Stafford left a legacy as a senator from a small state whose political career had a major influence on the nation's environmental and education policies.

★

Stafford's papers are held in Special Collections, University of Vermont (Burlington). For information on Stafford's career, see Dwight Garner, "The Bob Stafford Way," *Middlebury*, 63 (Winter 1989): 8–15; Howard Coffin, "Vermonter of the Year," *Sunday Rutland Herald and Times Argus* (18 Dec. 1988);

and Peter Freyne, "The Changing of the Guard," *Vanguard Press* (24 Nov.–1 Dec. 1988). Obituaries are in the *New York Times* and *Washington Post* (both 24 Dec. 2006), the *Rutland Herald* (24 Dec. 2006 and 7 Jan. 2007), and the *Burlington Free Press* (7 Jan. 2007).

Travis Beal Jacobs

STANTON, Frank Nicholas (*b.* 20 March 1908 in Muskegon, Michigan; *d.* 24 December 2006 in Boston, Massachusetts), broadcasting executive who helped build the Columbia Broadcasting System (CBS) from a fledgling radio network into a dominant worldwide television and multimedia communications company, serving as president from 1946 to 1974.

Stanton was the son of Frank Cooper Stanton, a woodworking and mechanics teacher, and Helen Josephine (Schmidt) Stanton, who left teaching to raise the couple's two children. Growing up in Dayton, Ohio, Stanton was interested in radios and other electronics. He built his first receiver while in grade school and enjoyed operating a ham radio transmitter with his younger brother. On his

Frank Stanton, 1960. CBS PHOTO ARCHIVE/GETTY IMAGES

own initiative, he worked at a downtown department store beginning at age twelve until graduating from Steele High School in 1926. He attended Ohio Wesleyan University, majoring in zoology and psychology, and won early admission to the University of Michigan medical school as a college junior. But a summer job at a Philadelphia advertising agency convinced him that he had found his true vocation. In the fall of 1929, his senior year, he began to search for openings on Madison Avenue, the center of the advertising world in New York City. In November the stock market crashed, wiping out the job market overnight. He then accepted a teaching fellowship at Ohio State University in Columbus, where he earned an MA (1932) and PhD (1935) in psychology. Stanton married Sarah Ruth Stephenson, a childhood friend, on 31 December 1931. The marriage ended with her death in 1992. They did not have children.

Focusing on the emerging specialty of mass psychology, Stanton wrote a master's thesis exploring the effects of paper surfaces and tints on the behavior of readers. For his doctoral work, he turned his attention to radio, specifically the issue of the audience—who was listening and why. In 1934 Stanton wrote to the two network broadcasting companies, asking for permission to observe their audience research techniques. The National Broadcasting Company (NBC), a division of the Radio Corporation of America (RCA), promptly refused but suggested he send his findings. CBS, by far the smaller of the competitors, might not have replied at all if not for the personal interest of Paul W. Kesten, a marketing executive, who invited Stanton to the company's New York headquarters. Stanton spent several months at CBS and then returned to Columbus to complete his dissertation, "A Critique of Present Methods and a New Plan for Studying Radio Listening Behavior." He sent a copy to Kesten as a gesture of gratitude, and Kesten responded by offering him a job. In the summer of 1935 Stanton moved to New York City, where he lived all but the final years of his life.

Among his prominent early achievements at CBS was development of the Stanton-Lazarsfeld Program Analyzer, a device that could be attached to a radio to accurately record usage. It was a milestone in the development of the ratings system that became the economic cornerstone of commercial radio and television broadcasting. In a meteoric rise through the CBS executive ranks, Stanton was promoted to director of research (1938), director of advertising (1941), and vice president and general manager (1942). Four years later, at age thirty-eight, he was appointed president of CBS, putting him at the right hand of board chairman William S. Paley, whose family had saved the company from bankruptcy in 1928. Paley and Stanton ran CBS in tandem for a quarter-century. They were a study in contrasts: Stanton was an earnestly intellectual, public-spirited midwesterner who oversaw the details of management, Paley a wealthy Philadelphia socialite who reveled in relationships with celebrities and cultivated the image of an impresario. The clash of styles was complemented by clashes over substance, which increased over time. They nonetheless guided the company past its once indomitable rival, NBC, to make CBS the most profitable, powerful, and prestigious U.S. broadcasting company during the second half of the twentieth century.

Stanton's many talents, interests, and credentials were CBS assets. The only top-echelon executive in broadcasting who had played a role in pioneering audience measurement, he kept CBS at the cutting edge of the field, helping to transform it from the also-ran of network radio into the "Tiffany Network" of the television age. From the 1950s to the 1970s CBS shows dominated the television ratings in almost every genre of programming. A portion of the spectacular profits generated by the entertainment division was used to subsidize the news division, enabling its reputation as the finest commercial broadcast journalism organization in the world. An early proponent of what is now called branding, Stanton adopted the "CBS eye" (designed by William Golden in 1951) as the company logo, placing it as a corporate signature on all network programming and promotion. This had the effect of creating an aura of excellence around a television schedule dominated by comedies and dramas not known for their high quality—but that generated the bulk of company profits.

Possessing the language, manners, and diplomas of an academician, Stanton befriended and collaborated with innovative, influential scholars, such as Paul Lazarsfeld of Columbia University, Hadley Cantril of Princeton University, and Robert Elder of the Massachusetts Institute of Technology. Lazarsfeld and Stanton were especially productive. After collaborating on their radio measurement device, they coauthored three books that became early classics in the study of communications. Through Stanton, CBS became the corporate patron of a new academic discipline that would provide it (and the industry) with ongoing access to the latest advances in audience research. In addition, these new university programs—to which CBS and other corporations could make tax-deductible donations—would serve to train future executives.

Within CBS, Dr. Stanton, as he was referred to by everyone who worked there, promoted the career of the physicist Peter Goldmark, leading to his appointment as head of CBS Laboratories in 1954. Goldmark was in large part responsible for ending the long monopolistic dominance that RCA (NBC's parent) enjoyed over home entertainment technologies. Goldmark's research and development efforts brought more than 150 products and devices to market for CBS, including video equipment chosen for the U.S. space program. While RCA Victor was heavily investing in the 45-rpm record, Goldmark invented the "long-playing" (LP) 33 1/3-rpm phonograph record, an achievement that especially pleased Stanton. CBS's Columbia Records division

trademarked the LP in 1948, gradually establishing it as the disk of choice for phonograph music.

Stanton applied his personal tastes and theories wherever he saw fit in company operations. When CBS planned a new midtown Manhattan corporate headquarters building during the early 1960s, he persuaded Paley, who had been leaning toward a gaudier design, to select the sleek, angular skyscraper, which came to be known as Black Rock, designed by the architect Eero Saarinen. He then took personal charge of the interior design, specifying mazes of cubicles compatible with his views on industrial psychology. Under the Paley-Stanton regime, CBS diversified to encompass such enterprises as publishing (Holt, Rinehart and Winston), toy manufacturing (Creative Playthings), and professional sports (the New York Yankees baseball team).

Stanton's prominence in broadcasting history is most pronounced in the area of news and public affairs. While Paley tired of the many controversies (and low returns) generated by CBS News, Stanton continued to encourage journalistic excellence and to seek new roles for broadcasting in American democracy. In 1960 he successfully petitioned the Federal Communications Commission (FCC) to suspend its "equal time" rule so that the Nixon-Kennedy presidential election debates could be aired. (The equal time rule compelled a broadcaster who gave free air time to one candidate to give an equal amount of time to all opponents for that office. Suspension of the rule freed the networks to invite only the two major party candidates, Kennedy and Nixon, to appear together in nationally televised debates, instead of requiring the inclusion of minor party candidates as well.) No incident is more characteristic of his legacy than the 1971 controversy surrounding *The Selling of the Pentagon*, a CBS News documentary presented on the prime-time *CBS Reports* series. The hour-long program, aired during the later phase of the Vietnam War, is an exposé of military mismanagement and corruption in the handling of funds. Members of congressional oversight committees, who had long regarded the military's relations with private contractors as a national security concern, and thus off-limits to the press, accused CBS News of distorting the issue by doctoring footage.

In hearings before the House Interstate Commerce Committee, Stanton was the star witness. Representative Harley Staggers, the committee chair, demanded that Stanton turn over, in evidence, all production notes and all footage shot for the program, including outtakes. Stanton refused. As he later noted, "I felt very deeply that, under the First Amendment, Congress could keep its cotton-picking fingers off us. It was what my mother taught me." When a federal agent arrived at Stanton's office to serve him with a subpoena, Stanton was prepared to go to jail rather than turn over the materials. But the agent had been instructed not to arrest him, pending a vote of the entire House on whether to cite Stanton for contempt of Congress. The measure was defeated, and the committee backed down. In an industry not known for defying the government that licenses it, the CBS president had taken a stand on behalf of extending constitutional press protections to the electronic media.

As Stanton approached age sixty-five, he expected Paley to propose a board waiver of the company's mandatory retirement policy. But Paley did not do for Stanton what he had done for himself. Stepping down as president in 1971, Stanton served as vice chairman of the CBS board until 1973 (and retained a seat on the board—at arm's length from real power—until 1987). Stanton's rare combination of executive power and academic credibility (enhanced over time by personal wealth) made him an attractive figure to foundations and institutes hoping to influence the nation's cultural direction and educational policies. While CBS president, he also served as chair of the Rand Corporation (1961–1967) and held directorships and trusteeships on the boards of more than thirty first-tier nonprofits, including the Ford Foundation, Rockefeller Foundation, Center for Advanced Study in the Behavioral Sciences, and Lincoln Center for the Performing Arts. After retiring from CBS, he began a six-year term as president of the American Red Cross, and in 1978 he became the first nonalumnus elected to the Board of Overseers of Harvard University.

Harvard, where he took on advisory positions and pursued projects for several campus institutions, became the focal point of his many interests and the chief object of his philanthropy for the remainder of his life. As travel became more difficult with age, he relocated to Boston in 1998. Among the positions he endowed at Harvard are a chair in urban and policy planning in honor of his wife; the directorship of the Health Communication Center, where he was an active collaborator in the project that first promoted the concept of "designated driver"; and the Frank Stanton Professor of the First Amendment at the Kennedy School. Among the many honors bestowed on Stanton were five George Foster Peabody Awards and the National Academy of Television Arts and Sciences Lifetime Achievement Award, which describes him as "the conscience of broadcasting." He died in his sleep at age ninety-eight.

Stanton's seamless synthesis of academic proclivities and entrepreneurial talents, unusual during most of his lifetime, suggests a prototype for the executive intellectual of the information age, a period he helped to shape during his decades of leadership at CBS. What is perhaps most remarkable about Stanton is that power and wealth did not play their most familiar tricks on him. He continued to enjoy the satisfactions of transforming worthwhile ideas into productive actions until he died.

★

Stanton's spoken recollections are available in oral history archives at Syracuse University, Columbia University, and the John F. Kennedy Presidential Library and Museum at the University of Massachusetts at Boston. William J. Buxton and Charles R. Acland, "Interview with Dr. Frank N. Stanton: Radio Research Pioneer," *Journal of Radio & Audio Media* 7, no. 2 (Jan. 2000): 474–503, focuses on his experiences in the early days of radio audience research. Alfred Baik, "'Riding Two Horses': Radio at Television's Creation—An Interview with Dr. Frank N. Stanton," *Journal of Radio & Audio Media* 15, no. 1 (Jan. 2008): 103–114, focuses on the condition of radio at the advent of the television age. Stanton is a pervasive presence in several memoirs and accounts of CBS, including Robert Metz, *CBS: Reflections in a Bloodshot Eye* (1975); Paley, *As It Happened: A Memoir* (1979); Robert Slater, *This—Is CBS: A Chronicle of 60 Years* (1988); and Corydon B. Dunham, *Fighting for the First Amendment: Stanton of CBS vs. Congress and the Nixon White House* (1997). An obituary is in the *New York Times* (26 Dec. 2006).

David Marc

STAPLETON, (Lois) Maureen (*b.* 21 June 1925 in Troy, New York; *d.* 13 March 2006 in Lenox, Massachusetts), highly respected stage, screen, and television actress who was acclaimed for playing an array of complex, deeply human heroines and who was honored with critical raves and numerous Academy, Tony, and Emmy awards and nominations.

Stapleton was born in a midsize city in upstate New York. Her father, John Stapleton, was never steadily employed; his jobs included railroad worker, speakeasy operator, and bartender. He also was an alcoholic. Stapleton's mother, Irene (Walsh) Stapleton, was a New York State government worker. Stapleton had a younger brother. Her parents constantly fought and separated when Stapleton was five. She was a chunky, despondent child who passed long hours in local movie houses immersed in the fantasy worlds portrayed on-screen, and she longed for an acting career. Despite her heft—by the time she reached her teens, she weighed 180 pounds—Stapleton dreamed of becoming the new Barbara Stanwyck or Jean Harlow. Among male stars she favored Joel McCrea, Clark Gable, and Robert Taylor.

After graduating from Troy's Catholic Central High School in 1942, Stapleton took night courses at Siena College. She toiled as a clerk and in a munitions factory, and she hoarded her pennies. The following year, with $100 in savings, she moved to New York City, where she lived in an apartment that cost $45 per month and worked as an artist's model, a salesgirl, a waitress, and a hotel clerk. Stapleton attended the New School in Greenwich Village, where she studied with the famed acting teacher Herbert

Maureen Stapleton, 1978. AP IMAGES

Berghof. Eventually she joined the Actors Studio to learn method acting.

Gradually Stapleton began winning stage roles, appearing in Broadway revivals of *The Playboy of the Western World* (1946) and *Antony and Cleopatra* (1947) and touring in *The Barretts of Wimpole Street* (1947). On 22 July 1949 she married Max Allentuck, the general manager for the stage producer Kermit Bloomgarden. The couple had two children.

In the meantime, the quality of Stapleton's roles steadily increased. She played showy supporting parts on Broadway in Sidney Kingsley's *Detective Story* (1949) and Arthur Laurents's *The Bird Cage* (1950). Then she won the prime role of Serafina delle Rose, a lonely Sicilian-American widow, in Tennessee Williams's *The Rose Tattoo* (1951). Williams wanted to cast Anna Magnani, the famed Italian star, but Magnani refused because of her lack of command of English. (Magnani played Serafina in the 1955 screen version.) Harold Clurman, director of *The Bird Cage*, recommended Stapleton. She was auditioned, and a Broadway star was born.

Stapleton's casting was just one of many opportunities she would have to play characters far older than her actual age. She won rave reviews, the first of her six Tony Award nominations, and the first of her two Tony Awards. *The Rose Tattoo* ran for 300 performances before beginning a six-month road tour.

Stapleton's success, however, came with an exorbitant price. The pressure of instant fame, and of playing a demanding role onstage night after night, resulted in her continuous drinking. While claiming that she imbibed liquor only after performing, Stapleton often became physically ill right before going onstage. Since childhood she had been terrified of riding in elevators and of flying; when she needed to cross the United States or to journey abroad, she traveled by rail or by ship. She became convinced that while she was performing, an unknown assailant would murder her. After completing the *Rose Tattoo* tour, Stapleton entered therapy. She may have been recognized in her social circle for her sincerity and her devilish wit, but her fears—and her drinking—consumed her for her entire life.

Meanwhile, Stapleton's career steadily ascended. She replaced Beatrice Straight as Elizabeth Proctor on Broadway in Arthur Miller's *The Crucible* (1953), played Lady Anne opposite José Ferrer and Vincent Price in William Shakespeare's *Richard III* (1953), played Masha opposite Montgomery Clift in Anton Chekhov's *The Seagull* (1954), and appeared in Williams's one-act play *27 Wagons Full of Cotton* (1955). She starred as Lady Torrance, an embittered shopkeeper, in Williams's *Orpheus Descending* (1957)—a role that Magnani had also declined. The play earned so-so notices, but Stapleton won critical kudos. Then she turned to comedy, winning a Tony nomination as a matchmaker in S. N. Behrman's *The Cold Wind and the Warm* (1958).

Stapleton also spent the 1950s accepting guest roles on television anthology series and earned an Emmy nomination as Sadie Burke, Willie Stark's secretary-mistress, in a *Kraft Television Theatre* presentation of *All the King's Men* (1958). Stapleton then made her screen debut in *Lonelyhearts* (1959), playing a frustrated seductress, and she won her first Academy Award nomination, for best supporting actress. That same year she and Allentuck divorced, and she became romantically involved with David Rayfiel, a writer.

Magnani replaced Stapleton in *The Fugitive Kind* (1959), the screen adaptation of *Orpheus Descending*, but Stapleton appeared in an underwritten supporting role as a sheriff's softhearted wife. She returned to Broadway as Carrie Berniers opposite Jason Robards in Lillian Hellman's *Toys in the Attic* (1960), winning yet another Tony nod, and accepted roles on such diverse New York City–based television series as *Naked City*, *East Side/West Side*, and *Car 54, Where Are You?* She also appeared in screen adaptations of Miller's *A View from the Bridge* (1962), playing a long-suffering wife, and the musical *Bye Bye Birdie* (1963), cast as a meddlesome mother.

Stapleton and Rayfiel wed in July 1963. However, Stapleton blamed herself for the failure of her first marriage and escaped into alcohol. Her drinking led first to hospitalization and then to voluntary confinement in a psychiatric facility. Meanwhile, Stapleton starred onstage as Amanda Wingfield, one of Williams's faded southern belles, in a revival of *The Glass Menagerie* (1965). Stapleton and Rayfiel divorced the following year. She never remarried but became involved in a series of ill-fated relationships. One was with the stage director George Abbott. It lasted a decade and began when he was eighty-one and she was forty-three.

Following her second divorce, Stapleton replayed Serafina in a stage revival of *The Rose Tattoo* (1966). For the next fifteen years she appeared in coveted roles in A-list plays, films, and television movies, and rarely did she give a less-than-stellar performance. Stapleton earned an Emmy playing a spinster in a television adaptation of Truman Capote's *Among the Paths to Eden* (1967). She returned to Broadway, displayed her flair for comedy playing three characters in Neil Simon's *Plaza Suite* (1968), and emerged with another Tony nomination. She copped an Oscar nod as the worried wife of a bomb smuggler in *Airport* (1970) and earned her second Tony playing an alcoholic singer in Simon's *The Gingerbread Lady* (1970).

Stapleton then replayed one of the characters she created onstage in the screen version of *Plaza Suite* (1971). She was cast as the drab Georgie Elgin in a Broadway revival of Clifford Odets's *The Country Girl* (1972), won an Emmy nomination as a widow starting life anew in the television movie *Queen of the Stardust Ballroom* (1975), replayed Wingfield in another Broadway revival of *The Glass Menagerie* (1975), played Big Mama opposite Laurence Olivier in a made-for-British-television version of Williams's *Cat on a Hot Tin Roof* (1976), earned another Emmy nomination as the estranged wife of a dying man in the TV movie *The Gathering* (1977), replaced Jessica Tandy on Broadway in D. L. Coburn's *The Gin Game* (1978), earned another Oscar nod playing a vivacious widow in Woody Allen's *Interiors* (1978), and won another Tony nomination as the genteel Birdie Hubbard in her final Broadway appearance, a revival of Hellman's *The Little Foxes* (1981).

Stapleton played the anarchist Emma Goldman in Warren Beatty's *Reds* (1981)—a performance that earned her a fourth Oscar nomination. This time she emerged victorious. At this juncture she began receiving lifetime achievement awards. In 1980 she was given the Actors Studio Award for her contributions to the theater. The following year she was inducted into the Theatre Hall of Fame, and Hudson Valley Community College, located in her hometown, named a 350-seat theater for her.

In the 1980s Stapleton joined Bette Davis, Angela Lansbury, and other luminaries in *Little Gloria... Happy at Last* (1982), a television miniseries. Stapleton accepted supporting roles in such prestigious Hollywood fare as *Johnny Dangerously* (1984), *Cocoon* (1985), *Heartburn* (1986), *Nuts* (1987), and *Cocoon: The Return* (1988) and in the independent features *Made in Heaven* (1987) and *Sweet Lorraine* (1987).

In the late 1980s Stapleton settled in Lenox, to be near her daughter and two grandchildren. She enjoyed a quiet country life and regularly lent her name to local charitable functions. Only rarely did she accept acting jobs. Stapleton earned three more Emmy nominations, for appearances in *Road to Avonlea* (1989), *B. L. Stryker* (1989), and *Miss Rose White* (1992). Easily her best late-career film was *The Last Good Time* (1994), in which she played a chatty widow. Her last screen roles were minor, from *Addicted to Love* (1997), a forgettable romantic comedy starring Meg Ryan and Matthew Broderick, to *Living and Dining* (2004), Stapleton's final credit, an obscure independent feature.

Stapleton died at age eighty in her Lenox home. She was a longtime smoker, and the cause of death was chronic obstructive pulmonary disease. She is buried in Saint Mary's Cemetery in Troy.

Throughout her life Stapleton suffered from demons that terrified her and drove her to alcoholism. Nevertheless, she was one of the finest and most respected actresses of her time, effortlessly moving from the Broadway stage to the Hollywood soundstage. She was a commanding presence and was much honored for her work. Her varied roles allowed her to elude her demons by escaping into the fantasy of make-believe—much to the delight of audiences.

★

Stapleton published an account of her life, *A Hell of a Life: An Autobiography* (1995), written with Jane Scovell. The only substantive Stapleton biography is Jeannie Marlin Woods, *Maureen Stapleton: A Bio-Bibliography* (1992). Obituaries are in the *New York Times*, *Albany Times Union* and *Washington Post* (all 14 Mar. 2006) and the *Guardian* (15 Mar. 2006).

Rob Edelman

STUDDS, Gerry Eastman (*b.* 12 May 1937 in Mineola, New York; *d.* 14 October 2006 in Boston, Massachusetts), twelve-term U.S. representative from Massachusetts; first openly gay member of Congress; chairman of the House Merchant Marine and Fisheries Committee.

Studds, son of Elbridge Gerry (pronounced Gary) Eastman Studds and Beatrice (Murphy) Studds, was born on Long

Gerry Studds, 1995. AP IMAGES

Island in Mineola, New York, but he spent his youth growing up in Cohasset, Massachusetts, along with his brother, Colin, and sister, Gaynor. His father's side of the family descended from Elbridge Gerry—a member of the Continental Congress, signer of the Declaration of Independence, governor of Massachusetts, and U.S. vice president. Studds's mother graduated from Miss Walker's School (Simsbury, Connecticut) and his father, a Yale-trained architect, had managed a Park Avenue firm that consulted in the development of what would become Franklin D. Roosevelt Drive along the East River in New York City. After the family relocated to Cohasset, Studds attended the local public schools and Derby Academy in Hingham, Massachusetts. He graduated in 1959 from Yale University with a BA in American studies. Studds earned an MAT in history from Yale two years later.

As a young man, Studds cut his political teeth during the John F. Kennedy administration. He joined the U.S. State Department as a foreign service officer from 1961 to 1963, eventually working as an executive assistant and congressional liaison for the Domestic Peace Corps Task Force. He subsequently joined the office of Senator Harrison Williams of New Jersey as a legislative assistant. He left Washington in 1965 to teach at Saint Paul's School in Concord, New Hampshire, but he remained politically active. In March 1968 Studds was a key strategist in Senator Eugene McCarthy's strong New Hampshire primary showing, developing an action plan that allowed the candidate to reach 75 percent of voters in a twelve-day swing through the state. "We had statistical information in our heads which we knew the administration forces never had," Studds recalled. McCarthy nearly won on his anti–Vietnam War platform, finishing a few percentage points behind President Lyndon Johnson and prompting Johnson's decision not to seek reelection.

In 1970 Studds made his first bid for elective office when he challenged the six-term Republican incumbent Hastings Keith in a Massachusetts district that swept along the south shore suburbs of Boston, and encompassed Martha's Vineyard and Nantucket, before curving northeastward up Cape Cod. The district, which included Studds's hometown of Cohasset, depended heavily on the commercial fishing industry and tourism. In the general election Studds pushed Keith to the limit, falling just 1,522 votes (about 1 percent of the vote) short of ousting the incumbent.

Reapportionment and redistricting in 1971 led the Democratic-controlled state legislature to carve several Republican strongholds out of the district. Keith chose to retire. Studds, who had never ceased to campaign after the 1970 election, made inroads by learning to speak Portuguese, the native language of many of the local fishermen. He ran against U.S. military intervention in Southeast Asia, and in the general election defeated William Weeks by a slim margin of 1,206 votes. Studds became the first Democrat to represent the district since 1915. He was subsequently reelected to eleven more consecutive terms, running without opposition in two elections and usually winning by solid majorities of between 61 and 75 percent.

When Studds was sworn into the House in January 1973, he received assignments on the Merchant Marine and Fisheries Committee and the Public Works Committee—two prime positions from which to tend to the economic and environmental details of his district. Representing a district uniquely dependent on commercial fishing, he remained on Merchant Marine and Fisheries until it was disbanded after Republicans seized control of the House in the 104th Congress (1995–1997). After the committee chairman died in 1992, Studds chaired the full panel for the final years of its existence. When many of its oversight duties were subsumed by the new Resources Committee, Studds joined that panel and served as the ranking member on the subcommittee, which encompassed some of his old committee's jurisdictions. Midway through the Ninety-fourth Congress (1975–1977), he left his Public Works assignment for a seat on the International Relations Committee (later renamed Foreign Affairs). In 1991 he left Foreign Affairs to serve on the influential Energy and Commerce Committee. Studds also served on the Outer

Continental Shelf Committee (an ad hoc panel that later became a select committee), and the Select Committee on Aging.

For two decades Studds had a large hand in congressional initiatives to husband maritime resources and improve coastal environments. Known for his acerbic wit, keen mind, and mastery of legislative detail, he kept a low profile and immersed himself in committee business. As chairman of the Fisheries, Wildlife Conservation, and Environment Subcommittee he played a leading role in passage of oil spill legislation in the wake of the 1989 *Exxon Valdez* disaster in Alaska. He also was a decisive player behind successful bills to expand U.S. territorial waters to a 200-mile limit, to prohibit oil drilling in the Georges Bank fishing grounds, and to extend the Marine Mammals Protection Act of 1972. Throughout, he remained a faithful defender of the watermen who populated the Massachusetts coastline, seeking to advance the economic interests of an industry damaged by overfishing—in one instance by initiating a boat buyback program to help cash-strapped watermen. Among one of his signal accomplishments was the Atlantic Striped Bass Conservation Act of 1984, which he authored. When enacted it helped restore one of the East Coast's most storied (and depleted) fisheries. One colleague recalled that Studds claimed "his pivotal role in the revival of the striped bass was not in legislating...but in his inability to catch any." As a show of respect for his collective work, Congress eventually renamed the Stellwagen Bank National Marine Sanctuary for him.

Studds's years of quiet, effective labor on maritime issues were overshadowed when he was implicated in a congressional sex scandal. On 18 July 1983, after a yearlong investigation, the House Committee on Standards of Official Conduct recommended that Studds, along with Representative Daniel Crane of Illinois, be reprimanded for engaging in "improper sexual conduct" with House pages (high school-age couriers). Crane had sex with a seventeen-year-old female page in 1980. During the course of the committee's investigation, a former male page testified that he had had a sexual relationship with Studds in 1973. The day the allegations became public, Studds spoke on the House floor. "It is not a simple task for any of us to meet adequately the obligations of either public office or private life, let alone both," Studds said. "But these challenges are made substantially more complex when one is, as I am, both an elected public official and gay." Studds admitted the relationship was "a very serious error in judgment on my part." He insisted, however, it "was mutual and voluntary; without coercion; without any preferential treatment, express or implied; without harassment of any kind," and failed to meet the committee's definition of improper sexual conduct. Some representatives insisted on expulsion, arguing that a reprimand—which was the least punitive form of punishment the committee could have imposed—

did not go far enough. Newt Gingrich of Georgia argued that the "moral authority" of the institution was in danger, and that his colleagues should "clean up the Capitol" by expelling both men. On 20 July the full House instead censured Studds by a vote of 420 to 3. Along with Crane, he became one of just twenty-two individuals in House history dating to 1789 to receive such a punishment. Studds stood in the well of the House as the Speaker read the censure condemning his behavior. Additionally, he lost his chairmanship of the Coast Guard and Navigation Subcommittee.

House censures often irreparably damaged their recipients' political careers. Undeterred, Studds held a series of unscripted, town-hall meetings in which he addressed constituents' concerns about the censure episode. He had the additional burden of running for reelection as the first openly gay candidate in congressional history. "My sexual preference," he asserted at the time, "has nothing to do with my ability to do this job well or to do it badly." He staved off two primary opponents in 1984, including the Plymouth County sheriff Peter Flynn, who accused Studds of "seducing a young child." Studds prevailed, winning majorities in all but four towns. In the general election, the Republican Lewis Crampton refused to attack Studds frontally on the censure issue, though he did remark it would undermine Studds's influence in the House. Burnishing his credentials as caretaker of the local fishing industry, Studds carried coastal precincts and won reelection with 56 percent of the vote. A respected political almanac summed up his postcensure career as "a how-to book on political survival." Of his five remaining elections, Studds won four with majorities of between 61 and 69 percent. He turned back a strong challenge in 1990 when the Republican Jon Bryan tapped into an anti-incumbent mood and cast himself as a "family values" conservative. Studds was held to just 53 percent of the vote, but he was reelected twice more even though the Republican-controlled state legislature removed his New Bedford base from the district.

After constituents returned him to the House, Studds worked assiduously to regain his influence. He reasserted himself on maritime issues, reclaiming the Coast Guard and Navigation Subcommittee chairmanship in 1985 and, two years later, winning the gavel of the Subcommittee on Fisheries, Oceans, and Wildlife. On issues related to gay rights, he followed the legislative style he had long before established—working tirelessly behind the scenes and avoiding the limelight. Nevertheless, Studds fought to expand funding for HIV/AIDS research, pushed President Bill Clinton to repeal the ban on gays in the military, and opposed the Defense of Marriage Act.

After declaring he would not seek reelection to Congress in 1995, Studds settled into quiet retirement in Boston with his longtime partner, Dean Hara. In 2004, shortly after Massachusetts legalized same-sex marriages, Studds and Hara wed. Studds collapsed while walking his dog on 3 October 2006 in Boston. Diagnosed with a vascular disease, he passed away on 14 October from a blood clot. Hundreds of friends and family attended a memorial service at the John F. Kennedy Library and Museum in early December 2006.

Studds's political career spanned a pivotal era when American society became incrementally more accepting of gays and lesbians. Respected for his work on maritime and environmental policy, this intensely private man became a reluctant trailblazer who, like earlier congressional pioneers, embodied a symbolic significance that transcended his legislative work. "It was very important to see, for young people in particular, somebody as capable and talented as he be openly gay," observed his Massachusetts colleague Barney Frank, who himself disclosed that he was gay several years after Studds. "That gave a lot of people the courage to say, 'I can survive this business being honest about who I am.'"

★

An oral history interview with Studds is part of the Oral History of Groton School Collection at the Groton School Library in Groton, Massachusetts. Charles Kaiser, *1968 in America* (1988), discusses Studds's role as a key McCarthy strategist in the New Hampshire primary. Obituaries are in the *Boston Globe* (14 Oct. 2006) and the *New York Times* and *Washington Post* (both 15 Oct. 2006).

Matthew A. Wasniewski

William Styron, 1985. AP IMAGES

STYRON, William Clark, Jr. (*b*. 11 June 1925 in Newport News, Virginia; *d*. 1 November 2006 in Oak Bluffs, Martha's Vineyard, Massachusetts), Pulitzer Prize–winning novelist, essayist, and major figure in the literary generation that came to prominence following World War II.

Styron was the only child of William Clark Styron, a marine engineer and low-level manager at the Newport News naval shipyard, and Pauline Margaret (Abraham) Styron, the daughter of a wealthy owner of a Pennsylvania coke and coal company. Styron's mother had studied voice in Vienna and prior to her marriage had taught music in the Pittsburgh public schools and in Pueblo, Colorado. Among Styron's lasting memories of her—she died of breast cancer when he was fourteen—was her singing operatic arias as she went about her household tasks, a memory that one day would save his life.

By his own account, Styron had a comfortable childhood in the middle-class world of Hilton Village on the James River just outside Newport News. The river, he wrote, "was the absolute and dominating physical presence" of his youth—not only as a playground (he learned to sail its waters) but as a visible reminder that a great part of his family's history—and America's—had taken place in Tidewater Virginia. Styrons had resided there and in North Carolina since the early 1700s, and as a boy Styron heard his grandmother tell stories of his grandfather's service in the Confederate army, the Union troops' destruction of her family's cotton plantation in 1862, and the loss of her family's slaves in 1865.

Styron attended the segregated Newport News public schools where he was a mediocre student, consistently undisciplined, unfocused, and lazy. In 1940 his father transferred him from Morrison High School to the private Christchurch School for boys in Christchurch, Virginia. He graduated in 1942 and, despite low passing grades, entered Davidson College in Davidson, North Carolina. Midway through freshman year, he enlisted in the Marine Corps Reserve, and following his eighteenth birthday in June 1943, he was assigned to the V-12 Program at Duke University—a wartime program offered on 131 campuses nationally that was designed to give potential officers in the navy and the Marine Corps four to seven semesters of college education.

As a V-12 student Styron was on active duty, in uniform, subject to military discipline, and required to spend nine and a half hours weekly in rigorous physical training that, in a year, added several pounds of muscle to his once skinny six-foot frame. Given the opportunity to select electives, Styron took a writing course with Professor William Blackburn, who drew from him his first solid academic work and in the postwar years played a significant role in directing his writing career. Styron left Duke in late October 1944 for boot camp at Parris Island, South Carolina, where he was quarantined for several weeks in a naval hospital after a doctor mistakenly diagnosed him as syphilitic when he was actually suffering from trench mouth. Years later Styron wrote a dark comedy about his hospital stay called *In the Clap Shack*, which premiered at the Yale Repertory Theatre in New Haven, Connecticut, on 15 December 1972.

Commissioned a second lieutenant in July 1945, Styron was on board a ship in the Pacific headed for the invasion of Japan when the war was ended by atom bombs. Discharged in December 1945, he returned to Duke (and Professor Blackburn) a serious student of literature and a voracious reader. Earning a BA in literature in 1947, he headed to New York to become a writer. With Blackburn's help, he found a job as a manuscript reader in the trade book division of McGraw-Hill, and with Blackburn's assistance, enrolled in Hiram Haydn's creative writing class at the New School for Social Research in lower Manhattan. Early in 1948, bored with his job and showing it, Styron was fired from McGraw-Hill. Now free to write full time—and receiving financial support from his father—he had two short stories published in *American Vanguard* (1948 and 1950). Haydn, the New York–based fiction editor for Bobbs-Merrill, told him the story form was too constricting for his talent and urged him to write a novel.

The result was *Lie Down in Darkness*, published in 1951 to mostly favorable reviews. Set in Tidewater Virginia, it is the harrowing account of a middle-class family torn apart by adultery, alcoholism, and insanity. The story—developed through a series of flashbacks—begins and ends with a suicide. Styron employs techniques that owe a considerable debt to the writers William Faulkner and James Joyce and to a lesser extent Ernest Hemingway and F. Scott Fitzgerald; but the voice throughout is clearly his own, as are the characters, many of them composites of people from his past. Several reviewers found the writing overblown and the plot too melodramatic, but generally the book was praised as a remarkable first novel, and several critics hailed the author as the new Faulkner.

In 1952 the American Academy in Rome gave Styron its coveted Rome Prize, which provided him with a year in Italy. Stopping in Paris on his way to Rome, he met George Plimpton and Peter Matthiessen and joined them in founding the *Paris Review*. He wrote the manifesto for the first edition (Spring 1953), setting forth the publication's intention to publish "the good writers and good poets" and to examine the myriad ways writers write. In Rome on 4 May 1953, Styron married Rose Burgunder, a poet and later a civil rights activist, whom he had met in her native Baltimore a year earlier. Together they had four children in a marriage that lasted until his death. On their return to America in 1954, they settled briefly in Manhattan but found the city too noisy and distracting, so in 1955 they purchased a farmhouse on twelve acres in rural Roxbury, Connecticut, within driving distance of New York.

Once settled in the country, Styron was guided by a motto from the French writer Gustave Flaubert inscribed on the wall of his writing studio: "Be regular and ordinary in your life like a bourgeois, so that you may be violent and original in your work." For most of his writing life he adhered to a schedule that had him sleeping until late morning or noon, lunching at one o'clock in the afternoon, walking for an hour with his dog (to "unlock the unconscious"), and listening for an hour or so to classical music in preparation for writing. He wrote undisturbed in "complete noiseless privacy" from four o'clock to eight o'clock, took dinner at nine o'clock, and spent the night into the early morning hours listening to music, reading, drinking, and talking with guests. He was in bed by dawn.

He wrote in longhand with a pencil on yellow legal pads. It was a slow process; on a good day he might produce as many as three pages. He was what the critic Malcolm Cowley called "a bleeder"—his output limited, Styron said, "by a neurotic need to perfect each paragraph." Claiming that "writing is hell," he nonetheless acknowledged he was "happiest . . . when I'm writing. [It is] the only time I feel completely self-possessed." In all, he produced five novels, one memoir, a single collection of short stories, and three collections of nonfiction essays that first appeared in such publications as the *American Scholar*, *Harper's* magazine, *Esquire*, the *New York Review of Books*, *Vanity Fair*, and the *New York Times Book Review*.

In 1956 Styron followed his first novel with the novella *The Long March*, a fictionalized account of two incidents at Parris Island in 1951 during the Korean War when the Marine Corps recalled Styron and other reserve officers to duty. While he awaited a medical discharge for poor eyesight, Styron learned of the accidental killing of several reservists by a stray shell during training and of a brutal forced march ordered by a sadistic colonel. Styron used the incidents to examine the moral universe of the military and its world of violence in a book reviewers praised for the clarity of its prose and its strongly limned characters.

Styron's third book, *Set This House on Fire* (1960), was greeted by a barrage of negative reviews in the United

States but favorable criticism in France, where it was a best seller. Set in Europe at the end of World War II, it is a sprawling novel as well as an angry indictment of American violence and materialism about three degenerate Americans living in Italy and the spiritual redemption of one of them following a rape and murder.

The Confessions of Nat Turner, the most celebrated and controversial of Styron's novels, was published in October 1967 to the acclaim of critics and readers alike. It tells the story of Nat Turner, the slave leader of the Southampton Insurrection of 1831 in which fifty-five white men, women, and children were massacred by seventy-five black slaves. Styron tells the story of the uprising from Nat's point of view in the first person, with long interior monologues in a dialect Styron himself constructed. He begins the book with the condemned man in prison awaiting execution, the event that brought him there revealed through a series of flashbacks. The novel is not so much a history as it is an extended meditation on the anguish and ambiguities of slavery, race, and violence in the American South. It is Styron's tour de force, and historians and critics everywhere praised the book as superb. It won the Pulitzer Prize for Fiction in 1968 and reached a broad audience.

It also produced a stinging rebuke from a number of black intellectuals (and some whites) who protested that Styron had stolen the African-American heritage, in the bargain demeaning Turner by means of cruel racial stereotyping. In *William Styron's Nat Turner: Ten Black Writers Respond* (1968) the writers condemned the book as hateful, error-filled, and simply another racist tract. Two black writers, John Hope Franklin, the historian of slavery, and James Baldwin, who had urged his friend Styron to write the book, came to his defense as did a number of prominent historians, including Eugene Genovese and C. Vann Woodward. Several of the collected essays in Styron's *This Quiet Dust* (1982), his first nonfiction book, are devoted to problems he faced before and after he chose to write about Turner. Other essays are devoted to Styron's political activism in the 1960s and beyond.

His fifth and final novel, *Sophie's Choice* (1979), is a story of the Holocaust, of a non-Jewish survivor of Auschwitz, a Polish Christian woman, who faces the loss of her two children in the death camp and undergoes a series of changes and humiliations both in the camp and in Brooklyn, where she lives in a Jewish boardinghouse. The woman is modeled after a displaced woman Styron met briefly in the apartment house where he lived when he first came to New York. As with Nat Turner, *Sophie's Choice* begins in the fictional present of 1947 after the events in the death camp occurred; the narrative then moves back and forth in time, gradually revealing the horror of the woman's past, a narrative device consistent with Styron's belief that the past is never dead but lives on to shape the present. As in his other novels, his subject is humanity's capacity for evil and violence linked to its search for redemption and survival. *Sophie's Choice* won the American Book Award and was made into a motion picture starring Meryl Streep in 1982.

As he turned sixty Styron developed clinical depression, the full extent of which became apparent in October 1985. He was in Paris to receive the French literary award, the Prix Mondial Cino Del Duca, and marred the ceremony and formal dinner with erratic behavior. Returning the next day to the United States, he descended into a months' long siege—in his words—of "dank joylessness," marked by relentless insomnia and bouts of paranoia. One evening in early 1986, as he was preparing to commit suicide, Styron turned on the television in time to hear a sudden soaring passage from the Brahms *Alto Rhapsody* that his mother had occasionally sung in his youth. It reduced him to tears and waking his wife, he begged to go to the hospital. Years later, in recovery, he wrote an essay for *Vanity Fair* (1989) describing in electrifying and powerful prose the course of his illness and the near miracle of his recovery. Expanded into a book, *Darkness Visible: A Memoir of Madness* (1990) was a critically acclaimed best seller.

Styron published two last books: an enlarged edition of *This Quiet Dust* (1993) and *A Tidewater Morning: Three Tales from Youth* (1993), a collection of three short stories from *Esquire* that center on autobiographical themes of loss, race, and memory. A nonfiction volume, *Havanas in Camelot: Personal Essays*, was assembled posthumously by Rose Styron and Styron's biographer James L. W. West III (2008).

Styron died of pneumonia in Martha's Vineyard Hospital. He is buried in West Chop Cemetery in Vineyard Haven, Massachusetts. A memorial service—"A Celebration of the Life of William Styron"—was held at Saint Bartholomew's Church in New York City on 2 February 2007. Among the speakers were family members and friends, including Senator Edward Kennedy and former President Bill Clinton. Robert Loomis, his longtime editor at Random House, summed up Styron's writing career by saying that his greatest achievement was his skill in creating human characters: "unique creations destined to live as long as books are available.... [It's] an accomplishment that happens all too rarely in this world."

★

The William Styron Papers are in the Rare Book, Manuscript and Special Collections Library, Duke University. An inventory of the collection's 22,500 items is online at http://library.duke.edu/digitalcollections/rbmscl/styron/inv/. The Manuscript Division of the Library of Congress holds the holograph manuscripts, typescripts, and galleys of four Styron novels. Part of his editorial correspondence is in the Random House Papers at Special

Collections, Butler Library, Columbia University. Styron, *This Quiet Dust* (1982, enlarged 1993) and *Havanas in Camelot* (2008) offer autobiographical essays. See also James L. W. West III, *William Styron: A Life* (1998). Among the numerous interviews with Styron are "An Interview with William Styron" by Victor Strandberg and Balkrishna Buwa in *Sewanee Review* 99, no. 3 (Summer 1991): 463–477; an interview with Peter Matthiessen and George Plimpton in *Writers at Work: The* Paris Review *Interviews*, Malcolm Cowley, ed. (1958); and *Conversations with William Styron*, James L. W. West III, ed. (1985). Reviews and assessments of Styron's work are in *The Critical Response to William Styron*, Daniel W. Ross, ed. (1995) and *Critical Essays on William Styron*, Arthur D. Casiato and James L. W. West III, eds. (1982). Obituaries are in the *New York Times* (2 Nov. 2006) and *Vineyard Gazette* (3 Nov. 2006).

Allan L. Damon

T

TEMPLETON, John Marks (*b.* 29 November 1912 in Winchester, Tennessee; *d.* 8 July 2008 in Nassau, Bahamas), investment guru and pioneer in both financial investments and philanthropy.

Templeton was the son of Harvey Maxwell Templeton, a committed Presbyterian and the town lawyer who also sold real estate, and Vella (Handly) Templeton. Precocious as a high school student, he taught himself and then his classmates the fourth-year math that Yale University required and that his school, Central High School, was unable to provide. Templeton gained admission to Yale, but because of financial difficulties due to the Depression, after a year he could no longer pay the fees. Nevertheless, he stayed, working his way through, partly with his poker winnings, graduating with an AB in 1934. He received a Rhodes Scholarship to Balliol College, Oxford, and graduated in 1936 with an MA in law.

After completing his time at Oxford, Templeton spent several months traveling the world with a friend before moving to New York in 1937 to work as an investment adviser. He recalled, "I couldn't find any counselors who specialized in helping people invest outside America. So I saw a wide-open opportunity." On 7 April 1937 Templeton married Judith Dudley Folk; they had three children. Folk died in 1951, and Templeton married a second time, on 31 December 1958, to Irene Reynolds Butler; Butler died in 1993.

Templeton's first major success was to borrow $10,000 when the German army invaded Poland in 1939 and to invest $100 in each of the 100 stocks on the New York Stock Exchange valued at under $1 a share. All but four made a profit. Templeton counted on war driving up

profits. In 1940 he opened his own fund management company, Templeton, Dobbrow & Vance, Inc.

Templeton was very successful during those early years and in 1954 started the Templeton Growth Fund. Thousands of investors entrusted their money to him, and it is estimated that $10,000 invested at that time would have been worth $7 million by 1992. The growth funds were sold in 1992 to Franklin Resources. Templeton continued to invest for himself and a few others. His insightfulness was put to the test when he liquidated technology stocks. His gamble paid off when the dot-com bubble burst.

From this success many corporations, funds, and foundations were cultivated. Templeton held the position of director, president, or chairman of many of these. They included Templeton Growth Fund Canada (1954–1985), Templeton Damroth Corporation (1959–1962), First Trust Bank Ltd. in the Bahamas (1963), Templeton Funds, Inc. (1977–1986), Templeton Global Funds, Inc. (1981–1986), and Templeton Galbraith & Hansberger Ltd. (1986–1992).

Templeton was a man who had a "following." Fund meetings in Toronto were very popular. These meetings, as did all of Templeton's business meetings, started with a prayer. It was, he said, not a plea for success but a way of calming the mind. He reasoned, "If you begin with prayer, you will think more clearly and make fewer mistakes."

In 1968 Templeton moved to Lyford Cay, Nassau, renouncing his American citizenship and taking British citizenship. This decision had tax advantages, but taxes were not his primary motive for the move. He argued that he was able to make better investment decisions away from the pressures of Wall Street. He lived a relatively modest life in a large house close to the sea, driving old cars and communicating with his office primarily by fax,

John M. Templeton. LYNN PELHAM/TIME LIFE PICTURES/GETTY IMAGES

thus showing two of the most important recurrent themes of his life: modesty and humility.

In 1972 Templeton established the Templeton Prize for Progress in Religion. The annual Templeton Prize grew out of his belief that an honor equivalent to a Nobel Prize should be bestowed on living innovators in spiritual action and thought. Mother Teresa of Calcutta was the first recipient in 1973, followed later that decade by the evangelist Billy Graham and the writer Aleksandr Solzhenitsyn. Other prize winners include Pandurang Shastri Athavale, William "Bill" Bright, Paul Davies, George Ellis, Charles Townes, John Barrow, Nikkyo Niwano, Michael Heller, and Bernard d'Espagnat. Representatives of all of the world's major religions have been on the panel throughout the prize's history, and recipients have included Christians, Jews, Muslims, Buddhists, and Hindus.

The John Marks Templeton Foundation was established in 1987, continuing the work and ideals of the Templeton Prize as well as other important philanthropic work. The mission of the foundation is to encourage exploration into the laws of nature and the universe, and "the nature of love, gratitude, forgiveness and creativity." Critics argued, however, that Templeton's grants for research to discover "spiritual realities" sought to manipulate science to foster religion.

Templeton's awards and honors were numerous. For his work in Great Britain, he was decorated Knight Order of the British Empire, Knight of Saint John by Queen Elizabeth II (1987). Other significant awards include International Churchman of Year (1981), a Centennial Medal from the New York Mayflower Society (1987), a National Business Hall of Fame Award (1996), an Interfaith Gold Medallion from the International Council of Christians and Jews (1997), and an Abraham Lincoln Award (1997).

Templeton's involvement in social, civic, and academic organizations demonstrated his drive and dedication to his personal philosophy. He was a trustee of Englewood Hospital (1953–1956), chairman of the board of trustees of Princeton Theological Seminary (1967–1973 and 1979–1985), a trustee for the restoration of Westminster Abbey (1991–2008), a member of the Board of Visitors of the Harvard Divinity School (1981–1988), and a member of the advisory board for the Harvard Center for the Study of World Religions (1975–1989). He was also an active member of numerous clubs and societies.

Templeton wrote, coauthored, or edited nearly thirty books on investing, philosophy, religion, and science. Notable titles include *The Humble Approach* (1981), *Global Investing* (1988), *Riches for the Mind and Spirit* (1990), *Agape Love: A Tradition Found in Eight World Religions* (1999), *Simple Asset Allocation Strategies* (2000), and *Wisdom from World Religions* (2002). Templeton died of pneumonia at Doctors Hospital. He is buried at Lakeview Memorial Gardens and Mausoleums in Nassau.

Templeton was "arguably the greatest global stock-picker of the century." His investment philosophy was that "bull markets are born on pessimism, grown on skepticism, mature on optimism and die on euphoria. The time of maximum pessimism is the best time to buy." He is remembered for his financial successes and his philanthropic efforts, as well as for funding research into the connection between science and religion.

★

For additional information about Templeton's life, see Robert L. Herrmann, *Sir John Templeton: Supporting Scientific Research for Spiritual Discoveries*, rev. ed. (2004). Obituaries are in the *Daily Telegraph*, *South Florida Sun-Sentinel*, and *New York Times* (all 9 July 2008).

Joan Goodbody

TERKEL, Louis ("Studs") (*b.* 16 May 1912 in New York City; *d.* 31 October 2008 in Chicago, Illinois), Pulitzer Prize winner for nonfiction, radio broadcaster, storyteller, actor, political activist, and oral historian of American life.

Terkel was the son of Russian Jewish immigrants, Samuel, a tailor, and Anna (Finkel) Terkel, a seamstress and hotel manager. In 1920 the Terkel family moved to Chicago, where they soon purchased the Wells-Grand Hotel on the North Side. Terkel's father was in poor health, and so the task of running the family business fell to his mother. With the coming of the Great Depression, jobless guests often had little to do but sit in the lobby trading stories and telling tall tales as the young Terkel listened. He also was a habitué of "Bughouse Square" (Chicago's Washington Square Park), a place where the soapbox orators gathered to speak their minds.

In 1928 Terkel graduated from McKinley High School. He enrolled in the University of Chicago, earning a BA in 1932 and a law degree from its law school two years later. Instead of taking up a law practice, however, he worked for the Federal Emergency Rehabilitation Administration and then moved on to the Works Project Administration's Federal Writer's Project, composing radio scripts, announcing

Louis (Studs) Terkel. © BETTMANN/CORBIS

news and sports, and occasionally acting. Soon he adopted the name "Studs" after James T. Farrell's *Studs Lonigan* character in his novelistic trilogy of Irish life in Chicago. On 2 July 1939 Terkel married Ida Goldberg. The couple would go on to have a son.

During World War II, Terkel served for a year in the U.S. Air Force (1942–1943) before receiving a medical discharge for perforated eardrums. Soon after, in 1944, he hosted his own radio show, the *Wax Museum*, where he played various kinds of music, ranging from jazz, gospel, and blues to folk and opera. In 1949 he landed a television program, *Studs' Place*. Set in a fictional tavern, the weekly comedy began as a local broadcast but then was picked up by the National Broadcasting Company (NBC) before being canceled following its second season. Working initially one day a week without pay for Chicago's WFMT radio station and afternoons as a disc jockey for another radio station, Terkel also acted in radio shows and performed in plays such as Clifford Odets's *Waiting for Lefty* and *Detective Story*. In 1952, on WFMT, he produced *Studs Terkel's Almanac* and later *The Studs Terkel Show*, which eventually became the prize-winning *The Studs Terkel Program*. The show ran during the zenith of Senator Joseph McCarthy's anticommunist witch hunts. Terkel was accused of harboring left-wing sympathies, the show was canceled, and Terkel blacklisted. To these charges, he pleaded guilty. He also refused to "name names" of the other leftists he had known.

Remaining true to his leftist sympathies, in 1984, thirty years after the McCarthy era, Terkel narrated *The Good Fight*, about Americans who volunteered for combat with the Abraham Lincoln Brigade for the Loyalist government during the Spanish civil war (1936–1939). In 1956, after being blacklisted, Terkel, a dedicated jazz lover, wrote his first book, *Giants of Jazz*.

On the *Studs Terkel Show*, he interviewed an incredibly diverse group of people, from the famous to the unknown. When asked the secret of his questioning technique he answered, "to make people feel needed. . . . It isn't an inquisition. It's . . . an exploration into the past. So . . . the gentlest question . . . is, 'And what happened then?'" Much of Terkel's work was based on his desire to encourage Americans never to forget their personal and historical pasts. Too many of us, he remarked in the documentary film *Anthem: An American Road Story* (1997), have "no yesterday, no memory." The writer Garry Wills, a frequent guest on Terkel's show, called him "the best prepared interviewer I have ever met."

Terkel always credited the editor and publisher André Schiffren, then at Pantheon Books and later at his new publishing house, the New Press, with first urging him to work on oral histories. Schiffren suggested Terkel look about Chicago and talk with a wide variety of its residents, the famous and not-so-famous. The result was his first oral history, *Division Street: America* (1967). Approximately seventy people were interviewed: housewives, renters, landlords, and people living in public housing projects, old-timers and newcomers. One of them, a thirty-four-year-old woman had abandoned a small town in Pike County, Kentucky, with her sick husband and six children and moved to Chicago in search of a better life. "Nothin's there now," she said of her former home. "The mines are all worked out."

Terkel's *Hard Times: An Oral History of the Great Depression* (1970) is fueled by those who suffered and those who managed to escape the era's misery. Replete with life stories often overlooked by historians, it is a dramatic retelling of that desperate period. One woman recalled home evictions, a former six-day bicycle rider remembered the gangsters and bootleggers who came to the bike events until the collapse of the stock market when "the bike game went out of business," and a Republican congressman explained why he opposed Franklin D. Roosevelt and the New Deal. Terkel much regretted the loss of historical knowledge. "Ours, the richest country in the world, may be the poorest in memory," he wrote. "Perhaps the remembrances of survivors of a time past may serve as a reminder to others. Or to themselves."

His *Working: People Talk About What They Do All Day and How They Feel About What They Do* (1972) dealt with work, "[which] is by its very nature, about violence—to the spirit as well as the body." Accidents, illnesses, fights, nervous breakdowns, and daily embarrassments: "To survive the day is triumph enough for the walking wounded among the great many of us." His interviewees were farm laborers, strip miners, receptionists, models, prostitutes, actors, sanitation workers, washroom attendants, doormen, police officers, taxi drivers, athletes, steel workers, and many more among the voiceless and anonymous.

Terkel continued to appear in motion pictures. He commented briefly in the documentary *Sacco and Vanzetti* (2007), the story of two Italian-born anarchists who were convicted and executed for murder in 1927. Perhaps his most memorable film appearance was in John Sayles's *Eight Men Out* (1988), about the 1919 Black Sox scandal.

For his *"The Good War": An Oral History of World War II* (1984), Terkel was awarded a Pulitzer Prize for Nonfiction in 1985. He deliberately placed quotation marks around "The Good War" because, he wrote, "the adjective 'good' mated to the noun 'war' is so incongruous." In the book, war veterans recall their experiences. Eugene B. Sledge, a former marine, said, "There was nothing macho about the war at all. We were a bunch of scared kids who had to do a job." U.S. Rear Admiral Gene LaRocque, veteran of World War II and Vietnam, believed that "World War Two has warped our view of . . . things. . . . The twisted memory of it encourages . . . my generation to be willing, almost eager, to use military force anywhere." A retired postal worker and former marine

recalled a day in September 1945, following the atomic bombing of Nagasaki, Japan, when he and his buddies went into that devastated city. Looking back, he told Terkel, "We didn't drop those two [atomic bombs] on military installations. We dropped them, on women and children." In Moscow, Terkel met Grigori Baklanov, a veteran turned novelist, who told him he was "the only one from our class of all the boys who went to the front who remained alive after that war. What else is there to say?"

Terkel also received the National Medal of Humanities in 1997 and the Presidential National Humanities Medal in 1999. He died at home with his son at his side. His body was cremated.

★

Terkel's recordings and personal papers are housed in the Chicago History Museum, where he had been named the first distinguished scholar-in-residence. Obituaries are in the *Chicago Tribune* and *New York Times* (both 31 Oct. 2008).

Murray Polner

THARP, Marie (*b.* 30 July 1920 in Ypsilanti, Michigan; *d.* 23 August 2006 in Nyack, New York), geologist and oceanographic cartographer whose charting of the world ocean floor contributed to the understanding of continental drift and plate tectonics.

Tharp was the daughter of William Edgar Tharp, a surveyor for the U.S. Department of Agriculture, and Bertha Louise (Newton) Tharp, a language teacher. During her early years the family moved frequently, as her father's job preparing soil-classification maps took him around the country. By her estimation she attended two dozen public schools before entering Ohio University, where she changed majors frequently, graduating with a BA in English and music and four minors in 1943. As a woman, Tharp's career options at the time were limited, but her father had encouraged her throughout her early years to find her "life's work." During World War II, with many young men in military service overseas, the University of Michigan recruited women for its master's program in geology, linking a graduate degree with the promise of a job in the petroleum industry. Tharp received an MS from Michigan in 1944 and went to work for Stanolind Oil & Gas in Tulsa, Oklahoma. Because fieldwork was restricted to men, Tharp was assigned the task of preparing maps and reports using geological data. She attended night school at the University of Tulsa and received a second bachelor's degree, in mathematics, in 1948.

That year she set out for New York City in the hope of finding more challenging work. She went first to the

Museum of Natural History but was dissuaded from pursuing a career there after speaking with a paleontologist engaged in the time-consuming endeavor of fossil research. She next tried Columbia University, where her drafting experience was of interest to the geologist Maurice Ewing, whose focus on oceanographic research was based on the conviction that an understanding of Earth required an understanding of the 70 percent of it covered by water. Ewing hired her as a research assistant, and in 1949, when he became the founding director of Columbia's Lamont Geological Observatory (now the Lamont-Doherty Earth Observatory), Tharp continued on as part of his team at the observatory in Palisades, New York. By 1952, promoted to research geologist, Tharp was working closely with the geologist Bruce C. Heezen, who had entered Columbia as a graduate student of Ewing's. For the next twenty-five years the pair undertook the unprecedented endeavor of mapping the world's seafloor.

When Tharp and Heezen began their collaboration, little was known about the geology, topography, and evolution of the ocean floor. Navigators throughout the centuries had relied on rudimentary techniques such as the lead line to measure discrete depths, but it was only with the advent of remote-sensing technology in the early twentieth century that a continuous depth profile of the seafloor could be produced. Echo sounders measured the time it took for a sound wave to make the circuit from ship to ocean bottom and back again, making it possible to record differences in bottom relief along a ship's track.

These soundings, gathered by Heezen during oceanographic fieldwork and collected by institutions including the U.S. Navy, were Tharp's raw material. Because contour maps were classified by the navy until 1962, Tharp and Heezen set about creating a physiographic display of the Atlantic basin. The science writer John Noble Wilford describes this technique as rendering "a landscape as it might be sketched in perspective by an observer from a great height, but rendered more maplike with the addition of coordinates and scale." Tharp meticulously plotted the echo-sounder readouts, proceeding by degrees of latitude and longitude across the ocean floor. She used the available data to present the basin's topographical forms, seamounts, valleys, and ranges stretching thousands of miles in a map of the North Atlantic basin, published in 1957 as a supplement to Bell Telephone System's *Technical Journal* and reprinted in 1959 by the Geological Society of America. The map both opened up a new frontier and sparked a challenge to the prevailing scientific view that Earth's surface was largely fixed. Tharp had diagrammed a rift valley running between the Atlantic's most notable known feature, the Mid-Atlantic Ridge, a finding that lent support to the theory of continental drift.

Tharp and Heezen went on to produce maps of the South Atlantic (1961), the Indian Ocean (1964 and 1967), the Pacific (1968), and the Arctic (1975), published by the Geological Society of America and the National Geographic Society, culminating in the creation of the World Ocean Floor panorama, released in 1977 by the U.S. Navy Office of Naval Research. The product of some 5 million miles of ocean soundings and a vast accumulation of geophysical data, the World Ocean Floor map was both a work of art (it was painted by the landscape artist Heinrich Berann) and science. It shows a line of mountains, continuous with the Mid-Atlantic Ridge, complete with rift valley, running through all the oceans. This Mid-Ocean Ridge girds the globe; seismographical data showed that the ridge coincided with earthquakes, a finding that was crucial to the development of the theory of plate tectonics. Tharp and Heezen were honored with the National Geographic Society Hubbard Award for their achievement in 1978.

Tharp's collaboration with Heezen extended to their personal lives; they entertained as a couple in Tharp's riverfront home in South Nyack, New York, on the Hudson, and a *New York Times* tribute remarked that upon Heezen's death in 1977 she was a "widow in all but name." Associates described their partnership as platonic, a relationship in which two intellectuals shared wide-ranging interests and sometimes achieved consensus through heated argument.

Women were barred from sailing on the Lamont Observatory's research vessel until the mid-1960s, but thereafter Tharp joined excursion teams on oceanographic research trips as far afield as Africa and Australia. Tharp retired from Lamont-Doherty in 1983, and in her later years operated a map-distribution business in South Nyack and was a consultant to oceanographers. She kept Heezen's papers and worked with the Library of Congress in cataloging the Tharp-Heezen Collection, which contains more than 23,000 pieces and spans four decades. She received the Women Pioneers in Oceanography Award from the Woods Hole Oceanographic Institution in 1999 and the first Lamont-Doherty Earth Observatory Heritage Award in 2001. Tharp died of cancer, at the age of eighty-six, at Nyack Hospital. Her body was donated to science at her request.

Although her career was launched at a time when many doors were closed to women in professional life, Tharp will be remembered for her work in opening up a vast new landscape: the ocean floor. "I worked in the background for most of my career as a scientist," she said in 1986, "but I have absolutely no resentments." Indeed, her pioneering maps put her at the forefront of scientists who have furthered an understanding of Earth's formation and evolution. Referring to the discovery of the 40,000-mile Mid-Ocean Ridge, considered her most notable contribution, she commented: "You can't find anything bigger than that, at least not on this planet."

★

Tharp's recollections of her cartographic career are in Tharp and Henry Frankel, "Mappers of the Deep: How Two

Geologists Plotted the Mid-Atlantic Ridge and Made a Discovery that Revolutionized the Earth Sciences," *Natural History* (Oct. 1986). For the historical context of her achievement see John Noble Wilford, *The Mapmakers* (2000), chapter 19. A tribute, "The Contrary Map Maker," by Stephen S. Hall, is in the *New York Times Magazine* (31 Dec. 2006). Obituaries are in the *New York Times* (26 Aug. 2006) and *Los Angeles Times* (4 Sept. 2006).

Melissa A. Dobson

THERING, Rose Elizabeth (*b.* 9 August 1920 in Plain, Wisconsin; *d.* 6 May 2006 in Racine, Wisconsin), scholar, teacher, and activist Sister of Saint Dominic who cofounded the National Christian Leadership Conference for Israel and whose early research influenced the Second Vatican Council's 1965 official statement that the Jews were not responsible for the killing of Christ.

Thering was the sixth of eleven children born to Albert Thering, a dairy farmer, and Elizabeth (Lins) Thering, a homemaker, both German-American Roman Catholics. She attended Catholic schools until 1936, when she entered the convent in Racine's Saint Catherine of Siena Center to train to become one of the Sisters of Saint Dominic. As an adult she decided to pursue her education, receiving a bachelor's degree in 1953 from the Dominican College of Racine and a master's degree in 1957 from the College of Saint Thomas in Saint Paul, Minnesota. Thering then began working toward a doctorate. During these years she also taught in Catholic elementary and high schools.

Thering's doctoral research focused on the way in which Catholic textbooks portrayed other faith communities. To her dismay, she discovered that the textbooks were rife with hostility toward Jews, including accusations that Jews bore collective guilt for the death of Jesus and thus were accursed and rejected by God. These texts framed the centuries-long persecution of Jews as God's punishment for their participation in the death of Christ. In 1961 Thering earned her PhD from St. Louis University in St. Louis. Her research inspired her lifelong dedication to championing the fight against anti-Semitism by challenging Christian prejudices against Jews and Judaism.

Thering's research played an important part in the Second Vatican Council (1962–1965), often referred to as Vatican II. Relying in part on her work, the American Jewish Committee requested that the Roman Catholic Church issue an authoritative statement against the religious roots of anti-Semitism. Augustin Cardinal Bea consulted her dissertation when drafting portions of the

Nostra Aetate, the document released on 28 October 1965 that formally stated that Jews should not be presented as rejected or accursed by God as this was not a teaching present in the Holy Scriptures. Thus through Vatican II one long-term result of her work was the removal of negative teachings about Jews from Catholic school textbooks. As Thering later observed about the document's statement on Jews, "They were fifteen lines in Latin, but they changed everything."

In 1968 Thering joined the Menorah Studies Program, an outreach program of the newly established Institute of Judaeo-Christian Studies at Seton Hall University in South Orange, New Jersey, which was under the directorship of Monsignor John M. Oesterreicher. The institute was dedicated to promoting the education of a generation of Catholic students, teachers, and clergy that would be free from religious anti-Semitism by raising awareness that the tradition of the Catholic faith had its roots in Judaism. In 1970, together with Rabbi Marc H. Tanenbaum, Thering hosted a conference at Seton Hall University to explore whether the teachings of *Nostra Aetate* had been implemented in Catholic high schools and colleges. In 1972 she planned and directed the first Menorah Institute to Israel, sponsored by the Institute of Judaeo-Christian Studies. This was the first of more than fifty trips she made to Israel.

In 1973 Thering joined the faculty at Seton Hall University as a professor of education specializing in Jewish-Christian studies. In 1974 she presented a menorah to Pope Paul VI. In 1978, along with the Reverend Doctors Franklin Littell, David Lewis, Arnold Olson, and Bill Harter, she cofounded the National Christian Leadership Conference for Israel (NCLCI). She traveled to Poland in 1982 to visit the Nazi death camps. That same year Governor Thomas Kean appointed her to the New Jersey Holocaust Education Commission. She helped to pass a bill making Holocaust education mandatory in New Jersey elementary and high schools. In 1986 she traveled to Austria to protest the inauguration of President Kurt Waldheim because of his Nazi affiliations during World War II. A year later she traveled to the Soviet Union to protest the government's treatment of Russian Jews.

Thering became professor emerita of Jewish-Christian Studies at Seton Hall University in 1988. Five years later the university established the Sister Rose Thering Endowment for Jewish Studies to foster understanding between Christians and Jews through education and cooperation. In 1986 Thering became the executive director of NCLCI, retiring from that position in 1995 but remaining as vice president of its board of directors until she died. In 1992 she became a member of the Advisory Council of the Tanenbaum Center for Interreligious Understanding.

In 2001 Thering received an award from the International Liaison Committee of the Holy See's Commission on Relations with Jews and the International Jewish Committee for Interreligious Consultations. In 2004 she received both the American Jewish Committee's Jan Karski Moral Courage Award and the Anti-Defamation League's Cardinal Bea Interfaith Award, and she was honored the following year by the International Raoul Wallenberg Foundation. Her work in forging positive Jewish-Catholic relations was the subject of a thirty-nine-minute documentary, *Sister Rose's Passion*, which won the 2004 Tribeca Film Festival award for best documentary short and was nominated for the 2005 Academy Award in the same category.

Thering retired from Seton Hall University in 2005 and moved back to Racine. She died of renal failure at the age of eighty-five at the Saint Catherine of Siena Center of the Sisters of Saint Dominic. She is buried at the Dominican order's cemetery in Racine.

Thering dedicated her life to fighting religious anti-Semitism. As a pioneer in Catholic-Jewish relations, she transformed the way in which the Jews were characterized in Roman Catholic textbooks. Her research influenced the Second Vatican Council's *Nostra Aetate*, the document that formally declared that the Jews were not responsible for the death of Jesus—a declaration that had worldwide repercussions. As an educator she was instrumental in training generations of post–Vatican II Catholics to view Judaism as the root of their religious tradition. Symbolizing her dedication to this goal, around her neck she wore a Star of David fused with a cross.

★

Judith Banki, "Pivotal Figure: The Woman Behind 'Nostra Aetate,'" *Commonweal* 133, no. 12 (16 June 2006): 11–12, offers a personal recollection of Thering by a colleague. *Sister Rose's Passion* (2004), directed by Oren Jacoby, is a vital source of information about Thering and her work. Obituaries are in the *New York Times* (8 May 2006) and *National Catholic Reporter* (19 May 2006).

Caroline Fuchs

THOMAS, Craig Lyle (*b.* 17 February 1933 in Cody, Wyoming; *d.* 4 June 2007 in Bethesda, Maryland), rancher, power company executive, state representative, U.S. congressman, and U.S. senator, who became a spokesman for the rural West and a respected conservative advocate for preserving national parks and managing public lands.

Born in Wyoming and raised on a ranch near Cody, Thomas was the son of Craig E. and Marge Thomas, both teachers, and had one sister. In the summer the Thomas

Craig L. Thomas. AP IMAGES

family operated a small dude ranch near Yellowstone National Park. Thomas often credited those summers with establishing his love of natural spaces and his dedication to America's national park system. He attended the rural public schools in the Wapiti Valley of Wyoming and graduated from Cody High School in 1951. He studied agriculture and animal husbandry at the University of Wyoming, earning a bachelor's degree in 1955 and received an LLB from La Salle Extension University, a correspondence school, in 1968. Following graduation from college, Thomas served in the U.S. Marine Corps from 1955 to 1959; he was stationed in Japan and attained the rank of captain.

Thomas settled in Casper after completing military service. He invested in local real estate, purchasing a small hotel in Torrington, Wyoming, which prompted his interest in the state's tourist industry. In 1966 he joined the Wyoming Farm Bureau in Laramie as a claims adjuster, rising to the level of executive vice president and serving until 1975. That year he became the natural resources director for the American Farm Bureau in Washington, D.C., and later served as general manager of the Wyoming Rural Electric Association in Casper. In 1975 he met Susan Roberts, a high school teacher of children with special needs. They married and had three sons and one daughter.

In the 1970s Thomas turned his attention to political office. He ran unsuccessfully for state treasurer in 1978 and failed again to gain that office in 1982. He won a seat in the Wyoming state legislature, representing Natrona County, in 1984. Five years later he saw an opportunity for election to the U.S. Congress when Wyoming's at-large representative in the U.S. House of Representatives, Dick Cheney, was appointed secretary of defense by President George H. W. Bush. The National Republican Congressional Committee placed a high priority on keeping the seat under Republican control in the wake of several high-profile election losses and offered funding and organizational support to Thomas throughout his campaign to win the special election on 26 April 1989. He campaigned successfully on a theme of "continuity of conservative leadership" to "provide the kind of environment where business will prosper." Thomas ran against the Democrat John P. Vinich and two third-party candidates and won the election by a nearly ten-point margin, 52.5 percent to 42.9 percent. The campaign to replace Cheney exhibited in Thomas a tenacity and independence that became a trademark during his career. He was reelected in 1990 with 55 percent of the vote, and again in 1992 with 57 percent of the votes cast. In the House of Representatives Thomas served on the Committees on Government Operations; Interior and Insular Affairs; and Banking, Finance, and Urban Affairs.

In 1994 the three-term Wyoming senator Malcolm Wallop announced his retirement, and Thomas chose to run for Wallop's Senate seat. Facing the popular two-term Democratic governor Mike Sullivan in the election, Thomas campaigned across sparsely populated Wyoming with a message of smaller government and less regulation and support for a balanced-budget amendment and for a line-item veto for the president. During the 1994 campaign, many Republican candidates for the House of Representatives signed a "Contract with America," a campaign pledge to pursue a reform agenda in a Republican-controlled Congress that included such measures as the balanced-budget amendment, anticrime legislation, reduced federal regulation, and strengthened national security. Although Thomas did not agree with all elements of the contract, he, along with other Republican candidates for the Senate, took advantage of public disapproval with policies of the administration of President Bill Clinton and the popular appeal of the Contract with America to win the 1994 election. Thomas began his Senate career by supporting a cut in taxes for the middle class, health-care reform, and an overhaul of the Medicare system, all aspects of the Contract with America, but he quickly took up issues that were of vital importance to Wyoming. He noted that public lands policy, for example, would be among his top priorities. Representing a state where more than 48 percent of the land is owned by the federal government presents special challenges. Thomas told his constituents that he would be watching Secretary of the Interior Bruce Babbitt "like

a hawk," indicating that he would protect public access to government-owned land.

In the Senate, Thomas served on the Committees on Finance and Foreign Relations and the Select Committee on Ethics, but his most dedicated service came on committees of special importance to his Wyoming constituents. These included the Committees on Energy and Natural Resources, Environment and Public Works, Indian Affairs, and Agriculture, where he established a legislative record in areas such as public land management, agricultural policy, and rural health care. Perhaps his most important committee assignment was service on the Subcommittee on Parks, Historic Preservation, and Recreation, a subcommittee of Energy and Natural Resources. He remained on the subcommittee throughout his Senate career, serving as chairman twice, from 1997 to 2001 and again from 2003 to 2007. From this position, Thomas worked diligently on policy governing the protection and management of national parks. In 1997 he began a series of hearings to explore the broad range of challenges facing the National Park Service. Such efforts culminated in his proposal of "Vision 2020: The National Parks Restoration Act," which became known as the National Parks Omnibus Management Act, signed into law in 1998 (PL 105-391). This legislation established new criteria for management of park land, resources, and concessions and included a controversial plan to promote private-sector funding of park maintenance and restoration. In 1998 he was honored by the National Parks Conservation Association, receiving the William Penn Mott, Jr., Park Leadership Award for his service in improving accountability and promoting scientific research throughout the park system. In 2003, following several catastrophic wildfires in western states, Thomas successfully sponsored legislation for forest management and restoration of the fire-ravaged area to healthy conditions.

Thomas was often unpopular with environmentalists, however, and his efforts to open the Arctic National Wildlife Refuge in Alaska to energy exploration and to revise the Endangered Species Act, making it more difficult to add an animal to the protected list, often brought criticism from activists who supported his efforts to protect the national parks. He favored land use and management, reflecting the majority opinion of his Wyoming constituents who wanted to maintain access to the state's vast holding of government-owned land. Throughout his public career, Thomas sought a balance between those who favored access and those who sought protection, between those who favored development and those who wanted to maintain a pristine environment. Wyoming is home to the nation's first national park, the first national forest, and the first national monument, he often said, but it is also home to some of the largest reserves of coal, oil, and natural gas. He spoke frequently of the need to find a workable compromise. He wrote in 2001, "we can achieve a balance between our environmental goals and provide a level of public land access that many of us desire." Among his last legislative efforts were the Grand Teton Land Expansion Act of 2007, which added nearly fifty acres to the park (S. 277, 1/12/2007), establishment of the National Day of the American Cowboy (S. Res. 130, 3/28/2007), and the Snake Headwaters Legacy Act of 2007, a bill to designate as "wild and scenic" more than 400 miles of rivers and streams in northwest Wyoming (S. 1281, 5/3/2007).

On 5 November 2006, on the final day of campaigning for reelection, Thomas fell ill during church services in Casper and was hospitalized with pneumonia. Canceling campaign activities, he flew back to Washington that evening and entered the National Naval Medical Center in Bethesda, Maryland, where he was diagnosed with acute myeloid leukemia and began chemotherapy treatments. In his typical upbeat fashion, Thomas issued a statement: "I certainly didn't expect this diagnosis, but I will be back by the January session ready for full service in the new Congress." While hospitalized, Thomas monitored the election as Wyoming voters reelected him to a third Senate term with 70 percent of the vote. As promised, Thomas returned to the Senate in January to resume his senatorial duties. The leukemia proved resistant to treatment, however, and Thomas died at the Naval Medical Center in Bethesda on 4 June 2007. He is buried in Riverside Cemetery in Cody.

As a U.S. senator, Thomas was a fiscal conservative who called for a smaller, more efficient federal government, while promoting issues of importance to sparsely populated Wyoming, particularly rural health care policy, promotion of energy and clean coal technology, and protection of the national parks. His quiet and humble demeanor often masked a tough competitor not afraid to take on legislative battles.

Following his death, Thomas's Senate colleagues passed legislation naming a new visitors center at Grand Teton National Park in his honor. The Craig Thomas Discovery and Visitor Center opened on 11 August 2007, a lasting legacy to Thomas's dedication to America's national park system. In 2008, Susan Thomas established the Craig and Susan Thomas Foundation to serve the needs of Wyoming's disadvantaged and at-risk children through scholarships and leadership programs.

★

Thomas wrote many op-ed pieces during his Senate career, including "National Parks in Dire Need of Repairs," *Denver Post* (27 Sept. 1998); "Clean Environment or Public Access Is False Choice," *Hill* (4 Apr. 2001); "Finding a Balance: Energy and Environment," *Hill* (19 Sept. 2001); and "The Time Is Now for Energy Security, Electricity Reform," *Hill* (19 Mar. 2003). Following his death, his congressional colleagues issued a volume of tributes, *Memorial Addresses and Other Tributes Held in the Senate and House of Representatives of the United States Together with a Memorial Service in Honor of Craig Thomas, Late a Senator from Wyoming* (S. Doc. 110-5, U.S. GPO, 2007). Obituaries are in the *New York Times, Chicago Sun-Times, Los Angeles Times,* and *Casper Star-Tribune* (all 5 June 2007), and the *Wyoming Tribune-Eagle* (9 June 2007).

Betty K. Koed

TIBBETS, Paul Warfield, Jr. (*b.* 23 February 1915 in Quincy, Illinois; *d.* 1 November 2007 in Columbus, Ohio), U.S. Air Force officer who piloted the airplane that dropped the atomic bomb on Hiroshima, Japan, during World War II.

Tibbets was the son of Paul Tibbets, Sr., a wholesale grocery salesman, and Enola Gay (Haggard) Tibbets, a homemaker. In 1924 the family, which included a younger sister, settled in Miami, where his father founded a wholesale confectionery firm. The young Tibbets was introduced to the "delightfully incurable disease," as he described it, of flying as a passenger in an open-cockpit biplane dropping Baby Ruth candy bars over Hialeah racetrack. He graduated from Western Military Academy in Alton, Illinois, in 1933, then enrolled in the University of Florida. Two years later, Tibbets began premed studies at the University of Cincinnati, but his love of flight led to enlistment in the U.S. Army Air Corps (later the Air Force) as a cadet in early 1937.

Commissioned in 1938 after finishing at the top of his class, Tibbets opted not to fly fighters and was assigned to the Sixteenth Observation Squadron at Fort Benning, Georgia. He married Lucy Wingate on 19 June 1938; they had two sons. Tibbets quickly accumulated flying hours, including service as General George Patton's personal pilot and multiengine time in the obsolete B-10 bomber. In 1941 he was reassigned to fly high-performance A-20 aircraft with the Ninetieth Attack Squadron at Savannah, Georgia. There Tibbets honed his low-level-formation flying skills and furthered his reputation as a disciplined and capable leader.

Following the Japanese attack on Pearl Harbor on 7 December 1941, Tibbets transferred to the Twenty-ninth Bomb Group and flew daylight antisubmarine patrols along the East Coast in the B-18 bomber. At this time the army increased production of the B-17 Flying Fortress, and Tibbets took command of the Fortieth Bomb Squadron (Heavy) at MacDill Field, Florida, to prepare it for combat using this plane. By midsummer 1942 the unit was deployed to RAF Polebrook, a Royal Air Force airfield in England, where Tibbets became executive officer to the

Ninety-seventh Bomb Group commander. Tibbets's airmanship resulted in his selection as command pilot for the first American daylight heavy bomber mission over Europe.

In the fall of 1942 Tibbets flew General Mark Clark on a secret mission to Gibraltar, a British territory and important British military base at the tip of the Iberian Peninsula, in advance of Operation Torch, the British-American invasion of North Africa, then controlled by the French. He also flew General Dwight Eisenhower to the same location on the eve of the Allied invasion, in November 1942. Tibbets then led B-17 raids from Algeria against Axis positions to the east. On one mission, a German 88-millimeter shell went through the wing of his bomber, *Red Gremlin*, but did not explode. In early 1943 Tibbets returned stateside to work on the B-29 Superfortress project. While the program languished for months, he became skilled in instrument flying with the Nineteenth Transportation Group.

For nearly a year Tibbets conducted important test flights of the B-29, one of the largest aircraft used during World War II. By qualifying two Women Airforce Service Pilots (WASPs) to fly the giant plane, he persuaded B-29 aircrew trainees that the plane was safe to fly. In September 1944 he was selected to join the Manhattan Project, America's top-secret effort to develop an atomic bomb. Commanding the 509th Composite Group, a unit of 1,800 men at Wendover Field in Utah, Tibbets, not yet thirty years old and with the relatively junior rank of lieutenant colonel, was given extraordinary authority to organize and train a force to deliver the weapon. Demands for maintaining secrecy were extreme and, as Tibbets later acknowledged, put a strain on his marriage that led to divorce in 1955.

While awaiting A-bomb delivery, Tibbets tirelessly trained his crews in navigation, bomb dropping, and post-release evasive maneuvers. Beginning in May 1945 the 509th, with eighteen modified B-29s, deployed to Tinian Island in the Northern Mariana Islands in the West Pacific. The group then flew twelve "special missions" over Japan using nonatomic, high-explosive bombs to perfect tactics. Once the atomic attack was approved for 6 August 1945, Tibbets named his bomber *Enola Gay*, in honor of his mother. At the preflight briefing for the seven aircrews involved in the mission, Tibbets remarked, "it is possible that history will be made." After an uneventful flight, the primary target of Hiroshima was visually acquired and the bomb called Little Boy released; destruction was immediate and complete. Upon return to Tinian, Tibbets was presented with the Distinguished Service Cross by General Carl Spaatz, and he became an instant celebrity at home. The 509th's second atomic mission, on 9 August 1945, dropped the "Fat Man" bomb on Nagasaki. Japan surrendered on 15 August 1945. Tibbets and his unit were subsequently reassigned to Roswell, New Mexico.

Tibbets relinquished command in early 1946 but remained as technical adviser for the A-bomb test at Bikini Atoll, part of the Marshall Islands in Micronesia. Following staff school, Tibbets became involved in the development of the B-47, the first all-jet-engine bomber, and remained in the United States for the duration of the Korean conflict (1950–1953). A Hollywood film about Tibbets's World War II experience, *Above and Beyond*, was released in 1952. After completing Air War College in 1954, Tibbets was assigned to the North Atlantic Treaty Organization in Paris. While in France, he met Andrea Quattrehomme. They were married on 4 May 1956 in the Hunter Air Force Base chapel in Savannah, Georgia. Also in 1956 he took command of the low-performing 308th Bomb Wing at Savannah, Georgia, and turned it around. Tibbets's leadership led to air division command at MacDill, with accompanying promotion to brigadier general.

Known as a problem solver, Tibbets lead the Air Force Office of Strategic Analysis, then in 1964 was assigned to the U.S. Military Assistance Group in New Delhi, India, as second in command. He retired from active duty in 1966. Tibbets joined Executive Jet Aviation (later NetJets), an innovative business-jet taxi service headquartered in Columbus and served as its president from 1976 until 1986. In 1994 a planned fiftieth-anniversary exhibit of parts of the *Enola Gay* (which had been in storage for decades) at the Smithsonian Institution's National Air and Space Museum in Washington, D.C., proved controversial. Veterans' groups, along with some members of Congress, expressed outrage at the text accompanying the exhibit, which they felt was a negative and unfair portrayal of the American forces. Tibbets shared their outrage but did not take an active role in the controversy, which led to congressional hearings, the resignation of the museum's director, and a revamped exhibit. Tibbets died after a period of declining health due to a variety of ailments; his body was cremated and his ashes scattered in the English Channel.

Tibbets was an exceptional airman whose abilities led to command of the most secretive mission in American military history. Linked forever with the advent of the atomic age, Tibbets suffered the jealousies of peers who hampered his military advancement as well as a lifetime of vilification and scorn by antiwar activists. Yet Tibbets never wavered in his belief that his actions saved lives, of both friend and foe, by helping to end World War II without a ground invasion of Japan. In the end, Tibbets slept well at night, harboring no animosity or guilt over his role in the Manhattan Project.

★

The Air Force Historical Research Center, Maxwell Air Force Base, Alabama, holds Tibbets's personal papers. His autobiography is *The Return of the* Enola Gay (2005), an updated edition of *The Tibbets Story* (1978). Bob Greene, *Duty: A Father, His Son, and the Man Who Won the War* (2000), a memoir of the author's father, a World War II veteran, is also a biographical treatment, with interviews, of Tibbets as well as an ode to the World War II generation. The Air Force Association's *Enola Gay Archive: The Enola Gay and the Smithsonian*, which documents the controversy surrounding the exhibit of the plane, is available from www .afa.org/media/enolagay. Obituaries are in the *New York Times* (1 Nov. 2007) and *Columbus Dispatch* (2 Nov. 2007). Tibbets appears in a television documentary, *Men Who Brought the Dawn* (1995), which marked the fiftieth anniversary of the Hiroshima bombing.

William E. Fischer, Jr.

TOGURI, Ikuko ("Iva"; "Tokyo Rose") (*b.* 4 July 1916 in Los Angeles, California; *d.* 26 September 2006 in Chicago, Illinois), broadcaster of propaganda for Japanese radio during World War II who was convicted of treason but who was later pardoned by President Gerald Ford.

Toguri was the daughter of Jun Toguri, who came to the United States in 1899 and ran a small mercantile establishment; her mother arrived in 1913. Most of Toguri's schooling was completed in Los Angeles. She spent a year

Iva Toguri, 1945. HULTON ARCHIVE/GETTY IMAGES

at Compton Junior College and then entered the University of California, Los Angeles, graduating with a BS in zoology in 1940. Her intention was to return to school to study medicine, but until June 1941 she helped her father in his store. During her youth she used a more American-sounding nickname, Iva.

Despite her Japanese ancestry, Toguri seemed to be the ideal American teen. She was raised a Methodist and was a Girl Scout. In high school she was a member of the varsity tennis team. Like many children, she took piano lessons. She once listed her pastimes as sports, hiking, and swing music. In the 1940 election she registered and voted as a Republican.

Toguri's life changed dramatically when her mother's sister in Japan became ill and Toguri went to Japan to represent the family. Without time to get an American passport, she carried a certificate of identification and sailed on the *Arabia Maru* in July 1941. In September of that year she applied for a passport at the American consulate in Japan. Refusing to accept the certificate as proof of her American birth, the consulate sent her file to the U.S. State Department. When Pearl Harbor was attacked, Toguri's application was still pending. Japan considered her an "enemy alien" but refused her request to be interned with other Americans; she was not included in the group that was repatriated.

In the meantime Toguri's pro-American attitude caused difficulties with her Japanese relatives and neighbors. On more than one occasion, she was investigated and harassed by the Kempeitai, Japan's military police. She registered for classes in Japanese language and culture to become more acclimated. Now on her own, Toguri needed to support herself, and she took a job as a typist for Domei News; later she added similar work for Radio Tokyo. There a small group of American and Australian prisoners of war (POWs) were being used to broadcast pro-Japanese propaganda. When it was decided to add a female voice to the program, she was one of several American-sounding women who made broadcasts. *Zero Hour* aired weekdays and Saturdays from 6:00 p.m. to 7:15 p.m. (Tokyo time). The scripts were written by the POWs. When Toguri was on the air, she spoke for about twenty minutes under the pseudonym "Orphan Ann"; the remainder of the time was devoted to popular American music.

Toguri sympathized with the men with whom she worked and scrounged the black market to find food, clothing, and medicine for them. Her American views caused serious problems with coworkers at Domei, so she quit that job and worked part time at the Danish consulate. Taking part of her pay in luxuries from the consulate store, she traded these on the black market for additional food for the POWs. She also met and in 1945 married Felipe D'Aquino, a Portuguese citizen of Portuguese-Japanese ancestry.

When Japan surrendered, American reporters went to the country with the army of occupation. Harry Brundidge, a correspondent for *Cosmopolitan*, wanted to find the notorious "Tokyo Rose," the general nickname for Radio Tokyo's female broadcasters. He offered $250 for her identity; when Toguri's name turned up, he offered her $2,000 for an exclusive interview. *Cosmopolitan* refused to provide the funds, so she was never paid. Instead Brundidge turned his information over to the military. Toguri was arrested on 17 October 1945 and was investigated by the Federal Bureau of Investigation (FBI) and army counterintelligence. Toguri was held at Sugamo Prison in the wing for war criminals. The investigators concluded that there was not enough evidence to prosecute and released her in October 1946.

When press reports reached the United States, the American Legion mounted a national campaign for Toguri's arrest and trial; this was championed by the noted columnist Walter Winchill. The Justice Department asked for the FBI records and sent an attorney and Brundidge to Japan for another investigation; Brundidge persuaded one of his contacts to commit perjury. The U.S. attorney in San Francisco convened a grand jury, which charged Toguri with eight counts of treason. She was only the seventh American ever charged. Transported to the United States on a troop ship, she was immediately arrested by the FBI.

Toguri's trial, which lasted thirteen weeks, was the most expensive to that time, costing the government $750,000. Witnesses were flown from Japan for the prosecution; Toguri's expenses were paid by her father. The judge, who later admitted his prejudice against Toguri, ruled that Brundidge and his suborning of perjury could not be admitted because he did not testify. Witnesses in Toguri's favor were ruled irrelevant. When the jury could not reach a verdict, the judge sent them back, instructing them under the Allen Rule, noting that the huge expenses would have to be repeated in a new trial and imploring them to reach a verdict. On 29 September 1949 Toguri was found guilty on one count. On 6 October she was fined $10,000 and sentenced to ten years at the Federal Reformatory for Women in Alderson, West Virginia.

The prison reports indicate that Toguri was a model prisoner, always active; they calculated her IQ at 130. Assigned to the prison hospital as a clerk, she soon was performing duties as a nurse, a laboratory technician, and a physician's assistant. She also reorganized the dental records. As there was no staff dentist at that time, from books she learned how to do temporary medicinal fillings and even made some dentures. When a dentist was added, he praised her intelligence and work. Toguri was released on 28 January 1956 and spent two years fighting a deportation order. Meanwhile, she worked in her father's import business in Chicago. Her mother, a diabetic, had died on the way to internment as a West Coast Japanese at Gila River, Arizona.

In 1976 various news reporters, including Morley Safer of the Columbia Broadcasting System program *Sixty Minutes*, ran stories casting doubt on the circumstances of Toguri's trial and conviction. These efforts led to Toguri's official pardon by President Gerald R. Ford on 19 January 1977, Ford's last day in office. Because her husband was always denied permission to come to the United States, Toguri reluctantly divorced him in 1980. (In January 1948 she had given birth to a baby, who died almost immediately.) In 2005 a veterans group awarded Toguri the Edward J. Herlihy Citizenship Award. She was still operating the family business when she died. Toguri is buried in Montrose Cemetery in Chicago.

The story of Toguri is that of a young woman caught in the maelstrom of war and forced to survive on her own. A victim of her Japanese ancestry in the racist climate of the time, she was railroaded into prison as a traitor to a country she loved despite its flaws.

Biographies include Melvin Belli and Danny Jones, *Trial of Tokyo Rose* (1960), and Masayo Umezomo Duus, *Tokyo Rose: Orphan of the Pacific* (1979). For a brief account, see J. Kingston Price, "They Called Her Traitor," *American History* 37, no. 4 (2002): 22–28; and Erling Hoh, "Iva Tells Her Tale," *Far Eastern Economic Review* (26 June 2003). Obituaries are in the *New York Times* and *Los Angeles Times* (both 28 Sept. 2006).

Art Barbeau

TOLEDANO, Ralph de (*b.* 17 August 1916 in the International Zone, Tangier, Morocco; *d.* 3 February 2007 in Bethesda, Maryland), prominent conservative author.

Toledano's father, Haim Toledano, was a Paris-educated newspaperman, translator, and businessman; his mother, Simy (Nahon) Toledano, was a correspondent for Latin American and Moroccan newspapers. When he was five, his parents, who were American citizens, brought him to New York City. He attended Horace Mann School and then Fieldston School in the Riverdale section of the Bronx, New York City, from which he graduated in 1934. Enrolling at Columbia College, he won literary awards and served on the staff of several college publications. Under his editorship in the academic year 1937–1938, the *Columbia Jester* won the Intercollegiate Cup as the best college humor magazine in the nation. While in college he added "de" to his name.

Ralph de Toledano. **COURTESY OF COLUMBIA COLLEGE TODAY**

Upon receiving his BA in 1938, Toledano cofounded *Jazz Information*, the nation's first serious jazz publication. He worked for various leftist journals and radio stations and from 1938 to 1939 was an editor at Lex Publications in New York City. From 1940 to 1943 he was the associate editor of the *New Leader*. This weekly publication was the voice of the "old guard" wing of the Socialist Party, a segment of the political left that opposed Communism. In addition to writing news stories, music columns, political gossip columns, feature pieces, book reviews, and editorials, he also helped put the magazine together to be ready for printing. During this time, as a jazz aficionado he wrote music criticism for the *American Mercury*. In 1940 he married Nora Romaine, a painter and writer; they had two sons. Divorced in 1968, he married Eunice Godbold, a legal secretary, on 19 April 1979; she died in 1999.

Entering the army as a private in March 1943, Toledano rose to the rank of staff sergeant. He was first trained as an antiaircraft gunner, then assigned to the Office of Strategic Services, a U.S. intelligence agency formed during World War II and the predecessor of the Central Intelligence Agency, for intensive instruction in Italian. Deemed

too anti-Communist to work with Italian leftists, he was sent to San Juan, Puerto Rico, where, as chief of section of the Information and Educational Service, he edited army newspapers. Upon leaving the service he returned to New York, where in 1946 he briefly edited the *Standard*, the monthly of the American Ethical Union. From 1946 to 1947 he was the managing editor of *Plain Talk*, a new monthly devoted to exposing Soviet goals of expansion and Communist subversive activities in the United States. During the following two years he was the publicity director of the Dress Joint Board, one of the largest units of the International Ladies' Garment Workers' Union.

From 1948 to 1960 Toledano was employed by *Newsweek*, beginning as assistant editor and rising to assistant Washington bureau chief. His reporting on the 1949 perjury trial of Alger Hiss, a U.S. State Department official accused of spying for the Soviet Union, led to his best seller, written with Victor Lasky, *Seeds of Treason: The True Story of the Hiss-Chambers Tragedy* (1950; revised and updated, 1962). The Hiss case also led him to the closest of friendships with Whittaker Chambers, an American writer who became a Soviet spy but later renounced Communism and testified against Hiss. Their correspondence was later published under the title *Notes from the Underground* (1997). The Hiss-Chambers affair, a significant episode during the cold war era, also drew him close to Richard Nixon, then a California congressman, about whom Toledano wrote two friendly accounts, *Nixon* (1956; revised and expanded, 1960) and *One Man Alone: Richard Nixon* (1969). From this focus Toledano moved on to wider subjects: *Spies, Dupes and Diplomats* (1952), a book accusing American leaders of being responsible for Communist gains in the Far East, and *The Greatest Plot in History* (1963), covering major atomic spies. Over the course of his career he contributed to such journals as the *Freeman, Collier's, Reader's Digest, Coronet, Saturday Review, Commonweal, Commentary*, and the *American Scholar*.

After leaving *Newsweek*, Toledano held many journalistic posts, among them as a columnist with Hearst's King Features Syndicate (1960–1971), editor in chief of the weekly tabloid *Washington World* (1960–1961), and president of the National News-Research Syndicate (1971–1974). He also worked for the Copley News Service (1974–1999) and Heritage Features Syndicate. In 1956 he began almost a half-century of writing for *National Review*, a journal founded by the conservative thinker William F. Buckley, Jr., joining its masthead as contributing editor in 1960 and becoming both its music critic and Washington correspondent.

Toledano was also prolific as an author of books. His *Day of Reckoning* (1955) was a fictional account of real events surrounding the murder of the Italian anarchist Carlo Tresca, a personal friend, by Communist assassins. In his memoir *Lament for a Generation* (1960), he explains how the Moscow Trials, sham trials in the 1930s that resulted in the execution of many political opponents of the Soviet leader Joseph Stalin, and Russia's role in the Spanish civil war led him to turn away from his early radicalism; Vice President Nixon wrote the foreword. In *The Winning Side: The Case for Goldwater Republicanism* (1964) and *The Goldwater Story* (1964), he argued that conservative Republicans were being continually betrayed by their liberal Republican counterparts. Several of his biographies were quite critical of their subjects, among them his study of Senator Robert F. Kennedy, *R.F.K.: The Man Who Would Be President* (1967); *Claude Kirk: Man and Myth* (written with Philip V. Brennan, Jr., 1970); and his study of the migrant organizer César Chávez, *Little Cesar* (1971). In his book *Hit & Run: The Rise—and Fall?—of Ralph Nader* (1975), Toledano claimed that Ralph Nader had falsified evidence concerning the Corvair automobile; Nader brought a successful libel lawsuit against Toledano for that charge.

In contrast to his critical biographies was the admiring study *J. Edgar Hoover: The Man in His Time* (1973). *Let Our Cities Burn* (1975; reprinted as *The Municipal Doomsday Machine*, 1976), with a foreword by Senator Jesse Helms, attacked public-service unions. The versatile Toledano also wrote another novel, *Devil Take Him* (1980), and two books of poems, *Poems: You and I* (1979) and *The Apocrypha of Limbo* (1994). He was the editor of *Frontiers of Jazz* (1947); *The Conservative Papers* (with Karl Hess, 1964); and *America, I Love You* (1968), an anthology of his articles and speeches. In his last book, *Cry Havoc! The Great American Bring-down and How It Happened* (2006), he discusses what he sees as a national moral crisis rooted in the work of the neo-Marxist thinkers known as the Frankfurt school.

Toledano was vice chairman of the American Conservative Union (1965–1966), received three Freedoms Foundation Awards (1950, 1961, 1974) and an award from the Veterans of Foreign Wars (1953), and was made a distinguished journalism fellow of the Heritage Foundation. He died of cancer at the age of ninety. He is buried at Shearith Israel Cemetery in Queens, New York.

Descended from a line of Sephardic rabbis, Toledano himself possessed something of a mystical strain, as evidenced by his musical and literary tastes. He was indeed a man of general cultural sophistication, at home equally in the world of politics, poetry, and jazz. His passionately conservative and anti-Communist views had a major influence on the development of the conservative movement.

★

The bulk of Toledano papers are at the Hoover Institution, Stanford University, and Boston University. The best examination of Toledano's work is George H. Nash, "Forgotten Godfathers: Premature Jewish Conservatives and the Rise of *National Review*," *American Jewish History* 87, nos. 2–3 (June and Sep. 1999):

123–157. Obituaries are in the *Washington Times* (5 Feb. 2007), *New York Times* (6 Feb. 2007), *Washington Post* (7 Feb. 2007), and *National Review* (5 Mar. 2007).

Justus D. Doenecke

TONER, Roberta Denise ("Robin") (*b.* 22 May 1954 in Chester, Pennsylvania; *d.* 12 December 2008 in Washington, D.C.), national political correspondent for the *New York Times* and the first woman to hold that position.

Toner, known as "Robin," was one of six children of Charles R. Toner, an oil refinery supervisor, and Mary Louise (Zern) Toner, a homemaker. During World War II her father had been a pilot, her mother a riveter in an aircraft factory. She grew up in Chadds Ford, Pennsylvania, and attended Syracuse University in New York State. After graduating summa cum laude in 1976 as a political science and magazine journalism major, Toner found her first reporting job at the *Charleston Daily Mail* in West Virginia. Among her assignments for that paper was covering a coal miners' strike. She then worked for the *Atlanta Journal-Constitution*, reporting on the 1984 presidential bid of the civil rights activist Jesse Jackson.

In 1985 Toner was hired by the *New York Times*. In 1988 she covered the presidential campaign of the Massachusetts governor Michael Dukakis. Her supervisors appreciated her dedication to her work and her understanding of politics and the people involved, and she rose through the ranks quickly. Toner and Michael Oreskes served in the paper's Washington bureau as co-national political correspondents until 1990, when Toner became the sole reporter in that post. In 1992 she was assigned to cover the presidential campaign of Bill Clinton, and in that role she entered the ranks of top political reporters in the nation. Along with her colleagues Adam Clymer and Robert Pear, in 1993 Toner reported on the Clinton administration's health-care reform initiative and the debate surrounding this major political issue. Writing of the struggle to implement health-care reform she wrote, "reality often seemed to be just another subject for debate"; after the Clinton plan failed she observed that "a variety of experts are quietly noting that the problems that promoted the health care struggle are still, ahem, very much here."

In 1996 Toner married Peter Gosselin, then a reporter for the *Boston Globe*. They were the parents of twins, a girl and a boy.

Toner became chief of correspondents at the *Times* national desk in New York in the late 1990s. She oversaw reporters nationwide in their coverage of state legislatures, budget deficits, scandals, crises, and crime. Later she returned to the Washington bureau, where she held the rank of senior writer and covered issues such as abortion, racial justice, and judicial nominations.

Over the course of her twenty-three-year career at the *Times*, she reported on five presidential campaigns and many congressional and state contests as well as the full range of domestic matters, such as taxes, welfare, Social Security, immigration, and health-care policy. Toner respected hardworking politicians who did not always win the spotlight; in her reporting on political contests, she looked for the story that might emerge from the underdog's perspective. In a 2003 profile, Toner wrote that Richard Gephardt's legislative record hindered his presidential aspirations; politicians such as he, she wrote, were "sin eaters, too loaded up with baggage and compromise for the message-driven simplicity of a modern presidential campaign." She had an appreciation for the way race and class remain a factor in American politics, for instance pointing out the dominance of white men in the 2004 race to become the Democratic nominee on the presidential ticket. She called one of those candidates, Senator John Edwards, "Atticus Finch with an attitude."

Toner died at home of complications from colon cancer.

Toner relished the game of politics and often took a wry view of political machinations. *New York Times* editors praised Toner for her elegant writing and accurate assessments of politics and policy issues. She was known for her scrupulous fact-checking of her own articles. The *Times* printed only half a dozen corrections for over 1,900 articles under her byline. Her astute and hard-hitting coverage of presidential politics, as well as many other issues, earned her enduring respect in the field of journalism.

Obituaries are in the *Washington Post* and *New York Times* (both 13 Dec. 2008).

Sheila Beck

TRUMAN, (Mary) Margaret (*b*. 17 February 1924 in Independence, Missouri; *d*. 29 January 2008 in Chicago, Illinois), concert singer, radio and television personality, best-selling author, and daughter of the thirty-third president of the United States.

Truman was the only child of Elizabeth "Bess" (Wallace) Truman and Harry S. Truman, a Jackson County judge (at that time in Missouri, an administrator, not a judicial officer). Born at home in the spacious Victorian house built by her mother's maternal grandfather, Truman was raised by an adoring father, a stern but loving mother, and

Margaret Truman, 1951. © BETTMANN/CORBIS

numerous doting aunts and uncles. Her childhood, she said years later, was "nearly perfect."

Truman initially attended the local public schools, but following her father's election to the U.S. Senate in 1934, she was schooled in Independence during the fall term, and from January to June, while Congress was in session, she attended Gunston Hall, a private girls' school in Washington, from which she graduated in 1942.

Truman was a junior at George Washington University (GWU) when her father, the recently elected vice president, succeeded to the presidency of the United States upon the death of Franklin Delano Roosevelt on 12 April 1945. The full understanding of how her life had changed came slowly. "Before everything happened"—as she always put it—she had traveled alone to GWU. Now she was driven daily to and from her classes in a White House limousine, accompanied by Secret Service agents who never left her side. The university, too, guarded her privacy, keeping away reporters and photographers. Off campus, the Washington press pursued her everywhere, reporting where she went, whom she saw, how she dressed.

As the first presidential daughter to live in the White House since Woodrow Wilson's three daughters nearly thirty years earlier, Truman became a subject of gossip and rumor, "a sitting pigeon for critics and busy bodies," she said. Though she had been trained since childhood to act with tact and discretion, she nevertheless soon discovered that the most innocent acts of a president's daughter could have unintended public consequences. When she refused potatoes at a Washington restaurant, the potato-growers association flooded the White House with letters of protest. Similarly, she piqued the ire of milliners across the country when she was photographed wearing a head-scarf instead of the more customary (and, according to many, proper) hat.

Following her graduation in June 1946 with a BA in history, Truman set out to have a career, something few or no White House daughters before her had done. Given a baby grand piano when she was eight, she had taken up voice lessons at sixteen. She dreamed of being a concert singer, and for a time she trained with Helen Traubel, the Metropolitan Opera star. At twenty-three she was sure she was ready.

A coloratura soprano, Truman made her professional debut with the Detroit Symphony Orchestra on 15 March 1947 in a nationwide radio broadcast. Her stage debut followed in August before 20,000 people at the Holly-wood Bowl, Eugene Ormandy conducting. She made her New York debut at Carnegie Hall on 20 November 1949. In the summer of 1951, joined by the Robert Shaw Chorale, Truman recorded "American Songs" for RCA Victor Red Seal Records. She toured off and on in major cities until 1953, drawing mostly approving audiences but generally tepid reviews.

Five feet, five inches tall and slender, with blue-green eyes and ash-blond hair, Truman had an attractive stage presence, and most critics treated her gently and with restraint—save perhaps for Paul Hume of the *Washington Post*, who wrote a dismissive account of her concert at Constitution Hall on 5 December 1950. In his review, he opined that she "cannot sing very well" and was "too much of a vocal beginner to appear in public"—a caustic assessment that elicited an inflammatory, handwritten response from the president, who threatened Hume with bodily harm for his "lousy review" were the two men ever to meet. The letter was front-page news across the country, and hundreds of parents sent letters to the president, some 80 percent of them supporting his defense of his daughter.

Truman made her network television debut on 29 October 1950 on *Toast of the Town*, the Sunday night show hosted by Ed Sullivan on the Columbia Broadcasting System (CBS) television network. Beginning in February 1951, having signed a contract with the National Broadcasting Company (NBC), she was a frequent guest on a number of the network's variety programs, including *Your Show of Shows* with Sid Caesar and Imogene Coca, and the *Texaco Star Theater* with Milton Berle. On 27 May 1955, sitting in for Edward R. Murrow on his CBS program *Person to Person*, Truman interviewed her parents.

Beginning in November 1955 Truman was paired with Mike Wallace on *Weekday*—an NBC radio program featuring news briefs, human interest stories, and interviews with well-known personalities and entertainers. The show was favorably reviewed, and Truman received plaudits for her sense of humor and relaxed demeanor, but she abruptly left the program in early February 1956 to marry Clifton Daniel, a star foreign correspondent (and later managing editor) for the *New York Times*. The couple was wed on 21 April 1956 in Independence, Missouri. They would go on to have four sons.

In May of that same year, McGraw-Hill published Truman's *Souvenir: Margaret Truman's Own Story*, a memoir written with Margaret Cousins, an editor at *Good Housekeeping*. The first of the thirty-two books Truman would write, *Souvenir* sold more than a million hardcover copies. Her financial position much improved (she had received nearly $100,000 in advances), Truman purchased an apartment on Park Avenue near East 76th Street, where she and her family would live until just before her death.

Truman returned briefly to broadcasting in 1966 with *Authors in the News*, a series of five-minute interviews with well-known writers heard daily on more than 100 radio stations. In 1969 she completed *White House Pets*, an anecdotal history of first-family animals. She now turned to writing full time.

Over the next three years, Truman completed her biography of her father with the assistance of the historian Thomas Fleming. *Harry S. Truman* (1972) was a Book-of-the-Month Club selection and sold in excess of 1 million copies. Reviewers faulted its analyses of events as simplistic but praised Truman's human portrayal of the thirty-third president. Fleming also assisted Truman with her next book, *Women of Courage: From Revolutionary Times to the Present* (1976), sketches of twelve women, including Elizabeth Blackwell, the first female graduate of an American medical school; the singer Marian Anderson; and Senator Margaret Chase Smith of Maine. Truman went on to edit *Letters from Father: The Truman Family's Personal Correspondence* (1981) and *Where the Buck Stops: The Personal and Private Writings of Harry S. Truman* (1989). Her own memories and the letters of her father informed her best-selling biography, *Bess W. Truman* (1986). Her last two historical books were *First Ladies: An Intimate Group Portrait of White House Wives* (1995) and *The President's House: A First Daughter Shares the History and Secrets of the World's Most Famous Home* (2003).

Something of a lark, Truman's long-running "Capital Crime" mystery series won her a large and enthusiastic audience of faithful readers who made many of her twenty-three titles best sellers. Penned over twenty-seven years, the series opened in 1980 with *Murder in the White House*, an immediate hit and the template for each succeeding volume: a dead body, a few clues interpreted by amateur sleuths, and insider details about the murder site and Washington's political culture. There were twenty-two subsequent murders, each at a Washington landmark: *Murder on Capitol Hill* (1981), *Murder in the Supreme Court* (1982), *Murder in the Smithsonian* (1983), *Murder on Embassy Row* (1984), and so on until the final *Murder on K Street* (2007).

It was a genre beyond the reach of critics, and after the first book, Truman was rarely reviewed; her books sold on the strength of her name alone. No one mistook her for a master of detective fiction. Truman was not in that class, but she was a competent writer and storyteller, she knew the world she described, and she provided just what her legion of readers demanded: light, escapist fiction, as comforting and familiar as an old friend.

In early 2007 Truman sold her home in New York and moved to Chicago to live with her son Clifton. Within the year, she became ill and spent her final days in an assisted living facility on a respirator. She died of natural causes and was cremated. Her ashes and those of her husband, Clifton Daniel, who died 21 February 2000, were interred near her parents' graves at the Harry S. Truman Library and Museum in Independence.

Having come of age in the glare of the White House spotlight, Truman carved out the multiple careers that she wished to have and became an admired woman in her own right, respected for her talents, candor, and grace—the goals she had set in her youthful memoir.

★

The papers of E. Clifton Daniel and Margaret Truman Daniel—and the personal and family papers of Bess Truman—are in the Truman Library and Museum. A useful memoir is Truman's *Souvenir: Margaret Truman's Own Story* (1956, 2007). For more about Truman, see Beth Furman, "Margaret Truman, Career Girl," the *New York Times Magazine* (8 Sept. 1946). President Truman's original letter to Paul Hume is in private hands, but a copy is in the Truman Library and online at http://www.trumanlibrary.org/trivia/letter.htm. Obituaries are in the *New York Times*, *Washington Post*, and *Los Angeles Times* (all 30 Jan. 2008).

Allan L. Damon

U

UPSHAW, Eugene Thurman (''Gene''), Jr.
(*b.* 15 August 1945 in Robstown, Texas; *d.* 20 August 2008 in Lake Tahoe, California), Hall of Fame left guard for the National Football League's (NFL) Oakland Raiders and later executive director of the National Football League Players' Association (NFLPA).

Upshaw grew up in rural east Texas, where his father, Eugene Upshaw, Sr., worked as an oil company meter reader, and his mother, Cora (Riley) Upshaw, labored as a domestic for white families. The Upshaw family picked cotton to help make ends meet, but Upshaw's father, who played semiprofessional baseball, allowed him and his younger brother Marvin to escape the fields if the boys played baseball. Marvin, however, proved the superior athlete, and Upshaw earned only one high school letter in football.

Though he failed to attract a college scholarship offer following his high school graduation in 1963, Upshaw's family prevailed upon him to attend predominantly black Texas A&I University in nearby Kingsville, Texas. Studying to be a teacher, Upshaw tried out for the college football squad and was offered a scholarship. During his time at Texas A&I, Upshaw grew from five feet, ten inches tall, and 185 pounds, to six feet, five inches, and 255 pounds. He played a number of positions, including fullback and tight end, earning National Association of Intercollegiate Athletics (NAIA) All-American honors. Upshaw graduated in 1968 with a BS degree.

Upshaw was projected as a third-round draft pick until his outstanding performances at the 1967 Senior Bowl and College All-Star Game drew the attention of professional football scouts. Al Davis, owner of the Oakland Raiders, selected Upshaw in the first round of the 1967 American Football League (AFL) draft, believing that as an offensive guard Upshaw would be able to thwart the Raiders' nemesis, defensive lineman Buck Buchanan of the Kansas City Chiefs. Davis, however, had first to convince Upshaw that the controversial Raiders were not too rowdy for the young Texan. He told Upshaw that he had enough "tough" players on the team. What he was looking for was leadership.

The match proved to be an excellent one, and Upshaw emerged as the team leader Davis had hoped for, earning the title "The Governor" from his teammates and coaches for his political skills. For fifteen seasons, Upshaw played starting left guard and was instrumental in securing the club's Super Bowl victories in 1976 and 1980. From 1973 to 1982, Upshaw also served as offensive team captain. During his NFL career, Upshaw played in seven American Football Conference title games, in addition to his three Super Bowls (the first, during his rookie season, was a loss), and was selected to six NFL Pro Bowls.

In addition to his success on the playing field, Upshaw was active in the Democratic Party, serving in 1970 as a member of the Democratic Central Committee of Alameda County, California. He was recognized for his community service with the 1980 NFLPA Whizzer White Humanitarian Award. He served as the Raiders representative to the NFLPA from 1969 to 1975, and in 1976 he was elected to the NFLPA Executive Committee. From 1967 to 1973 Upshaw served with the U.S. Army Reserve. On 30 December 1967 Upshaw married Jimmye Hill. The couple would go on to have a son but divorced in 1986.

Gene Upshaw, 1981. NFL/NFL/GETTY IMAGES

Retiring from professional football following the 1981 season, Upshaw remained active as president of the NFLPA, serving as a loyal lieutenant to Ed Garvey, the controversial executive director of the players' union. During the 1982 collective bargaining sessions and subsequent strike, which cost two months of the season, Upshaw earned a reputation for aggressive negotiating tactics, threatening those players who failed to fully support the union's positions.

When Garvey resigned in 1983, Upshaw was selected as his replacement, earning him a spot on the AFL-CIO Executive Council and making him the most influential African-American labor leader in the nation. On 13 September 1986 Upshaw married Teresa Buich, whose parents of Irish and Yugoslav ancestry did not approve of her relationship with an African American fifteen years her senior. Nevertheless, the union produced two sons and lasted until Upshaw's death.

In 1987 Upshaw led the NFLPA into a strike in which ownership used replacement players as strikebreakers. In response, Upshaw decertified the union and moved the dispute from labor law into the arena of antitrust where ownership was arguably more vulnerable. The result was a 1993 settlement of the *Reggie White v. NFL* case that established free agency with a team salary cap. Player salaries rose dramatically, and by 2008 players were earning approximately 60 percent of total team revenues.

Despite these successes, Upshaw was not without his critics. In 2006 more than 300 retired players complained that the union was not concerned about their disability benefits. Upshaw appeared insensitive when he insisted that he worked for the current players rather than the retired veterans. He even threatened to break the neck of former Buffalo Bills guard Joe DeLamielleure, who advocated for increased pension benefits. In April 2008 the player representative Matt Stover of the Baltimore Ravens called for new leadership in the NFLPA.

Upshaw, however, planned to continue in his role as union leader, announcing that he would hold a briefing on labor negotiations before the 2008 season opener. He was unable to fulfill this promise. On 17 August 2008, while vacationing at his Lake Tahoe home, Upshaw was diagnosed with pancreatic cancer and died just three days later. The noted sportscaster John Madden, and one of Upshaw's former coaches, proclaimed, "He was respected by everyone, because as a player . . . [and] union head he was a tough guy. But he . . . could compromise, and he could make things happen."

Overviews of Upshaw's life and career can be found in Alan Ross, *Away from the Ball: The NFL's Off-the-Field Heroes* (2008); Nathan Aaseng, *Football's Crushing Blockers* (1982); John Madden, *Hey, Wait a Minute (I Wrote a Book!)* (1984); and Frank Deford, "Bonus Piece: The Guard Who Would Be Quarterback," *Sports Illustrated* (14 Sept. 1987). An obituary is in the *New York Times* (22 Aug. 2008).

Ron Briley

V

VALENTI, Jack Joseph (*b.* 5 September 1921 in Houston, Texas; *d.* 26 April 2007 in Washington, D.C.), head of the Motion Picture Association of America who previously served as special assistant to President Lyndon B. Johnson.

Valenti was the son of Joseph Valenti, a clerk at the county court house, and Josephine (De George) Valenti. He and his younger sister grew up in a Greek and Italian neighborhood of Houston, where his paternal grandparents, immigrants from Sicily, owned a grocery store, and his maternal grandfather was a leader of the local Sicilian community. Educated in public schools, he was an honor student who loved books, reading novels, history, philosophy, and fables. When he was ten years old he gave an impromptu campaign speech during an election rally for a local sheriff, beginning a lifelong love of politics. He graduated from Sam Houston High School at the age of fifteen.

During high school Valenti found his first job at a movie theater, working part time as an usher and hanging movie posters. After high school he did odd jobs for another theater and then went to work as an office boy at Humble Oil Company (a precursor to ExxonMobil), a coveted day job that paid seventy-five dollars a month, which the sixteen-year-old Valenti saw as a fortune. He worked his way up to the advertising and marketing department and also served on the editorial staff of the company newsletter. In September 1938 he enrolled at the University of Houston, working to pay his tuition during the day and taking classes at night. However, his college career was interrupted by U.S. involvement in World War II.

In January 1942, one month after the Japanese attack on Pearl Harbor, Valenti tried to enlist in the U.S. Naval Air Corps but was rejected because of a heart murmur discovered during his physical. He then enlisted in the U.S. Army Air Corps (later the Air Force), becoming a B-25 bomber pilot. During his service in Italy, Valenti flew fifty-one combat missions, receiving several decorations, including the Distinguished Flying Cross.

After the war Valenti resumed his studies, earning a BA from the University of Houston in 1946. He then earned an MBA from Harvard Business School in 1948. In 1953 Valenti and his friend Weldon Weekley formed the advertising agency Weekley and Valenti, Inc. One of their clients was the Texas Democratic Party; Valenti got to know the Texas Senate majority leader, Lyndon Baines Johnson, whom John F. Kennedy chose as his running mate in the 1960 presidential election. Valenti became part of the vice president's inner circle, writing speeches and political memos pro bono. On 1 June 1962 Valenti married Mary Margaret Wiley, a secretary to Johnson; the couple would have three children.

In 1963 the firm of Weekley and Valenti was put in charge of the Texas press schedule for President Kennedy's trip to Dallas. On 22 November 1963 Valenti was riding several cars behind the president's in the presidential motorcade when Kennedy was assassinated. He was with Johnson on Air Force One when Johnson was sworn in as Kennedy's successor. President Johnson immediately appointed Valenti his special assistant. In his three years in that role, Valenti worked as a liaison between the White House and Congress and provided candid advice and friendship to Johnson.

In February 1966 Valenti received a visit in his White House office from two Hollywood executives.

Jack Valenti, 1989. **PAM FRANCIS/GETTY IMAGES**

Lew Wasserman, chairman of MCA/Universal, and Arthur Krim, chairman of United Artists, asked Valenti to become the head of the Motion Picture Association of America (MPAA), a powerful consortium of major studio owners. He accepted, beginning a thirty-eight-year tenure as a powerful figure in the movie industry.

Valenti's most significant accomplishment as MPAA head was the implementation of the ratings system. He pushed to eliminate the Hays Production Code, a set of self-censoring rules dating from the 1930s according to which films could not include nudity, profanity, or other content considered "morally questionable." Arguing that the code was outdated and restricted artistic freedom, Valenti devised a film ratings system that would allow filmmakers to make films as they chose and help viewers decide if a film was suitable for children or family viewing. The system would also prevent the censorship of films by local review boards. Determined to free Hollywood from the Hays code, Valenti also, as he put it, "emphasized that freedom demanded responsibility." By this voluntary ratings system, instituted in 1968, a studio submits a film to a ratings board, assembled and paid by the MPAA, to receive a G, PG (another category, PG-13, was added later), R, or X (later changed to NC-17) rating. As a lobbyist, Valenti also championed the intellectual property

rights of filmmakers and television producers. In his last decade with the MPAA, he devoted himself to fighting digital piracy. Valenti, with his slight frame and snow-white hair, was a familiar figure to many Americans through his annual speech at the Academy Awards.

Valenti stepped down as head of the MPAA on 1 September 2004. He continued to work on world health issues as well as consulting with the entertainment industry on parental control of objectionable television material. Throughout his life he remained a loyal and ardent admirer of Johnson. He wrote a book about Johnson, *A Very Human President* (1975), as well as a collection of essays, a guide to public speaking, and a novel. He died of complications of a stroke at age eighty-five at his home. He is buried in Arlington National Cemetery in Arlington County, Virginia.

Valenti, a decorated war veteran, was equally at home in the worlds of politics and moviemaking. His loyalty to Johnson became legendary, and the president valued Valenti's devotion. An eloquent public speaker fond of grand and complicated phrases, he relished his role as advocate for the film industry as well as the company of movie stars. Throughout his years as MPAA head, Valenti drew on his earlier political experiences and connections to bridge the gap between Hollywood and Washington.

★

Valenti's memoir, *This Time, This Place: My Life in War, the White House, and Hollywood* (2007), was published shortly before his death. George Wayne, "A Politician Oscar Could Love," *Vanity Fair* (27 Apr. 2007), is an interview with Valenti covering the many aspects of his career. Obituaries are in the *Washington Post*, *New York Times*, and *Los Angeles Times* (all 27 Apr. 2007).

Steven Wise

VAN ALLEN, James Alfred (*b.* 7 September 1914 in Mount Pleasant, Iowa; *d.* 9 August 2006 in Iowa City, Iowa), physicist and space scientist who discovered the radiation belts in Earth's upper atmosphere that now bear his name.

Van Allen was the second of four sons born to Alfred Morris Van Allen, a second-generation Iowan and a small-town lawyer, and Alma E. (Olney) Van Allen, who taught in a one-room schoolhouse but gave up that career to be a full-time homemaker. Except for his academic excellence, Van Allen spent his youth like many boys in the small-town Midwest. He raised chickens and chopped wood, in addition to working in the family's large kitchen garden.

James A. Van Allen. © THE PRINT COLLECTOR/ALAMY

In the summer there was grass to cut; the winter meant shoveling snow.

Van Allen was interested in almost anything mechanical. His favorite reading materials were *Popular Mechanics* and *Popular Science*. These two magazines showed ways to build scientific and semiscientific instruments using inexpensive or discarded materials. With the knowledge gained from those sources, Van Allen built motors and crystal radios. He had brothers on whom to test the results; his mother was less sure of his demonstrations of a Van de Graaff generator that he built. When he graduated from Mount Pleasant High School in 1931, he was class valedictorian. As the Great Depression deepened, he attended Iowa Wesleyan College; as a hometown school, it was an inexpensive choice.

Van Allen's commitment to science was evident from the start, and for some time he wavered between majoring in physics or chemistry; at Wesleyan each subject had only a single teacher. In the end Van Allen chose physics because his teacher, Thomas Poulter, offered him a position as a part-time student assistant. As an undergraduate

Van Allen took four years of physics, chemistry, and math. To these he added a single class in astronomy and a summer class in geology fieldwork. As Poulter's assistant he helped create and build the instruments for Admiral Richard Byrd's second polar expedition; Poulter was the head scientist on that expedition. Van Allen and a friend built their own instruments to study meteor trails during the Perseid meteor shower of 1932. In 1935 Van Allen graduated summa cum laude with a BS.

The next year Van Allen began graduate studies at the University of Iowa, and in 1936 he was awarded an MS in physics. He earned a PhD from the same institution in 1939. When he attended a conference and read a paper on his dissertation project, the physicist and later Nobel laureate Hans Bethe pointed out some flaws in the equipment Van Allen had used, confirming that poorly designed equipment can skew the results of experiments.

Van Allen moved to Washington, D.C., and went to work as a research fellow for the Carnegie Corporation until 1942, when the Applied Physics Laboratory of Johns Hopkins University took over the project. When he began that work, war was already going on in Asia and soon broke out in Europe. Van Allen was assigned to work on proximity fuses. Antiaircraft fire was highly unreliable; the proximity fuse was intended to detonate the charge when the shell was within reasonable distance of the target. Though Van Allen developed a promising fuse using photoelectric cells, the main focus of the work had turned to radio-controlled fuses.

The new fuses needed to be tested in the field, and Van Allen was commissioned as a lieutenant junior grade in the U.S. Naval Reserve. Within a week of being commissioned, he was sent to the Pacific for field testing, and for the next eight months he served on various islands and aboard ships. Combat testing demonstrated two weaknesses: The fuses had too short a battery life, and key components failed to hold up to the heat and humidity of the South Pacific. Van Allen returned to Washington to work out solutions to the problems and then returned to the Pacific with the modified fuses. At the end of the war Van Allen was on inactive service as a lieutenant commander in the naval reserve. On 13 October 1945 he married Abigail Fithian Halsey; they subsequently had three daughters and two sons.

Following the war Van Allen continued work for the Applied Physics Laboratory, developing a strong interest in high-altitude and atmospheric research using V-2 rockets that had been captured from the German military or were copies of these. With Ernst Krause, Van Allen launched forty-eight V-2 rockets. The two scientists then developed an entirely new rocket called the Aerobee; twenty of these rockets were used in their research. By 1950 Van Allen had become disappointed because the research was under contract with the Office of Naval Research, and officials were no longer interested in academic research. Around that time friends encouraged Van Allen to apply for head of the physics department at the University of Iowa. Though he was the second choice of the selection committee, Van Allen got the position when the first choice turned down the job. With his wife and two young daughters, he moved back to Iowa and settled into temporary housing that the navy had constructed there during the war.

At Iowa, Van Allen continued his high-altitude research by using balloons to carry instruments up to 50,000 feet; a small grant from the private Research Corporation provided the funds. Then assistance from the Office of Naval Research allowed him to use rockets launched from the balloons to achieve heights of 250,000 feet. In 1952 he was able to carry out his first series of tests in the Arctic, and by 1953 he was able to demonstrate that the luminosity of the aurora was caused by electrons in the upper atmosphere. Van Allen spent fifteen months in 1953–1954 at Princeton University, where he helped in the planning for the International Geophysical Year of 1957–1958; funding for this work was provided by the National Science Foundation.

Van Allen is best known for his involvement with the satellites that were launched into space beginning in 1958. On 31 January 1958, *Explorer 1* was launched; using data provided by the satellite, Van Allen was able to identify the radiation belts circling Earth, which became known as the Van Allen belts. He was honored for this discovery with a *Time* magazine cover story. Subsequently, Van Allen participated in three other Explorer probes along with Pioneer probes and Mariner probes.

During Van Allen's tenure, the laboratories at the University of Iowa continued to excel in the production of instruments for high-altitude and space research. The first Explorer mission might have been delayed if Iowa had not already created the research instruments it would carry. The Explorer series of launches studied solar X-rays and solar energetic particles. The Injun launches concentrated on examining plasma and wave phenomena. The aptly named Hawkeye launch of 1974 studied the geomagnetic field over the polar cap. The Mariner series used instruments from the University of Iowa to probe for radiation belts around Mars and Venus but did not get close enough to either planet to detect them. However, *Pioneer 10* and *Pioneer 11* carried the instruments close enough to Jupiter to show the existence of electromagnetic radiation there, before going on to fly past the other outer planets. Finally, Van Allen's facility provided much of the instrumentation for the orbiting geophysical laboratory.

Though he officially gave up the position as head of the physics department in 1985, Van Allen continued his work there as Carver Professor of Physics, Emeritus. In all Van Allen was involved in at least twenty-four satellite and planetary missions. His supremacy in the field was recognized by thirteen other academic institutions that

awarded him honorary degrees. Van Allen died of heart failure.

Van Allen was one of a handful of scholars who, through their life's work, created an entirely new field of endeavor—in Van Allen's case, planetary and space science. At the midpoint of his career Van Allen turned away from what could have been a very lucrative future in military technology to pursue knowledge for its own sake, and he greatly advanced what is known about the electromagnetism of the solar system. One of his greatest contributions was to supervise the creation of a huge array of new scientific instruments. In this regard, one is reminded of another pioneer, Galileo Galilei, who also demonstrated that science cannot exceed its ability to measure and record.

Van Allen's papers are in the archives of the University of Iowa. Van Allen wrote an interesting and short autobiography, "What Is a Space Scientist? An Autobiographical Example," *Annual Review of Earth and Planetary Sciences* 18 (1990): 126. A useful biography is Abigail Foerstner, *James Van Allen: The First Eight Billion Miles* (2007). An obituary is in the *New York Times* (10 Aug. 2006).

Art Barbeau

VIERECK, Peter Robert Edwin (*b.* 5 August 1916 in New York City; *d.* 13 May 2006 in South Hadley, Massachusetts), philosopher, teacher, historian, and poet who founded a conservative movement in the United States and won numerous awards, including a Pulitzer Prize.

Viereck was the older son of the poet and novelist George Sylvester Viereck and Margaret Edith (Hein) Viereck, a homemaker. George Viereck was born in Munich and, although his family immigrated to New York City in 1896, he maintained close ties with Germany. His support of National Socialism estranged his family.

Peter Viereck enrolled at Harvard University and achieved distinction by winning both the Garrison Prize for the best undergraduate verse and the Bowdoin Prize for the best prose. He graduated summa cum laude with a BS in 1937 and did graduate work at Christ Church, Oxford, as a Henry Fellow. Returning to Harvard, Viereck earned an MA (1939) in European history. In addition to studying, he was writing for newspapers and magazines. In 1940 his five-thousand-word manifesto "But—I'm a Conservative" was published in the *Atlantic Monthly*. As an undergraduate, Viereck started work on a book that would be the basis for his PhD dissertation that was published in 1941, three months before the attack on Pearl

Harbor. *Metapolitics: From the Romantics to Hitler*, a study of the origins of Nazism, was praised for its historical scholarship and psychological insight. He earned a PhD in European history at Harvard in 1942.

When America entered the war in December 1941, Viereck's younger brother volunteered, and fifteen months later Viereck was drafted. Because their father had been convicted and imprisoned for conspiring with the Nazis, neither brother was allowed to become an officer or to serve in the Office of Strategic Services. Stationed in Africa, Viereck became a propaganda analyst for the Army Psychological Warfare Branch. Because he was fluent in German, he analyzed documents, but in his free time he wrote poetry. Several poems were published in the *New Yorker* under the byline Sergeant Peter Viereck. Later, stationed in Italy, Viereck met and in 1945 married Anya de Markov, a Russian who had been a resistance fighter. They would have two children. Returning home after the war, Viereck taught briefly at Harvard and at Smith College. He was wooed by the University of Chicago, but, impressed by the beauty of its campus, chose to teach at Mount Holyoke College in South Hadley.

Viereck taught at Mount Holyoke from 1948 until his retirement in 1987, but continued to teach his survey of Russian history course until 1997. His final lecture, titled "The Messiness of History," warned students of the dangers of trying to democratize the world. Students in Viereck's classes soon realized his demeanor as the stereotypical "absent-minded professor" was misleading; in addition to his extraordinary knowledge of history, his facility with languages, as he easily shifted from English to French to German, kept students on their toes. Viereck was also writing. Within a series of books published during the late 1940s and early 1950s, he continued to develop his political philosophy and became known as a founder of American conservatism.

In *Conservatism Revisited: The Revolt Against Revolt, 1815–1949* (1949) Viereck challenged the concept of conservatism representing a bias favoring business and a preference for minimal government. He defined conservatism in the context of a humane civilization with an appreciation for the need for moral and other restraints. Rather than business and finance setting the tone for society, Viereck wished to reawaken humankind's higher, moral-spiritual nature and argued for the existence of universal moral values. Later conservatives, such as William F. Buckley, censored Viereck for his refusal to denounce the New Deal and his objection to McCarthyism. Viereck shunned extremism of all types. His book *Conservatism: From John Adams to Churchill* (1956) became required reading on many college campuses.

While developing his political philosophy and teaching, Viereck was also writing poetry. His first book of poems, *Terror and Decorum: Poems 1940–1948* (1948), won the Pulitzer Prize for Poetry in 1949. Viereck's poetry is characterized by adherence to form and wit. His delight in language is evident in his tone and word choice. Subject matter ranges from a satiric commentary on man's roles in society in "To a Sinister Potato" to the elegy "Vale from Carthage," written in memory of his brother who was killed in action. The poem "Kilroy" is both about the role of the American soldier in time of war and the human spirit, finding its way through chaos. Other volumes of poetry followed regularly. Not only did Viereck write poetry, he critiqued it in a number of essays. He also welcomed poets, such as Dylan Thomas, Robert Lowell, and Robert Frost, to his home in South Hadley.

In the mid-1960s Viereck stopped writing about politics to focus solely on poetry and the study and teaching of history. He achieved the rare distinction of being awarded a Guggenheim Fellowship in both history and poetry. His deep interest in Russian history resulted in trips to the Soviet Union. He was instrumental in bringing the Soviet rebel poet Joseph Brodsky to the United States and to Mount Holyoke. There they cotaught the class "Poets Under Totalitarianism," which Viereck dubbed "Rhyme and Punishment."

Viereck divorced his wife; they remarried and again divorced in 1970. He married Betty Martin Falkenberg in 1972. Until his death he continued to write, both original work and revisions of previously published books for new editions. Viereck died in his home in South Hadley, following a lingering illness. His ashes are buried in Evergreen Cemetery in South Hadley. On his gravestone are verses from his poetry, chosen by Viereck. One line defines a poet as "someone who skims ever weightier stones ever farther over water," in effect, Viereck himself.

Viereck published eight books of prose (one of them a slightly revised and retitled version of *Conservatism*), eight books of poetry, and a number of articles. Joseph Ellis, Pulitzer Prize–winning historian and Mount Holyoke colleague, proclaimed Viereck "one of the most original and influential American thinkers of the mid-twentieth century." Not only did Viereck help launch the conservative movement in the United States, but he was also a renowned poet. In addition, Viereck was a scholar and both a challenge and an inspiration to generations of students.

★

Viereck's papers are at Columbia University; some materials are at Mount Holyoke College. The one book on Viereck, *Peter Viereck* (1969), by Marie Henault, is principally on his poetry. Lengthy articles on Viereck include Tom Reiss, "The First Conservative," *New Yorker* (24 Oct. 2005) and Claes G. Ryn, "The Legacy of Peter Viereck: His Prose Writings," *Humanitas* 19, nos. 1–2 (2006): 38–49. Obituaries are in the *Boston Globe* and *New York Times* (both 19 May 2006).

Marcia B. Dinneen

VOGT, Marguerite Maria (*b*. 13 February 1913 in Berlin, Germany; *d*. 6 July 2007 in La Jolla, California), cell biologist whose work made the polio vaccine possible. Vogt also contributed considerable knowledge to an understanding of cancer genetics.

Vogt was the youngest daughter of Oskar Vogt and Cécile (Mugnier) Vogt, who were well-known neuroscientists in Berlin, Germany, where Oskar Vogt was at one time the director of the Kaiser Wilhelm/Max Planck Institute. The Vogts not only insisted that their children—Marthe and Marguerite—become scientists, they reputedly also determined what the girls' areas of specialties would be.

Most of Vogt's early work, which was focused on fruit flies, went unknown for decades. She supposedly published her first paper at age fourteen and accumulated considerable knowledge on the genetics of mutated fruit flies. However, the combination of German-language publications and Adolf Hitler's regime conspired to keep her early work largely undiscovered until after she passed away.

Vogt received her MD from the University of Berlin in 1937. For a while, she worked on fruit fly research in Paris. However, when her parents were forced to leave the Planck Institute due to their political views (they had many Jewish friends and close ties to Russia), Vogt returned to Germany. She joined her parents in a private institute they founded in the Black Forest, near Neustadt.

The trauma of the Nazi regime left a deep impression on the young woman, one that stayed with her for her entire life. In Hitler's Germany she refused to date, saying later on that she felt she could not trust any man in those days, for fear he would turn out to be a Nazi. Once in the United States, Vogt reportedly refused to speak German with visiting scientists from her country of origin. She did speak French (her mother's native tongue) with visiting French scientists.

In 1950, probably as a result of her earlier work in France, Vogt received a job offer from the California Institute of Technology (Caltech). Though it meant giving up fruit fly research, she jumped at the chance to leave Europe and its unpleasant memories behind. She arrived in the United States bringing with her only her piano. In 1958 Vogt became an American citizen.

Vogt first worked with Max Delbrück, who was later the winner of the 1969 Nobel Prize in Physiology or Medicine. When a young scientist named Renato Dulbecco started working on a method to culture the polio virus, Delbrück suggested Vogt switch projects and assist Dulbecco. Because the polio virus was immensely feared prior to the advent of the polio vaccine, Vogt and Dulbecco were told to take their project out of Caltech into a windowless lab in the basement of Huntington Hospital. Vogt would not even tell her parents she was working with live polio since she feared it would upset them too much.

Vogt had, by all accounts, a fantastic talent for tissue culturing and a brilliant scientific mind. She and Dulbecco were able to culture polio and purify it in the lab. They showed that polio formed distinct plaques in tissue culture. They also showed that each plaque was attributed to a single virus, and therefore it was possible to create purified lines of the polio virus. In addition, Dulbecco and Vogt showed that the number of plaques correspond to the concentration of the virus in the tissue. Their work transformed the science of human virology, which became a practical rather than theoretical science. It was also an important step in understanding the disease and enabling the development of a polio vaccine.

Dulbecco and Vogt went on to work on viral transformation of cells in cancer. They studied the polyoma virus first in hamsters, and showed that the virus inserts its deoxyribonucleic acid (DNA) into the hamster cell's DNA, transforming the cell into a cancerous one that keeps producing virus particles. The work shed the first light on the process of cell transformations into cancer, and the genetic basis of cancer. For his work on such cell transformation, Dulbecco shared the 1975 Nobel Prize in Physiology or Medicine with David Baltimore and Howard Temin. Vogt's contribution was never widely acknowledged, though in an interview after her death Dulbecco acknowledged her work should have been more broadly recognized. This opinion is supported by other scientists who knew her work.

In 1962, while still working on their cell transformation project, Dulbecco was invited to work for the newly founded Salk Institute for Biological Studies in La Jolla, and Vogt moved with him. It is interesting to note that these two scientists, both with identical degrees, equally bright, and only a year apart in age, had such different career tracks. Vogt became a full research professor at the Salk Institute in 1973, while Dulbecco had held an equivalent position since the time of their polio work. Vogt was aware of the different treatment she received as a woman scientist, but she refused to let it bother her. Her colleagues have said she was always looking to the future and was happy to be able to carry out her research. Vogt went on to study the genetics of cell aging and cancer cell immortality, particularly the role that telomeres play in this process. (Telomeres are found at the ends of each chromosome, and they get shorter as a cell ages.)

Vogt died of natural causes at the age of ninety-four. She embodied the spirit of the old-fashioned scientist, completely dedicated to science for the sake of the pursuit and discovery of knowledge, not the fame that may come with it. She remained largely anonymous to the world at large, which suited her just fine. In a *New York Times* interview in 2001 she stated, "When you get too famous, you stop being able to work." She published her last paper in 1998 at age eighty-five, and she continued to show up for work at the Salk Institute until shortly before her death. Throughout a career that spanned some eighty years, Vogt trained countless scientists, including four who became

Nobel Prize winners. She never married or had children, feeling she could be either a scientist or a mother, but not both (she reflected that her mother was an exception, able to play both roles). Though this sentiment may make her a controversial role model for women scientists in the twenty-first century, she is highly regarded and emulated for her ethics, dedication, and the selfless nurturing of her colleagues.

★

A profile of Vogt is in the *New York Times* (10 Apr. 2001). Obituaries are in the *New York Times* (18 July 2007) and the Salk Institute's "InsideSalk" (Nov. 2007). A memorial tribute is available online, "Remembering Marguerite Vogt," http://www-rcf.usc.edu/forsburg/vogt.html (accessed 18 Nov. 2008).

Adi R. Ferrara

VONNEGUT, Kurt, Jr. (*b.* 11 November 1922 in Indianapolis, Indiana; *d.* 11 April 2007 in New York City), prolific writer of fiction and nonfiction best known for his absurdist antiwar novel *Slaughterhouse-Five*.

Kurt Vonnegut, 1979. **AP IMAGES**

Vonnegut was the youngest of three children born to Kurt Vonnegut, Sr., a second-generation German-American architect, and Edith Lieber, the daughter of an Indianapolis brewery owner. Vonnegut attended the private Orchard School between 1928 and 1936, but because of the family's failing fortunes during the Great Depression he attended the public Shortridge High School. It was there that he had his first experiences as a writer, serving as a reporter and editor on the school's daily newspaper, the *Daily Echo*.

After graduating from high school in 1940, Vonnegut went to Cornell University, where he majored in chemistry and served as a writer and editor for the student newspaper, the *Cornell Daily Sun*. However, before Vonnegut could finish his undergraduate work, World War II intervened, and he enlisted in the army in 1943. The military assigned him to the Carnegie Institute of Technology (now Carnegie Mellon University) in Pittsburgh and the University of Tennessee to study mechanical engineering. While Vonnegut pursued his studies, his mother, who had suffered from chronic depression, committed suicide on 14 May 1944, which, perhaps not coincidentally, was Mother's Day.

In 1944 Vonnegut was shipped to Europe to serve with the 106th Infantry Division. In the winter of 1944–1945 he briefly saw combat at the Battle of the Bulge, a Nazi offensive late in the war that resulted in 19,000 U.S. soldiers killed and an estimated 80,000 injured. His harrowing experience during this bloody battle would

profoundly shape his political vision and his subsequent work as a writer. The young private was serving as a battalion scout when he and several other soldiers wandered behind enemy lines; they were captured by the Nazis on 22 December and interned at a former meat-processing center near Dresden. Although the beautiful city held little military significance, the British and American air forces detonated tons of firebombs there between 13 and 15 February 1945, resulting in the deaths of as many as 135,000 noncombatant German citizens. Vonnegut was among the few Americans to witness the fire-bombing on the ground and to survive to write about it, most famously in the novel *Slaughterhouse-Five* (1969), named for the meat locker in which he was housed. After the attack the Germans put him to work gathering horribly charred bodies for mass burial and other cleanup details; but by then the Nazi Wehrmacht (the German armed forces) was seriously weakened, and Vonnegut was eventually freed by Russian army troops in May 1945. That same month, he was returned to the United States and awarded the Purple Heart, a military honor for those who have been wounded or killed while serving.

Vonnegut immediately set about making a life for himself back home. On 1 September 1945 he married his childhood sweetheart, Jane Marie Cox, with whom he had three children. He found work as a reporter for the Chicago City News Bureau and also enrolled in the graduate program in anthropology at the University of Chicago. He left the program the following year when his thesis, titled "On the Fluctuations Between Good and Evil in Simple Tales," was unanimously rejected by the anthropology faculty.

In 1947 he moved to Schenectady, New York, taking a job in public relations for the General Electric Company, where his brother, Bernard Vonnegut, worked as a research scientist. At the same time he began writing short fiction, and his first success came when *Collier's* magazine published his short story, "Report on the Barnhouse Effect," in its 11 February 1950 issue. The magazine market for short fiction was thriving during the postwar period, and after placing more of this work in such lucrative venues as the *Saturday Evening Post*, Vonnegut decided in 1951 to leave his job at General Electric, move his young family to Cape Cod, and devote himself full time to his writing.

A big break came two years later in 1952, when Charles Scribner's Sons published the thirty-year-old writer's first novel, *Player Piano*. This science-fiction novel presented a dystopian (inhuman and bleak) world in which corporate bureaucrats and scientists have devised ways to replace most human workers with machines. It received brief, favorable reviews in a number of national periodicals, including the *New York Times Book Review* and *Saturday Review*. Over the next two years the book appeared abroad, became a special edition published by the Doubleday Science Fiction Book Club, and was issued as a Bantam paperback under the title *Utopia 14*. Yet despite this impressive debut Vonnegut did not have another book published until *The Sirens of Titan* in 1959; that novel, along with its immediate successors, *Mother Night* (1961) and the short-story collection *Canary in a Cathouse* (1961), appeared as paperback originals and were overlooked by mainstream reviewers. To supplement his income, Vonnegut worked at a variety of jobs on Cape Cod, including teaching English, writing advertising copy, and opening the second Saab automobile dealership in the United States. The late 1950s also brought personal calamities. Vonnegut's father died in 1957, and the following year, his sister, Alice, died of cancer at the age of forty-two, just twenty-four hours after her husband, John Adams, was killed in a train crash. In addition to their own three children, Vonnegut and his wife adopted and raised three of his sister's children.

By the early to mid-1960s, Vonnegut's literary fortunes began to look much brighter. *Cat's Cradle* appeared in 1963, his first book in hardcover in more than a decade, and was favorably reviewed in the *New York Times Book Review* and the *Spectator*. The novel presents a dark comic vision of the end of the world brought on by the irresponsible use of technology. Although the book sold only modestly at the time of its publication, it has come to be regarded as among Vonnegut's best works. In fact, in 1971, more than twenty-five years after his thesis was rejected, the University of Chicago decided to award him the master's degree in recognition of the book's contribution to the field of cultural anthropology.

His next novel, *God Bless You, Mr. Rosewater; or, Pearls Before Swine* (1965), was significant for two reasons: it became his first widely reviewed book, and it introduced his best-known recurring character, Kilgore Trout, the science-fiction hack writer who serves as Vonnegut's alter ego (a literary second self) in many of the works to follow. In 1965, too, Vonnegut was sufficiently well known to be offered a two-year appointment as writer-in-residence at the University of Iowa's prestigious Writers' Workshop.

In 1967 Vonnegut was awarded a Guggenheim Fellowship, which he used to return to Dresden after more than twenty years to do research for a book about his wartime experiences there. That book, published in March 1969, was *Slaughterhouse-Five* (containing a comically long subtitle of some eighty words), which has consistently appeared on lists of the best American novels ever written. Climbing to number one on the *New York Times* best-seller list, it launched Vonnegut to international prominence. The autobiographical novel tells the story of Billy Pilgrim, an emotionally fragile chaplain's assistant, who, like Vonnegut, is captured behind enemy lines during World War II and imprisoned at a Dresden slaughterhouse. The book is remarkable for a variety of reasons. Although its tone is almost childlike in its simplicity, the narrative effectively projects the horror and absurdity of war, an idea that stands in stark contrast to the glorification of World War II and its soldiers found in most postwar novels and popular films. Moreover, this book marks the full emergence of Vonnegut's trademark style—telling a story out of chronological sequence in short narrative bursts, with ordinary, everyday elements mixed in with absurdly imaginative elements (for example, space beings from the planet Tralfamadore). Although set during an earlier war, the book became a rallying point for youth then protesting America's involvement in Vietnam. "So it goes"—the novel's often-repeated catchphrase, used whenever someone or something dies—became the slogan of a generation.

Vonnegut's long-awaited literary success seemed to make him depressed and restless. In 1970 he separated from his wife after twenty-five years of marriage. He also asserted that he would not write another novel and instead tried his hand at a variety of other political, artistic, and academic endeavors. In January 1970 he traveled to Biafra, a war-torn region of Nigeria suffering from mass starvation. Later that year he was appointed to the faculty of Harvard University's creative writing program, and in October his play *Happy Birthday, Wanda June* opened off-Broadway in New York City to mixed reviews. In 1973 he was appointed the distinguished professor of English prose at the City University of New York. That year, having abandoned his vow not to write another novel, he published his most bizarre book, *Breakfast of Champions.* Although it proved to be a commercial success, many of the reviewers who so enthusiastically embraced *Slaughterhouse-Five* were confused by, even hostile toward, this new work. Critics also expressed disapproval of his next book, *Slapstick; or, Lonesome No More* (1976), which was notable only for the fact that on its cover he began to identify himself simply as "Kurt Vonnegut," dropping the "Jr." tag that he had used since the beginning of his career.

In the late 1970s things were looking a bit brighter for Vonnegut, both personally and professionally. His first grandchild was born in 1977, and in 1979, his divorce from his first wife finalized, he married the photographer Jill Krementz, with whom he had been living since his separation in 1970. The couple adopted an infant daughter in 1982. Also in 1979, *Jailbird*, his comic novel about the Watergate political scandals, was published, drawing modest praise, and a musical version of *God Bless You, Mr. Rose-water*, written by Vonnegut's daughter Edith, premiered at the Entermedia Theatre in New York. He then published three new books in quick succession: *Sun Moon Star* (1980), a children's book with illustrations by Ivan Chermayeff; *Palm Sunday: An Autobiographical Collage* (1981), a collection of essays and reviews; and *Deadeye Dick* (1982), which, for personal reasons, he considered his best work but which failed to excite readers or critics. In 1984 depression set in again, and the famed author made an unsuccessful suicide attempt with alcohol and sleeping pills.

Rebounding in 1985, Vonnegut published *Galapagos*, which some reviewers and many readers believed was his best work in years. Another end-of-the-world novel, this one takes place over the span of a million years and playfully makes use of Charles Darwin's principles of evolution to envision a new humanity. Critical reception of the book was the best since *Slaughterhouse-Five* had come out sixteen years earlier. Yet just two years later, when *Bluebeard* (1987) came out, respected periodicals such as *Newsweek*, the *New York Review of Books*, and the *Times Literary Supplement* (of the London *Times*) refused to review it. Interestingly, as elite reviewers began to shun Vonnegut, charging the author with repeating tired themes, techniques, and characters, popular culture continued to embrace him. He had a comic cameo in Rodney Dangerfield's film *Back to School* (1986); the Showtime cable channel aired dramatized versions of several short stories under the title *Kurt Vonnegut's Monkey House* (1991), with Vonnegut himself providing brief introductions; and film versions of *Mother*

Night (1996) and *Breakfast of Champions* (1999) were released. Moreover, Vonnegut's work remained popular in high school and college classes. He published two more novels, *Hocus Pocus* (1990) and *Timequake* (1999), as well as several collections of new and previously published short pieces, including *Fates Worse Than Death: An Autobiographical Collage of the 1980s* (1991), *Bagombo Snuff Box* (1999), *God Bless You, Dr. Kevorkian* (2000), *A Man Without a Country* (2005), and the posthumously published *Armageddon in Retrospect* (2008).

In 2000 Vonnegut was hospitalized for smoke inhalation after a fire broke out at his home. After his recovery, he took a position teaching advanced writing at Smith College in Northampton, Massachusetts, and was named state author of New York. Vonnegut died at Mount Sinai Hospital in New York City at the age of eighty-four, after a fall at his Manhattan home several weeks earlier had left him with irreversible brain damage. A memorial service was held on 21 April 2007 at the Algonquin Hotel in New York, and interment details remained private.

Out of a long career in which he wrote many works of fiction and nonfiction, it was the inventive style, unique approach to telling a story, black humor, and antiwar theme of *Slaughterhouse-Five* that made Vonnegut a hero to American counterculture youth in the early 1970s and a literary idol to subsequent generations. Some view him as a starry-eyed philosopher, others as a gentle, tragicomic critic of all that is wrong in the world. He remains a voice that inspires idealism and for that reason continues to be taught in high schools and universities worldwide.

★

For the best autobiographical statements, see the author's own nonfiction collections: *Wampeters, Foma & Granfalloons* (1974), *Palm Sunday: An Autobiographical Collage* (1981), *Fates Worse Than Death* (1991), *God Bless You, Dr. Kevorkian* (2000), *A Man Without a Country* (2005), and *Armageddon in Retrospect* (2008). Several good biographies have appeared since the early 1970s, notably Peter J. Reed, *Kurt Vonnegut, Jr.* (1972); Stanley Schatt, *Kurt Vonnegut, Jr.* (1976); James Lundquist, *Kurt Vonnegut* (1977); Jerome Klinkowitz, *Kurt Vonnegut* (1982); and John Tomedi, *Kurt Vonnegut* (2004). Marc Leeds, *Vonnegut Encyclopedia* (1995), is a useful companion to the writer's universe. For an overview of academic and mass-media criticism, see Leonard Mustazza, *The Critical Response to Kurt Vonnegut* (1994); for an excellent assessment of Vonnegut's influence over the years, see Klinkowitz, *The Vonnegut Effect* (2004). Obituaries are in the *New York Times* and *Los Angeles Times* (both 12 Apr. 2007) and the *Guardian* (13 Apr. 2007).

Leonard Mustazza

WADE, Richard Clement (*b.* 14 July 1921 in Des Moines, Iowa; *d.* 19 July 2008 in New York City), widely regarded as the father of urban history in the United States whose book *The Urban Frontier: The Rise of Western Cities, 1790–1830* (1959) reshaped the understanding of the westward movement.

Although born in Iowa, Wade grew up in an Irish-American family in the northern suburbs of Chicago. His father was an attorney. In Chicago, Wade starred as a tennis player at New Trier High School and became a member of the Midwest Junior Davis Cup team. He then entered the University of Rochester, where he not only excelled as a student but reached the round of sixteen in the National Collegiate Athletic Association national championship tennis competition in 1939, played varsity basketball for three seasons, and also competed in track, baseball, and football. After earning his undergraduate degree at Rochester, Wade moved on to Harvard University, where he studied with Arthur Schlesinger, Sr., and became a lifelong friend of Arthur Schlesinger, Jr. His dissertation was on the early settlement of the Ohio River Valley and focused on five communities: Pittsburgh, Pennsylvania; Cincinnati, Ohio; Louisville and Lexington, Kentucky; and St. Louis, Missouri. His conclusion was that the famous frontier thesis of Frederick Jackson Turner was wrong—farmers did not rub up against savages as the line of settlement moved west. Rather, cities were in place before the farmers arrived; they were the spearheads of the frontier.

After receiving his PhD in history from Harvard in 1954, Wade returned to the university as an assistant professor of history. He moved briefly to Washington University in St. Louis from 1961 to 1962 and then

joined the faculty of the University of Chicago in 1963 as professor of history. His nine-year tenure at that institution proved to be one of the most remarkable in the history of American higher education. His unusual combination of humor, insight, idealism, liberalism, and enthusiasm for his subject inspired hundreds of students to change their attitudes toward history and politics. In addition to the dozens of dissertations he sponsored, he launched the *Urban Life in America* series, which brought into print other studies that did not originate in his seminars.

Wade wrote many other books of seminal importance. His *Slavery in the Cities: The South, 1820–1860* (1964), argued that the peculiar institution of human bondage was ill suited to a crowded environment, in part because the very nature of city living made "discipline" difficult to enforce and administer and in part because the practice of "hiring out" and "living out" undermined slavery in places such as Charleston, South Carolina, so that bondage was declining in urban areas even before the Emancipation Proclamation and the Union army obliterated it in rural areas. Finally, *Chicago: Growth of a Metropolis* (1973), written with the geographer Harold M. Mayer, was unusual for its focus on outlying neighborhoods rather than the central business district, and for its use of photographs as part of the argument, not as gratuitous illustrations.

Wade did not play sports at an advanced level during his academic career, but he threw himself into politics with abandon. He was always unusual among historians for his near obsession with contemporary affairs. Even while teaching full time, he involved himself in speech writing and campaign strategy for those with whom he agreed. He commuted to New York in 1964 to manage the Empire State campaign of Robert F. Kennedy for the U.S. Senate, and he was among the small circle of admirers who advised George McGovern during his run for president in 1972. On more familiar turf, Wade served as a commissioner for the Chicago Housing Authority from 1967 to 1971, chaired the New York Governor's Commission for Historic Preservation from 1974 to 1978, and chaired the New York State Commission on Libraries from 1989 to 1993.

A founder and the first president of the Urban History Association, Wade was married three times—to Louise Carroll Wade, an urban historian who later taught at the University of Oregon; to Cynthia Hyla Whitaker, a Russian historian who chaired the history department at Baruch College in Manhattan; and to Liane (Wood-Thomas) Wade, who survived him. He had no children of his own but served as a surrogate father to the children of Whitaker. Wade died in New York City of natural causes at the age of eighty-seven. As per his request, his ashes were scattered at the south end of Roosevelt Island at the site of the future New York City memorial to President Franklin D. Roosevelt.

Wade was a close adviser and friend of dozens of powerful politicians at the federal, state, and local level. But he never sought office for himself. Rather, his goal was to overcome what he saw as the racist heritage of the United States, and to move the nation toward the full equality that he felt was the right of every citizen.

★

An obituary is in the *New York Times* (25 July 2008).

Kenneth T. Jackson

WAGONER, Porter Wayne (*b*. 12 August 1927 in South Fork, Missouri; *d*. 28 October 2007 in Nashville, Tennessee), country music superstar credited with popularizing the genre for a national audience through his recordings, performances, and work in television.

Wagoner was the fifth and last child born to Charles Wagoner and Bertha (Bridges) Wagoner, a farming couple. Working alongside his parents, two brothers, and two sisters on the family farm, near the town of West Plains, he ended his education in the seventh grade. His passion for music having surfaced at an early age, he raised money for his first guitar by selling pelts from rabbits he had caught himself. In 1943, at age sixteen, Wagoner married Velma Johnson, but they divorced a year later. In 1946 he married Ruth Olive Williams, with whom he had a son and two daughters.

When financial difficulties forced Wagoner's parents to sell their land and move to West Plains, Wagoner found work at a butcher shop. His employer soon discovered the young man's talent, enlisting Wagoner and his band, the Blue Ridge Boys, to sing jingles for the business on local

Porter Wagoner. RCA RECORDS/GETTY IMAGES

radio station KWPM in 1950. By 1951 Wagoner had made the transition to bigger and better venues, working at the Springfield, Missouri, radio station KWTO, where in 1952 Steve Sholes, a record producer for Radio Corporation of America and the man credited with signing Elvis Presley to his first record deal, offered Wagoner and his band their first recording contract. The Porter Wagoner Trio consisted of Wagoner on guitar and vocals, Don Warden playing steel guitar and singing harmony, and Herschel "Speedy" Haworth on the rhythm guitar.

Wagoner's performing costumes garnered a considerable amount of attention. In 1953 Wagoner bought his first "Nudie suit," named after the outfit's designer, Nudie Cohn. These flashy suits were decked out in rhinestones and wagon-wheel stitching. Wagoner's suits had the word "Hi" sewn into the coat's linings so that he could open his jacket to greet photographers or fans who approached him. Wagoner's musical and personal style came to be known as "hillbilly deluxe." He had his first commercial success with three Top Ten hits on the country music charts: "Trademark" (1953), written by Wagoner and performed by Carl Smith, which reached number two; and two songs written by others that Wagoner performed, "Company's Comin'" (1954), which reached number seven, and "A Satisfied Mind" (1955), which reached number one. He appeared for a year on American Broadcasting Company television's *Ozark Jubilee* (1955–1956), and moved with his family to Nashville in 1956.

Among his more than eighty hits to reach the charts, twenty-nine were Top Ten singles, including "Green, Green Grass of Home" (1965), "Skid Row Joe," and "The Cold Hard Facts of Life" (1967). One of his songwriting trademarks was a surprising ending to the story lines told by the lyrics. "Albert Erving" (2007), for example, spun the tale of a man who created a portrait of a woman he loved, yet the song's ending revealed that the woman was only a figment of the artist's dreams. Such lonely, despairing lyrics certainly characterized much of country music from Wagoner's era, yet his work proved to be unique and enduring. Wagoner was credited with introducing the "concept album" to country music. His 1967 *Soul of a Convict* garnered significant acclaim and commercial success, paving the way for work by such notable artists as Johnny Cash and Marty Stuart. He received numerous awards and honors, including three Grammy awards for gospel collaborations with the Blackwood Brothers in 1966, 1967, and 1969. In 1966 Wagoner and his wife became formally separated, though they did not obtain an official divorce until 1986.

Perhaps Wagoner's best-known contribution to country music was his television program, *The Porter Wagoner Show*, which aired from 1960 until 1981. After the departure of his previous singing partner in 1967, Wagoner introduced a talented twenty-year-old singer from Tennessee, Dolly Parton. Wagoner and Parton went on to record a number of duets, including fourteen Top Ten songs and the number-one hit "Please Don't Stop Loving Me" in 1974. The pair embarked on a number of national tours, and they won the Country Music Association's Group of the Year Award in 1970 and Duo of the Year in 1971.

After Parton left the show in 1974, she and Wagoner spent six years in court battling over such professional issues as ownership of songs on which the two collaborated. Rumors swirled about the nature of their partnership, including allegations of a romantic relationship that jeopardized the marriages of both stars. Parton said that Wagoner served as the inspiration for her 1974 hit, "I Will Always Love You," yet she and Wagoner always insisted that their relationship was purely platonic.

Wagoner officially retired from touring in 1976, focusing instead on music production and work with the Grand Ole Opry. In 1979 he arranged the Opry appearance of the soul singer James Brown, who performed country standards as well as his own "Papa's Got a Brand New Bag." Switchboard operators at the Opry were said to have fielded a variety of complaints after Brown's appearance, and the *New York Times* labeled those "riled" by the performance unnamed "country traditionalists." Wagoner also ventured into Hollywood during this period, making a brief appearance in Clint Eastwood's 1982 film *Honkytonk Man*.

Wagoner had been a frequent performer at the Grand Ole Opry from his first appearance in 1960, and in 1992,

upon the death of Roy Acuff, he stepped into the role of unofficial spokesman. In the 1990s he also cohosted the Nashville Network's *Opry Backstage* with Bill Anderson. Wagoner was inducted into the Country Music Hall of Fame in 2002, and he continued performing up until the last year of his life. He released his final gospel album, *Gospel 2006*, in 2006, and a country album, *Wagonmaster*, in 2007. In July 2007 he served as the opening act for the rock band the White Stripes at Madison Square Garden in New York City.

Wagoner, who struggled with health problems in the later years of his life, died of lung cancer at Alive Hospice in Nashville at the age of eighty. A public funeral honored Wagoner's musical and personal legacy at the Grand Ole Opry on 1 November 2007. He is buried at the Woodlawn Cemetery in Nashville.

Wagoner made his mark not only as a singer and songwriter but also as a true entertainer who connected with audiences. He helped develop the careers of other future stars, notably Parton, and always celebrated the country music traditions he was steeped in. His television show brought country to huge numbers of viewers, many of whom were hearing this music for the first time. Familiar as the blond man in the rhinestone-studded suit, he was one of the major figures of country music.

Steven Eng, *A Satisfied Mind: The Country Music Life of Porter Wagoner* (1992), an official biography, remains the primary source of information on his personal and professional lives. Parton's autobiography, *Dolly: My Life and Other Unfinished Business* (1994), includes interesting information regarding the volatile relationship between the two stars. Obituaries are in the *Los Angeles Times* (29 Oct. 2007), *New York Times* (30 Oct. 2007), and *Tennessean* (30 Oct. 2007).

Kimberly K. Little

WALD, Florence Sophie Schorske (*b.* 19 April 1917 in New York City; *d.* 8 November 2008 in Branford, Connecticut), nurse, dean of the Yale School of Nursing, and founder of the first hospice program in the United States.

Wald was the younger of two children of Theodore Alexander Schorske, a banker, and Gertrude (Goldschmidt) Schorske, who worked in the shipping industry. Despite her father's ties to banking, both parents were members of the Socialist Party and were committed to social activism, concentrating their efforts toward helping immigrants adjust to American life. Wald's older brother became an eminent European intellectual historian at

Princeton University. Wald was raised and educated in Scarsdale, New York, graduated from Mount Holyoke College with a BS in 1938, and received a master's degree in nursing from Yale University in 1941. She then took at job as a staff nurse at Children's Hospital in Boston and worked there between 1941 and 1942. In 1942 Wald returned to New York City to pursue her nursing career. She became a staff nurse for the Visiting Nurse Service of New York, a research assistant at the Columbia University College of Physicians and Surgeons, and an instructor at the Rutgers University School of Nursing.

During World War II, Wald served as a research technician with the U.S. Army Signal Corps; there she met Henry Wald, a participant in the study, who proposed marriage. She declined, but later in life Henry Wald, by then a widower with two young children, renewed the offer, and the two were married in 1959; they would have a son and a daughter. In 1956 Florence Wald received a second master's degree from Yale, in mental health nursing, and became an instructor in the school's nursing program. She rose to become dean of the school in 1959, a position she held until 1966. She continued to hold a faculty position in the Yale Nursing School and was promoted to full professor in 1980.

In 1963 Wald attended a lecture at Yale given by the English physician Cicely Saunders, an innovator in the hospice field. The lecture's focus on palliative care for terminally ill cancer patients energized Wald, who remarked that "until then I had thought nurses were the only people troubled by how a terminal illness was treated."

Wald soon devoted her career to the hospice movement. She visited Saunders twice in England, spending a one-month internship at Saint Christopher's Hospice in London, the institution founded by Saunders. Wald's husband accompanied her and then reframed his career by enrolling in a Columbia University program in hospital planning and creating a plan for the Connecticut Hospice in his graduate thesis in 1971. Wald worked for several years with a team of doctors, clergy, and nurses before opening the first hospice in the United States in Branford. At first the program offered only home care, but by 1980 a forty-four-bed facility had opened in Branford. Disagreements with the governing board of the hospice forced Wald to resign just before the facility opened. Her program at Branford inspired similar efforts around the country. By 1980 Medicaid had begun to pay for hospice care, spurring further development. By 2008 there were more than 3,000 hospice programs in the United States, serving approximately 900,000 patients. Among those who benefited from Wald's innovations were her college and graduate roommate, Elsie Russell Hodges, and her husband, the Reverend Graham Rushing Hodges.

Wald's experiences in working with hospice patients also led to her support of euthanasia. "There are cases in which either the pain or the debilitation the patient is experiencing is more than can be borne, whether it be economically, physically, emotionally or socially," she said. She argued that "a range of options," including assisted suicide, should be available to terminally ill patients.

Wald turned her attention to establishing the hospice movement in the American prison system. She traveled extensively on a research project for the National Prison Hospice Association, an organization founded in Boulder, Colorado, in 1991. Wald promoted use of the hospice methods for prison inmates, training them to help one another or to arrange compassionate leave outside of prisons for the terminally ill. In an interview with the *Journal of the American Medical Association*, she said that the needs of prisoners are different because they face death knowing that they have not had successful lives. She found that inmates serving as hospice volunteers gained confidence from the experience. "It shows that even in this terrible situation, something good can happen, a sense of possibility emerges," she said.

Among many honors, Wald received a Founders Award from the National Hospice Association and the American Academy of Nursing's Living Legends Award in 2001. The Connecticut Nurses' Association established an award in her name for outstanding contributions to the field of nursing. In 1996 Wald was inducted into the American Nurses Association Hall of Fame, followed by induction into the National Women's Hall of Fame in 1998 and the Connecticut Hall of Fame in 1999. In 2004 she received the Connecticut Treasure Award. Henry Wald died in 2000. Wald died at her home in Branford at age ninety-one. A funeral service was held at Battell Chapel of Yale University on 12 November 2008.

When Wald received an honorary doctorate from Yale in 1996, she was introduced as "the mother of the American hospice movement." In a characteristic show of modesty, she responded, "That's a completely incorrect description. . . . There were many, many people in those days who were just as inspired and motivated as I was." In November 2007 the Connecticut Department of Veterans' Affairs dedicated the Florence and Henry Wald House to provide a peaceful temporary home for families involved with hospice care at the facility.

★

Wald's papers are housed in the Yale University Library Archives. Wald's interview about prison hospice is in M. J. Friedrich, "Hospice Care in the United States: A Conversation with Florence S. Wald," *Journal of the American Medical Association* 281 (1999): 1683–1685. Obituaries are in the *New York Times* and *Los Angeles Times* (both 14 Nov. 2008).

Graham Russell Gao Hodges

WALGREEN, Charles Rudolph, Jr. (*b.* 4 March 1906 in Chicago, Illinois; *d.* 10 February 2007 in Northfield, Illinois), son of the founder of Walgreens, the largest drugstore chain in the United States, who succeeded his father as the company's president in 1939 and who guided the firm for thirty-seven years during a period of rapid growth and innovation.

Walgreen was the second of three children born to Charles R. Walgreen, Sr., president of the drugstore chain Walgreens, and Myrtle (Norton) Walgreen, a homemaker. Walgreen's father was born to Swedish immigrants in Rio, a farm hamlet outside of Galesburg, Illinois. In 1887 the Walgreen family moved to Dixon, Illinois. There Walgreen's father worked at the largest drugstore in town for nearly two years. After moving to Chicago in 1893 to seek his future, he worked at a variety of drugstores and in 1897 passed the Illinois State Board of Pharmacy practical examination, becoming a registered pharmacist. Four years later he opened the first Walgreens drugstore at 4134 South Cottage Grove Avenue on Chicago's South Side.

Charles R. Walgreen, Jr. BLOOMBERG NEWS/LANDOV

Growth of the Walgreens chain over the next twenty-five years was steady, and innovations were measured. By 1915 there were five stores in the Chicago area; each had a soda fountain and a lunch service as a way to differentiate Walgreens from the competition. By the mid-1920s the chain had sixty-five stores, fifty-nine of which were in Chicago and its suburbs, and annual sales reached $1.2 million. Charles Walgreen, Sr., then accelerated the pace of expansion, and by 1930 the number of stores approached 400 with total annual sales of about $4 million. In 1939, when the younger Walgreen became president shortly before his father's death, the company had over 500 stores nationwide. The ascendancy of Walgreens during the elder Walgreen's thirty-eight years of leadership earned Charles Walgreen, Sr., a designation as one of the country's foremost entrepreneurs.

In his youth the younger Walgreen gave every indication that he would spend his adult life working in the drugstore business. At age nine he was making deliveries from one of his father's stores, and at age eleven he carried his mother's homemade soups to the store's lunch counter. As a senior at the University of Chicago High School, however, the young Walgreen showed unusual adeptness in design and architectural drawings. In 1923, after graduating from high school, he entered the University of Michigan as a liberal arts major, intent on becoming an architect. At about that time the Illinois legislature passed a law requiring any corporate officer, owner, or manager of a drugstore to be a licensed pharmacist. After a lengthy conversation with his father about his future, Walgreen changed his course of study to pharmaceutical chemistry, graduating with a PhC in 1928. In 1933 he married Mary Ann Leslie; she would die in 1983, shortly before the couple's fiftieth wedding anniversary. The Walgreens had three children. During the late 1920s and through the 1930s, Walgreen worked at a variety of in-store and corporate jobs with the company. He succeeded his father as president in 1939, a position he held until 1963, when he became chairman of the board of directors, a post from which he retired in 1976.

Not content to preserve the status quo, Walgreen spent his thirty-seven years as the head of Walgreens turning the company into America's drugstore. He made expansion an integral part of the company's corporate culture. During his tenure annual sales increased from $72 million to nearly $1 billion, and the number of stores topped 700. At the time of Walgreen's death, the company was operating approximately 6,700 stores, serving 5 million customers per day, and filling over 600 million prescriptions per year, with annual sales of nearly $50 billion. Walgreen not only made Walgreens bigger; he also made it better.

From his firsthand experiences in the 1930s, Walgreen was well aware of the long hours and the hard work expected of pharmacists, and he resolved to improve the working conditions and the professional stature of those who gave their all to the mortar and pestle. At the time of his ascendancy to company president, pharmacists in the United States typically worked between sixty and seventy hours per week, and their compensation was based in part on commissions from nonpharmaceutical sales and on kickbacks from brand manufacturers of consumables. Almost single-handedly Walgreen gradually reduced pharmacists' hours at his stores from an industry norm of sixty to forty per week, and he discontinued practices that compensated pharmacists for tasks not directly related to their professional expertise. These changes helped to improve the professional image of pharmacists, putting it on a par with that of doctors, attorneys, and accountants.

In addition to his innovations in human resource management, Walgreen pioneered other business practices. Early in the 1950s Walgreens led the way to self-service shopping from clerk-assisted merchandising. A longtime member of Rotary International, Walgreen, in 1955, incorporated that organization's "Four-Way Test" into a code of conduct for the corporation; it still forms the ethical foundation of the company. The test asks that any business action or decision produce an affirmative response to four fundamental questions: Is it the truth? Is it fair to all concerned? Will it build goodwill and better friendship? Will it be beneficial to all concerned?

After his retirement Walgreen continued to work two or three days a week into his nineties, but his focus shifted to other activities. In 1971 he passed all of the U.S. Coast Guard exams required to earn an unlimited ocean captain's license. Thereafter he spent much of his time sailing the world. In 1995, at age eighty-nine, he traveled to the Walgreen Coast, a 1,000-mile stretch of Antarctica shoreline so named by Admiral Richard E. Byrd for Charles Walgreen, Sr. Six years later with his second wife, Jean, and a crew including professional nurses, Walgreen sailed his new 127-foot yacht, the *Sis W.*, to the East Coast, the Panama Canal, and the Galapagos Islands. A generous benefactor particularly of his alma mater, Walgreen was recognized in 2005 for his philanthropy when the University of Michigan named a new drama center in his honor.

Walgreen could have merely maintained the business his father built; instead he strove to make something good even better, and did so with considerable success. He died three weeks shy of his 101st birthday, leaving behind a leadership legacy based on a blend of compassion, integrity, and panache.

★

Extensive biographical information is in Herman Kogan and Rick Kogan, *Pharmacist to the Nation* (1989), and John U. Bacon, *America's Corner Store* (2004). Each book also contains a business history of Walgreens. For additional facts about the Walgreen family and business, see Daniel I. Dorfman, "Focus: Influential Families: Walgreen," *Crain's Chicago Business* (17 Oct. 2005), and "Legacy of the Walgreen Jr. Years," *Drug Store News* (19 Mar. 2007). Obituaries are in the *Chicago Tribune* (11 Feb. 2007), *Chicago Sun-Times* (12 Feb. 2007), *New York Times* (13 Feb. 2007), and *Drug Store News* (5 Mar. 2007).

James Cicarelli

WALLACE, David Foster (*b*. 21 February 1962 in Ithaca, New York; *d*. 12 September 2008 in Claremont, California), metafiction and postmodern writer, most famous for penning *Infinite Jest*, a 1,004 page novel about addiction and tennis.

Wallace was one of two children born to James Donald Wallace and Sally Foster Wallace, both college teachers. As a young child he lived in Champaign, Illinois; when he was in fourth grade his family moved to Urbana, Illinois. There he attended Yankee Ridge school. He went to Amherst College, his father's alma mater, and graduated summa cum laude with a BA in English and philosophy in 1985. He received an MFA in creative writing from the

David Foster Wallace. ©GARY HANNABARGER/CORBIS

University of Arizona. While growing up in Illinois, Wallace was a regionally ranked tennis player, a life experience that would later find its way into his novel *Infinite Jest*, the book that would put him on the literary map.

In 1987 he published his debut novel, *The Broom of the System*, a book that drew comparisons from critics to the work of John Irving, Thomas Pynchon, and Stanley Elkin. Concerning a switchboard operator who deals with the disappearance of her great-grandmother and twenty-five other members of a nursing home, a sexless love affair with her boss, the stardom of her talking cockatiel, and a search for self-determination that leads to life complications, *The Broom of the System* established Wallace's style of filling his pages with arcane and valuable information on myriad topics. He drafted footnotes that could take up a full page of text, and he created sentences that were both convoluted and expansive.

Despite suffering bouts of severe depression, Wallace was unflaggingly prolific throughout his career and was in print from 1987 until his untimely death. He published many short pieces in magazines and literary journals, notably "Lyndon" (1987), "Other Math" (1987), "Here and There" (1987), "Solomon Silverfish" (1987), "Say Never" (1987), "John Billy" (1988), "Fictional Futures and the Conspicuously Young" (1988), "Late Night" (1988), "Little Expressionless Animals" (1988), "Everything Is Green" (1988), "Church Not Made with Hands" (1990), "Forever Overhead" (1991), "Tennis, Trigonometry, Tornadoes" (1991), and "Order and Flux in Northampton" (1991). The story collection *Girl with Curious Hair* was published in 1989. In it, Wallace took on such diverse topics as President Lyndon Johnson, game-show hosts, late-night comedians, and a clash between punk nihilism and young Republicans.

The following year saw the appearance of *Signifying Rappers: Rap and Race in the Urban Present*. Wallace attended Harvard University as a graduate student in philosophy but left his studies to teach literature at Boston's Emerson College in 1991. In 1992 the literary scholar Steven Moore, an expert in metafiction, encouraged Wallace to apply for a teaching position in English at Illinois State University. Work on his second novel, *Infinite Jest* had begun in 1991, and by 1993 Wallace was ready to submit a draft of it. The book appeared to great acclaim in 1996. At thirty-four years old, Wallace had completed his last novel. He began to write short fiction for the top American magazines and publications—the *New Yorker*, *Harper's*, *Esquire*, and *Best American Short Stories*, among numerous others.

The following year saw another short-story collection, *A Supposedly Fun Thing I'll Never Do Again*. In it Wallace took on tennis, philosophy, postmodern literary theory, and the film director David Lynch. Also in 1997 Wallace won the prestigious "genius grant" from the MacArthur

Foundation. Meanwhile, his output only increased; he contributed to *Mid-American Review*, *Parnassus: Poetry in Review*, *Harper's*, *Ploughshares*, and *McSweeney's Quarterly*, among many others. The story collection *Brief Interviews with Hideous Men* appeared in 1999. In 2002 Wallace became the first Roy E. Disney Professor of Creative Writing and Professor of English at Pomona College in Claremont, California.

During the first decade of the twenty-first century Wallace continued to produce a steady stream of nonfiction, short stories, essays, and articles. Among these was the nonfiction *Everything and More* (2003) and *Oblivion* (2004), a short-story collection. On 27 December 2004, Wallace married Karen L. Green. They had no children. In 2005 Wallace published an essay collection, *Consider the Lobster and Other Essays*.

At the time of his death by suicide Wallace was at work on a third novel, *The Pale King* (projected 2010). The publisher Michael Pietsch assembled the manuscript from thousands of draft pages, notes, and outlines. The story is set in an Illinois Internal Revenue Service facility. Wallace, the ever-meticulous researcher, enrolled in an accounting course to familiarize himself with the subject. His passing left a hole in the development of the metafiction genre.

★

Critical studies of Wallace's work can be found in Stephen Burn, *David Foster Wallace's* Infinite Jest: *A Reader's Guide* (2003); Marshall Boswell, *Understanding David Foster Wallace* (2003); Greg Carlisle, *Elegant Complexity: A Study of David Foster Wallace's* Infinite Jest *(2007); and Stefan Hirt, The Iron Bars of Freedom: David Foster Wallace and the Postmodern Self* (2008). Obituaries are in the *New York Times* and *Los Angeles Times* (both 14 Sept. 2008).

Vincent LoBrutto

WALSH, William Ernest (''Bill'') (*b*. 30 November 1931 in Los Angeles, California; *d*. 30 July 2007 in Woodside, California), professional football coach and architect of the San Francisco 49ers' National Football League (NFL) dynasty whose mastery of the passing game had a profound effect on offensive football at all levels of the game.

Walsh was the son of William Archibald Walsh, a manual laborer who worked mainly in automobile production, and Ruth (Mathers) Walsh, a homemaker. Walsh spent most of his youth in the Los Angeles area before moving to northern California's East Bay area when he was fifteen. At Hayward Union High School, he was a fine multisport athlete, best known for quarterbacking the football team.

Bill Walsh, 1988. MICHAEL ZAGARIS/GETTY IMAGES

After graduation in 1949, Walsh was hoping for an athletic scholarship, but one never materialized. Family finances did not permit his matriculating at a four-year college, so he took advantage of California's liberal higher education system and enrolled at San Mateo Junior College for two years, earning an AA in 1952. He then entered San Jose State University, where he majored in physical education and got a BA in 1954. A bit "street tough," Walsh participated in Golden Gloves boxing and came close to becoming a sparring partner for the then heavyweight champion Rocky Marciano. However, Marciano's upcoming opponent was a large, plodding fighter, and Walsh's quick-hitting and elusive style was deemed unsuitable. Walsh's friend George Coakley hinted that the decision may have been lucky for Marciano, noting that "Bill had a killer left hook."

At San Jose State, injuries curtailed Walsh's playing time. Walsh had hoped to be a quarterback, but his coaches played him—when they played him—as an offensive end. However, despite sporadic playing opportunities, Walsh absorbed enough of the game to realize that coaching was

a possible future calling. He stayed on at San Jose State after graduation and took an MA in education in 1959.

Walsh served briefly with the U.S. Army during the closing months of the Korean War. In 1955 he married Geri Nardini, whom he had met while he was a graduate student at San Jose State. They had three children.

Walsh made enough of an impression on the San Jose State coach, Bob Bronzan, that he was hired as a graduate assistant the same year he got married. After a year as a graduate assistant (a low-pay or no-pay position) with the Spartans, Walsh secured his first full-time job, as head football coach of Washington Union High School in Fremont, California. Before sending Walsh off to his first head coaching job, a prescient Bronzan said that Walsh would one day "become the outstanding football coach in the United States."

Walsh, who coached under three Pro Football Hall of Fame coaches—Paul Brown, Al Davis, and Marv Levy—would later single out Bronzan as the individual "who most greatly influenced" his philosophy and methods as a coach. With an innovative and far-reaching passing game, Walsh brought a conference championship to Washington Union in his third season at the helm. The year before Walsh arrived, Washington Union had won only one game.

In 1960 Walsh made the leap to major college football. He was hired by the head coach Levy as defensive coordinator at the University of California, Berkeley. Three years later Walsh began a long and fruitful association at Stanford University under John Ralston as the Cardinals' defensive coordinator. It may seem odd that the man termed "the Genius" for his offensive innovations began his college coaching career as a defensive coordinator, but Walsh credited his understanding of defense with helping his mastery of the offensive side of the game. Walsh also served as Ralston's recruiting coordinator.

Continuing his climb, Walsh moved to the Oakland Raiders as Al Davis's backfield coach in 1966. At the time the Raiders were members of the American Football League. During that time Walsh completed the requirements for an MBA from Stanford.

In 1968 the legendary coach Brown tapped Walsh to be his quarterbacks coach and offensive coordinator with the American Football League expansion Cincinnati Bengals. Walsh stayed in Cincinnati for eight seasons, experiencing the best of times and the worst of times. He developed many of the principles of what would become known as the West Coast offense, while developing the quarterbacks Virgil Carter, the star-crossed Greg Cook, and the unheralded Ken Anderson. West Coast "wrinkles" included the scripting of the game's opening offensive plays. Initially only about the first six plays were scripted on Thursdays and Fridays to be run on Sundays, but eventually the number of scripted plays grew to twenty-five. Walsh felt that it was better to decide the plays in an unhurried manner during practice sessions than to try to formulate a plan of attack during the heat of battle. These plays included tactics almost exclusive to the Bengals—quick quarterback "reads"; three, four, or five receivers quickly out for passes; precision pass routes and precision timing between the quarterback and the receiver; and the use of running backs as receivers. While all of these tactics would eventually become common at all levels, including high school, college, and professional football, in the 1960s they were departures from the traditional strategies.

Walsh was gaining a reputation as a potential NFL head coach, but Brown could be as vindictive as he was innovative. Brown discouraged those teams who inquired about Walsh's availability and went so far as to refuse Walsh permission to interview for the Houston Oilers' head coaching job. The original thinking was that Brown wanted Walsh as his own successor. However, when Brown resigned on New Year's Day in 1976, Walsh was not elevated to Bengals head coach. Brown chose another assistant, Bill "Tiger" Johnson. Walsh, who heard about Johnson's hiring "through a sportswriter, not Brown," was obviously hurt as well as stunned and left the Bengals to become Tommy Prothro's assistant with the San Diego Chargers. In San Diego, Walsh helped develop the young Dan Fouts into a future Pro Football Hall of Fame quarterback. After one season in San Diego, Walsh became head coach at Stanford University and produced a 17–7 record over two seasons.

Finally, in 1979, at age forty-eight, Walsh was tapped as an NFL head coach. Unfortunately, he was hired by the San Francisco 49ers, the dregs of the league. The team Walsh took over had gone 2–14 the previous season. In five prior seasons, the neophyte owner Eddie DeBartolo, Jr., had gone through six head coaches. Before being fired, DeBartolo's general manger Joe Thomas had left the franchise bereft of talent through egocentric player personnel decisions and trades. Walsh quickly replenished the talent pool. Over the next few years, through the draft and wise trades, Walsh secured the services of such stars as Dan Bunz, Dwight Clark, Roger Craig, Randy Cross, Fred Dean, Ronnie Lott, Joe Montana, Jack "Hacksaw" Reynolds, and Jerry Rice.

Walsh's magic, though, was not so quickly evident. He, too, took the 49ers to a 2–14 record in his first season. In 1980 the team improved to 6–10, but still there were few believers. That situation changed in 1981. The franchise posted a regular season record of 13–3 and shocked the Dallas Cowboys, and much of the pro football world, by winning the National Football Conference championship game 28–27. The play that won the game is known simply as "the catch." In the final minute Clark raced along the back of the end zone, leaped, and pulled down

Montana's high desperation pass. The 49ers were off to Detroit for Super Bowl XVI; they faced the Bengals, who were no longer coached by Johnson.

To loosen the team, Walsh donned a bellman's uniform and helped unsuspecting players with their luggage at the team hotel in Detroit. Montana, not recognizing Walsh, put up a momentary struggle when Walsh tried to take Montana's briefcase. The game was not as close as the score (San Francisco 26–Cincinnati 21) indicated. It was said at the time that the most often told lie in the Bay Area was, "I've always been a Niners' fan."

As "the Team of the Eighties," San Francisco won Super Bowl XIX in 1985 and Super Bowl XXIII in 1989 under Walsh. Citing football as "a very stressful occupation," Walsh retired in 1989 with a record of 102–63 and put in two seasons as a television analyst for the National Broadcasting Company.

The coaching bug bit Walsh in 1992, and he returned to Stanford for two seasons. After that he was a consultant to the 49ers, taking over as general manager in 1999. In 2001, at age seventy, he retired fully. After a three-year battle with leukemia, Walsh succumbed at his home. His remains were cremated, and his ashes were scattered in Monterey, California.

Steve Young, a Pro Football Hall of Fame quarterback whom Walsh acquired to supplant Montana, said of Walsh, "He was the most important person in football in the last twenty-five years—no debate." At the time of Walsh's death, twenty of the NFL's thirty-two franchises could trace their coaching lineage back to Walsh.

While publicly Walsh appeared cerebral and professorial, his tantrums and tirades were legendary inside the 49ers organization. Dubbed "the Genius," Walsh, who was inducted into the Pro Football Hall of Fame in 1993, irritated some by the ease with which he accepted the moniker. Others thought he gave little or no credit to his assistants and players. Tom Gadd, who successfully used Walsh's West Coast offense at Bucknell University, however, succinctly sized up Walsh when he said, "He knew the passing game and how to coach it."

★

Walsh authored *Finding the Winning Edge* (1998), with Brian Billick and James A. Peterson. Other works about Walsh and his coaching methods include Lowell Cohn, *Rough Magic: Bill Walsh's Return to Stanford Football* (1994); Susan M. Moyer, *Remembering "The Genius": 1931–2007* (2007); and David Harris, *The Genius: How Bill Walsh Reinvented Football and Created an NFL Dynasty* (2008). Obituaries are in the *New York Times* and *San Francisco Chronicle* (both 31 July 2007).

Jim Campbell

WASSERSTEIN, Wendy Joy (*b*. 18 October 1950 in New York City; *d*. 30 January 2006 in New York City), playwright and author known for her portrayals of women's issues, humorous style, and advocacy of theater, and recipient of the Pulitzer Prize and many other honors in American drama.

Wasserstein was the youngest of four children born to Polish-born Jewish immigrants. Her father, Morris Wasserstein, was a textile and novelty manufacturer, and her mother, Lola (Schleifer) Wasserstein, was a dancer and homemaker. Wasserstein was also the granddaughter of the Polish playwright Solomon Schleifer. In the early 1960s this family of high achievers moved from Brooklyn to the Upper East Side of New York City, where Wasserstein graduated from the private Calhoun School in 1967. She studied dance at the June Taylor Dance School and attended Saturday matinees, beginning her lifelong love of theater. Wasserstein graduated from Mount Holyoke College in 1971 with a BA in history; while there she took playwriting courses at nearby Smith College and Amherst College. She continued her education at City College, part of the City University of New York, and graduated in 1973 with an MA in creative writing. After completing her MA she applied to and was accepted by both the Columbia University Business School and the Yale School of Drama. Wasserstein chose to study at Yale and received an MFA in 1976.

Wasserstein's thesis for her degree at City College, *Any Woman Can't*, is a satirical play about a woman's dance audition. The play was produced off-Broadway in 1973. Playwrights Horizons, an organization that, particularly under the artistic director André Bishop, became Wasserstein's second home was connected with the production. *Happy Birthday, Montpelier Pizz-zazz*, which depicts a college party scene, was produced at Yale in 1974, while *When Dinah Shore Ruled the Earth*, a play exposing beauty pageants, was produced at Yale in 1975. The play was coauthored by the playwright and actor Christopher Durang, Wasserstein's lifelong friend whom she met at Yale. In the School of Drama at Yale, Wasserstein also met and became friends with the actress Meryl Streep and the playwright Albert Innaurato. Wasserstein's *Uncommon Women and Others* was first performed at Yale in 1977 as her one-act thesis project. She then revised and expanded the play for the National Playwrights Conference at the Eugene O'Neill Theater Center in Waterford, Connecticut. With its descriptive subtitle, "A Play About Five Women Graduates of a Seven Sisters College Six Years Later," this episodic work was set in two periods with a male narrator and several songs (features that appear in her other works). The play was also produced by the Phoenix Theatre group at the Marymount Manhattan Theatre in New York City in 1977 and as a made-for-television movie that was released by the Public Broadcasting Service in 1979 with Streep. For the play Wasserstein won the Drama-Logue Award, Joseph Jefferson Award, and Inner Boston Critics Award.

Applying clarity and wit to her own background and incorporating aspects of her forceful mother, Wasserstein wrote *Isn't It Romantic*. The play was commissioned by the Phoenix Theatre in New York City in 1981; its first production did poorly. After extensive revisions, the play was produced at Playwrights Horizons in 1983 and the Lucille Lortel Theater in 1984. Observing the relationship of college graduates Janie Blumberg, a young Jewish woman loosely based on Wasserstein, and Janie's friend Harriet Cornwall, a WASP daughter of a successful businesswoman, the play highlights mother-daughter relationships. Wasserstein's technique of introducing ideas with humor as a way of diffusing pain was admired by some reviewers and criticized by others.

At the Marathon 1983 Festival of One-Act Plays, presented by the Ensemble Studio, Wasserstein produced *Tender Offer*, a work about a father-daughter relationship. Her dramatic adaptation of Anton Chekhov's short-story *The Man in a Case* was one of the seven plays commissioned by the Acting Company for *Orchards* at the Lucille

Wendy Wasserstein, 1985. AP IMAGES

Lortel Theater in 1985. Wasserstein also won a Guggenheim Fellowship in 1983, wrote for numerous periodicals, and traveled abroad.

While in London, England, on a British American Arts Association grant, Wasserstein wrote what would become her most acclaimed work, *The Heidi Chronicles.* The play explores educated women's choices and relationships with realistic dialogue and flashbacks from the 1960s to the late 1980s. Centered on the art historian Heidi Holland, the play was first performed at the Seattle Repertory Theatre, premiered at Playwrights Horizons in 1988, and moved to the Plymouth Theatre on Broadway in 1989 for more than 550 performances. In 1989 the play won Wasserstein a Pulitzer Prize for Drama, Antoinette Perry Award (Tony Award; marking the first sole woman playwright to receive the award) for best play, Drama Desk Award for outstanding new play, New York Drama Critics' Circle Award for best new play, Dramatists Guild Award, Susan Smith Blackburn Prize, and the Hull-Warriner Award. Despite this impressive amount of recognition, reviewers criticized the play for lacking a central plot. Many feminists also disapproved of the play, because at the end, Heidi, single and feeling "stranded," adopts a baby. A 1994 version of the work included a coda. A cable television adaptation aired on Turner Network Television in 1995.

Following the success of *The Heidi Chronicles,* Wasserstein's next play, *The Sisters Rosensweig,* had a record-breaking advance when it went to Broadway. Also developed at the Seattle Repertory Theatre, the play opened at the Lincoln Center for the Performing Arts Mitzi E. Newhouse Theater in fall 1992, was moved to the Ethel Barrymore Theater for another 574 performances, and won the Outer Critics Circle Award for best play. The play emulated qualities of the works of Chekov and Neil Simon, both of whom Wasserstein admired. *The Sisters Rosensweig* is not merely autobiographical; the author noted, "My plays are my art and not just self revelation." Yet Sara Goode, the central and oldest sister in the play, is based on Wasserstein's sister Sandra (thirteen years her senior), a twice-divorced pioneering executive. "Gorgeous" is middle sister Georgette's nickname, and the youngest sister, Pfeni, is a writer. Set at a birthday celebration, this comedic drama focuses on Jewish identity as much as it does on women's identity. The play differs from Wasserstein's other plays by being less episodic and involving middle-aged characters as opposed to younger ones. It was, in the author's words, "a play about possibilities," as was most of her work.

During the 1990s Wasserstein experienced personal difficulties when her sister Sandra died of cancer. At the same time she was struggling, as her character Heidi does, with her views on motherhood. In 1999, at the age of forty-eight and after ten years of effort, she became the single mother of a daughter, Lucy Jane, who was born

prematurely. Wasserstein was also an advocate for theater. Believing that "a society is defined by its culture and that culture begins in early education," she introduced a group of students from DeWitt Clinton High School in the Bronx, New York City, to theater. This 1998–1999 experiment providing underprivileged students with the opportunity to experience live theater was taken over by the Theater Development Fund as its Open Doors project.

Influenced by political events, Wasserstein wrote *An American Daughter,* a play about a would-be female surgeon general and daughter of a senator; it was first performed at the Seattle Repertory Theatre in 1996. The next year it was produced at the Lincoln Center for the Performing Arts and was moved to Broadway during the same year. The Lincoln Center for the Performing Arts was also the site of the opening of several other plays by Wasserstein, including *Old Money* (2000) and *Third* (2005). Wasserstein's other plays include *Waiting for Philip Glass* (1999), which was performed as one of seven plays by other authors in the production *Love's Fire,* and *Psyche in Love* (2004). Her additional writing includes two collections of revealing personal essays, mostly written for varied periodicals; two musicals, the self-written *Miami* (1986), and "Smart Women/Brilliant Choices," part of *Urban Blight* (1988); a children's book, *Pamela's First Matinee* (1996); several television scripts and film screenplays, including *The Object of My Affection* (1997); and a posthumously published book, *Elements of Style: A Novel* (2006), a parody of the Upper East Side wealthy elite. Besides writing and producing plays, Wasserstein taught at the Young Playwrights Festival, Columbia University, Cornell University, and New York University. Known for a warm and humorous manner, she frequently spoke at all-girls schools as a role model.

The Council of Dramatists Guild, Educational Broadcasting Company, MacDowell Colony, Playwrights Horizons, Young Playwrights, and the Breast Cancer Research Foundation were just a few organizations of which Wasserstein was an active or board member. The Mount Holyoke College Alumnae Association honored Wasserstein with the Mary Lyon Award in 1985 and a doctorate of humane letters in 1990. She received the William Inge Award for Distinguished Achievement in the American Theatre (also in 1990), and a doctorate of fine arts from Bates College (2002). She was posthumously inducted into the American Theatre Hall of Fame.

Wasserstein died of lymphoma at Memorial Sloan-Kettering Cancer Center in New York City at age fifty-five, leaving six-year-old Lucy Jane in the care of Wasserstein's brother Bruce, a prominent businessman. Wasserstein's private funeral was followed by two events in her honor at the Lincoln Center for the Performing Arts. The 5 March 2006 benefit, which included a reading of *The Sisters Rosensweig,* raised more than $1 million for the center, while a 13 March 2006 memorial service was attended by more than

1,000 people. To honor Wasserstein's memory, the Dramatists Guild established a $25,000 prize for an emerging female playwright.

Wasserstein was an outstanding dramatist, more humanist than feminist. Nevertheless, she was a major role model for educated women of her generation. A female playwright who wrote about women's concerns and created important theatrical roles for women, she embodied her belief, onstage and off, that women have valid voices and that friendship and relationships of various kinds are important. She was an observant social critic who used wit and humor without rancor to illuminate the search for identity. Strong yet not strident, she was an advocate for theater and the arts. Balancing her writing with an active personal life, this plump, cheerful woman had many friends. Besides winning various awards, Wasserstein portrayed and influenced issues of the women's movement of the late twentieth century and had a major effect on the American stage.

★

Wasserstein's papers (1967–2005) are archived at Mount Holyoke College, South Hadley, Massachusetts. *Bachelor Girls* (1990) and *Shiksa Goddess; or, How I Spent My Forties: Essays* (2001), collections of Wasserstein's forthright and humorous essays, explore her thoughts on family, theater, diet, and politics. *Wendy Wasserstein: A Casebook*, edited by Claudia Barnett (1999), contains analysis of several of Wasserstein's works and an interview with her. Gail Ciociola, *Wendy Wasserstein: Dramatizing Women, Their Choices, and Their Boundaries* (1998), is an academic study that explores the complexity of women's lives. Extensive interviews also appear in *Interviews with Contemporary Women Playwrights* (1987), compiled by Kathleen Betsko and Rachel Koenig; Esther Cohen, "Uncommon Woman: An Interview with Wendy Wasserstein," *Women's Studies: An Interdisciplinary Journal* 15, no. 3 (1988): 257–270; and Laurie Winer, "The Art of Theater No. 13: Wendy Wasserstein," *Paris Review* 142 (Spring 1997): 164–188. Obituaries are in the *New York Times*, *Seattle Times*, and *Playbill* (all 31 Jan. 2006).

Rachel Shor

WEAVER, (William) Dennis (*b.* 4 June 1924 in Joplin, Missouri; *d.* 24 February 2006 in Ridgway, Colorado), Emmy-winning actor known for his roles in a succession of television series beginning with *Gunsmoke*.

Weaver, known as Bill or Billy when he was growing up, was the fourth of Walter Leon Weaver and Lenna Leora (Prather) Weaver's five children. His father retained his job with the local electric company throughout the 1930s, but after the nation's economic collapse wiped out his savings the Weavers moved to a ten-acre farm near

Joplin to supplement their income. In 1934 drought forced them to give up the farm. His father remained in Joplin while for several years his mother sought seasonal employment in Oregon and California, taking the children with her. Weaver spent the eighth grade with his sister and brother-in-law in Manteca, California, where he worked in a theater. The movies he saw there and the Saturday matinee Westerns he enjoyed in Joplin inspired him to become an actor.

After graduating in 1941 from Joplin High School, where he excelled in drama and sports, Weaver attended Joplin Junior College. During his second year he left school to volunteer for the navy's V-5 Flight Preparatory program. By the time he was inducted and completed training, World War II was almost over. En route to the Pacific when Japan surrendered in 1945, Ensign Weaver was discharged. Back home, on 20 October 1945 he married Gerry Stowell, whom he had met in 1942 at a college dance. He then enrolled in the University of Oklahoma at Norman, where he majored in drama, on an athletic scholarship and the GI Bill. In 1948 he earned his BFA and also qualified for decathlon tryouts for the London Olympics being held in New Jersey. Sixth out of thirty-six contestants, Weaver felt he could have made the team had he not spent the night before in the New York theater district.

Instead of returning to Oklahoma, where his wife had remained with her family, Weaver remained in New York, working various jobs and obtaining occasional roles in plays, television, and commercials. After joining the Actors' Equity labor union, Weaver decided to use the name "Dennis Weaver" to avoid a name conflict with another actor. He returned to Oklahoma briefly for the birth of his first son in 1949, but by that time he was securing enough work and favorable notice to encourage him to continue pursuing his acting career. Although his financial situation remained precarious, after landing a role in the play *They Shall Not Die* Weaver brought his wife and son to New York. Following one performance, Lee Strasberg, the acting teacher who influenced three generations of actors and directors, visited the struggling performer backstage and told him he was in the right profession. Weaver later studied with Strasberg at the prestigious Actors Studio.

A role in the 1950 play *Come Back, Little Sheba* provided income for a year, but a contract with Universal Studios for $125 a week persuaded him to move to Los Angeles in 1952. The next year he appeared in fourteen movies, but the studio did not renew his contract. Periodic appearances on the television series *Dragnet*, occasional roles in other television productions, and odd jobs provided a meager income. In 1953 the Weavers' second son was born with a rare immune system disorder that required extended hospitalization. With financial assistance from friends and a part-time delivery job at his aunt's flower shop, Weaver was barely getting by when he landed a part in a Columbia Broadcasting System (CBS) series in 1955. Cast as Chester Goode in *Gunsmoke*, television's first Western series made for adult audiences, he began earning enough to support his family. He played the sidekick of Marshal Matt Dillon for nine seasons, earning an Emmy as best supporting actor in a dramatic series in 1959. He also directed many *Gunsmoke* episodes and appeared in other TV series and movies. In 1958 he played the nervous night manager of a motel in Orson Welles's classic film noir *Touch of Evil*. The next year the Weavers' third son was born.

Weaver left *Gunsmoke* in 1964 for the title role in *Kentucky Jones*, a series about a widowed veterinarian who has adopted a Chinese orphan. The show was canceled after a single season. Weaver appeared in several movies in 1966 and 1967, including the starring role in *Gentle Giant*, a film about a Florida game ranger who rescues a bear. He continued the role on television in *Gentle Ben*, a highly rated television series from 1967 to 1969. The next year he was cast in the series *McCloud* as the title character, a New Mexico lawman who comes to New York City to learn big-city police procedure. His fish-out-of-water role was the most satisfying of his acting career and changed his image from the limping Chester Goode to the galloping Sam McCloud. The show ran for seven years, during which time he also appeared in other programs and television movies, including a role as the traveling salesman confronted by a menacing truck in *Duel*, the first movie Steven Spielberg directed. He also served as president of the Screen Actors Guild from 1973 to 1975. After *McCloud* three more series followed: *Stone* (American Broadcasting Company [ABC], 1979–1980), *Emerald Point, N.S.A.* (CBS, 1983–1984), and *Buck James* (ABC, 1987–1988). In 1991 he hosted *Backstage at the Zoo*, a twelve-part syndicated series about the world's zoos, emphasizing conservation.

Weaver's talent and interests were not confined to acting. In the early days of *Gunsmoke*, he and other cast members formed a musical group called the Gunsmoke Trio. Later, he released several albums of country and spiritual music, including songs he had written. He appeared frequently on *Hee Haw*, the *Sonny and Cher Comedy Hour*, and the *Dean Martin Show*. During the economic downturn of the early 1980s, Weaver, his wife, and the actress Valerie Harper organized Love Is Feeding Everyone (LIFE), a charity that provided food for the Los Angeles homeless. Alarmed about pollution, Weaver built a solar-powered home that he called Earthship in Colorado, and in 1993 he established the Institute of Ecolonomics (a term he coined) to encourage development of sustainable, nonpolluting energy. His concern led him to endorse hybrid vehicles and promote production of crops that required little water. Weaver continued acting and crusading for lifestyle changes to preserve the environment almost until his death from cancer. His remains were cremated. In 2007 Dennis Weaver Memorial Park was opened in Ridgway, on land donated by Weaver's widow to the town.

In a career that spanned six decades, Weaver proved himself a versatile and popular actor as well as a dedicated spokesman for causes he sincerely cared about. Later in his career he chose roles that focused public attention on social issues, including adult illiteracy, battered women, divorce, and the treatment of Vietnam veterans. He is also remembered for his efforts to raise awareness of the need for alternative energy sources.

Weaver's autobiography, *All the World's a Stage* (2001), sketches his life and explores his outlook and efforts to preserve the environment. Ramifications of Weaver's ecolonomics are discussed in Jack A. Brill, "Teaching the Nuts 'n Bolts of Ecolonomics," *In Business* (Mar./Apr. 1996). Obituaries are in the *New York Times*, *Los Angeles Times*, and *Denver Post* (all 28 Feb. 2006).

Brad Agnew

WEINBERG, Alvin Martin (*b.* 20 April 1915 in Chicago, Illinois; *d.* 18 October 2006 in Oak Ridge, Tennessee), influential nuclear scientist and leading advocate for the commercial use of nuclear power.

Weinberg was the son of Jacob Weinberg, a tailor, and Emma (Levinson) Weinberg, a homemaker. Although his original interest was chemistry, he received his AB (1935) and MS (1936) in physics and his PhD in mathematical biophysics (1939) from the University of Chicago. He became an environmentalist, urging national scientific laboratories to serve as tools for social progress. On 14 June 1940 he married Margaret Despres, with whom he had two sons; she died in 1969. He married Genevieve DePersio on 20 September 1974.

After completing his doctorate Weinberg became a research associate at the Metallurgical Laboratory (Met Lab) at the University of Chicago. The Met Lab was part of the World War II–era Manhattan Project, a U.S. government project to develop an atomic bomb. Weinberg's group developed the first nuclear reactor. In 1945 he joined the Oak Ridge National Laboratory (ORNL) in Tennessee, also part of the Manhattan Project, where he helped produce materials for the U.S. nuclear arsenal; these materials were used in the first atomic bombs. He became director of ORNL's physics division in 1948. During his first years at ORNL he received his first patent of many, on light-water reactor technology. As early as 1945, Weinberg foresaw the advantage of nuclear

Alvin M. Weinberg. STAN WAYMAN/TIME LIFE PICTURES/GETTY IMAGES

The information gathered from the HRE led to design and operation of the Molten Salt Reactor Experiment, which was the first reactor to use uranium-235 as fuel and which set a record for continuous use of a reactor. Weinberg called it "a chemist's reactor."

With Eugene P. Wigner (who in 1963 became a Nobel laureate in physics), he wrote what became the standard text on nuclear chain reaction theory, *The Physical Theory of Neutron Chain Reactors* (1958). In 1959 he was elected president of the American Nuclear Society, a group whose formation he had proposed. Weinberg's opinions were often sought by federal lawmakers. In 1960, under the Dwight Eisenhower administration, he began to serve on the President's Science Advisory Committee. In 1961 he was chairman of President John F. Kennedy's Panel of Science Information. This panel issued what was known as the Weinberg Report, a landmark study of how best to inform both specialists and the general public about science. In 1964 Weinberg was pleased that the General Electric company catalog offered guaranteed prices on boiling water reactors. Cheap nuclear power had arrived.

Weinberg, who coined the term *Big Science* to refer to nuclear power and other projects funded by government and research institutions, had two major goals regarding nuclear energy: to ensure an unlimited and safe source of energy through the development of breeder reactors, and to apply nuclear energy to solve political and social problems—what he termed the "technology fix." One such fix was the use of giant reactors by the agro-industrial complex to provide cheap electricity and desalinated water to overpopulated and underfed countries. In 1965 he was also vice president of Union Carbide Corporation's Nuclear Division.

An ardent environmentalist, Weinberg oversaw tremendous growth at the ORNL Biology Division, which was dedicated to understanding how radiation interacts with living things and to find ways to help organisms survive radiation damage, such as in bone marrow transplants. In 1970 he started the first bioecology project in the United States, the National Science Foundation's Research Applied to National Needs program. Weinberg published *Energy: Future Alternatives and Risks* (1974) with the National Academy of Sciences, and edited *Economic and Environmental Impacts of a U.S. Nuclear Moratorium, 1985–2010* (1979).

In 1974 the Richard M. Nixon administration fired Weinberg from ORNL because he continued to advocate for increased nuclear safety and molten-salt reactors rather than the Liquid Metal Fast Breeder Reactor, promoted by the Atomic Energy Commission's Reactor Division. Weinberg's firing halted progress on the meltdown-proof Molten Salt Reactor and the use of thorium as a nuclear fuel. That year Weinberg was named director of the U.S. Office of Energy Research and Development. In 1975 he helped found the Institute for Energy Analysis, a federal

energy to power fleets of submarines and extend U.S. naval power into the Arctic and other remote regions.

Weinberg became research director at ORNL in 1948 and director in 1955, a position he held until 1974. Weinberg helped guide ORNL through the cold war, emphasizing the necessity of increasing public confidence in the safety of commercial reactors. Admiral Hyman Rickover, following Weinberg's suggestion that the Nautilus submarine be powered by a pressurized water reactor, oversaw the development of the nuclear navy. This led to the development of commercial nuclear power plants. Weinberg had the materials testing reactor converted into a mock-up of a real reactor called the Low Intensity Test Reactor, or "Poor Man's Pile," which led to the design of pressurized water and boiling water reactors, the most dominant reactor types in commercial nuclear plants. The Homogeneous Reactor Experiment (HRE), also called Alvin's 3P Reactor (for its pot, pipe, and pump), used liquid fuel instead of solid fuel. The HRE operated for 105 days in 1950 before it was closed down. Despite leaks and corrosion, it was a safe and simple reactor to control.

consortium, at Oak Ridge Associated Universities, and initiated studies of reactor safety, carbon dioxide emissions, and other subjects related to national energy use, such as global warming. At the institute, where he was director until 1985, he advocated increasing the number of commercial reactors so as to cut emissions of heat-trapping gases. After the 1979 accident at Pennsylvania's Three Mile Island nuclear power plant, which resulted in the release of low-level radiation, he noted that "Three Mile Island ought become the salvation of nuclear energy" precisely because a large-scale meltdown was averted. The prevention of this potential disaster would bolster public confidence in the safety of commercial reactors.

After stepping down as director of the Institute for Energy Analysis, Weinberg became a distinguished fellow at Oak Ridge Associated Universities. His book *The Second Nuclear Era: A New Start for Nuclear Power* (1985) examined the possibility of designing completely safe reactors. He wrote that "to deny rebirth of nuclear energy is to deny human ingenuity and aspiration.... This struggling ingenuity will be equal to the task of creating the Second Nuclear Era."

In 1992 Weinberg published *Nuclear Reactions: Science and Trans-Science*. That same year he was named chairman of the International Friendship Bell Committee, which arranged for the installation of a Japanese bell at Oak Ridge. Weinberg personally raised a major share of the funds. During President Bill Clinton's administration in the 1990s, the report *Science in the National Interest* proposed that 3 percent of the federal budget be used for research and development, but it was not taken seriously. Interviewed in 1995, Weinberg observed that "one of the prices of nuclear energy is the commitment of certain pieces of real estate in perpetuity to nuclear activity including waste disposal." He reasoned that this was not a huge commitment, given that the United States has only eighty-five reactor sites and fifty other nuclear-related sites.

Weinberg was a primary planner of the 4 May 1996 Symposium on Non-Use of Nuclear Weapons, which addressed how to avoid future war. He received the Atoms for Peace Award (1980), the Harvey Prize (1982), and the Enrico Fermi Award (1980). He was a member of the National Academy of Sciences, National Academy of Engineering, American Academy of Arts and Sciences, and American Philosophical Society.

Weinberg died at his home in Oak Ridge of heart disease on 18 October 2006. His remains were cremated.

Weinberg believed that nuclear energy could be used to benefit society. He stressed the need to avoid the further use of nuclear weapons as well as to prevent harm to the environment. Throughout his career he pressed the scientific community to focus on safety, even when that stance was unpopular among fellow supporters of nuclear energy. He was an influential adviser to presidents and a spokesman to the public on scientific matters.

★

Weinberg wrote two memoirs, *Reflections on Big Science* (1967) and *The First Nuclear Era: The Life and Times of a Technological Fixer* (1994). Obituaries are in the *New York Times* (21 Oct. 2006) and *Washington Post* (22 Oct. 2006).

Louise B. Ketz

WEINBERG, John Livingston (*b.* 5 January 1925 in Scarsdale, New York; *d.* 7 August 2006 in Greenwich, Connecticut), senior partner and chairman of Goldman Sachs Group (1976–1990) who preserved Wall Street's last major partnership in the 1980s while refusing engagement in the era's hostile takeovers.

Weinberg, the younger of two brothers, was born to Sidney James Weinberg, who began as a janitor's assistant in 1907 and became senior partner and chairman of Goldman Sachs (1930–1969), a banking and equity house, and Helen (Livingston) Weinberg, the daughter of a prominent apparel manufacturer. Although Weinberg was raised in an affluent Scarsdale home, he rejected pretentiousness, instead emulating his father's humble origins and work ethic.

Weinberg graduated from Deerfield Academy in Deerfield, Massachusetts. He earned a BA from Princeton University in 1947 and an MBA from Harvard Business School in 1950. Weinberg served as a lieutenant in the U.S. Marine Corps in the Pacific during World War II and was promoted to captain during the Korean War. His father hired him only after sending him to meet the heads of the rival banks J. P. Morgan, Morgan Stanley, and First Boston. Another contact, the wealthy lawyer and industrialist Floyd Odlum, recommended to Weinberg the book *Extraordinary Popular Delusions and the Madness of Crowds* (1841) by Charles Mackay, which Weinberg placed on his desk; prophetic words for the 1980s from the book were: "Watch for the excesses. No one is going to tell you what they are or when they will arise; each time they will look different."

Weinberg reflected, "I worked for my father all my business life, but he never made it easy for me. No strawberries for lunch, he used to say to me." Weinberg was an associate (1950–1956), a partner (1956–1976), a senior partner (1976–1990), cochairman, with John C. Whitehead (1976–1984), and chairman of the Management Committee (1984–1990), concluding forty years of investment banking. After his retirement Weinberg volunteered, providing fifty-two years' total service. He maintained close relationships with chief executive officers of America's landmark companies, including Ford Motor Company, Sears, and the Bronfman family, which ran Seagram, and he served on numerous corporate boards, including Seagram,

Knight-Ridder, Kraft, Providian Financial Corporation, Yum! Brands, and DuPont (1986–1995).

Plainspoken and a man of straight talk, Weinberg delivered earthy maxims to deflate other bankers' egos. He commanded a warm, sincere personality that his colleagues respected. Described as "a block of a man with the battered square-jawed appearance of an ex-boxer," he was well-built, kept his hair closely cropped, and had thick jowls and a kind face. Modest in dress, he selected off-the-rack suits and wore his socks slightly low.

Weinberg's modest standards were reflected at work. Art and artifacts decorated the halls, as long as they were neither costly nor extravagant. Partners' offices were equipped with identical desks and cabinets, so that if someone vacated, a few well-appointed framed family photos and two or three files could easily be removed. The partners' dining room retained old furnishings, featuring instead healthful food.

Weinberg continued the firm's dedication to client service, emphasizing teamwork, loyalty, and business expansion garnered by trust. He disdained arrogance and egotism. Even his own managers felt Weinberg's egalitarianism when they discovered that he had canceled their 4:30 p.m. limousine service. When a young trader photocopied Weinberg, "I did this trade," Weinberg bluntly replied, "At Goldman Sachs we say 'we,' we never say 'I.'" Goldman Sachs employees realized that they were a team of contributors.

As a leader Weinberg faced trials and triumphs. In 1970 Penn Railroad defaulted on $87 million worth of commercial paper, with backing of only $53 million of the forty-five partners' capital. Weinberg met with angry creditors, offering them fifty cents on the dollar. While his effort failed, he brought the firm through an embarrassing bankruptcy. In 1981 Weinberg presided over the $120 million purchase of the commodities trading firm J. Aron. In August 1986 he negotiated a limited partnership with a $500 million investment from Sumitomo Bank, the third-largest bank in the world. Weinberg reported that the deal would "assist Goldman Sachs in meeting capital requirements for our rapidly growing worldwide businesses." This partnership was opportune because it helped Goldman Sachs to weather the stock market crash of 19 October 1987.

Goldman Sachs met Black Monday with a $100 million trading loss, as underwriter of the sale of 32 percent of British Petroleum. Weinberg knew Goldman's record. Capital earnings of $200 million in 1980 had increased to $1 billion by 1986, with an 80 percent return on equity, far exceeding other major competitors. Never relenting, Weinberg addressed syndicate bankers: "Gentlemen, Goldman Sachs is going to do this. . . . [T]hose of you who decide not to do it, you won't be underwriting a goat house. Not even an outhouse."

Weinberg, civic leader and philanthropist, was a trustee of Deerfield Academy; Princeton University (1987–1995); Teachers College, Columbia University; and the Whitehead Foundation. He funded a sports pavilion at Vassar College, was honorary chairman of the John L. Weinberg Center for Corporate Governance at the University of Delaware, and was a contributor to the New York Public Library, Boy Scouts of America, the UJA-Federation of New York, and the Jewish Museum. He was director of the DeWitt Wallace Fund for the Memorial Sloan-Kettering Cancer Center and served for more than forty-five years as a trustee of New York Presbyterian Hospital, where he helped create the Sue and John L. Weinberg Cystic Fibrosis Center, the Sue and John L. Weinberg Inpatient Rehabilitation Medicine Center, and the Sue and John L. Weinberg Medical Intensive Care Unit. Weinberg was a Republican Party supporter and served on the National Republican Congressional Committee, the National Republican Senatorial Committee, and the Council on Foreign Relations. Weinberg and his wife of more than fifty years, Sue Ann Gotshal, shared their concerns for civic causes. They had a son and a daughter. Weinberg died of complications from a fall.

Rarely seen is someone like Weinberg, who integrated his values of humility, teamwork, and client-based relationships beyond the boardroom. His constancy was furthered by devotion to family, community, and country. Weinberg showed how life is best lived—by giving of oneself to better others' lives.

★

There is no biography of Weinberg. Lisa Endlich, *Goldman Sachs: The Culture of Success* (1999), is a carefully referenced analysis, effectively describing the history of the firm, its leaders, including Weinberg, and its growth. Nils Lindskoog, *Long-Term Greedy: The Triumph of Goldman Sachs* (1998), is a first-hand account by the author, a corporate mergers and acquisitions professional, who worked closely with Goldman Sachs and Weinberg in the 1980s and early 1990s. Among the numerous tributes are Christopher Cole, "Weinberg 81, Built Goldman Foundation," *Daily Princetonian* (6 Aug. 2006), and Henry M. Paulson, "Statement of Treasury Secretary Henry M. Paulson on John L. Weinberg," *Press Room: U.S. Department of the Treasury* (9 Aug. 2006). Obituaries are in the *New York Times* (9 Aug. 2006) and the *Times* (London; 14 Aug. 2006).

Sandra Redmond Peters

WEINBERGER, Caspar Willard (*b*. 18 August 1917 in San Francisco, California; *d*. 28 March 2006 in Bangor, Maine), cabinet member under three presidents and the architect of an unprecedented military buildup as secretary of defense in the Reagan administration.

Caspar W. Weinberger. TIME LIFE PICTURES/PIX INC./TIME LIFE PICTURES/GETTY IMAGES

"I learned many lessons from that and felt keenly the necessity of adequate training of men and procurement of personnel," he later wrote.

Back in San Francisco after the war, Weinberger became a clerk for a U.S. appeals court judge and then joined a law firm. Finding this work tedious, he turned to his real passion, politics. He successfully ran for an open California state assembly seat in 1952 and won reelection in 1954 and 1956. He lost the 1958 race for state attorney general but remained on an upward trajectory in Republican politics, becoming the party's state chairman in 1962. In 1968 Governor Ronald Reagan appointed him as state finance director to lead a series of tax reforms and budget cuts that formed the hallmark of the governor's fiscally conservative administration.

In 1969 newly elected President Richard Nixon brought Weinberger to Washington to serve as chairman of the Federal Trade Commission. Weinberger's next assignment, as deputy director and then director of the newly formed Office of Management and Budget, earned him the nickname "Cap the Knife" as he oversaw Nixon's directive to slash federal spending. The president then tapped him as secretary of the Department of Health, Education, and Welfare (HEW), putting him in charge of the nation's vast portfolio of social services.

After Nixon's resignation in 1974 following the Watergate scandal, Weinberger remained briefly in his HEW post under President Gerald Ford. In 1975 he returned to California to become vice president and general counsel of the Bechtel Group Inc., an international construction and engineering firm.

When Reagan became president in 1981, he named Weinberger secretary of defense. Committed to Reagan's policy of "peace through strength," Weinberger set out to reverse the deterioration of the military during the preceding administration of Jimmy Carter. In contrast to his earlier reputation as a relentless budget cutter, Weinberger nearly doubled defense spending, implementing modernization of weaponry, transport, electronic warfare, and intelligence gathering. He also energized the all-volunteer military, increasing salaries and benefits in an attempt to boost self-esteem and professionalism within the armed forces. Known for his skillful navigation of the bureaucracy, Weinberger protected the Pentagon from spending cuts and emphasized the military buildup as the most important element of Reagan's foreign policy. He considered the Soviet Union the greatest threat, "militarily and morally," to the United States and vigorously championed the Strategic Defense Initiative, a space-based antimissile system nicknamed "Star Wars."

Weinberger felt military force should be deployed only as a last resort. He directed a U.S invasion of the Caribbean island of Grenada in 1983 to confront a radical Marxist regime and rescue more than 600 American

Weinberger, known as "Cap" from early childhood and throughout his life, was the younger of two sons of Herman Weinberger, an attorney, and Cerise (Carpenter Hampson) Weinberger, a violinist and teacher. An inquisitive child, he developed an early passion for politics and closely followed the national political conventions of the 1920s and 1930s, favoring Republican over Democratic philosophies. After graduating from public high school, he attended Harvard University, where he began to overcome his childhood shyness as a member of the debate team and an editor on the Harvard *Crimson*, to which he contributed conservative editorials. He graduated magna cum laude with an AB in 1938, then completed Harvard law school in three years.

Weinberger passed his bar exam in 1941 and enlisted in the U.S. Army. After attending Officer Candidate School, he was shipped to the Pacific. En route he met army nurse Rebecca Jane Dalton, whom he quietly married in Australia in 1942 in defiance of army regulations. They would have two children. Weinberger was an infantry platoon leader and later served as a captain on General Douglas MacArthur's intelligence staff. During his years of service Weinberger was disturbed by what he saw as the lack of U.S. preparedness. He and other recruits trained with wooden rifles and blocks of wood labeled as grenades.

students at a medical school on the island. However, he opposed sending U.S. Marines as peacekeepers to Lebanon; in 1983 the terrorist group Hezbollah claimed responsibility for the bombing of the Marine Corps barracks in Beirut that killed 241 Americans. In 1986 the United States ordered air strikes in Libya in response to Libyan terrorist attacks in Europe.

The Iran-Contra scandal, which emerged in 1986 during the second Reagan administration, was devastating for Weinberger. Reagan, acting on the advice of National Security Adviser Robert McFarlane, had permitted shipments of U.S.-made missiles to Iranian moderates in the hopes of obtaining the release of several U.S. hostages and paving the way for a friendly regime in Iran. But Reagan repeatedly insisted that the arrangement was not a direct arms-for-hostages swap. Nor, he said, was he aware of the most explosive element of the deal: the use of profits from the sale of those arms to illegally finance U.S.-backed rebels, known as Contras, fighting to overthrow the leftist regime in Nicaragua. Weinberger vigorously opposed the arms shipments, arguing that they would be interpreted as the payment of ransom for hostages, a violation of administration policy.

On 23 November 1987 Weinberger, citing his wish to spend time with his wife during her treatment for cancer, resigned as defense secretary and returned to private life. Reagan's term ended in 1989, and during the subsequent administration of George H. W. Bush, an investigation of the Iran-Contra deal and alleged cover-up was conducted by an independent counsel. In 1992 a grand jury indicted Weinberger on five counts of lying under oath and concealing more than 1,700 pages of diary notes about the arms sale. Weinberger called the indictment a "moral and legal outrage." He was preparing to stand trial when President Bush, in one of his final acts as president, granted him a Christmas Eve pardon in 1992. Weinberger wrote Bush a thank-you note on every subsequent Christmas Eve. He continued to advocate a strong defense posture and believed the military buildup he helped launch during the Reagan years contributed to the collapse of the Soviet Union in 1991.

Following his years as defense secretary, Weinberger became publisher of *Forbes* magazine in 1989 and later rose to chairman of Forbes Inc. At his home in Maine, he developed complications from pneumonia and died at the Eastern Maine Medical Center at the age of eighty-eight. He is buried at Arlington National Cemetery.

★

Weinberger's papers are in the Library of Congress. His comprehensive autobiography is *In the Arena: A Memoir of the 20th Century* (2001). He also recounted his experiences as defense secretary in *Fighting for Peace: Seven Critical Years in the Pentagon* (1990). Other memoirs and biographies from the Reagan era offer glimpses of Weinberger from varying perspectives: Reagan, *An American Life* (1990); Reagan, *The Reagan Diaries*, edited by Douglas Brinkley (2007); James A. Baker III, *Work Hard, Study—And Keep Out of Politics! Adventures and Lessons from an Unexpected Public Life* (2006); Anatoly Dobrynin, *In Confidence: Moscow's Ambassador to America's Six Cold War Presidents (1962–1986)* (1995); and Richard Reeves, *President Reagan: The Triumph of Imagination* (2005). Obituaries are in the *Washington Post* and *New York Times* (both 29 Mar. 2006).

Dave Montgomery

WELLER, Thomas Huckle (*b.* 15 June 1915 in Ann Arbor, Michigan; *d.* 23 August 2008 in Needham, Massachusetts), virologist, tropical medicine specialist, and Nobel Prize winner whose work led to breakthroughs in the study and prevention of polio and the German measles.

Weller was the son of Carl Vernon Weller, a University of Michigan Medical School pathologist, and Elsie (Huckle) Weller. His grandfather was a general practitioner. Weller graduated from Ann Arbor High School in 1932. He was a devoted bird-watcher with a strong interest in natural history. His first scientific paper, published in his third year of college, was on blue jays. Weller received his AB in zoology from the University of Michigan in 1936. He earned his MS in medical zoology, also in 1936, for his work on fish parasites over two summers at the University of Michigan Biological Station.

Weller studied under two distinguished parasitologists when he arrived at Harvard Medical School in 1936, and his interests shifted. He was accepted as a tutorial student by the leading microbiologist and immunologist John Franklin Enders. Enders introduced Weller to the field of virus research and to the use of tissue-culture techniques as a method to study infectious disease, launching his lifelong interest in tropical diseases. Weller earned his MD from Harvard in 1940. His clinical training at the Children's Hospital in Boston was interrupted when he joined the U.S. Army Medical Corps in 1942. He spent most of World War II at the Antilles Medical Laboratory in San Juan, Puerto Rico, as head of the army's campaign to control malaria at its Caribbean bases. After the war he left the army with the rank of major. He married Kathleen Fahey on 18 August 1945. The couple had two sons and two daughters. Weller returned to Harvard in 1946, continued his training at Children's Hospital, and was a founding member, with Enders, of Harvard's infectious diseases research department. The pediatrician and virologist Frederick C. Robbins, whom Weller had first met in medical school, joined the center in 1948.

In the 1940s and 1950s, the polio virus was running rampant in the United States. Its victims mostly were children who ended up in iron lungs and on breathing machines, filling hospital wards. Polio often resulted in paralysis or death. Nearly 600,000 Americans suffered from polio in the twentieth century. At the peak of the epidemic, in 1952, around 58,000 cases were reported. Healthy children were kept indoors by terrified parents. In 1949 Weller was named assistant director of the infectious diseases department at Children's Medical Center. Also that year Weller, Enders, and Robbins grew the polio virus for the first time outside human or monkey nerve cells. Using human embryonic skin and muscle tissue, they disproved the going theory that the polio virus fed on nerve tissue, finding instead that it attacked muscle tissue. They reported their findings in the October 1949 issue of *Proceedings of the Society for Experimental Biology and Medicine*.

The discovery was an incredible breakthrough in the study of the virus, and within a few years, Jonas Salk and Albert Sabin developed vaccines for the disease. Weller, Enders, and Robbins shared the Nobel Prize for Physiology or Medicine for their work in 1954. That year there were 28,000 cases of polio in the United States. Less than a decade later, there were 121. In the highly competitive world of medical research, Weller, Enders, and Robbins had combined their resources. Upon winning the prize, Enders reflected the spirit of the team: "No discovery in the scientific world is due to the work of any one man, but always results from the work of many people." In 1955 Weller also isolated and grew the causative agent of chicken pox and shingles.

Adult-onset rubella (German measles) tore through in Europe and the United States during the mid-1960s, causing thousands of miscarriages, stillbirths, and therapeutic abortions for women with intrauterine infections, and life-threatening organ disorders for infants who survived. Weller was working on the virus when he learned of competing researchers at Walter Reed Army Institute of Research. Neither team had made any headway. Again in the spirit of goodwill and public benefit, Weller exchanged virus samples with the other team, resulting in breakthroughs for both. They published their findings back-to-back in the same journal in 1962. In 1963 Weller and three other researchers discovered the virus that causes German measles, using a urine sample from his own son, who had conveniently developed the virus as his father was conducting his research. Today the vaccine that resulted from Enders's breakthrough is part of the standard measles, mumps, and rubella immunization given to American children.

Weller was also accomplished and respected in the field of tropical medicine. He was a professor of tropical medicine at the Harvard School of Public Health from 1954, achieving emeritus status in 1985. From 1953 to 1959 he directed the Armed Forces' Commission on Parasitic Diseases. From 1954 to 1981 he headed the Department of Tropical Health at Harvard and was president of the American Society of Tropical Medicine and Hygiene; he was awarded that organization's Walter Reed Medal in 1996. He was a consultant to the World Health Organization, the Pan American Health Organization, and the International Health Organization of the Rockefeller Foundation. Despite his close contact with disease in the United States and abroad—he worked in Trinidad, Egypt, Thailand, South Africa, Saudi Arabia, Kuwait, and rural areas of Brazil—Weller never contracted any of the diseases he studied. He died in his sleep.

★

Weller wrote an autobiography, *Growing Pathogens in Tissue Cultures: Fifty Years in Academic Tropical Medicine, Pediatric, and Virology* (2004). A short, thorough biography is in *Les Prix Nobel* (1954), the Nobel Foundation's yearbook. Obituaries are in the *Boston Globe* (25 Aug. 2008) and the *New York Times* and *Los Angeles Times* (both 27 Aug. 2008).

Brenna Sanchez

WEXLER, Gerald ("Jerry") (*b.* 10 January 1917 in New York City; *d.* 15 August 2008 in Sarasota, Florida), record producer, journalist, songwriter, and record label executive who most notably worked with Ray Charles, Aretha Franklin, and Bob Dylan, and who coined the phrase "rhythm and blues."

Wexler was born in the Bronx borough of New York City to Harry Wexler, a Polish immigrant who worked as a window washer, and Elsa Spitz, a bakery employee who became a homemaker upon marriage; the couple later had a second son, Arthur. Elsa pushed her firstborn in his studies, and though uninterested in schoolwork, Wexler nonetheless graduated from New York's George Washington High School in 1932 at age fifteen.

Wexler was a keen music fan and ventured into Harlem to buy records and see shows, when he was not hanging out at local pool halls. He attended City College for two semesters before dropping out. His mother then enrolled him at Kansas State College of Agriculture and Applied Science (later Kansas State University) in Manhattan, Kansas, but Wexler again neglected his studies, preferring to investigate the jazz scene in nearby Kansas City, Missouri. He dropped out in his second year.

Returning to New York, Wexler worked for his father. In 1941 he married Shirley Kampf (whom he had met in 1936, when she was in high school); the couple would go on to have three children. A year later, he entered the army and served stateside until 1946. He then returned to Kansas State and completed a degree in journalism. In

Jerry Wexler, 1979. **AP IMAGES**

1947 he was back in New York. His first job in the music industry was as a copywriter for the performing rights organization Broadcast Music, Inc (BMI). A referral from a BMI employee landed him a writing job at *Billboard*, the music industry publication. Wexler came up with the term *rhythm and blues* (R & B) as the new name of the magazine's "Race Records" chart, "a label more appropriate to more enlightened times," he wrote in the *Saturday Review of Literature*. In 1951 he left *Billboard* to work as promotions director for the Big Three, the music publishing arm of Metro-Goldwyn-Mayer.

The following year, Ahmet Ertegun, who ran the jazz/blues label Atlantic, offered Wexler a job doing promotions, but Wexler was only interested in a partnership. A year later, when Atlantic's cofounder Herb Abramson entered the army, he was offered such a position. Atlantic wanted to serve the burgeoning African-American market, with no initial thought of attaining "crossover" success on the pop—that is, white—charts. But Atlantic records soon began to enjoy success in both the pop and R & B charts through recording artists such as Ruth Brown, LaVern

Baker (the first artist Wexler produced), the Coasters, and the Drifters.

Ray Charles, who Wexler called a "genius," was the most notable artist on Atlantic in the 1950s. Wexler (with Ertegun) coproduced Charles's first number-one R & B hit, "I Got a Woman," based on a gospel hymn; by the end of the decade, Charles had crossed over to pop mainstream with such hits as "What'd I Say," "Georgia on My Mind," and "Hit the Road, Jack."

In the 1960s Wexler became drawn to the bluesy southern music scene, setting up a distribution deal with the Memphis-based Stax label. Wexler produced Wilson Pickett's mid-1960s string of soul classics at both Stax's studio (where "In the Midnight Hour" was recorded), and the Fame Studios in Muscle Shoals, Alabama (where "Land of 1,000 Dances" was recorded).

In 1967 Wexler signed Aretha Franklin to Atlantic. Franklin had previously been at Columbia as a pop and jazz singer, finding little success. Wexler encouraged her to return to her gospel roots (as well as to play piano on her recordings), a strategy that resulted in four Top Ten hits in 1967 alone: "I Never Loved a Man (the Way I Love You)" (to which Wexler also contributed lyrics), "Respect" (which won Wexler a Grammy for Best Rhythm & Blues Recording), "Baby I Love You," and "(You Make Me Feel Like) A Natural Woman." Wexler was named Record Executive of the Year for his role in refashioning Franklin into the "Queen of Soul."

In the fall of 1967, Atlantic was sold to Warner Bros.–Seven Arts (later Warner Communications) at Wexler's recommendation. Though the buyout enabled Wexler and Ertegun to continue working at Atlantic, Wexler later felt the buyout fee ($17.5 million) had been too low.

Another notable Wexler production of the era was Dusty Springfield's *Dusty in Memphis* album; though not a commercial success on its release in 1969, it is now regarded as a white soul classic. During the sessions, Springfield also tipped off Wexler about a new U.K. hard rock act, Led Zeppelin. Wexler beat out Columbia and Warner Bros. for the band's signature, and Led Zeppelin would become Atlantic's biggest selling act of the 1970s. Wexler's continuing interest in southern rock led to Atlantic serving as distributor of Capricorn Records, based in Macon, Georgia, enjoying success with artists such as the Allman Brothers Band and the Marshall Tucker Band.

Wexler's work as producer of the Broadway cast album of *The Wiz* won Wexler a 1975 Grammy in the Best Cast Show Album category. But that same year, unhappy with his decreasing influence at Atlantic, Wexler quit the company. His retirement was short-lived; in 1977 he became a vice president of Warner Bros. Records, heading up the East Coast A&R department, signing the B-52s, Gang of Four, the Roches, and Dire Straits (whom he also produced), among others.

Wexler continued producing artists on other labels as well, including Bob Dylan's Christian-themed album *Slow Train Coming*, released in 1979, enjoying the irony of a "born again" artist working with, in Wexler's words, "a sixty-two-year-old confirmed Jewish atheist." He also produced Dylan's follow-up album, *Saved*.

Wexler acknowledged that his devotion to work caused problems in his personal life. His marriage to Shirley ended in divorce in 1972. He married Renee Pappas, whom he had met when she worked for the Beach Boys, in 1973; the marriage ended in 1981. In 1985 he married the playwright and novelist Jean Arnold. Four years later, in 1989, he suffered the loss of his daughter, Anita, who died of AIDS-related causes.

In 1987 Wexler was inducted into the Rock and Roll Hall of Fame in the Non-Performer category; the same year he was inducted in the Alabama Music Hall of Fame, and received the Sammy Cahn Lifetime Achievement award from the Songwriters Hall of Fame. Wexler continued producing into the 1990s, working with Carlos Santana and Etta James; he also won the 1992 Grammy in the Liner Notes category for Aretha Franklin's *Queen of Soul: The Atlantic Recordings* box set.

Wexler eventually retired to Florida, where he had lived off and on since the 1970s. He died at his home in Sarasota from congestive heart failure.

★

Wexler's memoirs (cowritten with David Ritz) can be found in *Rhythm and the Blues: A Life in American Music* (1993). The story of Atlantic Records is detailed in Ertgun, *What'd I Say? The Atlantic Story: 50 Years of Music* (2001), which also features essays by Greil Marcus, Perry Richardson, and Nat Hentoff. Wexler's Atlantic years are covered in Dorothy Wade and Justine Picardie, *Music Man: Ahmet Ertegun, Atlantic Records, and the Triumph of Rock 'n' Roll* (1990), and Charlie Gillett, *Making Tracks: Atlantic Records and the Growth of a Multi-Billion-Dollar Industry* (1974). Obituaries are in the *New York Times* (15 Aug. 2008) and *Rolling Stone* (18 Sept. 2008).

Gillian G. Gaar

WEYRICH, Paul Michael (*b.* 7 October 1942 in Racine, Wisconsin; *d.* 19 December 2008 in Fairfax, Virginia), leader of political and social conservative movements, newspaper and radio reporter and pundit, and founder and president of the Heritage Foundation and the Free Congress Research and Education Foundation.

Weyrich was born to a German immigrant, Ignatius Weyrich, who worked for fifty years stoking the furnace in a Catholic hospital, and to Virginia Weyrich. Ignatius

instilled in his son strong political and religious ideas. When Weyrich was a teenager, his interest in trains and politics prompted him and his friends to launch a grassroots campaign to save a train route from Milwaukee to Chicago. He studied journalism at the University of Wisconsin–Madison, though he did not take a degree. At the same time, he enhanced his political experiences further by participating in the Racine Young Republican Party from 1961 to 1963.

On 6 July 1963 Weyrich married Joyce Anne Smigun. They remained married until his death. The couple would go on to have five children.

With both journalism and politics under his belt, Weyrich ventured further into the political arena in 1964, working on the presidential campaign of the archconservative Barry Goldwater, who went down to crushing defeat against President Lyndon Johnson in that year's presidential cycle. Nevertheless, the experience had a lasting effect on Weyrich and further sparked his interest in politics.

Over the next few years Weyrich found work in both radio and television, beginning with WAXO-FM radio in Kenosha, Wisconsin, where he served as a news director, announcer, and program director from 1960 to 1963. A year later, he was a reporter covering city hall and state politics for the *Milwaukee Sentinel* from 1963 to 1964. As a political reporter and weekend anchor for Columbia Broadcasting System Milwaukee from 1964 to 1965 and as a news director for KQXI in Denver, Colorado, in 1966, he combined his two careers: journalism and politics.

Weyrich came to Washington, D.C., in 1966, initially handling the press relations and other assignments for Senators Gordon L. Allot of Colorado and Carl T. Curtis of Nebraska. He began to develop structures and organizations that were instrumental in forming the conservative movement. While on the Hill, he worked on the Republican Study Committee, an advocacy group that seeks to ensure loyalty among Republicans in Congress to conservative policies. He also served on the Conservative Working Group, a strategy group for lobbyists and staffers.

In 1973 Weyrich cofounded and served as the first president of the Heritage Foundation, a conservative think tank. As a strategist, he was credited with bringing religious conservatives into the Republican Party. Among other organizations either founded or led by Weyrich were the American Legislative Council (1975–1978) and the Coalition for America (1978–2008). Through this work and his commitment to conservative causes, Weyrich demonstrated his leadership ability and his dedication to the movement.

Relying on his experiences as a political reporter and news director, Weyrich became a prolific writer. His work appeared in the *New York Times*, *Washington Post*, and *Wall Street Journal* and included policy reports, columns, and journal articles on a variety of conservative topics. In

1984, with Connaught Marshner, he compiled *Future 21: Directions for America in the 21st Century*. Among Weyrich's more notable undertakings was his work with the Kreible Institute from 1989 to 1996. In that role, he was responsible for assisting various recently independent states—particularly those that had splintered off of the former Soviet Union—to develop stable democratic institutions. The outcome of this work led to his serving on the board of directors of the Russian Freedom and Democracy Institute from 1997 to the time of his death in 2008. A final book-length work, *The Next Conservatism* was published posthumously in 2009.

In 1999, after years of working on behalf of conservative causes, Weyrich became disillusioned with the "Moral Majority" and penned a statement to that effect that disappointed many of his supporters. The Republican-led Congress, he thought, was failing on cultural issues. He believed that conservatives could no longer be supportive of legislation that was aimed at the cultural and social concerns of conservatism.

In the final years of his life, Weyrich suffered from generally poor health. In 2001 and until the time of his death he was confined to a wheelchair due to a combination of illnesses and a fall on black ice that injured his spine. In 2005 both of his legs were amputated because of complications from diabetes. Weyrich died from unspecified complications from diabetes at Inova Fair Oaks Hospital in Fairfax. He was interred in Fairfax Memorial Park Cemetery on 22 December 2008.

Weyrich received the Heritage Foundation's Clare Boothe Luce Award in 2005. He was described by the *Economist* as "A vigorous thinker of the conservative movement." Additionally, he was voted by the readers of the *Conservative Digest* from 1981 to 1983 as one of the top three "most popular conservatives in America not in Congress." Finally, *Regardie's Magazine* named him one of the "100 most powerful Washingtonians."

★

Obituaries are in the *New York Times* (18 Dec. 2008) and the *Los Angeles Times* and *Washington Post* (both 19 Dec. 2008).

Ann E. Pharr

WHITESIDE, Lawrence W. ("Larry") (*b.* 19 September 1937 in Chicago, Illinois; *d.* 15 June 2007 in Brighton, Massachusetts), journalist known for his coverage of baseball and pioneering efforts as one of the first African-American sportswriters to work for a major newspaper.

Whiteside was the son of Alonzo Whiteside, Sr., and Myrtis (Wells) Whiteside. He graduated with an AA from Wilson Junior College in 1957 and went on to Drake University, earning a BA in 1959. While at Drake he began covering sports for the *Des Moines Register* and also worked for the Johnson Publishing Company as a researcher. After graduation, he worked for the *Kansas City Kansan* as sports reporter and assistant editor. From 1963 to 1965, as a sportswriter for the *Milwaukee Journal*, he covered the Milwaukee Braves (before the franchise moved to Atlanta), writing about future Hall of Famers Hank Aaron, Eddie Mathews, and Warren Spahn. Also for that paper, from 1970 to 1973 he covered the Brewers, then owned by Bud Selig, who two decades later would become the commissioner of Major League Baseball. Selig noted that he and Whiteside started in baseball together. Whiteside also worked for the *Milwaukee Sporting News* as correspondent from 1970 to 1974. He married Elaine Fain, with whom he had a son.

Whiteside, known as "Sides" to friends and colleagues, joined the *Boston Globe* in 1973, becoming the only African-American reporter covering a Major League Baseball team, the Boston Red Sox, for a major metropolitan newspaper. He was also the first African-American beat writer in the *Boston Globe* sports department. He gained the respect of his colleagues in what was then a very white department, in a city troubled with racism. In his writing and in the newsroom, he called attention to racism in sports.

Whiteside covered some of the most memorable moments in Red Sox history, including Bucky Dent's home run in the 1978 American League East playoff game, the team's collapse in game six of the 1986 World Series against the New York Mets—as he wrote, "the demons of 68 years' worth of failure will haunt the Red Sox for at least another day"—and Roger Clemens's second twenty-strikeout game in 1996. Known for having left the ballpark during Clemens's no-hitter on 29 April 1986 to attend the National Basketball Association playoff game that day with the Boston Celtics, he was chatting with Clemens after the 1996 game when the pitcher remarked, "Thanks for sticking about this time, Larry."

Throughout his career Whiteside was known for his role as a mentor who helped others grow in their careers. In 1971 he began the "Black List," a list of African-American journalists—then only eight or nine names—covering sports. As it grew, the list served as a network to aid editors in hiring black journalists. He would produce the list whenever anyone complained they were unable find qualified African Americans for positions. By 1985, when the number of names had reached between eighty-five and ninety, he ceased keeping the list.

Among his many awards, Whiteside was honored as Wisconsin Sportswriter of the Year by the Milwaukee

Press Club in 1973. In 1980 he became the first African-American Baseball Hall of Fame voter, and in 1987 he became the first sportswriter to win the Knight Fellowship, a journalism fellowship at Stanford University. The National Association of Black Journalists honored him with a Lifetime Achievement Award in 1999 and later established the Larry Whiteside Scholarship, for an enrolled college student pursuing a career in sports journalism. Also in 1999, owing to his depth of knowledge of the Negro Leagues, he served on the committee for selecting the All Century Team. The Sports Museum of New England awarded him its Legacy Award in 2002. He served three terms as chairman of the Boston chapter of the National Association of Baseball Writers, which awarded him the Dave O'Hara Award for service to the chapter. He was one of the first American journalists to follow baseball in countries other than the United States, traveling to Japan and Australia to cover games there. In 2008 he was posthumously awarded the J. G. Taylor Spink Award, the highest honor of the Baseball Writers Association of America, making him only the third African-American journalist to be so honored.

Whiteside left the *Globe* in 2004 when Parkinson's disease made it impossible for him to continue working. He died of the disease at Kindred Hospital–Boston. He is buried in Newton Cemetery in Newton, Massachusetts, where he resided for most of his life.

Whiteside was universally praised as a man of good humor, goodwill, and humility. Despite his role as a pioneering African-American journalist, he did not want to be the story, only to report it. Owing to his deep knowledge of baseball, many called him a walking history. At a time when there were many more black players on the field, he worked to bring more black sportswriters into the newsroom. After his death, the Boston Red Sox honored him by observing a moment of silence before the start of a game in Fenway Park.

★

Howard Bryant, *Shutout: A Story of Race and Baseball in Boston* (2002), contains numerous references to Whiteside and his role as an African-American sportswriter in Boston. An obituary is in the *Boston Globe* (16 June 2007).

Kim Laird

WIDMARK, Richard (*b.* 26 December 1914 in Sunrise, Minnesota; *d.* 24 March 2008 in Roxbury, Connecticut), Academy Award–nominated film, television, and stage actor celebrated for his characterizations of antiheroes and villains in 1940s and 1950s film noir such as *Kiss of Death* (1947).

Widmark was one of two children born to Carl Henry Widmark, owner of a general store, and Ethel Mae Barr in a small farming community north of Minneapolis–Saint Paul near the Wisconsin border. After his father sold his store to become a traveling salesman, Widmark endured an itinerant childhood. At various times, the family lived in South Dakota, Illinois, and Missouri. In 1932 Widmark graduated from Princeton High School in Princeton, Illinois, where he discovered that he could be a captivating public speaker. Although cinema and acting became one of his earliest passions thanks to his frequent trips to the movies with his grandmother, Widmark's initial career choice was to be a lawyer. He secured an athletic-academic scholarship and enrolled at Lake Forest College near Chicago as a prelaw student. It was during his time at Lake Forest that he became a favorite of the drama coach Russell Tomlinson and won first prize in the McPherson Oratory Contest. In 1936 he graduated with a BA in speech and political science.

After graduation, Widmark and his friend Fred Gottlieb toured Germany on their bikes and, while there, shot a documentary about the Hitler youth camps. Widmark then returned to Lake Forest to teach speech and drama, but he hated the job and decided to go to New York to try his hand at acting. He soon landed parts in radio shows such as *Aunt Jenny's Real Life Stories*, *Front Page Farrell*, and Orson Welles's *Mercury Theatre on the Air*. A perforated eardrum prevented Widmark from fighting in World War II. On 5 April 1942 he married the actress and screenwriter Jean Hazlewood in Evanston, Illinois; the couple would go on to have a daughter. After their marriage, Richard and Jean settled down in New York, where Widmark made his Broadway debut in March 1943 in *Kiss and Tell*. Widmark worked steadily in radio and on Broadway until 1947, at which time he made his Hollywood debut in the role of the psychopath Tommy Udo in Henry Hathaway's *Kiss of Death*. The Twentieth Century–Fox producer Darryl F. Zanuck apparently cast Widmark after seeing his screen test, rejecting Hathaway's own choice, something that initially made the working relation between the actor and the director a difficult one. Despite this, both contemporary reviewers and later critics are unanimous in their assessment of Widmark's characterization as one of the most stunning and poignant first performances in American cinema. Widmark received an Academy Award nomination for best supporting actor and greatly contributed to the success of the film.

Following the Hollywood habit of typecasting an actor after a successful role, the studio employed the newly discovered star to play slight variations on Udo's sadistic character in William Keighley's thriller *The Street with No Name* (1948), Jean Negulesco's melodrama *Road House* (1948), and Joseph L. Mankiewicz's *No Way Out* (1950) opposite Sidney Poitier. However, two other films shot in 1950 offered Widmark the chance to depart from his psychopath screen persona. In Jules Dassin's *Night and the City* the actor gave a memorable performance as a wrestling promoter pursued by gangsters through the streets of London. In *Panic in the Streets*, the director Elia Kazan made Widmark's transition to positive characters complete casting him as Clint Reed, a New Orleans doctor facing a gang of criminals that threatens to spread bubonic plague.

For his part, Widmark was never entirely at home in the several "good-guy" roles that as a contract actor he was forced to accept, the majority of them in war movies such as *Halls of Montezuma* (1950), *The Frogmen* (1951), and *Destination Gobi* (1953) and in the Westerns *Red Skies of Montana* (1952), *Broken Lance* (1954), and *Garden of Evil* (1954). In spite of his transition to the good side, he still displayed his best acting in more ambiguous roles, such as in the violent cold war thrillers *Pickup on South Street* (1953) and *Hell and High Water* (1954). In *Pickup on South Street*, for example, Widmark played a sleazy pickpocket who accidentally steals some intelligence secrets and negotiates with the Communists to pass them on. His final decision not to sell them is not the result of the character's patriotism, but rather of his desire for revenge.

In the mid-1950s, Widmark—no fan of the studio system—refused to renew his contract with Fox in order that he could choose his roles more freely. Despite this move, he continued to play mainly tough and uncompromising heroes in Westerns such as John Ford's *Two Rode Together* (1961) and *Cheyenne Autumn* (1964); Edward Dmytryk's *Alvarez Kelly* (1966), opposite William Holden; and Andrew McLaglen's *The Way West* (1967). Widmark also starred in big-budget, all-star films such as *Judgment at Nuremberg* (1961), in which he played a prosecutor trying Nazis at the end of World War II, and *Murder on the Orient Express* (1974), in which he added yet another to his gallery of villains. His best performance before his retirement in 1990 was in Don Siegel's thriller *Madigan* (1968), playing the titular police officer. The film formula proved so successful that Widmark agreed to shoot several television films based on the same character.

Two years after the death of his first wife in 1997, Widmark married Susan Blanchard. He died in his home in Roxbury after a long illness. For his contribution to the motion-picture industry, Widmark was given a star on the Hollywood Walk of Fame.

Widmark's dramatic range was a limited one. He was unsuitable for comedies, and he was unconvincing as the amiable blue-eyed and muscular blond that he played in several films. Yet his aloof style made him perfect for Westerns and his inclination toward ambiguity rendered his name synonymous with the genre of film noir and its chilling villains.

★

A detailed look at Widmark's life and work can be found in Kim Holston, *Richard Widmark: A Bio-Bibliography* (1990). Further information about his movies and their critical and popular reception is in Allen Hunter, *Richard Widmark: The Man and His Movies* (1985). Obituaries are in the *New York Times*, *Independent*, *Guardian*, and *Washington Post* (all 27 Mar. 2008).

Luca Prono

WILLIAMSON, John Stewart ("Jack") (*b.* 29 April 1908 in Bisbee, Arizona Territory; *d.* 10 November 2006 in Portales, New Mexico), writer and teacher famed as one of the stars of the golden age of science fiction in the 1930s as well as for his long literary career.

Williamson was one of four children born to Asa Lee Williamson and Lucy Betty (Hunt) Williamson, both of whom had careers as school teachers and farmers. Teaching jobs were often hard for his parents to find, so they tried to homestead in newly available lands in the western United States. Their farms had to be nearly self-sufficient, with even underwear being stitched by Lucy out of flour sacks. The family produced eggs and cream that were sold to pay for shoes, overalls, coffee, and flour.

Williamson met his future wife, Blanche Slaten, in school in 1921, but he was too shy to approach her. Williamson drove for the first time that year. The school bus driver was sick, and having watched the driver closely, Williamson tried his hand at driving the bus, steering somewhat wildly along roads. It was typical of him to try his hand at something new, and it was his fascination with things mechanical and the physical laws that governed them that inspired him to acquire much of his scientific knowledge. His education after high school was haphazard. He studied chemistry at Canyon College for two years (1928–1930). In about 1932 he briefly attended the University of New Mexico. He tried to attend the University of California, Berkeley, but was not admitted because he refused to take a Shakespeare class as part of his academic requirements. In spring 1957 his received his BA in English from Eastern New Mexico University (ENMU); he chose English because it had a fellowship available whereas his preferred subjects of chemistry and physics did not. In the fall of that same year, he received his MA in English from ENMU. He accepted a teaching job at a military school and in 1960 joined the faculty at ENMU, while working on his PhD at the University of Colorado. In 1964 he became an assistant professor of English at ENMU, where he pioneered the teaching of science fiction as literature. He received his PhD later that year; his dissertation focused on the author H. G. Wells.

Williamson's mother occasionally wrote small pieces that were published, and Williamson may have been inspired to write because of her interest in writing. Williamson often retreated from emotional pain into daydreams, and by the time he left high school he wanted to write about his dreams of a wonderful future inspired by advances in technology. His first published story, "The Metal Man," appeared in *Amazing Stories Quarterly* in December 1928. He worked with the author Miles J. Breuer, learning to tie his fantasies to realistic situations and collaborated with Breuer on the novel *The Girl from Mars* (1929).

In spite of his growing popularity as an author, Williamson was deeply troubled by his inability to emotionally connect with women. He had read a book by the psychoanalyst Karl Menninger, and he wrote to Menninger to ask for help. He spent most of 1933 in Topeka, Kansas, in the Menninger Clinic, undergoing psychotherapy. He sold little during that year and had to leave because he could not afford to stay. Later in the 1930s, he would continue psychotherapy off and on in California, and he later credited the therapy with helping him to resolve his anxieties.

Although he seems to have thought of himself as a withdrawn personality, he was actually an adventurer who embraced physical challenges. Often, he and the science-fiction writer Ed Hamilton would travel together across the United States and Mexico. Williamson had an uncle who owned a ranch in Mexico, which had become self-sufficient to survive the Great Depression, and Williamson and his friends visited it for months at a time, working in a wild land among sometimes dangerous people.

In 1942 Williamson was drafted into the U.S. Army, reporting to Fort Bliss, Texas, for active service on 5 August. Ever interested in science, Williamson applied to be an army weatherman, serving in the army's weather service from 1942 to 1945. He rose to the rank of staff sergeant but was treated by pilots with more respect than most enlisted men because of his importance to their flight plans and hope for survival. He trained in weather observation for eleven weeks at Chanute Field, Illinois. He took and passed a test that allowed him to enter training in weather forecasting at Chanute Field, a stint lasted twenty-two weeks from July to November 1943. In 1944 he was stationed at Hobbs Army Air Field in New Mexico. On 19 April 1945 Williamson arrived at Tacloban in Leyte, an island in the Philippines. His duties often put him in harm's way, but his worst injury was a hernia caused by packing weather gear; he suffered from many infections. In 1946 he had surgery to repair his hernia and two surgeries to repair an abdominal blockage that nearly killed him.

Slaten had married when Williamson was seventeen years old, and she had children, but when Williamson saw her in July 1947, she was again single. She owned a shop in Portales where she sold products for babies and small children. A mutual friend thought she would play matchmaker and bring the two together; they were smitten with each other and were married on 15 August 1947, and Williamson thereafter referred to her children and grandchildren as his own. He and Blanche traveled much of the world after she retired in the 1980s, but she was killed in an car accident on 5 January 1985 while Williamson was driving; although he could not remember the accident, he always blamed himself for causing it.

Williamson was much loved by science-fiction fans, but he had trouble breaking into the mainstream market until the publication of the novel *The Reefs of Space* (1964), a collaboration with Frederik Pohl. He and Pohl frequently collaborated on novels and stories; typically, Williamson wrote the first draft and Pohl revised or sometimes rewrote the draft and took care of the marketing of the novels and stories. A publisher persuaded Williamson to write his autobiography, *Wonder's Child*, which was published in 1984 and won a Hugo Award in 1985. His novella *The Ultimate Earth* (2000) won a Hugo Award (2001) and a Nebula Award (2001). His novel *Terraforming Earth* (2001) won the John W. Campbell Memorial Award for Best Science Fiction Novel. Williamson influenced such luminaries as Isaac Asimov and Robert Heinlein and was respected among authors and fans alike for his kindness and for the sense of wonder that was the hallmark of his fiction.

Williamson died of natural causes at his home at the age of ninety-eight. A memorial service was held on 16 November 2006 at ENMU. The speakers included the author Connie Willis.

★

Williamson's papers are in the Jack Williamson Science Fiction Library at Eastern New Mexico University. The best source for information about Williamson's life is his autobiography, *Wonder's Child: My Life in Science Fiction* (updated 2005). An obituary is in the *Portales News-Tribune* (11 Nov. 2006).

Kirk H. Beetz

WILLIS, William Karnet ("Bill") (*b.* 5 October 1921 in Columbus, Ohio; *d.* 27 November 2007 in Columbus, Ohio), college football All-American who was one of four African Americans to break the modern "color line" in professional football a year before Jackie Robinson broke the color barrier in Major League Baseball in 1947.

Willis was born to Clement Willis, a railroad porter, and WilAnna Willis, a housekeeper. Growing up in Ohio's state capital, Willis had a rather ordinary youth, playing the games of youngsters and participating in various youth sports, as did his older brother, Claude. Claude was such an outstanding scholastic athlete at Columbus's East High School that Willis almost did not enroll there.

From a family that stressed character, both Willis and his brother were called "Deke" (short for "Deacon") because of their straight-arrow personalities. At East High School, Willis excelled in football, basketball, and track and field before graduating in 1941. His coach, Ralph Webster, tried to interest the University of Illinois in offering the rangy, speedy tackle a football scholarship, but then a fortuitous coaching change occurred at Ohio State University. Paul Brown, a scholastic coaching legend, was hired to take over the Buckeyes. Willis related, "Brown had a reputation for fairness. . . . [H]e had many Negro players while coaching at [Washington High School in] Massillon, [Ohio]. . . . [H]e said yes he would let me play at Ohio State."

In his sophomore year (1942), Willis, a stalwart two-way tackle, helped the Buckeyes to a national championship. He continued to use his speed and quickness to have another fine season in 1943 and climaxed a career that would qualify him for enshrinement in the College Football Hall of Fame as a consensus All-American in 1944. Not surprisingly, with the National Football League's (NFL) "gentlemen's agreement" on no blacks still in effect, Willis—despite being an All-American from a top school in the nation's top conference (Big Ten)—went undrafted by the pro league.

After graduation from Ohio State in 1945 with a BA in education (he would later work toward an MA), Willis accepted the positions of head football coach and athletic director at Kentucky State College, a historically black school. Willis took the team to a 4–2–4 record.

A rival pro football league, the All-America Football Conference, was formed and was slated to begin play in 1946. The league's Cleveland franchise, named the Browns, was to be coached by none other than Brown. Willis said, "After one season at Kentucky State, I got the urge to play pro football. I felt I might have a chance in the new league, especially with . . . Brown as coach." Willis drove to Cleveland to meet with Brown and expressed his interest in playing. Willis said of the meeting that Brown "knew of nothing that would keep Negroes out of the new league. I felt encouraged."

At the same time, the Canadian Football League was also competing for U.S. football talent. Coach Lew Hayman of the Montreal Alouettes contacted Willis.

To get ready for the season, Willis had an old knee injury repaired. For all of the spring and much of the summer, Willis initially heard nothing from either coach.

He was about to use Coach Hayman's plane ticket and fly to Montreal. Finally and indirectly, Brown, using the sportswriter Paul Hornung as a go-between, invited Willis to the Browns' training camp—two weeks after it started.

Willis, who stood six feet, two inches tall and weighed 210 pounds, made an immediate impression with his speed and quickness. He was thrust into a scrimmage at middle guard, a position where he played directly over the center. In this case the center was Mike "Mo" Scarry, a player reputed to have "the fastest hands in football." All Willis did on the first play was to get past Scarry and nail the quarterback Otto Graham in his tracks. Surprised and frustrated, Scarry yelled, "Hey! Check the offsides!" The Browns assistant Blanton Collier checked out Willis. He was playing within the rules. The next three plays produced the same result: Willis went through, over, and around Scarry and dropped Graham before he could pull away from center. Having seen enough and wanting to preserve team morale, Brown called off the rest of the practice session. Later Willis stated, "That night coach Brown signed me to a contract—$4,000." In short order Brown also signed the fullback Marion Motley. Willis and Motley, along with Kenny Washington and Woody Strode of the Los Angeles Rams, were pro football's modern African-American pioneers. Both Willis (1977) and Motley (1968) were inducted into the Pro Football Hall of Fame.

Such was Willis's speed and quickness that the Browns' press guide offered this tip to photographers: "If you want to take stop-action photographs of Willis, you need to set your shutter speed at 1/600th of a second." Willis and the Browns tore through the All-America Football Conference, winning championships in each of the league's four seasons of competition, while losing just four games. When the Browns were merged into the NFL in 1950, the dominance continued. For the four seasons Willis played before retiring after the 1953 season, the Browns were in the NFL championship game—winning in 1950 and 1953. Willis was All-Pro in seven of his eight seasons.

After his playing days Willis turned to a career helping youngsters—first with Cleveland's Recreation Department and then as longtime director of the Ohio Youth Commission. With the Youth Commission he established a program whereby incarcerated youths received credit at public schools for courses taken while they were detained. Education was always a high priority for Willis and his wife, W. Odessa Porter, whom he married in 1948 and with whom he had three sons. Willis died of complications of a previous stroke. He is buried at Forest Lawn Memorial Garden in Columbus.

Paul Zimmerman of *Sports Illustrated*, perhaps the leading authority on long-ago NFL football, declared Willis to be "the fastest interior lineman ever to play the game." The Pro Football Hall of Fame center Clyde "Bulldog" Turner said of Willis, "About the first player to ever convince me I couldn't handle anybody I met was Bill Willis." A vast number of people also remember the courtly and dignified Willis for the countless youngsters he helped get back on the right track to productive and meaningful lives.

★

Willis's career is discussed in Myron Cope, *The Game That Was: The Early Days of Pro Football* (1970); Don Smith, *Pro Football Hall of Fame All-Time Greats* (1988); Donald Steinberg, *Expanding Your Horizons: Collegiate Football's Greatest Team* (1992); and Ron Smith, *Heroes of the Hall* (2003). Obituaries are in the *New York Times* and *Columbus Dispatch* (both 29 Nov. 2007).

Jim Campbell

WINTERS, Shelley (*b.* 18 August 1920 (?) in St. Louis, Missouri; *d.* 14 January 2006 in Beverly Hills, California), Academy Award–winning actress known for her roles in *A Place in the Sun, The Diary of Anne Frank, Alfie,* and *Lolita.*

Born Shirley Schrift on 18 August 1920 (though some sources note her birth year as 1922) to Rose (Winter)

Shelley Winters, 1963. ©BETTMANN/CORBIS

Schrift, an opera singer, and Jonas Schrift, a pattern maker, Winters had one sibling, an older sister. When she was young the family moved to Brooklyn, New York. From an early age Winters was bent on stardom. She captured the lead in a junior high school production and began skipping school to attend matinees on Broadway, to which she would return on weekends. While a student at Thomas Jefferson High School, she supported her acting ambitions by working at Woolworth's and as a model. Lying about her Actors' Equity membership, Winters auditioned for the national company of *Pins and Needles* and garnered a part.

After winning a prize at a Major Bowes Amateur Competition, Winters dressed the part of a southern belle complete with accent (however tainted by having moved to Brooklyn) and auditioned during a nationwide search to play Scarlett O'Hara in *Gone with the Wind* (1939). The producer David O. Selznick and a Metro-Goldwyn-Mayer (MGM) talent scout began to laugh, but the director George Cukor advised Winters to study acting and speech and to apprentice on the New York stage. Following Cukor's advice, Winters took acting classes at the New Theatre School and played comedic roles in summer stock in the Catskills. She landed a part in a Shubert Organization production that allowed her to join Actors' Equity in earnest.

Max Reinhardt auditioned her for the English version of Johann Strauss's operetta *Die Fledermaus (Rosalinda)*. Winters earned a small part in the 1944 production and was billed as Shelley Winter (the "s" in her last name was added later). The Columbia Pictures mogul Harry Cohn ventured backstage and offered Winters a screen test. When the studio tyrant viewed Winters in slip, black stockings, and a negligee he became interested in the actress's sexy and comedic persona, perceiving her to fit in the blonde bombshell category. Winters was given a contract at $100 a week.

Winters reported to Hollywood to appear in the film *Cover Girl* (1944) while her husband, Captain Mack Paul Mayer, whom she had married 1 January 1942, left for Europe to serve in World War II. Winters and her new friend Norma Jean Baker (soon to be Marilyn Monroe) became roommates.

The actress's rebellious streak quickly emerged in a fight against studio powers. When she was offered a role in the Samuel Goldwyn production of Kurt Weill's *Knickerbocker Holiday* (1944), Cohn went ballistic having already cast her in *Nine Girls* (1944). An arrangement was made and Winters got her way. Soon she was back at Columbia playing a harem girl in *A Thousand and One Nights* (1945). Cohn had not succeeded in creating a new sex goddess, and Winters was let go.

After meeting the tough guy Lawrence Tierney, who was the first in a long list of torrid affairs including Errol Flynn, Burt Lancaster, Marlon Brando, and William Holden, she was offered the role of a nightclub singer in

The Gangster (1947). She also picked up an agent who got her work in *New Orleans* (1947), an MGM musical. When her MGM screen test was viewed by the executives, hope of a contract died. Lewis Milestone wanted Winters for the war drama *A Walk in the Sun* (1945); then Cukor cast her in *A Double Life* (1947), in which she delivered a highly credible performance. Winters's marriage to Mayer dissolved in 1948. She landed a role in the Broadway production of *Oklahoma!*, but she left the musical for a role in Paramount's *The Great Gatsby* (1949).

Winters studied Shakespeare with Charles Laughton to improve her diction. Her breakthrough performance was in *A Place in the Sun* (1951), directed by George Stevens. In the role of Alice Tripp, the proletarian wife of George Eastman (Montgomery Clift), she is allowed to drown by her husband, who is romantically obsessed with the socialite Angela Vickers (Elizabeth Taylor). Winters was nominated for an Academy Award for a performance that was characterized by vulnerability and pathos and that highlighted the range of her acting abilities.

While in Europe she met her second husband, the Italian actor Vittorio Gassman, with whom she had her only child, a daughter born 14 February 1953. Universal Studios was angry about the marriage, fearing a scandal similar to Ingrid Bergman's liaison with the Italian director Roberto Rossellini. Winters had been cast in Universal Studios Western *Untamed Frontier* (1952); Universal lent her to MGM for *Executive Suite* (1954). Winters was a member of an ensemble cast in *Mambo* (1954) that included her husband, but when Gassman had an affair during a stage production of *Hamlet*, the marriage crumbled and led to a divorce.

One of Winters's most prestigious projects was *The Night of the Hunter* (1955), directed by Charles Laughton, in which she played victim to Robert Mitchum's maniacal conman, expanding her range as a pathetic and manipulated wife. During this period she also did a live-television broadcast of *Sorry, Wrong Number* (1954), a long monologue acting tour de force, and the film *I Am a Camera* (1955).

Winters had a keen capacity for self-promotion and rolled with the punches to maintain her career as her offbeat beauty faded and her body expanded. By the late 1950s she was considered a character actor and was cast in the film adaptation of *The Diary of Anne Frank* (1959). She won an Oscar for her portrayal of the self-centered and materialistic Mrs. Van Daan. During this period Winters had a third tumultuous marriage to the actor Anthony Franciosa, which ended in divorce in 1960.

During the 1960s Winters was active in political issues. An avid supporter of President John F. Kennedy, she was invited to his inauguration during the filming of *Lolita* (1962). The film's director, Stanley Kubrick, was furious at the disruption, which threw the production into chaos. In the end, she gave a convincing performance as Charlotte Haze, the clawing, man-chasing mother of the title character. Winters appeared in *The Chapman Report* (1962), which was inspired by the work of the sexologist Alfred Kinsey. In 1963 Winters entered the theater of the absurd on film in an adaptation of Jean Genet's *The Balcony*.

Winters finished out the turbulent 1960s with roles in *The Greatest Story Ever Told* (1965); *A Patch of Blue* (1965), for which she won her second Oscar; *The Three Sisters* (1966); *Alfie* (1966); *Enter Laughing* (1967); *Wild in the Streets* (1968); and *Buona Sera, Mrs. Campbell* (1968).

In the 1970s Winters worked often, acting in, among others, *Bloody Mama* (1970), featuring a young Robert DeNiro; *Flap* (1970); the blockbuster disaster movie *The Poseidon Adventure* (1972; for which she garnered an Oscar nomination); and *Next Stop, Greenwich Village* (1976). By the 1980s the former blonde bombshell and dame of theater had aged before a changing audience, and Winters had fewer roles. Films included *S.O.B.* (1981), *The Delta Force* (1986), and *An Unremarkable Life* (1989).

Throughout her career Winters was involved with the renowned Actors Studio, where she studied Method acting. She appeared in many Broadway plays, including *A Hatful of Rain* (1955), *The Night of the Iguana* (1961), *Minnie's Boys* (1970), and *The Effect of Gamma Rays on Man-in-the-Moon Marigolds* (1978). She also wrote the semiautobiographical trilogy of one-act plays *One Night Stands of a Noisy Passenger* (1970).

Winters made numerous appearances on television, including *Two Is the Number* (1964), for which she won an Emmy, *Batman* (1966), *Here's Lucy* (1968), and *Weep No More, My Lady* (1992). In the 1990s she played the recurring role of Roseanne Barr's grandmother in the hit show *Roseanne*.

During the 1990s Winters continued to appear in films, including *The Pickle* (1993), *The Silence of the Hams* (1994), *Heavy* (1995), and *The Portrait of a Lady* (1996). After fifty years in motion pictures and theater, she kept herself in the public eye with frequent appearances on the television talk-show circuit, vamping for a new generation of viewers.

Winters suffered a heart attack in October 2005 and died of heart failure 14 January 2006 at the Rehabilitation Centre of Beverly Hills. Winters married, though it was not a legally binding union, for the fourth and last time to Gerald DeFord just hours before her passing. The couple had lived together for nineteen years. Her last film, released in 2006, was *A-List*, in which she played herself, a fitting end to a remarkable life in the theater, television, and on the silver screen.

★

Winters wrote two tell-all autobiographies, *Shelley: Also Known as Shirley* (1980), and *Shelley II: The Middle of My Century* (1989). Obituaries are in the *New York Times* and *Los Angeles Times* (both 15 Jan. 2006).

Vincent LoBrutto

WOLFSON, Louis Elwood (*b.* 28 January 1912 in St. Louis, Missouri; *d.* 30 December 2007 in Bal Harbour, Florida), industrialist, financier, and philanthropist who was a pioneer in the formation of conglomerates and in dramatic proxy battles.

Wolfson was one of eight children of the Lithuanian-born Morris David Wolfson, who operated a junkyard, and the Baltimore native Sarah (Goldberg) Wolfson, a homemaker. The impoverished Jewish family moved to Jacksonville,

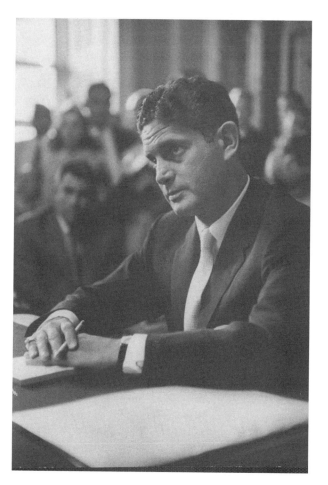

Louis E. Wolfson, 1955. GEORGE SKADDING/TIME LIFE PICTURES/GETTY IMAGES

Florida, when Wolfson was an infant, and Wolfson began his business career at the junkyard. Growing up in a mostly black neighborhood, Wolfson was a gifted athlete at Andrew Jackson High School, where he graduated in 1930. He won a football scholarship to the University of Georgia at the onset of the Great Depression. However, a serious injury curtailed his varsity career, and the economic insecurity of his family forced him to drop out of the university in 1932 and return to the scrap metal business.

Wolfson's first break came near Starke, Florida, when Wolfson and his older brother bought discarded plumbing supplies and resold them for huge profits. The Florida Pipe and Supply Company that the brothers formed was soon earning as much as $4.5 million a year, and by the age of twenty-eight, Wolfson had become a millionaire. He went on to acquire shipyards in Jacksonville and Tampa, Florida. Most important, in 1949 he acquired the New York Shipbuilding Corporation, a subsidiary of Merritt-Chapman & Scott. Two years later Wolfson became the chairman of its board and its president. This construction and marine salvage conglomerate built tunnels, bridges, roads, and ships throughout the world. The Priest Rapids and the Glen Canyon dams built in the 1950s constituted the largest construction projects that a single contractor had ever assumed up to that point. Within five years the company's net income after taxes had quadrupled. Wolfson's controlling interest in the New York Shipbuilding Corporation, located in Camden, New Jersey, gave him management of the third-largest shipyard in the United States. In 1960 the company launched the USS *Kitty Hawk*, a supercarrier that by the end of the twentieth century was second only to the USS *Constitution* in the duration of active status in the U.S. Navy.

In 1950 Wolfson moved from Jacksonville to Washington, D.C., where he acquired the municipal bus system, Capital Transit Company. Accused of valuing the dividends of stockholders ahead of the needs of the passengers, Wolfson moved to Miami Beach, Florida, in 1952. He remained there until his death.

Wolfson married Florence Monsky in 1936; they had four children. Lean and handsome, Wolfson carried 190 pounds on a six-feet, two-inch frame. He rarely drank, nor did he socialize heavily, preferring to work very long hours on his business ventures from his home overlooking Biscayne Bay, Florida. By the mid-1950s Wolfson's wealth was estimated at about $250 million, and he controlled over two dozen corporations. Nevertheless, he remained loyal to relatives and friends from the earlier Jacksonville phase of his life, and he inspired devotion from his closest associates.

Wolfson's close associates consisted of eight men known as "the Wolfsons," though only two of them (two of Wolfson's brothers) bore that surname. This group specialized in identifying companies that did not fit into any cohesive pattern but were pegged at prices on the stock exchange below what the Wolfsons believed to be their actual worth. The companies that were acquired were diverse. Wolfson's investments ranged from paint companies to movie chains and from oil wells to steel mills. In 1955, when the journalist John Gunther described Wolfson as an "ambitious and fiercely energetic young promoter," Wolfson tried to acquire the nation's second-largest mail-order house, Montgomery Ward. The proxy battle was waged with such conspicuous energy that Wolfson put himself at the center of the most enthralling media event in American business that year. The Wolfsons gained only three seats on the nine-person board, however, and Wolfson himself resigned from the directorship of Montgomery Ward in 1956. An effort to challenge the management of American Motors under George Romney failed as well.

By the beginning of the 1960s, Wolfson's flamboyant business practices had attracted the attention of the Securities and Exchange Commission (SEC) and the Department of Justice; much of that decade was spent in legal battles. Wolfson was accused of fraud in the manipulation of stock in Merritt-Chapman & Scott, but those charges were eventually dropped. He was also indicted for selling unregistered stock in Continental Enterprises, one of his companies located in Jacksonville. No one since 1933, when the SEC regulation was promulgated, had ever faced criminal penalties for such a violation. Wolfson was convicted under the SEC statute, despite his insistence that he had been unaware that any law had been broken. He had even reported the sale on his income tax returns. In 1969 the U.S. Supreme Court refused to consider his appeal, and he spent nine months in a federal minimum-security prison near Pensacola, Florida.

In 1965 the legal difficulties of Merritt-Chapman & Scott led Wolfson to meet the Washington attorney Abe Fortas, who was impressed with the Wolfson Family Foundation, which devoted itself mostly to medical and Jewish charities in Jacksonville. There the foundation had established a children's clinic at the Baptist Memorial Hospital and proclaimed that all races and religions could expect care—even in the age of jim crow—without discrimination.

Later in 1965, as President Lyndon B. Johnson was appointing Fortas to the Supreme Court as an associate justice even as Wolfson's own legal troubles were mounting, the jurist agreed to accept an annual retainer from the foundation. The arrangement was $20,000 a year for consulting on racial and religious issues, for as long as Fortas lived; should Fortas's wife, the tax attorney Carolyn Agger, outlive her husband, she would receive the same annual amount. By 1968 Fortas's liberal opinions from the bench had aroused the hostility of Republicans in the U.S. Senate, and they succeeded in an unprecedented filibuster to block Fortas's appointment as chief justice

upon the retirement of Earl Warren. The withdrawal of the nomination did not satisfy the new president, Richard M. Nixon, however, and his administration orchestrated efforts to remove Fortas from the Supreme Court entirely. In 1969 the revelation that he had accepted such a financial arrangement from the Wolfson Family Foundation, though he had resigned from it in 1966 and had returned the first and only check half a year later, created such a furor that Fortas felt compelled to resign from the Supreme Court. No other member of the Court in the modern era had ever been forced to step down to quell controversy.

Wolfson's first wife died in 1968, and on 30 December 1972 Wolfson married Patrice Jacobs, the daughter of the celebrated racing horse trainer Hirsch Jacobs. In 1959 Wolfson had bought Harbor View Farm, near Ocala, Florida, for the purpose of breeding and racing Thoroughbreds. The investment paid off in 1978, when Affirmed won the Triple Crown. Affirmed was only the eleventh horse since 1919 to win the Kentucky Derby, the Preakness, and the Belmont Stakes.

Wolfson's business career had largely evaporated when he entered prison. Nevertheless, he continued to champion liberal political causes, such as the presidential campaign of Senator George S. McGovern. Such financial support led to the inclusion of Wolfson's name on President Nixon's enlarged "enemies list" that the White House turned over to the Internal Revenue Service for proposed audits in 1972. The Wolfson Family Foundation, of which Wolfson was chairperson for over a third of a century, was also unusual in deliberately exhausting itself in charities. The causes were mostly medical and educational, in Jacksonville, such as the student center at Jacksonville University and the River Garden Hebrew Home for the Aged. The foundation had ceased to exist by the beginning of the twenty-first century. Wolfson was personally committed to the Anti-Defamation League of B'nai B'rith as well, and the problem of anti-Semitism was the aspect of his own Jewish heritage that touched him most deeply. Wolfson usually attended religious services only on the High Holidays. Zionism did not interest him, probably because of the gratitude that his own father had felt toward an America that had offered such economic opportunities. Despite his unwavering claim that his prison sentence had been unjust (as well as unprecedented), Wolfson was fervently patriotic. Suffering from Alzheimer's disease, Wolfson died of colon cancer at age ninety-five. He is buried at the cemetery of Congregation Ahavath Chesed in Jacksonville.

Wolfson's dazzling early achievements in business exemplified the "creative destruction" that the economist Joseph Schumpeter believed to be integral to capitalism. Wolfson sought to take charge of companies that he deemed sclerotic and to streamline their management. He was among the first of the "corporate raiders," though the term had not yet been coined when he engaged in hostile takeovers. In Merritt-Chapman & Scott he consolidated the first postwar conglomerate, that is, a corporation characterized by diverse, often unrelated, and even random interests. Unlike later takeover artists, however, Wolfson and his associates generally risked their own money rather than raise it from passive investors and institutions.

★

For information on Wolfson, see Harold H. Martin, "Florida's Fabulous Junkman," *Saturday Evening Post* (24 July 1954), and Herbert Brean, "It's Easier to Make a Million than a Hundred Thousand," *Life* (22 Nov. 1954). The most complete analysis of Wolfson's effect upon the highest appellate court is in Bruce Allen Murphy, *Fortas: The Rise and Ruin of a Supreme Court Justice* (1988). Obituaries are in the *New York Times* and *Florida Times-Union* (both 2 Jan. 2008). The William E. Wiener Oral History Library of the American Jewish Committee holds an oral history, also on deposit at the New York Public Library. The interviews were conducted in 1977.

Stephen J. Whitfield

WU, Ray Jui (*b.* 14 August 1928 in Beijing, China; *d.* 10 February 2008 in Ithaca, New York), pioneering biochemist and genetic engineer who modified rice to withstand environmental stress, and who is widely regarded as one of the founders of plant genetic engineering.

Wu was born the third of five children to Hsien Wu, a biochemist and professor at Peking Union Medical College (PUMC), and Daisy (Yen) Wu, a teaching associate who assisted in Hsien Wu's experiments. His mother later founded a private elementary school, the Ming Ming School.

In 1931 the Japanese invaded China, leading to years of turmoil and oppression. Wu, however, was largely protected from this because PUMC, established by America's Rockefeller family, was considered U.S. property and thus was not subject to the whims of the Japanese occupiers. In 1939 Wu entered the Yu Ying School, considered one of the best secondary schools in Beijing. He played on the basketball team and was known for his skill at the piano.

In 1942 the Japanese declared war on the United States and ordered PUMC to close. Faculty members were forced to leave, and some were sent to detention camps. Wu's father left for Chungking (Chongqing), the new wartime capital of China, to assist in establishing the Chinese Research Institute of Health there.

After the Japanese surrendered in 1945, Wu entered Fu Jen Catholic University but soon transferred to Yenching University in Beijing, where he studied chemistry. He came

to the United States three years later, in 1948, at the urging of his father, who was attending a scientific meeting in San Francisco. In 1950 he earned a BS in chemistry from the University of Alabama; he followed this with a doctoral degree from the University of Pennsylvania in 1955. From 1955 to 1966 he conducted research with the Public Health Research Institute of the City of New York. On 12 August 1956 he married Christina Chan. In 1961 he became a naturalized citizen of the United States.

In 1966 Wu became an associate professor at Cornell University, where he would spend the rest of his professional life. In 1972 he became a professor, and in 2004 he was named Liberty Hyde Bailey Professor of Molecular Biology and Genetics. From 1976 to 1978 he was department chair of Cornell's Section of Biochemistry, Molecular and Cell Biology. During his long career at Cornell, he also served as a senior visiting investigator in the Biochemistry Department at Stanford University; a National Science Foundation senior fellow at the MRC Laboratory in Cambridge, England; and a visiting associate professor in the Department of Biology and Chemistry at the Massachusetts Institute of Technology. During a sabbatical in 1989, he was director of the Institute of Molecular Biology of Academia Sinica in Taipei, Taiwan. He served as an honorary professor, and later as an adjunct professor, at Peking University. Wu was editor or coeditor of nine volumes of the *Recombinant DNA* book in the Methods of Enzymology series, from 1979 to 1993. He wrote over 300 scientific papers and held five patents on genetic engineering methods.

In 1970 Wu developed the first method for sequencing deoxyribonucleic acid (DNA), as well as other tools used in cloning. His DNA sequencing method is known as the "location-specific primer approach," a process that, though improved through subsequent research, would soon be used by genetic scientists around the world. The location-specific primer approach allowed scientists to determine the DNA sequence of the entire genome of rice, as well as humans and other organisms, leading to innovations in agriculture and medicine, among other fields.

Wu's efforts in genetic engineering were focused on the goal of alleviating world hunger, specifically by modifying rice plants. Rice, a staple for over half the world's population, is subject to crop failure caused by drought and excessive salinity in the soil. Wu worked to modify rice plant genes to create plants that could withstand both. Later, he added traits for resistance to insect pests and low temperatures.

In addition to protecting plants grown in optimal environments, this genetic modification allows farmers to harvest crops from land that would otherwise be unusable because of arid or saline soil. Wu's work was broadened by other researchers, who used his methods to modify the genes in corn, wheat, oats, moss, and other plants.

As a scientific adviser to both China and the United States, Wu coordinated the China-U.S. Biochemistry

Examination and Administration (CUSBEA) program. Operative from 1982 to 1989, CUSBEA brought over 400 Chinese students to the United States for graduate training; more than 100 of them later became faculty members at major universities or worked in key positions in industry. These scientists, along with others from the Chinese Academy of Sciences, founded the Ray Wu Society to promote the life sciences.

From 1982 to 1995 Wu was a scientific adviser to the China National Center for Biotechnology Development. He also chaired several committees, including the Scientific Advisory Committee for the Transgenic Plant Program; National Science Council, Taiwan; and the Board of Scientific Advisors of the International Center for Genetic Engineering and Biotechnology.

In 1999 Wu established the Ray Wu Graduate Fellowship in Molecular Biology and Genetics. He funded the scholarship over the following five years and created a permanent annual endowment to support one graduate student in the field of molecular biology and genetics.

In 2002 Wu was awarded the Frank Annunzio Award in Science and Technology, which includes a $50,000 prize. In 2003 he became a fellow of the American Academy for the Advancement of Science; he was also a fellow of the Chinese Academy of Engineering.

Wu died at Cayuga Medical Center in Ithaca, New York, of heart failure. Throughout his life, those who knew him remarked on his unwavering commitment to help feed the immense number of people in the world who depend on rice for their lives. Wu was known for his gentle, respectful manner, his positive approach to solving both scientific and interpersonal problems, and his financial support of promising students. His work in alleviating world hunger endures to this day and is continually being elaborated upon and refined by subsequent generations of researchers, many of whom he trained.

★

A detailed discussion of Wu's family and life in China can be found in Yu-fei Shen, *Science in China Series C: Life Sciences* (2009). An account of his work appeared in Andy Coghlan, *New Scientist* (30 Nov. 2002). Obituaries are in the the *Scientist* (19 Feb. 2008) and *New York Times* (25 Feb. 2008).

Kelly Winters

WYMAN, Jane (*b.* 4 January 1917 in Saint Joseph, Missouri; *d.* 10 September 2007 in Rancho Mirage, California), film and television actress best remembered for her roles in the film *Johnny Belinda* (1948) and the television series *Falcon Crest*; former wife of President Ronald Reagan.

Jane Wyman, 1981. CBS/LANDOV

Wyman was born Sarah Jane Mayfield, the only child of Manning Jefferies Mayfield, a meal-company laborer, and Gladys Hope (Christian) Mayfield, an office assistant. Her parents divorced in 1921, and the following year her father died of pneumonia. Her mother moved to Cleveland, Ohio, leaving Sarah Jane in the care of Richard D. Fulks, a county collector and chief of detectives, and Emma (Reise) Fulks, a homemaker. Unofficially adopted by the couple, she took their surname. She was unhappy in the strict Fulks home and later reflected, "I have always felt that I was essentially alone at the beginning of my life—and that I will be essentially alone at the end of it." Richard Fulks died when Wyman was eleven, and Emma Fulks, who had two grown children in Los Angeles, took Wyman to live there for a time. They returned to Missouri in 1930. Wyman attended Lafayette High School in Saint Joseph for two years and then went back to Los Angeles, where she completed another year of high school.

Wyman claimed to have attended the University of Missouri, entering in 1935, but like some other information she provided about herself over the years, this appears to have been untrue. She denied having married Ernest Eugene Wyman on 8 April 1933, when she was sixteen; but according to Edmund Morris's 1999 memoir of

Ronald Reagan, the marriage certificate is on file with the state of California. Her second marriage, to which she did admit, was to Myron Futterman, a dress manufacturer, on 29 June 1937; she divorced him in 1938. At some point in the mid-1930s Wyman was a radio singer (under the name Jane Durrell), and from 1936 to 1938 Wyman worked as a model, switchboard operator, waitress, manicurist, and secretary. At the same time she made the rounds of casting calls in Hollywood and dealt with the harsh realities of sexual exploitation. A close friend said she became "a hard-boiled show girl."

With assistance from Leroy Prinz, a Hollywood choreographer and the son of her childhood dancing teacher, Wyman got her first part as a Goldwyn Girl (a dancing female employed by the producer Samuel Goldwyn) in the 1932 film *The Kid from Spain*. Although never considered a Hollywood beauty, at five feet, ten inches and 110 pounds Wyman displayed a gamine quality with big dark eyes, a puckish nose, and long dancer's legs. Her chorus girl friends dubbed her "Button Nose," and the actor William Demarest nicknamed her "Dog Puss."

She signed her first contract as Jane Wyman with Warner Bros. on 6 May 1936. She costarred with Ronald Reagan in *Brother Rat* (1938) and four other films. They married on 26 January 1940; they had a daughter and adopted a son. In 1947 Reagan was hospitalized with a life-threatening case of viral pneumonia. Wyman, pregnant at the time, delivered prematurely, and the baby died; she was devastated by the loss. The couple divorced in 1949. During Reagan's political career, first as governor of California and then two-term president of the United States, she never publicly discussed him. Only upon his death in 2004 did she state that "America has lost a great president and a great, kind, and gentle man."

Critics recognized Wyman's dramatic talent when she appeared in the role of Helen St. James in the 1945 film *The Lost Weekend* (1945). In 1947 she was nominated for an Academy Award for Best Actress for her role in *The Yearling* (1946). In 1949 she won that award for her portrayal of Belinda, the deaf-mute rape victim in *Johnny Belinda* (1948); that year she also won a Golden Globe for best motion-picture actress. She won critical acclaim for her role in *The Glass Menagerie* (1950) and over the next few years was honored several more times, winning the Golden Globe for world film favorite awarded to a female (1951) and the Golden Globe for best motion-picture actress awarded in drama (1952), and being nominated for the best actress Oscar for *The Blue Veil* (1951) and *Magnificent Obsession* (1954). In *Here Comes the Groom*

(1951) she sang with Bing Crosby in the Academy Award–winning song "In the Cool, Cool, Cool of the Evening."

Wyman married the musician Freddie Karger on 1 November 1952; they divorced in 1954. That year Wyman converted to the Roman Catholic faith. Her actress friend Loretta Young explained that Wyman's newfound faith gave her balance. On 11 March 1961 she married Karger for the second time, and in 1965 for the second time divorced him. She never remarried, telling friends, "I guess I just don't have a talent for it."

Beginning in 1955 Wyman immersed herself in television. In 1957 she was nominated for an Emmy for best continuing performance by an actress in a dramatic series for *Jane Wyman Presents The Fireside Theatre*. From 1981 to 1990 she gained wide popularity as the matriarch Angela Channing in *Falcon Crest*; she was nominated twice for a Golden Globe for best performance by an actress in a television series in drama and won the award in 1984. After appearing on *Dr. Quinn, Medicine Woman* in 1993, she retired from acting.

Wyman, who developed arthritis, devoted twenty years of philanthropic service to the Arthritis Foundation. She died at home in her sleep of natural causes. She is buried in Forest Lawn Mortuary and Memorial Park in Cathedral City, California.

Wyman overcame her shyness and a difficult childhood to achieve success as a career-driven performer. She appeared in more than eighty films and forged a second career when she moved to television. Equally adept at comedy and drama, she also exhibited her talent for singing and dancing. As the former wife of a U.S. president, Wyman maintained an absolute reserve when approached for stories or gossip about her years with Reagan. She is remembered as a hard-working and gifted Hollywood star.

★

Daniel Bubbeo, *The Women of Warner Brothers: The Lives and Careers of 15 Leading Ladies, with Filmographies for Each* (2002), offers insight into Wyman's personal life, while following her career chronologically. Joe Morella and Edward Z. Epstein, *Jane Wyman: A Biography* (1985), contains an analysis of her relationship with Reagan. She is also one of the subjects of James Robert Parish and Don E. Stanke, with Roger Greene and Thomas Nocerino, *The Forties Gals* (1980). Lawrence J. Quirk, *Jane Wyman, the Actress and the Woman: An Illustrated Biography* (1986), is based on lengthy interviews with Wyman. An obituary is in the *New York Times* (11 Sept. 2007).

Sandra Redmond Peters

Directory of Contributors

Agnew, Brad
Northeastern State University
CROWE, WILLIAM JAMES, JR.
HIGHTOWER, ROSELLA
WEAVER, (WILLIAM) DENNIS

Allen, Howard
Brooklyn College, City University of
New York (Retired)
COHEN, PAUL JOSEPH

Amerman, Don
Freelance Writer, Bethlehem, Pa.
ANDERSON, ROBERT ORVILLE
BREWER, TERESA
FIELDS, FREDDIE
HARTFORD, (GEORGE) HUNTINGTON,
II
HEINZ, W(ILFRED) C(HARLES)
JORDAN, (WILLIAM) HAMILTON
MCWHORTER
KRULAK, VICTOR HAROLD
NEWMAN, ARNOLD ABNER
SHELDON, SIDNEY

Anderson, Dave
New York Times
BERG, PATRICIA JANE ("PATTY")

Arakaki, Jon S.
State University of New York, College
at Oneonta
RIZZUTO, PHILIP FRANCIS ("PHIL")

Aurand, Harold W.
Pennsylvania State University,
Schuylkill
RINGO, JAMES STEPHEN ("JIM")
SCHEMBECHLER, GLENN EDWARD, JR.
("BO")

Bamberger, Robert L.
Producer/Host, "Hot Jazz Saturday
Night," WAMU-FM (88.5),
Washington, D.C., and NPR
Worldwide
STAFFORD, JO

Barbeau, Art
West Liberty State College
DIXON, FRANK J(AMES)
FIROR, JOHN WILLIAM, JR.
GLUECKSOHN-WAELSCH, SALOME
TOGURI, IKUKO ("IVA"; "TOKYO
ROSE")
VAN ALLEN, JAMES ALFRED

Baumann, Mary
U.S. Senate Historical Office
EAGLETON, THOMAS FRANCIS

Beck, Sheila
Queensborough Community College,
City University of New York
JASTROW, ROBERT
TONER, ROBERTA DENISE ("ROBIN")

Beetz, Kirk H.
Author and Educator
BISHOP, JOEY
LAY, KENNETH LEE ("KEN")
WILLIAMSON, JOHN STEWART ("JACK")

Bosky, Bernadette Lynn
Olympiad Academia
BRUCCOLI, MATTHEW JOSEPH
IVINS, BRUCE EDWARDS

Breskin, Ira
State University of New York,
Maritime College
CAREY, RONALD ROBERT ("RON")
FELKER, CLAY SCHUETTE

Briley, Ron
Sandia Preparatory School,
Albuquerque, N. Mex.
JORDAN, WINTHROP DONALDSON
LIPSET, SEYMOUR MARTIN
UPSHAW, EUGENE THURMAN, JR.
("GENE")

Byrne, John J.
Bronx Community College
OLSEN, TILLIE LERNER

Campbell, Jim
Bucknell University (Retired)
BAUGH, SAMUEL ADRIAN
("SAMMY")
WALSH, WILLIAM ERNEST
("BILL")
WILLIS, WILLIAM KARNET
("BILL")

Carstensen, Fred
University of Connecticut
RUKEYSER, LOUIS RICHARD

Carstensen, Mildred G.
Freelance Writer
FREEDMAN, JAMES OLIVER

Castañeda, James Agustín
Rice University
NELSON, (JOHN) BYRON, JR.

543

Chen, Jeffrey H.
Cambridge University Press
JACOBS, JANE
PAGE, BETTIE MAE

Cicarelli, James
Roosevelt University–
Schaumburg, Ill.
HURWICZ, LEONID
WALGREEN, CHARLES RUDOLPH, JR.

Cicarelli, Julianne
Freelance Writer, Arlington
Heights, Ill.
BAVARIA, JOAN
HELMSLEY, LEONA

Cooksey, Gloria
Independent Scholar, Sacramento
County, Calif.
KIRKPATRICK, JEANE DUANE
JORDAN

Cox, Patrick L.
Dolph Briscoe Center for American
History, University of Texas at
Austin
BENTSEN, LLOYD MILLARD, JR.

Crawford, Scott A. G. M.
Eastern Illinois University
FRANCE, WILLIAM CLIFTON, JR.
("BILL")
OERTER, ALFRED ADOLPH, JR.
("AL")

Crispell, Brian Lewis
Florida College
SMATHERS, GEORGE ARMISTEAD

Damon, Allan L.
Horace Greeley High School (retired),
Chappaqua, N.Y.
BUCKLEY, WILLIAM F(RANCIS), JR.
JOHNSON, CLAUDIA ALTA TAYLOR
("LADY BIRD")
STYRON, WILLIAM CLARK, JR.
TRUMAN, (MARY) MARGARET

Davidson, Abraham A.
Tyler School of Art, Temple
University
HARTIGAN, GRACE
LEWITT, SOL

Davis, Robert E.
DeSantis Center for Motion Picture
Industry Studies, Florida Atlantic
University
MANN, DELBERT MARTIN, JR.
("DEL")

Dinneen, Marcia B.
Bridgewater State College
CHARISSE, CYD
MOFFO, ANNA
VIERECK, PETER ROBERT EDWIN

Dobson, Melissa A.
Freelance Writer, Bristol, R.I.
GALLO, ERNEST
THARP, MARIE

Doenecke, Justus D.
New College of Florida
LEOPOLD, RICHARD WILLIAM
TOLEDANO, RALPH DE

Dorinson, Joseph
Long Island University
BUTTONS, RED

Drobnicki, John A.
York College, City University of New
York
HUNT, LAMAR

Dyer, Leigh
Charlotte Observer, N.C.
IVINS, MOLLY TYLER

Edelman, Rob
Writer and Editor
BROWN, JAMES JOSEPH, JR.
FORD, GWYLLYN SAMUEL NEWTON
("GLENN")
GRIFFIN, MERVYN EDWARD, JR.
("MERV")
KERR, DEBORAH JANE
MAC, BERNIE
NEWMAN, PAUL LEONARD
PARKS, GORDON ROGER ALEXANDER
BUCHANAN
STAPLETON, (LOIS) MAUREEN

Ennis, Lisa A.
Lister Hill Library of the Health
Sciences, University of Alabama at
Birmingham
INGRAM, VERNON MARTIN
JONASSON, OLGA

Farrelly, Maura Jane
Brandeis University
HUMBARD, (ALPHA) REX EMMANUEL
MICHAELS, JAMES WALKER

Fermaglich, Kirsten
Michigan State University
FRIEDAN, BETTY

Ferrara, Adi
Freelance Writer, Bellevue, Wash.
SHUMWAY, NORMAN EDWARD, JR.
VOGT, MARGUERITE MARIA

Fischer, William E.
Westland High School, Galloway,
Ohio
OLDS, ROBIN
TIBBETS, PAUL WARFIELD, JR.

Fitzpatrick, Jane Brodsky
Mina Rees Library, City University of
New York Graduate Center
DITH PRAN
GOWDY, CURTIS EDWARD ("CURT")
GRAY ADAMS, VICTORIA ALMETER
JACKSON
HARDWICK, ELIZABETH BRUCE
SEAMAN, BARBARA

Fitzpatrick, John
Miklós Rózsa Society
HESTON, CHARLTON

Flannery, Maura C.
St. John's University, New York
KORNBERG, ARTHUR
LEDERBERG, JOSHUA
MERRIFIELD, (ROBERT) BRUCE
PALADE, GEORGE EMIL

Flynn, Joseph G.
State University of New York College
of Technology, Alfred
AGEE, PHILIP BURNETT FRANKLIN

Frick, Lisa
Freelance Writer, Columbia, Mo.
BUTCHER, SUSAN HOWLET
OWENS, ALVIS EDGAR, JR. ("BUCK")

Friedwald, Will
New York Sun
O'DAY, ANITA

Frisch, Paul A.
Our Lady of the Lake University, San
Antonio, Tex.
O'BRIEN, (WILLIAM) PARRY, JR.

Fuchs, Caroline
Cuny Graduate Center Special
Collections
THERING, ROSE ELIZABETH

Furguson, E. B., III
Writer, Annapolis, Md.
ABERCROMBIE, THOMAS JAMES

Gaar, Gillian G.
Independent Scholar
BARBERA, JOSEPH ROLAND
GOULET, ROBERT GERARD
SCHEIDER, ROY RICHARD
SNYDER, THOMAS JAMES ("TOM")
WEXLER, GERALD ("JERRY")

Gao, Yunxiang
Ryerson University
HO, DONALD TAI LOY ("DON")

Goodbody, Joan
U.S. Patent and Trademark Office
SCHWARTZ, ANTHONY
TEMPLETON, JOHN MARKS

Goodstein, Judith R.
California Institute of Technology
BENZER, SEYMOUR

Griffith, Clark C.
Independent Scholar
PUCKETT, KIRBY

Harmond, Richard P.
St. John's University, New York
BENCHLEY, PETER BRADFORD
FELT, (WILLIAM) MARK

Healy, John David
Drew University
ALLYSON, JUNE
AVIS, WARREN EDWARD
DARMAN, RICHARD

Hirsch, Foster
Brooklyn College, City University
of New York
ALTMAN, ROBERT BERNARD
HART, KITTY CARLISLE

Hlavaty, Arthur D.
Freelance Writer and Editor, Yonkers,
N.Y.
ELLIS, ALBERT

Hodges, Graham Russell Gao
Colgate University
PATTERSON, FLOYD
WALD, FLORENCE SOPHIE SCHORSKE

Hoogenboom, Lynn
New York Times News Service
BUCHWALD, ARTTHUR ("ART")
COMDEN, BETTY

Howlett, Charles F.
Molloy College
COFFIN, WILLIAM SLOANE, JR.

Jackson, Kenneth T.
Columbia University
WADE, RICHARD CLEMENT

Jacobs, Travis Beal
Middlebury College
STAFFORD, ROBERT THEODORE

Johnson, Kathleen
Independent Scholar, Silver Spring,
Md.
DRINAN, ROBERT FREDERICK
MCFALL, JOHN JOSEPH

Keen, W. Hubert
Farmingdale State University of New
York
KRUSKAL, MARTIN DAVID
MCKUSICK, VICTOR ALMON

Ketz, Louise B.
Louise B. Ketz Agency
LAWFORD, PATRICIA KENNEDY
POLSBY, NELSON WOOLF
WEINBERG, ALVIN MARTIN

Koed, Betty K.
U.S. Senate Historical Office
THOMAS, CRAIG LYLE

Laird, Kim
Library of Michigan
WHITESIDE, LAWRENCE W. ("LARRY")

Lankevich, George J.
City University of New York
APPLE, RAYMON WALTER, JR.
("JOHNNY")
ROSENTHAL, A(BRAHAM) M(ICHAEL)
("ABE")

Lauer, Josh
University of New Hampshire
CHANDLER, ALFRED DU PONT, JR.

Lawlor, William
University of Wisconsin–Stevens
Point
GIROUX, ROBERT

Leab, Daniel J.
Seton Hall University
HUNT, E(VERETTE) HOWARD, JR.
MOTT, STEWART RAWLINGS
SMITH, ROGER BONHAM

Lewis, Jane Amler
Iona College
KUNITZ, STANLEY JASSPON
PALEY, GRACE GOODSIDE

Lille, Dawn
Juilliard School of Music
HAYDEN, MELISSA ("MILLY")
KIDD, MICHAEL ("MIKE")

Link, William A.
University of Florida
HELMS, JESSE ALEXANDER, JR.

Linkletter, Karen
California State University, Fullerton
FRIEDMAN, MILTON
HUFFINGTON, ROY MICHAEL
KELLER, GEORGE MATTHEW
LEONARD, JOHN DILLON

Little, Kimberly K.
Ohio University
LEDGER, HEATHCLIFF ANDREW
("HEATH")
L'ENGLE, MADELEINE CAMP
MESSNER, TAMARA FAYE LAVALLEY
("TAMMY FAYE")
PLESHETTE, SUZANNE
WAGONER, PORTER WAYNE

Lo Brutto, Vincent
School of Visual Arts, New York City
ELDER, WILL
HERBERT, DONALD JEFFREY ("DON")
WALLACE, DAVID FOSTER
WINTERS, SHELLEY

Luft, Eric v. d.
State University of New York, Upstate
Medical University
RORTY, RICHARD MCKAY

Lydon, Michael
Writer and Musician, New York City
DIDDLEY, BO

Maggin, Donald L.
Freelance Writer, New York City
DUNHAM, KATHERINE
ROACH, MAXWELL LEMUEL ("MAX")

Mancini, Candice
Freelance Writer, Missoula, Mont.
BOYD, EDWARD FRANCIS
FOSSETT, JAMES STEPHEN ("STEVE")

Marc, David
Freelance Writer and Editor, Syracuse,
N.Y.
CARLIN, GEORGE DENIS PATRICK
DOUGLAS, MIKE
MCKAY, JIM
SPELLING, AARON
STANTON, FRANK NICHOLAS

Markley, Patricia L.
Siena College
KNOTTS, JESSE DONALD ("DON")
KORMAN, HARVEY HERSCHEL

Markoe, Lauren
Center for Political Accountability
LIBRESCU, LIVIU

McElwaine, James
Purchase College, State University of
New York
BRECHT, GEORGE
KITT, EARTHA
PITNEY, GENE FRANCIS ALLAN

Meckna, Michael
Texas Christian University
ARNOLD, RICHARD EDWARD
("EDDY")
FERGUSON, (WALTER) MAYNARD
LAINE, FRANKIE

Mieczkowski, Yanek
Dowling College
FORD, GERALD RUDOLPH, JR.

Miller, Michael C.
Austin History Center
BASS, PERRY RICHARDSON

Mitchell, Nicole
University of Alabama at
Birmingham
SKIPPER, HOWARD EARLE

Molyneaux, Gerard
La Salle University
BOYLE, PETER LAWRENCE
MULLIGAN, ROBERT PATRICK
POLLACK, SYDNEY IRWIN

Montgomery, Dave
Fort Worth Star-Telegram
SMITH, ANNA NICOLE
WEINBERGER, CASPAR WILLARD

Moore, William Howard
University of Wyoming
FALWELL, JERRY LAMON
GREENGLASS, RUTH LEAH PRINTZ
HINCKLEY, GORDON BITNER

Murray, Michael D.
University of Missouri–St. Louis
BRADLEY, EDWARD RUDOLPH, JR.
("ED")
RUSSERT, TIMOTHY JOHN, JR. ("TIM")

Murray, Paul T.
Siena College
CLARK, JAMES GARDNER, JR. ("JIM")
HILL, OLIVER WHITE, SR.
ODETTA

Mustazza, Leonard
Pennsylvania State University
CRICHTON, (JOHN) MICHAEL
ERTEGUN, AHMET MUNIR
VONNEGUT, KURT, JR.

Nagel, Miriam C.
Freelance Writer
DAVIS, RAYMOND, JR.
FOLKMAN, (MOSES) JUDAH
GAJDUSEK, DANIEL CARLETON
LAMB, WILLIS EUGENE, JR.
MACDIARMID, ALAN GRAHAM
MILLER, STANLEY LLOYD
SCHWARTZ, MELVIN

Nelson, Murry R.
Pennsylvania State University
ARIZIN, PAUL JOSEPH
MEYER, RAYMOND JOSEPH ("RAY")
NEWELL, PETER FRANCIS, JR. ("PETE")

Neuman, Johanna
Author and Journalist, Washington,
D.C.
CHANDLER, OTIS

Neumann, Caryn E.
Miami University of Ohio
KNIEVEL, ROBERT CRAIG, JR. ("EVEL")
METZENBAUM, HOWARD MORTON
PAIK, NAM JUNE
SCHOENFELD, GERALD

O'Malley, Brendan
Graduate Center of the City University
of New York
LEVINE, LAWRENCE WILLIAM

Pach, Chester
Ohio University
FRANK, (ISRAEL) REUVEN
HALBERSTAM, DAVID

Peters, Sandra Redmond
Crowder College
WEINBERG, JOHN LIVINGSTON
WYMAN, JANE

Pharr, Ann E.
Good Samaritan Foundation
DEAVER, MICHAEL KEITH
WEYRICH, PAUL MICHAEL

Polner, Murray
Freelance Writer, Great Neck, N.Y.
SHULMAN, MARSHALL DARROW
TERKEL, LOUIS ("STUDS")

Polster, Joshua
Emerson College
GEERTZ, CLIFFORD JAMES

Porter, David L.
William Penn University
AUERBACH, ARNOLD JACOB ("RED")
BAVASI, EMIL JOSEPH ("BUZZIE")
HASKINS, DONALD ("DON")

Prono, Luca
Independent Scholar
MENOTTI, GIAN CARLO
WIDMARK, RICHARD

Rice, Bradley R.
Clayton State University
KING, CORETTA SCOTT
SHOULDERS, JAMES ARTHUR ("JIM")

Riley, James A.
Negro Leagues Baseball Museum
O'NEIL, JOHN JORDAN, JR. ("BUCK")

Roberts, Priscilla
University of Hong Kong
ASTOR, (ROBERTA) BROOKE RUSSELL
GALBRAITH, JOHN KENNETH
HUNTINGTON, SAMUEL PHILLIPS
SCHLESINGER, ARTHUR MEIER, JR.

Rocco, John
State University of New York,
Maritime College
DASSIN, JULES
PALANCE, JACK
SPILLANE, MICKEY

Rollyson, Carl
Baruch College, City University of
New York
JOHNSON, (CHARLES) VAN DELL
MAILER, NORMAN KINGSLEY

Sanchez, Brenna
Freelance Writer, Los Angeles, Calif.
ALPHER, RALPH ASHER
GOHEEN, ROBERT FRANCIS
MONDAVI, ROBERT GERALD
WELLER, THOMAS HUCKLE

Savage, Steven P.
Eastern Kentucky University
HARTACK, WILLIAM JOHN, JR. ("BILL")

Scharnhorst, Gary
University of New Mexico
FEIGNER, EDDIE
RICHARDS, (DOROTHY) ANN WILLIS

Scherer, John L.
Minneapolis, Minn.
SCHRECKENGOST, VIKTOR SEBRING

Sheidlower, Scott
York College, City University of
New York
GITTINGS, BARBARA

Shor, Rachel
Queens Borough Public Library, New
York City
WASSERSTEIN, WENDY JOY

Smalls, F. Romall
Journalist and Media Consultant,
Jersey City, N.J.
  BUTLER, OCTAVIA ESTELLE

Smallwood, James M.
Oklahoma State University
  ROBINSON, EDWARD GAY ("EDDIE")

Smith, James F.
Pennsylvania State University, Abington
  HAYES, ISAAC LEE, JR.
  PICKETT, WILSON, JR.
  RAWLS, LOUIS ALLEN ("LOU")

Smith, Michael
Walter P. Reuther Library, Wayne State
University
  FRASER, DOUGLAS ANDREW ("DOUG")

Smith, Patrick S.
Freelance Writer, Pittsburgh, Penn.
  ADAMS, EDIE
  CASSINI, OLEG LOLEWSKI
  CLAIBORNE, ANNE ELISABETH JANE
    ("LIZ")
  HUTTON, BETTY

Smith, Whitney
Indianapolis Star
  BARNES, CLIVE ALEXANDER
  ROSTROPOVICH, MSTISLAV
    LEOPOLDOVICH
  SILLS, BEVERLY

Spatt, Hartley S.
State University of New York,
Maritime College
  BUSCH, FREDERICK
  CROSSFIELD, (ALBERT) SCOTT, JR.
  HILL, PHILIP TOLL, JR. ("PHIL")

Su, Di
York College, City University of New York
  CALDWELL, SARAH

Sumner, Jim L.
Historian, Raleigh, N.C.
  BEARD, RALPH MILTON, JR.

Takooshian, Harold
Fordham University
  DULLES, AVERY ROBERT

Tamborrino, Victoria
St. John's University, New York
  LAUTERBUR, PAUL CHRISTIAN
  SCHIRRA, WALTER MARTY,
    JR.("WALLY")

Tassinari, Edward J.
State University of New York,
Maritime College
  FISCHER, ROBERT JAMES ("BOBBY")
  GIARDELLO, JOEY
  PEP, WILLIE

Thompson-Feuerherd, Jennifer
New York Institute of Technology
  BROWNE, ROSCOE LEE

Tomasino, Adriana C.
Ph.D. Candidate, City University of
New York
  BRENNER, CHARLES
  DEBAKEY, MICHAEL ELLIS
  KANTROWITZ, ADRIAN
  LEAVITT, HAROLD JACK
  MURRAY, ELIZABETH
  SONNENBLICK, EDMUND HIRAM

Traflet, Janice M.
Bucknell University
  LEVITT, THEODORE ("TED")

Trombe, Carolyn
New York State Education Department
  COLLINS, DOROTHY YVONNE WILTSE
    ("DOTTIE")

Turner O'Hara, Laura
Washington, D.C.
  LANTOS, THOMAS PETER ("TOM")

VanDoren, Sandra Shaffer
  ARPINO, GENNARO PETER ARTHUR
    ("GERALD")

Vorperian, John
Concordia College
  KUHN, BOWIE KENT

Waldman, Michael
Baruch College, City University of
New York
  LADER, LAWRENCE POWELL

Wasniewski, Matthew
Greenbelt, Md.
  HYDE, HENRY JOHN
  MONTGOMERY, GILLESPIE V.
    ("SONNY")
  STUDDS, GERRY EASTMAN

Wedge, Eleanor F.
Writer and Editor, New York City
  D'HARNONCOURT, ANNE JULIE
  EPSTEIN, BARBARA ZIMMERMAN
  PELIKAN, JAROSLAV JAN, JR.
  RAUSCHENBERG, ROBERT

Weisblat, Leigh Bullard
Independent Art Historian, New York
City
  OLITSKI, JULES

Whitfield, Stephen J.
Brandeis University
  LEVY, LEONARD WILLIAMS
  WOLFSON, LOUIS ELWOOD

Winegrad, Dilys Pegler
Arthur Ross Gallery, University of
Pennsylvania
  MEYERSON, MARTIN

Winters, Kelly
Freelance Writer, Bayville, N.Y.
  MATHIAS, ROBERT BRUCE ("BOB")
  WU, RAY JUI

Wise, Steven
Sueltenfuss Library, Our Lady of the
Lake University
  FENDER, FREDDY
  VALENTI, JACK JOSEPH

Womack, Malcolm
University of Washington
  NICHOLAS, FAYARD ANTONIO

Yalom, Marilyn
  MIDDLEBROOK, (HELEN) DIANE WOOD

Young, Hope E.
York College, City University of New
York
  MORRIS, HENRY M(ADISON)

Occupations Index, Volumes 1–8 and Thematic Volumes

See also the Alphabetical List of Subjects beginning on p. 613. Note that the Sports *and* 1960s *thematic series each comprise two volumes. Thus, for example, a citation for "1960s-2" means that the subject is found in Volume 2 of the* 1960s *thematic set.*

ACTING TEACHER

ACTOR

Jastrow, Robert — 8
Sagan, Carl Edward — 4
Van Allen, James Alfred — 8
Von Braun, Wernher — 1960s-2

ATHLETE (AUTO RACING)

Andretti, (Gabriele) Mario — Sports-1
Bernstein, Kenneth Dale ("Kenny") — Sports-1
Earnhardt, (Ralph) Dale — 6, Sports-1
Foyt, A(nthony) J(oseph), Jr. — Sports-1
France, William Henry Getty, Sr. ("Bill") — Sports-1
Garlits, Don(ald) — Sports-1
Gordon, Jeff — Sports-1
Gurney, Dan(iel) Sexton — Sports-1
Hill, Philip Toll, Jr. ("Phil") — 8
Johnson, Robert Glenn, Jr. ("Junior") — Sports-1
Muldowney, Shirley Roque — Sports-2
Oldfield, Berna Eli ("Barney") — Sports-2
Parsons, Johnnie — 1
Penske, Roger S. — Sports-2
Petty, Lee Arnold — 6
Petty, Richard Lee — Sports-2
Unser, Al(fred), Jr. — Sports-2
Unser, Al(fred), Sr. — Sports-2

ATHLETE (BASEBALL)

Aaron, Henry Louis ("Hank") — 1960s-1, Sports-1
Alexander, Grover Cleveland — Sports-1
Alston, Walter Emmons — 1
Anderson, George Lee ("Sparky") — Sports-1
Anson, Adrian Constantine ("Cap," "Pop") — Sports-1
Appling, Lucius Benjamin, Jr. ("Luke") — 3
Ashburn, Don Richard ("Richie") — 5
Averill, Howard Earl ("Rock") — 1
Banks, Ernest ("Ernie") — Sports-1
Bell, James Thomas ("Cool Papa") — 3, Sports-1
Bench, Johnny Lee — Sports-1
Berra, Lawrence Peter ("Yogi") — Sports-1
Black, Joseph, Jr. ("Joe") — 6
Bonds, Barry Lamar — Sports-1
Boudreau, Louis ("Lou") — 6
Brett, George Howard — Sports-1
Brock, Lou(is Clark) — Sports-1
Brown, Mordecai Peter Centennial — Sports-1
Bunning, James Paul David ("Jim") — Sports-1
Campanella, Roy — 3, Sports-1
Carew, Rod(ney) Cline — Sports-1

Carlton, Steven Norman — Sports-1
Cartwright, Alexander Joy, Jr. — Sports-1
Chadwick, Henry — Sports-1
Chandler, Albert Benjamin ("Happy") — Sports-1
Charleston, Oscar McKinley ("Charlie") — Sports-1
Chesbro, John Dwight ("Jack") — Sports-1
Clemens, (William) Roger — Sports-1
Clemente, Roberto Walker — 1960s-1, Sports-1
Cobb, Ty(rus) Raymond — Sports-1
Cochrane, Gordon Stanley ("Mickey") — Sports-1
Collins, Dorothy Yvonne Wiltse ("Dottie") — 8
Collins, Edward Trowbridge ("Eddie") — Sports-1
Comiskey, Charles Albert — Sports-1
Conigliaro, Anthony Richard ("Tony") — 2
Conlan, John Bertrand ("Jocko") — 2
Connors, Kevin Joseph Aloysius ("Chuck") — 3
Coveleski, Stanley Anthony ("Covey") — 1
Cronin, Joseph Edward — 1
Dancer, Faye Katherine — 6
Dandridge, Raymond Emmett ("Squatty") — 4, Sports-1
Day, Leon — 4
Dean, Jay Hanna ("Dizzy") — Sports-1
Dean, Paul ("Daffy") — 1
Dickey, William Malcolm ("Bill") — 4, Sports-1
DiMaggio, Joseph Paul ("Joe") — 5, Sports-1
Doby, Lawrence Eugene ("Larry") — 7, Sports-1
Drysdale, Donald Scott ("Don") — 3, 1960s-1, Sports-1
Durocher, Leo Ernest — 3, Sports-1
Ewing, William ("Buck") — Sports-1
Feller, Robert William Andrew ("Bob") — Sports-1
Fingers, Roland Glen ("Rollie") — Sports-1
Flood, Curt(is) Charles — 5, Sports-1
Ford, Edward Charles ("Whitey") — Sports-1
Foster, Andrew ("Rube") — Sports-1
Fox, Jacob Nelson ("Nellie") — Sports-1
Foxx, James Emory ("Jimmie") — Sports-1
Frick, Ford Christopher — Sports-1

Frisch, Frank Francis ("Frankie") — Sports-1
Garciaparra, (Anthony) Nomar — Sports-1
Gehrig, (Henry) Lou(is) — Sports-1
Gehringer, Charles Leonard ("Charlie") — 3, Sports-1
Giamatti, A(ngelo) Bartlett ("Bart") — Sports-1
Gibson, Josh(ua) — Sports-1
Gibson, Pack Robert ("Bob") — Sports-1
Gomez, Vernon Louis ("Lefty") — Sports-1
Gray, Peter Wyshner ("Pete") — 6
Greenberg, Henry Benjamin ("Hank") — 2, Sports-1
Griffey, (George) Ken(neth), Jr. — Sports-1
Griffith, Clark Calvin — Sports-1
Grimes, Burleigh Arland — 1
Grove, Robert Moses ("Lefty") — Sports-1
Gwynn, Anthony Keith ("Tony") — Sports-1
Henderson, Rickey — Sports-1
Herman, Floyd Caves ("Babe") — 2
Herman, William Jennings ("Billy") — 3
Hornsby, Rogers ("Rajah") — Sports-1
Hoyt, Waite Charles ("Schoolboy") — 1
Hubbard, (Robert) Cal — Sports-1
Hubbell, Carl Owen — 2, Sports-1
Huggins, Miller James — Sports-1
Hunter, James Augustus ("Catfish"; "Jim") — 5, Sports-1
Jackson, Joseph Jefferson Wofford ("Shoeless Joe") — Sports-1
Jackson, Reginald Martinez ("Reggie") — Sports-1
Jackson, Travis Calvin ("Stonewall") — 2
Jeter, Derek Sanderson — Sports-1
Johnson, Randall David ("Randy") — Sports-1
Johnson, Walter Perry ("The Big Train") — Sports-1
Johnson, William Julius ("Judy") — 2, Sports-1
Kaline, Al(bert) William — Sports-1
Keeler, William Henry — Sports-1
Kelly, George Lange ("Highpockets") — 1
Kelly, Michael Joseph ("King") — Sports-1
Killebrew, Harmon Clayton, Jr. — 1960s-1, Sports-1
Kiner, Ralph McPherran — Sports-1
Klem, William Joseph ("Bill") — Sports-1
Kluszewski, Theodore Bernard ("Ted"; "Big Klu") — 2

Forte, Fulvio Chester, Jr. ("Chet") 4
Frazier, Walt, II ("Clyde") Sports-1
Fulks, Joseph Franklin ("Joe") Sports-1
Gaines, Clarence Edward, Sr.
 ("Bighouse") Sports-1
Gates, William ("Pop") 5
Hannum, Alex 6
Haskins, Donald Lee
 ("Don") 8, Sports-1
Havlicek, John Joseph Sports-1
Hawkins, Cornelius L.
 ("Connie") Sports-1
Hayes, Elvin Ernest Sports-1
Haynes, Marques Oreole Sports-1
Holdsclaw, Chamique
 Shaunta Sports-1
Holman, Nathan ("Nat") 4, Sports-1
Holzman, William ("Red") 5
Iba, Henry Payne ("Hank") Sports-1
Iverson, Allen Ezail Sports-1
Jackson, Philip Douglas
 ("Phil") Sports-1
Johnson, Earvin, Jr. ("Magic") Sports-1
Jones, K. C. Sports-1
Jordan, Michael Jeffrey ("Air") Sports-1
Knight, Robert Montgomery
 ("Bob") Sports-1
Krzyzewski, Michael William
 ("Mike") Sports-1
Kurland, Robert ("Bob") Sports-1
Lapchick, Joseph Bohomiel
 ("Joe") Sports-2
Lemon, Meadow George
 ("Meadowlark") Sports-2
Leslie, Lisa DeShaun Sports-2
Lieberman-Cline, Nancy Sports-2
Lobo, Rebecca Rose Sports-2
Luisetti, Angelo Enrico
 ("Hank") 6, Sports-2
Malone, Karl Anthony Sports-2
Malone, Moses Eugene Sports-2
Maravich, Peter Press
 ("Pistol Pete") 2, Sports-2
Meyers, Ann Elizabeth Sports-2
Mikan, George Lawrence, Jr. 7, Sports-2
Miller, Cheryl DeAnn Sports-2
Miller, Reginald Wayne
 ("Reggie") Sports-2
Monroe, Earl Vernon, Jr.
 ("the Pearl") Sports-2
Mourning, Alonzo Harding, Jr. Sports-2
Murphy, Calvin Jerome Sports-2
Naismith, James Sports-2
Newell, Peter Francis, Jr.
 ("Pete") 8, Sports-2
Olajuwon, Hakeem Abdul Sports-2
O'Neal, Shaq(uille) Rashaun Sports-2

Pettit, Robert E. Lee, Jr.
 ("Bob") Sports-2
Pippen, Scottie Sports-2
Pollard, James Clifford
 ("Jim") Sports-2
Reed, Willis, Jr. Sports-2
Riley, Pat(rick) James Sports-2
Ripley, Elmer Horton 1
Robertson, Oscar Palmer Sports-2
Robinson, David Maurice Sports-2
Rupp, Adolph Frederick Sports-2
Russell, William Felton
 ("Bill") 1960s-2, Sports-2
Schayes, Adolph ("Dolph") Sports-2
Smith, Dean Edwards Sports-2
Staley, Dawn Sports-2
Stern, David Sports-2
Stockton, John Houston Sports-2
Summitt, Pat(ricia) Head Sports-2
Swoopes, Sheryl Denise Sports-2
Tatum, Reece ("Goose") Sports-2
Thomas, Isiah Lord, III Sports-2
Thompson, David O'Neal Sports-2
Thompson, John Robert, Jr. Sports-2
Walton, William Theodore, III
 ("Bill") Sports-2
Weatherspoon, Teresa Sports-2
West, Jerry Alan Sports-2
Wilkens, Leonard Randolph
 ("Lenny") Sports-2
Woodard, Lynette Sports-2
Wooden, John Robert Sports-2
Worthy, James Ager Sports-2
Yardley, George Harry, III
 ("the Bird") 7

ATHLETE (BOWLING)

Carter, Don(ald) James Sports-1
Nagy, Steve Sports-2
Varipapa, Andrew ("Andy") 1, Sports-2
Weber, Pete Sports-2

ATHLETE (BOXING)

Ali, Muhammad
 (Cassius Clay) 1960s-1, Sports-1
Armstrong, Henry Jackson, Jr. Sports-1
Conn, William David, Jr.
 ("Billy") 3, Sports-1
Corbett, James John Sports-1
D'Amato, Constantine
 ("Cus") Sports-1
Dempsey, William Harrison
 ("Jack") 1, Sports-1
Dundee, Angelo Sports-1
Frazier, Joseph William
 ("Joe") 1960s-1, Sports-1
Futch, Eddie 6

Gavilan, Kid 7
Giardello, Joey 8
Graham, William Patrick ("Billy") 3
Graziano, Rocky 2, Sports-1
Greb, Edward Henry
 ("Harry") Sports-1
Griffith, Emile Alphonse Sports-1
Hagler, Marvin Nathaniel Sports-1
Hearns, Thomas Sports-1
Jack, Beau 6
Jeffries, James Jackson Sports-1
Johnson, John Arthur ("Jack") Sports-1
Ketchel, Stanley Sports-1
King, Don(ald) Sports-1
LaMotta, Jake Sports-2
Leonard, Benny Sports-2
Leonard, Ray Charles
 ("Sugar Ray") Sports-2
Liston, Charles
 ("Sonny") 1960s-1, Sports-2
Louis, Joseph ("Joe") 1, Sports-2
Marciano, Rocky Sports-2
Moore, Archibald Lee
 ("Archie") 5, Sports-2
Patterson, Floyd 8, 1960s-2, Sports-2
Pep, Willie 8, Sports-2
Rickard, George Lewis
 ("Tex") Sports-2
Robinson, Ray
 ("Sugar Ray") 2, Sports-2
Saddler, Joseph ("Sandy") 6
Sharkey, Jack 4
Sullivan, John Lawrence Sports-2
Tunney, James Joseph
 ("Gene") Sports-2
Tyson, Michael Gerard
 ("Mike"; "Iron Mike") Sports-2
Walcott, "Jersey Joe" 4
Walker, Edward Patrick
 ("Mickey") 1, Sports-2
Zale, Tony 5, Sports-2

ATHLETE (CHESS)

Fischer, Robert James ("Bobby") 8

ATHLETE (CRICKET)

Wright, William Henry
 ("Harry") Sports-2

ATHLETE (CYCLING)

Armstrong, Lance Sports-1
LeMond, Greg(ory) James Sports-2
Taylor, Marshall Walter
 ("Major") Sports-2

ATHLETE (DOG RACING)

Butcher, Susan Howlet 8

ATHLETE (FIGURE SKATING)

Albright, Tenley Emma	Sports-1
Boitano, Brian Anthony	Sports-1
Button, Richard Totten ("Dick")	Sports-1
Fleming, Peggy Gale	1960s-1, Sports-1
Hamill, Dorothy Stuart	Sports-1
Hamilton, Scott Scovell	Sports-1
Heiss Jenkins, Carol Elizabeth	Sports-1
Henie, Sonja	Sports-1
Jenkins, David Wilkinson	Sports-1
Jenkins, Hayes Alan	Sports-1
Kwan, Michelle Wing	Sports-1
Yamaguchi, Kristi Tsuya	Sports-2

ATHLETE (FOOTBALL)

Aikman, Troy Kenneth	Sports-1
Albert, Frank Culling ("Frankie")	6
Allen, Marcus LeMarr	Sports-1
Alworth, Lance Dwight	Sports-1
Baker, Hobart Amory Hare ("Hobey")	Sports-1
Battles, Clifford Franklin ("Gyp")	1
Baugh, Samuel Adrian ("Sammy")	8, Sports-1
Bednarik, Charles Philip ("Chuck")	Sports-1
Bell, DeBenneville ("Bert")	Sports-1
Berry, Raymond Emmett	Sports-1
Blaik, Earl Henry ("Red")	Sports-1
Blanchard, Felix Anthony, Jr. ("Doc")	Sports-1
Blanda, George Frederick	Sports-1
Bowden, Robert Cleckler ("Bobby") Sports-1	
Bradshaw, Terry Paxton	Sports-1
Brown, James Nathaniel ("Jim")	1960s-1, Sports-1
Brown, Paul Eugene	Sports-1
Brown, Roosevelt H., Jr. ("Rosey")	7
Bryant, Paul William ("Bear")	Sports-1
Buchanan, Junious ("Buck")	Sports-1
Butkus, Richard Marvin ("Dick")	Sports-1
Camp, Walter Chauncey	Sports-1
Campbell, Earl Christian	Sports-1
Campbell, Milton Gray ("Milt")	Sports-1
Canadeo, Anthony Robert ("Tony")	7
Carter, Cris D.	Sports-1
Conerly, Charles Albert ("Charlie"), Jr.	4
Connor, George Leo, Sr. ("Moose")	7
Crisler, Herbert Orin ("Fritz")	1
Davis, Al(len)	Sports-1
Davis, Glenn Woodward	7, Sports-1
Dickerson, Eric Demetric	Sports-1

Ditka, Mike	Sports-1
Dodd, Robert Lee ("Bobby")	2
Dorsett, Anthony Drew ("Tony")	Sports-1
Elway, John Albert	Sports-1
Engle, Charles Albert ("Rip")	1
Ewbank, Wilbur Charles ("Weeb")	Sports-1
Favre, Brett Lorenzo	Sports-1
Fears, Thomas Jesse ("Tom")	6, Sports-1
Fish, Hamilton	3
Friedman, Benjamin ("Benny")	1
Gibbs, Joe Jackson	Sports-1
Gifford, Frank Newton	Sports-1
Gillman, Sid(ney)	Sports-1
Graham, Otto Everett, Jr.	7, Sports-1
Grange, Harold Edward ("Red")	3, Sports-1
Greene, Charles Edward ("Mean Joe")	Sports-1
Gregg, (Alvis) Forrest	Sports-1
Groza, Louis Roy ("Lou")	6, Sports-1
Halas, George Stanley	Sports-1
Hannah, John Allen	Sports-1
Harmon, Thomas Dudley ("Tom")	2, Sports-1
Harris, Franco	Sports-1
Hart, Leon	6
Hayes, Robert Lee ("Bob")	6
Hayes, Wayne Woodrow ("Woody")	Sports-1
Heffelfinger, William Walter ("Pudge")	Sports-1
Hein, Mel(vin) John	Sports-1
Heisman, John William ("Johnny")	Sports-1
Hirsch, Elroy Leon ("Crazylegs")	7, Sports-1
Hornung, Paul Vernon	Sports-1
Hubbard, (Robert) Cal	Sports-1
Hunt, Lamar	Sports-1
Hutson, Don(ald) Montgomery	5, Sports-1
Jones, David ("Deacon")	Sports-1
Jones, Jerral Wayne ("Jerry")	Sports-1
Kinard, Frank Manning ("Bruiser")	1
Lambeau, Earl Louis ("Curly")	Sports-2
Lambert, John Harold ("Jack")	Sports-2
Landry, Thomas Wade ("Tom")	6, Sports-2
Lane, Richard ("Dick"; "Night Train")	6, Sports-2
Lanier, Willie E.	Sports-2
Largent, Steve	Sports-2

Layne, Robert Lawrence ("Bobby")	2, Sports-2
Leahy, Francis William ("Frank")	Sports-2
Lillard, Joseph ("Joe")	Sports-2
Lilly, Robert Lewis ("Bob")	Sports-2
Lombardi, Vincent Thomas ("Vince")	Sports-2
Lott, Ronald Mandel ("Ronnie") Sports-2	
Luckman, Sid(ney)	5, Sports-2
Lujack, John Christopher, Jr. ("Johnny")	Sports-2
McElhenny, Hugh Edward, Jr.	Sports-2
McNally, John Victor ("Johnny Blood")	1, Sports-2
Marchetti, Gino John	Sports-2
Marino, Daniel Constantine, Jr. ("Dan")	Sports-2
Marshall, George Preston	Sports-2
Matson, Oliver Genoa, II ("Ollie")	Sports-2
Maynard, Don(ald) Rogers	Sports-2
Mitchell, Robert Cornelius, Sr. ("Bobby")	Sports-2
Montana, Joseph Clifford ("Joe")	Sports-2
Motley, Marion	5, Sports-2
Nagurski, Bronislau ("Bronko")	2, Sports-2
Namath, Joseph William ("Joe")	1960s-2, Sports-2
Nevers, Ernest Alonzo ("Ernie")	Sports-2
Nitschke, Ray(mond) Ernest	5, Sports-2
Noll, Charles Henry ("Chuck")	Sports-2
Nomellini, Leo Joseph	6
Olsen, Merlin Jay	Sports-2
Osborne, Thomas William ("Tom")	Sports-2
Page, Alan Cedric	Sports-2
Parcells, Duane Charles ("Bill")	Sports-2
Parker, James Thomas ("Jim")	7, Sports-2
Paterno, Joseph Vincent ("Joe")	Sports-2
Payton, Walter Jerry	5, Sports-2
Peabody, Endicott ("Chub")	5
Pollard, Frederick Douglass ("Fritz")	2, Sports-2
Rice, Jerry Lee	Sports-2
Ringo, James Stephen ("Jim")	8, Sports-2
Robinson, Edward Gay ("Eddie")	8, Sports-2
Robustelli, Andrew ("Andy")	Sports-2
Rockne, Knute Kenneth	Sports-2

Rooney, Arthur Joseph
("Art"), Sr. Sports-2
Rote, (William) Kyle, Sr. 6
Rozelle, Alvin Ray ("Pete") Sports-2
Sanders, Barry Sports-2
Sanders, Deion Luwynn Sports-2
Sayers, Gale Eugene Sports-2
Schmidt, Joseph Paul ("Joe") Sports-2
Selmon, Lee Roy Sports-2
Shula, Don(ald) Francis Sports-2
Simpson, Orenthal James
("O. J.") Sports-2
Smith, Emmitt James, III Sports-2
Stagg, Amos Alonzo, Sr. Sports-2
Starr, Bryan Bartlett ("Bart") Sports-2
Staubach, Roger Thomas Sports-2
Strode, Woodrow Wilson Woolwine
("Woody") 4
Tarkenton, Fran(cis) Asbury Sports-2
Taylor, Lawrence Julius
("LT") Sports-2
Thorpe, James Francis ("Jim") Sports-2
Tillman, Patrick Daniel ("Pat") 7
Tittle, Y(elberton)
A(braham), Jr. Sports-2
Trippi, Charles Louis
("Charley") Sports-2
Turner, Clyde Douglas
("Bulldog") 5, Sports-2
Unitas, John Constantine
("Johnny") 6, 1960s-2, Sports-2
Upshaw, Eugene Thurman, Jr.
("Gene") 8, Sports-2
Van Brocklin, Norm(an)
Mack 1, Sports-2
Van Buren, Stephen Wood
("Steve") Sports-2
Walker, (Ewell) Doak, Jr. 5, Sports-2
Walsh, William Ernest
("Bill") 8, Sports-2
Warner, Glenn Scobey
("Pop") Sports-2
Waterfield, Robert Staton
("Bob") 1, Sports-2
Weinmeister, Arnold George
("Arnie") 6
White, Byron Raymond 6
White, Reginald Howard
("Reggie") 7, Sports-2
Wilkinson, Charles Burnham
("Bud") Sports-2
Willis, William Karnet ("Bill") 8
Winslow, Kellen Boswell Sports-2
Young, Claude, Jr. ("Buddy") 1
Young, Jon Steven ("Steve") Sports-2
Zuppke, Robert Carl ("Bob") Sports-2

ATHLETE (GOLF)

Armour, Thomas Dickson
("Tommy") Sports-1
Berg, Patricia Jane ("Patty") 8, Sports-1
Demaret, James Newton ("Jimmy") 1
Didrikson Zaharias, Mildred Ella
("Babe") Sports-1
Gibson, Althea 7, Sports-1
Hagen, Walter C. Sports-1
Hogan, William Benjamin
("Ben") 5, Sports-1
Inkster, Juli Simpson Sports-1
Jones, Robert Tyre, Jr.
("Bobby") Sports-1
Lopez, Nancy Marie Sports-2
Middlecoff, (Emmett) Cary ("Doc") 5
Nelson, (John) Byron, Jr. 8, Sports-1
Nicklaus, Jack
William 1960s-2, Sports-2
Ouimet, Francis DeSales Sports-2
Palmer, Arnold Daniel
("Arnie") Sports-2
Sarazen, Gene 5, Sports-2
Snead, Samuel Jackson
("Sam") 6, Sports-2
Stewart, (William) Payne 5
Suggs, (Mae) Louise Sports-2
Trevino, Lee Buck Sports-2
Vare, Glenna Collett 2
Vines, Henry Ellsworth, Jr.
("Elly") Sports-2
Watson, Thomas Sturges
("Tom") Sports-2
Woods, Eldrick ("Tiger") Sports-2

ATHLETE (GYMNASTICS)

Conner, Bart Sports-1
Karolyi, Béla Sports-1
Miller, Shannon Lee Sports-2
Retton, Mary Lou Sports-2
Rigby, Cathy 1960s-2, Sports-2

ATHLETE (HOCKEY)

Abel, Sidney Gerald ("Sid") 6, Sports-1
Baker, Hobart Amory Hare
("Hobey") Sports-1
Bossy, Michael Dean ("Mike") Sports-1
Boucher, Frank Xavier Sports-1
Brimsek, Francis Charles
("Frank") 5, Sports-1
Brooks, Herb(ert) P. Sports-1
Chelios, Chris ("Chel") Sports-1
Clarke, Robert Earle
("Bobby") Sports-1
Delvecchio, Alex Peter ("Fats") Sports-1
Esposito, Phil(ip) Anthony Sports-1

Gretzky, Wayne Douglas
("The Great One") Sports-1
Hall, Glenn Henry Sports-1
Howe, Gordon ("Gordie") Sports-1
Hull, Brett Sports-1
Hull, Robert Marvin, Jr.
("Bobby") Sports-1
Jagr, Jaromir Sports-1
Leetch, Brian Sports-2
Lemieux, Mario Sports-2
Lindsay, Robert Blake Theodore
("Ted") Sports-2
Mikita, Stan Sports-2
Mullen, Joseph ("Joey") Sports-2
Orr, Robert Gordon
("Bobby") 1960s-2, Sports-2
Parent, Bernard Marcel
("Bernie") Sports-2
Patrick, (Curtis) Lester Sports-2
Potvin, Denis Charles Sports-2
Sawchuk, Terrance Gordon
("Terry") Sports-2
Schmidt, Milt(on) Conrad Sports-2
Shore, Edward William
("Eddie") 1, Sports-2

ATHLETE (HORSE RACING)

Arcaro, George Edward
("Eddie") 5, Sports-1
Atkinson, Theodore Frederic ("Ted") 7
Cordero, Angel Tomas, Jr. Sports-1
Fitzsimmons, James Edward
("Sunny Jim") Sports-1
Hartack, William J.
("Bill") 8, Sports-1
Haughton, William Robert
("Billy") 2
Jacobs, Hirsch Sports-1
Krone, Julieanne Louise
("Julie") Sports-1
Longden, John Eric
("Johnny") 7, Sports-2
Pincay, Laffit Alegando, Jr. Sports-2
Sande, Earl Sports-2
Shoemaker, William Lee
("Bill") 7, 1960s-2, Sports-2
Sloan, James Forman ("Tod") Sports-2
Stephens, Woodford Cefis
("Woody") Sports-2

ATHLETE (POLO)

Hitchcock, Thomas, Jr.
("Tommy") Sports-1

ATHLETE (RODEO)

Canutt, Enos Edward ("Yakima") 2
Shoulders, James Arthur ("Jim") 8

ATHLETE (ROWING)

Kelly, John Brendan, Sr.
("Jack") — Sports-1

ATHLETE (SAILING)

Conner, Dennis W. — Sports-1
Hart, Marion Rice — 2
Jobson, Gary — Sports-1
Mosbacher, Emil, Jr. ("Bus") — Sports-2
Shields, Cornelius — 1

ATHLETE (SKIING)

Fraser, Gretchen Claudia — Sports-1
Johnson, William D. ("Bill") — Sports-1
Kidd, William Winston
("Billy") — Sports-1
Mahre, Phil(ip) — Sports-2
Street, Picabo — Sports-2

ATHLETE (SOCCER)

Akers, Michelle Anne — Sports-1
Hamm, Mariel Margaret
("Mia") — Sports-1
Lalas, Alexi — Sports-2
Lilly, Kristine Marie — Sports-2
Meola, Tony — Sports-2
Rote, Kyle, Jr. — Sports-2

ATHLETE (SOFTBALL)

Feigner, Eddie — 8

ATHLETE (SPEED SKATING)

Blair, Bonnie — Sports-1
Heiden, Eric Arthur — Sports-1
Jansen, Dan — Sports-1

ATHLETE (SURFING)

Kahanamoku, Duke — Sports-1

ATHLETE (SWIMMING AND DIVING)

Babashoff, Shirley — Sports-1
Biondi, Matt(hew) — Sports-1
Bleibtrey, Ethelda — Sports-1
Chadwick, Florence May — 4, Sports-1
Counsilman, James Edward
("Doc") — Sports-1
Crabbe, Clarence Linden
("Buster") — 1, Sports-1
De Varona, Donna — 1960s-1, Sports-1
Ederle, Gertrude Caroline
("Trudy"; "Gertie") — 7, Sports-1
Evans, Janet — Sports-1
Holm, Eleanor Grace Theresa — 7
Kahanamoku, Duke — Sports-1
Kiphuth, Robert John Herman
("Bob") — Sports-1
Louganis, Greg(ory) Efthimios — Sports-2
McCormick, Pat(ricia) Joan — Sports-2

Nyad, Diana — Sports-2
Sanders, Summer Elisabeth — Sports-2
Schollander, Don(ald) Arthur — Sports-2
Spitz, Mark Andrew — Sports-2
Weissmuller, Peter John
("Johnny") — 1, Sports-2

ATHLETE (TENNIS)

Agassi, Andre Kirk — Sports-1
Ashe, Arthur
Robert, Jr. — 3, 1960s-1, Sports-1
Betz, Pauline May — Sports-1
Budge, John Donald
("Don") — 6, Sports-1
Connolly, Maureen Catherine
("Little Mo") — Sports-1
Connors, James Scott
("Jimmy") — Sports-1
Davenport, Lindsay — Sports-1
Evert, Christine Marie
("Chris") — Sports-1
Gibson, Althea — 7, Sports-1
Gonzales, Richard Alonzo
("Pancho") — 4, Sports-1
Jacobs, Helen Hull — 5, Sports-1
King, Billie Jean
Moffitt — 1960s-1, Sports-1
Kramer, John Albert ("Jack") — Sports-1
McEnroe, John Patrick, Jr. — Sports-2
Marble, Alice — 2, Sports-2
Navratilova, Martina — Sports-2
Riggs, Robert Larimore
("Bobby") — 4, Sports-2
Sampras, Pete — Sports-2
Tilden, William Tatem, Jr.
("Bill") — Sports-2
Trabert, Marion Anthony
("Tony") — Sports-2
Vines, Henry Ellsworth, Jr.
("Elly") — Sports-2
Williams, Venus Ebone Starr — Sports-2
Wills (Moody), Helen
Newington — 5, Sports-2

ATHLETE (TRACK AND FIELD)

Ashford, Evelyn — Sports-1
Beamon, Robert Alfred
("Bob") — Sports-1
Boston, Ralph — Sports-1
Calhoun, Lee Quency — Sports-1
Campbell, Milton Gray
("Milt") — Sports-1
Connolly, Harold V. ("Hal") — Sports-1
Cunningham, Glenn V. — 2, Sports-1
Didrikson Zaharias, Mildred Ella
("Babe") — Sports-1
Dillard, Harrison — Sports-1

Ewell, Henry Norwood
("Barney") — Sports-1
Fixx, James Fuller — 1
Fosbury, Richard Douglas
("Dick") — Sports-1
Glickman, Martin Irving
("Marty") — 6
Griffith Joyner, Florence Delorez
("Flo Jo") — 5, Sports-1
Hayes, Robert Lee ("Bob") — 6, Sports-1
Jenner, (William) Bruce — Sports-1
Johnson, Michael — Sports-1
Johnson, Rafer Lewis — 1960s-1, Sports-1
Jones, Marion Lois — Sports-1
Joyner-Kersee, Jacqueline
("Jackie") — Sports-1
Lewis, Frederick Carlton
("Carl") — Sports-2
Liquori, Martin William, Jr.
("Marty") — Sports-2
Mathias, Robert Bruce
("Bob") — 8, Sports-2
Matson, James Randel
("Randy") — Sports-2
Metcalfe, Ralph Horace — Sports-2
Moses, Ed(win) Corley — Sports-2
O'Brien, (William)
Parry, Jr. — 8, Sports-2
Oerter, Al(fred) Adolph, Jr. — 8, Sports-2
Owens, James Cleveland
("Jesse") — Sports-2
Prefontaine, Steve Roland
("Pre") — Sports-2
Richards, Robert Eugene
("Bob") — Sports-2
Rodgers, William Henry
("Bill") — Sports-2
Rudolph, Wilma
Glodean — 4, 1960s-2, Sports-2
Ryun, James Ronald
("Jim") — 1960s-2, Sports-2
Shorter, Frank Charles — Sports-2
Thorpe, James Francis ("Jim") — Sports-2
Tyus, Wyomia — Sports-2
Warmerdam, Cornelius Anthony
("Dutch") — Sports-2
Whitfield, Mal(vin) Greston — Sports-2

ATHLETE (VOLLEYBALL)

Chamberlain, Wilt(on)
Norman — Sports-1
Kiraly, Karch — Sports-1

ATHLETE (WEIGHTLIFTING)

Anderson, Paul Edward — Sports-1
Davis, John Henry — Sports-1
Kono, Tommy Tamio — Sports-1

ATHLETE (WRESTLING)

AUTHOR (CHILDREN'S LITERATURE)

AUTHOR (COMIC BOOK AND STRIP)

AUTHOR (COOKBOOK)

AUTHOR (DRAMA)

AUTHOR (FICTION)

Monroe, Earl Vernon, Jr.   Sports-2
Murray, Kathryn Hazel   5
North, John Ringling   1
Paley, William Samuel   2
Roach, Harold Eugene ("Hal")   3
Ruby, John ("Jack")   1960s-2
Sackler, Howard Oliver   1960s-2
Schoenfeld, Gerald   8
Spector, Philip Harvey ("Phil")   1960s-2
Steel, Dawn Leslie   5
Stein, Julian Caesar ("Jules")   1
Tartikoff, Brandon   5
Tisch, Laurence Alan ("Larry")   7
Tisch, Preston Robert ("Bob")   7
Valenti, Jack Joseph   8
Wallis, Harold Brent ("Hal")   2
Wasserman, Lewis Robert ("Lew")   6
Wilson, Flip   5
Wood, Robert Dennis   2

BUSINESS EXECUTIVE (ENTREPRENEUR)

DeVos, Richard Marvin, and
    Jay Van Andel   1960s-1
Fisher, Avery Robert   4
Gardner, Edward George   1960s-1
Grace, J(oseph) Peter, Jr.   4
Kroc, Raymond Albert
    ("Ray")   1, 1960s-1
McLean, Malcom Purcell   6
Rosenberg, William ("Bill")   6
Sassoon, Vidal   1960s-2
Thomas, Rex David
    ("Dave")   6, 1960s-2
Vernon, Lillian   1960s-2
Wackenhut, George Russell ("Russ")   7

BUSINESS EXECUTIVE (FINANCIAL SERVICES INDUSTRY)

Bavaria, Joan   8
Fossett, James Stephen ("Steve")   8
Templeton, John Marks   8
Weinberg, John Livingston   8
Wolfson, Louis Elwood   8

BUSINESS EXECUTIVE (FOOD INDUSTRY)

Austin, John Paul   1
Black, William   1
Bunker, Ellsworth   1, 1960s-1
Busch, August Anheuser, Jr.
    ("Gussie")   2
Carvel, Thomas Andrew   2
Chen, Joyce   4
Cohen, N(ehemiah) M(yer)   1
Gallo, Julio Robert   3
Goizueta, Roberto Crispulo   5

Heinz, Henry John, II ("Jack")   2
Husted, Marjorie Child   2
Knott, Walter   1
Kroc, Raymond Albert
    ("Ray")   1, 1960s-1
Lay, Herman W.   1
Lewis, Reginald Francis   3
Lichine, Alexis   2
Mack, Walter Staunton, Jr.   2
Magowan, Robert Anderson   1
Maris, Roger
    Eugene   1, 1960s-2, Sports-2
Marriott, J(ohn) Willard   1
Mars, Forrest Edward, Sr.   5
Morton, Thruston Ballard   1
Parks, Henry Green, Jr.   2
Perdue, Franklin Parsons ("Frank")   7
Pillsbury, Philip   1
Redenbacher, Orville   4
Rosenberg, William ("Bill")   6
Samuels, Howard Joseph   1
Sanders, Harlan David
    ("Colonel")   1960s-2
Seabrook, Charles Courtney   7
Simon, Norton Winfred   3
Smucker, Paul Highnam   5
Thomas, Rex David
    ("Dave")   6, 1960s-2
Woodruff, Robert Winship   1

BUSINESS EXECUTIVE (FOOD SERVICES)

Cantalupo, James Richard   7
Lippert, Felice Sally   7
Rosenberg, William ("Bill")   6

BUSINESS EXECUTIVE (FRANCHISE INDUSTRY)

Carvel, Thomas Andrew   2
Kroc, Ray(mond) Albert   1, 1960s-1
Marchetti, Gino John   Sports-2
Murray Arthur   3
Murray, Kathryn Hazel   5
Rosenberg, William ("Bill")   6
Sanders, Harlan David
    ("Colonel")   1960s-2
Thomas, Rex David
    ("Dave")   6, 1960s-2

BUSINESS EXECUTIVE (GREETING CARD INDUSTRY)

Hall, Joyce Clyde   1

BUSINESS EXECUTIVE (HOTEL INDUSTRY)

Bates, Clayton ("Peg Leg")   5
Helmsley, Leona   8
Johnson, Wallace Edward   2

Marriott, Alice Sheets   6
Marriott, J(ohn) Willard   1
Pritzker, A(bram) N(icholas)   2
Pritzker, Jay Arthur   5
Wilson, (Charles) Kemmons, Jr.   7

BUSINESS EXECUTIVE (INSURANCE INDUSTRY)

Groza, Louis Roy ("Lou")   6
Kemper, James Scott   1
Kemper, James Scott, Jr.   6
Kennedy, William Jesse, Jr.   1
Roosevelt, James   4
Stone, W(illiam) Clement   6

BUSINESS EXECUTIVE (MANUFACTURING INDUSTRY)

Adams, Charles Francis   5
Baldrige, (Howard) Malcolm   2
Blough, Roger Miles   1, 1960s-1
Callaway, Ely Reeves, Jr.   6
Castro, Bernard   3
Clay, Lucius Dubignon, Sr.   1960s-1
Donner, Frederic Garrett   2
Foerstner, George Christian   6
Ford, Henry, II ("Hank the Deuce")   2
Fuller, S. B.   2
Handler, Ruth   6
Hart, Leon   6
Houghton, Arthur Amory, Jr.   2
Jarvis, Howard Arnold   2
Johnson, Samuel Curtis ("Sam")   7
Ling, James Joseph   1960s-1
Ludwig, Daniel Keith   3
Spanel, Abram Nathaniel   1
Tandy, Charles David   1960s-2
Tupper, Earl Silas   1
Wilson, Joseph Chamberlain   1960s-2
Zamboni, Frank Joseph, Jr.   2

BUSINESS EXECUTIVE (MINING INDUSTRY)

Crown, Henry   2
Hirshhorn, Joseph Herman   1

BUSINESS EXECUTIVE (MUSIC INDUSTRY)

Asch, Moses ("Moe")   2
Ellington, Mercer Kennedy   4
Ertegun, Ahmet Munir   8
Fisher, Avery Robert   4
Gordy, Berry, Jr.   1960s-1
Graham, Bill   3
Hammond, John Henry, Jr.   2
Jackson, George Anthony   6
Jones, Quincy Delight, Jr.   1960s-1
Mayfield, Curtis Lee   5

Rauh, Joseph Louis, Jr.   3
Rustin, Bayard Taylor   2, 1960s-2
Sagan, Ginetta Teresa Moroni   6
Scott, Hazel Dorothy   1
Seale, Robert George
    ("Bobby")   1960s-2
Seaman, Barbara   8
Shabazz, Betty Jean   5
Shilts, Randy Martin   4
Snyder, Mitch(ell) Darryl   2
Sullivan, Leon Howard   6
Taylor, Telford   5
Washington, Chester Lloyd, Jr.
    ("Chet")   1
Washington, Harold   2
Wheeler, Raymond Milner   1
White, Ryan   2
Wilkins, Roy   1, 1960s-2
Williams, Hosea Lorenzo   6
Young, Andrew Jackson, Jr.   1960s-2

CLERGY (BAPTIST)

Abernathy, Ralph David   2
Cox, Harvey Gallagher, Jr.   1960s-1
Jackson, Jesse Louis   1960s-1
King, Martin Luther, Jr.   1960s-1
King, Martin Luther, Sr.
    ("Daddy King")   1
Ladd, George Eldon   1
Mays, Benjamin Elijah
Powell, Adam Clayton, Jr.   1960s-2
Robertson, Marion Gordon
    ("Pat")   1960s-2
Sullivan, Leon Howard   6

CLERGY (CHRISTIAN CHURCH)

Hargis, Billy James   1960s-1

CLERGY (CHURCH OF GOD)

Armstrong, Herbert W.   2

CLERGY (CHURCH OF THE BRETHREN)

Richards, Robert Eugene
    ("Bob")   Sports-2

CLERGY (CONGREGATIONALIST)

Bainton, Roland Herbert   1
Cleage, Albert Buford, Jr.   6
Young, Andrew Jackson, Jr.   1960s-2

CLERGY (CONSERVATIVE JUDAISM)

Kelman, Wolfe   2

CLERGY (DUTCH REFORMED)

Chino, Wendell   5
Peale, Norman Vincent   3

CLERGY (EASTERN ORTHODOX)

Meyendorff, John   3

CLERGY (EPISCOPALIAN)

Allin, John Maury   5
Fletcher, Joseph Francis, III   3
Murray, Anna Pauline ("Pauli")   1
Pike, James Albert, Jr.   1960s-2
Stokes, Anson Phelps, Jr.   2

CLERGY (EVANGELICAL SYNOD OF NORTH AMERICA)

Niebuhr, Reinhold   1960s-2

CLERGY (JEWISH)

Baron, Salo Wittmayer   2
Finkelstein, Louis   3
Kahane, Meir   2, 1960s-1
Kelman, Wolfe   2
Lelyveld, Arthur Joseph   4
Prinz, Joachim   2
Schindler, Alexander Moshe   6
Schneerson, Menachem Mendel   4
Soloveitchik, Joseph Baer   3

CLERGY (LUTHERAN)

Preus, Jacob Aall Ottesen, Jr. ("Jake")   4

CLERGY (METHODIST)

Lord, John Wesley   2
Mueller, Reuben Herbert   1
Peale, Norman Vincent   1960s-2
Roberts, Oral   1960s-2

CLERGY (MORMON)

Kimball, Spencer Woolley   1

CLERGY (PENTECOSTAL)

Roberts, Oral   1960s-2

CLERGY (PRESBYTERIAN)

Blake, Eugene Carson   1
Coffin, William Sloane, Jr.   8, 1960s-1
McIntire, Carl Curtis   6
Naismith, James   Sports-2

CLERGY (ROMAN CATHOLIC)

Bernardin, Joseph Louis   4
Berrigan, Daniel Joseph, and Philip
    Francis Berrigan   1960s-1
Berrigan, Philip Francis   6
Brown, Raymond Edward   5
Campion, Donald Richard   2
Carberry, John Joseph   5
Cody, John Patrick   1
Cooke, Terence James   1
Drinan, Robert Frederick   8
Dulles, Avery Robert   8

Egan, John Joseph ("Jack")   6
Ellis, John Tracy   3
Groppi, James Edmund   1, 1960s-1
Hartdegen, Stephen Joseph   2
Healy, Timothy Stafford   3
Hesburgh, Theodore Martin   1960s-1
Illich, Ivan   1960s-1
Judge, Mychal Fallon   6
Krol, John Joseph   4
Manning, Timothy   2
Medeiros, Humberto Sousa   1
O'Connor, John Joseph   6
Perry, Harold Robert   3

COACH. SEE SPORTS COACH.

COMEDIAN (SEE ALSO ACTOR)

Adams, Edie   8
Allen, Stephen Valentine Patrick
    William ("Steve")   6, 1960s-1
Allen, Woody   1960s-1
Backus, James Gilmore ("Jim")   2
Ball, Lucille Désirée   2
Belushi, John
Berle, Milton   6
Bishop, Joey   8
Bruce, Lenny   1960s-1
Burnett, Carol   1960s-1
Burns, George   4
Buttons, Red   8
Candy, John Franklin   4
Carlin, George Denis Patrick   8
Carson, John William
    ("Johnny")   1960s-1
Cavett, Richard Alva ("Dick")   1960s-1
Coca, Imogene   6
Dangerfield, Rodney   7
Diller, Phyllis Ada   1960s-1
Farley, Chris(topher) Crosby   5
Foxx, Redd   3
Gilford, Jack   2
Gleason, Herbert John ("Jackie")   2
Gobel, George Leslie   3
Goulding, Ray(mond) Walter   2
Gregory, Richard Claxton
    ("Dick")   1960s-1
Hackett, Buddy   7
Harris, (Wanga) Phillip ("Phil")   4
Hartman, Phil(ip) Edward   5
Hope, Leslie Townes
    ("Bob")   7, 1960s-1
Jessel, George Albert ("Georgie")   1
Kaufman, Andrew Geoffrey ("Andy")   1
Kaye, Danny   2
King, Alan   7
Kirby, George   4

Styne, Jule 4
Warren, Harry 1
Willson, (Robert Reiniger) Meredith 1

COMPOSER (POPULAR)

Arlen, Harold 2
Calloway, Cab 4
Carmichael, Howard Hoagland
  ("Hoagy") 1
Fain, Sammy 2
Gleason, Herbert John ("Jackie") 2
Hayes, Isaac Lee, Jr. 8
Jenkins, Gordon Hill 1
Jones, Quincy Delight, Jr. 1960s-1
Kaye, Sylvia Fine 3
Loewe, Frederick 2
Mancini, Henry Nicola 1960s-2
Marks, John D. ("Johnny") 1
Martin, Freddy 1
Nilsson, Harry Edward, II 4
Riddle, Nelson Smock, Jr. 1
Schwartz, Arthur 1
Styne, Jule 4
Van Heusen, James ("Jimmy") 2
Warren, Harry 1
Willson, (Robert Reiniger) Meredith 1

COMPOSER (RADIO AND TELEVISION)

Bennett, Robert Russell 1
Bernstein, Elmer 7
Gleason, Herbert John ("Jackie") 2
Gould, Morton 4
Jenkins, Gordon Hill 1
Jones, Quincy Delight, Jr. 1960s-1
Mancini, Henry Nicola 4, 1960s-2
Riddle, Nelson Smock, Jr. 1

COMPUTER SCIENTIST

Atanasoff, John Vincent 4
Church, Alonzo 4
Cocke, John 6
Cray, Seymour Roger 4
Dertouzos, Michael Leonidas 6
Diebold, John Theurer 7
Eckert, J(ohn Adam) Presper, Jr. 4
Elias, Peter 6
Hopper, Grace Brewster Murray 3
Kemeny, John George 3
Licklider, J(oseph) C(arl) R(obnett) 2
Molnar, Charles Edwin 4
Newell, Allen 3
Noyce, Robert Norton 2, 1960s-2
Piore, Emanuel Ruben ("Mannie") 6
Postel, Jonathan Bruce 5
Simon, Herbert A(lexander) 6
Stibitz, George Robert 4

Tukey, John W(ilder) 6
Wang, An 2

CONDUCTOR. SEE MUSICIAN (CONDUCTOR).

CONGRESSMAN/WOMAN. SEE POLITICIAN (UNITED STATES REPRESENTATIVE).

CONSULTANT (PUBLIC RELATIONS)

Bernays, Edward L. 4
Schwartz, Anthony 8

CONSUMER ADVOCATE

Furness, Elizabeth Mary ("Betty") 4
Nader, Ralph 1960s-2
Peterson, Esther 5
Warne, Colston Estey 2

COOK. SEE CHEF.

COSTUME DESIGNER

Cashin, Bonnie Jeanne 6
Head, Edith 1

CRIME FIGURE (MURDERER)

Beckwith, Byron De La, Jr. ("Delay") 6
Bundy, Theodore Robert ("Ted") 2
Abbott, Jack Henry 6
Dahmer, Jeffrey Lionel 4
Gacy, John Wayne, Jr. 4
McVeigh, Timothy James 6
Manson, Charles Milles 1960s-2
Oswald, Lee Harvey 1960s-2
Price, Cecil Ray 6
Ray, James Earl 5, 1960s-2
Ruby, John ("Jack") 1960s-2
Salvi, John C., III 4
Sirhan, Sirhan Bishara 1960s-2
Speck, Richard Benjamin 3
Williams, Stanley Tookie, III 7

CRIME FIGURE (ORGANIZED CRIME)

Accardo, Anthony ("Big Tuna") 3
Bonanno, Joseph ("Joe Bananas") 6
Giancana, Salvatore ("Sam") 1960s-1
Gigante, Vincent ("the Chin") 7
Gotti, John Joseph 6
Lansky, Meyer 1
Marcello, Carlos 3
Patriarca, Raymond 1
Provenzano, Anthony ("Tony Pro") 2
Trafficante, Santo, Jr. 2

CULT LEADER

Applewhite, Marshall Herff, Jr.
  ("Herff"; "Do") 5
Koresh, David 3

CULTURAL CRITIC

Barrett, William Christopher 3
Elkin, Stanley Lawrence 4
Goodman, Paul 1960s-1
Jackson, J(ohn) B(rinckerhoff) 4
Jacobs, Jane 8, 1960s-1
Kirk, Russell Amos 4
Lasch, Christopher 4
Leonard, John Dillon 8
Lerner, Max 3
Lynes, (Joseph) Russell, Jr. 3
Macdonald, Dwight 1, 1960s-2
McLuhan, (Herbert) Marshall 1960s-2
Mills, C(harles) Wright 1960s-2
Mitford, Jessica ("Decca") 4
Mumford, Lewis Charles 2
Packard, Vance Oakley 4
Patterson, Louise Alone Thompson 5
Roszak, Theodore 1, 1960s-2
Sontag, Susan 1960s-2
Trilling, Diana Rubin 4
Whyte, William Hollingsworth, Jr. 5
Wills, Garry 1960s-2

CYTOLOGIST

Stern, Curt 1

DANCE INSTRUCTOR

Ailey, Alvin 2, 1960s-1
Balanchine, George 1, 1960s-1
Danilova, Alexandra Dionysievna
  ("Choura") 5
Gennaro, Peter 6
Graham, Martha 3
Greco, Costanzo ("José") 6
Hightower, Rosella 8
Holm, Hanya 3
Joffrey, Robert 2, 1960s-1
Kelly, Eugene Curran ("Gene") 4
Le Clercq, Tanaquil ("Tanny") 6
Murray, Arthur 3
Murray, Kathryn Hazel 5
Primus, Pearl Eileen 4
Shook, Karel Francis Antony 1
Verdon, Gwyneth Evelyn ("Gwen") 6

DANCER

Ailey, Alvin 2, 1960s-1
Arpino, Gennaro Peter Arthur
  ("Gerald") 8
Astaire, Adele Marie 1
Astaire, Fred 2
Balanchine, George 1, 1960s-1
Bates, Clayton ("Peg Leg") 5
Bennett, Michael 2
Bolger, Ray(mond) Wallace 2
Bruhn, Erik Belton Evers 2

Woodcock, Leonard Freel 6
Yost, Charles Woodruff 1
Young, Andrew Jackson, Jr. 1960s-2

DIRECTOR (FILM)

Abbott, George Francis 4
Allen, Woody 1960s-1
Altman, Robert Bernard 8
Axelrod, George 7
Beatty, (Henry) Warren 1960s-1
Brooks, Richard 3
Canutt, Enos Edward ("Yakima") 2
Capra, Frank 3
Carnovsky, Morris 3
Clavell, James duMaresq 4
Cukor, George 1
Dassin, Jules 8
Dmytryk, Edward 5
Eames, Ray 2
Eastwood, Clinton, Jr. ("Clint") 1960s-1
Ephron, Nora Louise 1960s-1
Ferrer, José 3
Foreman, Carl 1
Fosse, Robert Louis ("Bob") 2
Frankenheimer, John Michael 6, 1960s-1
Freleng, Isadore ("Friz") 4
Fuller, Samuel Michael 5
Hannah, John Frederick ("Jack") 4
Henson, James Maury ("Jim") 2
Hill, George Roy 6
Hitchcock, Alfred Joseph 1960s-1
Hopper, Dennis 1960s-1
Huston, John Marcellus 2, 1960s-1
Kanin, Garson 5
Kazan, Elia 7
Kelly, Eugene Curran ("Gene") 4
Kidd, Michael ("Mike") 8
Kramer, Stanley Earl 6
Kubrick, Stanley 5, 1960s-1
LeRoy, Mervyn 2
Lewis, Jerry 1960s-1
Logan, Joshua Lockwood, III 2
Lorentz, Pare 3
Lumet, Sidney Hopper, Dennis 1960s-1
Lupino, Ida 4
Mamoulian, Rouben Zachary 2
Mankiewicz, Joseph Leo 3
Mann, Delbert Martin, Jr. ("Del") 8
May, Elaine 1960s-2
Meredith, (Oliver) Burgess 5
Milland, Ray 2
Minnelli, Vincente 2
Montgomery, Robert 1

Mulligan, Robert Patrick 8
Nichols, Mike 1960s-2
Pakula, Alan Jay 5
Parks, Gordon Roger Alexander Buchanan 8, 1960s-2
Peckinpah, David Samuel ("Sam") 1, 1960s-2
Penn, Arthur Hiller 1960s-2
Poitier, Sidney 1960s-2
Pollack, Sydney Irwin 8
Preminger, Otto Ludwig 2
Redford, (Charles) Robert, Jr. 1960s-2
Ritt, Martin 2
Roach, Harold Eugene ("Hal") 3
Robbins, Jerome 5
Schaffner, Franklin James 2
Scott, George C(ampbell) 1960s-2
Siegel, Don 3
Sirk, Douglas 2
Steiner, Ralph 2
Streisand, Barbra 1960s-2
Sturges, John 3
Vidor, King Wallis 1
Warhol, Andy 2, 1960s-2
Webb, John Randolph ("Jack") 1
Welles, Orson 1
Wilder, Samuel ("Billy") 6
Wise, Robert 7
Wiseman, Frederick 1960s-2
Wyler, William 1
Zinnemann, Alfred ("Fred") 5

DIRECTOR (STAGE)

Abbott, George Francis 4
Adler, Stella 3
Ashman, Howard Elliot 3
Beck, Julian 1, 1960s-1
Bennett, Michael 2
Burrows, Abe 1
Caldwell, Sarah 8
Carnovsky, Morris 3
Champion, Gower Hopper, Dennis 1960s-1
De Cordova, Frederick Timmins ("Fred") 6
de Mille, Agnes George 3
Drake, Alfred 3
Ferrer, José 3
Fosse, Robert Louis ("Bob") 2
Gordone, Charles 4, 1960s-1
Hill, George Roy 6
Houseman, John 2
Kanin, Garson 5
Le Gallienne, Eva 3
Logan, Joshua Lockwood, III 2
Ludlam, Charles 2

Mamoulian, Rouben Zachary 2
Meisner, Sanford 5
Meredith, (Oliver) Burgess 5
Montgomery, Robert 1
Nichols, Mike 1960s-2
O'Horgan, Thomas ("Tom") 1960s-2
Papp, Joseph 3, 1960s-2
Penn, Arthur Hiller 1960s-2
Perkins, Anthony 3
Preminger, Otto Ludwig 2
Quintero, José Benjamin 5
Robbins, Jerome 5, 1960s-2
Schechner, Richard 1960s-2
Schneider, Alan 1
Sillman, Leonard Dexter 1
Strasberg, Lee 1
Welles, Orson 1
Yannopoulos, Konstantinos ("Dino") 7

DIRECTOR (TELEVISION)

De Cordova, Frederick Timmins ("Fred") 6
Forte, Fulvio Chester, Jr. ("Chet") 4
Frankenheimer, John Michael 6, 1960s-1
Hewitt, Don S. Hopper, Dennis 1960s-1
Hill, George Roy 6
Hitchcock, Alfred Joseph 1960s-1
Landon, Michael 3
Leonard, Sheldon 5, 1960s-1
Liebman, Max 1
Lumet, Sidney Hopper, Dennis 1960s-1
Lupino, Ida 4
Montgomery, Robert 1
Mulligan, Robert Patrick 8
Peckinpah, David Samuel ("Sam") 1, 1960s-2
Penn, Arthur Hiller 1960s-2
Ritt, Martin 2
Ritts, Herbert, Jr. ("Herb") 6
Schaffner, Franklin James 2
Siegel, Don 3
Walker, Nancy 3
Webb, John Randolph ("Jack") 1

DOCTOR. SEE PHYSICIAN.

DRAMATIST. SEE AUTHOR (DRAMA).

ECOLOGIST

Hutchinson, G(eorge) Evelyn 3
Ripley, S(idney) Dillon, II 6

ECONOMIST

Ackley, H(ugh) Gardner 5
Adams, Walter 5

Gates, John 3
Greenfield, Mary Ellen ("Meg") 5
Gruening, Ernest 1960s-1
Hearst, William Randolph, Jr. 3
Hobby, Oveta Culp 4
Kahane, Meir 1960s-1
Kirkpatrick, Clayton ("Kirk") 7
Knight, John Shively 1
Lacy, Samuel Harold ("Sam") 7
McGill, Ralph Emerson 1960s-2
Maynard, Robert Clyve 3
Oakes, John Bertram 6
Pope, Generoso Paul, Jr. 2
Pope, James Soule, Sr. 1
Reston, James Barrett
 ("Scotty") 4, 1960s-2
Rosenthal, A(braham) M(ichael)
 ("Abe") 8
Salisbury, Harrison Evans 3, 1960s-2
Shapiro, Karl Jay 1960s-2
Sheppard, Eugenia 1
Smith, Hazel Brannon 1960s-2
Sutton, Carol 1
Washington, Chester Lloyd, Jr.
 ("Chet") 1
Wechsler, James Arthur 1
Wiggins, James Russell ("Russ") 6

EDUCATIONAL REFORMER

Adler, Mortimer J(erome) 6
Fannin, Paul Jones 6
Howe, Harold, II ("Doc") 6

EDUCATOR

Ackley, H(ugh) Gardner 5
Adams, Walter 5
Albion, Robert G. 1
Alvarez, Luis Walter 2, 1960s-1
Ambrose, Stephen Edward 6
Anderson, Carl David, Jr. 3
Anfinsen, Christian Boehmer 4
Arbus, Diane 1960s-1
Archibald, Nathaniel
 ("Nate"; "Tiny") Sports-1
Arendt, Hannah 1960s-1
Armour, Richard Willard 2
Arrington, Leonard James 5
Aserinsky, Eugene 5
Asimov, Isaac 3
Atanasoff, John Vincent 4
Bailey, Thomas A. 1
Bailyn, Bernard 1960s-1
Bainton, Roland Herbert 1
Baker, Carlos Heard 2
Baker, George Pierce 4
Bardeen, John 3

Barnett, A(rthur) Doak 5
Barnett, Marguerite Ross 3
Barnouw, Erik 6
Baron, Salo Wittmayer 2
Barr, Stringfellow 1
Barrett, William Christopher 3
Barth, John Simmons 1960s-1
Barzun, Jacques Martin 1960s-1
Baskin, Leonard 6
Bate, Walter Jackson 5, 1960s-1
Beadle, George Wells ("Beets") 2
Bell, Daniel 1960s-1
Bell, Terrel Howard 4
Berberova, Nina Nikolaevna 3
Berenson Abbott, Senda Sports-1
Bernard, Anna Jones 1
Biggers, John Thomas 6
Billington, Ray Allen 1
Bishop, Hazel Gladys 5
Black, Fischer Sheffey 4
Black, Joseph, Jr. ("Joe") 6
Bloch, Felix 1
Bloch, Konrad Emil 6, 1960s-1
Bloom, Allan David 3
Bloom, Benjamin Samuel 5
Boulding, Kenneth Ewart 1960s-1
Boyer, Ernest LeRoy, Sr. 4
Boyle, Katherine ("Kay") 3
Branscomb, (Bennett) Harvie 5
Breuer, Marcel 1
Brewster, Kingman, Jr. 2, 1960s-1
Brodie, Fawn McKay 1
Brodsky, Joseph (Iosif or Josip
 Alexandrovich) 4
Brooks, Cleanth 4
Brown, Raymond Edward 5
Brozen, Yale 5
Bundy, McGeorge 4, 1960s-1
Bunting-Smith, Mary Alice Ingraham
 ("Polly") 5
Burke, Kenneth Duva 3
Burns, Arthur Frank 2, 1960s-1
Buscaglia, Felice Leonardo ("Leo") 5
Busch, Frederick 8
Byrnes, Robert Francis 5
Calvin, Melvin 5, 1960s-1
Campbell, Joseph John 2, 1960s-1
Carnovsky, Morris 3
Chall, Jeanne Sternlicht 1960s-1
Chandrasekhar, Subrahmanyan
 ("Chandra") 4
Chomsky, (Avram) Noam 1960s-1
Church, Alonzo 4
Clampitt, Amy 4
Clark, Kenneth Bancroft 7, 1960s-1
Clark, Mark Wayne 1

Clarke, John Henrik 5
Cochran, Thomas Childs 5
Cohen, Audrey C. 4
Coleman, James Samuel 4, 1960s-1
Collins, John Frederick 4
Commager, Henry Steele 5
Cooley, Denton Arthur 1960s-1
Cooper, Irving Spencer 1
Cori, Carl Ferdinand 1
Cormack, Allan MacLeod 5
Corner, George Washington 1
Cox, Harvey Gallagher, Jr. 1960s-1
Cram, Donald James 6
Creeley, Robert White 7
Cremin, Lawrence A(rthur) 2, 1960s-1
Cunliffe, Marcus Falkner 2
Curti, Merle Eugene 4
Dallin, Alexander 6
Dangerfield, George 2
Davis, (William) Allison 1
Davis, Angela Yvonne 1960s-1
Dawidowicz, Lucy Schildkret 2
DeBakey, Michael Ellis 8, 1960s-1
de Kooning, Elaine Marie Catherine 2
Delany, Sarah Louise ("Sadie") 5
Deloria, Vine Vincent, Jr. 7, 1960s-1
de Man, Paul 1
Dickey, James Lafayette 5
Dickey, John Sloan 3
Dirac, Paul Adrien Maurice 1
Dmytryk, Edward 5
Doisy, Edward Adelbert 2
Dorris, Michael Anthony 5
Drake, (John Gibbs) St. Clair 2
Drucker, Peter Ferdinand 7
Dubos, René Jules 1
Dulles, Avery Robert 8
Edel, (Joseph) Leon 5
Eisenhower, Milton Stover 1
Eliade, Mircea 2
Elias, Peter 6
Elkin, Stanley Lawrence 4
Ellis, John Tracy 3
Ellmann, Richard David 2
Engel, A. Lehman 1
Engle, Paul Hamilton 3
Erikson, Erik Homburger 4
Fairbank, John King 3
Fall, Bernard B. 1960s-1
Farmer, James Leonard, Jr. 1960s-1
Farrell, Eileen Frances 6
Fehrenbacher, Don Edward 5
Feshbach, Herman 6
Festinger, Leon 2
Feyerabend, Paul Karl 4

JOURNALIST (FASHION COLUMNIST)

Donovan, Carolyn Gertrude Amelia ("Carrie")   6
Sheppard, Eugenia   1
Vreeland, Diana   2, 1960s-2

JOURNALIST (FILM CRITIC)

Canby, Vincent   6
Crowther, (Francis) Bosley, Jr.   1
Fidler, James Marion ("Jimmy")   2
Kael, Pauline   6
Lorentz, Pare   3
Macdonald, Dwight   1, 1960s-2
Siskel, Eugene Kal ("Gene")   5

JOURNALIST (FOREIGN CORRESPONDENT)

Halberstam, David   8, 1960s-1
Lewis, Flora   6
Szulc, Tadeusz Witold ("Tad")   6

JOURNALIST (GOSSIP COLUMNIST)

Fidler, James Marion ("Jimmy")   2
Graham, Sheilah   2
Skolsky, Sidney   1
Sullivan, Edward Vincent ("Ed") 1960s-2
Wilson, Earl   2

JOURNALIST (MAGAZINES)

Ace, Goodman   1
Amory, Cleveland ("Clip")   5
Bancroft, Mary   5
Buckley, William
   F(rancis), Jr.   8, 1960s-1
Chamberlain, John Rensselaer   4
Clurman, Richard Michael   4
Cousins, Norman   1960s-1
Cowles, Gardner ("Mike")   1
Deford, Frank   Sports-1
Ephron, Nora Louise   1960s-1
Feather, Leonard Geoffrey   4
Fitch, James Marston   6
Fuller, Samuel Michael   5
Garson, Barbara   1960s-1
Gellhorn, Martha Ellis   5
Gill, Brendan   5
Greenfield, Mary Ellen ("Meg")   5
Gruening, Ernest   1960s-1
Halberstam, David   8, 1960s-1
Haley, Alexander Murray Palmer
   ("Alex")   1960s-1
Hazlitt, Henry Stuart   3
Hemingway, Mary Welsh   2
Hentoff, Nathan Irving
   ("Nat")   1960s-1
Hersey, John Richard   3
Hersh, Seymour M.   1960s-1

Hobson, Laura Kean Zametkin   2
Howe, Irving   1960s-1
Hughes, Emmet John   1
Huie, William Bradford   2
Ingersoll, Ralph McAllister   1
Johnson, Robert Edward   4
Karnow, Stanley   1960s-1
Kempton, (James) Murray   5
Kraft, Joseph   2
Lerner, Max   3
Lippmann, Walter   1960s-1
Luce, Clare Boothe   2
Lynes, (Joseph) Russell, Jr.   3
Maas, Peter Guttrich   6
McCarthy, Mary Therese   2,1960s-2
Macdonald, Dwight   1, 1960s-2
McGinnis, Joseph ("Joe")   1960s-2
Mailer, Norman Kingsley   8, 1960s-2
Mannes, Marya   2
Martin, John Bartlow   2, 1960s-2
Michaels, James Walker   8
Mitchell, Joseph Quincy   4
Mohr, Charles Henry   2
Murray, James Patrick ("Jim")   5
Packard, Vance Oakley   4
Parks, Gordon Roger Alexander
   Buchanan   8, 1960s-2
Phillips, William   6
Porter, Sylvia Field   3
Ryskind, Morrie   1
Samuelson, Paul Anthony   1960s-2
Schaap, Richard Jay ("Dick")   6
Schell, Jonathan Edward   1960s-2
Shepley, James Robinson   2
Sontag, Susan   1960s-2
Southern, Terry Marion, Jr.   4
Stein, Aaron Marc   1
Steinem, Gloria Marie   1960s-2
Stone, I. F.   1960s-2
Strout, Richard Lee   2
Thompson, Hunter
   S(tockton)   7, 1960s-2
Trilling, Diana Rubin   4
Updike, John Hoyer   1960s-2
Vreeland, Diana   2, 1960s-2
Whitaker, Rogers E(rnest) M(alcolm)
   ("E. M. Frimbo")   1
White, Theodore Harold
   ("Teddy")   2, 1960s-2
Whitney, Ruth Reinke   5
Whyte, William Hollingsworth   5
Wolfe, Thomas Kennerly, Jr.   1960s-2

JOURNALIST (MUSIC CRITIC)

Feather, Leonard Geoffrey   4
Schonberg, Harold Charles   7

Slonimsky, Nicolas (Nikolai
   Leonidovich)   4
Thomson, Virgil Garnett   2

JOURNALIST (NEWSPAPER)

Alsop, Joseph Wright, V   2, 1960s-1
Amory, Cleveland ("Clip")   5
Anderson, Jack Northman   7
Apple, Raymon Walter, Jr. ("Johnny")8
Ashmore, Harry Scott   5
Atkinson, (Justin) Brooks   1
Attwood, William Hollingsworth   2
Baldwin, Hanson Weightman   3
Bancroft, Mary   5
Barnes, Djuna Chappell   1
Benson, Mildred Wirt   6
Bigart, Homer William   3
Bingham, (George) Barry, Sr.   2
Bishop, James Alonzo ("Jim")   2
Bombeck, Erma Louise Fiste   4
Browne, Malcolm Wilde   1960s-1
Broyard, Anatole Paul   2
Buchwald, Artthur ("Art")   8
Buckley, William
   F(rancis), Jr.   8, 1960s-1
Caen, Herb Eugene   5
Canham, Erwin Dain   1
Catledge, Turner   1
Chamberlain, John Rensselaer   4
Chase, Mary Coyle   1
Childs, Marquis William   2
Claiborne, Craig Raymond   6
Cowles, Gardner, Jr. ("Mike")   1
Cronkite, Walter Leland, Jr.   1960s-1
Crowther, (Francis) Bosley, Jr.   1
Dabney, Virginius   4
Daniel, (Elbert) Clifton, Jr.   6
Daniels, Jonathan Worth   1
Dedmon, Emmett   1
Del Olmo, Frank   7
Denby, Edwin Orr   1
Douglas, Marjory Stoneman   5
Drury, Allen Stuart   5
Ephron, Nora Louise   1960s-1
Evans, Rowland, Jr. ("Rowly")   6
Fidler, James Marion ("Jimmie")   2
Frick, Ford Christopher   Sports-1
Garson, Barbara   1960s-1
Gates, John   3
Gellhorn, Martha Ellis   5
Gilbreth, Frank Bunker, Jr.   6
Goode, Malvin Russell
   ("Mal")   4, 1960s-1
Graham, Katharine Meyer   6
Graham, Sheilah   2
Greenfield, Mary Ellen ("Meg")   5

Burger, Warren Earl   4, 1960s-1
Celebrezze, Anthony Joseph   5
Coleman, J(ames) P(lemon)   3
Daniel, Price Marion   2
Ervin, Samuel James, Jr.   1
Ferguson, Homer Samuel   1
Fortas, Abraham ("Abe")   1, 1960s-1
Friendly, Henry Jacob   2
Gabel, Hortense Wittstein   2
Garrison, Earling Carothers
    ("Jim")   3, 1960s-1
Garrity, W(endell) Arthur, Jr.   5
Goldberg, Arthur Joseph   2
Greene, Harold Herman   6
Haynsworth, Clement
    Furman, Jr.   2, 1960s-1
Higginbotham, A(loysius) Leon, Jr.   5
Hoffman, Julius Jennings   1960s-1
Hofheinz, Roy Mark   1
Jessup, Philip Caryl   2
Johnson, Frank Minis, Jr.   5
Kaufman, Irving Robert   3
Kerner, Otto, Jr.   1960s-1
Landis, Kenesaw Mountain   Sports-2
Lausche, Frank John   2
McCree, Wade Hampton, Jr.   2
Marshall, Thurgood   3, 1960s-2
Matthews, Burnita Shelton   2
Medina, Harold Raymond   2
Mills, Wilbur Daigh   3
Motley, Constance Juanita Baker
    ("Connie")   7
Page, Alan Cedric   Sports-2
Parsons, James Benton   3
Powell, Lewis Franklin, Jr.   5
Ribicoff, Abraham Alexander   5
Rothwax, Harold J(ay)   5
Sirica, John Joseph   3
Smith, William French   2
Stewart, Potter   1
Trías Monge, José   7
Wallace, George Corley   5
White, Byron Raymond   6
Wisdom, John Minor   5
Wyzanski, Charles Edward, Jr.   2
Yarborough, Ralph Webster   4

LABOR LEADER

Abel, I(orwith) W(ilbur) ("Abe")   2
Beck, David   3
Bellamy, Ralph Rexford   3
Boyle, William Anthony ("Tony")   1
Bridges, Harry   2
Carey, Ronald Robert ("Ron")   8
Chaikin, Sol (Chick)   3
Chávez, César Estrada   3, 1960s-1

Curran, Joseph Edwin   1
de Mille, Agnes George   3
Dubinsky, David   1
Fasanella, Raphaele ("Ralph")   5
Feldman, Sandra   7
Fitzsimmons, Frank Edward   1
Fraser, Douglas Andrew ("Doug")   8
Galarza, Ernesto, Jr.   1
Gleason, Thomas William ("Teddy")   3
Heston, Charlton   8, 1960s-1
Hoffa, James Riddle ("Jimmy")   1960s-1
Kirkland, (Joseph) Lane   5
Koontz, Elizabeth Duncan   2
Korshak, Sidney Roy   4
Lovestone, Jay   2
McBride, Lloyd   1
Miller, Arnold Ray   1
Miller, Marvin Julian   Sports-2
Montgomery, Robert   1
Murphy, George Lloyd   3
Peterson, Esther   5
Petrillo, James Caesar   1
Presser, Jackie   2
Provenzano, Anthony ("Tony Pro")   2
Quill, Michael Joseph
    ("Mike")   1960s-2
Reagan, Ronald Wilson   1960s-2
Reuther, Victor George   7
Reuther, Walter Philip   1960s-2
Riesel, Victor   4
Shanker, Albert ("Al")   5, 1960s-2
Upshaw, Eugene Thurman, Jr.
    ("Gene")   8, Sports-2
Van Arsdale, Harry, Jr.   2
Ward, John Montgomery   Sports-2
Weinmeister, Arnold George
    ("Arnie")   6
Williams, Roy Lee   2
Woodcock, Leonard Freel   6
Wurf, Jerome   1

LAWYER

Abram, Morris Berthold   6
Abzug, Bella   5, 1960s-1
Agnew, Spiro Theodore   4, 1960s-1
Albert, Carl Bert   6
Alioto, Joseph Lawrence   5
Allott, Gordon Llewellyn   2
Anderson, Robert Bernerd   2
Austin, John Paul   1
Baldwin, Raymond Earl   2
Ball, George Wildman   4
Barnett, Ross Robert   1960s-1
Belli, Melvin Mouron   4
Berman, Emile Zola   1
Bernard, Anna Jones   1

Bible, Alan Harvey   2
Bird, Rose Elizabeth   5
Blackmun, Harry Andrew   5
Blough, Roger Miles   1, 1960s-1
Boudin, Leonard B.   2
Bradley, Thomas ("Tom")   5
Brannan, Charles Franklin   3
Brennan, William J., Jr.   5, 1960s-1
Brewster, Kingman, Jr.   2, 1960s-1
Brooke, Edward William, III   1960s-1
Brown, Edmund Gerald ("Pat")   4
Brown, John R.   3
Brown, Ron(ald) Harmon   4
Brownell, Herbert, Jr.   4
Burch, (Roy) Dean   3
Burdick, Quentin Northrop   3
Burger, Warren Earl   4
Cannon, Howard Walter   6
Casey, Robert Patrick ("Spike")   6
Casey, William Joseph   2
Celebrezze, Anthony Joseph   5
Celler, Emanuel   1
Chalk, (Oscar) Roy   4
Chandler, Albert Benjamin
    ("Happy")   3
Cherne, Leo   5
Clark, Joseph Sill, Jr.   2
Clark, (William) Ramsey   1960s-1
Clifford, Clark McAdams   5, 1960s-1
Cochran, Johnnie L., Jr.   7
Cohen, Benjamin Victor   1
Cohn, Roy Marcus   2
Colby, William Egan   4
Coleman, J(ames) P(lemon)   3
Collins, John Frederick   4
Collins, (Thomas) LeRoy   3
Connally, John Bowden, Jr.   3
Connor, John Thomas ("Jack")   6
Cooper, John Sherman   3
Corcoran, Thomas Gardiner   1
Cosell, Howard   4, Sports-1
Cotton, Norris Henry   2
Cox, Archibald   7
Curtis, Carl Thomas   6
Cutler, Lloyd Norton   7
Daniel, Price Marion   2
Dash, Samuel   7
Dean, Arthur Hobson   2
Dickey, John Sloan   3
DiSalle, Michael Vincent   1
Dixon, Julian C.   6
Dulles, Allen Welsh   1960s-1
Edley, Christopher Fairfield, Sr.   7
Ehrlichman, John Daniel   5
Ervin, Samuel James, Jr.   1

Comden, Betty   8
Harburg, Edgar Yipsel ("Yip")   1
Larson, Jonathan   4
Lerner, Alan Jay   2
Rado, James, and Gerome
    Ragni   1960s-2
Ryskind, Morrie   1
Sessions, Roger Huntington   1, 1960s-2
Willson, (Robert Reiniger) Meredith   1

LINGUIST

Chomsky, (Avram) Noam   1960s-1
Greenberg, Joseph H(arold)   6

LITERARY CRITIC

Baker, Carlos Heard   2
Brooks, Cleanth   4
Burke, Kenneth Duva   3
Campbell, Joseph   2
Ciardi, John Anthony   2
Cowley, (David) Malcolm   2
de Man, Paul   1
Edel, (Joseph) Leon   5
Ellmann, Richard David   2
Fadiman, Clifton Paul   5
Fiedler, Leslie Aaron   7
Gardner, John Champlin, Jr.   1
Hardwick, Elizabeth Bruce   8
Heilbrun, Carolyn   7
Hicks, Granville   1
Howe, Irving   3, 1960s-1
Janeway, Elizabeth Ames   7
Kazin, Alfred   5
Kosinski, Jerzy Nikodem   3
Leonard, John Dillon   8
McCarthy, Mary Therese   1960s-2
Macdonald, Dwight   1, 1960s-2
Mizener, Arthur Moore   2
Nemerov, Howard   3
Podhoretz, Norman Harold   1960s-2
Riding, Laura   3
Said, Edward W.   7
Sontag, Susan   7, 1960s-2
Trilling, Diana Rubin   4
Trilling, Lionel   1960s-2
Warren, Robert Penn   2
Wellek, René Maria Eduard   4, 1960s-2
Williams, Sherley Anne   5

LYRICIST

Ashman, Howard Elliot   3
Berlin, Irving   2
Caesar, Irving   4
Cahn, Sammy   3
Comden, Betty   8
Dietz, Howard   1

Ebb, Fred   7
Gershwin, Ira   1
Green, Adolph   6
Harburg, Edgar Yipsel ("Yip")   1
Kaye, Sylvia Fine   3
Larson, Jonathan   4
Lerner, Alan Jay   2
Mercer, John Herndon
    ("Johnny")   1960s-2
Miller, Roger Dean   3
Rado, James, and Gerome
    Ragni   1960s-2
Sondheim, Stephen   1960s-2
Willson, (Robert Reiniger) Meredith   1

MADAM

Stanford, Sally   1

MAGICIAN

Scarne, John   1

MANAGEMENT THEORIST

Deming, W(illiam) Edwards   3
Diebold, John Theurer   7
Drucker, Peter Ferdinand   7, 1960s-1

MARINE CORPS OFFICER

Boyington, Gregory ("Pappy")   2
Carl, Marion Eugene   5
Chapman, Leonard Fielding, Jr.   6
Day, James Lewis   5
Glenn, John Herschel, Jr.   1960s-1
Krulak, Victor Harold   8, 1960s-1
Lee, William Andrew   5
Puller, Lewis Burwell, Jr.   4
Shoup, David Monroe   1, 1960s-2
Sitter, Carl Leonard   6
Walt, Lewis William   2
Wilson, Louis Hugh, Jr.   7

MARITIME WORKER

Hoffer, Eric   1

MATHEMATICIAN

Atanasoff, John Vincent   4
Chandrasekhar, Subrahmanyan
    ("Chandra")   4
Church, Alonzo   4
Cohen, Paul Joseph   8
Debreu, Gerard   7
Goldstine, Herman Heine   7
Harsanyi, John C.   6
Hoffmann, Banesh   2
Hopper, Grace Brewster Murray   3
Kahn, Herman Bernard   1, 1960s-1
Kemeny, John George   3
Kruskal, Martin David   8

Neyman, Jerzy   1
Pople, John Anthony   7
Robinson, Julia Bowman   1
Shannon, Claude Elwood   6
Tarski, Alfred   1
Tukey, John W(ilder)   6
Ulam, Stanislaw Marcin   1
Weil, André   5

MAYOR. SEE POLITICIAN (MAYOR).

MEDIA THEORIST

McLuhan,
    (Herbert) Marshall   1960s-2

MEDICAL ADMINISTRATOR

Thomas, Lewis   3

METEOROLOGIST

Charney, Jule Gregory   1
Fitch, James Marston   6
Sloane, Eric   1
Suomi, Verner Edward   4

MICROBIOLOGIST

Bunting-Smith, Mary Alice
    Ingraham ("Polly")   5
Dubos, René Jules   1
Friend, Charlotte   2
Hilleman, Maurice Ralph   7
Ivins, Bruce Edwards   8
Luria, Salvador Edward   3
Nathans, Daniel   5
Niel, Cornelis Bernardus van   1
Palade, George Emil   8

MINISTER. SEE CLERGY.

MISCELLANEOUS

Greenglass, Ruth Leah Printz   8
Schiavo, Theresa Marie ("Terri")   7

MISSIONARY

Judd, Walter Henry   4

MOUNTAINEER

Lowe, Steward Alexander ("Alex")   5

MUSEUM CURATOR

d'Harnoncourt, Anne Julie   8
Geldzahler, Henry   4

MUSEUM DIRECTOR

Barr, Alfred Hamilton, Jr.   1
Sweeney, James Johnson   2

MUSEUM FOUNDER

Burden, William Armistead Moale   1
Getty, J(ean) Paul   1960s-1

Whitney, Betsey Maria Cushing 5
Whitney, John Hay 1
Woodruff, Robert Winship 1

PHILOSOPHER

Adler, Mortimer J(erome) 6
Arendt, Hannah 1960s-1
Barrett, William Christopher 3
Bloom, Allan David 3
Boulding, Kenneth Ewart 1960s-1
Chomsky, (Avram) Noam 1960s-1
Church, Alonzo 4
Feyerabend, Paul Karl 4
Friedrich, Carl Joachim 1
Harsanyi, John C. 6
Hoffer, Eric 1
Hook, Sidney 2
Kirk, Russell Amos 4
Kristeller, Paul Oskar 5
Kuhn, Thomas Samuel 4
Lamont, Corliss 4
Langer, Susanne Katherina 1
Marcuse, Herbert 1960s-2
May, Rollo Reece 4
Nagel, Ernest 1, 1960s-2
Nisbet, Robert Alexander 4
Nozick, Robert 6
Rand, Ayn 1, 1960s-2
Rawls, John Bordley 6
Rorty, Richard McKay 8
Salmon, Wesley C(harles) 6
Tarski, Alfred 1
Weiss, Paul 6

PHOTOGRAPHER

Abbott, Berenice 3
Abercrombie, Thomas James 8
Adams, Ansel Easton 1
Arbus, Diane 1960s-1
Avedon, Richard 7
Cadmus, Paul 5
Eisenstaedt, Alfred 4
Feininger, Andreas Bernhard Lyonel 5
Hinton, Milton John ("Milt") 6
Horst, Horst Paul 5
Kertész, André (Andor) 1
Lerner, Nathan Bernard 5
Liberman, Alexander Semeonovitch 5
McCartney, Linda Louise Eastman 5
McDowall, Roderick Andrew
   Anthony Jude ("Roddy") 5
Mapplethorpe, Robert 2
Newhall, Beaumont 3
Newman, Arnold Abner 8
Parks, Gordon Roger Alexander
   Buchanan 8, 1960s-2

Ritts, Herbert, Jr. ("Herb") 6
Scavullo, Francesco 7
Siskind, Aaron 3
Steiner, Ralph 2
VanDerZee, James Augustus Joseph 1
Welty, Eudora Alice 6
Winogrand, Garry 1
Wojnarowicz, David Michael 3

PHOTOJOURNALIST

Abercrombie, Thomas James 8
Dith Pran 8
Eisenstaedt, Alfred 4
Onassis, Jacqueline Lee Bouvier 4
Parks, Gordon Roger Alexander
   Buchanan 8, 1960s-2

PHYSICIAN

Albright, Tenley Emma Sports-1
Alpher, Ralph Asher 8
Benzer, Seymour 8
Calderone, Mary Steichen 5
Cooley, Denton Arthur 1960s-1
Cooper, Irving Spencer 1
Corner, George Washington 1
Cournand, André Frederic 2
Crichton, (John) Michael 8
DeBakey, Michael Ellis 8, 1960s-1
Garcia, Hector Perez 4
Geschwind, Norman 1
Gruentzig, Andreas Roland 1
Harken, Dwight Emary 3
Hartline, Haldan Keffer 1, 1960s-1
Heiden, Eric Arthur Sports-1
Hornberger, H(iester) Richard, Jr.
   (Richard Hooker) 5
Huggins, Charles Brenton 5, 1960s-1
Jenkins, David Wilkinson Sports-1
Jonasson, Olga 8
Jones, Georgeanna 7
Judd, Walter Henry 4
Kelsey, Frances Kathleen
   Oldham 1960s-1
Lillehei, C(larence) Walton ("Walt") 5
Luria, Salvador Edward 3, 1960s-1
Margulies, Lazar 1
Masters, William Howell 1960s-2
Merrill, John Putnam 1
Moore, Francis Daniels, and
   Thomas Earl Starzl 1960s-2
Nathans, Daniel 5
Ochsner, (Edward William) Alton 1
Percy, Walker 2, 1960s-2
Rock, John Charles 1
Rous, (Francis) Peyton 1960s-2
Rusk, Howard Archibald 2

Sabin, Albert Bruce 3, 1960s-2
Salk, Jonas Edward 4
Spock, Benjamin McLane 5
Stein, Julian Caesar ("Jules") 1
Taussig, Helen Brooke 2
Terry, Luther Leonidas 1
Thomas, Lewis 3
Wheeler, Raymond Milner 1
White, Jack Edward, Sr. 2
Wiliams, William Carlos 1960s-2
Zoll, Paul Maurice 5

PHYSICIST

Alvarez, Luis Walter 2, 1960s-1
Anderson, Carl David, Jr. 3
Bardeen, John 3
Békésy, Georg von ("György") 1960s-1
Bethe, Hans Albrecht 7
Bloch, Felix 1
Bradbury, Norris Edwin 5
Brattain, Walter Houser 2
Chandrasekhar, Subrahmanyan
   ("Chandra") 4
Cormack, Allan MacLeod 5
Dirac, Paul Adrien Maurice 1
Feshbach, Herman 6
Feynman, Richard Phillips 2, 1960s-1
Firor, John William, Jr. 8
Fletcher, Harvey 1
Fowler, William Alfred 4
Gell-Mann, Murray 1960s-1
Glaser, Donald Arthur 1960s-1
Goeppert-Mayer, Maria 1960s-1
Hagen, John Peter 2
Hall, Theodore Alvin 5
Hoffmann, Banesh 2
Hofstadter, Robert 2, 1960s-1
Hughes, Vernon Willard 7
Jastrow, Robert 8
Kahn, Herman Bernard 1, 1960s-1
Kendall, Henry Way 5
Kilby, Jack St. Clair 7
Kruskal, Martin David 8
Kuhn, Thomas Samuel 4
Kusch, Polykarp 3
Lamb, Willis Eugene, Jr. 8
Libby, Leona Woods Marshall 2
Livingston, M(ilton) Stanley 2
McMillan, Edwin Mattison 3
McNair, Ron(ald) Erwin 2
Mulliken, Robert Sanderson 1960s-2
Pais, Abraham 6
Piore, Emanuel Ruben ("Mannie") 6
Purcell, Edward Mills 5
Rabi, I(sidor) I(saac) 2
Rainwater, (Leo) James 2

Spock, Benjamin McLane
("Dr. Spock")   5
Steinem, Gloria Marie   1960s-2
Taylor, Peter Hillsman   4
Tree, Mary Endicott Peabody
FitzGerald ("Marietta")   3
Vidal, Gore   1960s-2
Wald, George David   5
Wechsler, James Arthur   1
Welch, Robert Henry Winborne, Jr. 1
Weyrich, Paul Michael   8
Wojnarowicz, David Michael   3
Young, Coleman Alexander   5

POLITICAL ADVISER

Adams, (Llewellyn) Sherman   2
Atwater, Harvey Leroy ("Lee")   3
Ball, George Wildman   1960s-1
Blaisdell, Thomas Charles, Jr.   2
Bliss, Ray Charles   1
Brown, Ron(ald) Harmon   4
Brownell, Herbert, Jr.   4
Bundy, McGeorge   1960s-1
Burch, (Roy) Dean   3
Burns, Arthur Frank   2
Casey, William Joseph   2
Clifford, Clark McAdams   5, 1960s-1
Cohn, Roy Marcus   2
Dean, Arthur Hobson   2
Deaver, Michael Keith   8
De Sapio, Carmine Gerard   7
Ehrlichman, John Daniel   5, 1960s-1
Galbraith, John Kenneth   8, 1960s-1
Gavin, James Maurice   2, 1960s-1
Goldman, Eric Frederick   2
Green, Edith Starrett   2
Haldeman, H(arry) R(obbins)
("Bob")   1960s-1
Harlow, Bryce Nathaniel   2
Harriman, W(illiam) Averell   2
Heller, Walter Wolfgang   1960s-1
Hilsman, Roger   1960s-1
Hughes, Emmet John   1
Jordan, Barbara Charline   4
Kahn, Herman Bernard   1, 1960s-1
Keeny, Spurgeon Milton ("Sam")   2
Kennedy, Robert Francis   1960s-1
Keyserling, Leon Hirsch   2
Kleindienst, Richard G.   6
Lodge, Henry Cabot, Jr.   1, 1960s-1
Logue, Edward Joseph   6
Lowenstein, Allard Kenneth   1960s-1
McCloy, John Jay   1960s-2
Martin, John Bartlow   2, 1960s-2
Minow, Newton Norman   1960s-2
Mitchell, John Newton   1960s-2

Neustadt, Richard Elliott   7, 1960s-2
O'Brien, Lawrence Francis
("Larry"), Jr.   1960s-2
Phillips, Kevin Price   1960s-2
Revelle, Roger Randall Dougan   3
Rostow, Walter Whitman
("Walt")   1960s-2
Samuelson, Paul Anthony   1960s-2
Schlesinger, Arthur
Meier, Jr.   8, 1960s-2
Shriver, (Robert) Sargent, Jr. 1960s-2
Shulman, Marshall Darrow   8
Smith, William French   2
Sorensen, Theodore Chaikin
("Ted")   1960s-2
Stein, Herbert   1960s-2
Taylor, Maxwell Davenport   1960s-2
Thompson, Llewellyn E., Jr.
("Tommy")   1960s-2
Wallis, W(ilson) Allen   5
Wiesner, Jerome Bert   1960s-2

POLITICAL SCIENTIST

Barnett, Marguerite Ross   3
Bloom, Allan   3
Dallin, Alexander   6
Fall, Bernard B.   1960s-1
Friedrich, Carl Joachim   1
Gay, Peter ("Jack")   1960s-1
Harrington, (Edward) Michael 1960s-1
Hartz, Louis   2
Hook, Sidney   2
Huntington, Samuel Phillips   8
Kirkpatrick, Jeane Duane Jordan   8
Kissinger, Henry Alfred   1960s-1
Kraemer, Fritz Gustav Anton   7
Lipset, Seymour Martin   8
Lubell, Samuel   2
Moos, Malcolm Charles   1
Neustadt, Richard Elliott   7, 1960s-2
Padover, Saul Kussiel   1
Perkins, James Alfred   5, 1960s-2
Polsby, Nelson Woolf   8
Pool, Ithiel de Sola   1
Shulman, Marshall Darrow   8
Simon, Herbert A(lexander)   6
Voorhis, Horace Jeremiah ("Jerry")   1
Wildavsky, Aaron Bernard   3

POLITICIAN

Hicks, Louise Day   7

POLITICIAN (GOVERNOR)

Adams, (Llewellyn) Sherman   2
Agnew, Spiro Theodore   1960s-1
Aiken, George David   1, 1960s-1
Arnall, Ellis Gibbs   3

Baldwin, Raymond Earl   2
Barnett, Ross Robert   2, 1960s-1
Benson, Elmer Austin   1
Blanton, (Leonard) Ray   4
Bowles, Chester Bliss
("Chet")   2, 1960s-1
Bricker, John William   2
Brown, Edmund Gerald ("Pat")   4
Casey, Robert Patrick ("Spike")   6
Chafee, John Hubbard   5
Chandler, Albert Benjamin
("Happy")   3
Chiles, Lawton Mainor, Jr.   5
Clements, Earle C.   1
Coleman, J(ames) P(lemon)   3
Collins, (Thomas) LeRoy   3
Connally, John Bowden, Jr.   3
Daniel, Price Marion   2
Davis, James Houston ("Jimmie")   6
DiSalle, Michael Vincent   1
Exon, John James, Jr.   7
Fannin, Paul Jones   6
Faubus, Orval Eugene   4
Ferré, Luis Alberto ("Don Luis")   7
Folsom, James   2
Foss, Joseph Jacob ("Joe")   7
Freeman, Orville Lothrop   7
Furcolo, (John) Foster   4
Grasso, Ella Rosa Giovanna Oliva
Tambussi   1
Harriman, William Averell   2, 1960s-1
Hildreth, Horace Augustus   2
Hughes, Harold Everett   4
Johnson, Paul Burney   1
Jordan, Leonard Beck ("Len")   1
Kerner, Otto, Jr.   1960s-1
Landon, Alf(red) Mossman   2
Lausche, Frank John   2
Lee, J(oseph) Bracken ("Brack")   4
Lodge, John Davis   1
McCall, Thomas William Lawson   1
Maddox, Lester Garfield   7
Meyner, Robert Baumle   2
Muskie, Edmund Sixtus   1960s-2
Nelson, Gaylord Anton   7
Ogilvie, Richard Buell   2
Pastore, John Orlando   6
Peabody, Endicott ("Chub")   5
Perpich, Rudolph George ("Rudy")   4
Ray, Dixy Lee   4
Reagan, Ronald Wilson   7, 1960s-2
Rhodes, James Allen ("Jim")   6
Richards, (Dorothy) Ann Willis   8
Ribicoff, Abraham Alexander   5
Rockefeller, Nelson Aldrich   1960s-2
Romney, George Wilcken   4

Ruppert, Jacob   Sports-2
Russell, Richard Brevard, Jr.
  ("Dick")   1960s-2
Shivers, (Robert) Allan   1
Spence, Floyd D(avidson)   6
Stennis, John Cornelius   4
Stokes, Carl Burton   1960s-2
Taft, Robert, Jr.   3
Unruh, Jesse Marvin   2
Vinson, Carl   1
Wagner, Robert Ferdinand   3
Wallace, George Corley   5, 1960s-2
Washington, Harold   2
Yorty, Samuel William   5
Young, Coleman Alexander   5

POLITICIAN (UNITED STATES REPRESENTATIVE)

Abzug, Bella   5, 1960s-1
Adams, Brockman ("Brock")   7
Albert, Carl Bert   6
Arends, Leslie Cornelius   1
Aspin, Les(lie), Jr.   4
Bentsen, Lloyd Millard, Jr.   8
Bingham, Jonathan Brewster ("Jack") 2
Blanton, (Leonard) Ray   4
Boland, Edward Patrick   6
Bono, Salvatore Phillip ("Sonny")   5
Bowles, Chester Bliss ("Chet")   2
Brown, George Edward, Jr.   5
Bunning, James Paul David
  ("Jim")   Sports-1
Burdick, Quentin Northrop   3
Burton, Phillip   1
Case, Clifford Philip   1
Celler, Emanuel   1
Chisholm, Shirley Anita   7, 1960s-1
Clements, Earle Chester   1
Cotton, Norris Henry   2
Curtis, Carl Thomas   6
Diggs, Charles Coles, Jr.   5
Dirksen, Everett McKinley   1960s-1
Dixon, Julian C.   6
Drinan, Robert Frederick   8
Ervin, Samuel James, Jr.   1
Fascell, Dante Bruno   5
Fenwick, Millicent Hammond   3
Fish, Hamilton   3
Ford, Gerald Rudolph, Jr.   8
Fulbright, J(ames) William   4, 1960s-1
Furcolo, (John) Foster   4
Gonzalez, Henry Barbosa   6
Gore, Albert Arnold, Sr.   5
Grasso, Ella Rosa Giovanna Oliva
  Tambussi   1
Green, Edith Starrett   2

Halleck, Charles Abraham   2
Hays, (Lawrence) Brooks   1
Hays, Wayne Levere   2
Heinz, Henry John, III   3
Hill, (Joseph) Lister   1
Hruska, Roman Lee   5
Hyde, Henry John   8
Jackson, Henry Martin
  ("Scoop")   1, 1960s-1
Javits, Jacob Koppel   2
Johnson, Lyndon Baines   1960s-1
Jordan, Barbara Charline   4
Judd, Walter Henry   4
Lantos, Thomas Peter ("Tom")   8
Largent, Steve   Sports-2
Lewis, John Robert   1960s-1
Lindsay, John Vliet   6, 1960s-1
Lodge, John Davis   1
Lowenstein, Allard Kenneth   1960s-1
Luce, Clare Boothe   2
McCarthy, Eugene Joseph   1960s-2
McFall, John Joseph   8
McGovern, George Stanley   1960s-2
Madden, Ray John   2
Magnuson, Warren Grant   2
Mansfield, Michael Joseph ("Mike") 6
Mathias, Robert Bruce
  ("Bob")   8, Sports-2
Matsunaga, Spark Masayuki
  ("Sparkie")   2
Metcalfe, Ralph Horace   Sports-2
Mills, Wilbur Daigh   3
Mink, Patsy Matsu Takemoto   6
Moakley, John Joseph ("Joe")   6
Montgomery, Gillespie V. ("Sonny") 8
Morton, Thruston Ballard   1
Nixon, Richard Milhous   1960s-2
O'Neill, Thomas Philip, Jr. ("Tip") 4
Osborne, Thomas William
  ("Tom")   Sports-2
Passman, Otto Ernest   2
Pepper, Claude Denson   2
Powell, Adam Clayton, Jr.   1960s-2
Pucinski, Roman Gordon   6
Randolph, Jennings   5
Reuss, Henry Schoellkopf   6
Rhodes, John Jacob, Jr.   7
Ribicoff, Abraham Alexander   5
Rodino, Peter Wallace, Jr.   7
Roosevelt, James   3
Roth, William Victor, Jr.   7
Ryun, James Ronald ("Jim")   1960s-2
Scott, Hugh Doggett, Jr.   4
Simon, Paul Martin   7
Smathers, George Armistead   8
Smith, Margaret Chase   4

Sparkman, John Jackson   1
Spence, Floyd D(avidson)   6
Stafford, Robert Theodore   8
Staggers, Harley Orrin   3
Stratton, William Grant   6
Studds, Gerry Eastman   8
Taft, Robert, Jr.   3
Thomas, Craig Lyle   8
Tsongas, Paul Efthemios   5
Udall, Morris King   5
Ullman, Al(bert) Conrad   2
Velde, Harold Himmel   1
Vinson, Carl   1
Voorhis, Horace Jeremiah ("Jerry") 1
Washington, Harold   2
Whitten, Jamie Lloyd   4
Williams, John Bell   1
Wylie, Chalmers Pangburn   5
Yates, Sidney Richard   6
Yorty, Samuel William   5
Young, Andrew Jackson, Jr.   1960s-2
Young, Stephen M.   1

POLITICIAN (UNITED STATES SENATOR)

Adams, Brockman ("Brock")   7
Aiken, George David   1, 1960s-1
Allott, Gordon Llewellyn   2
Baldwin, Raymond Earl   2
Benson, Elmer Austin   1
Bentsen, Lloyd Millard, Jr.   8
Bible, Alan Harvey   2
Bradley, William Warren
  ("Bill")   1960s-1
Bricker, John William   2
Brooke, Edward William, III   1960s-1
Bunning, James Paul David
  ("Jim")   Sports-1
Burdick, Quentin Northrop   3
Cannon, Howard Walter   6
Case, Clifford P.   1
Chafee, John Hubbard   5
Chandler, Albert Benjamin
  ("Happy")   3
Chiles, Lawton Mainor, Jr.   5
Church, Frank Forrester   1
Clark, Joseph Sill, Jr.   2
Clements, Earle C.   1
Cooper, John Sherman   3
Cotton, Norris Henry   2
Coverdell, Paul Douglas   6
Cranston, Alan MacGregor   6
Curtis, Carl Thomas   6
Daniel, Price Marion   2
Dirksen, Everett McKinley   1960s-1
Eagleton, Thomas Francis   8

POLITICIAN (VICE PRESIDENT OF THE UNITED STATES)

POLITICIAN (VICE-PRESIDENTIAL CANDIDATE)

PREACHER. SEE CLERGY.

PRESIDENTIAL ADVISER

Brett, George Howard — Sports-1

Busch, August Anheuser, Jr. ("Gussie") — 2

Carpenter, Robert Ruliph Morgan, Jr. — 2

Chandler, Albert Benjamin ("Happy") — 3

Collins, Edward Trowbridge ("Eddie") — Sports-1

Comiskey, Charles Albert — Sports-1

Cronin, Joseph Edward — 1

Finley, Charles Oscar ("Charlie") — 4

Foster, Andrew ("Rube") — Sports-1

Frick, Ford Christopher — Sports-1

Gehringer, Charles Leonard ("Charlie") — 3, Sports-1

Giamatti, A(ngelo) Bartlett ("Bart") — 2

Greenberg, Henry Benjamin ("Hank") — 2, Sports-1

Griffith, Calvin Robertson — 5

Griffith, Clark Calvin — Sports-1

Hofheinz, Roy Mark — 1

Hubbard, (Robert) Cal — Sports-1

Hubbell, Carl Owen — 2, Sports-1

Kauffman, Ewing Marion — 3

Kiner, Ralph McPherran — Sports-1

Kroc, Ray(mond) Albert — 1, 1960s-1

Landis, Kenesaw Mountain — Sports-2

Lane, Frank Charles — 1

Lemon, Robert Granville ("Bob") — 6

Mack, Connie — Sports-2

MacPhail, Leland Stanford, Sr. ("Larry") — Sports-2

Martin, Alfred Manuel, Jr. ("Billy") — 2

Mathewson, Christopher ("Christy") — Sports-2

Richards, Paul Rapier — 2

Rickey, Branch Wesley — Sports-2

Robinson, Frank, Jr. — 1960s-2

Ruppert, Jacob — Sports-2

Steinbrenner, George Michael, III — Sports-2

Stoneham, Horace — 2

Veeck, William Louis, Jr. ("Bill") — 2, Sports-2

Williams, Edward Bennett — 2

Wright, William Henry ("Harry") — Sports-2

SPORTS EXECUTIVE (BASKETBALL)

Auerbach, Arnold ("Red") — 8, Sports-1

Baylor, Elgin — Sports-1

Blazejowski, Carol Ann — Sports-1

Cunningham, William John ("Billy") — Sports-1

Hannum, Alex — 6

Irish, Edward Simmons, Sr. ("Ned") — 1

Jordan, Michael Jeffrey ("Air") — Sports-1

Lieberman-Cline, Nancy — Sports-2

Mikan, George Lawrence, Jr. — Sports-2

Monroe, Earl Vernon, Jr. — Sports-2

Newell, Peter Francis, Jr. ("Pete") — 8, Sports-2

O'Brien, Lawrence Francis, Jr. ("Larry") — 2, 1960s-2

Reed, Willis, Jr. — Sports-2

Schayes, Adolph ("Dolph") — Sports-2

Stern, David — Sports-2

Thomas, Isiah Lord, III — Sports-2

West, Jerry Alan — Sports-2

SPORTS EXECUTIVE (FOOTBALL)

Bell, DeBenneville ("Bert") — Sports-1

Brown, Paul Eugene ("P. B.") — 3

Davis, Al(len) — Sports-1

DeBartolo, Edward John, Sr. — 4

Graham, Otto Everett, Jr. — Sports-1

Halas, George — 1, Sports-1

Hein, Mel(vin) John — Sports-1

Hirsch, Elroy Leon ("Crazylegs") — Sports-1

Hunt, Lamar — Sports-1

Jones, Jerral Wayne ("Jerry") — Sports-1

Lane, Richard ("Dick"; "Night Train") — 6, Sports-2

Lombardi, Vincent Thomas ("Vince") — 1960s-1

Marshall, George Preston — 1960s-2, Sports-2

Mitchell, Robert Cornelius, Sr. ("Bobby") — Sports-2

Murchison, Clint(on) Williams, Jr. — 2

Parcells, Duane Charles ("Bill") — Sports-2

Rooney, Arthur Joseph — 2, Sports-2

Rozelle, Alvin Roy ("Pete") — 4, 1960s-2, Sports-2

Starr, Bryan Bartlett ("Bart") — Sports-2

Thorpe, James Francis ("Jim") — Sports-2

Van Brocklin, Norm(an) Mack — Sports-2

Walsh, William Ernest ("Bill") — 8, Sports-2

Williams, Edward Bennett — 2

Young, Claude, Jr. ("Buddy") — 1

SPORTS EXECUTIVE (HOCKEY)

Clarke, Robert Earle ("Bobby") — Sports-1

Delvecchio, Alex Peter ("Fats") — Sports-1

Esposito, Phil(ip) Anthony — Sports-1

Lemieux, Mario — Sports-2

Patrick, (Curtis) Lester — Sports-2

Schmidt, Milt(on) Conrad — Sports-2

Shore, Edward William ("Eddie") — 1, Sports-2

SPORTS EXECUTIVE (SOCCER)

Hunt, Lamar — Sports-1

SPORTS EXECUTIVE (TENNIS)

Hunt, Lamar — Sports-1

King, Billie Jean Moffitt — 1960s-1

Kramer, John Albert ("Jack") — Sports-1

SPORTS EXECUTIVE (VOLLEYBALL)

Chamberlain, Wilt(on) Norman — Sports-1

SPORTS MANAGER (BASEBALL)

Alston, Walter Emmons — 1

Anderson, George Lee ("Sparky") — Sports-1

Anson, Adrian Constantine ("Cap," "Pop") — Sports-1

Appling, Lucius Benjamin, Jr. ("Luke") — 3

Bell, James Thomas ("Cool Papa") — 3, Sports-1

Berra, Lawrence Peter ("Yogi") — Sports-1

Boudreau, Louis ("Lou") — 6

Bunning, James Paul David ("Jim") — Sports-1

Charleston, Oscar McKinley ("Charlie") — Sports-1

Cobb, Ty(rus) Raymond — Sports-1

Cochrane, Gordon Stanley ("Mickey") — Sports-1

Collins, Edward Trowbridge ("Eddie") — Sports-1

Comiskey, Charles Albert — Sports-1

Cronin, Joseph Edward — 1

Dickey, William Malcolm ("Bill") — 4

Durocher, Leo Ernest — 3

Ewing, William ("Buck") — Sports-1

Foster, Andrew ("Rube") — Sports-1

Frisch, Frank Francis ("Frankie") — Sports-1

Griffith, Clark Calvin — Sports-1

Grimes, Burleigh Arland — 1

Herman, William Jennings ("Billy") — 3

Hornsby, Rogers ("Rajah") — Sports-1

Huggins, Miller James — Sports-1

Johnson, Walter Perry ("The Big Train") — Sports-1

Kelly, Michael Joseph ("King") — Sports-1

Lajoie, Nap(oleon) — Sports-2

Lemon, Robert Granville ("Bob") — 6

Lindstrom, Frederick Charles, Jr. ("Lindy") — 1

Lloyd, John Henry ("Pop") — Sports-2

Lopez, Alfonso Ramon ("Al"; "El Señor") — 7

Lyons, Theodore Amar ("Ted") — 2

McCarthy, Joseph Vincent
("Joe")   Sports-2
McGraw, John Joseph   Sports-2
Mack, Connie   Sports-2
Martin, Alfred Manuel, Jr. ("Billy")   2
Mathewson, Christopher
("Christy")   Sports-2
O'Neil, John Jordan, Jr. ("Buck")   8
Ott, Mel(vin) Thomas   Sports-2
Richards, Paul Rapier   2
Rickey, Branch Wesley   Sports-2
Robinson, Frank, Jr.   1960s-2
Rose, Peter Edward ("Pete")   Sports-2
Sisler, George Harold   Sports-2
Spahn, Warren Edward   Sports-2
Spalding, Albert Goodwill
("A. G.")   Sports-2
Speaker, Tris(tram) E.   Sports-2
Stengel, Charles Dillon
("Casey")   Sports-2
Terry, William Harold
("Memphis Bill")   2, Sports-2
Torre, Joseph Paul ("Joe")   Sports-2
Traynor, Harold Joseph
("Pie")   Sports-2
Ward, John Montgomery   Sports-2
Wells, Willie James   Sports-2
Williams, Theodore Samuel
("Ted")   Sports-2
Wright, William Henry
("Harry")   Sports-2

SPORTS OFFICIAL (BASEBALL UMPIRE)
Conlan, John Bertrand ("Jocko")   2

SPORTS PROMOTER (FOOTBALL)
Hunt, Lamar   8
Rooney, Arthur Joseph   2

SPORTS TRAINER (BOXING)
Arcel, Ray   4
D'Amato, Constantine
("Cus")   1, Sports-1
Dundee, Angelo   Sports-1
Futch, Eddie   6
Jack, Beau   6
Saddler, Joseph ("Sandy")   6

SPORTS TRAINER (HORSE RACING)
Fitzsimmons, James Edward
("Sunny Jim")   Sports-1
Jacobs, Hirsch   Sports-1
Jones, Horace Allyn ("Jimmy")   6
Shoemaker, William Lee
("Bill")   Sports-2
Stephens, Woodford Cefis
("Woody")   5, Sports-2

SPORTSWRITER. SEE JOURNALIST (SPORTSWRITER).

SPY. SEE ESPIONAGE AGENT.

STATISTICIAN
Deming, W. Edwards   3
Gallup, George Horace   1
Jacoby, Oswald ("Ozzie")   1
Kuznets, Simon Smith   1
Neyman, Jerzy   1

STUNT MAN
Canutt, Enos Edward ("Yakima")   2

SUPREME COURT JUSTICE
Blackmun, Harry Andrew   5
Brennan, William
Joseph, Jr.   5, 1960s-1
Burger, Warren Earl   4, 1960s-1
Fortas, Abraham ("Abe")   1, 1960s-1
Goldberg, Arthur Joseph   2
Marshall, Thurgood   3, 1960s-2
Powell, Lewis Franklin, Jr.   5
Rehnquist, William Hubbs   7
Stewart, Potter   1
Warren, Earl   1960s-2
White, Byron Raymond   6

SURGEON
Albright, Tenley Emma   Sports-1
Cooley, Denton Arthur   1960s-1
DeBakey, Michael Ellis   8, 1960s-1
Folkman, (Moses) Judah   8
Hornberger, H(iester) Richard, Jr.
(Richard Hooker)   5
Huggins, Charles Brenton   5, 1960s-1
Jonasson, Olga   8
Judd, Walter Henry   4
Kantrowitz, Adrian   8
Lillehei, C(larence) Walton ("Walt")   5
Merrill, John Putnam   1
Moore, Francis Daniels, and
Thomas Earl Starzl   1960s-2
Ochsner, (Edward William) Alton   1
Shumway, Norman Edward, Jr.   8
Stein, Julian Caesar ("Jules")   1
White, Jack Edward, Sr.   2

SWIMMER. SEE ATHLETE (SWIMMING AND DIVING).

TEACHER. SEE EDUCATOR.

TELEVISION PERSONALITY
Allen, Stephen Valentine Patrick
William ("Steve")   6, 1960s-1
Allison, Fran(ces)   2
Arnaz, Desi   2

Arnold, Richard Edward ("Eddy")   8
Ball, Lucille Désirée   2
Belushi, John   1
Berle, Milton   6
Bishop, Joey   8
Bombeck, Erma Louise Fiste   4
Bono, Salvatore Phillip
("Sonny")   5, 1960s-2
Borge, Victor   6
Bradley, Edward Rudolph, Jr. ("Ed")   8
Brinkley, David McClure   7
Broun, Heywood Hale ("Woodie")   6
Buckley, William
F(rancis), Jr.   8, 1960s-1
Burnett, Carol   1960s-1
Carson, John William
("Johnny")   7, 1960s-1
Cavett, Richard Alva ("Dick")   1960s-1
Cerf, Bennett Albert   1960s-1
Child, Julia Carolyn   7
Clooney, Rosemary   6
Coca, Imogene   6
Como, Pierino Ronald ("Perry")   6
Cooke, Alistair   7
Cosell, Howard   4, Sports-1
Cronkite, Walter Leland, Jr.   1960s-1
Daly, John Charles, Jr.   3
Day, Dennis   2
Day, Doris   1960s-1
Diller, Phyllis Ada   1960s-1
Douglas, Mike   8
Edwards, Ralph Livingstone   7
Evans, Dale   6
Evans, Rowland, Jr. ("Rowly")   6
Falwell, Jerry Lamon   8
Farley, Chris(topher) Crosby   5
Ford, Ernest Jennings
("Tennessee Ernie")   3
Foxx, Redd   3
Francis, Arlene   6
Frederick, Pauline   2
Funt, Allen   5
Furness, Elizabeth Mary ("Betty")   4
Garland, Judy   1960s-1
Garroway, David Cunningham   1
Gleason, Herbert John ("Jackie")   2
Gobel, George Leslie   3
Godfrey, Arthur (Morton)   1
Gowdy, Curtis Edward ("Curt")   8
Graham, Virginia   5
Graziano, Rocky   2
Griffin, Mervyn Edward, Jr. ("Merv")   8
Hart, Kitty Carlisle   8
Hartman, Phil(ip) Edward   5
Herbert, Donald Jeffrey ("Don")   8
Hobson, Laura Kean Zametkin   2

Alphabetical List of Subjects, Volumes 1–8 and Thematic Volumes

Haley, Alexander Murray Palmer
  ("Alex")   3, 1960s-1
Haley, William John, Jr. ("Bill")   1
Hall, Glenn Henry   Sports-1
Hall, Gus   6
Hall, Joyce Clyde   1
Hall, Theodore Alvin   5
Halleck, Charles Abraham   2
Halper, Albert   1
Halston   2, 1960s-1
Hamill, Dorothy Stuart   Sports-1
Hamilton, Margaret   1
Hamilton, Scott Scovell   Sports-1
Hamm, Mariel Margaret
  ("Mia")   Sports-1
Hammer, Armand   2, 1960s-1
Hammond, E(dward) Cuyler   2
Hammond, John Henry, Jr.   2
Hampton, Lionel   6
Hancock, Joy Bright   2
Handler, Ruth   6
Hanks, Nancy   1
Hanna, William Denby ("Bill")   6
Hannah, John Allen   Sports-1
Hannah, John Frederick ("Jack")   4
Hannum, Alex   6
Hansberry, Lorraine Vivian   1960s-1
Hansen, Al(fred) Earl   4
Hanson, Duane Elwood   4
Hanson, Howard Harold   1
Harburg, Edgar Yipsel ("Yip")   1
Hardwick, Elizabeth Bruce   8
Hargis, Billy James   7, 1960s-1
Haring, Keith Allen   2
Harken, Dwight Emary   3
Harkness, Rebekah West   1, 1960s-1
Harlow, Bryce Nathaniel   2
Harmon, Thomas Dudley
  ("Tom")   2, Sports-1
Harriman, Pamela Beryl Digby
  Churchill Hayward   5
Harriman, William Averell   2, 1960s-1
Harrington, (Edward)
  Michael   2, 1960s-1
Harris, Franco   Sports-1
Harris, Patricia Roberts Fitzgerald   1
Harris, (Wanga) Phillip ("Phil")   4
Harris, Sydney Justin   2
Harsanyi, John C.   6
Hart, Kitty Carlisle   8
Hart, Leon   6
Hart, Marion Rice   2
Hartack, William John, Jr.
  ("Bill")   8, Sports-1
Hartdegen, Stephen Joseph   2
Hartford, (George) Huntington, II   8

Hartigan, Grace   8
Hartke, Rupert Vance   7
Hartline, Haldan Keffer   1, 1960s-1
Hartman, Phil(ip) Edward   5
Hartz, Louis   2
Haskins, Donald Lee ("Don")   8, Sports-1
Hassenfeld, Merrill Lloyd   1960s-1
Hassenfeld, Stephen David   2
Hatcher, Richard Gordon   1960s-1
Hathaway, Starke Rosecrans   1
Haughton, Aaliyah Dana. *See* Aaliyah.
Haughton, Daniel Jeremiah   2
Haughton, William Robert ("Billy")   2
Haupt, Enid Annenberg   7
Havlicek, John Joseph   Sports-1
Hawkins, Cornelius L.
  ("Connie")   Sports-1
Hawkins, Erskine Ramsay   3
Hawkins, Frederick ("Erick")   4
Hay, Henry, Jr. ("Harry")   6
Hayakawa, S(amuel) I(chiye)   3, 1960s-1
Hayden, Melissa ("Milly")   8
Hayden, Thomas Emmett
  ("Tom")   1960s-1
Hayek, Friedrich August von   3
Hayes, Elvin Ernest   Sports-1
Hayes, Helen   3
Hayes, Isaac Lee, Jr.   8
Hayes, Robert Lee ("Bob")   6, Sports-1
Hayes, Wayne Woodrow
  ("Woody")   2, Sports-1
Haynes, Marques Oreole   Sports-1
Haynsworth, Clement
  Furman, Jr.   2, 1960s-1
Hays, (Lawrence) Brooks   1
Hays, Lee Elhardt   1
Hays, Wayne Levere   2
Hayworth, Rita   2
Hazlitt, Henry Stuart   3
Head, Edith   1
Healy, Timothy Stafford   3
Hearn, Francis Dayle (Chick)   6
Hearns, Thomas   Sports-1
Hearst, Randolph Apperson   6
Hearst, William Randolph, Jr.   3
Hecht, Harold   1
Heffelfinger, William Walter
  ("Pudge")   Sports-1
Heflin, Howell Thomas   7
Hefner, Hugh Marston   1960s-1
Heidelberger, Michael   3
Heiden, Eric Arthur   Sports-1
Heifetz, Jascha   2
Heilbroner, Robert Louis   7
Heilbrun, Carolyn   7
Hein, Mel(vin) John   Sports-1

Heinlein, Robert Anson   2
Heinz, Henry John, II ("Jack")   2
Heinz, Henry John, III   3
Heinz, W(ilfred) C(harles)   8, Sports-1
Heisman, John William
  ("Johnny")   Sports-1
Heiss Jenkins, Carol Elizabeth   Sports-1
Heller, Joseph   5, 1960s-1
Heller, Walter Wolfgang   2, 1960s-1
Hellman, Lillian Florence   1
Helms, Jesse Alexander, Jr.   8
Helms, Richard McGarrah   6
Helmsley, Henry Brakmann
  ("Harry")   5
Helmsley, Leona   8
Hemingway, Margaux   4
Hemingway, Mary Welsh   2
Henderson, Joseph A. ("Joe")   6
Henderson, Leon   2
Henderson, Lyle Russell Cedric
  ("Skitch")   7
Henderson, Rickey   Sports-1
Hendrix, James Marshall ("Jimmy";
  "Maurice James"; "Jimi")   1960s-1
Henie, Sonja   Sports-1
Henry, Aaron Edd Jackson   5
Henson, James Maury ("Jim")   2
Henson, Paul Harry   5
Hentoff, Nathan Irving
  ("Nat")   1960s-1
Hepburn, Audrey   3, 1960s-1
Hepburn, Katharine Houghton   7
Herbert, Donald Jeffrey ("Don")   8
"Herblock." *See* Block, Herbert
  Lawrence.
Herlihy, James Leo   1960s-1
Herman, Floyd Caves ("Babe")   2
Herman, William Jennings ("Billy")   3
Herman, Woody   2
Herrnstein, Richard Julius   4
Hersey, John Richard   3
Hersh, Seymour M.   1960s-1
Hershey, Alfred Day   5, 1960s-1
Hesburgh, Theodore Martin   1960s-1
Heston, Charlton   8, 1960s-1
Hewitt, Don S.   1960s-1
Hewlett, William Redington
  ("Bill")   6, 1960s-1
Hewlett, William Redington ("Bill"),
  and David Packard   1960s-1
Hexter, J. H. ("Jack")   4
Hibbler, Albert George ("Al")   6
Hickerson, John Dewey   2
Hickey, James Aloysius   7
Hicks, Granville   1
Hicks, Louise Day   7

Mark, Herman Francis	3
Markham, Dewey ("Pigmeat")	1
Marks, John D. ("Johnny")	1
Marriott, Alice Sheets	6
Marriott, J(ohn) Willard	1
Mars, Forrest Edward, Sr.	5
Marshall, Burke	7
Marshall, E(dda) G(unnar)	5
Marshall, George Preston	Sports-2
Marshall, Thurgood	3, 1960s-2
Marston, Robert Quarles	5
Martin, Agnes Bernice	7
Martin, Alfred Manuel, Jr. ("Billy")	2
Martin, Dean	4, 1960s-2
Martin, Donald Edward ("Don")	6
Martin, Freddy	1
Martin, John Bartlow	2, 1960s-2
Martin, Mary Virginia	2
Martin, William McChesney, Jr.	5, 1960s-2
Martinez, Pedro Jaime	Sports-2
Marvin, Lee	2
Mas Canosa, Jorge	5
Mason, (William) Birny J., Jr.	5
Massey, Raymond Hart	1
Masters, William Howell	6, 1960s-2
Masters, William Howell, and Virginia Eshelman Johnson	1960s-2
Mathews, Edwin Lee ("Eddie")	6
Mathewson, Christopher ("Christy")	Sports-2
Mathias, Robert Bruce ("Bob")	8, Sports-2
Matson, James Randel ("Randy")	Sports-2
Matson, Oliver Genoa, II ("Ollie")	Sports-2
Matsunaga, Spark Masayuki ("Sparkie")	2
Matthau, Walter	6, 1960s-2
Matthews, Burnita Shelton	2
Mature, Victor John	5
Mauldin, William Henry ("Bill")	7, 1960s-2
Maxwell, Vera Huppé	4
Maxwell, William Keepers, Jr.	6
May, Elaine	1960s-2
May, Rollo Reece	4
Mayer, Maria Goeppert. *See* Goeppert-Mayer, Maria.	
Mayfield, Curtis Lee	5
Maynard, Don(ald) Rogers	Sports-2
Maynard, Robert Clyve	3
Mayo, Virginia	7
Mayr, Ernst Walter	7
Mays, Benjamin Elijah	1

Mays, William Howard, Jr. ("Willie")	1960s-2, Sports-2
Meader, (Abbott) Vaughn	1960s-2
Meadows, Audrey	4
Means, Gardiner Coit	2
Medeiros, Humberto Sousa	1
Medina, Harold Raymond	2
Meeker, Ralph	2
Meisner, Sanford	5
Mellon, Paul	5
Menninger, Karl Augustus	2
Menotti, Gian Carlo	8
Menuhin, Yehudi	5
Meola, Tony	Sports-2
Mercer, John Herndon ("Johnny")	1960s-2
Mercer, Mabel	1
Meredith, (Oliver) Burgess	5
Meredith, J(ames) H(oward)	1960s-2
Merman, Ethel	1
Merriam, Eve	3
Merrick, David	6
Merrifield, (Robert) Bruce	8
Merrill, James Ingram	4
Merrill, John Putnam	1
Merrill, Robert	7
Merton, Robert K(ing)	7
Messick, Dale	7
Messner, Tamara Faye LaValley ("Tammy Faye")	8
Metcalfe, Ralph Horace	Sports-2
Metzenbaum, Howard Morton	8
Meyendorff, John	3
Meyer, Raymond Joseph ("Ray")	8
Meyers, Ann Elizabeth	Sports-2
Meyerson, Martin	8
Meyner, Robert Baumle	2
Michaels, James Walker	8
Michener, James Albert	5
Middlebrook, (Helen) Diane Wood	8
Middlecoff, (Emmett) Cary ("Doc")	5
Middleton, Drew	2
Mies van der Rohe, Ludwig	1960s-2
Mikan, George Lawrence, Jr.	7, Sports-2
Mikita, Stan	Sports-2
Milanov, Zinka	2
Milgram, Stanley	1
Milland, Ray	2
Millar, Kenneth. *See* Macdonald, Ross.	
Miller, Ann	7
Miller, Arnold Ray	1
Miller, Arthur Asher	7, 1960s-2
Miller, Carl S.	2
Miller, Cheryl DeAnn	Sports-2
Miller, Marvin Julian	Sports-2

Miller, Merton Howard	6
Miller, Reginald Wayne ("Reggie")	Sports-2
Miller, Roger Dean	3
Miller, Shannon Lee	Sports-2
Miller, Stanley Lloyd	8
Miller, William Mosely	2
Mills, C(harles) Wright	1960s-2
Mills, Wilbur Daigh	3
Milstein, Nathan	3
Mink, Patsy Matsu Takemoto	6
Minnelli, Vincente	2
Minnesota Fats (Rudolf Walter Wanderone, Jr.)	4
Minow, Newton Norman	1960s-2
Mitchell, (John) Broadus	2
Mitchell, Joan	3
Mitchell, John James, Jr.	1
Mitchell, John Newton	2, 1960s-2
Mitchell, Joseph Quincy	4
Mitchell, Robert Cornelius, Sr. ("Bobby")	Sports-2
Mitchum, Robert Charles Durman	5
Mitford, Jessica ("Decca")	4
Mize, John Robert ("Johnny")	3
Mizell, Jason William. *See* Jam Master Jay.	
Mizener, Arthur Moore	2
Moakley, John Joseph (Joe)	6
Modigliani, Franco	7
Moffo, Anna	8
Mohr, Charles Henry	2
Molnar, Charles Edwin	4
Momaday, N(avarre) Scott	1960s-2
Mondavi, Robert Gerald	8
Monette, Paul Landry	4
Monge, José Trías. *See* Trías Monge, José.	7
Monk, Thelonious Sphere	1, 1960s-2
Monroe, Earl Vernon, Jr	Sports-2
Monroe, Marilyn	1960s-2
Monroe, Marion	1
Monroe, Rose Leigh Will	5
Monroe, William Smith ("Bill")	4
Montagu, Ashley	5
Montana, Joseph Clifford, Jr. ("Joe")	Sports-2
Montgomery, Elizabeth	4
Montgomery, Gillespie V. ("Sonny")	8
Montgomery, Robert	1
Moody, Helen Wills. *See* Wills (Moody), Helen Newington.	
Moog, Robert Arthur	7
Moore, Archibald Lee ("Archie")	5, Sports-2

Moore, Francis Daniels, and Thomas Earl Starzl 1960s-2
Moore, Garry 3, 1960s-2
Moore, Jack Carlton ("Clayton") 5
Moore, Mary Tyler 1960s-2
Moore, Paul, Jr. 7
Moore, Stanford 1
Moorer, Thomas Hinman 7
Moos, Malcolm Charles 1
Moreno, Rita 1960s-2
Morgan, Henry (Lerner von Ost) 4
Morgan, Henry Sturgis ("Harry") 1
Morgan, Joe Leonard Sports-2
Morganfield, McKinley. *See* Waters, Muddy.
Morison, Elting Elmore 4
Moross, Jerome 1
Morris, Henry M(adison) 8
Morris, Richard Brandon 2
Morris, Robert 1960s-2
Morris, William Weaks ("Willie") 5
Morrison, James Douglas ("Jim") 1960s-2
Morse, Wayne Lyman 1960s-2
Morton, Thruston Ballard 1
Mosbacher, Emil, Jr. ("Bus") Sports-2
Mosconi, William Joseph ("Willie") 3
Moses, Edwin Corley Sports-2
Moses, Robert 1
Moses, Robert Parris 1960s-2
Moss, Frank Edward ("Ted") 7
Motherwell, Robert 3
Motley, Constance Juanita Baker ("Connie") 7
Motley, Marion 5, Sports-2
Mott, Stewart Rawlings 8, 1960s-2
Mourning, Alonzo Harding, Jr. Sports-2
Moynihan, Daniel Patrick ("Pat") 7, 1960s-2
Mueller, Reuben Herbert 1
Muhammad, Elijah 1960s-2
Muldowney, Shirley Roque Sports-2
Mullen, Joseph ("Joey") Sports-2
Mulligan, Gerald Joseph ("Gerry") 4
Mulligan, Robert Patrick 8
Mulliken, Robert Sanderson 2, 1960s-2
Mumford, Lawrence Quincy 1
Mumford, Lewis Charles 2
Murchison, Clint(on) Williams, Jr. 2
Murphy, Calvin Jerome Sports-2
Murphy, George Lloyd 3
Murphy, Joseph Samson 5
Murray, Anna Pauline ("Pauli") 1
Murray, Arthur 3

Murray, Elizabeth 8
Murray, James Patrick ("Jim") 5, Sports-2
Murray, Kathryn Hazel 5
Murrow, Edward Roscoe 1960s-2
Musial, Stanley Frank ("Stan the Man") Sports-2
Muskie, Edmund Sixtus 4, 1960s-2
Myer, Dillon Seymour 1
Nabokov, Vladimir 1960s-2
Nabrit, James Madison, Jr. 5
Nader, Ralph 1960s-2
Nagel, Ernest 1, 1960s-2
Nagurski, Bronislau ("Bronko") 2, Sports-2
Nagy, Steve Sports-2
Naismith, James Sports-2
Namath, Joseph William ("Joe") 1960s-2, Sports-2
Nash, Gerald David 6
Nash, Graham. *See* Crosby, Stills, and Nash.
Nason, John William 6
Nathans, Daniel 5
Navratilova, Martina Sports-2
Nearing, Helen Knothe 4
Nearing, Scott 1
Neel, James Van Gundia 6
Nef, John Ulric 2
Negri, Pola 2
Nelson, (John) Byron, Jr. 8, Sports-2
Nelson, Eric Hilliard ("Rick") 1
Nelson, Gaylord Anton 7
Nelson, Harriet Hilliard 4
Nemerov, Howard 3
Neuberger, Maurine Brown 6
Neumann, Vera Salaff ("Vera") 3
Neustadt, Richard Elliott 7, 1960s-2
Nevelson, Louise 2, 1960s-2
Nevers, Ernest Alonzo ("Ernie") Sports-2
Newell, Allen 3
Newell, Peter Francis, Jr. ("Pete") 8, Sports-2
Newfield, Jack 7
Newhall, Beaumont 3
Newhart, George Robert ("Bob") 1960s-2
Newhouse, Caroline Herz 7
Newhouser, Harold ("Prince Hal") 5
Newman, Arnold Abner 8
Newman, Paul Leonard 8, 1960s-2
Newton, Huey Percy 2, 1960s-2
Neyman, Jerzy 1
Nicholas, Fayard Antonio 8
Nicholas, Harold Lloyd 6

Nichols, Mike 1960s-2
Nicholson, Jack 1960s-2
Nicklaus, Jack William 1960s-2, Sports-2
Niebuhr, Reinhold 1960s-2
Niel, Cornelis Bernardus van 1
Nikolais, Alwin Theodore ("Nik") 3, 1960s-2
Nilsson, Harry Edward, III 4
Nin, Anaïs 1960s-2
Nirenberg, Marshall Warren 1960s-2
Nisbet, Robert Alexander 4
Nitschke, Ray(mond) Ernest 5, Sports-2
Nitze, Paul Henry 7
Nixon, Pat(ricia) 3
Nixon, Richard Milhous 4, 1960s-2
Nizer, Louis 4, 1960s-2
Noguchi, Isamu 2
Noll, Charles Henry ("Chuck") Sports-2
Nomellini, Leo Joseph 6
Norris, Clarence 2
Norstad, Lauris 2
North, John Ringling 1
Northrop, John Howard 2
Northrop, John Knudsen ("Jack") 1
Norvo, Joseph Kenneth ("Red") 5
Notorious B.I.G. ("Biggie Smalls") 5
Noyce, Robert Norton 2, 1960s-2
Nozick, Robert 6
Nyad, Diana Sports-2
Oakes, John Bertram 6
Oates, Joyce Carol 1960s-2
O'Brien, Lawrence Francis, Jr. ("Larry") 2, 1960s-2
O'Brien, (William) Parry, Jr. 8, Sports-2
O'Brien, William Joseph, Jr. ("Pat") 1
Ochs, Philip David 1960s-2
Ochsner, (Edward William) Alton 1
O'Connor, Carroll 6
O'Connor, Donald David Dixon Ronald 7
O'Connor, Flannery 1960s-2
O'Connor, John Joseph 6
O'Day, Anita 8
Odell, Allan Gilbert 4
Odetta 8, 1960s-2
O'Dwyer, (Peter) Paul 5
Oerter, Alfred Adolph, Jr. ("Al") 8, Sports-2
O'Farrill, Arturo ("Chico") 6
Ogilvie, Richard Buell 2
Ogilvy, David Mackenzie 5
O'Hair, Madalyn Murray 4, 1960s-2
O'Horgan, Thomas ("Tom") 1960s-2

Okada, Kenzo   1
O'Keeffe, Georgia Totto   2
Olajuwon, Hakeem Abdul   Sports-2
Oldenburg, Claes Thure   1960s-2
Oldfield, Berna Eli ("Barney")   Sports-2
Olds, Robin   8
Olin, John Merrill   1
Oliphant, Patrick Bruce ("Pat")   1960s-2
Olitski, Jules   8
Olsen, Merlin Jay   Sports-2
Olsen, Tillie Lerner   8
Onassis, Jacqueline Lee Kennedy ("Jackie")   4, 1960s-2
O'Neal, Shaq(uille) Rashaun   Sports-2
O'Neil, John Jordan, Jr. ("Buck")   8
O'Neill, Thomas Philip, Jr. ("Tip")   4
Onsager, Lars   1960s-2
Oppen, George   1
Orbach, Jerome Bernard ("Jerry")   7
Orbison, Roy Kelton   2, 1960s-2
Ormandy, Eugene   1
Orr, Robert Gordon ("Bobby")   1960s-2, Sports-2
Osborne, Adam   7
Osborne, Thomas William ("Tom")   Sports-2
O'Sullivan, Maureen   5
Oswald, Lee Harvey   1960s-2
Ott, Mel(vin) Thomas   Sports-2
Ouimet, Francis DeSales   Sports-2
Owens, Alvis Edgar, Jr. ("Buck")   8
Owens, James Cleveland ("Jesse")   Sports-2
Owings, Nathaniel Alexander   1
Paar, Jack Harold   7
Packard, David. *See also* Hewlett, William Redington, and David Packard.   4
Packard, Vance Oakley   4
Padover, Saul Kussiel   1
Page, Alan Cedric   Sports-2
Page, Bettie Mae   8
Page, Geraldine   2
Page, Ruth Marian   3
Paige, Leroy Robert ("Satchel")   1, Sports-2
Paik, Nam June   8, 1960s-2
Pais, Abraham   6
Pakula, Alan Jay   5
Palade, George Emil   8
Palance, Jack   8
Paley, Grace Goodside   8
Paley, William Samuel   2
Palmer, Arnold Daniel ("Arnie")   Sports-2
Palmer, James Alvin ("Jim")   Sports-2

Palmer, R(obert) R(oswell)   6
Palmieri, Carlos Manuel, Jr. ("Charlie")   2
Papp, Joseph   3, 1960s-2
Parcells, Duane Charles ("Bill")   Sports-2
Paredes, Américo   5
Parent, Bernard Marcel ("Bernie")   Sports-2
Parish, Dorothy May Kinnicutt ("Sister Parish")   4
Parker, James Thomas ("Jim")   7, Sports-2
Parker, Thomas Andrew ("Colonel")   5
Parks, Bert   3
Parks, Gordon Roger Alexander Buchanan   8, 1960s-2
Parks, Henry Green, Jr.   2
Parks, Rosa Louise   7
Parnis, Sarah Rosen ("Mollie")   3
Parsons, Elizabeth Pierson ("Betty")   1
Parsons, James Benton   3
Parsons, Johnnie   1
Parton, James   6
Passman, Otto Ernest   2
Pasternak, Joseph Herman ("Joe")   3
Pastore, John Orlando   6
Paterno, Joseph Vincent ("Joe")   Sports-2
Patriarca, Raymond   1
Patrick, (Curtis) Lester   Sports-2
Patterson, Floyd   8, 1960s-2, Sports-2
Patterson, Louise Alone Thompson   5
Pauley, Edwin Wendell   1
Pauling, Linus Carl   4, 1960s-2
PayCheck, Johnny   7
Payton, Walter Jerry   5, Sports-2
Peabody, Endicott ("Chub")   5
Peale, Norman Vincent   3, 1960s-2
Pearl, Daniel ("Danny")   6
Pearl, Minnie   4
Peck, (Eldred) Gregory   7
Peckinpah, David Samuel ("Sam")   1, 1960s-2
Pedersen, Charles John   2
Peerce, Jan   1
Pei, I(eoh) M(ing)   1960s-2
Pelikan, Jaroslav Jan, Jr.   8
Pendleton, Clarence Mclane, Jr.   2
Penick, Harvey Morrison   4
Penn, Arthur Hiller   1960s-2
Penske, Roger S.   Sports-2
Pep, Willie   8, Sports-2
Peppard, George   4
Pepper, Claude Denson   2
Percy, Walker   2, 1960s-2

Perdue, Franklin Parsons ("Frank")   7
Perkins, Anthony   3
Perkins, Carl Lee   5
Perkins, Dexter   1
Perkins, James Alfred   5, 1960s-2
Perkins, (Richard) Marlin   2
Perlmutter, Nathan   2
Perls, Laura   2
Perot, H(enry) Ross   1960s-2
Perpich, Rudolph George ("Rudy")   4
Perry, Harold Robert   3
Perry, Lincoln. *See* Fetchit, Stepin.
Persichetti, Vincent Ludwig   2
Peter, Laurence Johnston   2, 1960s-2
Peter, Paul, and Mary   1960s-2
Peterson, Esther   5
Peterson, Roger Tory   4
Petrillo, James Caesar   1
Petry, Ann Lane   5
Pettit, Robert E. Lee, Jr. ("Bob")   Sports-2
Petty, Lee Arnold   6
Petty, Richard Lee   Sports-2
Pforzheimer, Walter Lionel   7
Philbrick, Herbert Arthur   3
Phillips, John Edmund Andrew   6, 1960s-2
Phillips, Kevin Price   1960s-2
Phillips, Marjorie Acker   1
Phillips, Samuel Cornelius ("Sam")   7
Phillips, William   6
Phoenix, River Jude   3
Piazza, Michael Joseph ("Mike")   Sports-2
Pickering, William Hayward   7
Pickett, Wilson, Jr.   8, 1960s-2
Picon, Molly   3
Pidgeon, Walter   1
Piel, Gerard   7
Pierce, Samuel Riley, Jr.   6
Pike, James Albert, Jr.   1960s-2
Pillsbury, Philip Winston   1
Pincay, Laffit Alegando, Jr.   Sports-2
Piñero, Miguel   2
Piore, Emanuel Ruben ("Mannie")   6
Pippen, Scottie   Sports-2
Pitney, Gene Francis Allan   8
Plath, Sylvia   1960s-2
Platt, Lewis Emmett ("Lew")   7
Pleshette, Suzanne   8
Plimpton, George Ames   7
Plough, Abe   1
Podhoretz, Norman Harold   1960s-2
Pogue, Forrest Carlisle   4
Poitier, Sidney   1960s-2
Pollack, Sydney Irwin   8

Simon, Paul Martin 7

Simon, William E(dward) 6

Simone, Nina 7

Simpson, Adele Smithline 4

Simpson, Alan 5

Simpson, Orenthal James ("O. J.") Sports-2

Simpson, Wallis Warfield. *See* Windsor, Wallis Warfield (Simpson), Duchess of.

Sinatra, Francis Albert ("Frank") 5

Singer, Isaac Bashevis 3, 1960s-2

Sirhan, Sirhan Bishara 1960s-2

Sirica, John Joseph 3

Sirk, Douglas 2

Sisco, Joseph John ("Joe") 7

Sisk, Mildred Elizabeth. *See* Gillars, Mildred Elizabeth Sisk ("Axis Sally").

Siskel, Eugene Kal ("Gene") 5

Siskind, Aaron 3

Sisler, George Harold Sports-2

Sitter, Carl Leonard 6

Skelton, Richard Bernard ("Red") 5

Skinner, B(urrhus) F(rederic) 2

Skipper, Howard Earle 8

Skolsky, Sidney 1

Slaughter, Enos Bradsher (Country) 6

Slayton, Donald Kent ("Deke") 3

Slick, Grace Wing 1960s-2

Sloan, James Forman ("Tod") Sports-2

Sloane, Eric 1

Slonimsky, Nicolas (Nikolai Leonidovich) 4

Smalley, Richard Errett 7

Smathers, George Armistead 8

Smith, Ada Beatrice Queen Victoria Louisa Virginia. *See* Bricktop.

Smith, Anna Nicole 8

Smith, C(yrus) R(owlett) 2

Smith, David Roland 1960s-2

Smith, Dean Edwards Sports-2

Smith, Emmitt James, III Sports-2

Smith, Hazel Brannon 1960s-2

Smith, Henry Nash 2

Smith, Howard K(ingsbury) 6

Smith, John William Sports-2

Smith, Joseph 3

Smith, Kathryn Elizabeth ("Kate") 2

Smith, Margaret Chase 4

Smith, Osborne Earl ("Ozzie") Sports-2

Smith, (Charles) Page (Ward) 4

Smith, Ralph Corbett 5

Smith, Robert Emil ("Buffalo Bob") 5

Smith, Robert Weston. *See* Wolfman Jack.

Smith, Roger Bonham 8

Smith, Walter Wellesley ("Red") 1, 1960s-2, Sports-2

Smith, William French 2

Smothers, Thomas ("Tom"), and Richard ("Dick") Smothers 1960s-2

Smucker, Paul Highnam 5

Snead, Samuel Jackson ("Sam") 6, Sports-2

Snell, George Davis 4

Snelling, Richard Arkwright 3

Snider, Edwin Donald ("Duke") Sports-2

Snow, Clarence Eugene ("Hank") 5

Snyder, James ("Jimmy the Greek") 4, Sports-2

Snyder, John Wesley 1

Snyder, Mitch(ell) Darryl 2

Snyder, Thomas James ("Tom") 8

Soloveitchik, Joseph Baer 3

Solti, Georg 5

Sondheim, Stephen Joshua 1960s-2

Sonnenblick, Edmund Hiram 8

Sonny and Cher 1960s-2

Sontag, Susan 7, 1960s-2

Sorensen, Theodore Chaikin ("Ted") 1960s-2

Sosa, Samuel Peralta ("Sammy") Sports-2

Sothern, Ann 6

Soule, Gertrude May 2

Southern, Terry Marion, Jr. 4, 1960s-2

Soyer, Raphael 2

Spahn, Warren Edward 7, Sports-2

Spalding, Albert Goodwill ("A.G.") Sports-2

Spanel, Abram Nathaniel 1

Sparkman, John Jackson 1

Speaker, Tris(tram) E. Sports-2

Speck, Richard Benjamin 3

Spector, Philip Harvey ("Phil") 1960s-2

Spelling, Aaron 8

Spence, Floyd D(avidson) 6

Sperry, Roger Wolcott 4

Spiegel, Sam(uel) 1

Spillane, Mickey 8

Spitz, Mark Andrew Sports-2

Spock, Benjamin McLane ("Dr. Spock") 5

Stack, Robert 7

Stacy, Jess Alexandria 4

Stafford, Jo 8

Stafford, Robert Theodore 8

Stagg, Amos Alonzo, Sr. Sports-2

Staggers, Harley Orrin 3

Staley, Dawn Sports-2

Stanford, Sally 1

Stanley, Kim 6

Stans, Maurice Hubert 5

Stanton, Frank Nicholas 8

Stanwyck, Barbara 2

Stapleton, (Lois) Maureen 8

Stargell, Wilver Dornel ("Willie") 6

Starr, Bryan Bartlett ("Bart") Sports-2

Starzl, Thomas. *See* Moore, Francis Daniels, and Thomas Earl Starzl.

Stassen, Harold Edward 6

Staubach, Roger Thomas Sports-2

Steber, Eleanor 2

Steel, Dawn Leslie 5

Stegner, Wallace Earle 3

Steiger, Rodney Stephen ("Rod") 6, 1960s-2

Stein, Aaron Marc 1

Stein, Herbert 5, 1960s-2

Stein, Julian Caesar ("Jules") 1

Steinbeck, John Ernst 1960s-2

Steinberg, Saul 5

Steinbrenner, George Michael, III Sports-2

Steinem, Gloria Marie 1960s-2

Steiner, Ralph 2

Stella, Frank Philip 1960s-2

Steloff, (Ida) Frances 2

Stengel, Charles Dillon ("Casey") Sports-2

Stennis, John Cornelius 4

Stephens, Woodford Cefis ("Woody") 5, Sports-2

Sterling, J(ohn) E(wart) Wallace 1

Stern, Curt 1

Stern, David Sports-2

Stern, Isaac 6

Stern, William ("Bill") Sports-2

Stevens, Brooks 4

Stevenson, Adlai Ewing 1960s-2

Stewart, Ellen 1960s-2

Stewart, James Maitland ("Jimmy") 5

Stewart, Leroy Elliott ("Slam") 2

Stewart, (William) Payne 5

Stewart, Potter 1

Stibitz, George Robert 4

Stills, Stephen. *See* Crosby, Stills, and Nash.

Stockdale, James Bond 7

Stockton, John Houston Sports-2

Stoessel, Walter John, Jr. 2

Stokes, Anson Phelps, Jr. 2

Stokes, Carl Burton 4, 1960s-2

Stokes, Colin 1

Stone, Edward Durell 1960s-2

Stone, I. F. 2, 1960s-2

Stone, Irving 2

For Reference

Not to be taken from this room

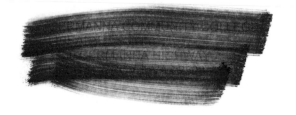